THE ILLUSTRATED

FAMILY

ENCYCLOPEDIA

THE ILLUSTRATED
FAMILY
ENCYCLOPEDIA

Colour Library Books

CLB 2270
This edition published 1989 by Colour Library Books Ltd
Godalming Business Centre, Catteshall Lane,
Godalming, Surrey GU7 1XW

Original material © 1975-1987 Marshall Cavendish Ltd
This arrangement © 1989 Marshall Cavendish Ltd

Prepared by Marshall Cavendish Books Ltd, 58 Old Compton Street,
London W1V 5PA

Printed in Italy

ISBN 0 86283 725 1

CONTENTS

PART 1: THE NATURAL WORLD   7

The Earth   8

The Age of the Earth 10
Earthquakes 14
Volcanoes 18
Mountain Building 22
Minerals 26
Metal Ores 30
Coal 35
Petroleum 38
The Fossil Record 42
The Sea at Work 47
The Ocean Floor 52

Plants   56

The Plant Kingdom 58
The Evolution of Plants 62
Algae 66
Fungi 70
Plant Partnerships 74
Parasitic and Climbing Plants 78
Carniverous Plants 81
Flowering Plants 84
Flowering Trees and Shrubs 90

Animals   94

The Animal Kingdom 96

Insects 102
Butterflies and Moths 108
The Bird Kingdom 112
Bird Migration 116
Marsupials 120
Hedgehogs, Moles and Shrews 124
Bats 128
Elephants and Hyraxes 132
Rhinos and Tapirs 136
Hippos, Pigs and Peccaries 140
Giraffe and Okapi 144
Snakes and Lizards 148
Turtles and Crocodiles 152
Amphibians 156
The Big Cats 161
Pandas, Raccoons and Badgers 166
Seals, Walruses and Sea Cows 170
Whales 174
Gibbons and Orang-utans 178
Old World Monkeys 181
Gorillas and Chimpanzees 184

The Human Body   188

Sight 190
Taste and Smell 194
Hearing 198
The Nervous System 202
Touch 206
The Brain 209
The Skeleton 212
Muscles 215
The Essence of Blood 218
Blood Circulation 221

CONTENTS

The Cardiovascular System 224
The Lymphatic System 227
The Heart 230
The Hormone System 234
Respiration 238
Digestion in the Mouth 242
Digestion in the Stomach 246
The Pancreas, Liver and Gall Bladder 250
The Small Intestine 254
The Large Intestine 258
The Kidneys 262
Skin 266
Hair and Nails 269

PART 2: SCIENCE AND TECHNOLOGY   273

Matter and Energy   274

Atoms and Molecules 276
Elementary Particles 280
Electricity and Magnetism 285
Light and Sound 290
Foundations of Chemistry 294
Elements of Nature 298

Transport and Technology   302

Aircraft 304
Helicopters and Autogyros 308
Hovercraft and Hydrofoils 312
Bicycles and Motorcycles 316

Cars, Trucks and Buses 320
Railways 324
Rockets and Missiles 328

Applied Science and Technology   332

Space Flight 334
Space Shuttle 338
The Nature of Mathematics 342
Scientific Analysis 346
Optics 350
Radar 354
Navigation 358
Nuclear Power 362
Gas Production 366
Electricity Supply 370
Water Supply 374
Batteries and Fuel Cells 378
Internal Combustion Engines 382
Steam Engines and Turbines 386
Jet and Gas Turbines 390
Medical Technology 394
Calculators 398
Computers 402
Telephone and Telegraph 406
Radio 412
Cameras and Film 416
Sound Recording 420
Sound Reproduction 424
Cinema 430
Lasers 435
Satellites 440

Index   444

PART 1
THE
NATURAL
WORLD

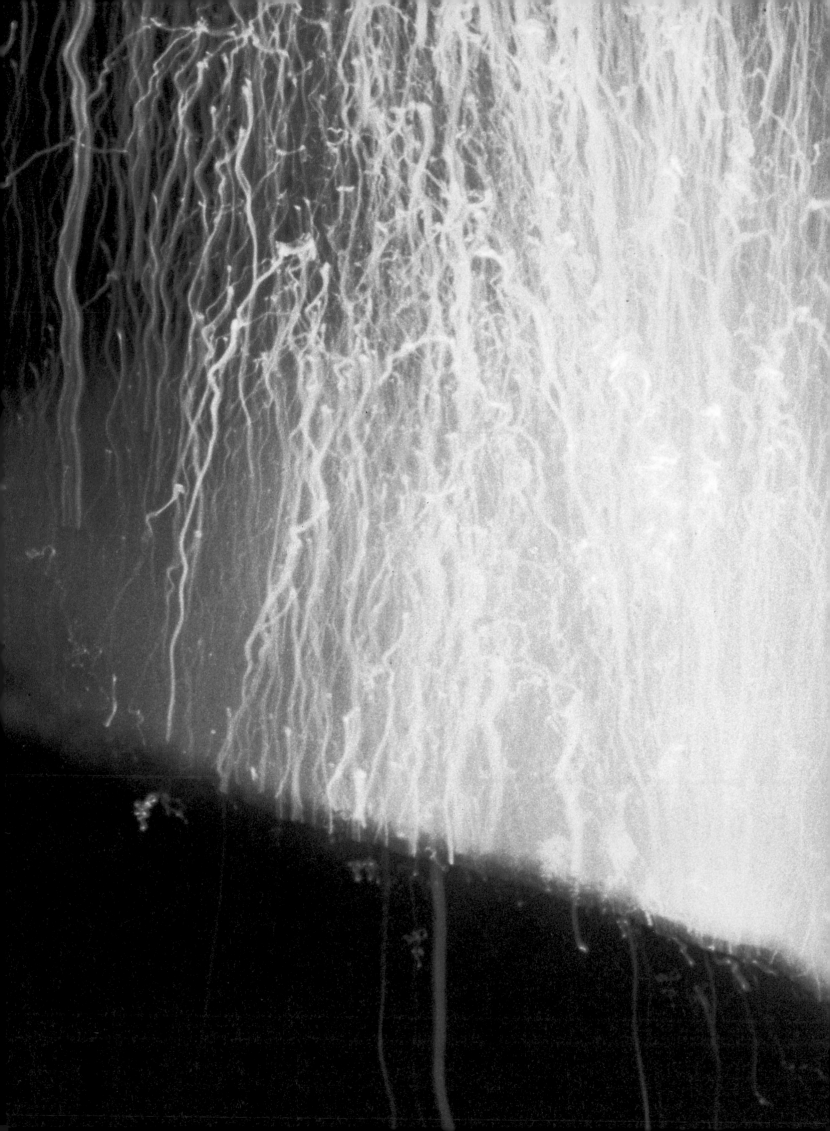

THE
EARTH

The Age of the Earth

The longstanding argument about the age of the earth was finally resolved by a breakthrough in a field of science quite separate from geology. In 1895, Henri Becquerel, a French physicist, realized that a mysterious form of energy was given out by certain substances independently of any external action. What Becquerel had discovered was the energy released by the spontaneous disintegration of the atoms of certain substances, the *radioactive elements*, into atoms of a different, stable element.

The process by which an unstable element spontaneously breaks up to form a second element is called *radioactive decay*. From the moment they exist, all radioactive elements are subject to decay from one form, or *isotope*, to isotopes of other, stable elements. The isotopes of an element differ in the number of particles in their atomic nucleii. They are therefore labelled according to this number. For example, uranium has two important radioactive isotopes—U^{235} and U^{238}. These *parent* atoms change slowly to the *daughter* lead (Pb) isotopes Pb^{207} and Pb^{206} respectively.

Just ten years after Becquerel's discovery of radioactivity, the pioneer English nuclear physicist Ernest Rutherford suggested that radioactive minerals such as uranium could be used to date rocks. Although the spontaneous decay of an individual atom is unpredictable, the overall rate of decay of the large number of atoms of uranium, as in all radioactive material, is constant and can be measured. Knowledge of this constant and of the ratios of parent to daughter isotopes provides geologists with a 'clock'.

The half-life

The intervals of time involved are enormous. It is more meaningful to express the rate of decay as the *half-life*, the time required for half the atoms in a specimen to have changed to the daughter isotope. Uranium-235, for example, has a half-life of 713 million years. This means that if there were 1,600 atoms of U^{235} in a specimen at the start, after one half-life there will be 800 atoms of U^{235} and 800 of Pb^{207}. After the next half-life of 713 million years, 400 atoms of U^{235} will remain and 1,200 atoms of Pb^{207} will have formed. The process of disintegration is effectively infinite, for as the radioactive material declines in abundance, its decline becomes progressively slower. The proportion of lead formed from decay indicates the length of time since decay began, and thus the age of the mineral.

Early results from this method were unreliable. Difficulties existed in measuring the proportions of the minute amounts of the isotopes. The development in the 1950s of the *mass spectrometer*, a machine capable of isolating different isotopes, meant a vast improvement in precision. Today, the isotopic decays that are valuable in determining geologic age include not only uranium to lead, but also thorium to lead, rubidium to strontium, potassium to argon, and carbon to nitrogen.

RADIOCARBON DECAY

0 years – death of plant

5,570 years – 50% remains

11,140 years – 25% remains

16,710 years – 12.5% remains

22,280 years 6.25% remains

55,700 years – 0.1% remains

Above: The rate at which radioactive carbon isotopes (C^{14}) decay to nitrogen isotopes (N^{14}) is shown here. All living plants and animals absorb radiocarbon from the atmosphere. This decay rate is known and the approximate time of death can be calculated by measuring the amount of C^{14} remaining in a specimen.

Above right: The enormous Columbia ice fields in Jasper National Park in western Canada, an area where long sequences of glacial deposits allow a count going back thousands of years. Seasons of melting and freezing are clearly marked in the graded layers or varves (right) deposited in lake floors formed by melting ice.

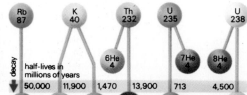

Rb 87	K 40	Th 232	U 235	U 238

half-lives in millions of years

decay

50,000	11,900	1,470	13,900	713	4,500

6He 4 7He 4 8He 4

| Sr 87 | Ar 40 | Ca 40 | | Pb 207 | Pb 206 |

Above: These isotopes are used by geologists in absolute dating. The original radioactive materials are shown with their half-lives and end-products. As the half-lives are millions of years long, the decay rates are used to calculate the ages of rocks and fossils—and the earth's age, estimated to be 4,500 million years.

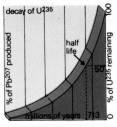

decay of U^{235}

% of Pb^{207} produced

half life

% of U^{235} remaining

millions of years 713

Above: Half-life decay follows the same curve, which can be plotted on a graph, for all radioactive materials. The curve remains constant although the rates vary considerably. Half the radioactive material decays quite early in the specimen's existence. The remainder decays by half again for each half-life period.

Right: The yearly growth of trees in spring is marked by a series of annual tree-rings in the wood. When counted these reveal the tree's age.

Below: The bristlecone pine, the world's oldest living thing, survives in the cold, dry White Mountains of California. Pines nearly 5,000 years old have been found.

PRE-CAMBRIAN SHIELD

Arctic Ocean

GREENLAND SHIELD

site where oldest known rock found

CHURCHILL

Hudson Bay

CORDILLERAN MOUNTAIN BELT

CENTRAL STABLE REGION

SUPERIOR

GRENVILLE

APPALACHIAN MOUNTAIN BELT

Atlantic Ocean

CANADIAN SHIELD

Above: A Pre-Cambrian map of North America indicates the Canadian shield, the age of granite rocks and location of the oldest rock. Pre-Cambrian rocks form the core or shield area of all the continents. The three provinces of the Canadian shield are drawn on the basis of radioactive ages. The oldest is the Superior province where most rock ages are close to 2,500 million years. The average ages of the Churchill and Grenville provinces are about 1,700 and 900 million years respectively. Today they may be covered by glacial and other deposits.

Left: The oldest rock in the world was found in western Greenland, where this amitsoq gneiss crystallized some 3,800 million years ago.

Two isotopes of uranium, U^{235} and U^{238}, occur in minerals. The rate of decay of U^{235} to Pb^{207} (with a half life of 713 million years) is much greater than that for U^{238}, which slowly decays to Pb^{206} with a half-life of 4,500 million years. Since the two are found together in minerals, this permits geologists to make a third measurement of age by comparing the ratio of Pb^{207} and Pb^{206}.

The element thorium also produces lead—changing from its single natural isotope Th^{232} to Pb^{208} with a half-life of 13,900 million years. As with uranium decay, the disintegration of thorium releases helium gas. The best of these methods is U^{238} decay, for Pb^{206} makes up 95 per cent of the lead developed by radioactive decay or *radiogenically* and hence can be determined with the best precision.

Even in carefully controlled experiments, the ages determined by the three decay processes may be different. One correction often required, though usually small, arises from the presence of 'common lead' not produced by the decay being measured. Unless allowed for in the calculation, this will inflate the value of Pb^{206} and Pb^{207} and the age of the sample.

The ratio of the abundances of uranium isotopes can be used to estimate roughly the age of the earth. The result given is 5,400 million years. From the ratios of lead isotopes in certain minerals, the composition of lead existing at the origin of the earth can be calculated and this leads to another estimate of the earth's age. Early calculations gave around 4,000 million years but higher figures have been obtained more recently.

Certain meteorites, rock masses which have fallen to earth from space, contain a mineral known as troilite which is virtually uranium-free. Any lead they contain is considered to represent the original mix or ratio in the planetary system, a ratio frozen through time since their creation. Using this primaeval lead isotope ratio and applying it to terrestrial rocks gives an age for the earth of 4,500 million years. Intensive analysis of meteorites also revealed none older than 4,500 million years.

The ages of moon rocks given by uranium-lead and other methods range from 3,100 to 4,500 million years. Some lunar rocks have given slightly greater ages, but probably these result from special processes operating on the moon. In contrast, the oldest rock on earth found so far is about 3,800 million years old. The fact that maximum ages for the earth, moon and meteorites give the same date— 4,500 million years—suggests to scientists that a major event occurred at that time throughout the solar system.

Finding the ages of rocks
The lead isotope methods have not proved very useful for dating crustal rocks. The elements are relatively rare, only a few minerals being suitable for analysis. These include zircon, monazite, sphene, uranite and pitchblende, the first substance to be analysed by Rutherford in 1904. Other techniques have been more widely used. The value of the rubidium-strontium method is that it can be applied to several common rock-forming minerals. The rubidium isotope Rb^{87} decays to strontium isotope Sr^{87} with a half-life of about 50,000 million years, giving useful age data for the oldest rocks including the oldest meteorites and moon rocks.

Above: This meteorite contains the virtually uranium-free mineral troilite. It offers scientists the chance to measure what is considered to be the 'primaeval' or original ratio of lead isotope Pb^{207} to Pb^{206}. Using this ratio gives a maximum age of 4,500 million years, the age of earth, for all meteorites.

Below: Information gathered from the face of the moon is immensely valuable in dating the rocks on earth. Moon rocks, which are as old as 4,500 million years, have escaped the weathering, erosion and transformation processes which occur on earth, where rocks older than 3,800 million years have probably all been lost.

This method is not so useful for younger rocks, but has provided valuable information on the source of igneous rocks, allowing a distinction to be made between igneous materials derived from the mantle and those from the crust. Extension of this idea has indicated to geologists the possibility that the crust has accumulated at a more or less consistent rate throughout geological time.

There are several factors that can cause dates derived from radioactive dating methods to be incorrect. On one hand, for example, the unnoticed presence of a 'common' or original isotope has exaggerated the findings. On the other, the escape of daughter elements may reset the 'clock' to zero or reduce the ages given. Argon is the gas given off in small amounts by decay of potassium isotope K^{40}, which has a half-life of 11,900 million years. The meaningfulness of results from this method is limited because the gaseous argon isotope Ar^{40} can be lost in some later, perhaps mild, heating of the rock. However, using carefully chosen materials, this method has yielded good results, and is applicable to a wide range of rocks and minerals containing sufficient potassium.

The long half-lives of all these radioactive elements restrict their use in dating to the distant past. This is exactly the period of the earth's history, however, about which relative dating methods can reveal little because of the lack of fossils. Pre-Cambrian rocks in which fossil evidence is rare form the cores of the continents, the so-called *shield areas*. Thousands of age determinations have been made, revealing provinces which are distinct in space and time. The Canadian shield, for example, contains three such provinces—Superior, Churchill and Grenville. Each is essentially the product of a cycle of sedimentation, volcanism, folding, metamorphism and igneous intrusion, and each took several hundred million years to complete. Provinces of comparable ages have been located on other continents, and geological maps drawn up which reveal the ancient history of the land masses.

In general, the most reliable radioactive dates are obtained from igneous and metamorphic rocks, in which the mineral crystallization provides a relatively sharp starting point in time.

Dating the recent past

For younger dates, much use has been made of the *radiocarbon* method, which measures the decay of carbon to nitrogen. All living plants and animals absorb the carbon isotope C^{14} in the form of carbon dioxide in their food cycles. The amount in organic bodies is the same as the small fixed proportion in the atmosphere, and remains constant through the life of the plant or animal. But when an organism dies, the intake of carbon ceases and the C^{14} slowly decays to nitrogen isotope N^{14}, starting a radioactive decay clock which can be applied to wood, peat, shells and certain limestones and bone materials.

The results can be subject to serious error. Contamination from other forms of carbon can upset the clock, and great care has to be exercised. One assumption which is basic to this method is that the concentration of C^{14} in the atmosphere, and thus in plants and animals, has remained constant through geological time. This assumption is now being questioned and corrections to some early radiocarbon dates have been made using age correlations with tree-ring dating.

Long-living trees like the bristlecone pine, found in California, Utah and Nevada in the United States, provide in their annual growth rings a precise method of dating for the last 8,000 years or so. Dates obtained by radiocarbon methods have been revised or *calibrated* both by tree-ring dating and by the yearly cycle of deposits left by melting ice. These deposits, called *varves*, mark the seasonal melting and freezing of ice as recorded in the debris deposited in lakes left behind by retreating ice sheets. The glaciers of the last ice age, in Scandinavia, for example, have created a time sequence of varves stretching back some 11,000 years.

One major contribution of radioactive methods has been to date the eras and periods included in the Geologic Column. This time-scale was constructed in the 19th century by correlating rock strata and fossil evidence, without any real idea of the dates of major earth events. Disputes as to the age of the earth are now substantially resolved and agreement exists that the earth's crust was created about 4,500 million years ago.

Man appears as no more than an afterthought, with an abruptly short record of existence. It has been calculated that if one thinks of the entire history of the earth as having occurred in one year, the first known living things would have appeared about 240 days before the end of the year. Early man would have appeared some 5 hours before the end of the very last day, and modern man some five minutes before midnight.

12

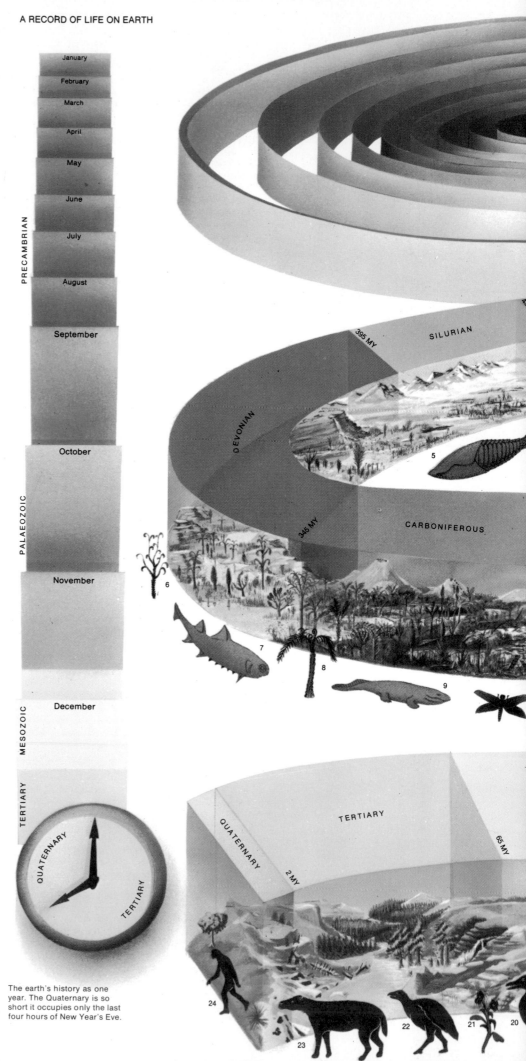

A RECORD OF LIFE ON EARTH

PRECAMBRIAN

January
February
March
April
May
June
July
August
September
October

PALAEOZOIC

November
December

MESOZOIC

TERTIARY

QUATERNARY

The earth's history as one year. The Quaternary is so short it occupies only the last four hours of New Year's Eve.

SILURIAN
DEVONIAN
CARBONIFEROUS
395 MY
345 MY

TERTIARY
QUATERNARY
65 MY
2 MY

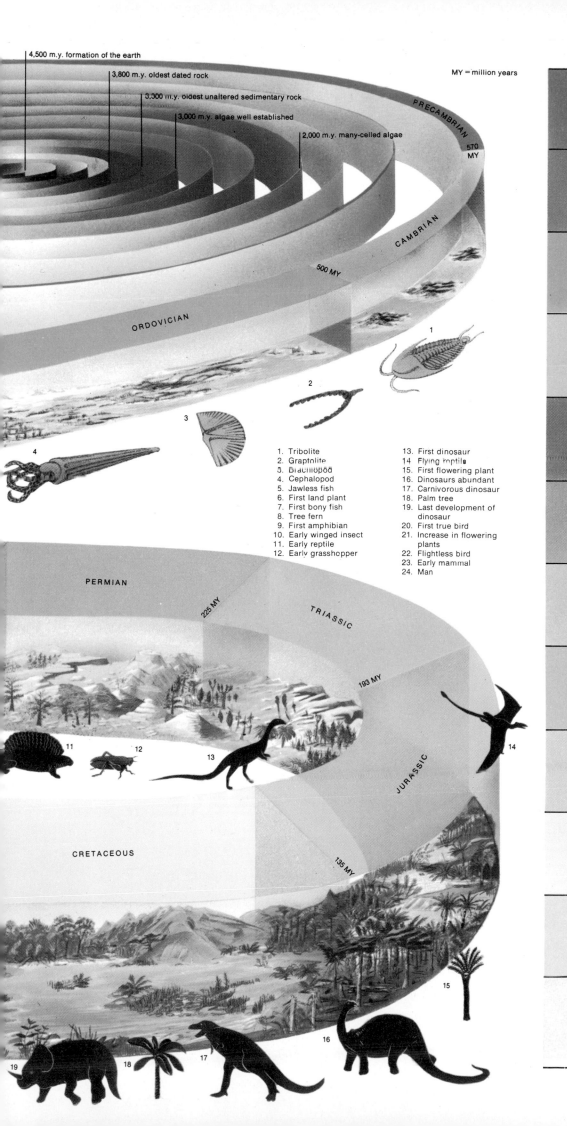

4,500 m.y. formation of the earth

3,800 m.y. oldest dated rock

3,300 m.y. oldest unaltered sedimentary rock

3,000 m.y. algae well established

2,000 m.y. many-celled algae

MY = million years

PRECAMBRIAN
570 MY

CAMBRIAN
500 MY

ORDOVICIAN

PERMIAN
225 MY

TRIASSIC
193 MY

JURASSIC
135 MY

CRETACEOUS

1. Tribolite
2. Graptolite
3. Brachiopod
4. Cephalopod
5. Jawless fish
6. First land plant
7. First bony fish
8. Tree fern
9. First amphibian
10. Early winged insect
11. Early reptile
12. Early grasshopper
13. First dinosaur
14. Flying reptile
15. First flowering plant
16. Dinosaurs abundant
17. Carnivorous dinosaur
18. Palm tree
19. Last development of dinosaur
20. First true bird
21. Increase in flowering plants
22. Flightless bird
23. Early mammal
24. Man

PRE-CAMBRIAN
The greatest part of geological time is represented by the Pre-Cambrian. The crust, land masses and seas formed and great volcanic activity occurred. Pre-Cambrian rocks form shield areas of all the continents. Traces of life are generally rare.

CAMBRIAN
The transition to the Cambrian is notable for the sudden appearance of abundant fossils. This marks the beginning of the Palaeozoic (ancient life) era. In the widespread shallow seas, early marine life proliferated. Tribolites were particularly common.

ORDOVICIAN
Much of the earth enjoyed a mild climate and seas still covered most of the surface. There was continuing sedimentation and important mountain-building occurred. Reef-building algae were notable and corals, sponges and molluscs such as cephalopods abundant.

SILURIAN
A dramatic development in earth's history came with the evolution of jawless fish, the first vertebrates (animals with backbones), which first appeared in the Ordovician. The late Silurian saw another important step — the growth of the first land plants.

DEVONIAN
Mountain-building movements reached a peak early in the Devonian but this was notably a period of explosive evolution. Land was colonized by the earliest seed plants. Fish grew in variety and size and the first land creatures — amphibians — evolved.

CARBONIFEROUS
Mountain building, folding and erosion continued. Richly forested swamps and deltas in North America and Europe were submerged and formed large coal measures. Extensive glaciation gripped the southern continents. Insects thrived. The first reptiles appeared.

PERMIAN
Desert conditions prevailed over much of Panagaea, the giant land mass made from all the drifting continents. The reptiles spread widely and modern insects evolved. Several marine creatures became extinct but new land flora, including conifers, developed.

TRIASSIC
As the Mesozoic era opened, Pangaea began breaking up. On land conifers became the dominant plants. This was a period of great diversity among the reptiles and the first dinosaurs and giant marine reptiles appeared. Small primitive mammals also evolved.

JURASSIC
Considerable volcanic activity was associated with the opening of the Atlantic Ocean. On land the dinosaurs reigned supreme and the air was first conquered by flying reptiles and later by primitive birds. There are traces of the earliest flowering plants.

CRETACEOUS
During the maximum extension of the seas of the world, great deposits of chalk formed in Britain. Dinosaurs remained dominant until they and many large reptiles became extinct at the end of the period. First true birds and early mammals became numerous.

TERTIARY
The opening of the Cainozoic (recent life) era heralded an explosive growth of mammals. Many large species evolved but some died out. Flowering plants increased rapidly and as climates later cooled grasslands appeared. Considerable uplift of land occurred.

QUATERNARY
This, the latest geological period, continues up to and including the present day. It is marked by climatic changes in which four major ice ages alternated with warmer intervals. Mammals increased and adapted and man evolved to dominate the earth.

Earthquakes

Earthquakes are movements within the earth caused by natural or man-made stresses. Many are so slight that they can barely be detected but others can be violent and catastrophic. In 1960 the Agadir earthquake in Morocco killed 12,000 people and nearly 50,000 died as a result of the Peruvian earthquake of 1970.

There are some parts of the world, *seismic* regions, where earthquakes are common occurrences. These lie along relatively narrow and unstable sections of the earth's crust which are also often areas of volcanic activity.

At these points a constant build-up of stress is released by sections of rock shifting along fault planes—cracks in the earth. These movements, known as *tectonic* events, are usually felt over a wide area and can be prolonged. In the San Fernando earthquake in 1971 small aftershocks went on for more than three days after the main shock.

Sometimes old fault areas can be briefly reactivated, causing minor earthquakes in *aseismic* regions such as Britain where they do not normally occur. The stresses which cause major earthquakes, however, build up along the edges of the plates or layers which form the earth's outer crust.

When rocks yield under stress a series of shocks radiate in all directions. If they are strong enough to reach the earth's surface the ground trembles, and ripples may be produced so that cracks, or fissures, open and close.

At the beginning of an earthquake there will be minor shocks which may be barely felt, then several more violent tremors spaced from a few seconds to a few hours apart. These are followed by small aftershocks, which can continue for several days or even weeks, while the disturbed rocks in the region of origin readjust and settle down.

Earthquakes quite frequently accompany or anticipate volcanic eruptions. Although they may have disastrous effects in the immediate vicinity, these die out rapidly away from the eruption.

Apart from the immediate effects of collapsed buildings, the earthquake can create havoc by burying settlements under landslides, destroying coastal regions with tidal waves, and causing fires from damaged cables, gas mains and petrol storage tanks. It is these secondary effects that most often cause the appalling loss of life associated with an earthquake. In the San Francisco earthquake of 1906 fire caused 400 million dollars worth of damage, and destroyed 700,000 homes in the Tokyo earthquake of 1923. The destruction of sewage systems and water supplies also tends to lead to epidemics breaking out in the disaster area.

Many earthquakes occur in coastal regions or under the ocean floor, resulting in a sudden shift in the level of the sea bed. Huge waves or *tsunami* are created by the water displacement and their effect may be felt for hundreds of miles. In the open ocean these waves are hardly noticeable and make no impression on passing vessels. As the wave nears shore and reaches shallower water, however, it gets larger and larger and travels at great speed. The 'tidal' wave may surge far

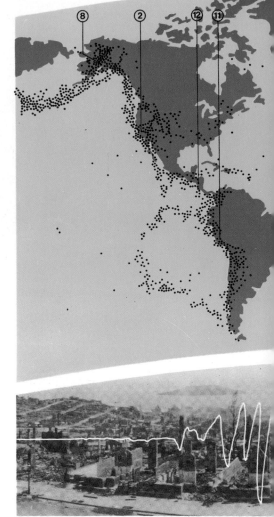

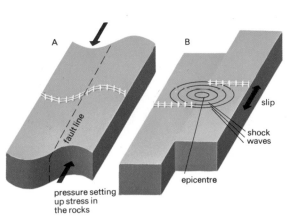

Above: Movement of the San Andreas fault in 1906 produced an earthquake which destroyed large areas of San Francisco. Much of the damage was caused by fires that broke out as gas mains fractured. The seismograph tracing of the vibrations was recorded in Albany, New York, 4,830 km (3,000 miles) away.

Left: These two views of the Peruvian village of Yungay show how it looked before and after an earthquake in 1970. The shock dislodged snow and ice from Nevados Huascarán, highest peak in Peru. A massive avalanche careered along the Santa valley at 480 km (298 miles) per hour, devastating Yungay.

Left: The two sides of a fault have bonded since the last earthquake. As stress builds up around the bond, rocks bend to accommodate it in A. In B the bond fails and the rocks fracture. The stress is relieved and the rocks spring back causing vibrations from the spot, or focus, where the bond failed.

Right: Earth movements caused by earthquakes. A road in Hachinohe, Japan, has been partially destroyed by vertical subsidence. All the railway lines in Niigata, Japan (far right) were buckled by an earthquake in 1964. Undulatory features of this type are characteristic of earthquake damage and are often caused by soil liquefaction.

A

B

fault line

slip

shock waves

epicentre

pressure setting up stress in the rocks

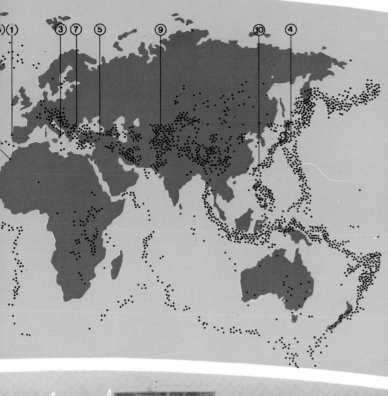

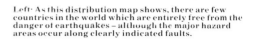

Left: As this distribution map shows, there are few countries in the world which are entirely free from the danger of earthquakes – although the major hazard areas occur along clearly indicated faults.

inland, more especially along coasts with long narrow inlets. A tsunami can affect a region far removed from an earthquake. People have been drowned in Hawaii as a result of an earthquake in the Aleutian trench, over 3,000 km (1,900 miles) away in the North Pacific Ocean.

One of the most disastrous earthquakes in history, and one which first excited some scientific curiosity, was the Lisbon earthquake of 1 November 1755 in Portugal. This was felt over a wide area as witnessed by the account in *Gentleman's Magazine* of March 1756 by Mr Stoqueler, the Hamburg consul in Lisbon, who was about 30 km (19 miles) to the west-north-west of the city that day. 'The day broke with a serene sky, the wind continuing east; but at 9 o'clock the sun began to grow dim, and about half an hour after 9, we heard a rumbling like that of carriages, which increased so much as to resemble the noise of the loudest cannon; and immediately we felt the first shock, which was succeeded by a second, third and fourth.' In Lisbon itself, the first shock brought down many buildings while worshippers were at church—thousands were crushed. Many more were killed by the fires and tsunami which then swept parts of the city. The effects were felt, with diminishing intensity, as far away as Switzerland and Scotland where water levels in various lakes oscillated slightly. The resultant tsunami created noticeable waves in the North Sea and reached Martinique in the Caribbean.

While many in Europe found evidence

Left: Earthquakes under the sea or in coastal regions set up great waves, or tsunami, which can cause devastation far away from the earthquake site. Boats were flung inland at Kodiak by waves created by the Alaskan earthquake of 1964. A Pacific early warning system is now in operation.

Right: 'The Great Wave of Kanagawa', a Japanese print, shows a tsunami. Tsunamis are caused by rapid rise or fall of the sea floor during an earthquake. In open sea tsunami, often hundreds of miles long, may pass unnoticed. When they reach the continental shelf close to land, water piles up to heights of 12m (40ft).

Left: Another example of earth movement can be seen in this orange grove which was offset along the San Jacinto fault in California during the Imperial Valley earthquake of 1940. The photograph was taken 19 years later.

Right: The intensity of an earthquake diminishes from a zone of maximum effect, the *epicentre*, which is directly over its origin or *focus*, to areas where its effects can no longer be felt. The lines of equal intensity or *isoseismic* lines are arranged concentrically around the epicentre. The numerals show the intensity and the arrows show the movements of P and S waves and the two types of surface waves.

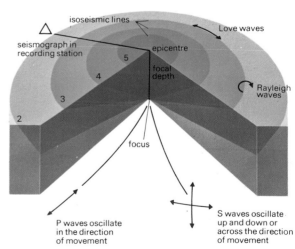

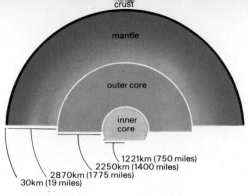

of God's or the Devil's work in these events, a small number of scientists pursued their own investigations. Thus Mr Stoqueler noted some of the local effects away from the city, such as springs drying up and new ones appearing, a swampy lake uplifted to form dry land, and the sea retreating so that 'you walk almost dry to places where before you could not wade'.

More importantly, as a result of collecting as many observations on the effect of the earthquake as possible, John Mitchell (1724-1793) suggested that an initial explosive shock could have given rise to waves spreading out through the rocks in all directions. This fundamental realization heralded an increasingly scientific approach to the study of earthquakes, or seismology.

Measurement of earthquakes

There are two main methods of measuring the strength of earthquakes—the Mercalli scale which relies on the comparison of eye-witness accounts of the effects of the earthquake and the Richter scale. In 1935 C. F. Richter, an American seismologist, devised a formula for calculating the strength of an earthquake from instrumental recordings of its magnitude. This is related to the total amount of energy stored in the rock under stress and released during an earthquake shock by the initial rock fractures at the point of origin, or *focus*.

The depth of the focus can be calculated. Shallow earthquakes have a focus above the boundary between the earth's crust and the deeper mantle. This boundary, known as the Moho after the Yugoslav seismologist Mohorovicic who discovered it, is 35 km (22 miles) deep. Intermediate

Above and below: The course of earthquake waves as they pass through the earth indicates its structure. The progress of the waves suggests a change in density and composition between the *crust* and the *mantle*. P and S waves that have travelled through the earth are registered on seismographs

through an arc of 0°-103° from the epicentre. Both then disappear into the *shadow zone*. P waves alone, noticeably bent, reappear at 143°. This suggests a liquid outer core, since S waves cannot travel through liquids. Increased speed of P waves through the central part of the core suggests that the inner core is solid.

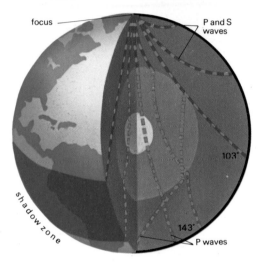

earthquakes have a focus between the Moho and a depth of 300 km (190 miles). Deep earthquakes have a focus below this, usually between 500 and 700 km (310 to 435 miles) from the surface.

A single earthquake produces three main types of shock wave, referred to as P, S and L waves. P or 'Primae' or 'Push and Pull' waves are analogous to sound waves in which each particle of rock vibrates longitudinally or parallel to the direction of the wave. S or 'Secundae' or 'Shear' waves are more like light waves in that each particle of rock has a shear motion, across the direction of movement of the wave. While P waves can pass through solids, liquids and gases, S waves pass through solids only. P waves also travel more quickly than S waves and therefore are picked up first by a distant seismograph.

A third, even slower set of waves are L or 'Long' waves which pass only through the earth's crust and are the last to be picked up by a seismograph. Conversely they are more easily detected than P and S waves at great distances from the source as they lose their energy more slowly. Surface waves set up by very large earthquakes have been recorded after they have travelled around the earth six times. There are two main types of L waves: Rayleigh waves and Love waves, which oscillate rather like P and S waves respectively.

A global network of seismological stations coupled with rapid exchange of information means that the focus, magnitude and *epicentre*, or the area of maximum effect, of an earthquake are quickly calculated. It also allows the study of the internal structure of the earth, using the

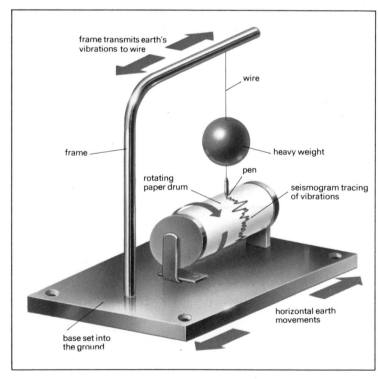

Above: A seismograph is a device for detecting and recording seismic waves. It consists of a spring suspended weight or pendulum and a clockwork-operated rotating drum. The frame of the device is set in bedrock. Seismic waves set up a horizontal motion which moves the frame backwards and forwards. The pen

attached to the pendulum moves in the same way, marking the movements on the rotating drum. This produces a seismogram which indicates the duration and severity of the earth tremors. The record of an earthquake is a wavy line; when there is no movement the seismogram shows a straight line.

Right: The Mercalli scale uses observations of an earthquake's effect at a point on the earth's surface to assess its intensity. The scale is subjective and a reading can be exaggerated, for example, by the collapse of badly constructed buildings. However, it has given much useful information on the nature of earthquakes.

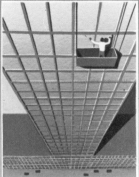

Point 2: Very slight. Felt by people on the upper floors of buildings and others favourably placed to sense tremors, such as those at rest.

Point 5: Quite strong. Small articles fall, liquids spill, sleepers wake, bells tinkle, doors swing open and closed. Noticed out of doors.

Point 7: Very strong. General alarm. Fall of loose plaster and tiles. Some buildings crack. Noticed by people driving vehicles.

various shock waves to 'X-ray' the structure. The behaviour of the various types of wave can be used, for example, to study the nature and relative thickness of the earth's crust in different regions. A natural progression from this is the creation of small, man-made seismic shocks to study the structures within the crust when looking for oil.

Earthquake distribution
The overall pattern of distribution of earthquake epicentres follows closely the regions of the last two major periods of mountain building during the Tertiary (between ten and 70 million years ago) and Recent (the last 11,000 years) eras, the rift valleys of Central and East Africa and the submarine mid-oceanic ridges. The distribution of active and recently extinct volcanoes is very similar. The pattern fits well with the arrangement of crustal plates which cover the surface of the globe. Such a distribution indicates stresses build up at the places where the crustal material is being formed at the mid-oceanic ridges and where the plate edges are moving against one another or plunging back down into the mantle.

The distribution of earthquake focusses is even more instructive. The deeper focus earthquakes, over 200 km (120 miles) deep, are limited to the ocean trench and island arc systems, such as the Japanese islands. They appear to originate in the zones where one crustal plate is being forced beneath another. The pattern of focusses indicates that the inclination of these zones is about 45°. The zones were discovered by the American seismologist, Hugo Benioff, and are known as Benioff zones or subduction zones.

Man-made earthquakes
Significant man-made earthquakes are created by nuclear explosions, major constructions such as dams and reservoirs, and by liquid injection into underground reservoirs. The energy released by a nuclear explosion can equal that of a moderately strong earthquake, although the pattern of shock waves is different and can be distinguished from that of natural earthquakes. In regions of structural instability sudden changes in water level of a reservoir may lead to earthquakes. The pumping of liquid waste into deep wells near Denver, Colorado, and of water under pressure in the Rangely oil-field, Colorado, have both triggered off earthquakes in previously quiet areas.

Earthquake prediction and control
It is unlikely that inhabitants of the major earthquake zones could ever be moved out permanently, especially in view of the fertility and wealth of some regions, but it may prove possible to protect people from major disasters. Attempts have been made to recognize physical changes prior to a major earthquake. This work is still in its infancy, but several lines are possibly worth pursuing.

In Japan and the Soviet Union slight changes in the inclination of the ground have been detected prior to an earthquake. Changes in the pattern of microearthquakes, which form the normal background seismic activity have sometimes been observed before a major shock. Possibly the most important observation is the local change in the earth's magnetic field which has sometimes been detected prior to an earthquake.

Another recent discovery suggests that there is a marked variation in the velocity of P waves recorded from microquakes during quite long periods prior to major earthquakes. According to this theory, observations suggest that San Francisco and central California will remain free from major earthquakes for at least the next 25 years.

The modification of earthquake patterns to avoid a major disaster may soon prove scientifically possible. Small earthquakes have been induced by injecting fluids into faulted areas. From this it has been inferred that strains built up along faults such as the San Andreas fault in California could be released in a relatively controlled manner by artificially triggering small earthquakes. This could prevent a major natural earthquake which would otherwise appear to be unavoidable along the Californian fault.

The reduction of loss of life is already being tackled in other ways. Specially designed modern buildings can withstand significant tremors. In the Tokyo earthquake of 1923, for example, the Imperial Hotel designed by Frank Lloyd Wright suffered little damage. Further research is being conducted on building resistance in Tashkent in the Soviet Union where there are empty apartment blocks with machines on their roofs to induce vibrations and thus test resistance of the buildings to stresses and strains. Populations are also slowly being educated to take sensible shelter indoors instead of running into the open streets where debris from collapsing buildings may cause them injury. By taking such precautions it may be possible to minimize the devastation and loss of life caused by earthquakes in the future.

Far left: The earthquake that hit Anchorage in Alaska in 1964 caused relatively little damage to timber buildings. The brick building on the left has suffered considerable damage; in the timber house even the windows are intact.

Left: These buildings in Niigata, Japan were built to withstand earthquakes. When strong tremors shook the city in 1964 the structures survived— there was not even a hair line crack in the walls. They toppled because certain soils lose their rigidity and 'liquefy' as a result of repeated seismic shocks. Few structures can survive this process— the ground simply slides away beneath them.

Above: The earthquake that struck Alaska in March 1964 was one of the most severe ever recorded and caused hundreds of millions of dollars-worth of damage. Landslides wrecked buildings, roads and railway lines. The houses shown here were smashed by a landslide with a front 2.4 km (1½ miles) long.

Right: Chang Heng, a Chinese astronomer, first recorded distant earth tremors in 132AD. His seismoscope contained a pendulum which moved in a particular direction when an earthquake set up vibrations in the casing. This tipped one of the metal balls from the side of the seismoscope.

Point 8. Destructive. High chimneys and bell towers collapse, statues move. Most buildings crack and branches are torn from trees.

Point 10: Disastrous. Most buildings destroyed. Landslides and large cracks in the ground. Tsunami flood coastal regions.

Point 12: Catastrophic. Near total destruction. Major distortions and changes of ground level. Loose objects are hurled into the air.

Volcanoes

A volcano behaves like a giant chimney, conducting material from shallow depths in the earth up to the surface. When a volcano erupts, hot liquid rock, called *lava,* gases and rock fragments are spewed on to the surface through its opening. This 'chimney' may take the form of a tall mountain *cone.* Volcanoes, however, may also appear as gently-sloping domes, or even as long, low-lying slits through which lava oozes out to produce a flat lava field.

A volcanic eruption starts deep down in the earth's *crust* or in the upper *mantle*—the thicker under-lying layer. Here rocks melt to form *magma,* essentially a mixture of volcanic gases dissolved in liquid lava. Underground pressure from the weight of the surrounding rocks forces the magma towards the surface.

As the magma wells up, sometimes into an underground reservoir, or *magma chamber,* under the volcano, the pressure drops and the gases start to bubble out of the liquid. The gases consist mainly of steam, most of which comes from water seeping through the rocks of the upper crust to meet the rising magma. They also contain carbon dioxide, nitrogen, sulphur dioxide and small quantities of such noxious gases as hydrogen sulphide and hydrogen chloride.

Eventually magma finds its way to the surface in a volcanic eruption, either through an existing vent or fissure from a previous eruption, or by forcing its way up through new cracks in the crust. On the flanks and around the base of an existing cone, secondary vents often produce small 'pimples' known as *parasitic cones.* Mount Etna on Sicily, for example, has 200 such satellite cones.

Quiet eruptions

The thickness of the magma—whether it is thin and syrupy or tacky like toffee—depends on its temperature, pressure and chemical nature. This consistency determines how easily the volcanic gases will be able to escape into the atmosphere before or during an eruption.

In fluid, fairly flat magma—usually basaltic—that wells slowly up the central *vent* of a typical volcano, what little gas there is has plenty of time to separate peacefully from the magma. The gas-free lava collects in the funnel-shaped cup or *crater* at the summit of the volcano. When the crater is full, the lava spills over the edge and flows rapidly down the side of the cone in fiery rivers of *lava flows.*

When very liquid lava oozes out of a central vent or a big fissure it tends to spread out over a wide area, forming either huge plateaux or thin sheets of lava on the typically-gentle sloping dome of a *shield volcano.* Mauna Loa in Hawaii, the world's largest volcano with a base 100 km (62 miles) in diameter and rising 10,000 metres (32,820 feet) above the sea floor, is a perfect example of a shield volcano built up over the years.

When the lava first reaches the surface it is very hot and fluid at temperatures between 800°C and 1200°C. It quickly starts to cool and solidify into volcanic or *igneous* rock. As the molten lava cools, the different minerals it contains crystallize, just like ice crystals freezing in water.

Gordon Gahan, Photo Researchers

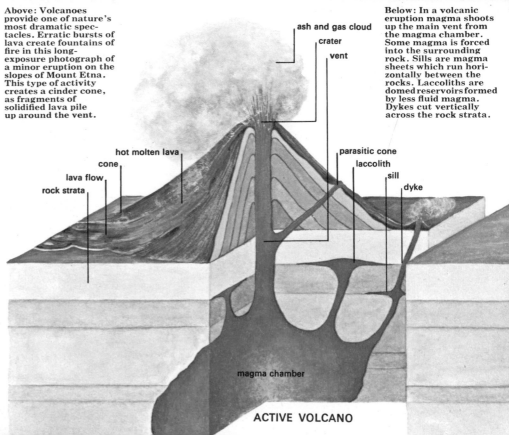

Above: Volcanoes provide one of nature's most dramatic spectacles. Erratic bursts of fire in this long-exposure photograph of a minor eruption on the slopes of Mount Etna. This type of activity creates a cinder cone, as fragments of solidified lava pile up around the vent.

Below: In a volcanic eruption magma shoots up the main vent from the magma chamber. Some magma is forced into the surrounding rock. Sills are magma sheets which run horizontally between the rocks. Laccoliths are domed reservoirs formed by less fluid magma. Dykes cut vertically across the rock strata.

ash and gas cloud
crater
vent
hot molten lava
cone
lava flow
rock strata
parasitic cone
laccolith
sill
dyke
magma chamber

ACTIVE VOLCANO

Left: Mt Fuji, the highest mountain in Japan, is a dormant volcano which last erupted in 1707. It has a perfect conical shape, with a summit crater. Volcanic cones of this type, also seen at Etna, Vesuvius and Stromboli, are strato volcanoes, formed by alternating layers of lava and ash.

Right: Cerro Negro in Nicaragua, a cinder cone built up over an older terrace of lava flows. Vast dark clouds of ash are disgorged when gases escape carrying minute particles of cooled lava powder. Eventually a rain of ash falls from the spreading cloud, burying settlements and countryside.

Left: Fumaroles are small vents in the ground from which volcanic gases and steam escape.

Right: Cooler fumaroles are called solfataras. The steam they emit has a high sulphur content, and mineral deposits are formed as the water evaporates.

Left: Bird's eye view of a volcanic crater, surrounded by liquid basalt flows.

Above right: Molten lava sweeps down from an Icelandic volcano. Lava flows can reach speeds of up to 100 km (62 miles) per hour, but usually they move more sluggishly.

Below: A composite cone is built of layers of lava and pyroclasts. If the main vent grows too high or becomes plugged by lava, a parasitic cone forms. The vents of a dormant or extinct volcano are plugged by lava. Pressure may build under a dormant volcano causing it to erupt after a long period of inactivity.

Below: The lava plug may remain as a hill after the rest of the cone has been eroded. Edinburgh's Castle Rock, for example, is the plug of one vent of the Arthur's Seat volcano, active 325 million years ago. Erosion also reveals the existence of sills and dykes when ash and rock has worn away.

Right: Pahoehoe is highly fluid lava, spread in sheets, which drags the cooling surface layer into folds.

Below right: 500 million year-old pillow lavas formed underwater now lie above sea level. Rapid cooling creates bulbous shapes inside a glassy skin.

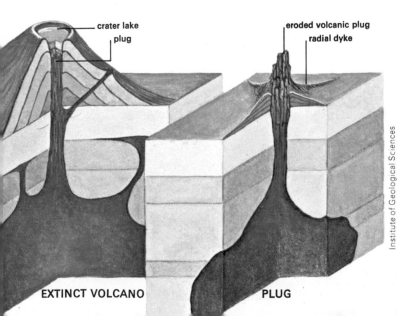

crater lake
plug

eroded volcanic plug
radial dyke

EXTINCT VOLCANO   **PLUG**

TYPES OF ERUPTIONS

Icelandic: Quiet eruption of lava from fissures builds up horizontal lava flows.

Hawaiian: Fluid lava erupts quietly and builds up huge shield volcanoes.

Strombolian: Minor explosions throw out lava which cools into pyroclasts.

Vulcanian: Explosive escape of gas from viscous magma. Clouds of volcanic ash form.

Vesuvian: Violent eruption produces huge quantities of ash. A vast cloud develops.

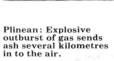

Pelean: Violent eruption of highly viscous magma. Hot gas cloud forms.

Plinean: Explosive outburst of gas sends ash several kilometres in to the air.

Thin sheets of lava cool quickly into fine grained rocks in which individual mineral crystals are invisible to the unaided eye. The more slowly the lava cools the larger the crystals grow before setting. Thicker blocks of lava take a long time to cool—they may still be too hot to touch several months after the eruption—and therefore form larger grained rocks. If the lava is chilled instantly, there is no time for this crystallization process to occur. Instead, it forms a volcanic glass called *obsidian*. This happens particularly in underwater eruptions, or where a stream of hot lava pours down into the sea.

Angry mountains
Where magma is of a slightly stickier consistency, the gas bubbles wind their way to the surface more slowly, growing as they climb and as more gas separates out of the rocky solution. These large bubbles burst when they reach the surface, splashing up a shower of lava spray that cascades over the sides of the vent in a spectacular natural fireworks display. The blobs of liquid lava clot quickly as they fly through the air, forming fragments of hard lava called *pyroclasts*. These missiles range in size from fine *dust* and *ash* to small pebble-sized particles called *lapilli* and large boulders or *bombs*. Bombs spin as they travel through the air, solidifying into characteristic shapes or spindle bombs. Breadcrust bombs on the other hand, have a zigzag pattern of cracks over the surface caused by the lava forming a solid skin which is broken by expansion and the escape of gas. Such bombs often shatter as they hit the ground.

A small pile of pyroclasts begins to form a *cinder cone* around the vent. The typical volcanic cone shape develops because most particles and all the larger, heavier fragments land near the vent, while smaller, lighter pieces are thrown further away. Consequently the volcanic mound grows more quickly nearer the vent, creating the classically rising slopes of a volcanic cone. Occasionally the globules of lava do not solidify in the air and form a *spatter cone* as they land.

In contrast to the fluid lavas, very tacky lavas barely flow at all but are squeezed out of the vent like toothpaste from a tube, forming steep-sided volcanic *domes* of hot lava in the crater. Sometimes a pocket of hotter, thinner lava forces its way through a crack in the dome creating a tall pinnacle of solid lava called a *spine* that towers over the vent. The spine of Mont Pelée on the island of Martinique in the Caribbean rose to the imposing height of 300m (984 ft) during its period of activity in 1902, before it cracked around the base and crumbled into the crater.

Thick lavas also tend to congeal in the vent and together with rubble from the crater form a plug that blocks the exit. Tremendous pressure builds up as gases are trapped under the plugged vent until the volcano literally 'blows its top' in a violent explosion.

Violent explosions, like the famous blast at Krakatoa in 1883, shoot vast quantities of rock, lava, gas and ash into the air. In the shock of the drop of pressure, the gases froth in the lava, but because of the thickness of the lava they are unable to burst free. If the lava drops back into the sea it sets very quickly, trapping the gas bubbles permanently into a petrified foam called

pumice, which floats on water.

During a particularly violent eruption, the magma chamber may be completely emptied, leaving the central part of the cone unsupported. Often under such circumstances the crater and walls of the vent collapse into the hollow chamber, creating a large saucer-shaped depression known as a *caldera* across the summit of the volcano, which may be as much as several kilometres in diameter. An explosive eruption may cause the entire cone to fall into the magma chamber. After Krakatoa erupted, an underwater caldera 7 km (4.3 miles) in diameter was formed.

Life and death of a volcano
The sudden rise of a cinder cone called Parícutin on 20 February 1943—in the field of a surprised Mexican farmer—provided scientists with a rare opportunity to observe a volcano from its birth. In the first day of intense activity, it produced a huge glowing cloud of hot ash and a cone of pyroclasts 40 m (131 ft) high. After this astonishing effort, fissures opened around the base and lava seeped across the field. Eruptions continued with decreasing intensity until, when the volcano ceased eruption in 1952, the cone was 410 m (1,344 ft) high.

Library of Congress

The life-span of a volcano ranges from a few months to many thousands of years. Activity may vary greatly during that time. Of the 500 or so active volcanoes in the world today only a small number erupt each year. A few volcanoes, like Stromboli in the Lipari Islands off Italy, erupt continuously with successive bursts. The majority, however, erupt only irregularly and spend most of their time 'asleep'.

During these periods of inactivity, however, it is impossible to tell whether the volcano is really *extinct*—that is, stopped erupting for ever—or merely *dormant*, undergoing a temporary period of rest. Generally volcanoes are classified as extinct when no eruption has been noted in 'recorded history'.

Yet even then they may be potentially active, one day to wake up in a fresh eruption, with devastating results. Vesuvius, overlooking the Italian port of Naples, was thought to be extinct before its catastrophic eruption in 79AD which completely destroyed the Roman cities of Pompeii and Heraculaneum.

Causes of volcanic activity
Volcanoes are distributed in areas where conditions are suitable for the formation of magma. The concept of plate tectonics

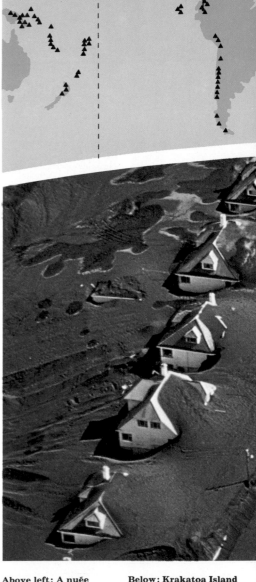

Above left: A nuée ardente, a glowing cloud of dust and gas, erupted from Mt Pelée in the island of Martinique at 7.50 am on 8 May 1902. The city of St Pierre, with its 30,000 inhabitants, was destroyed in seconds. The surge of gas that headed the cloud was hot enough to melt metal and glass.

Below: Krakatoa Island in the East Indies was formed by a group of volcanic cones built up from a prehistoric caldera. In 1883 a huge eruption destroyed most of the island and left a 300 m (1,000 ft) crater in the sea bed. The explosion, heard as far away as Australia, had worldwide effects. A tidal wave killed

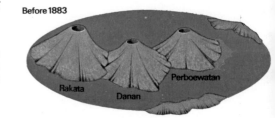

Before 1883

Rakata   Danan   Perboewatan

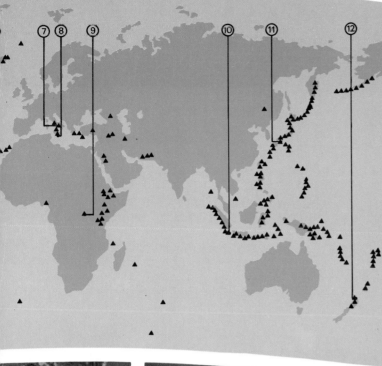

DISTRIBUTION OF VOLCANOES

Some of the world's major sites of volcanic activity are shown on the map:

1. Kilauea, Hawaii
2. Katmai, Alaska
3. Paricutin, Mexico
4. Cotopaxi, Ecuador
5. Pelée, Martinique
6. Surtsey, Iceland
7. Vesuvius, Italy
8. Etna, Italy
9. Nyamuragira, Zaire
10. Krakatoa, Indonesia
11. Sakurajima, Japan
12. White Island, New Zealand

Most active volcanoes are concentrated in a belt around the Pacific and one that extends through Indonesia and New Guinea. Indonesia has the greatest concentration of volcanoes with 29 actively emitting gases and 78 eruptions since records began.

provides an explanation of the distribution of active volcanoes. The earth has a cool rigid crust which consists of a dozen or so plates which are free to move in relation to each other and to glide relatively freely over the earth's surface.

The mantle of the earth, the layer below the crust, is solid and its temperature is normally not high enough to start the melting which forms magma. Pressure here also prevents melting. Heat from the earth's interior does, however, cause the slow circulation of the mantle, or *mantle convection*.

A constructive plate margin, such as the mid-Atlantic ridge, is one where new crustal material is formed by rising magma. Lower pressure in these places allows the hot mantle to melt and produce magma. This rises and forms new oceanic crust and volcanoes at the plate margins. Iceland is an area that experiences this process.

At destructive plate margins, usually at oceanic boundaries such as the trenches around the Pacific Ocean, the edge of one plate is forced beneath that of another, or *subducted*. Oceanic crust is carried down into the mantle and starts to melt. It then rises and heats the overlying continental material and may cause further independent melting. These various kinds of magma reach the surface and produce the different types of volcano found around the perimeter of the Pacific and in the island arcs of Indonesia, West Indies and Japan.

Hawaii, lying in the centre of the Pacific plate, does not fit this pattern. The islands are thought to overlie a 'hot spot' or *plume* of rising mantle which provides the magma for eruptions.

Effects of volcanic activity

Volcanic activity is the main process by which material from the interior of the earth reaches the surface, and it must have contributed to the formation of the atmosphere and the oceans. Volcanic gases, for example, include carbon dioxide which is vital to life on earth. Fertile soils develop from the weathering of volcanic ash and lava, and are extensively cultivated even on the lower slopes of active volcanoes.

Crushed lavas make suitable roadstone. Pumice is used industrially and domestically as an abrasive, and, along with perlite, volcanic glass which expands when heated, for insulation in buildings. Volcanic pipes of an unusual rock, called kimberlite, are the source of diamonds, and sulphur is exploited in the volcanic areas of Japan and Sicily. Volcanic activity provides hot water for central heating in Iceland and steam-generated electricity in New Zealand, Italy and the United States.

The death and destruction inflicted by some volcanic eruptions makes the task of predicting eruptions one of real concern. The start of an eruption can be forecast fairly accurately by monitoring the temperature, pressure and composition of the gases within a volcano. Minor earth tremors, caused by movement of magma within a volcano, are recorded by seismometers positioned at selected sites, and portable machines can determine the exact location of an expected eruption. Observatories have been established on many volcanoes but it is still not possible to predict the intensity or duration of an eruption.

Left: The eruption of Eldfjell on the Icelandic island of Heimay in 1973 partly buried the town of Vestmannaeyjar in dust and ash. Volcanic areas may be quiet for many years—the only known volcano on Heimay last erupted 5,000 years ago—and then come suddenly and violently to life.

Above: The volcanic island of Surtsey appeared off Iceland on 15 November 1963. First eruptions were explosive as sea water entered the vent. When the cone was large enough to prevent this, lava flows were erupted. Surtsey was 2.3 sq km (1 sq mile) in area and 410 m (1344 ft) high by 1965.

Below: Anak Krakatoa, meaning the 'child of Krakatoa', has emerged on the site of the old island in the Sunda Strait between Sumatra and Java. Pressures from a lava pocket in the old volcano threw up a new submarine cone which reached the surface in 1928. A year later a geyser began to spout steam.

36,000 Indonesians and was recorded in the English Channel. For several years volcanic dust drifted around the earth in the upper atmosphere, causing brilliant red sunsets and reducing the earth's temperature by partly blocking the sun's rays. Recent volcanic activity has produced the tip of a new island.

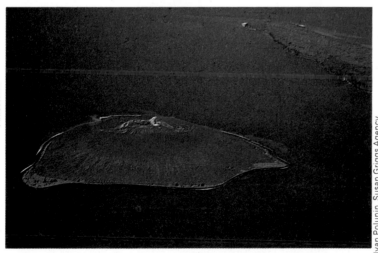

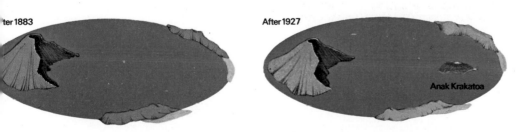

After 1883

After 1927

Anak Krakatoa

21

Mountain Building

There are two great chains of mountains on earth. One includes the South American Andes, the Rocky Mountains and other ranges encircling the Pacific; the other runs eastwards from the Alps of Southern Europe right across to the Himalayas and beyond. This system of 'linear' mountain belts appears to be unique to the planet earth.

Extending across the planet's surface for hundreds and even thousands of kilometres in continuous tracts, these mountains rise in places to peaks many kilometres above sea level. Their height means that most are snow covered. Frost-shattered fragments may break away to form jagged peaks surrounded by slopes covered in rock debris. Fast flowing streams cut gullies and gorges which are gradually widened and deepened, and may be cut still more savagely by glaciers flowing down from snow fields near the summit. Over millions of years such agents of erosion give mountains their characteristic features. Yet how did they originally form, and what forces were at work to create them?

Movements in the earth's crust

From the patterns revealed by volcanic and earthquake activity it has become clear that the earth's great mountain chains lie over unstable areas of the planet's crust. Indeed these mountains are not merely surface features, but are expressions of fundamental structures in the earth's crust. And it is this that has led scientists to regard mountain-building (known as *orogeny*) as part of an activity beginning beneath the earth's surface.

The earth can create mountains in a number of different ways, yet the great linear belts are an example of by far the most important mechanism, one which has been at work since early in the earth's history. These vast mountain chains of folded rock originate where the earth's crustal 'plates' converge, forcing layers of rock into great arcs which may rise far above sea level.

Investigation of the rocks of an 'orogenic' mountain belt like the Himalayas shows that over millions of years they have undoubtedly suffered severe distortion and displacement from their original position. The layers of sediment, deposited in the sea long ago and hardened to form sedimentary rocks, contain fossilized remains of marine animals. When these fossils are found in rock strata of mountain folds thousands of metres above sea level it is clear that astonishing forces have pushed the layers upwards. The flat and continuous layers originally formed have been shaped into huge folds, tilted into vertical layers, or broken and stacked in a series of slabs. Such was the force of compression when the Indian continental plate met the vast plate of Asia that the Himalayas were formed.

The effect of this convergence of plates does vary from place to place. For example, it is particularly where the leading edges of both plates consist of 'continental' crustal material—which is less dense than crust of 'oceanic' type—that the

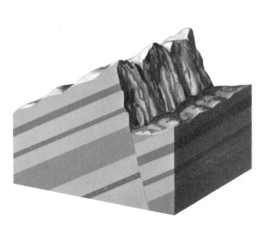

Left: Some of the world's most spectacular peaks are those formed by volcanic action. The classical shape of a volcanic cone is produced by the steady eruption of ash, pyroclasts and sticky lava from a central vent. Most volcanoes are located on the margins of the continental plates at mid-ocean ridges and deep sea trenches.

Right: The snow-capped peak of Mount Osorno reaches 2,660 metres into the South American skyline. A perfect example of a volcanic cone, Osorno is part of the Andes mountain range, formed when the Pacific plate was thrust under the South American plate.

Left: Most mountain ranges are the product of continual pushing and compression of the earth's surface. Sideways pressure on layers of sedimentary rock can produce fold mountains of a simple, open shape, as in parts of the Jura range in France and Switzerland. In more complex belts like the Alps and Himalayas, distorted folds—overturned and recumbent—are more common.

Right: The Himalayan range contains the highest peaks in the world. They are formed by the compression and uplift of a land area between the colliding mass of Asia and the subcontinent of India.

Left: Under strong compression blocks of surface rocks may fracture rather than bend, producing a fault rather than a fold. Normal faulting produces a mountain with a steep fault face raised above a plain and a gentle dip slope on the other side.

Right: The Sierra Nevadas are a good example of 'tilt block' mountains, formed by the uplift of a tilted fault block. This view shows the steep eastern face—up to 3,000 metres high—rising above the floor of the Great Basin of eastern California and western Nevada. The Sierra slope coincides with a major fault area, which includes the San Andreas fault.

Left: Some mountains are geological 'remnants' rather than 'constructions'. A mass of hard igneous rock such as granite intrudes into pre-existing rock, pushing up into the layers. Later, erosion of the softer surrounding rock leaves the igneous mass exposed as a dome or block-shaped mountain.

Right: Mighty Half Dome in the Yosemite Valley of California is a spectacular example of an intrusive mountain. Its tough granite face has resisted erosion better than the rock which once enclosed it. The sheer north-west face—now a mountaineer's delight—was carved by glaciation.

Picturepoint

Left: Mount Ararat in eastern Turkey is a volcanic cone, 5,000 metres high. It lies in a 'collision zone' where volcanic and earthquake activity are caused by collision between the African and Eurasian plates. According to Biblical legend, Noah's Ark came to rest on Mount Ararat after the great flood.

Below: The sunlit slopes of Mount Ngauruhoe in New Zealand's Tongariro National Park. The mountain is a recently active volcano, the cone surmounted by an explosion crater which is still giving off gases. Mount Ngauruhoe lies on the fringe of the great 'linear' mountain belt that encircles the Pacific.

Colorific

Below: The Elborz mountains near Teheran were formed by local tilting and faulting in an area of compression. They show a regular pattern of folding and deformation.

Below right: Diagram showing the features of a simple fold, created by horizontal pressure.

Right: Twisted layers of rock are clearly evident beneath the snow on a ridge along the western cwm of Everest, between Lhotze and Nuptse, at about 7,500 metres. These twisted strata indicate the kind of localized folding which produces minor anticline and syncline features in an area of compression.

John Cleare

Robert Harding Associates

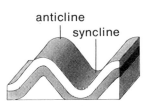

anticline

syncline

Picturepoint

Above: The uplifted fault scarp of the tilt block of the Teton range forms a majestic panorama for visitors to the Grand Teton National Park in

Wyoming, USA. Weathering processes have continually attacked the uplifted block, producing the present topography of sharp, angular peaks.

Picturepoint

Left: A view of the Yosemite Valley from 3,000 metres up. Glacial action has smoothed a rounded valley in the granite rock, about 11 km long. The natural features of the area—sculptured granite cliffs and majestic waterfalls— are typical of heavy glaciation.

Right: The massive mountain dome overlooking Narssaq Harbour in Greenland. The slightly irregular shape is due to glaciation and frost action—exposure to extremes of temperature results in the fracturing of the rock which leaves jagged outlines and slopes which may be covered in a mass of rock debris.

Picturepoint

flat lying strata symmetrical asymmetrical overturned isoclinal series recumbent

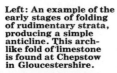
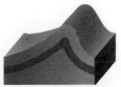

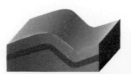

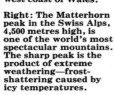

Left: An example of the early stages of folding of rudimentary strata, producing a simple anticline. This arch-like fold of limestone is found at Chepstow in Gloucestershire.

Below left: The more advanced stages of folding in which many minor anticlines and synclines occur within a larger complex anticline. This example is on Anglesey, an island off the north-west coast of Wales.

Right: The Matterhorn peak in the Swiss Alps, 4,500 metres high, is one of the world's most spectacular mountains. The sharp peak is the product of extreme weathering—frost-shattering caused by icy temperatures.

IGS

John Watney

John Cleare

forces of compression and uplift lead to formation of mountain belts. Where one of the plates consists of 'oceanic' crustal material, this may be overridden by the more buoyant continental plate, creating such features as oceanic trenches and volcanic island arcs. The Andes, the North American Cordilleras and the island arcs of Japan, the Philippines and Indonesia are products of the over-riding of the Pacific floor by the American and Asian continental plates.

The Geosyncline

Large parts of the world's orogenic mountain belts are carved from rocks which originated below the sea. Over periods of at least 100,000,000 years, marine sediments accumulated to thicknesses of ten or more kilometres on the sites of the belts. Most of these show features which indicate their accumulation in shallow seas and it is assumed that in the distant past, throughout the period of deposition, the sea-floor gradually subsided to make room for them. Such a well-defined region of long-continued subsidence of the earth's crust is called a *geosyncline*. For example, where the Appalachian Mountains (an 'orogenic' belt of mountains formed some 400 million years ago) now stand, a thick pile of sediment once lay beneath the sea. And this led two American geologists, Hall and Dana, to infer a connection between the development of a geosyncline and the subsequent operation of mountain-building forces.

The accumulation of great thicknesses of sedimentary and volcanic rocks in many such geosynclinal troughs has, however, been punctuated by phases of

crustal instability and volcanic activity. In these periods portions of the trough filling were raised above sea level and subjected to erosion. The successive layers visible today as mountain belts may therefore have gaps which reflect erosion at several different periods. Lower layers, for example, may show folds developed before the accumulation of the most recent deposits.

In many belts, the continued deposition of sediment ended with the collision of two continental plates. As a consequence, the 'geosynclinal' sea was eliminated as the layers folded upward to form the mountain belt. This mountain-building stage at the plate margin is marked by severe distortion of the deposits. Other changes are associated with the great heat generated in the active zone. For example, where rocks undergo slow deformation, and especially where they are weakened by high temperatures, they yield like plastic to give gigantic folds. Where forces uplift as well as compress the layers, sedimentary rock strata may break away and cascade down to pile up at lower levels in flat-lying or *recumbent* folds.

On the other hand, where deformation is rapid and the rocks cold or strong, fracturing of the layers is common. As a result folds may be severed from their roots and piled up again, together with slabs wrenched from the underlying basement. By all these means, the orderly layers of sedimentary rocks and lavas laid down one by one on the geosynclinal floor may be disturbed, reversed or disrupted. In the Alps, for instance, the characteristic structures are recumbent folds or thrust-slices piled one above the

Above: A view of the last 900 metres of Everest. Man's greatest mountaineering challenge, the peak was first conquered by Sir Edmund Hilary in 1953.

Below: The mechanism that is thought to have formed the Appalachian Mountains is illustrated by these six stages. (1) Some 600 million years ago the North American and African continents were parted by a spreading rift. (2) The Atlantic ocean opens up and sediments are laid down on the continental margins, their weight causing subsidence of the sea bed and the formation of *geosynclines*. (3) The ocean begins to close and a trench is formed adjacent to the North American continent as the lithosphere is re-absorbed into the earth's hot mantle. This underthrusting compresses the North American geosyncline into folds, so creating the ancient Appalachians. An upthrust of magma and volcanic activity is triggered, so creating an intrusion of hard granite and surface volcanic mountains. (4) The Atlantic is now fully closed, so compressing the geosynclines of both continents and leaving only a vertical fault line. The two continents were joined in this way between 350 and 225 million years ago. (5) About 180 million years ago the Atlantic ocean began to open again along the old fault line, new oceanic crust material being formed as the continents drifted apart. (6) Today the rate of sea-floor spreading is some three centimetres per year, and new geosynclines are thought to be forming at the margins of the continents.**

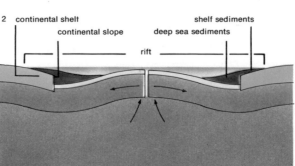

1 North America   Africa
rift

2 continental shelf   shelf sediments
continental slope   deep sea sediments
rift

3 granite
trench

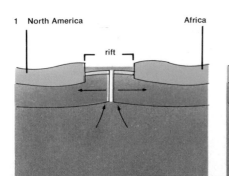
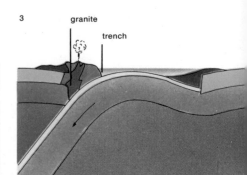

TYPES OF FAULTS

unfaulted blocks   normal   reverse   strike-slip   oblique-slip   hinge

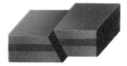

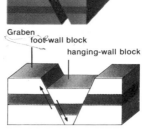

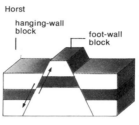

Left: A faulted anticline of shales and sandstones near Saundersfoot in Pembrokeshire. The shale core has been eroded, leaving a cave.

Below: Close-up of a section of rock from Trevaunance Cove, in Cornwall, showing small faults in layers of grit and shale.

Right: A rift valley, or *graben*, is formed when the centre of an anticline slips down along fault lines.

Below right: A block mountain, or *horst*, is produced by a reverse movement—the middle block is forced up along fault lines. Erosion tends to round the rock surfaces.

Left: The Grampian mountains in Scotland, an ancient, heavily-eroded mountain area. But crustal movements are still taking place—as erosion lessens a mountain's mass, it triggers movements to maintain a balance between the mountain's height and the depth of its 'roots' which lie in the molten mantle.

other.

Intense heat in the mountain-building belt results in two things: firstly, modifications, or the *metamorphism*, of the deformed rocks themselves; secondly, the rise of magma which is generated by partial melting of rocks at great depths. Chemical reactions during metamorphism lead to new minerals such as micas, garnet and hornblende. Different degrees of metamorphism also produce different rock types. For example, low intensities may produce slates, while higher intensities produce schists and gneisses whose parallel crystalline structure is related to the direction of the deforming forces.

The rise of granite is the dominant form of igneous activity during the mountain-building stage. The granite magma is derived largely from melting of rock near the base of the continental crust. Intrusive masses of up to several hundred kilometres in length occupy much of the interior of the Andes and the western Cordilleras of North America. Where one crustal plate over-rides another in a collision zone, magma may rise to the surface to build volcanic island arcs or volcanic mountain belts.

Mountain roots
The crumpling and disruption of rocks in a mountain-building belt do not only lead to a shortening of the belt, but also, in many instances, to a thickening of the crustal layer forming the belt. Like an iceberg in water, the mountain belt rises to a height above sea level which is balanced by a 'root' projecting deep into the denser material of the earth's mantle. This adjustment is the final stage in the mountain-building cycle, and is known as

the *isostatic* stage.

Mountain massifs may be the product of forces other than the collision of crustal plates. Blocks of the earth's crust for example, may rise vertically along deep faults in response to abnormal temperatures at great depth. At first this kind of block-uplift tends to give level-topped plateaux. But the effects of erosion on the plateaux, and especially at the boundary faults, may transform them into spectacular landscapes. The Colorado Plateau in the US and the Drakensberg Mountains of South Africa, are both the result of such forces at work.

Volcanic mountains, on the other hand, are built up by the extrusion of lava and ash from volcanic vents or fissures. The symmetry of the volcano depends on the style of volcanic activity. For example, eruptions from a single centre give conical mountains; eruptions through cracks or fissures in the earth's surface result in irregular ridges or lines of cones. Yet volcanic activity is so commonly associated with deep fracturing that the resulting mountains may reflect several processes. In the African Rift Valley, for instance, central volcanic cones such as Mounts Kenya, Elgon and Kilimanjaro rise in a highland plateaux which is the result of the uplift of a block along deep fault lines.

Erosion over millions of years
The emergence of all new mountain massifs, whatever their origin, is accompanied by intense erosion. Millions of years pass before a new mountain range emerges and long before it has ceased to rise the rock is subject to heavy erosion. The Brahmaputra and Indus rivers, for

example, which cross the Himalayas from sources in the Tibetan plateau, were able to deepen their valleys at the same time as the mountains rose, and so maintained their southward course to the sea. Continued denudation by the forces of erosion not only lowers the general level but also ultimately flattens out the topographical irregularities of the surface. The end-product may be a *peneplain* of low relief and broad contours which exposes rocks and structures originally formed many kilometres below the surface.

The removal of rock-material as a result of erosion, however, also triggers off new crustal movements. This is because the isostatic balance is upset; the equilibrium is restored by a further rise of the eroded regions, which in turn stimulates further erosion. Many mountain terrains have been 'rejuvenated' more than once by this and other mechanisms. The Grampian Highlands of Scotland, for example, are the product of a mountain building belt 400 million years old which was rejuvenated comparatively recently. Successive cycles of erosion have revealed the roots of the old belt, made of deformed metamorphic rocks.

Indeed the forces which create and destroy mountains are at work all the time. Although uplift may occur at the rate of a metre or more in 100 years, erosion begins very rapidly, only slowing down as the elevation of the land diminishes. No highland area on the earth's surface can be regarded as 'stable'. All will change in some degree within a matter of a few hundred years. Within a hundred million years, the earth's surface will again be transformed.

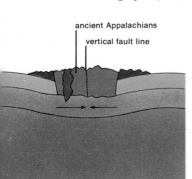

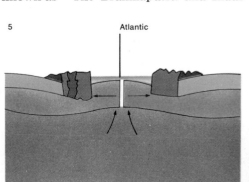

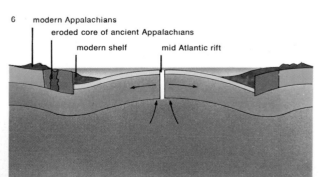

ancient Appalachians
vertical fault line

5   Atlantic   6   modern Appalachians
eroded core of ancient Appalachians
modern shelf   mid Atlantic rift

Minerals

Minerals are the building bricks of rocks. They are the basis of every rock except those of organic origin, like coal and chalk. A mineral is defined as any solid substance with a definite chemical composition occuring naturally in the earth, but which is not derived from plants or animals. By popular definition, anything that is mined is called a mineral, but the fossil fuels—coal, natural oil and gas—are excluded from the geological definition as they are formed from the remains of plant and animal life. One usual exception to the rule that a mineral must be solid is quicksilver, which is mercury in its native, liquid state.

Just as rocks are made up of combinations of minerals, the minerals themselves are composed of different fusions of chemical elements. Some minerals, however, such as gold or naturally-occurring copper and sulphur, contain only one element. The most common elements found in minerals, in descending order of occurrence, are oxygen, silicon, aluminium, iron, magnesium, calcium, potassium, and sodium. These are only eight of the 90 naturally-occurring elements, but they make up nearly 99 per cent by weight of the earth's crust. Oxygen and silicon alone account for nearly three quarters of the crust's constituents.

Secrets of atomic structure

The smallest particle of an element is a single atom. Examination of most minerals reveals that the atoms of the constituent elements have arranged themselves into a distinct and regular three-dimensional framework. These frameworks, known as *crystals* are geometric forms with their flat faces arranged symmetrically. Most minerals have this ordered atomic structure and are termed *crystalline*.

Under certain conditions that allow a crystalline mineral to grow without interference, it may form regular-shaped crystals. Silica, for example, may crystallize into perfect trigonal crystals of quartz. But if the growing crystals interfere with each other, then they may be distorted into mis-shapen grains of quartz which do not display regular crystal faces. Alternatively silica may develop into chalcedony, a *cryptocrystalline* mineral in which clusters of crystals are invisible except under the most powerful magnification. Finally, silica may take the form of opal, an *amorphous* or non-crystalline mineral, in which there is no regular arrangement of atoms. Each of these different manifestations of silica has a different atomic structure—directly affecting the crystal structure and thus the shape of each mineral.

How minerals are classified

Crystalline structure is an important clue in distinguishing one mineral from another. There are seven basic shapes of structural unity, and this gives rise to seven categories or *crystal systems*. Each mineral crystallizes in a particular system and can be identified accordingly. For example, a diamond belongs to the cubic system, whereas a ruby has a hexagonal crystal system.

Minerals display a dazzling variety of

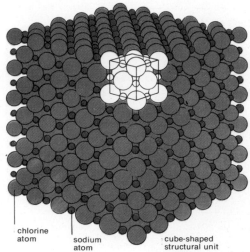

chlorine atom   sodium atom   cube-shaped structural unit

Above: Common table salt (sodium chloride) consists of finely ground crystals of a mineral called halite. When a crystal is magnified 100,000,000 times, its atomic structure is revealed. The large green circles represent chlorine atoms; the smaller red ones are sodium atoms. A 'detail' from the atomic structure model (right) outlines the molecular building block, or structural unit of the crystal. In this case it is the shape of a perfect cube.

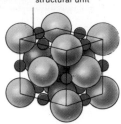

Below: A scanning electron micrograph of a common salt crystal, magnified 800 times. Even in small quantities the cubic crystal structure is recognizable.

Alan Windle

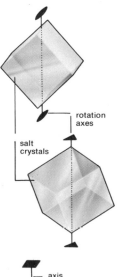

rotation axes

salt crystals

axis

crystal

An important clue in identifying one mineral from another is symmetry—a property which allows a crystal to be spun on an axis and to appear identical twice or more before it has rotated one full turn. The number of axes of symmetry in a crystal are then counted. The cube of a common salt crystal, for example, reveals three axes of symmetry.

Top left: Rotated on an axis taken through the centres of diagonally opposite edges, the cube appears identical twice in a complete rotation of 360°. This is termed a two-fold axis of symmetry. There are six such axes on a cube.

Centre left: On an axis taken through the opposite corners, the cube looks the same three times in a complete rotation, and reveals four three-fold axes.

Left: In the same way there are three four-fold axes of symmetry emerging through the centres of the faces of a cube. Minerals can be categorized into seven distinct systems determined by their crystal symmetry.

CRYSTAL SYSTEM	STRUCTURAL UNIT
	AXES OF CRYSTAL SYMMETRY UNIQUE TO EACH SYSTEM

CUBIC
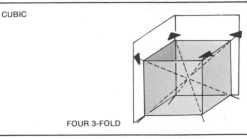
FOUR 3-FOLD

TETRAGONAL
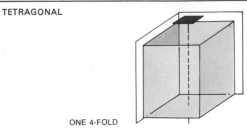
ONE 4-FOLD

ORTHORHOMBIC
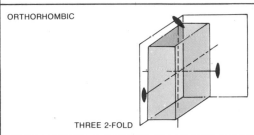
THREE 2-FOLD

MONOCLINIC
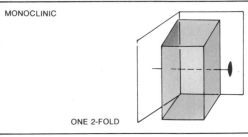
ONE 2-FOLD

TRICLINIC
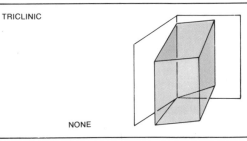
NONE

HEXAGONAL
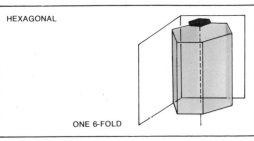
ONE 6-FOLD

TRIGONAL
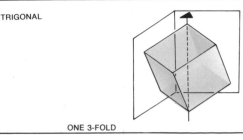
ONE 3-FOLD

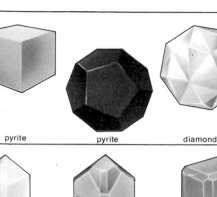
pyrite

pyrite

diamond

1. A mineral belonging to the cubic system is pyrite which occurs with either 12 faces (left in photograph) or as a cube with six faces (right). Other examples of this system are diamond, galena and garnet.

ircon

rutile

idocrase

2. Wulfenite is included in the tetragonal system and has fine orangish-yellow crystals. The mineral is found in zones of lead deposits. Its lustre varies but it leaves a distinctive white streak.

rolite

baryto

olivine (peridot)

3. Topaz crystallizes as orthorhombic crystals. This attractive gemstone is typically yellow but can also be colourless, skyblue, or even pink if subjected to heat. However, its streak is always colourless.

pyroxene

amphibole

orthoclase

4. Orthoclase occurs as white, pink, yellow or brown coloured monoclinic crystals. Most of the common rock-forming minerals are in the system. Orthoclase is important as a constituent of igneous rocks.

uoise

5. A fine example of a stone in the triclinic system is turquoise although it rarely forms perfect crystals. Normally it is found as an amorphous mineral. Two examples of polished turquoise are shown.

high quartz

corundum

6. Beryl (below) forms emerald when shaded green by impurities of chromium. Ruby and sapphire are types of corundum which also crystallize as hexagonal minerals, as do certain types of quartz (above).

lcite

tourmaline

7. Herkimer quartz (left) is a trigonal crystal of gem quality. Quartz crystals occur in two systems and some authorities consider the hexagonal and trigonal systems as one. Dolomite (right) also occurs in two systems.

The symmetry of the structural unit controls the symmetry of the crystal structure. Since the structure governs the crystal shape, the symmetry of the whole crystal is an exact indication of the shape of the structural unit. The cubic structural units of the mineral pyrite can build two crystal shapes. In both cases the symmetry requirements —four 3-fold axes— are satisfied.

Above and below left: Cube-shaped iron pyrite (iron sulphide).

Above and below right: An eight-sided pyrite crystal, galena (lead sulphide).

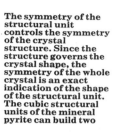

Paul Brierley

colour, which is determined both by their structure and by the presence of impurities. But colour is not always a reliable clue to identity. Many minerals are commonly white or colourless and others, such as quartz or calcite, may occur in a whole range of colours.

The most reliable colour indicator is obtained by scraping the mineral against unglazed porcelain. This leaves a finely powdered trail, the colour of which is the mineral's *streak*. In this way, for example, crystals of haematite, which have a red streak, can be distinguished from those of magnetite which leave a black streak—although the crystals appear as the same colour.

The way in which a specimen affects light is another important clue to its identity. Minerals reflect light in different ways; this characteristic, known as *lustre*, ranges from the dull quality of clay to the adamantine lustre of diamond.

Hardness and *specific gravity* are two other reliable diagnostic properties. Hardness is actually rated in terms of the resistance of a mineral to scratching, arranged in ascending order from talc, which is easily crushed by a finger-nail, to diamond, the hardest mineral known to man. The hardness of a mineral is measured in terms of Mohs' Scale—an arbitrary scale with very irregular intervals, devised in 1822 by Mohs, an Austrian mineralogist.

The specific gravity of a mineral is the ratio between its weight and the weight of an equal volume of water. Taking the specific gravity of water as 1.0, the great majority of minerals have a specific gravity ranging between 2.2 and 3.2. Only those minerals which are as light as graphite (1.9) or as heavy as gold (15.0 to 20.0 according to purity) can be distinguished by their specific gravity when held in the hand.

The world's great mineral deposits

The geological processes in which minerals are formed determines both the distribution and the type of mineral deposits. *Magmatic* minerals are those

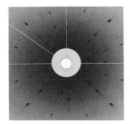

Above: The action of a crystal on X-rays is an important means of mineral identification. This X-ray diffraction photograph of common salt shows how the atoms deflect and reflect X-rays; the 4-fold rotation symmetry shown by the pattern of spots indicates that the atoms are packed in a cubic arrangement.

Paul Brierley

Paul Brierley

Left: A glowing piece of fluorite demonstrates the property of fluorescence. This refers to the way particular specimens of certain minerals emit visible light while bombarded with invisible radiation such as ultra-violet or X-rays. Fluorite, calcite and diamond all have this property.

Right: The vast salt deposits in the Danakil region of Ethiopia. This is an area where hot springs bring up minerals in solution —solid deposits are left behind when the solution evaporates.

Below: The 'Big Hole' at Kimberley in South Africa—one of the world's richest diamond mines.

George Gerster/John Hillelson

fracture   cleavage

Left: The atoms of the mineral mica are strongly bonded in layers, but between the layers the bonds are very weak. The crystal will thus split smoothly between the layers— this is known as its cleavage tendency. Where the bonding is strong, across the horizontal layers, it fractures irregularly.

Paul Brierley

Left: A spectacular formation of magnetite, a common example of a magnetic mineral—one which is strongly attracted by an iron magnet. Magnetite also has the property of exerting and retaining its own magnetic field; in the form of 'lodestone' it was used by the ancients as a compass.

ZEFA

Right: A number of diamond stones can be polished simultaneously using modern methods. The extreme hardness of diamonds gives them an important industrial role, in glass-cutting tools, rock-drilling and cutting equipment.

Below: Flint hand axes, some 250,000 years old, were one of man's first uses of minerals.

De Beers

Michael Holford

which crystallize from molten magma as it cools to form igneous rock. The first minerals to crystallize in the cooling period—silicates with a high proportion of iron and magnesium—are free to grow without interference and form well-shaped crystals. For example, the important mineral chromite, used for toughening steel, was concentrated in enormous quantities in the huge Bushveld igneous complex of South Africa by this process.

As magma cools further, more minerals are formed until only a little 'residual liquid' is left between grains of rock. This liquid may be rich in volatile components and in elements that form valuable minerals, and may either be trapped in cavities known as *geodes, drusies* or *vugs* in which beautifully shaped crystals grow in towards the centre, or be violently squeezed out by pressure from solidifying minerals into cracks and fissures in surrounding rock. There it solidifies to form *hydrothermal veins* in which mis-shapen crystals of quartz grow, along with a wide variety of other minerals. These are commonly-mined deposits, as they often form at shallow depths.

Mineral deposits may also be of *sedimentary* or *metamorphic* origin. Deep down in the earth's crust, or near hot magma, metamorphic minerals are formed from pre-existing minerals in solid rock by intense heat and pressure. Most sedimentary rocks are the product of minerals weathered by wind, water and chemical action from igneous and metamorphic rocks and are consolidated in layers, such as shale and calcite-rich limestone. Other minerals, such as rock salts and gypsum, are *evaporites*, caused by evaporation in shallow seas or lakes.

1. As magma cools and forms igneous rock, minerals also form. Fine crystallized minerals, such as quartz, amethyst, galena and tourmaline, as well as feldspar and pyrite, occur in rock cavities called drusies, vugs and geodes. Diamonds from the Kimberley mine come from Kimberlite, an igneous rock.

2. River alluvial deposits have sometimes provided prospectors with easy pickings. Precious stones and metals may accumulate in places from the weathering and erosion of different types of rocks. Panning and dredging are used to sort out the potentially rich deposits from other sediments.

3. Limestone altered by heat-metamorphism and igneous gases is an important source of commercially valuable ores like copper, gold, 'fools gold' (pyrite), iron, lead and zinc.
4. Where heat has metamorphosed shale, minerals found include garnet, chiastolite, biotite and cordierite.

5. Hydrothermal veins are heavily mined for their rich supplies of gold and silver, as well as the silver- and lead-bearing galena, gems such as opals, emeralds and tourmaline, and sulphide minerals like pyrite and chalcopyrite. Secondary minerals like copper-bearing azurite and malachite occur.

HOW AND WHERE MINERALS OCCUR

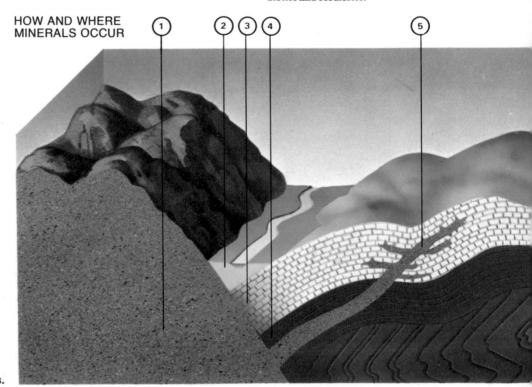

Right: A variety of agate known as Mexican Lace, typical of the fantastic and colourful structures which make agate popular as an ornamental stone. Agate is in fact a variety of chalcedony, a mixture of quartz and opal.
Left: Panning gravel for diamonds in Borneo, a prospecting method still used today.

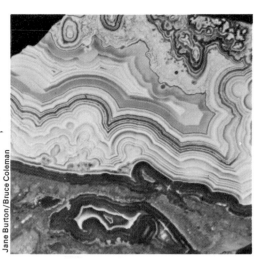

Left: An asbestos suit in action in an industrial test. As well as withstanding heat, asbestos has a high electrical resistance and is immune to chemical action. Chrysotile (above) is one of a number of minerals which occur as long fibrous crystals which can be spun to form asbestos.

Above: A crystal of diamond, as it occurs in Kimberlite, the igneous rock which forms the famous South African 'diamond pipes'.
Left: The breath-taking Kohinoor diamond, originally found in India. It was cut in 1852 and is now part of the British crown jewels. This is one of the world's largest diamonds.

MOHS SCALE OF MINERAL HARDNESS

HARDNESS	MINERAL	TEST
1	talc	can be scratched by fingernail
2	gypsum	
3	calcite	
4	fluorite	can be scratched with steel point
5	apatite	
6	orthoclase	
7	quartz	will scratch glass easily
8	topaz	
9	corundum	
10	diamond	will scratch any other material

6. Beach sand and gravel retain deposits eroded from rocks and sorted by the continual action of waves. For example, chalcedony and calcite are eroded from limestone and sandstone, and pyrite and marcasite from shale. Some normally rare minerals like monazite may be concentrated here.

7. Ancient metamorphic rock, subject to great pressure and change, is the setting for garnet, asbestos, talc, serpentine, turquoise and some emeralds.
8. Sedimentary strata contain large deposits. Dolomite is an example of a constituent of many sedimentary rocks. Others are gypsum and halite.

Some rare minerals are very hard and have an unusually attractive colour and lustre. Those of greatest rarity, and therefore of greatest monetary value, are the precious gemstones, diamond, emerald, ruby and sapphire. Platinum, gold and silver, the precious metals, have also acquired great value because of their beauty, rarity and durability. These three metals together with copper and iron are the only metals to occur as *native*, or uncombined, elements in nature.

The precious minerals are both hard and, except for silver, chemically unreactive. When rocks bearing minerals of high specific gravity are exposed to weathering, the lighter material is gradually eroded away while the heavier, chemically stable minerals are concentrated in *placer* deposits.

Such deposits are called *residual* if they have remained at or near their original position, *eluvial* if they have been concentrated by rain-wash and gravity, and *alluvial* if they have been formed by streams. The famous deposits which sparked off the 1849 gold rush to California were alluvial placers. The discovery of diamond-bearing gravels caused a similar great rush to Lichtenburg in South West Africa in the 1920s.

Finding precious stones is still largely a matter of luck. Most occur in close association with particular types of rock, but suitable geological locations only rarely contain precious minerals and only exceptionally are these of gem quality. The most productive diamond mines are at Kimberley in South Africa, where the stones crystallized in an igneous rock called kimberlite. Other major producers are Angola and Zaire.

The weight of precious minerals is measured in *carats*, one carat weighing a mere 200 milligrams. Stones of gem quality are closely inspected for flaws and weaknesses, before being carefully cut and used in jewelry. The emerald, for example, owes its great value to the rarity of flawless crystals. This dark green variety of the mineral beryl occurs in highly metamorphosed shales called mica-schists. The finest emeralds come from near Bogota in Columbia, but other important deposits have been found in the Ural Mountains in the Soviet Union and in Austria, Norway and Australia.

The world's supply of fine rubies has come largely from the Mogok mines in Upper Burma, where they occur in metamorphosed limestone. The presence of minute quantities of chromium causes the red colour of ruby in the mineral corundum. Another gem variety of the colourless corundum is the sapphire, tinted blue by iron and titanium impurities. Fine sapphires are found in gravels in Sri Lanka, Thailand and Kashmir.

Technological progress in exploiting minerals has determined the growth of civilization. The Stone Age began when the first crude but handy tools were fashioned from flint. From the Copper Age—when man first discovered a method of isolating metal from its natural mineral state—through the successive Bronze, Iron and Atomic Ages, man's activities and well-being have been affected by his increasingly sophisticated use of earth materials. The industrial and technological revolution which has reshaped society in every continent relies massively on a continued supply and large-scale exploitation of the earth's mineral wealth.

Metal Ores

The search for metals dates back almost to the beginning of civilization. Ores are minerals from which metal can be extracted, yet the first metal to be recognized by man was undoubtedly gold—which occurs naturally in a metal state and needs no extraction. Unaffected by weathering and other chemical processes, gold occurs in veins in rocks or as flakes and nuggets in river gravels. Gold was prized by the ancients for its unrivalled colour and lustre and for the ease with which it could be worked into objects of beauty and value. The Egyptians believed that gold had divine significance and established a state industry to exploit the metal over 4,000 years ago.

The Middle East also saw the beginnings of *metallurgy*, the extraction of metals from their ores. Archaeological excavations in Iran and Afghanistan have revealed that around 5,000 BC copper was being extracted from its easily-smelted ore, the beautiful emerald-green mineral malachite. The Greeks and Romans controlled extensive mining industries and their empires owed much of their pre-eminence to their wealth in metals.

In response to the needs of the technological revolution came a more scientific understanding of the formation of ores and their distribution patterns. Geologists now realize that nearly all the metals used in industry are very scarce. Copper forms 0.007 per cent of the earth's crust, tin 0.004 per cent, lead 0.0016 per cent, uranium 0.0004 per cent, silver 0.00001 per cent and gold a mere 0.0000005 per cent.

Usable ore deposits are therefore extremely rare features because they require a concentration of metals to as much as a million times their average distribution. There are two main processes by which ore deposits are formed. They may be concentrated within rocks formed by cooling magma or deposited by surface processes of erosion.

When magma cools slowly, insulated by the thickness of surrounding rocks, the minerals crystallize out in a particular order. Some minerals separate out early and sink to the bottom of the magma to form *magmatic segregations* such as the enormous quantities of chromite found in southern Africa. The remaining liquid then becomes more concentrated in other ore minerals and contains large amounts of dissolved gases and water vapour. At a late stage of the cooling process, the liquid may squeeze into cracks and fissures in the igneous rock to form *pegmatite* deposits.

The crystallizing minerals of pegmatite may grow very large. In the Black Hills of South Dakota, USA, for instance, one crystal of the lithium-aluminium mineral spodumene measuring over 15 metres in length and weighing over 90 tonnes was taken out of the pegmatite mine. Many of the rarer and more exotic minerals are found in pegmatites, including monazite, an ore of the radioactive metal thorium.

The solutions remaining in the late stages of separation are under great pressure and are chemically highly reactive. As they stream into the surrounding rocks they may react with them and deposit the metals they hold in solution as *pneumatolytic* mineral deposits. Deposits

Paul Brierley

Above: A polished example of malachite. This beautiful emerald-green mineral is often a result of secondary enrichment. Metallic copper was extracted from this easily-smelted ore as long ago as 5000BC.

RTZ

RTZ

IGS

Above: Bauxite (top) is the only important ore of aluminium. The rich specimen of copper ore (above) came from the Palabora mine in South Africa.

Above right: Dark red crystals of cinnabar, the ore of mercury. The white mass of crystalline calcite (right) is rich in gold flakes.

Above: These copper ingots, probably used as a trading currency, came from the oldest known shipwreck, dated 1000 BC, off the coast of Turkey.

Below: Geophysical techniques are used in the search for ores. The operator in this crew using a portable ground system carries a coil. This measures the responses to signals from an electromagnetic source.

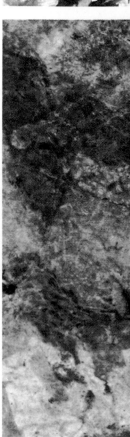

IGS

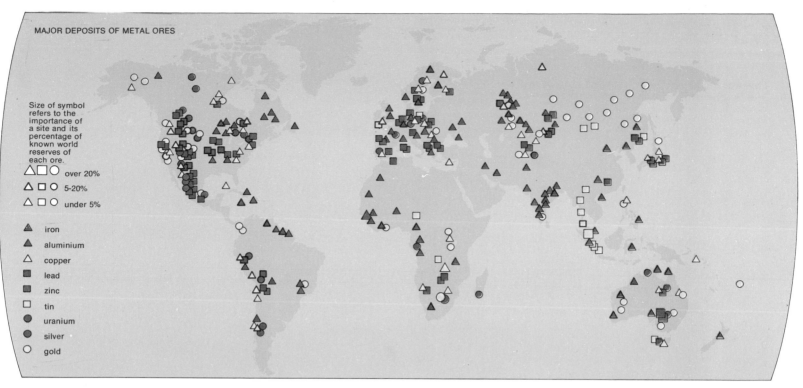

MAJOR DEPOSITS OF METAL ORES

Size of symbol refers to the importance of a site and its percentage of known world reserves of each ore.

△ □ ○ over 20%
△ □ ○ 5-20%
△ □ ○ under 5%

▲ iron
▲ aluminium
△ copper
■ lead
■ zinc
□ tin
● uranium
● silver
○ gold

Above: The world map indicates the known distribution of major metal ore deposits. There are several thousand minerals but only about a hundred are of economic value. Distribution and production of the most important metal ores are detailed (right).

Below: This spectacular photograph of the southern half of Rhodesia was taken at a height of 500 miles from an orbiting NASA satellite. The picture emphasizes certain bands of the light spectrum and reveals many large-scale geological features unrecognizable on the ground. The long green strip is the Great Dyke, a major source of chromite ore.

Iron is the fourth most plentiful element in the earth's crust and rich ores are widely spread. This is fortunate for the world uses over 800 million tonnes annually. USSR, USA, Australia and Brazil produce the most.

Aluminium is the most abundant metal in the earth's crust, but production is only 15 million tonnes, mostly from USA, USSR, Japan, Canada and Norway.

Copper production is some 6.6 million tonnes a year. Two-thirds comes from Chile, Zambia, Zaire and Peru whose economies largely depend on copper.

Tin is mined in large quantities in only a few areas in Asia, Africa and Bolivia. Low output—under 200,000 tonnes—makes tin an expensive metal.

Lead and **Zinc** usually occur together. Lead production is some 4 million tonnes annually, mostly from USA, USSR, Canada and Australia. The 6 million tonnes of zinc come mainly from the same four countries.

Gold is associated with South Africa which produces two-thirds of the world total of less than 1,500 tonnes. Other major sources are USSR and Canada.

Silver is also valuable but less rare. Leading producers are Mexico and Peru followed by USSR, Canada and USA. Annual supply is under 1,000 tonnes.

Uranium ore of a high-grade is of limited supply. Estimated consumption is 30,000 tonnes a year. Rich deposits occur in Canada, Australia and Africa.

of the tin ore cassiterite in Cornwall in southwest England, once a major source of the metal, are of this type.

The final stage of the formation of ore deposits of magmatic origin involves the watery hot, liquid residues called *hydrothermal* solutions. Under the right conditions, these solutions can move great distances and, being chemically and physically so different from the rocks in their path, they react with them to deposit their load of ore minerals. In cavities and fissures, *lodes* and *veins* are formed, while in the minute spaces between the grains of rocks, *impregnations* result.

Hydrothermal deposits are classified according to their temperature of formation. The Morro Velho gold mine in Brazil, still worked after two centuries of mining, is an example of the highest temperature deposits which formed nearest to the magma source. This is known because some of the minerals accompanying the gold only form at high temperatures.

Many of the world's great copper ore deposits are considered to have formed at a more moderate temperature. The enormous copper deposits found in the geologically-young mountain chains of the Andes, for example, are typically

great masses of igneous rock peppered through with copper minerals. The world's largest copper mine is at Chuquicamata, some 3,000 metres up in the Andes. The richest mercury mine in the world is at Almaden in Spain. This is an example of the coolest hydrothermal deposits, usually formed at shallow depths.

The second major group of mineral deposits includes those formed by sedimentary processes. The action of rivers, seas and wind on rocks gradually wears them down and the heavier, ore minerals become concentrated together to produce deposits, such as the beach sand deposits along the eastern coastline of Australia, mined for titanium and zirionium.

Sedimentary deposits have also been formed by chemical or organic action. Many important iron ore deposits, such as the ironstones of the English Midlands and of Alsace-Lorraine in France, were formed by the action of acidic water on iron-bearing rocks.

More often, the chemical action of weathering produces new minerals. Under intense tropical weathering conditions, clays are broken down to leave their constituent aluminium minerals. The extensive layers of bauxite (aluminium oxide combined with water), like those

Left: Sinking a shaft at a diamond mine in Cape Province, South Africa. The deepest shafts extend over 3 km (2 miles) down into the earth at the Witwatersrand gold mines. Problems of water pumping, intense heat (rock temperatures increase 1°C for every 60 metres in depth) and high humidity have to be overcome before mining is possible.

Below: The gold mine at West Driefontein in South Africa is one of the world's largest. The tower on the right lies over the shaft. Winding gear hauls the skips of ore to the surface. The ore is then crushed at the plant in the centre and gold extracted. Waste is carried away by conveyor belt.

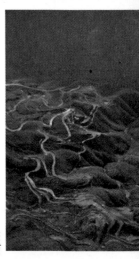

Above: The open-cast Toquepala copper mine in the Peruvian Andes. The open-cast method is suitable for mining large tonnages of low grade ore. First the barren rock or over-burden is removed and then each terrace or bench is mined back into the sides of the pit. After blasting, the ore is scooped up with mechanical shovels into waiting trucks. Ores with as little as 0.3% copper—once rejected as waste—can now be profitably mined.

Right: The residual deposits of gernierite on the Pacific island of New Caledonia form one of the world's most valuable reserves of nickel. It is mined by an open-cast method called strip-mining.

found in Jamaica which built up in this way, form residual deposits of virtually the only ore of aluminium.

Ore deposits, like other rocks, are also subject to chemical weathering at their surface outcrops. Water percolating through rocks often contains acid which attacks the ore and forms a metal-bearing solution. *Secondary enrichment* is the term applied to ore deposits carried downward in solution and later solidified in rich concentrations.

Exploration for the world's deposits
Many of the world's major ore fields have been discovered by chance. The great nickel deposits of Sudbury, Ontario, were found accidentally in the 1880s by workmen on the Canadian Pacific railway. Before the development of modern ex-

ploration techniques, minerals were located by prospecting. This involved searching directly for ore deposits on the surface, as in gold-panning, or indirectly by looking for the tell-tale signs of buried ore deposits. These signs include the *gossans* or 'iron hats' of rusty, spongy rock which sometimes cap sulphide ore deposits, or the staining of rocks by traces of the brightly coloured minerals of some metals.

Modern exploration involves searching an area in a much more elaborate way. Mining companies spend millions of pounds every year on exploration, with only very small chances of success. It has been estimated that perhaps one in a thousand prospects examined ever leads to a major ore discovery and an eventually productive mine.

Exploration usually follows a set sequence. First, a large area is selected because the right rock types and structure exist for a particular type of ore deposit. For example, rock fractures such as joints or faults may provide channels of easy access for metal-bearing hydrothermal solutions. At each stage in his exploration the geologist will build up knowledge of the type and distribution of rocks in the area by making geological maps. Here, he may be aided by aerial photographs. By careful interpretation, an enormous amount of information can be gained about the rocks and structure of the area which would otherwise take a great deal of time and work on the ground to obtain. A development of this technique on an even greater scale is the use of satellite photographs.

RTZ

Colorific

Above: Most of the world's tin is mined from alluvial deposits of cassiterite (tin oxide) in South-East Asia. This dredger operating in Malaysia slowly works up and down a shallow lake. It is fitted with a large bucket-wheel which scoops up the tin-bearing gravels from the bottom. Malaysia is the world's largest tin producer.

Below: Molten gold poured from the furnace cascades into a set of moulds. After cooling, these ingots contain almost 99% pure gold but they are then even further refined to extract some of the valuable by-product metals. The gold in this picture was originally dispersed through many tonnes of rocks.

Gold generally occurs as the native metal, often mixed with silver and other precious minerals. Probably no metal has had more influence on the economics, politics and history of man than gold. Its principal use has been as a backing for currency but sizeable amounts go into jewellery.

Paul Brierley

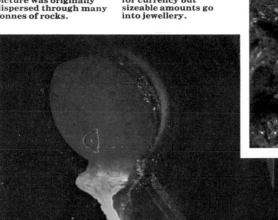

Consolidated Gold Fields

Right: The tough shell of an Apollo spacecraft and the complex equipment carried are made of a variety of metals. Aluminium alloys for the hull are toughened with small amounts of other metals to enable it to withstand great heat. Tiny quantities of gold are used in some electronic components.

Above: This specimen of meteoric iron was found at Krasnoyarsk in Siberia. Meteorites are material from outer space which have broken through the earth's atmosphere to fall on the earth's surface. They provide important clues to geologists of material and metals that exist on other planets.

Right: Copper is an excellent conductor of electricity and some 60% of all copper extracted goes to the electrical industry. Several kilometres of copper wire were used in this modern telephone exchange system. Copper is also an essential ingredient of the alloys brass and bronze.

BASF

Direct geological observations are supplemented by the techniques of geochemistry and geophysics. Geochemistry utilizes the fact that traces of the metals in minerals can work their way to the surface, carried there by the water which circulates through the rocks. These metals then become dispersed in the soils carried into the sediment of streams and rivers or are even taken up by trees and plants. Geophysics depends on the fact that the physical properties of concentrations of ore minerals are measurably different from those of surrounding rocks. Instruments have been developed to detect the minutely different electrical, magnetic and gravitational response of ore bodies.

Both geochemistry and geophysics can only give a hint of what lies beneath the surface. Many features other than ore deposits can give rise to false indications and the real test of whether an ore deposit exists is to probe beneath the surface. The most widely used technique is *diamond drilling*. The cutting action of the rotating diamond-tipped drill bit produces a cylindrical *core* of rock. This is hauled up at intervals and examined.

Drilling can provide the first direct evidence of ore minerals. Using a grid pattern of drill holes over an area containing a deep-seated deposit, it is possible to get an estimate of a deposit's shape, size and grade of the ore even before the first tunnel is driven into the deposit.

Detailed exploration work provides enough information about the ore deposit for an entire modern mining operation to be planned and designed several years before mining actually starts. Advances in mining technology have meant that very low grade ores can be worked economically, provided the tonnages mined are sufficiently large. The bulk of the major, large-tonnage, new mines brought into production are enormous quarrying operations called *open cast*.

For ores deposited in veins or narrow layers, as well as for those lying too deep or at too steep an angle, underground mining methods have to be used. Shafts are sunk and horizontal tunnels driven at different levels into the ore deposit. The deposit is then explored from subsidiary tunnels. Alluvial deposits which are not amenable to either underground or open cast mining are extracted by dredging. For example, large dredgers scoop up tin-bearing gravels in lakes in Malaysia.

Coal

Coal is a unique deposit. No other rock (for coal is as much a rock in the geological sense as sandstone, limestone or granite) has played such an important role in the development of major industrial countries. Without coal, many modern technologies would be impossible, or prohibitively expensive. For example, coal is not only a fuel, but also—in the form of coke—an essential ingredient of steel. In addition, through making coke, many useful chemical by-products are generated.

The formation of coal

Coal is formed from the compacted and deeply buried remains of trees and plants which grew in forests millions of years ago. It is usually found in layers, or seams, each covering a large area, often hundreds of square kilometres, and ranging from one or two centimetres to several metres thick.

The oldest coal occurs in rocks of the Upper Devonian period, some 360 million years old, and is found subsequently in rocks of all ages up to the Tertiary period, which began 70 million years ago. However, most coals of economic importance were formed in the latter part of the Carboniferous period (the name means coal-bearing) some 265-290 million years ago. In this period conditions were just right for the prolific growth of forests, whose later burial led to the formation of the coalfields of North America, Europe and USSR. The climate was tropical and the trees grew in extensive swamps similar to the present-day jungles in such places as the Amazon basin and the Irrawaddy Delta of Burma.

Under these conditions, growth is very rapid. Dead trees and plant debris falling into the swamps quickly become water-logged, and accumulate on the bottom. The stagnant swamp waters contain little oxygen, inhibiting the action of bacteria which would normally cause the vegetation to decay. Instead, the leaves and other soft parts gradually turn into a dark, jelly-like *humus*. This impregnates the harder, more woody plant debris until the end result is a layer of peat. (In present day swamps, peat layers 10 m (30 ft) thick have been found.) This is the first stage in the development of true coal. During peat formation, the weight of the upper layers compacts the lower layers, squeezing out some of the water. Chemical reactions accompany this compaction and result in the gradual enrichment of the peat with carbon. At the same time *methane*, or marsh-gas, is released.

To turn peat into coal, it must be buried and compacted still further beneath a thick pile of sediments. The consequent increase in pressure and slight rise in temperature results in progressive chemical changes. Water, methane, and other gases (known as *volatiles*) are further driven off and increasing carbon enrichment occurs until, ultimately, coal is formed. Such a decrease of volume takes place that a layer of peat more than 10-15 metres thick will produce only 1 metre of coal.

In Upper Carboniferous times, when coal formation was at its peak, the earth was in a general state of unrest. Fluctuating periods of earth movement caused

Above: Reconstruction of a typical coal-forming forest in the Carboniferous period reveals the luxuriant vegetation. Giant club-mosses, 'horsetails' and a dense undergrowth of smaller fern and creeper-like plants flourished in swampy terrain similar to the tropical jungles found in the Amazon basin.

Below: The types of plants which grew in coal-forming forests are known because of fossilized remains commonly found in the rocks near coal seams. These well-preserved fossil ferns came from a coal measure in Yorkshire. Dead ferns and trees accumulated in the swamp to form peat and, later, coal.

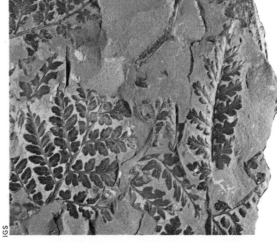

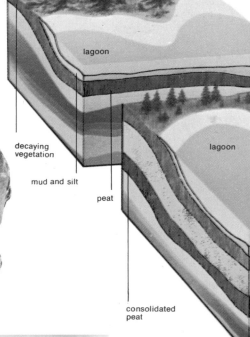

Left: Peat forms also in temperate climates. In this hilly area of Scotland, with poor drainage, thick peat deposits have formed from fallen trees, heather and mosses. After digging and stacking to dry, the peat is used by local people as fuel but it gives off little heat and much smoke.

MAJOR DEPOSITS OF COAL

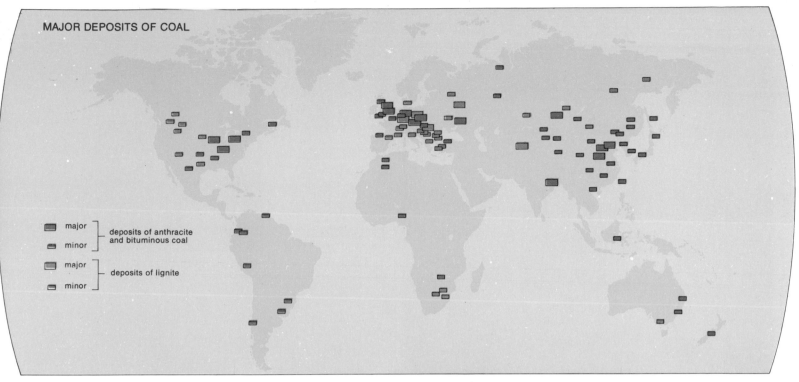

major ⟶ deposits of anthracite
minor ⟶ and bituminous coal

major ⟶ deposits of lignite
minor ⟶

Below: Three stages in the formation of coal seams are shown. Dead vegetation falls into the swamp to form peat. After subsidence, water floods the forest and deposits a sedimentary layer of mud and silt which buries the peat to form coal eventually. As the water recedes, new forests grow and a new cycle begins.

Above: Coal deposits are widely distributed throughout the world and will offer a continuing supply of fuel to an energy-hungry world for many centuries. It is estimated that remaining resources are some 2.9 million million tonnes. Annual production is 3,000 million tonnes.

Right: The three main types of humic coal are classed by their degree of alteration. Lignite (right) is a soft coal, dark brown in colour, with a woody texture. Coals are broadly made up of carbon, hydrogen and oxygen. With high rank coals, carbon content increases. Lignite is typically 70% carbon.

LIGNITE

BITUMINOUS

Left: Bituminous coal is the type most commonly used in the home. It is black and brittle with alternating bands of shiny vitrain and dull durain layers. Anthracite (below) is the highest rank coal produced by the greatest degree of alteration. It is very hard and has a 96% carbon content.

ANTHRACITE

FORMATION OF COAL

new forest

sedimentary layer

fresh layer of peat

lagoon

consolidated peat

lignite coal

gradual subsidence of the coal-forming forests, with occasional periods of rapid subsidence in which the sea frequently flooded the forests and accumulating peat beds.

The forests occupied vast areas of swampland through which rivers and streams flowed. When they reached the sea, the rivers formed extensive deltas which were also colonized by forests. As rapid subsidence took place, the plants became submerged, and thick mud was deposited on top of the forests, burying and compacting the peat. When rapid subsidence ceased, the sea level remained much the same, but the waters became shallower as rivers carried down more sediments.

Eventually, so much sediment accumulated that sand-banks and mud flats appeared above water level. These were quickly colonized by plants and soon became new swampy forests. Peat formation started again, continuing until another rapid subsidence flooded the area, starting the whole cycle over again. Such a sequence of events is known as *cyclic sedimentation.*

Types of coal

Coals which have formed in seams by the process outlined above are known as *humic* coals and may be classed by the degree of alteration which the original peat has undergone. This is known as their *rank*. A whole range of coals can occur, but the main types are *lignite*, *bituminous coal*, and *anthracite*.

Lignite is a softish coal which is dark brown in colour. Nearest to peat in composition, it gives off a lot of smoke when burnt, without a great deal of heat. There are extensive deposits in central Europe and North America. Bituminous coal, on the other hand, is the type with which most people are familiar. It is black and brittle, with a tendency to fracture along one or two vertical planes, forming straight-sided blocks of coal.

Bituminous coals usually have horizontal bands of alternating shiny and dull layers. These represent different types of

35

J. Pfaff/Zefa

Daily Telegraph Colour Library

Left: Open-cast mining for low quality brown coal up to a depth of 50 metres near Cologne in Germany. This method is applied to shallow seams and vast excavating machines are used to mine a deep pit.

Right: For deeper deposits, underground mining is required. Miners working at the coal face are hampered by dirty and dangerous conditions. Modern mining techniques involve increasing use of mechanization.

Below: A plan of a typical coal mine shows the tremendous amount of careful planning and costly machinery needed to extract coal from deep coal seams.

A cutaway section through the unmined coal shows the machinery used in longwall mining at work. The arrow shows the direction of mining into the coal face

Fan-house, with powerful fan to extract the foul air

The top of the upcast shaft is housed in a sealed building, to ensure that the fan operates efficiently in removing used air from the whole underground area

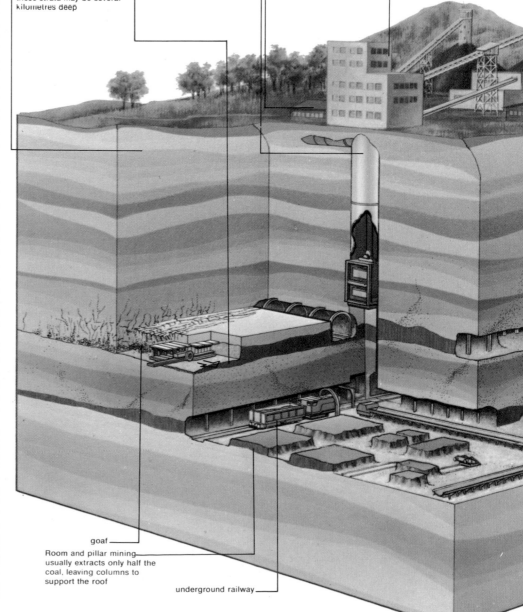

Intermediate rock strata. The diagram is not to scale — these strata may be several kilometres deep

Upcast shaft is used to bring coal, loaded in buckets called skips, to the surface

goaf

Room and pillar mining usually extracts only half the coal, leaving columns to support the roof

underground railway

original plant debris. The hard shiny, almost glassy, layers are known as *vitrain*. Microscopic examination shows that they consist of highly compressed bark and woody material. The dull layers are called *durain* and are formed mainly of the smaller and more resistant plant debris, such as spore-cases. Neither durain nor vitrain soil the fingers when touched. It is the presence of *fusain* that makes coal dirty to handle. Fusain is a soft and friable substance resembling charcoal, and was most probably formed from dead branches and trunks exposed to the air.

Anthracite is the highest rank of coal. Durain and vitrain bands are both present, but rarely fusain, and so anthracite is clean to handle. It burns with a very hot flame with hardly any smoke.

By contrast with the humic coals, the *sapropelic* coals are a group which do not appear to have formed from extensive tropical forest peat. There are two main types: *cannel coal* (the name is probably a corruption of 'candle' since it burns with a bright, smokey flame) is unbanded and breaks like glass. It is thought to have originated from the accumulation of fine floating plant material, such as spores. The remains of algae often form some of the constituents. *Boghead* coals, on the other hand, are dark brown or black, and resemble tough leather. They consist mainly of the remains of algae, which probably lived in large, well-oxygenated lakes.

The process of repeated seam formation leads to a great thickness of coal-bearing sediments being built up. These are given the general term *coal measures* and may reach a thickness of at least 1500 m, containing 20-30 main coal seams between one and three metres thick and many additional, much thinner ones. Their original horizontal layers, however, have often been disturbed by folding, tilting and faulting as a result of earth movements during the hundreds of millions of years in which they formed. Where coal-measures outcrop at the surface, an exposed coalfield is found but, over many

Left: American coal mining is carried out on a large scale. Here an automatic loader is picking up the coal cut from the seam face and loading it on to a transporter. This is driven through the underground tunnels to a central conveyor belt.

Below left: Two types of drilling bit are commonly used in coal exploration. An open-hole bit simply bores a hole through the rock. A coring bit is hollow with numerous industrial diamonds set in the rim. It retains a core of rock which is analysed for traces of coal seams. Often the borehole drilling rig is small enough to be mounted on a truck and moved from site to site.

Right: The Industrial Revolution began in Britain when the steam engine, fuelled by coal, replaced the water-driven wheel. This quiet valley town in Wales, now centred around the winding gear of a coal mine, grew rapidly in the 19th century as its rich seams were exploited.

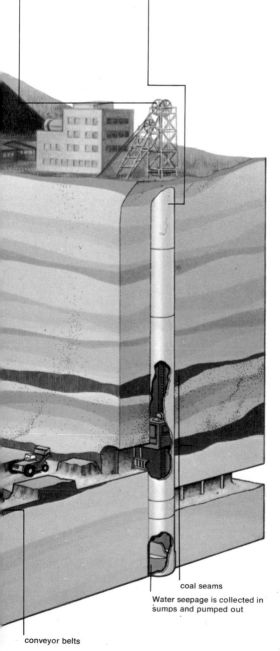

The headgear of the downcast shaft is made of an open lattice of steel girders, so that fresh air can enter to ventilate the mine

Downcast shaft is fitted with a cage, used to convey man and equipment into and out of the mine

coal seams

Water seepage is collected in sumps and pumped out

conveyor belts

areas, erosion has removed all trace of the coal. In other regions, younger rocks cover the coal measures completely, resulting in a concealed coal field at depth.

The search for coal

In completely unknown country, a thorough geological survey normally reveals coal deposits of some importance. The geologist will often employ aerial photography to help him with surface mapping but to prove the existence of a concealed coalfield boreholes have to be sunk.

The cores which are taken from the boreholes are analysed to determine their physical and chemical properties. These will indicate whether it would be economic to mine. Open-hole boreholes can also provide useful information, using a remarkable new technique called *electrical logging*. This involves lowering various instruments on a cable down the hole. These send back electrical impulses which vary according to the nature of the strata and the type of probe used. The results are recorded on graph-charts which build up an accurate picture of the borehole.

A comparatively new technique in coal field exploration is *seismic* surveying, although it has been used for many years in the search for oil. This kind of survey is carried out by drilling a line of shallow holes three metres deep. A small quantity of explosive is loaded into each hole, and then fired in succession. This produces a series of miniature earthquakes whose shock waves pass down into the ground. The different layers of rock reflect the waves back up again with different intensities, and these are picked up on the surface by special microphones, called *geophones*. The resulting picture built up shows different types of strata and, more importantly, the *structures*—for example, the folding or faulting of the layers.

Mining methods

Coal is extracted by the open-cast method where coal is near the surface, or by deep mines underground. The average depth of British open-cast mines is 37 metres (120

ft); the deepest-ever site of 213 metres (700 ft) was at Westfield, Scotland. All overlying soil and rocks ('overburden') are removed by large draglines and excavators while mining, but later British Coal refurbishes its sites.

The main method of mining, however, is by fully mechanized *longwall* extraction. Two parallel tunnels or roadways, usually about 200 m apart, are driven into the coal seam. These are connected at right angles by a third tunnel, the height of the seam, which forms the coal face. Successive strips of coal are cut from the face, advancing it forward. Simultaneously the two roadways at each end are lengthened, to keep pace with the coal face.

The coal is cut by an electrically operated machine, mounted on a special armoured steel conveyor running along the length of the face. It pulls itself along the conveyor track by a chain and sprocket arrangement, cutting a strip of coal from the face, which falls onto the conveyor to be taken to one end of the face. There, it is loaded onto a belt conveyor which transports it to the mine shafts, where it is lifted to the surface.

Longwall *retreat* mining differs from advance mining in that the two parallel roadways are initially driven right to the furthest extent of the coal panel. The coal face is formed at the far end and retreats back towards the mine shafts. By 'blocking out' the panel in this way, any geological hazard like a fault can be assessed before the face starts production.

The world's remaining coal resources are estimated at 2,900,000,000,000 tonnes, of which only some 12 per cent can be economically worked by present day mining methods. Techniques such as *in-seam gasification* (which obtains energy by igniting the coal in its seam), however, may enable some of the energy of the remaining 88 per cent to be tapped. But in the meantime, much research is being carried out into methods of using coal more wisely and efficiently. The world is using coal many hundreds of thousands of times faster than it took to form—and the supply is not inexhaustible.

Petroleum

Petroleum, defined broadly to include crude oil, inflammable natural gas and the semi-solid black substance known as asphalt or bitumen, has been exploited on a small scale for centuries. Bitumen, for example, was used more than 5,000 years ago in waterproofing ships and as a mortar for bricks. But these early uses relied on natural escapes or *seepages* of oil and gas to the earth's surface and on hand-dug shafts near such places. Oil had also been recovered from the surface of some rivers, again provided by seepages, and small amounts had been found to contaminate wells drilled for water.

In Pennsylvania, on 27 August 1859, a retired railway guard named Edwin L. Drake sank a steam-powered drill into the ground, to produce petroleum commercially for the first time. Drake struck oil at a depth of only 21 metres (69 feet). Today, however, advanced technology enables oil and gas to be produced from depths well in excess of 6,000 m (20,000 ft), and the deepest well drilled to date in search of oil is 9,583 m (31,441 ft). Oil and gas fields have been developed in more than 60 countries, as well as offshore in many parts of the world, with wells in some cases more than 275 km (170 miles) from land and in depths of water of over 140 m (450 ft).

The Origin of Petroleum

The origin of crude oil and natural gas is still a subject of investigation and debate. However, most geologists now believe that oil and gas formed from changes in the remains of a variety of animals and plant life. This organic matter is thought to have been deposited with inorganic minerals as sediments on the bottom of ancient seas and lakes, most commonly in shallow, calm tropical seas. The organic matter generally constituted only a small amount of the total sediment, which was buried deeper by successive deposits of sediment and turned into rock.

The organic remains, imprisoned in the mud and sand, then underwent considerable change. They were partially modified by the action of bacteria and, after biochemical changes ceased, the total organic complex was slowly acted upon by heat. As the sedimentary strata were buried progressively deeper in the earth's crust, they entered zones of greater pressure and higher temperature. This heating, never strong, caused changes in which *hydrocarbons*—compounds of carbon and hydrogen—and other petroleum components were formed directly or developed by further alteration of previously released compounds.

Many of these changes may have taken place over several millions of years and at temperatures not more than about 180°C. In the process, an entire range of products—including crude oil and natural gas—were released. In the early stages in particular, the products will have been influenced by the nature of the parental matter. For example, coaly type organic matter is prone to give methane gas, and not the decidedly heavier hydrocarbons characteristic of crude oils. Like coal, which is also derived from organic material, oil and natural gas are known as *fossil fuels*.

Picturepoint

Above: Excess petroleum gas is burnt off at a field in Abu Dhabi. Much of the natural gas which occurs with oil is burnt off at the point of production, because of the cost and difficulty of transporting it to areas of consumption great distances away.

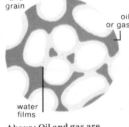

Right: Edwin Drake drilled the first ever well in a specific search for oil at Titusville, Pennsylvania in 1859. The Pennsylvania Oil Company, founded in the same year, was the ancestor of the international oil companies of today. Drake was lucky—he picked a spot where oil lay just 21 metres below the surface.

Drake Museum

FAULT TRAP

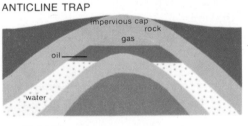

impervious rock · impervious rock · fault · gas · oil · impervious cap rock · water

ANTICLINE TRAP

impervious cap rock · gas · oil · water

SALTDOME

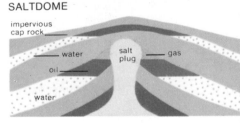

impervious cap rock · water · salt plug · gas · oil · water

and grain · oil or gas · water films

Above: Oil and gas are trapped between the pores of reservoir rock—the mineral grains are usually surrounded by a thin film of water.

Above right: Pools of iridescent colour created by natural seepage from a Venezuelan oil field. If petroleum leaks from underground, via a fault or crack, it floats on top of surface water.

Left: Three examples of the natural traps in which oil may be found. Oil is formed from microscopic marine organisms which died and sank to the bottom of water, becoming trapped beneath mud. Oil then rises until it reaches impervious rock.

Picturepoint

THE WORLD'S SUPPLY OIL AND GAS

Middle East · Communist countries · Afr

56% · 38% · 16% · 19% · 9%

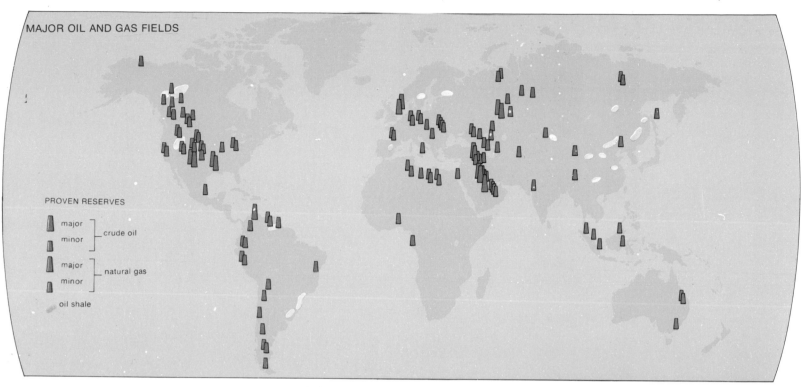

MAJOR OIL AND GAS FIELDS

PROVEN RESERVES

major ⎤
minor ⎦ crude oil

major ⎤
minor ⎦ natural gas

oil shale

Where petroleum is found

Organic matter is generally deposited in greatest abundance in fine-grained rocks such as clays. Because only a small proportion of it is split off to give hydrocarbons, its concentration in these, the *source rocks*, is very low. Quite early it was recognized that, in order for oil or gas to accumulate to form a *field* or pool, the hydrocarbons must have moved away from their point of origin and that certain rocks with significantly different physical characteristics to those of the source rocks must be present. This movement, or *migration*, is caused by the pressure from the weight of overlying sediments.

Water trapped in the source rock is squeezed out and carries the petroleum with it into porous *reservoir rocks*, where the openings between the mineral grains allow fluid to percolate towards the surface. As the fluid slowly migrates through the porous rocks, the less dense petroleum separates from the salt water, which then accumulates below the crude oil and natural gas or occupies parts, sometimes as much as 20 per cent, of the pores in which the oil and gas occur.

Crude oils range widely in their physical and chemical properties. The colours range from green and brown to black with rare examples of straw-coloured oils. When they reach the surface, some oils are more fluid than water, yet others may be as viscous as treacle. The principal elements in their composition are carbon and hydrogen, with appreciable amounts of sulphur, oxygen and nitrogen, and yet smaller amounts of metallic elements, among which nickel and vanadium are outstanding. Natural gas is largely com-

posed of methane in most cases, but small amounts of ethane and propane are commonly present. In addition some gases contain significant amounts of nitrogen, carbon dioxide, hydrogen sulphide and, more rarely, helium.

The most common reservoir rocks are sandstones and various types of limestones. Especially in the latter, some storage space is provided by openings other than inter-grain or inter-crystal openings, some of which may be decidedly larger than the pores between the sand grains. These are openings inside fossils, or between irregular fossil fragments; spaces are also formed by the solution or replacement of minerals, and by open fractures. Fractures are especially important in the finer-pored rocks, not so much because of the 'storage space', but because they make the rock mass much more permeable.

Accumulations occur when the petroleum is trapped in the reservoir rock by an overlying layer of suitably shaped impervious rock. This is known as the *cap rock*. Shales, clays, salt, gypsum and anhydrite are the principal cap rocks. Any pores in these rocks are much smaller than those in reservoir rocks, and are occupied by water. There is little if any penetration of the oil or gas into the cap rock. Natural gas may collect above salt water without the presence of oil. Free gas may also occur in a *gas cap* overlying crude oil containing dissolved gas. This in turn rests on the main body of salt water. On the other hand, some accumulations of petroleum have no associated gas cap, but do have dissolved gas in the oil. Various geological formations can produce traps.

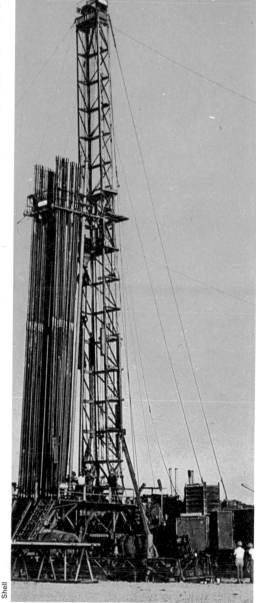

Right: An exploratory drilling rig. Mud is pumped down the drill shaft to lubricate the drill bit. Drilling mud disappearing below ground is a sign of porous rock and this in turn means there is possibly oil present. The cutting bit of the drill is rotated by turning the whole length of the pipe.

Shell

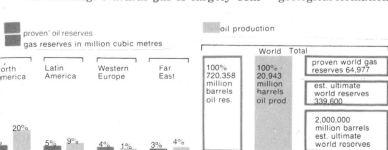

proven oil reserves
gas reserves in million cubic metres

oil production

	Latin America	Western Europe	Far East			World Total	
orth merica				100% 720,358 million barrels oil res.	100% 20,943 million barrels oil prod.	proven world gas reserves 64,977	
						est. ultimate world reserves 339,600	
20%	5% 9%	4% 1%	3% 4%			2,000,000 million barrels est. ultimate world reserves	

Right: A crude-oil processing refinery in Britain producing petro-chemicals to make plastics.

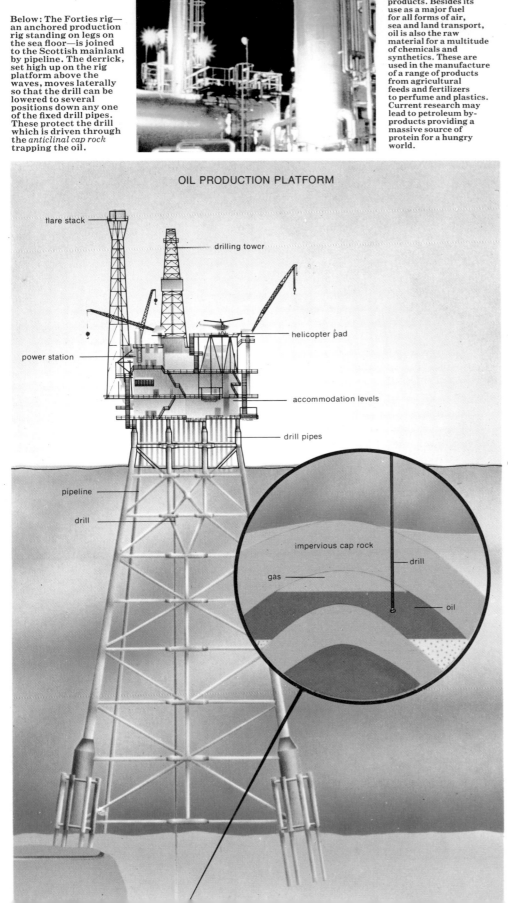

ATO Chemical Products (UK) Ltd

Below: The Forties rig—an anchored production rig standing on legs on the sea floor—is joined to the Scottish mainland by pipeline. The derrick, set high up on the rig platform above the waves, moves laterally so that the drill can be lowered to several positions down any one of the fixed drill pipes. These protect the drill which is driven through the *anticlinal cap rock* trapping the oil.

Right: A giant torch lights up a North Sea oil rig as excess gas is burnt off during production tests. Natural gas occurs both alone and with oil; its principal component is methane, an important raw material for the chemical industry.

Below right: The massive Esso refinery at Fawley on Southampton Water, is one of the largest in the world. Crude oil is refined into a vast number of primary products. Besides its use as a major fuel for all forms of air, sea and land transport, oil is also the raw material for a multitude of chemicals and synthetics. These are used in the manufacture of a range of products from agricultural feeds and fertilizers to perfume and plastics. Current research may lead to petroleum by-products providing a massive source of protein for a hungry world.

Shell

OIL PRODUCTION PLATFORM

flare stack

drilling tower

helicopter pad

power station

accommodation levels

drill pipes

pipeline

drill

impervious cap rock

drill

gas

oil

Esso

Some arise from the way the layers of sediment were at first deposited. Others are *structural traps,* formed by the folding or faulting of the earth as in *anticlinal* or *fault* traps, or by intrusions of different rocks, of which the *salt dome* is an example. Fields can also be dependent on more than one trapping feature. In the North Sea, for example, 'Leman Bank', a large gas field, is a broad, gentle, faulted anticline, while 'Indefatigable' has several pools on separate fault blocks.

The quantity of oil and gas in commercial accumulations varies widely and always exceeds the recoverable amount (known as reserves) sometimes by as much as 20 times. Yet changes in the economic climate and technical advances may quickly alter the amount of designated reserves. Commercial viability simply requires that the exploration, development and operating costs of the field shall be amply covered by the income from the sale of the oil and gas. What constitutes a commercial oil field depends on many factors and these

Right: In fractional distillation, crude oil is heated in an enclosed fractioning column. The lighter fractions boil off before the heavier ones and rise to the top. The fractions are drawn off as liquids at various levels of the column. Fresh crude oil is added continuously.

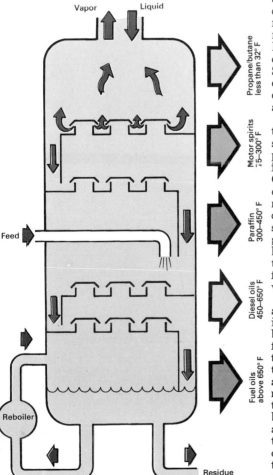

Above: The giant oil tanker *Esso Scotia*, launched at Bremen in 1969, capable of carrying almost half a million tons of crude oil.

accumulations are formed.

Drilling is an expensive operation, particularly in marine areas. Success is not assured even after extensive geological and geophysical surveys, because for various reasons traps can lack hydrocarbons, or contain quantities of hydrocarbons which are too small to justify commercial development.

The cuttings and other rock samples from a test drilling are carefully examined. These reveal the nature of the rocks penetrated and their fluid contents, and checks are kept on the returning mud for evidence of oil or gas. In addition, instruments are lowered into the hole from time to time to make electrical, radioactivity and other measurements. From these results, geologists can assess the type of rock, its porosity and the content of gas, oil or salt water. When hydrocarbons are recognized or thought to be present in exploratory wells, further special tests are made to check whether oil or gas can be produced at adequate rates. All of this is done before finally deciding to complete the well for production or to abandon it. Additional wells are normally needed to estimate the approximate size of the accumulation before embarking on full development, which includes the costly installation of pipe lines, storage and other major facilities.

To bring oil or gas to the surface, oil producers largely rely on the great pressure to which the petroleum at the bottom of a well is subjected. This pressure is reduced by opening surface valves or by other means, permitting fluids as a whole in the reservoir rock to expand, with gas coming out of solution in the oil, and the fluid itself being forced into and up the well.

Wells commonly produce oil unaided, for a time at least, but later many have to be helped in some manner, such as by pumping, in order to bring oil to the surface. Oil reaching the surface, as well as being accompanied by gas, is sometimes also associated with salt water, especially as the wells grow older. Gas, oil and water have to be separated before the saleable products are dispatched from the fields.

As the reserves of known accumulations of liquid hydrocarbons are used up, other sources become increasingly important. One such source—still so expensive that full exploitation lies in the future—are rocks impregnated with extremely viscous petroleum which will not flow into wells. These are referred to as *tar sands*, and include an enormous accumulation, known as the Athabasca Tar Sands of northern Canada. Special means, amongst which are excavation and washing, have to be employed in order to utilize these deposits. Such operations are commercially viable only rarely at present.

Another potential source may be the oil obtainable from *oil shales*. These are rocks rich in solid organic matter called kerogen, but not in free oil. However, by heating these shales at temperatures of several hundred degrees centigrade, the organic matter breaks down to yield considerable amounts of oil. This oil differs in various ways from crude oil, but may be refined by similar procedures although environmental problems arise from the disposal of large amounts of baked rock produced as waste. However, very extensive oil shale deposits exist, and they are potential sources of large volumes of oil, at a price.

include the quality of the oil, the current price of oil and the depth of the reservoir.

Among the highest known reserves are the 66,500 million barrels of oil at the Ghawar field in Saudi Arabia and 65 million million cubic feet of gas under Slochteren in Holland. (One barrel of oil is about 0.16 cubic metres and contains 35 gallons. Gas reserves are in volumes calculated at atmospheric pressure and temperature.) Field areas vary from over 2,800 sq km (1,100 sq miles) to as little as 2.5 sq km (1 sq mile) for some pools. Individual well producing rates range from more than 20,000 barrels a day to less than 100 at the peak, and gas wells may flow at rates of tens of millions of cubic feet per day. There are, however, inevitable declines as the fields and wells are depleted.

There is no means of recognizing with certainty whether masses of oil or gas exist at depth before wells have been drilled. However, geologists can make reasonable predictions on the basis of rock forms which could constitute traps. In some areas, the surface rocks give clues to the different rock layers at depth. Surface mapping, often aided by the examination of aerial photographs, will often dictate accurately the positions of anticlines and faults at depth.

Where surface rocks are not a guide to the position of underground geological structures, or at underwater sites, geophysical techniques must be used to indicate the sites of structures at depth. One method uses readings of the intensity of the earth's gravitational pull. This may show where denser, and hence commonly older, rocks are nearer the surface than elsewhere. This indicates to geologists that violent earth movements have occurred in the past and could imply the existence of an anticline or point to a fault, both of which are capable of providing traps.

Seismic surveys are carried out as an alternative technique, or to confirm other indications. Pulses of energy, generated by explosives or other means, travel down from the earth's surface and, after reflection or refraction at boundaries between the rock layers, return to the surface and are detected by seismometers. Measurement of the travel times and the recognition of what are apparently the same boundaries from a series of observations allow the shapes of sub-surface boundaries to be plotted. In this way trapping forms can be recognized. Aeromagnetic surveys throw light on the broader features of sedimentary basins in which oil and gas

Vapor Liquid

Feed

Reboiler

Residue

Propane/butane less than 32° F

Motor spirits 75-300° F

Paraffin 300-450° F

Diesel oils 450-650° F

Fuel oils above 650° F

The Fossil Record

The term *fossil* originally referred to any object dug from the ground, but its use is now limited to the remains of once-living animals and plants. Although the study of the fossil record often seems of distant relevance to the practicalities of modern life, it does in fact have great importance. One outstanding example is the use of fossil evidence by geologists in their search for sources of fuel. Most importantly, however, its study provides us with a fascinating glimpse of the colourful assortment of life on earth during its long history. 'Glimpse' is, unfortunately, the most appropriate word, for the fossil record is far from complete and much of the existing record remains poorly explored by *palaeontologists*, the scientists who study fossils.

The fossil record depends on how much has survived the ravages of time. Only the hard parts, such as the bones and shells of animals, the tree trunks or leaf cuticle of plants, are normally preserved in the rocks. Consequently, information about the function of the hard and soft parts has to be deduced from the skeletal remains.

Completely soft-bodied animals usually leave little or no direct evidence of their former existence. However, certain 'freak' sediments, such as the Burgess Shale (Cambrian) of British Columbia, preserve such creatures and give a fleeting impression of the real diversity of life hundreds of millions of years ago. In addition, many animals burrowed into sediment, or briefly rested on it, or bored into a hard sea floor. The traces of these activities are preserved surprisingly often as *trace fossils*.

Even fossil excreta are found and can sometimes be attributed to a particular kind of animal living long ago. Evidence of damage during life, or of disease, are also often visible. Palaeontologists have found such examples as ammonites that have patched up tears in their shell and dinosaurs that suffered rheumatoid arthritis.

The fossil record is biased towards the marine realm because the seas and oceans have always been the main area of deposition of sediment. Because land areas are essentially regions of weathering and erosion, even those animals with backbones, the *vertebrates*, may have been poorly preserved on land. The remains of many vertebrates—amphibians, reptiles, mammals and many birds—are rare except at certain limited geological levels or *horizons* where non-marine deposits have been preserved.

Fossils can provide an immense amount of information. Historically, it is their role in the correlation of rock strata that was first appreciated, but they are also used in the interpretation of past environments, in studying the rates, processes and paths of evolution, and in testing alternative models of plate movement and continental drift. The correlation of rocks by the fossils they contain—a key principle in *stratigraphy*, the study of rock strata—reflects the evolution of life through time. The stratigrapher collects

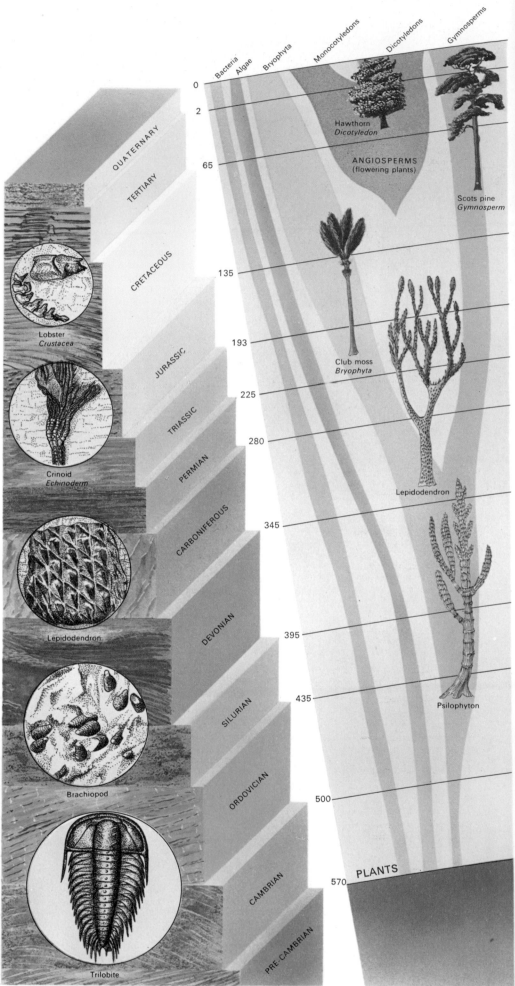

REPRESENTATIVE FOSSILS

million years ago

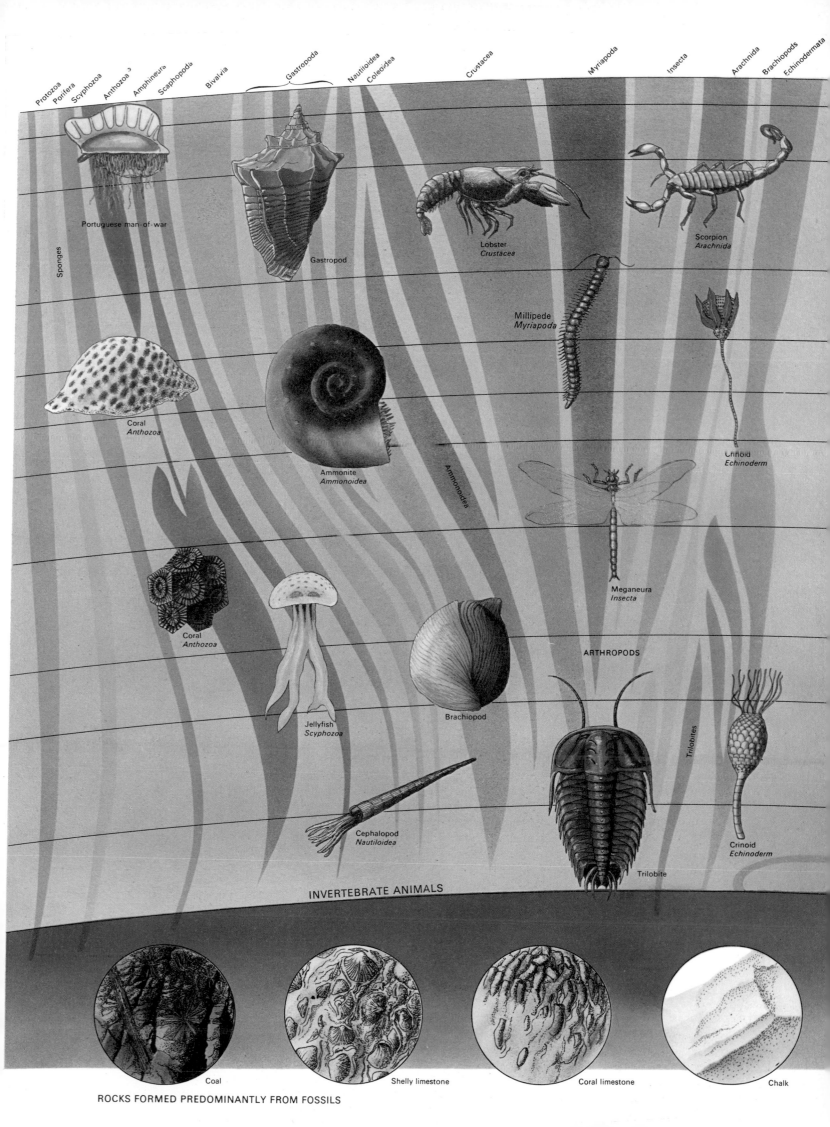

Protozoa Porifera Scyphozoa Anthozoa? Amphineura Scaphopoda Bivalvia Gastropoda Nautiloidea Coleoidea Crustacea Myriapoda Insecta Arachnida Brachiopods Echinodermata

Sponges

Portuguese man-of-war

Gastropod

Lobster
Crustacea

Scorpion
Arachnida

Coral
Anthozoa

Ammonite
Ammonoidea

Ammonoidea

Millipede
Myriapoda

Crinoid
Echinoderm

Coral
Anthozoa

Jellyfish
Scyphozoa

Brachiopod

Meganeura
Insecta

ARTHROPODS

Cephalopod
Nautiloidea

Trilobites

Trilobite

Crinoid
Echinoderm

INVERTEBRATE ANIMALS

Coal

Shelly limestone

Coral limestone

Chalk

ROCKS FORMED PREDOMINANTLY FROM FOSSILS

Hemichordata
Urochordata
Cephalochordata
Cyclostomes
Elasmobranchs
Cephalochordata
Teleosts
Crossopterygii
Lung fishes
Urodeles
Apoda
Anura
Chelonia
Crocodilia
Ophidia
Aves

Acorn worms

Herring
Teleost

Newts

Legless lizards

Turtles

Snakes

Lizards

Birds

Archaeopteryx
Aves

Rays

Bony fishes

Sharks

Turtle
Chelonia

Ornithopods

Theropods

Sauropoda

Ichthyosauria

Acorn worm

Coelacanth
Crossoptergii

Holosteans

Lungfish
Dipterus

Protosuchus
Crocodilia

Shark
Elasmobranch

Chondrosteans

Ichthyosaur
Icthyosauria

Sea squirt
Urochordata

Acanthodires

Rachitomes

Ichthyostega

REPTILES

Agnatha

Ostracoderms

Cheirolepis
Chondrostean

Lepospondyls

Dipterus

Pteraspidomorph
Ostracoderm

Amphioxus
Cephalochordata

Acanthodes
Acanthodire

CHORDATES

VERTEBRATE ANIMALS

Pterosaur

Ceratopsian

Sauropod

Carnosaur

Ichthyosaur

Plesiosaur

Pliosaur

Dominant reptiles of
the age of Dinosaurs

Nautiloid dies

Sediment settles

Earth Movements

Erosion exposes fossil

THE STORY OF A FOSSIL

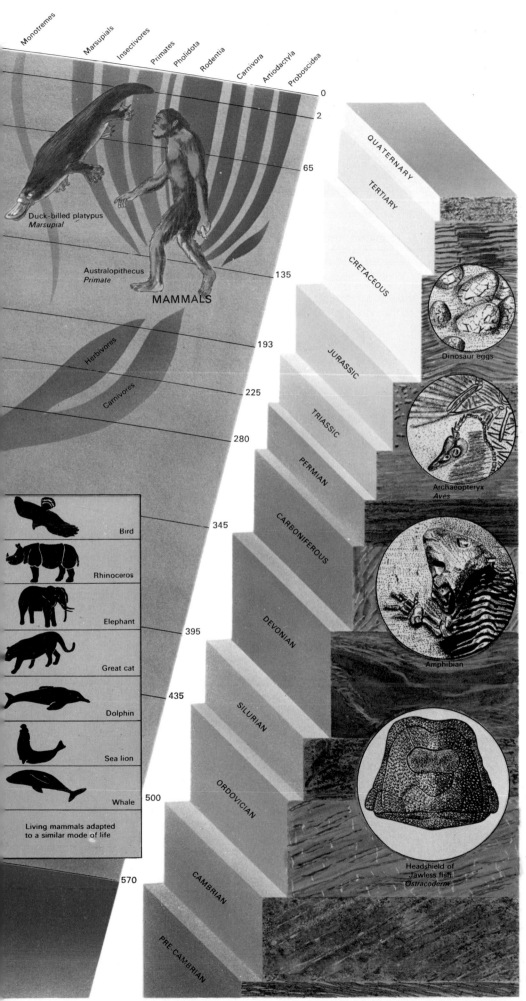

Duck-billed platypus *Marsupial*

Australopithecus *Primate*

MAMMALS

Monotremes · Marsupials · Insectivores · Primates · Pholidota · Rodentia · Carnivora · Artiodactyla · Proboscidea

Herbivores

Carnivores

Bird
Rhinoceros
Elephant
Great cat
Dolphin
Sea lion
Whale

Living mammals adapted to a similar mode of life

QUATERNARY
TERTIARY
CRETACEOUS
JURASSIC
TRIASSIC
PERMIAN
CARBONIFEROUS
DEVONIAN
SILURIAN
ORDOVICIAN
CAMBRIAN
PRE-CAMBRIAN

0 · 2 · 65 · 135 · 193 · 225 · 280 · 345 · 395 · 435 · 500 · 570

Dinosaur eggs

Archaeopteryx *Aves*

Amphibian

Headshield of Jawless fish *Ostracoderm*

million years ago

REPRESENTATIVE FOSSILS

fossils layer by layer to establish the time-sequence of the various forms, and then recognizes that any rock succession containing the same sequence of species spans the same period of geological time —no matter how different the rock types themselves may be. In this way the relative geological time scale was built up.

The *palaeoecologist* studies the relationship of a fossil animal or plant to the environment in which it lived. Study of whole *fossil assemblages*, the complete entity or number of fossils in an area, can indicate differing depths of sea water, while research into the geographical distribution of fossil organisms, the study of *palaeobiogeography*, sheds light on ancient climates or geography.

Fossils and evolution

The present is simply a brief cross-section of geological time. Biologists build up much of their understanding of the processes and result of evolution by studies in such fields as the comparative morphology, embryology, genetics and biochemistry of living forms. But present-day life represents only the culmination of over 3,500 million years of evolution, the direct evidence of which is locked into our fossil record. Charles Darwin (1809-82), in his celebrated work *The Origin of Species*, was fully aware of the potential importance of fossils in testing his evolutionary theories, but he stressed the many imperfections of the record. Since Darwin's day our knowledge has vastly expanded and a more rigorous approach has demonstrated definite patterns in evolutionary processes, though these are certainly not to be regarded as 'laws' of evolution.

The most spectacular pattern is that of *explosive evolution*. On several occasions through geological time there have been relatively sudden bursts in the evolution of major groups of animals and plants. One instance is the rapid diversification or *radiation* of fish during the Devonian period nearly 400 million years ago. Such bursts interrupted the more usual, slow or *progressive evolution* within individual groups, and often seem to be associated either with periods of major extinctions or with significant environmental changes such as the flooding of extensive areas of continental margins to form shallow shelf seas.

Explosive evolution often affected unrelated groups of animals or plants at the same time. The sudden diversification of a group to exploit an environmental change is called an *adaptive radiation* because it usually results in a great variety of new forms evolving. Some of these prove to be successfully adapted to live in the new environment, but others quickly become extinct.

For periods of more normal, progressive evolution, *rates of evolution* can be worked out. Although absolute rates have rarely been calculated, there has long been tacit recognition among palaeontologists that some fossil groups evolved faster than others. The most rapidly changing groups have always been used as *zone fossils*, those fossil species which are used to characterize a particular horizon and are restricted to it in time.

Rates of evolution can apparently vary considerably within any division of the animal kingdom, or *phylum*. Some bivalve species, for example, apparently lasted at least six times as long as contemporaneous

Above: These extinct ammonites date from the Jurassic. Some species lived for less than half a million years before evolving into another species and their sequence gives an accurate relative time scale for Jurassic and Cretaceous rocks.

Left: Trilobites are extinct marine arthropods which superficially resemble woodlice. They are zone fossils, used in the age correlation of rocks, for the Cambrian and Ordovician periods.

Below: These shellfish are brachiopods. Living examples are quite rare but they are significant as zone fossils from the Ordovician period to the Permian.

ammonites during the Cretaceous, yet both belong to the phylum *Mollusca*. However, some authorities point out that the rate of evolution of some groups may appear faster simply because they have more characters which can vary and are therefore more readily divided into chronological 'species'. This reflects the problem that affects every palaeontologist. He is dealing not with a single slice of time but with a continuum, and therefore has to distinguish both contemporaneous and chronological species.

Evolutionary convergence is known from both the fossil and modern records. It is the tendency of completely unrelated groups to give rise to similar looking forms, usually reflecting a similar mode of life. Thus the fossil plesiosaur developed into a form very much like a fish although it was a reptile. Repeated or *iterative*

evolution is a similar tendency which occurs in related organisms. Many different ammonites, for example, give rise to tightly coiled shells at the end of their evolutionary lineages.

Extinction of fossil species

While many fossil species became 'extinct' simply by evolving into another species, there were periods when whole groups disappeared. Such wholesale extinctions are quite common in the geological record and, as explained earlier, their occurrences have been linked with bursts of explosive evolution. Indeed, the boundaries between our major divisions of Phanerozoic time—the Palaeozoic, Mesozoic and Cainozoic eras—and to a lesser extent the boundaries between the geological periods were based essentially on the recognition of major periods of extinction followed by bursts of evolution.

Some of the extinctions were spectacular. Some were so impressive, as for example the disappearance of the giant reptiles about 65 million years ago at the end of the Cretaceous period, that external catastrophies, such as changes in the sun's radiation or collision with a huge meteorite, have been invoked. However, more thorough study has demonstrated that most extinctions and evolutionary radiations actually occurred over a period of time, though accelerated in relation to more normal periods of evolution and extinction. The changes probably reflect major but progressive changes in the environment, such as extensive marine retreats or advances, or significant changes in the world's climate.

The progress of life through time

Despite its major imperfections, the fossil record, when properly interpreted, provides an immense amount of information on the progression of life through geological time. The record starts very early in the earth's history. Indeed, so-called *chemofossils*, minute agglomerations of organic acids possibly of living origin, are known from rocks almost 4,000 million years old, and algae were well established by 3,000 million years ago. Much more advanced, though soft-bodied, animals are known from a variety of late Pre-Cambrian rocks and trace fossils of this age are common. All are *invertebrates*, animals without a backbone, but some are difficult to assign to their correct phylum.

Invertebrate fossils are common from the beginning of the Cambrian period (some 570 million years ago) onward. This resulted from the development of hard shells, initially often chitinous but soon mainly calcareous, by most invertebrate phyla at that time. With one exception—the *Archaeocyatha*, a group of extinct marine forms—all the phyla which had appeared by the end of the Cambrian still flourish today, though many of the early forms look very different from their modern descendants.

The phylum *Arthropoda* probably originated in the Pre-Cambrian and is represented at first by marine creatures called *trilobites*. These became extinct during the Permian period of 280 to 225 million years ago, but the phylum is by then represented by many other forms including abundant crustaceans—a group represented today by such creatures as crabs, lobsters and shrimps. 'Modern' crabs originated some 100 million years later during the Jurassic. To the palaeontologist some of the most important crustacean arthropods are the microscopic *ostracods* which originated late in the Cambrian and are of importance as zone fossils in the correlation of rock strata of Silurian and later age. An equally important group for this purpose are the *foraminifera*, a division of the single-celled phylum *Protozoa*. The phylum must have had a long Pre-Cambrian history, and foraminifera appeared early in the Cambrian.

The phylum, *Coelenterata*, which includes present-day corals, sea-anemones and jelly-fish, is represented in the Pre-Cambrian by the traces of jelly-fish and in many later systems by the skeletons of fossil corals. The latter often formed reefs in ancient tropical areas. The phylum *Mollusca* has reached its peak today, but its fossil record is varied and impressive. The *cephalopod* molluscs, forms with chambered shells, appeared at the end of the Cambrian and radiated rapidly at the beginning of the Ordovician 500 million years ago. They gave rise during the Devonian, 100 million years later, to the *ammonoid* cephalopods, whose shells are so common in some Mesozoic sediments.

Another cephalopod group, the *belemnites*, appeared in the Carboniferous and are ancestral to the modern squid and cuttlefish. Other molluscan groups include the *bivalves*, which are rare until the Silurian, 400 million years ago, but then become increasingly common to achieve enormous diversity today, where they include the common cockles, mussels and scallops. The *gastropod* molluscs, common today as snails, slugs and whelks, have coiled shells and a geological history similar to that of the bivalves.

The phylum *Brachiopoda* is another shellfish group. In contrast to the Mollusca they are relatively insignificant now, although their geological record, especially from Ordovician to Permian times, was much more important. The phylum *Echinodermata* also originated in the Cambrian or earlier, and its two major fossil groups are the *Crinoidea* (sea lilies) and the *Echinoidea* (sea urchins). The former were most important in the distant Palaeozoic where their skeletal remains are sometimes important rock builders, while the latter diversified during the Mesozoic to reach a peak in the Cretaceous.

The *graptolites* appeared in the Ordovician and became extinct 200 million years later in the Carboniferous. They are colonial organisms that were once classified with the Coelenterata but are now placed among the most primitive members of the phylum *Chordata*, which includes the vertebrates. The first true vertebrates, the fish, evolved in the Ordovician. Land was first colonized in the Devonian, when amphibians as well as the first land plants appeared, to be followed by reptiles in the early Carboniferous.

The conquest of land left only one realm to be fully occupied—the air. Flying insects were well established by the Carboniferous, and the first flying reptiles are of Triassic age (over 200 million years ago). Some 50 million years later, true birds appeared in the late Jurassic, by which time many forms of life were taking on a modern appearance while the land was roamed by the dinosaurs, now long extinct. Man appeared only about 2.5 million years ago, at about the beginning of the Pleistocene epoch.

The Sea at Work

The seas make a constant assault on our coasts. Yet the pounding action of the waves is not only destructive, for while cliffs and other coastal landforms are being eroded, the resulting rock debris (often quickly reduced to fine material like sand) may be deposited by that same wave action elsewhere.

The power of waves

Most coastal changes occur under storm conditions, when the destructive powers of waves are at their greatest. The energy of a wave depends on its *length* (the distance from crest to crest), its *height* (the distance from trough to crest) and its swiftness or *celerity* (measured by the period of time between waves). Variation in any one of these characteristics will change the ability of a wave breaking on a coast to erode and move material.

However, the most important factor in the power of a wave is its height. Because this depends in part on wind speeds, the highest waves most commonly occur in storms, when gales whip the sea into a furious assault on the coast. The crash of storm waves on a cliff traps pockets of air in the rock cavities and compresses them. Then as waves fall back, the air expands explosively, throwing spray, pebbles and shattered rock high into the air. Further erosion is the result of the *corrasive* action of the debris hurled by waves against the coasts. The material itself is worn into smaller particles by the constant grinding or *attrition*.

The immense amount of damage that can be caused by storm waves was dramatically illustrated in January 1953 along the coasts of the North Sea. Under strong northerly winds and the high tide, a surge of water was forced into the southern part of the North Sea. The effect was devastating. In many places along the eastern coast of England, the beach was completely washed away by the sea, and once this protection was lost, the cliffs were exposed to rapid erosion. In some areas of Lincolnshire, low cliffs were cut back by more than 10 m (33 ft).

The sea can also change a shoreline considerably without actually eroding the cliffs or beach. On tropical coasts, for example, huge waves are generated by violent hurricanes. In 1960 Hurricane Donna in two days shifted an estimated 5,000,000 m³ (176,500,000 cubic ft) of sand from one part of the Florida coast to another. Under normal conditions it would take about 100 years to transport that amount. Although very little erosion —that is, breakdown of material—had occurred, at the end of the storm, each resort had an entirely new beach similar in all respects to the pre-storm beach.

Cliffs

Perhaps the clearest example of the erosive action of the sea is the way a cliff is undercut by wave action, and then eventually recedes as the unstable slope above collapses. Cliffs are undoubtedly the most striking landform to be seen along a coast, and although their height is entirely determined by the relief of the land, the sea can have dramatic effects. In England, for example, some parts of the Isle of Sheppey are retreating by more

Phatri

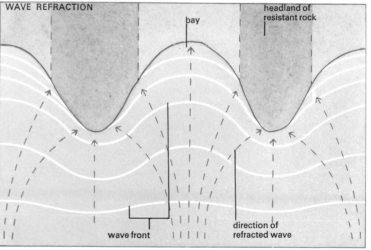

WAVE REFRACTION

bay · headland of resistant rock · wave front · direction of refracted wave

Above: Waves breaking on the rocky shore of Oregon's Pacific coast. The cliffs are fairly low (about 10 m high) but their vertical faces indicate active erosion by waves. Weaknesses in the rock have been exploited to create an attractively varied coastline of capes and bays. Outcrops of more resistant rock have produced an intertidal island (centre right of the photograph) and a curving arch (bottom). Rock debris and driftwood are deposited at the cliff-base by the gentle swell waves.

Right: Waves tend to reach the shore at right angles. As they approach the coast, the waves 'feel' the sea bottom. The increased friction slows the waves as they bear down on the protruding headlands. Initially, the brunt of the sea's attack is borne by the headlands and the less disturbed conditions in the bay offer safer anchorage for shipping. However, since the sea-floor is uneven, waves will advance more quickly into the bays where the water is deepest and a wave front becomes curved as the water shallows. The bending, or *wave refraction*, increases until, at the moment of wave break, the front is almost parallel to the coastline.

Right: Aerial photograph of Sakonnet Point on Rhode Is. (USA) showing waves being refracted as they near the coast. In the lee of the offshore rocks the waves produce an interference pattern.

Dr. John S. Shelton

47

than three metres (10 feet) every year. On another part of the eastern coast of England, the cliffs are being eroded even further—as much as 10 metres (33 feet) a year.

Yet the sea can attack the cliffs only within a very restricted vertical range, in effect up to a level reached by the highest waves. Concentrated at the base of the cliff, the sea's erosive force obviously varies with the strength of the waves. In sheltered locations, for example, cliffs are eroded much more slowly than those on exposed coasts. However, the other major factor affecting the rate of erosion is the geology of the area. Cliffs composed of soft rocks, such as clays or glacial sands, can be attacked and the rock debris washed away very quickly.

Cliffs of harder rock such as granite offer much greater resistance to the pounding force of the sea, even along exposed shores such as Land's End at the tip of southwest England and the stormy Cape Horn of South America. Where harder rocks alternate with softer ones, the sea often carves out *bays* and *coves* in the less resistant rocks, leaving the harder ridges jutting into the sea as *headlands*. Straight shorelines are characteristic only of faulted coasts and those formed of rocks of generally uniform resistance to erosion. Along the English Channel, for example, the famous White Cliffs of Dover and the Seven Sisters coast near Eastbourne are composed of chalk of very even texture.

Marine erosion at the cliff-base occasionally creates unusual landforms. Most hard rocks have fault joints and other lines of weakness which are exploited by the sea, sometimes cutting *inlets* and *caves* deep into the cliffs. The explosive pressure of trapped air and surging water inside a cave may be sufficient to erode upwards through the roof to form an opening known as a *blowhole* from which clouds of spray may shoot upwards. Quite often, caves hollowed on both sides of a headland join up to form a natural arch. In time, when the top of the arch collapses, the remnant of the headland stands as a detached pillar, known as a *stack*. All tall, off-shore rock pinnacles are called stacks, irrespective of how they were formed. Many well-known examples occur around the coasts of Britain, such as the chalk pinnacles known as the Needles off the Isle of Wight, and the Old Man of Hoy, a 137 m (450 ft) high pillar of Old Red Sandstone, in the Orkney Islands of Scotland.

Beaches

A beach is a deceptively transient feature, a sloping accumulation of loose material —which may consist of boulders, *shingle* (coarse gravel), pebbles, sand, mud and shells—along the sea-shore. Movement of material both up and down and along the beach ensures that it is constantly changing. Beaches may be removed overnight by a violent storm, as occurred in 1953 along the Lincolnshire coast—but they usually build up again during long periods of calm weather. Often, a thin layer of material is moved nearly continuously, being deposited at one end of the beach, washed by *longshore drift* along the length of it, and carried out the other end.

The continuous interplay of waves and this loose material contributes to the

Dr. John S. Shelton

Picturepoint

Left and right:
The changing appearance of beaches from one season to another is familiar to people who live near sandy sea-shores. Usually a beach loses sand during storms when the waves are highest and most destructive, and regains it during calmer periods. These two photographs of the same part of Boomer Beach near La Jolla, California, show a dramatic gain and loss of sand. In summer (right) gentle swell waves carry material up to the shore, building up a soft sandy beach. In winter (left) storm waves wash away the easily-moved, fine material such as sand, carrying it out to sea, and expose the coarse fragments at the base of this beach.

Right: Waves thump against the protective sea-wall at Portmellon in Cornwall. In winter the south-western corner of England often suffers storm waves swept across the Atlantic Ocean. Such waves possess a large amount of energy and can bring major changes to shorelines in a very short time. It has been estimated that Atlantic storm waves pound exposed coasts with an average force of 10,000 kg per square metre (2,000 lb/sq ft).

Far right: Tidal mud-flats at Dawlish on Devon's south coast. In sheltered coastal areas such as this where waves are feeble, deposition dominates over erosion. Fine silt and sand are laid down by the sea and rivers add their alluvium. Salt-tolerant vegetation tends to colonize the flat ground and this helps to trap more silt. In tropical areas, mud-flats support mangrove swamps.

Below: This former island in the Scottish sea-loch Eriboll is joined to the mainland by a *tombolo*, a linking deposit of sand and shingle.

Picturepoint

Picturepoint

CAPE COD, MASSACHUSETTS

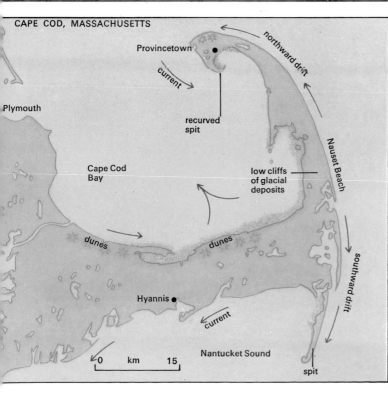

northward drift

Provincetown

current

Plymouth

recurved
spit

Cape Cod
Bay

low cliffs
of glacial
deposits

Nauset Beach

dunes

dunes

Hyannis

current

southward
drift

Nantucket Sound

spit

0 km 15

Above: Miami Beach, the
tourist and convention
centre in south-eastern
Florida (USA), is built
on an offshore sand-bar.
Separated from the
mainland by shallow
Biscayne Bay, the island
was a mangrove swamp
until developed and
joined to Miami proper
by causeways in 1912.
The growth of coastal
deposits such as
bars and spits depends
on sizeable longshore
drift of material along
an irregular coastline.
Here the drift is from
the south, as shown by
the sand trapped on the
near-side of the groynes,
low walls or jetties
built to protect the beach
from further erosion.

Left and right: At Cape
Cod on the coast of
Massachusetts, the
easily-eroded glacial
debris is gradually
drifting both north and
south along Nauset
Beach. Long bands of
shingle and sand, known
as *spits*, are extending
the length of the beach.
Spits are formed by
longshore drift, which
occurs when waves arrive
obliquely at a beach
(right). Material carried
both up and along the
beach by the swash is
pulled straight down the
slope by the backwash.

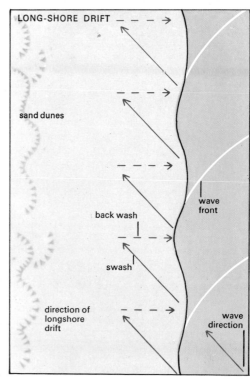

LONG-SHORE DRIFT

sand dunes

back wash

swash

direction of
longshore
drift

wave
front

wave
direction

great variety of beaches. Sand and shingle may be washed up from the sea-floor and a small amount of debris is provided by cliff erosion, but most of the material comes from sediment carried to the sea by rivers and then transported along by the waves and currents. The river Nile, for example, is responsible for nearly all the beach sediments in the south-east corner of the Mediterranean Sea. The remains of shells, corals and other organisms may be a further source of beach material.

It is often possible to trace the varied origins of material. For example, at Cap Griz Nez, near the French Channel port of Calais, the beach consists of huge boulders more than a metre (39 in) across, which have fallen from thick limestone bands in the cliff face. Flint cobbles the size of a fist are found on Chesil Beach in Dorset, having been eroded from the chalk on the Channel floor, then washed up by the waves.

Coarse sand is common in the beaches of Cornwall, having been eroded from the granite rocks inland, while extremely fine sands from the Old and New Red Sandstone areas provide a popular holiday beach at Weston super Mare on the Bristol Channel coast.

On all beaches, eroded material is gradually broken down into smaller pieces by the constant pounding of the sea. The surge or *swash* of waves pushes pebbles and sand up the beach, while the *backwash* (the return of seawater down a beach after a wave has broken) or underwater currents drag the material down the slope. Generally, the coarser the material, the steeper the beach slope will be. The steep profile of the shingle beach at Chesil Beach, for example, is partly due to the large size of the flints, whereas the beach at Weston-super-Mare slopes gently because of its fine sand. Where a mixture of sediment sizes occurs, as at many beaches of East Anglia, the coarser material tends to gather at the highest part, and there is usually a marked change in slope between this and the finer sediments towards the low water level.

The shape of a beach is also affected by

Aerofilms

Bruce Coleman

Above: The *cuspate foreland* at Dungeness on the English Channel is one of the best examples of this very unusual feature. Its origins are unclear but shingle has been added to the foreland in a sharply defined series of beach ridges. Many fine ridges were destroyed by the construction of the Nuclear Power Station.

J. Rufus/Robert Harding

Above: Seastacks and a rocky shore platform project out to sea at a cove near Hartland Quay on the north coast of Devon. The gently inclined *platform* was built and extended as the cliffs were eroded back. Debris from the cliff face has fallen onto the platform, to be swept away by the waves. On coasts like this— battered by strong storm waves—mechanical erosion by the sea picks out the weaknesses in the rock strata. Harder rocks resist destruction and many cliffed coasts end in a series of offshore rocks or *sea stacks* on which lighthouses are often built. Well-known examples include the Needles off the Isle of Wight.

NORTH ATLANTIC TYPE PLATFORM

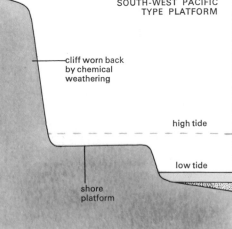

cliff

high tide

low tide

shore platform

undercutting leads to cliff collapse

beach material

SOUTH-WEST PACIFIC TYPE PLATFORM

cliff worn back by chemical weathering

high tide

low tide

shore platform

Above and right: There are two basic types of shore platform. The North Atlantic type (above) has an inclined surface stretching from the cliff-base to beyond the low-water mark. It is typical of storm wave coasts, where erosion by the sea leads to undercutting of the cliff. The abrasive and quarrying action of the waves is usually concentrated into joints and cracks in the rock, producing an irregular surface, as seen at Hartland Quay. The SW Pacific type (right) is characterized by a near-horizontal platform that ends abruptly at a low tide cliff. Here chemical weathering is important. The sea merely removes loosened material.

Above: These inspiring arches on the coast of the Algarve, Portugal, are known locally as the 'bridges of piety'. Natural arches are an attractive feature of many cliffed coasts. They are most likely to form where horizontally bedded rocks are cut by major vertical joints. Limestones and basalt are particularly suitable.

Right: A fountain of spray shoots out of a *blowhole* on Española or Hood Is. in the Galapagos. Blowholes occur where a chimney extends from the cliff top down to a sea cave. As waves enter the cave, usually at high tide, air is forced up the chimney, carrying water with it, usually with a great roaring noise.

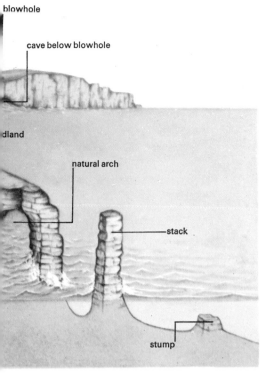

blowhole

cave below blowhole

dland

natural arch

stack

stump

Above: Some of the most striking features along a cliffed coast are those sculpted by the ceaseless battering of the sea. Caves occur quite commonly at weak points in the rock face; for once the sea has cut a hole in the rock, it enlarges it by compression and erosion. Collapse of the cave roof may produce a blowhole. If two caves develop on opposite sides of a headland, the waves may erode through their back walls to carve a natural arch. The sea will continue to erode the arch. When the roof of the arch gives way and debris is carried away by the waves, a large pillar or stack is left offshore. Further erosion may leave a stump, only revealed at low tide.

variations in the movement of waves. Once the direction of prevailing waves or the swash and backwash change, the beach is modified, either by erosion or deposition. If the beach is battered by high waves, as often occurs in winter, the loose material raked from the beach is carried back to the sea, producing a more gentle slope (often separated from the beach beyond the level of wave attack by a small sand or shingle cliff). By contrast, when these steep waves are replaced by more gentle *swell waves* (those which are not driven by winds) material tends to be built up and the beach slope is increased. This produces the generally steeper, larger beaches of summer.

Waves tend to approach the shore at right angles. This is true even of a cape and bay coastline, for as the waves approach the shore, they first encounter the shallower water opposite the headlands, and are slowed down. Opposite the bays, however, the water usually remains deep, so that the waves advance more rapidly. As they too begin to 'feel bottom' they slow and a swinging effect, known as *wave refraction*, occurs by which the line of advance of the waves becomes generally parallel to the shore so that they break head-on.

In many places, however, waves are not fully refracted, and approach at an angle to the coast. This results in *longshore drift*: the movement of shingle and sand along a coastline. Where longshore drift is strong, an abrupt change in the direction of the coast or the entry of a river can produce a *spit*, a narrow ridge of sand, gravel and pebbles piled up by the waves.

Orford Ness on the Suffolk coast is a shingle spit which first sealed off the estuary of the River Alde and then extended southwards for several kilometres across the mouth of the River Butley. The town of Orford lies inland between the two rivers, but 750 years ago it was a port facing the open sea. The curiously shaped triangular beach known as a *cuspate foreland*, and found for example at Dungeness in Kent and at Cape Kennedy (Canaveral) in Florida, is the

result of material adjusting to a particular pattern of wave or current action.

Man has attempted to arrest the drift of material along some beaches by constructing barriers or *groynes*. While they may prove a temporary success, groynes all too frequently upset the natural relationship between beach supply, wave action and sediment transport, so that at the end of the protected zone serious erosion occurs. As an alternative to this a number of attempts have been made to artificially replenish beaches by dumping material of an appropriate size. For example, Portobello beach near Edinburgh—robbed of its sand by a long history of erosion—has received this treatment with some success and the technique has been quite widely adopted in California and Florida.

Shore platforms

Along rocky coasts, a level rock shelf or *shore platform* extends seawards from the cliff-base. Shore platforms show almost as much variety as beaches but two basic forms can be recognized. The first, typical of storm wave coasts where mechanical erosion is dominant, consists of an inclined surface stretching to low tide and below. The second consists of a near-horizontal platform that ends abruptly at what is called a *low tide cliff*. This form is typical of tropical and warm temperate areas, such as the New South Wales and Victoria coasts of Australia, where chemical weathering is important.

The surface form of the platform owes much to the waves and the underlying geology, but it also depends on the processes by which a platform is eroded. Alternating hard and soft sands in shore platforms are eroded at differing rates so that miniature scarps and vales are produced. Biological activity is often a notable feature of shore platforms and in warm seas becomes very important. A continuous sea-weed cover tends to protect the platform surface, but a variety of intertidal organisms cause erosion. Some creatures such as piddocks survive by drilling a hole into the platform surface, enlarging it as they grow. Others, like the sea urchin, excavate a shallow hollow or cave. On limestone rocks a number of animals, as for example the limpet, create a variety of hollows by exuding acids which eat into the rock. In these limestone areas, chemical solution is often an important weathering process. But, inevitably, it is slow and its effects may be overtaken by other, more powerful, erosive processes such as the pounding of storm waves.

Below: Robin Hood's Bay in Yorkshire, created by the rapid erosion of cliffs of soft rock. In many such cases, the sea actually erodes very little material, but it encourages mass movement processes to operate on the cliff and then removes material that slumps onto the beach—as in happening in the foreground.

Heather Angel

Alphabet & Image

51

The Ocean Floor

Like the back of the moon, the floor of the ocean was almost entirely unknown until a few years ago. In the days of the great circum-global expedition of HMS *Challenger* in 1872-1876 the depth of the ocean was still being determined by line sounding. This was achieved by laboriously unwinding a line with a weight attached to the end until it touched the ocean bottom. As the ocean is commonly 5,000 m (3 miles) deep, this was very time consuming and required careful judgement.

During and after the First World War, echo sounding was introduced. At first it consisted of letting off a single sound pulse into the ocean and 'listening' for its echo from the bottom. Knowing the speed of sound in water and the time taken for the echo to return to the surface, the depth of water could then be determined.

Under the stimulus of the Second World War continuously recording deep-sea echo sounders were developed which synchronized the repeated firing of a sound pulse with a recording device, such as an electrically-activated 'pen' scanning a moving paper roll. These echo sounders produced a continuous profile of the ocean floor along the line of the ship's course.

Because of this invention we now have a comprehensive and detailed idea of the morphology of the floors of seas and oceans—comprehensive because it can be obtained automatically whenever a ship is under way; detailed because it can provide precision within 2 m (6 ft) or so in depths of 5,000 m (3 miles) of water. For maximum accuracy it is necessary to actually measure the temperature of the ocean water from top to bottom, because this, together with salinity (saltiness) and pressure, affects the precise speed of transmission of sound.

Other methods similar to echo sounding include *continuous seismic profiling*, which can also be obtained from a moving vessel. However, this method uses a more powerful and lower frequency sound source than echo sounding. This will not only reflect back off the immediate ocean floor, but also in part penetrate through it, to be reflected back by underlying sediment layers and rock surfaces. In this way more information is gained about the structure of the rocks beneath the sea bed.

The *sidescan sonar* is a further advance, as it can look obliquely sideways from a ship, instead of vertically downwards, and therefore cover a broad band across the ocean floor. It is particularly good at picking out the pattern of rock layers which outcrop on the sea floor.

Ocean floor provinces

From all this wealth of information we can conclude that the ocean floor has just as varied a 'landscape' as the surfaces of the continents. The floor is made up of a series of major 'provinces', each with its own special characteristics. Working outwards from the coast, the first is known as the *continental shelf*, followed by the *continental slope* and the *continental rise*, and then out on to the *abyssal plains* and *hills*. However, at destructive plate margins, where the oceanic crust is subducted below the continental crust at the foot of the continental slope, deep *ocean trenches* are

THE OCEAN FLOOR

volcanic island — seamount — transform fault — flat-topped seamount (guyot) — mid-oceanic ridge — ocean trench

Above: This idealized panorama of the ocean floor illustrates the major sea-floor features to be expected in any ocean basin. In order to show these features clearly, the vertical scale is greatly exaggerated and the features have been grouped closer together than they are actually found. The depths are shown as if they were illuminated, although in reality there is little light below 200 m and it is completely dark below 1,000 m in the oceans.

Right: Recent pillow lavas on the mid-Atlantic ridge. Where molten lava erupts underwater, the leading edges of the flow cool very quickly and solidify into these pillow-like masses. Sediment is often trapped between the pillows and this helps to date the period of eruption. Unfortunately, chemical reactions between the fresh lava and seawater often make the usual radioactive methods of age determination unreliable, but the oldest known sediments brought up from beneath the ocean floor are 165 million years old.

Lamont Doherty Geological Observatory

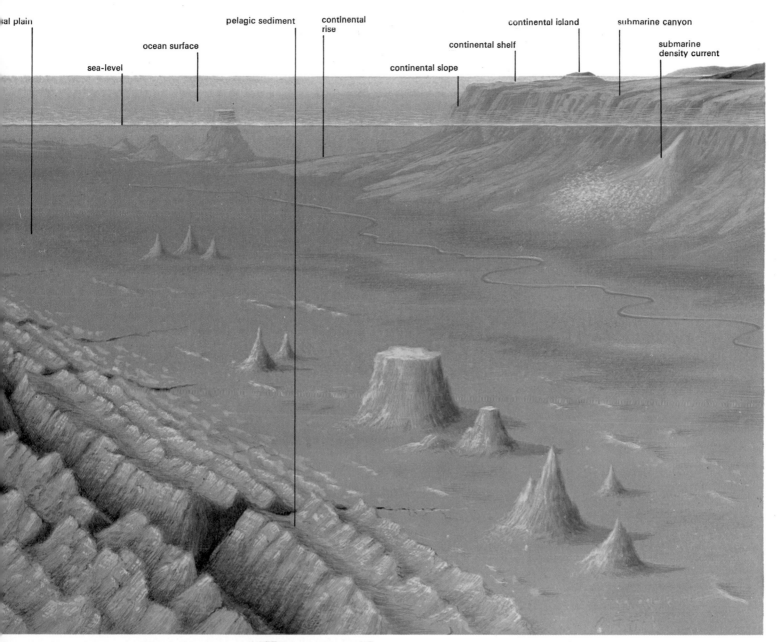

sal plain

ocean surface

pelagic sediment

continental rise

continental shelf

continental slope

continental island

submarine canyon

submarine density current

sea-level

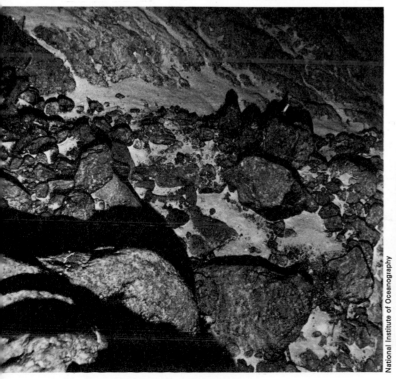

Left: In the ocean, as well as on land, rocks are often broken by large fractures or faults and form cliffs or escarpments. In this photograph, taken at a depth of 3,390 m (1,850 fathoms), boulders up to a metre across and other smaller angular blocks of rock can be seen at the bottom of a bare rock slope, on Palmer Ridge in the NE Atlantic. Samples of rock can often be obtained by dredging the sea floor.

Below: This picture shows ripples (about 20 cm from crest to crest) produced by currents passing over calcareous sands (rich in calcium carbonate) between outcrops of basaltic rock on top of a seamount, on the Carlsberg Ridge in the Indian Ocean. The photograph was taken 2,500 m down. Despite the conditions of darkness and great pressure, animals still thrive. A sea lily (or crinoid) is visible, its branched arms open to catch small organisms on which it feeds.

National Institute of Oceanography

National Institute of Oceanography

53

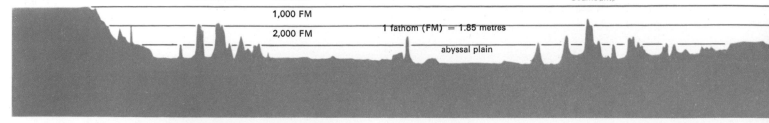

Kelvin seamounts   sea-level   Corner Seamounts

1,000 FM

2,000 FM   1 fathom (FM) = 1.85 metres

abyssal plain

Above: A cross-section of the bottom of the N Atlantic. The topographical profile shown is of the sea floor from Martha's Vineyard, Massachusetts (USA) to Gibraltar, 5,600 km away. An accurate picture of the undersea 'landscape' is given by modern devices such as this echo-sounding machine (left), which is producing a trace of the sea-floor off the Canary Islands in the Atlantic as the sounding ship moves over it. Each line records the echoes from one sound pulse.

developed instead of a continental rise. The final major province of the ocean floor comprises the flanks and crest of the *mid-oceanic ridges* or *rises*.

The *continental shelves* are the submerged edges of the continents. The water over them is usually no more than about 200 m (660 ft) deep. Because of its shallowness the sea bottom here is strongly affected by tidal and other currents which disturb and transport the sandy, clayey and shelly sediments produced by coastal erosion and by the growth of plants and animals in these shallow ocean waters. The width of the continental shelves varies in different parts of the oceans, from 2 km (1.25 miles) or less off the coast of Chile, to 320 km (200 miles) off Land's End in England, to over 1,200 km (750 miles) off the Arctic coast of Siberia.

At the seaward limit of the shelf there is usually an abrupt change in slope, and the sea bottom then descends steeply towards the deep ocean floor. This steep slope is known as the *continental slope*. It often declines at a rate of between 1 in 40 and 1 in 6 (the latter comparable with the steeper hillsides on land) from a depth of about 200 m (660 ft) to around 3,000 m (about 2 miles) deep. In parts of the ocean it is covered by a mantle, sometimes unstable, of clay and silty clay. Elsewhere it consists of the more or less cut-off edges of the layers of sediment making up the continental shelves. It is the continental slope, not the coastline, that marks the true boundary of each continent.

Many continental slopes are incised with vast steep-sided *submarine canyons* that cut back into the continental shelves —often nearly to the coast itself. Sometimes they occur directly off the mouths of major rivers: one, for example, has been discovered directly in front of the mouth of the River Congo in Africa. The canyons cut deep into the sea-floor, usually emerging somewhere near the foot of the continental slope, where there is often a fan-shaped sedimentary deposit on the deep-sea floor. These troughs are the result of submarine erosion by sediment en route more or less directly from the near-shore to the deep-sea floor.

At the base of the continental slope there is generally a more gently inclining province (sloping at a rate of 1 in 100 to 1 in 700) known as the *continental rise*, which takes the sea-floor down gradually to truly oceanic depths of 4,000 to over 5,000 m (16,500 ft). The rise is made up of sediments brought down by dense, heavy flows of sediment-laden water called *submarine density currents*, sometimes along submarine canyons from the adjacent continent, thereby building up the ocean floor above its normal level. The rise represents the coarser deposits of slowing density currents. Beyond it are the extensive *abyssal plains*.

The almost flat, featureless abyssal plains have been called 'the smoothest surfaces on earth'. Their actual inclinations are between 1 in 1,000 and 1 in 10,000. Beneath them is the irregular igneous basaltic crust. Over them are deposited the finer suspended debris which ultimately settle out from the larger density currents.

Mainly in the Pacific Ocean, beyond the influence of density currents, the ocean floor is composed of a series of gently moulded *abyssal hills*. The undulations reflect the original unevenness of the igneous basement. On these abyssal hills rain the slowly accumulating remains of planktonic (floating) plants and animals, which lived in the surface waters, but whose skeletons fall to the depths to form a fairly uniform blanket of sediment. In the narrower Atlantic Ocean, however, the abyssal plains stretch right out to the flanks of the *mid-oceanic ridge*.

The mid-oceanic ridge consists of a crestal region adjacent to the centre line along which new igneous crustal material (basalt) is being injected, and a flank region in which the crust very gradually subsides as it cools and is pushed away from the centre line. A slow-spreading ridge often has a characteristic median rift valley, as in the Atlantic, with peaks rising thousands of metres on either side of a fissure on average 50 km (30 miles) wide. Some points along the crest may actually project above sea-level as an island, such as Iceland, or as a sub-aerial volcano, such as Tristan da Cunha in the South Atlantic. Faster-spreading ridges, as in the south-east Pacific, generally lack such a central rift valley and have a lower profile.

The mid-oceanic ridges or rises are the site of formation of new ocean floor. Old ocean floor is consumed by underthrust-

Above and below: Echo sounders beam sound waves to the bottom and measure the time taken for the echo to be reflected back to the ship. A major advance came with seismic surveying, which uses more powerful low-frequency equipment to penetrate the sea floor and record underlying sediment layers and rock. By towing the array of devices, interference from ship-board noises can be avoided. These seismic reflection profiles (above) across the Bay of Biscay show that great thicknesses of sediment have accumulated under abyssal plain conditions. Multilayered profiles are often an indication that numerous episodes of deposition have occurred, by deep-sea density currents.

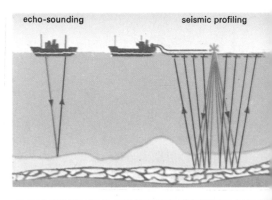

echo-sounding   seismic profiling

Above: A diver inspects the wreck of the sunken *Cooma* in the shallow waters of the continental shelf of Australia.

Right: The radiating feeding tracks on this abyssal plain (more than 5,500 m deep) indicates an animal buried in the soft calcareous *Globigerina* ooze. A sea lily can also be seen.

Left: This NASA shot of the Atlantic coast off Cape Hatteras shows the extent of the continental shelf off the NE United States beneath the ocean waters. The line of puffy clouds marks the junction between the colder water covering the shelf and the warmer Gulf Stream waters further out. The shelf is an average 120 m deep.

Right: The very slow rates of sediment accumulation on the deep-sea floor may leave very resistant remains, such as whales' earbones and sharks' teeth, at or near the surface of sediment for very long periods. This now-extinct shark's tooth was dredged in the Pacific from a depth of over 4,000 m by HMS *Challenger* in 1874.

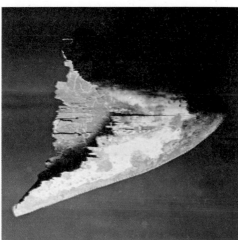

ing, either beneath continents, or beneath other pieces of oceanic crust. At the point where the ocean floor is deflected downwards by crustal activity an *ocean trench* is formed. It is in these trenches that the greatest depths on the deep ocean floor are found. A depth of 11,033 m (36,198 ft) was recorded by echo sounding from the Marianas Trench off the Philippines.

Composition of the ocean floor

New ocean floor, freshly created at the mid-ocean ridges, is made of basaltic igneous rock. This may be either extruded onto the ocean floor as pillow lavas, or intruded as horizontal sills or vertical dykes into pre-existing sediments or igneous rocks. These rocks form the crest of the mid-ocean ridges. They also form the foundations of individual volcanoes or chains of volcanoes, and of their submerged counterparts, the volcanic *seamounts*. Seamounts are isolated peaks rising from the ocean floor, and are especially numerous in the Pacific Ocean. Here, in the Tonga Trench between Samoa and New Zealand, is the highest known seamount, its summit being some 8,690 m (28,500 ft) above the sea bed.

The original surface of the volcanic mid-oceanic ridge crest is very rugged. In time the depressions get filled in with *pelagic sediment* (mostly the skeletal remains of planktonic organisms) which is often re-deposited by slumping off the steep slopes of the surrounding volcanic rocks. The deposit in these so-called sediment 'ponds' is likely at first to be calcareous, because of the calcium carbonate content of the remains of the microscopic algae called *coccolithophores*, and the microscopic animals called *foraminifers*. In time the whole of the original surface will be blanketed by these deposits, known as *calcareous ooze*, and this is generally the case on the upper flanks of mid-ocean ridges.

At greater depths the ocean floor passes below the level (4,000 to 5,000 m) at which calcium carbonate dissolves. Here the sediment consists only of insoluble clay or the remains of siliceous (silica rich) organisms such as *diatoms* and *radiolarians*. Therefore drilling through those parts of the ocean floor covered by the oldest sediments will often reveal a sequence of non-calcareous, then calcareous sediments, then volcanic basalt rock.

From the shallowest water to the greatest depths, the ocean floor is almost universally colonized by animals of one kind or another. In soft sediment they live by burrowing into the sediment, on hard rock attached to the surface. Where currents run near the bottom it may be patterned by ripple marks, and near areas influenced by the past and present polar ice caps are found sand, silt and blocks of erratic rock, carried and eventually dropped by drifting icebergs. In fact the ocean floor is a veritable repository of the entire history of our planet.

Seaphot

National Institute of Oceanography

Alphabet & Image

PLANTS

The Plant Kingdom

To help understand the living world it is convenient to divide it into distinct groups of similar organisms; each group having certain combinations of features which are common to it alone and which separate it from all other groups. These groups can then be divided into sub-groups or combined to make super-groups—a process which highlights both the similarities and differences between different organisms. The science of classifying living organisms is known as *taxonomy*. Once an organism has been correctly classified it is possible to succinctly summarize a great deal of knowledge about it simply in its name.

The fundamental unit of classification is the *species*. A species is a group of plants or animals which reproduce among themselves to give the same type of plant or animal. Generally the common names used to describe animals and plants refer to particular species such as tomato,

Lycopersicum esculentum, and man, *Homo sapiens*. Each species is then grouped in larger groups which in ascending order are: *genus* (the first name in the two-part Latin name), *tribe*, *family*, *order*, *class*, *phylum*, and finally *kingdom*. Just two kingdoms are generally accepted—the plant kingdom and the animal kingdom.

Bacteria, blue-green algae and fungi

Although classification is an indispensable aid to study, all divisions above species are entirely artificial. (This explains why whether one group is called, say, a class or a phylum is often in dispute). Many animals and plants are extremely difficult to classify satisfactorily. In particular there are a large number of organisms which cannot be

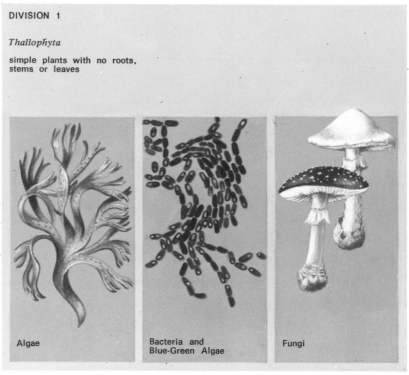

DIVISION 1

Thallophyta

simple plants with no roots, stems or leaves

Algae

Bacteria and Blue-Green Algae

Fungi

DIVISION 2

Bryophyta

plants with leaves and stems but no true roots

Mosses

Left: A group of pennate diatoms, *Striatella*, clustered on the red alga, *Polysiphonia*. Algae are the predominant group of marine plants and vary from simple single-celled species to large complex seaweeds.

Below: *Mycena inclinata*, a fungus, growing on a fallen oak tree. Fungi do not have chlorophyll and are not related to any other plant groups. Some botanists claim they should be classified in a separate kingdom from plants or animals.

Above: The plant kingdom. All life developed originally in the seas and the earliest life forms were probably similar to the *prokaryotic* bacteria and blue-green algae. When the first *eukaryotic* cell (with

specialized organelles) developed is not known, but it is probable that it was much like the simple single-celled algae of today. From the algae all higher plant forms have evolved by improved adaption to life on land.

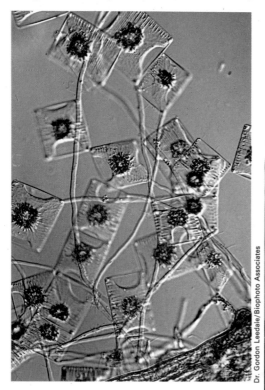

Dr. Gordon Leedale/Biophoto Associates

Heather Angel

DIVISION 3

Pteridophyta

plants with roots, stems
leaves and water conducting
tissue

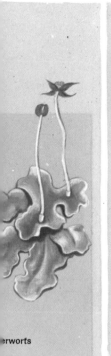

erworts

Ferns

Horsetails

Clubmosses

DIVISION 4

Spermatophyta

seed - bearing plants with roots,
stems, leaves and water
conducting tissue

Gymnosperms
(coniferous trees)

Angiosperms
(flowering plants)

Below: The Royal fern, *Osmunda regalis.* **In many ways ferns resemble higher plants. They have a dominant sporophyte—the gametophyte being an inconspicuous filament many times smaller than the sporophyte.**

Right: A species of silver fir, *Abies,* **clearly showing the red mature cones. Firs are coniferous trees—the most distinctive group of the** *Gymnospermae,* **which also includes yews and the tropical cycads and ginkgos.**

Giuseppe Mazza

Family

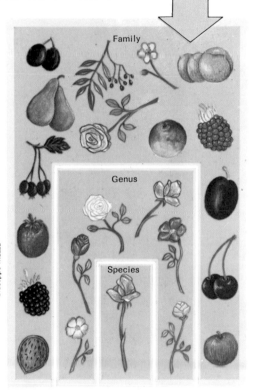

Genus

Species

Right: Plants are classified into groups each of which has a set of characteristic features which distinguishes it from other groups. The family, *Rosaceae,* **illustrated here, includes the** *genera,* *Malus* **(apples),** *Pyrus* **(pears) and** *Rubus* **(raspberries and blackberries) as well as** *Rosa* **(roses).** *Rosa* **are further divided into species such as** *Rosa canina,* **the dog rose, and** *Rosa odorata,* **the tea rose.**

conveniently accommodated in either the plant or animal kingdoms. A vast group of such organisms are the *prokaryotes* which includes bacteria and blue-green algae. Their distinctive characteristic— they do not have cells with specialized structures or *organelles*—divides them so completely from all other organisms that many authorities consider them as a kingdom in their own right.

Another group, the *Fungi,* are normally considered to be plants but differ from the majority of plants by one factor—the absence of chlorophyll. Hence, all fungi lack the ability to make their own food. They obtain their nourishment in the same way as animals do by feeding on other living organisms (*parasitism*) or on their dead remains (*saprophytism*).

The three main classes of fungi are the *Phycomycetes,* the *Ascomycetes* and the *Basidiomycetes.* They differ in the way they produce their spores. Some species of phycomycetes have free-swimming *zoospores* though not all do so. The others such as pin-mould, *Mucor,* reproduce by non-mobile spores which are either enclosed inside a spore case (*sporangium*) or are unenclosed so that they can be blown away by the wind. Another characteristic of phycomycetes is that the young cells do not possess crosswalls.

In the *Ascomycetes* the cells have cross-walls and characteristically they also produce eight spores in special sporangia, called *asci,* which are often grouped within cup- or flask-shaped fruiting bodies. Ascomycetes also form

Heather Angel

59

Above: *Quercus*, the oak. There are 450 species of oak—two of which, *Quercus robur* and *Quercus petraea*, are native to Britain and 60 to North America. Before extensive cultivation, oak forest was the dominant vegetation of Europe. The success of oak and other genera of trees relies upon their ability to lay down wood in thickened growths—a process known as *secondary thickening*. Secondary growth allows the tree to produce a tall, dense leaf canopy which suppresses other plants by overshadowing them.

Right: Flowers in their many forms are the distinguishing feature of the phylum *Angiospermae*, the flowering plants, which are by far the largest group, in both numbers and species, of plant forms today. These flowers belong to the beech, *Fagus sylvatica*.

Below: *Chionochloa flavescens*, an alpine grass growing in New Zealand. Grasses are a most important family of the sub-phylum *Monocotyledonae*. Monocots have only one seed leaf (*cotyledon*) which develops inside the seed. The cotyledon of grasses absorbs food from another part of the seed (the *endosperm*) and passes it on to the developing plant. In other plants it is a food storage organ itself (as in legumes) or develops with the young plant to become the first green photosynthesizing leaf.

the fungal part of the fungus-alga association which comprises a lichen. Two examples of an ascomycete are yeast (*Saccharomyces*) and *Penicillium notatum* from which penicillin is produced.

The third group of fungi, the *Basidomycetes*, includes the mushrooms and toadstools. All these have a spore-bearing structure, called a *basidium*, which swells at the end to form a spore, rather as a glass bulb is blown at the end of a piece of glass tubing.

Algae
The majority of plants, however, differ from animals primarily in their ability to manufacture their own food by photosynthesis. The simplest form of plants which do this are the *Algae*. Algae have no roots, stems, leaves or water-conducting tissue and are all totally dependent on water. Almost all are aquatic.

Colour is the most distinguishing characteristic of algae and the group is divided up into classes according to the predominance of one pigment or another in their cells. In the diatoms (*Chrysophyta*), which constitute the major element of marine plankton upon which all marine life ultimately depends for food, the predominant colour is brown. In the green algae, *Chlorophyta*, however, the green pigment, chlorophyll, is not disguised by the presence of other colouring matter. This class includes the majority of the simple fresh water algae such as *Chlamydomonas* as well as filamentous forms such as *Spirogyra*.

The brown algae, *Phaeophyta*, are almost all seaweeds and are probably the best known algae, owing to the size and complexity which many of them attain

and the extraordinary abundance in which they occur along the coasts. The brown/green colour of their body structure (*thallus*) results from the fact that they contain a brown pigment, *fucoxanthin*, as well as chlorophyll. Treatment with hot water, which dissolves the fucoxanthin, has the effect of turning brown seaweeds green.

Land plants
The simplest land plants are the *Bryophyta* which possesses many features which must have been common to the first land plants. They have an outer layer of cells, the *epidermis*, which surrounds the plants and to some extent prevents drying out. Nevertheless they are highly dependent on water for their reproduction and hence are limited in the habitats they can colonize. Nor do they have a well-developed conducting system for transporting food or water and thus their maximum size is also restricted.

The bryophytes are divided into two classes, the liverworts (*Hepaticae*) and the mosses (*Musci*). In both classes the gamete-producing generation (the *gametophyte*) is dominant over the spore-producing generation (the *sporophyte*). In the liverworts the gametophyte is a flat, green, ribbon-like thallus which grows horizontally with root-like *rhizoids*, while the sporophyte, which develops from a fertilized egg in the gametophyte, remains as a small simple structure dependent on the gametophyte for its nutrition.

The moss gametophyte is not unlike a higher plant. It has a vertical stem with simple leaves, but rhizoids, not roots, anchor it to the ground. Again the

sporophyte is simple, and at least partly dependent on the gametophyte for its food, but it is generally more complex than the sporophyte of the liverworts. Despite this, the structure of the moss gametophyte is quite different from that of the corresponding generation of higher plants, and so mosses and liverworts may be regarded as an isolated group, highly developed in their own way, but with no near affinities to other groups of plants.

This is not true of the ferns (*Filicinae*), the largest class of the phylum *Pteridophyta*. In ferns the situation is reversed with respect to the two generations. The sporophyte is dominant while the gametophyte is small and little more than a structure for producing sex organs and gametes. (Nevertheless it leads an independent life unlike the gametophyte of more advanced plants.) The ferns and their relations, the clubmosses and the horsetails, further resemble higher plants in possessing a sporophyte with roots, leaves and stems and also woody conducting tissue (*vascular tissue*) for transporting water and food. Unlike advanced plants, however, fern male gametes are mobile *spermatozoids*, similar to those of the bryophytes, which must swim to the female sex organs in a water film on the plant surface. Ferns, therefore, are still very dependent on water.

Though they have vascular tissue none of the existing pteridophytes possess the ability to lay down wood in annual rings (*secondary growth*) as do the flowering plants. Secondary growth, however, did occur in pteridophytes of the past and these were possibly related to the early ancestors of the flowering plants.

The *Gymnospermae* are further

advanced. In these plants secondary growth is usual, allowing the formation of trees like pine (*Pinus*), fir (*Pseudotsuga*) and spruce (*Picea*). Gymnosperms are also the oldest group of living plants which produce true seeds and in which the male gametophyte is reduced to a nucleus in small wind-borne spores (pollen). Unlike the flowering plants, however, the egg cells of gymnosperms are naked and not enclosed in *ovaries* and gymnosperms do not have flowers. The sporophyte gymnosperms of today are woody trees mostly with evergreen foliage and are particularly abundant as individuals, if not species, in the mountains and cool temperate regions of the world.

Flowering plants

A more recently evolved phylum than the *Gymnospermae* is the *Angiospermae* or flowering plants. This phylum contains the bulk of the present world flora. Like the gymnosperms, angiosperms do not have mobile gametes and hence they are not so dependent on water as the ferns and lower plants. This factor is responsible for their success in a great number of habitats including near deserts.

The characteristic feature of flowering plants is that the egg-bearing ovules are enclosed in an ovary which is usually crowned by a pollen-receiving surface, the *stigma*, borne on a stalk, the *style*. The pollen is produced on nearby reproductive structures called *anthers*. Both the ovary and anthers are then enclosed by special modified leaves, *petals*, and the whole constitutes a flower.

Flowering plants are divided into two sub-phyla: the *Dicotyledonae* which possess two seed leaves (*cotyledons*) and are mainly broad-leaved plants with branching leaf veins, and the *Monocotyledonae* which possess one seed leaf, and have long narrow leaves with parallel veins. Monocotyledons do not undergo secondary growth so all flowering trees are dicotyledons. A major class of the *Monocotyledonae* are the *Graminae*, which include all grasses and cereals.

Classification of the angiosperms is on the basis of the structure of the flowers, fruits and seeds, and a large array of families have been distinguished. Their diversity and adaptability are indicated by the many varied habitats they have invaded. Forms such as cacti and other succulent plants have colonized deserts and the salt sand of sea shores. Water storage tissue and thick wax layers around these plants help to conserve water. Others, such as mistletoe, *Viscum album*, have lost the ability to photosynthesize and have become parasitic.

Finally, a very few angiosperms have returned to the sea from which all plants originated. For example, *Poseidonia* grows on the bed of the sea in warm parts of the world. Thus the group of plants which have become the dominant vegetation of the world because of their success as land plants are now recolonizing the sea and may become a dominant group of marine plants as well. Nevertheless, the dominance of angiosperms cannot be expected to be unending. It is probable that another group of plants, possibly developing from some obscure and unimposing species, will in the future supersede the angiosperms just as they have superseded the ferns and gymnosperms of 300 million years ago.

Above: An example of a monocot flower—the lily, Royal Gold. Monocots are easily distinguished from dicots by their leaves which have parallel veins. Lilies and irises are monocots. Most other flowers are dicots with branched veins on their leaves.

Below: *Papaver rhoeas*, the common field poppy. Poppies are a family of simple dicot flowers with petals which are separated from each other. Some complex flowers, like those of daisies, *Compositae*, consist of many simple flowers fused to form a tube.

Giuseppe Mazza

The Evolution of Plants

Throughout much of geological time, plants have been preserved as fossils in sedimentary rocks. Today this fossil record provides evidence of some of the major steps in the evolution and astonishing diversification of the plant kingdom. But the usefulness of this record goes far beyond the palaeobotanist's interest in the ancient history of plant life. Buried in this fossil record, there are clues to the origin of life itself.

Indeed, research into the Pre-Cambrian fossil record has been encouraged by the advances in space exploration. For, in anticipation of finding some primitive form of life on other planets, earth scientists are examining the oldest and most primitive remains of life on earth.

The first evidence of life

At present the oldest known remains of cellular organisms are found in the Fig Tree chert (black, glassy rocks made of silica) in Swaziland, which is some 3,100 million years old. The simple morphological structures are presumed to be bacteria because of their size and shape. From the same rocks scientists have also extracted many different kinds of complex organic substances which are the essential biochemical constituents of living matter. These include, for example, certain familiar amino acids and carbohydrates.

The search has been extended to other slightly younger rocks. This has shown that as the age decreases so cellular structure and chemical complexity increase. For instance, 2,800 million year old rocks in the Bulawayan Group from Rhodesia contain fossils of multi-cellular organisms, thought to be the remains of colonial algae which form reef-like calcareous banks called *stromatolites*. These are easily preserved as fossils because of the hard calcareous dome-shaped mats which the algal cells secrete.

Very similar organisms still survive today and grow in profusion in the quiet intertidal zones of western Australia. These *procaryotes* (lacking a true nucleus) are among the simplest known organisms. Their occurrence 2,800 million years ago marks the beginning of plant life as we know it, and the start of the development of greater complexity by living things.

The next major stage in the increasing sophistication of the fossil plant record is found in Canada. Certain blue-green algae have been identified in the 1,900 million year old Gun Flint chert. These still have simple procaryotic organization, but they are more complex than the algae which produced the stromatolites because their cells are ordered into filamentous chains. Once again, the specimens that have been found in these old rocks are very similar to types of blue-green algae that grow in ponds and lakes today.

More and more of these very old fossils are being discovered every year, particularly in Australia, where suitably preserved sediments a little younger than 1,000 million years old are quite common. The best known are from Bitter Springs where large numbers of multi-cellular photosynthetic organisms have been

Dr Michael Boulter

Left: About 400 million years ago, plants first made the transfer from sea to land. The oldest known vascular plant (with fluid-conducting cells) is *Cooksonia* (shown beside tall fern) which grew up to 10 cm high at the edge of the water. The fossil (above) shows the simple branching of the stem and the spore capsules. Many other very simple fern-like plants also colonized the land and some grew to over 1 m high. Intertidal zones continued to support the dome-shaped mats of secretions from various blue-green algae, which form the easily fossilized stromatolites. These vary from a few centimetres to several metres across. (Below) Section of a stromatolite dome. Stromatolites date back to 2,800 M.Y. ago.

discovered. These fossils are among the oldest records of *eucaryotes*, organisms with highly organized cytoplasm, the earliest of which gave rise through evolution to all other types of plants. These more sophisticated organisms become widespread in younger fossil-bearing deposits and, though they often occur alongside the simpler procaryotes, they begin to dominate the vegetation from about that time.

Until about 400 million years ago, single-celled, colonial and filamentous algae formed the basis of plant life on this planet. Much of today's land surface was covered with water.

An environmental change enabling plants to adapt to new forms came over 400 million years ago. During the Silurian period, the seas retreated from earlier continental coastal regions. Palaeobotanists believe that multi-cellular algae began to colonize the new intertidal areas and to have differentiated into forms of plants that could best survive away from the seas. The new land environments had many advantages: they offered a stable base, a source of food in the newly developing soil and a warm humid atmosphere, with some concentration of oxygen for more efficient respiration.

Jane Burton/Bruce Coleman

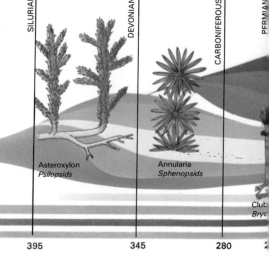

PRE-CAMBRIAN | CAMBRIAN | ORDOVICIAN | SILURIAN | DEVONIAN | CARBONIFEROUS | PERMIAN

Asteroxylon
Psilopsids

Annularia
Sphenopsids

Club
Bryc

570   500   435   395   345   280

Left: Carboniferous swamp forests contained many large ferns and other pteridophytes such as *Calamites* which grew to a height of 60 metres. Their large soft stems bore rosettes of branches arranged in a simple symmetrical manner with leaves at the nodes. The fossil *Calamites* (below) clearly reveals its original stem shape although the leaves and branches have been broken off and the stem is preserved only as an impression in the rock.

Right: These tree trunks grew in Arizona over 200 M.Y. ago. The organic constituents have been replaced by minerals to produce petrified wood. Plants are preserved mainly by petrification or carbonization, as occurs in coal measures.

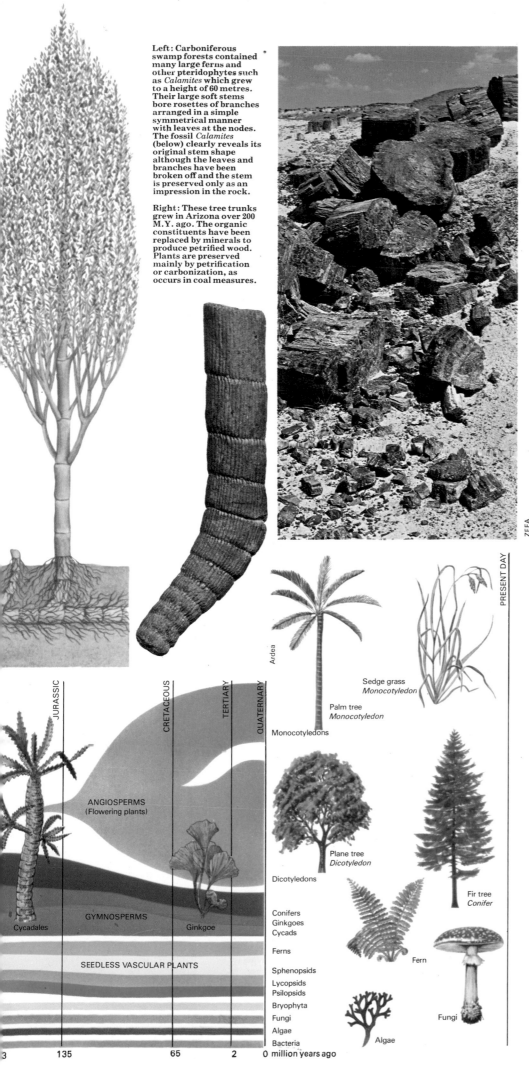

ZEFA

PRESENT DAY

Ardea

Sedge grass
Monocotyledon

Palm tree
Monocotyledon

Monocotyledons

Plane tree
Dicotyledon

Dicotyledons

Fir tree
Conifer

Conifers
Ginkgoes
Cycads

Ferns

Fern

Sphenopsids
Lycopsids
Psilopsids

Bryophyta

Fungi

Algae

Fungi

Bacteria

Algae

JURASSIC · CRETACEOUS · TERTIARY · QUATERNARY

ANGIOSPERMS
(Flowering plants)

GYMNOSPERMS

Cycadales

Ginkgoe

SEEDLESS VASCULAR PLANTS

3 · 135 · 65 · 2 · 0 million years ago

At the end of the Silurian, there began a rapid burst of evolution within the plant kingdom. Within just 25 million years—a very short length of geological time—land plants evolved complex vascular systems to transport food all over the plant body, leaves which specialized in photosynthesis, roots and stems for support, and, most dramatically of all, *sporangia* (in which spores were produced) and even seeds for reproduction. Moreover, the biochemical, physiological and genetical processes needed to support such complex organisms developed too.

Plants of the past

These events occurred during the Devonian—a period when much land surface was exposed—and now recognized as being one of the two intervals of greatest expansion in plant evolution. Consequently, at the end of the Devonian, 345 million years ago, not only were there diverse types of marine and freshwater algae, but also a huge variety of spore-bearing plants such as ferns, tree-ferns, horse-tails, club-mosses and many now unfamiliar little plants with simple stems and small sporangia.

All these plants are now extinct, though modern ferns, club-mosses and horse-tails do survive as rare representatives of the ancient lineages. Particularly unfamiliar to us would be the Devonian pro gymnosperms which are thought to have grown up to 25 metres (88 feet) in height with woody trunks, conifer-like leaves and simple seeds which were fertilized by wind-blown pollen.

A similarly unfamiliar, completely extinct group of plants was particularly common during the Carboniferous period that followed. These were the *pteridosperms*, with fern-like leaves, underground stems and very simple large seeds hanging loosely from the leaves. They relied on the wind blowing large pollen grains over the mouth of the seed for pollination to take place. Because this was a very inefficient process which encouraged inbreeding, they quickly became extinct. For a time, however, they achieved some success and are commonly found as fossils in the Carboniferous coal measure deposits.

The equatorial swamps of North America and Europe, then joined as a single land mass, also supported forests of very large *pteridophytes*. These plants reproduced by spores, like modern ferns, and were formed of very soft parts with a high water content. The best known of these is *Lepidodendron* which grew up to 35 metres (115 feet) in height and had a stem over 1 metre (39 in) in diameter. Just as common were giant horse-tails such as *Calamites* and ferns similar to, but larger than, those of modern times. These very warm, wet and humid swamps were environments in which plant life flourished, and where the rate of growth has been shown to have been considerable.

The relatively sudden and major changes in world environment that took place at the end of the Carboniferous period marks the end of this botanical paradise. Climatic and other changes forced an end to the profusion of the luxurious forest swamps, and large numbers of once abundant plants became extinct very quickly. The environmental changes enabled those plants with the more sophisticated seed reproduction systems, the *gymnosperms* (which include the conifers and their relatives), to win over those with the simpler sporangia. Their woody nature also proved to be most suitable for the drier environments that were to follow.

The periods of the Mesozoic era saw a great diversification of these plants. Gymnosperms with short hard trunks and crowns of hard waxy leaves up to four metres (13 feet) long were commonplace. For 150 million years, until some 100 million years ago, the plant kingdom diversified more than it had done before. Trees with naked seeds relying on wind for pollination, ferns, and relatively few smaller pteridophytes formed the basis of the floras of the world. As in the Carboniferous, plants were able to consolidate on this type of structure once they had become established within a reasonably stable environment.

World vegetation during the Mesozoic was based on four separate floras, whose origins can be traced back to Carboniferous times. The Euramerican flora occupied most of Europe and North America, the *Glossopteris* flora most of what was Gondwanaland in the south, the Angaran flora most of northern Asia, whilst the Cathaysian flora occupied what is now central Asia, China and S.E. Asia.

The Glossopteris flora was the most distinctive. Alone, it has representatives of another quite extinct group of plants, which had veined spear-shaped leaves and complex seeds. Moreover, plants from this flora have been recognized for many years from South America, southern Africa, India, Australasia and Antarctica. They provided one of the major proofs that these land masses formed a single continent 280 million years ago.

Many recent studies of these Mesozoic floras have involved not only examination of the fossilized leaves, stems and seeds, but also of their pollen grains. Since these are well preserved (they are formed of *sporopollenin* which is one of the most stable and resistant chemical substances known) they are easily observed with a microscope. And since they are more readily obtained in narrow bore-hole samples than large fossils, the recognition of pollen is particularly important in the exploration for oil and other minerals. Most of the oil deposits in the North Sea, for example, are of Mesozoic age, and have been discovered with the help of fossil pollen studies to identify the age of the sediments.

The success of flowering plants

The Cretaceous period some 100 million years ago saw the second really large explosion of evolutionary activity in the plant kingdom. The environmental circumstances that were responsible for this event are more controversial than those for the Devonian expansion as many more factors were operating to cause the changes. But the effect of this second revolution was that the dominating gymposperms of the Mesozoic were replaced by the much more successful *angiosperms*, or flowering plants, with their widely varied morphology and specialized seeds enclosed in a protective carpel.

One current explanation for this dramatic evolutionary growth is that during the relative stability of the Mesozoic plants had been able to build up a large reserve of genetic facility, needing only the opportunity to use it. Whether this opportunity was afforded by the sudden expansion of insects during the Cretaceous (most angiosperms are pollinated by insects) or whether the particular climate and environmental circumstances of the Cretaceous were suddenly favourable is not fully understood.

The effect of this evolutionary explosion of plant life was far reaching. The first groups of flowering plants succeeded so well that they caused the greater number of Mesozoic gymnosperms to become extinct quite quickly. The disappearance of others has been more gradual, and even today there is one surviving species of the *Ginkgoales*, a few species of *Cycads* in isolated parts of the world and many conifers, though the last are restricted to extreme environments such as deserts and cool temperate regions. These are the only survivors. Today most areas of the world are more or less dominated by angiosperms.

The continuing debate on the evolutionary origin of the angiosperms remains the one most substantial unanswered question in palaeobotany. One difficulty is that there are very few fossil remains of early angiosperm plants, possibly because they first appeared on mountain tops where erosion has destroyed all evidence. Another is that so many advanced gymnosperm groups, such as the members of the Glossopteris flora, have leaves and other organs that are very similar to what the earliest angiosperms may have resembled. Also, many of the parts of simple angiosperms are likely to have been very soft and so unlikely to survive as fossils. But fossil pollen grains may hold important clues since they are distinctive and easily preserved. Current research suggests that discoveries of very primitive angiosperm pollen from Cretaceous rocks from southeast Asia and Africa may represent some of the first appearances of the flowering plants.

Once they had developed, angiosperms became established very quickly. The fossil record of 90 million years ago shows few traces. Yet at the end of the Cretaceous 25 million years later they form the dominant group of plants in most fossil floras. So rapid was the rate of change that, by the beginning of the Tertiary 65 million years ago, the characters of primitive angiosperms were giving way to the relatively advanced features recognizable in modern plants.

The last 60 million years

The last 60 million years of history of the plant kingdom have been dominated by climatic fluctuations in most parts of the world. These have helped create a wider range of ecological niches and thus an increase in the potential for plant evolution to produce more species. The climax occurred just two million years ago with the beginning of the extensive ice ages, when ice at the poles produced a maximum range of climate from north to south.

The climate of the whole planet had been fluctuating from the beginning of the Tertiary. Successive waves of cooling were directed from the poles towards the equator. These changes in temperature had themselves caused a pattern of plant migration away from the poles for most of the temperate plants living in what are now polar regions, 50 and 60 million years ago. At the same time, substantial climatic changes were being caused by the effects of sea floor spreading and continental drift.

Scientists are in the process of trying to piece together the fossil evidence to explain the details of these effects of plant migration. Not only were subsequent generations of the same species of plants migrating as the climate changed, but new forms were also evolving and others were becoming extinct. One difficulty is that we know little enough of modern plants, particularly those that grow in the unexplored tropical parts of the world, to make adequate comparisons with the fossils that we might luckily find. From the huge variety of environmental and genetical factors influencing their development, it seems as though the last 50 million years in the history of plants are the hardest to understand.

Dr Michael Boulter

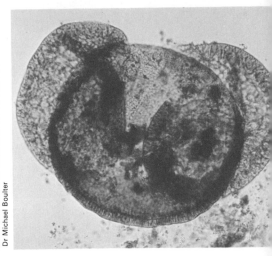

Dr Michael Boulter

Left: This fossil moss grew in Derbyshire in the English midlands, then enjoying a warm climate, about 8 M.Y. ago. Its perfect preservation shows many botanical features though no living moss is quite the same. It is one of the few fossils that record the warm climate of the time and like them it is extinct.

Below: A fossil pollen grain from an extinct species of silver fir. The grain is only 0.1 mm long but its delicate features are revealed under a microscope to aid in identifying the plant. *Palynology*, the study of pollen grains, is widely used in oil exploration to determine the age of sediments found in boreholes.

DISTRIBUTION OF REDWOODS 70 MILLION YEARS AGO

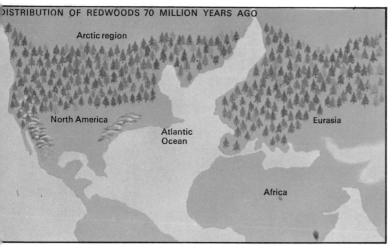

Arctic region

North America

Atlantic Ocean

Eurasia

Africa

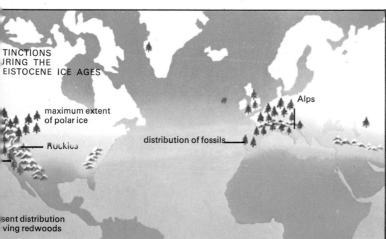

TINCTIONS
URING THE
EISTOCENE ICE AGES

Alps

maximum extent
of polar ice

Rockies

distribution of fossils

sent distribution
ving redwoods

Left: At the end of the Cretaceous, 70 M.Y. ago, when the Arctic was in a different position on the globe, the world's major mountain chains were not fully formed. Arctic regions supported temperate vegetation, of which many fossils remain. During the Tertiary period the east-west mountain chains of Europe and Asia were uplifted as the drifting continents collided. These formed a barrier to the plants trying to migrate south to escape the colder climates produced by advancing polar glaciations (below left). Many plant species became extinct. But in North America, where the mountain chains lie north-south, no such barrier existed and fewer species became extinct. Thus the modern flora of western North America represents a more ancient lineage than that of Europe. The redwoods of California, like these giants from Yosemite (below), survive today but their European and Asian counterparts from the Tertiary have long been extinct.

Dr Michael Boulter

Below: Fossil plants closely related to the present-day Californian redwood have been found in Tertiary rocks from many parts of the northern hemisphere. These portions of 8 M.Y. old trunks were found particularly well preserved in Miocene clays in Derbyshire. They have been identified as an extinct species of the *Sequoia* family by looking at thin sections of wood under a light microscope (left). The leafy shoots from the deposits (below) have similar botanical characters to the modern Californian forms, such as two types of leaves and a cone. Other fossil material from similar plants is found in many parts of the world.

Dr Michael Boulter

Barnaby's

65

Algae

Algae are simple aquatic or semi-aquatic plants widely distributed in large numbers in most ponds, lakes, streams and the surface waters of oceans. They are perhaps the most numerous of all plants, forming, with small animals, the plankton of the seas which is the primary food source of fish.

They do not possess roots, stems or leaves, yet vary greatly in size from single cells one micron (0.001 mm) in diameter, through colonies and filaments, to large fronded seaweeds which may be up to 100 m (300 ft) in length. In evolutionary terms this variation is thought to indicate the course of the development of the higher plants which are generally supposed to have originated from the green algae.

Colour

Algae are among the simplest plants in which the different functions carried out by the cell occur in specialized structures called organelles—that is they are *eukaryotic*. (Blue-green algae are an exception: they are more closely related to bacteria than to other algae and their cells do not contain discrete organelles.) In particular, algal cells have structures called *chromatophores*, containing various pigments. Most important of these is the green pigment *chlorophyll*, which occurs in chromatophores called *chloroplasts*. Chlorophyll, together with the other pigments, is able to trap the energy of

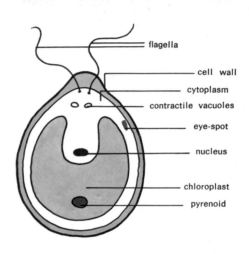

Dr. Gordon Leedale/Biophoto Associates

Left: A species of the *Euglena* group of green algae, seen under a light microscope at a magnification of about 1000 times. The plant has been squashed during preparation, causing it to release mucilage which is seen as yellow globules around the edge of the cell. Also visible are the central nucleus, two rings of paramylon —stored carbohydrate— and many green chloroplasts.

Right: *Ptilota plumosa*, a red alga. Red algae are generally small (rarely over a few centimetres in length), many-celled seaweeds with many filaments often arranged in intricate feather-like shapes as shown here.

Right: The single-celled green alga *Chlamydomonas*, found in both freshwater and seawater, showing the organelles within the cell, each with a different function. The centre of the cell is the nucleus containing the genetic material DNA. Around this is the cup-shaped *chloroplast* containing a structure known as a *pyrenoid* in which starch is stored. The *contractile vacuole* is used to force out water which continuously enters the alga from the outside.

flagella

cell wall

cytoplasm

contractile vacuoles

eye-spot

nucleus

chloroplast

pyrenoid

Below: Green algae blooming round a soda spring in the Rift Valley of East Africa. The colour is produced by the photosynthetic pigment, chlorophyll.

Right: Two different algae taken from the Mediterranean. The long reddish-brown strands are part of a filamentous red alga, *Rhodophyta*, while the circular structure in the centre of the picture is a centric diatom—one of the *Bacillariophyta*. Most oceans, lakes and ponds contain diatoms.

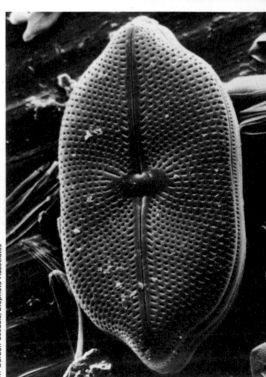

Lee Lyon/Bruce Coleman

Dr. Gordon Leedale/Biophoto Associates

Below: Two types of reproduction in the single-celled green alga, *Chlamydomonas*.
1. Asexual reproduction, in which the cell splits into two halves to produce two identical daughter cells.
2. Sexual reproduction, in which the plant produces several sex cells (gametes) by repeated division. These gametes do not have a thickened cell-wall. When they are released they fuse with gametes, often from another plant, to form first a zygote with four flagella and then a *zygospore* with a thickened cell-wall able to withstand the cold of winter. On germination the zygospore divides to produce 4 new plants.

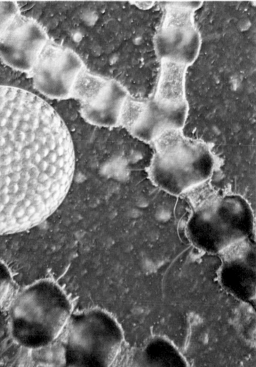

Left and below: Two diatoms as seen by the scanning electron microscope—about 1000 times actual size. *Navicula monilifera* (left) is common on sandy beaches around British coasts. Here it is seen in 'valve view' showing the central *raphe* slit. The secretion of mucilage through the raphe is known to produce movement. Because of the silica in the *frustule* ('shell'), it is very long-lasting. The fossil (below), *Melosira sulcata*, is a marine diatom many millions of years old. A gritty deposit, *diatomite*, formed from the accumulation of millions of frustules is used in polishes.

Giuseppe Mazza

1

2

gametes

zygote

zygospore

sunlight and use it to build chemicals needed by the cell. This is the well-known process of *photosynthesis*.

The shape and number of chloroplasts varies from one alga to another. For example, *Chlorella*, a unicellular alga, has a single cup-shaped chloroplast. *Spirogyra*, on the other hand, consists of a long filament of cells each having one or a few spiralling, ribbon-shaped chloroplasts. Other algae may have plate-like or star-like chloroplasts.

The colour given to algae by these various pigments is one of their distinctive characteristics. Each group has a particular range of pigments in a particular combination. Because of this, algae have traditionally been divided into groups by colour: the green algae, *Chlorophyta*; the red algae, *Rhodophyta*; and the brown algae, *Phaeophyta*. Other groups include diatoms, *Bacillariophyta*, and dinoflagellates, *Pyrrophyta*.

Ecology

Algae can exist in almost any environment provided it is damp. They occur in salty, brackish and fresh water, though not many species are found in all three. They can grow in hot springs and on snow or ice. Some exist in just a film of water and

so can live in the soil or on sand, rocks, wood and other plants. The seaweeds anchor themselves to rocks by a structure known as a *holdfast* and are not easily dislodged. Other species intermingle with fungi to form lichens which are composite plants composed of both algae and fungi.

Light is a dominant factor in determining where algae live. The different coloured pigments of the algae trap light of different wavelengths. Water absorbs red light more strongly than other (shorter) wavelengths: only green and ultra-violet light penetrate to any depth. Red algae contain the pigment *phycoerythrin* which absorbs green and ultraviolet light, and so they can live at greater depths—up to 200 m (600 ft)—than green algae. On the other hand, the green algae (which absorb more red light) can live only in the upper or shallow zones.

The chemistry of the water can also determine which species can grow in it. The lack of only one chemical element may be decisive; for example, the single-celled diatoms need a considerable amount of silica. In lakes, during the spring, the light intensity and the temperature increase and algae grow well. If the nutrient content of the lake is high, the growth in the spring may be so great that the water appears to turn green—a phenomenon known as *algal bloom*.

The large seaweeds occupy a unique habitat, the shoreline, part land and part water. The plants must be pliable and resilient, yet tough and leathery to survive beating by the waves and intermittent drying. The height of tides determines how long the algae are dried in the air. To protect themselves in this environment seaweeds often produce large quantities of *mucilage*—a slimy substance secreted by the plant cells. Distinct zones of seaweeds form on the shore—the less adaptable species below the low tide line and the more adaptable higher in the intertidal zone.

Single-celled algae

The green alga *Chlorella* ia a good example of a single-celled alga. It consists of a cell with a nucleus, containing the genetic material DNA, and chloroplasts containing chlorophyll. The cell is surrounded by a cell wall, which in the case of *Chlorella* contains cellulose.

Some single-celled algae are able to move and have one or more *flagella*—whip-like appendages of the cell growing through the cell wall—to propel them through the water. For example, most of the dinoflagellates, present in both marine and freshwater plankton, have one flagellum housed in a transverse furrow and a second flagellum in a longitudinal furrow. Many mobile algae also have an *eye-spot*, an orange-red structure often located near the base of the flagella, usually within a chloroplast. It may be light sensitive and is thought to be used in direction finding.

Diatoms are enclosed in a shell-like case called a *frustule* which is composed of silica and consists of two sections, like the two halves of a box. A special band, the *girdle band*, holds the two halves of the frustule together. The top and bottom sections of the two halves are known as *valves*. When describing a diatom it is usual to say whether it is in 'valve view' or 'girdle view' because the same diatom can look quite different in these two views. Most diatoms look rectangular in

Left: A semi-tropical green seaweed, *Caulerpa prolifera*. *Caulerpa* has many nuclei but is not sub-divided by cell-walls into individual cells. This represents one possible way in which large many-celled plants may have evolved from a primeval, single-celled algal ancestor.

Right: The common shore seaweed, *Fucus vesiculosus*. Male plants have red, while females have dark green, reproductive swellings on the tips of fronds.

Below: Infra-red photography produces a sharp contrast between seaweed (*Fucus*) and surrounding rocks. Chlorophyll in the seaweed appears purple in infra-red light.

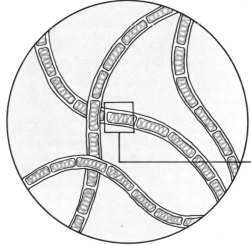

Left and below: The filamentous green alga *Spirogyra*. The bulk of the plant is taken up by a *vacuole*—a large space filled with water containing dissolved substances. Each *chloroplast* is a flat ribbon spiralling round the edge of a cell and dotted with *pyrenoids* surrounded by stored starch.

chloroplast

nucleus

vacuole

cytoplasm

girdle view but appear different in valve view. Diatoms like *Melosira* which are circular, rather like a cheese box, are called *centric*. Others are very variable and can be sausage-shaped, S-shaped, wedge-shaped or broadly oval, and are called *pennate*.

All the diatoms have elaborate and distinctive patterns of pores on the surface of the frustule, but the pennate diatoms often have an additional feature, the *raphe*. This is a furrow extending lengthways through the wall of the valve. Pennate diatoms with raphes are able to move by means of mucilage secreted from the raphe.

The *desmids*, a group of the green algae, also have cells in two halves—though in some species this is not conspicuous—but they differ from the diatoms in having a cell wall which contains cellulose, as in the higher plants. In most desmids the two halves are joined by a narrow neck of tissue, giving the alga a dumb-bell shape. Often the cell wall is decorated with ribs, spines and warts, and the chloroplasts are complex lobed structures, one in each semi-cell.

Many-celled algae

Single-celled algae can clump together to form colonies in which each cell acts more or less independently and there is no specialization of cells within the group to form structures with a specific function, like, for example, reproduction. More complex colonies can be formed by flagellate cells in mucilage. Such colonies have a variety of shapes. For instance, they may be plate-like or spherical. Other algae, particularly the diatoms, form long chains. More genuinely filamentous algae are found attached to rocks, like *Oedogonium*, or are free-floating, like *Spirogyra*.

The larger algae vary considerably in structure. In the common green seaweed *Cladophora* for example, the cells are arranged in highly branched filaments. Red algae are formed of numerous filaments joined together in a wide variety of shapes and structures. And in the common shore seaweeds *Fucus* and *Laminaria* the thalli are formed of many-celled true tissues.

Reproduction

Algae have a great variety of life histories depending on the ways in which they reproduce. In vegetative reproduction new plants are produced by simple fragmentation of the plant into one or more parts. This is different from asexual reproduction where specialized cells or groups of cells produce spores which in turn go on to produce new plants. Many different kinds of spores are involved, in particular the swimming *zoospore*. Zoospores have one, two or more flagella and often contain eye-spots to help them in their direction finding. Their mobility enables them to spread the species throughout any stretch of water. Sometimes a special spore is produced with a particularly thick wall, and this enables the plant to survive harmful conditions such as drought.

Most algae also reproduce sexually. In sexual reproduction, the zygote—formed from the fusion of the haploid male and female sex cells (gametes)—either undergoes immediate reduction division before producing new plants or produces a plant (the *sporophyte*) having a double set of chromosomes in each cell which subsequently produces asexual spores each having a single complete set of chromosomes. (Cells with a double set of chromosomes are known as *diploid*, while those with a single set are called *haploid*.) The asexual spores then go on to produce a second generation of haploid plants, known as *gametophytes*. Two stages of reproduction are therefore involved in the

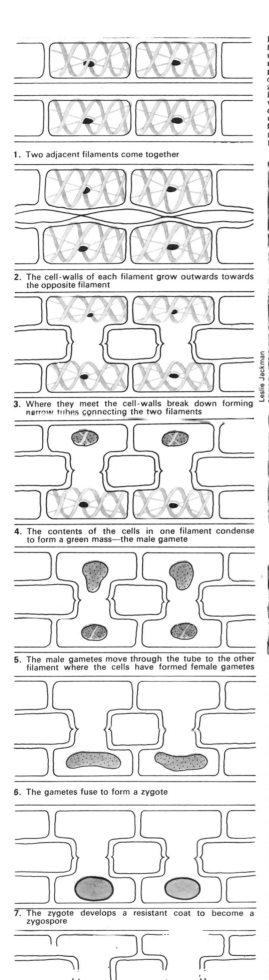

1. Two adjacent filaments come together

2. The cell-walls of each filament grow outwards towards the opposite filament

3. Where they meet the cell-walls break down forming narrow tubes connecting the two filaments

4. The contents of the cells in one filament condense to form a green mass—the male gamete

5. The male gametes move through the tube to the other filament where the cells have formed female gametes

6. The gametes fuse to form a zygote

7. The zygote develops a resistant coat to become a zygospore

8. The filament dies, releasing the zygospore

Left: Two adjacent filaments of *Spirogyra* undergoing sexual reproduction by the process of *conjugation*. The zygospores are covered in a resistant case which can withstand drought, cold and heat until conditions are favourable. Then they germinate, each producing one new plant.

Right: The brown seaweed *Fucus vesiculosus*. It consists of flat blades (*laminae*) attached by a *stipe* to the holdfast which anchors the plant to the sea-bed.

Below: An example of a brown seaweed, 'tangle' (*Laminaria digitata*). The photograph, taken at low-tide, reveals the anchoring holdfasts.

air bladders (to give buoyancy)

reproductive swellings

midrib (to give support and to transport nutrients)

holdfast

Below: One of the uses of algae is the purification of sewage. The sewage is sprayed over beds of clinker on which the algae grow. While the sewage percolates through the clinker it dissolves oxygen produced during photosynthesis by the algae and so allows further purification by bacteria.

latter type of life cycle, as in the higher plants, and the process is called *alternation of generations*.

This occurs in all brown and red algae and a few green algae. In some algae, such as the many celled red algae, these two plant generations are similar in appearance but in others they show marked differences. In the more complex algae, as in higher plants, the sporophyte is dominant and the gametophyte generation is greatly reduced. In the common large seaweed *Laminaria*, for example, the gametophyte generation is reduced to microscopic filaments of a few cells which produce either sperm or eggs. Fertilized eggs develop into the sporophyte.

Algae and man

Despite the great importance of algae as the primary food source of the oceans, their direct use by man is limited. Nevertheless, they can be eaten, for example, *Porphyra*, the lava bread of Wales, or fed to animals. In particular the mucilage from the large seaweeds, such as *Macrocystis*, is processed to make animal foodstuffs. The reproduction of algal cells has been studied to give a guide to the cause of cancer and algae are also used for oxidizing sewage and for pro-

ducing oxygen during space flights.

A jelly, known as *agar-agar*, is produced from some red algae such as *Gelidium*. It is widely used in bacterial and fungal culture, in confectionary, dentistry, in cosmetics and in baked foods. *Carageenin* extracted from the red alga *Chondrus crispus* is used in toothpaste. Other substances, *alginates*, produced from brown algae, are used as emulsifying agents in the treatment of latex for rubber tyres, and in ice-cream, coal briquettes, and paints. The alginates are extracted by disintegrating the plants in acid and then adding calcium carbonate (lime) to settle out the alginate.

Algae are used as food and in the preparation of processed foods. But they can also be harmful. Some are poisonous to animals; more importantly they may produce toxins which can spoil water supplies wanted for domestic use. Alternatively the death and decay of large numbers of algae following an algal bloom can use up all the available oxygen in water turning it fetid and causing fish to die. Despite this, the photosynthesis of the billions of algae in the sea is responsible in no small part for the production of the life-giving oxygen in the atmosphere.

Fungi

From the bright red 'Fly Agaric' toad-stool to the mould growing on an old boot, fungi can be found in practically every environment where life is possible. They are the main rivals of bacteria, in both the variety and the quantity of the materials they decompose.

By far the greatest part of a fungus, called the *mycelium*, remains unseen beneath the surface of the growing medium, be it woodland soil or shoe-leather. The visible parts are merely the reproductive organs of the fungus. The mycelium is a network of narrow, tubular branches, called *hyphae*, which extend in all directions, secreting enzymes to break down organic materials for food. The breakdown products are absorbed into the hyphae along with vital mineral salts and water.

Fungi are unable to build structural materials from simple chemical compounds like carbon dioxide using energy from chemical oxidations or the Sun (photosynthesis). They must, therefore, live on organic material from other living things, whether alive or dead. In other words they are all either parasitic or saprophytic.

Although the mycelium is perhaps the most important part of a fungus, it does not vary much from one species to the next. As a result, the classification of fungi is based largely on their reproductive structures, which are much more diverse. Fungi are usually divided into three groups. The first is called the *Phycomycetes*, literally 'algal fungi', because its members show some similarities to the green algae. The second and third groups have reproductive structures quite unlike anything else known in the plant kingdom. The *Ascomycetes*—cup fungi and their allies—characteristically produce spores, usually in groups of eight, in a special sac, the *ascus*, which explodes violently at maturity, shooting out the spores. The *Basidiomycetes*, to which toadstools and mushrooms belong, characteristically produce four spores on four projections from a special cell, the *basidium*. These spores are shot into the air when they are ripe.

Phycomycetes
The 'water moulds' are among the most interesting of Phycomycetes. Like green algae, most of them live in fresh water or damp soil. *Synchytrium* and *Olpidium* are examples of the simpler type of water mould. They are different from most other Phycomycetes in that they consist of single rounded cells, not of mycelium. Both produce free-swimming spores, *zoospores*, rather like those of green algae, except that they have only a single flagellum. Both are parasitic, either upon algae or on the roots of plants. *Olpidium brassicae* is the fungus whose zoospores transmit virus diseases such as tobacco necrosis virus. *Synchytrium endobioticum* is well known as the organism responsible for the grotesque malformations called 'wart disease' which sometimes afflict potatoes.

Every gardener who raises his own seedlings will be familiar with *damping-off disease*, which causes seedlings suddenly to topple over and die. The disease spreads from plant to plant in a widening

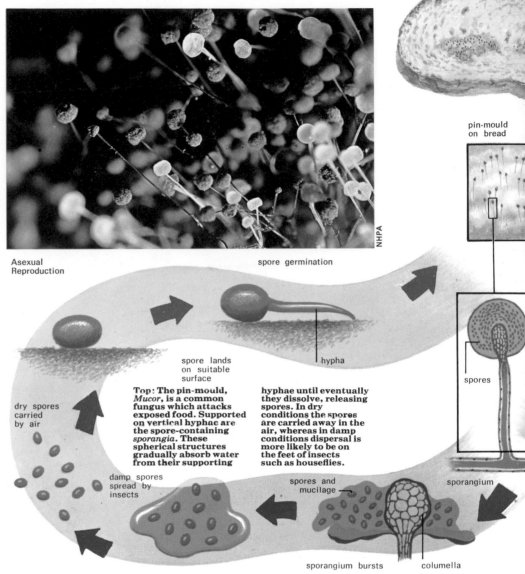

Asexual Reproduction

spore germination

pin-mould on bread

spore lands on suitable surface

hypha

dry spores carried by air

spores

Top: The pin-mould, *Mucor*, is a common fungus which attacks exposed food. Supported on vertical hyphae are the spore-containing *sporangia*. These spherical structures gradually absorb water from their supporting

hyphae until eventually they dissolve, releasing spores. In dry conditions the spores are carried away in the air, whereas in damp conditions dispersal is more likely to be on the feet of insects such as houseflies.

damp spores spread by insects

spores and mucilage

sporangium

sporangium bursts

columella

Right: Often referred to as 'grey mould', *Botrytis* is a common ascomycetous fungus which attacks a variety of plants including tomato, lettuce and raspberry as well as vines. Nowadays crops are often treated with fungicides to prevent damage such as this.

circle, usually in the centre of the seed-box where the soil tends to be most moist. This damping-off is usually caused by another of the Phycomycetes, *Pythium*.

Pythium mycelium grows between the cells of the seedling and bursts through the skin into the surrounding soil. On the surface of the seedling the tips of the hyphae swell into little sacs surrounded by a cell wall. The multinucleate cell completes its growth and then travels through a germ-tube at the tip of the sac. It remains there surrounded by a very thin membrane while each nucleus, with a small piece of cytoplasm, develops into a separate zoospore with two flagella. The zoospores begin to move about within the membrane, becoming increasingly agitated, until they burst free and swim away, in the soil moisture, in search of other seedlings.

Pythium can also reproduce by a sexual process. Two hyphae fuse together—a small specialized one which is called 'male' and a large, equally specialized one which is regarded as 'female'. A thick wall is then secreted around the fertilized 'egg', which enables it to withstand unfavourable conditions, such as drought and frost. On the arrival of

NHPA

BASF

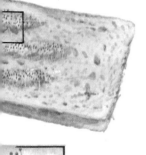

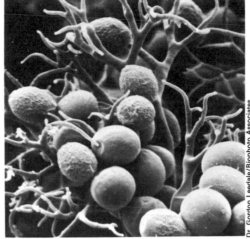

Dr. Gordon Leedale/Biophoto Associates

Left: Sporangia of the fungus *Peronospora parasitica* magnified about 400 times. This fungus is a 'downy mildew' which attacks such plants as turnips, cauliflowers, brussels sprouts and wallflowers. The sporangia appear as a white 'fur' on the swollen stems and under the leaves of the afflicted plant. The picture was taken with a scanning electron microscope (SEM) which has a much greater depth of field than other microscopes.

Below: On a forest floor in Thailand, the corpse of a fly is attacked by a fungus (seen as white patches on its thorax and abdomen). Like bacteria, fungi perform a useful function in breaking down dead organic matter.

C. B. Frith/Bruce Coleman

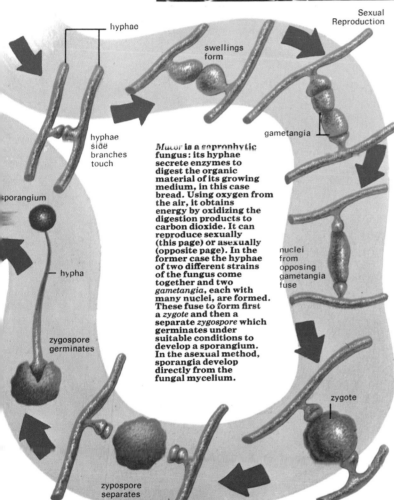

hyphae

hyphae side branches touch

sporangium

hypha

zygospore germinates

zypospore separates

swellings form

gametangia

Sexual Reproduction

nuclei from opposing gametangia fuse

zygote

Mucor is a saprophytic fungus: its hyphae secrete enzymes to digest the organic material of its growing medium, in this case bread. Using oxygen from the air, it obtains energy by oxidizing the digestion products to carbon dioxide. It can reproduce sexually (this page) or asexually (opposite page). In the former case the hyphae of two different strains of the fungus come together and two *gametangia*, each with many nuclei, are formed. These fuse to form first a *zygote* and then a separate *zygospore* which germinates under suitable conditions to develop a sporangium. In the asexual method, sporangia develop directly from the fungal mycelium.

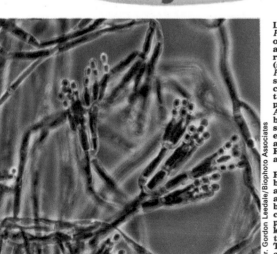

Dr. Gordon Leedale/Biophoto Associates

Left: Fungi of the genus *Penicillium* are common on all kinds of decaying animal and plant remains. Seen here (stained blue) is *Penicillium notatum*, the species which is used commercially to produce the well known penicillin antibiotics. At the tips of the branching hyphae can be seen the *conidia*, which eventually split off and grow into new fungi. Reproduction is always asexual.

Right: Colonies of a bacterium which contains a red pigment when alive. *Penicillium* has been introduced at the centre of the dish: the penicillin it produces kills the bacteria in the central colonies. The outlying colonies are unaffected.

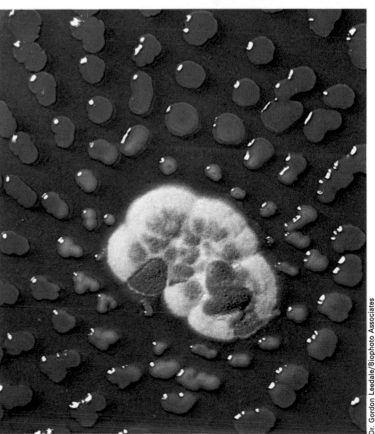

Dr. Gordon Leedale/Biophoto Associates

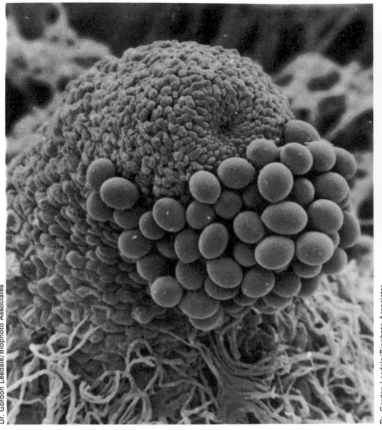

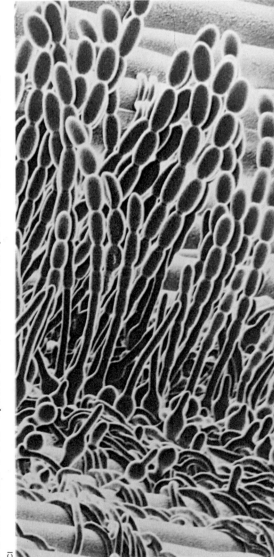

Above: A clump of ascospores on the fruiting body of *Sordaria macrospora*, an ascomycetous fungus. Fungi belonging to the genus *Sordaria* are often found on the dung of plant-eating animals for their ascospores will only germinate readily after passing through the gut of an animal.

Above right: The spore-bearing structure of *Aspergillus niger*, an ascomycetous fungus common in most soils. The spores (conidia) are carried at the ends of the radiating branches. This picture and the one above left were taken with a SEM at magnifications of about 1,800 and 360 respectively.

suitable soil conditions, it germinates to produce zoospores which infect new seedlings.

Among other common phycomycetous fungi are the pin-moulds, such as *Mucor*, the downy mildews, such as *Peronospora*, and the parasitic fungus *Phytophthora*, which is responsible for potato blight, perhaps the most notorious of all plant diseases.

Potato blight

Phytophthora is similar to *Pythium* but is less dependent on moisture. It was introduced into Europe in about 1840 from South America, the original home of the potato, and in the succeeding five or six years spread over the entire continent, including the British Isles.

Whereas the South American native potatoes were resistant to the disease, breeding of the potato in Europe, aimed at giving higher yields, had resulted in loss of resistance in the European varieties. From the appearance of the first few dark green blotches on the leaves of a single susceptible European potato to the time when whole fields were reduced to a blackened mass of rotting vegetation was only a matter of days.

As a direct result of the potato famine, the population of Ireland was reduced from eight million in 1845 to six million a decade later. Many people died and many more were forced to emigrate, mostly to the US. Apart from the direct human suffering, the reduction of the working population was on a scale that no country could afford, and it had long-term economic and political consequences. Fortunately, fungicides are now available to combat potato blight.

Ascomycetes

Ascomycetes and Basidiomycetes, the remaining two groups of the true fungi, are typical land creatures. They can grow and reproduce in the most exposed situations, like the tops of tall trees and the surfaces of rocks. In neither of these two groups is there any free-swimming stage in the life-cycle and the mycelium itself, perhaps from the unique construction of its cell walls, is much better able to resist dry conditions.

Ascomycetes are mostly saprophytic, but an interesting parasitic species is *Taphrina deformans*. This fungus causes the well-known leaf-curl disease of peaches, apricots and almonds. Leaves of peach trees permeated by the mycelium of *Taphrina* swell up and become discoloured and twisted in much the same way as the 'warts' on the potato caused by *Synchytrium*. If examined carefully, the leaves seem to be dusted with a white powder. This discolouration is caused by special spore-containing sacs which protrude through the skin of the leaf. Each of these sacs is a short cylindrical cell, the ascus, formed by the fusion of two cells of the mycelium in much the same way as the sexually produced spore of *Pythium*.

Within the young ascus the male and female nuclei first fuse and then immediately divide again to produce uninucleate spores. When the spores are ripe, pressure generated in the ascus causes it to burst, ejecting the spores. These are then carried by the wind and, if they happen to come to rest on the developing bud of a peach tree, they become trapped between the growing bud-scales where they remain until the spring. They

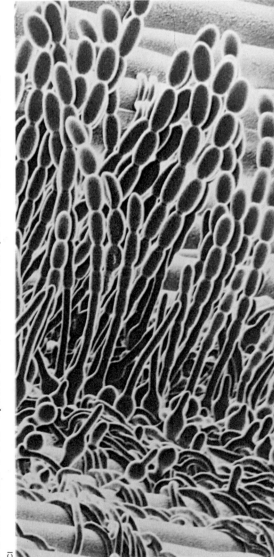

72

BUDDING OF YEAST

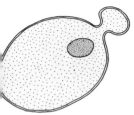

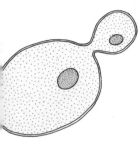

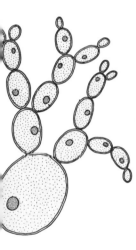

Above: Commonly called yeasts, the members of the genus *Saccharomyces* are among the most important fungi from a commercial point of view. They are used in both the baking and the brewing industries. By the process known as *alcoholic fermentation* yeast converts sugar into carbon dioxide and alcohol in the absence of oxygen. As shown here, yeasts reproduce by *budding*. A constriction forms in the parent cell, a nucleus moves into the bud and the constriction closes. Sometimes the buds do not separate from the parent cell, so large branching colonies develop.

Left: Powdery mildews can cause considerable damage to crops like wheat and barley. They get their name from their appearance on the surface of the host plant. This SEM picture shows a powdery mildew growing on barley— the hyphae and conidia are clearly visible.

Right: The toadstool-like fruiting body of the ascomycetous fungus *Helvella crispa*. The asci are formed in the 'head' of the fungus.

Giuseppe Mazza

Above: Regarded as a great delicacy, the Périgord truffle, *Tuber melanosporum*, is found in parts of France. It is the fruiting body of an ascomycetous **fungus which develops underground in association with the roots of oak trees. Having a strong and distinctive smell, truffles are often** **sniffed out by specially trained dogs or pigs. Another much sought after truffle is the white truffle, *Tuber magnatum*, from Piedmont in Italy.**

Dr. Gordon Leedale/Biophoto Associates

germinate as soon as the peach bud begins to burst, and as the young leaves escape from the bud, the germ-tube of the spore enters the leaf and a new infection begins. This method of reproduction necessitates the production of thousands of spores since most of them fail to reach a developing peach and are wasted. Nevertheless it eliminates the need for free water.

Ascomycetes of the genus *Penicillium* are very common on all kinds of decaying animal and vegetable remains. *Penicillium glaucum* is a green mould frequently found growing in these situations. The green colour is not due to chlorophyll, which no fungus contains, but to a non-photosynthetic pigment. *Penicillium glaucum* produces millions of asexual spores, called *conidia*, on special upright hyphae. The tips of these hyphae are repeatedly forked, each final branch ending in a bottle-shaped, spore-bearing cell. The spores emerge in a long chain from the neck of each bottle, so that the whole conidium-producing structure looks like a minute paint brush. Conidia are detached by the wind or other agency and spread all over the Earth's surface and even up into the stratosphere.

On particularly nutritious substrates, *Penicillium glaucum* reproduces sexually as well. A special thin and flexible male hypha grows spirally round a thick female branch. Then a small hole develops in the cell walls at the point of contact of the two. The contents of the male hypha pass into the female, leaving the male as an empty shell. The male and female nuclei move towards each other, but do not immediately fuse. The fertilized female cell then begins to branch and divide and eventually a small knot of cells is formed. In the centre of this knot the asci develop, and at once the descendants of the paired nuclei fuse. The double nucleus immediately divides again to produce *ascospores*, which are spherical with thin flanges around them, reminiscent of the planet Saturn with its rings. If an ascospore encounters suitable conditions it germinates to produce a mycelium with slightly different properties from its parent, and so some variation is maintained within the species.

Many other species of Ascomycetes, however, including most of the penicillia, have lost their ability to reproduce sexually, or do so so rarely that it has never been observed. Some such fungi are used in industrial processes. One of them, *Fusarium graminiarum*, is grown for its high protein content and is used as an additive to human and animal foods —the fibrous texture of the mycelium makes it more acceptable as a human food than other vegetable proteins made from bacteria or soya meal. Another, *Saccharomyces cerevisiae*, is the well-known yeast used in the baking and brewing industries.

One interesting process is concerned with recycling. An enzyme produced by *Trichoderma viride*, another asexual fungus, breaks down cellulose into its constituent glucose molecules. It has been shown that in this way a very high yield of sugar can be obtained from old newspapers. The printing ink and other impurities are not acted upon by the enzyme and are left behind as a black sludge in the bottom of the tank, and the rich syrup can be used without further purification.

73

Plant Partnerships

It is often accepted as the 'law of nature' that all living things live directly or indirectly by exploiting others. This is true of all life forms incapable of producing their own food from inorganic substances—that is, of everything except green plants. Nevertheless few plants live entirely independently; each forms part of a living community, the different organisms and species of which are interdependent on one another. The greatest degree of interdependence occurs when two plants of different species live attached to one another in an association known as *symbiosis* which is beneficial to both organisms. Symbiosis is the opposite of *parasitism* in which one partner benefits at the expense of the other.

Lichens

One very common group of plants has been used since the middle of the nineteenth century as an example of symbiosis. These are the *lichens*, the small grey, brown or sometimes brightly coloured plants which grow on walls, rocks and tree-trunks, often appearing as no more than a circular crust 1-2 cm across. Under the microscope a lichen can be seen to be two completely different types of plant—a fungus and an alga—living together in a close symbiotic relationship. The lichen consists of an interwoven network of fungal filaments (*hyphae*) packed together to form a *mycelium*. The mycelium has a number of distinct layers, in one of which, near the upper surface of the lichen, the hyphae are intermingled with cells of an alga which contain chlorophyll and can perform photosynthesis, in which the energy of sunlight is used to produce carbohydrate. Together the fungus and the alga form one unit, the *thallus* of the lichen.

The lichen fungus is usually a member of the group *Ascomycetes*, while the algal partner is most often a species of *Trebouxia*, a green alga, or *Nostoc*, a blue-green alga important because of its ability to *fix* nitrogen from the atmosphere—making it available to the fungus. A few lichens include both green and blue-green algae as well as the fungus, showing that symbiosis may include three types of plant living together.

The fungus and the alga can be seen to be living together in a lichen, but it is more difficult to show that both partners receive some benefit from the association. However, lichens grow on bare rock surfaces or walls where there is no decomposing organic matter, on which fungi normally live. The fungi of a lichen could survive in such conditions only if they obtained carbohydrate from the algae and experiments have verified that this is what happens—up to 70% of the carbohydrate produced by photosynthesis in the alga is released from the algal cells and enters the fungal mycelium. The carbohydrate is usually released as a chemical called a *polyhydric alcohol*, though some types of lichen algae release glucose. The alga benefit by receiving moisture, containing inorganic nutrients dissolved by the fungal mycelium.

Rod Borland/Bruce Coleman

Jacques Six

Above: Lichens growing on rock at Cape Cross, South West Australia. Lichens are most commonly greyish in colour (bottom left of picture) but may be brightly coloured like the orange species here.

Right: *Cladonia sylvatica*, a very common lichen on moorland, on rocks and walls. *Cladonia* produces cup-shaped *podetia*, up to 1 cm in height, around the edge of which are borne small wind-dispersed spores or *soredia*.

There are more than 18,000 species of lichen in the world; about 1,400 have been found in the British Isles alone. They can be divided according to thallus structure into three groups: *crustose* lichens, which form flat, scaly circular thalli, *foliose* lichens, in which the thallus has the form of a leaf, often with root-like structures growing out underneath, and *fruticose* lichens, in which the thallus is branched like a miniature tree. Wall lichens are commonly crustose, while foliose lichens are found on trees or (like reindeer moss, *Cladonia rangiferina*) covering the ground in tundra regions.

Little is known for certain about the reproduction of lichens. Some species of lichen fungi reproduce sexually, by means of *ascospores*, but these contain no algal cells. But an ascospore could grow into a new lichen thallus by combining with cells of the appropriate alga—which would be difficult, since neither fungus nor alga is likely to survive for long by itself. It is more likely that lichens normally reproduce either vegetatively, by *fragmentation*, when small pieces of the thallus break away and later begin to grow by themselves, or asexually by the dispersal of *soredia*, which are small groups of algal cells surrounded by fungal

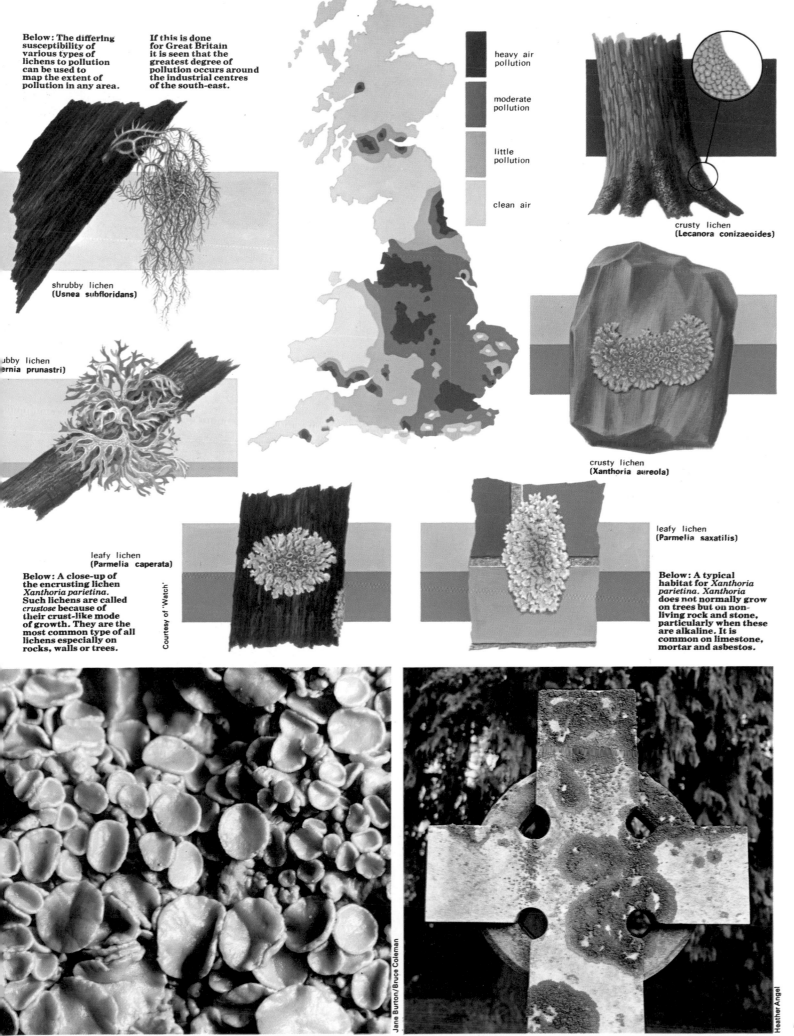

Below: The differing susceptibility of various types of lichens to pollution can be used to map the extent of pollution in any area.

If this is done for Great Britain it is seen that the greatest degree of pollution occurs around the industrial centres of the south-east.

heavy air pollution

moderate pollution

little pollution

clean air

shrubby lichen
(Usnea subfloridans)

ubby lichen
ernia prunastri)

crusty lichen
(Lecanora conizaeoides)

crusty lichen
(Xanthoria aureola)

leafy lichen
(Parmelia caperata)

leafy lichen
(Parmelia saxatilis)

Courtesy of 'Watch'

Below: A close-up of the encrusting lichen *Xanthoria parietina*. Such lichens are called *crustose* because of their crust-like mode of growth. They are the most common type of all lichens especially on rocks, walls or trees.

Below: A typical habitat for *Xanthoria parietina*. *Xanthoria* does not normally grow on trees but on non-living rock and stone, particularly when these are alkaline. It is common on limestone, mortar and asbestos.

Jane Burton/Bruce Coleman

Heather Angel

75

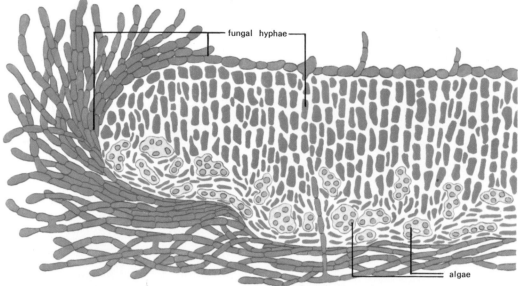

fungal hyphae

algae

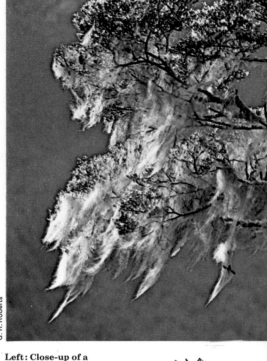

G. R. Roberts

Above: Stylized section through the body of a lichen (the *thallus*) showing the two types of plant—fungus and alga—which together combine to form a third type—the lichen. The alga and fungus do not intermingle randomly in the lichen, but the lichen is divided up into layers which are more or less distinct from one another. Three of these layers are composed of a network of intertwining fungal filaments, or *hyphae*, while the fourth layer contains the algae. The algae contain chlorophyll and can photosynthesize, and a few fungal hyphae grow into the alga layer and obtain carbohydrate produced by them.

Leslie Jackman

Left: Close-up of a *fruticose* lichen. These lichens have a many branched body, producing a shrub-like or antler-like structure. Most are very small—no more than several centimetres in size—but some tropical forms may be up to a metre in length, hanging from trees.

hyphae. Soredia are often visible as a powdery deposit on the surface of a lichen thallus. They are light, and can be blown around by the wind.

In the laboratory, it is possible to grind up the lichen thallus, separate the fungus and alga, and grow them separately. The fungus grows into a simple colony quite unlike the complex structure of a lichen thallus, and the alga no longer releases carbohydrate. The obvious next experiment—taking the separate cultures of fungus and alga and trying to recombine them to form a lichen—has, however, proved to be almost impossible. This may be because it is difficult in a laboratory to simulate the harsh natural environment of a lichen, where growth is limited by low levels of nutrients and the frequent drying-out of the thallus.

Root nodules

Farmers have known for centuries that the fertility of their soils could be maintained by including in their crop rotations a planting of clover or beans. These plants, and others such as the widespread group of tropical trees, *Acacia*, are in a family called *Leguminosae* (legumes). During the nineteenth century it was discovered that the increase in soil fertility was the result of the ability of legumes to absorb nitrogen from the atmosphere and fix it—that is, convert it into the organic forms contained in plant and animal tissues. Later still it was found that this process, called *nitrogen fixation*, is carried out not by the plants alone, but with the help of bacteria present in *nodules* (swellings) on their roots. This is an example of symbiosis involving a higher plant and a bacterium.

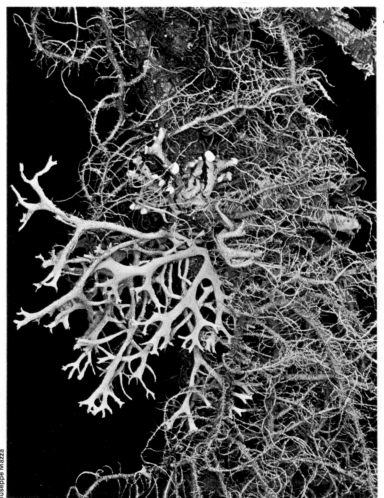

Giuseppe Mazza

Rothamsted Experimental Station

Above: An early woodcut of the root of the broad bean, *Phaseolus vulgaris*, showing the nitrogen-fixing nodules on the root. Beans provide a very cheap source of protein because they do not need large dressings of expensive nitrogen fertilizer—nitrogen being provided by the root nodules. In contrast to the action of symbiotic bacteria in root nodules the industrial process used to manufacture nitrogen fertilizer requires a temperature of 450°C and a pressure of 200 atmospheres—and correspondingly consumes large amounts of energy and money.

Above right: Nodules on the root of alder, *Alnus glutinosa*. Unlike the legumes, the nitrogen-fixing organism in the nodules of alder is probably a fungus and not a bacterium.

Left: Two different fruticose lichens of the groups *Evernia* (left) and *Usnea*. Usnea lichens form long tangled masses—often up to 15 cm (6 in) long—and are commonly called 'old man's beard'.

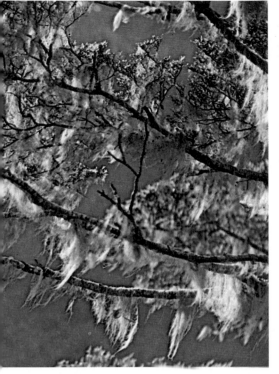

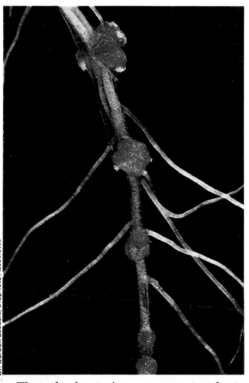

Dr. Gordon Leedale/Biophoto Associates

NHPA

Above left: Large growth of lichen hanging from a tree in a beech forest in the Eglinton valley of New Zealand. A plant which uses another merely for support, as the lichen does here, is called an *epiphyte*. Epiphytism benefits one partner alone, but only rarely harms the other plant.

Above: The common woodland fungus, the fly agaric, *Amanita muscaria*. Woodland fungi appear to be growing independently but are often in fact symbiotic with the roots of trees such as pine or birch. The fungus is connected to the tree by a mass of fungal filaments in the soil.

That the bacteria are separate plants from the legumes in which they are growing is shown by the fact that legumes grown from seed in sterile soil do not have nodules and do not fix nitrogen. Instead, nodules develop only after the bacterium, *Rhizobium*, normally present in the soil, infects the roots of the young legume. Inside the nodule the bacteria enlarge to form modified bacterial cells called *bacteroids*.

The bacteroids fix nitrogen using an enzyme called *nitrogenase* which catalyzes the reaction by which nitrogen is converted to ammonia—free-living *Rhizobium* does not have nitrogenase and cannot fix nitrogen. This ammonia is then used by the legumes to synthesize amino acids and ultimately protein used in the construction of plant tissue. Root nodules are thus of great value to the legume as

nitrogen is an essential nutrient, often in short supply.

Numerous plants other than legumes are now also known to have nitrogen-fixing root nodules. Among these are alder, *Alnus*, sea buck thorn, *Hippophäe*, bog myrtle, *Myrica*, and a tropical tree called *Casuarina*. These plants, however, differ from legumes as the symbiotic organism is probably a fungus and not a bacterium.

Mycorrhizas
A further example of a symbiotic association occurring between the roots of higher plants and fungi is called a *mycorrhiza*. In these, common woodland fungi are connected, through extensive networks of hyphae in the soil, to the roots of trees. Mycorrhizal relationships are in fact extremely common; most common temperate trees including birch, beech, eucalyptus, spruce and larch are known to form mycorrhizas with several species of fungi. Scots pine, *Pinus sylvestris*, forms mycorrhizas with more than 100 species of fungi.

In one type of mycorrhiza, called *ectotrophic*, the fungus forms a sheath of hyphae covering the fine absorbing roots of the tree. This gives the tree a greatly increased area of absorbing root and thus it is able to absorb greater amounts of mineral nutrients such as nitrogen, phosphorus and potassium. Experiments have shown that in its turn the fungus receives a supply of carbohydrate from the tree.

In nutrient-rich soils mycorrhizas are of little value to the tree and the fungus is virtually a parasite on the tree. However, in most soils at least one nutrient is

in short supply and a tree with ectotrophic mycorrhizas will grow faster than an uninfected tree.

A completely different type of mycorrhiza is called *endotrophic*. In this, the fungal hyphae grow inside (instead of outside) the cells of the higher plant. Such mycorrhizas are found in all orchids and in many other plants—indeed possibly in *all* higher plants. In orchids, the mycorrhizal fungus, usually of the group *Basidiomycetes*, infects the roots as they begin to grow from the germinating seed. The hyphae grow into the cells of the root and form coils inside each cell. Later, some of the orchid cells digest the hyphae within them, releasing fungal nutrients for the benefit of the orchid. Because of this a young orchid can grow underground for several years, unable to perform photosynthesis, but obtaining a supply of carbohydrate from its fungal partner.

Eventually most orchids produce leaves and photosynthesize their own carbohydrate, some of which may be passed on to the fungus—a mutually beneficial association. A few orchids, however, never produce leaves and are therefore always dependent on their fungus; in such cases the orchid is a parasite on the fungus.

On plants other than orchids, endotrophic mycorrhizas are often formed with a fungus called *Endogone* from the same group, *Phycomycetes*, as the familiar pin mould, *Mucor*. The fungal hyphae grow into the root cells, branching within them to form structures called *arbuscules* (because of their tree-like appearance) and also thick-walled swellings called *vesicles*. Because of this, this type of mycorrhiza is sometimes called *vesicular-arbuscular*.

Experiments have compared the growth of plants, such as strawberries and tomatoes, with and without endotrophic mycorrhizas, and have shown that the fungus can help to supply the plant with mineral nutrients if these are in short supply in the soil. In most cases the fungus also benefits by receiving a supply of carbohydrate from its partner. This is obviously of vital importance to the most common mycorrhizal fungus, *Endogone*, as it will not grow except as a mycorrhizal partner.

Other kinds of symbiosis
Many other cases are known of associations between different kinds of plant which may be instances of symbiosis. In practice, it is often difficult to discover whether both plants benefit from the presence of their partners, so botanists tend to use the term symbiosis when neither plant is harmed by the other. Examples of possible symbiosis exist between the blue-green alga, *Nostoc*, and cycads (a group of primitive plants like giant ferns) and between green algae and the moss, *Sphagnum*, which forms peat bogs. Much research would be needed in every case to discover whether the association was or was not true symbiosis; whether nutrients are transferred between the two plants, and whether the association is necessary for the survival of either or both partners. Nevertheless, it is clear from an understanding of lichens, root nodules and mycorrhizas that symbiosis is an extremely widespread phenomenon, essential to the normal functioning of nearly all plant communities.

Parasitic and Climbing Plants

Higher plants are generally the *producers* of the world. All other life forms are *consumers*, dependent on the food which plants manufacture during photosynthesis. But in a few species and families of plants this normal pattern is upset. These plants are themselves dependent. They are *parasites* and *climbers*, dependent to a greater or lesser extent upon a host plant.

Parasitic and climbing plants, although different in many ways, have several features in common. Both groups use neighbouring plants to aid them to grow —either as a prop to enable a climber to reach the light, or as a source of food for the parasitic plant. Indeed, many species, like dodder, *Cuscuta*, are both climber and parasite.

Additionally, although particular species in both groups are confined to specific areas of the world, they are all largely non-specific in relation to their choice of host: the neighbouring plant used as a support or food source will simply be that which was nearest to the germinating seed of the climber or parasite. The only exception to this is the observation that parasitic plants, only rarely, and then usually unsuccessfully, parasitize monocot plants. The reasons for this selectivity, however, are not clearly understood.

Parasitic plants

Despite the fact that most plants are producers synthesizing their own food, it is wrong to think that parasitism among plants is rare. Two extremely large and important groups of plants, *fungi* and *bacteria*, are all either parasites or organisms that live on the dead remains of others (*saprophytes*). Even among the higher plants parasites are not all that uncommon, particularly in the tropics. Four families, the *Loranthaceae*, the *Balanophoraceae*, the *Orobanchaceae* and the *Rafflesiaceae* are composed entirely of parasitic plants. Other families, such as the *Convolvulaceae* and the *Lauraceae*, contain both parasitic and non-parasitic members.

Parasitic plants obtain water and food from the host plant through specially developed organs, called *haustoria*, which secure the parasite to the host and grow into the host's tissue, particularly its vascular tissue. Most parasites have a multiplicity of these connections with their host, but some have only a single primary connection. Indeed there are many levels of parasitism in the several families containing parasitic plants, and several forms of growth.

The extent to which a parasite is dependent on its host largely determines its vegetative form. True parasites, such as the dodders, *Cuscuta* and *Cassytha*, are entirely devoid of chlorophyll and rely entirely on the host as a food source. In this case the vegetative parts are very small—the leaves are present only as tiny scales on the thin, weak stem which itself possesses only poorly developed vascular tissue.

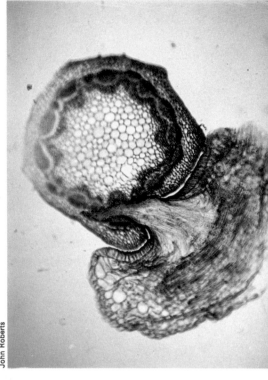

John Roberts

Above and below left: The common climbing parasite, dodder, *Cuscuta*. Dodder twines around the plant which it parasitizes—its *host*—and extracts nutrients and water from it through specialized organs called *haustoria*. These can be seen (below left) as small foot-like pads growing into the host stem; one is more clearly shown in the cross-section above. Here the dodder is located beneath the stem of the host plant. The projection from the dodder into the host is the haustorium.

Below: The red fruits of the tropical mistletoe *Viscum minimum*.

Dr. G. Leedale/Biophoto Assoc.

Nevertheless, dodders are quite conspicuous, varying in colour from bright yellow to red. After emerging from seed the seedling immediately begins to grow in a circular fashion, searching for another plant around which to twine. Once a suitable host is found, the thin stem of the dodder then twines round the host's stem in a manner similar to that of the related climber, bindweed, *Convolvulus*. Unlike bindweed, however, the dodder stem has haustorial pads which become attached to and grow into the host stem. These pads break through the epidermis of the host stem into its interior, where they branch and form connections with the xylem and phloem. In the mature dodder the initial connection with the ground then withers away. The dodder is then entirely dependent on its host.

Other parasites, such as the toothwort, *Lathrea*, and the broomrape, *Orobanche*, are parasitic on the roots of other plants, rather than their stems. Correspondingly these plants are generally less conspicuous than dodders for most of their vegetative parts are usually below ground. Normally, the only growths above ground are flowering parts. Some root parasites, however, such as *Gaiadendron*, appear as a substantial bush above ground. In such cases the plants are almost certainly not entirely parasitic, but also manufacture some of their own food.

A well known example of a partial parasite is mistletoe, *Viscum*, which grows as a cluster of branches hanging from trees, commonly apple or poplar in Britain. The mistletoe produces a haustorium which connects with the host's xylem and extracts water and mineral nutrients, but it also has green leaves capable of producing much of the food it requires in the same way as other green plants. The host plant is used chiefly as a support but also as a 'root', as the mistletoe has no roots of its own.

In contrast to mistletoe, the tropical *Rafflesiaceae* are completely dependent on their hosts. Although *Rafflesia* bear the largest flowers of all plants, there is virtually no visible trace of the vegetative parts, which are buried in the tissues of the host (normally a liana). These consist of slender filaments, resembling the mycelium of a fungus. Like a fungus, too, these filaments are frequently only single-celled strands. The only large masses of cells are the *floral cushions*, groups of cells which give rise to the massive flowers.

The *Rafflesiaceae* are perhaps the ultimate example of the parasitic tendency to minimize all but the reproductive parts. All that remains of the varied structure of a higher plant is the reproductive apparatus. Such parasitic plants, relieved of the need to produce an elaborate vegetative structure, are able to devote most of the energy extracted from their host to the production of seeds.

Climbing plants

Although climbing plants live on their hosts, and in many cases harm them, they are not, strictly speaking, parasites. They do not obtain nourishment from their host but use it merely as a means of support. Nevertheless, this is no mean benefit. It enables climbers to grow high up in a dense vegetation canopy so that

Above: The bird's nest orchid, *Neottia nidus-avis*, is white because it lacks chlorophyll. It is normally regarded as a saprophyte but, though its food ultimately comes from dead remains in the forest litter, it obtains them parasitically through a mycorrhizal *Basidiomycete* fungus.

Below: The largest flower of any plant belongs to a parasite, *Rafflesia arnoldii* (shown here). The flowers can be up to 1m (3 ft) in diameter and weigh up to 6 kg (15 lb).

Right: The common European mistletoe, *Viscum album*. The white berries ripen in winter and are eaten by birds, especially thrushes, but the sticky seeds cling to the birds' beaks. The birds wipe them off on to the boughs of trees, such as apple, so dispersing them. The germinating seedling then connects itself to the host's water conducting tissue (*xylem*) through a haustorium.

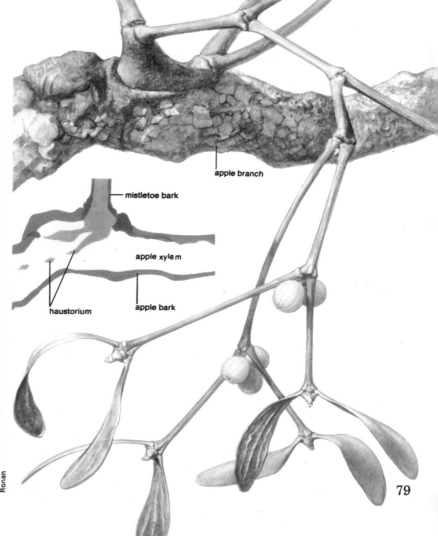

apple branch

mistletoe bark

apple xylem

apple bark

haustorium

79

their leaves receive more light and their fruits can be more easily dispersed by the wind.

Climbers have these advantages without the need to produce the structural tissues that their hosts must produce. This enables them both to grow faster than their hosts and to devote more of their energy to the production of flowers and fruits. If a climber fails to find a host, however, it has little chance of survival.

The simplest climbers, such as bramble, *Rubus*, or goosegrass, *Galium aparine*, have stems which are provided with curved hairs, all with tips pointed downwards. These hairs hook the plant on to its support. Goosegrass has single-celled hook-hairs, which are very small and not easily seen, though they are quite effective in aiding the plant to cling to any available support. Brambles, on the other hand, have large multicellular hairs, or thorns.

The hairs of the runner bean *Phaseolus multiflorus* are especially interesting. They do not all grow downwards but are arrayed in all directions. The cells at the base of the hairs are flexible. They allow the hooked tips to twist in different directions around the base, so that purchase may be obtained in several directions at once.

A more specialized method of gaining support is the use of *tendrils*. There are several kinds of tendrils, though most are modified leaves or leaf parts. In the *Leguminosae*, well illustrated by the sweet pea, *Lathyrus odoratus*, leaflets of the compound (*pinnate*) leaf blade serve as tendrils, while leaf-like structures in the bud axils (the *stipules*) are enlarged to

compensate for the loss of photosynthetic surface. In extreme cases, as in the meadow vetchling, *Lathyrus aphoca*, the whole of the leaf blade is transformed into a tendril—in which case the large stipules provide the major photosynthetic surface.

A less common form of tendril is produced by old man's beard, *Clematis*. Here the leaf stalk (*petiole*) rather than the leaf blade forms the tendril. In yet another group of climbers, including the virginia creeper, *Ampelopsis veitchi*, and the passion flower, *Passiflora*, the tendril, known as a *branch-tendril*, grows directly from the stem. In virginia creeper the tendrils grow from opposite each leaf, while in the passion flower they grow from the axils of the leaves.

The most tightly attached climbing plants, however, are those in which the plant itself behaves as a 'tendril' and twines about its support. Good examples are bindweed, *Convolvulus*, and honeysuckle, *Lonicera*. Initially the shoots of these plants grow up unsupported, but after some time the tip leans over and begins to revolve until it finds some support about which to twine. The climber then continues to twine up the stem of the support. In most species the direction of twining is always the same. For example, honeysuckle always twines clockwise while larger bindweed, *Calystegia sepium* twines anti-clockwise. A few species, however, like woody nightshade, *Solanum dulcamara*, have no fixed twining habits.

Entwining climbers have one particular adaptation to this life style. The growing point (*apex*) of most plants is surrounded by a cluster of expanding young leaves. These would tend to interfere with the encirclement of the supporting plant. The apex of entwiners, however, is surrounded by only very small leaves and the stem immediately below the apex grows particularly quickly so that there are large spaces (*internodes*) between the leaves.

Disadvantages
The advantage to a plant of the climbing life-style is that it enables it to grow high up in a plant canopy without producing a massive stem. Paradoxically, the lack of a large stem is also a major problem. It is difficult to transport enough water over the often long distances from ground to tip through the thin stem, and consequently small amounts of vascular tissue, of the climbing plant.

To overcome this problem climbing plants have adapted by increasing the efficiency of each individual xylem vessel. Resistance to the flow of water through the xylem is largely caused by the adhesion of water to the walls of the vessels and this is comparatively reduced if the cross-section of the vessels is larger. The vessels in the stems of climbers are very wide in comparison to those of other plants. Indeed they are occasionally visible to the naked eye.

Parasitic plants, dependent as they are on other plants, are of little value to man, but several species of climbers are of major economic importance. These include important pulses, such as peas, *Pisum sativum*, and beans, *Phaseolus*. Other climbers enhance man's enjoyment of life. For many life would not be so pleasant without the grape vine, *Vitis vinifera*, or the hop, *Humulus lupulus*.

Above: An unusual form of support. *Ampelopsis crampons* (shown here) uses *suckers* which grow on a short branch from the stem and hold the plant to its host. Also unusual, and superficially similar, are the *adventitious* roots which grow from the stem of ivy, *Hedera helix*, and hold it to its support.

Below: A more usual way of climbing is by means of downward growing hairs. This electron micrograph (about 50 times life size) is of the stem of goosegrass (or cleavers), *Galium aparine*. Poultry, and geese in particular, like to eat this plant which explains the origin of its name.

Jean-Pierre Bourret

Dr. G. Leedale/Biophoto Assoc.

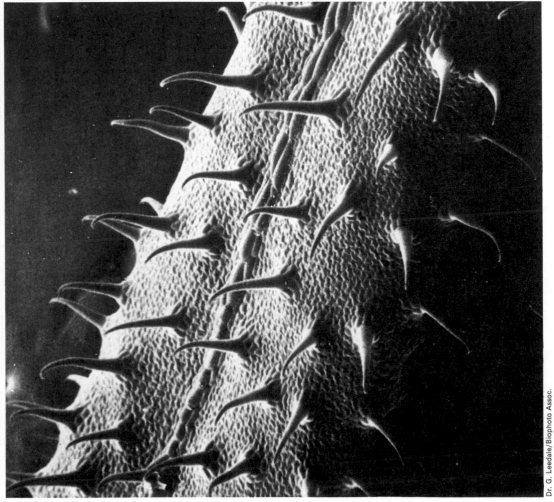

Carnivorous Plants

Carnivorous plants live by capturing insects, digesting them and absorbing the products through the leaf surface. By obtaining essential nutrients in this way they are able to grow successfully in poor, mineral-deficient habitats. Carnivorous plants are surprisingly widespread—there are some 450 species distributed between six families—and they grow all over the world and in all sorts of conditions.

The sundew, *Drosera*, and the butterwort, *Pinguicula*, grow in cold acidic bogs, while the Dutchman's pipe pitcher plant, *Nepenthes*, is common in the hot, moist rain forests of South-East Asia. Pitcher plants are not confined to tropical forests. The huntsman's horn, *Sarracenia*, the cobra plant, *Darlingtonia*, of North America and *Cephalotus* of Australia all grow in warm acidic bogs, and *Heliamphora* is confined to mist-enshrouded swamps in Venezuela. Many species of the largest carnivorous plant genus, the bladderworts, *Utricularia*, grow, as does *Aldrovanda*, in pools of slightly acidic water, while several others are found on wet tree trunks in tropical jungle, or in marshy waterlogged soils.

Carnivorous plants have five distinct mechanisms for catching their prey—pitcher traps, snap traps, adhesive traps, suction traps and lobster-pot traps—but there is no correlation between the type of trap and any particular family. Thus, plants with pitcher trap mechanisms are found in three separate families, whereas within one family, *Lentibulariaceae*, four forms of trap occur.

Pitcher plants

Pitcher plants capture their prey by means of modified, cup-shaped leaves or 'pitchers' which contain digestive fluid. Insects are induced to land inside the pitcher where they lose their footing, fall into the pool of fluid below and drown. The traps vary considerably in size and construction. In the genera *Sarracenia* and *Heliamphora*, for example, they are 10 to 60 cm (4 to 24 in) long and are formed from a whole leaf, whereas in *Nepenthes* and *Cephalotus* they are 5 to 40 cm (2 to 16 in) long and are formed by a tendril-like growth from the leaf tip. The simple, conical traps of *Heliamphora* have only a narrow rim, while *Sarracenia* has a wide, decorated lip, the *peristome*.

Both *Nepenthes* and *Cephalotus* have ridged peristomes which may develop vanes, as in *Nepenthes villosa*, or a *cornice* of large, downward-pointing spines inside the pitcher, as in *Nepenthes raja* and *Cephalotus*. In many species the mouth of the pitcher shelters under a lid, while in *Darlingtonia* and *Sarracenia psittacina* the top of the pitcher curls right over forming a hood.

To attract insects, the rim and the inner wall of the pitcher are often a bright red colour, and many pitchers secrete a viscous sugary fluid on to the peristome and the underside of the lid as an added attractant. The lip of *Sarracenia* is covered with long hairs and red veins leading downwards to the mouth of the

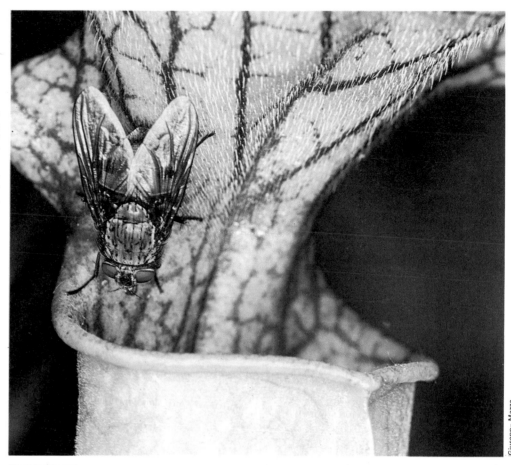

Left: A pitcher plant, *Nepenthes pervillei*, from the Seychelles. The pitcher traps, which have lids, form at the ends of the leaves.

Above: A fly in danger of its life at the mouth of a pitcher trap of *Sarracenia drummondii*. All *Sarracenia* species come from N America.

trap. Below the lip is a zone of shorter hairs and then a much smoother area. Just above the water level is another zone of long, downward-pointing hairs. This is all designed to prevent an insect from getting a grip on the pitcher walls.

It is difficult to explain why insects that reach the lip do not fly away before entering the pitcher proper. *Nepenthes*, usually found climbing in forests, catches numerous ants, but the prey of *Sarracenia* is usually winged. Possibly the sugary secretion covering the walls and lip contains a narcotic which drugs the prey, or perhaps the insects become disoriented by the lid overhanging the pitcher.

The lower part of the inner surfaces of the pitchers are lined with small glands which are responsible for the digestive processes. *Nepenthes* secretes a slightly acidic fluid into the pitcher, and this becomes gradually more acidic as the plant matures due to the secretion of hydrochloric acid. The glands also secrete special proteins, called *enzymes*, into the fluid. These compounds speed up the breakdown of the insect bodies, and they function most efficiently in acid conditions. The small molecules produced by the digestion process are easily absorbed by the pitcher wall glands.

One of these enzymes is *nepenthesin*, a protease which breaks down proteins into their constituent amino acids. These compounds provide the pitcher plant with a source of nitrogen which is often lacking in its wet, tropical habitats. Nepenthesin is similar to *pepsin*, which breaks down proteins in the strongly acidic mammalian stomach. The other potential source of nitrogen is the insect's exoskeleton, composed entirely of the virtually indestructible substance *chitin*, and another of the enzymes produced by *Nepenthes* is capable of slowly breaking down this tough material. The digestive fluid of *Nepenthes* also has enzymes to break down fats and nucleic acids.

Despite this prodigious digestive capacity there are some insects which are able to live within the pitchers. Larvae of the mosquito *Wyeomyia smithii* live in the pitcher of *Sarracenia purpurea*, and the adults have no difficulty alighting on the walls or flying out of the pitcher. Other larvae and a host of protozoa all live unharmed within the pitcher fluid, while the spider *Misumenops nepenthicola* spins a web inside the mouth and so is able to move about within the pitcher—an ideal location for catching insect prey.

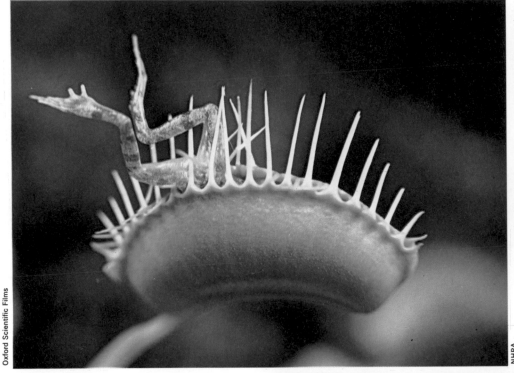

Above: A small frog caught by a Venus's flytrap, *Dionaea*, provides an unusual meal. Although the trap is not designed for such large prey, it will close whenever two trigger hairs inside the leaf lobes are touched.

Right: A Venus's flytrap with both open and closed traps. The inner surfaces of the leaf lobes carry bright red digestion glands. The red colour, caused by an *anthocyanin* pigment, serves to attract insects to the plant.

Above: A fly is trapped by a British species of sundew, *Drosera rotundifolia*. Each unusual-looking leaf carries many slender tentacles, each with a globule of sticky, sugary fluid which sticks to the prey.

Snap traps

The Venus's flytrap, *Dionaea muscipula*, is a small terrestrial plant having rosettes of six to eight leaves bearing traps 1 to 3 cm (0.4 to 1.2 in) long. The trap itself forms on the end of the leaf, the leafstalk forming a hinge and the remainder of the leaf tissue two lobes. The edges of the lobes are equipped with a number of long spines. The spines of opposite lobes intermesh when the leaf closes.

Located in a triangle on each lobe are three stiff hairs. These are about 1.5 mm (0.06 in) long and serve to trigger off the closing of the leaf. An insect moving over the leaf surface will brush against one of the hairs. Movement of the hair compresses a constricted zone of cells at its base causing an electric charge to be established, but the trap remains open. The hinge is activated only when a second hair movement increases the potential to a fixed discharge level.

The electric discharge, which now activates the hinge, moves across the leaf as fast as a nerve impulse, although there is no specialized nervous tissue. Furthermore, the second hair movement can be at the same hair or any one of the other hairs. The Venus's flytrap may have developed this 'double action' trigger to avoid fruitless closing of the trap by, for example, a raindrop. Once triggered, the trap closes very quickly—within one fifth of a second.

When the lobes come together the spines intermesh but do not completely close the gap, and if the trapped insect is very small it can escape and the trap will reopen. In this way valuable digestive fluid is not wasted on prey which will yield less nutrient than is used digesting it. If, however, the prey is sufficiently large the trap closes slowly over several hours, finally crushing it.

Adhesive traps

The traps of the sundews, *Drosera* and *Drosophyllum*, the butterworts, *Pinguicula*, and the rainbow plants, *Byblis*, all use a sticky mucilage to ensnare insects. The leaf surfaces are covered with two types of gland, *stalked* and *sessile*. The stalked glands, in the form of hairs or 'tentacles' secrete a highly viscous sugary fluid which attracts insects and holds them fast once they have landed on the plant. As the prey struggles to escape neighbouring hairs bend towards it and it becomes even more firmly held.

The sessile glands are responsible for producing digestive enzymes. Within one to two days of an insect becoming trapped by the plant, enzymes can be detected and after four days digestion of the prey is at its most active.

Suction traps

The bladderworts, *Utricularia* and *Polypompholyx*, grow free-floating or rooted in ponds and streams. They have branched stems with tight crowns of leaves, and the traps are small bladders from 0.3 to 5 mm (0.01 to 0.19 in) long located on the leaves. The prey consists mainly of water fleas, protozoa and insect larvae.

The pear-shaped bladders are attached to the leaf by a short stalk and have an opening which is closed by a trap door, a free-hanging structure with a hinge at one side and a second hinge three-quarters of the way down. Just below the second hinge are two long, rigid *trigger hairs*. The bottom of the door rests on an inclined semi-circular collar, the *threshold*. A second, much more flexible door rests against the base of the trap door and

BLADDERWORT

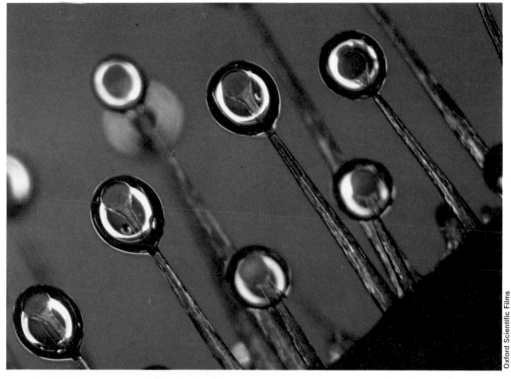

Oxford Scientific Films

Below: A bladderwort, *Utricularia*. An aquatic plant, it catches its prey, typically water fleas, by means of small bladders carried by the leaves. Each bladder, closed by a hinged 'trap door', is first emptied of most of its water by means of special glands. When trigger hairs near the entrance are touched, the door springs open and water floods in, carrying the prey with it. The door then closes to prevent escape, and digestion begins.

Left: The pink butterwort, *Pinguicula lusitanica*, catches its prey by means of sticky tentacles carried by the upper leaf surfaces. The captured insects supply nitrogen, which is usually lacking in its boggy habitat.

Above: A close-up of the stalked glands of a sundew, *Drosera*. The globules of sticky fluid are plainly visible. Glands on the leaf surface secrete enzymes to digest the prey once it has been caught by these tentacles.

Natural Science Photos

the threshold, thus ensuring a water-tight fit. Two long antennae curve down over the entrance and numerous stiff bristles surround the trap door.

Bifid and *globular* glands, which are located on the inner side of the threshold and on the outer surface of the trap respectively, pump water from the interior of the bladder in order to set the trap. Up to 90 per cent of the original water is expelled so that the door is pressed tightly against the threshold by external water pressure. Glands located on the outer surface of the door and threshold secrete a sugary mucilage which attracts prey and seals the door. The bristles guide prey towards the door until, by pushing against the trigger hairs, the lower part of the door levers open. Within 0.0015 sec the pressure forces the door inwards and both water and prey are sucked in. The door then springs shut, ensuring that the prey cannot escape, and water is pumped out so that digestion can begin.

Lobster-pot traps

Genlisea grows as a small free-floating rosette partially submerged in shallow water and is often found with bladderworts. The trap-leaves, only a few centimetres long, have a short stalk which divides into two tubes. These hang down into the water. A slit runs in a spiral all the way down the tubes, and along the inner edge of this is a row of inward-pointing hairs. The outer edge is covered in glands which secrete mucilage. Small aquatic animals can easily find their way past the hairs and get into the trap, but then cannot find the entrance and are caught. The inner surface has numerous glands similar in appearance to those of bladderworts.

bladder trap (cutaway)

digestive glands

trigger hairs

water flea

entrance

bladder trap (section)

Flowering Plants

Over the last 100 million years one group of plants has become dominant on the Earth, both in numbers and species. Called the *Angiospermae*, the flowering plants, the group includes well over 200,000 species, more than a hundred times as many as the next major group, the gymnosperms. It contains most of the trees grown by man for timber and almost all of the plants grown for food.

The dominance and variety of the flowering plants is closely linked with the three features used to distinguish them from other groups, such as the gymnosperms. These features are flowers, seeds enclosed in fruits, and a well-developed conducting system. Flowers encourage *cross-pollination* (fertilization with pollen from another plant rather than the same plant) by insects or other animals; seeds enclosed in fruits encourage widespread dispersal; and a fully developed system of conducting tissues means the efficient transport of water and nutrients within the plant.

Origin of the flowering plants

It is probable that the angiosperms evolved from the gymnosperms, though this can never be known for certain as most species of gymnosperms are known only as fossils. Plants have no skeleton and so plant fossils give only a limited picture of the appearance of the living plant. It is difficult, therefore, to deduce the important details of reproduction and development from a fossil. Nevertheless, it seems that the angiosperms are most like a group called the *pteridosperms*, the seed ferns. These plants, which have been extinct for at least 100 million years, were similar to the *cycads*, a few species of which still survive.

The earliest angiosperm fossils date from the Lower Cretaceous period (100-135 million years ago). Some of these are very similar to present day flowering plants; but the great explosion in the number of species of flowering plants probably took place more recently, during the early Tertiary period (about 80 million years ago). At that time, insects such as bees and butterflies, which are important pollinators, evolved to their present day forms. It is easy to relate the amazing diversity of flowering plants to the equally remarkable diversity of their insect pollinators.

Flowers

Flowers vary enormously in their size, colour and structure. When a flower is described, the first things normally mentioned are the *sepals* and *petals*. The petals are the brightly coloured structures that make flowers attractive to people, and, more important as far as the plant is concerned, to the insects or other animals that pollinate the flower. The sepals are a ring of smaller, leaf-like structures outside the petals. They enclose and protect the flower bud before it opens. All the sepals together are called the *calyx*, and all the petals together the *corolla*. In a few flowers, such as lilies (*Liliaceae*), the calyx is as large and

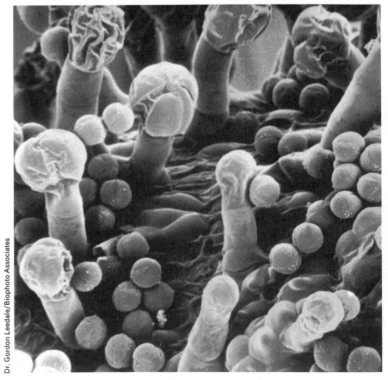

Above: The beautiful forms, colours and perfumes of flowers exist not to be aesthetically pleasing to man but as an attraction to bees and other insects. In their hunt for both pollen and *nectar* (a sugary substance produced by some flowers in glands, *nectaries*, on the petals) insects become covered by pollen produced by the male sex organs (*anthers*). This pollen is then transferred to the female sex organ(s) (*stigma*) of another plant. The pollen of one flower therefore fertilizes the eggs of a second flower—a process known as *cross-pollination*—which produces a plant with characteristics slightly different from either parent and a total population of plants each slightly different from the other. Such a variable population allows the gradual adoption of favourable characteristics by natural selection.

Right: The surface of a stigma (magnification about 500 times) showing *epidermal hairs* and pollen grains between them.

Dr. Gordon Leedale/Biophoto Associates

A-Z

84

The fragile fuchsia, seen
in cross section. The
pollen tube, stamen and
stigma are exposed (see
diagram, page 87).

Above: The Swedish botanist, Carl von Linné (1707-78) whose system of classification, based on flower structure, was a great help to early botanists.

Above right: Nodding (or musk) thistle, *Carduus nutans*. Thistles are members of the daisy family, *Compositae*. Each

'flower' is in fact an inflorescence of many small flowers and is called a *capitulum*.

Below right: Flower of the tulip tree, *Liriodendron tulipifera*. Tulip and tulip tree flowers look similar but the plants are not closely related. Tulip trees are dicots, tulips (*Tulipa*) are monocots.

brightly coloured as the corolla, and the term *perianth* is then used to describe both calyx and corolla.

It was realized in very early times that pollination is necessary for seed and fruit production; Assyrian kings performed a ceremonial pollination of date palms. However, the discovery that plants have two sexes is credited to Rudolph Jacob Camerarius (1665-1721). He realized that, less conspicuous than petals and sepals, there are male and female reproductive structures at the centre of a flower.

The male structures are called *stamens*. Each normally consists of a stalk supporting a bright yellow or orange head, the *anther*, which contains thousands of *pollen* grains, inside which are contained the male gametes. The female parts of the flower are more variable. The essential features, however, are the *ovules*, each of which contains one female gamete; the *ovary*, which contains the ovules; and the *style*, an elongated projection from the ovary. The style carries at its tip a flattened, often sticky, surface called the *stigma*.

A flower may have one or several styles and stigmas, and the ovary may be a single structure or be composed of a number of separate parts. When a pollen grain finds its way on to a stigma, it germinates to form a *pollen tube* which grows down through the style and into the ovary where fertilization—the fusion of male and female gametes—takes place. Each fertilized ovule develops into a seed.

The structure of flowers and the details of the reproductive organs in flowering plants are different from anything found in other plants. Flowering plants do, however, have a life-cycle with an alter-

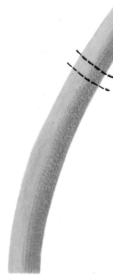

Right: Cross section of a typical flower. *Pollen grains*, deposited on the *stigma*, each produce a *pollen tube* which grows down through the style and into the *ovule* through a small pore, the *micropyle*. Inside the ovule is an *embryo sac* typically containing 8 nuclei—*antipodals, polar nuclei, synergids,* and the *female egg*. The pollen tube discharges two *sperms* which fertilize the ovule—one fuses with the egg, the other with the two polar nuclei. The other nuclei usually disintegrate.

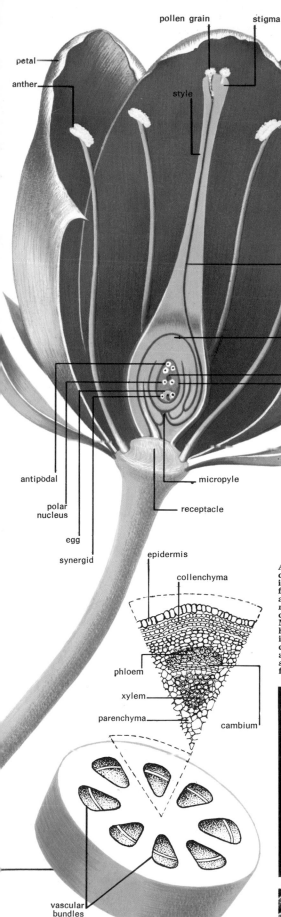

pollen grain

stigma

petal

anther

style

stamen

pollen tube

ovule

sperm

antipodal

polar nucleus

egg

synergid

micropyle

receptacle

embryo sac

sepal

epidermis

collenchyma

phloem

xylem

parenchyma

cambium

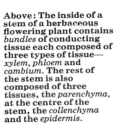

vascular bundles

Above: The inside of a stem of a herbaceous flowering plant contains *bundles* of conducting tissue each composed of three types of tissue—*xylem, phloem* and *cambium*. The rest of the stem is also composed of three tissues, the *parenchyma*, at the centre of the stem, the *collenchyma* and the *epidermis*.

Above right: The characteristic inflorescence of the family *Umbelliferae* is a lot of small flowers radiating out from a central main stalk. Most *Umbelliferae* also have a *tap root*, which in many cases, such as carrot, *Daucus carota*, and parsnip, *Pastinaca sativa*, is swollen to form a food store.

Below: Flowering plants also reproduce vegetatively. A *bulb* is a modified stem (the darker yellow portion at the base) from which grow fleshy *scale leaves* in which food is stored. An onion, *Alium cepa*, is an example of a bulb eaten for its food. This bulb, however, is the daffodil, *Narcissus*.

Right: Roots differ from stems in having no leaves or buds and in possessing conducting tissue arranged in a central core rather than in vascular bundles. The absorbing area of roots is greatly increased by thousands of tiny root hairs which are in intimate contact with the soil particles.

Jean Pierre Bourret

Leslie Jackman

G. R. Roberts

nation of generations, like mosses, ferns and gymnosperms, though one generation is hardly noticeable. The plant as we see it is the sporophyte. The gametophytes are so much reduced in size and complexity that only careful research shows that they are actually present. The male gametophyte, consisting of only three cells, develops inside the pollen grain. The female gametophyte remains buried within the ovule and is never released from inside the sporophyte.

The flower of an angiosperm is different in appearance from the cone of a gymnosperm, but the processes of pollination and fertilization are much the same. The most important difference is indicated by the word *angiosperm*, which means 'covered seed'. In gymnosperms the seed is exposed, whereas in flowering plants it is contained within the ovary. In some plants, as the seed forms, the ovary and other parts of the flower expand to form a *fruit*, surrounding the seed.

Another distinctive feature of many flowering plants is the way the flowers are arranged together in groups called *inflorescences*, giving a large patch of colour which may help to attract pollinating insects. Inflorescences are also useful to the botanist: the different types are often an easy way of recognizing the family to which a plant belongs.

Stems, roots and leaves

Flowers, being conspicuously colourful and varied in structure, are probably the most immediately interesting part of a flowering plant. Nevertheless, the growth and flowering of plants depends on intricate structures and complex processes which occur within stems, roots

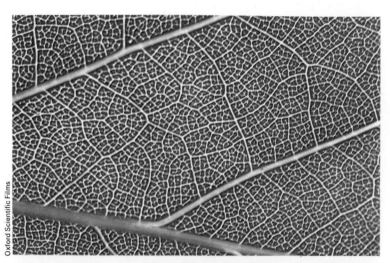

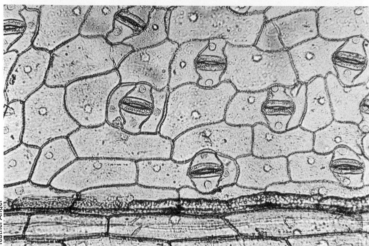

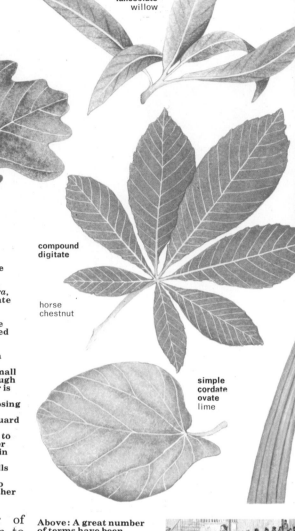

simple
lanceolate
willow

simple lobed
oak

compound
digitate

horse
chestnut

simple
cordate
ovate
lime

Above left: Intricate pattern of the leaf veins of a tulip tree, *Liriodendron tulipifera*, showing the elaborate branched network of dicotyledons. In monocotyledons the veins are unbranched and parallel.

Left: A close-up of a leaf of *Tradescantia* (x50) showing the small pores, *stomata*, through which water vapour is lost from the plant. The opening and closing of each stoma is controlled by two guard cells at its mouth. These cells respond to changes in the water pressure (*turgidity*) in the cell. As water is lost the pressure falls and the guard cells close the stomata so preventing any further loss of water.

and leaves. The non-flowering parts of plants are by no means always similar: they vary in an almost infinite number of ways.

The stem of a plant provides the framework to which are attached the leaves and flowers. Within it are contained two types of tissue, *xylem* and *phloem*, specially modified for conducting water and nutrients from one part of the plant to another. Xylem consists of long tubes, called *vessels*, formed from dead cells with missing end walls and thickened side walls. It provides the pathway along which water and inorganic nutrients pass upwards from the roots to the leaves. Phloem, on the other hand, consists of two kinds of living cells, *sieve tube cells* and *companion cells*, and is concerned with the transport of organic nutrients—particularly *sucrose* (sugar)—downwards from the leaves to the roots.

Sieve tube cells are elongated cells linked together but separated by perforated end walls to form a tube. The smaller companion cells are arranged alongside the sieve tube cells and apparently control their activity. Additionally, between the xylem and phloem, are a few layers of narrow cells called the *cambium*. Cambium cells continuously form new cells which replace aging xylem and phloem cells.

In the stems of herbaceous plants, xylem and phloem run alongside one another in *vascular bundles*, each of which forms a cylinder of conducting tissue running from the roots up into the leaves. The vascular bundles are either arranged regularly in a ring towards the outside of the stem (in *dicotyledons*), or they are scattered irregularly throughout the stem

(in *monocotyledons*). The number of bundles also varies—from about ten to more than a hundred in some species.

The vascular tissue of roots is not arranged like that of stems. In roots the xylem and phloem are gathered together into a single vascular cylinder running down the centre of the root. Externally, however, root systems vary quite considerably. For example, some plants have a *tap root*, a main root which grows downwards with smaller roots branching off it. A carrot, *Daucus carota*, is a swollen tap root containing a reserve supply of nutrients for the carrot plant. Other plants, such as grasses, have a relatively shallow network of small fibrous roots, which are efficient in extracting water and nutrients from the upper region of the soil.

Leaves are attached to the stem at places called *nodes*: if there is a single leaf at each node the leaves are called *alternate*; if there is a pair of leaves, they are called *opposite*. In either case, each leaf consists of a flat blade attached to the stem by a leaf-stalk, the *petiole*, through which runs a vascular bundle which begins in the stem. (New vascular bundles are created along the length of the stem by the branching of old bundles, thus keeping the total number of bundles in the stem roughly constant.) The vascular bundle of the leaf-stalk branches within the leaf to form *leaf veins*.

Internally, a leaf's structure is related to its function as the main site of photosynthesis. The surface layer of cells, the *epidermis*, is perforated by pores called *stomata*. Stomata allow air, containing carbon dioxide, to enter the intercellular spaces within the leaf, and so reach the

Above: A great number of terms have been coined to describe the various shapes of leaves. Among other things, these terms may describe leaf blade composition, like *simple* (all parts of the blade in one piece) or *compound* (composed of separate leaflets); the general shape of the leaf, such as *linear* (several times longer than broad) or *reniform* (kidney-shaped); or the margin of the leaf, such as *entire* (no indentations) or *serrated* (saw-like indentations).

simple ovate alder

simple triangular lombardy poplar

compound pinnate rowan

simple linear grass

simple ovate-assymetric elm

simple palmate sycamore

simple oval beech

Right: Except for deserts, mountains, towns and coniferous forests, the land surface of the Earth is covered with flowering plants. This is part of a sub-tropical rain forest in Queensland, Australia.

Below right: Another use of flowering plants —Kenyan women picking *pyrethrum* flowers used to make the insecticide, *pyrethrum*. Pyrethrum, in the concentrations used in insecticides, is non-toxic both to plants and higher animals and is widely used on livestock and on edible plants. Though once regarded as a genus in their own right, these plants are now classified as a species of the genus *Chrysanthemum*.

Eric Crichton

Alphabet & Image

Left and below: The importance of flowering plants as food sources is inestimable. They are the basic food of virtually all life outside of the oceans. They are also of major economic importance in other ways. The most significant of these is timber production but other uses include textiles, drugs, dyes, resins, and perfumes. These women (left) are sorting roses for perfume manufacture (France 1891), while (below) vegetable dyes are exhibited for sale in India.

cells where photosynthesis takes place. Stomata may be found on the upper, lower or both surfaces of the leaf, although it is most usual to find them only on the lower surface.

Water is lost from the plant by diffusion from the intercellular spaces through the stomata—a process, called *transpiration*, which can be controlled by opening and closing the stomata. Water loss by evaporation from the epidermis is reduced by a layer of waxes, called the *cuticle*, which extends over the whole of the above-ground surface of the plant.

Monocotyledons and dicotyledons

The English botanist John Ray (1627-1705) was the first person to recognize the fundamental division of the flowering plants into two groups, the *Monocotyledonae* and the *Dicotyledonae*. They are divided by four obvious differences. Firstly, monocots, as their name implies, have only one seed leaf (*cotyledon*), while dicots have two. (Cotyledons are the simple leaves that appear first when a seed germinates, although in some plants they remain inside the seed.) Secondly, monocots have leaves with parallel, unbranched veins while in dicots the veins form a branched network. Thirdly, though the form of the flowers in both groups is very variable, as a general rule monocots have three or six of each flower component, for example three or six petals and three or six stamens, while dicots have their flower parts in fours or fives or in much larger numbers. Finally, although some monocots, such as palms and bamboos, appear woody, none show the *secondary thickening* by which woody dicots increase in girth each year.

As examples, buttercups (*Ranunculaceae*) and cabbages (*Cruciferae*) are familiar plants with obvious dicot features, while lilies (*Liliaceae*) and irises (*Iridaceae*) are monocots. The division into dicots and monocots reflects evolution; the dicots are probably more like the earliest angiosperms than the monocots.

Success of the flowering plants

Flowering plants are successful because of their flowers, their fruits and their efficient water-conducting systems. Many are also successful because they are *herbaceous* (not woody). Herbaceous plants can grow from seed to flower within a very short time—sometimes only a few weeks. This means that they can spread more rapidly than trees which may grow for decades before flowering and producing seed. One extreme example, the herbaceous desert plant, *Boerhaavia repens*, can produce seed eight days after germination. Such adaptation is of great advantage in harsh environments where to survive it is necessary to produce seed quickly before short-lived favourable conditions pass away.

In inhospitable environments the adaptability of the flowering plants has enabled them to grow where other plants would not be successful. In favourable conditions this same adaptability has resulted in a diversity of forms which together dominate the vegetation of the Earth—from tropical rain forest to the upland meadows of the Alps. The scenery of the Earth is largely the scenery of flowering plants. More importantly, they provide food, shelter and clothing for most of the world's population.

Flowering Trees and Shrubs

The naturally dominant vegetation of any moderately wet and fertile area is forest. Trees are capable of producing a tall leaf canopy which overshadows other plants. In colder northern regions these trees are normally gymnosperms, but in more hospitable warm temperate and tropical areas they are almost always angiosperms. They are dicots, but have retained the tree characteristics which were probably normal among the earliest flowering plants, rather than evolving into herbaceous forms.

The trunks and branches that form the framework of trees and shrubs are built up over years of growth, with a gradual increase in girth. Typically this increase is about 25 mm (1 in) a year (measuring around the trunk at 1.5 m (5 ft) above the ground.) Some species grow much faster than this, in particular species of *Eucalyptus*. Others, including horse chestnut, *Aesculus hippocastanum*, and the common

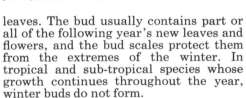

Above left: Female catkins of the common sallow (goat willow), *Salix caprea*. Members of the willow family, *Salicaceae*, which also includes poplars, *Populus*, have flowers in catkins but each plant has flowers of one sex only. Willows may be large trees, such as the cricket bat willow, a variety of *Salix alba*; shrubby trees, such as osier, *Salix viminalis*; or dwarf shrubs like creeping willow, *Salix repens*. Poplars are often large, fast growing trees, such as some varieties of black poplar, *Populus nigra*.

Left: Cork oak, *Quercus suber*. Its thick rugged bark is the world's principal source of cork.

lime, *Tilia × europea*, grow more slowly. Young trees usually grow more rapidly than average; old trees more slowly.

The growth of a woody trunk or stem involves a process known as *secondary thickening*. In both dicots and gymnosperms there is a ring of vascular bundles in the stem towards the outer surface. In older stems and branches this ring of individual vascular bundles becomes a continuous ring of conducting tissue, with phloem on the outside, xylem on the inside, and a layer of cambium in between. The cells of the cambium continue to divide to produce new xylem and phloem cells and the stem grows outwards by the laying down of successive layers of xylem tissue. In cold and temperate regions the xylem cells produced in spring are relatively large, with thin walls, but as the growing season progresses the new cells are smaller, with thicker, darker walls. Thus over a number of years the wood comes to have a series of *annual rings*, each being a band of darker *autumn wood* separated by the lighter *spring wood*. When a tree trunk is sawn across, these rings are clearly visible and by counting them the age of the tree can be found. Trees growing in the tropics, without pronounced seasons, have either irregular rings, corresponding to periods of good and bad weather rather than to years of age, or no rings at all.

Increase in the height or spread, rather than the girth, of a tree or shrub takes place by a different process, called *terminal growth*, which occurs at the tips of the branches. In the autumn, growth ceases and *winter buds* form. Each bud consists of a growing point covered by a number of *bud scales* which are modified leaves. The bud usually contains part or all of the following year's new leaves and flowers, and the bud scales protect them from the extremes of the winter. In tropical and sub-tropical species whose growth continues throughout the year, winter buds do not form.

Temperate tree families
There is no hard-and-fast dividing line between dicot families which include trees and shrubs and those which include only herbaceous plants. Many families include both—suggesting that, if herbaceous plants evolved from woody plants, then this evolution must have taken place on many separate occasions. Nevertheless, many families consist predominantly of trees and shrubs.

The tree family that contains plants probably most similar to the earliest angiosperms is the magnolia family, *Magnoliaceae*. Like the simple herbaceous family, the water-lilies, *Nymphaeaceae*, they have flowers with many separate petals and stamens. The flowers are valued by gardeners for their large size and delicate pink or cream colouring.

Beeches, *Fagus*, sweet chestnuts, *Castanea*, and oaks, *Quercus*, all belong to one family, the *Fagaceae*. These are mostly

90

G. R. Roberts

Left: The majestic English elm, *Ulmus procera*. Unfortunately elm trees are susceptible to a fungal disease, 'Dutch' elm disease, *Cerotocystis ulmi*, spread by a bark beetle, *Scolytus scolytus*. Periodic outbreaks have killed large numbers of trees. For example, one such outbreak, which started in 1970, killed most of the prominent hedgerow elms in large areas of England. Chemical control of the disease is impracticable for the millions of trees growing in the countryside and in the long term it is probably better to reduce the impact of epidemics by planting different trees to replace the elms.

Right: Common (or European) beech, *Fagus sylvatica*. Beeches, oaks, *Quercus*, and sweet chestnuts, *Castanea*, all belong to the same family, the beech family, *Fagaceae*.

Below: Scanning electron micrograph (about 700 times life size) of the *xylem* (wood) of lupin, *Lupinus*. The thickened rings around the xylem vessels give strength to the wood.

Giuseppe Mazza

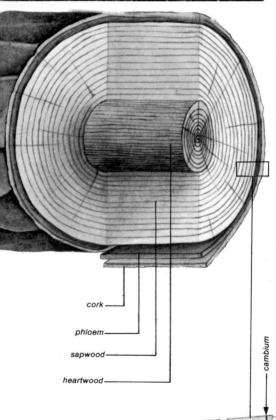

cork

phloem

sapwood

heartwood

cambium

Dr Gordon Leedale/Biophoto Associates

Above left and below: Wood is made up of *annual rings* of xylem produced by a thin layer of cells, the *cambium*, between the phloem and xylem. The cells of the xylem continue to function as water-conducting tissue for 20-30 years. During this time, however, they eventually become *lignified*—filling up with a substance, called *lignin*, which gives strength to the wood but prevents the passage of water. The outer, functional xylem forms a pale zone called the *sapwood*. The central lignified zone, often darker in colour, is called the *heartwood*. The *cork* (bark) is a protective layer of dead impermeable cells.

deciduous forest trees, with simple leaves and separate male and female flowers on the same tree. The flowers are grouped into inflorescences of petal-less flowers, called *catkins*, and appear early in the year, often before the leaves. The pollen is carried by the wind from male to female catkins, making cross-pollination very likely where a number of trees of the same species are present. After fertilization the female flowers produce *nuts*, hard-walled fruits dispersed by the animals which use them as a source of food.

Over 450 species of oak grow in Europe, Asia or America. Two are native to Britain and Northern Europe. The sessile oak, *Quercus petraea*, has acorns carried directly on the twigs (which is what the word 'sessile' means), while the pedunculate oak, *Quercus robur*, has stalked acorns. Pedunculate oak is often planted in areas where sessile oak is the naturally occurring wild-growing species and, since the two species interbreed freely, intermediate types are common.

Beeches, *Fagus*, are also widespread. They are particularly common on steep, chalk-based hillsides, such as the Chiltern hills in southern England, although they are found in most north temperate regions; while a related genus, the southern beeches, *Nothofagus*, are common in the southern hemisphere. Beech nuts (*mast*) are enclosed in a prickly husk. 'Copper beech' is a variety of the most common northern species, *Fagus sylvatica*, but has dark, purplish foliage.

Elms, *Ulmus*, belong to another family, the *Ulmaceae*. They are important timber trees but are perhaps more important for their contribution to the scenery in both Europe and North America. They are particularly common hedgerow trees, and, although elm flowers have inconspicuous greenish petals, the stamens have bright red filaments, so that the branches of an elm in flower appear red at a distance. The flowers are wind-pollinated, and the fruits, consisting of a seed surrounded by a circular papery wing, are dispersed by the wind. However, the fruits are often sterile. Most elm trees originate

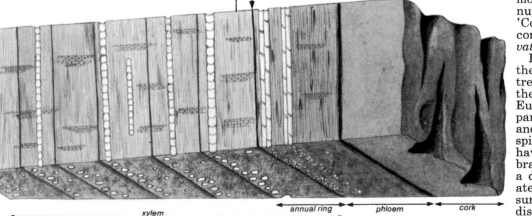

xylem

annual ring

phloem

cork

91

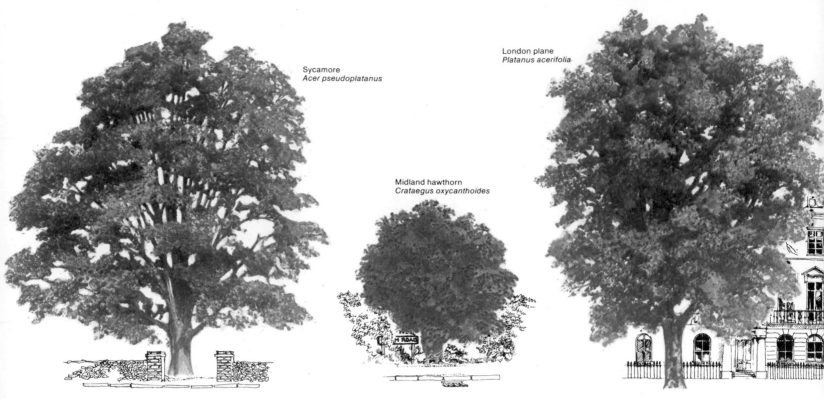

Sycamore
Acer pseudoplatanus

London plane
Platanus acerifolia

Midland hawthorn
Crataegus oxycanthoides

Above: Trees are capable of enlivening a drab urban scene. These six trees are common in British towns:— *Sycamore* is sometimes regarded as an urban weed as it produces masses of winged seeds which often germinate in unlikely places. *Midland hawthorn* is generally planted as a hedging plant, mainly because of its 3 cm (1 in) thorns. *London plane* for many epitomizes the town tree, thriving in central London. Characteristically the dark soiled bark peels off in strips, revealing pale new bark beneath. *Lime*, though often mutilated and 'lollipopped', is in fact a stately tree with yellow-green, heart-shaped leaves. *Flowering cherry* unfailingly produces a mass of colour in the spring. The variety 'Kanzan' is grown by grafting buds on to a rootstock of wild cherry, *Prunus avium*. *Red horsechestnut* is a hybrid between white horsechestnut, *Aesculus hippocastanum*, and American red buck-eye, *Aesculus pavia*.

Left: A group of alders, *Alnus*, in their most common habitat—beside water. Alders, which are members of the birch family, *Betulaceae*, have two remarkable features: they are the only flowering trees to produce 'cones', and they have symbiotic nodules on their roots. The 'cones' are not true cones as produced by gymnosperms but fruits which develop from the fertilized female catkins. The root nodules, probably formed by an *Actinomycetes* fungus, provide the alder with a supply of nitrogen which may be in short supply in the poor, boggy soils in which the tree grows.

Below: *Anthocyanins* in the leaves of sugar maples, *Acer saccharum*, turns them golden red in autumn. Maples, *Aceraceae*, occur in America, Asia and Europe. Sugar maples are native to North America, particularly New England. The most common European maples are sycamores, *Acer pseudoplatanus*, and Norway maples, *Acer platanoides*.

as suckers thrown up by neighbouring trees.

The family with the hardiest of all flowering trees is the birch family, *Betulaceae*, which includes alder, *Alnus*, and birches, *Betula*. One especially hardy birch is the dwarf birch, *Betula nana*, a small shrub with glossy, circular leaves which grows at high altitudes in northern Europe. Birches generally are small, fast-growing trees which are often the first to colonize open areas of land.

A closely related family to the birches is the *Corylaceae*, which includes hornbeam, *Carpinus betulus*, and hazel, *Corylus avellana*. Hornbeam is somewhat similar in appearance to beech, but its leaves have serrated rather than smooth edges, and the fruit is a cluster of winged seeds rather than a nut.

A final family of temperature woody plants is the heath family, *Ericaceae*, important more for shrubs than for trees. Most members of the family are evergreen shrubs, including *Rhododendron*, and many different kinds of heather, *Calluna* and *Erica*. Heathers and other dwarf ericaceous shrubs are the dominant plants over large areas of heathland, a vegetation type that is widespread in temperate areas and which also occurs on mountains in the tropics.

Tropical food trees
Several woody families include tropical plants from which are obtained food or drinks. Tea comes from the shrub *Cam-*

ellia sinensis of the family *Theaceae*. It has been cultivated in China for at least 3,000 years. Both ordinary black teas and green teas are made from its leaves, but by different processes of withering (drying), roasting, fermentation and pressing. Coffee comes mainly from *Coffea arabica* (family *Rubiaceae*) which originally grew wild in Ethiopia. Another species, *Coffea canephora*, produces the inferior 'robusta' coffee. Coffee plants carry red berries, and the 'coffee beans', which are the seeds, are extracted from inside the berries.

Cocoa, a native of tropical America, but now widely grown in West Africa, comes from a small tree called *Theobroma cacao* (family *Sterculiaceae*). The tree is unusual in that the flowers and fruits grow directly from the trunk and main branches rather than on side branches. The cocoa beans, of which 40-60% is a fat called *cocoa butter*, are enclosed in red or yellow pods. They can be processed in several ways: to make cocoa for drinking, in which case part of the fat is removed; or to make chocolate, in which case extra cocoa butter, sugar and milk are added.

Many tropical trees yield edible fruits, but the papaya, *Carica papaya* (family *Caricaceae*), is unusual in several ways. The trees grow rapidly from seed and bear fruit in the first year. After 3-4 years they may reach a height of 6 m (20 ft), but their fruit-bearing then declines and they must be replaced. Male and female flowers are borne on separate trees. The female trees produce an edible fruit, something like a melon, which is a greenish-yellow outside but has orange flesh. The sap is also useful. It contains an enzyme, *papain*,

Common lime
Tilia x europea

Flowering cherry
Prunus "Kanzan"

Red horsechestnut
Aesculus x carnea

HPA

Eric Crichton

G. R. Roberts

Left: Two ghost gums, *Eucalyptus papuana*, growing near Alice Springs in central Australia. The name 'eucalyptus' comes from the Greek *eu*, well, and *kalyptos*, covered. It refers to the cap, formed from the joined sepals and petals, which covers the stamens while the flower is in bud. This cap falls off when the flower opens.

Right: Two fruits: (top) sweet chestnut, *Castanea sativa*; (bottom) mango, *Mangifera indica*. The sweet chestnut (family *Fagaceae*) is a common woodland species in north temperate regions but, although once planted it grows well in northern regions, it is really a warm temperate species—it does not produce ripe seed further north than the Midlands of England. The mango (family *Anacardiaceae*) is a large evergreen tree up to 27 m (90 ft) tall —though cultivated varieties may be smaller—producing the fruit sometimes known as the 'tropical apple'. The fruit is eaten raw, cooked as an ingredient of chutney, or occasionally canned.

which can break down protein. Papain is collected on a commercial scale and used, among other things, to tenderize meat.

Tropical and sub-tropical timber trees
Other tropical families contain species which are valuable for their timber. Among the better known of these timbers are mahogany, from *Swietenia mahogani* (family *Meliaceae*), teak, from *Tectona grandis* (family *Verbenaceae*) and ebony, from *Diospyros ebenum* (family *Ebenaceae*). In sub-tropical areas, species of *Eucalyptus* (family *Myrtaceae*) are becoming increasingly important as timber trees. Eucalypts, or gum trees, are native to Australasia, and are unusual in that they have two kinds of foliage. The foliage found on young plants consists of large rounded leaves clasping the stem. The adult foliage has smaller, lanceolate

(long and narrow), stalked leaves. Eucalypts can grow extremely quickly, up to 10 m (33 ft) a year; one species, *Eucalyptus regnans*, grows to more than 105 m (340 ft), making it the tallest of all flowering trees.

The baobab, *Adansonia digitata* (family *Bombacaceae*) does not grow as fast as *Eucalyptus*, but is one of the oddest-looking trees, having a massive trunk up to 40 m (130 ft) in girth, surmounted by a comparatively sparse crown, as if it had been stuck into the ground with its roots waving in the air. For this reason, it is sometimes called the 'upside-down-tree'. The largest baobabs are around 1,000 years old, and old trees are treated with some reverence—but not by elephants, which frequently kill them. The trunks of baobabs store water and may contain over 100,000 litres (20,000 gallons).

Other uses of flowering trees
Flowering trees are important for food and for their timber. They also have a number of other uses, such as the production of cork, rubber and tannin. Further uses are more exotic. Around the Red Sea, for example, a small twisted tree, *Boswellia thurifera*, (family *Burseraceae*) produces a resin which is collected by making an incision in the tree's trunk. As the resin oozes out it gradually hardens and after about three months can be scraped off as hard, translucent lumps, 1-2 cm ($\frac{3}{8}$-$\frac{3}{4}$ in) across. These lumps are the most important constituent of frankincense, which for thousands of years has been an important item of commerce in the Middle East. It is burnt in houses and churches all over the world. A high-yielding incense tree may be the jealously guarded property of a Somali family.

93

ANIMALS

The Animal Kingdom

Probably the best known division in the animal kingdom is that between the animals which have backbones, the vertebrates, and those which do not, the invertebrates. The vertebrates claim a larger share of human attention since man himself is a vertebrate—it is easier for us to relate to animals that are built more or less on the same body plan. Also, the vertebrates are the largest of animals.

Whatever the invertebrates may lack in size is more than compensated for in numbers. They are so numerous that their combined weight, or *biomass*, is far greater than that of the vertebrates. As proof of this, it is only necessary to think of the structure of a typical food chain and its associated pyramid of numbers. The organisms at each level of the pyramid, which form the food of those at the level above, must have a greater biomass than their predators. For example, on the African plains the breeding population of antelopes and zebra must have a greater biomass than the population of lions which it supports.

The invertebrates also dominate the animal world in numbers of species. As zoologists tend to disagree about the details of classification their estimates vary, but well over a million species of living animals are known and only about 40,000 of these are species of vertebrates. All the others are invertebrates, including three-quarters of a million arthropods, a group which might be judged the most successful of all. Insects are arthropods and just one group of insects, the beetles, outnumber the living species of vertebrates by over 7 to 1, for almost 300,000 species of beetles are known.

Animal groups

The animal kingdom is made up of 24 or 25 major subdivisions, or *phyla*. The members of a particular phylum will all have certain features in common at one time or another in their life histories, even though they may look very different as adults. It would be hard to imagine two more different animals than men and sea squirts, yet we both belong to the same phylum, the *Chordata*. The tadpole-like larva of the sea squirt has the three typical chordate features: a *notochord* running dorsally along the body, gill slits in the pharynx and a nerve chord lying centrally above the notochord. These features are also observed in the human embryo, but, except for the nerve chord, they do not last for long.

The construction of a family tree to show the relationships between the various phyla and the order of their evolution is bound to be somewhat speculative—evolution is a slow process and has taken place over many millions of years. The family relationships and ancestry of a particular animal may be established by a number of methods. Firstly it must be compared in all stages of development with other animals. If there is a strong similarity between, say, the larvae of two animals this may indicate a close family relationship. On the other hand it may simply mean that the two

Left: The protozoan *Amoeba*. The first members of the animal and plant kingdoms originated from a common ancestor whose properties can only be guessed at. It probably contained chlorophyll, the green pigment responsible for photosynthesis in plants. At a very early stage in their evolution, almost all animals lost chlorophyll. It is still found in some protozoans such as the colonial *Volvox*. Although the single-celled *Amoeba* is relatively simple it must have undergone many changes in the course of evolutionary history.

Below: Jewel anemones, *Corynactis viridis*. Coelenterates like these probably developed from a group of protozoans.

Below: An earthworm, *Lumbricus terrestris*. In common with other annelids, the earthworm has a segmented body. Although most of the segments are alike, some are specialized for particular functions. The saddle-like bulge (the clitellum) visible in the picture plays an important role in reproduction.

Left: An African grasshopper in mid-air. Along with crustaceans and spiders, insects belong to the enormous phylum *Arthropoda*. Although arthropods have segmented bodies like annelids, specialization is much more extreme. The third thoracic segment, for example, carries powerful legs, and wings.

Below: An edible snail, *Helix pomatia*. Unlike annelids and arthropods, molluscs are not segmented, and it therefore seems likely that they branched off from the evolutionary tree before segmentation arose. There is, however, a striking similarity between the trochophore larvae of molluscs and those of annelids.

A lioness with zebra kill, in South West Africa. The vigilance of the zebra herd forces lions to make combined rushes, or lie in ambush for their prey.

grasshopper

butterfly

beetle

wasp

louse

flea

centipede

bluebottle

peripatus

silverfish

woodlouse

scorpion

spider

mite

man

chimpanze

jaguar

land snail

earthworm

lobster

squid

sea snail

sea slug

syncarida

nautilus

sea butterfly

agworm

copepod

rotifer

cockle

bry

leech

barnacle

chiton

nematode worm

brachiopod

deuterost

stony coral

protostomia

tapeworm

turbellaria

jellyfish

graptolite (extinct)

gastrula

hydrozoan

blastula

morula

tabulata (extinct)

simple cell

COELENTERATES　　　　FLATWORMS　　　　ANNELIDS　　　　ARTHROPODS　　　　NEMATODES　　　　MOLLUSCS

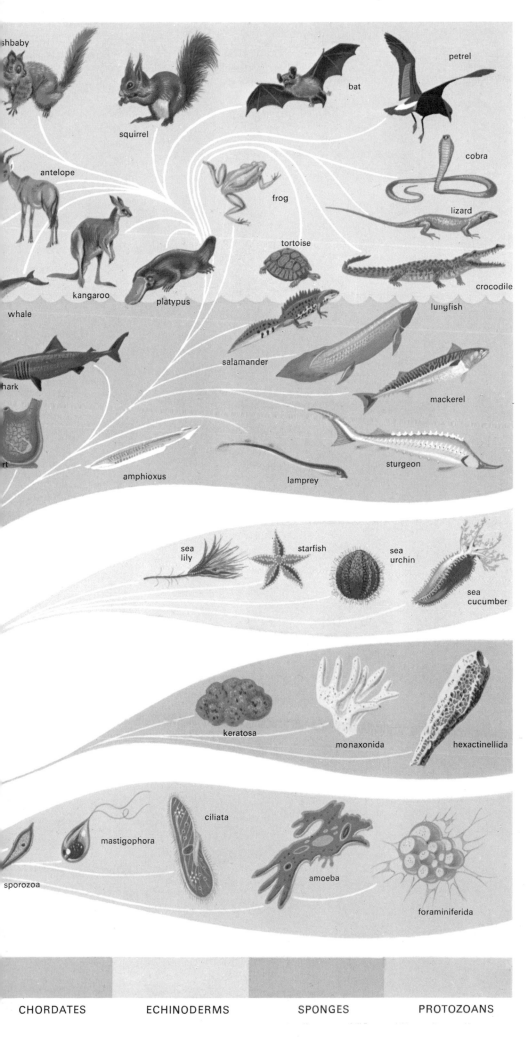

larvae have adapted in the same way to similar living conditions. It is always important to look at all the evidence rather than a single clue. Further indications of an animal's ancestry can sometimes be found in its development from egg to adult, particularly in the way the cells divide and the way the mouth and anus are formed.

Fortunately we do not have to rely only on what we can glean from living species, for fossil remains provide direct evidence of animals which lived in prehistoric times. Indeed fossils provide the most satisfactory evidence of an animal's ancestry. Usually the most ancient fossils are found in the lower rock strata and the most recent ones in the upper strata.

Some of the best fossil lineages are provided by the molluscs. Snails with backwardly coiled shells, straight-shelled cephalopods (related to the present day nautilus) and bivalves were already common in the Ordovician seas of 450 million years ago, and since that time molluscs have been a dominant group in the sea. At one time the sea was populated by great numbers of these early molluscs called *ammonites*, and today their relatives the squids and cuttlefish are important open sea creatures. Sea urchins and starfish have a good fossil history but some other groups, notably the arthropods, are not so well represented and it is more difficult to understand their relationships with the other invertebrates.

Early characteristics

Two important features, observed in almost all animals, probably arose at a very early stage in evolutionary history: bilateral symmetry and the presence of a mesoderm layer between the inner and outer body walls. The former condition may have come about as an adaptation to feeding on the seabed. The development of the mesoderm layer paved the way for the appearance of an internal body cavity surrounding the gut, a necessary preliminary to the development of more specialized organs. The way in which the mesoderm is formed in an embryo or larva provides an important distinction between animals on the two main lines of animal evolution, known as the arthropod and the chordate lines.

The development of the body cavity was a significant improvement in the body plan. Muscles could press against such a fluid-filled cavity to push the animal through the mud without interfering with the operation of the mouth or any other activities of the gut. Organs could become bigger and more complex in an internal body cavity. Several worms evolved with body cavities that fulfilled these functions but they were not identical in structure.

The earthworm's body cavity is called a *coelom*. Its ancestors probably had an open cavity so the animal was just two long tubes, one inside the other. The earthworm, however, is segmented and so the coelom is divided up. The animal

Left: An evolutionary tree of the animal kingdom. The scheme begins with a simple cell, the supposed ancestor of plants as well as animals. The single-celled animals, the protozoans, probably developed directly from this. Cell division led to more complex structures: the morula, blastula and gastrula.

In the last of these an inner wall of cells is present and the animal has developed radial symmetry. It is likely that the ancestors of the coelenterates and the sponges developed from animals modelled on the gastrula plan as did the forerunners of the chordate and arthropod lines. Most extinct animals are not shown.

CHORDATES   ECHINODERMS   SPONGES   PROTOZOANS

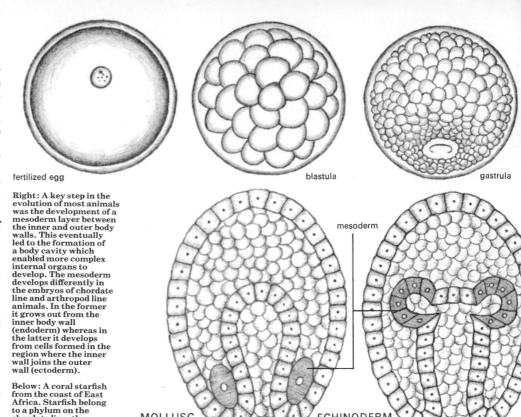

fertilized egg

blastula

gastrula

mesoderm

MOLLUSC EMBRYO

ECHINODERM EMBRYO

moves with one of its pointed ends going first, so the segments at this end become modified so as to become a sort of reconnaissance party, with the main outward-looking sense organs and an important nerve centre. In other words, a simple head develops.

In the arthropods the process has gone further and the head is distinct. So distinct, in fact, that its original segmented nature has been modified almost beyond recognition. Vertebrates, too, are segmented but in a different way. The segmentation can be seen in the repetition of the vertebrate and the spinal nerves.

The arthropod body plan

In the arthropod body plan segmentation is retained and the exoskeleton appears for the first time. In evolving an external skeleton the arthropods have produced an outstandingly effective answer to a number of problems. The arthropod skeleton provides support for the body, protection from enemies and, often, protection against the loss of such important substances as water. As compared with the internal vertebrate skeleton the arthropod skeleton is not only more useful in these ways, but also stronger. As any engineer knows, a hollow tube is stronger than a solid rod of the same material and equivalent weight.

The external skeleton is a major factor in the success of the arthropods, but it also imposes severe limitations upon them. It limits their size and, because an external skeleton cannot grow as easily as an internal one, arthropods must moult as they grow. Moulting is a hazardous process. For a short while, until its new, larger skeleton expands and hardens, the moulting arthropod is defenceless.

Another factor which limits arthropod size is the manner in which they supply oxygen to their internal tissues. In some arthropod groups, including the insects, tracheae—tiny branching tubes—carry air to all parts of the body. Air moves through the tracheae at least in part by diffusion, a process which is inadequate to supply oxygen to the middle of a large organism. The bulkiest insect, the Goliath beetle, uses muscular pumping to help ventilate the tracheae, but even so it is less than 15 cm (6 in) long when fully grown.

Appearing before the vertebrates on the chordate line of evolution are the echinoderms. One reason they appear on this branch of the plan is that, in the embryo, the mesoderm layer develops in the same way as in the chordates.

Vertebrates

By far the most important chordates are the vertebrates—animals with backbones. The first vertebrates probably appeared about 450 million years ago. They were fish which looked rather like an armoured version of the present-day lamprey and they had neither jaws nor pairs of fins. They used the gill slits in the pharynx to strain food from the water. From these early vertebrates fish called *placoderms* developed, which had both jaws and paired pectoral and pelvic fins and sometimes a series of smaller fins between these. The placoderms gave rise to the cartilagenous fish such as sharks. These and the bony fish were able to colonise freshwater and marine habitats as successfully as the molluscs and arthropods. Their shape, pattern and colour was

Right: A key step in the evolution of most animals was the development of a mesoderm layer between the inner and outer body walls. This eventually led to the formation of a body cavity which enabled more complex internal organs to develop. The mesoderm develops differently in the embryos of chordate line and arthropod line animals. In the former it grows out from the inner body wall (endoderm) whereas in the latter it develops from cells formed in the region where the inner wall joins the outer wall (ectoderm).

Below: A coral starfish from the coast of East Africa. Starfish belong to a phylum on the chordate line, the *Echinodermata*.

ACORN WORM LARVA

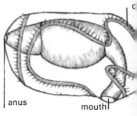

anus

mouth

Far left: A grass snake, *Natrix natrix*. Snakes are descended from a group of lizards and their ancestors may have been burrowing animals. This is suggested not only by the loss of limbs but also by the structure of their eyes and ears. The remnants of hind legs can still be seen in some snakes such as boas and pythons.

Left: A puffin, *Fratercula arctica*, with two newly caught fish. Like the mammals, birds are descended from reptiles. They developed very rapidly at the end of the Mesozoic era about 65 million years ago. Their success was no doubt helped by the rapid spread of insects and flowering plants at that time. These provided a plentiful supply of food.

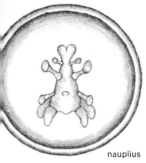

nauplius

larva

Left: The development of a lobster from egg to larva. One way to learn about an animal's ancestry is to study the growth of its embryo. In the case of a lobster there is a three-limbed nauplius stage which is characteristic of all crustaceans, even of the sedentary barnacles which do not outwardly look like crustaceans.

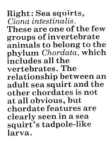

Right: Sea squirts, *Ciona intestinalis*. These are one of the few groups of invertebrate animals to belong to the phylum *Chordata*, which includes all the vertebrates. The relationship between an adult sea squirt and the other chordates is not at all obvious, but chordate features are clearly seen in a sea squirt's tadpole-like larva.

Below: A grayling, *Thymallus thymallus*. Present day fish developed from jawless ancestors which were the first vertebrate animals. The fish's body is supported by its backbone but is able to flex from side to side. It is movements of this sort that propel the fish through the water.

Heather Angel

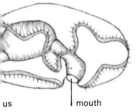

ECHINODERM LARVA

us

mouth

Left: Although there is hardly any resemblance between an adult chordate and an adult echinoderm, the larvae shown here are very much alike. Acorn worms belong to a phylum which is closely related to the chordates. This sort of similarity often helps to establish relationships between otherwise quite different animals.

Above: A brightly coloured toad, *Bufo periglenes*. Amphibians have changed considerably since they first ventured from the sea about 350 million years ago, but most of them still must return to the water to breed. Amphibians have adapted to many habitats. Some frogs have toe pads for climbing trees.

Below: Cheetahs, *Acinonyx jubata*, are the fastest mammals. They can keep up a speed of about 100 kph (62 mph) over a distance of 600 m (660 yd). Like birds, mammals are warm-blooded and this enables them to lead more active lives than other animals like reptiles whose blood temperature varies with the surroundings.

John Dominis, Time/Life/Colorific!

modified to suit the conditions they colonised, but their success depended in each case on a body plan with an internal supporting skeleton.

The bony fish fell into two groups—those whose bones and muscles remained within the body wall and those whose bones and muscles extended into the fins. A group of these latter 'lobe-finned' fish were probably the first vertebrates to venture on to land: they became the first amphibians. The lobe fins were gradually transformed into legs.

The early amphibians would have been able to feed on a variety of invertebrates which had preceded them on to land, indeed it may have been the presence of this new food source that first attracted them from the water. Amphibians could not, however, stray far from water. They needed a moist environment to keep down the loss of water from their bodies by evaporation and they could not breed in the absence of water. Their larvae were aquatic.

A group of amphibians gave rise to the reptiles which were much better equipped for life on land. A waterproof outer layer of the skin eliminated the problem of water loss and they were able to colonise dry areas of the land. Extra membranes in the reptiles' eggs kept the embryo bathed in fluid and allowed it to develop on dry land.

The Mesozoic era, with the coming of the giant dinosaurs, was the heyday of the reptiles. One such animal, the brontosaurus, must have weighed about 20 tonnes, reaching a length of 18 m (60 ft). It was the largest land animal that has ever lived. By the end of the Mesozoic era, about 65 million years ago, the reptiles were on the decline and the dinosaurs had become extinct.

From two groups of the many reptiles that once existed, the birds and the mammals evolved. Some reptilian features, such as the scaly skin on their legs, are still evident in birds. Both birds and mammals differ from reptiles in one fundamental respect: they are warm-blooded. In order to lead an active life the conversion of food into energy must proceed at an adequate rate in the animal's body. The biochemical reactions involved, like most chemical reactions, are very dependent on temperature—if the temperature is too low they will proceed relatively slowly. Thus reptiles, being cold-blooded, cannot keep moving for long periods even though they can move very swiftly for a short time; at night, when their body temperature is low, they are very sluggish. Birds and mammals, on the other hand, have both developed mechanisms for keeping the body temperature at a suitable constant level and so are capable of sustained periods of activity.

In mammals there are three main structural departures from the reptilian body plan. Firstly, the limbs are rotated so that they become located underneath the body rather than projecting from the sides. This is a much improved arrangement for an animal that lives on land, for much less effort is required to support the body weight—it is transmitted directly through straightened legs to the ground. Secondly, the jaws of mammals are much simpler than those of reptiles and thirdly, the teeth of mammals are divided into three basic types, incisors, canines and molars, while the teeth of a reptile are all very much alike.

Insects

The insects are undoubtedly the largest and one of the most successful groups of animals. There are more than 750,000 species inhabiting a vast range of habitats on land and in water. The only environment that insects have failed to colonize to any great extent is the sea; they are completely absent from deep sea water. In the air, on the other hand, they are present up to heights of 2,000 metres (6,600 ft), forming an aerial 'plankton' on which many birds depend for food.

Insects owe their success to a number of features, perhaps the most important of which is the development of a waterproof layer on the outside of their hardened cuticle. This has liberated them from the restrictive damp environments of the onychophorans, centipedes and millipedes and, coupled with the development of flight, has enabled them to escape more easily from predators and to explore and colonize new habitats. Another important feature of the insect success story is their tremendous reproductive potential.

Insects are built on the basic arthropod design. The body is divided into three quite distinct regions. A head of six joined segments bears the feeding and sensory apparatus and is connected by a very short 'neck' to a thoracic region of three segments which bear the wings and three pairs of walking legs. The third region is an abdomen of eleven segments, either with no limbs at all or with small specialized limbs for purposes other than walking.

Wingless insects

Not all insects have wings, and they are thus divided into two groups: the wingless *Apterygota* and the winged *Pterygota*. The former contains those groups like the springtails, *Collembola*, and the bristletails, *Thysanura*. In these species some of the other features typical of insects are also poorly developed.

The springtails are small cosmopolitan, insects with a unique forked jumping organ at the bottom end of a short abdomen of five or six segments. They have a 'spring' fastened to the end of the abdomen by a 'catch' which when released allows the spring to move suddenly downwards, striking the ground and throwing the insect into the air. Since their cuticle is not waterproofed they only thrive in damp environments, in leaf mould, soil and rotting wood. It has been estimated that in an acre of English meadowland there may be as many as 250,000,000 rounded green springtails, *Sminthurus viridis*.

Bristletails derive their name from three bristle-like projections at the end of the abdomen and their long bristle-like antennae. They are about 2 cm (0.8 in) long and their legs are well developed for swift running. Although they are found throughout the world, they also are restricted to damp environments. The best known bristletails are the silverfish, *Lepisma*, and the firebrat, *Thermobia domestica*. The silverfish is so called since the division of the body into three parts is not obvious, giving a fish-like form and the body of the adult is covered with silvery scales which easily rub off. They are frequently found in larders, cup-

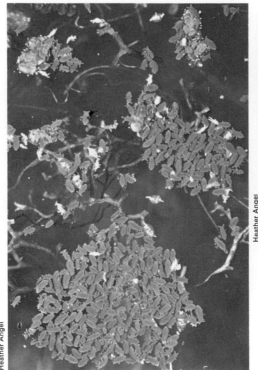

Left: Springtails, *Podura aquatica*, clustering on the surface of a pond. Springtails are primitive wingless insects which are usually very small. They have a spring mechanism formed from a pair of abdominal limbs. On each side of the head there is a group of simple eyes rather than the compound eye of most insects.

Above: Well camouflaged bristletails, *Petrobius maritimus*, on a stone. These animals get their name from the three jointed filaments at the tail end of the abdomen. Like the springtails, bristletails are primitive insects and cannot fly. They are usually found among rotting wood or leaves and under stones.

Below: The mating of two damselflies. The male grasps the female's thorax with claspers at the end of his abdomen. Like most insects damselflies have two pairs of wings carried on the second and third thoracic segments. Damselflies carry their wings parallel to their abdomens when they are not in flight.

Right: A close-up of the head of a dragonfly, *Aeshna cyanea*, showing the enormous compound eyes. They are composed of almost 30,000 separate light-sensitive units and cover most of the head. Compound eyes are found in most insects although in some (infants, for example) they may be composed of as few as 50 units.

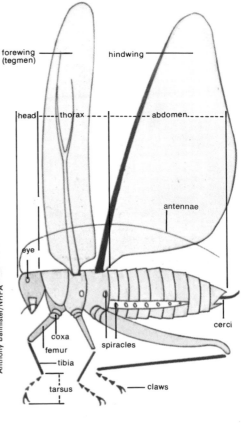

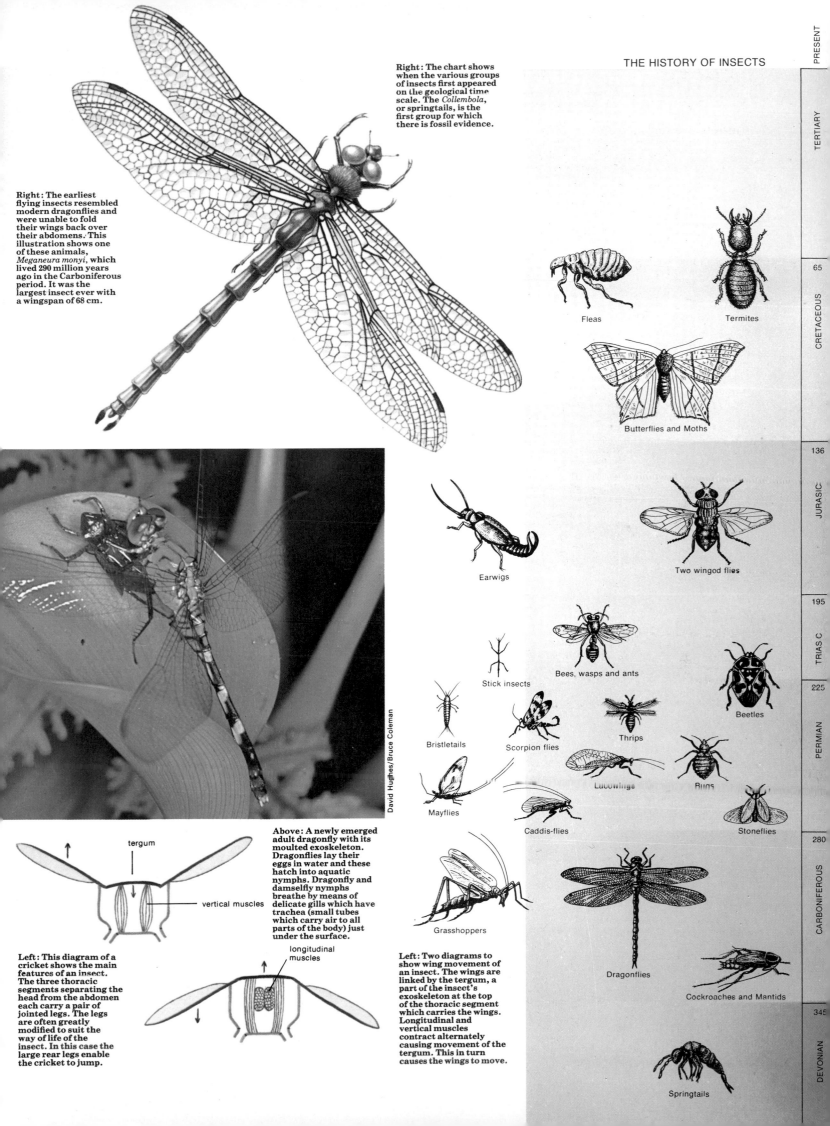

Right: The earliest flying insects resembled modern dragonflies and were unable to fold their wings back over their abdomens. This illustration shows one of these animals, *Meganeura monyi*, which lived 290 million years ago in the Carboniferous period. It was the largest insect ever with a wingspan of 68 cm.

Right: The chart shows when the various groups of insects first appeared on the geological time scale. The *Collembola*, or springtails, is the first group for which there is fossil evidence.

David Hughes/Bruce Coleman

Above: A newly emerged adult dragonfly with its moulted exoskeleton. Dragonflies lay their eggs in water and these hatch into aquatic nymphs. Dragonfly and damselfly nymphs breathe by means of delicate gills which have trachea (small tubes which carry air to all parts of the body) just under the surface.

tergum

vertical muscles

Left: This diagram of a cricket shows the main features of an insect. The three thoracic segments separating the head from the abdomen each carry a pair of jointed legs. The legs are often greatly modified to suit the way of life of the insect. In this case the large rear legs enable the cricket to jump.

longitudinal muscles

Left: Two diagrams to show wing movement of an insect. The wings are linked by the tergum, a part of the insect's exoskeleton at the top of the thoracic segment which carries the wings. Longitudinal and vertical muscles contract alternately causing movement of the tergum. This in turn causes the wings to move.

PRESENT

TERTIARY

65

CRETACEOUS

Fleas

Termites

Butterflies and Moths

136

JURASIC

Earwigs

Two winged flies

195

TRIAS C

Bees, wasps and ants

Stick insects

Beetles

225

Bristletails

Scorpion flies

Thrips

PERMIAN

Lacewings

Bugs

Mayflies

Caddis-flies

Stoneflies

280

Grasshoppers

CARBONIFEROUS

Dragonflies

Cockroaches and Mantids

345

DEVONIAN

Springtails

boards and behind skirting boards of houses and in books where they can cause damage to the binding material. Firebrats occur in large numbers around fireplaces, boilers and bakery ovens.

It is probable that the winged insects arose from a bristletail-like stock 400 million years ago in the Devonian era. The first winged insects could not fold back their wings over their abdomen when at rest. These insects are known as the *Palaeoptera* and are represented by the present day dragonflies and damselflies (the *Odonata*) and mayflies (the *Ephemeroptera*).

Dragonflies, damselflies and mayflies

Dragonflies, or 'devils darning needles' as they are sometimes known, derive their name from their long, brilliantly coloured scaly body. They are completely harmless to man although males patrolling their territory can be a nuisance when they try to drive away human intruders. They are among the largest living insects; a Borneo dragonfly, *Tetracanthagyna plagiata*, has a wing span of 18cm (7.1 in) and a length of about 13 cm (5.1 in). A 300 million year old fossil dragonfly from the Carboniferous era had a wing span of about 68cm (26.8 in) making it the largest known insect. The *Odonata* have two pairs of large wings with a complex system of veins supporting the wing membrane. Although the wings are only capable of simple up and down movements, dragonflies can travel at speeds estimated at up to 96 kph (60 mph) which makes them one of the fastest flying insects. Damselflies, however, have a much slower, fluttering flight which, with their more slender body, easily distinguishes them from dragonflies.

Both dragonflies and damselflies mate near water, and the males are distinguished from females by their colour. In some damselflies there is even a form of courtship. The method of mating is unique among insects. The male transfers sperm from the opening of the male glands at the end of the abdomen to an accessory organ near the front of the abdomen. He then alights on the back of a female and holds her head (male damselflies hold the female's thorax) with a pair of claspers at the end of his abdomen. The female curls her abdomen round so that her posterior reproductive opening is in contact with the male accessory organ and sperm is transferred.

Damselflies and some dragonflies insert their eggs into the stems of water plants and some dragonflies bury them in sand or gravel at the water's edge. Most dragonflies, however, shed the eggs directly into the water while flying over it with the tip of their abdomen under the surface. The eggs hatch into nymphs which, like the adults, are carnivorous. Young fish, other aquatic insects and tadpoles are caught by a unique method. The lower lip, the *labium*, is enlarged and is rapidly extended to seize the prey in its pincer-like hooks. The labium is then retracted bringing the victim within reach of the jaws.

Damselflies spend at least a year and dragonflies two years as nymphs. In this time they form a very important source of food for fresh-water fish. After this they climb up a water plant into the air and undergo a final moult to become winged adults which live for only a few summer months.

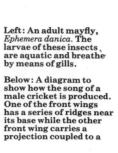

Chaumeton/Jacana

Left: An adult mayfly, *Ephemera danica*. The larvae of these insects are aquatic and breathe by means of gills.

Below: A diagram to show how the song of a male cricket is produced. One of the front wings has a series of ridges near its base while the other front wing carries a projection coupled to a membrane. When the wings are rubbed together the projection is drawn across the ridges so generating the characteristic song which is amplified by the membrane.

Right: The head of a bush cricket. These insects have mouthparts which are designed for biting and chewing.

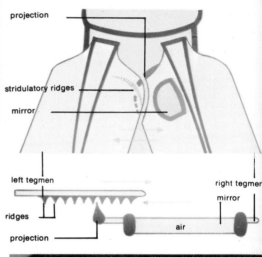

projection

stridulatory ridges

mirror

left tegmen

right tegmen

mirror

ridges

projection

air

Below: The nymph of a stonefly. These animals are aquatic and only live in clean water. Their presence therefore means a low level of pollution. They breathe by means of gills. The adult flies have two pairs of large membranous wings but are poor fliers and usually prefer to run from place to place.

Right: A lubber grasshopper, *Phymateus purpurascens*, displaying the vivid colours of its hind wings.

Far right: The bizarre toad grasshopper is wingless and normally well camouflaged against its background. It is found in the dry and semi-desert regions of Southern Africa.

Heather Angel

Jane Burton/Bruce Coleman

Below: Locusts often migrate in enormous numbers either on the ground as bands of nymphs, called hoppers, or as flying insects. Locusts may either be in a migratory or a solitary phase and during these phases differ both in structure and physiology. A solitary locust is identical to a grasshopper.

Right: A front leg (above) and back leg (below) of a grasshopper. Insect legs have four main sections: the coxa which connects the leg to the thorax; the femur which in the back leg of a grasshopper is enlarged to contain the muscles needed for jumping; the tibia, and the tarsus which terminates in claws.

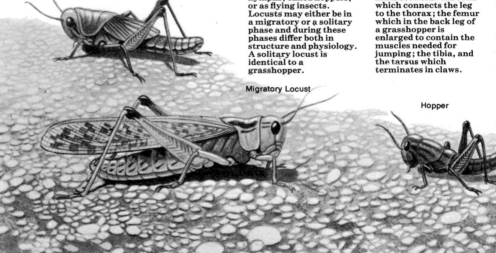

Grasshopper

Migratory Locust

Hopper

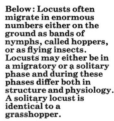

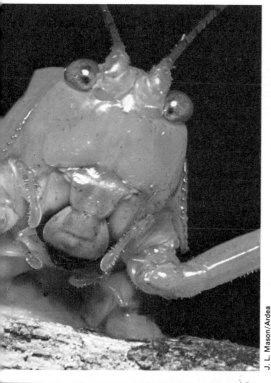

The group known as *Ephemeroptera* to which the mayflies belong, is so called because of the 'ephemeral' life of the adult fly. It usually lives only long enough to reproduce. This may take a few hours or at the most a few days after the transition from an aquatic nymph stage that may last for up to four years. The adult has two pairs of finely veined wings; the first pair is larger than the hind pair which may be absent in some species. The legs are small and weak; the abdomen ends in three, or sometimes two, long filaments or *cerci*. The antennae are greatly reduced but the compound eyes are very well developed, suggesting great dependence on sight. This also seems to be the case in the free-swimming nymphs which orientate themselves by the direction from which light reaches their eyes. If illuminated from below they will swim upside down. The nymphs breathe by means of gills along each side of the abdomen and are herbivorous. The mouth parts of the adult, however, are rudimentary and the adult is incapable of feeding. The front part of the gut can be filled with air to reduce the body weight and make flight easier.

The aquatic nymph of a mayfly first changes into a terrestrial *subimago* stage whose wings are dulled by a covering of extremely fine hairs. After a few hours this stage moults to the true adult, or *imago*, stage. The emergence of adults is synchronized so that great numbers appear together, the males gathering in large dancing swarms which attract the females. The male dies immediately after mating and the female soon after dropping her eggs into the water. Adult mayflies are a favourite food of fish, especially trout, and artificial flies are made by anglers as lures to catch them. The sub-imagos are called 'dun' and the adults 'spinners'.

From the original *Palaeoptera* there also arose insects, probably in the early Carboniferous era, which were able to fold their wings over the abdomen when at rest. They are called the *Neoptera* and were able to explore such new environments as areas of dense foliage, to hide under stones and logs, and even to burrow. The early *Neoptera* were probably similar to the present day stoneflies and give rise to the group containing the grasshoppers and crickets, the *Orthoptera*. In this group the immature forms are known as nymphs and generally resemble the adult form except in size and degree of wing development. They gradually change into the adult imago stage through a series of up to twenty moults. They also inhabit the same general environment as the adult and eat the same type of food. Insects with this development are *exopterygote* insects.

A second more specialized evolutionary line from the early neopteran stock led to the flies, butterflies, bees and beetles where the young, known as *larvae*, do not resemble the adult and usually occupy a very different environment, feeding on different foods. After a number of moults the larvae pass through a quiescent *pupal* phase where extensive alteration of larval tissue precedes the emergence of a winged adult. These are the *endopterygote* insects to which about 80 per cent of present-day insects belong.

Grasshoppers, crickets and cockroaches

The *Orthoptera* include such insects as grasshoppers, katydids, crickets, cock-

Above: A desert locust just after moulting. Locusts are a type of grasshopper and sometimes migrate in swarms causing enormous damage to the surrounding countryside and crops. A medium sized swarm may contain 1,000,000,000 insects and consume as much as 3,000 tonnes of vegetable material in a single day.

Below: Front and side views of the head of a grasshopper. The animal has three simple eyes (ocelli) as well as the two large compound eyes. The mouthparts, designed for biting and chewing, are equipped with two pairs of sensory organs, or palps, which help the insect to distinguish one sort of food from another.

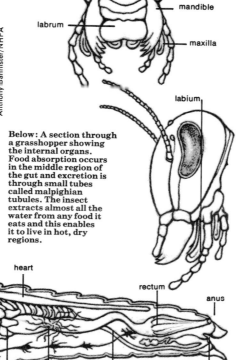

ocelli

antenna

compound eye

labrum

mandible

maxilla

labium

Below: A section through a grasshopper showing the internal organs. Food absorption occurs in the middle region of the gut and excretion is through small tubes called malpighian tubules. The insect extracts almost all the water from any food it eats and this enables it to live in hot, dry regions.

trochanter

tibia

femur

pretarsus

tarsus

coxa

ocellus

brain

ovarian tabules

heart

rectum

anus

optic ganglion

labium

labrum

salivary gland

crop

gastric caeca

nerve cord

malphigian tubules

oviduct

genital pore

ovipositor

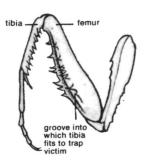

tibia — femur

groove into
which tibia
fits to trap
victim

Right and above: A praying mantis and a diagram of one of its forelegs. The leg is specially adapted for seizing prey. The prey is grasped between the femur and the tibia which have spiny inside edges for the purpose. The innermost section of the leg, the coxa, is much larger than that of a grasshopper.

Below: A well camouflaged praying mantis eating a fly. These insects lie in wait for their prey, seizing the victim very rapidly when it strays within reach of the forelegs. These insects get their name from the way they carry their forelegs (see the picture on the right) which looks rather like an attitude of prayer.

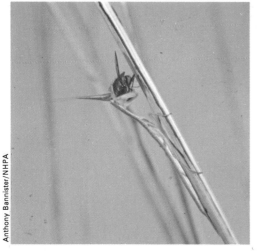

Anthony Bannister/NHPA

Natural Science Photos

Below and right: It is often almost impossible to see stick insects in their natural habitats, so well do they blend in with their backgrounds. The stick insect in the photograph on the right even has spines resembling the prickles of the bramble on which it lives. Stick and leaf insects are sluggish animals, often remaining **stationary for long periods. They are herbivorous, usually feeding on leaves. The longest living insect is a tropical stick insect which can grow to more than 30cm (1 ft). Because female stick insects can produce fertile eggs without mating, males are very rare and possibly do not exist in some species.**

Jacana

roaches, mantids and stick insects. Cockroaches and mantids however are now generally placed in a separate group, the *Dictyoptera*, and the stick insects in the *Phasmida*. Typically, they have two pairs of wings although they may be reduced or absent as in some crickets and the common British cockroach. The male of this cockroach has reduced wings, the female is almost wingless, and both sexes are incapable of flight. The fore wings of orthopterans are leathery and when folded cover and protect the delicate membranous hindwings which are the flight wings. The large head has well developed compound eyes and strong chewing mouth parts.

There are about 3,500 species of cockroaches living mostly in the tropics but some have been accidentally transported throughout the world and are now cosmopolitan. In Britain there are six such imported species; the most common are the brown-black common cockroach, *Blatta orientalis*, the yellow brown German cockroach, *Blatta germanica*, and the reddish brown American cockroach, *Periplaneta americana*.

Cockroaches are nocturnal scavengers feeding on a very wide range of dead animal and plant material. In houses they will devour any kind of human food and although the amount eaten is relatively small the remainder is fouled. Females lay 16 eggs enclosed in a hard dark brown purse-like capsule, the *ootheca*, which is deposited in crevices. The eggs hatch after about two to three months, the ootheca splitting to let out the white wingless nymphs. As they grow, they become brown in colour and reach maturity in 6 to 12 months. In the German cockroach the ootheca contains up to 45 eggs and is carried by the female until about a day before hatching.

Grasshoppers are the most numerous of the *Orthoptera*. They prefer a grassy habitat and have greatly enlarged hindlegs which enable them to jump considerable distances when disturbed. The male attracts the female to mate by rubbing a row of very small projections on a hindleg joint against the veins of the forewing to produce the familiar chirping song, or *stridulation*, of grasshoppers. The song varies from species to species. Eggs are laid in pods in the soil, each pod containing up to 14 eggs. Grasshoppers are herbivorous, and when they occur in very large numbers can cause damage to crops.

Crickets and bush crickets, sometimes known as 'long-horned grasshoppers' or in America 'katydids', are cosmopolitan and resemble grasshoppers in possessing long, though less powerful hind legs for jumping. Their antennae, however, are long, they stridulate by rubbing the wing edges together and are nocturnal. Specialized organs, the *tympani*, are developed to receive soundwaves. Grasshoppers have a pair on the first abdomenal segment but in crickets they are on the forelegs. Crickets are herbivorous but bush crickets can be carnivorous. Eggs are laid singly in slits made in plant stems by a well developed blade-like or tubular organ called an *ovipositer*. Like grasshoppers there is one generation a year. Of particular interest is the mole cricket which is now rare in Britain. It does not have jumping legs, but the forelegs are powerful and armed with cutting edges which enable it to tunnel through the soil in a mole-like fashion.

A common grasshopper. This is an example of the variety which appears most widely in meadows and fields.

Butterflies and Moths

Of all the insects the butterflies and moths have been the most admired and popular. Butterflies are large and very beautiful but although we can understand the functioning of their colours it is difficult to explain why they should be so bright and exuberant. While the butterflies belong to a single well defined group, the popular name 'moth' covers a diversity of insects both large and small. Most moths are sombre-coloured and nocturnal although there are some that resemble butterflies inasmuch as they are brightly coloured and are active during the day. Butterflies and moths belong to the insect order *Lepidoptera*, a name which refers to their scaly wings, and there are about 100,000 different species.

The scales which are characteristic of butterflies and moths are hollow, flattened hairs covered with minute grooves and ridges. They usually contain pigment or give colour by reflecting and scattering

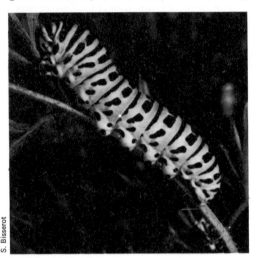

S. Bisserot

light. Sometimes the scales are shed, leaving the wings transparent as in the clearwing moths, which look like wasps or other members of the insect order *Hymenoptera*.

The colours of lepidopterans serve a number of purposes, for example to help members of the same species recognize each other and to camouflage them against predators. Butterflies carry their wings vertically when they are at rest, and the undersides of the wings are often coloured in such a way as to conceal the insect. For instance, the underside of the wing of the Indian leaf butterfly, *Kallima*, looks remarkably like a dead leaf and the grayling butterfly, *Eumenis semele*, even leans to one side when it is on the ground so that its shadow is minimized.

Unlike butterflies, most moths hold their wings flat over their backs when at rest, but these are also often cryptically patterned so that the moth blends into its background. Such moths as the yellow underwings, *Triphaena comes*, for example, have brightly coloured hind wings which provide flashes of colour as the insect flies along. When the moth settles the flashing suddenly stops and this can be confusing to predators as well as entomologists. Another method of defence

Above: Three pictures showing the egg, larva (caterpillar) and pupa (chrysalis) of a swallowtail butterfly.

Left: The caterpillar of a swallowtail butterfly. It has a curious forked organ behind its head which it shoots rapidly in and out to disperse an unpleasant smell when disturbed.

Above: A swallowtail butterfly, *Papilio machaon*, newly emerged from its chrysalis. This is the only member of the *Papilionidae* family which is a permanent resident in Britain.

Above right: A swallowtail with its wings spread out. More usually they are held vertically.

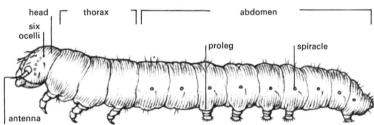

head · six ocelli · thorax · abdomen · proleg · spiracle · antenna

Above: A diagram to show the main features of a caterpillar of the cabbage white butterfly. Each of the thoracic segments carries a pair of legs, and five of the abdominal segments have pairs of fleshy extensions called prolegs. The outermost layer of the body, the cuticle, is quite soft but is able to act as an exoskeleton because the caterpillar's blood pressure is sufficiently high to keep it taut. The head does not have antennae or compound eyes. There are six simple eyes (ocelli) on each side. The animal has strong biting mandibles for chewing cabbage leaves.

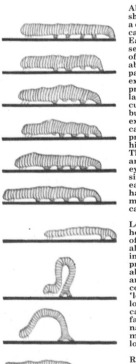

Left: Diagrams to show how two different types of caterpillar crawl along. The most important organs are the prolegs which are alternately retracted and extended by contracting and relaxing 'locomotor' muscles. The lower diagrams show how caterpillars of the family *Geometridae* (the name means 'earth measuring') proceed by looping movements.

Right: The eggs of a privet hawk moth.

Heather Angel

against predators is shown by the peacock butterfly, *Nymphalis io*, and the eyed hawk moth, *Smerinthus ocellatus*. These insects have markings on their wings called 'eye spots' which look rather like the eyes of mammals. The eye spots are suddenly displayed when the insect is disturbed and may confuse or frighten off a predator.

Some of these insects, like the burnet moths, have bright colours to advertise the fact that they are unpalatable or poisonous and in many cases other, palatable species very closely resemble them, so gaining protection. It was from such observations a century ago that the British naturalist H. W. Bates first put forward his theories on the phenomenon of mimicry, now known to be widespread among insects. The milkweed butterflies, which belong to the family *Danaidae*, are distasteful and are very widely mimicked by other palatable butterflies. For the mimic to gain protection it has to be less common than the model, otherwise birds will learn that the common pattern means palatable rather than unpalatable prey. In the swallowtail butterfly *Papilio dardanus* there are five different-looking varieties of female, and four of these mimic four different species of distasteful butterfly. By this means the species maintains a larger population than if it mimicked only a single species.

Some butterflies show colour variations according to the season. The comma butterfly, *Polygonia c-album*, in Britain shows different colours in spring and summer broods, the spring generation being much paler and brighter than the summer one. The African butterfly *Precis octavia* is also well known for its marked seasonal forms. Some moths, particularly those species which rest during the day on rocks or soil, show variation in colour with geographical area. The peppered moth *Biston betularia*, for example, has a normal pale speckled form in rural areas, while a black, or *melanic*, form has become common in industrial areas where the lichens on trees have been killed and soot deposited. Experiments have shown that birds will mainly feed on the more conspicuous form: in cities the speckled form and in the country the black form. This phenomenon of industrial melanism has been much studied in the last 20 years or so and has given valuable information about how evolution takes place in nature and the rate at which it can become effective.

Migration

Butterflies and moths are usually strong fliers, although they may not always travel very far. Marking experiments in the Scilly Isles demonstrated that meadow brown butterflies remained in their own area of bramble and bracken and did not even fly the short distance across a grassy area to another bracken and bramble area inhabited by other meadow browns. In a few species such as the early moth, *Theria rupicapraria*, and the winter moth, *Operophtera brumata*, the male is normally winged but the female has very small wings or, in some species, none at all. After emerging from the pupa the female has to climb up the trunk of a tree to lay her eggs. In spite of these flightless varieties, however, the *Lepidoptera* contains some of the most powerfully flying insects and a number are known to be migratory.

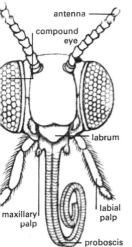

antenna
compound eye
labrum
maxillary palp
labial palp
proboscis

Right: A map to show the migrations of the bath white butterfly, *Pontia daplidice*, and the silver Y moth, *Plusia gamma*, in Europe.

Left and bottom left: Drawings of the heads of a butterfly and a moth. These insects feed on nectar and their mouth parts are specially adapted for this. The two maxillae are much longer than in other insects and they are joined together by a series of hooks and spines to form a tube called the proboscis through which the nectar is drawn. Feeding on fluids, butterflies and moths have no need for the cutting mandibles of insects like locusts, and these organs are very small or absent.

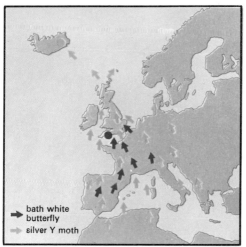

bath white butterfly
silver Y moth

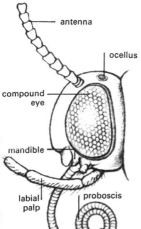

antenna
ocellus
compound eye
mandible
labial palp
proboscis

Above and right: A privet hawk-moth, *Sphinx ligustri*, and its caterpillar. The bodies and wings of butterflies and moths are covered with scales which not only give rise to the characteristic iridescent colouring of the wings, but also serve to conserve body heat by enclosing an insulating layer of air.

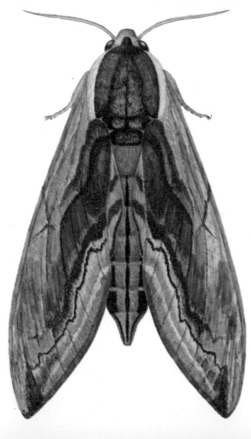

109

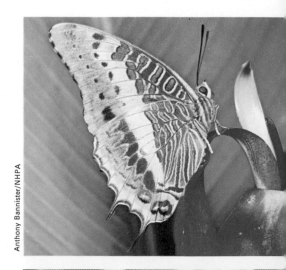

Left: A pearl-bordered fritillary butterfly, *Argynnis euphrosyne*. In order to show the wing markings, the picture was taken with the insect's wings in the uncharacteristic spread position. This butterfly, like most others, has antennae which are enlarged, or 'clubbed', at their tips. Both butterflies and moths have a well developed sense of vision and can distinguish one colour from another. This is important in feeding and mating for both flowers and potential mates are recognized by sight.

Right: An African butterfly, *Charaxes saturnis*.

Below: The beautiful golden emperor moth of India.

In recent years it has been shown that the other two great migratory groups of insects, the locusts and the aphids, are both passively carried along with the prevailing wind, even though some of their short term flights appear oriented. The situation with butterflies and moths is far from clear. Pioneer work on butterfly migration was carried out by C. B. Williams who showed that many of the butterfly species that migrate to the British Isles in the summer return in the autumn, although it is the offspring of the original migrants that make the return. The red admiral, *Vanessa atalanta*, was the first species that was shown to make this return, but since then it has been demonstrated that other species do the same. It is characteristic of most butterflies when migrating to fly in a constant, clearly oriented direction. They do not seem to fix their direction by reference to wind, temperature or magnetic factors, and it has recently been argued that the Sun is the reference point. This is by no means impossible since other insects navigate by reference to the Sun.

The best known migratory species is the milkweed butterfly *Danaus plexippus*. It breeds in the northern USA and Canada during the summer and then migrates south in swarms in the late summer to California, Florida or New Mexico. Marked individuals have been recovered that have flown nearly 3,200 km (2,000 miles). The butterflies spend the winter in trees, using the same ones year after year, forming something of a tourist attraction. In the spring a northerly journey begins. As with other butterfly migrations the return flight is more scattered, with individuals flying singly rather than in a swarm. On the way back the insects lay their eggs and the species becomes spread throughout the northern part of its range. A number of moths also migrate, notable visitors to Britain being the humming-bird hawk moth, *Macroglossum stellatarum*, and the silver Y moth, *Plusia gamma*. The latter seems to show oriented flight early in its adult life when it flies by day, but later, nocturnal flights are downwind. It seems likely that prevailing winds bring it all the way from North Africa. The humming-bird hawk moth is an immigrant to Britain from southern Europe, and arrives from June onwards.

Flight

Moths and butterflies have their fore and hind wings coupled together, though the method of coupling varies from species to

species as does the rate of wing beat and speed of flight. The wings of moths are typically linked by a bristle which projects from the hind wing and engages a hook from a vein of the fore wing. Wing speed and flight may be quite rapid: a hawk moth may beat its wings 70 times a second and reach a speed of 55 kph (35 mph). In butterflies the wings merely overlap at the base. They flap about 12 times every second, giving the insect a top speed of about ten kph (six mph). Large butterflies can glide quite effectively, especially in the sheltered conditions of woodland.

A remarkable feature of some nocturnally flying moths is their ability to avoid bats. Bats detect their prey by an 'echo sounding' system of ultrasonic squeaks that reflect from any object such as a flying moth. Some moths have a pair of hearing organs called *tympanal organs* set at the sides of the base of the abdomen which can detect these ultrasonic signals. Thus the moth can tell when a hunting bat is nearby and even determine its angle of approach. Different moth species respond in different ways—some swing violently off course, some zig-zag and others drop to the ground. This manoeuvring brings to mind the technological warfare of our own species.

A very few moths can make audible sounds—the death's head hawk moth, *Acherontia atropos*, for example, squeaks when disturbed—but this is rare. Sight is important to most butterflies and moths, and the compound eyes are well developed. Antennae act as smell receptors and in some species the front legs are used for tasting. Many butterflies have small forelegs which are no use for walking but are important organs of taste.

Above: The caterpillar of a puss moth, *Cerura vinula*, in its defence posture. Normally the caterpillar is well camouflaged against its background, and irregular purple markings on its green back break up the body outline. When attacked, however, the animal rears up to expose the vivid 'face' markings seen in the picture and lashes out with the threads attached to its tail. If this fearsome display is not enough to deter the predator, the caterpillar will squirt strong formic acid from a gland in its thorax.

Above right: A convolvulus hawk moth, *Herse convolvuli*, feeding on tobacco flowers. The long, uncoiled proboscis can be seen probing one of the flowers for nectar. There is a slight bend in the proboscis about one third of the way along its length, and this 'knee joint' allows the insect to feed whatever the angle of the flower. A moth picks out flowers by sight rather than smell, and the accuracy with which it can 'aim' its tongue shows just how good its sight must be.

Left: A scarlet windowed moth which lives in the Himalayan region of India is well disguised as a leaf. There is even a dark line running from one wing tip to the other to represent the mid-rib of the leaf.

Right: The broken irregular pattern and colour of this hawk moth, *Deilephila merii*, camouflage it against a background of foliage. The outline of the insect is broken by the pale band which extends across both wings and the front of the abdomen.

Below: The head of a buff-tip moth, *Phalera bucephala*. When at rest with its wings folded back, this insect looks exactly like a freshly broken twig covered with lichen.

Stephen Dalton/HNPA

W. Harstrick/Bavaria

Anthony Bannister/NHPA

W. Harstrick/ZEFA

Left: Three methods of avoiding predators. A moth from Trinidad, *Syssphinx molina*, (top, left and right) exposes eye spots on its hind wings when it is attacked. Superficially these resemble the eyes of mammals and when suddenly displayed they startle predators such as birds. The bee hawk moth, *Hemaris tityus*, and the lunar hornet moth, *Sphecia bembeciformis*, (centre, left and right) mimic stinging insects to escape the attention of predators. The peppered moth, *Biston betularia*, is normally a pale colour (bottom left) to camouflage it against lichen covered trees. In smoke-blackened industrial areas, however, a black variety (bottom right) has become common.

Right: The small yucca moth, *Pronubia yuccasella*, is vital for the survival of the yucca plant (and itself depends on the plant) in the southern parts of North America. The moth pollinates the plant, and in return the plant produces enough seeds both to feed the moth's larvae and ensure its own survival.

Life history

The life history of lepidopterans is well-known: the egg, a plant-eating caterpillar (the larva), an immobile chrysalis (the pupa) and finally the adult insect. In some species the virgin female produces a scent which attracts males from a considerable distance. The French entomologist J. H. Fabre described this phenomenon, and Victorian collectors used it to collect large numbers of lepidopterans like male emperor moths. Today a similar method is used to control populations of the gypsy moth, a forest pest; a synthetic female scent attracts males to a death by insecticide.

Caterpillars are soft-bodied and mostly found on plants; they are an important source of food for birds. Caterpillars protect themselves against their predators in a number of ways. Some are camouflaged by their green body colour while others resemble twigs. Several caterpillars are distasteful to birds and they generally have bright and characteristic markings to advertise the fact. The cinnabar moth, *Hypocrita jacobaeae*, for example, is marked with vivid black and yellow bands along its entire length, and birds soon learn to avoid the hairy caterpillars (often called 'woolly bears') of the tiger moth, *Arctia caja*. Many caterpillars suffer from parasites like ichneumon flies or other parasitic members of the insect group *Hymenoptera*.

Some moths are of considerable economic value to man. The silk from the pupal cocoon of certain species has been used to produce the fabric of that name from ancient times. Indeed, the silk moth, *Bombyx mori*, is a highly bred flightless species not found in the wild. However, wild silk is produced from such species as the giant atlas moth, *Attacus atlas*. Some species are also economically valuable because they pollinate night scented flowers like tobacco, a crop of immense commercial importance.

Conversely, caterpillars can cause enormous agricultural losses by feeding on crops. For example, the caterpillar of the codling moth, *Cydia pomonella*, damages apple orchards, the pink bollworm, *Platyedra gossypiella*, can reduce the yield of a cotton crop by as much as 25 per cent, and the maize stem borer, *Busseola fusca*, can completely destroy African maize crops. In marked contrast, the well named *Cactoblastis cactorum* was instrumental in the destruction of the great cactus plague in Australia. The *Lepidoptera* are an order that touches man in many ways.

The Bird Kingdom

Before studying any group of animals, particularly a group as large and diverse as the birds, it is helpful to put the various members into subgroups which reflect evolutionary trends and affinities. Unfortunately, the fossil record is frequently far from complete so that the reconstruction of the various branches of the evolutionary tree must to some extent be a matter of guesswork. Although this is certainly true of the bird kingdom, it is nevertheless possible to classify birds in a reasonably satisfactory manner.

Where the classification of animals or plants is concerned, much is owed to the great Swedish naturalist, Carl von Linné (1707-1778), often known as Linnaeus, who introduced what is known as the binomial system of scientific or Latin names. His system involves the use of two Latin names—one for the genus and one for the species. The genus is a purely artificial concept whereby species which are assumed to be close relatives are grouped together under a single name. Most surface-feeding ducks, for example, are put together into the genus *Anas*. The species, on the other hand, is a fundamental unit because it refers to a particular animal that exists in nature, for example *Anas platyrhynchos*, commonly known as the mallard.

Families and orders

Higher classification involves the grouping of genera into families and families into orders. For completeness the name of the first person to describe the animal scientifically may be placed after the name of the species. Thus in the case of the mallard (which was described by von Linné) its classification would be given as follows: order *Anseriformes*, family *Anatidae* (which is simply the Latin name for the duck family), genus *Anas* and species *Anas platyrhynchos* Linné. If the describer's name is shown in brackets the species has been transferred from the genus in which it was originally placed. For example the rock thrush, was first named by von Linné as *Turdus saxatilis* Linné, but further study showed that it resembled birds in the genus *Monticola* rather than those in the genus *Turdus*. The same bird is now known as *Monticola saxatilis* (Linné).

Both internal and external features of a species are taken into account when classifying it into a particular genus, family or order. Often, though by no means always, members of the same order are so very alike, for example the owls (order *Strigiformes*), that classification presents few difficulties.

Just as no two humans are exactly alike no two specimens of a species are ever exactly alike, although no one would doubt that they are of the same kind and should be classified together. How then is a species to be defined when individual characteristics vary? A suitable definition might be that it is a group of similar animals occupying a well defined geographical area and breeding with each other but not with those that differ from them either physically or in behaviour.

Jacana

Hans Reinhard/Bruce Coleman

Left and above: A purple heron, *Ardea purpurea*, with its young, and a bluethroat, *Luscinia svecica*. The herons constitute one of six families belonging to the order *Ciconiiformes*, the others being the shoebills, the storks, the hammerheads, the ibises and the flamingos. All these birds have long legs and live close to water. They move about in the shallows with slow, deliberate steps. The bluethroat is a typical member of the order *Passeriformes*, the perching birds.

Below: A blue-footed booby, *Sula nebouxii*, with its young. These birds belong to the order *Pelecaniformes*. One of the features which characterize members of this order is the curious structure of their feet which, in addition to being webbed, have a forward pointing hind toe. This is a clear distinction from ducks and geese. Most *Pelecaniformes* are large or medium-sized birds which obtain their food from the sea, often by diving. Gannets may dive from heights of 15 m (50 ft) or more.

Right: A peregrine falcon, *Falco peregrinus*, with its young. Birds of prey belong to the order *Falconiformes* and they are easily distinguished from other birds by their short, hooked beaks and powerful talons. They have very keen eyesight. These characteristics are adaptations for seizing and feeding on living prey. Peregrine falcons are perhaps the most effective of all birds of prey. They can reach speeds of nearly 320 kph (200 mph) when swooping on their prey.

Eric Hosking

R. Fieselmann/Bavaria

Left: A bird of paradise, *Diphyllodes magnificus,* from New Guinea. These are perching birds belonging to the order *Passeriformes.* In the classification of birds, genera with very similar features are placed in the same family, and families which broadly resemble each other will belong to the same order. Sometimes members of the same order may look so very different from each other that it is difficult to see how they can be related. They will, however, have at least one characteristic in common, perhaps the structure of part of the skeleton, which to a scientist definitely relates them. Passeriformes have feet designed for perching. Four toes project from the same point of the leg—three forwards and one backwards. The design of the bony palate is characteristic of the order, and is only rarely seen in other birds. More than a fifth of all living bird species are *Passeriformes.*

Right: The brown pelican, *Pelecanus occidentalis.* Pelicans belong to the order *Pelecaniformes* as do a number of other sea birds, such as gannets and cormorants, which nest in colonies.

Marc Lelo/Jacana

Okapia

Bavaria

Right: The razor-billed auk, *Alca torda,* is a sea bird which inhabits the shores and islands of the North Atlantic. It belongs to the order *Charadriiformes* along with a wide variety of wading birds, gulls and terns. Although members of this order come in many different forms and sizes, they are related by internal similarities and by the composition of their blood albumin. The auk family, which also includes the guillemots and puffins, feeds mainly on small fish and invertebrates.

Below: The golden eagle, *Aquila chryseatos,* is the most powerful of all birds of prey. Its victims include other birds, young deer, foxes (as in this picture) and even wolves. It is a typical member of the order *Falconiformes.* Eagles of the genus *Aquila* (there are nine different species) are found in all parts of the world except South America. The largest of these, the golden eagle, has a wingspan of about 2.1 m (7 ft), the females being slightly larger than the males.

This is by no means a perfect definition, but it is perhaps the closest to the facts as they are observed in nature.

Sub-species

Within any individual species, particularly one with a wide distribution, a further problem may be the existence of separate, distinctive populations. These are called sub-species or geographical races. They are distinguished by the addition of a third scientific name added to the name of the species. Thus it has been shown that the mallard of Greenland is slightly different from that found in Europe. The form occurring in Europe is therefore named *Anas platyrhynchos platyrhynchos* Linné while the Greenland variant is called *Anas platyrhynchos conboschas* Brehm. The naturalist C. L. Brehm was the first to distinguish the Greenland mallard from the common European variety.

In most cases sub-species of birds differ from each other only in slight variations in their colour and size. It is often necessary to examine a specimen very closely before it can be distinguished from allied races with any degree of certainty. Indeed, there are some ornithologists who do not consider that these minor differences should be recognized by name, in the belief that it is quite enough to note the localities where the variants live.

Excluding the various sub-species, there are something like 8,600 species of birds living in the world today. Ornithologists hold diverse opinions as to the number of orders and families that these represent, but the system of classification most widely adopted today is that of the American ornithologist J. L. Peters, based on the system of his fellow American Alexander Westmore. This system recognizes 27 orders and about 150 families. In the chart that follows the English equivalent of the family name is used.

Visage/Jacana

THE ORDERS AND FAMILIES OF BIRDS

Struthioniformes
Ostrich

Rheiformes
Rhea

Casuariiformes
1. Cassowary
2. Emu

Apterygiformes
Kiwi

Tinamiformes
Tinamou

Sphenisciformes
Penguin

Gaviiformes
Diver

Podicipediformes
Grebe

Procellariiformes
1. Albatross
2. Shearwater
3. Storm petrel
4. Diving petrel

Pelecaniformes
1. Tropicbird
2. Pelican
3. Gannet
4. Cormorant
5. Darter
6. Frigate bird

Ciconiiformes
1. Heron and bittern
2. Shoebill
3. Hammerhead
4. Stork
5. Ibis and spoonbill
6. Flamingo

Anseriformes
1. Screamer
2. Swan, goose and duck

Falconiformes
1. Condor and king vulture
2. Osprey
3. Hawk, buzzard, kite, eagle and Old World vulture
4. Falcon and caracara
5. Secretary bird

Galliformes
1. Mound bird
2. Curassow
3. Grouse, ptarmigan, capercaillie and prairie chicken
4. Pheasant, quail and partridge
5. Guineafowl
6. Turkey
7. Hoatzin

Gruiformes
1. Mesite
2. Buttonquail
3. Plainswanderer
4. Crane
5. Limpkin
6. Trumpeter
7. Rail
8. Sungrebe
9. Kagu
10. Sunbittern
11. Seriema
12. Bustard

Charadriiformes
1. Jacana
2. Painted snipe
3. Oystercatcher
4. Plover
5. Sandpiper
6. Avocet
7. Phalarope
8. Crab plover
9. Thick-knee
10. Courser
11. Seed snipe
12. Sheathbill
13. Skua
14. Gull and tern
15. Skimmer
16. Auk

Ostrich **Struthioniformes**

Rhea **Rheiformes**

Cassowary **Casuariiformes**

Albatross **Procellariiformes**

Pelican **Pelecaniformes**

Flamingo **Ciconiiformes**

Parrot **Psittaciformes**

Crane **Gruiformes**

Gull **Charadriiformes**

Pigeon **Columbiformes**

Mousebird **Coliiformes**

Humming bird **Apodiformes**

THE 27 ORDERS OF LIVING BIRDS

Kiwi
Apterygiformes

Tinamou
Tinamiformes

Penguin
Sphenisciformes

Diver
Gaviiformes

Goose
Anseriformes

Grebe
Podicipediformes

Secretary bird
Falconiformes

Turaco
Cuculiformes

Curassow
Galliformes

Owl
Strigiformes

Frogmouth
Caprimulgiformes

Roller
Coraciiformes

Trogon
Trogoniformes

Toucan
Piciformes

Crow
Passeriformes

Columbiformes
1. Sandgrouse
2. Pigeon

Psittaciformes
Parrot

Cuculiformes
1. Turaco
2. Cuckoo

Strigiformes
1. Barn owl
2. Typical owl

Caprimulgiformes
1. Oil bird
2. Frogmouth
3. Potoo
4. Owlet frogmouth
5. Nightjar

Apodiformes
1. Swift
2. Crested swift
3. Humming bird

Coliiformes
Mousebird

Trogoniformes
Trogon

Coraciiformes
1. Kingfisher
2. Tody
3. Motmot
4. Bee-eater
5. Cuckoo roller
6. Roller
7. Hoopoe
8. Wood hoopoe
9. Hornbill

Piciformes
1. Jacamar
2. Puffbird
3. Barbet
4. Honeyguide
5. Toucan
6. Woodpecker

Passeriformes
1. Broadbill
2. Woodhewer
3. Ovenbird
4. Antbird
5. Antpipit
6. Tapaculo
7. Pitta
8. Asity
9. New Zealand wren
10. Tyrant flycatcher
11. Manakin
12. Cotinga
13. Plantcutter
14. Lyrebird
15. Scrub bird
16. Lark
17. Swallow
18. Wagtail
19. Cuckoo shrike
20. Bulbul
21. Leafbird
22. Shrike
23. Vanga
24. Waxwing
25. Palmchat
26. Dipper
27. Wren
28. Mockingbird
29. Accentor
30. Thrush, gnatcatcher,
    warbler and babbler
31. Tit
32. Nuthatch
33. Treecreeper
34. Flowerpecker
35. Sunbird
36. White eye
37. Honeyeater
38. Bunting
39. American warbler
40. Honeycreeper
41. Vireo
42. Oriole
43. Finch
44. Weaver finch
45. Weaver and sparrow
46. Starling
47. Drongo
48. Wattlebird
49. Magpie lark
50. Wood swallow
51. Magpie
52. Bowerbird
53. Bird of paradise
54. Crow

115

Bird Migration

Migration is fairly common in the animal kingdom—some species of fish, whales, turtles, insects, bats and land mammals (including man) all migrate. But birds are unique among the migratory animals; their powers of flight give them exceptional mobility and they have a remarkable ability to navigate over immense distances.

Bird migration is a seasonal shift in the centre of gravity of a population; a regular move both in season and direction involving a 'round trip'. In many cases the entire population of the species moves from a winter to a summer range separated by hundreds or even thousands of kilometres: these are called total migrants. Sometimes, however, the summer and winter ranges overlap or only part of the population migrates. Birds which follow this pattern of migration are known as partial migrants.

Some groups that regularly disperse at a particular season are not, strictly speaking, migrants at all because there is no mass movement in any particular direction; the population simply becomes more scattered. Some British seabirds arrive with great regularity each spring at their coastal colonies and depart again when breeding is over, but during the winter they wander widely. Kittiwakes, *Rissa tridactyla*, for example, range extensively over the Atlantic, reaching as far south as 40°N (the latitude of Madrid), westwards to the Grand Bank of Newfoundland and north to Greenland, while others may remain in home waters.

The reasons for migration

Apart from the enormous physical demands they make, these journeys can only be hazardous—they lead birds across hostile environments and, especially in the case of young birds, to unfamiliar habitats. For those species which do migrate, however, the risks involved in doing so are clearly less than those involved in staying put; were it not so, natural selection would have eliminated the migrating habit.

Migration is therefore concerned with survival and with food supply, and in the case of those species such as swallows, *Hirundinidae*, swifts, *Apodidae*, and flycatchers, *Muscicapidae*, which feed on flying insects, to remain in colder climates in winter would be impossible. Because the long cold winter night of the Arctic is an impossibly harsh environment for all but a very few highly specialized birds, many residents migrate southwards after feeding on the myriads of insects which flourish in the short summer.

The reasons for some migratory patterns, however, are less obvious. Many European swallows winter north of the equator, where there is evidently an adequate supply of insect food. Yet British breeding swallows fly on for thousands of kilometres to winter in the extreme south of Africa. What benefit they derive from this further journey is a mystery.

Equally perplexing is the case of the lapwing, *Vanellus vanellus*. This familiar bird is a partial migrant which suggests that the balance of advantage between staying put and migrating is a delicate

one and not yet firmly resolved one way or the other. Each year countless lapwings from northern and central Europe come to winter in Britain and Ireland, escaping the snow-covered landscape which deprives them of access to food. In Britain, and especially in Ireland, the snow cover is usually brief, so the advantage to the immigrant lapwings is obvious. The odd thing is that perhaps half of all British lapwings migrate to spend the winter in the south of France and Spain, their places being taken by the immigrant lapwings from the North.

The evolution of migration

The wheatear, *Oenanthe oenanthe*, is one of the clearest examples of the evolution of migration. Primarily a bird of rocky uplands, the population breeding in western Europe has a relatively simple journey southward into Africa, where it winters in semi-desert country to the south of the Sahara. At some time after the last ice age, however, the species colonised first Iceland, then Greenland, and finally northeast Canada. Remarkably, these pioneering populations retained the same winter home in Africa, their migratory journeys getting longer and longer with each stage. In the process of evolution these northern birds have grown bigger and longer winged than their southern relatives, so becoming better equipped to face the long overseas flights.

It seems probable that a number of species originally made rather short simple migratory journeys which subsequently became much longer as they extended their range. The pied flycatcher, *Ficedula hypoleuca*, appears to have evolved in the west of Europe; it migrates from there southwards to Spain and Africa each autumn. A successful species, it has spread eastwards in the course of history and now breeds well to the east of Moscow. One might suppose that these eastern birds would follow a simple southward route into Africa, yet ringing has shown that they travel in a south westerly direction and first fly to the

Right: One of the most remarkable migrants is the wheatear, Oenanthe oenanthe. Colonies are found in Alaska and Greenland, and both groups spend the winter in Africa. Curiously they migrate to their winter home by quite different routes. The Alaskan birds travel westwards across Asia while the Greenland group travel eastwards by way of Iceland and western Europe.

Below: It is not only large species like the pintail duck, Anas acuta, that are capable of migration. The tiny ruby-throated humming bird, Archilochus colubris, migrates each year across the Gulf of Mexico from the eastern United States to central America.

D. N. Dalton/NHPA

Pintail duck

Ruby-throated humming bird

Below: Golden plovers, Pluvialis apricaria, on migration. The golden plover nests in northern Europe and Canada, migrating to southwest Europe, North Africa and South America for the winter. It is a wading bird but prefers drier land than its cousins the curlews, sandpipers and snipe.

Frank Lane

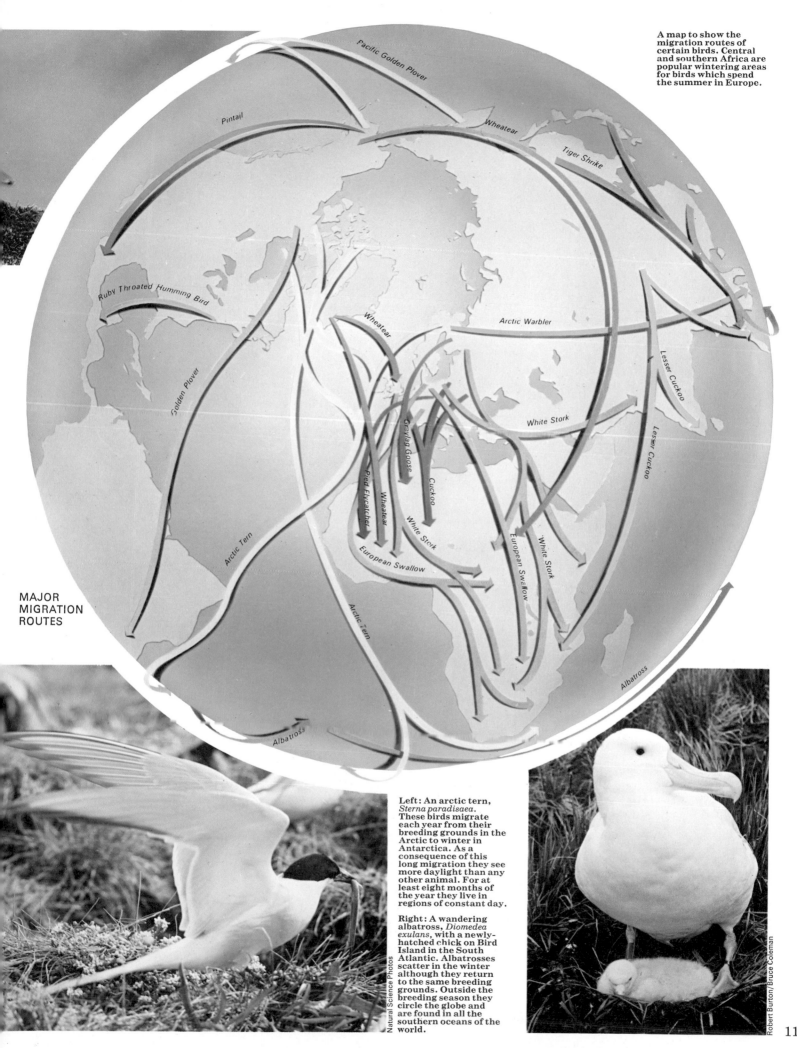

A map to show the
migration routes of
certain birds. Central
and southern Africa are
popular wintering areas
for birds which spend
the summer in Europe.

Pacific Golden Plover

Pintail

Wheatear

Tiger Shrike

Ruby Throated Humming Bird

Wheatear

Arctic Warbler

Golden Plover

Lesser Cuckoo

White Stork

Lesser Cuckoo

Greylag Goose

Arctic Tern

Pied Flycatcher

Wheatear

Cuckoo

White Stork

European Swallow

White Stork

European Swallow

MAJOR
MIGRATION
ROUTES

Arctic Tern

Albatross

Albatross

Left: An arctic tern,
Sterna paradisaea.
These birds migrate
each year from their
breeding grounds in the
Arctic to winter in
Antarctica. As a
consequence of this
long migration they see
more daylight than any
other animal. For at
least eight months of
the year they live in
regions of constant day.

Right: A wandering
albatross, *Diomedea
exulans*, with a newly-
hatched chick on Bird
Island in the South
Atlantic. Albatrosses
scatter in the winter
although they return
to the same breeding
grounds. Outside the
breeding season they
circle the globe and
are found in all the
southern oceans of the
world.

Natural Science Photos

Robert Burton/Bruce Coleman

117

coast of Portugal before heading south.

Migration is, of course, part of an annual cycle. Into each twelve month period every bird must fit a breeding season, rarely lasting less than six to eight weeks and sometimes many months. There is also a period of moult, during which the bird replaces all its worn plumage with a new set of feathers. Then, for the migrants, there has to be time for two travel seasons.

The timing of migration

Most birds moult immediately after breeding is completed but some migratory species postpone the process until they have reached their winter quarters. In just a few species which breed in the extreme north, where the summer season is very short, the moult starts on the breeding grounds, is suspended for migration and is then resumed and completed further south. One species, the tiny willow warbler, *Phylloscopus trochilus*, actually undertakes two complete moults in the year, one immediately after breeding in the autumn and one in Africa before the start of the spring migration. A moult may last for six weeks or even longer in some species and, since birds normally do not moult and migrate at the same time, migration has to be fitted into those parts of the year not affected by breeding and moulting.

A migrating bird covers its long journey in a series of stages, and the time spent feeding at each 'staging post', and therefore the amount of fat deposited seems to depend on the length of the stage ahead. Thus a small insect-eating bird might leave southern Britain (most departures occur at dusk) with sufficient reserves for a flight of several hundred kilometres. There may be two or more such stages, but then for migrants travelling to tropical Africa comes the critical phase of the journey across the Sahara—a flight stage of not less than 1,600 km (1,000 miles). Remarkable though such a flight may seem, there is strong circumstantial evidence that many species take off from Spain or even from France, flying over both the Mediterranean and the Sahara in a single stage. Since their flying speed in still air is generally between 30 and 40 kph (20 to 24 mph) it is evident that many of them must fly uninterruptedly for 60 hours or more—a prodigious feat of endurance.

Navigation

One fascinating aspect of migrating birds is their ability to navigate with great precision. Using identification rings, it has been established that adult swallows and swifts, which winter south of the Sahara, tend to return to the same nest each year throughout their lives, while young ones normally return at least to the district of their birth. By taking the eggs of migratory species from the wild, hatching them in incubators and hand rearing them in isolation from others of their kind, it has been proved that young birds inherit not only a knowledge of the direction in which they must fly in autumn, but also the ability to determine that direction. Young cuckoos, *Cuculus canorus*, also travel alone to southern West Africa, departing a month or two after the adults.

Navigators require some means of holding a steady course across the featureless ocean and, before the invention of the

Frank Lane

Above and right: The greylag goose, *Anser anser*, lives in central and northern Europe, migrating to southern and western Europe and Africa for the winter. As in other birds, the yearly cycle of migration is controlled by a biological 'programme' in each bird. This releases into the bloodstream at the correct times of year the hormones responsible for migration, breeding and moulting. The V-shaped flight formation is typical of many wild geese. The leading birds will probably have been on several previous migrations, so they will have learnt to recognize landmarks on the route. Younger birds will lie at the back of the group.

Ken Fink/Ardea

Left: A North American screech owl, *Otis asio*. A European owl belonging to the same genus, the scops owl, *Otis scops*, is a night migrant. Each year it makes its way under cover of darkness to winter in equatorial Africa.

Below: A curlew sandpiper, *Calidris ferruginea*. Many birds interrupt their long migratory journeys to build up strength for the next stage. Curlew sandpipers can be seen feeding around the coasts of Britain in the spring and autumn as they break their northerly and southerly journeys. Staging posts of this sort are vital to migrants which have to fly long distances over sea or desert. Many species seem to use traditional 'fattening areas' in southern Europe in the autumn and central Africa in the spring. These areas are vital for their survival.

Above: Starlings, *Sturnus vulgaris*, depend at least partly on the sun for their navigational skill. When the sun is shining they are able to orient themselves without difficulty, but on an overcast day their movements are much more random. Pigeons also need to see the sun for accurate navigation.

Ardea

cuckoo

white stork

swallow

Three species which spend the winter in Africa: the European white stork, *Ciconia ciconia*, the swallow, *Hirundo rustica*, and the cuckoo, *Cuculus canorus*. The swallow is common in Britain during the summer but in the winter months it may be found as far south as the southern tip of Africa.

Right: In order to study the movements of birds it is necessary to mark individuals and this is usually done by means of light aluminium rings fixed around the right leg. The bird being ringed in this picture is a whinchat, *Saxicola rubetra*, which migrates from Europe to Africa for the winter.

Below: Adelie penguins, *Pygoscelis adeliae*, move each spring from the pack ice to the Antarctic mainland for breeding. They not only return to the same colony each year but individual birds even occupy the same nest site year after year. Among other penguin migrants are the crested penguins, *Eudyptes*.

Frank Lane

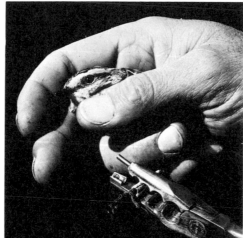

Eric Hosking

compass, primitive man made use of both the sun and the stars. Many years ago it was noted that migrating birds tend to become disoriented when the sky is totally overcast, and this observation prompted experiments which proved that birds, too, make use of the sun to set their course. However, many migrants set off at dusk and must be able to steer in darkness. At first it was thought that they might somehow 'remember' the position of the setting sun, but the true explanation proved more remarkable. It was discovered that birds kept in a windowless room could, when taken outdoors, nevertheless 'read' the night sky. This observation led to a series of studies involving placing living birds in planetaria, from which it was deduced that while they may recognize certain constellations, they make use of the north-south axis about which the night sky appears to rotate.

Thus it seems that in determining direction birds primarily use celestial clues. Recently, however, it has been discovered that some species are apparently able to use the earth's magnetic field to guide them. Even more surprising is an Italian discovery that some birds' ability to orientate is impaired if their olfactory nerves are severed. This new evidence presents two difficulties. Firstly, because the olfactory lobes in the brains of birds are very poorly developed it has always been thought that they have very little sense of smell; secondly, even if they do have a sense of smell, it is very difficult to see how it could help them navigate.

One feature which is undoubtedly important in helping birds to navigate is their 'built-in clock'. (Human navigators need chronometers to determine the exact longitude of any position.) This clock is so accurate that even if a bird is confined for several weeks in a cellar, whose lighting bears no relation to that outside, they still follow a normal 24-hour rhythm.

Although birds do inherit a sense of direction, their navigational ability also depends to some extent on learning details of the migratory route. It is significant that most young birds fly in the company of adults; this ensures that they will arrive safely at their destination in spite of their inexperience. On the way they learn to recognize landmarks, feeding grounds and the position of their winter home. In this way some essential aspects of navigation and the geographical positions of their summer and winter homes are passed on from one generation to the next.

Ardea

Marsupials

The largest and best known members of the order *Marsupialia*, or pouched mammals, are the kangaroos of Australia. They were first discovered by a Dutch explorer, Francisco Pelsaert, in 1629 but his report of strange new animals did not arouse much interest in Europe. It was not until more than 140 years later, in 1770, when kangaroos were rediscovered by Captain James Cook, that naturalists first took notice of the new family of animals. Several years later the first live specimens to reach Europe caused a considerable stir when they were put on show in London. Although their upright gait and powerful hind legs immediately distinguish kangaroos from other animals, it is their unusual method of reproduction—the young develop in a pouch on the mother's abdomen—that makes them fundamentally different from non-marsupial animals.

The offspring of most mammals (placental mammals) reach a fairly advanced stage of development while still inside the mother's womb. The growing embryo receives oxygen and nourishment from its mother's bloodstream by means of a connecting organ called the *placenta* and the umbilical cord. Kangaroos, however, like most other marsupials, have no placenta and the embryo feeds on the yolk-sac of the egg. Although the marsupial egg is much larger than that of placental mammals, the food supply provided by the yolk-sac does not last for very long, and so marsupials are born at a very early stage in their development. The embryonic kangaroo when born is extremely small and hardly resembles its parent at all, but it is nevertheless able to crawl to its mother's pouch and there to find one of the nipples.

This is a remarkable feat for an animal which weighs only 0.9 gm (0.03 oz) at birth as compared with 25 kg (55 lb) for an adult kangaroo, and not surprisingly the newly born animal is specially adapted for the climb. Its fore limbs and shoulder region are relatively well developed and the digits are equipped with sharp curved claws for clinging to its mother's fur.

Once in the pouch the young animal finds the nipple by trial and error; as soon as the teat is touched it stops moving and takes hold. If it fails to find a nipple to supply it with milk, as may happen if there are already other young in the pouch, the young kangaroo is doomed to starvation. Once on the nipple the young does not release its grip and, because it is unable to suckle by itself, the muscles of the mother's mammary gland regulate the flow of milk. The epiglottis, which in placental mammals covers the trachea (the tube leading to the lungs), is extended upwards to form a tube leading into the nasal chamber. Thus a continuous passage is formed from the nostrils to the trachea so that air passes down to the windpipe as milk flows to the gullet.

All marsupials share the kangaroo's basic method of reproduction, with only minor variations from species to species. The group includes the wombats and marsupial moles, which are tunnellers, the gliding possums which are the only aerial representatives, the tree-dwelling

Rat opossum

Above: A South American marsupial, the Ecuador rat opossum, *Caenolestes fuliginosus.*

Right: A view inside the pouch of an Australian brush-tailed possum, *Trichosurus vulpecula*, shows a young possum clinging to its mother's teat. The picture clearly shows how undeveloped newly born marsupials are. As soon as it is born the tiny and virtually helpless animal crawls into its mother's pouch to suckle. At this stage it is unable to feed for itself and muscles in the mother's milk gland control the flow of milk to her offspring. The young possum will remain in its mother's pouch for about five months.

Left: The common opossum, *Didelphis marsupialis*, lives in both North and South America. It was the first marsupial to be discovered by Europeans (in 1520) and in the years after its discovery its then unique method of reproduction aroused considerable interest.

Below: A ringtail possum, *Pseudocheirus*, from Australia. The animal usually curls the end of its tail into a ring, and this accounts for its name. Ringtail possums are nocturnal animals and they feed on fruit and leaves as well as small vertebrates such as lizards. They are solitary animals and, as this picture suggests, they live in trees.

koala bears and a variety of surface land animals ranging in size from the marsupial mice to the kangaroos.

The ancestors of the marsupials separated from the main evolutionary line of mammals about 100 million years ago. Since then both marsupials and placental mammals have evolved a wide variety of adaptations to different ways of life, and it is surprising how similar these adaptations are. The kangaroo, for example, is the marsupial equivalent of the antelope. There are also marsupial versions of the mouse, the wolf, the mole, the cat and the anteater, and these animals look remarkably like their placental mammal counterparts. Although today most marsupials are quite small, this was not always the case: one extinct marsupial, *Diprotodon*, was as big as a rhinoceros.

Right: The koala bear, *Phascolarctos cinereus*, is one of the most familiar marsupials. It feeds exclusively on eucalyptus leaves and this makes it a difficult animal to keep in captivity outside Australia. A curious feature of this diet is that young eucalyptus leaves and shoots often contain lethal amounts of hydrogen cyanide, especially in winter, and this accounted for many deaths among the first zoo animals in Australia. In the wild, koalas avoid the young shoots, feeding almost exclusively on the more mature leaves. Only a century ago there were many millions of koalas in Australia, but today the total population must be measured in thousands. They have completely disappeared from southern and western Australia, exterminated by hunting and by natural epidemics. In 1927 alone more than half a million koala furs were exported from the state of Queensland. Fortunately the animals are now protected and the population is on the increase. Koalas have been reintroduced in some areas.

Left: A female rabbit bandicoot, *Macrotis lagotis*, with her young. These animals get their name from their long rabbit-like ears and their habit of building long burrows to a depth of 1.5 m (4.8 ft) or more. They are beneficial to man because they have a large appetite for pests such as insect larvae and mice.

Below: A young long-nosed bandicoot, *Perameles nasuta*, climbs into its mother's pouch. Most burrowing marsupials, like the bandicoots, have pouches which open to the rear. Bandicoots are found in most parts of Australia and some species, such as the spiny bandicoots, live in New Guinea.

Long-nosed bandicoot

The geographical distribution of the marsupials is unusual—they are found only in Australia and South America (except for a few opossums which have spread to North America relatively recently). The reason for this odd distribution is obscure—possibly Antarctica once formed a bridge between the two continents so that their animal populations merged. At any event it seems likely that competition from placental mammals drove them out of all other regions of the world (fossils of marsupials have been found in both North America and Europe). Marsupials were most successful in Australia where such competition was least.

Australian marsupials

Of the nine marsupial families, seven are exclusively Australian: the kangaroos, *Macropodidae*, the carnivorous marsupials, *Dasyuridae*, the phalangers, *Phalangeridae*, the wombats, *Vombatidae*, the bandicoots, *Peramelidae*, the marsupial anteaters, *Myrmecobiidae*, and the marsupial moles, *Notoryctidae*.

The word 'kangaroo' is often restricted to the three members of the genus *Macropus* (the word means great foot): the red kangaroo, *Macropus rufus*, of the plains, the great grey kangaroo, *Macropus giganteus*, of the open forests, and the stocky, powerful wallaroo, *Macropus robustus*, of the rocky mountain ranges. The many smaller species of the kangaroo family are usually called 'wallabies'.

Kangaroos and wallabies occupy the same ecological niche as the grazing animals such as deer and antelopes of other lands. Like ruminants (animals which chew the cud) they have specialized bacteria in their stomach to break down the cellulose in the sparse vegetation which forms their diet. Some species have even developed the ability to regurgitate food and chew the cud like cattle. Because they can digest plant material efficiently kangaroos and wallabies can survive in the most inhospitable environments.

The long tapering tail is used as a balance and rudder for leaps and turns. At high speed the tail does not hit the ground with every bound, but is used more to help turning. The tail is so powerful that the animal may actually stand upon it and take its hind legs off the ground. Large kangaroos can achieve speeds of about 50 kph (30 mph) for short bursts and can sustain a speed of 40 kph (25 mph) for some time. An adult grey kangaroo may stand over two metres (seven feet) tall and weigh 90 kg (200 lb) or more.

The family *Phalangeridae* contains a wide variety of marsupials, including the koala, *Phascolarctos cinereus*, the slow moving cuscuses, *Phalanger*, with prehensile (grasping) tails and big eyes, the flying possums, *Petaurus*, which glide from tree to tree like flying squirrels, and the doormouse possums, *Cercartetus*. The solitary koala 'bear' is one of the most interesting and attractive of all marsupials. It is rarely seen in zoos outside Australia because it thrives only on a diet of leaves from the native eucalyptus tree, which have a high oil content. Koalas seldom drink water, apparently deriving sufficient moisture from the eucalyptus leaf diet and dew. The reproductive rate of koalas is low. The female produces a single young every two years

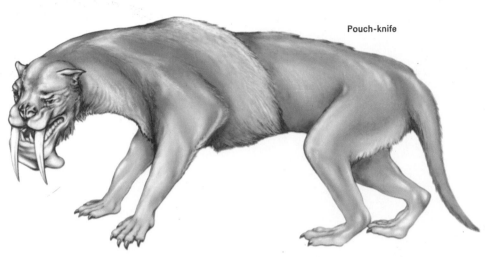

Pouch-knife

after a pregnancy of about a month. At birth the young koala weighs only about five grams (0.2 oz) and, after reaching its mother's pouch, it remains there for six months being suckled. As in many other marsupials such as the Tasmanian wolf and the wombats the koala's pouch opens to the rear. After weaning, the young koala clings to its mother's back until it is able to fend for itself.

Bandicoots are shy nocturnal animals which inhabit New Guinea as well as Australia. They range in size from that of a rat to that of a badger and have pointed noses. They feed on insects and roots which they scratch from the ground. Wombats are stocky rodent-like animals which live in burrows; they are solitary and feed mainly on roots.

Marsupial moles have adapted to a burrowing existence in just the same way as the placental mammals of the same name, and this has resulted in a striking resemblance between the two groups. Although they are quite unrelated the marsupial mole, *Notoryctes*, is outwardly very like the African golden mole, *Chrysochloris*; it has fine silky fur varying in colour from white to a rich golden red.

Carnivorous marsupials

The largest and rarest of the flesh-eating marsupials is the marsupial wolf, *Thylacinus cynocephalus*, which lives in caverns among the rocks in the most mountainous part of Tasmania. Very few of these creatures survive today and unless drastic steps are taken to protect them they will shortly become extinct. The animal looks like a dog with chocolate coloured stripes across its lower back. Most of the day is spent in a lair from which it emerges at dusk in search of prey, hunting either singly or in pairs. Its natural food consists of wallabies and smaller marsupials, rats and birds.

Another carnivorous marsupial is the Tasmanian devil, *Sarcophilus harrisi*, which is still quite common in Tasmania. It received its unfortunate name after early reports of its aggressive temperament. In fact it is no more aggressive than many other animals, but it will use its powerful jaws to defend itself if attacked. The Australian native cats, *Dasyurus*, are slender carnivores which look rather like martens and feed on birds, small mammals and lizards.

The rare marsupial anteater or numbat, *Myrmecobius fasciatus*, is sometimes placed with the marsupial carnivores in the family *Dasyuridae* rather than in a separate family of its own. It has a pointed

Above: *Thylacosmilus*, a large carnivorous marsupial which once roamed the forests of South America. Its similarity to the sabre-toothed tiger is remarkable because the two animals were quite unrelated. Evidently both animals evolved in the same way to meet similar environmental conditions.

Right: An albino brush wallaby, *Wallabia*. Members of the kangaroo family normally produce only a single young at a time, and twins, as seen here, are rare. Albinism, the absence of body pigmentation, is a genetically produced condition and, although not common, it occurs in many mammals, including man.

Douglas Baglin/NHPA

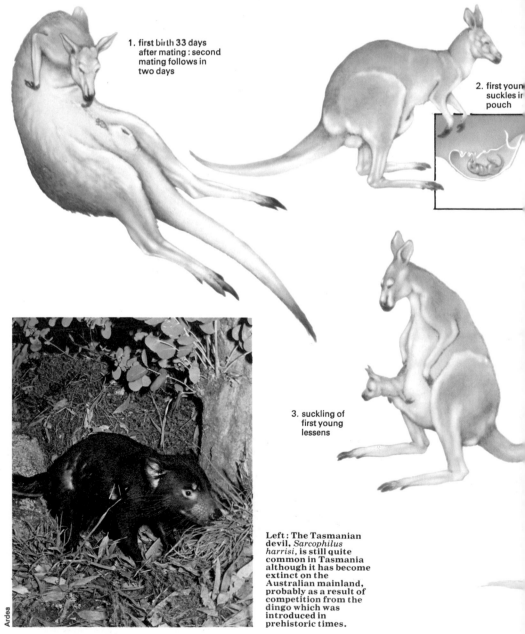

1. first birth 33 days after mating: second mating follows in two days

2. first young suckles in pouch

3. suckling of first young lessens

Left: The Tasmanian devil, *Sarcophilus harrisi*, is still quite common in Tasmania although it has become extinct on the Australian mainland, probably as a result of competition from the dingo which was introduced in prehistoric times.

Ardea

Left: Illustrations to show the characteristic hopping movement of kangaroos. The very powerful hind legs and long slender feet enable the animals to move extremely rapidly by a series of jumps which may measure nine metres (30 ft) or more.

Above: Matschie's tree kangaroo, *Dendrolagus matschiei*. This strange animal lives in the forests of northern Australia and New Guinea feeding on fruit and leaves. It is not at all well adapted to its tree-dwelling existence, but this does not seem to matter because it has no natural enemies and food is plentiful.

Right: An Australian 'tiger cat', *Dasyurus maculatus*, devouring a crimson rosella parrot. These carnivorous marsupials are excellent climbers and they prey on lizards, fish and small mammals as well as birds. They were once slaughtered in large numbers for raiding chicken coops and are now quite rare.

4. second birth after first young has left pouch: about seven months after second mating

. second young suckles in pouch and first young returns to suckle occasionally

NHPA

Left: A typical breeding sequence for the red kangaroo, *Macropus rufus*. After the first young is born (the mother leans back as the tiny embryo crawls up into her pouch) mating takes place for the second time. The fertilized egg, however, only begins to develop when the suckling of the first young has lessened. By the time the second animal is born, the first will have left the pouch, although it may still return to suckle occasionally.

snout, long hair and a long bushy tail. Its diet consists mainly of termites which it extracts from crevices and rotten wood with its long tongue. It lives only in a few small regions of central and southern Australia.

American marsupials

The two American marsupial families are the rat opossums, *Caenolestidae*, and the opossums, *Didelphidae*. There are only three species of rat opossums. They are small animals found in the forests of the Andes from Venezuela to southern Chile. Fossil evidence suggests that they are the survivors of a much larger marsupial group which flourished in the Tertiary period.

The most widely distributed member of the opossum family is the common opossum, *Didelphis marsupialis*, which is found from Argentina to Canada. It inhabits forests at all altitudes, feeding on insects and small mammals, but avoids grasslands and the high plains of the Andes. Opossums are solitary, nocturnal animals; they spend the hours of daylight in dens or nests taken over from other species. Despite their fairly large size— about 75 cm (2.5 ft) from head to tail— opossums do not live long. The average lifespan from weaning has been estimated to be only 1.3 years and the longest four years, so few opossums live beyond the summer following their birth. Even though females become mature at six months, they rarely breed more than once in a lifetime.

The water opossum, *Chironectes minimus*, of South America has the distinction of being the only marsupial adapted to an aquatic existence although its cousin the thick-tailed opossum, *Lutreolina crassicaudata*, is also a good swimmer. It lives on the banks of ponds and rivers feeding on shellfish, spawn and crayfish. The pouch of the water opossum, which opens to the rear, is equipped with a muscle so that it can be closed off when the animal dives, ensuring that the young remain dry while their mother searches for food.

Hedgehogs, Moles and Shrews

Hedgehogs, moles, shrews and a number of other small insect-eating mammals all belong to the order *Insectivora*. The grouping is largely one of convenience because its various members do not have many structural features in common: they are linked more by their way of life than anything else. Insectivores are small animals—none is larger than a rabbit and most are considerably smaller—which lead secret, often nocturnal, lives hidden in the undergrowth and the earth. It is not therefore surprising that although they are quite common they are only rarely seen.

The insectivores are placental mammals: they differ from both monotremes (such as the duck-billed platypus) and marsupials (such as kangaroos) in a number of important ways. The main distinction is that the young are retained within the mother's womb until an advanced stage of development and are nourished through a connecting organ called the placenta, a complex system of blood vessels and tissue. This arrangement provides maximum protection and a controlled environment for the growing embryo. Another important feature seen in placental mammals but not monotremes or marsupials is the *corpus callosum*, a bundle of nerve fibres which connects the left and right cerebral hemispheres of the brain providing improved co-ordination.

Hedgehogs and moles

Altogether there are more than 350 known species of insectivores and these are normally divided into eight families. The family *Erinaceidae* contains the hedgehogs and the moon rats. Hedgehogs are found throughout Europe, Africa and Asia, north to the latitude of Oslo and east as far as Borneo. They will inhabit any region where they can find food and dry shelter: hollow trees, the bases of hedges and cavities underneath farm buildings make popular living quarters. They line their nests with moss, leaves and grass but only rarely dig burrows of their own.

The most familiar feature of the hedge-

Hans Reinhard/Bruce Coleman

Above: A group of young European hedgehogs, *Erinaceus europaeus*, at the base of a tree. Hedgehogs are most active in the evening and early in the morning, probing among leaves and moss and under stones with their sensitive noses. They feed on insects, snails and even mice. In the autumn when the outside air temperature drops to around 10°C (50°F) hedgehogs begin their hibernation. First they burrow into their nest material and roll themselves into a ball to minimize heat loss. Then the body processes slow down: the breathing rate falls to about seven per minute and the heart rate to 20 per minute. The blood temperature falls dramatically although it is never allowed to drop below about 2°C (36°F). With the onset of warmer weather in the spring, the animal 'wakes' and immediately begins feeding.

Right: A common mole, *Talpa europaea*, feeding on an earthworm.

Below: The bizarre star-nosed mole, *Condylura cristata*, from North America.

Heather Angel

P. Morris

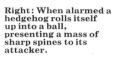

Left: The pen-tailed tree shrew, *Ptilocercus lowii*, belongs to the family *Tupaiidae*. Members of this group were once regarded as insectivores—there are some affinities with the elephant shrews—but are now normally classified with the primates, the order which includes lemurs, monkeys and man.

Right: When alarmed a hedgehog rolls itself up into a ball, presenting a mass of sharp spines to its attacker.

Left: The bones in the hand of a mole are specially adapted to equip the animal for its burrowing way of life.

Below right: The lesser tenrec, *Echinops telfairi*, from Madagascar is a typical insectivore. It lives in gardens, the drier forests and sandy areas where it forages for snails, worms, insects and lizards. The sense of smell is well developed and the animal uses its long snout as well as its claws to uncover food.

Below: An elephant shrew, *Elephantulus brachyrhynchus*, eating an insect. Most elephant shrews, which inhabit central and southern Africa, have longer trunk-like snouts than this species. Their long hind legs enable them to jump and hop rapidly for considerable distances, and this, together with their long snouts, distinguishes them from other insectivores.

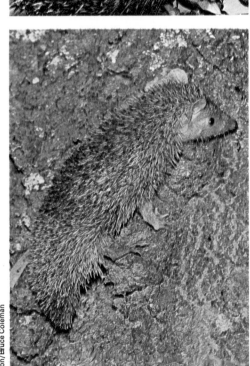

Left: The bicoloured white-toothed shrew, *Crocidura leucodon*, is common in central and southern Europe. It inhabits the undergrowth of hedges, fields and gardens, and like most insectivores it feeds mainly on invertebrate animals such as insects and earthworms. The smallest of all mammals is a shrew—Savis' pygmy shrew, *Suncus etruscus*—which measures only about 7 cm (2.7 in) from nose to tail.

Right: A Cape golden mole, *Chrysochloris asiatica*. It belongs to a different family from the European moles but has a similar way of life, constructing long burrows just below the surface and feeding on insects and earthworms.

hog is its covering of spines—as many as 16,000 extend over the animal's back and sides from its forehead to its rump. On the face and underside of the body is a covering of soft hair. The spines provide an almost impregnable defence against possible predators such as foxes, for when a hedgehog is alarmed it curls up into a tight ball by contracting its well developed skin muscles so that the soft parts of the body are protected and the spines point outwards. Hedgehogs are fairly agile and will eat almost anything, from insects, slugs and snails (their preferred diet) to fruit and berries, the young of nesting birds and amphibians and reptiles.

Some of the stranger habits of hedgehogs are not fully understood, including the peculiar habit of anointing the spines with saliva when chewing strong-smelling food, be it a toad or carrion. This behaviour may be to do with grooming or it may simply be a way of disguising the animal's own scent. Not surprisingly the many spines make grooming a difficult operation, and as a result hedgehogs are frequently plagued with parasites. Almost all wild hedgehogs are infested with fleas, *Archaeopsylla erinacei*, and many also carry ticks, mites and nematode worms.

Hedgehogs are remarkably resistant to poisons that would prove deadly to other mammals. It is well known that the European hedgehog will tackle a large adder; the snake has little chance of biting because of the hedgehog's spines and defence tactics. Hedgehogs eat blister beetles, which contain the powerful poison cantharidin, with no harmful effect and reputedly can tolerate 7,000 times as much tetanus toxin as a human. In the same family as the hedgehogs are the moon rats which are large opossum-like insectivores with striking black and white markings. They are nocturnal creatures and live in the lowland and mangrove forests of Malaysia.

The moles are classified in the family *Talpidae*. Among the several sub-families are the shrew moles of South East Asia, the desmans of east and southwest Europe, the Old World moles of Europe and Asia and the star-nosed moles of North America. The diversity of animals within one family is typical of the insectivores.

Moles, especially those of the genus *Talpa*, are well adapted to an underground life. The forelimbs and the hands are specialized; in the most extreme types, like the European mole, *Talpa europaea*, the shoulder girdle is shifted close to the neck and the front joint of the breast plate is prolonged forward and broadened to give a large area for the attachment of digging muscles. The size of the hand is increased by a special sickle-shaped bone and there is an equivalent bone in the feet which probably helps the animal to get a grip on the sides of its burrow. Most species of mole throw out the excavated earth from their burrows as 'molehills', pushing it up from below with the palms of the hands. The nest, made of dry leaves and grasses, is usually below ground and covered with a particularly large mound of earth known as a 'fortress'.

Most moles eat earthworms, and stocks of immobilized worms with their heads cut off are often kept as a food store. This diet is supplemented with insects while some of the North American moles eat large quantities of vegetable matter. Although moles have a poor sense of smell and poor eyesight, they make up for this by having extremely sensitive tactile organs located on the snout, as well as sensitive hairs on the nose and wrist. The extraordinary star-nosed mole of North America has a ring of 22 fleshy tentacles surrounding its nostrils. No doubt these help the animal to feel its way through the earth and locate its prey.

Shrews
The shrews form the largest family of insectivores (*Soricidae*) with over 300 species. They are found in most parts of the world, being absent only from Australasia and the southern part of South America. Shrews forage in and under the leaf litter and undergrowth of woods where they construct runs and shallow burrows. They are forever on the move and are extremely aggressive little animals, communicating with each other by high-pitched squeaks and twitterings. Like bats, they probably use echo location to help detect each other and their prey. Although they eat all kinds of insects, shrews will also tackle any other prey that they can overpower. The European common and pygmy shrews appear to favour woodlice, while the diet of some North American shrews includes a high proportion of vegetable matter.

To maintain their high metabolic rate, shrews have to eat a great deal of food, indeed their life is one continuous meal. The food consumed each day often exceeds the animal's body weight and digestion is very rapid, the gut being emptied in three hours. Common shrews are often found lying dead during the autumn; the cause of death most probably being cold and starvation. The reason why so many are found is that their skin contains strong-smelling glands which make them unpalatable to most carnivorous mammals which would otherwise eat them. The main predators of shrews are birds of prey, particularly owls.

It is easy to think of shrews as typical of European woodlands but they have an immense range and the 300 forms are spread throughout most of the world, with many species confined to the remote mountain streams of Tibet and eastern Asia. The strangest of all are the armoured shrews of tropical Africa. These medium-sized shrews show no outward appearance of anything unusual but their internal anatomy is quite extraordinary; the details of the vertebral column are like nothing found in any other mammal. The dorsal and many of the lumbar vertebrae are large and have a complex system of extensions, so that most of the backbone

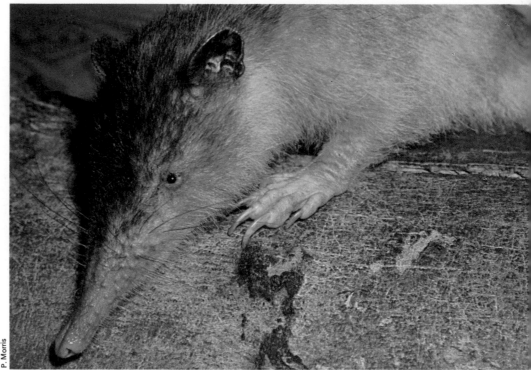

P. Morris

MOLE'S NEST COMPLEX

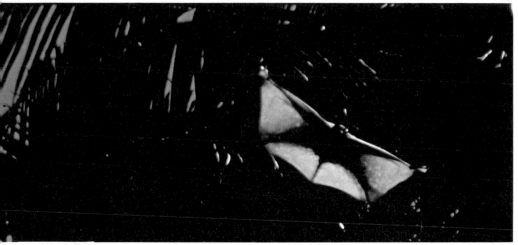

Left: A solenodon, *Solenodon paradoxus,* from Haiti. Solenodons are not as defenceless as they look for they have very large incisors and also poisonous salivary glands (an unusual feature for a mammal) which they use to subdue large prey such as rodents. They are now quite rare and face extinction.

Above: A colugo, *Cynocephalus volans,* from the Philippines. Unlike other mammals which have developed the ability to glide, these animals have a web of skin stretching between the hind legs and the tail. Often misleadingly called 'flying lemurs', they are classified in an order of their own, the *Dermoptera.*

Below: All insectivores have much the same way of life. They live under the ground or on the surface sheltered by the undergrowth, feeding mainly on small invertebrates such as insects and earthworms. In this illustration of a typical insectivore habitat can be seen a European hedgehog, *Erinaceus europaeus,* a common mole, *Talpa europaea,* and its young, and a common European white-toothed shrew, *Crocidura russula.* Many beetle grubs lie buried in the ground—they will probably fall prey to moles. The inset shows how a mole's nest is surrounded by a network of tunnels. It often lies under a large mound of earth.

forms a strong braced girder. The purpose of this strange fortified backbone remains a mystery but illustrates the unusual make-up of many insectivores.

The elephant shrews belong to a separate insectivore family, the *Macroscelididae.* They look like long-nosed rodents, and have large eyes, long legs and a stance and way of moving that is unlike other insectivores. Most elephant shrews (they get their name from their long, mobile snout) are about the size of a mouse and they live in the rocky scrub areas of northern Algeria and Morocco as well as in central and southern Africa. Some members of the group, like the giant elephant shrews, *Petrodromus* and *Rhynchocyon,* are forest dwellers and differ from the others in having only four toes on the hind feet. Elephant shrews feed almost exclusively on ants which they prise out of rotting wood and other crevices with their long snouts.

Other insectivore families

The smallest insectivore family, the *Solenodontidae,* contains only two rare species which are found on the islands of Cuba and Hispaniola (Haiti and the Dominican Republic) in the West Indies. Solenodons are odd-looking mammals about the size of a guinea pig, with long pointed snouts bristling with sensitive hairs. They have large naked ears and an equally naked rat-like tail. Solenodons live in rocky, wooded country where they hunt smaller mammals, reptiles and ground-nesting birds as well as the more usual insect diet.

Another group of island insectivores is the family *Tenrecidae* found only in Madagascar and the nearby Comoro Islands in the Indian Ocean. Most of the twenty or so species are nocturnal and dig their own burrows and nests. The tenrec, *Tenrec ecaudatus,* is the largest living insectivore and the most widely distributed and commonest member of the family. It has a long snout and a coat of mixed hairs and spines. The spines, mostly on the nape of the neck, are raised when the animal is alarmed giving this small mammal a ferocious appearance.

Closely related to the large family of tenrecs are the otter shrews of the family *Potamogalidae* which live on the mainland of Africa. As their name suggests, these aquatic insectivores look and behave like miniature otters. There are only three species of which the giant African otter shrew, *Potamogale velox,* is the largest. It inhabits lowland equatorial West Africa whereas the other two species (of the genus *Micropotamogale*) live only in the mountain streams of West Africa. All have a broad, flat head, small eyes and short soft fur, and they feed on a variety of prey such as fish, amphibians and crustaceans.

The golden moles make up the final family of insectivores, the *Chrysochloridae.* Although looking superficially like the true moles, these animals are more exotic in appearance: their fur is thick with a dense soft underfur and has an iridescent bronzy sheen of green, violet, yellow or red. The forelimbs are very powerful and have four digits, the outer ones small but the central two very large and armed with huge pointed claws. There is a hard leathery pad on top of the snout. They live in Africa south of the equator where they feed on insects, earthworms and lizards. The prey is held by the long fore-claws while being eaten.

127

Bats

Bats inhabit almost every corner of the globe. Only in Antarctica, the Arctic tundra and a few remote islands are they unknown. The total number of individuals runs into tens of billions and there are more than 1,200 known species and sub-species. They belong to the order *Chiroptera* and, second only to the rodents (order *Rodentia*), constitute the largest population of mammals on earth.

Their small furry bodies and large membranous wings make bats instantly recognizable. They are the only mammals that can fly, although a number of creatures, such as the flying squirrels of West Africa, are able to glide from tree to tree. In most respects bats are typical placental mammals: their young are born alive and feed on their mother's milk. The group is divided into two sub-orders: the *Megachiroptera*, fruit-eating bats with large eyes, a clawed thumb and second finger and a small or non-existent tail, and the *Microchiroptera*, mainly insect-eating bats with claws only on the thumbs, a tail forming part of the wing and the ability to find their prey by echo location, or 'sonar'.

Bats are nocturnal, and this way of life suits them in several respects. Firstly, most species are tropical so daytime activity would expose the thin skin of their wings to the harmful effects of the ultra-violet radiation in sunlight. Also, the heat would increase the rate of water loss from these large surfaces, and so would restrict bats to feeding grounds close to water sources. For most bats, however, the most important advantage of a nocturnal lifestyle is that it makes available the enormous food supply of night-flying insects. During the day bats roost in caves or trees, hanging upside down from suitable perches.

Bats usually mate in the autumn before hibernating. The sperm from the male remains in the female's fallopian tubes

FLYING FOX (Pteropus)

radius · sternum · clavicle · scapula · humerus · ilium · ulna · femur · pubis · tibia

pectoral muscles · thigh muscles · calcar · tail · foot

Left: The skeleton of a flying fox, *Pteropus*. It has long arms and particularly long fingers for supporting the wings. The breast bone (sternum) has a keel to which the powerful flight muscles are attached. Ignoring those features which are special adaptations for flight, bats resemble the insectivores, such as shrews and moles.

Right: A nectar bat, *Leptonycteris sanborni*, feeds on the pollen and nectar of an agave flower and pollinates the plant. These bats have long tongues for probing flowers, but they also feed on insects. During the day they cluster together in groups in the hollows of cliffs and trees.

Above: A flying fox, *Pteropus*, partly cut away to show the wing-structure and the arrangement of the muscles. The short first digit, or thumb, can be seen projecting from the front edge of each wing. The animal uses these for climbing. The wing membrane, or patagium, is joined to the fore and hind limbs.

Above: A long-tongued fruit bat, *Macroglossus logichilus*, from South East Asia. This species is the smallest of all fruit bats, having a body length of only about 6 cm (2.4 in).

Left: A flying fox, *Pteropus*, from the Seychelles. During the day, fruit bats like the flying fox roost in trees, wrapping their wing membranes around their bodies.

Right: An Indian short-nosed fruit bat, *Cynopterus sphinx*, feeds on a banana.

Oxford Scientific Films

Right: A false vampire, *Vampyrum spectrum*, from South America. It eats insects, mice and birds but is not a bloodsucker like true vampire bats.

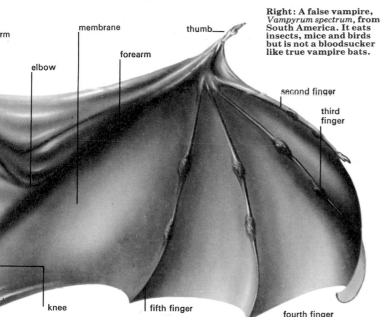

arm

elbow

membrane

forearm

thumb

second finger

third finger

knee

fifth finger

fourth finger

P. Morris/Ardea

until the following spring, when the first egg is produced. A single foetus develops from the fertilized egg and the baby is born in the summer. At birth the young bat is naked and blind, and it clings to its mother's body to keep warm, travelling with her when she leaves the roost at night to feed. As the bat grows older it becomes less dependent on its mother, flying behind her at night and hanging next to her during the daytime rest period. Insect-eating bats develop quickly and are able to fly at an early age; they are fully grown in no more than eight weeks. Unlike birds, young bats seem to inherit their skill at flying, for they fly well from the beginning without any practice flights.

Flight

The wings of a bat are formed of skin and in this respect they resemble prehistoric flying reptiles like the pterodactyl more than birds. The design of the wings is essentially the same in all bats: there is a short, stout upper arm, a long, slender forearm and extremely long fingers which support the skin of the wing. The second finger extends along the leading edge of the wing; immediately behind it is the third and longest finger; and behind that are the fourth and fifth fingers, which are

well spaced out and serve as 'struts' to support and control the shape of about half of the wing membrane. The wing extends between the fingers and continues beyond the fifth finger to the side of the body and leg. It consists of upper and lower layers of skin enclosing a network of fine blood vessels. The animal's thumb, or first finger, projects from the front edge of the wing and carries a claw; it plays no part in supporting the wing.

Bats usually roost upside down. As they approach a landing they flip over in full flight, throw their hind claws against the roost, grasp it and hang. To take off they simply release their grip, fall for a short distance and begin to fly. A few heavier bats, such as the flying foxes, flap their wings to raise the body to a horizontal position before releasing their hold. Many bats do not fly more than two kilometres or so from their roost, although some species may cover 100 km (60 miles) or more on a round trip. A few species are known to migrate; the nectar bat, *Leptonycteris*, for example, travels from Mexico to Arizona for the summer. Bats fly at altitudes of anything up to about 300 m (1,000 ft); insect-eaters will naturally tend to fly at the same height as their insect prey.

Senses

The expression 'as blind as a bat' is very much misplaced. Many bats can see very well, and their eyes have become adapted to operating in extremely dim light. Bats that feed on fruit or flowers no doubt also use their sense of smell to detect their food. One of the most remarkable features of bats, however, is their sonar system which enables them to catch their prey and avoid obstructions such as trees and buildings when it is almost completely dark. Only one genus, *Rousettus*, of the sub-order *Megachiroptera* possesses it, but all members of the other sub-order *Microchiroptera* have this ability.

The bat sends out a series of high-pitched squeaks as it flies along, and the pattern of sounds in the echo tells it what objects are ahead, how far away they are and whether or not they are moving. The squeaks are short and intense, but their pitch (wave frequency) is too high to be heard by the human ear. However, bats also emit audible sounds as they fly about at dusk catching their prey. These sounds lie at the high frequency end of the human hearing ability and are more easily heard by children than adults. The sounds are emitted through the animal's mouth or nostrils, depending on the species. Those

129

Above: Common pipistrelle bats, *Pipistrellus,* **clinging to a wall. Insect-eaters are smaller than fruit-bats, and they have the advantage of a 'sonar system'.**

Left: A long-eared bat, *Plecotus auritus.* **These creatures belong to the largest of the bat families, the** *Vespertilionidae,* **and they are common throughout Europe. The enormous ears help give the animal the keen sense of hearing needed for its sonar system.**

Right: A tomb bat, *Taphozous melanopogon,* **from Malaya. The genus was first discovered in ancient Egyptian tombs by French naturalists in the late 18th century.**

bats that emit sound nasally usually have a large nose 'leaf' which probably acts rather like a reflector to 'aim' the sound in a particular direction. Bats which emit sound orally, on the other hand, usually form their mouth and lips into a megaphone shape to project the sound. The squeak of a bat is not a continuous sound but rather a series of individual sound pulses and the pitch of each pulse varies depending on whether the animal is cruising or closing in on a target.

Flying foxes
The largest of all bats are the flying foxes, *Pteropus,* from India, South-East Asia and Australia, which can weigh up to 1.5 kg (3.3 lb) and have a wingspan of up to 1.5 m (5 ft). They have a fox-like face and long sharp canine teeth, but despite their forbidding appearance they are strictly vegetarian. They use their teeth for tearing husks or even cracking coconuts. Flying foxes belong to the sub-order *Megachiroptera* and they have prominent well-developed eyes but no sonar system. Flying foxes live in colonies of many thousands of individuals. They roost in high trees during the day, moving to food trees, which they detect mainly by smell, in the evening. After returning to their roost the following morning they fly noisily around for several hours before settling down for the day. The roost is not a permanent site, for the bats will always rest close to a suitable source of food.

Insectivorous bats
Insect-eating bats are smaller than fruit bats. One of the smallest, *Pipistrellus nanulus,* from West Africa, has a body length of only four centimetres (1.6 in) when fully grown. Among the larger families of insect-eating bats are the horseshoe bats, *Rhinolophidae,* which are found from Western Europe across Asia to Australia; the Old World leaf-nosed bats, *Hipposideridae,* of Africa, southern Asia and Australia; and the New World leaf-nosed bats, *Phyllostomatidae,* of the southern United States and northern South America. The largest family of all

A BAT IN FLIGHT

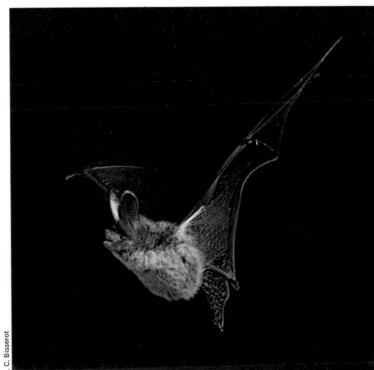

Above: A series of illustrations of a bat in flight.

Left: A Bechstein's bat, *Myotis bechsteini,* **is frozen by the camera in mid-flight. This is one of about 60 species of mouse-eared bats (genus** *Myotis***) which are found in most parts of Europe. This particular species has larger ears than most other members of the genus. Mouse-eared bats roost together in large colonies, and their summer and winter quarters may be separated by as much as 200 km (120 miles). They hibernate in natural or artificial chambers such as caves and buildings.**

Right: A diadem round-leaf bat, *Hipposideros diadema.* **The strange shape of the nose has to do with the transmission of the ultrasonic 'squeaks' of the animal's echo location system. As with other leaf-nosed bats, the squeaks are emitted from the nostrils and not the mouth. Closely related to the leaf-nosed bats are the horseshoe bats which also have nostrils surrounded by skin growths.**

S. C. Bisserot

Below: A bat emits 'squeaks' at frequencies of up to 100,000 Hz (the limit of human hearing is 20,000 Hz) and the character of the echoes reflected back provides information about what lies in its path—how far away it is, its size and so on.

A BAT'S 'SONAR SYSTEM'

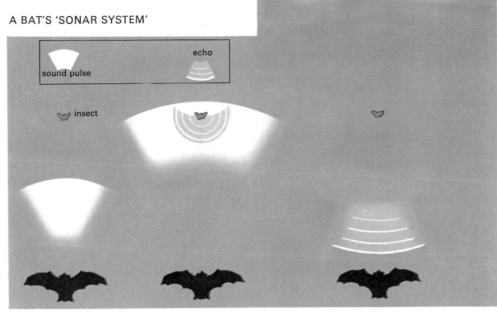

echo

sound pulse

insect

Left: A dog-faced fruit bat, *Cynopterus brachyotis*, roosting in a tree. As its name suggests, this bat's diet consists mainly of fruit: figs, bananas, guavas and mangos are popular food items. It inhabits the forests of India and South-East Asia. Very few predators feed on bats to any great extent; one that

does is the bat hawk, *Machaeramphus alcinus*, from the tropics. Occasionally a bat will be taken by an owl, a mammal predator or a snake, but this is rare. Bats do, however, suffer from the attentions of parasites, particularly fleas, lice, ticks and mites. One family of wingless insects is found only on bats.

S. C. Bisserot

is the *Vespertilionidae* which is world-wide in its distribution.

Many insect-eating bats have adapted themselves to other food sources in order to supplement their diet. One of the most remarkable examples of this is the fishing bulldog bat, *Noctilio leporinus*, of Mexico and Central America. It uses its echo location system to detect fish under the water and then flies down to the surface and rakes the water with its long claws. In this way it usually succeeds in impaling a fish which it transfers to its mouth while in flight. If it is a long way from its roost the bat may chop up the fish with its teeth and store the pieces in its cheeks until it can eat them at leisure.

Another curious group of bats are the false vampires of the family *Megadermatidae*, which are strongly built animals with long, razor-sharp teeth. In addition to their normal diet of insects they prey on birds, smaller bats (though never their own species) and other small mammals. The African species *Lavia frons* is a dove-grey colour with pink wings and nose while the ghost bat of Australia, *Macroderma gigas*, has white wings, large white ears and a very pale body. These creatures are far removed from the popular conception of bats as dark, sinister animals.

Vampire bats

The notorious vampire bats belong to the family *Desmodontidae* and are related to the leaf-nosed bats. They are found only in the tropics and sub-tropics of the Americas and feed exclusively on the blood of vertebrate animals such as cattle, horses, dogs, poultry and even humans. Their prey is almost always warm-blooded. They are not particularly large bats, but have a broad skull and enormous incisor and canine teeth. The two upper incisors are curved and extremely sharp, the upper canines are large and pointed and the back molar and lower teeth are small.

The common vampire, *Desmodus rotundus*, lives in darkened caves which shelter many other kinds of bats. It feeds at night on the blood of cattle, landing very lightly on its victim. First of all it licks the spot it intends to bite, and this may serve as an anaesthetic since animals rarely stir when they are bitten. If the animal does wake the bat will immediately fly off. The wound is made by the front incisors and the tongue is extended and curled over at the edges. In conjunction with a deep groove in the lower lip, this forms a sort of 'straw' through which the blood is channelled. An anticoagulant in the bat's saliva prevents the blood from clotting while it is feeding.

The usual nightly consumption is about 30 g (1 oz). This may be taken from a single animal such as a cow, which may be bitten on the neck, ears or anal region, or from several smaller animals. Small birds are known to have been drained of blood by a vampire bat and so killed. Although the amount of blood taken by a single bat is relatively little, even quite a small colony may consume a considerable amount: 1,000 bats will need about 70 litres (15 gallons) of blood every night. Humans are attacked only rarely and when they are, the fingers, toes, ears, forehead or lips are usually the areas singled out. The loss of 30 g of blood is very unlikely to be serious, but vampire bats are carriers of the deadly disease of rabies and so a bite can be dangerous.

Elephants and Hyraxes

Man's association with the elephant dates from the earliest times. Many thousands of years ago the elephant and its relatives were a prized source of food: if a band of Paleolithic hunters could kill an elephant or a mammoth they would not need to hunt again for many days. More recently elephants have been hunted for their tusks, and countless animals were slaughtered in the 18th century and the first half of this century. Fortunately the ivory trade is now strictly controlled in most countries, so the pressure on the elephant population has been eased.

The Carthaginians were probably the first people to train elephants—they were used in the Punic Wars against the Romans. The Carthaginian general Hannibal took 38 elephants with him when he crossed the Alps with his army in 218 BC. Trained elephants are still used today in the forests of India and Burma for handling timber.

The elephant's closest living relatives are much less familiar creatures. They are the hyraxes, which belong to the order *Hyracoidea*, and the sea cows, which belong to the order *Sirenia*. The hyraxes are small furry animals looking rather like large guinea pigs, while the sea cows are aquatic mammals which resemble seals. From its outward appearance the hyrax would seem an unlikely relative of

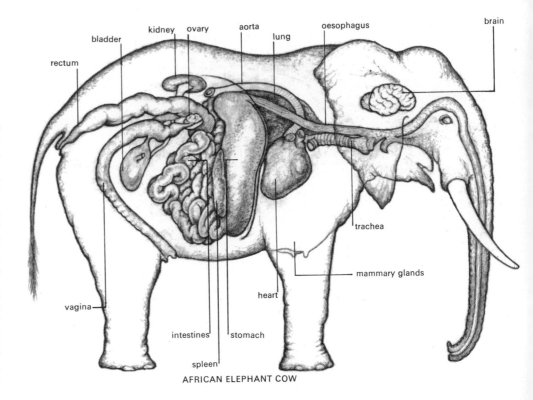

AFRICAN ELEPHANT COW

Above: A body plan of a female African elephant, *Loxodonta africana*, showing most of the main body organs. The brain is larger than that of any other land mammal, and research has shown that elephants have a well developed learning ability. There may therefore be some truth in the saying 'elephants never forget'.

Below: Only rarely will elephants charge in earnest; usually they halt or veer off before reaching their target, but wounded animals can be very dangerous. The African elephant was once found throughout Africa, but the ivory trade drastically reduced the population and now they are rarely found outside reserves.

Su Gooders/Ardea

Norman Myers/Bruce Coleman

Above: An Indian elephant feeding on bamboo in the Chitwan National Park of Nepal. An elephant's digestive system is inefficient; about half of what it eats is excreted undigested. To allow for this, elephants must eat even more food than the already enormous amount their bodies actually need.

Below: The great weight of an African elephant enables it to fell sizeable trees without much difficulty. It does this to get at the leaves near the top of the tree, which would otherwise be out of reach. A herd of elephants can quite quickly demolish whole stands of trees in this manner.

Frank Lane

Left: An Indian elephant, *Elephas maximus*, at work lifting rocks. Although the species is in decline, wild Indian elephants are still hunted and put to work in such countries as Burma. The hunt, called a *khedda*, may involve as many as 2,000 drivers and 50 tame work elephants. A herd of wild elephants is slowly surrounded by this army of hunters and driven into a strong wooden enclosure. Once caught, the elephants are easily trained, and each animals will have just one keeper and driver, the *mahout*, throughout its working life.

Below: A herd of African elephants on the march. These animals can migrate hundreds of kilometres to escape from regions of drought, often negotiating formidable obstacles in their path. They have been known to swim across more than one kilometre of open ocean to get from one island to another—they swim with their trunks held above their heads like a snorkel. Steep slopes present few problems for elephants; even large bulls are surefooted.

Sylva/Tierbilder Okapia

Des Bartlett/Bruce Coleman

mature cow

immature cow

immature bull

young

mature bull

Left: A herd of elephants has a well defined structure. The main part of the herd is led by a large cow elephant and is composed only of females, immature animals and calves. Mature bulls live apart from the herd, and the oldest bulls, which are often very bad tempered, are completely solitary.

the elephant, but scientists have shown that the two animals must have had a common ancestor in comparatively recent times. Skeletal features such as the crossing of the bones of the forelimb and the flattening of the bones below the wrist are shared by animals in both groups.

Evolution

Elephants are descended from a small animal, *Moeritherium*, which lived in what is now Egypt about 45 million years ago. This creature was only about 60 cm (2 ft) high and had no trunk. In the course of time its descendants grew larger and developed long trunks and tusks. They colonised all the continents of the world except Australia, Antarctica and much of South America.

The closest and most recent of the elephant's ancestors were the mammoths, *Mammuthus*, and the mastodons, *Mammut*. Mammoths flourished only in cold climates: during periods of glaciation they inhabited central and southern Europe, but during interglacial periods they would retreat northwards with the ice. The largest of these creatures was the mammoth *Mammuthus imperator*, an enormous animal with a shoulder height of around 4.5 m (15 ft), which roamed the southern half of North America.

We know a considerable amount about the woolly mammoth, *Mammuthus primigenius*, which inhabited Europe and Asia and probably died out less than 10,000 years ago in Siberia. Paintings of the animal, made in French caves by its Paleolithic hunters, show a creature outwardly like an elephant but with very long hair, long curved tusks and a huge hump at the back of the neck. These drawings are now known to be remarkably accurate, for the remains of complete animals 'deep frozen' in the Siberian ice have the same features. The excellent state of preservation of many of these frozen mammoths has allowed a detailed study of them—even the contents of their stomachs have been found intact.

The evolution of the hyraxes has been much less varied than that of the elephants. The group probably branched from the same evolutionary line as the elephants in the late Paleocene epoch about 55 million years ago. Fossils found in Africa show that hyraxes have existed in more or less their modern form at least since the Oligocene epoch 35 million years ago.

Hyraxes

Hyraxes are alert, energetic animals, rather fat with pointed muzzles and small rounded ears. They are about the same size as a rabbit and have brown fur with a patch of yellow, white or black fur surrounding a scent gland in the middle of the back. Like elephants they are herbivores and feed on leaves, climbing trees to reach them, and grass. There are eleven species divided between three genera. The members of two genera (*Heterohyrax* and *Procavia*) are called rock hyraxes while the members of the third (*Dendrohyrax*) are known as tree hyraxes. Hyraxes are found only in Africa, Arabia and Syria.

Rock hyraxes live in colonies of from 30 to 60 individuals. They are found in the dry, semi-arid areas bordering deserts and also high up mountains, such as Mount Kenya, in the rain and mist. They are unable to burrow for themselves and make their homes in existing holes beneath the

133

Left: A group of African elephants (cows and young) leaving a water hole. A young elephant is protected not only by its own mother but also by other cows in the herd. Sometimes 'kindergarten' groups composed of several young animals and one or two adult cows will split off from the main body of the herd.

Right: An Indian elephant bathing in a river. Elephants usually bathe several times each day; it helps them to cool off as well as providing an opportunity to drink. They can drink about 50 litres on each occasion, sucking the water up into the trunk and then squirting it into the mouth.

Below: A newly born African elephant is helped to its feet for the first time by its mother. It weighs about 100 kg (220 lb) and is about 1 m (3 ft) tall.

rocks. Normally they are careful to choose holes with small entrances so that they can escape from their chief predator, the leopard. As its name implies the tree hyrax is arboreal—it inhabits the great rain forests of West Africa. It is a solitary animal, an extremely agile climber and lives in hollow trees.

Elephants

Only two species of elephant (order *Proboscidea*) survive today: the Asiatic elephant, *Elephas maximus*, and the African elephant, *Loxodonta africana*. The African elephant is the larger of the two, a mature bull standing 3.4 m (11 ft) or more at the shoulder and carrying tusks between 1.8 and 2.4 m long (6-8 ft). The largest elephant ever recorded was shot in Angola in 1955: it measured 4 m (13 ft) at the shoulder and weighed nearly 11 tonnes.

The Asiatic elephant seldom stands more than three metres (10 ft) at the shoulder and its tusks are usually between 1.2 and 1.5 m long (4-5 ft). While female African elephants have long, if slender tusks, females of the Asiatic species are either tuskless or have very small tusks, known as 'tushes', which do not project beyond the jaw. The females of both species weigh between one and two tonnes less than the males.

In side view the two species look very different. The ears are the most obvious distinguishing feature, being so large in the African species that they cover the whole of the neck and shoulders and reach as low as the breast; the ears of the Asiatic species are relatively small. The back of the African elephant has a marked dip between the fore and hind quarters,

B. Laidmann/Bavaria

Left: The woolly mammoth, *Mammuthus primigenius*, was one of the more recent relatives of the modern elephant. It flourished in the late Ice Age and had a thick coat of long hair to resist the cold. It was hunted by prehistoric man for its flesh and hide, and died out less than 10,000 years ago.

Above: An African elephant dusting itself. This behaviour may help to keep down the number of insects, such as elephant lice, which live in the many folds of the animal's skin. An elephant's skin is quite sensitive and the animal quickly feels uncomfortable if it is carrying too many parasites.

whereas the back of the Asiatic elephant tends to be slightly humped. The trunks of the two species are also slightly different: in the African elephant it is marked by horizontal ridges and ends in two fleshy outgrowths or 'fingers', but in the Asiatic species it is relatively smooth and has only a single outgrowth.

Next to its size the elephant's most distinctive feature is its trunk. This is an extremely sensitive organ both of touch and smell, and is ideally suited to searching for food. It has evolved from the animal's upper lip rather than its nose, although it does enclose the nostrils which open at its tip. An elephant uses its trunk not only to search for food but also to transfer the food to its mouth. It grasps leaves and grass by coiling its trunk around them or by holding them between the fingerlike outgrowths at the tip of the trunk. When drinking, water is sucked into the trunk and then squirted into the mouth. The trunk also acts as an amplifier for a variety of different sounds expressing pleasure, dislike, apprehension and so on. Elephants produce a distinctive trumpeting sound when they are excited and this is actually created in the trunk itself rather than the larynx.

Elephants have to learn how to use their trunks; it is not an instinctive skill. Baby elephants evidently find their trunk a considerable inconvenience—not only do they have no use for it at first (they drink and feed with their mouths) but also it gets in their way and they tend to trip over it. They solve the problem by curling it up or holding it to one side.

Feeding

Elephants are herbivorous animals, feeding mainly on grass and leaves. As with other plant-eating mammals their molar teeth are particularly suited to grinding vegetable material. During its life an elephant develops 24 of these molars, although only one or two on each side of each jaw are ever in use at the same time. While the first group of four are being worn down, four new teeth are growing behind them; these gradually move forward to replace the old teeth, which are eventually shed. Each successive tooth is larger than the last, and when the sixth and largest tooth, which may be 30 cm (one foot) long and weigh 4 kg (9 lb), has passed through each half of each jaw no further teeth can be grown. It is the rate of deterioration of these final teeth that determines an elephant's maximum lifespan, for it cannot survive without them. Normally they will be very worn by the time the animal is 60 and elephants rarely live beyond this age.

Not surprisingly, elephants eat an enormous quantity of food. A fully grown elephant in a zoo will eat about 45 kg (100 lb) of hay every day. Zoo animals are usually females, however, and a large bull might be expected to eat twice as much. An elephant's thirst matches its appetite; the daily water intake for an adult animal is between 130 and 230 litres (30 to 50 gallons).

Social behaviour

Elephants are gregarious animals and live in herds. The herd is composed of a number of distinct family groups, each consisting of a matriarch, her daughters and her grandchildren. Males, except for the younger ones, are not normally tolerated within these groups and they spend much of their time alone or in small groups some way off from the rest of the herd. For communal activities such as bathing or drinking, however, the herd becomes more integrated, while females will temporarily leave the family group for mating. Bull elephants become bad tempered and unpredictable in their old age and they then live entirely alone.

Pregnancy in elephants lasts for between 19 and 22 months, and at birth the calf weighs about 100 kg (220 lb) and is about 85cm (34 in) high. Sometimes other females in the family group assist the birth by removing the foetal membrane and then helping the calf to its feet. After about 20 minutes the baby elephant can stand on its own. The mother will help her clumsy offspring while it is very young by moving obstacles such as fallen trees out of its way or even lifting it over them. All the cows in the family group are attentive to the young; they fondle them, wash them and protect them from danger. The bulls rarely come into contact with the calves and have nothing to do with their upbringing.

When the herd is on the move the elephants travel in single file. The cows usually go first, their calves trotting behind, while the young males form separate contingents. Normal marching speed is about 10 kph (6 mph) but this can be raised in an emergency to a fast shuffle of 25 kph (15 mph) or more. An elephant walks on its toes—its 'knee' joint is really the equivalent of our wrist—and its legs are ideally adapted to support its vast bulk. Elephants can neither trot nor gallop, but they can move through the jungle very quietly.

Left: A group of Cape hyraxes, *Procavia capensis*, resting on a rock. They live in small colonies and one or two animals act as guards while the remainder of the group feed or rest. The main predators are eagles and leopards. Cape hyraxes feed on grass and shrubs during the day, spending the night in holes and crevices among the rocks.

Right: A common tree hyrax, *Dendrohyrax arboreus*, from East Africa. Unlike rock hyraxes, tree hyraxes are nocturnal and solitary animals. They proclaim their territory at night by loud and penetrating calls each consisting of a succession of screams.

Tierbilder Okapia

Jane Burton/Bruce Coleman

135

Rhinos and Tapirs

The largest living land mammal after the elephant is the rare square-lipped rhinoceros of Africa: adult males may stand over 1.8 m (6 ft) at the shoulders and weigh more than three tonnes. Their huge size and strange 'armoured' appearance have long fascinated Europeans: Dürer's well known woodcut of an Indian rhino, executed in 1515, aroused a great deal of interest. The large pointed horn on the rhino's snout has earned the animal an undeserved reputation for fierceness—in fact this timid creature will charge an intruder only if suddenly alarmed.

The rhino's nearest relatives are the tapirs. They have much the same body shape as rhinos, but are considerably smaller, lack the rhino's horn and have a generous coat of hair. Rhinos and tapirs, together with their more fleet-footed cousins the horses and zebras, belong to the order *Perissodactyla*. Members of this group have a number of important features in common: they are all plant-eaters and have noticeably elongated skulls to accommodate the continuous row of broad cheek teeth needed to cope with their diet of grass and leaves. Their feet have an odd number of toes, the weight of the body being carried mainly or entirely by the third toe of each limb, which terminates in a hoof.

Tapirs

The tapirs living today are the survivors of a much larger group, which in its heyday populated much of the globe. Fossil remains from that time (the Miocene epoch, which began about 26 million years ago) show that tapirs have remained almost unchanged for many millions of years: the modern species look very much the same as their ancestors must have done. But they are now found only in Central and South America and Malaya.

Tapirs are solitary jungle animals with short legs, rounded ears, small eyes and a short proboscis or trunk formed by an extension of the upper lip and the nose. They are animals of habit, keeping to well-used paths through the thick undergrowth where they browse on leaves and shoots. Like many forest dwellers they have poor eyesight, but make up for this by good hearing and an acute sense of smell.

Tapirs are particularly fond of water and frequently wallow in river shallows. Bathing probably helps them to get rid of irritating parasites such as ticks and other biting insects. In the wild tapirs often defecate in or near their favourite water hole; possibly this serves as a recognition signal to others of the species. Rhinos behave in the same way. There is only one genus of tapirs, *Tapirus*, with four species of which one is Asiatic and three South American.

The Malayan tapir inhabits the Malay peninsula and the island of Sumatra and is the largest of the four species, having a nose to tail length of around 2.5 m (8 ft). The body markings of the adult animal are unusual: the head, shoulders, limbs

Left: Albrecht Dürer's famous woodcut of an Indian rhinoceros, executed in 1515. Dürer clearly shows the heavy 'armour' of this huge beast which, unlike the African rhinos, normally has one horn only. Dürer cannot have drawn from life, for he also shows a small extra horn on this rhino's back.

Right: A young black rhino, *Diceros bicornis*. The two large horns characteristic of this species are only partly formed. Black rhinos are found only in Africa, where they were once widely distributed. Today their numbers are seriously depleted—a 1967 estimate gave a total of about 12,000, of which almost one-third were in Tanzania.

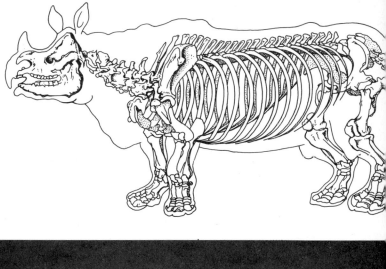

Right: The skeleton of an Indian rhinoceros. The anatomical structure has changed very little in the last million years. The vertebral column acts like a girder balanced on the front legs, and the weight of the body is carried almost entirely by the third toe of each foot, which ends in a kind of hoof.

Below: Black rhinos rarely travel in groups of more than five; when two are found together they will usually be a bull and a female, or a mother and her young. It was once thought that the birds which follow rhinos picked the ticks from their skin, but it now appears they are interested only in the insects stirred up by the animals walking.

Mansell

Giuseppe Mazza

136

and belly are black, while the back and flanks are white. The young, like those of all tapirs, are strikingly marked with a series of horizontal stripes and dots. Both the adult's body pattern and that of the young has a camouflaging effect, breaking up the animal's outline and making it difficult to detect in the changing light and shade of the jungle.

The three South American tapirs all have a uniform brownish coat with slight differences in shade, thickness and texture between the species. The Central American tapir is the largest mammal of the American tropics and also has the distinction of being one of the rarest. The second species, the lowland tapir, is the most common, and inhabits the forests of the northern part of South America. The mountain tapir is the rarest of all and lives in the northern Andes at altitudes between 1,800 and 3,600 m (6,000 to 12,000 ft). It has a thicker coat than its lowland relatives to protect it from exposure and extremes of temperature.

Being solitary and rather shy animals, tapirs avoid areas which are inhabited by man, retreating further into the forest whenever a part of their territory is cleared for cultivation. Consequently, the populations of all tapir species are declining as their jungle habits are eroded, and this trend will only be halted if areas of tropical forest are set aside as sanctuaries, free from development by man.

Rhinos

The rhinos are the only surviving large perissodactyls. Like tapirs they are mainly nocturnal and timid creatures, though they will charge when threatened, especially when protecting their young. The skin is characteristically thick and has little hair. The horns are composed entirely of hair-like growths set above thickenings of the nasal bone and (in two-horned species) the frontal bones. They are not attached to the skull, and may even be torn off in fighting; when this happens they quickly grow again.

The largest rhinoceros is the square-lipped rhino, *Ceratotherium simum*, from Africa. The upper lip is very broad, having evolved to equip the animal for grazing. This rhino is a gregarious creature, living in small herds on the open savannah, and at one time it occupied most of the open grassland south of the Sahara. In the Pleistocene epoch, about one million years ago, it could be found as far north as Algeria and Morocco.

There are two surviving races of square-lipped rhino, separated by more than 1,200 miles (2,000 km). The northern race lives in southwest Sudan, Uganda and Zaire, and it is seriously threatened with extinction—only about 300 individuals still survive in the wild. Early white settlers pursued the animal for its tasty flesh and for its hide, and nowadays it is poached for its horn, which the Chinese value for its undeserved reputation as a powerful aphrodisiac. The southern race, which lives in Natal, South Africa, is more fortunate. Although it is found only in a relatively small region, it has been protected there since 1897 and its future seems assured.

The black rhino, *Diceros bicornis*, is smaller than the 'square lip', standing less than 1.5 m (5 ft) at the shoulder. It is a browser rather than a grazer and has a prehensile upper lip which it uses for reaching and stripping off foliage from

Tierbilder Okapia

Left: Black rhinos mating. During their courtship, the animals sniff at each others' mouths, frequently uttering gurgling noises. The female will often charge the male, butting hard into his flanks. Black rhinos can conceive at any time of year; the gestation period is about 15 months.

Below: Black rhinos are mainly nocturnal, and spend most of the day sleeping in sand or dust-filled hollows. Sometimes seen in mountain forests as high up as 2,100 m (7,000 ft), their normal habitat is the open plain, with mixed vegetation. Their pointed upper lip is used for stripping foliage from shrubs and bushes. They have no incisors or canine teeth.

Jacana

Frank Lake

Frank Lake

Jacana

1

2

3

4

Above: *Dicerorhinus sumatrensis,* the Sumatran rhino, is the smallest and hairiest species. It is now extremely rare and expected to become extinct, for its natural habitat is being destroyed by the timber and rubber industries. Moreover, the Chinese believe powdered rhino horn to be aphrodisiac, and poaching has proved impossible to reduce significantly.

Left: The great Indian rhino, *Rhinoceros unicornis,* is found today only in protected areas. Large folds divide the skin into sections marked by flat bumps which look like rivets. Despite its appearance, the skin is not very thick, and many bulls carry large scars caused by fighting.

Above: Four related species of perissodactyls. Remains of the whoolly rhino (1), now extinct, have been found as far apart as China, Russia and Spain. The Javan rhino, (2) *Rhinocerus sondaicus,* is practically extinct. (3) *Tapirus bairdi,* the Central American tapir. (4) The mountain tapir, *Tapirus pinchaque.*

Left: *Ceratotherium simum,* the square-lipped rhinoceros, is better known as the 'white' rhino—a mistranslation of the Afrikaans work *wijde,* meaning 'wide'. The largest of all rhinos, they reach a height of some 2 m, and weigh up to 3 tonnes. Their horns are attached rather loosely to the skin and are easily torn off, but quickly grow again.

Right: *Tapirus terrestris,* the most common of the tapir species. All young tapirs have horizontal stripes and dots on their coats; these usually take about a year to disappear. The projecting upper lip is adapted for tearing off leaves and shoots from trees and bushes.

138

Giuseppe Mazza

Left: The Malayan tapir, *tapirus indicus*, is easily identified by its distinctive markings. These are ideal for camouflage in the changing patterns of light and shade of its natural forest habitat. They break up the outlines of the body so that, lying down in the daytime, the tapir looks just like a pile of stones.

Below: Past and present distribution of tapirs and rhinos. The South American lowland tapir and the African black rhino are the only species with a good chance of survival, although both their populations have been seriously reduced in recent years. Rhinos are hunted for their meat and their horns, which are prized for their supposed medicinal properties. The animal is rarely found today outside protected areas. Tapirs live mainly in forested regions and their habitats are being progressively destroyed by timber companies and rubber plantations. They are hunted for meat and for their skins, which can be tanned and cut into long straps for reins and whips. They are often killed as pests.

Bruce Coleman

shrubs and bushes. It was once widely distributed in Africa, from Cape Province to eastern Africa and as far north as the Sudan, but only scattered populations remain today. Although not classed as endangered its status is vulnerable.

The black rhino spends much of its life within a well defined home range which may vary from 8 to 50 sq km (3 to 20 sq miles) in area and changes according to the seasons and consequent food supply. When they meet their neighbours in overlapping parts of their ranges black rhinos are not usually aggressive, but determined trespassing is not tolerated and a large intruder may be suddenly charged.

The largest of the Asiatic rhinos is the great Indian rhino, *Rhinoceros unicornis*, which can approach the size of a square-lipped rhino. Unlike its African relatives it has only a single horn. The upper lip is prehensile and the lower jaw contains a large pair of incisor teeth which have developed into tusks and are used with great effect for self-defence.

The Indian rhino once inhabited a wide tract of country in northern India and Nepal, from the foothills of the Hindu Kush to the Burmese border, but today less than 1,000 individuals remain in eight reserves in India and Nepal. This impressive animal lives a slow and quiet existence in secluded swampy areas where there is an abundance of tall grass and reeds. Its diet includes a large number of food plants, including many agricultural crops.

The Javan rhinoceros, *Rhinoceros sondaicus*, is the rarest of all rhinos. It looks like a smaller version of the Indian rhino, but the skin folds are slightly different and the male's horn is shorter—it is absent altogether in females. The Javan rhino's favourite food has been reported to be the peculiar 'tepus' plant, one of the ginger family which throws up 5.5 m (18 ft) broad-leaved spikes but carries its red flowers at or below ground level. The horn trade has wiped out all but a few of these creatures and it seems likely that the population of Javan rhinos is now too small for the species to survive, and it will probably soon be extinct.

The smallest and hairiest rhino is the Sumatran rhino, *Dicerorhinus sumatrensis*. Small isolated populations occur in widely separated areas of Asia from Burma southeast through Thailand to Sumatra and Borneo. It has two horns—the front one reaches a length of up to a foot (30 cm) while the back one is usually no more than a slight hump.

Sumatran rhinos favour forested hill country and are extremely agile: they can climb up steep mountain slopes with no apparent difficulty. They browse on twigs and leaves, invariably feeding in virgin forest or very old regenerated jungle. Like the Javan rhino they are very rare and the principal cause of their decline has been over-hunting. In 1972 a single rhino carcass was worth more than 2,000 US dollars, many times the annual earnings of most local farmers, so it is hardly surprising that the animals are so ruthlessly hunted.

Responsibility for the survival of both rhinos and tapirs rests with man. Conservation areas, such as the famous Chitwan National Park in Nepal (where there is now a good stable population of Indian rhinos), are likely to play an increasingly important role as the animals' natural habitats are destroyed.

SENT DISTRIBUTION OF
PIRS

PAST AND PRESENT DISTRIBUTION OF
RHINOS

AFRICA

INDIA

SOUTH-EAST ASIA

SOUTH AMERICA

BORNEO

SUMATRA

JAVA

MALAYA

SUMATRA

○ Present populations

Lowland Tapir
Mountain Tapir
Central American Tapir
Malayan Tapir

Javan Rhino
Sumatran Rhino
Great Indian Rhino
African Rhino

Bruce Coleman

Hippos, Pigs and Peccaries

The most prolific large mammals living today are the members of the order *Artiodactyla*. These are hoofed animals with an even number of toes on each foot and they rely on speedy running or sheer bulk as a defence against predators. The group includes the camels, deer, antelopes, cattle, goats and sheep, as well as pigs, peccaries and hippopotamuses. One of the key factors in their success is the ability to make efficient use of the most readily available of all food sources—plants.

All artiodactyls have highly developed digestive systems which can break down cellulose, the main structural material of plants, and most have evolved the habit of ruminating, or chewing the cud, which further improves the digestion process. Pigs, peccaries and hippopotamuses, however, are non-ruminants and they have changed relatively little since the first artiodactyls appeared about 45 million years ago.

Pigs

The artiodactyls' remote ancestors were not plant-eaters, but were related to the ancestors of the modern carnivorous mammals. With this ancestry it is not surprising that the surviving members of the pig family are by no means purely herbivorous. Their molar and premolar teeth have low, rounded cusps not unlike those of other omnivorous mammals, such as man, and certainly pigs have omnivorous tendencies, feeding on such things as small animals, roots and fruit. Most omnivorous mammals, such as brown rats or bears, are basically either herbivores or carnivores but are simply not very fussy about what they eat. Pigs, however, like our own order, the primates, seem to have been omnivorous throughout their history.

For hoofed animals, pigs have relatively short legs. They have four toes on each foot, the thumb and big toe being absent as is always the case in artiodactyls. The two middle toes are the largest and usually carry all the weight, the hoofs on the outside toes coming into use only on marshy ground or very uneven surfaces. Pigs are not very fleet-footed: the wart hog, for example, has a maximum speed of about 18 kph (11 mph). Because they are not very tall, however, pigs are able to run beneath branches, and their heavy bodies are ideal for crashing through thick undergrowth. This is more important to them than sheer speed, for pigs are typically inhabitants of forests and bush. They are also good swimmers.

One rather unusual feature of the pig family is the way in which they keep their bodies warm. Almost all land mammals are kept warm by their hair, the skin being only loosely joined to the body, rather than bound to it by layers of fatty tissue. But examination of a rasher of bacon reveals that immediately beneath a pig's skin there is a great deal of fat, an excellent insulator but more commonly found in aquatic mammals such as seals and whales. Apart from pigs the only other land mammals primarily insulated

Bruce Coleman

Above: A female wart hog, *Phacochoerus aethiopicus*, with her young. The wart hog inhabits the savannahs and bush country of Africa south of the Sahara. Unlike most members of the pig family, wart hogs are only active during the day; at night they sleep in dens which are usually the abandoned homes of other animals such as aardvarks. The long curved canine teeth are formidable weapons and can inflict very severe injuries on predators such as lions and leopards.

Right: A wild boar, *Sus scrofa*, in a West German forest. In cultivated areas the wild boar can cause considerable damage to crops by its continual rooting in the ground, but in forests it assists growth by feeding on tree parasites such as sawfly larvae and by loosening the soil.

Below: Two African bush pigs, *Potamochoerus porcus*. Like most pigs, these creatures eat a wide variety of both animal and plant food. In South Africa they sometimes damage peanut and fruit crops.

ZEFA

Keith Dowson/Natural Science Photos

Above: The breeding capacity of the pig was undoubtedly one of the factors which led to its domestication. A Danish sow is on record as having given birth to as many as 34 young in a single litter, the largest number for any mammal. In the wild, where infant mortality is high, large litters are a great advantage.

Above: In France the keen sense of smell of a trained domestic pig enables it to sniff out truffles. All domestic pigs are descended from wild boars.

Below: The babirusa, *Babyrousa babyrussa*, is a strange-looking pig from the Celebes Islands of South-East Asia. In males the canine teeth of both the upper and lower jaws are particularly long and curved. The survival of the species is threatened by the clearing of forested areas for cultivation.

Above: Although these collared peccaries, *Tayassu tajacu*, from Texas look like the wild pigs of Europe, Asia and Africa, they are only distant relations.

by subcutaneous fat are human beings. In each case the reason is obscure.

Wild pigs usually feed by rooting in the ground and they have a keen sense of smell. The domestic pigs in France which are trained to smell out truffles (rare fungi considered a delicacy since classical times), which grow beneath the ground, behave in a very natural way for members of the pig family. The only thing that they have to be taught to do is to indicate the presence of truffles to their human trainers, rather than digging them up and eating them on their own account.

Wild pigs root in the ground for fungi, roots, bulbs, tubers and earthworms, and also eat leaves, fruits and nuts, and sometimes small vertebrates and carrion. They are gregarious animals, living in herds of up to 50, although male wart hogs are often observed on their own. When not feeding or resting, they often wallow in mud to keep their skins in good condition. Contrary to popular belief, wild pigs (and properly kept domestic ones) are clean in their habits, and not notably greedy.

Wild boars

There are eight living species in the pig family, and by far the most widely distributed of these is the wild boar, *Sus scrofa*. Before man reduced its range the wild boar was found in most parts of Europe; it only became extinct in Britain in the early 17th century. It still inhabits parts of central Europe as well as North Africa and Asia, from its western border to Java, Sumatra, Formosa and Japan. A male wild boar may weigh as much as 200 kg (440 lb) and, although flight is its normal defence, it can be a fierce adversary. Hunting wild boar with lances, as was once the custom in India, was by no means a one-sided sport. A wounded or cornered wild boar uses its teeth in self-defence, and they are formidable weapons. The constantly growing tusks, which are canine teeth, are razor sharp, and the molar and premolar teeth have great biting power. A bite from a wild boar is said to be worse than a bite from a lion.

Wild boars are prolific breeders, and the female may have up to 12 young in a litter. They are born after a pregnancy of about 115 days and, in contrast to the brindled brown appearance of the adults, have boldly striped markings which provide good camouflage in dappled shade. No doubt it was the wild boar's breeding capacity combined with its ability to thrive on almost anything edible that caused man to domesticate it.

The domestic pig is so similar to the wild boar from which it was derived that it is regarded as belonging to the same

hippopotamus

Left: A hippopotamus, *Hippopotamus amphibius*, wallowing in mud. These creatures spend much of their time lying on the muddy shores of lakes and rivers or standing almost entirely submerged in the water. In this way the animal's legs are spared the effort of supporting the enormous body weight (it is not uncommon for a hippo to weigh as much as three tonnes).

Right: A pygmy hippopotamus, *Choeropsis liberiensis*. As its name suggests, it is a much smaller animal than its more abundant relative. Being very shy, the pygmy hippo is difficult to study in its swampy forest homeland and little is known about its way of life in the wild.

Below: A herd of hippos in the Virunga National Park, Zaire. Within the herd mother and child groups live slightly apart from the other animals, and young hippos usually stick very close to their mothers. Old aggressive males live very much on their own.

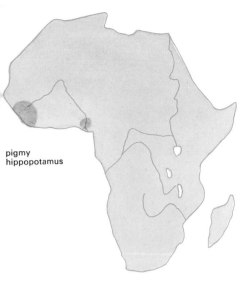

pigmy
hippopotamus

Geoffrey Kinnis/Natural Science Photos

Above left and above: Maps to show the distribution of the hippopotamus and the pygmy hippopotamus (brown areas). Although pygmy hippos inhabit only small areas and are regarded as rare, it may be that they were never very common. Hippos were found in Egypt up to the early 19th century.

Right: A hippo's lower canine teeth grow throughout the animal's life, to become formidable tusks. A male animal threatens its rivals by opening its mouth to display these enormous teeth. Fights between males are not uncommon and sometimes one of the combatants is killed by his opponent.

species, *Sus scrofa*. However, selective breeding by man has resulted in greater efficiency in producing meat. The heaviest domestic pig can weigh twice as much as a wild boar, a large part of this increase being in the form of fat, and domestic sows have even larger litters than their wild cousins.

Closely related to the wild boar and very similar in appearance, are three Asian species which are much less widely distributed. These are the rare pygmy hog, *Sus salvanius*, of southern Asia, the Javan pig, *Sus verrucosus*, of Java, Celebes, and the Philippines, and the Bornean pig, *Sus barbatus*, of Borneo and the Philippines.

Another species from the same part of the world, the babirusa, *Babyrousa babyrussa*, of Celebes and neighbouring small islands is remarkable for the development of the canine tusks of the males. In addition to the lower tusks which emerge from the side of the mouth and curve upwards, the upper tusks protrude from the top of the snout and curve upwards and backwards. These tusks are too long to be kept sharp by wear and have no apparent function except as distinguishing characteristics of males. The native legend that babirusas sleep hanging from branches hooked on by means of their tusks is certainly untrue.

The remaining species of wild pigs live in Africa. The most common is the wart hog, *Phacochoerus aethiopicus*, which owes its popular name to thickenings of the skin in front of the eyes of males. Unlike most other pigs, wart hogs are mainly active by day, and they live in grasslands as well as the open forests of Africa south of the Sahara. The giant forest hog, *Hylochoerus meinertzhageni*, inhabits only thick equatorial forests. This is the only kind of pig with glands on the face, immediately in front of the eye. These glands are probably scent glands, used in signalling. The bush pig, or water hog, *Potamochoerus porcus*, usually lives in long grass of southern Africa and Madagascar. It is the hairiest of the pigs, has extremely sharp canine teeth and long ear tufts.

Peccaries

Wild pigs have never existed in America. Here their place is taken by the peccaries, which have evolved from the same ancestors as the pigs but have a long history of their own; they have evolved their pig-like characteristics quite separately as an adaptation to much the same way of life. They are therefore placed in a different family. They look very much like small, rather densely-haired pigs but have shorter tusks, those of the upper jaw growing downwards rather than upwards or outwards.

There are two species. The collared peccary, *Tayassu tajacu*, is distinguished by a band of lighter hair round the neck, and inhabits semi-deserts and dry woodlands from Texas to Patagonia, while the white-lipped peccary, *Tayassu pecari*, lives in rain forests from southern Mexico to Paraguay. Peccaries have scent-glands producing a strong musky odour on their backs. They breed less prolifically than pigs, usually only having two young at a time, and rarely more than four.

Hippopotamuses

Although fossil hippopotamuses occur in Europe, parts of Asia including Sri Lanka (Ceylon) and Madagascar, the surviving members of the family are found only in Africa. In many ways they are like large pigs, but in order to support their weight on soft ground they have four large toes on each foot and, because of the difference in their feeding habits their muzzles are not at all like pigs' snouts. Both their incisor and canine teeth grow continuously throughout life, the incisors pointing forwards and being rounded in section, while the canines, especially the lower canines, form formidable, sharp tusks. They have three-chambered stomachs, but do not chew the cud.

The common hippopotamus, *Hippopotamus amphibius*, can weigh over four tonnes, and is therefore one of the heaviest of all land animals. However, common hippos are amphibious, spending much of their time in the water where they are almost weightless, and perhaps

should be judged among such aquatic mammals as the whales: in this company they are but small fry

The position of the eyes, ears and slit-like, closeable nostrils on the upper surface of a hippo's head is typical of the way these organs are placed in amphibious animals, permitting breathing, seeing and hearing when the animal is almost completely submerged. Hippos spend much of the day in rivers and lakes, diving for as long as ten minutes at a time in search of the water plants on which they feed. When they surface they expel the air from their lungs with a snort that can be heard many hundreds of metres away. They have huge appetites and in order to satisfy them they also feed for part of the night, coming ashore to graze. Although hippos are normally placid animals, they will sometimes attack humans; old hippos are notoriously bad tempered and aggressive. Attacks usually occur when the animals are grazing on land and suddenly find their retreat to the water cut off.

Hippos live in herds of up to 40 animals. Large male hippos defend territories, scent-marking by means of their faeces, which are scattered by vigorous wagging of the short brush-like tail, in order to warn rivals to keep clear. When necessary they fight, using their bulk and their tusks. Females have only one young at a time, giving birth in the water after a pregnancy of up to 240 days. Young hippos weigh about 40 kg (90 lb) at birth, and can swim before they can walk. They are mature at about 3 years, and may live to be 40 or 50.

The pygmy hippopotamus, *Choeropsis liberiensis*, is less aquatic in its habits, and is found only in the dense forests and swamps of Ivory Coast, Liberia and Sierra Leone in West Africa. Apart from having a rounder head and circular nostrils, it looks very much like a smaller version of the common hippo, but is no bigger than a large pig, weighing up to 240 kg (540 lb). Pygmy hippos seem to live singly or in pairs, but they are shy and partly nocturnal in their habits and difficult to study in the wild.

Giraffe and Okapi

Gawky and ungainly though it may appear, the giraffe has survived where many members of its family have not. It has only a single living relation, the okapi, an inhabitant of the impenetrable equatorial forests of Africa so secretive that it was unknown until early this century. Both animals belong to the family *Giraffidae*, which is part of the great mammalian order *Artiodactyla*. They are cud-chewing, hoofed animals found only in the continent of Africa, although they once lived in eastern Europe and many parts of Asia.

Fossil remains of the giraffe have been found in Greece, southern Russia, Asia Minor, India and China, and it is thought that the ancestors of the modern species entered Africa about one million years ago. In more recent times giraffes were brought to Europe in about 46 BC by Julius Caesar to feature as an attraction in the Roman arenas. The giraffe is by far the tallest mammal, reaching a height of almost six metres (20 ft).

Like other ruminants (animals that chew the cud), giraffes and okapis feed exclusively on plants, which they are able to digest very efficiently. They have large back teeth for grinding up their plant diet, but no teeth in the front of the upper jaw. A giraffe's tongue is prehensile and very long (often 45 cm, 18 in); it is used to draw leaves and twigs into the mouth where they are cut off by sharply twisting them over the lower front teeth (incisors).

Giraffes

The most obvious distinguishing feature of the giraffe is its enormously long neck and limbs, clearly an advantage to an animal which browses on the foliage of trees. This arrangement does, however, present some physiological problems. In particular, a high blood pressure is needed to maintain the flow of blood to the head, and the creature has to have a special system of blood channels to prevent a brain haemorrhage when it lowers its head the six metres (20 ft) or so down to the ground to graze or drink. These channels are controlled by reflex muscles and they automatically 'short circuit' the blood flow to stop any rush of blood to the head.

Surprisingly, the neck contains no more bones than that of most other mammals: the same seven cervical vertebrae (bones of the spine) are present in both man and the giraffe, but in the latter they are enormously long. Similarly, the leg bones are basically the same as in man but again they are very long. The forelegs are longer than the hind legs and the shoulder is deep, so accounting for the downward slope of the giraffe's back. All four limbs end in two hoofed toes, each forefoot being about 30cm (one foot) across.

The giraffe's back legs are its chief defence against predators. Few carnivores will take on anything so large as a giraffe, but lions do occasionally attack them if other game is scarce. A single blow from the hind leg of a giraffe is powerful enough to kill a lion and encounters between the

Left: This short-necked giraffe, *Sivatherium*, became extinct in the Pleistocene epoch. It was a large, sturdy animal and its flattened horns were much larger than those of its modern relatives. Although they now live only in Africa, giraffes originated in Asia and Europe. This creature inhabited southern Asia.

Above: Giraffes feed on the leaves and twigs of trees such as acacia and mimosa. They have long, prehensile tongues to tear the foliage from the branches.

Left and above: The giraffe's enormous height is a distinct disadvantage when it comes to drinking. It must either splay its front legs wide apart (left) or bend them in a rather ungainly way (above) to reach the water. Giraffes are very vulnerable to attacks from predators when drinking.

Frank Lane

Frank Lane

Above: A giraffe gallops away from danger in the Kenyan bush. Because it is such a large animal it cannot keep up this pace for long, but its chief predators, lions, usually give up the chase early if they do not succeed right away. Giraffes pursued for long distances have been known to collapse and die of heart failure.

Above and above right: Male giraffes, using their heads and necks as clubs, fight for the possession of females. Each animal tries to swing its head against the opponent's neck or shoulders. Although these contests are normally fairly harmless, they sometimes result in serious injuries and even death.

Hans Reinhard/Bruce Coleman

Left: The giraffe, *Giraffa camelopardalis*, has keen eyesight, unlike its relation the okapi. Also, because it is so tall it has an excellent field of view and these two factors make it a difficult animal for a lion to stalk successfully. Even by night giraffes are watchful, rarely lying down or sleeping.

Giraffes may have anything between two and five 'horns'. The main horns are situated above the eyes and are crowned with tufts of hair. Any additional horns are simply bony protuberances. The animals shown here have three (above) and five (below) horns.

two animals quite often end in the death of the hunter rather than the hunted. Although adult giraffes do not normally attack lions, they will do so if young animals in the herd are threatened.

Giraffes have at least two short 'horns' located above the eyes. These are bony protuberances covered with hairy skin and structurally they resemble deer's antlers more than the horns of antelopes or cattle. Unlike a deer's antlers, however, which are shed and replaced each year, a giraffe's horn is permanent. Moreover the bony part of the horn develops separately from the skull at first but becomes joined to it as the animal grows older. Some giraffes possess four horns and occasionally, in certain northern races, there is a central swelling between the eyes which is almost as long as the horns. In southern races this swelling is so small as to be hardly noticeable.

The giraffe's pale, buff coloured coat is covered to a greater or lesser extent with reddish brown spots that range from regular geometric designs to irregular, blotchy shapes. Various methods of classifying giraffes into species, subspecies and even sub-subspecies have been devised but none is very satisfactory because the animals vary so much; giraffes with different colours and patterns can sometimes be observed even within a single herd. Nowadays a single species is normally recognized, *Giraffa camelopardalis*, with many different forms. Broadly these fall into two types—the reticulated giraffes with clear geometric markings, and the blotched giraffes with irregular or leaf-shaped markings—but there are many intermediate forms.

In the equatorial regions of Africa, where most reticulated giraffes live, there are sharp contrasts between the bright sunlight and deep shadows, so the distinct light and dark markings of the animals' coat blend in well with its natural background. Blotched giraffes are normally larger than the reticulated variety and they have a wider range extending over most of Africa south of

145

the Sahara. Their markings are more suited to the softer light and less well defined shadows of non-equatorial regions.

The giraffe lives in open country; dry bush regions with scattered acacia and mimosa trees are favourite haunts. It never moves to the forest since its long legs and neck would make movement through the dense trees and creepers difficult, and wet forest swamps would be deadly traps for its long legs.

Because trees for forage are often scattered over a wide area, giraffes are nomadic. They travel in herds of 20 to 30 animals, the herds usually being composed of an old bull, females and calves. Younger bulls usually keep a small distance apart from the rest of the herd, but when sufficiently mature they may challenge for the leadership of the herd. Giraffes can trot, run or gallop and when in full flight the legs on each side of the body move together though not quite simultaneously. When galloping they can reach a speed of about 50 kph (30 mph).

Mating occurs at any time of the year, and there is considerable competition between the bulls for the females. The bulls fight each other by swinging their heads against the neck and shoulders of their opponent. Since a giraffe's head weighs something like 45 kg (100 lb) and the neck is about two metres (6 ft 6 in) long the blows are severe and can quite easily cause a broken or dislocated neck. Usually, however, these fights do not end in death, merely the exhaustion of one or both animals.

The young are born about 14 months after mating and they are on their feet within 20 minutes of birth. Normally only a single young is produced at one time but occasionally twins are born. The lifespan of the giraffe may be as much as 30 years in captivity, but is probably considerably less than this in the wild.

As with many other animal species, man is the most dangerous enemy of the giraffe. The natives of Africa and the early European settlers prized the giraffe for its palatable flesh and also for its hide which is as much as 2.5 cm (one inch) thick and was used to make the long reins needed for teams of six or eight horses. As a result of indiscriminate killing the numbers were severely reduced and the giraffe has disappeared from large areas of northern, western and southern Africa. It is still fairly numerous in East Africa where it is a protected species, but populations elsewhere are small.

Okapis

The only living relative of the giraffe is the okapi, *Okapia johnstoni*. It is a rare mammal, native to the dense tropical forests of central equatorial Africa, and it has changed little since, like the giraffe, it migrated to Africa from Europe and Asia in prehistoric times. The okapi rarely emerges from its forest home and has hardly ever been seen in the wild.

When European explorers like Henry Stanley penetrated central Africa at the end of the nineteenth century they found that the pygmies of the region were not surprised at the sight of their horses and claimed that similar animals were to be found in the local forests. At first little attention was paid to these reports but when Sir Harry Johnston, governor of Uganda, obtained a skin and several skulls in 1901 the existence of a new species was confirmed. Zoologists were

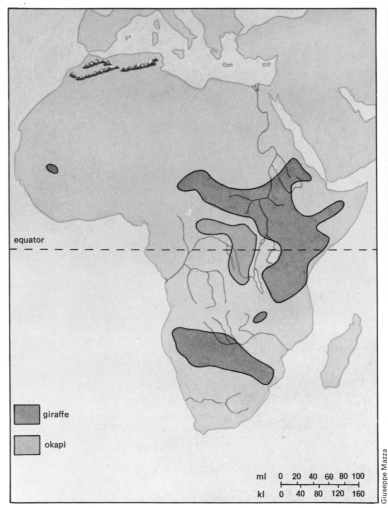

giraffe

okapi

| ml | 0 | 20 | 40 | 60 | 80 | 100 |
| kl | 0 | 40 | 80 | 120 | 160 | |

Giuseppe Mazza

Above: A map showing the distribution of giraffes and okapis in the wild. Giraffes were once much more wide-ranging than they are today, particularly in western Africa. Even within their present ranges there are large areas where the animals have disappeared. Little is known of the former range of the okapi.

Below: The Masai giraffe with its leaf-shaped body markings is a typical blotched giraffe. Young giraffes are about 2 m (7 ft) tall at birth and they are on their feet within 20 minutes. The young animal suckles for about six months and during this time it never strays far from its mother.

Right: A water hole in Africa attracts all sorts of animals from the surrounding area, both predators and their prey. Because giraffes are so vulnerable when drinking, one of the older members of the herd keeps watch while the remaining animals quench their thirst and feed on leaves.

Giuseppe Mazza

ZEFA

Left: A reticulated giraffe has sharply outlined geometrical markings so that it blends in with its background when seen from a distance.

Below: A white giraffe. Unusual colours and markings do sometimes occur, but albinos, with pure white coats and pink eyes, are rare.

Above: The okapi, *Okapia johnstoni*, which lives in the equatorial forests of central Africa has rarely been seen in the wild, but it is not uncommon in zoos. Although the first okapis to reach Europe were infested with worms and soon died, a healthy, breeding zoo population has now been established.

immediately struck by the resemblance between the new species and the extinct short-necked giraffe, *Helladotherium*, which inhabited Europe and Asia over ten million years ago.

It was surprising that such a large animal could have remained undiscovered for so long, and expeditions were soon mounted to capture an okapi alive. Although several animals were caught in the early 1900s they soon died and it was not until 1928 that one reached a European zoo (Antwerp) and survived there. Today okapis flourish in various zoos throughout the world, and something like half the zoo population has been bred in captivity.

The most obvious points of resemblance between the okapi and its relative the giraffe are the long front legs and the shape of the head. Like the giraffe, the okapi has bony 'horns' above the eyes. These grow independently of the skull but become joined to it as the animal matures. The horns, however, are present only in male animals. An adult okapi stands about 1.8 metres (6 ft) high. Its coat is a rich plum colour over most of the body but the hindquarters and the upper parts of all four limbs are horizontally striped with black and white. The lower parts of the legs, from hock to hoof, are white.

Whereas the giraffe lives in herds, the okapi lives in small family groups of one male and one or two females with their calves: life in the dense tropical forests would be difficult for larger groups of animals. Okapis have rather poor eyesight but they compensate for this by having keen senses of hearing and smell which in fact are much more useful in the jungle where vision is in any case limited. Because okapis are so shy and their habitat so inaccessible it is difficult to estimate their population with any accuracy, and until they have been studied more closely in the wild it will be impossible to say whether or not they are an endangered species. Certainly any attempt to clear their jungle homes for cultivation would threaten their survival.

Natural Science Photos

Snakes and Lizards

For about 150 million years reptiles were the dominant form of life on earth. The best known prehistoric reptiles are the often enormous dinosaurs of the Jurassic and Cretaceous periods. The plant-eating *Brontosaurus*, for example, was the largest land animal that ever lived, reaching a length of 18 m (60 ft) and a weight of 20 tonnes. Preying on the many plant-eating species were a variety of carnivorous dinosaurs, the most ferocious being *Tyrannosaurus rex* which walked on its two hind legs, reached a height of about 5 m (17 ft) and had almost 1,000 teeth.

About 65 million years ago, at the end of the Cretaceous period, a profound change both on land and in the sea drastically reduced the number of reptiles, and dinosaurs became extinct. Just what these sudden changes were is not known. Possibly some widespread climatic change affected the plant life on which all dinosaurs ultimately depended for their survival. Today, of the many groups of reptiles which flourished in prehistoric times only four remain: the turtles and tortoises, *Chelonia*, the crocodiles and alligators, *Crocodilia*, the beak-nosed reptiles, *Rhynchocephalia*, of which only one species survives, and the snakes and lizards, *Squamata*.

Snakes

The oldest fossil snakes date from about 65 million years ago. They resembled modern boas and pythons in being stout-bodied and large. Undoubtedly the loss of the limbs, elongation of the body and joined eyelids were originally adaptations to a burrowing lifestyle, though the increase in size probably represents a subsequent adaptation to life above the ground, feeding on the increasing numbers of rodents which developed during the Eocene period. The smaller predecessors of these snakes might not be expected to leave a significant fossil record.

Adapting to a life above ground must have raised enormous problems of locomotion for a legless animal, but it was a problem the snakes overcame well. There are three important methods of movement. The main method is by waves of muscular contraction which produce a side to side undulation from head to tail. In water, their movement is almost identical to that of a fish.

On land, snakes can also move by using ventral (underneath) plates which extend from the throat to the junction of the tail. These overlapping plates cover much of the body and are attached to pairs of ribs by muscles. Since the near edges are free, the muscles can move the plates forwards and backwards and to some extent up and down. Thus, a plate may be lifted, moved forward, lowered and moved backwards. Waves of movement of such plates pass along the body from front to rear, producing a slow crawl which enables snakes to climb steep gradients or squeeze through narrow apertures. For example, the corn snake, *Elaphe guttata*, which can climb vertically up the trunks of trees, uses this method.

Anthony Bannister/NHPA

Left: A royal or ball python, *Python regius*, constricting a mouse. Pythons do not have poison glands; they kill their prey by preventing expansion of the lungs or even the heart. They are found in India and parts of south-east Asia. This is one of the smaller members of the group, reaching a maximum length of about two metres (six feet). The record length for any python is 10 m (32ft).

Right: A king cobra, *Ophiophagus hannah*, rears up and spreads its hood in a threat display. King cobras are the largest poisonous snakes in the world, reaching lengths of up to five metres (16 ft). Their venom is extremely toxic. They feed mainly on other snakes, including poisonous ones.

Below and below left: The skull of an African spitting cobra, *Naja nigricollis*, and diagrams to show how a snake opens its mouth to swallow very large prey. The spitting cobra is one of ten African cobras. They are not as venomous as their Indian cousins.

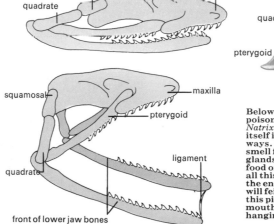

Supratemporal — quadrate — nasal

squamosal — maxilla — pterygoid — quadrate — front of lower jaw bones joined only by ligament — ligament

squamosal — quadrate — pterygoid — parietal — maxilla — fang — dentary

Below: The non-poisonous grass snake, *Natrix natrix*, defends itself in a number of ways. It will emit a foul smell from special stink glands, regurgitate food or defecate. If all this fails to deter the enemy, the snake will feign dead, as in this picture, with its mouth open and tongue hanging out.

Right: Although they look like snakes and move in the same way, slow worms, *Anguis fragilis*, are really legless lizards. Rather than lay eggs, slow worms give birth to live young and this enables them to survive in colder climates than egg-laying reptiles. They are common in most parts of Europe.

Anthony Bannister/NHPA

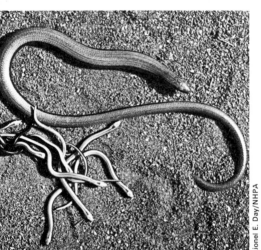

Lionel E. Day/NHPA

Michael Morcombe/NHPA

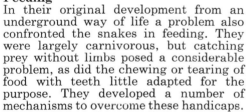

Adrian Warren/Ardea

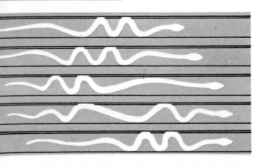

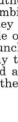

Another method of movement is known as 'side-winding'. This may be used for moving rapidly on very loose soil or in desert conditions. In sidewinding a grip is maintained with a sideways loop. The head is arched forwards so that the front part of the body does not touch the ground. It is then put down in a sideways loop and the back of the body is drawn up. Perhaps the most famous snake to move in this way is the American rattlesnake, or side-winder, *Crotalus cerastes*.

These varied methods of movement have allowed snakes to colonise a wide range of habitats and thus contributed to their success and variety. Burrowing snakes such as the desert leaf-nosed snakes, *Phyllorhynchus*, have large shields on their snouts, and some also have a spine or flat shield on the tail to act as a brace when burrowing. Examples of these include the American mud snakes, *Farancia*, and the shield-tailed snakes of southern India, *Uropeltidae*. Some tree-climbing snakes are almost able to glide. They hold the body rigid and the underside of the body slightly concave as they launch themselves from a tree. In this way they glide from one tree to another and are also able to slow down any fall to the ground.

Feeding

In their original development from an underground way of life a problem also confronted the snakes in feeding. They were largely carnivorous, but catching prey without limbs posed a considerable problem, as did the chewing or tearing of food with teeth little adapted for the purpose. They developed a number of mechanisms to overcome these handicaps.

Because they have no limbs, snakes do not require a shoulder girdle or pelvis and this made it possible for them to develop a means of swallowing prey larger than their own body diameter. To allow the victim's body to pass through the mouth, a flexible joint was developed in the middle of each lower jaw, and the brain became completely encased in bone to protect it during swallowing. Snakes have well developed ribs which can enlarge to accommodate the swallowed prey.

To swallow, the teeth take a good grip on the prey. The outer rows of upper teeth are alternately moved forwards and outwards and pulled back again into position, in such a way that the curved teeth drag the prey back to the throat. The lower teeth are only used to hold the prey while the upper teeth are freed and refastened but otherwise play no part in the swallowing. As the bulk of the prey enters the throat, the jaws spread out and the neck muscles start to push the prey onwards to the stomach. Once past the head, spine movements help in further swallowing. The process can be slow: it often takes 30 minutes or more to swallow large prey.

Such a slow swallowing process requires the prey to be at least subdued, if not dead. The larger snakes such as boas,

Boinae, or pythons, *Pythoninae*, strike at their prey, seizing it in their jaws and then throwing one or more coils around the prey killing it by constriction.

Smaller snakes developed an even more effective way of subduing prey—poison. The evolution of this means of killing prey occurred by modification of some salivary glands into venom glands and the development of fangs. The group with the most specialized fangs include the vipers and the pit vipers, where the fang is situated well forward in the upper jaw. It is not rigid as in other snakes but can be swivelled to lie flat in the mouth when not in use. The venom is forced through an enclosed duct running through the tooth rather than just trickling down a groove in the fang as in some other snakes. This arrangement, like a hypodermic needle, allows the prey to be killed quickly with a minimum amount of venom, thus reducing the risk to the snake.

Among the most venomous snakes in the world are the taipan, *Oxyuranus scutulatus*, of Australia and the banded krait, *Bungarus fasciatus*, from south-east Asia. The latter, however, is virtually harmless for much of the time because it very rarely, if ever, bites during the day, even if severely provoked.

Reproduction

In the breeding season many snakes go through a form of rivalry and courtship. They do not stake out territory, but some species such as vipers indulge in protracted combat in which their heads rear up and each snake tries to push over his rival. The male snake trails a female by picking up the scent left by secretions of her skin. He does this by using not only his nose but also a special organ, called Jacobson's organ, which opens into the mouth and is situated above it. The Jacobson's organ probably acts as a sensor for substances picked up by the snake's tongue as it flicks in and out. Certainly it is common during courtship for the male to rub his chin along the female's back while playing his tongue in and out.

For the act of coitus the two snakes lie extended side by side, and the process frequently lasts for several hours. Eggs are usually deposited in clutches, under stones or in rotting vegetation. Female pythons incubate their eggs in the coils of their bodies. Only a few snakes such as the sea snakes, *Hydrophiinae*, give birth to live young like mammals.

Many snakes hibernate in groups; there are, for example, numerous accounts of rattlesnake dens in the US. How long they live varies greatly from one species to another; large pythons probably live the longest and some have been recorded as living for more than 25 years.

Lizards

The lizards are closely related to the snakes, but there are obvious differences. Snakes have neither limbs nor eardrums, their eyes are covered by a transparent film and a single row of wide scales run along the belly. The 'typical' lizards on the other hand, have four limbs, moveable eyelids, a visible eardrum and many scales

Above and below: A European chameleon, *Chamaeleo chamaeleon*, and a brightly coloured South African species. Chameleons clamber about among the branches of trees, anchoring themselves with their long prehensile tails. They feed mainly on insects which they catch with their long sticky tongues.

Bottom: Diagrams to show how a lizard like a chameleon alters the colour of its skin. Impulses from the spinal cord are transmitted through nerve fibres to melanophore cells which then disperse a black pigment. Thus the colour observed through the outermost layer of the skin (epidermis) darkens.

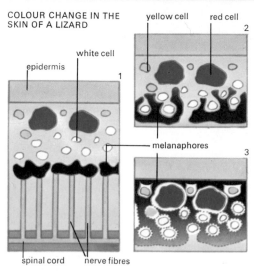

Above: A giant monitor, *Varanus giganteus*, from Australia. These animals reach a maximum length of about 2.4 m (7 ft). Monitors prey on smaller animals such as birds, rats, snakes and frogs. Like snakes, but unlike other lizards, they can drop the lower part of the jaw when swallowing large prey.

Below: A flying lizard, *Draco volans*, from south-east Asia. These animals have ribs which extend outside the body wall and support a membrane of skin in much the same way as the ribs of an umbrella support its fabric. By spreading this apparatus on each side of its body, the lizard is able to glide from tree to tree in search of insects.

COLOUR CHANGE IN THE SKIN OF A LIZARD

yellow cell

red cell

white cell

epidermis

melanaphores

spinal cord   nerve fibres

Above, left to right: Most lizards run on all fours to escape their enemies, but for short rapid bursts some species such as the zebra-tailed lizard, *Callisaurus draconoides*, of North America run on their hind legs alone, using the tail as a balance. All reptiles are cold-blooded animals: they have no mechanism for regulating their blood temperature. Most therefore prefer hot climates where they can raise their body temperature in the sun. The warmer the blood the more active the animal can be. At night reptiles are normally very sluggish.

Below: A gecko from Madagascar, *Phelsuma madagascariensis*. Unlike other geckos these lizards are active during the day and are brightly coloured. They live in trees and have a call like the croak of a frog.

Heather Angel

Left: The tuatara, *Sphenodon punctatum*, is the only surviving species of the reptile group *Rhynchocephalia*. It lives only on a few small islands off the coast of New Zealand and is strictly protected. Curiously, tuataras prefer a much lower temperature than other reptiles, and they live longer.

Below: Lizards usually move about with their bellies sliding along the ground. Undulating movements of the body help to push the animal along. In moments of crisis when they have to move rapidly the body is lifted off the ground even though, because of the position of the legs, this needs considerable effort.

Right: The strange-looking moloch, *Moloch horridus*, of central Australia. Despite its forbidding appearance, the moloch is quite harmless. It feeds on black ants. A store of fat under its spiny skin helps it to survive in the desert. When water is available tiny canals in the skin lead it to the animal's mouth.

NHPA

Anthony Bannister/NHPA

on their undersurface. They differ from mammals in having legs which stick out on each side of the body rather than under it. The belly usually rests on the ground and the legs push the lizard along, helped by undulating or wriggling movements.

Lizards found in tropical climates are often spectacular. The geckos, *Gekkonidae*, are small lizards with flattened bodies and curious adhesive pads on their toes which enable them to run easily on vertical or overhanging surfaces. Most geckos are partly nocturnal, appearing in the evenings when they can be seen stalking insects on walls—they are often seen lying in wait close to electric lights where insects collect. There are also some geckos that live in the desert, and many of these have enlarged tails which probably act as a food reserve.

Perhaps the most spectacular, however, are the huge monitor lizards which look like incarnations of mythical dragons. Inhabiting a number of Indonesian islands, the largest of these creatures is appropriately named the Komodo dragon, *Varanus komodoensis*, and can reach a length of 3 m (10 ft). Monitor lizards are predatory; they feed on invertebrates and smaller vertebrates, including snakes, and sometimes raid poultry farms killing chickens and stealing eggs. They are fierce animals and defend themselves vigorously with teeth, claws and by using their powerful tails. Often confused with the monitor lizards are the iguanas, large lizards which live in the Americas.

Lizards are sexually mature when they are two years old and are fully grown at four or five years. The average lifespan is about 10 years although some, such as the slow worm, will live for up to 50 years.

Turtles and Crocodiles

Many reptiles have found the key to survival in the evolution of body armour to protect them from their enemies. Perhaps no other reptiles, however, have armoured themselves so completely as those of the group *Chelonia*. This order includes the typical land tortoises, the amphibious terrapins and marine turtles. It is an ancient order, the members of which have undergone little change since the late Triassic 200 million years ago.

Turtles and tortoises

All turtles and tortoises have shells consisting of two main pieces, the *carapace* above and the *plastron* below. These are usually joined in the middle region of each side, leaving apertures in front and behind for the head, legs and tail. The shell is made up of two materials, an outer layer of horny *scutes*, and an inner layer of bony plates. The skeleton is enclosed in the shell and is partly joined to the carapace. To compensate for the resulting rigidity of the trunk, the neck is long and mobile, and in most species the head can be drawn back until it is almost hidden by the carapace.

The most numerous of the group are the sea turtles and of these the leatherback turtle, *Dermochelys coriacea*, is the largest, reaching a length of over two metres (6.5 ft), a width of about 3.6 m (12 ft) across the front paddles and a weight of over 675 kg (1,500 lb). Like all reptiles they evolved on land, but they have since reverted to an aquatic life. They are a small but fascinating group found in the world's tropical and subtropical seas. To equip them for this life, turtles have evolved special glands around the eyes to dispose of excess salt, their fingers are joined together to form paddles and, compared with those of tortoises, their shells are light and streamlined. The front paddles are considerably longer than the hind ones, allowing turtles to swim well despite their considerable bulk. When swimming, the paddles sweep gracefully up and down with a motion that has been compared to a bird's wings. On land, marine turtles are very clumsy and, like tortoises, have great difficulty in righting themselves when turned on their backs. This is not too much of a disadvantage because they rarely come out of the sea except to lay their eggs.

Turtles often make prodigiously long sea journeys to lay their eggs, returning to the same beaches on remote islands. Whereas there is an obvious advantage to laying their eggs in sparsely populated

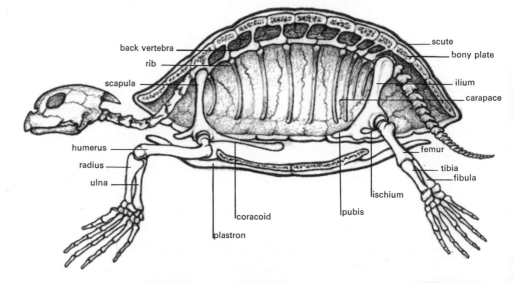

Above: The skeleton of a turtle. The shell of a turtle or tortoise is made up of two main pieces, the carapace above and the plastron below. It is composed of two materials, an outer layer of horny scutes and an inner layer of bony plates. The skeleton is enclosed in the shell and is partly joined to the carapace.

Right: A brightly marked terrapin, *Pseudemys dorbicny*. Terrapins live in ponds and rivers, particularly in North and South America. They are often seen basking in the sun on logs or tree stumps. Terrapins are often kept as pets, but these usually die from malnutrition before reaching maturity.

Below, left to right: A female turtle digs a nest hole in the sand before laying her eggs. The young turtles all hatch out together and begin to dig upwards. On reaching the surface they head for the sea.

Above: The extraordinary Mata-mata turtle, *Chelys fimbriatus*, of South America. The turtle's shell is irregular and its head and limbs are covered with folds of skin which

undulate in the currents of water to camouflage it. It lies in wait on a river bottom until a fish touches the skin near the mouth. Instantly the Mata-mata's mouth springs open and the fish is swept in.

Below right: Newly hatched leatherback turtles, *Dermochelys coriacea*, on a beach. Leatherbacks are the largest species of turtle and they have the widest range of any of the world's reptiles.

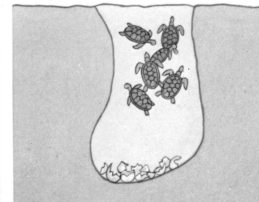

Heather Angel

Above and left: Giant tortoises, *Geochelone elephantopus*, from the island of Isabela in the Galápagos archipelago. These creatures were made famous by Charles Darwin after he had visited the islands in the 1830s. The tortoises spend most of their time in the warm dry lowlands of the islands, but they make regular journeys to the volcanic highlands in search of fresh water. The pool in the picture above lies in the crater of an extinct volcano. A curious feature of some local plants is that they germinate much more effectively if the seeds have first passed through the gut of a giant tortoise. The tortoises feed on all kinds of vegetation.

Heather Angel

S. C. Bisserot

Above: An Indian star tortoise, *Testudo elegans*. Star tortoises rest in the middle of the day when the sun is hottest, being most active in the early morning and late afternoon. Curiously, they still rest at noon even when kept in captivity in cool climates.

Left: The alligator snapping turtle, *Macroclemys temminckii*. It lies with its mouth open and part of its tongue is filled with blood to resemble a worm. A fish that tries to take the 'worm' will be caught instantly.

Below: A newly hatched green turtle, *Chelonia mydas*. Its shell is still curved to fit the eggshell and a yolk ball protrudes from its belly. In 24 hours the shell will be straight and the yolk absorbed.

Below right: A map to show the movement of turtles in the Caribbean from the beaches of Costa Rica where many begin life.

Oxford Scientific Films

islands, it seems rather odd that islands so very far away should be chosen. The answer to this problem may lie in the antiquity of the group. Possibly millions of years ago the islands were lying only a short distance from the mainland. According to the theory of continental drift the land masses have moved, over millions of years, so possibly the turtles' nesting island gradually and imperceptibly drifted apart from the mainland. To each successive generation of turtles the distance was no more than on the previous visit but over millions of years inches became many miles.

The nesting patterns of turtles vary, but have many common features. The green turtle, *Chelonia mydas*, comes ashore on an incoming tide, using the waves and her paddles to beach as high as possible. After a few minutes rest she uses her front paddles, advancing both of them at the same time, to drag herself forward. The rear paddles acting in unison with the front ones also assist in pushing the turtle forward. The body is never raised clear of the sand but moves forward a few inches at a time by the pushing and pulling of the paddles. At first the female turtle takes frequent rests of several minutes but as she progresses further up the beach these become shorter. On reaching the softer dry sand, she stops and begins to use her paddles to dig into the sand at a chosen spot. After twenty minutes of digging the action of the rear paddles changes, digging more directly downwards and curving like hands to scoop out the sand.

When finished, the egg chamber is pear-shaped with a narrower neck region and a wider chamber below which will house most of the eggs. This egg chamber is around 40 cm (16 in) deep. The eggs are white and resemble table tennis balls; at first they are discharged singly into the chamber but later in twos, threes, or fours, until up to 500 eggs may lie in the chamber. After laying the eggs the turtle fills in the depression with her paddles, and then, with one strong series of flipper movements, toboggans down to the sea.

After several months the eggs hatch. When emerging from the eggs, the young turtles find themselves underground and it takes them several days to dig their way to the surface. Group effort plays an important part in the emergence of young turtles—the movement of the first to hatch stimulates the others to activity. When they near the surface, the leading turtles will stop moving if the sand is warm because to emerge during the day would leave them open to attack from predators. As the sand cools in the night, activity resumes and the lower turtles again respond to the efforts of those above. In this way most of the young from a particular clutch of eggs will break the surface at more or less the same time.

Frank Lane

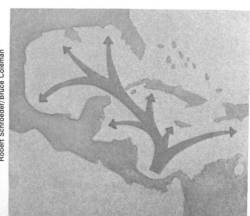

Robert Schroeder/Bruce Coleman

153

Late hatchers, without the benefit of the group effort, are doomed.

Once the hatchlings leave the nest they make rapid progress to the sea. However, even during this short space of time they are preyed upon by crabs, particularly the large ghost crab, and birds. This kind of predatory action on land is nothing compared with the hazards which the baby turtles face on entering the water, from attack by carnivorous fish. Those that survive will one day return to lay eggs of their own.

Crocodiles and alligators

In contrast to the generally placid tortoises and turtles are the group of reptiles familiarly known as crocodiles. Those alive today, formidable enough, are not as big as the crocodiles which lived at the time of the dinosaurs. One, called *Phobosuchus*, the 'terror crocodile', was about 14 m (45 ft) long and most probably preyed on the huge aquatic plant-eating dinosaurs. The present day crocodiles can be divided into three groups: the true crocodiles confined to the warmer parts of Africa, Asia and Australia, the alligators and caimans of North and South America and the long-nosed crocodiles called gharials or gavials from India.

There is one small difference between the true crocodile and an alligator: in crocodiles the fourth tooth of the lower jaw on each side fits into a notch in the upper jaw and is visible when the animal's mouth is closed. In alligators it fits into a pit in the upper jaw. The gharials have long slender jaws, very like a beak and set with small teeth.

The largest crocodile now living is the estuarine crocodile, *Crocodylus porosus*,

CAIMAN

ALLIGATOR

Above: The eyes of a crocodile are located high on the head so that the animal can see what is going on above the water level while still submerged.

Left: An American alligator, *Alligator mississippiensis*, emerging from the water. With the exception of a single Chinese species, all alligators live in North or South America. As in all reptiles, the limbs project from the sides of the body and are therefore not very good at supporting the body weight on land.

found in Asia, Southern China and Southern Australia. Although it is mature and can breed when about three metres (ten feet) long, it continues growing throughout its life. The largest one ever recorded was found in Bengal in India and measured 10 m (33 ft) in length and was nearly 4.2 m (14 ft) in girth at the middle of its body. Unfortunately hunting is widespread and consequently very few estuarine crocodiles reach any great age or size: specimens over six metres (20 ft) long are now very rare. The smallest species of crocodile is a South American caiman, *Caiman palperbrosus*, which barely reaches a length of 1.2 m (4 ft).

All crocodiles are adapted for life in water. The tail is flattened from side to side like an oar for efficient swimming and the nostrils are situated in a small dome or bump on top of the snout so that the animal can breathe when almost completely submerged. They can also spend a long period under the water without breathing: up to 5 hours in the case of the alligator. The teeth are conical

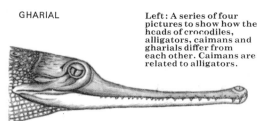

Left: A series of four pictures to show how the heads of crocodiles, alligators, caimans and gharials differ from each other. Caimans are related to alligators.

Jen & Des Bartlett/Bruce Coleman

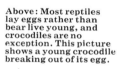

Above: Most reptiles lay eggs rather than bear live young, and crocodiles are no exception. This picture shows a young crocodile breaking out of its egg.

Left: A long-nosed crocodile or gharial, *Gavialis gangeticus*, from India. These animals are fish eaters and are not dangerous to man. Another type of gharial, the false gharial, *Tomistoma schlegelii*, lives only in the Malay peninsula and Sumatra. It is more closely related to true crocodiles than to its Indian namesake.

Ron Boardman

and pointed, designed for holding prey, not for chewing or cutting it up, so crocodiles have to swallow their food in large lumps. This does not help the digestion processes. Stones are often found in the stomachs of crocodiles, which might assist in digesting the food by crushing and grinding it. This is only a possibility however, since they may just be swallowed by accident.

Like most other reptiles, crocodiles lay eggs. These are laid on land and may be as large as geese eggs. The Nile crocodile, *Crocodylus niloticus*, of Egypt and Northern Africa, buries its eggs in the sand; others, including the estuarine crocodile, make a sort of nest consisting of a heap of water weeds and vegetable debris in which the eggs are buried. This not only helps to keep the eggs hidden, but also maintains them at a constant and fairly high temperature because of the heating effect of the moist, decaying vegetable matter. The mother crocodile guards the nest area until the young hatch out, but does not tend her offspring after they emerge. The nest-building habits of crocodiles are reminiscent of those of birds; indeed, crocodiles are their nearest living relatives.

The emerging crocodiles are miniature adults. They grow rapidly at first, especially if food is plentiful. Alligators, for example, grow about 30 cm (one foot) a year for their first four years of life, achieving sexual maturity after six years when they are around two metres long. Individual alligators and crocodiles are known to have lived for about 45 years, and some may well reach greater ages.

Characteristics of reptiles

All reptiles have a number of features in common. To begin with, like fishes and amphibians, they are all cold blooded, or *doikilothermic*. This means that they have no effective internal mechanism for regulating the body temperature; in conse-

quence it varies widely, depending mainly on the temperature of the environment. When the outside temperature is low, for example at night, a reptile will be very sluggish because the biochemical processes in its body will proceed only slowly.

Reptiles breathe air by means of lungs; they never possess gills like fish or amphibian larvae. The ventricle of the heart is usually only partly divided by a *septum* and, as a result, some mixing of arterial and venous blood occurs. This is an important point of distinction from adult birds and mammals where arterial and venous blood never mix.

The skin of a reptile is comparatively waterproof, being made up of an *epidermis* on the outside and an inner *dermis*. The epidermis forms the scales or scutes (in turtles) which are characteristic of reptiles and distinguish them from amphibians. The scales are composed of dead, horny tissue of which the protein *keratin* forms a large part. They are continually being shed from the surface of the body, either flaking off piecemeal or being sloughed off in one piece as in snakes. This loss is made good by the proliferation of living cells in the epidermis.

A reptile's teeth are shed and replaced throughout its life, instead of there being just one or two sets as in mammals. In some reptiles the replacement of teeth follows an alternating pattern. Between any two functional teeth there is often an empty space. As a new tooth grows in the empty space and begins to function, the teeth on either side of it are shed. This prevents the reptile from losing all its functional teeth at the same time. The teeth are capped with enamel, but its composition is different from that of mammalian tooth enamel.

Reptiles have a well developed sense of sight. The eyes are often brightly coloured, the iris being yellow or red, or sometimes blending in with the camouflage pattern of the rest of the animal. The sense of hearing varies considerably from one reptile group to another. Crocodiles and certain lizards, for example, have fairly keen hearing whereas snakes are almost deaf. Reptiles do not have an external ear and the exposed eardrum is often visible on the surface of the head behind the eyes. Whereas mammals have three bones for conducting sound from the eardrum to the inner ear, reptiles have only one.

Left: The spectacled caiman, *Caiman sclerops*, is common in the northern parts of South America. It rarely grows to more than 2 m (6 ft).

Right: One of the largest crocodiles is the Nile crocodile, *Crocodylus niloticus*. Once common in Africa it is now found only in isolated preserves.

Bavaria

Amphibians

The amphibians were the first group of vertebrate animals to have made a serious attempt at a life on land. Their history is long and complex from a fish-like ancestor to the three groups of modern amphibians, the *Anura* (frogs and toads), the *Urodela* (newts and salamanders) and the *Apoda* (worm-like animals called caecilians).

To trace the origin of the amphibians we must look back over 350 million years to the Devonian period, a time of seasonal drought and wet periods. Prototype amphibians are thought to have arisen from a fish-like ancestor related to the modern coelacanth. These ancient fish had primitive lungs and a skull structure resembling that of later amphibians; they were also probably capable of surviving the periods of drought.

Since the Devonian period many amphibians have evolved and adapted to terrestrial life while others have reverted to a mainly aquatic existence. *Ichthyostega* is the oldest and best known fossil form, resembling a cross between a fish and a salamander. It probably had the five-fingered (pentadactyl) limbs of all higher four-legged animals. *Ichthyostega* belonged to a large group of fossil amphibians called the *Labyrinthodontia*, named from the folded nature of the surface of their teeth. The most successful members of this group were the *Temnospondyli* which grew to a length of up to three metres (ten feet).

Another great branch of fossil forms were the *Lepospondyli*, generally small amphibians with salamander or limbless snake-like forms. Most inhabited the great swamps of the Carboniferous period in areas that now include Europe and North America. There are considerable gaps in our knowledge relating to the evolution of modern forms, but we do know that during the Carboniferous period hundreds of different amphibian forms roamed the swamps and that these

Heather Angel

Above: A tree frog, *Hyla arborea*, resting on the leaf of a *Poinsettia* plant. Clearly visible are the frog's toe pads which enable it to climb trees. Although very obvious in this picture, the frog would normally be well camouflaged by its bright green skin colour against tree foliage. These animals are sometimes found resting in the full glare of the tropical sun. Evaporation of moisture from their body surface helps to keep their bodies at a reasonable temperature.

Right: The eye of a tree frog, *Phyllomedusa trinitatis*. Unlike fish, but like many other land animals, sight is the dominant sense in most amphibians.

Oxford Scientific Films

Right: The mating of common frogs, *Rana temporaria*. The eggs are fertilized by the male (above) as soon as they are laid by the female. A mass of spawn can be seen in the background.

Left: An Argentine horned frog, *Ceratophrys ornata*, is well camouflaged against its background. Unlike most amphibians, these frogs are equipped with biting teeth. Their tadpoles have especially strong jaws and frequently prey on their own kind. The skin of frogs and toads contains poison glands for defence: one of the strongest poisons known comes from a tree frog, *Phyllobates bicolor*. It is used by South American Indians to poison arrowheads.

Jane Burton/Bruce Coleman

H. Rivarola/Bruce Coleman

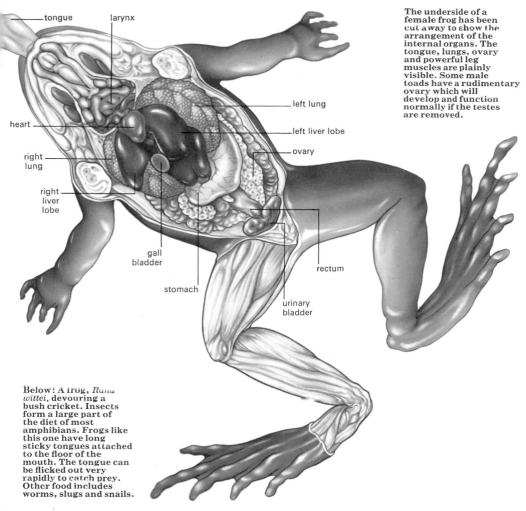

tongue — larynx

heart

right lung

right liver lobe

gall bladder

stomach

left lung

left liver lobe

ovary

rectum

urinary bladder

The underside of a female frog has been cut away to show the arrangement of the internal organs. The tongue, lungs, ovary and powerful leg muscles are plainly visible. Some male toads have a rudimentary ovary which will develop and function normally if the testes are removed.

Below: A frog, *Rana wittei*, devouring a bush cricket. Insects form a large part of the diet of most amphibians. Frogs like this one have long sticky tongues attached to the floor of the mouth. The tongue can be flicked out very rapidly to catch prey. Other food includes worms, slugs and snails.

creatures led easy lives with little competition from other animals and an abundance of fish and insect food.

The change from life in the water to that on land involved relatively few changes in the form and function of amphibians. Apart from caecilians, modern amphibians lost their fish-like scales and developed a soft naked skin that was kept moist to help respiration. This arrangement carried with it the danger of dehydration of the body tissues (water was easily lost by evaporation from the moist skin surface), but provided the amphibians kept to humid regions where the air was already laden with moisture the problem was not a serious one. For effective movement the body was raised off the ground by the development of a sturdy, lightweight skeleton and associated strong muscle systems. The skull lost its stiff connection with the pectoral girdle, giving better mobility. The hind limbs of frogs and toads became well developed for a swimming, and later jumping, habit and in both the anuran (frogs and toads) and urodele (newts and salamanders) groups the pentadactyl limbs became webbed for use as swimming paddles.

Frogs and toads

The anurans are the largest and most widely distributed amphibian group with over 2,500 species. They live in a wide variety of habitats from swamps and marshes to mountain streams and deserts.

Respiration in frogs is effected in three ways. In common with all higher vertebrates, frogs have paired airsacs or lungs. While breathing, the mouth is kept tightly closed and air is sucked in through the nostrils by lowering the floor of the mouth. Air is passed backwards and forwards several times between the lungs and the mouth before finally being exhaled. The skin and the lining of the mouth are also important for respiration. Both areas are richly supplied with blood vessels and are kept moist by secretions of mucous glands.

To help camouflage themselves many amphibians are able to change colour by

Below: A neotropical toad, *Bufo marinus*, calling to attract a mate. Frogs and toads were the first vertebrates to have a larynx and vocal cords. The inflated vocal sac under the mouth of the toad amplifies the sound and enables it to be heard from a distance of a kilometre or more.

Jane Burton/Bruce Coleman

Left: A series of diagrams to show how a frog leaps. The power for the jump comes from the well-muscled back legs which push the frog upwards and forwards. On landing, the back legs are once again drawn up against the body and the impact is taken by the front legs. The frog is then ready for another jump.

David Hughes/Bruce Coleman

expanding and contracting three layers of pigment cells in the skin. The skin is composed of several outer layers which are continuously renewed by moulting. It is often thickened as seen in the warty nature of toads. Apart from mucous glands to keep it moist, the skin contains poison glands used for defence. The poisonous secretion of toads contains substances which have a similar effect to the drug digitalis on the human heart.

The life history of the common frog, *Rana temporaria*, shows the change in body form (complete metamorphosis) common to anurans. Males and females congregate near ponds in early spring and sound is an important factor in bringing the sexes together. Both sexes have vocal cords but only those of the male are fully developed. The typical croaking call is produced by vibration of the vocal cords, a pair of folded membranes in the larynx. Prior to mating the male frog develops a horny 'nuptial pad' on its forelimbs which helps give a secure grip on the female when mating. The male grasps the female during the whole period of egg-laying which may last for several days.

The eggs are almost always fertilized externally by the male immediately after being laid and swell up on contact with water. A jelly-like covering acts as a food supply for the young tadpole and also as a protection against predators. The tadpoles differ greatly in form from their parents, they are completely aquatic and in the early stages are vegetarian. In early summer, young frogs emerge from the pond to feed on small insect prey.

While the common frog gives us an example of the typically amphibian dependence on water for breeding, some species have devised more ingenious methods to ensure the survival of the species. Asian tree frogs, *Rhacophoridae*, lay their eggs in a bubble mass of rainwater on leaves overhanging streams and pools, so that on hatching the young fall directly into the water to continue their development. The male European midwife toad, *Alytes obstetricans*, protects the eggs by carrying them in a string

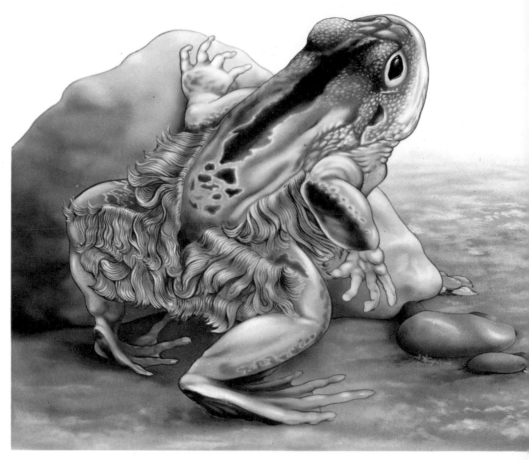

Above: The hairy frog, *Trichobatrachus robustus*. These curious amphibians are found in West Africa and they have small claws on several of their toes. The function of the vascular 'hairs', present only on male frogs, is uncertain. They may be for recognition, camouflage or other purposes.

Above: A pair of mating toads, *Bufo bufo*. Toads mate in much the same way as frogs, but their spawn is in the form of 'ropes' rather than a disorganized mass.

Left: A fire salamander, *Salamandra salamandra*. These amphibians are common in central Europe. They were thought by the ancients to be able to withstand the action of flames. The salamander secretes a milky poison from glands in its smooth skin, and the bright yellow and black markings serve as a warning to potential predators. Fire salamanders give birth to live young.

Right: Pyrenean mountain salamanders, *Euproctes asper*, during courtship.

Below: A male palmate
newt, Triturus
helveticus. The webbed
hind feet and slender
tail extension are
plainly visible. Male
and female newts are
easily distinguished
from each other,
particularly during the
breeding season. The
males are more vividly
coloured and have higher
crests on their backs.

Right: An axolotl,
Ambystoma mexicanum. In
their natural habitats
these amphibians remain
permanently in the
larval state although
they mature sexually.
The feather-like
external gills are
typical of salamander
larvae. Axolotls can be
induced to metamorphose
into salamanders by
treatment with iodine.

around his legs until just before hatching when he rushes down to a stream to allow the young tadpoles their freedom. In *Phyllobates* of South America, the tadpoles live on their father's back until they reach an advanced stage of development. The Seychelles frog, *Sooglossus*, goes one step further in parental care, for the tadpoles develop into young frogs while still on the father's back. An extreme short cut in the life history is shown by a few species. For instance in the marsupial frog, *Gasterotheca*. eggs are laid in a brood pouch on the mother's back and the young hatch out in a zipper-like fashion from the pouch. The young of the Surinam toad, *Pipa pipa*, emerge singly from honeycomb depressions on the female's back.

These examples show not only degrees of parental care, but also some independence of water for breeding purposes. Frogs and toads that live in the extremely dry conditions of the Australian desert can imbibe so much water after a rainstorm that Aborigines catch them during the dry season to drink their water store. These desert amphibians often spend the heat of the day in deep burrows and are able to breed almost immediately after a sudden downpour of rain. Since the rainy season is short, the embryos develop very rapidly.

Anurans range in length from a few centimetres to the giant goliath frog, *Gigantorana goliath*, of West Africa which measures up to 40 cm (16 in). Oddities of the group include the Borneo flying frog, *Rhacophorus pardalis*, which can glide from tree to tree and the hairy frog, *Trichobatrachus robustus*, of West Africa.

Newts and salamanders

Most of the 450 species of urodeles live in water or else hidden away in mossy retreats or other humid habitats like the rotting stumps of trees, in caves or under stones. They have long tapering bodies with weak legs, and the adult and larval forms differ little from each other. Urodeles are commonly found in mountainous regions with a temperate, moist climate and have their greatest distribution in the Northern Hemisphere.

The most familiar members are the newts which belong to the large group known as true salamanders. Newts have long, laterally flattened tails and often develop crests in the breeding season. Colour plays an important role in breeding and the gaudy nuptial colours of the males are particularly striking. The pattern of courtship varies with the species, but the secretions of 'hedonic glands' play an important role in initiating sexual response in all cases. These glands are located in the skin, especially in the cloaca and tail region. Among the more common European newts, the male deposits a packet of sperms called the *spermatophore* which is taken up by the female's cloaca. Eggs are commonly laid on the leaves of water plants and from these swimming larvae emerge with well developed feathery gills.

One curious phenomenon observed in many of these amphibians is a tendency for larval features to be retained in the adult. This is called *neoteny*. The giant Asian salamanders, *Andrias*, for example, lose their larval gills, but lack eyelids and retain their larval teeth. Still more modified are the mud puppies, *Necturus*, of North America which keep their larval gills throughout life and have very small lungs. Perhaps the most famous example of neoteny is the axolotl, *Ambystoma mexicanum*, found in Lake Xochimilco and a few other cold water mountain lakes around Mexico city. The axolotl hardly ever changes into the adult form in nature, although of course it does reach sexual maturity. It will, however, metamorphose into a salamander under experimental conditions after treatment with thyroid hormone, extract of pituitary gland (the gland that controls hormone activity in vertebrates) or iodine.

Many urodeles represent the last living species of a previously large and widely distributed group. Some 60,000,000 years ago during the Tertiary period, giant salamanders were found over much of Eurasia. Today there are only three living species confined to China and Japan.

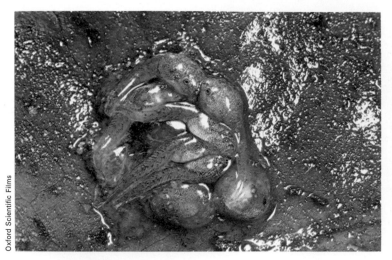

Oxford Scientific Films

Left: Some frogs have achieved a degree of independence from the water even for breeding. This picture shows young tadpoles of the frog *Phyllobates trinitatis* on a leaf. The tadpoles will eventually be carried on their father's back before being released into a pond or stream.

Below: Five stages in the development of a tadpole. Newly hatched tadpoles have external gills, suckers to help them cling to plants but no eyes. The eyes soon develop and the gills become covered by an operculum. They feed mainly on algae and other plant material. Later the back legs develop and finally the front legs grow out from the gill cavity.

3 external gills

2 suckers

2 days

anus

8 days

water to Internal gills

operculum covering internal gills

1 month

water from gills

2 months

3 months

Right and below: Tadpoles move through the water in a similar way to fish by side to side movements of the body and tail. Because most of the weight is concentrated in the body rather than the tail, the swimming action is not very efficient. The tail is absorbed in the final stage of metamorphosis.

Above: A South American caecilian, *Siphonops annulatus*. Caecilians are found in the same sort of habitat as earthworms and are often confused with them. They can, however, be distinguished from earthworms quite easily by their method of locomotion which is much more like that of a snake.

Right: A caecilian from the Seychelles burrows into the soil. Caecilians are blind: instead of eyes they have special sensory tentacles with which they find their way through the earth and locate their prey. They feed mainly on invertebrates, although larger species may eat snakes or small rodents such as mice.

Heather Angel

These relics grow up to 1.5 m (5 ft) in length and live on the bottom of fast-flowing streams. They are nocturnal and hunt a wide variety of prey from fish and frogs to smaller invertebrate animals.

Another relic group are the cave salamanders, *Hydromantes*. Although they are found above ground they prefer the damp and constant environment of caves. They move slowly, using their prehensile tails for climbing and hunt soft-bodied invertebrates which they catch with their extremely long tongues. The olm, *Proteus anguinus*, is another cave dweller, but this time aquatic. This blind larval urodele with pale unpigmented skin and orange feathery gills, lives in the underground water systems of Yugoslavia.

The largest urodele family is the *Plethodontinae* containing over 60 per cent of known species. These lungless salamanders are mostly found in North America, especially in the Appalachian mountain chain. Such lungless salamanders range from purely aquatic forms like the larger dusky salamanders to the tree-climbing salamander of California.

These creatures demonstrate that an animal can survive on land even without lungs. They breathe through their moist skin and through mucous covered membranes inside the mouth. To survive in this way it is obviously an advantage for the surface area of the body to be as large as possible for a given body weight, so plethodont salamanders are usually long and slender.

The Congo eels or *amphiumas* form another curious group of urodeles. Their common name is singularly inappropriate since they have no connection with eels and are not found in Africa. All amphiumas live in the south-eastern United States. They have long cylindrical bodies equipped with very small weak limbs, often only a few millimetres long.

Caecilians

The apodans are all blind, limbless, burrowing animals and are the least known of the three amphibian groups. They lack both shoulder and pelvic girdles and their long, ringed, worm-like bodies are often scaled. They range in length from several centimetres to the giant *Caecilia thompsoni* which grows to a length of 1.5 m (5 ft).

Caecilians are all confined to tropical and sub-tropical regions of the world, especially Africa and South America. The best known member is the Ceylonese caecilian, *Ichthyophis glutinosus*, a striking blue-black creature with a bright yellow longitudinal stripe. This species shows a curious feature in that parental care is often very well developed. After laying her eggs, the female wraps herself around them until the larvae hatch out. Other caecilians give birth to live young which hatch out from eggs inside the mother. The young larvae feed in the oviduct on 'uterine milk' consisting of oil droplets and sloughed-off cells from the oviduct.

Many amphibians have made a good attempt at a life on land and are not just a precarious remnant of a once more widely distributed group. In habitats like swamps and marshes and mountain streams, they are often quite numerous and have evolved into a variety of forms. However, their survival has often meant evasion rather than total adaption to the more severe conditions of a terrestrial life.

The Big Cats

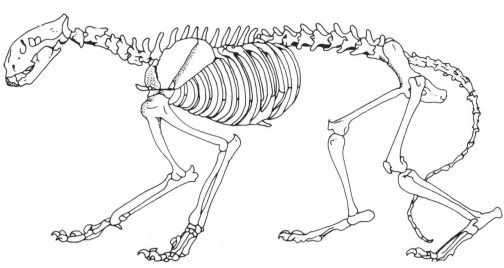

As long as animal life has existed on earth, most animals have eaten plants, leaving the way open for a fiercer minority to become meat-eaters. During the course of evolution a succession of carnivorous animals has appeared, and among the terrestrial mammals the cat family (*Felidae*) of the order *Carnivora* contains in many respects the most highly-developed and efficient carnivores of all.

Like the other members of their order they are descended from the weasel-like miacids that flourished about 50 million years ago, becoming a recognizable group on their own account about 35 million years ago. For most of the time since then there have been two very distinct types of cats, one of which, the sabre-tooths, died out only a few thousand years ago. With their huge fangs—those of the sabre-toothed tiger were up to 20 cm (8 in) long—the sabre tooths are thought to have hunted large plant-eating animals such as rhinoceroses by making slashing attacks.

The other group of cats, the one that survives today, relies instead on stealth. Moving on tip-toe with retracted claws, so that only the soft pads touch the ground, the typical cat approaches its prey silently, before springing, using the powerful muscles of the hind legs and back. The killing weapons are the claws and teeth. Cats have shorter jaws than any other carnivores, and this gives them great biting power. The pointed canine teeth are primarily used in killing, and the large last upper premolars and first lower molars (the *carnassial* teeth) for crushing and slicing the flesh before it is swallowed. Most cats hunt prey smaller than themselves, for there are many more small herbivores than large ones, but the biggest and most impressive cats of all usually hunt prey even larger than themselves.

Above: The skeleton of a tiger, *Panthera tigris*. It has a strong flexible backbone to enable it to pounce swiftly on its prey, and a long body with most of the weight carried by the front legs so that it can negotiate uneven ground and steep inclines with ease. Although tigers and lions look quite different from each other, their skeletons are almost identical and it takes an expert to tell them apart.

Right: A tiger cub. Normally a tigress gives birth to between two and four cubs after a gestation period of 105 days. They are born in a secluded den and are at first blind and helpless. Full maturity is not reached until the animals are more than three years old, but they learn to fend for themselves long before this.

Below: A sabre-tooth, *Machairodus lapidens*, which lived in the early Pleistocene epoch, less than 2,000,000 years ago. Sabre-tooths were members of the cat family but did not belong to the same sub-family as modern cats.

ZEFA

The big cats make up the genus *Panthera*, and apart from their size resemble each other in various ways. Unlike the smaller cats they have eyes with round pupils, and their larynxes or voice boxes are flexibly joined to the skull.

This may seem to be rather an unimportant anatomical detail, but it has important effects on sound production. Small cats yowl, but big cats roar, small cats can purr almost continuously, but when big cats purr they must pause for breath between each reverberation. Finally, in relation to their size the big cats have even larger heads than the small ones.

The first big cats evolved about a million years ago, as fossils from southern Europe and China prove. It may be that the arrival of this genus was a major cause of extinction of the sabre-tooths, for members of both groups hunted large prey, and may therefore have been in competition with each other. Travelling by land bridges, often temporary, which linked the major land-masses the big cats invaded Africa, the islands of southeast Asia, and (passing through North America) South America.

There were never very many species of big cats, but until man as a hunter com-

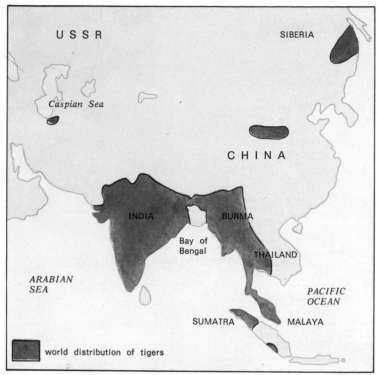

world distribution of tigers

Left: Tigers are much less common than they once were. Not only has their jungle habitat been cleared for cultivation in many places, but the animals themselves have been hunted for their skins and for 'sport'. Sometimes tigers become man-eaters and have to be hunted and destroyed, but this is relatively rare. Man-eaters are usually injured animals which can no longer catch their normal prey; the injury is often a gunshot wound or a porcupine quill lodged in one foot. A single man-eater has been known to kill more than 100 people in the course of its career.

Right: A cheetah, *Acinonyx jubatus*, feeding on the carcass of a Thomson's gazelle.

Below: The cheetah is the fastest of all mammals. It has a highly flexible backbone which allows the powerful back muscles as well as the leg muscles to be used in running. Hoofed animals such as zebras and antelopes have much more rigid backbones than cheetahs and rely on their leg muscles for running.

Jacana

P. Castel/Jacana

Left: The most distinctive feature of the tiger is its striped coat which blends in well with the strong shadows of the trees and grass in its jungle homeland. Tigers range from South-East Asia to Siberia, and their prey varies accordingly. Russian tigers hunt roe deer, elk, musk deer and sometimes wolves or bears, whereas in tropical Asia tigers pursue deer of other species, nilgai (large antelopes), wild boar and even young elephants. Throughout their range tigers will take domestic animals when they can.

Right: Unlike most members of the cat family, tigers are not afraid of water and are strong swimmers.

peted with them, in some cases exterminating their prey, every major part of the world except for Australasia and some remote islands, had its own big cat population. For example, there were lions in Europe until only a few thousand years ago. The lion *Panthera leo*, was the biggest cat of Europe, western Asia, and Africa, being replaced by the tiger, *Panthera tigris*, in more eastern regions of Asia. Over much of the Old World these two species coexisted with the leopard, *panthera pardus*, which, being slightly smaller and a better climber, was adapted for hunting different prey and was therefore not in competition with them. In the mountains of central Asia the snow leopard, *Panthera uncia*, was best adapted for the conditions, and the jaguar, *Panthera onca*, was the only

member of the group to find its way to America, where it lived in the warmer and more forested regions.

Human activity has whittled down the original ranges of the big cats. Not only have the lions gone from Europe, but more recently they have also become extinct in what was then Palestine and North Africa. Almost all surviving lions now live in Africa south of the Sahara Desert, but a few still live in the Gir Forest of north-east India.

Not all wild members of the same species are the same colour: the colour of lions' manes is very variable, ranging from black to tawny, and in both leopards and jaguars dark individuals are not uncommon in some parts of the world. These are very dark brown with black spots, and at a quick glance appear to be

plain black. A 'black panther' is simply a dark-haired leopard. Similarly, 'white' tigers, which have dark stripes and blue eyes are merely a paler version of the usual colouring. Like red hair in humans, these variations sometimes appear naturally in the wild.

Lions and tigers are the biggest members of the genus, tigers being slightly bigger than lions and can weigh up to 200 kg (440 lb) or more. Leopards and snow leopards are only a little shorter than the biggest cats, but much of their length consists of a long tail, useful in balancing on overhanging branches, and 45 kg (100 lb) is a good weight for either animal. Jaguars are superficially similar to leopards, and only a little shorter in overall length. However, they have shorter tails and are much more heavily

Above: A jaguar, *Panthera onca,* **with its prey—in this case a domestic goat. Jaguars are the only large cats** of the Americas, and they hunt deer, peccaries and some of the huge rodents of tropical America such as the sheep-sized capybara. The home range of a single jaguar may extend over 500 sq km (190 sq miles) or more.

Below: The clouded leopard, *Neofelis nebulosa,* **hunts such prey as deer and wild pigs in the forests of South-East Asia.**

built, weighing about 90 kg (200 lb). Being the only big cats of tropical America, they fill the ecological niches occupied in the Old World by both the lion or tiger and the leopard, and this may be the reason why jaguars are intermediate in size. Ecologically speaking, they are a compromise.

Most cats live and hunt on their own, and the majority of the big cats are no exception. Sometimes more than one individual of species such as the tiger are seen together, but these are almost certainly pairs during their brief courtship, or part of a growing family. There is no certain proof that any of the big cats defend fixed territories against other members of their own species, but it seems probable that they do, for all of them make scent marks using both dung and urine, and also scratch on trees or the ground. This sort of behaviour looks very much like territorial demarcation. Certainly a large carnivore must range over a wide area for it must not deplete the local population of prey animals faster than they can reproduce or it will eventually run out of food. Individual leopards range over an area of roughly 22 sq km (8 sq miles), and tigers range over about 65 sq km (25 sq miles). On scantier evidence the ranges of both jaguars and snow leopards are thought to be even larger.

Lion families

The lions of the grasslands of eastern and southern Africa live in groups known as prides whereas other big cats are solitary animals. This seems to be an adaptation to their environment, for of all the big cats lions are the only ones to live where their prey species occur in large herds. In order to outwit the combined vigilance of the herd, lions co-operate, making combined rushes, or lying in ambush for their prey. Because prey is usually numerous, the territory occupied by a pride is not particularly large—perhaps 33 sq km (13 sq miles). Although lions are the only big cats which are easy to observe in the wild, it is only very recently that detailed studies have been made of their social behaviour by zoologists working on the Serengeti Plain of Tanzania.

A typical pride consists of two or three adult males, perhaps twice as many mature lionesses, and their young. Before they become mature, at between 2 and 3 years old, the adolescent males

Above: The leopard, *Panthera pardus*, is an expert climber. It hunts antelopes, monkeys (including baboons), hyraxes and large rodents, often wedging the remains of a kill in the fork of a tree to protect it from hyenas, jackals and other scavengers. Leopards live in Africa and southern Asia and, as with other big cats, old or injured animals occasionally become man-eaters.

Right: The snow leopard, *Panthera uncia*, has the longest fur of all cats for it inhabits the cool plateaux and mountain slopes of central Asia. It ranges over a wide area, hunting small deer, mountain goats, ground squirrels and some domestic animals.

Below: A lion, *Panthera leo*, splashes through a shallow pool. This is an African lion, recognizable by its thick mane. A few hundred lions also live in north-east India: they are a different race of the same species and have noticeably shorter manes than their more numerous African cousins.

Above: A lioness with her cub. Lions are the only cats of the genus *Panthera* to live in family groups consisting of males, females and cubs. This is probably an adaptation to life on the open plains where prey animals live in large herds. Tigers, leopards and jaguars are solitary animals of the forest and bush.

Above right and right:
Within a pride of lions
hunting is normally
carried out by the
females, who kill
zebras, wildebeests and
other antelopes. Related
lionesses form the
permanent core of the
pride, for the males are
ousted every few years
by stronger males from
outside, thus ensuring
an influx of new blood.

and some of the females too are expelled by the adults. The females that are allowed to remain become part of the pride, but the others must live more solitary, less successful, and probably short lives. The young males wander in company, hunting on their own account, and growing powerful. When they are adult two or more of them will move in on another pride, take on the reigning males one at a time and kill or expel them, taking over the pride as their own. They kill the young cubs and, probably as a result of shock, any of the lionesses that are pregnant tend to lose their litters. Later the new males mate with the lionesses and sire their own cubs—in this way their social system is perpetuated and an influx of strong new blood ensured.

This life-style is very different from that of tigers, but nevertheless the two largest species of cats are quite closely related. In zoos hybrids between lions and tigers have been bred. They are called 'ligers' if a lion is the father and 'tygons' if a tiger is the father. Beyond this, the fact that the geographical ranges of the two species do not overlap indicates that they are both filling the same ecological niche—that of the strongest, and fiercest of predators.

Cheetahs

The cheetah, *Acinonyx jubatus*, is in many ways the most distinctive member of the otherwise rather homogeneous cat family. It is taller than a leopard, measuring about 90 cm (3 ft) at the shoulder, and nearly as long but is very lightly built weighing only about 54.5 kg (120 lb). Unlike those of the leopard and jaguar, the cheetah's spots are not grouped into rosettes, but are scattered singly all over the sandy-brown coat. Alone among the cats the adult cheetah is unable to retract its claws.

Other cats hunt by pouncing on the prey from close range, but the cheetah which is able to reach a speed of up to 100 kph (62 mph), catches its prey by sheer speed. However it has no stamina, and can maintain high speeds only over a few hundred yards or metres.

Cheetahs live in grasslands and semi-deserts of southern Asia and Africa. In many parts of their range, especially in Asia, they are now very rare. They hunt small, fleet-footed antelopes such as the Indian blackbuck and Thomson's gazelle of East Africa, and are usually most active early in the morning and in the evening. Either they stalk their prey, using the sparse cover that is available

before launching the attack from some dozens of metres away, or else they move towards the prey first at a walk, then a trot, and then a full-blooded gallop.

Living in herds, the prey species are watchful for such an attack, and usually stay well away from cover that could conceal a cheetah. If a sprinting cheetah succeeds in catching its prey (and often it does not), it bowls the animal over with its paws, and bites into the throat in order to kill.

Clouded leopards

Although smaller than some so-called 'small' cats, the clouded leopard, *Neofelis nebulosa*, is regarded as an intermediate species between the smaller cats and the big cats. Anatomically it possesses features of both major groups of cats in almost equal parts. It purrs like a small cat, and has neither round pupils (typical of big cats) nor vertical slit-like ones (like small cats), but horizontal oval ones. In relation to its size it has longer canine teeth than any other living cat. It lives in the forests of South-East Asia from Nepal to southern China and Sumatra, hunting quite large prey species, including deer and wild pigs—it has even been known to attack man.

165

Pandas, Raccoons and Badgers

The weasels and their relatives, which together make up the family *Mustelidae*, have the short legs and long muscular bodies which were typical of the remote ancestors of the carnivores. Although this shape is a primitive one it can, with just a little modification, be adapted to the varied life-styles of the small to medium-sized species that make up the family.

The typical weasels hunt through thick cover, sometimes pursuing their prey into burrows beneath the ground. The more heavily built badgers dig their own burrows. Martens chase squirrels through the treetops, catching their prey by a combination of speed and agility. With the addition of webbing between the toes, otters can swim fast enough to catch fish. It is not surprising that members of this family are successful in all parts of the world that they have been able to colonize: they are found in every continent except Australasia.

Mustelids are more closely related to dogs than to the specialized carnivores of the cat family. Like dogs they have relatively long jaws containing rows of molar and premolar teeth—typically three teeth of each type on either side of both the lower and upper jaws. Their eyesight is only fair, but they have keen hearing and an excellent sense of smell. They have five digits on each limb, and the claws are often partially retractable.

Females are usually appreciably smaller than males, and have a fixed breeding season. In some species the ovum, fertilized during mating, does not immediately implant itself on the wall of the uterus and start to grow. Instead it only becomes implanted after a delay of some months, making the gestation period very long— nearly a year in the case of some martens. A few mustelids, such as weasels and polecats, may have two litters in the same year, but most have only a single litter usually consisting of about four young. Sea otters generally have only one young one at a time.

Weasels and badgers

The *Mustelidae* is divided into five subfamilies, the first of which contains the most typical members of the family including the weasels, polecats, minks, ferrets and stoats of the genus *Mustela*, and the longer-tailed, arboreal martens of the genus *Martes*, about 30 species in all. Many members of the group inhabit cool climates of northern Europe, Asia, and America. Being small, long and slender their bodies do not hold heat well, and so the mustelids of northern climates have superbly soft, dense fur. It is no accident that some of the most expensive and sought-after furs used in the fashion trade come from members of this group. Like other mammals of cool climates, many mustelids grow especially thick winter fur and for this reason the early fur-trappers of the Canadian north used to ply their trade in winter.

Left: A stoat, or ermine, *Mustela erminea*, with its prey. Stoats hunt a wide variety of small animals, including insectivores, rodents, rabbits, birds, lizards and insects; only rarely do they eat any plant material. Stoats are territorial animals, marking stones, tree stumps and other prominent features in their home ranges with a strong-smelling secretion from scent glands to warn off their rivals. They move quickly, stopping from time to time to survey their surroundings, sometimes standing up on their hind legs.

Right: A spotted skunk, *Spilogale putorius*, performs a 'handstand' before spraying its scent at an enemy.

Right: The wolverine, *Gulo gulo*, is the largest member of the weasel sub-family. It lives in northern Asia and North America where it feeds mainly on carrion, eggs and insects. It is an efficient predator, especially in the winter months when it can move noiselessly across the snow, but it usually hunts only when carrion is scarce. The wolverine can successfully tackle prey as large and strong as elks and lynxes.

Below: A female polecat, *Mustela putorius*, with her young. The babies are born in early summer after a pregnancy of six weeks and are weaned at one month. By the end of the summer they will be fully grown.

Frank Lane

S. C. Bisserot

Frank Lane

The largest of the weasels is the wolverine or glutton, *Gulo gulo*, of northern pine forests and tundras, which weighs about 18 kg (40 lb). It has long dark brown fur with unique water-repellent qualities. For this reason the fur is used to line the edges of the hoods of Eskimos' parkas. The wolverine normally feeds on lemmings, although it occasionally also kills reindeer. It owes its reputation for gluttony to its habit of using its powerful scent-glands to mark uneaten kills, thus seeming to spoil the meat that it cannot immediately eat. Its smaller relatives feed mainly on rodents and birds: the European polecat, *Mustela putorius*, has a well-deserved reputation for raiding chicken runs. Members of the subfamily are common in Europe, Asia and North America, but also occur in

Hans Reinhard/Bruce Coleman

Below: One of the most familiar mustelids is the Old World badger, *Meles meles*. It is active mainly in the evening and at night when it searches for fruit, roots, insects and other small animals. Badgers live in dens, or *setts*, which consist of numerous chambers and tunnels, with several entrances.

Right: An African clawless otter, *Aonyx capensis*, devouring a fish. This species differs from most other otters in having no claws and only very short webs between the fingers. This makes it considerably more skilful at grasping prey and other objects in its front paws than other species.

Right: A sea otter, *Enhydra lutris*, breaks open shellfish by smashing them against a stone which it carries on its chest.

Below: The Canadian otter, *Lutra canadensis*, is found throughout most of Canada and the US. It feeds on fish, crustaceans, ducks, water voles and eggs.

South America and in Africa, where one of them, the zorilla, *Ictonyx striatus*, has paralleled the evolution of the skunks in its black and white coat and defense behaviour.

Placed in a sub-family of its own is the ratel or honey badger, *Mellivora capensis*, of Africa and southern Asia. This species is best known for its relationship with the indicator bird, which postures and chatters in order to lead the ratel to wild bees' nests. The ratel, heavily built and strikingly marked in black and grey, rips open the nest with its claws and feeds on the honey, incidentally providing food for the birds. This is a good example of *symbiosis*, a partnership between two species from which both benefit.

The badgers and the slightly smaller ferret badgers of southern Asia make up another sub-family which contains eight species. They are heavily built and usually eat both animal and plant food. For example, the common badger, *Meles meles*, of the woodlands of Europe and temperate Asia, which weighs about 13 kg (29 lb) and spends the day in extensive burrows, feeds on berries, roots, bulbs and acorns as well as invertebrates and mammals of up to the size of a rabbit. In North America it is replaced by a slightly smaller species, *Taxidea taxus*, which prefers open sandy plains.

Skunks and otters

The nine species of skunks are found only in the Americas, and make up the fourth sub-family. They too feed on a wide variety of plant materials as well as invertebrates and rodents. Presumably it is because they are among the least fierce of the carnivores that they have evolved their remarkable defensive system. Like many other mammals, mustelids have special scent-glands, which have primarily evolved as a means of signalling to other members of their own species. Like other glands in the skin, these glands tend to release their odour when the animal is under stress.

The paired scent-glands of the skunk, situated beneath the tail on either side of the anus, have become modified to serve as weapons of defence in situations where the animal feels threatened, and the scent itself has become virtually a poison gas. Armed in this way, and giving warning of their deterrent by means of bold black and white markings, skunks are quite fearless and rarely flee from potential enemies. If they are threatened they emphasize their markings by means of special displays: the spotted skunk, *Spilogale putorius*, of Central and North America performs handstands as a threat. Only if this does not deter the enemy is the secretion of its tail glands discharged, being squirted with considerable accuracy for up to 3.6 m (12 ft). Starting as a liquid, it rapidly becomes a poisonous and foul-smelling vapour. No enemy would willingly face an angry skunk twice.

The fifth mustelid sub-family contains the 18 species of otters. These have very thick fur which, even when the otter is swimming, always retains plenty of trapped air, forming a warm and flexible diving suit. In addition to the webbed feet, the powerful tail, which is horizontally flattened, is also used in swimming. Otters live near lakes and rivers, and sometimes on estuaries and sea coasts, in most parts of the world.

The Eurasian otter, *Lutra lutra*, occurs from Britain to North Africa and Sumatra, and is in many respects typical of the group. It weighs up to about 15 kg (33 lb) and feeds on invertebrates including crayfish, fish, frogs and small aquatic birds. The largest of the otters is the giant otter, *Pteronura brasiliensis*, of South America, which may be up to 2.2 m (7 ft) long and weigh 24 kg (54 lb). The rarest is the sea otter, *Enhydra lutris*, from the north Pacific which has been hunted almost to extinction for its fur. Sea otters live in groups on remote coasts, feeding on sea urchins, molluscs, crabs, fish and sea weed, and often swimming lazily on their backs.

Raccoons

The raccoon family, *Procyonidae*, is found only in the Americas. It contains 16 species, and its members are much more alike than those of the weasel family. Like mustelids and dogs, raccoons have long jaws, usually with four premolar teeth and two molars in each corner of the mouth. They have moderately long legs with five toes on each foot, and are usually plantigrade, the soles of the feet making contact with the ground at each step. The best-known member of the family is the North American raccoon, *Procyon lotor*, which lives in woods and forests, usually not far from water. The favourite food of this species is the fresh water crayfish.

The North American cacomistle, *Bassariscus astutus*, has a shorter nose and larger ears than the raccoon. It lives in woods and on dry, rocky hills, and is an efficient predator, catching small rodents

Above: A North American raccoon, *Procyon lotor*, searching for food near the edge of a lake. It will eat almost anything, from leaves and grass to snails, small mammals, fishes, crayfishes and occasionally birds. The habit of searching for food underwater with its fore-paws is retained in captivity: zoo animals place food items into water and then go through the motions of searching for them. This behaviour has led to the popular misconception that the raccoon washes its food.

Right: A ring-tailed coatimundi, *Nasua nasua*, from Brazil. Coatis spend much of their time on the forest floor searching for food, but seek refuge in trees when danger threatens.

with great skill. The coatimundis, *Nasua*, have long, pointed noses and live in the forests and bush of Central and South America. They travel in troops, poking their noses into the soil and into crevices in the bark of trees as they search for food. The most arboreal member of the family is the kinkajou, *Potos flavus*, which inhabits tropical forests and has a prehensile tail. It is nocturnal, and feeds primarily on fruit, using its long tongue in order to extract the pulpy flesh. The olingos, *Bassaricyon*, are very similar, but are unable to cling by means of their tails.

Pandas

The precise relationships of the two living species of pandas are still the subject of much argument among zoologists. When the giant panda, *Ailuropoda melanoleuca*, was first discovered on the remote, bamboo-covered plateaus of China by Père David, a French missionary, it was very understandably described as a black and white bear. Later, after a detailed examination of its anatomical features, it was classified as one of the raccoons. This was not such a startling change as it might appear to be, for the raccoons and the bears have evolved from the same ancestors, and a large raccoon will inevitably look bear-like. Today some zoologists once more believe that the giant panda rightly belongs to the bear family. It is no wonder that many experts, seeking to answer the problem of classification, place the pandas in a family of their own, the *Ailuropodidae*.

The giant panda's closest living

Below: The kinkajou, *Potos flavus*, is an expert climber and is the only member of the raccoon family to have a prehensile tail. Feeding mainly on fruit, such as wild fig, guava and mango, it occupies much the same ecological niche as the New World monkeys. It is, however, active at night rather than in the day.

Right: The lesser panda, *Ailurus fulgens*, lives in mountain forests and bamboo thickets from Nepal to western China. It is a nocturnal animal and feeds on bamboo shoots, grasses, fruit and occasionally insects and small mammals. When attacked the lesser panda defends itself efficiently with its long sharp claws.

Right: The giant panda 'Chia Chia' eating bamboo shoots at London Zoo. Giant pandas, *Ailuropoda melanoleuca*, have never been very common because they can thrive only in cool mountainous regions where bamboo is abundant. Today they live in the western part of Szechwan province in western China at altitudes of between 1,500 and 4,000 m (5,000 to 13,000 ft). In spite of their restricted distribution giant pandas are probably not in danger of extinction because the Chinese government conserves them with care.

Left and below: The curious 'playing' behaviour of the giant panda makes it a popular, if rare, zoo animal.

relation is undoubtedly the red panda, *Ailurus fulgens*, which looks much more like a raccoon than a bear. It is long-tailed and arboreal and lives in Asia on forested slopes of the Himalayas. The red panda is mainly active at dawn and dusk, when it feeds on lichens, acorns, and bamboo shoots. It spends much of the day sleeping either in the fork of a tree or in a hollow tree. Weighing only about 5 kg (11 lb) it is much smaller than the giant panda, but has the same pigeon-toed walk.

The giant panda eats a variety of foods, including some small animals, but the bulk of its diet consists of bamboo shoots which are like large, tough, woody grasses. It holds the shoots by means of a long wrist bone that works rather like a thumb. Its teeth are powerful, the molars having flattened crowns designed to crush and chew bamboo. Giant pandas need bulky bodies in order to be able to hold enough of their rather unpromising diet, and they weigh about 135 kg (300 lb). Despite their weight and their short tails, they can climb quite well, if rather clumsily, and climbing is their main defence against predators such as wolves.

It was not until the 1930s that giant pandas first appeared in zoos, and in the early 1970s they became instruments of diplomacy as the Chinese government presented pairs of them to zoos in Japan, the US, France and England. So far giant pandas have rarely bred in zoos outside their native continent, but the probability that they will soon do so is good. The female panda suckles her one or two young sitting up and holding them in her arms in a manner rather like that of primates.

169

Seals, Walruses and Sea Cows

Seals, sea lions and walruses are aquatic mammals belonging to the carnivore suborder *Pinnipedia*. This suborder is divided into three families: the true or earless seals, *Phocidae*, the eared seals, *Otariidae*, and the walruses, *Odobenidae*. The pinnipeds evolved from terrestial carnivores but it is not known exactly when the transformation took place. Although fossil remains of seals from each of the three modern families have been discovered (dating from the Miocene epoch some 20 million years ago) they are from animals which already closely resemble their modern relatives. Many zoologists believe that the true seals have a separate ancestry from the eared seals and the walruses: they suggest that true seals evolved from a creature resembling an otter while the other two families had a bear-like ancestor.

Modern pinnipeds are very well adapted for an aquatic existence. Their bodies are streamlined and the digits of both front and hind limbs are fused together to form paddles or flippers for swimming. Although able to spend considerable lengths of time at sea, all seals must come ashore, on to land or ice, in order to breed. A female normally gives birth to a single calf which is suckled on land from one or two pairs of nipples which are hidden from view in pouches on the underside of her body.

True seals

The true seals have no obvious external ears. Their bodies and limbs are covered with a pelt of short, coarse hair which is moulted annually. The hind flippers are directed backwards, beside the tail, and are no use at all when the creature is moving on land. In the water the hind flippers spread out sideways like the tail-flukes of a porpoise and are used to propel the seal forwards while the front flippers are used for steering. True seals are, at best, rather awkward on land, moving forward by a series of wriggling jerks involving muscular contractions of the whole body.

The largest of the true seals are the elephant seals of which there are two species. The southern elephant seal, *Mirounga leonina*, is a huge animal found in Antarctic waters. A large bull may be as much as 7.6 m (25 ft) long and weigh up to three tonnes. The cows are about half this size. Breeding colonies, called 'rookeries', form each year on many Antarctic islands. The cows arrive at the rookeries in September and shortly after this each gives birth to a single calf. The bulls begin arriving in October for the next mating season and each one takes possession of a 'harem' of cows. Rival bulls are constantly fighting over the ownership of the largest harem and the losers of these fights are often severely wounded. During the 19th century, elephant seals were hunted almost to extinction for the sake of their blubber which was processed to yield an oil.

True seals are most numerous in the Antarctic and the crab-eating seal, *Lobodon carcinophagus*, is particularly abundant.

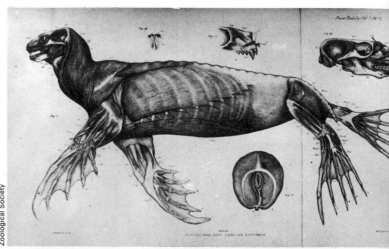

Right: This early anatomical illustration of a sea lion shows how the creature's outer muscles are arranged. Movement through the water is effected by flexing the body as well as moving the flippers.

Zoological Society

Below: A herd of walruses, *Odobenus rosmarus*, lying on a rocky shore on the coast of Alaska. These creatures are much less common than they were a century ago having been hunted by man for their skin, meat and blubber. Apart from man, they have few enemies for they can defend themselves very effectively with their huge canine teeth. Polar bears and killer whales occasionally take young walruses, but rarely molest adults.

Fred Bruemmer

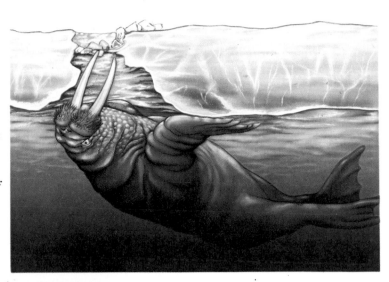

Left: A young walrus supports itself on one of its front flippers. Walruses, like sea lions, have quite well developed front limbs and can move about surprisingly rapidly on dry land.

Right: Walruses spend much of their time feeding beneath the pack ice, and they use their tusks to prevent breathing holes from freezing over. Walruses also use their tusks, which are enlarged upper canine teeth, to help haul themselves out of the water.

Below: The dugong, *Dugong dugon*, is found around the coasts of the Red Sea and the Indian Ocean as far east as northern Australia.

Allan Power/Bruce Coleman

Rex Features

Erik Pabst

Below: Bull elephant seals, *Mirounga angustirostris*, fight for the possession of females on the Pacific coast of Mexico. Elephant seals are so called because the nose of the male is long and pendulous and can be inflated with air to form a proboscis reminiscent of an elephant's trunk.

Right: A sea lion about to eat a fish. The majority of sea lions are found in the southern oceans where fish are plentiful, but a few species live in the Northern Hemisphere. The Californian sea lion, *Zalophus californianus*, for example, inhabits the rocky coastal areas of the US West Coast.

A survey in the early 1970s estimated the total population of these seals at between two and five million animals. It is a slender and fast moving seal with an unusual method of feeding. Whereas the majority of seals feed on a variety of fishes, cephalopods and crustaceans the crab-eating seal feeds only on a type of small, free-swimming shrimp, known as *krill*. When feeding the seal swims into a shoal of krill, takes in a mouthful of the shrimp-filled water and then squeezes the water out between its cheek teeth which are specially shaped to trap the shrimps within the seal's mouth. Weddell's seal, *Leptonychotes weddelli*, is another inhabitant of the Antarctic pack-ice. It is larger than the crab-eating seals and is capable of underwater dives of prodigious depth and duration.

Around the British coastline there are only two resident species of seal, the larger of these being the grey seal, *Halichoerus grypus*. An adult bull may be over 2.7 m (9 ft) long. Grey seals are gregarious and large rookeries exist on various rocky islands and beaches around Britain. Breeding takes place in the autumn, and the pups grow extremely quickly, doubling their size and weight within a week of birth. The pups are born with a shaggy coat of white fur which is moulted when they are weaned at about three weeks. At this early age the pups are deserted by their mothers and must thereafter fend for themselves. The other resident British seal is the common or harbour seal, *Phoca vitulina*, a small seal about 1.7 m (5.5 ft) long. Common seals are monogamous and less gregarious than grey seals. Breeding takes place in mid-summer on offshore sandbanks and secluded beaches.

Eared seals

The eared seals are divided into two sub-families—sea lions, *Otariinae*, and fur seals, *Arctocephalinae*—and they differ from true seals in having small but distinct external ears. Their hind flippers, as well as providing the main propulsive force in the water, can also be brought forward sideways to help the animal move about on land. The front flippers are larger and more supple than those of true seals and they can be flapped together underwater to provide some propulsion as well as providing steering power. On land the front flippers support the forward part of the body and are used as true walking legs. Eared seals are a great deal more mobile on land than true seals.

Steller's sea lion, *Eumetopias jubatus*,

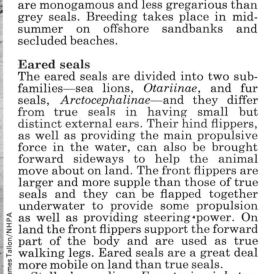

James Tallon/NHPA

171

Far left: An encounter
between sea lion cows
during the breeding
season. At this time of
year each of the older
bulls takes possession
of a harem of about 15
cows, and there is much
rivalry both between
cows and bulls.

Left: A sea lion uses
its rear flippers for
grooming as well as for
swimming.

Right: A female harp
seal, *Payophilus
groenlandicus*, resting
on the ice. Harp seals
are members of the
family *Phocidae* and
they are found in the
North Atlantic. Their
fur, particularly that
of pups, is much prized
by hunters, and because
they spend so much time
on the ice they make
easy targets.

is one of the largest species of seal, adult
males reaching a length of more than 3 m
(10 ft) and a weight of one tonne. Each
summer many thousands of these sea
lions migrate to the Aleutian Islands to
breed, the adult bulls arriving first, in
early May, to establish territories.
Pregnant females are the next to arrive
and almost immediately each one gives
birth to a single calf. The calves of sea
lions are suckled by their mothers for a
great deal longer than those of true seals;
weaning is rarely completed in less than
two or three months.

The Californian sea lion, *Zalophus
californianus*, is a smaller, more agile
species which inhabits the rocky coastal
areas of California. This is the sea lion
commonly seen in zoos and circuses
around the world. It is a playful and
intelligent animal and it appears to have
a natural talent for performing tricks
which require a fine sense of balance.

In their habits fur seals closely resemble
their relatives the sea lions. The Alaska
fur seal, *Callorhinus ursinus*, is found in
the northern Pacific and breeds only in
the fog-bound Pribilov Islands of the
Bering Sea. At the height of the summer
breeding season as many as two to three
million seals congregate at the Pribilov
rookeries. There are several other species
of fur seal belonging to the genus *Arctocephalus* from the Southern Hemisphere.

The walrus

The walrus, *Odobenus rosmarus*, is the
sole representative of the family *Odobenidae*. It has features in common with
both true seals and eared seals although
it is more closely related to the latter.
Like true seals, walruses have no external
ears, but they use both front and hind
flippers when walking on land like the
eared seals. The walrus inhabits the
shallow Arctic coastal waters of the
Atlantic and Pacific oceans, always living
close to land or ice. Adult males reach a
length of 3.7 m (12 ft) and weigh up to
1.5 tonnes, while the females are somewhat smaller and slimmer. Walrus skin is
enormously thick and wrinkled and
adults are almost completely hairless. In
both sexes the upper canine teeth are
greatly enlarged to form tusks which, in
old males, may reach a length of 76 cm
(30 in). Walruses feed mainly on shellfish,
the tusks being used when feeding to rake
the shellfish up off the sea-bed. Once
inside the mouth they are crushed
between massive cheek-teeth and the soft
contents are sucked out and swallowed.
Walruses breed during April and May.

Jacana

The bulls are polygamous and use their
tusks as formidable weapons when fighting for possession of the females; old bulls
are invariably heavily battle-scarred.
Young walruses are not fully weaned
until the end of their second year,
probably because they are unable to feed
properly until their tusks have grown.

Sea cows

Although sea cows are aquatic mammals
and superficially resemble seals in many
respects, they are quite unrelated and
belong to a different order, the *Sirenia*.
Indeed, the closest living relatives of sea
cows are elephants. The order *Sirenia* is
extremely ancient and sea cows were
widespread in the oceans of the world as
far back as the Eocene epoch some 40 to
50 million years ago. The order is divided
into two families: the manatees, *Trichechidae*, and the dugongs, *Dugongidae*.

Sea cows are completely aquatic and
they die very quickly if they become
stranded on land. They are shy, slow
moving creatures and they are entirely
herbivorous, feeding on various water
plants and sea-weeds. Their bodies are
bulky and the tail is flattened horizontally
to form a broad paddle, or 'fluke', which
is used to propel the animal through the

Above: A herd of South
African fur seals,
Arctocephalus pusillus.
Fur seals have a thick
coat of soft waterproof
underfur beneath their
coarse outer hair, and
this distinguishes them
from their relatives the
sea lions. Fur seals
were once vigorously
hunted for their fur,
but today hunting is
strictly controlled.

Below: A female hooded
seal, *Cystophora
cristata*, with her pup.
The hooded seal is
closely related to the
elephant seal and it
inhabits the drifting
ice floes of the Arctic.
Like elephant seals, the
male hooded seal can
inflate its nostrils
with air to form a
large bulbous air-sac
or hood.

Fred Bruemmer

Fred Bruemmer

water. The hind limbs have disappeared
completely and the front limbs are small
and oar-shaped. The eyes of sea cows are
very small and their faces are curiously
grotesque because the upper lip is huge
and mobile and adorned with a fringe of
stiff bristles. The skin of the sea cow is
thick and tough and beneath it is a layer
of fat or blubber which helps to insulate
the animal from the cold.

There are three species of manatee: the
Florida manatee, *Trichechus manatus*,
which is found in small numbers around
the Gulf of Mexico and the Caribbean, the
Amazonian manatee, *Trichechus inunguis*
from the northeastern coast of South
America and in the rivers Amazon and
Orinoco, and the West African manatee,
Trichechus senegalensis, which is very
rare and occurs along the tropical west

coast of Africa. Manatees vary in length
from 1.8 to 4 m (6 to 13 ft) and weigh from
270 to 900 kg (600 to 2000 lb). They are
slate grey or black in colour and the huge
upper lip is deeply divided in the centre
into two prehensile halves which can be
moved independently when gathering food
into the mouth. The tail fluke is smooth
and rounded and the flippers are sufficiently supple to be helpful in collecting
food. The flippers are equipped with short
nails and the body has a sparse covering
of short hairs.

There is one living species of dugong
and one species which became extinct
within the last 200 years. The dugong,
Dugong dugon, is found around the
coasts of the Indian Ocean. Dugongs are
slightly smaller than manatees and are
more highly adapted for aquatic life. The

upper lip has no cleft in it and the tail
fluke has a deep indentation in the centre.
The clawless flippers are less supple than
those of manatees and are no use in
feeding. The body is completely hairless
and male dugongs have two short tusks
in their upper jaws.

Steller's sea cow, *Hydrodamalis stelleri*,
an extinct member of the dugong family,
was first discovered in the cold Bering
Sea in 1741 by the German naturalist
Steller. It was a huge animal which grew
to a length of 7.6 m (25 ft). Its skin was
curiously rough and bark-like and instead
of teeth it had horny plates on the inside
of its mouth which it used to chew the
seaweed on which it fed. Within 17 years
of their discovery, the Steller's sea cows
had been completely exterminated by
hunters and traders.

Whales

Of all the mammals, both living and extinct, whales are the most perfectly adapted to an aquatic way of life. So perfect is this adaptation that, until comparatively recent times, naturalists mistakenly classified them as fish. Belonging to the order *Cetacea*, they are descended from four-legged, terrestrial mammals, although there is some uncertainty as to precisely which early mammals were their true ancestors. The change from terrestrial to aquatic habitat probably took place in the Palaeocene epoch some 65 million years ago.

Whales have streamlined, fish-shaped bodies and they lack a proper neck as a result of shortening or, in some cases, joining of the neck vertebrae. The body tapers smoothly towards the tail which is expanded out horizontally on both sides to form two flat, pointed tail flukes which provide the whale with propulsive power when they are beaten up and down in the water. Cetaceans show no trace of hind limbs and the front limbs have evolved to become smooth paddle-shaped flippers which are used for balancing and steering. Most whales have a dorsal fin positioned on the midline of the back which varies considerably in size and shape depending on the species.

Like all mammals, whales breathe air. Air is inhaled and exhaled through a special nasal opening known as the blowhole which is situated on the highest point of the head behind the snout.

Museum of Natural History/Leiden

P. Morris

The position of the blowhole allows the whale to breathe when only a small portion of its head and back are above the surface of the water. The blowhole has a characteristic shape for each species, and a few of the larger whales have two blowholes instead of the more usual one. Air is exhaled from the blowhole explosively, producing a blow or spout. The spout consists of mucus and water which forms as the whale's breath condenses in the air. The whale's windpipe is completely separated from its throat or pharynx so that it can open its mouth under water and breath at the same time.

The openings of the female's reproductive organs lie in a narrow slit on the underside of the body in front of the anus. The nipples are hidden in recesses on each side. When suckling, the nipples

Above: A Dutch engraving dating from about 1600 shows a stranded male sperm whale, *Physeter catodon*. The artist was clearly more interested in showing the size of the creature, which is slightly exaggerated, than in anatomical accuracy, for the eye (which is too large) and the flippers are wrongly positioned.

Right and far right: Sections through the skin of a dolphin and skin from a human palm. The dolphin's skin is perfectly smooth to reduce water resistance, and the dark cells (1) show through the outer transparent layer (2). It lacks the ridges (3) and sweat glands (4) which are typical of human skin.

Above: A pilot whale, *Globicephala scammoni*, from the Pacific Ocean. These animals are toothed whales and they live in herds of 100 or more individuals, feeding on fish and marine invertebrates, notably cuttlefish. They belong to the same subfamily as the killer whale and can grow to a length of 8.5 m (28 ft).

Right: The white whale, *Delphinapterus leucas*, is a close relation of the narwhal, and it is found in the oceans of the Northern Hemisphere. Although preferring Arctic waters, white whales are sometimes found along the coasts of northern Europe. The creature's blowhole and broad tail flukes are plainly visible in this picture.

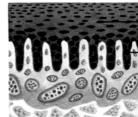

Right: A dolphin drives itself through the water by beating its tail flukes up and down with its powerful body muscles.

P. Morris

are protruded and milk is rapidly injected by the female directly into the calf's mouth. Suckling is rapid and takes place while both cow and calf are fully submerged. In the male the testes are internal and the penis lies beneath the abdominal skin in an almost coiled form. Beneath the skin, the whale's body is completely encased in an envelope of thick fat or blubber. For hundreds of years whales have been hunted by man for the sake of this blubber which, once refined, gives rise to a commercially valuable whale oil. Whale flesh is used in the manufacture of pet foods and is eaten by humans in some countries.

The whales are divided into two sub-orders: the baleen or whalebone whales, *Mysticeti*, which include the right whales, rorquals and humpback whales, and the toothed whales, *Odontoceti*, which include the sperm whales, beaked whales, narwhals, dolphins and porpoises.

Toothed whales

The *Odontoceti* or toothed whales are generally smaller than the whalebone whales and they have only a single blow-hole. Toothed whales feed on fish, squid and cuttlefish, and one species, the killer whale, also feeds on sea birds, seals and other whales. The behaviour of toothed whales is better known than that of whalebone whales because many of the smaller species are kept and studied at marine parks and oceanariums around the world. They are gregarious, playful animals and communicate with each other by means of clicks, whistles and quacking sounds.

Many, if not all, of the toothed whales are able to navigate in the dark by echolocation: the whale emits a pulse of ultrasonic clicks and then listens to the echoes of these clicks reflected off nearby objects. The pattern and quality of the returning echoes gives the whale detailed information about its surroundings and enables it to hunt for food in total darkness. As far as is known, whalebone whales cannot navigate by echolocation.

The sperm whale, *Physeter catodon*, is by far the largest of the toothed whales, adult males growing to a length of 18 m (60 ft). The females are considerably smaller. Each tooth is about 20 cm (8 in) long and weighs about 2.7 kg (6 lb). Sperm whales have a characteristic, domed forehead containing a large organ filled with a waxy substance called *spermaceti* which was once highly valued as an industrial lubricant and was also used in the manufacture of candles. The purpose of the spermaceti-producing organ is unknown but it may be involved in echolocation. Sperm whales were extensively hunted for their spermaceti and blubber, and in the days of sailing ships and hand-thrown harpoons the capture of these whales was a dangerous business. Unlike most other whales, sperm whales have been known to attack whaling boats, either ramming them

Below: A series of photographs showing the birth of a dolphin. Whales are born tail first, unlike most large mammals, and because they are born underwater they do not attempt to breathe at once. Only when the mother has nosed her newborn calf to the surface does it fill its lungs with air.

Below right: Bottle-nosed dolphins, *Tursiops truncatus*, are familiar performers at oceanariums throughout the world. They seem to delight in co-operating with their trainers and soon learn to perform the most remarkable tricks. They grow to a length of 3.6 m (12 ft) and come from the North Atlantic.

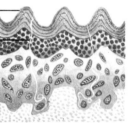

Below: Like all other whales, killer whales, *Orcinus orcas*, mate by swimming alongside each other belly to belly. Killer whales are the only cetaceans which regularly tackle warm-blooded prey such as dolphins, seals and penguins. Packs of 40 or more killer whales have even been known to overcome baleen whales.

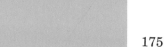

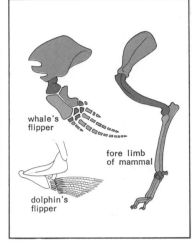

whale's flipper

fore limb of mammal

dolphin's flipper

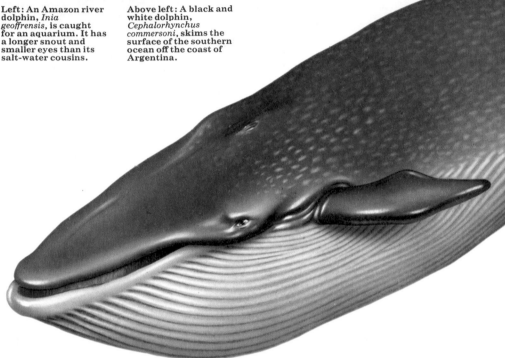

Left: An Amazon river dolphin, *Inia geoffrensis*, is caught for an aquarium. It has a longer snout and smaller eyes than its salt-water cousins.

Above left: A black and white dolphin, *Cephalorhynchus commersoni*, skims the surface of the southern ocean off the coast of Argentina.

with the snout or splintering them like matchwood between their massive jaws.

The narwhal, *Monodon monoceros*, is a peculiar, small whale inhabiting Arctic waters. Adult narwhals have only two teeth in the upper jaw, and in the male one of these teeth, usually the left one, is enormously enlarged to form a long, straight, spirally twisted horn or tusk which projects to a length of 2 m (6.5 ft) from the whale's snout. Although many suggestions have been made, it is not known how the narwhal uses its tusk.

Dolphins and porpoises

The dolphin family contains many species of small toothed whales. The largest of these is the killer whale, *Orcinus orca*, which grows to a length of 9 m (30 ft), has a striking black and white coloration and a very tall dorsal fin. Killer whales have about 50 sharp, conical teeth and are, as their name suggests, fierce predators. Their reputation as man-eaters, however, is probably undeserved for in captivity they have proved to be surprisingly gentle and co-operative.

The true dolphins are among the fastest of marine animals and are capable of reaching a speed of 25 knots in pursuit of the fish on which they feed. Dolphins usually travel around in large schools, sometimes containing hundreds of animals. They are natural acrobats and in the wild they frequently jump high out of the water when playing. Schools of dolphins often accompany ships at sea, positioning themselves at the front of the ship where they ride the bow-wave like surfers. They seem to enjoy this activity immensely and jostle each other for the best positions for wave riding.

Dolphins are curiously friendly towards humans and there are a few authenticated cases of dolphins attempting to rescue drowning swimmers by swimming underneath them and pushing them towards the surface. They will behave in the same way with injured members of their own species. In captivity, no dolphin, however severely provoked, has ever been known seriously to attack its trainer. In the wild, dolphins attack and kill sharks without hesitation and in the breeding season the males sometimes injure each other in fights, so there is little doubt that they could kill or maim a human if they wished to do so.

Many small toothed whales, dolphins included, have relatively large and complex brains and there seems to be little doubt among scientists that these are highly intelligent animals. Some zoologists who have studied dolphins firmly maintain that they must have a language of their own which is sufficiently complex to allow them to convey complicated instructions to each other. If this is true then dolphins must have an intellectual level comparable to man's and far above that of our nearest living relative, the chimpanzee which is highly intelligent, but has no language of its own.

The common porpoise, *Phocaena phocaena*, is one of the smallest whales, measuring 1.5 to 1.8 m (5 to 6 ft) in length. It is found in the North Atlantic and is one of the most familiar whales to be found along the coasts of Europe. Occasionally porpoises enter the mouths of large rivers, such as the Seine and the Thames, and they may travel upstream for several kilometres.

Whalebone whales

The most characteristic feature of a whalebone or baleen whale is its enormous mouth equipped with rows of whalebone plates which are used to strain food from the water. Each strip of whalebone is made up of thousands of long hairs which have grown together to form a single rigid plate with a fringe of stiff bristles

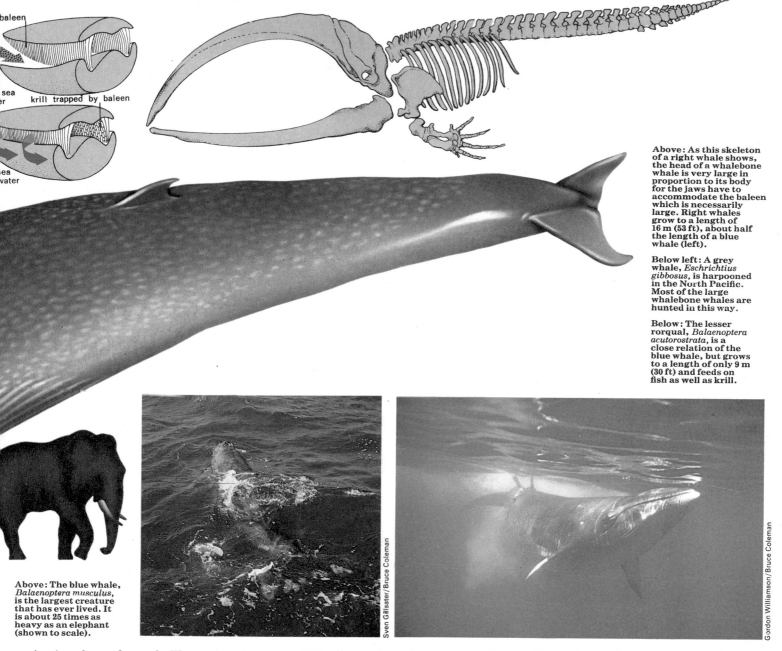

baleen

krill trapped by baleen

sea water

sea water

Above: As this skeleton of a right whale shows, the head of a whalebone whale is very large in proportion to its body for the jaws have to accommodate the baleen which is necessarily large. Right whales grow to a length of 16 m (53 ft), about half the length of a blue whale (left).

Below left: A grey whale, *Eschrichtius gibbosus*, is harpooned in the North Pacific. Most of the large whalebone whales are hunted in this way.

Below: The lesser rorqual, *Balaenoptera acutorostrata*, is a close relation of the blue whale, but grows to a length of only 9 m (30 ft) and feeds on fish as well as krill.

Above: The blue whale, *Balaenoptera musculus*, is the largest creature that has ever lived. It is about 25 times as heavy as an elephant (shown to scale).

projecting from the end. There may be hundreds of individual plates within the jaws of a single whale. The plates are rooted at their bases to the inside of the upper jaw and can be raised when the animal has its mouth closed to lie along the roof of the mouth. When the whale is feeding the plates are lowered to form a dense barricade, called the *baleen*, at the entrance to the mouth. The whalebone whales are filter-feeders and they use their baleens as gigantic sieves to extract shrimp-like organisms called *krill* from the water. After feeding, a large whale may have as much as ten tonnes of krill in its stomach.

Surprisingly little is known about the behaviour of whalebone whales. Most of them are migratory, spending the winter in tropical and temperate waters and migrating to the poles in summer, those in the Northern Hemisphere wintering in the arctic and those in the Southern Hemisphere in the Antarctic. Though occasionally observed on their own, these whales are sociable animals and are usually seen in pairs or small groups called *pods*. When migrating some species form huge schools of more than a thousand individuals. To communicate with each other, certain species produce an extraordinary 'song' made up of a series of peculiar squeals, grunts and moans. Many species migrate to specific areas in order to breed. Calves are born after a gestation period of about 11 months and are suckled by their mothers for from four to seven months depending on the species. Their rate of growth is astonishing: a whale calf may double its weight within the first week of life.

Right whales are unusual in having no dorsal fin and, unlike other whalebone whales, the right whale has no grooves on the underside of its throat. The mouth is a curious shape with the upper jaw being strongly arched and containing up to 600 plates of whalebone, each with a maximum length of 3.6 m (12 ft). Right whales formed the basis of the earliest whaling industries, indeed they are thought to have got their name simply because early whalers considered them the 'right' whales to hunt. They are unable to swim very fast and were successfully pursued and killed from rowing boats. The Greenland right whale or bowhead whale, *Balaena mysticetus*, is now very rare but still occurs in the Atlantic west of Greenland. It is dark grey in colour and grows to a length of 18 m (60 ft).

Rorqual whales are usually more slender and streamlined than right whales. The mouth is smaller and less grotesque, the back is equipped with a dorsal fin and there are conspicuous grooves on the throat. It is believed that these grooves enable the throat to expand when the whale is feeding so that a greater volume of water can be taken into the mouth. Until the advent of motorized whaling ships and harpoon guns, the rorqual whales were virtually unmolested by man because they are too swift to be pursued by a rowing boat. In this century, however, they have been the subject of a terrible slaughter and many are in danger of becoming extinct.

The blue whale, *Balaenoptera musculus*, is the largest of the rorquals and is also the largest animal which has ever lived. Blue whales sometimes reach a length of 33 m (110 ft) and a weight of 130 tonnes. Once widespread throughout the world, these whales are now exceptionally rare having been hunted almost to extinction by the whaling industry. Many scientists believe that the population of blue whales is now so drastically reduced that it has no hope of recovery and that the species will inevitably disappear in the near future.

Gibbons and Orang-utans

Of all living animals the true apes are the most closely related to man. As well as having large brains and being highly intelligent, they have the same number of teeth as we do and they lack tails. Nevertheless, in spite of these similarities, the relationship between apes and man must not be overstated: we are not descended from them. We should regard ourselves rather as cousins, for we are both descended from common ancestors who lived in the Miocene epoch, some 25 million years ago. Since that time the true apes and man have evolved along different lines, and it is therefore a mistake to think of apes simply as less perfect versions of ourselves. They are as highly adapted for their way of life as we are for ours.

All of the surviving apes live in or near the tropical forests of the Old World. The gorilla and chimpanzees live only in Africa, and the orang-utan and gibbons in Asia. Of these four groups of apes the gibbons are set rather apart from the others. Not only are they smaller, ranging in height from about 38 to 91 cm (15 to 36 in) when standing erect, but also, like the Old World monkeys, they have on their buttocks leathery patches which are useful when sitting on the tops of branches. The gibbons are therefore usually classified in a family of their own, the family *Hylobatidae*, which means 'tree walkers'.

Gibbons

On the ground gibbons are the only non-human primates which move only on their hind legs. Their arms are so long that in this erect posture their knuckles sometimes touch the ground and are used in rather the same way as crutches. The arms are often held rather awkwardly

Bruce Coleman

Below: The gibbon's lightly-built skeleton reflects its arboreal existence. Its arms are long and its hands act as hooks as it swings from branch to branch.

Norman Tomalin/Bruce Coleman

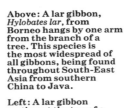

Above: A lar gibbon, *Hylobates lar*, from Borneo hangs by one arm from the branch of a tree. This species is the most widespread of all gibbons, being found throughout South-East Asia from southern China to Java.

Left: A lar gibbon resting at the top of a tree. Gibbons have dense fur which they keep spotlessly clean and free of parasites by constant grooming. Having such thick coats they can thrive in surprisingly cold climates. Several European zoos keep gibbons in outdoor enclosures or on islands in the middle of lakes for much of the year.

Right: The siamang, *Symphalangus syndactylus*, from Sumatra and the Malay peninsula is the largest and strongest of the gibbons. Siamangs produce a loud and characteristic 'song' at dawn and dusk. The sound is amplified by the creature's throat sac and probably denotes the ownership of territory. Siamangs are considerably less agile than the true gibbons of the genus *Hylobates*.

P. Morris

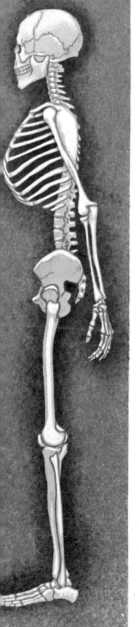

Below: The most obvious features of the human skeleton, when compared with that of a gibbon, are the larger skull, longer legs, shorter arms and wider pelvis.

Above: A gibbon can move through the forest very swiftly by swinging hand over hand from one tree to the next. This mode of progression, using the arms rather than the legs, is called *brachiation*, and is typical of the apes.

Left: A large male orang-utan like this one may weigh as much as 150 kg (330 lb). The huge cheek flaps are seen only in males and appear after the animal has reached maturity.

Below: Orang-utans, *Pongo pygmaeus*, live in the forests of Borneo and Sumatra. Although they come from the same part of the world as the gibbons, they are in fact more closely related to the gorillas and chimpanzees of equatorial Africa. Now on the brink of extinction in the wild, orangs were once quite common throughout eastern Asia. Their remains have been found in excavations as far north as Peking. In the last few thousand years orangs have become smaller—early remains show that orangs as large as gorillas once lived on the Asian mainland.

P. Morris

Okapia

clear of the ground when the animal runs. However, wild gibbons spend almost all their time in trees, and when they run along branches on two legs, grasping with their opposable big toes, their arms are extended as balancing organs. More often gibbons climb by *brachiation*, swinging on their long arms beneath the horizontal branches. The length of their arms is an adaptation to this mode of progression, and usually they swing hand over hand, although sometimes both arms are used in unison. They are capable of leaping across gaps up to 9 m (30 ft) wide, and can cover 3 m (10 ft) with a single reach of the arms. In gripping the branches the four fingers of each hand are held together and used as grappling hooks. The thumbs are small and are not brought into play. Moving fast and at considerable heights above the ground, it is not surprising that gibbons sometimes miss a hand-hold and fall. Usually they are saved from injury by the lower branches which act as safety nets, but injuries do occur from time to time. Sampling of some wild populations has shown that about one gibbon in three has suffered from a broken limb at some time in its life. Like the other apes, gibbons cannot swim.

The study of the behaviour of wild primates and especially apes is a popular branch of zoological science. The early hope that these studies would throw light on aspects of human behaviour has been fulfilled only in part. It seems that behaviour evolves more rapidly than anatomy, and in their behaviour wild apes differ much more than they do in bodily form. For example, the behaviour of gibbons, first studied in the wild in the 1930s, is in some ways more like that of many birds than that of other mammals. This is not as remarkable as it seems for gibbons, like many birds, live in the trees of dense forests, and have had to overcome much the same problems. Adult gibbons live in monogamous pairs. Each pair defends a territory and, being unable to see the neighbouring pairs, does so primarily by means of vocal signals, uttering loud, ringing and whooping calls. These carry over long distances, and are directly comparable to bird-song. Each pair of gibbons is accompanied by up to four of their young of differing ages, but on reaching maturity at perhaps six years of age the young are driven from the group.

Females give birth to usually only a single young one after a pregnancy of about 200 days. Like other young primates, young gibbons are at first almost completely helpless, able only to suckle and to cling to the mother's breast as she moves through the trees. At night the family sleeps huddled together, sitting erect on branches, with their limbs tucked up against their bodies. Early in the morning there is a burst of noisy territorial defence, and then the group moves round the territory feeding on leaves, buds, fruits and some insects. Some species also eat small birds, which they snatch from the air with remarkable dexterity. When drinking, gibbons usually dip their hands into the water, and then lick the moisture from them. As with other primates, part of the day is spent in social grooming. How long gibbons live in the wild is not certain, but in zoos many individuals have lived for more than 20 years.

sia, but in historic times the species has been found only in Borneo and Sumatra. Even in these islands they are now rare, and the total population numbers only a few thousand. The populations of the two islands are very similar in appearance, both having the same reddish brown, rather sparse hair, but there are differences. Sumatran orangs are on the average slightly larger, while male Bornean orangs have larger cheek flaps. For these and other reasons the two races are regarded as separate sub-species. The present rarity of orangs is chiefly the result of man's destruction of their native forests, both for timber and to make way for plantations. Also, orangs are too often caught as zoo specimens and pets, although this is now illegal. Attempts are now being made to conserve them in the wild: illegally caught young orangs are being rehabilitated for release in the wild, and reputable zoos no longer seek wild-caught specimens, having learned to breed their own orangs. However, economic pressures for forest destruction are strong, and the survival of the orang-utan is by no means certain.

The forests in which orangs live are usually dense, with some very tall trees and little or no undergrowth, and the forest floor is often swampy. Orangs are found in the trees at all heights, and at night they sleep in nests of branches and leaves about 20 m (66 ft) above the ground. The same nest is occupied for only a few nights before a new one is built elsewhere. The ability to make nests appears to be at least partly instinctive. When it rains they cover themselves with large leaves. Orang-utans mainly feed on fruit, especially that of the durian tree, which is their staple diet from August to December, but they also eat some leaves, seeds, bark and birds' eggs.

The gestation period is between eight and nine months, and almost always only one young is born at a time. The average weight at birth is 1.5 kg (3.3 lb) and the young orang clings tightly to its mother with its long arms. It may suckle for several years, but grows up at almost twice the speed that humans do. Orangs can breed when they are about seven years old, and are full-grown at about ten years. More information is needed, but it seems likely that the potential life-span is comparable to that of chimpanzees and gorillas, about 30 or 40 years.

Although orangs can move with surprising speed when they want to, their movements are normally slow and deliberate. Compared with chimpanzees they appear to be slow and introverted, so it is often believed that they are less intelligent than chimpanzees. There is however, no firm foundation for this view for most of the scientific intelligence testing that has been carried out on apes has been on chimpanzees, whose seeming fondness for showing off makes them co-operative, at least when they are immature. Orang-utans are certainly very intelligent: their brains are about as large as those of chimpanzees, being up to 450 cc (27 cu in) in volume. In captivity orangs show greater mechanical aptitude than chimpanzees do, being able to undo nuts and bolts that would fool a chimpanzee. They use their hands with great dexterity, but because their palms are long, the rather short thumb is less useful than the human thumb for many purposes.

Bruce Coleman

Okapia

Above: The social behaviour of the orangs is quite unlike that of the other great apes. Females and juveniles live in small, widely scattered groups, each keeping to its own home range, while adult males travel, mostly on their own, through a large territory visiting the various groups it contains. Pictured here is a group of young animals in a Sumatran forest. The territorial males father some but not all of the young. Less mature and less assertive males also visit the females when opportunity offers.

Left: A young orang. Like human babies, newborn orangs are almost completely helpless. They are suckled for between three and four years, but are fed some pre-chewed solid food from an early age.

Below: A female orang stands erect and carries her baby in her arms.

In appearance individuals of the typical gibbon genus, *Hylobates*, vary considerably. Even within a single species the thick, shaggy fur of some individuals may be black and that of others brown or silver-grey. The six species are therefore not easy to distinguish. Most often seen in zoos is the lar gibbon, *Hylobates lar*, found throughout South-East Asia, which can be identified by the white fur on the hands and feet and round the face. The hoolock gibbon, *Hylobates hoolock*, of Assam, Burma, and south-western China has prominent white eyebrows and an especially penetrating call. The smallest of the gibbons is *Hylobates klossi*, which is found only on the Mentawai Islands, off the west coast of Sumatra.

Orang-utans

Although it is the only Asian representative of the great ape family, *Pongidae*, the orang-utan, *Pongo pygmaeus*, is more closely related to the gorilla and chimpanzees than it is to the gibbons. Orangutan means 'old man of the woods' in the Malay language, and in facial appearance orangs are the most like humans of all the apes.

Fossil remains of orangs are widely
distributed in southern China and Malay-

Old World Monkeys

The monkeys of Africa and Asia belong to the same infraorder, *Catarrhina*, as the great apes and man himself. Although some of them can walk upright on their hind legs for short distances they generally walk on all fours. They have flattened nails on all fingers and toes, and, like all primates except tree shrews, they are able to grasp objects between the thumb and forefinger. Many Old World monkeys have long tails to help them balance when moving through the trees, but these are never prehensile as they are in many African monkeys. Also, the nostrils of Old World monkeys are closer together than they are in their American cousins.

All monkeys and apes are thought to have originated from a family of lower primates, the *Omomyidae*, which inhabited Europe and North America in the early Tertiary period some 60 million years ago. Descendants of these creatures migrated southwards, probably about 50 million years ago in the Eocene epoch, from North America to South America and from Europe to Africa and southern Asia. The two groups thus became geographically separated and evolved along slightly different lines to produce the zoologically distinct New and Old World monkeys we know today.

The African and Asian monkeys are

Above: Rhesus monkeys, *Macaca mulatta*, enjoy the protection of a temple at Kathmandu, Nepal. Grooming, as seen here, is an important activity for most monkeys; it not only rids them of parasites but also serves as a constant reminder of social position—high ranking animals receive the most attention.

Below: The pig-tailed macaque *Macaca nemestrina*, from South-East Asia is one of the largest macaques. The males have longish muzzles and look rather like baboons. This particular animal, from Singapore, has been trained to shin up coconut palms and pick the fruits for its human masters.

divided into two families, the *Cercopithecidae* which includes the macaques, baboons, guenons, drills and mandrills, and the *Colobidae* which includes the colobus monkeys, the proboscis monkey and the langurs. Man has been attracted by monkeys from the earliest times, the obvious resemblances to humans making them particularly fascinating. Two species of baboon were regarded as sacred by the ancient Egyptians and one of them, *Papio anubis*, still bears the name of their god of the dead, Anubis. Monkeys have always been popular research animals. As long ago as the second century AD the Greek physician Galen dissected baboons and other monkeys in the hope that he would learn about human anatomy.

Macaques

Macaques are found in southern and central Asia from India to Japan. They are heavily built monkeys reaching a maximum weight of about 13 kg (29 lb), and their fur is usually a yellowish brown colour. Like many Old World monkeys they have conspicuous pads of hard, hairless skin on the buttocks which develop after puberty and are often reddish in colour.

One of the best known macaques is the Barbary ape, *Macaca sylvana*, which gets its misleading name from the fact that, like the true apes, it has no tail. Living in North Africa and Gibraltar, it is the only macaque to be found outside Asia. Whether it was introduced to Gibraltar by man or whether it has always been a resident there is uncertain, but fossil remains of similar monkeys have been found in various parts of Europe. They live in family troops and are quite bold even in their North African habitat where they frequently raid gardens and fields. This behaviour has, not surprisingly, made them unpopular with the human population and they are killed as pests in some regions.

Another well known macaque is the rhesus monkey, *Macaca mulatta*, from northern India, China, Burma and Thailand. Their true homes are the forests of

Right: With its arms and legs outstretched and its tail curled upwards behind it, a silvered leaf monkey, *Presbytis cristatus*, prepares to land on a tree in western Malaysia. These monkeys move with great agility when they are disturbed, covering as much as 10 m (33 ft) with a single leap.

both lowland and highland areas, but nowadays they have become adapted to, and even seem to prefer, man-made environments. In some parts of India, where monkeys are protected by religious laws, only about 15 per cent of the total rhesus monkey population lives in the forest, the remaining 85 per cent preferring villages, cities, temples and other human habitations.

Of all monkeys, the rhesus monkey is most commonly seen in zoos. It has played a vital role in medical research for many years, the most important contribution being the identification of the rhesus factor, a blood characteristic which occasionally appears in both rhesus monkeys and man. The unborn offspring of a rhesus negative mother and a rhesus positive father has a high risk of being stillborn because antibodies in the mother's blood tend to destroy the red corpuscles in the blood of the foetus if the latter should prove to be rhesus positive. Nowadays, thanks to research on rhesus monkeys, this dangerous condition can be detected early and the child's life saved by a blood transfusion.

Baboons and mandrills
The baboons, *Papio*, are a group of ground-dwelling monkeys from Africa. They are heavily built animals, reaching a maximum weight of about 50 kg (110 lb), and have well developed teeth, the canines being exceptionally long and pointed. As well as the usual plant diet, baboons eat eggs and small animals. One of the baboon's chief enemies is the leopard, and although the predator usually overcomes its prey in the end, this is by no means always the case. Large male baboons can defend themselves very effectively and will often drive off a marauding leopard; there are even cases of leopards being killed by baboons.

Baboons are active in the day and they spend much of the time in open grasslands close to herds of antelopes and zebra where they feed and groom each other. As well as keeping them free from parasites, grooming is an important social

Above: A troop of baboons on the move. The dominant males travel at the centre of the troop with the main group of females and young. Acting as a guard for this central group are the remaining adult males and females. The juveniles travel at the edge of the group but retreat inwards when danger threatens.

Right: When a dominant male baboon encounters rivals he 'yawns' to display his teeth. Because the size and condition of his teeth, particularly the canine teeth, are a good indication of his physical strength, the 'yawning' threat is a clear demonstration of his high social standing in the troop.

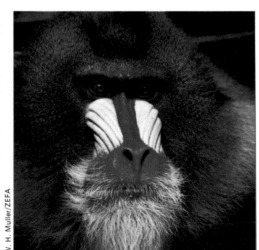

activity and is an indicator of a particular animal's rank: a dominant male will be groomed more frequently than other members of the troop. At night, when predators like hyenas and leopards are active, baboons climb trees for security, and several of the males take it in turn to keep watch throughout the night.

The mandrill, *Mandrillus sphinx*, is another large African monkey. It comes from the rain forests of central West Africa and is easily recognized by its extraordinary face: its long nose is covered by reddish skin and is flanked on either side by patches of pale, often bluish skin which have longitudinal grooves running along them from the eyes to the nostrils. The creature's buttocks are also hairless and brightly coloured. These areas of pigmented skin act as threat

Left: The mandrill, *Mandrillus sphinx*, is easily recognized by its bizarre face markings. Although it lives in the equatorial rain forests of West Africa, it spends most of its time on the ground searching for roots, fallen fruit, insects and frogs. It uses the same 'yawning' threat display as the baboon (above).

Below: A southern black-and-white colobus monkey, *Colobus polykomos*, from the coast of East Africa. At the beginning of this century colobus monkeys were shot in large numbers for their fur, and they became quite rare in some places. Nowadays their chief enemies are leopards and eagles.

W. H. Muller/ZEFA

Natural Science Photos

signals to other mandrills for they become markedly more vivid when the animal is excited. They probably also play an important role in attracting mates. Like baboons, mandrills spend the day on the ground, climbing trees at night to sleep. They live in small troops and feed on a variety of plant and animal food. Of similar appearance and habits but less vividly coloured is the drill, *Mandrillus leucophaeus*, also from West Africa.

Guenons

Almost every region of Africa south of the Sahara is inhabited by one or more species of guenon monkey. Although most species are residents of the central African rain forests, some guenons are more at home in open country. Guenons are slender animals with long tails and they have well marked and often brightly coloured coats. One of the most common guenons is the vervet or green monkey, *Cercopithecus aethiops*, which prefers savannah to forest. Having greenish-grey fur, vervet monkeys live in small troops and are quite bold, approaching other animals and even tourists without apparent concern.

Like all monkeys, guenons breed throughout the year, one or, rarely, two young being born after a gestation period of about seven months. For the first weeks of its life the baby guenon clings to its mother's abdomen using its tail as well as its arms to help it hold on. This ability to grasp with its tail, so common among American monkeys, is soon lost as the young animal grows. By the time it is two months old the baby guenon is very active and eating its first solid food, and by four months it is fully weaned. It becomes sexually mature at the relatively advanced age of four years.

Colobus monkeys

These are the only leaf monkeys (members of the family *Colobidae*) to inhabit the African continent—they live in the equatorial rain forests south of the Sahara. There are four species of which the southern black-and-white colobus, *Colobus polykomos*, is perhaps the most striking. Its coat is mostly black but there are areas of long white hair on the tail, the flanks and the face. Although it is not a true brachiator (an animal which uses only its arms when moving through the trees) like the gibbons of South-East Asia, the black-and-white colobus is very agile and it does use its arms and hands more than many other monkeys as it moves from branch to branch. This probably explains its lack of thumbs, for these digits appear to hinder brachiation.

Colobus monkeys live high in the forest canopy where they feed on leaves. Unlike that of most other monkeys (except leaf monkeys) the colobus's diet is restricted almost entirely to leaves and shoots; surprisingly it eats very little fruit. To cope with their unpromising diet of leaves, colobus monkeys as well as the other leaf monkeys have compartmented stomachs rather like those of ruminants such as cattle or sheep. In the first two stomach compartments bacteria begin the digestion process by breaking down the cellulose in the leaves into smaller, more manageable carbohydrates. These compounds then pass to the gut proper for normal enzymic digestion.

Langurs and proboscis monkeys

The langurs of the genus *Presbytis* are the most common of the Asian leaf monkeys. They are slender, long-limbed monkeys which inhabit the forests of India, South-East Asia and southern China. Langurs have long tails which no doubt help them to balance as they jump from tree to tree. In fact langurs and the other leaf monkeys are not so restless as most Old World monkeys, but they nevertheless move with great agility when they need to, and can cover 10 m (33 ft) or so with a single jump.

One of the most remarkable leaf monkeys is the proboscis monkey, *Nasalis larvatus*, from Borneo. It is a large, strong monkey immediately recognizable by its long nose. An adult male may reach a length of 76 cm (30 in) from its nose to the base of its tail, and its large, bulbous nose may be 10 cm (4 in) long. Proboscis monkeys spend most of their time in the mangrove forests feeding on buds and leaves. They are reputed to be excellent swimmers. Closely related to the proboscis monkeys are the snub-nosed langurs, *Rhinopithecus*, from China and Tibet and the pig-tailed langur, *Simias concolor*, from Sumatra. These leaf monkeys also have long noses, but not so long as that of the proboscis monkey.

Ivan Polunin

Left: Guenons, genus *Cercopithecus*, can be distinguished from each other by their facial markings. Shown here are (1) the owl-faced guenon, *C.hamlyni*; (2) DeBrazza's monkey, *C.neglectus*; (3) the vervet monkey, *C.aethiops*; (4) the mona monkey, *C.monas*; and (5) the crowned guenon, *C.pogonias*.

There are often differences in colour and marking between the adults and young of the same guenon species. This may serve to prevent young animals from being attacked by the adult males (who tend to be aggressive) by making them easily distinguishable from other members of the family troop.

Below: The odd-looking proboscis monkey, *Nasalis larvatus*, is a native of the island of Borneo. Adult males have huge, bulbous noses which are important secondary sexual characteristics: in the breeding season females select the males with the largest noses. The females have short, turned-up noses.

Bruce Coleman

1
2
3
4
5

Gorillas and Chimpanzees

Popularly known as the great apes, the chimpanzees and gorillas, together with the orang-utan of South-East Asia, make up the family *Pongidae*. Of all primates these are the most closely related to man, whom they resemble in having no visible external tail, and in their well developed brains. Within the family the chimpanzees and gorillas, which live in Africa, are more closely related to each other than to the orang-utan, having diverged from a common ancestor perhaps seven million years ago.

Both chimpanzees and gorillas have the long arms associated with the arm-swinging method of climbing (*brachiation*) best seen in the gibbons of Asia, but because they are so large and heavy, adult chimpanzees and gorillas rarely brachiate for long. Gorillas spend most of their time on the ground, and chimpanzees spend only about half of their time in trees. One expert, Adriaan Kortlandt, has argued that the immediate ancestors of the chimpanzee were even more terrestrial, living in the African grasslands from which they have since been driven by mankind. This is far from certain. We know only that when chimpanzees were first discovered by Europeans they were living in the African forests.

Gorillas

The gorillas' reputation as savage monsters is entirely without foundation. They are shy vegetarians. During the day the dominant male leads the troop through a home range which has a total area of about 39 sq km (15 sq miles). Home ranges are not defended against other groups of gorillas—if two troops happen to meet, the adults usually ignore each other, although the juveniles may mix together briefly. This cool behaviour is typical of gorillas and reflects their aloof, introverted personalities.

The dominant male is allowed to rest in the most comfortable places, and gets the first choice of the food available without appearing to assert his massive authority. Only rarely, in defence of the troop against the gorilla's only serious enemy, man, or very occasionally when confronting rivals, does he launch into his threat display, hooting, rising on to his hind legs, beating his chest with his hands, and finally charging. Even then he is not very likely to attack; usually the charge is a bluff, and stops short of the intruder. More often at the first hint of danger the troop silently moves off, avoiding confrontation.

Such shy animals are difficult to observe in the wild and so, no doubt, a great deal remains to be discovered about gorillas' behaviour. As far as we know they are purely vegetarian, feeding on leaves, stems, bark, roots and fruit. Some of their favourite foods, for example, are stringy stems with about the consistency of celery. Like most other primates they eat quite a wide variety of foods, but are fussy as to which part of it they accept: before eating they examine their food carefully, pulling it apart, and

gibbon   orang-utan

gorilla   chimpanzee

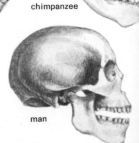
man

Below: A lowland gorilla. Gorillas are vegetarians and they spend much of their time feeding on shoots, leaves and the pith of stalks and branches. Because their food is so low in nutritional value, they have to eat a large quantity each day. Although they are good climbers, they generally remain on the ground.

Bottom: In the wild, gorillas live in groups like this one of about 15 animals. Led by a large silver-backed male, the group consists mainly of adult females with their young, juveniles and one or two other adult males. On reaching maturity most males leave the family group. These are mountain gorillas.

Above and right: The human cranium is larger and more rounded than that of any ape, for it has to accommodate a brain whose volume is about 1,500 cc. The brain sizes of gorillas, chimpanzees and orang-utans are about 500, 400 and 450 cc respectively. Man's weaker jaw accounts for many other differences.

Jacana

Bruce Coleman

184

Left: A large male gorilla in typical surroundings. Because they feed on bushes and small trees, gorillas prefer to live near the edge of the rain forest where the sunlight can penetrate. Whereas felling trees for timber often provides an ideal habitat for gorillas, wholesale clearing of the forest for cultivation reduces their range.

Below: The male gorilla's threat display can take a number of forms. Usually it begins with a series of hooting sounds and culminates in a chest-beating performance, but a variety of other gestures may intervene. Only very rarely is the threat display followed by a genuine attack.

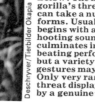

hooting

chest beating

running sideways

uprooting plants

rejecting any discoloured parts.

Gorillas sleep in nests, but even when tall trees are available these are constructed near the ground. Male gorillas, having nothing to fear from predators, usually make their nests in low bushes or even on the ground. An adult male gorilla standing on its relatively short hind legs may be up to 1.8 m (5.9 ft) tall, and has an arm span of up to 2.75 m (9 ft). Large males may weigh up to 275 kg (605 lb), but this is exceptional. The creature's head is particularly massive because it includes a tall bony ridge on top of the skull to which the powerful jaw muscles are attached. These give the gorilla a very strong bite used primarily to tear through the hard stems of some plants to get at the softer pith inside. Adult male gorillas are larger than the females and can be recognized by the greyish-white fur on their backs.

Females and juveniles climb more often than adult males do. No doubt the gorilla's ancestors were smaller and more arboreal than their modern descendants, for, apart from their size, they are well adapted for climbing, with long, grasping digits, opposable thumbs and big toes, long arms which are potentially useful for brachiation and good binocular vision. The ability to judge distance is essential to an active climber.

Gorillas have a discontinuous distribution in equatorial Africa. The western lowland gorilla inhabits forests of Cam-

Left: Like humans, chimpanzees use a whole range of facial expressions to indicate their emotions. This animal, with its gaping mouth and jutting upper lip, is expressing frustration. Chimpanzees also communicate with other group members by a variety of hoots and grunts, and, to some extent, by touch.

Below: Chimpanzees spend more time in trees than do gorillas. Every evening the adults build nests like the one shown here to provide protection from predators. The nests are made of bent and woven branches covered with a bed of smaller branches and leaves. They may be as much as 30 m above the ground.

Giuseppe Mazza

excitement

elation

Left: Chimpanzees, like the other apes, use their hands more than their feet for climbing about among the trees. As an adaptation for this method of locomotion, they have particularly long arms and relatively short legs. They walk with the soles of the feet flat on the ground and the upper part of the body supported on the knuckles.

Below: A chimpanzee extracts termites from a nest by using a twig stripped of its leaves. When the twig is poked into the nest, angry termites seize it and are drawn out of the nest. Although chimpanzees eat leaves, bark and insects, about 90 per cent of their diet consists of fruit.

eroun, Gabon, and western Zaire. Nearly 1,000 miles to the east, the eastern lowland gorilla inhabits forests from the Lualaba or upper Congo River to the foothills of the mountains beyond. Here on the slopes of the Virunga volcanoes and the mountains bordering Lake Kivu lives the mountain gorilla. These three populations differ slightly from each other in features of the skull and in certain other ways— mountain gorillas, for example, have slightly longer, thicker fur.

However, most zoologists now agree that there is only one species, *Gorilla gorilla*, and that the various forms are only subspecies. Lowland gorillas live in dense forest, preferring areas where fallen trees or rivers break the upper canopy, allowing the sunlight to encourage thick undergrowth, which is a rich source of their food. Mountain gorillas prefer more thinly wooded valleys where ferns and creepers abound. Sometimes they venture above the tree-line in search of bamboo shoots.

The gestation period of the gorilla is about nine months. At birth baby gorillas are even more helpless than those of most other primates. For the first month of life they cannot even cling to their mother, but have to be cradled in her arms. At three

months a baby gorilla may start to ride on its mother's back, and at six or seven months it can walk and climb on its own. However, the bond with the mother remains very strong until, three or four years later, she has another youngster. In the rate at which they mature, gorillas resemble chimpanzees. More data is needed, but it seems likely that they have a potential life-span of 40 or more years.

Chimpanzees

There are two main kinds of chimpanzees. The commoner of these, *Pan troglodytes*, is widely distributed in tropical Africa, and several different races or subspecies have been described. However, all chimpanzee populations are rather variable in appearance, and these differences are not very important. The most distinct of all chimpanzees is the pygmy chimpanzee, the only form to be found south of the Congo River. This is regarded by many authorities as a separate species, *Pan paniscus*. The pygmy chimpanzee is less heavily built than the common chimpanzee, which weighs up to 50 kg (110 lb) or more, adult females being almost as large as males.

Chimpanzees are far from being specialized feeders. In mature rain forests they

feed mainly on fruit, when it is available, although they also eat leaves and bark. In more open savannah woodland they make up for the smaller supply of vegetable foods by eating insects, and sometimes by hunting and eating other mammals, such as small antelopes. In some parts of West Africa chimpanzees have colonized rubbish dumps outside towns, where they feed on scraps.

Chimpanzees have developed a remarkable technique for obtaining termites, a popular item of diet. Picking a small twig or grass stem they remove all its side branches, and poke it into a termites' nest. Angry termites seize the intruding object with their jaws, and cling to it as the twig is withdrawn. The chimpanzee then pulls the twig through its lips, removing the termites. This action looks highly intelligent, but there is some evidence to suggest that it is purely instinctive. If they are given a slender twig, zoo-bred chimpanzees need little encouragement to poke it into holes, and also draw it through their lips.

One interesting aspect of this behaviour is that in preparing the twigs for use chimpanzees are essentially making tools. They also do this when crushing dry leaves before using them to soak up

fear

sadness

Left: Some common chimpanzee expressions.

Right: A female pygmy chimpanzee with her baby. Like the other apes, chimpanzees reproduce only slowly because the females cannot conceive while they are lactating. Since the female will nurse her young for between two and three years, she can produce only one (occasionally two) offspring every three years or so. The gestation period is between seven and eight months. This particular species, *Pan paniscus*, is found in equatorial Africa, south of the Congo River. The more common species, *Pan troglodytes*, is found throughout central and western Africa, from Senegal to Tanzania.

Tierbilder Okapia

Tierbilder Okapia

Above: Chimpanzees in captivity are enthusiastic painters, and their efforts resemble the early works of human children. They seem to have a rudimentary sense of symmetry for their compositions on paper are usually fairly well balanced. They rarely paint only down one side of the paper.

Below: The most significant difference between man and his nearest relatives, the apes, is his much greater mental capacity. The ability to learn and remember things made language possible and paved the way for logical thought. These spectators are watching a chess championship in the USSR.

Marc Riboud/John Hillelson Agency

water for drinking. This means that man is not unique as a toolmaker, and the attempts that were made a few years ago to use toolmaking ability to place man apart from all other animals are not based on fact. The truth is that no absolute distinction can be made between man and all other animals.

Chimpanzees are certainly intelligent. Experiments to determine intelligence have all been carried out with young chimpanzees, for adults are aggressive and uncooperative, and young animals learn more quickly than old ones. Once young chimpanzees have learned that by standing on a box they can reach higher objects—even such an obvious fact has to be learned—they swiftly put their knowledge to good use in obtaining fruit which is otherwise out of reach. Behaviour of this kind enables them to solve problems which could never be solved by instinct alone, and produces flexible behaviour which can be adapted to meet a variety of situations.

In the wild chimpanzees live in large, loosely-knit groups. About 80 animals may occupy an undefended home range of between 20 and 78 sq km (8 to 30 sq miles). They move equally well through the trees or on the ground, where they walk on all fours, touching the ground with the backs of their knuckles. Adult males travel further than the others, acting as scouts for the main party. When they find a tree laden with ripe fruit their drumming and loud hooting calls attract other chimpanzees from up to 3 km (2 miles) away to join in the feast. On these occasions chimpanzees belonging to neighbouring troops mix without hostility. Large males have high status,

and are treated with deference, but within the troop there is no rigid 'pecking order'. When conflicts arise between individuals they are usually solved when one of the individuals concerned moves off to join another troop.

The chimpanzee's essentially peaceable disposition is not even disturbed when the females come into breeding condition, as they do every month or so. At this time females have swellings in the region of the genital organs. They are promiscuous, and may mate with several males in succession. The gestation period is usually between seven and eight months, and at birth the young chimpanzee weighs about 1.9 kg (4.2 lb). For the first two years of life it is completely dependent upon its mother, but as it grows older it is supported by other members of the troop.

By playing with other juveniles it exercises its body, learns about its surroundings and, probably most important of all, becomes socialized and learns how to get on with other members of its species. Until about six years of age the young chimpanzee never goes far from its mother, but it then becomes more independent and, especially if it is a male, may begin to go off with other chimpanzees for increasingly lengthy periods. Chimpanzees are sexually mature at about 8 years, full-grown at about 12 years, and may live for 40 or more years unless they fall victim to a predator. Apart from man the chimpanzee's greatest enemy is the leopard. When threatened by such a predator, chimpanzees arm themselves with missiles and sticks, and confront it aggressively, the combined strength and resourcefulness of the troop being their main defence.

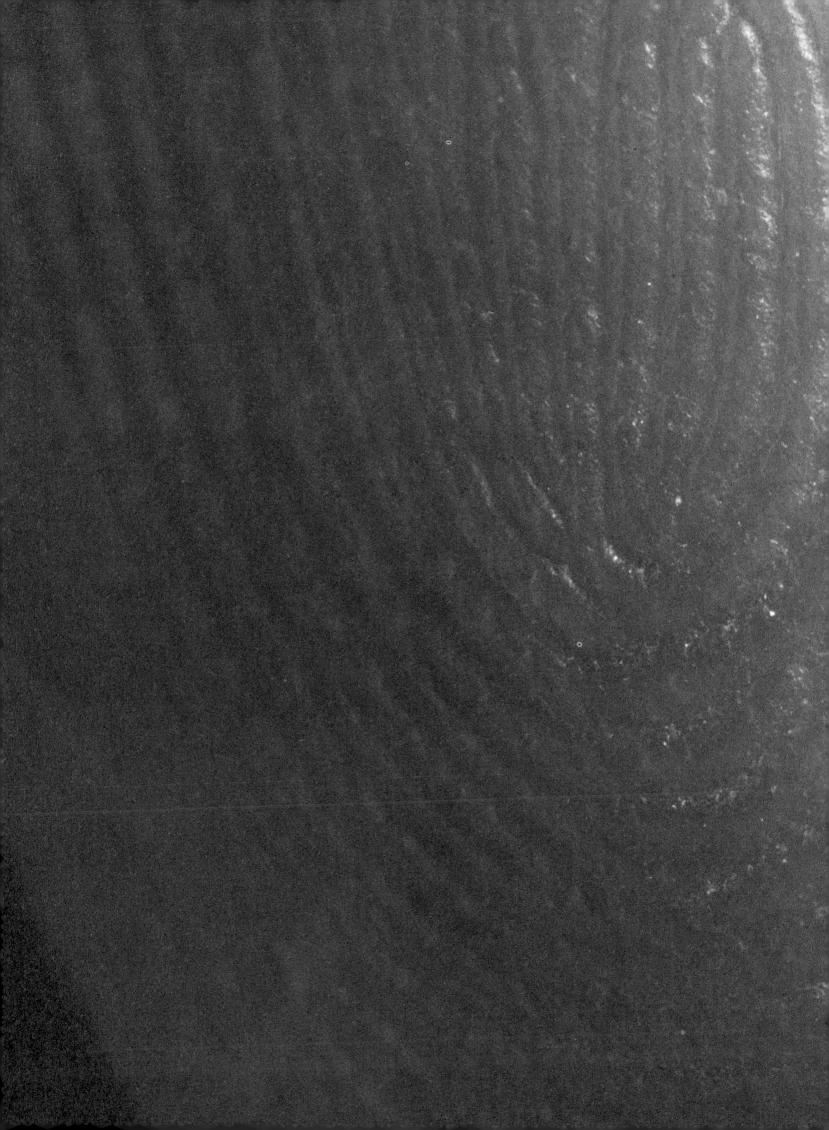

THE
HUMAN BODY

Sight

Man depends on sight more than upon any other sense to supply information about his environment. His upright posture, the mobility of his eyes and head and stereoscopic vision—vision from the two slightly different angles of the eyes—give man a panoramic view of the world, containing information on depth, distance, dimension and movement. Further, the adaptability of the eye and its sensitivity to colours and contours enables man to perform close and detailed tasks.

The eye has a highly complex structure. The *cornea*, the bulge at the front, is a transparent window that lets light rays into the eye and bends, or refracts, them. A flat, circular coloured membrane, the *iris*, lies behind the cornea and gives the eyes their characteristic colours. Between the cornea and the iris is a small compartment containing a clear fluid, the *aqueous humour*, which nourishes the cornea.

The iris governs the size of the *pupil*, a small hole in its centre that regulates the amount of light entering the eye. The *crystalline lens*, lying behind the pupil, further refracts the light to focus a sharp image on the *retina*. This thin, nerve-laden screen lining the back of the eye, transforms light energy into electrical messages that are transmitted to the brain by the *optic nerve* which runs from the back of the eye. A large compartment, containing a viscous fluid called the *vitreous humour*, lies between the lens and the retina and makes up most of the volume of the eyeball.

The case of the eyeball, apart from the transparent cornea at the front, is made from tough, white fibrous tissue called the *sclera*. The sclera contains fine blood vessels and when the eye is irritated, say by dust or disease, the blood vessels become enlarged and the 'white' of the eye appears pink or bloodshot.

Light and sight

Some light is always necessary for seeing. The human eye cannot perceive the image of an object unless it is carried by light rays. A luminous source, such as a candle, may either send light directly to the eye, or the rays may bounce off the surface of an object before reaching the eye.

Light rays, which normally travel in straight lines through air, are refracted or change direction slightly when they enter a denser medium such as water or glass. The eye uses refraction to focus the light rays it receives from the object on to the retina.

Light first passes through the cornea and, as this is denser than air, the rays are refracted. This begins the process of focussing an image on to the retina. Since the cornea bends the light rays more than any other part of the eye, it is referred to as the coarse focus.

The aqueous humour has hardly any effect on the light rays as it is of a similar density to the cornea. It is renewed every four hours but may occasionally have small impurities in it which cast shadows on the retina, creating 'spots before the eyes'. Pressure on the eyeball has a similar effect of causing coloured patterns. These arise because

Left: A light ray passing from air into a denser medium such as glass is bent or refracted. A light ray entering the eye is refracted slightly by the cornea. This starts the process of focussing the image on to the retina. The aqueous humour lying behind the cornea continues the process, which is completed by the lens.

Right: Astigmatism is a common visual defect caused by an imperfectly curved cornea. It results in blurred vision. Light rays entering the eye are refracted to a greater degree in either the horizontal or vertical plane. Astigmatism is corrected by lenses that compress the image in the direction opposite to that of the distortion.

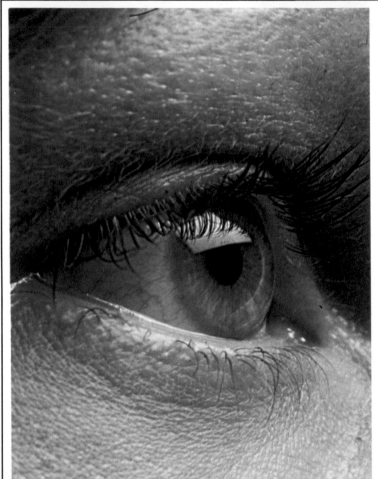

Left: Several features protect the eye.

Eyebrows prevent sweat running into the eye.

Eyelashes keep the eye clean and protect it from glare. Each eye has about 200 lashes and each lasts between three and five months.

Eyelids sweep dirt from the surface of the eye, protect it from injury and help distribute tear fluid.

Tears are sterile and constantly bathe the front of the eye and its thin, protective covering membrane, the *conjunctiva*. Though tear flow is continual, only about $\frac{1}{2}$ to $\frac{2}{3}$ of a gram of fluid is produced per day. This is drained off through a small duct leading from the inner corner of the lower eyelid and into the nose. Sometimes mucus and dust collect as 'sleep' in the inner corner of the eye.

The *eyeball*, together with the muscles that control eye movement, blood vessels, nerves and the lacrimal gland are lodged in a bony socket in the skull. The socket is lined with fat and has a volume five times as great as that of the eyeball.

Right: The structure of the eye.

NEAR SIGHT

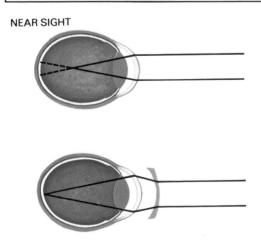

Top left and right: Short-sightedness or *myopia* occurs when the light rays from a distant object are focussed in front of the retina. If the eyeball is too long from front to back, or if the lens provides too great a degree of refraction, the focussed image falls short of the retina. Adolescents sometimes suffer from short-sightedness, as the eyeball becomes excessively long during uneven body growth.

Bottom left: Spectacles with concave glass lenses are worn to correct short sight. The lenses diverge the rays slightly so that they have to travel further through the eyeball and are focussed exactly on the retina.

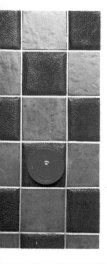

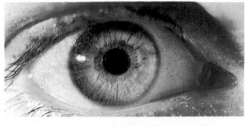

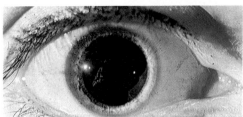

the eye can only interpret stimulation in terms of 'visual' signals.

Normally the aqueous humour is secreted behind the iris, circulates through the pupil and filters out between the iris and the cornea. If, however, the fluid is secreted faster than it can be reabsorbed into the veins, pressure rises and a condition known as *glaucoma* develops. If untreated, this will cause damage to the optic nerve fibres, and a gradual restriction of visual field.

Where the cause of this condition can be found, it is usually obstruction to the outlet of fluid, rather than excessive production of the aqueous humour. As a result, drugs can often be used to reduce the pressure—for example, by constricting the pupil and so relieving congestion of the fluid outlets.

Control of the amount of light entering the eye is essential if the retinal image is not to be blurred. The pupil determines the amount of light let in as a result of the contraction and expansion of the muscles of the iris. This control is particularly important for detailed work in which a special sharpness or *acuity* of vision is vital. In close work, such as reading, the pupil shrinks in order to sharpen the focus by limiting the access of light rays from a single point on the object. People who spend much of their time doing intricate work, such as artists, often look at their work through half-closed eyes to 'distance' it. Again, this cuts down the amount of light entering the eyes so that they see the shape and perspective more clearly.

Accommodation
The process of adjustment for near and distant vision is called *accommodation* and is controlled by the movement of the crystalline lens. The lens of the eye, although it resembles a piece of curved glass, differs from glass in that it does not have a uniform structure, but consists of 2,000 thin layers of tissue. As the light rays pass through each layer they are refracted to a minute degree.

The lens of the eye differs from a glass lens in another important way—it is more flexible. Whereas the lens of a camera, for example, has to be moved backwards and forwards until the correct focus is found, the lens of the eye simply changes shape.

The lens is supported by a sheath of transparent material, called the *suspensory ligament*. The eye adjusts its focus by changing the curvature or thickness of the lens. *Ciliary muscles* control the tension in the suspensory ligament which pulls the lens into different shapes. To focus on near objects, for example, the ciliary muscles contract, allowing the suspensory ligament to relax. This causes the pliable lens to become more spherical, decreasing its focal length and increasing its refractive power. Thus it is able to focus a clear image of a near object on to the retina. The pupil decreases in diameter at the same time to concentrate the light on to the central part of the lens where the accommodation changes are most marked.

For focussing on a distant object, the lens becomes flatter. Light rays from such an object are almost parallel by the time they reach the eye so there is no need for such a large degree of refraction as for the divergent rays from a near object. The lens therefore has less adjustment to

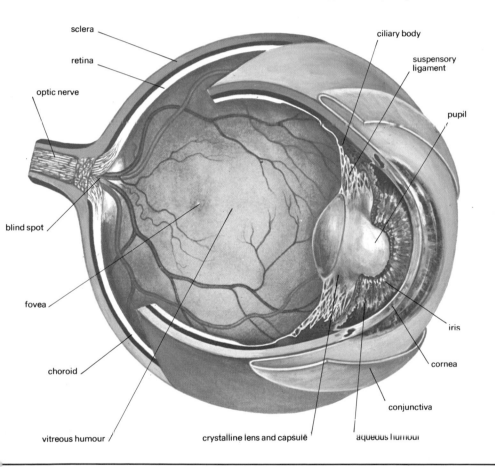

sclera
retina
optic nerve
blind spot
fovea
choroid
vitreous humour
crystalline lens and capsule
ciliary body
suspensory ligament
pupil
iris
cornea
conjunctiva
aqueous humour

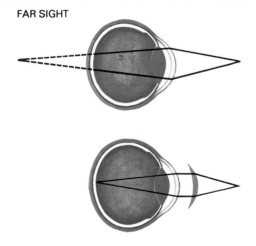

FAR SIGHT

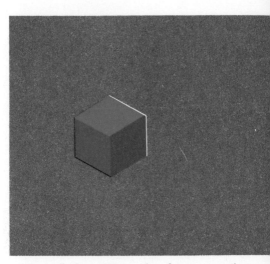

Left: The camera obscura, a dark room with a small hole in one wall, is like an eye. Light travelling in straight lines from a point on an object through the hole or pupil casts a sharp, inverted image on the far wall or retina. The image is upside down because the light rays cross at the aperture. The brain turns it up the right way.

Right: To find the blind spot, hold the page at arms' length. Close the left eye and focus the right eye on the left hand object. Bring the page slowly towards you until the object on the right vanishes. Its image has fallen on the point where the optic nerve leads from the back of the eye. There are no rods or cones here.

make when the rays have passed through the cornea.

The focussing power of the lens is influenced by the eye's rate of growth and age. An eye which has reached normal maturity can focus clear images of near and distant objects. Ageing makes the lens less pliant, however, and consequently less able to adjust its shape quickly for close and distant focus. Bifocal spectacles help to correct this condition—the upper half of the lens aids distant vision, and the lower half, near vision—and compensate for the overall rigidity of the lens.

The elderly are also far more prone to *cataract,* a condition causing opacity of the lens, than the young. This often results in complete or partial blindness. Sometimes this can be alleviated by removing the damaged lens and replacing it with thick-lensed spectacles. This operation is relatively simple but the effect, restoration of sight, is dramatic.

The cavity containing the vitreous humour lies behind the lens. The fluid keeps the retina in position and maintains the spherical shape of the eyeball. The density of the vitreous humour is similar to that of the lens so it does not interfere with light passing through it.

Rods and cones

The retina, the screen on which light rays are projected, is a network of more than 130 million tightly packed fibres, covering the transparent innermost layer of the eyeball. The nerve fibres are composed of two types of light sensitive receptors, *rods* and *cones.* There are two types because man exists in two visual worlds— day and night, light and dark. The clarity of an image depends on light intensity and the angle of perception. The seven million cones operate for detailed examination of an object in bright light; the rods are used for seeing in dim light.

The cones contain the chemical, *iodopsin,* and are sensitive to coloured light. Rods respond only to shades of black and white. They contain a chemical, *rhodopsin* or *visual purple,* allowing them to function in dim light only, when colours are much subdued and often lost completely. Bright light bleaches the chemical, reducing the sensitivity of the visual system to light. Consequently, when a person walks into a dark room from a sunny garden he is temporarily 'blinded' until the visual purple is formed again.

A mixture of cones and rods are distributed unevenly in the retina. In the centre of the retina, the *fovea* contains only cones and is used for accurate vision in bright light. This is why it is so difficult to read, for example, in a poorly lit room when the cones are not functioning efficiently.

The fovea has a limited field of view so the eyeball moves continuously to keep the image within this. There are also cones on the periphery of the retina but too few for sharp focus—they serve to alert man to movement and the eyeball shifts so that a sharp image falls on the fovea. Again this explains why it is impossible to read this page or do any detailed work out of the corner of an eye. Either the head or the eyes or both must be moved to face the object of interest before its image falls on the fovea and it comes into clear focus.

The fovea, because it contains only cones, is useless in dim light. To see an object in such light, the light rays have to fall outside the fovea and on to the area of rods. So instead of looking directly at the object under these conditions, a person tends to look to one side of it. Although this peripheral vision does not give as much clear detail about the object it does provide enough information to discern its basic outline.

Left and below: Stereo vision is vision from two slightly different angles. It is one of the means by which man perceives depth and distance. The stereoscope, a popular Victorian device, allows the viewer to see two pictures of the same scene taken from different angles, the difference corresponding to the distance between the eyes, which are set some 65mm or 2½in. apart. Viewed through a stereoscope the picture of the couple turns from a flat photograph into a three dimensional scene. Stereo vision can be demonstrated by opening and closing each eye alternately. Near objects will seem to shift in relation to distant objects.

Right: Double vision, or *diplopia,* is usually caused by paralysis or weakness of one or more of the six muscles that control the movement of each eye. With normal vision the eyes, when viewing an object, move to such a position that the two slightly different images received fall on corresponding parts of the retina and are therefore exactly superimposed. Failure of the muscles of one eye creates an imbalance which results in one clear image overlaid with a 'ghost' image. Double vision is also a symptom of several nervous diseases and of diphtheria. A temporary state is sometimes induced by an excess of alcohol.

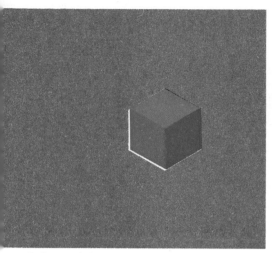

Colour vision

The way in which the eye distinguishes between the colours of the spectrum is not fully understood and there are several theories of the mechanism of colour vision. Currently, the most widely accepted theory that explains most of the facts is the Young-Helmholtz theory, the basis of which was laid in 1801 by the English physician and physicist, Thomas Young. It was developed in the mid-nineteenth century by the German scientist, Hermann von Helmholtz.

According to this theory, there are three types of cones, each of which is sensitive to either red, green or blue light, the three basic colours. Each type of cone has its own visual pigment, equivalent to the visual purple of the rods. Coloured light excites various proportions of the three types of cones and in this way, intermediate colours, combinations of the basic colours — are detected. Green light, for example, stimulates only green-sensitive cones, while yellow light stimulates both red and green units in equal amounts, producing the effect of yellow.

A similar process occurs in a colour television receiver. Pictures on a colour television screen are composed of thous-

Above and below: In the seventeenth century Sir Isaac Newton discovered that white light was composed of colours. Passing a narrow beam of light through a prism produced a spectrum of colours at the other side —starting with red at one end and going through orange, yellow, green, blue and indigo to violet at the other.

Light is the only source of colour and objects assume their colour because they absorb some of the colours of the spectrum and reflect others. A red rose chiefly reflects red rays and it is these which enter the eye and give the concept of redness. White surfaces reflect all the colours of the spectrum.

ands of minute dots, colour coded to appear in the correct patterns. In a similar way, the mosaic of cones on the retina sorts out the colour distribution in the image by reacting in differing degrees of sensitivity to light rays.

The German physiologist, Ewald Hering, challenged the Young-Helmholtz theory. His opponent-process theory holds that there are three pairs of sensory reaction—black-white, red-green and yellow-blue. No part of the last two pairs can be active at the same time though black and white can operate together, to allow perception of grey shades. Recent research suggests that both main theories of colour vision have validity.

Colour blindness, the inability to distinguish between certain colours, is a congenital abnormality which affects about six per cent of males and one per cent of females. In red-green colour blindness, which is the most common defect, a person is unable to tell the difference between red and green. It is not that red looks green or green looks red but that both look grey, blue or yellowish depending on the amount of the blue and yellow in the light. Exactly what goes wrong in the colour vision mechanism to make someone colour blind is not clear.

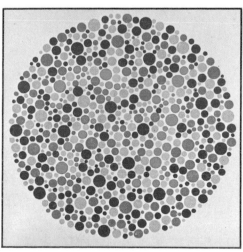

Left: What number do you see? People with normal colour vision perceive three basic colours—red, green and blue—and see the number 74. Individuals with red-green colour blindness, the most common type, cannot tell red from green and see the number 21. Totally colour blind people see no number.

Above: Focus on the dot for 20 seconds and then look at a white surface. Because red and green and blue and yellow share the same colour coding mechanism, and the removal of one stimulus temporarily triggers the other, an after image will appear, showing the other of the paired colours.

Taste and Smell

Ever since man first stood up on his hind legs and lifted his nose from the ground his sense of smell and the associated sense of taste have become relatively less important to his survival than they are to other animals. Increasingly he has come to rely on his sight, hearing and touch to provide information about his surroundings. Consequently taste and smell tend to be the least developed and most neglected of the human senses, reserved almost exclusively for the selection and appreciation of food and drink.

Taste and smell are both chemical senses. Unlike the eyes that are stimulated by light or the hearing mechanism that is excited by sound waves, the senses of taste and smell are triggered by the chemical content of substances in the environment. Chemical particles are picked up by receptor sites in the mouth and nose respectively and converted into nerve impulses for conduction to the brain.

Exciting the taste buds

The sense of taste is the least versatile of the five human senses, being strictly limited in the range and potential of its discoveries. In fact the tongue is able to detect only four 'basic' tastes. It can tell the difference between the sourness of lemon juice, the sweetness of syrup, the bitterness of coffee and the saltiness of bacon. There is no taste category for 'savoury' as such, for example, which is used to describe a multitude of different foods. Basically the impression of 'savoury' depends on the relative proportions and combinations of the four 'basic' tastes.

The sense of taste depends on the stimulation of taste receptors on the tongue. In order to be tasted the chemicals of the food must be in liquid form. Put a dry piece of food into a dry mouth and there is very little sensation of taste. Particles of dry food have to be dissolved in saliva before they can be detected by the taste buds, the organs of taste. Salt is picked up very quickly because it is highly soluble in water and rapidly dissolves in the saliva. More complex substances take slightly longer to dissolve and are therefore not picked up as quickly.

Taste buds are buried in shallow pits on the tip, sides and back of the upper surface of the tongue. Children usually have more taste buds than adults and consequently have a more highly developed sense of taste. Some of their taste buds are also distributed in the lining and roof of the mouth, cheeks and throat.

Although a particular food probably tastes roughly the same to most people, there are a few who suffer from taste 'blindness' to certain substances. A simple test with a chemical called phenylthiocarbimide (PTC) distinguishes between 'tasters', who detect a bitter taste, and 'non-tasters', for whom the liquid is tasteless. This ability or inability to detect PTC seems to run in families and therefore appears to be inherited. Such differences in the personal experience of tastes may well exist for other substances.

The combination of all the information received by the brain from the mouth about the nature of the food influences the way in which the brain interprets its chemical taste. Hot foods often taste different when they are cold and tough meat seems to have less taste than a tender cut. This is not because the taste buds react any differently to the chemicals in the food but because other sensory receptors in the mouth for temperature and touch are stimulated in different ways.

Confusion often arises between the detection of taste by the taste buds and the stimulation of temperature, pressure and pain receptors in the mouth. Peppermint, for example, 'tastes' cool because it excites temperature receptors on the tongue. In the same way, certain spices like curry and ginger 'taste' hot because they cause a burning sensation by stimulating the pain nerve endings. Curry paste has a similar effect if it is applied to soft skin on other sensitive parts of the body.

Touch and pressure receptors provide information about the texture of a food, whether it is crisp or creamy, hard or soft. The ears detect what sound it makes as it is chewed in the mouth. The jaw muscles used for chewing report on how much chewing it needs. The eyes report on the food's colour and presentation.

Colour and appearance of the food are two very important components of taste appreciation. Most people find it impossible, for example, to tell the difference between grapefruit and orange juice if they are blindfolded before the test and unable to see the different colours of the two liquids.

By far the greatest influence on the sense of taste is the sense of smell itself. What

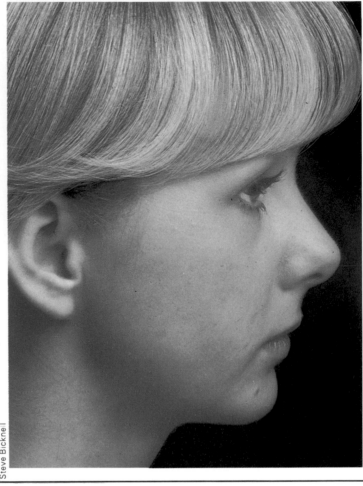

Steve Bicknel

Air flows up the nostrils into two chambers, the nasal cavities, behind the nose. The nasal cavities are lined with a thick mucous membrane which is richly supplied with blood vessels, nerves and glands. This nerve-laden lining is extremely sensitive to pain. The blood vessels of the nose can become dilated during menstruation and pregnancy, causing the distortion of the sense of smell, and when the air is hot, making the nose stuffy in an overly warm room. It is also one of these blood vessels that ruptures during a nose bleed. Glands in the mucous membrane secrete the mucus that keeps the lining of the nasal cavities moist. Over-activity of these glands results in excessive mucus production that can block the nose. The smell-detecting part of the lining of the nose is called the olfactory area. Tucked away in two small pits or olfactory clefts towards the roof of the nasal cavities, each patch covers about 2.5 sq sm (1 sq in) on either side. As air passes up the nose and into the nasal cavities it is warmed and moistened. Some of it is then deflected up over the olfactory area by the three bony turbinate plates on the walls of the chamber. Before an odour can be smelled it must be dissolved in the fluids coating the lining of the nasal cavity.

Right: The tongue is covered with tiny taste detectors, taste buds, which are buried in its surface. Food placed in the mouth dissolves in saliva and then washes over the taste buds, each of which is sensitive to one of the four basic tastes — bitter, sweet, salt and sour. Although taste buds sensitive to each are scattered all over the tongue, those sensitive to one particular taste tend to be concentrated in separate regions which can be mapped.

Bitter: The bitterness of black coffee, beer or the quinine in tonic water is chiefly detected at the back of the tongue. These liquids only really taste bitter when they hit the back of the throat as they are swallowed. Sweet: Sweetness is largely picked up by the tip of the tongue. Sipping sherry or licking a lollipop effectively concentrates their sugary sweetness on the tip of the tongue. A sugar lump placed in the centre of the tongue tastes far less sweet than if it is tested with the tip. Salt: Sensitivity to the saltiness of salted peanuts or bacon is greatest on the tip of the tongue. Salt dissolves quickly on the tongue and is almost instantly recognizable. Sour: Sourness is a characteristic of all acids such as the citric acid in grapefruit or acetic acid in vinegar and is mostly picked up by the sides of the tongue.

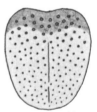

bitter

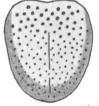

sweet

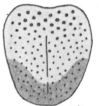

salt

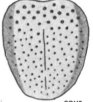

sour

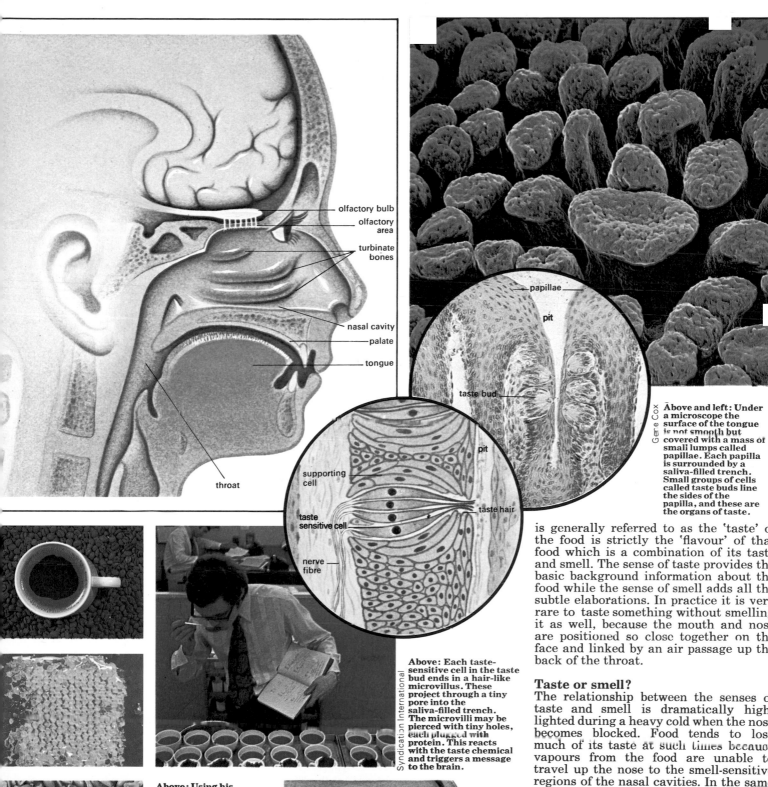

olfactory bulb

olfactory area

turbinate bones

nasal cavity

palate

tongue

throat

papillae

pit

taste bud

supporting cell

pit

taste sensitive cell

taste hair

nerve fibre

Above and left: Under a microscope the surface of the tongue is not smooth but covered with a mass of small lumps called papillae. Each papilla is surrounded by a saliva-filled trench. Small groups of cells called taste buds line the sides of the papilla, and these are the organs of taste.

Gene Cox

Lennart Nilsson, Time/Life

Above: Each taste-sensitive cell in the taste bud ends in a hair-like microvillus. These project through a tiny pore into the saliva-filled trench. The microvilli may be pierced with tiny holes, each plugged with protein. This reacts with the taste chemical and triggers a message to the brain.

Syndication International

Above: Using his highly-developed senses of taste and smell a professional tea taster can distinguish between many subtle blends of teas.

Right: Smells reach the smell-sensitive regions of the nose by two routes. During normal breathing most air passes straight through the nose into the wind pipe. Sniffing helps to break up the airflow, sending eddies of smell-laden air over the olfactory region, thus increasing the sense of smell. Vapours from food in the mouth can also escape via the throat into the nasal cavities. Smell is thus an important element in the appreciation of the flavour of food.

Gordon Roberton

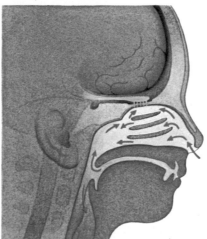

is generally referred to as the 'taste' of the food is strictly the 'flavour' of that food which is a combination of its taste and smell. The sense of taste provides the basic background information about the food while the sense of smell adds all the subtle elaborations. In practice it is very rare to taste something without smelling it as well, because the mouth and nose are positioned so close together on the face and linked by an air passage up the back of the throat.

Taste or smell?

The relationship between the senses of taste and smell is dramatically high-lighted during a heavy cold when the nose becomes blocked. Food tends to lose much of its taste at such times because vapours from the food are unable to travel up the nose to the smell-sensitive regions of the nasal cavities. In the same way it is almost impossible to tell the difference between finely-grated apple, potato or onion on the tongue without chewing, if your eyes are closed and your nose is blocked. Chewing the food would agitate some vapours up the back passage to the nose and hence to the olfactory region where they would be recognized as onion, potato or apple. On the tongue all taste slightly sweet.

A simple game with food mixtures illustrates how many different clues are used to identify a food. Three or four different foods are mixed together. Then someone is blindfolded, given a spoonful of the mixture and asked to name its constituents. The right answers are usually only reached after the food has been thoroughly tested and played with in the mouth.

195

Mixtures of foods also raise the question of the influence of one food's taste on that of another food. Sweet foods, for example, often tend to taste less sweet if eaten after some other sweet food. It appears that the taste buds get used to tasting sweetness and need a short break before they are able to pick it up again at full power.

To be smelly a substance must give off particles of the chemical of which it is made. In other words it must be volatile. A saucepan of chicken soup boiling on the stove smells more strongly of chicken than a plate of cold chicken because many more 'chicken' particles are escaping from the broth than they are from the cold meat. For the same reason a smell gets stronger closer to its source because the cloud of vapour gets denser.

The particles of a smelly substance must remain in the air so that they can be swept up into the nose where the sense of smell is located in the lining of the nasal cavities. Just like the sense of taste, the smelly substance must be soluble in water before it can reach its receptors. Travelling over the olfactory membrane some of the odour particles dissolve in the mucus layer and come into contact with the smell-sensitive surface of the mucous membrane.

Wetness also generally heightens smells. By definition a smelly substance is soluble in water. As the water evaporates from the wet surface of an object it carries some particles of the substance with it. A wet dog is smellier than a dry dog and wet earth smells more 'earthy' than when dry because of the water vapour rising from their surfaces.

Loss of smell

The sense of smell wanes rapidly with exposure to the odour. Someone working in a coffee shop would be oblivious to the strong smell of freshly-roasted coffee beans that greets the customers as they enter the shop. Similarly, it becomes possible to tolerate an unpleasant smell when one has got used to it. A person entering a crowded, stuffy room is often repulsed by the mixture of body odours and stale smoke. Yet after a comparatively short time he will probably become as unaware of these smells as the people already in the room.

This apparent change in a person's sensitivity to a smell arises because of the phenomenon of *adaptation* in which the odour receptors quickly become occupied by odour particles. The detection of a smell depends on the interaction between the chemical units of the smelly substance and their receptor sites in the nose. When all the receptor sites are filled, such an interaction can no longer take place. Consequently the olfactory region stops signalling to the brain that the smell exists.

Water is an exception to the rules of solubility and volatility of smelly substance. For although water is both soluble and volatile it is quite odourless. One theory suggests that the mucous membrane of the olfactory region is permanently adapted to the presence of water since it is bathed in the fluid all the time. Therefore it stops signalling the presence of water which is consequently odourless.

As with taste, other factors influence the way in which the brain interprets messages about a smell. The characteristic smells of ammonia or chlorine, for

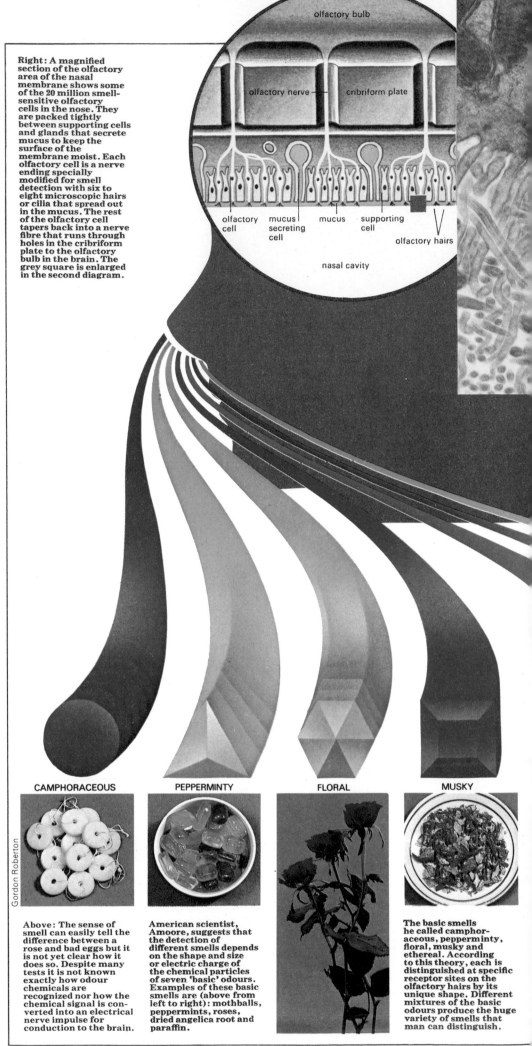

Right: A magnified section of the olfactory area of the nasal membrane shows some of the 20 million smell-sensitive olfactory cells in the nose. They are packed tightly between supporting cells and glands that secrete mucus to keep the surface of the membrane moist. Each olfactory cell is a nerve ending specially modified for smell detection with six to eight microscopic hairs or cilia that spread out in the mucus. The rest of the olfactory cell tapers back into a nerve fibre that runs through holes in the cribriform plate to the olfactory bulb in the brain. The grey square is enlarged in the second diagram.

olfactory bulb

olfactory nerve — cribriform plate

olfactory cell — mucus secreting cell — mucus — supporting cell — olfactory hairs

nasal cavity

Gordon Roberton

CAMPHORACEOUS

PEPPERMINTY

FLORAL

MUSKY

Above: The sense of smell can easily tell the difference between a rose and bad eggs but it is not yet clear how it does so. Despite many tests it is not known exactly how odour chemicals are recognized nor how the chemical signal is converted into an electrical nerve impulse for conduction to the brain.

American scientist, Amoore, suggests that the detection of different smells depends on the shape and size or electric charge of the chemical particles of seven 'basic' odours. Examples of these basic smells are (above from left to right): mothballs, peppermints, roses, dried angelica root and paraffin.

The basic smells he called camphoraceous, pepperminty, floral, musky and ethereal. According to this theory, each is distinguished at specific receptor sites on the olfactory hairs by its unique shape. Different mixtures of the basic odours produce the huge variety of smells that man can distinguish.

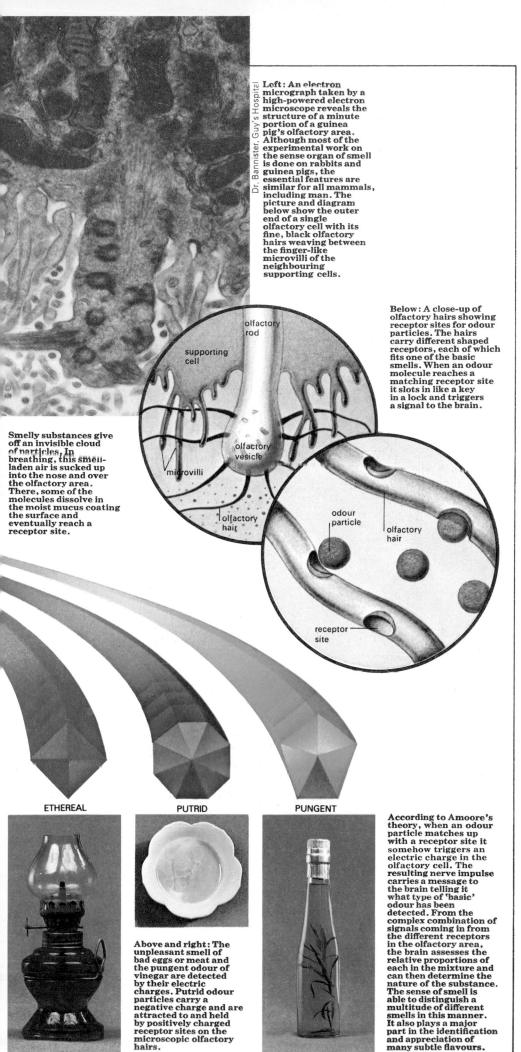

Left: An electron micrograph taken by a high-powered electron microscope reveals the structure of a minute portion of a guinea pig's olfactory area. Although most of the experimental work on the sense organ of smell is done on rabbits and guinea pigs, the essential features are similar for all mammals, including man. The picture and diagram below show the outer end of a single olfactory cell with its fine, black olfactory hairs weaving between the finger-like microvilli of the neighbouring supporting cells.

Dr. Bannister, Guy's Hospital

Below: A close-up of olfactory hairs showing receptor sites for odour particles. The hairs carry different shaped receptors, each of which fits one of the basic smells. When an odour molecule reaches a matching receptor site it slots in like a key in a lock and triggers a signal to the brain.

supporting cell

olfactory rod

olfactory vesicle

microvilli

olfactory hair

odour particle

olfactory hair

receptor site

Smelly substances give off an invisible cloud of particles. In breathing, this smell-laden air is sucked up into the nose and over the olfactory area. There, some of the molecules dissolve in the moist mucus coating the surface and eventually reach a receptor site.

ETHEREAL PUTRID PUNGENT

Above and right: The unpleasant smell of bad eggs or meat and the pungent odour of vinegar are detected by their electric charges. Putrid odour particles carry a negative charge and are attracted to and held by positively charged receptor sites on the microscopic olfactory hairs.

According to Amoore's theory, when an odour particle matches up with a receptor site it somehow triggers an electric charge in the olfactory cell. The resulting nerve impulse carries a message to the brain telling it what type of 'basic' odour has been detected. From the complex combination of signals coming in from the different receptors in the olfactory area, the brain assesses the relative proportions of each in the mixture and can then determine the nature of the substance. The sense of smell is able to distinguish a multitude of different smells in this manner. It also plays a major part in the identification and appreciation of many subtle flavours.

example, in cleaning fluids or at a swimming pool, are partly due to their caustic attack on the lining of the nose that stimulates pain receptors in the nasal cavity. Peppermints and the camphor in moth balls can also induce a feeling of coldness.

The senses of taste and smell are more than mere sensory decoration. They serve as valuable early warning systems in situations where there are no auditory or visual clues. It is possible, for example, to smell the smoke of the fire before the flames appear. A smell had to be added to odourless natural gas when it was introduced for domestic use because people were unable to see or smell the potentially dangerous gas leaks.

At a more primitive level, taste and smell are used for choosing food and avoiding poisonous substances. Most people are naturally repulsed by the smell and taste of bad eggs or rotting meat and will therefore not eat large quantities that might be harmful.

The message in smells

Throughout the animal world smells play an important part as a means of communication between individuals and as a way of influencing one another's behaviour. Such chemical signals are referred to as *pheromones*. Humans, too, use artificial smells like perfumes to express their sexuality. Certain scents are associated with women while others are considered more masculine. There may also be a primitive hidden language of odours between humans which they react to unconsciously but which nevertheless plays a part in exciting responses of fear, hostility or friendliness. Chemical compatability or incompatability may be an important aspect of a relationship.

Each person has his or her own distinctive natural smell. Body odour arises largely from the action of bacteria on the chemicals in sweat, producing a rank odour. There are basically two kinds of sweat glands on the body, those associated with cooling and temperature regulation that excrete mostly water and mineral salts. The others differ between the sexes and produce a fatty substance which the bacteria attack. Masking these natural body odours with deodorants and anti-perspirants may also smother the communication of fear, hostility, nervousness or sexual excitement to another person.

It is possible to identify and isolate the chemicals responsible for the characteristic tastes and smells of many different substances. These chemicals can be reproduced in the laboratory and substituted for the natural substance. Taste and smells are rapidly becoming an important branch of the chemical industry as the demand for artificial flavours and odours is growing all the time. There are pleasant smells to mask unpleasant smells, marketed as air fresheners, and 'old car' smells to spray in new cars to give them extra 'character'.

On the whole, tastes and smells are very memorable. The smell of a place or a person and the taste of a particular food are often evocative. They add an extra dimension to a scene, one that it is impossible to capture on film or in words. They tend to be very personal memories, experiences that cannot be shared with anyone else who has not experienced them for himself.

197

Hearing

A human being's sense of hearing involves a natural mechanism with awe-inspiring powers of sensitivity and range. In the hearing process an intricate chain of events operates in which sound waves are conducted through the ear and translated into electrical impulses. These impulses are then routed to the brain for decoding. Almost instantly the hearer can distinguish the meaning of these signals. A clackety-clack is recognized as a typewriter, a click of metal on metal is understood as the sound of a key in the lock, and the vibrations of human vocal chords are heard as a familiar voice.

Equally remarkable is man's ability, within limits, to select the focus of his listening attention. Many clearly audible sounds may scarcely be noticed while other slight sounds may alert the hearer's attention immediately. This selective process is important because life would be a nightmare if every sound in the environment forced itself into one's consciousness.

Sound itself is both a physical and psychological phenomenon. Waves of sound caused by a vibrating object are basically minute changes in air pressure. The waves have no meaning, no message until they reach the ear. There they are translated into nerve impulses for interpretation by the brain.

The three compartments of the ear

The ear is divided into three sections: the outer, middle and inner ear. The outer ear consists of the *auricle,* which is the visible shell of the ear, and the *ear canal* which leads to the eardrum. The functions of the outer ear are limited to concentrating and directing sound waves into the auditory canal where they are condensed, increasing the pressure of the higher frequency sounds, and conveyed to the eardrum.

The middle ear begins at the *tympanic membrane,* or eardrum. This cavity is air-filled, and the internal air pressure is maintained at the same level as the external atmosphere by means of the *Eustachian tube.* The tube leads from the ear to the throat and opens whenever a person swallows or yawns, to protect the most delicate parts of the ear from abrupt changes in the air pressure. Another protection of the hearing mechanism is operated by the muscles of the middle ear. These react automatically to extremely loud sounds, cutting down the volume by tightening the eardrum and pulling the bones of the middle ear back from the delicate inner ear.

The middle ear contains the *ossicles,* three tiny bones named for their distinctive shapes: the *malleus* (meaning hammer), *incus* (anvil) and *stapes* (stirrup). When a sound wave reaches the tympanic membrane it causes the tightly-stretched membrane to vibrate; this vibration is magnified in force by the action of the ossicles. It is picked up by the malleus and pushed on through the incus and stapes. From the ossicles the amplified vibrations of sound pressure are transmitted via a tiny membrane called the *oval window* to the fluid-filled inner ear.

The inner ear cavity houses the *cochlea,* a minute, coiled tube of two canals

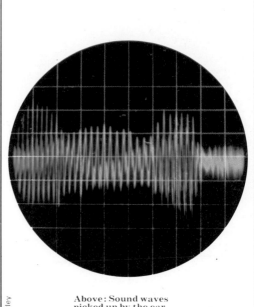

Paul Brierley

Above: Sound waves picked up by the ear when we hear someone speak can be recorded and visualized by an oscilloscope.

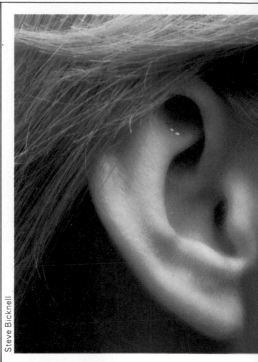

Steve Bicknell

David Levin

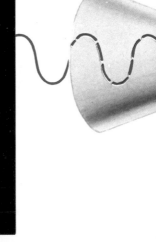

Left: As the clapper hits the sides of the bell it sets up tiny vibrations in the metal. The movements compress and separate surrounding air particles, causing a sound wave that is detected by the ear. The loudness and pitch of the bell's ringing are determined by the size and rapidity of the vibrations.

Right: It can be very difficult to pinpoint the source of a sound. The bird's song coming from behind reaches the man's ear a split second before the left ear picks it up. Sound waves coming from the tree ahead would reach the right and left ears with exactly the same time gap. Since his brain uses any minute time gap to assess where a sound is coming from, the man cannot distinguish between the two possible sources of sound. He has to move his head so that the relative positions of the real and imagined birds are changed. While the true source remains in the same place the shadow sound moves, indicating that the bird is indeed singing in the tree behind him.

Outer ear
The auricle, the visible ear flap, helps to direct sound into the ear canal, which is lined at its entrance with fine hairs and wax-secreting cells to protect the ear from dirt and dust. The canal leads down to the eardrum, the tympanic membrane, stretched across the mouth of the middle ear cavity.

Middle ear
This air-filled space is spanned by the ear ossicles, the malleus, incus and stapes (hammer, anvil and stirrup). These small hinged bones convey vibrations of the eardrum to the oval window of the inner ear. The Eustachian tube, connected to the back of the nose, balances air pressure with that of the middle ear. When ears 'pop' the tube has opened to equalize pressure inside and outside the ear.

Inner ear
This consists of the fluid-filled cochlea, the coil that houses the delicate hearing mechanism.

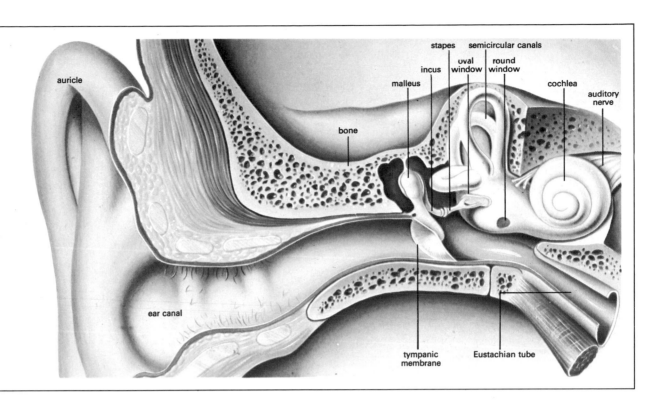

Right: The three tiny bones of the middle ear, the ossicles, serve as connecting links from the eardrum to the wall of the inner ear. The ossicles are connected to each other by hinges and act as mechanical levers to carry and push the vibrations of the ear drum forward to the flexible membrane of the oval window.

Above: The process of hearing really starts when the sound wave enters the ear canal. The wave motion sets the eardrum vibrating. The higher the pitch of the sound, the faster the membrane vibrates. The louder the sound, the greater the vibrations. These movements are then transmitted via the ossicles to the inner ear. The knocking of the stapes on the membrane of the oval window causes pressure waves in the fluid that travels through the cochlear coil. After their passage through the cochlea the waves are finally dispersed when they reach the membrane of the round window.

Below: An important characteristic of sound is its amplitude. This is the degree of a sound's loudness, and is measured in decibels (db). The hearing threshold—the point at which the average young adult can just detect sound from silence—is 0 db. 115-120 db is the threshold of pain.

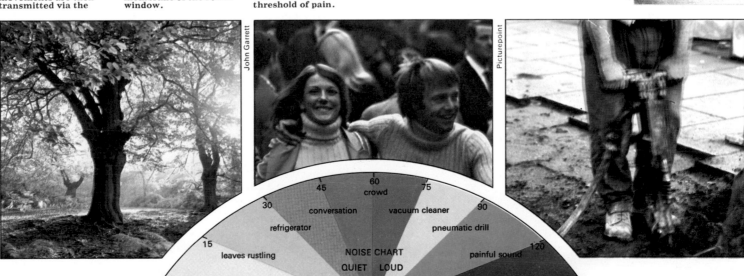

and a duct subdivided by a thin elastic membrane partition. Sound vibrations reaching the inner ear become waves of pressure which are transmitted through the fluid of the cochlear canals — the *vestibular canal* and the *tympanic canal* — and around the *cochlear duct* which separates them.

As the pressure of the waves flows over the *basilar membrane,* which is the vibrating wall of the cochlear duct, the fluid inside the duct is agitated. This agitation in turn stimulates the incredibly sensitive and highly-developed *organ of Corti* where pressure is converted into electrical impulses. After circuiting the cochlear route the pressure waves reach the *round window,* a membrane just below the oval window, where they are dissipated.

Research now seems to show that sounds of different frequencies produce maximal displacement at different points on the cochlear partition, and it is this factor which plays an important role in man's ability to discriminate pitch. Scientists, however, have not reached a complete understanding of how the complex and precise translation of information operates.

Sound also reaches the inner ear by bone conduction. If a tuning fork is struck and placed on the forehead its vibrations travel not only through the air passage to the inner ear, but also through the bones of the skull. When a person speaks he hears his voice simultaneously through these two routes of air and bone conduction. When a person hears his own voice from a tape recorder he often fails to recognize it, because he is hearing himself through air conduction alone.

Learning to distinguish sounds
The newborn baby can certainly hear, but he has not yet acquired the selective process of listening. Any loud noise will startle him, causing him to fling up his arms and legs. Gradually, as he begins to recognize the sounds around him, this reflex is inhibited.

By six weeks of age the sound of his mother's voice is familiar enough to give him pleasure on recognition, and by 20 weeks he can distinguish between speech sounds as similar as 'p' and 't'. As the child grows older he becomes able to recognize any one of hundreds of voices. His developing interests will cause him to concentrate on some occupation so hard that the sounds of a radio, passing cars or insistent calls from his mother will fail to disturb him. He will be able to choose which conversation he 'tunes into' in a crowd and switch from one to another, according to his interest.

Normal hearing plays a vital role in developing and maintaining communications with others through language. The young child with a hearing loss will attempt to match his own speech with the distorted utterances he hears from others, and he will need special training if his speech is to be intelligible.

In conversation a person needs to be able to hear his companion's words, although these alone do not convey understanding. Understanding of what one hears is aided by visual clues of expression and gesture, anticipation of what one is expecting to hear and, most importantly, experience of language. The use of telephones for communication relies on this

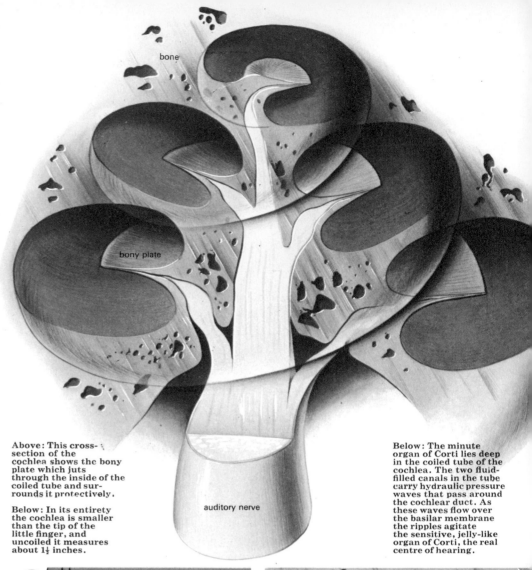

Above: This cross-section of the cochlea shows the bony plate which juts through the inside of the coiled tube and surrounds it protectively.

Below: In its entirety the cochlea is smaller than the tip of the little finger, and uncoiled it measures about 1¼ inches.

Below: The minute organ of Corti lies deep in the coiled tube of the cochlea. The two fluid-filled canals in the tube carry hydraulic pressure waves that pass around the cochlear duct. As these waves flow over the basilar membrane the ripples agitate the sensitive, jelly-like organ of Corti, the real centre of hearing.

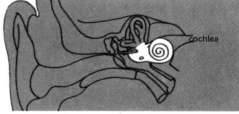

hearing experience because the frequency response of the telephone is limited. For example, the words 'socks' and 'fox' would be indistinguishable out of conversational context over the telephone. Hearing further relates to spoken language in that it enables the speaker to hear himself in order to monitor his own speech, in particular its inflection volume.

Conductive deafness is a failure of the sound waves to be conducted to the inner ear. For example, childhood middle ear infections can cause secretions which hamper the movement of the ossicles and prevent the Eustachian tube from acting as an airway. This is also often experienced with a heavy cold.

In middle and old age the ossicles may become progressively less mobile in a condition known as otosclerosis. The effect of these conditions is to dampen the subject's reception for sounds at all frequencies. He may speak quietly because he hears his own voice loudly and clearly by bone conduction but fails to hear sounds in the environment. Conductive deafness is treatable and amplification from a hearing aid also helps.

There is no cure for perceptive deafness, however, where there is damage to the sound-receiving centres of the inner ear. Most congenital deafness is of this

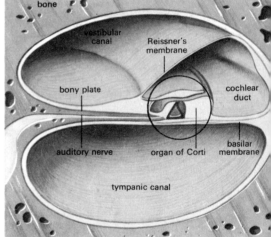

type. Usually the reception of high frequency sounds is more affected than the reception of low frequency sounds, such as vowels in speech, until the sufferer's speech develops poorly, lacking the high frequency consonants that he is failing to hear.

In modern, industrial societies an increasing amount of hearing loss seems to be caused by noise from the automated, urban environment, and such a loss is irreversible. The ingenious protective mechanism of the ear cannot cope with sudden or repeated sounds of very high intensity.

During the past fifteen years or so, researchers have been examining the effects of noise on people's hearing. A British study of workers in a forge found that about half the sample of 2,900 men tested had a mild hearing loss and ten per cent were suffering from occupational deafness to a serious degree. Many researchers have also pointed out the potential danger of rock music amplified to the borders of pain. Some have found significant hearing loss for high frequencies among group members, although others consider that the case against loud music as a specific cause of hearing loss, as so far established, is scientifically inconclusive.

In Western countries it is accepted that a deterioration in hearing may occur as a normal part of the ageing process. But recent studies of hearing among members of primitive tribes living in quiet isolation show no loss of hearing in elder tribesmen. A test of 500 African Mabaans revealed that nearly all of them, regardless of age, could hear a whisper over a distance as great as the length of a football field, an ability few Westerners could match. Such surveys indicate that the potential human range of hearing is far greater than that perceived in people who live against a background of constant noise from radios, traffic, typewriters, machinery and the babble of conversation.

Another cause for concern is that the sounds of an increasingly noisy environment may adversely affect a person's psychological state. It seems that noise may reduce work performance, disrupt sleep and cause annoyance and irritability, but sensitivity to noise varies considerably among individuals.

The selective listening process

Linguists have isolated the levels at which we analyze the sounds of language, and some ingenious experiments have been devised by psycho-linguists to show their psychological reality. In one study, for example, a brief click was superimposed on a tape recorded sentence. Subjects hearing the message were asked at which point the click occurred. There was a significant tendency for the subjects to report that they had heard the click at a grammatical juncture (the end of a phrase), although they were often sounds and even words off the correct spot.

Such experiments give some information about the way in which people manage to understand each other. Psychologists have also looked at the ability to select the focus of attention in what is called 'the cocktail party phenomenon'. How is it that loud voices all around do not significantly mask the interesting gossip one may be listening to over one's shoulder? In one experiment subjects had different messages played to each ear through headphones. It was found that with no prior instructions a subject's attention would be caught involuntarily by the loudest message. When instructed to pay attention to one particular message the subjects successfully reproduced the substance of the quieter message indicated, ignoring a louder one. However certain words — in particular the subject's own name — if embedded at equal volume in the rejected message, will cause him to switch his attention away from the task of following a selected message.

It seems that it is the fact that a human has two ears which enables him to localize different sound sources and to choose the message he will hear. For a microphone at a cocktail party acts as a single ear, and on listening to a tape recording of the conversations it becomes impossible to select one focus of attention. It is this natural human ability to pick up sounds from different directions that inspired the development of stereophonic equipment to reproduce a fuller, more natural effect in sound recording. Binaural, or two-eared, hearing is perhaps the most vital factor in the way in which a person perceives the world around him.

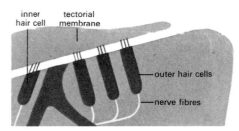

tectorial membrane   inner hair cell   arch of Corti   hairs   cells of Hensen

nerve fibres

basilar membrane

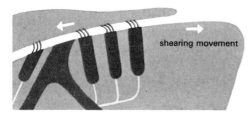

inner hair cell   tectorial membrane

outer hair cells

nerve fibres

Left: The motion of pressure waves through the cochlear fluid disturbs the tiny, hair-like protuberances from the cells in the organ of Corti, which in turn stimulate the auditory nerve endings. Nerve impulses are then relayed to the auditory centres in the brain for interpretation as specific sounds.

Left and below: Hair tips projecting from the organ of Corti brush against the tectorial membrane. As the organ of Corti bends with the pressure of waves the tectorial membrane bends in the opposite direction, creating a shearing motion against the hair tips which activates the hair cells.

shearing movement

Right: The surface of the organ of Corti is seen with its orderly multiple rows of inner (left) and outer (right) hair cells.

Below: This greatly-magnified photograph shows the delicate cilia, or hair tips, which protrude from each hair cell in the organ of Corti.

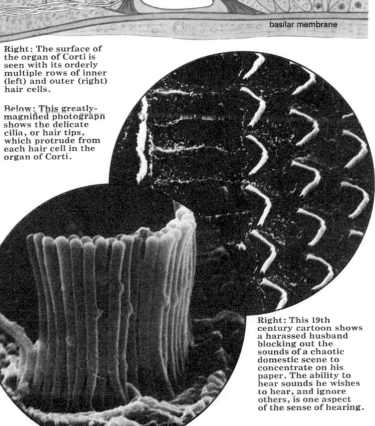

Right: This 19th century cartoon shows a harassed husband blocking out the sounds of a chaotic domestic scene to concentrate on his paper. The ability to hear sounds he wishes to hear, and ignore others, is one aspect of the sense of hearing.

The Nervous System

The nervous system is the most highly developed, and perhaps the most important, communication system of the human body. It receives information about the outside world and relays it to the organs, tissues and cells, so enabling them to adapt to external events.

Without this highly complex mechanism, man would be unable to relate or respond to the outer world and keep the cells and tissues of his inner world functioning healthily. If, for example, the body were unable to adapt to extremes of heat or cold, the welfare and development of the body as a whole would be threatened. The nervous system, therefore, maintains the delicate balance between the two environments.

The nervous system is made up of two parts: an outer system, sometimes referred to as the *somatic* system and an inner or *visceral* system. The somatic system consists of the sense organs—sight, hearing, taste, touch and smell—and the organs of motion, the muscles, bones and joints. The visceral system controls the internal organs such as the heart, glands, blood vessels and intestines. The activities of both are co-ordinated by the central nervous system, formed by the brain and spinal cord.

From the base of the brain 12 pairs of cranial nerves emerge, and 31 pairs of spinal nerves originate from either side of the spinal column. These are known as the *peripheral nerves* or the peripheral nervous system. They are made up of bundles of nerve fibres bound together with sheaths of connective tissue. A peripheral nerve may contain fibres which convey messages from the brain and spinal cord to the muscles in the head, neck, trunk and the limbs, known as *motor* or efferent fibres. Similarly, a peripheral nerve may contain *sensory* or afferent nerve fibres which convey information from the skin and the sense organs to the brain and spinal cord. Many peripheral nerves, however, contain both motor and sensory fibres.

The transmission of the electrical impulses from the skin and sense organs to the central nervous system is controlled by the parent cells of the nerve or *neurone*. Those which control the activity of the sensory nerve fibres are located just outside the spinal cord, buried in the bones of the vertebral column, while the parent cells of the motor nerves are situated within the matter of the brain and spinal cord. Neurones are of a variety of sizes and shapes—they may be spherical, star- or pyramid-shaped, or look like baskets of ferns. Each neurone has a cell-body, a central nucleus which controls the activities of the cell. This is covered with a fine membrane. Projecting from the cell-bodies of the neurones are one or more *axons*, the main conducting fibres. They may be as short as a fraction of a millimetre or as long as a metre: an axon projecting from its parent cell in the base of the spine may extend to a muscle in the foot. Extensive, thread-like branches (called *dendrites*) also project from the cell-body.

The intricate relay network

Neurones may be connected to each other in several different ways. A neurone may send its axon and dendrites to only one other neurone and receive the axon and dendrites of that particular neurone. But a neurone generally forms connections with hundreds of other neurones from which it also receives connecting axons and dendrites. The interconnections between an estimated 10 billion neurones, therefore, forms an extremely complex relay network.

Nerve cells are accompanied by other types of cells which supply them with food and energy. Those found in the brain and spinal cord are known as *neuroglia* while the cells which accompany the peripheral nerve fibres are called *Schwann cells*, after the researcher who first discovered them. Since neurones are the largest cells of the body—the longest stretching from the tip of the toes to the brain—they are dependent on the supporting cells for their survival. A neurone which loses contact with its supporting cell rapidly dies: neurones are so specialized that they are incapable of reproducing themselves.

The nerve fibre has to be insulated to ensure that the messages are conducted without interference and to protect it from damage. Each fibre is enclosed in a myelin sheath—a tube made of a fatty substance formed · of Schwann cells—except at intervals known as nodes of Ramvier. Damaged nerve fibres have the ability to heal themselves, provided the myelin sheath is intact. If the myelin sheath is cut or otherwise unable to restore itself, regeneration of nerve fibres cannot take place and they cease to function.

Nerve fibres have been likened to a telegraph system in that the function of both is to convey messages over long distances at great speed. For example, when we hold an object such as a pencil, the specialized touch receptors in our fingers respond to the size, weight, length, temperature and texture of the pencil and send this information, translated into electrical impulses, along the sensory nerve fibres to the central nervous system—spinal cord and the brain.

The number of impulses and the speed at which they are conveyed along the sensory nerves—which may be up to 100 metres per second, depending on the diameter of the sensory fibre—in a given time enables the brain, the most complex part of the nervous system, to

Left: Our ability to relate to the world around us is dependent on information received through the senses. Stimuli from the outside world are converted into pulses of electro-chemical energy by specialized receptors in the eyes, ears, nose, mouth and skin. These impulses are relayed to the brain for interpretation at a rate of a hundred million per second.

Far right: The central nervous system is made up of nerve cells or neurones specialized to transmit impulses. These neurones are grouped together into the brain and spinal cord, protected by the skull and the vertebrae. The cell-bodies of the neurones are housed within the brain and spinal cord. The axons, the main conducting fibres and their terminals, the dendrites, are spread throughout the body. Together they form the bundles of nerve fibres known as the peripheral nerves, containing sensory nerve fibres (which conduct impulses to the central nervous system) and motor fibres (which conduct impulses from the central nervous system to the internal organs).

Right and below: The tissue of the spinal cord. The H-shaped grey matter contains motor nerves which carry impulses from the brain, while the surrounding white matter contains sensory nerves which convey impulses to the brain.

SPINAL COLUMN

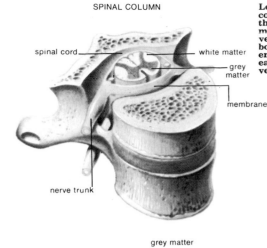
spinal cord
white matter
grey matter
membrane
nerve trunk

grey matter
white matter
central canal
sensory nerve root
motor nerve root
membraneous layer
membraneous layer
membraneous layer

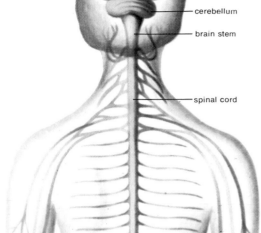

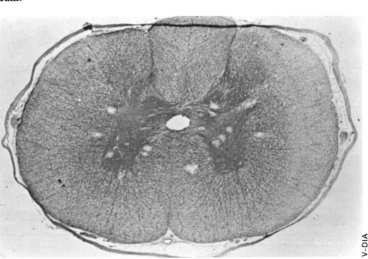
V-DIA

Left: The spinal cord is protected by three layers of membranes and the vertebrae, the spinal bones. The spinal nerves emerge in pairs from each side of the vertebrae.

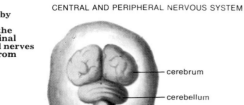
CENTRAL AND PERIPHERAL NERVOUS SYSTEM

cerebrum
cerebellum
brain stem
spinal cord
peripheral nerves

Right: The passage of sensory impulses to the central nervous system is generated by the receptors which are responsive to changes in the external environment. The interpreted message is then conducted along the motor pathways to the internal organs. Many situations, however, such as touching something excessively hot, demand immediate action. Information is then passed to motor neurones which activate the appropriate muscles without passing through the brain. The shortest neural pathway is the knee jerk: the single synapse between the sensory and motor neurone allows the leg to straighten instantly in response to a tap below the kneecap.

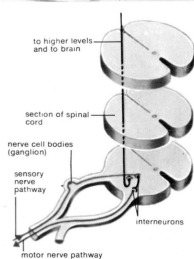
to higher levels and to brain
section of spinal cord
nerve cell bodies (ganglion)
sensory nerve pathway
interneurons
motor nerve pathway

203

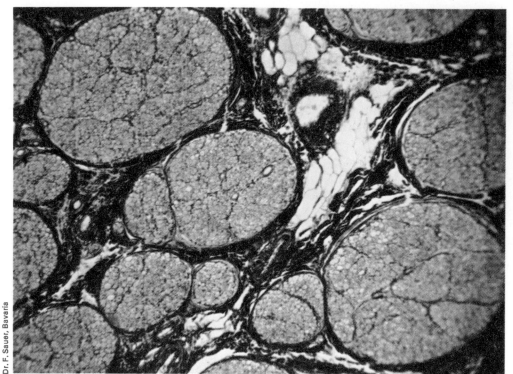

Dr. F. Sauer, Bavaria

Brian Bracegirdle

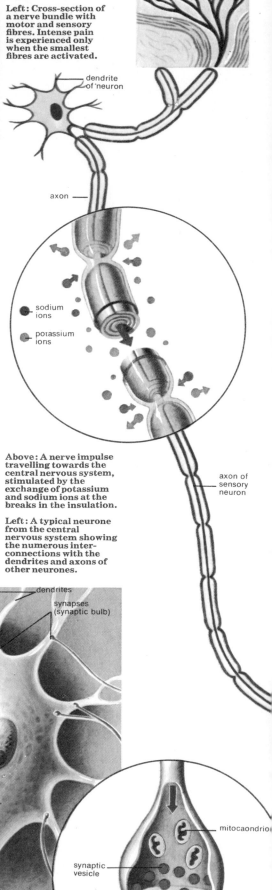

Right: Nerve endings in the skin. The receptors detect the nature, direction and intensity of external stimuli.

Left: Cross-section of a nerve bundle with motor and sensory fibres. Intense pain is experienced only when the smallest fibres are activated.

skin receptors

dendrite of neuron

axon

sodium ions

potassium ions

axon of sensory neuron

Above: A nerve impulse travelling towards the central nervous system, stimulated by the exchange of potassium and sodium ions at the breaks in the insulation.

Left: A typical neurone from the central nervous system showing the numerous inter-connections with the dendrites and axons of other neurones.

dendrites

synapses (synaptic bulb)

nucleus

mitocaondrio

synaptic vesicle

synaptic cleft

dendrite

axon

determine the nature of the events taking place in the world outside. These nerve inputs are interpreted by the brain with the aid of memory—impressions of sights, sounds, smells, textures and temperatures stored from past events.

Receptors—the vital link

The impulses conveyed to the central nervous system may be received through receptors (specialized cells connected to sensory nerve fibres) or through nerve fibres embedded in the skin or deeper tissues of the body.

Receptors are generally classified into various groups depending on the type of stimuli to which they respond. They give us information about changes in our external environment through sensation of different temperatures and atmospheres, by direct contact through touching external objects or from the specially adapted organs of sight, hearing, taste and smell. These receptors are highly sensitive to particular types of events—the receptors in the ear do not respond to changes in light intensity, nor do the retinal receptors in the eye respond to changes in temperature.

Receptors situated in the deeper tissues of the body supply information about the internal system of the body itself. Through them, the body is constantly monitoring changes such as the pressure within the blood vessels, bladder and gut and the temperature and chemistry of the blood and body fluids. Changes in the position and movements in the head and limbs are also monitored, enabling the body to relate to gravity and the space around it.

The transmission process

Unlike a telegraph system, which has electricity supplied to it and transmitted along it, the nerve fibre has to generate its own electrical current to enable the impulses to pass along it.

All animal and plant tissues contain fluids both inside each cell (*intracellular fluid*) and in the small spaces between the cells (*extracellular fluid*). In the neurone, these two fluids are separated by a mem-

Right: Nerve cell bodies in the C.N.S. connect with the axons of numerous other neurones. Impulses arriving from these neurones affect the action of the nerve cell body by either inhibiting or exciting it.

Far right: This is the junction between two neurones or a neurone and a muscle. Known as the synapse, it regulates the action of other neurones by releasing a chemical transmitter which passes across the synaptic cleft, thereby initiating an impulse in the stimulated cell. The chemical transmitter is released when a nerve impulse arrives at the synapse, this depends on the number and frequency of previous impulses.

brane composed of lipid (fats) and protein. The intracellular fluid contains a high concentration of potassium ions (electrically charged particles) and a low concentration of sodium ions; whereas the opposite concentrations are present in the extracellular fluid.

The differing concentrations of ions on opposite sides of the cell membrane imparts a negative electrical charge to the inside of the cell and a positive electrical charge to the outside. The potential difference between the outside and the inside of the cell is called the *membrane potential*. When the nerve fibre is in a resting state, this potential remains steady at about 70 millivolts (less than 1/20th of the voltage of a torch battery) and the cell membrane is said to be *polarized*.

However, when the nerve is conducting an impulse, a small region of the neurone's membrane temporarily changes its properties, acting as though the membrane had suddenly been punctured. The two fluids previously separated by the membrane begin to pass across it. These movements of electrically charged ions from one side of the membrane to the other alter the size of the membrane potential. For a short period of time (less than one millisecond) the inside of the cell becomes positively charged and the outside negatively charged. This brief reversal of the membrane potential is called an *action potential*.

When a small region of the nerve cell is made to generate an action potential an electrical current flows between this active region and the resting region immediately next to it. The process is

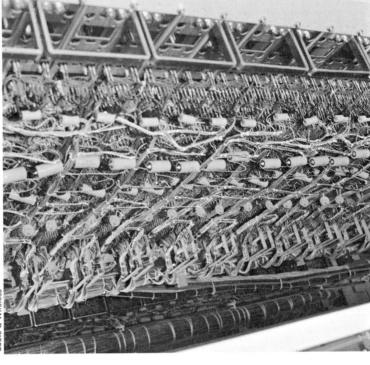

Below: The end plates connecting motor nerve fibres to the muscles direct them to contract or relax depending on the instruction they receive from the impulses. This is an all-or-nothing response, and to keep a muscle contracted a continual stream of impulses is required.

Cable & Wireless

Above: A telephone exchange is a simple example of a communications network. The body's nervous system, however, involves billions of interconnections.

similar to the chain reaction caused by lighting one end of a gunpowder trail, with the essential difference that the nerve cell membrane can be reactivated after a very short time.

This electrical charge from a nerve cell will allow an impulse, from a sense receptor, for example, to travel freely along its nerve fibre. The speed at which the impulse travels along the fibre depends on its thickness. The thickest fibres may conduct an impulse, such as the stimulus from touching something excessively hot, at 100 metres per second, while a sensation of actual pain may follow at one metre per second.

The Synapse

The electrical impulse travelling along the nerve fibre stops abruptly when it reaches the *synapse* at the end of the axon. The synapses are the junction points between individual neurones and each neurone is separated from its neighbours by a small gap, the *synaptic cleft*. The continuation of the nerve impulse requires a special mechanism to generate it across this gap. The terminals from the axon secrete particular chemicals—some of which are still unknown—which deliver a certain excitation to the cell membrane of the next neurone. The excitatory state induced by an impulse travelling along the fibre lasts only a short time. Since the cell membrane of the postsynaptic neurone is unable to maintain this charge for very long as it is a poor conductor, the current delivered leaks away as it spreads. The number of nerve impulses arriving at a neurone therefore, determines the degree to which it responds.

The number of impulses and the speed at which they eventually arrive by this process at the neurones in the central nervous system form the frequency code containing information about particular events. When the brain receives this coded message, it is able to begin its vital function of maintaining the balance between the external and internal environments.

Right: All nerve fibres are insulated against damage to prevent interruption of the neural transmission. The insulating material contains Schwann cells which supply the nerves with food and energy. Without these supporting cells, the neurones would die since they are too specialized to reproduce themselves.

interneuron

Schwann cell (nucleus)

motor neuron axis

node of Ranvier

myelin sheath

neurilemma

nerve cell bodies (ganglion)

sensory neuron axis

Above: Nerve impulses arriving at the spinal cord are routed by the interneurones to the brain or motor neurones.

Right: This diagram shows the pathway of a typical spinal reflex – known as the reflex arc. This is the shortest neural pathway.

motor neuron axis

interneurons

Touch

The sense of touch is the most basic means by which a person makes contact with the world around him. The ability to feel shapes and textures provides the brain with more precise information about the environment than is perceived through sight and hearing. The sensations of temperature and pain inform the brain of dangers to the body—often before the individual is consciously aware of such sensations—so that the body can immediately react to protect itself. Personal communication is also heightened by touch, which may be used to express a whole range of emotions.

In many ways a human being's sense of touch is the sense in which he places the greatest faith. Often it is not until an object can actually be touched that a person is finally convinced of its existence. But why should the information from our touch receptors be more 'real' than from our other sensory systems? If touch were the first of our senses to evolve in infancy our dependence on it might be explained. However, recent research has shown that the infant's world is far from the 'buzzing, booming confusion' that early psychologists, such as William James, thought it was. Young babies have in fact quite sophisticated visual and auditory abilities.

The reality sense

There are two likely reasons why touch tends to be considered as the 'reality' sense. Unlike the other four senses—sight, hearing, taste and smell—touch responds to more than one type of energy stimulus: it is responsive to both temperature and pressure. Secondly, each of the other senses is localized in a particular organ of the body (eyes, ears, mouth and nose), whereas the sense 'organs' for touch are distributed all over the body. The sense of touch is in this way more than a single sense. Early experimenters tried to classify the sense of touch into various sensory modalities, or channels, of sensation. The 19th century German physiologist, Hermann von Helmholtz, for example, classified four such modalities—touch, heat, cold and pain—all of which can be experienced by simply bringing an object into contact with an area of skin.

The first theories to explain this complex mechanism were based upon the microscopic examination of nerve endings in the skin. These nerve endings were found to be of several types, differing in appearance and each type was thought to be responsive to a particular stimulus.

According to one theory, five different types of nerve ending, said to respond to the stimuli of different sensory modalities, were differentiated as: pain—free nerve endings; pressure—Pacinian corpuscles; cold—Krausse end bulbs; heat—Ruffini endings; and touch—Merckels discs and Meissner corpuscles. Pressure was defined as the sensation of feeling the 'weight' of an object pressed on the skin or the 'hardness' of something against the skin. Whereas touch proper was identified as the perception of a touch or stroke against the skin and the size and shape of objects felt.

206   However, this 'classical' approach to

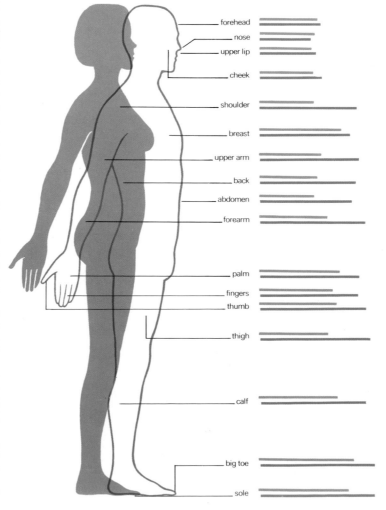

Left: The Pacinian corpuscles, the end-organs most receptive to pressure, not only form different patterns of distribution throughout the body but vary between men and women. Men are generally more tolerant of pressure sensations, indicated by the longer blue lines. The chart also shows the relative tolerance levels of various parts of the body. The back, for example, has fewer receptors and is capable of enduring more intense pressure than the forehead.

Above: Shaking hands with someone is a positive way of making contact which allows us to express our pleasure in getting to know them or renewing old friendship.

Right: The different forms of greeting expressed by different cultures are often reflections of social attitudes towards physical contact. The degree of intimacy permitted is subject to both the relationship and to the conventions of the society. Initial contact may be as distant as the Japanese bow (right) or as intimate as the embrace of the two Arabs (top right).

forehead
nose
upper lip
cheek
shoulder
breast
upper arm
back
abdomen
forearm
palm
fingers
thumb
thigh
calf
big toe
sole

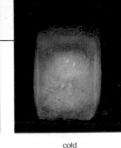

pain

cold

heat

Meissner corpuscle

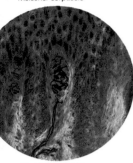

Pacinian corpuscle

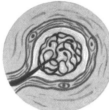

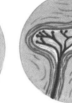

free nerve endings

Krausse end bulbs

Ruffini corpuscle

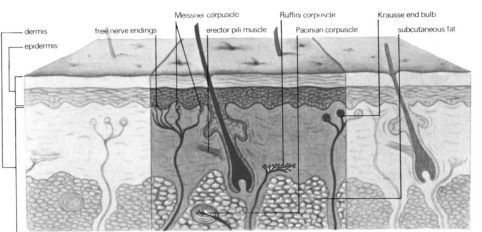

Meissner corpuscle   Ruffini corpuscle   Krausse end bulb

dermis — free nerve endings   erector pili muscle   Pacinian corpuscle   subcutaneous fat

epidermis

Left: The human skin contains receptors which are sensitive to outside stimuli. By reporting the nature, intensity and direction of the stimuli, the sense receptors enable the brain to make decisions about adapting the internal environment. Although there is a large spectrum of sensations, to which the sensory apparatus responds, some receptors are known to be particularly sensitive to certain types of stimuli.

A cross-section of the skin (bottom left) reveals that most of these specialized receptors are found in the dermis or innermost layer, and that they have a variety of forms. Free nerve endings, which are sensitive to pain, (above left) are the commonest form and have no special shape. The nerve endings most sensitive to cold and heat are fewer and less discriminating, so that heat and cold may be sensed simultaneously.

Far left: Pacinian corpuscles, which respond to pressure are highly concentrated in the fingertips, although they are widely distributed throughout the body. Meissner corpuscles, also more concentrated in the hands, are quite numerous in young babies but gradually decrease with age.

Keystone

Rene Burri, Magnum

the explanation of the sense of touch soon ran into difficulties. It was found that some of these sense organs in the skin respond to more than one type of stimulation. It also became apparent that the different end organs that early researchers had identified are not really completely distinct and that the sensations identified were but a few from the wide spectrum of stimuli which the end organs were capable of receiving.

Associated with each nerve ending is a 'receptive field', which is the area of the skin that can be stimulated to produce activity in that nerve. The receptive fields of sensory fibres overlap, so that by putting pressure on a particular point on the skin surface, several sensory nerves will be stimulated at the same time. Any particular sensory nerve may also be activated by both pressure and temperature changes in its receptive field.

Investigations have shown that nerve fibres respond continually to a variety of stimuli, but only those relating to temperature and pressure are intense enough to be detected. This is due to the fact that these particular stimuli cause a greater degree of excitation in the nerve fibre and the impulses are therefore conducted to the central nervous system at a greater rate. It has been suggested that it is the frequency rate of the firing of these nerves, that is, the rate at which impulses are conducted, which constitutes the message carried to the brain to tell it what type of stimulus is present.

The receptive fields vary around the body in degrees of sensitivity, depending on the concentration of nerve endings in different parts of the skin. The fine distinctions between these receptive fields of the skin do, strangely enough, change over a period of time. If the receptive fields for a certain area of skin are established, and then tested at a later date, it has been found that some of the receptive fields have disappeared and others have been created. It seems that the areas of skin over which a certain nerve can be stimulated are constantly changing, although it is not yet clear how or why this mysterious process happens.

The transmission process

The next stage in the process of transmitting touch information to the brain is accomplished when the individual nerve fibres leading from the end organs, which are actually receiving the stimuli, pass through somatic nerves—those nerves which carry sensory stimuli to the central nervous system. The fibres in these nerves are known to be of different thicknesses, which directly affects the speed with which messages can pass along them.

Experiments have been carried out to establish whether these different types of fibre carry messages about different kinds of stimuli. Various researchers have found that particular fibres transmit messages only when the skin is damaged, heated, pinched, and so on. Furthermore, a disease of the spinal cord called *syringomyelia* causes lesions which interrupt the nerve fibres carrying pain and temperature stimuli. People suffering from this disease may accidently handle objects which burn them or cut them without being aware of it. But they do not lose their actual sense of touch and still experience other tactile sensations.

These discoveries appear to verify those

Right: Information on the texture, shape and size of objects is vital in relating to and moving around in our environment.

Below: Sensitivity varies throughout the parts of the hand. Colour 5 represents the least sensitive part and Colour 1 the most sensitive.

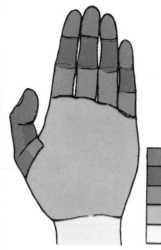

1
2
3
4
5

Right: In the ancient art of massage, both therapist and patient experience a variety of tactile sensations. Through techniques such as stroking, pressing, kneading and rubbing, the masseur can detect and treat discomfort from over-tensed muscles and stimulate blood flow to improve circulation.

Below: Most blind people rely on a developed secondary sense to compensate for loss of vision. Through his highly sensitive fingertips, a good braille reader can feel and interpret the small raised dots, set 2½ to 3mm apart, at the rate of 2,000 to 2,500 a minute, the equivalent of 100 words a minute.

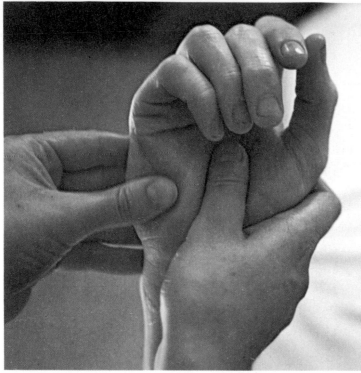

theories which attributed the role of responding to particular stimuli to specific end organs. However, it is not the end organ itself that responds in this way, but the nerve fibres later in the chain of the nervous system. The final stages of the touch transmission process carry the information from the somatic nerves into the spinal cord and from there to the brain.

It is no longer possible to explain the different sensations experienced by saying that they result from the stimulation of different sense organs found in the skin. Although there may be some types of nerve endings that are more responsive to certain kinds of external pressure, current theories assume that it is the firing rates and the distribution of impulses among the small and large nerve fibres which form a pattern which is then recognized as a particular sensation.

Besides providing information about the temperature, texture or weight of an object, the sense of touch also performs other functions. One of the most important sources of tactile stimulation is other human beings. The way in which a person is touched by others tells him a great deal about them, whether through a kiss, a pat on the back or a blow on the jaw. Even the feel of an initial handshake will colour one's attitude towards a stranger.

Equally, social psychologists have suggested that there is a definite 'hierarchy' of touch that defines human personal relationships. The minimal distance man tolerates between himself and another person depends on both the person's familiarity and the formality of the occasion.

A more serious example of the role of touch in communication between people has received attention in recent years. Mothers whose babies were placed in incubators or were not given to them immediately after birth were found to have problems in their attachment to their children later on. Mothers of babies who experienced periods of mutual touching, especially in the first hour after birth, were later found to have more satisfactory relationships than mothers and babies who had not had this experience.

There are other aspects of the sense of touch that are susceptible to social and cultural influences. Pain in particular is an area of touch sensation that seems to be dramatically modified by cultural factors. In certain cultures, for example, women in childbirth seem to tolerate the pain better and, to an onlooker, may appear to find it of only minor inconvenience.

Phantom limbs
The sensitivity of the sense of touch has more directly applicable advantages. The system of braille, for example, enables the blind to read through their fingertips. However, this sensitivity does have some consequences that can be unpleasant. After amputation of a limb a phenomenon known as a 'phantom limb' often occurs which can cause great distress and discomfort to a patient. This phantom limb feels to the person just like the one he has lost and although the physical limb is gone, the pain remains where it was, and is real to the sufferer. Eventually this exact replica fades; sometimes the 'limb' will disappear leaving only the sensation of the extremity, the hand or the foot, as a persistent phantom reminder.

The Brain

The human brain has been likened to a delicate flower perched on top of a slender stalk. The top three inches of the stalk, known as the brain stem, lie entirely within the skull, and are surrounded by the two bulging halves, or hemispheres of the brain. The spinal cord is the continuation of the brain stem outside of the skull.

The brain itself is a moist, pinkish-grey mass about the size of a grapefruit, and weighs less than three pounds. A shock-absorbing fluid cushions it against bumps and blows and its extra-tough outer envelope assists in its protection. Surrounding this is a crate of bone, called the cranium.

Although the human brain has often been compared to a computer, the comparison is a weak one, for the brain of an adult human being far outstrips any computer yet built by man. A computer can perform more than 4,000,000 additions of 36 figures in a single second, but the human brain, sometimes referred to as a biocomputer (biological computer), is still more versatile than the computers it builds.

An interesting fact about the brain is that its size is not related to intelligence. The French philospher Anatole France had a brain much smaller than average, but it in no way impaired his ability as a thinker. The largest brain ever weighed turned out to be that of a congenital idiot.

Electrical brain activity

Today, physiologists and neurologists have a considerable knowledge of the brain, yet the details of what actually happens in the brain when we think, remember, dream or imagine are still vague. It has been shown, for instance, that even when asleep, 50,000,000 'nerve messages' are being relayed back and forth between the brain and different parts of the body every second, but experiments have failed to isolate or identify the mechanism (or mechanisms) by which this balance is controlled and maintained.

Brain activity is mainly electrical. The brain sends and receives electrical currents from its own nerve cells to and from the many millions of nerves cells in various parts of the body. The basic nerve cell units which make up both the brain and the nervous system are called 'neurones'. Neurones differ in shape and size. They can be oval, round or spindle-shaped. Each neurone, which measures as little as 0.025mm (approximately 0.001 ins) across, has a tiny electrical charge even when it is not in use. This electrical charge is produced by the chemical difference between the interior of the nerve cell and the tissue which surrounds it. Touching and tasting, and other stimuli, alter this chemical balance and cause an electrical change which can be recorded. Physiologists refer to this as an electrochemical change.

An electrochemical change in a single neurone brings about a whole series of similar changes along the length of a

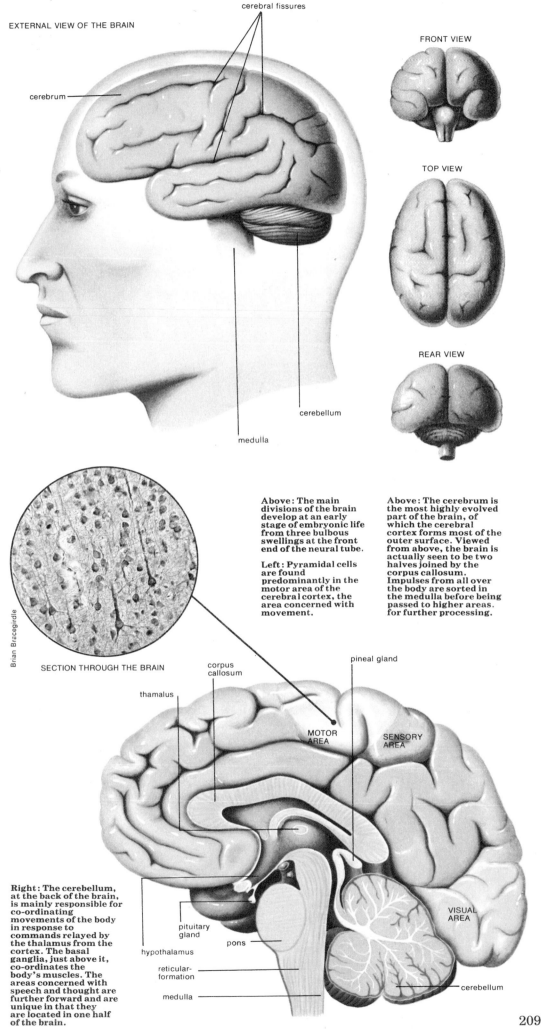

EXTERNAL VIEW OF THE BRAIN

cerebral fissures

cerebrum

cerebellum

medulla

FRONT VIEW

TOP VIEW

REAR VIEW

Brian Bracegirdle

SECTION THROUGH THE BRAIN

Above: The main divisions of the brain develop at an early stage of embryonic life from three bulbous swellings at the front end of the neural tube.

Left: Pyramidal cells are found predominantly in the motor area of the cerebral cortex, the area concerned with movement.

Above: The cerebrum is the most highly evolved part of the brain, of which the cerebral cortex forms most of the outer surface. Viewed from above, the brain is actually seen to be two halves joined by the corpus callosum. Impulses from all over the body are sorted in the medulla before being passed to higher areas. for further processing.

thamalus

corpus callosum

pineal gland

MOTOR AREA

SENSORY AREA

VISUAL AREA

cerebellum

pituitary gland

pons

hypothalamus

reticular-formation

medulla

Right: The cerebellum, at the back of the brain, is mainly responsible for co-ordinating movements of the body in response to commands relayed by the thalamus from the cortex. The basal ganglia, just above it, co-ordinates the body's muscles. The areas concerned with speech and thought are further forward and are unique in that they are located in one half of the brain.

nerve fibre, so causing an electrical impulse to flow like a spark along a fuse. When an electrical impulse is produced in this way, it is described as the *firing of a neurone*. The current initiated in one neurone often causes neighbouring neurones to undergo electrochemical changes, and they in turn fire to assist in the operation required. Millions of neurones are firing every second of our lives. The electrical impulses caused by this firing quickly find their way to the brain as 'coded messages', although many of them may be rejected as not belonging to 'priority categories'. For example, if message A is that the hand is in contact with something very hot, and message B is that a bird is singing, then the brain will select message A as the more important.

Seen under a microscope, a single brain cell may resemble the crown of a tree and a thin section of brain tissue looks remarkably like a collection of garden weeds. The communication system between neurones is composed of delicate fibres called 'dendrites'. But there is also another fibre attached to each neurone called the 'axon', and these link the brain with the whole of the body. A nerve fibre is made up of some thousands of axons. The overall communication system of the body is composed of over 13,000,000,000 neurones, yet such is the complexity of the brain that it alone contains 10,000,000,000 of these. The skin has some 4,000,000 special neurones which can detect pain, heat and cold. Other neurones throughout the muscles and organs of the body respond to leg and arm positions, stomach ache, the colour of a flower or the pitch of a note of music.

Interior and exterior control

The astounding versatility of the brain comes into focus when one considers that it is in charge of an interior environment as well as an exterior one. It keeps us alive by balancing the processes of growth and decay. Apart from the priority example given above, the brain is also deeply involved in the balance of itself as a mechanism. Because of this, it has to survey all the functions of the body simultaneously to ensure that each of its operations is co-ordinated. For example, sugar is one of the body's main energy-providing substances, and as human beings we must have just the right amount. It has been said that we walk a biological tight-rope between coma and convulsion, for only a slight change out of the ordinary in our blood-sugar level can send us in one direction or the other.

However, with the advance warning system of coded messages flooding into our brains every second, adjustments can be effectively made to ensure our survival. This leads us to the incomprehensible fact that our brains must 'know' that our required sugar level is about a 1/60th of an ounce for every pint of blood. Similar standards of control and regulation apply to breathing (we inhale and exhale 18 to 20 times per minute), to heartbeat rate (about 70 times per minute), and to body temperature (98.6° Fahrenheit).

When triggering impulses reach the brain from the sense organs, the brain adjusts to the outside world by dividing its operation into three parts: first it takes in the sense-impression messages, then organizes each input on the basis of past experience, present events and future

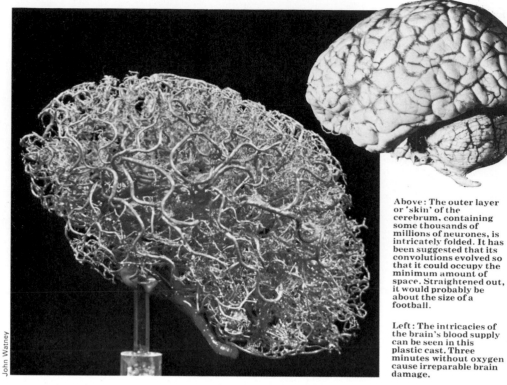

Above: The outer layer or 'skin' of the cerebrum, containing some thousands of millions of neurones, is intricately folded. It has been suggested that its convolutions evolved so that it could occupy the minimum amount of space. Straightened out, it would probably be about the size of a football.

Left: The intricacies of the brain's blood supply can be seen in this plastic cast. Three minutes without oxygen cause irreparable brain damage.

Right: Transverse section of the brain. (See diagram below). The spaces or ventricles formed by the folds of the cerebrum are filled with cerebro-spinal fluid, which protects the delicate tissue from shock or damage, resulting, for example, from a blow to the skull.

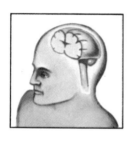

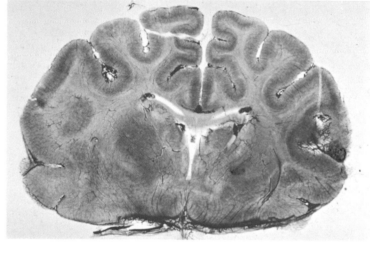

plans, and lastly selects and produces appropriate output as action or actions. The brain does relax in sleep (due to the reduction of sensory impressions) but as long as it is alive, it finds no actual rest.

The main mass of the brain rests snugly on a bony shelf inside the skull. The brain stem is connected to the brain through a hole in this shelf. At the direct centre of the brain stem reside many millions of neurones. This complex of neurones is called the *reticular formation*, which means 'like a net'. One of the most important recent discoveries has been that it is in this dense neurone-fibre centre that the brain's most important decisions are made. The many millions of messages which arrive at the brain are decoded by the reticular formation and put into order of importance. It is now also thought that this neurone-centre controls consciousness and awareness.

At the rear of the brain stem lies an elaborately folded area known as the *cerebellum*. It is from here that orders are sent down from the brain's higher levels to the muscles. For example, if someone is told to write the word 'man' with a pen, then the cerebellum co-ordinates the movements of the fingers.

The largest part of the brain, however, is the *cerebrum*, or fore-brain. The cerebrum is divided into two main halves or hemispheres and, like the cerebellum, is intricately folded. It has been suggested that the folds have evolved so that the entire mass can occupy as small a place as possible.

Two bands of neurones, separated by a deep cleft, run up, across, and down the cerebrum just above the ears. The band of neurones at the front controls the action of the muscles, and is called the *motor area*, while the band at the back receives messages from the skin, and is called the *sensory area*. In the motor area muscular reactions to stimuli are initiated and in the sensory area we sense the difference between warm and cold, the prick of a pin or the cut of a knife. Curiously enough, although the cerebrum can register pain or feeling within itself, it does not register pain or feeling when touched or cut during an operation.

Seeing is governed by the back part of the cerebrum. Messages arrive from the eyes via the retinas and optic nerves. The prime function of the eyes is to change light into a series of complex electrical impulses. The neurones at the

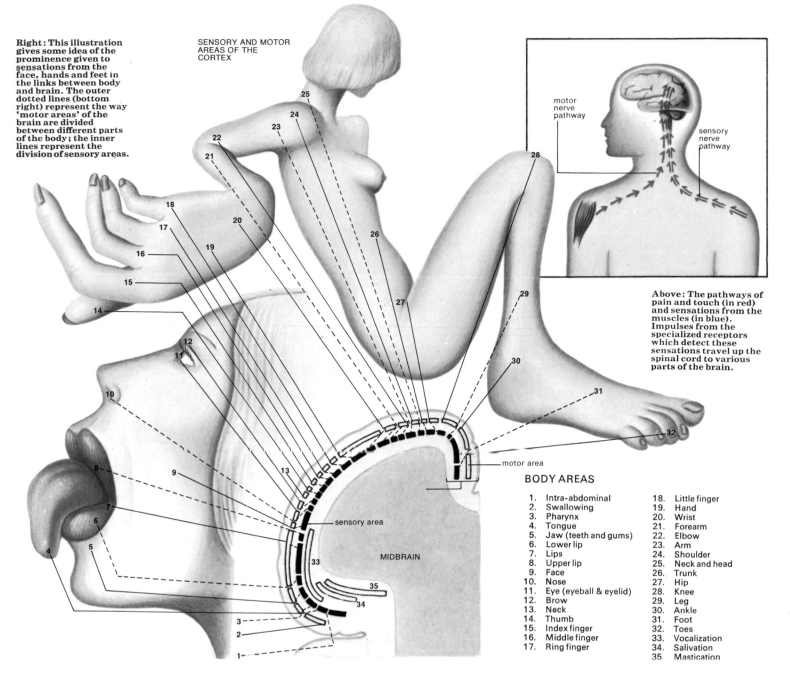

SENSORY AND MOTOR AREAS OF THE CORTEX

motor nerve pathway

sensory nerve pathway

Above: The pathways of pain and touch (in red) and sensations from the muscles (in blue). Impulses from the specialized receptors which detect these sensations travel up the spinal cord to various parts of the brain.

motor area

sensory area

MIDBRAIN

BODY AREAS

1.	Intra-abdominal	18.	Little finger
2.	Swallowing	19.	Hand
3.	Pharynx	20.	Wrist
4.	Tongue	21.	Forearm
5.	Jaw (teeth and gums)	22.	Elbow
6.	Lower lip	23.	Arm
7.	Lips	24.	Shoulder
8.	Upper lip	25.	Neck and head
9.	Face	26.	Trunk
10.	Nose	27.	Hip
11.	Eye (eyeball & eyelid)	28.	Knee
12.	Brow	29.	Leg
13.	Neck	30.	Ankle
14.	Thumb	31.	Foot
15.	Index finger	32.	Toes
16.	Middle finger	33.	Vocalization
17.	Ring finger	34.	Salivation
		35.	Mastication

back of the cerebrum translate this jumble of signals into meaningful patterns of light and dark, colour and shape.

One of the odd things about the cerebrum's functioning is that the neurones on its left side control muscle movements on the right side of the body, and vice versa. Why this is so is not yet known. The frontal area of the cerebrum, along with certain sections of the back and sides, show no electrical activity, and have been termed the 'silent areas'. Some researchers have suggested that it is in these silent areas that we 'know ourselves'. If, however, some of the neurones in these areas are destroyed, a person can quite often suffer from loss of judgement and initiative.

The human brain has evolved gradually, over many millions of years. The earliest forerunner of the brain in primitive creatures consisted of a slim, hollow tube of nerve tissue. A relic of this early brain can still be found in modern man, buried deeply in four hollow spaces at the base of the cerebrum. Just below these spaces is a small mass of brain divided into two lobes. This is the *thalamus*, or 'preliminary sorting office' for messages going to the cerebrum.

Although termed a sorting office, the thalamus can only tell us, for example, that something 'warm' is touching part of the body, but it is the cerebrum which must decide which part of the body, and the nature of the object. It is thought by physiologists that the thalamus is responsible for the general feeling of well-being.

Just below the thalamus is the *hypothalamus*, a tiny mass of nerve tissue which controls the functioning of the pituitary gland. The pituitary hangs down from the hypothalamus on a small stalk. As the 'master gland' of the body, the pituitary governs, in turn, the thyroid and other glands through the secretion of hormones. This includes the secretion of sex hormones. The hypothalamus is involved in the way our bodies react to situations; it exerts control over the pituary, adjusting the quantities of hormones which are secreted by this gland. When we have a dry mouth, sweaty hands or a pounding heart, it is the hypothalamus which is directing these body activities.

The brain's complexity can be approached through an understanding of how computers work. The computer's memory is based on the two-number

system. As with the brain, a computer is a highly complex mechanism, parts of which are either transmitting an electrical current or not. Two wires in a computer's circuit can transmit four different messages in code: off-off; off-on; on-off, and on-on. This corresponds to the firing of two neurones in the nervous system. If, however, we consider a computer circuit with three wires (or neurones), then we are faced by an operation of eight coded messages: off-off-off; off-off-on; off-on-off; off-on-on; on-off-off; on-off-on; on-on-off and on-on-on. The permutation of 'off' and 'on' doubles each time the circuit of wires or neurones is increased by one. As the human brain and nervous system contain over 13,000,000,000 neurones, or computer wires, then the number of possible 'on' and 'off' permutations becomes staggering.

This information, however, does not help us to understand how the brain decodes the messages it receives in meaningful terms, nor how it makes 'decisions'. Dreaming, feeling, emotion, reasoning and thinking creatively are also puzzles which have not yet been unravelled, although there are indications that a breakthrough is imminent.

The Skeleton

The skeleton is a masterpiece of architectural and mechanical design. It is the structural support system for the body, enabling us to run, jump and contort ourselves with a freedom unknown amongst our mechanical creations. The 206 bones of the average adult work together with the muscles and connective tissues to move, support and protect the vital organs making up the human body. The individual bones are carefully contoured to fulfil their role in this system, ranging in size from the powerful thigh bone or *femur*—about 500 mm (20 inches) long and more than 25 mm (1 inch) across at mid-shaft—to the *pisiform*, the smallest of the wrist bones, found at the base of the little finger and shaped like a split pea.

The skeleton as a whole consists of *bone*, *cartilage*, *tendons* and *ligaments* having a remarkable external and internal design. The femur, for example, must withstand great weight and pressure—at times up to 1200 pounds per square inch (83 bar) during walking. Its shaft is shaped like a hollow cylinder to give maximum strength with minimum bulk; internally it is filled with cross-hatching of bone combining great resistance to pressure with very light weight. Another example of functionalism appears in the *vertebrae* of the spinal column. To help bear the weight of the body they are formed as solid cylinders with a bony ring at the back to provide a protected passage for the nerve cord. Behind the ring three spurs protrude, to join with the ribs and anchor the muscles of the back.

The rib cage provides an excellent example of the versatility of joints and the protective function of the skeleton. It must protect the delicate tissues of the lungs and heart, whilst being able to expand and contract to bring in fresh supplies of air. Cartilage joins the ribs to the breastbone in the front, providing a movable elastic connection. At the back, the ribs are fitted onto the vertebrae by tiny gliding, rotating joints permitting individual movement and allowing the rib cage to adopt different rhythms of breathing. In contrast to these tiny joints is the large ball-and-socket joint of the hip, which holds the rounded end of the femur in a self-lubricating socket. The flexibility of this joint can be seen in the movements of a ballerina, or the contortions of a gymnast.

Movement is restricted to certain planes by the action of other joints. For example, the knee joint makes certain that the leg only bends in one way like a simple hinge; the shoulder has a shallow ball-and-socket joint restricting its movement (as anyone who has suffered from a dislocated shoulder will testify). The head rotates on the two top vertebrae in the neck. These are known as the *atlas* (named after the Greek god who carried the world on his shoulders) and the *axis*, which pivots the head and the atlas. The movements of these joints enables us to shake, nod and turn our heads.

The composition of bone

Bones have a complex internal structure. The structure of the femur, for example, varies from the thick-walled middle sections of the shaft, to the thin, expanded end parts. Here, the surface is contoured to accommodate the many insertions of ligaments and muscles concerned with joint action. Underneath the expanded ends is a delicate tracery of small bone filaments which have the appearance of foam. Although they look delicate, they are orientated to take the forces which act on the end of the bone giving the strength and lightness which is characteristic of the skeleton. The spaces in the centre of the bone are filled with *marrow* which supplies most of the blood components and aids the bone's nutrition.

Closer examination of bone reveals a basic structure of fibrous protein (*collagen*) twisted like a rope, surrounded and impregnated with needle-like crystals of *apatite* (a phosphate of calcium). In the embryo these fibrils of collagen are tangled up more or less at random, whilst in older bones they are arranged in very thin sheets. This difference is due to the quick build-up of bone during the embryonic stage, and the later erosion of these tangled fibres to expand the size of the bone when a child is born and begins to move about. Transferring the fibrous protein from the centre to the outside, and laying it down in sheets, gives the bone its characteristic hard cylindrical structure. Any growth or change of shape takes place either by the laying down of new bone on an already existing surface, or by the erosion of pre-formed bone and its transference to the outside of the bone.

By this method of eroding and laying down of new bone, a complex system of canals is formed, known as the *Haversian canals*, which contain the blood vessels and nerves. Bone is, in fact, well supplied with blood. If we strip away the outermost layer blood oozes out of the minute pores on the surface.

Unlike the shells of animals like snails, bone is very much alive. It is full of bone cells called *osteocytes*, which live entombed in tiny caverns called *lacunae*, and actually form the hard parts of the bone. These cells can communicate with each other through small tubes containing slender extensions of the cells. Blood

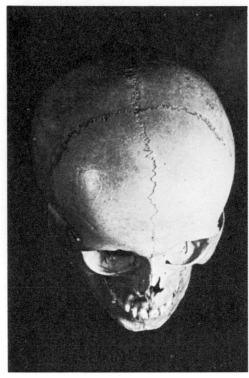

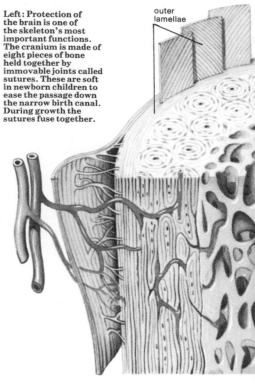

Left: Protection of the brain is one of the skeleton's most important functions. The cranium is made of eight pieces of bone held together by immovable joints called sutures. These are soft in newborn children to ease the passage down the narrow birth canal. During growth the sutures fuse together.

outer lamellae

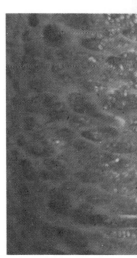

Right: This microscopic photograph shows the growth area of bone. Cartilage (shown here in blue) is formed first by the cartilage cells; this attracts a deposit of calcium which covers the protein fibres. The cartilage cells are now known as osteoblasts (bone-formers) and cause apatite crystals to be deposited around the calcium, thereby forming hard bone (shown here in white). Cartilage can be seen changing to hard bone at the centre of the photograph. Hundreds of cartilage and bone-forming cells can be seen clustered around this area—the epiphyseal plate—between the end of the bone and its shaft, the major site of bone expansion.

Picturepoint

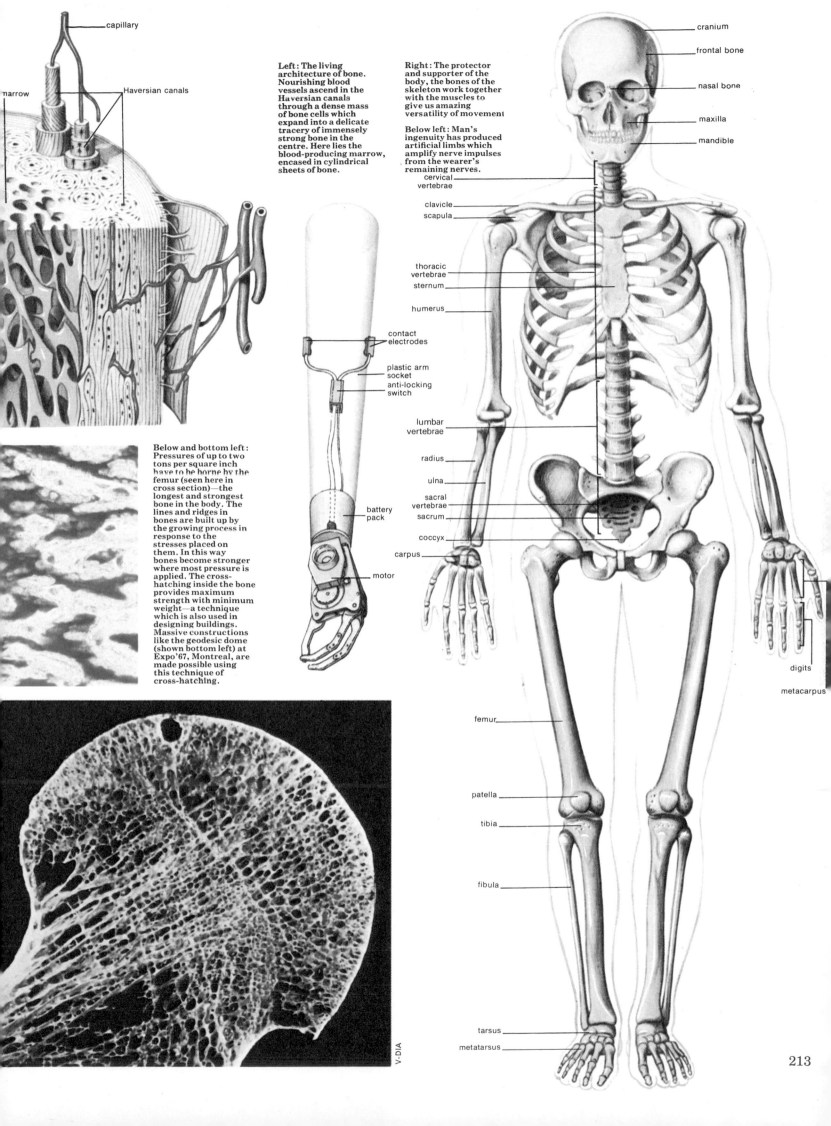

capillary

marrow

Haversian canals

Left: The living architecture of bone. Nourishing blood vessels ascend in the Haversian canals through a dense mass of bone cells which expand into a delicate tracery of immensely strong bone in the centre. Here lies the blood-producing marrow, encased in cylindrical sheets of bone.

Right: The protector and supporter of the body, the bones of the skeleton work together with the muscles to give us amazing versatility of movement

Below left: Man's ingenuity has produced artificial limbs which amplify nerve impulses from the wearer's remaining nerves.

Below and bottom left: Pressures of up to two tons per square inch have to be borne by the femur (seen here in cross section)—the longest and strongest bone in the body. The lines and ridges in bones are built up by the growing process in response to the stresses placed on them. In this way bones become stronger where most pressure is applied. The cross-hatching inside the bone provides maximum strength with minimum weight—a technique which is also used in designing buildings. Massive constructions like the geodesic dome (shown bottom left) at Expo'67, Montreal, are made possible using this technique of cross-hatching.

contact electrodes

plastic arm socket

anti-locking switch

battery pack

motor

cranium

frontal bone

nasal bone

maxilla

mandible

cervical vertebrae

clavicle

scapula

thoracic vertebrae

sternum

humerus

lumbar vertebrae

radius

ulna

sacral vertebrae

sacrum

coccyx

carpus

femur

patella

tibia

fibula

tarsus

metatarsus

digits

metacarpus

V-DIA

213

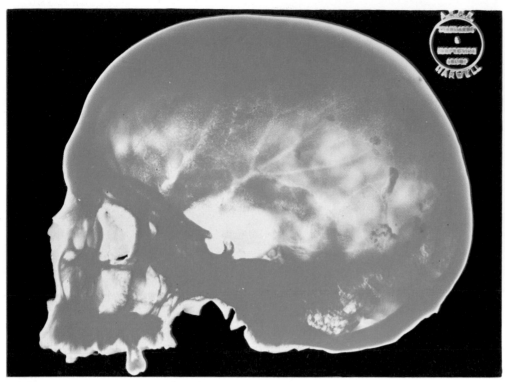

The structure of joints

Cartilage is found mainly in the joints. For example, its rubbery nature makes it an ideal protective padding between the vertebrae of the spinal column. It eases the movement of the small bones and helps to absorb the shocks being transmitted along the spine every time we take a step forward. The ends of the bones making up joints, like the ball-and-socket of the hip and the hinge of the knee, are also covered by a smooth, protective layer of cartilage which persists for life. Our joints work so smoothly and effortlessly that only when there is some malfunction do we notice them. Inflammation and swelling, or wear and tear on the cartilage of the weight-bearing joints in particular, often causes crippling pain. A slipped-disc, another painful malfunction, is the result of one of the thick pads of cartilage separating the vertebrae becoming dislodged and protruding onto a nerve.

The space between the bones in a joint is filled with a small amount of lubricating fluid, known as *synovial fluid*. Like the oil in a car engine, it reduces the friction between the moving parts. The whole joint is enclosed in a protective bag and prevented from moving too far by the *ligaments* which are strong bands of collagen connecting the two bones at the joint, so preventing dislocation.

In both the male and female pelvis, the bones are tightly bound together by joints made entirely of cartilage, but in the female, during the last stage of pregnancy, these joints loosen and separate slightly to enable the large head of the child to emerge more easily. The bone plates making up the skull of a newborn child are soft and able to move over each other slightly. This too makes it easier for the child's head to negotiate the narrow birth canal. The skull plates actually fix together as the child grows, to form a strong protective helmet for the delicate tissues of the brain.

Fractures and the growth of bone

Although the femur is able to withstand pressures up to 20,000 pounds per square inch during the landing from pole-vaulting, if a fraction of that pressure is applied at right angles to the shaft of the bone it will break. The cylindrical shape and hard, brittle material are designed to withstand great pressures applied to the ends, not to the sides. This makes bones vulnerable to fractures, especially through a blow or fall. (The healing process, however, can soon make these undetectable.)

The healing process begins immediately with the formation of a large blood clot between the broken ends of the bone. After a few days the minerals from the sharp ends of the bone are completely absorbed into the bloodstream leaving only the rubbery collagen fibres. Meanwhile a fibrous network of connective tissue grows through the blood clot holding the fragments together. Osteocytes migrate from inside the bone and begin to produce new hard bone at the fracture site. In two to three weeks this soft, calcium-rich bone has formed a callous, bridging the gap between the bone ends. The callous hardens and the bone is ready to perform its supportive functions. Over a number of years remodelling removes all trace of the callous.

Above: An X-ray photograph (radiogram) of a 300 year old skull. The photograph has been artificially coloured to show the different densities. Information about the diet, conditions and physique of past humanity can be found from the study of skeletal remains, some of which are over 2 million years old.

Below: The knee joint, the largest joint in the body, is shown here in cross-section. It is held together by muscles and ligaments, and enclosed in a capsule containing fluid which lubricates the joint. The patella (knee-cap) protects the joint and anchors the tendons coming from the powerful leg muscles.

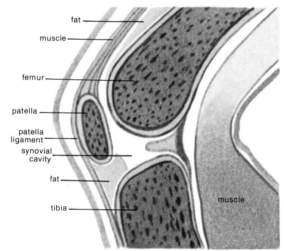

fat
muscle
femur
patella
patella ligament
synovial cavity
fat
tibia
muscle

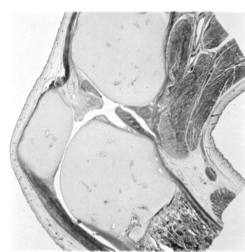

Brian Bracegirdle

vessels, which permeate the bone, provide nutrients for the cells and a means by which the 'metabolized' products can be expelled. Even so, osteocytes in patches of bone may die, leaving empty lacunae which fill with mineral deposits. These act as a storehouse for the body's mineral reserves.

Throughout the body's life bone is being continually laid down and removed in response to stresses placed upon it. This results in the building up of bone where it is under pressure around the joints, and the removal of unnecessary bumps. Should, for example, a child break a femur which is then wrongly aligned, the healing will look initially unsightly due to the formation of a large *callous*. This will be removed in a couple of years by remodelling of the bone.

Both the volume and density of bone can be made to increase by doing extra work and subjecting the skeleton to increased loads. Cavalrymen have been known to acquire bones in their buttocks and thighs, for example, quite distinct from the normal hip and femur bones. These have arisen entirely as a result of the cavalrymen's continual work on horses. Conversely, by leading a sedentary life bone is lost, so people kept in bed for long periods suffer from thin, weakened bones. Astronauts on prolonged flights have similar problems due to the lack of gravity which reduces stress on the skeleton. The sudden return to normal gravity, and the rigorous effort of moving again in a world of normal weight, causes new strains on the weakened skeleton.

All the parts of the skeleton are made of collagen fibres, except that in bone the collagen is surrounded and impregnated with mineral deposits which give it its strength. By dissolving away most of these mineral components, the remaining collagen resembles a dog's rubber bone; in fact a long bone like the femur can be tied in a knot. If the collagen part of the bone is removed by burning or decay, the result will be a dry, brittle, hard object with the strength of reinforced concrete.

Muscles

The muscles of a fully developed adult male can produce sufficient power to lift a weight of about 25 tonnes. This muscular power-house is totally contained in 42 per cent of a man's body weight. (In a woman, muscles make up 36 per cent of body weight.) It consists of 620 muscles working together to move the 206 bones of the human skeleton. A further 30 or so muscles are needed to ensure the passage of food through the intestines, to circulate the blood round the body and operate certain internal organs.

In man, three different types of muscle can be found: *skeletal* (or *striated*) muscle which is used for locomotion, *smooth* muscle which lines the various organs and intestine, and *heart* (*cardiac*) muscle. They all operate in the same general way —they contract and they relax. This action is possible because the fibres which make up the muscles are able to shorten their length by 30 to 40 per cent.

With very few exceptions (such as the blinking of the eye) single muscles never contract by themselves: rather, whole sets of muscles contract together or in sequence. To produce the complex movements necessary for even the simplest handling task there must be a correspondingly subtle control mechanism. This is the job of the nervous system: it neutralizes the actions of the muscles that are not required, and causes the contraction of muscles which are required. The brain and spinal cord exercise this control through the motor nerve fibres.

Each muscle, however, does not have a 'private line' from the central nervous system (CNS). Impulses travel down the nerve axon from the CNS, branching off to supply a group of muscles which contract together. In order to co-ordinate movement, the CNS must be supplied with information about the length of the muscle and the tension of the *tendons* which attach it to the skeleton.

For example, if we wish to pick up an object our CNS must know the present tension, length and position of the arm muscles in order to cause the correct amount of contraction to move the arm. The CNS must stop increasing the contractions when the arm reaches the object, maintain sufficient contraction to hold the object, and then cause the muscle contractions required to move the arm away. This information is provided by special sense organs called *muscle spindles*, which measure the strain in the muscles, and can be used to pre-set the tension of the muscles.

The control of muscles
Skeletal muscles must contract rapidly in response to messages from the CNS and they must develop tension at the same time to produce an effective mechanical force. Examination of skeletal muscle reveals a junction between the nerve fibre and the muscle surface. This gap (the *end plate*) acts as a kind of amplifier, increasing the effect of the tiny current coming down the nerve fibre to stimulate the much larger muscle fibre.

On the arrival of the nerve impulse, a chemical (known as *acetylcholine*) is released from the motor nerve ending and passes across the gap to stimulate the

Below: This illustration shows the operation of pairs of opposed muscles in the arm. It is the biceps of the upper arm that contract to raise the arm. When the triceps contract and the biceps relax, the arm is lowered. During the contraction, a muscle can shorten its length by up to 40%.

FLEXION

triceps

biceps

EXTENSIONS

triceps

biceps

Below: These remarkable anatomical drawings were published in 1543 by Vesalius. Unlike his contemporaries he made his own detailed examinations rather than rely on already established dogma, so setting new standards in biological studies. These pictures show muscle distribution in the body.

Alphabet & Image

Alphabet & Image

Right: The major skeletal muscles of the body, seen from the front. Posture and movement are the result of the combined action of these muscles and the skeleton. Muscles work together in groups contracting and relaxing to produce the fine control needed to do even simple tasks like writing one's name.

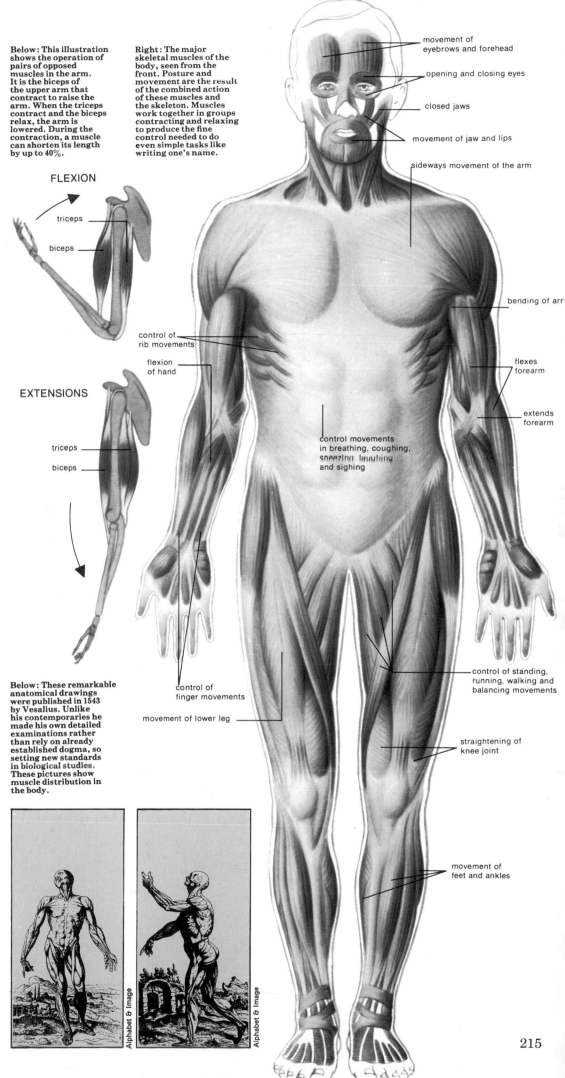

movement of eyebrows and forehead

opening and closing eyes

closed jaws

movement of jaw and lips

sideways movement of the arm

bending of arm

flexes forearm

extends forearm

control of rib movements

flexion of hand

control movements in breathing, coughing, sneezing, laughing and sighing

control of finger movements

movement of lower leg

control of standing, running, walking and balancing movements

straightening of knee joint

movement of feet and ankles

215

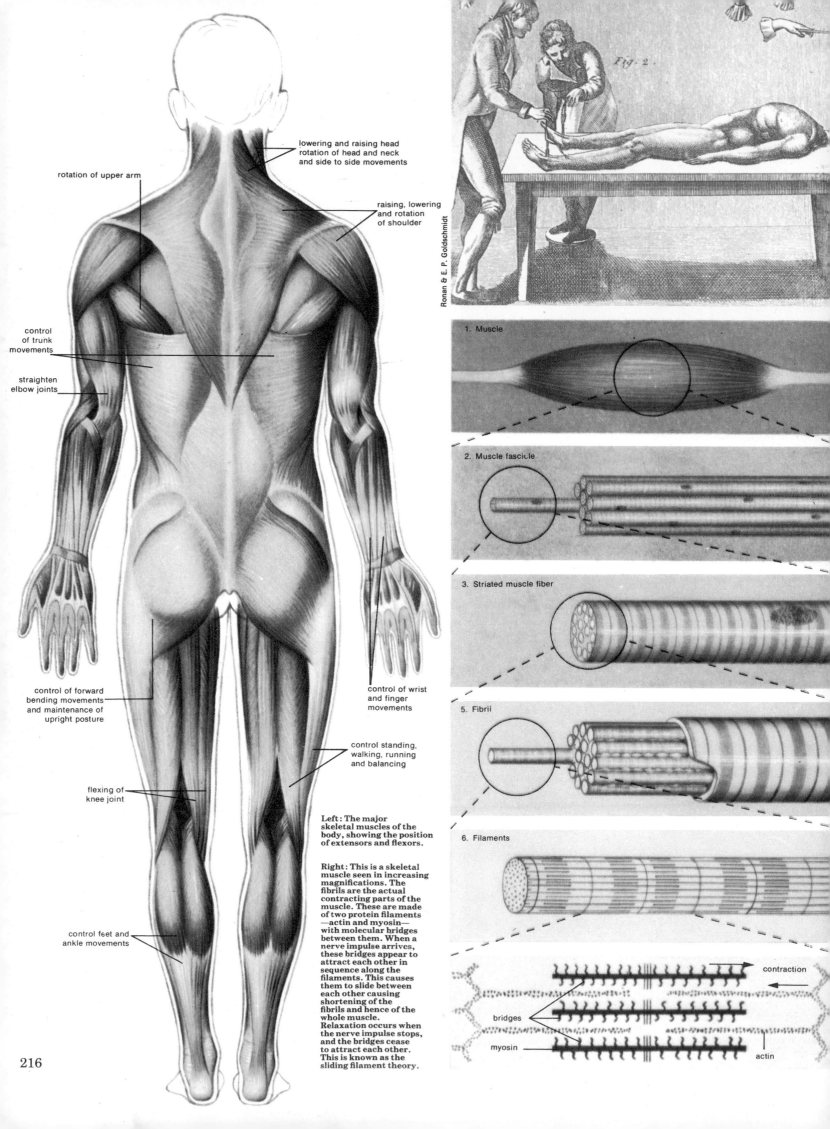

rotation of upper arm

lowering and raising head
rotation of head and neck
and side to side movements

raising, lowering
and rotation
of shoulder

control
of trunk
movements

straighten
elbow joints

control of forward
bending movements
and maintenance of
upright posture

control of wrist
and finger
movements

control standing,
walking, running
and balancing

flexing of
knee joint

control feet and
ankle movements

Ronan & E. P. Goldschmidt

Fig. 2.

1. Muscle

2. Muscle fascicle

3. Striated muscle fiber

5. Fibril

6. Filaments

contraction

bridges

myosin

actin

Left: The major
skeletal muscles of the
body, showing the position
of extensors and flexors.

Right: This is a skeletal
muscle seen in increasing
magnifications. The
fibrils are the actual
contracting parts of the
muscle. These are made
of two protein filaments
—actin and myosin—
with molecular bridges
between them. When a
nerve impulse arrives,
these bridges appear to
attract each other in
sequence along the
filaments. This causes
them to slide between
each other causing
shortening of the
fibrils and hence of the
whole muscle.
Relaxation occurs when
the nerve impulse stops,
and the bridges cease
to attract each other.
This is known as the
sliding filament theory.

216

Left: The conduction of electricity through a corpse making the muscle of a frog's leg (inserted in the corpse's leg nerve) twitch. Galvani in 1771 first discovered the connection between electricity and muscle contraction.

Below: The Jivaro tribe in Ecuador

uses curare tipped darts to paralyse their prey. Curare blocks the chemical nerve transmitter acetylcholine, so stopping impulses from reaching the muscles. Curare is made by boiling certain vines. The picture shows the darts and the gourd in which curare is carried.

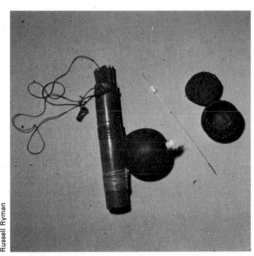

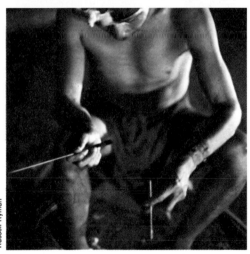

Below: The pictures are photographs taken through a microscope of the different types of muscles found in the body. Both skeletal and heart muscle are striated, meaning they are regularly divided into bands of protein filaments which slide over each other to cause contraction. Smooth muscle is made of small cells which do not have

the protein filaments. It is not yet understood how these contract. Heart and smooth muscle have their own internal pacemakers and contract without needing instructions from nerve impulses. Experiments have shown that heart muscle removed from the body and kept alive will continue to beat for a short period of time.

membrane of the muscle fibre. This stimulation is in the form of an electric current which passes along the surface of the muscle, causing it to contract. It takes one millisecond (1/1000th of a second) for the current to pass along the surface of the muscle fibre, the contraction being an all-or-nothing response. Then the fibre relaxes unless another impulse arrives. (If this chemical mechanism is blocked, the result would be paralysis.) And indeed many South American Indian hunters use a poison which effectively does just that and paralyses their prey. The poison, which is called *curare*, is smeared on arrows and spears, and when it enters an animal's bloodstream it instantly blocks the action of acetylcholine.

Heart muscle differs slightly from skeletal muscle because it has a built-in mechanism to maintain the necessary rhythmical contraction quite independently of any nervous connections. A turtle's heart, for instance, entirely removed from its body, can keep on beating for a long time; even small pieces of human heart muscle, kept alive in special solutions, may continue to contract rhythmically.

Smooth muscles react much more slowly to stimulation than skeletal muscles. The nerves, when present, alter the activity of the muscle rather than initiating it. This is in some respects similar to the heart muscle. Contraction takes place rhythmically without direct control from the CNS, and the impulses for contraction come from within the muscle itself.

The mechanics of contraction

To the unaided eye, skeletal muscles have a grainy appearance because they are made up of small fibres. Examination of the fibres through a microscope shows them to be cylinders, which may be several centimetres long, with regular bands (*striations*) dividing them into sections, rather like coins stacked in a pile. The fibres themselves are made up of many cylindrical subunits, the *fibrils*, and these are the structures that actually contract.

Further examination of the fibrils has revealed that they are made of two types of protein—*actin* and *myosin*—which are in the form of long *filaments*, thick ones consisting of myosin and thin ones made of actin. These filaments interlock and are able to slide over each other, so that when the muscle is stretched the filaments tend to be pulled apart like two pieces of a telescope. During shortening they slide into one another. During this contraction

it appears that cross-links are made between the actin and myosin filaments. These are almost instantaneously broken and new links set up slightly further along the filaments. So, by a process of making and breaking these cross-links, the two filaments move towards one another and the whole muscle shortens. This process, of course, takes place very rapidly.

Heart muscle has a similar appearance to skeletal muscle; it has striations and is thought to contract in the same way as skeletal muscle. Smooth muscle has no striations and is composed of small spindle-shaped cells totally lacking in filaments. The mechanism of contraction in smooth muscle still remains a mystery.

The chemistry of contraction

The muscles are biological machines which convert chemical energy into force and mechanical work. The energy for contraction, as for all the other life processes, comes from the chemical reaction between the foodstuffs that we eat and the oxygen that we breathe. Muscles therefore need a good blood supply to bring the essential food and oxygen, and to remove waste products. The actual chemical process involves the breakdown of *glucose* to carbon dioxide and water, thereby releasing energy which is used by the muscle proteins to cause contraction. This chemical reaction requires a very liberal supply of oxygen which is often not available; even during fairly moderate exercise the blood supply is often insufficient to carry enough oxygen to the muscles. To overcome this problem the muscles are able to convert the glucose into a substance called *lactic acid*, without the use of oxygen, which still gives the necessary release of energy.

There is, of course, a limit to the intensity with which we can exercise our muscles. Beyond this limit movement becomes painful and finally impossible. This is due to the accumulation of lactic acid which eventually fatigues the muscles and causes cramps. Removal of the lactic acid requires oxygen; this causes the familiar panting after exercise which brings in oxygen as rapidly as possible to pay off the *oxygen debt*.

Muscles are in fact able to store glucose in the form of *glycogen* (a *carbohydrate*) granules and it is this store which is used during exercise. It has in fact been worked out that if the total amount of fat on the average adult male (about one gallon) were to be converted into muscular energy, this would be enough to cycle 2,000 miles.

Cardiac

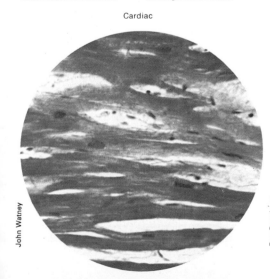

Striated

Smooth

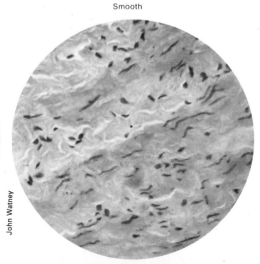

The Essence of Blood

Blood is truly 'the essence of life' for this vital fluid carries to every living cell in the body the nutrients necessary for providing energy and the raw materials needed for tissue growth, maintenance and repair.

It is vital, too, in clearing away from the cells all the waste products of their various activities, particularly the carbon dioxide produced when food is burned with oxygen for energy.

And blood has a third essential role: it acts as the body's policeman, destroying or neutralizing any potentially-dangerous foreign invaders like bacteria or other germs.

The average man has some five litres (10 pints) of blood in his body; women have about 15 per cent less. Blood makes up about 1/14th of the total weight of the human body. Around 45 per cent of the blood volume is composed of various types of specialized cells each adapted for its particular task. These cells—the most important are called *red cells* or *red corpuscles*, and *white cells* or *white corpuscles*—are suspended in a pale yellow liquid called *plasma*. They are so small that just one drop of blood will contain as many as 250,000,000 red cells and 400,000 white ones.

The transporting medium

The body contains slightly more than three litres of plasma, much of which is water. Its main task is to transport round the body a variety of substances in solution, some of which are salt, proteins and glucose.

Most nutrients in food are absorbed into the blood through the walls of the small intestine; some of them can be taken directly to cells; others first have to be processed into more useful compounds by

Mansell

John Watney

Left: Blood-letting was a popular method of treatment until the last century (and is still used in some parts of the world). Ill health was believed to be caused by an imbalance of the body humours due to a surfeit of blood. Some heart conditions are still treated by reducing the amount of blood to relieve strain on the circulation.

Above and top: Haemophilia, a disease which prevents blood from clotting, was common amongst European royal families —10 princes descended from Queen Victoria were affected. The normal clotting process is shown above—the thread-like fibrins mesh around the blood cells and eventually form a solid clot.

the specialized 'chemical factories' of the body—that is the liver and other glands. Some of these chemicals, called *hormones*, regulate body processes, while others, such as *enzymes*, act as catalysts for various chemical reactions in the cells.

The capillaries, the smallest branches of the blood vessels allow water, sugars for energy, amino-acids (the constituents of proteins which are themselves the building blocks of living matter) and various other chemicals to seep through their walls. Big molecules like the plasma proteins, however, cannot readily squeeze through the capillary walls. At the beginning of the return journey to the heart, the pressure in the capillaries has dropped and the waste products of the cells' activities are drawn in. Blood is continually being 'washed' by the kid-

neys: they extract the waste products which are finally disposed of in the urine.

The plasma proteins are called *albumin*, *globulin* and *fibrinogen*. The main task of the most abundant one, albumin, is in maintaining the blood's *osmotic pressure*. It is this pressure—acting in the opposite direction to that exerted by the heart—which pulls in water and the cells' waste products as the blood begins its journey back through the veins. Antibodies, special compounds which neutralize foreign invaders such as germs, are made of gamma-globulin proteins. They are formed in the spleen or lymph nodes in response to specific infections and they continue to circulate in the blood after the initial infection has been conquered, so providing *immunity* against further attack. Fibrinogen is responsible for blood clotting and like albumin, is manufactured in the liver.

The oxygen carriers

Red blood cells get their colour from a special pigment called *haemoglobin*—formed from a protein and an iron compound. Each cell is very small, about .008 cm (three-thousandths of an inch) in diameter and is shaped like a round cushion, with a hollow on each side. The haemoglobin picks up oxygen from the lungs and transports it to every cell in the body. On releasing its oxygen cargo—and changing from bright red to a dark red or purplish colour in the process—the red cell picks up carbon dioxide which is deposited on the next circuit through the lungs.

Red cells are manufactured in the bone marrow and have a life span of some 120 days. When they wear out—and it is a staggering fact that something like five million red cells are being destroyed in our bodies every second—they are broken down into their constituent parts, some of which can be used again in the manu-

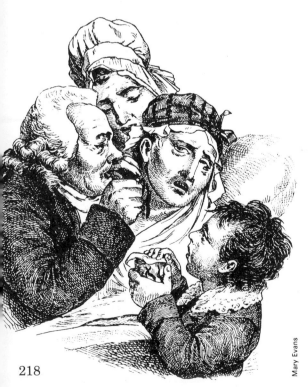

Mary Evans

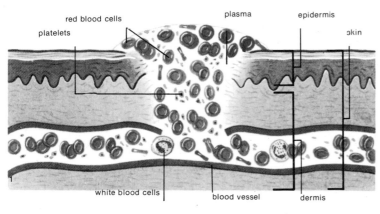

red blood cells | plasma | epidermis

platelets | skin

white blood cells | blood vessel | dermis

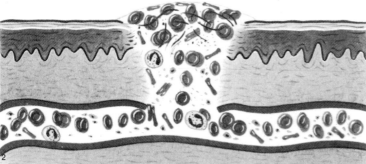

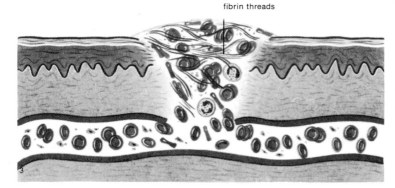

fibrin threads

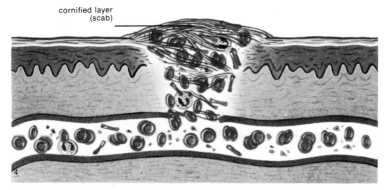

cornified layer
(scab)

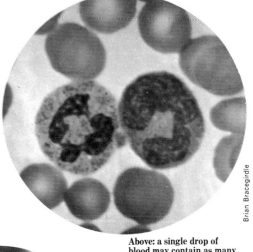

Left: The blood clotting mechanism, the process by which bleeding is arrested and tissues restored. (1) Bleeding releases an enzyme called thromboplastin from the damaged tissue cells which combines with the calcium and prothrombin in the blood. (2) Together these interact with fibrinogen, also present in the blood, to form fibrin, which forms threads around the red and white cells sealing the opening and fighting off any bacteria. (3) The resulting mesh of threads solidifies. The top layer of cells eventually die, becoming conified, so forming the scab. (4) Underneath the scab or protective layer, new cells are being formed. When damaged cells are completely replaced, the scab drops off.

Above: a single drop of blood may contain as many as 250,000,000 red cells and 400,000 white ones. A greater number of red cells are required for the vital task of transporting oxygen from the lungs to the tissues of the body. The oxygen is actually carried by the haemoglobin, the pigment which gives the cells their red colour.

Left: White blood cells are primarily concerned with combatting infection and disease. These granulocytes are in the process of engulfing and destroying bacteria. Other types of white cells appear to be particularly concerned with allergies and in providing the body with immunity through the formation of antibodies.

PER LITRE OF NORMAL ADULT BLOOD

Right: A litre of blood taken from a normal, healthy adult should contain all of the ingredients in the quantities listed in the table. Excessive amounts or deficiencies can cause problems: too much cholesterol may cause circulation problems in later life, and too little calcium can impede the growth of bone and also clotting.

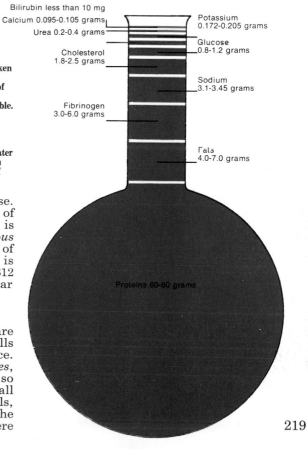

Bilirubin less than 10 mg
Calcium 0.095-0.105 grams
Urea 0.2-0.4 grams

Potassium 0.172-0.205 grams

Glucose 0.8-1.2 grams

Cholesterol 1.8-2.5 grams

Sodium 3.1-3.45 grams

Fibrinogen 3.0-6.0 grams

Fats 4.0-7.0 grams

Proteins 60-80 grams

facture of new red cells.

There are many diseases due to deficiencies of red cells and they are collectively known as *anaemia*. *Haemolytic anaemia*, for example, is due to excessive destruction of red cells, which may be caused by poisoning, by a disease like malaria, or by an inherited condition. There is also a special type of haemolytic anaemia which sometimes occurs in newborn babies.

Iron is essential for the manufacture of haemoglobin and although the body usually has good stores, a slow but steady loss of blood—as, say, from an ulcer—can cause anaemia. Women seem to be more vulnerable than men, and excessively heavy periods can make the problem worse. In pregnancy, too, when the mother is supplying iron to her baby,

she may not have enough for her own use. Anaemia is sometimes a symptom of malnutrition, especially if the diet is lacking in iron and folic acid. *Pernicious anaemia*, in which large numbers of abnormally large red cells are made, is due to a lack of proper absorption of B12 but is now easily controlled by regular injections of the vitamin.

The disease fighters
White cells, known as *leukocytes*, are spherical, slightly bigger than red cells and form the body's disease fighting force. There are two main types: *granulocytes*, also formed in bone marrow and so called because they contain many small granules scattered throughout their cells, and *lymphocytes* which are formed in the lymphatic system and in the spleen. There

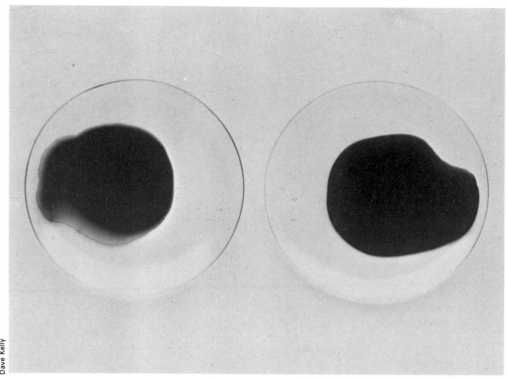

Dave Kelly

are about three times as many granulocytes as lymphocytes.

Granulocytes attack invaders such as bacteria by engulfing and consuming them. They are geared for instant action and congregate quickly at the appearance of an infection or injury. Lymphocytes act more slowly and are involved in the production of antibodies. There are actually more lymphocytes outside the blood than in it, living in all tissue. In fact, white cells seem to use blood only as a means of transport and unlike red cells they can seep out of blood vessels into surrounding tissue.

There is a considerable increase in white cell production when the body is invaded. Bacterial infection, for example, may cause them to multiply their numbers by three or four times. A *blood count*, in which a small quantity of blood is examined to find out the numbers and types of cell present, can therefore be a valuable aid to diagnosis. For example, in a patient suffering from an ill-defined stomach ache, large numbers of white cells might indicate appendicitis rather than indigestion. Haemoglobin levels can be checked in blood counts, too, and powerful modern microscopes make possible visual examination of any physical abnormalities in the cells.

Sometimes white cells proliferate needlessly, producing a cancer-like condition called *leukaemia* and chronic over-production of granulocytes leads to a similar condition called chronic leukaemia.

Bone marrow is sensitive to various poisons and to radiation, which can hinder the production of both red and white cells, leading to a dangerous but rare condition called *aplastic anaemia*.

The *pus* which may arise from inflammation is a mixture of dead white cells and the micro-organisms they have engulfed. White cells may also break down and dispose of inanimate invaders, even something as large as a wood splinter or a thorn. They also carry away clotted blood and dead tissue after wounds have healed.

Above: The blood sample on the left is arterial blood. It is bright red when it has just left the lungs, where the haemoglobin particles absorb oxygen, forming oxyhaemoglobin, but as it passes through the tissues, giving up the oxygen, it returns to the dark red colour of the sample of blood on the right.

Below: An experiment to test the viability of a form of artificial blood for emergency purposes. The mouse was suspended in the oxygen-carrying liquid to determine the amount of oxygen in it. When removed from the liquid after a few hours the mouse continued to breathe normally and suffered no ill effects.

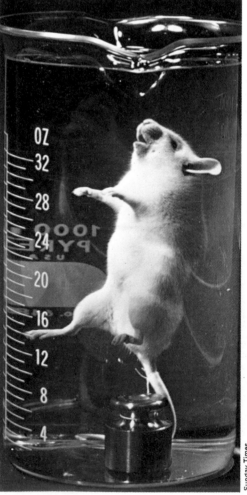

Sunday Times

The clotting process

Obviously so essential a fluid as the blood must be guarded against losses. Although we can lose up to 15 per cent without any ill-effects, a greater loss can be serious and often fatal.

Loss of blood from the circulation—either internally or externally—is called *haemorrhage*. Slow sustained bleeding leads to anaemia and rapid bleeding causes *shock*, resulting from a fall in pressure to a level inadequate to maintain blood flow to the heart. While most body organs can function for a time with reduced blood supply, the brain cannot and this is the lethal factor following serious injury or acute illness.

The body has a built-in system to prevent blood loss: the *clotting mechanism*, and specialized cells called *platelets* play a vital role in the process. Platelets, also made in the bone marrow, are much smaller than red cells. There are some 15 million of them in each drop of blood. When a blood vessel is damaged, platelets congregate and stick to the site of the injury and to each other, forming a plug. As they stick together platelets release substances essential to set the clotting mechanism going (the injured tissue itself also releases similar substances).

Clotting is fundamentally a change in that soluble plasma protein fibrinogen to an insoluble, thread-like protein, *fibrin*—more than a dozen factors are involved in this conversion, but they cannot come into operation until those substances are released by the platelets. The fibrin strands mesh around blood cells and then contract, squeezing a clear yellowish fluid called *serum*, and forming a solid clot.

The platelets help to control blood loss in yet another way. They release a hormone called serotonin which stimulates blood vessels to contract, thus reducing the flow.

Abnormal bleeding is a characteristic of a number of diseases, scurvy, epidemic meningitis (spotted fever) and the Black Death (bubonic plague) among them. Poisoning or radiation may affect the bone marrow and interfere with platelet production. Sometimes the number of platelets falls for no apparent reason. Surgical removal of the spleen often cures the trouble, but it is not yet certain why this is successful.

Vitamin K is essential for the formation of some of those dozen or so clotting factors but it cannot be absorbed into the bloodstream unless there is bile in the intestine. In some types of jaundice, when the bile flow is obstructed, clotting is affected.

The best-known of all clotting diseases, however, is *haemophilia*, an inherited disease from which only men suffer, although women may be carriers and pass it on to their sons. Its notoriety is due to its effects on members of Queen Victoria's family, notably the last Tsarevitch of Russia, but it is a relatively rare disease, affecting about one boy in 10,000.

It is caused by the absence of one of the clotting factors, a plasma protein known as anti-haemophiliac globulin or Factor VIII. The slightest injury can lead to uncontrolled bleeding and, in the past, few haemophiliacs survived childhood. Blood transfusions and now, injections of the vital factor, which can be extracted from plasma, can, however, give haemophiliacs some semblance of normal life.

Blood Circulation

The main functions of the circulatory system are to carry oxygen and nutriments, particularly glucose, to the tissues and to carry away carbon dioxide and other waste products produced by metabolic processes in the cells.

The most important unit in the circulatory system is the heart. The heart is a muscular pump which propels oxygenated blood to the tissues of the body through thick-walled vessels called arteries. The arteries branch into smaller vessels called arterioles through which much of the control of the circulation is achieved —the muscle cells in their walls can contract and thus alter the flow of blood. The arterioles further sub-divide and the blood eventually passes into the capillaries, the finest of the vessels, which have a diameter of only 0.006 mm.

The total surface area of capillary walls in the body is over 6,000 square metres; it is through this enormous area that the exchange of nutriments and oxygen for waste products takes place between the blood and the cells of the tissues. The blood becomes darker in colour as it gives up its oxygen. This deoxygenated or venous blood then flows into slightly larger vessels called venules which, in turn, drain into the veins which take the blood back to the heart. The lining of the walls of the veins is folded at intervals to form one-way venous valves which prevent the backflow of blood to the tissues.

The returned blood is then pumped by the heart through the pulmonary arteries to the capillaries of the lungs. The acquired carbon dioxide is given up, to be breathed out, and as fresh oxygen is taken in the newly oxygenated blood returns via the pulmonary veins to the heart ready for another trip round this double circuit.

The circulatory system does a prodigious amount of work. At rest, blood is pumped round the body at a rate of five litres per minute, but during violent exercise the amount pumped can increase to over 25 litres per minute. It has been calculated that during a man's lifetime a total of 500,000,000 litres of blood is pumped round the body.

The distribution of blood throughout the body is neither even nor fixed, since the basic requirements of different tissues vary. Under normal conditions the liver receives 28% of the total cardiac output; the kidneys receive 24%, the skeletal muscles 15%, the brain 14% and the heart 5%. However, these are only average figures and nervous control of the size of the arterioles allows extra blood to be diverted to particular areas in times of need. During exercise, for example, the increased cardiac output is directed mainly to the skeletal muscles to provide them with fuel. At the same time, the blood flow to the skin is increased so that the extra heat generated by the body can be radiated to the atmosphere—the effect responsible for the familiar reddening of the face during exertion—particularly when running, or playing energetic games such as squash.

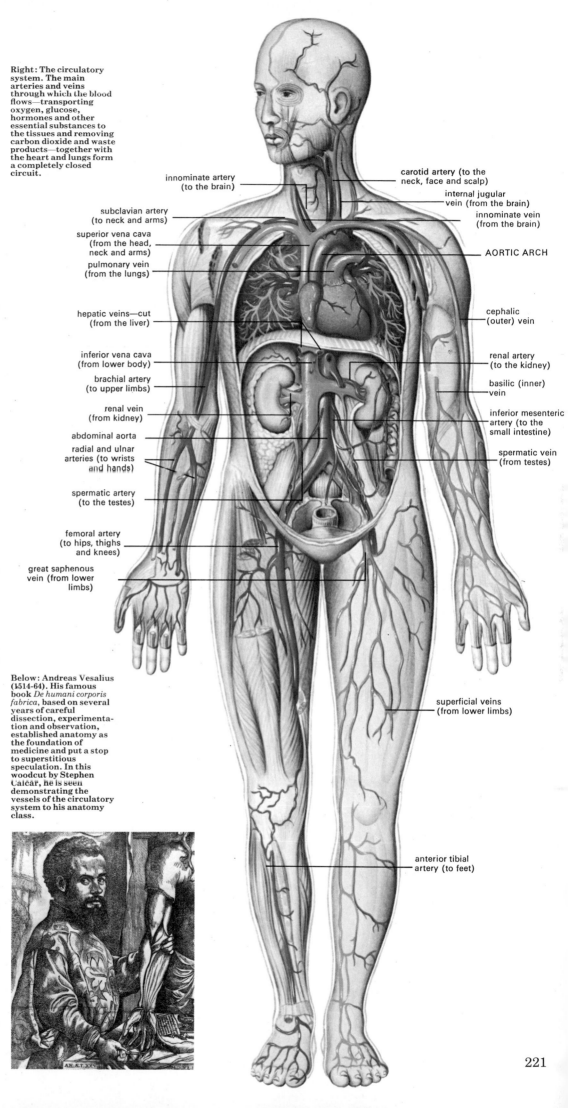

Right: The circulatory system. The main arteries and veins through which the blood flows—transporting oxygen, glucose, hormones and other essential substances to the tissues and removing carbon dioxide and waste products—together with the heart and lungs form a completely closed circuit.

innominate artery (to the brain)

subclavian artery (to neck and arms)

superior vena cava (from the head, neck and arms)

pulmonary vein (from the lungs)

hepatic veins—cut (from the liver)

inferior vena cava (from lower body)

brachial artery (to upper limbs)

renal vein (from kidney)

abdominal aorta

radial and ulnar arteries (to wrists and hands)

spermatic artery (to the testes)

femoral artery (to hips, thighs and knees)

great saphenous vein (from lower limbs)

carotid artery (to the neck, face and scalp)

internal jugular vein (from the brain)

innominate vein (from the brain)

AORTIC ARCH

cephalic (outer) vein

renal artery (to the kidney)

basilic (inner) vein

inferior mesenteric artery (to the small intestine)

spermatic vein (from testes)

superficial veins (from lower limbs)

anterior tibial artery (to feet)

Below: Andreas Vesalius (1514-64). His famous book *De humani corporis fabrica*, based on several years of careful dissection, experimentation and observation, established anatomy as the foundation of medicine and put a stop to superstitious speculation. In this woodcut by Stephen Calcar, he is seen demonstrating the vessels of the circulatory system to his anatomy class.

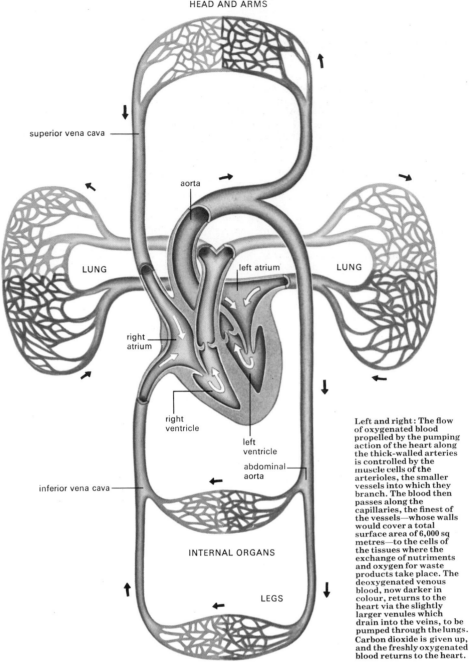

HEAD AND ARMS

superior vena cava

aorta

LUNG

left atrium

LUNG

right atrium

right ventricle

left ventricle

abdominal aorta

inferior vena cava

INTERNAL ORGANS

LEGS

Artery

Arteriole

Capillary

Venule

Vein

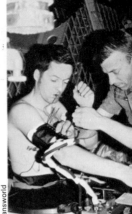

Left and right: The flow of oxygenated blood propelled by the pumping action of the heart along the thick-walled arteries is controlled by the muscle cells of the arterioles, the smaller vessels into which they branch. The blood then passes along the capillaries, the finest of the vessels—whose walls would cover a total surface area of 6,000 sq metres—to the cells of the tissues where the exchange of nutriments and oxygen for waste products take place. The deoxygenated venous blood, now darker in colour, returns to the heart via the slightly larger venules which drain into the veins, to be pumped through the lungs. Carbon dioxide is given up, and the freshly oxygenated blood returns to the heart.

Right: Resin is injected into the circulatory network of a foetus to demonstrate the complexity of veins, arteries and capillaries.

Below: Skylab, the orbiting laboratory, where astronauts spent up to 84 days in training. Blood pressure and heart functions were checked for stress.

Right: The eye photographed with an ophthalmoscope, showing the retinal blood vessels through which we see the world and the blind spot where the vessels and nerves leave the eyeball.

Below: Thermographic pictures demonstrate how smoking constricts blood vessels and so reduces the amount of heat radiated. Black, at the extreme left of the colour code, represents the lowest temperature, white the highest and the colours in between a rising scale each representing 0.5°C. The picture on the left shows the normal amount of heat radiated before smoking. The picture on the right, taken after smoking, shows the drop in temperature in several parts of the hand.

Control of the circulation

The flow of any fluid through a tube is determined by the diameter of the tube and the force behind the fluid. The flow rate in the circulatory system is governed by the alteration of the diameter of the arterioles and by control of the force and rate of the heartbeat. The muscle in the arteriolar walls is acted upon by a chemical, *noradrenaline*, released from the endings of their nerves, to produce constriction of the arteriole. Similarly, the heart rate is increased by noradrenaline released from the endings of the cardiac nerves. Thus, it is the nervous system which is largely responsible for the control of the circulation.

Since the brain is more sensitive to a lack of oxygen than any other organ in the body, and its function is so vital to life, its blood flow must be maintained at all costs. For this reason, the body has developed a system called 'autoregulation' by which various nerves act to maintain the flow to the brain even if the flow to the rest of the body falls dramatically, as in the case of a severe haemorrhage.

At a more general level, the autonomic nervous system is constantly receiving messages from the brain and spinal cord to adjust the flow to the various organs. For example, when a person stands up quickly this system operates immediately to counteract the effect of gravity which would retain the blood in the lower parts of the body. Occasionally, the system may be a little slow: the result is the type of giddiness or fainting that may be experienced after a hot bath.

There is also a mechanism for maintaining blood flow through the kidneys. If the blood flow falls, a substance called *renin* is released from the kidney. This causes the formation of another chemical called *angiotensin* in the blood. Angiotensin acts directly on the muscles of the arterioles. It also stimulates the release of the hormone, *aldosterone*, from the adrenal glands, which acts to increase the blood volume and hence raise the blood flow to the kidney. The increased flow then shuts off the secretion of renin. This system is an example of what engineers call a negative feedback loop and serves to maintain the status quo.

Another hormone, *adrenaline*, is produced by the adrenal gland in response to the emotion of fear. Adrenaline causes the redistribution of blood pressure, as a preparation for either fighting or fleeing. The sensations of a thumping heart and

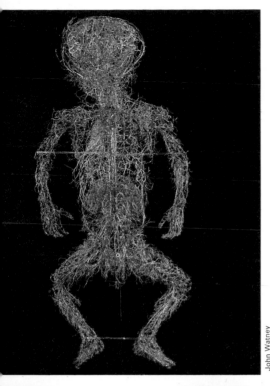

John Watney

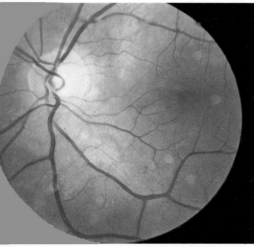

Transworld

cold, clammy skin are the well-known results of an unpleasant fright.

Blood clotting

Blood is a complex mixture of cells and dissolved proteins. The clotting or co-agulation system serves to minimize blood loss through any damaged vessel. It begins when exposure of blood cells to the air, or tissue damage, causes the release of substances which initiate a chain of reactions which result in the solidifying of the blood as a clot to block the wound. Under normal circumstances, clotting of the blood does not occur, first because the initiators of clotting are not available and secondly because some blood cells contain *heparin*, an acid, which prevents accidental clotting.

Very occasionally, a clot does form in the circulation—the accidental process called *thrombosis*. However, when a vessel is blocked by a clot, blood can often bypass the blockage by using alternative vessels which are, in this situation, called a *collateral circulation*. Clots can also be dissolved by the fibrinolytic system, continually in operation inside the vessels.

Blood pressure

The pressure of the blood in arteries and arterioles reaches a peak, called the *systolic* pressure, with each contraction of the heart and then gradually decreases to a minimum, the *diastolic* pressure, before the next contraction. Blood pressure is always expressed as two figures, for example, 120/80 in healthy young adults, representing respectively the systolic and diastolic pressures in millimetres of mercury.

Blood pressure may be increased for short periods by anxiety or exercise; it is also increased by a number of diseases and increases gradually with age. An individual is regarded as having high blood pressure if the systolic pressure consistently exceeds 100 + his age, or if the diastolic is greater than 100. The lower limit of normal adult blood pressure is 80/40. However, there is actually no such thing as a 'norm'. Blood pressure is a continuum in which the higher it goes, especially the diastolic, the more harmful the effects are likely to be.

Abnormally low blood pressure will occur, for example, after the loss of a large amount of blood, after a heart attack and in the terminal stages of many diseases. When the blood pressure is very low insufficient blood, and hence oxygen, reaches the brain and other vital organs and death is imminent. Drugs which contract the muscular walls of blood vessels and thus raise blood pressure are an effective short-term treatment until the cause of the low pressure can be treated directly, by such methods as transfusion to compensate for blood loss.

Abnormally high blood pressure may be due to an excess of adrenaline, the hormone which causes constriction of arterioles, and is produced by a tumour of the adrenal gland called a *phaeochromocytoma*. It may also be due to damage to one or both kidneys, causing them to release too much renin—this raises blood pressure by forming angiotensin which constricts blood vessels. In the vast majority of cases, however, no obvious cause for the high blood pressure can be found; this condition is referred to as idiopathic hypertension.

Yet whatever the reasons for high blood pressure, if the condition is not treated it leads to an early death. The pressure damages the walls of arteries which during healing, scar and narrow, thus raising the pressure still further and reducing the flow of blood to the body tissues. The kidney may be damaged and so contribute to a further rise in pressure by releasing renin. This may result in heart failure—as the pressure puts an excessive strain on the heart which will be unable to pump blood out of the lungs to the body. The pressure may also burst a blood vessel in the eye or the brain and cause blindness or a stroke.

Effective treatment can greatly reduce the risk of these complications. Surgical removal of an adrenal tumour or a single diseased kidney will return the blood pressure to normal. Idiopathic hypertension can be treated with drugs which prevent the action of the noradrenaline released by the sympathetic nervous system which, in health, maintains blood pressure by controlled contraction of the muscle in arteriolar walls. Different drugs decrease the production, release or effectiveness of noradrenaline so that in each case the blood vessels can release and dilate, thereby increasing blood flow and decreasing blood pressure.

The affluent disease

In Western civilization the most common disease of the arteries is *atherosclerosis* or hardening of the arteries. The process starts with the deposition and accumulation of fat on the inside of the vessel walls. Small blood cells, called platelets, then stick to the irregular accumulation within the vessels. These changes cause scarring, and by continuing platelet and fat accumulation the vessel walls become thick so the internal diameter of the arteriole is reduced. The whole process contributes to the rise of blood pressure with age and can itself be partly caused by high blood pressure. No single cause for atherosclerosis can be given but it seems to be inherited and to occur most frequently in those who are overweight, take too little exercise, are under stress or smoke cigarettes.

The most serious effect of atherosclerosis is that it eventually blocks arteries and therefore prevents sufficient blood being pumped to various parts of the body. For example, if the arteries supplying the heart are narrowed by atherosclerosis, it may not be able to get enough blood to fulfil its oxygen requirements during exercise. In this case, pain in the chest, angina pectoris, will result because the heart muscle, like other muscles, can only survive on very low oxygen for a while. It does this by using glucose in a way that produces lactic acid, and this is what causes pain. On stopping exercise, the heart then receives sufficient oxygen, the lactic acid is destroyed and the pain is relieved. Indeed the blockage of any artery is dangerous, since without an adequate blood supply tissue will die.

Poor circulation can have other consequences. For example, if the valves in the superficial veins of the legs are defective the blood cannot flow efficiently back to the heart. Instead it remains in the veins causing them to swell and occasionally burst. This condition is known as *varicose veins*. Treatment involves support of the swollen veins with elastic stockings which have a gentle, squeezing effect or, in severe cases, their surgical removal.

Cardiovascular System

The second century AD blessed the scientific world with the 'divine' teachings of Galen, the last of the great biologists of antiquity. His observations, right and wrong, halted scientific progress for 1,500 years. He did, however, recognize the structural differences between the arteries and veins, and successfully demonstrated that the arteries contain blood not air—a belief which had been held for 400 years. Galen taught that blood was made in the liver and reached the various parts of the body in a manner rather like the tidal movements of the sea: ebbing and flowing.

It was not until the seventeenth century when an Englishman, William Harvey, looked into the mechanics of circulation that any further progress in biology began to be made. He discovered that the blood flows in one direction only, controlled by the valves in the veins and the pumping of the heart. Unfortunately he never managed to pin-point the place where the blood ceased moving away from the heart and began moving towards it. This was left to the Italian physiologist Marcello Malpighi who discovered the tiny network of capillaries linking the veins and arteries in the lungs of a frog, finally establishing the circulation of the blood.

The heart of the average adult pumps something like 9,000 litres (2,000 gallons) of blood along almost 100,000 km (60,000

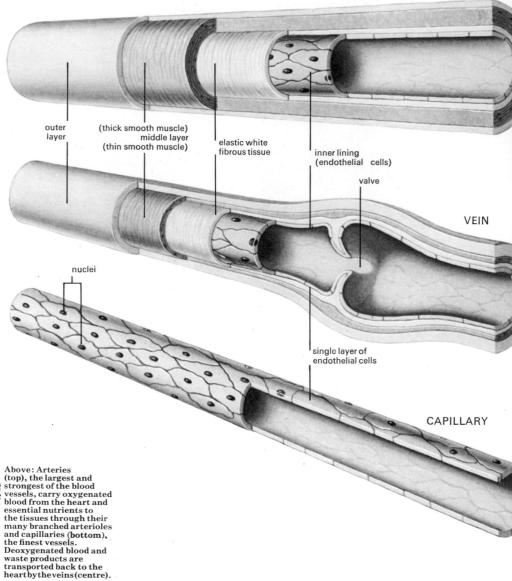

ARTERY

outer layer — (thick smooth muscle) middle layer (thin smooth muscle) — elastic white fibrous tissue — inner lining (endothelial cells)

valve

VEIN

nuclei

single layer of endothelial cells

CAPILLARY

Above: Arteries (top), the largest and strongest of the blood vessels, carry oxygenated blood from the heart and essential nutrients to the tissues through their many branched arterioles and capillaries (bottom), the finest vessels. Deoxygenated blood and waste products are transported back to the heart by the veins (centre).

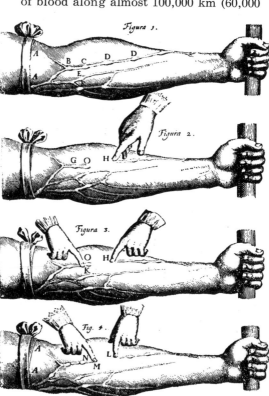

Figura 1.

Figura 2.

Figura 3.

Fig. 4.

Above: Illustrations from *De Motu Cordis,* written by the 17th century biologist, William Harvey, who discovered how the blood circulates round the body. The figures demonstrate by pressing on the veins how the direction of the blood flowing towards the heart is maintained by the valves.

Right: Transverse section of the liver showing the complexity of the capillary network, the finest vessels in the circulatory system. Efficient blood flow to the liver is particularly important since it is the only organ apart from the brain which stores glucose for energy.

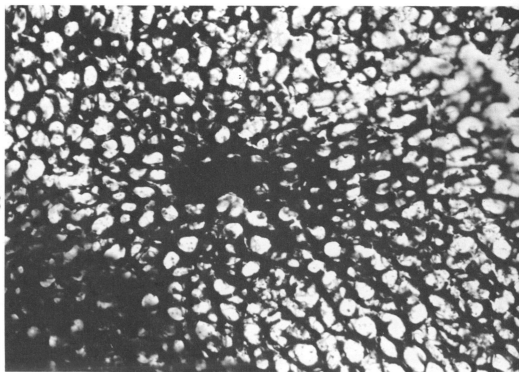

John Watney

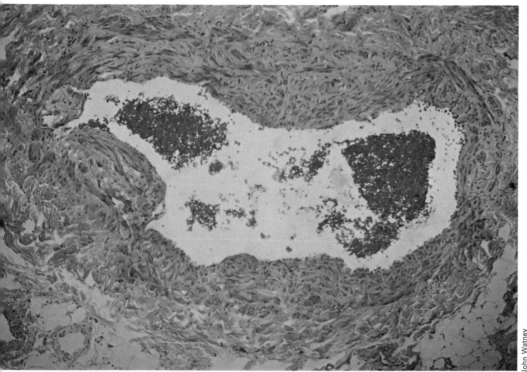

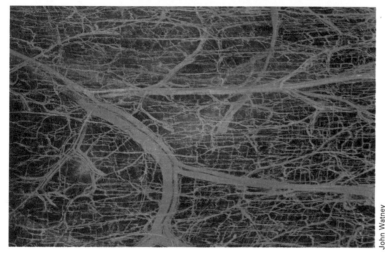

Above: A transverse section of an artery shows how the red cells have clotted together. Since a constant supply of blood is essential to the body's functioning, especially the brain, a clot which cannot be dispersed by the fibrolinytic system may deprive the surrounding tissues of oxygen, resulting in a stroke, or death if the brain is deprived of oxygen for more than three minutes.

Right: The capillary network permeates every tissue of the body. The capillaries are only .0018cm in diameter, but the action of the heart allows the body's 5 litres of blood to be pumped through their 100,000 km in a few minutes.

maintaining a suitable environment for the cells.

Some capillaries perform the sole function of joining up the arterial system with the venous system. These are more numerous in the skin. They help to regulate the body temperature by vasodilatation when the body is too hot—this increases the volume of blood available to be cooled by the air. Other capillaries deliver nutrients to the body cells through their thin walls which act as *semipermeable membranes*, allowing some, but not all, substances to pass through them.

Two processes, *diffusion* and *osmosis*, allow the passage of materials through the capillary walls. When two gases of different composition come into contact they intermingle. The air we breathe out, for example, has more carbon dioxide and less oxygen than the air we breathe in. However, this expired air does not float around the room as a separate portion of air, it diffuses into the rest of the air so that eventually the whole room contains less oxygen and more carbon dioxide. This same process of diffusion takes place between the blood inside the capillary walls and the tissue fluid outside them. It is also responsible for the exchange of oxygen, carbon dioxide, glucose and other nutrients. Osmosis is the passage of water from a weak solution to a stronger one through a semi-permeable membrane, a process which eventually makes the two solutions of equal strength. The two processes of diffusion and osmosis together enable the body cells to take what they need from the blood, and to deliver wastes and synthesized products to the blood for removal.

The veins
The blood, now deoxygenated and dark red, begins its journey back from the tissues to the heart. The blood from the capillaries flows into the venules, slightly larger vessels, then into the larger veins.

The walls of the veins are much thinner than those of the arteries: they do not contract to any noticeable extent and are not involved in adjusting the blood flow through the body tissues. They do, however, possess their own pumping mechanism which is really a by-product of the action of the muscles working in close proximity to the veins. These muscles squeeze the veins, forcing the blood through the vessels towards the heart. The direction of flow is maintained by pocket shaped valves, formed from the endothelium and strengthened by connective tissue, which only allow the blood to travel in one direction. The venous system has, in fact, quite a lot of work to do, returning blood from the lower parts of the body where gravity drags the blood away from the heart. The driving pressure caused by the heart beat is very low after having passed through the intricacies of the microcirculation, so the pumping mechanism of the venous system is essential in the return process.

Cardiovascular control
Any bodily system with a job as important as the supply of oxygen and nutrients to body tissues must be able to work at a fairly constant rate, despite changing internal and external conditions.

Total blood flow will be affected by two factors: cardiac output and arterial vessel resistance. The latter is determined by size and both are controlled by a variety

miles) of tubing in the circulatory system every day. This ceaseless activity takes place without our conscious knowledge, controlled by the central nervous system and the body's chemical co-ordinators.

The heart, veins, arteries and capillaries are collectively known as the cardiovascular system. All the blood vessels except the tiny capillaries have the same basic structure. They are made of three types of tissue: the endothelium—an inner lining made up of a single layer of flat cells resembling irregular stones fitted together in a smooth pavement—sheathed in a layer of muscle cells, interwoven with a layer of fibrous tissue. The muscle cells give the vessel a certain amount of elasticity, which allows the expansion and contraction of the vessels following the surge of blood from the pumping of the heart. The wall of the tube is so thin that it is only visible as a thin line when magnified 1,000 times. In fact it is less than .3025 cm (.0001 inch) thick.

The arteries leaving the left side of the heart branch off into smaller vessels, the arterioles, losing some of the elastic content of their walls as they do so. The arterioles play the major role in regulating the blood flow and pressure through the capillaries. Contraction of the thick muscular wall of the arterioles causes them to close up, reducing the blood flow through them (*vasoconstriction*); relaxation of the wall opens the arterioles, allowing the blood to flow easily through them (*vasodilatation*).

It is essential that at all times the heart and brain receive an adequate blood supply in order to carry out their vital functions; lack of blood to these organs will result in death in a matter of minutes. Skin cells, however, are able to survive short periods without blood, so that during periods of exertion blood can be diverted away from the skin to the gut or other areas of most need. This is carried out by alteration of the size of arterioles in different areas of the body which consequently alters the blood flow to these areas.

The microcirculation
The real purpose of the cardiovascular system is to carry to the cells of the body the substances needed for their metabolism and regulation, and to take away synthesized and waste products. The heart, veins and arteries are really only assistants in this task; it is the capillaries which permeate the tissues of the body

225

of mechanisms, both neural and hormonal. For example, nerves of the autonomic branch of the nervous system travel from the medulla, an area at the back of the brain, to both veins and arteries. The function of these nerves is to maintain the blood pressure in the arteries and distribute blood according to the functions and needs of the different organs.

Different areas of the body contain different concentrations of the nerve endings leading to the medulla. Regional blood flow may therefore be controlled and altered by central mechanisms. But local mechanisms also operate. Local nerve reflexes, hormones such as histamine and angiotensin, the concentration of metabolic products in nearby tissues and the amount of blood gases, such as oxygen and carbon dioxide, affect regional blood flow by causing local vasodilatation or vasoconstriction.

However efficiently these control systems of regional blood supply operated, they would be of little use without some system which ensured that the overall arterial pressure within the cardiovascular system remained constant. For this purpose the main arteries contain within their walls specialized nerve endings which are highly sensitive to changes in

pressure. These nerve endings, known as *pressoreceptors* or *baroreceptors*, are most numerous in the arteries running up the sides of the neck. They convey information concerning changes in pressure up to the medulla.

In the medulla there is a complex neuronal system which collects all the information relating to the cardiovascular system, somehow assesses the relative importance of this information, and sets into operation various processes which will keep the system stable. Exactly how this is done, or even which parts of the medulla are most active, is not yet known.

It has been discovered that the stimulation of arterial baroreceptors resulting from a rise in blood pressure causes the medulla to alter cardiac output and peripheral resistance through the autonomic nervous system, so that blood pressure falls again. Young ladies of the Victorian era were expected to show their good breeding by fainting if anything distressing or embarrassing occurred. Those who were not naturally so delicate were taught to induce the faint by clasping their hands to their necks. By pressing on the blood vessels at the side of the neck, the arterial baroreceptors are stimulated, and the consequent reductions in cardiac

output and blood pressure result in a faint.

Changes in external conditions may also have profound effects on the functioning of the body, and man has had to find ways of adapting to such changes. For example, when the Spaniards conquered the Incas, mountain dwellers of South America, both they and their horses suffered a variety of ills caused by the reduced atmospheric pressure which accompanies increased altitude. Symptoms ranged from mild irritability and lassitude to violent nausea, vomiting and headaches. Yet the Incas showed no such reactions since they had lived at those heights for generations and had therefore become well acclimatized.

Most of the symptoms of mountain sickness fade over a period of several weeks. Breathing becomes faster so that more oxygen can enter the blood stream, there is an increase in the number of red blood cells, the circulation increases and the way in which oxygen is actually used by the tissues becomes more efficient. But full acclimatization takes a long time and the Spanish living among the Incas suffered a low birth rate for many years.

Obviously there are limits to the natural adaptations that are possible, and if man wishes to survive under still more extreme conditions he must resort to artificial protective devices. For example, sudden or extreme drops in atmospheric pressure may be encountered both by deep sea divers who return to the surface very quickly, and by airmen who make rapid ascents. In each case the falling pressure may cause gases dissolved in the blood, especially nitrogen, to come out of solution and form bubbles. The victim may suffer from intolerable pain in the joints and limbs and feel forced to keep his arms and legs bent. Hence the condition is called 'the bends'. It can be fatal if vital vessels in the brain or heart are obstructed by the bubbles, unless treatment is given immediately. Airmen must return to normal altitudes and divers must be put in compressed air chambers with a pressure as high as that existing at the depth to which they descended. The air pressure must then be very gradually reduced, so that the gas in the blood can escape slowly and harmlessly.

Space flights present human physiology with particularly difficult problems. Oxygen must be supplied and maintained at a steady pressure despite enormous changes outside the space capsule. In attempting to leave the earth the spaceship must accelerate rapidly enough to break free of gravitational forces. The astronaut's body is thus exposed to very high G forces. If his head points towards the top of the rocket, the blood will pool in his feet and he will lose consciousness (blackout). With his head pointing the other way, the blood will pool in his head and although the vessels supplying the brain will be unaffected because the skull and cerebrospinal fluid protect them, the vessels in the eyes may rupture (redout). So the astronaut must lie transversely (cross-wise) to the line of flight. Even so his body will be made much heavier by the acceleration, prohibiting him from performing any delicate tasks.

Having left the atmosphere he is faced by the opposite problem—weightlessness. Future travellers may need vigorous exercise to avoid total breakdown with the subsequent return to earth gravity.

The Lymphatic System

In very simple animals such as the jelly-fish there is really very little difference between the internal and external environments. All the cells of the jellyfish are bathed in seawater and can take up nutrients and give out waste products directly by diffusion from their surroundings. As animals move up the evolutionary ladder, however, cells and groups of cells become more specialized, so more sophisticated systems for ensuring nutrition and waste removal are necessary. In man, as in other mammals, these systems have become very sophisticated indeed.

The cells of the human body, like the cells of the jellyfish, are surrounded by fluid, known as *interstitial* fluid, which is the direct source of nutrition. The composition of this interstitial fluid varies under different conditions and in different parts of the body; it is quite similar to blood plasma although its protein content is very small. In fact most of the interstitial fluid originates from the blood in the capillaries, and may diffuse back into it.

Other materials have diffused from the cells bathed by the fluid, and these too may diffuse into the blood in the capillaries. Some substances, particularly those composed of large molecules such as proteins, can leave the blood capillaries and enter the interstitial fluid, but cannot return because the pressure difference between blood vessels and extracellular fluid is too great. An extra drainage system is required to collect up these proteins and other substances and return them to the bloodstream. This drainage is provided by the lymphatic system.

Secondary transportation

Most parts of the body contain a set of lymphatic capillaries, which are completely separate from the network through which the blood flows.

They are somewhat similar to blood capillaries in that their walls are composed of similar kinds of cells, and they form a dense network of vessels to provide maximum contact with body tissues. But they differ in several aspects: for example, lymph vessels form a closed system and their terminal branches end blindly with rounded or swollen ends; they are irregular in shape, and very difficult to follow in their course through the body. The flow of lymph within them is very slow because there is no pumping force such as that provided in the blood system by the heart.

Indeed, it appears that lymph flow depends almost entirely on forces external to the system, such as the mechanical squeezing of the lymphatics by contraction of the muscles through which they course. The one-way flow is assured by the presence of valves like those found in larger veins. Directly above each pair of valves the vessel may show prominent layers of smooth muscle cells, which probably contract and help to propel the lymph onwards.

The lymph is collected from all over the body into progressively larger lymphatic vessels formed by the union of smaller

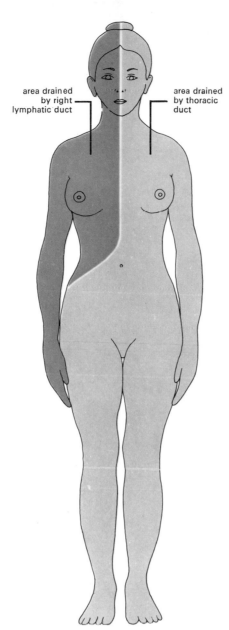

area drained by right lymphatic duct

area drained by thoracic duct

Below: The lymphatic system performs the vital function of acting as a secondary transport system. It supports and complements the circulatory system—which operates within a closed circuit—by collecting from the tissues all over the body the fluid squeezed out of the blood capillaries, recycling it and returning it to the circulation.

Above: The tissue fluid collected by the lymph vessels is emptied into two main ducts. The right lymphatic duct collects from the upper half of the right side of the body while the thoracic duct drains the remaining body area. Both ducts enter the large veins at the root of the neck by which the lymph is returned to the circulatory system.

John Watney

Above: Blood vessels at the root of the neck where lymph is returned to the circulation. The white 'sausage' shapes are the lymphatic vessels and the spaces are the valves.

Below: Diagram showing how the lymphatic system works. The tissue fluid squeezed out of the capillaries contains some large molecules which cannot re-enter the capillaries because of the different pressures inside and outside the blood vessels. This fluid passes through the lymph nodes where masses of lymphocytes engulf and destroy bacteria and toxins and large particles are broken down. The clear lymph fluid is drawn back into the capillary by osmosis.

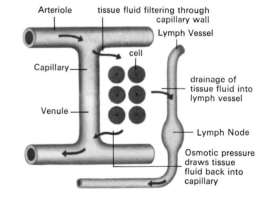

Arteriole

tissue fluid filtering through capillary wall

Lymph Vessel

cell

Capillary

Venule

drainage of tissue fluid into lymph vessel

Lymph Node

Osmotic pressure draws tissue fluid back into capillary

Erich Lessing/Magnum

227

ones. Most eventually empties into the thoracic duct which enters the large veins at the root of the neck on the left side. Lymph collected from the right upper half of the body enters the great veins via the right lymphatic duct. Back flow of venous blood into the lymphatic system is prevented by valves at the openings of the ducts.

It is unclear why the two main drainage points between the lymphatic and venous systems should serve such different size areas, but the thoracic duct alone empties from 4 to 10 mls of lymph into the veins every minute. If this lymph is drained away instead of being allowed to reach the blood, plasma protein begins to fall and blood volume decreases. In the course of a day 60 per cent of plasma volume and 50 per cent of the total amount of protein circulating in the blood is lost from the capillaries and returned to the bloodstream by the lymphatic system.

As is predictable from its relationship to both blood and interstitial fluid, lymph is similar in composition to plasma although not identical. In general it contains less protein than plasma, although regional differences in protein content are marked so that lymph from the liver contains similar amounts to plasma, far more than that from the skin. It also contains a variety of substances derived from cell metabolism and cell secretion, including enzymes, hormones and metabolites. Most importantly, however, the lymphatic system picks up bacteria and other foreign bodies which escape from the capillaries, playing a vital role in keeping the body free from disease.

The fight against disease
Lymphocytes, a type of white cell found in large numbers in the lymphatic system, aid in the manufacture of antibodies and the destruction of invading organisms. Although these white cells are rather large, they seem to be able to move quite freely in and out of both blood and lymphatic capillaries, by actually wriggling between the cells of the vessel walls with an amoeba-like movement.

Lymph is also involved, perhaps surprisingly, in one aspect of food transport: it picks up small globules of fat from the intestines and delivers them to the blood via the thoracic duct. Shortly after a meal, the lymph changes from its ordinary yellowish transparent colour to a milky colour due to the presence of the fat globules. The inner structure of the intestines contains a rich supply of lymphatic vessels which become quite visible as very fine white lines after digesting food. These lymphatics are called *lacteals* and their contents are known as *chyle*.

Certain other substances which have large molecules such as cholesterol, hormones and enzymes, may be transported directly from their sites of origin to the blood stream via lymphatic tissues. Others, which are found in much smaller concentrations, are probably returned to the bloodstream, having leaked out of capillary walls. Lymph can be seen as a clear yellowish fluid seeping from damaged tissues, especially near a pimple.

At points along the larger lymph vessels are lumpy enlargements of tissue which form the lymph nodes; all the lymph passes through at least one lymph node before it reaches the bloodstream. Several

Right and below: The lymph nodes or glands are collected in specific groups at the sides of the neck, in the armpits and groin, at the root of the lungs and near the large veins of the abdomen and pelvis. They may become inflamed as a result of containing bacterial infection and preventing it from spreading.

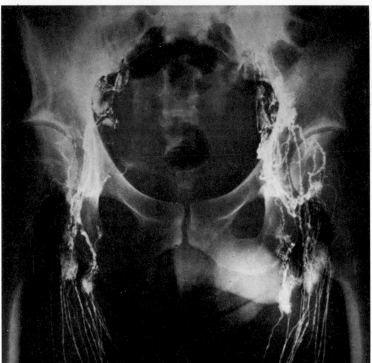

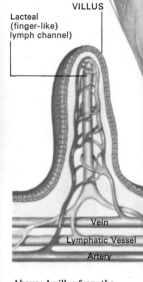

Complex network of lymph vessels

Lymph Node

VILLUS

Lacteal (finger-like) lymph channel)

Vein

Lymphatic Vessel

Artery

Above: A villus from the small intestine. It absorbs soluble food products of digestion, and sugars and amino acids are passed into the blood. The lacteals, the finger-like lymph channels, absorb fats, giving them a milky appearance. The fats are then conducted through the lymphatic vessels to the thoracic duct.

vessels will enter into a small cavity (sinus) around the node and valves at the entrances prevent backflow of the lymph. Within the node, the lymph passes through cell-lined sinusoids which filter out solid particles. By this process white cells in the node can ingest and destroy foreign particles, bacteria and dead tissue cells.

Lymphocyte production
The nodes are centres for the production and storage of the lymphocytes and other antibody-manufacturing cells. When the lymph has slowly percolated through the tissues of the node, and has been cleansed of impurities, it leaves the node through a single lymphatic vessel. The lymph nodes near the lungs of city dwellers are often black with soot and dust particles carried there by macrophage cells. This gradual clogging up of the nodes may help to explain why people who are constantly exposed to atmospheric pollution by smoke and industrial waste find it harder to resist lung and chest infections.

During any kind of infection the lymphatic nodes may become swollen and sore as they attempt to deal with both invading organisms and white cells destroyed by the infection. Those just beneath the ear, under the jaw, and in the armpits and groin, are most obvious when enlarged.

The number of lymphocytes in the body normally remains fairly constant, but may rise (lymphocytosis) or fall (lymphopenia) under certain conditions. For example, in the disease known as glandular fever the body produces many times the number of white cells, including lymphocytes, in an effort to combat the

infection. Lymphopenia is only likely to occur in response to stresses such as starvation or debilitating conditions.

The body's drainage system
The lymphatic system has several functions which complement the functions of the blood circulatory system in many important ways. It returns body fluid and protein to the blood, it transports substances with large molecules such as fats, hormones and enzymes from their manufacturing sites to the bloodstream, it filters out foreign particles and it helps to combat infection. Although animals with much simpler body structures seem to manage without a separate drainage and defensive system, its importance in the higher animals is easily demonstrated by the widespread problems which accompany its malfunction.

In some people the system fails to develop properly at birth, causing gradual swelling of the affected part, as water and proteins accumulate in the tissues. This swelling, known as *oedema*, is characteristic of lymphatic malfunction. It may be temporary, such as the swelling of the ankles experienced by people on very long coach rides which quickly subsides when they begin to move about again and the action of the muscles squeezes the lymph into movement. The oedema can be permanent and crippling if the lymphatic vessels themselves become blocked or destroyed.

The evolutionary puzzle
In evolutionary terms the lymphatic system is a fairly new one and, since biologists tend to study the smaller and

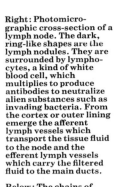

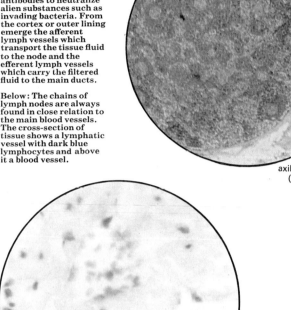

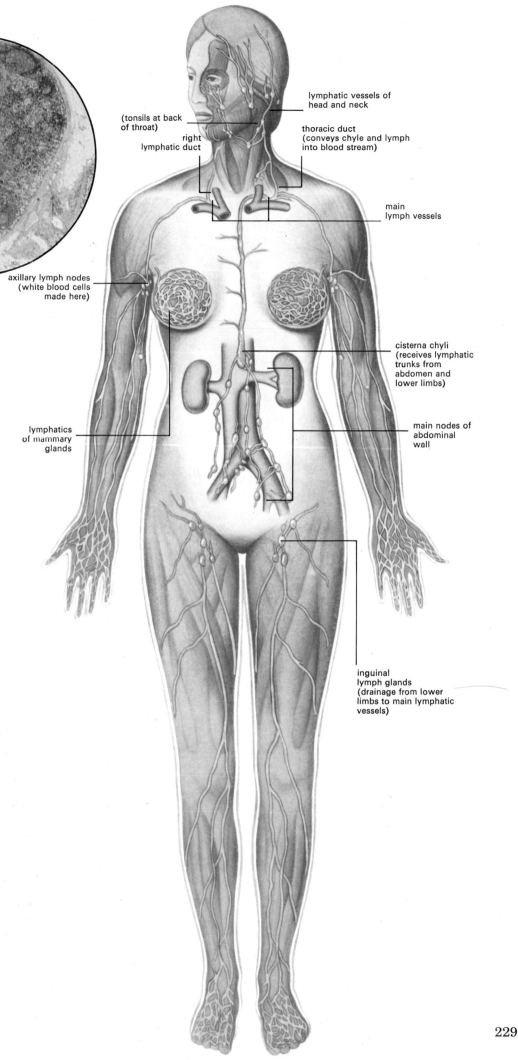

(tonsils at back of throat)

right lymphatic duct

lymphatic vessels of head and neck

thoracic duct (conveys chyle and lymph into blood stream)

main lymph vessels

axillary lymph nodes (white blood cells made here)

cisterna chyli (receives lymphatic trunks from abdomen and lower limbs)

lymphatics of mammary glands

main nodes of abdominal wall

inguinal lymph glands (drainage from lower limbs to main lymphatic vessels)

simpler animals in preference to the larger and more complex ones, its functioning was very poorly understood until comparatively recently.

For many years it was thought a great puzzle that nature had bothered to evolve this other circulatory system. But consideration of the nature of the blood supply in mammals demonstrated its necessity.

The cardiovascular system in those animals, including man, is a closed system operating under very high pressures. The pressure ensures that all organs and tissues are completely perfused with blood, but it also means the system is prone to leaks. It was formerly thought that substances of high molecular weight such as proteins could only escape from blood capillaries with great difficulty, or if the vessels had been damaged in some way. As we have seen this assumption was quite wrong, and plasma protein levels and total blood volume can only be maintained for as long as this drainage system collects up substances leaked from the blood capillaries.

Modern research indicates it may play an important regulatory role in a number of conditions in which no lymphatic involvement was previously suspected. For example, it seems that lymphatic drainage of the kidneys is vital in maintaining their ability to balance the water content of the body. This may explain why patients who have undergone kidney operations pass very dilute urine. Surgery may have damaged local lymph vessels, reducing their capacity for drainage and interfering with the reabsorption of water by the kidneys.

The Heart

Blood is the major transportation system within the vast complex of the human body. Its flow is maintained by a series of pumping mechanisms throughout the cardiovascular system; the most important of which is the heart, whose ceaseless rhythm pushes our blood through more than 1,000 complete circuits every day of our lives.

The work done by the heart seems out of all proportion to its size. Even while we are asleep the heart steadily pumps about two ounces of blood with every beat—341 litres (75 gallons) every hour, enough blood, in fact, to fill an average petrol tank nine times every hour. Moderate exercise doubles this output, and during strenuous activity, such as running a race, the heart may pump up to 2,273 litres (500 gallons) per hour. All this from an organ no bigger than a fist.

The fact that the blood actually circulated in a closed system was not realized in the West until William Harvey the 17th century English physician calculated that the heart must act as a pump which recycles the same blood again and again, knowledge which was available to the Chinese some 3,000 years earlier. A medical treatise of that time reported that 'the heart regulates all the blood of the body . . . . The blood current flows continuously in a circle and never stops', but this discovery was unfortunately overlooked by later peoples, until Harvey rediscovered it.

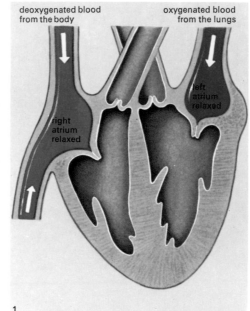

deoxygenated blood from the body

oxygenated blood from the lungs

right atrium relaxed

left atrium relaxed

1

Below: A 13th-century English manuscript showing some of the Greek physician Galen's ideas of how the internal organs worked. Despite gross errors in his observations, most of his theories were unchallenged until 1,500 years after his death when the English physician William Harvey calculated that the heart must act as a pump, recycling the same blood over and over again—a fact which the Chinese had established some 3,000 years earlier.

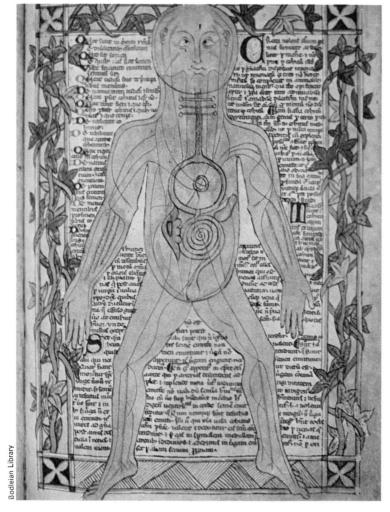

230

The design

The heart is really two separate pumps, placed side by side, welded together by the *septum*, a thick dividing wall. The reason for this oddity lies in the course of evolution. Our double heart evolved by the gradual separation of a single heart: the right heart pumps blood to the lungs via the *pulmonary artery*, and the left heart pumps the refreshed blood out through the *aorta*, the main artery, to the body tissues.

Each side of the heart consists of an ante-chamber, the *atrium*, and a larger chamber, the *ventricle*. Dark red blood from the body—low in oxygen and high in carbon dioxide—first enters the right atrium which serves as a reservoir for the larger and stronger ventricle below it. Relaxation of the ventricle (an action known as *diastole*) causes blood from the atrium to surge into it, and contraction of the atrium completes this transfer.

The thick muscular wall of the right ventricle performs systolic action—it contracts rapidly—which pumps the blood upwards out of the heart and into the

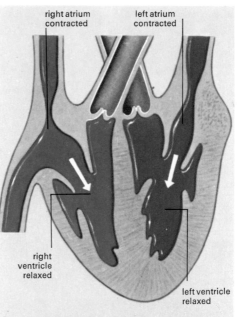

right atrium contracted

left atrium contracted

right ventricle relaxed

left ventricle relaxed

2   VENTRICULAR DIASTOLE

Above left: The beginning of the cardiac cycle which takes place during a single heartbeat. The atria fill with blood from the lungs (through the pulmonary veins) and from the head, neck, arms and chest (through the inferior venae cavae). The valves to the ventricles are forced open by the pressure and they fill with blood. (Left) The atria contract pushing the remaining blood into the ventricles whose walls become distended. A wave of muscular contraction sweeps over them and (below) the valves are snapped shut by the difference in the pressure between the ventricles and the atria. As the valves are closing, blood is forced out of the ventricles into the aorta or the pulmonary artery from which it travels to all parts of the body except the lungs. (Right) The pressure in the ventricles falls and they relax. The period during which the atria and ventricles fill is known as the diastole, and the contraction period as the systole.

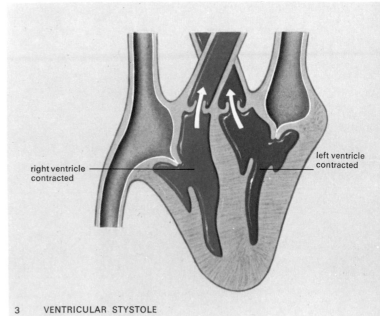

right ventricle contracted

left ventricle contracted

3   VENTRICULAR STYSTOLE

large pulmonary artery. The blood is forced through the capillaries of the lungs where carbon dioxide is unloaded, and oxygen is taken up, turning the dark red blood bright red. The return to the left heart is made via the *pulmonary vein*. The oxygen-rich blood is conducted into the left atrium, by the relaxation of the left ventricle, and is ready to be thrust out into the aorta and round the body.

The wall of the left ventricle is much thicker than that of the right: it has to pump harder to distribute the blood throughout the fine network of vessels in the body. The blood is not simply pushed out of the ventricles, it is wrung out of them by the action of the spiral muscles circling around them. The muscles are arranged in several layers of spiral and circular bands enclosing the ventricles in a common envelope.

The two ventricles pump almost simultaneously ensuring that each side of the heart ejects an equal volume of blood. This is necessary to prevent congestion or depletion of one side of the heart by the other side pumping too much or too little blood. The septum helps the effectiveness of the pumping action by becoming rigid just before contraction, acting as a fixed point for muscle band contraction.

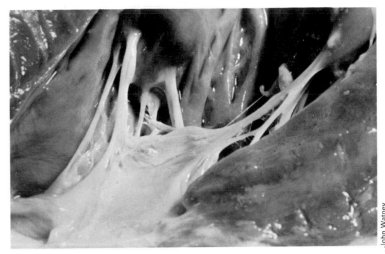

Left: The heart of a sheep showing the tendons known as chordae tendineae. These are responsible for preventing the ventricular valves from being forced back into the atria by the pressure of blood filling up the ventricles. The chordae tendineae are anchored to the papillary muscles in the ventricle walls.

John Watney

Below: Longitudinal section of the heart, centre of the blood circulation system that combines the vital functions of central heating, drainage, air conditioning, water main and food supply. Basically a muscular tube, the heart has slowly developed into a four-chambered organ as evolutionary survival demanded greater complexity and efficiency.

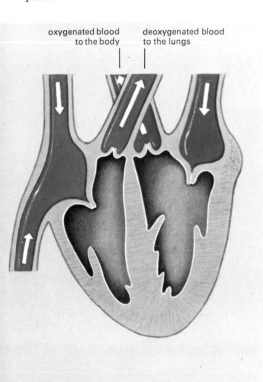

oxygenated blood to the body

deoxygenated blood to the lungs

Before birth, an opening known as the *foramen ovale* in the septum allows blood enriched with oxygen from the mother to flow directly from the right to the left atrium, bypassing the lungs which do not function until the moment of birth. The *foramen ovale* normally closes at birth, but very occasionally it remains open, resulting in poor circulation through the lungs where it fails to take up enough oxygen, causing the skin of the new-born child to turn blue (an indication of serious oxygen starvation). This condition is known as a hole in the heart, and can quite often be repaired by surgery. Especially small holes may remain undetected for years.

The blood is prevented from rushing back into the atrium by the flaplike valves between the atrium and ventricle which

Camera Press

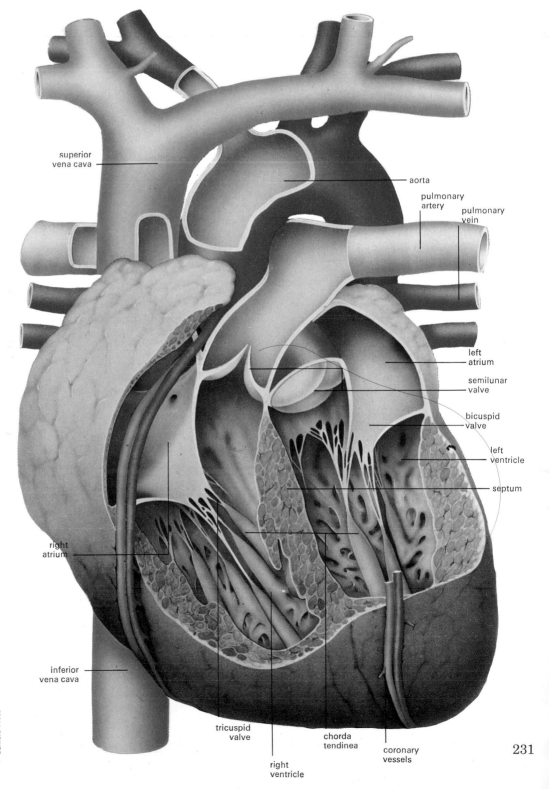

superior vena cava

aorta

pulmonary artery

pulmonary vein

left atrium

semilunar valve

bicuspid valve

left ventricle

septum

right atrium

inferior vena cava

tricuspid valve

chorda tendinea

coronary vessels

right ventricle

231

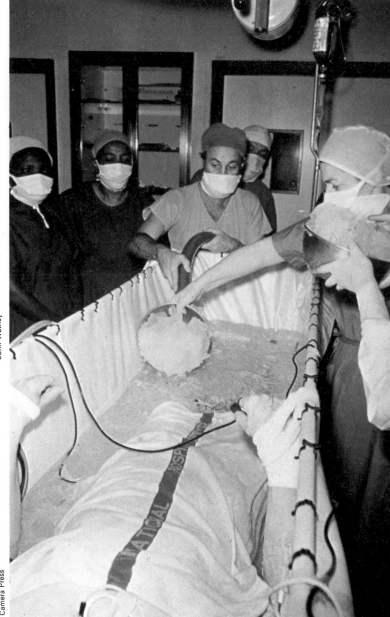

are forced shut by the pressure as the
ventricle begins to contract. The slamming shut of the valves can be heard
through a doctor's stethoscope as a dull
'boom'. Shortly afterwards, three smaller,
crescent-shaped valves open to allow the
blood to flow into the main arteries
leaving the heart. Then, as the muscles
relax, the pressure in the chambers falls,
and the outlet valves close preventing the
expelled blood from returning to the
heart. As they close, these valves make a
shorter, higher, almost clicking sound
which is distinctly audible with a stethoscope.

Safety factors of the heart

The presence of the atria in the heart
appears on first examination to contradict
the usual biological rule of maximum
efficiency and utilization of all the parts.
The atria seem to unnecessarily compli-
cate the cardiac pump, since the ventricles
are capable of performing the pumping
task by themselves. However, they do
provide a safety factor, necessary in this
vital organ. Under normal circumstances
the atria play a relatively minor role in
the filling of the ventricles, but when
disease narrows the valve openings
between the atria and the ventricles,
their pumping action is then essential to
drive the blood through the restricted
openings.

A heart completely deprived by disease
of the use of the right ventricle has the
amazing ability to continue pumping
blood through the lungs to the left ventricle. It is even possible to divert the
blood flow so that it bypasses the right
heart, and still maintain an efficient
circulation.

As for the left ventricle, this has such
large margins of safety that it can
function as a good pump when as much as
half of its muscle mass is dead. These
kinds of safety factors are indispensable
to organs such as the heart on which
immense strains are placed, particularly
through stress in urban societies.

There are also inbuilt safety factors in
the valves, whose function is to maintain

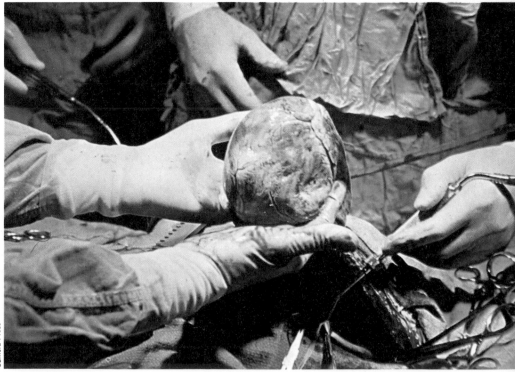

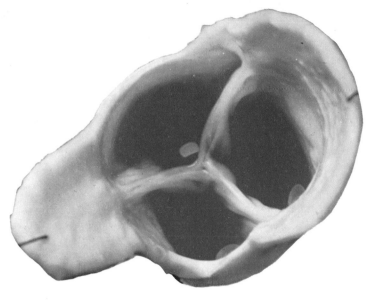

Above right: A heart valve taken from a dead person, freeze-dried and stored in a sterile 'organ bank'. This valve has been selected for its size (there are 13 sizes from 2cm to 4cm in diameter), revived in warm water and penicillin for about 20 minutes, trimmed to fit and made leakproof with a few drops of antibiotic solution. Valves are absolutely vital in the heart to ensure blood flow only in one direction.

Left: The valve is joined to the wall of the aorta by about 50 stitches and begins work instantly.

Below left: An artificial valve being stitched into a patient. Now widely used in heart surgery, they have a longer life than transplanted ones.

The heart's blood supply

Surprisingly, the heart has a very low margin of safety in one particular aspect —its oxygen supply. The coronary arteries supply oxygen to the heart, and are of immense importance since blockage of one of these vessels results in death. Unlike other body tissues, which use as little as one fourth of the oxygen supplied to them, the heart removes over 75 per cent of the oxygen from the blood brought to it. The blood supply is therefore of critical importance to the heart, especially when its workload is increased by exercise of various types.

Two large coronary arteries pipe oxygen-rich blood to the heart muscles. They curl around the surface of the heart, dividing almost immediately into two branches supplying different sections of heart muscle. The surface vessels divide repeatedly until they penetrate deep into the walls of the heart, surrounding the muscle elements with very fine capillaries which give up their oxygen to the muscle cells. Eventually three systems of veins return the blood to the right heart to be pumped back to the lungs.

Sudden blockage of any one of the coronary arteries will result in complete lack of blood to the area served by that artery. The muscles, deprived of blood, will soon stop contracting, die and be replaced by non-functional scar tissue, considerably weakening the pumping power of the heart. It has been noticed that, particularly in young people, the block of a main coronary artery over a number of years does not always result in death of the muscle it serves. It appears that vessels from other arteries can take over the area of supply, growing into the muscle tissue to form a collateral circulation. This, however, can only occur over a long period, although experiments indicate that the development of a collateral circulation takes place faster if exercise is taken regularly.

Heart muscle is able to survive without oxygen for periods up to ten minutes, whilst brain cells have a survival limit of about three minutes without oxygen. This involves doctors in an important moral problem when they are involved in cases of drowning or heart failure. It is often possible to restart the heart even after considerable brain damage has occurred, so that after the heart has stopped beating for three minutes the doctor has to decide whether or not to revive the patient who may then no longer be a human being in the normal sense.

the forward movement of the blood through the chambers. Doctors have long known that patients with serious leaks in the heart valves are able to maintain a good circulation simply by harder pumping of the heart. There are two main safety factors involved in this compensatory pumping: one is known as 'Starlings Law' which, in brief, says that the more a heart muscle is stretched, the more vigorously it responds, within its own limits, so that when the inlet or outlet valves of the ventricles leak, they fill with an excess of blood. This stretches the heart muscle, causing it to pump harder, and compensate for the loss of blood backward through the valves. The other safety factor is provided by the spiral arrangement of the deep bands of muscle around the ventricles which tend to direct the flow of blood forward rather than backward through the leaky valves.

Unfavourable circumstances sometimes conspire to reduce the force of the heart's contraction, but fortunately drugs like *digitalis* can often restore a failing heart by heightening muscle contractions.

The sounds produced by the slamming shut of the heart valves and the turbulence in the blood as it flows into the chambers give doctors valuable information about the working of the valves. When a valve leaks, the distinct thud as the valve shuts is accompanied by a 'murmur' like the sigh of a gust of wind coming through a leaking window-pane. The timing, quality and position of the murmur indicate the type of heart complaint. Constriction of the valve openings, for example, will cause a characteristic hissing sound similar to the noise made by water coming out of the constricted nozzle of a hosepipe.

The Hormone System

The specialized organs and cells of the human body which both control the conditions and generate the materials essential to our continued well-being have to be controlled and balanced. Any deviation from 'normality' has to be immediately remedied, otherwise life itself can be endangered. To do this, both the nervous system and the chemical 'messenger service' known as the hormone system, work together.

The hormone system at its simplest works like the thermostat in any heating system. Just as room temperature may fall, the body temperature may also fall and make adjustment necessary. The thermostat may instruct the central heating to switch on and, when the temperature rises, the thermostat again comes into operation and switches the system off. In this sense the temperature controls the thermostat as much as the thermostat controls temperature. And in the same way the hormone system controls conditions in the human body as much as it is itself controlled by them. This analogy, however, is over simple. The body's hormone system controls numerous positive-negative systems which keep the 'weather' inside the body stable whatever outside conditions or circumstances prevail.

It is this constant fine control that makes the hormone system so elegant. The hormone that controls the excretion of water, for example, is itself controlled by the amount of water in the body. If that were constant, the output of the hormone would be constant and the water excretion constant. In fact, all three vary a little during every 24 hours and in extreme conditions they can vary widely —whether during a long evening drinking in a bar or a march across a dry desert. It is a rare emergency when the hormone system cannot cope, restoring the delicate balance of conditions inside the body. If, for example, too little water is present in your body several mechanisms come into action and among the hormones that are released is one that helps to stimulate you to drink. Or if danger threatens, as part of the general 'fight or flight' mechanism ordered by the brain, the hormone *adrenaline* will be released to prepare the skeletal muscles for violent action.

The endocrines

The many hormones present in the body and the glands that produce them, are collectively known as the *endocrine* system. The vital fact about an endocrine gland is that it releases its secretion, the hormone, into general circulation to act where it can; other glands, which direct their secretion down some path to a particular place, are called *exocrine*. The sex glands, for example, are endocrine because they secrete sex hormones into the blood to be carried all over the body to produce a variety of effects. The same is true of the *thyroid*, the *adrenals*, and several other glands. Indeed, even when the target of the hormone is quite small and near the gland, the hormone may

Below: The endocrine system. The human body is controlled by two types of activity, electrical and chemical. The nervous system, which exerts electrical control, is integrated with the chemical control of the endocrine system to maintain the body in a balanced state. The endocrine system has glands which release chemical messengers, called hormones, which are carried by the blood to specific 'targets' in the body. The target organs are provoked into releasing substances essential to the development and maintenance of life.

- anterior pituitary
- posterior pituitary

1. TSH (thyroid stimulating hormone)
2. ACTH (adenocorti-cotrophic hormone)
3. FSH (follicle stimulating hormone)
4. LH (leuteinising hormone)

Many glands which control these activities are themselves controlled by the pituitary (Fig.1 and inset) which is, in turn, regulated by the hypothalamus at the base of the brain. The pituitary, known as the master gland (Fig.2), is attached to the hypothalamus by the pituitary stalk. The anterior lobe secretes hormones when stimulated by the hypothalamus. The posterior lobe stores hormones from the hypothalamus.

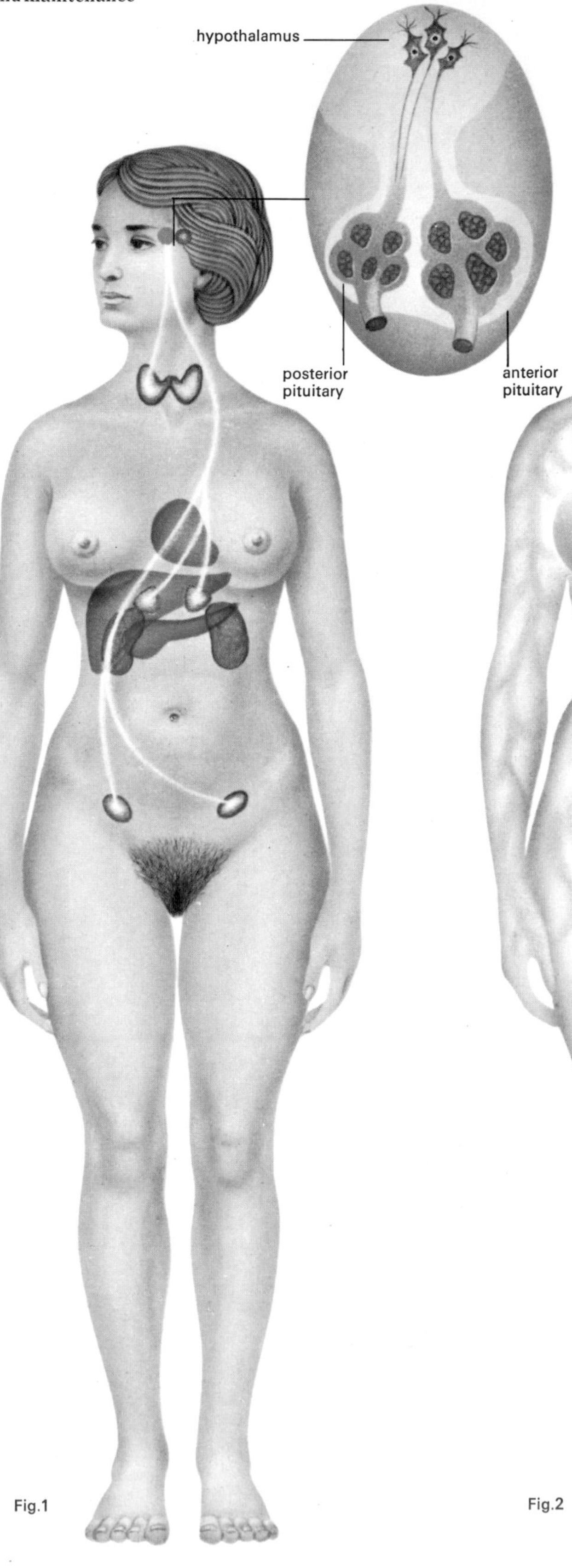

- anterior pituitary
- posterior pituitary
- Oxytocin
- Vasopressin (ADH)
- Prolactin
- Growth hormone

hypothalamus

posterior pituitary

anterior pituitary

Fig.1

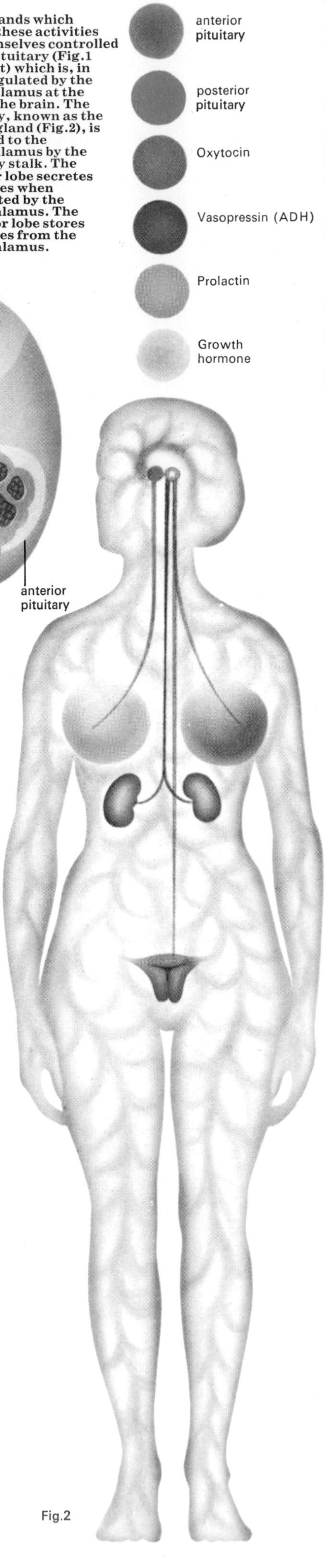

Fig.2

The release of the hormones is either stimulated or inhibited by the hypothalamus, depending on the information it receives about body needs. The hypothalamus itself produces only two hormones, vasopressin and oxytocin (Fig.2) which are sent to the posterior pituitary to be stored until the body requires them. Vasopressin (or ADH) is released when receptors in the hypothalamus sensitive to changes in the water level, inform it that the blood has too much or too little water. ADH stimulates the tubules of the kidney to absorb more or less water so that the balance is restored.

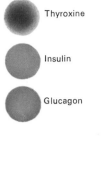

Thyroxine

Insulin

Glucagon

The action of oxytocin, which causes contraction of the uterus during labour and expulsion of milk from the breasts after birth, is triggered by nerve impulses from the uterus to the brain via the spinal cord. The anterior pituitary produces six hormones which, with the exception of growth hormone, stimulates particular endocrines. The adrenals (Fig.4) secrete adrenaline which stimulates the heart and the whole body (shown only in the right adrenal) and other hormones which act on the kidneys and also on the whole body to maintain salt levels (shown only in the left adrenal).

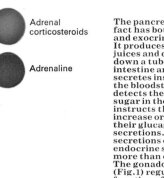

Adrenal corticosteroids

Adrenaline

The pancreas (Fig.3) in fact has both endocrine and exocrine functions. It produces digestive juices and delivers them down a tube into the intestine and also secretes insulin into the bloodstream. It detects the amount of sugar in the blood and instructs the cells to increase or decrease their glucagon secretions. Many of the secretions of the endocrine system have more than one function. The gonadotropins (Fig.1) regulate the function of the gonads which produce the female sex hormone, oestrogen, and the male, testosterone. These determine secondary sexual characteristics like body shape (Fig.5).

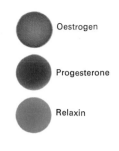

Oestrogen

Progesterone

Relaxin

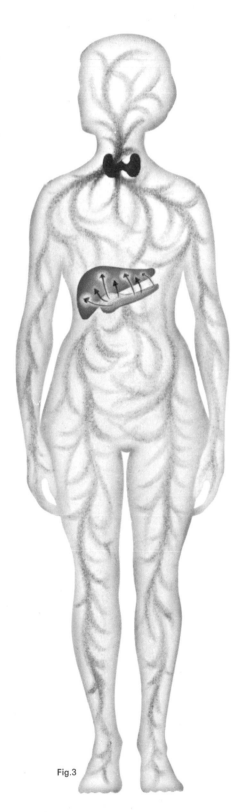

Fig.3

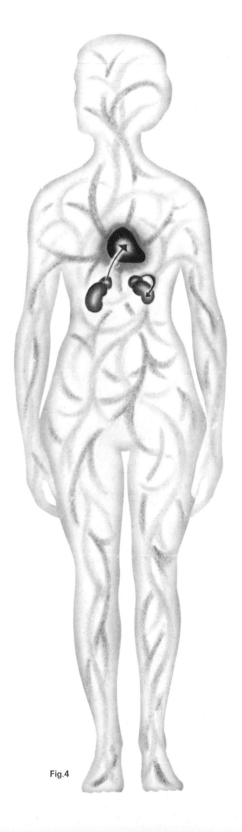

Fig.4

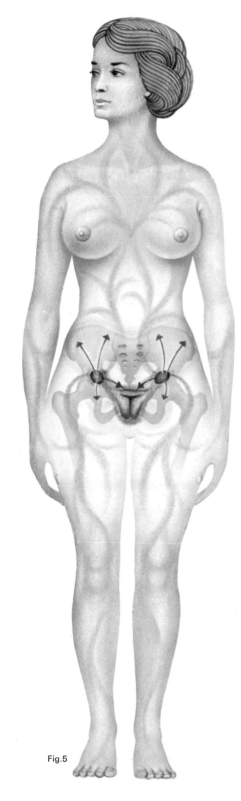

Fig.5

235

still travel right round the bloodstream—as, for example, do hormones produced in the stomach to act in another part of the stomach.

An exocrine gland, in contrast, is a simple and crude local worker. Saliva comes straight from the (exocrine) *salivary* glands into the mouth; wax from the (exocrine) *sebaceous* glands of the skin go on to its surface; and tears from the (exocrine) *lachrymal* glands go directly into the eye.

Some glands, however, may be both exocrine and endocrine. The cells of the *pancreas*, one of whose jobs is to produce digestive juices, do so in a simple exocrine fashion; they produce the juices and deliver them down a tube into the intestine. But the pancreatic cells responsible for controlling the amount of sugar in the blood have a more complicated job. They need to influence cells in many other parts of the body, increasing or decreasing their rate of sugar use or conservation. So they produce a hormone called *insulin* and secrete it into the bloodstream. Then when they detect an excess of sugar in the blood they can produce more, instantly signalling to all relevant tissues the need to take sugar out of circulation.

A number of classic techniques have been evolved to investigate the nature of a gland and determine whether or not it is endocrine. First, the gland is removed to determine the effects of stopping the gland's secretions. (Most of the experiments described are performed on animals, but there are also occasions when the same effect can be observed in man.) An extract of a fresh gland can then be prepared and injected into the animal to see whether the ill-effects, if any, disappear.

This initial test, however, will only establish that the gland is in fact a gland. It does not prove that the gland is endocrine. To do that, the gland from one animal is removed and, when it shows symptoms of abnormality, its blood circulation is connected to that of another animal which has not had the gland removed. If the gland-less animal recovers from its symptoms the blood of the other animal must have been responsible. Therefore, we can assume that the gland removed was an endocrine gland which secreted hormones throughout the body. Alternatively, the gland can be transplanted within the same animal from one place to another. In the new site it will soon build up a blood supply but will lack all other former connections: if the whole body system does not suffer, its secretion must, therefore, be endocrine.

But experiments on a gland like the pancreas, which is both endocrine and exocrine, have to be more sophisticated and such techniques are available today. Modern methods of analysis can, for example, measure hormones in quantities too small to be imagined: down to one part in a million million. The chemical identification of hormones, complex as they are, has also largely been achieved. This has opened the door to experimentation with pure molecules, as well as to powerful hormone replacement drugs, in larger quantities and at cheaper cost than is possible with the use of animal extracts.

To understand how the endocrine system works, we must first of all look at the *pituitary* and at the part of the brain called the hypothalamus which controls it. These two must come first because they

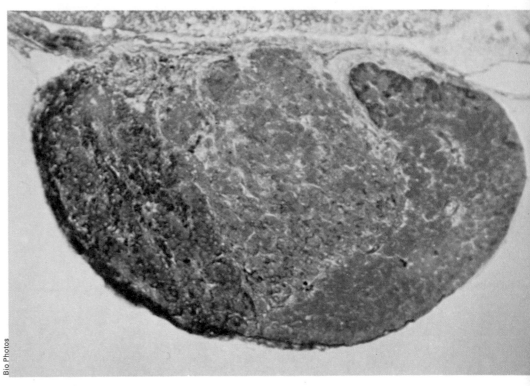

Bio Photos

not only produce hormones, but also release substances to control production of hormones from the other endocrine glands.

The master gland

The pituitary, a small gland situated at the base of the brain, is traditionally called 'the conductor of the endocrine orchestra'. If that analogy applies, however, then an even grander one must be found for the hypothalamus since this part of the brain controls the pituitary. It is here that the nervous system and the endocrine system are co-ordinated.

The anterior part of the pituitary produces no fewer than six different hormones and is controlled by hormone-like 'releasing factors' which come via a special blood vessel link from the hypothalamus. The posterior pituitary, producing just two hormones, is controlled by nerves, rather than chemical secretions, but their source is again the hypothalamus.

Four of the six hormones produced by the anterior pituitary are tropic (or trophic) hormones, that is, they regulate the action of other endocrine glands. *Thyroid-stimulating hormone* (THS) stimulates the thyroid to produce its hormones. *Adrenocorticotrophic hormone* (ACTH) does the same for the part of the adrenal gland that produces aldosterone, which regulates electrolyte metabolism (salt balance). *Follicle-stimulating hormone* (FSH) and *luteinising hormone* (LH) are both gonadotropins—hormones that stimulate development and hormone synthesis in the reproductive system. FSH promotes the development of the spermatazoa in the male and the ova in the female. LH stimulates the secretion of the male sex hormones, testosterone and one of the female sex hormones, oestradiol. Another anterior pituitary hormone, *prolactin*, stimulates the secretion of milk from the breasts. The sixth and final anterior hormone is growth hormone.

The hypothalamus receives inputs from all parts of the body including the emotional centres of the brain. If, for example, it detects that there is a need

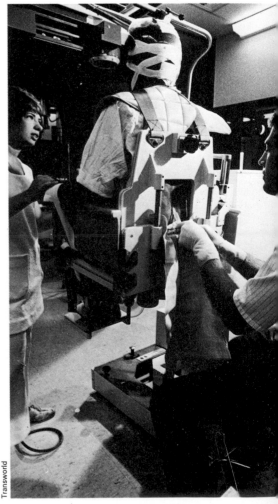

Transworld

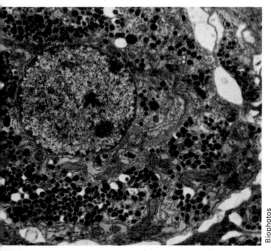

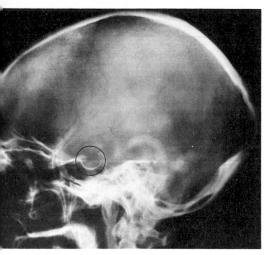

for more cortisol, it produces corticotropin releasing factor; this stimulates the pituitary to release some of its store of corticotropin (ACTH), which in turn stimulates the release of cortisol from the adrenal glands down by the kidneys. There is a releasing factor for each of the anterior pituitary hormones. In some cases, especially prolactin and growth hormone, there is also an inhibiting factor which the hypothalamus releases when it requires the pituitary to stimulate the system less.

Three of these pituitary hormones—growth hormone (anterior), antidiuretic (water retaining) hormone and oxytocin (posterior)—are slightly more important than the rest since their effects are more direct than the tropic hormones.

Growth hormone is still rather a mystery. Its job is to stimulate growth, therefore it plays its most important role in the growing years. But it works on many systems of the body and its effects do not stop after adolescence. Only recently have some of its actions been partially understood.

Growth hormone encourages the growth of cartilage at the ends of bones—the cartilage that forms the matrix for new bone to be laid down. It increases the rate of protein production by the body's growing cells and it increases the amount of energy-giving sugar and fat in the bloodstream.

In many of its effects growth hormone interacts with other hormones such as insulin, which regulates blood sugar by instructing body cells to increase or decrease their secretion of glucagon. At various times of life the thyroid hormones

and the sex hormones share a growth-promoting role. But the overall influence of growth hormone is shown when its secretion is abnormal. Too little is occasionally a cause of dwarfism—today preventable by treatment with growth hormone—while too much causes a person to grow to an unusual height and to have an abnormal bone structure.

The functions of the two posterior pituitary hormones are more specific. *Antidiuretic hormone* (ADH), sometimes called *vasopressin* because in artificial conditions it can cause constriction of blood vessels and hence a rise in blood pressure, is responsible for the regulation of water loss from the kidneys. (Diuresis means the production of a flow of urine; antidiuresis means the prevention of water loss into urine.) So it is clear from the hormone's name that it exerts a braking effect.

In the first stage of urine production in the kidneys, a large amount of water is skimmed off the blood along with all the waste products for excretion. If that first mixture were to flow out as urine, too much water would usually be lost. Therefore at a second stage a different part of the kidney reabsorbs some of the water, leaving the eventual urine less dilute. Under the influence of antidiuretic hormone the kidney will reabsorb a lot of water. If, on the other hand, the body contains too much water this situation will be assessed by the hypothalamus which will signal to the pituitary to release less ADH. With its reabsorbing system receiving less stimulus, the kidney will allow more water through into the urine.

ADH secretion is influenced by other factors than the quantity of body water: for example, alcohol depresses it, so the drinker tends to lose even more fluid than he takes in. Dehydration may be one of the contributary causes of the hangover.

The other posterior pituitary hormone, *oxytocin*, is most important during childbirth and breast feeding although it may exert minor effects on the reproductive system at other times.

During labour, oxytocin production increases, causing the uterus to contract. It is interesting that at the same time the uterine muscle becomes abnormally sensitive to the hormone. Many women have their labour induced or helped by oxytocin which they receive intravenously.

In breast feeding, oxytocin encourages the expulsion of milk from the nipple. A baby does not suck milk out of the nipple by its own power, as it has to from a bottle. The sucking of the child's mouth stimulates nerves in the breast which are linked to the hypothalamus. The hypothalamus sends a nerve message to the pituitary, which releases oxytocin into the bloodstream. When it reaches the breast, oxytocin, causes the milk within it to be carried along the ducts towards the nipple then forcibly ejected.

Hormones, rivalled only by the nervous system to which they are wedded, are one of the best examples of the genius of nature's design. They make up the 'weather' inside our bodies but, unlike the weather outside, they are reliable. They keep our internal machine neither too wet nor too dry, neither too warm nor too cold and function smoothly through the many complex stages of our lives from birth to death.

Left: above and below: A unique method of speeding up the diagnosis of brain disorders which in this case has outlined the pituitary gland. The patient is strapped into a rotating chair (left) and air is injected into the spine. The chair is than rotated in a full circle (below) to regulate the movement of air up the spine into the brain. The air distributes itself in the brain (above) filling up the ventricles (spaces) and outlining parts of the brain, (here, spaces around the pituitary show up clearly) allowing the medical team to view any abnormal growth of tissue, or lesions, more clearly. The use of TV monitoring and videotape also make examination easier.

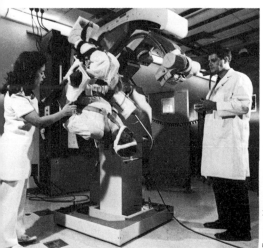

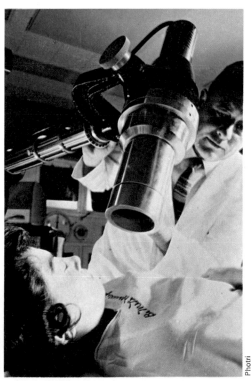

Above right and right: One of the methods of detecting glandular malfunction of the thyroid. Radioactive iodine (iodine which gives off radiation) is injected into the patient's bloodstream. It accumulates in the thyroid, where iodine is a natural component of its hormone, thyroxin. The radiation levels from the radioactive iodine can be picked up by a gamma ray detector and the resulting pattern of accumulation screened to show its distribution (right). The scanner plots the iodine content of the thyroid in colours according to local concentration. Radiation treatment can sometimes be used to control over-production.

237

Respiration

Respiration does not simply mean 'breathing'—it is used to describe all the processes associated with the release of energy in the body. Oxygen is supplied via the blood to the cells of all tissues. Cells need oxygen to break down such substances as carbohydrates and fats to obtain energy, at a rate which varies according to the activity involved. During normal quiet breathing an adult uses about 8,000 ml (15 pints) of air per minute, but sprinting to catch a bus would use much more—because the body muscles are working harder and more fuel is being oxidized to provide the necessary energy.

Breathing has to convey oxygen from the atmosphere to the haemoglobin inside the red blood cells, and carry the unwanted carbon dioxide from the plasma to the atmosphere, in such a way that the gas concentrations in the blood remain within the narrow range vital to health.

As the required amount of gas exchange ranges from just enough to keep the body quietly ticking over to providing extra supplies for energetic activity, a large reserve capacity is essential. Furthermore, a balance has to be constantly maintained between the rate and depth of breathing and the flow of blood through the lungs. These requirements have resulted in *alveoli* which provide a large surface area, to bring air and blood into contact, and a very sensitive system of sensory and motor nerves to control ventilation of the lungs and blood flow.

The respiratory organs

The respiratory system includes the upper respiratory passages in the head and neck, the two lungs with their air passages, arterial, venous, lymphatic and nervous systems, and the thoracic cage with its bones and muscles, of which the diaphragm is especially important.

The nose and mouth form the upper respiratory passages. They join at the back where the soft palate acts like a swinging door to shut off one or the other. Lining the nose are hairs, ciliated cells and a mucous membrane, each of which remove irritants and contamination from the air. The cilia are small whip-like 'hairs' which protrude from the cell surfaces. They beat in unison in a liquid medium, wafting mucus and captured particles into the throat to be swallowed. The spaces, or *sinuses*, in the bases of the cheeks and forehead, also lined with a mucous membrane and ciliated cells, open into the nasal passages. The mouth also has a mucous lining, so air passing through the nose or mouth is moistened to trap dust and other particles, as well as being warmed in preparation for entering the lungs.

Just beyond the junction of the oral and nasal passages, the air passage branches forward into a short passageway known as the *larynx*, or voicebox, while the *oesophagus*, or food passage, continues downwards behind it. The top of the larynx is closed off when swallowing by a cartilage plate, the *epiglottis*, which prevents food and liquid from going down the wrong way. Extending beyond the larynx is the *trachea*, or windpipe, a wide, single tube which divides into the right and left main *bronchi* at the

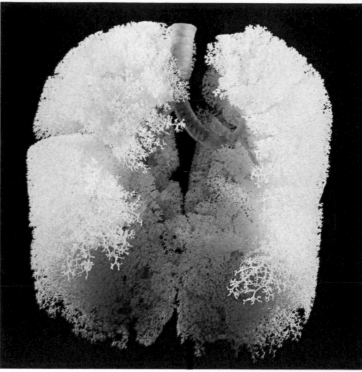

Picturepoint

level of the upper angle of the breastbone, or *sternum*. The main bronchi, accompanied by the left and right pulmonary arteries, enter the lungs. Soon after they divide into smaller secondary bronchi, one for each lobe of the lung; the left lung has two, the right lung has three. Branching continues, the airways becoming smaller and smaller as they pass from *bronchioles* to terminal bronchioles.

This bronchial 'tree' divides the air into about 30,000 separate jets in the gas exchange zone. Any air still contained in the airways at the end of a breath cannot take part in gas exchange and is regarded as 'dead space', air which just has to be exhaled again. It amounts to about 100 to 200 ml (between 0.2 and 0.4 pints). Approximately the first five divisions of the bronchi are held open by cartilage and are lined with a mucous membrane.

In the gas exchange part of the lung the bronchioles begin to have small sacs of *alveoli* in their walls. As the divisions continue more alveoli appear, until eventually there are so many that they form clusters. A mature pair of lungs contains about 300 million alveoli, presenting a total surface area up to about 50 times that of the body surface.

Each bronchus and bronchiole is accompanied by a pulmonary arterial branch which breaks up into capillaries when it reaches the alveoli. These capillaries form a network within the alveolar wall with air on each side. The blood is then separated from the air by only two layers of cells—one of which lines the capillary, the other lining the alveolus—and a variable amount of connective tissue in between. This amounts to a distance of about 0.01 mm across which oxygen and carbon dioxide have to diffuse.

The pulmonary arteries carry oxygen-depleted or venous blood from the right side of the heart to the lungs to be replenished. After picking up the oxygen, the blood passes through the tributaries of the pulmonary veins back to the left side of the heart to be pumped to the body's organs (including the lungs themselves

Alphabet & Image

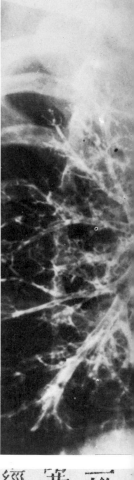

Left: These lungs were injected with plastic under pressure and then placed in a chemical to dissolve the tissue, leaving a model of the airways. Part of the trachea, or windpipe, can be seen branching into the two main bronchi. The coral-like mass consists of bronchioles terminating in 300 million alveoli.

Right: Bronchograms are used to locate blockages in the bronchial tree in the lungs. A small quantity of very mildly radioactive particles is inhaled into the lungs, and then filmed.

Below: A diagram of the lungs from a Chinese book of 1607. Although the windpipe was a good guess, the six lobes of the lung, looking like leaves, were sadly inadequate.

Below right: This machine measures the carbon dioxide exhaled during respiration so that the amount of oxygen used can be calculated. Strenuous activity burns up more fuel, so extra supplies of oxygen must reach the body's cells.

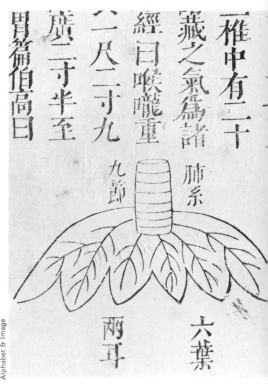

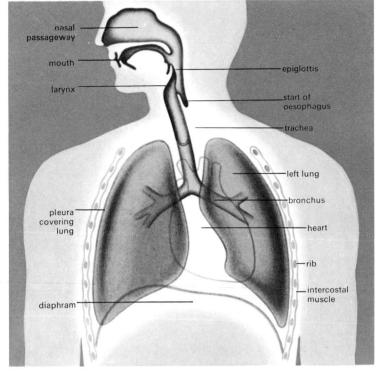

- nasal passageway
- mouth
- larynx
- epiglottis
- start of oesophagus
- trachea
- left lung
- bronchus
- pleura covering lung
- heart
- rib
- intercostal muscle
- diaphram

which are supplied by a separate set of bronchial arteries). There is also a turnover of tissue fluids which drain through lymphatic channels from the lungs to the lymph glands near the origins of the main bronchi.

Each lung is enclosed and protected by a shiny membrane, the *pleura*, which also lines the inner surface of the chest wall. Between each pleural membrane is a narrow space, the pleural cavity, which contains a small amount of fluid. This acts as a lubricant, preventing the lung and chest wall surfaces from sticking together during breathing. In pleurisy, a painful illness, the membranes become so inflamed that they rub against each other during breathing.

Even with this well-planned system, without the necessary muscular action we would be unable to breathe. The muscles concerned with breathing lie between the ribs (the intercostal muscles) and between the thorax and abdomen (the diaphragm). The job of these muscles is to assist breathing in, or *inspiration*, and breathing out, or *expiration*.

For air to flow into the lungs, the pressure inside the lungs must be less than atmospheric pressure. This is achieved by increasing the volume of the lungs. In

Right: Three pumping systems are associated with the working of the lungs: the thorax, which moves about 8,000 ml of air in and out every minute; the heart's right ventricle pumping blood, high in carbon dioxide, into the pulmonary capillaries to be oxygenated, after which it travels to the third pump, the left ventricle, which sends it to the body's organs. The right ventricle receives venous, or carbon dioxide-rich, blood from every part of the body, and then pumps it into the pulmonary artery, which divides finally into millions of thin-walled capillaries, so tiny that only one red blood cell can pass at a time.

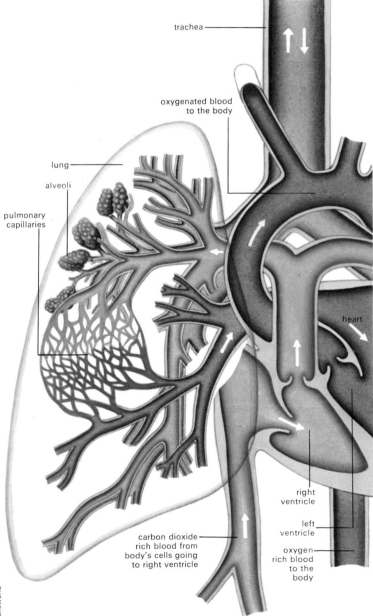

- trachea
- oxygenated blood to the body
- lung
- alveoli
- pulmonary capillaries
- heart
- right ventricle
- left ventricle
- oxygen rich blood to the body
- carbon dioxide rich blood from body's cells going to right ventricle

Transworld

239

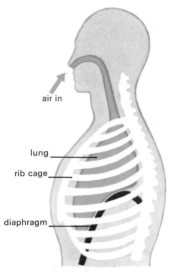

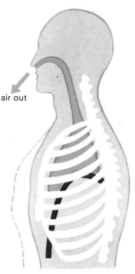

air in

air out

lung

rib cage

diaphragm

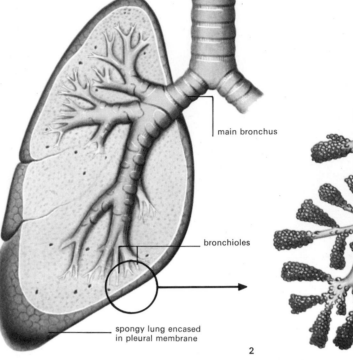

trachea

main bronchus

bronchioles

spongy lung encased
in pleural membrane

1

2

order to do this the muscles must work to create a negative pressure, or partial vacuum, between the chest wall pleura and the pleura covering the lung. The diaphragm contracts, flattening its dome-shaped protrusion into the thorax, and the intercostal muscles lift the ribs forwards and upwards. This increases the size of the thoracic cavity, the pressure falls and the lungs are sucked out by the partial vacuum. Air now flows in through the nose or mouth and down into the 300 million alveoli, flowing into the upper parts of the lung first.

At the end of inspiration the muscles relax and the elasticity of the pulmonary tissue allows the alveoli to close, so in quiet expiration the air flows out passively. However, there are also muscles to assist expiration during violent respiration or when parts of the body are diseased.

Central control

Breathing is controlled by centres in the brain, the main one being the *respiratory centre* which is found in the *medulla oblongata*. From here the nerve impulses are sent to the respiratory muscles, causing them to expand or contract. Information about oxygen and carbon dioxide levels is obtained directly from the concentrations in the blood. If, for example, the concentration of carbon dioxide rises, the centre increases both ventilation (in other words we breathe deeper and faster) and pulmonary blood flow so that the carbon dioxide is blown off. However, if too much carbon dioxide is removed, the centre causes ventilation to decrease.

The respiratory centre and other vital centres in the brain actually depend on carbon dioxide for their own stimulation. It is possible to overbreathe deliberately—sustained rapid breathing blows off carbon dioxide so that these vital centres switch off and the person falls unconscious. This curtails the voluntary over-breathing and, after a short period without taking a breath (known as *apnoea*) the carbon dioxide content rises again and the vital centres restart.

It is because the respiratory centre has connections with the cerebral cortex that man can voluntarily alter his breathing pattern and perform such feats as holding his breath while swimming underwater. However, when the level of carbon dioxide reaches a critical point, no amount of effort can stop the involuntary control centres taking over and breathing starting again.

Above: Breathing in and out. Muscular action increases the size of the chest cavity and the air pressure inside the chest falls. This causes air from outside to enter the lungs to equalize external and internal air pressures. The muscles relax, the cavity grows smaller, and the carbon dioxide-rich air is forced out.

Brian Bracegirdle

Above: A transverse section cut from a piece of dried lung and magnified x50. The lung was dried out under vacuum, leaving it rather like a bath sponge. The section shows the air spaces in the alveoli and a reticulum created by groups of alveoli. This tissue normally is very elastic.

1. A diagram of the lung showing the trachea encircled by a series of cartilage rings, the main bronchus passing into the lung, and part of the bronchioles. As these airways become smaller the cartilage rings are replaced by cartilage plates until finally in the bronchioles the walls are only muscle.

2. Looking rather like a bunch of grapes, the bronchioles terminate in numerous alveoli or air sacs.
3. A greatly enlarged diagram showing the terminal bronchioles proliferating into alveoli which are covered with a network of blood capillaries. These come from the pulmonary artery and

Right: In this section, cut from a piece of fresh lung, the areas stained red are the arterial capillaries containing carbon dioxide rich blood. The green areas are the venous capillaries which carry oxygenated blood back to the heart. The gaps are air spaces in the alveoli, and the red 'canal' is an arteriole.

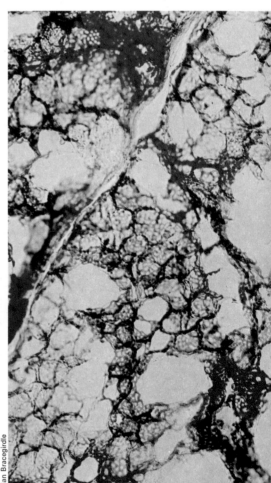

Brian Bracegirdle

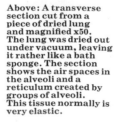

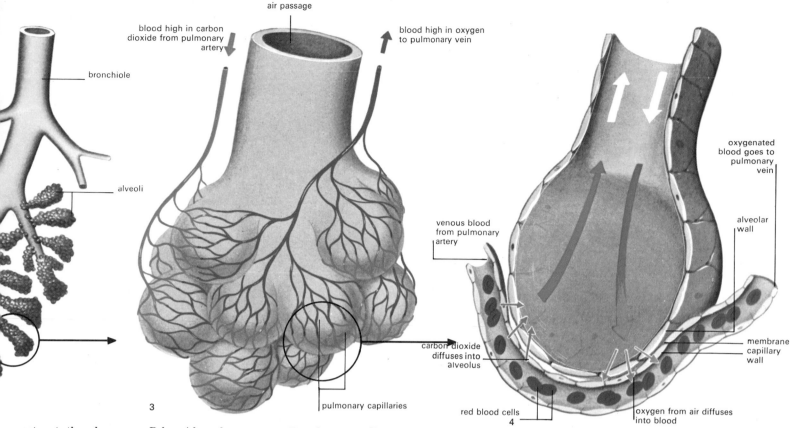

air passage

blood high in carbon dioxide from pulmonary artery

blood high in oxygen to pulmonary vein

bronchiole

alveoli

carbon dioxide diffuses into alveolus

pulmonary capillaries

3

venous blood from pulmonary artery

red blood cells

4

oxygenated blood goes to pulmonary vein

alveolar wall

membrane capillary wall

oxygen from air diffuses into blood

return to the pulmonary vein. Laid end to end, these capillaries would stretch for miles.
4. Oxygen in the air in the alveolus diffuses swiftly through the alveolar tissue, the basement membrane and the capillary tissue, to enter red blood cells, while carbon dioxide moves into the alveolus to be expired.

Below: A bronchoscope, here held outside the body with a narrow sucker for clearing mucus, is used to examine the interior of the lungs. It consists of a telescope and a light guide of glass fibres to allow a strong outside light source to be used.

Bottom right: A view of the bronchial region.

Respiratory disease in some people produces prolonged high carbon dioxide levels and low oxygen concentrations in the blood. In this case the oxygen level may take over as the driving force, instead of carbon dioxide. Thus, if the oxygen concentration was suddenly raised by breathing higher concentrations than the 20% found in air, the respiratory centre would switch off, with fatal results.

Information about the degree of expansion in the lungs reaches the brain from the *stretch receptors* in the alveolar walls and others in the respiratory muscles. The muscles themselves are activated by motor nerves which are partly under voluntary control and partly under involuntary control. There are also smooth muscle fibres in the walls of the larger bronchi and bronchioles which can alter the size of these airways. It is the contraction of these muscles, causing the airways to close off, that gives asthmatics their attacks of breathlessness. There are also muscle fibres in the arterial walls, allowing blood flow to be altered. However, they are not under voluntary control.

The cough reflex

The brain also responds to irritating stimuli. Immediately something gets stuck in the windpipe it stimulates the cough reflex. It forces a deep breath followed by the vocal cords coming together to close the larynx. Forced breathing out then builds up pressure in the bronchi until it is suddenly released by relaxing the vocal cords. The sudden expulsion of air, the cough, is often enough to dislodge the irritant.

Minor stimuli, such as small particles of dust or irritant gases, are dealt with by the mucus. The cilia sweep the mucus steadily up towards the oesophagus, where it is swallowed. Extra mucus is secreted if there is serious irritation or inflammation in the upper or lower air passages, in the case of a heavy cold, for example. But only particles smaller than 0.005mm ever reach the gas exchange part of the lung, and they are captured by scavenger cells within the alveoli.

Irritation in the nasal passages often causes sneezing—a spasmodic contraction of muscles, forcing air from the lungs.

How a baby starts breathing

The respiratory system develops early during the growth of a foetus in the womb. By the sixteenth week after fertilization, the branching pattern of the airways and arteries is complete. The gas exchange part of the lungs, however, develops much more slowly and is only completed in childhood, by the age of about eight. It remains filled with fluid until the baby is born.

At about 28 weeks, cells which secrete a wetting agent, or *surfactant*, start to appear in the alveolar walls. This is essential for when breathing starts. The surfactant prevents the alveolar walls from sticking together by surface tension. Otherwise the new-born baby, lacking the strength, would be unable to separate them to fill the alveoli with air. This is, in fact, one of the major difficulties with premature babies since an inadequate supply of surfactant results in poor ventilation and thus poor oxygenation.

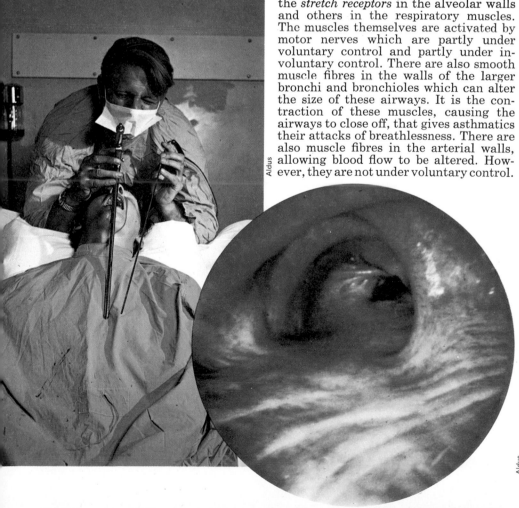

241

Digestion in the Mouth

All living things require food in order to survive. Oxygen inhaled from the atmosphere is not enough by itself to provide the raw materials for maintenance and repair and for the supply of energy. Most of the food for human consumption is derived from plants and animals, since they have already built up the complex molecules of carbohydrates, proteins and lipids (fats).

Food in this form, however, is difficult for living creatures to absorb and must be turned into a soluble form in order to reach the cells which require it. In simple animals like the worm this is accomplished when the food is taken in at one end of the body and passed along a tube, through the walls of which *enzymes* (chemicals which speed up reactions in the organism) flow, mixing with the food. It is then broken down and absorbed through the walls of the tube or tract and the residue of rejected materials passes out the other end. The larger the animal, however, and the larger the portions of food it is capable of taking in, or ingesting, the more complex the mechanism required to make the breakdown process possible.

The development of digestion

In man the simple tube, or *alimentary canal*, has lengthened in the course of evolution to provide the maximum area along which the food can be exposed to the enzymes. In this way, the greatest amount of necessary materials can be derived with the minimum amount of wastage.

Food spends possibly the shortest time of the whole process in the opening of the alimentary canal, the *mouth*. Nevertheless, it is one of the most important parts of the digestive process since it is here that the food undergoes its first stage of conversion into a substance which can eventually be more readily absorbed by the cells of the body.

Even in simple animals like the worm a band of muscle is necessary at the entrance to the digestive tube which can contract and stop the food from falling out. In man, the circular band of muscle known as the *orbicularis oris* (little circle around the mouth) serves this function. Strictly speaking, the mouth is the entrance to the alimentary canal which is visible as the orbicularis oris relaxes, and the lower jaw drops, but the outer layer of tissue covering that circle of muscle, the lips, is generally included in that term.

The lips have several functions, but they are primarily concerned with manipulating the food into the mouth in the most economical way possible. The thin outer membrane covers an abundant supply of blood vessels, giving the lips their red colour. They are also well supplied with nerve endings, making them highly sensitive to the size, texture and temperature of the food they are handling.

The movement of the food around the mouth so that it can be chewed requires skilfully co-ordinated movements of all the parts involved in the process—the tongue, jaws and the muscles of the cheeks. As soon as an adequate portion of food has been taken into the mouth, the muscles of the lips and cheeks stiffen, to assist the tongue in moving the food around the mouth and to prevent it escaping from the chewing action of the teeth. The movements of the jaw during the chewing of the food are reflex actions, but they can be voluntarily controlled by conscious direction from centres in the brain. The movements of the muscles are extremely important since they are responsible for aligning the top and bottom teeth to pulverize the food without damaging the tongue or the other tissues of the mouth, or indeed, the teeth themselves.

Humans are provided with two sets of teeth during their lives. The first set— the *deciduous* or milk teeth—are temporary and come through the gums during the first two years of life. From the sixth year onwards, they are gradually replaced by permanent teeth, about 32 of them by the time adulthood is reached. The permanent teeth have slightly different shapes and sizes, depending on their function in the eating process. The eight incisors at the front of the mouth (four on the top set, four on the bottom) are

Rank Xerox

Above: A dramatic view of the bones and tissue of the head and neck. The xeroradiography technique uses very low doses of X-rays and a photocopying process to produce the image, giving much greater definition than the conventional X-ray photo. The patient has an artificial plate in his skull.

Below: A warrior of the Txukahamae in the Amazon appears to have no difficulty eating with a large lip-plate. Accentuating the lips is thought by many peoples to enhance beauty. The lips, however, have a highly practical function, being very sensitive to the texture and temperature of food.

Transworld

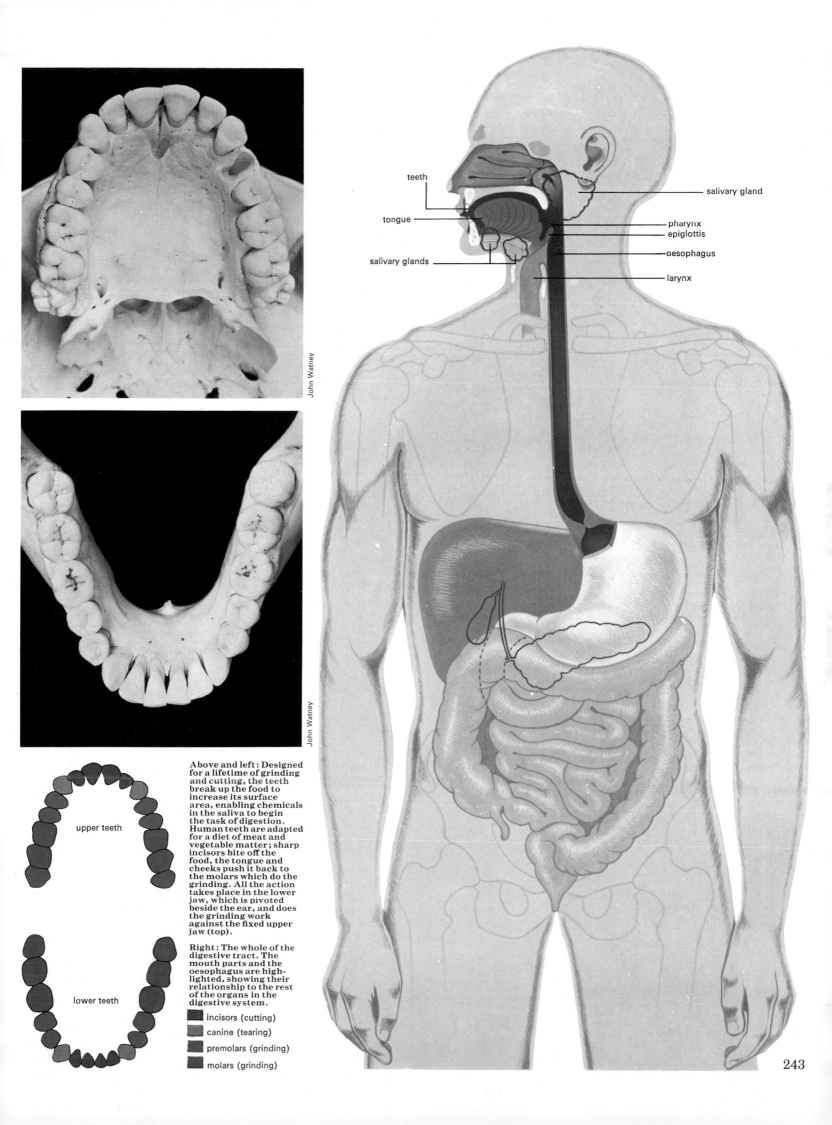

John Watney

John Watney

teeth

tongue

salivary glands

salivary gland

pharynx
epiglottis

oesophagus

larynx

upper teeth

lower teeth

Above and left: Designed
for a lifetime of grinding
and cutting, the teeth
break up the food to
increase its surface
area, enabling chemicals
in the saliva to begin
the task of digestion.
Human teeth are adapted
for a diet of meat and
vegetable matter; sharp
incisors bite off the
food, the tongue and
cheeks push it back to
the molars which do the
grinding. All the action
takes place in the lower
jaw, which is pivoted
beside the ear, and does
the grinding work
against the fixed upper
jaw (top).

Right: The whole of the
digestive tract. The
mouth parts and the
oesophagus are high-
lighted, showing their
relationship to the rest
of the organs in the
digestive system.

■ incisors (cutting)

■ canine (tearing)

■ premolars (grinding)

■ molars (grinding)

243

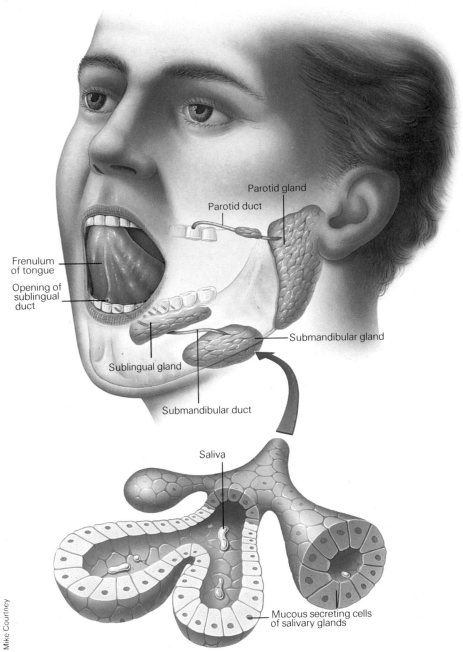

Parotid gland

Parotid duct

Frenulum of tongue

Opening of sublingual duct

Sublingual gland

Submandibular gland

Submandibular duct

Saliva

Mucous secreting cells of salivary glands

Mike Courtney

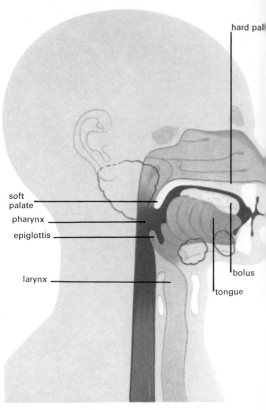

hard pal

soft palate

pharynx

epiglottis

larynx

bolus

tongue

Left and above: The location of the salivary glands is shown left. The position of the mouth parts prior to swallowing is shown above, the bolus of food being manoeuvered by the tongue and cheeks into the pharynx. During swallowing (above right) the tongue rises against the palate, forcing the food down the pharynx which continues the process by reflex action. Movement of the soft palate closes the nose, the larynx rises and the epiglottis seals off the larynx. This stops food from entering the air passages. The opening to the oesophagus is widened, and the bolus is forced down to the stomach by muscular action.

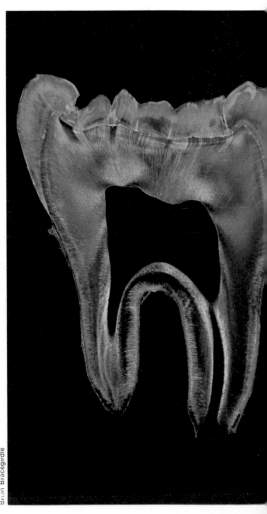

Brian Bracegirdle

chisel-shaped with sharp, bevelled edges for cutting the food; the four canines, one on each side next to the incisors, tear the food (meat off a bone, for example) while the eight premolars (small 'double' teeth) and the 12 molars at the back of the mouth near the throat grind the food up.

Grinding the food up is essential in the digestive process to increase the surface area of the food so that chemicals (enzymes) in the saliva can begin the task of breaking down the food into smaller molecules. Three pairs of salivary glands secrete *saliva* into the mouth. Saliva is a slightly sticky substance made up of about 98 per cent water and containing enzymes one of which is *amylase*. This works on the carbohydrates (starch) in the food converting them into simple sugars.

A small amount of saliva is secreted into the mouth, even when eating is not taking place, to keep the tongue, teeth and cheeks from rubbing against each other during speech and causing irritation. Another of the enzymes in the saliva, *lysozyme*, which has an anti-bacterial action, is useful in keeping the mouth free from infection.

The mouth is particularly susceptible to infection during fever when salivary secretion is suppressed to conserve water.

The lips, teeth and mouth become coated with dead cells, food particles and dried mucus (the substance which gives saliva its stickiness) and if it is not cleaned the mouth becomes infected. Secretion is also reduced during exercise, emotional stress and dehydration; one result is the sensation of thirst.

The flow of saliva is instantly increased at the sight, smell or even thought of food. The glands are stimulated by the reflex action of parasympathetic nerves. They release the saliva through between 10 and 20 small ducts. In the case of the walnut-sized *submandibular* gland under the back teeth, these ducts open out at either side of the tongue. The *sublingual* gland, the smallest of the three, opens out in the floor of the mouth behind the chin. The saliva from the *parotid* gland at the root of the cheekbone in front of the ear emerges from the duct which opens into the cheek.

The salivary glands are supplied with both sympathetic and parasympathetic nerves, although the exact distribution and function of these nerves is not yet fully understood. Parasympathetic stimulation through the *chorda tympani nerve*, however, is known considerably to increase the blood flow through the gland

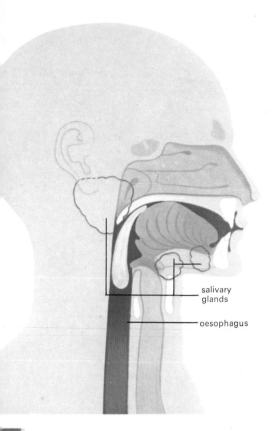

salivary glands

oesophagus

oesophagus

circular muscles contracted

bolus

oesophagus

longitudinal muscles contract

cardiac sphincter

bolus

and to produce a profuse secretion of saliva, consisting mainly of water and salts.

Stimulation of the sympathetic nerve, on the other hand, reduces blood flow and the volume of secretion is less and low in protein, mucus and enzymes. It is these nerves which are stimulated when we are frightened and contribute to the sensation of a dry mouth; even in less frightening situations, acute nervousness can produce the same effect, interfering with the ability to speak; but little is known about the psychological factors involved in the composition and flow of saliva.

As much as 1,500 mls (2.5 pints) of saliva are secreted each day and one of its functions is to maintain the level of acidity in the mouth so that enzymes can be effective. If sugar becomes lodged in the teeth after salivary flow has stopped, bacterial action can increase the acidity level. At this point the calcium in the teeth begins to dissolve and is lost.

The organic constituents

The main organic constituents of saliva are the glycoprotein, *mucin*, which gives saliva its viscous and lubricating properties, and the enzymes, *ptyalin*, which breaks down starch, and *lysozyme*, which destroys bacteria. Some dissolved gases, urea, uric acid, albumin and globulin are also present in small amounts. The water in saliva dissolves some of the food's components so that the digestive reactions can take place. Bicarbonates and phosphates keep the acidity level of the mouth constant. The blood groups of about 80 per cent of the population can also be determined from their saliva, since it usually contains some of the substance essential to blood clotting, known as the *ABO* soluble polysaccharides or blood agglutinogens (meaning to stick together).

The swallowing process

When the food has been chewed, moistened and to some extent broken down by enzymes, the tongue shapes it into a ball or *bolus* ready to be swallowed. The act of swallowing only takes a few seconds and is, in fact, a highly complex action requiring accurate co-ordination. The tongue firstly pushes the bolus to the back of the mouth and into the pharynx. At this point there is the danger of food entering the trachea instead of the oesophagus as they both open into the pharynx. Food entering the trachea by mistake immediately initiates the cough reflex, an important protective device which expels the food from the trachea back into the mouth to prevent choking.

During swallowing respiration is inhibited. The larynx rises to meet the epiglottis (a piece of cartilage behind the tongue) which seals off the entrance to the trachea. The rear entrance to the nose is closed by the soft palate, and the tongue, assisted by other throat muscles, acts as a plunger, pushing the bolus backwards with considerable force into the oesophagus connecting the mouth with the stomach.

The act of swallowing involves many muscles, their controlling motor nerves and a specialized centre in the medulla at the base of the brain. It is nevertheless a voluntary one. But once the bolus has entered the oesophagus a different set of mechanisms, involuntarily controlled, come into play to ensure its safe passage into the stomach.

Cruickshank's vivid illustration (1835) of the effects of bad eating habits. These can cause an imbalance of acids in the stomach, leading to *dyspepsia* and *ulcers*. Proper digestion of proteins in the stomach is achieved mainly by the enzyme *pepsin*.

Digestion in the Stomach

Digestion includes all the activities of the digestive tract, involving the preparation of foods to be absorbed by the body and the rejection of the residues. Some constituents of food such as glucose, water and soluble salts require no digestion, but the bulk of the components need to be considerably changed to enable them to pass through the lining of the intestine and into the blood or lymph transportation systems.

Foods, as we know them, are a mixture of nutrients, and to maintain health the human diet must contain certain proportions of proteins, carbohydrates, fats, salts, vitamins and water. All of these can be obtained from either plant or animal sources.

Different species of animals have widely different methods of obtaining their foodstuffs; for instance, horses, cattle and sheep eat only vegetable products and are known as *herbivores*. Some species like pigs and man will eat both animal and vegetable foods and are known as *omnivores*. Obviously, in order to deal with the various forms of diet, different species have specialized digestive systems and it is interesting that both pigs and man have a similar and relatively unspecialized digestive tract.

The process of digestion begins at the lips and ends at the rectum. Once the preliminary breaking up, moistening and chemical breakdown of the food has taken place in the mouth, the next stage is the transfer of the food from the mouth to the stomach. This process is initiated by the

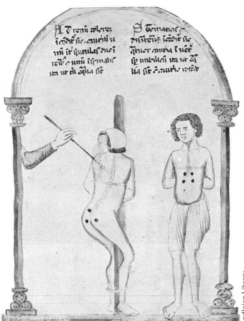

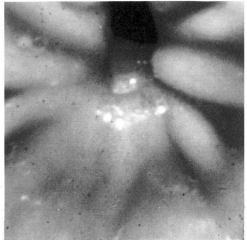

Below: The interior of the stomach lies in folds called rugae, which allow it to expand to hold large quantities of food. As the stomach distends the rugae smooth out.

Right: A wave of peristalsis, seen in the centre of this X-ray of the stomach, squeezes food down to the pyloric sphincter, into the intestine.

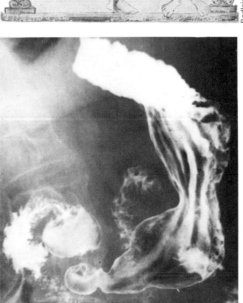

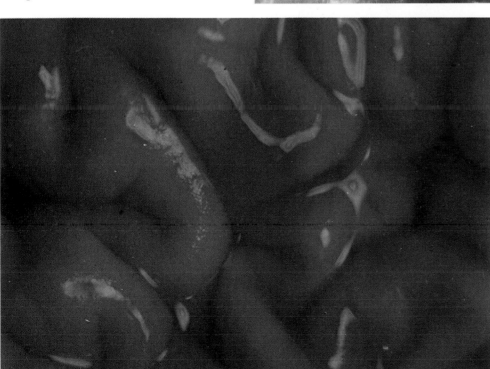

reflex action of swallowing, which pushes the bolus of food down the pharynx and into the oesophagus.

The oesophagus is a muscular tube with special rings of muscle known as *sphincters* at either end which are capable of opening and closing. The *oesophageal sphincter* opens as food is passed from the pharynx; it then closes and a wave of muscular contraction pushes the food down the oesophagus.

This wave of muscular contraction is known as *peristalsis* and is the basis of the movement of food through the whole of the digestive tract. The mechanism of peristalsis works independently of gravity; this enables us to eat and drink standing on our heads and allows astronauts to function for long periods in space without gravity.

Contraction of the circular muscles lying just above and around the top of the bolus, coupled with contraction of longitudinal fibres lying around the bottom of the bolus, forces the food down the oesophagus. These contractions are repeated in a wave moving towards the stomach, and movement of the bolus is made easier by secretion of mucus from glands in the wall of the oesophagus.

The food has now arrived at the lower end of the oesophagus where a valve, the *cardiac sphincter*, controls entry to the stomach. A sphincter is an opening with a circular set of muscles around it; when these contract the opening closes and when released the passageway opens. The fact that the stomach contents are at a higher pressure than those of the oesophagus presents a potential problem, in that the acid contents of the stomach might reflux up into the oesophagus when the passageway is open. However, there is one small portion of the smooth muscle of the oesophagus which contracts just as food is about to enter the stomach, raising the pressure sufficiently to prevent this reflux of the stomach contents, and the cardiac sphincter opens just long enough to permit the passage of the bolus into the stomach.

Belching, or *eructation*, is socially unacceptable in many cultures but in fact it plays a useful role in the digestive process. Stomach gas, derived from air swallowed with the food or drink, builds

247

up in the upper part of the stomach until the cardiac sphincter allows it to escape into the oesophagus; from there it is expelled through the mouth by an active muscular contraction.

The process of vomiting is a complex nervous process involving an area in the base of the brain called the *vomiting centre*. Vomiting—usually only found in carnivores (meat-eaters)—has a wide range of causes. It takes place after the hind part of the stomach has closed off and the oesophageal end has relaxed. The main force for vomiting comes from violent abdominal contractions forcing the stomach against the diaphragm which then forces food up the oesophagus and into the mouth.

The stomach and its secretions

The most obvious and important function of the stomach is to act as a store for ingested food. It also provides a site where digestive processes can occur, and where chemicals which cause the breakdown of the foodstuffs are secreted. Local 'messenger' chemicals (hormones) for other parts of the gut are also secreted in the stomach. Despite these many functions the stomach is not absolutely essential to life and there are many reported instances of total removal of the stomach (although the operation does produce an increased burden for the rest of the digestive system).

The stomach consists of a J-shaped bag which can be divided into three functional parts: the *cardiac area*, the *fundic area* and the *pyloric area*. These three areas are quite distinct from one another; they not only have a distinctive microscopic structure but also produce different secretions. The stomach as a whole has a muscular coat enabling it to produce a churning action which breaks up the food particles and mixes them with the secretions which cause chemical breakdown of the food. This muscular contraction is under the control of the nervous system, particularly the *vagus nerve*, which also controls the production and secretion of the digestive chemicals. The net result of this activity is that the food is mixed up into a milky liquid known as *chyme*.

The secretions produced by the stomach can be divided into different components each having specific functions. Perhaps the best known component is *hydrochloric acid*. The stomach is unique in the body in that it produces large amounts of strong acid from cells known as *parietal cells* present in the fundus region of the stomach. Hydrochloric acid is very important in digestion as it activates enzymes (biological catalysts) which are released from other cells. It also helps in the digestion of protein, sterilization of the ingested food and destruction of bacteria.

In man, however, hydrochloric acid is well known for the problems it can cause in relation to *dyspepsia* and *ulcers*. These problems usually arise when acid is produced in the wrong quantity at the wrong time as a result of bad eating habits. We usually resort to treating this inbalance by taking alkali substances (such as bismuth, sodium bicarbonate or other alkaline salts) which neutralize the acid, or by taking drugs (such as atropine) to suppress impulses travelling along the vagus nerve which stimulate the stomach secretions. Too much acid can erode parts of the stomach wall, causing ulcers; in

some cases surgery may be necessary to remove the damaged portion to prevent the damage spreading to a blood vessel, resulting in a possibly fatal haemorrhage.

The principal chemical activity of the stomach is to begin the digestion of proteins. In adults this is mainly achieved by the enzyme *pepsin*, which is produced by *chief cells* in the fundic region.

Pepsin starts the breakdown of the long chain-molecules of proteins into *proteoses* and *peptones*, which are smaller fragments of the original proteins. However, the food does not remain in the stomach long enough for this breakdown to be completed.

The function of the enzyme pepsin is to digest proteins, which poses the question of why the stomach does not digest itself, since all living cells are composed, in part, of proteins. Pepsin, when first secreted, is in an inactive form called *pepsinogen*, to prevent it from digesting the cells which produce it. Hydrochloric acid is necessary to convert pepsinogen into active pepsin, and this does not occur until pepsinogen is free within the stomach. The stomach cells are protected by a coating of mucus secreted by *mucous cells* which forms a barrier between the gastric juice and the cells. Failure of the protective mucus

barrier allows the pepsin and hydrochloric acid to eat a hole (a gastric ulcer) in the stomach wall.

One other component of gastric secretion is the enzyme *renin* which may be familiar as a milk-curdling agent. Its function is to break up the molecular chains of the protein *casein* which is found in milk. The product of this partial digestion reacts with calcium to form *curds*, the remainder being known as *whey*. Renin is important in the infant digestive processes, but is probably not used in adults since it works better in the much more alkaline environment of the infant stomach. Hydrochloric acid takes over the job of milk-curdling in adults.

The third enzyme of the stomach, which again operates best in the less acidic infant stomach, is *gastric lipase*. This acts on the butterfat molecules of milk, splitting them into smaller parts. Adults rely on an enzyme found in the small intestine to perform this function.

Gastric secretion is under nervous and hormonal control. Initially secretions are produced by nervous stimulation as a result of the thought, sight, taste and smell of food. The stomach is thus prepared to receive the food in advance, but problems may well occur if the promised

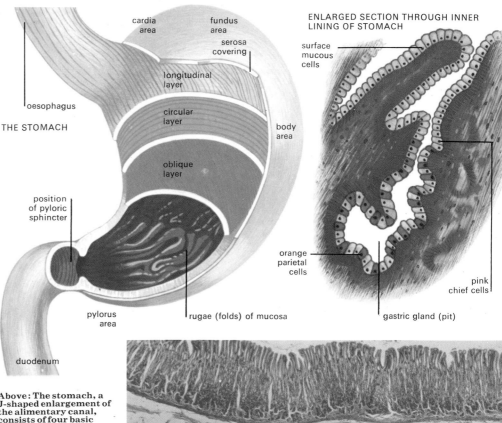

THE STOMACH

cardia area · fundus area · serosa covering · longitudinal layer · circular layer · body area · oblique layer · oesophagus · position of pyloric sphincter · pylorus area · duodenum · rugae (folds) of mucosa

ENLARGED SECTION THROUGH INNER LINING OF STOMACH

surface mucous cells · orange parietal cells · pink chief cells · gastric gland (pit)

Above: The stomach, a J-shaped enlargement of the alimentary canal, consists of four basic layers, the inner one being folded to enable it to expand. Layers of muscle are arranged to allow it to contract to churn, break down and mix together food and gastric juices. Microscopic examination of the inner layer, the mucosa, (above right and far right) reveals columns of cells containing pits, known as gastric glands, lined with three types of cells: chief cells secrete digestive enzymes into the stomach; parietal cells secrete hydrochloric acid to activate one of the enzymes; the mucous cells secrete mucus to protect the stomach from self-digestion.

Picturepoint

food does not materialize, as the acid present in the stomach will be undiluted by food. Further secretion is stimulated by the presence of food in the stomach. This secretion is initiated by the local production of a hormone called *gastrin*—which is secreted by the pyloric region of the stomach when protein foods are present—and by the activity of nerves which are stimulated by the presence of any type of foods.

When the food is thoroughly mixed and in the form of chyme, vigorous peristaltic waves beginning about the middle of the stomach push the partly digested food towards the *pyloric sphincter*, another valve formed by a muscular ring, preventing food passing into the duodenum (the first part of the small intestine). When the pressure in the stomach is greater than that in the duodenum, chyme is forced through the pyloric sphincter. The pressure in the stomach is increased mainly by peristaltic waves (about two to five millilitres of chyme pass into the duodenum with each wave of peristalsis). It takes from two to six hours for the stomach to empty all its contents; foods rich in carbohydrates leave in a few hours, followed by protein foods; fatty foods are the last to leave.

The stomach itself does very little in the way of absorption of foods into the blood. Only some water, salts, certain drugs and alcohol pass through the stomach wall—which explains why we notice the effects of intoxication so soon after drinking. The major breakdown and absorption processes take place in the small intestine, the next stage in the digestive system.

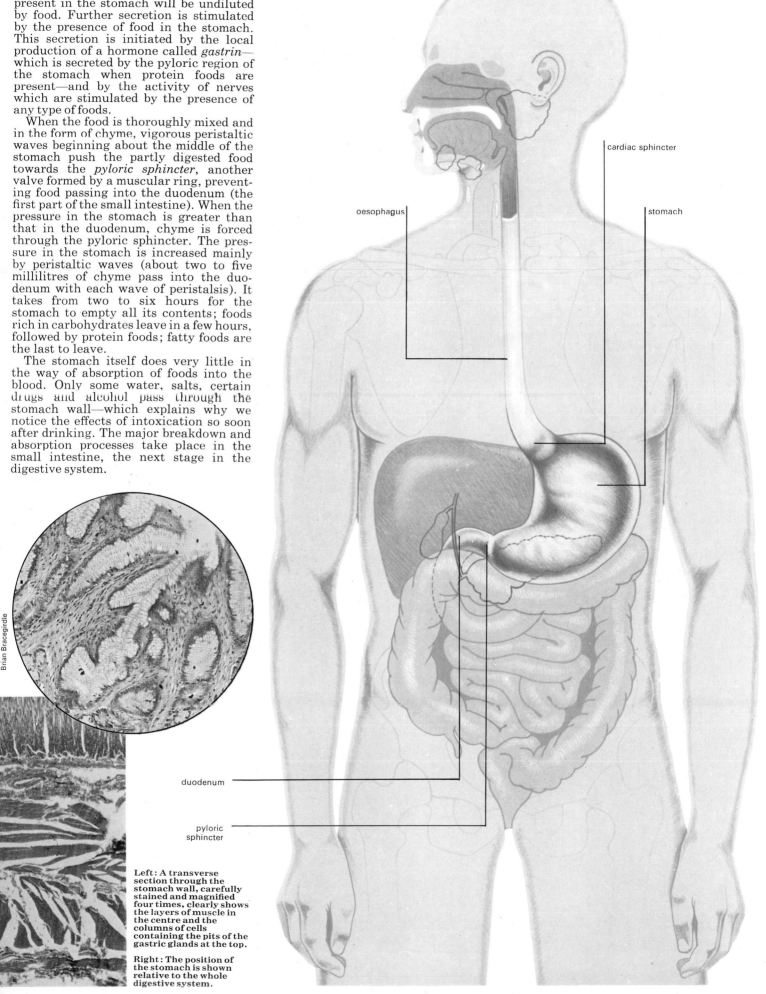

Left: A transverse section through the stomach wall, carefully stained and magnified four times, clearly shows the layers of muscle in the centre and the columns of cells containing the pits of the gastric glands at the top.

Right: The position of the stomach is shown relative to the whole digestive system.

oesophagus

cardiac sphincter

stomach

duodenum

pyloric sphincter

Pancreas, Liver and Gall Bladder

Reduced to a thin liquid called *chyme*, thoroughly mixed with digestive juices and partly digested, food is squirted out of the stomach and into the first part of the small intestine—the *duodenum*—to continue its journey through the digestive system. The acid and fat content of the chyme stimulates cells lining the wall of the duodenum to produce a number of hormones, some of which travel to their target organs the *pancreas*, *liver* and *gall bladder*, bringing into play the full functioning of these accessory organs in the digestive process.

Storage by the gall bladder

One of these hormones, *cholecystokinin*, released into the blood when acid and fat together come into contact with the hormone secreting cells of the *duodenum*, acts on the gall bladder—a pear-shaped bag attached to the underside of the liver. This stimulus causes the gall bladder to contract, squeezing its contents of a yellow/green liquid (*bile*) into a tube (*the common bile duct*) which opens into the duodenum a few centimetres below the stomach. This sudden rush of bile flows past a valve called the *sphincter of Oddi*, located in the common bile duct. Normally closed, under stimulation from the hormone cholecystokinin this valve opens to allow the bile into the duodenum.

Once in the duodenum, with the characteristic split-second timing of the body, bile meets the chyme, swamping it with bile salts which split the fats into tiny droplets (a process known as *emulsification*)—the first stage in their breakdown process.

The gall bladder does not manufacture bile, but receives it from the liver and stores it ready for release when food enters the duodenum. Each day the liver secretes about 800 to 1000 cc (about 2 pints) of watery bile, consisting of water, *bile salts*, *bile acids*, *cholesterol* and two pigments. One of these pigments *bilirubin*, is eventually broken down in the intestine and gives faeces its characteristic brown colour.

Bile trickles down the common bile duct from the liver to the sphincter of Oddi; if this valve is closed, the small intestine is empty and bile is not required, so it accumulates in the duct and is forced into the gall bladder to be stored. The gall bladder is far too small to hold the 1000 cc of bile produced daily by the liver, so to overcome this problem it has the ability to concentrate the bile up to 20 times. This attribute is brought about by the inner walls of the gall bladder which consist of a *mucus membrane* able to absorb water from the bile. This produces a strong sticky fluid which is accommodated in a similar fashion to the stomach—by expansion of the folded walls (*rugae*) of the inner lining of the gall bladder. The wall also has a middle muscular coat which is able to contract, squirting the concentrated bile towards the duodenum.

Under normal conditions concentration of the bile takes place to produce a deposit-free liquid, the bile salts keeping the cholesterol dissolved. However, if for

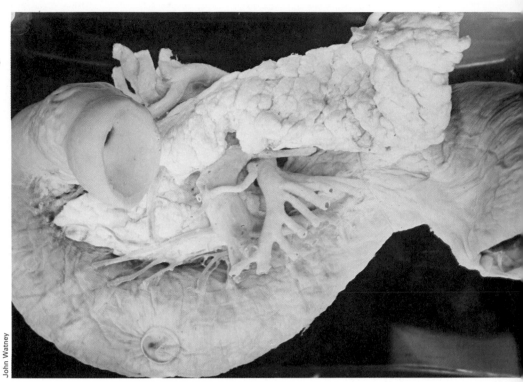

John Watney

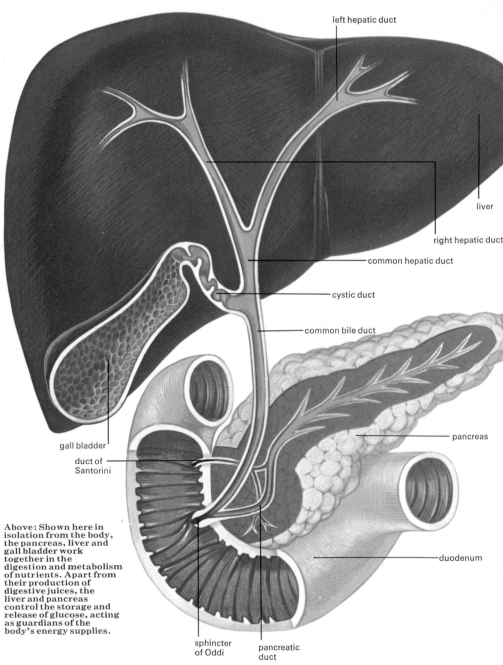

left hepatic duct

liver

right hepatic duct

common hepatic duct

cystic duct

common bile duct

pancreas

gall bladder

duct of Santorini

duodenum

sphincter of Oddi

pancreatic duct

Above: Shown here in isolation from the body, the pancreas, liver and gall bladder work together in the digestion and metabolism of nutrients. Apart from their production of digestive juices, the liver and pancreas control the storage and release of glucose, acting as guardians of the body's energy supplies.

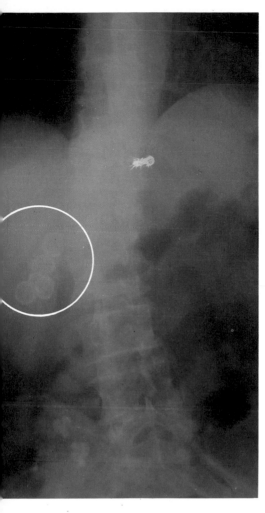

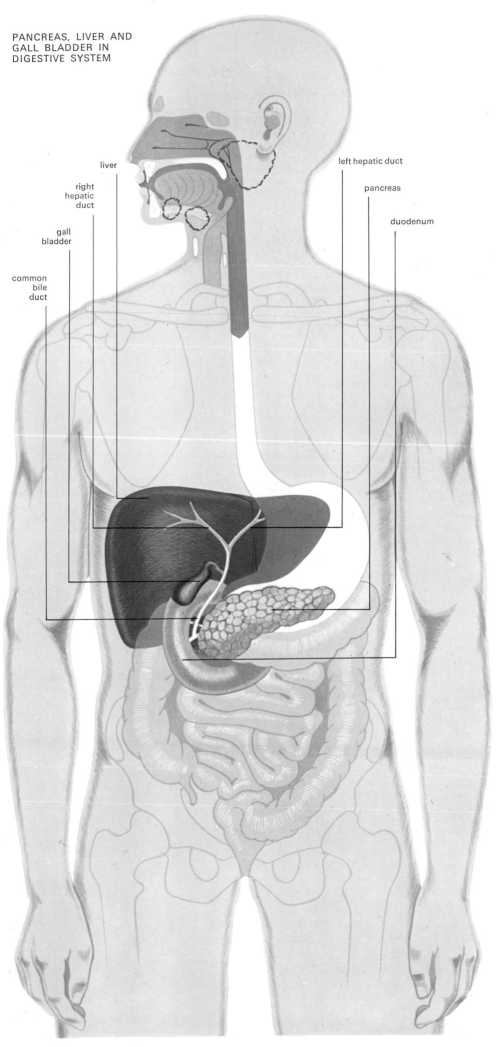

liver

right
hepatic
duct

gall
bladder

common
bile
duct

left hepatic duct

pancreas

duodenum

Above left: Secreting the most powerful digestive enzymes in the body, the pancreas avoids digesting itself by relying on the duodenum to activate its enzymes.

Above and below: Gallstones can form when the bile is being concentrated in the gall bladder. Consisting of cholesterol, calcium and bile pigments, they can grow to the size of a goose egg, preventing the flow of bile to the duodenum, resulting in jaundice. The X ray above shows five fairly large stones in the gall bladder, which may be dislodged as bile is squeezed out. A section through a gallstone is shown below.

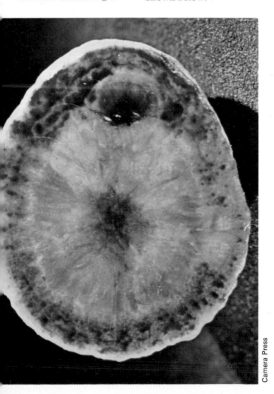

Camera Press

some reason the proportions are changed, the result can be that crystals of cholesterol are deposited inside the gall bladder. These crystals combine with the bile salts and bile pigments to produce *gallstones*—beautiful yellow-green tinted stones ranging in size from tiny crystals to a large stone weighing as much as five hundred grams (one pound). Three times as common in women than men, gallstones can pass out of the intestine without causing any problems, but they occasionally become lodged in the duct leading to the duodenum, particularly during times of festivity when the duodenum is flooded with fats. Obstruction of the duct stops the flow of bile—a painful and potentially dangerous condition if left untreated.

The many roles of the liver

The liver itself is an amazing chemical factory within the body, underrated and grossly abused by many people, it has such margins of safety that three quarters of it can be destroyed before life is threatened and, even when badly damaged, its cells have enormous powers of regeneration. Not only is it the body's most important biochemical organ, it is also the largest. Weighing about 1.4 kgs (4 lbs) in the average adult, it lies just below the diaphragm in the right quarter of the abdomen. The two lobes of the liver are supplied with oxygen-rich blood from the *hepatic artery*, and deoxygenated blood, rich in newly digested nutrients, from the *hepatic portal vein*. These two large blood vessels divide and subdivide into a network of thousands of tiny capillaries weaving their way between the millions of specialised cells of the liver. These cells are themselves arranged in functional groups called *lobules*.

All the products of digestion and oxygen are therefore brought to each liver cell, providing them with the raw materials and fuel to fulfil their biochemical role.

The formation of bile is only one of the many functions of the liver cells. It is made inside the cells and secreted into small channels (*bile ducts*) running between the columns of cells. It eventually

empties into the duct leading to the gall bladder for storage, or directly into the duodenum. Some of the components of bile are identical in concentration to that of the blood plasma which indicates that the liver cells simply filter the blood plasma, allowing molecules and ions of a certain size to pass through, and holding back the larger proteins. Other constituents are actively secreted by the liver cells; they include the *bile salts* which are responsible for breaking globules of fats into tiny droplets, and the pigment *bilirubin* which is removed from the body in the bile.

The normal life of red blood cells is about 120 days and, when they are worn out, certain cells of the liver break them down releasing bilirubin (a golden yellow colour) to be excreted. If for some reason the liver is unable to remove bilirubin from the blood, or there is an obstruction of the bile ducts, preventing excretion of the bilirubin in the bile, large amounts of this golden-yellow pigment will accumulate in the bloodstream. This in turn will collect in other tissues of the body, including the skin and eyes, giving them the yellow colour characteristic of the condition known as *jaundice*.

The bile salts are not lost after fulfilling their role in the digestive process, but are reabsorbed from the intestine where they pass into the *hepatic portal vein* and are carried back to the liver to be re-secreted into the bile. This type of action illustrates the efficiency of the digestive system which is so finely balanced that it recycles even the very small amount (3 to 4 gms) of bile salts present in the adult.

Besides being responsible for the destruction of worn out red blood cells, the liver has the task of supplying certain proteins to the blood plasma, and *heparin*, a chemical which prevents blood clotting inside the vessels. The liver also produces *fibrinogen*, one of the plasma proteins, which plays an essential part in the formation of blood clots.

All the absorbed nutrients from digestion pass through the biochemical factory of the liver. Carbohydrates arrive here as

simple sugars where they are immediately converted to glucose—the body's most direct source of energy. If the cells require immediate energy, the liver releases some of the glucose back into the bloodstream to be carried to the cells. The remaining glucose presents a small problem in that the liver cannot store it. To overcome this the liver changes it into a larger carbohydrate molecule—*glycogen*—which can be stored in the liver and in some of the skeletal muscle cells. When all the glycogen storage areas are filled up the liver transforms the remaining glucose into fat which can be stored below the skin and in other areas of the body. Later, when more energy is required, the glycogen and fat can be converted back to glucose. Even proteins can be converted into glucose by the liver should all the other energy sources be used up, but this

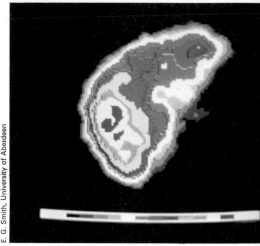

Above and below left: Measuring the amount of a radioactive substance taken up by the liver gives the remarkable picture shown above. Radioactive isotopes injected in very small quantities into the blood accumulate in organs like the liver where the blood flow is slow. By measuring the gamma radiation emitted (shown below left) a colour scan is produced, the colours representing the amount of the isotope absorbed by a normal liver. Obstruction to the blood supply is shown as a light colour, dark areas show fast blood flow.

Below: Over indulgence in fatty foods can cause fat droplets like these to accumulate in the liver.

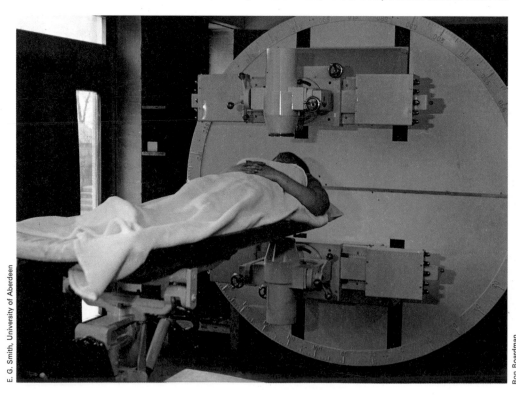

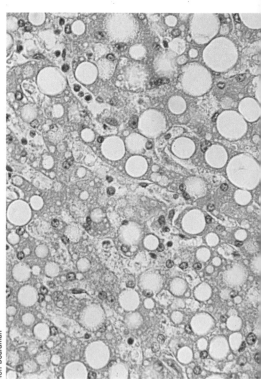

is unusual on a large scale; it produces poisonous waste products which the liver rapidly converts into *urea*. Moderate amounts of urea are harmless and are excreted by the kidneys into the urine, and in the sweat.

All these conversions of carbohydrates, proteins and fats illustrate the interchangeability of biological chemicals; they do, however, require certain enzymes to make them take place, and the liver has the proper enzymes to carry out these processes.

Glycogen, then, occupies most of the storage space of the liver, but other materials are also stored; notably the *vitamins A, D, B*^{12} and *iron*. One interesting example of the liver's storage of vitamin A can be seen in the liver of the polar bear, whose rich diet of fish gives it a very large store of the vitamin. When

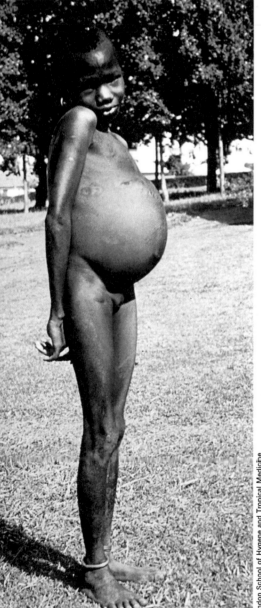

Above and right: Often mistaken for malnutrition, an enlarged abdomen can be caused (as in this case) by cysts in the liver making it swell to gross proportions. This Turkana child from Kenya had the hydatid cysts (shown right) removed from her liver. Hydatid cysts are formed by the larval stage of a tapeworm whose mature form exists in dogs. Man in this case plays the role of intermediate host for the tapeworm, and is infected by the embryo worm if the dog contaminates his food or licks his hands. The mature worm is very small in dogs, but the encysted form in man can become the size of a football before becoming dangerous.

London School of Hygene and Tropical Medicine

the liver has been eaten by humans it has led to severe poisoning and even death.

The liver also secretes certain poisons which cannot be broken down by the body. *DDT*, for example, is found in high levels in the livers of animals and humans who eat sprayed fruits and vegetables. Other poisons like *strychnine, nicotine*, some *barbiturates* and, of course, *alcohol* are destroyed by the liver. Although the liver's capacity for dealing with substances like alcohol is very great, prolonged and excessive intake will damage the cells making regeneration necessary to replace them. If this repair is to be extensive, or is continued over long periods of time, fibrous connective tissue replaces the normal liver cells, causing scarring. This condition is known as *cirrhosis* and, if left untreated, will prevent the liver carrying out its normal functions resulting in jaundice and eventually coma.

The pancreas

Situated behind and just below the stomach is the most important producer of digestive juices in the whole alimentary canal—the *pancreas*. This organ resembles a flask lying on its side, and secretes a variety of the most powerful digestive enzymes in the body. These are essential for the breakdown of carbohydrates, proteins and fats.

Each day the pancreas produces 1200 to 1500 cc (about 2.5 pints) of a clear, colourless liquid called *pancreatic juice* which pours down the *pancreatic duct*, to join with the common bile duct from the liver and gall bladder, and into the duodenum. The pancreas is well prepared for the surge of chyme into the duodenum, for as soon as food enters the mouth, the taste buds send impulses to the brain which responds by stimulating the pancreas (via the *vagus nerve*) to secrete its juice.

This, however, is only a preliminary preparation. The main secretions begin when the acidic chyme comes into contact with the hormone-producing cells of the duodenum. These cells secrete two hor-

mones into the blood which act on the pancreas: *secretin*, which stimulates the pancreas to make pancreatic juice rich in sodium bicarbonate, and *pancreozymin*, which stimulates the production of enzyme-rich pancreatic juice. Sodium bicarbonate neutralises the acid of the chyme, thereby creating the proper environment for the rest of the enzymes in the smaller intestine to work.

Pancreatic juice has five main enzymes. Three of these complete the digestion of proteins begun in the stomach; the others are *amylase*, which digests carbohydrates, and *lipase*, the only fat digesting enzyme in the body, which works on the tiny fat droplets prepared by the bile.

The main protein digesting enzyme, *trypsin*, is potentially a very dangerous chemical. To prevent it digesting the proteins in the cells of the pancreas it is secreted in an inactive form, to be activated when it comes into contact with one of the intestinal enzymes in the duodenum. If the pancreatic duct becomes blocked, the pressure of the juices which are unable to escape can rupture the trypsin producing cells, releasing active trypsin which proceeds to digest the pancreatic tissue and the blood vessels.

Apart from its digestive function, the pancreas produces the essential hormones *insulin* and *glucagon* from groups of cells (the *islets of Langerhans*) scattered throughout the organ. Glucagon accelerates the conversion of glycogen to glucose in the liver in response to the blood sugar level—as the blood sugar level falls, glucagon is secreted to raise it. Insulin, on the other hand, opposes glucagon, decreasing the blood sugar level by accelerating the transport of glucose into the cells and increasing the rate of conversion of glucose to glycogen in the liver. Working together these two hormones exercise control over the body's energy supplies.

Although we are hardly aware of them, these so-called accessory organs perform a phenomenal multiplicity of biochemical functions unequalled by any other organs in the body.

London School of Hygene and Tropical Medicine

The Small Intestine

About 90 per cent of the absorption of the food constituents into the bloodstream takes place in the segment of the gastro-intestinal tract known as the small intestine, which connects the stomach to the large intestine. By the time it reaches the small intestine, food from the mouth, lubricated and chewed into a ball to enable it to pass down the oesophagus into the stomach, has been reduced by the action of digestive juices to *chyme* and is almost entirely fluid. Digestion, however, is far from complete.

In the mouth carbohydrates are not fully broken down, and further digestion takes place in the stomach before the nutrients pass on. Similarly, although proteins are broken down into short chains of *amino acids* (the molecules which are chemically linked to form proteins, the essential stuff of all living tissue) in the stomach, further breaking down takes place in the small intestine until the molecules can be properly absorbed.

The pyloric sphincter, the muscular valve between the stomach and the small intestine, prevents the passage of partially digested food, or chyme, until it is sufficiently broken down and mixed by the stomach. When the food finally passes into the *duodenum*, the first of the three convoluted, winding tubes which make up the small intestine, it is again thoroughly mixed by the contraction of the muscular walls.

The longitudinal and circular muscles of the intestinal walls are capable of performing three different types of movement for different purposes. Contraction of the circular muscles firstly divides the tube into segments. Further contraction of the muscles between these segments occurs making smaller segments, then the first set of muscles relax. The resulting sloshing action, known as *rhythmic segmentation*, takes place between 12 and 16 times a minute. Together with the alternating contraction and relaxation of the longitudinal muscles, known as *pendular movements*, this action thoroughly mixes the chyme with the digestive juices. It is then propelled down the small intestine by *peristalsis*, a wave of contraction that flows from the duodenum to the *ileum*, the third part of the intestine.

Peristaltic action is made possible by the nervous organization of the intestinal walls. The walls contain tiny collections of nerve cells (ganglia) connected to one another, and to muscle cells, by nerve fibres, to form groups or *plexi*, which can operate by means of voluntary control to synchronize the contraction of groups of muscle fibres. Normal muscular activity of the intestine is not usually felt, although violent and painful spasms may occur if food contaminated with the toxin-producing bacteria which causes food poisoning is eaten. (Vomiting and diarrhoea, the two main symptoms of food poisoning, are both reactions to irritations of the stomach and bowel caused by toxic material. They are often early warning symptoms of certain diseases such as typhus and cholera.)

John Watney

The digestive juices

When the chyme enters the duodenum it is highly acidic. It contains a large proportion of hydrochloric acid from the stomach and enzymes which are necessary to break down the large molecules to a size more easily absorbed. The secretions released into the small intestine, however, contain bicarbonate, an alkaline substance, and they therefore neutralize the acid. These secretions come from special cells in the wall of the intestine and from the pancreas and gall bladder by way of the pancreatic duct.

The gall bladder secretions contain bile salts, originally produced in the liver, which act rather like detergents to emulsify the fatty acids and glycerides thus making very small particles which are readily absorbed by the walls of the small intestine.

The small intestine controls its digestive processes by hormones secreted into the bloodstream. The presence of food and hydrochloric acid in the duodenum and the first part of the *jejunum*, the second section of the intestine, stimulates the intestine to produce the hormones *secretin* and *pancreozymin* which stimulate the secretion of bicarbonate and enzymes from the pancreas. *Cholecystokinin* is another intestinal hormone which stimulates the contraction of the gall bladder and the release of bile into the pancreatic duct.

The absorption process

The structure of the small intestine is specialized so that the absorption of nutrients can proceed most efficiently. The wall of the intestine is quite thin but folded rather like the corrugated hose of a vacuum cleaner, providing a large inner surface area. The inner surface has special finger-like structures, called *villi*, which project into the intestinal contents.

The individual cells which line the villi have tiny villi of their own, increasing still further the surface area available for absorption. In an average adult this total area is over 20 square metres (200 sq ft).

In the small intestine, the tiny mole-

Above and above right: The surface of the mucosa or innermost layer of the small intestine (above magnified x 2, and above right x 400) is covered with minute, hair-like projections called villi. These greatly increase the surface area coming in contact with the food and contain specialized cells for absorbing it.

Right: The walls of the small intestine, formed from a mucous membrane and two layers of muscle cells. The muscle cells contract and expand, a movement ensuring that the food has maximum contact with the mucosal layer. The submucosal layer contains lymphoid tissues which destroy bacteria.

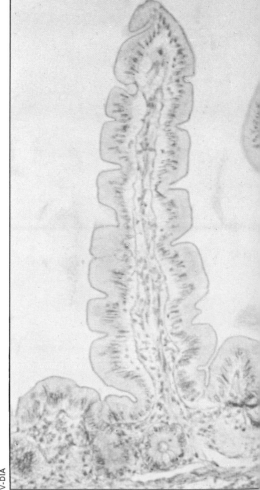

V-DIA

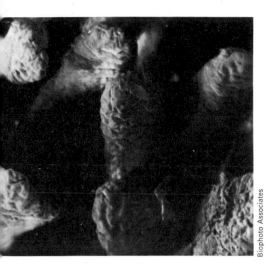

Biophoto Associates

Right: The small intestine—shown here in relation to the other digestive organs—fills the major portion of the abdominal cavity, its six-metre long tube tightly coiled into this small space. It is divided into three sequential sections: the *duodenum* starts at the pyloric sphincter, a valve which prevents the premature passage of food from the stomach, the slightly narrower *jejunum* and the *ileum*, ending at another valve, the *ileocaecal*, which joins it to the large intestine. The small intestine is largely concerned with the absorption of food into the bloodstream, for which its secretions and muscular structure are specially adapted.

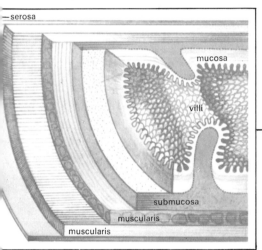

serosa

mucosa

villi

submucosa

muscularis

muscularis

Left and below: An electronmicrograph picture and a longitudinal section through a villus showing the network of blood capillaries through which protein products and carbohydrates are passed. They are then transported through the venules (into which the capillaries collect), the veins and the portal vein to the liver.

capillary network

villus

goblet cell

lacteal

lymph vessel

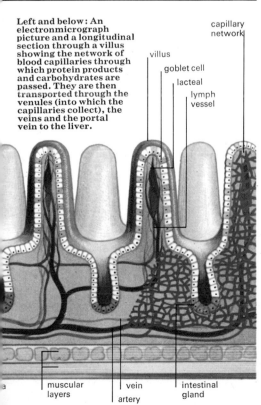

muscular layers

vein

artery

intestinal gland

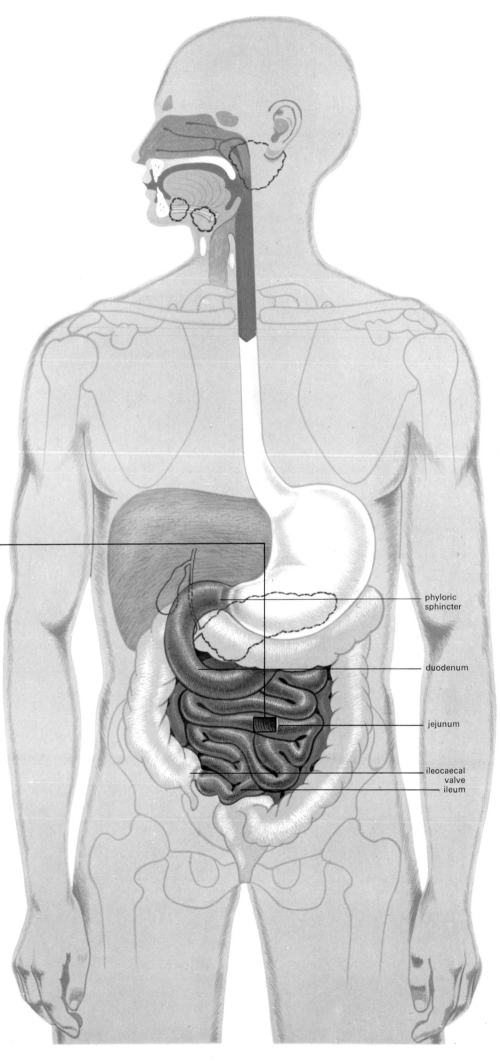

phyloric sphincter

duodenum

jejunum

ileocaecal valve

ileum

255

cules produced by breaking down carbohydrate and protein foods pass into the cells lining the villi and then travel into tiny blood capillaries which run into the small blood vessel draining each villus. These small vessels run into larger ones and then eventually into the *hepatic portal* (carrying) *vein* which leads to the liver, where the next steps of the breakdown processes continue before, finally, the nutrients are delivered to other cells in the body.

The products of fatty foods, on the other hand, do not enter the blood stream directly. They are absorbed from the gut through special ducts in the villi called *lacteals*. These connect with the lymphatics which eventually drain into the thoracic duct. This empties into the vena cava in the neck region, allowing the fats

into the blood stream so that they too can travel to the liver for further breakdown.

The small intestine, particularly the ileum, contains nodules of lymphoid tissue (known as 'Peyer's patches' after their discoverer). These nodules contain white scavenger cells or lymphocytes which may have a protective function by destroying bacteria. In some diseases, however, the patches themselves are attacked and in typhoid fever, for example, they may become intensely inflamed, damaging the intestinal wall as a result.

Parasites, such as tapeworms, are also found in the small intestine. Although common in tropical countries, tapeworms are now rare in most of Europe, but domestic animals like dogs and cats may still be infected. But not all the

inhabitants of our gut are dangerous parasites. Millions of mutually helpful, or *symbiotic*, bacteria live in our intestines and cause us no harm; they may indeed protect us from attack by harmful micro-organisms.

Absorption of the broken-down food constituents mainly takes place through the villi, the tiny-hair-like projections covering the inner surface of the small intestine. Depending on the size and complexity of their molecular structure, they may pass immediately into the bloodstream by simple diffusion, osmosis or by active transport systems through the cell membrane. The inner wall of the intestine is covered with a mucosal layer which will only allow lipid (fat) soluble substances to dissolve in it and diffuse into the blood vessels and lacteals. Specialized transport processes are present in the membranes of the mucosal cells which deal with larger soluble substances and ions.

Passive diffusion only enables the same concentration of substances to exist on either side of this semi-permeable membrane, since the diffusion can occur equally readily in either direction. But the active transport processes are like pumps, they only operate in one direction, and can concentrate the transported substance, amino acids for example, on the inside of the intestinal mucosa.

The proteins in the diet are absorbed mainly in the form of individual *amino acids* by these active transport systems. Some proteins can be absorbed in their natural, undigested form and many food allergies seem to develop because these proteins pass from the gut into the bloodstream, increasing sensitivity to future doses of food containing that particular protein. The nature of these proteins is not known, but many people appear to suffer violent reactions whenever they eat shellfish or other sea foods which may contain some specific absorbable protein.

Carbohydrates are absorbed in the form of *monosaccharides* (mainly fructose and glucose) by a separate, active transport process. Fats and lipids will passively pass through the intestinal mucosa as long as they are in sufficiently small droplets. As a result of the emulsifying action of the bile salts they are usually in the form of small droplets about 0.5u (0.00002 in) in diameter. The mucosal cells send out a small tentacle of cytoplasm which surrounds the droplet and takes it into the interior of the cell. This is very similar to the way in which an amoeba ingests food particles. About 94 per cent of the dietary fat is absorbed in this way as *triglycerides*.

Some aspects of the absorption of trace elements are still not fully understood, although they are vitally important to the body. For example, the importance of minute quantities of fluoride (found in the mineral structure of bone) for the health of the teeth is now recognized.

Once absorbed by the body, the broken down substances provide the raw materials for the building of longer and more complicated molecules better suited to human needs. They can be combined with oxygen to form water, carbon dioxide and nitrogen-containing wastes, so releasing vital energy for activity and regeneration. What remains of the food after assimilation then passes into the large intestine, where the final stage of the digestive process takes place.

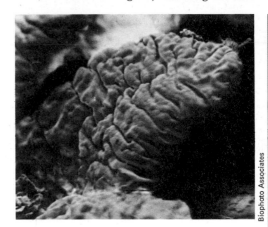

Biophoto Associates

Above: A section of tissue taken from a mouse's small intestine shows a single villus magnified 1,000 times. The outer surface is greatly folded to provide the maximum area for absorption.

Below: 'The cholic', a common digestive complaint, by a 19th-century cartoonist.

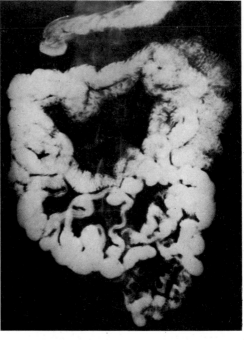

Right: This X-ray photograph shows the convolutions of the small intestine. Patients with suspected digestive disorders are given barium sulphate in a meal or an enema so that the intestines—which would usually be transparent on an X-ray plate—become opaque and can be seen in detail.

The Cholic

Mary Evans

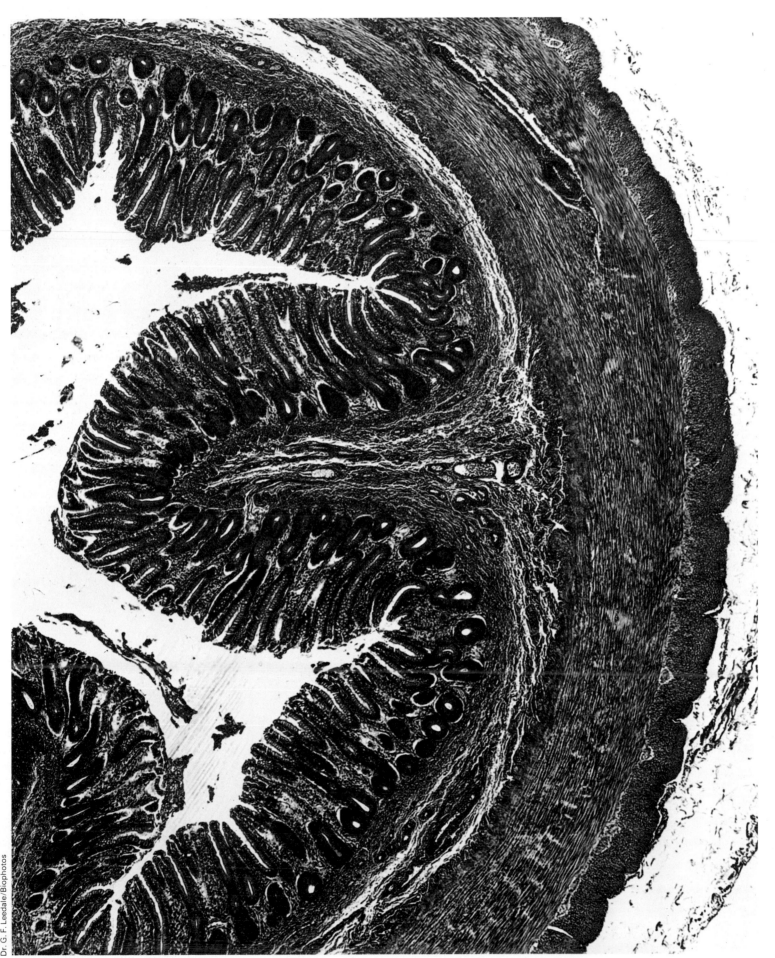

The small intestine photographed by light microscopy. The small intestine has a large surface area (over 20 square metres in the average adult) to enable nutrients to be easily absorbed.

The Large Intestine

By the time the contents of the gut reach the end of the small intestine—about five or six hours after leaving the stomach—the digestive processes are almost complete. The partly digested food passes from the ileum into the first section of the large intestine, to begin the final stages of digestion.

The structure of the large intestine

The large intestine is divided into four main sections: the *caecum, colon, rectum* (these are also known as the large bowel) and *anal canal*. Altogether it is about 1.5 metres (5 ft) long and 6.5 cms (2.5 ins) in diameter—three times the diameter of the small intestine. The caecum is a blind pouch hanging below the ileo-caecal valve, the sphincter separating the small and large intestines. The open end of the caecum joins the colon, a long tube which forms the greater part of the large intestine. The mucous membrane lining the colon—unlike the small intestine—is smooth and devoid of villi. A muscular coat surrounds the mucous layer, consisting of circular internal muscles and longitudinal external muscles, similar to the small intestine. These muscular walls contract to gather the colon into a large number of bulbous pouches called *haustra*, giving it a puckered appearance and creating an enormous capacity for expansion.

The colon terminates in the rectum, a passage about 12 centimetres (5 ins) long; the last three or four centimetres of the large bowel are the anal canal. The exterior opening, referred to as the anus, is held closed most of the time by a muscular valve—the anal sphincter.

The mucous membrane inside the anal canal is arranged in length-wise folds that contain a network of arteries and veins. Unlike the rest of the gastro-intestinal tract, the final part of the rectum and the anal valve are continuations of the skin and are very well endowed with sensory nerves—this is what makes inflammation and enlargement of the anal veins (known as piles or haemorrhoids) so painful.

A peculiar feature of the large intestine is a narrow, worm-like sac called the appendix, about eight cms (3 ins) long, connected to the caecum. This is a remnant from the time when man's ancestors were herbivores, living solely on plant foods. In herbivorous animals it plays a part in digesting the large quantities of cellulose found in plant material—the equivalent organ in a horse is about 1.25 metres (approx. 4 ft) long. But in man it no longer serves a useful function and has a tendency to become inflamed when irritating particles become lodged in it—sometimes resulting in the chronic or acute inflammation called appendicitis.

The activity of the large intestine

Chyme is squirted into the caecum through the ileo-caecal valve, which opens to allow only about two cc maximum through at a time. At this stage the fluid consists of undigested or undigestible food residues, water and secretions from the intestines. Water is extracted particularly

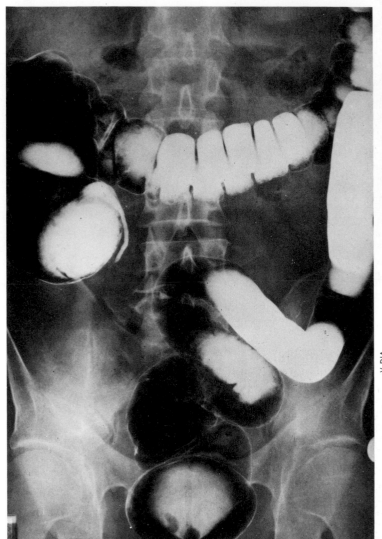

V-DIA

Above: A picture of the blood vessels supplying the large intestine. This rich collection of capillaries supplies the muscular walls with oxygen and nutrients, and also removes water, vitamins and minerals taken into the liver.

Left: An X-ray of the large intestine. The bulbous pouches called *haustra* are visible in the colon (top, left to right). The worm-like appendix can be seen (centre left) coming out of the caecum.

in the caecum and first part of the colon, so that the chyme becomes solid or semi-solid; in this state it is called *faeces*. Numerous cells secrete mucus from glands which line the walls of the large intestine, to lubricate the passage of the faeces and protect the walls from attack by any remaining digestive enzymes.

There is a constant to and fro movement of the chyme within the colon due to muscular activity known as *haustral churning*. The haustra are relaxed and stretched while they fill up with chyme, then at a certain point the wall contracts, squeezing the food residues into the next haustrum. Peristalsis also occurs, but at a much slower rate than elsewhere, culminating in a strong movement known as *mass peristalsis*, which pushes the colon's contents towards the rectum. This movement is brought about by the presence of food in the stomach; it empties the caecum ready for the newly digested chyme from the small intestine. Mass peristalsis, normally taking place three or four times a day, during or soon after a meal, is the cause of some of the 'rumblings' in the abdomen after eating.

The role of bacteria

The bacteria found in the large intestine play an essential role in nutrition and digestion. One of their most important functions is to synthesize several vitamins, particularly some B vitamins and vitamin K—which is vital in helping the liver to manufacture substances used in the blood-clotting process. The bacteria

Erich Lessing/Magnum

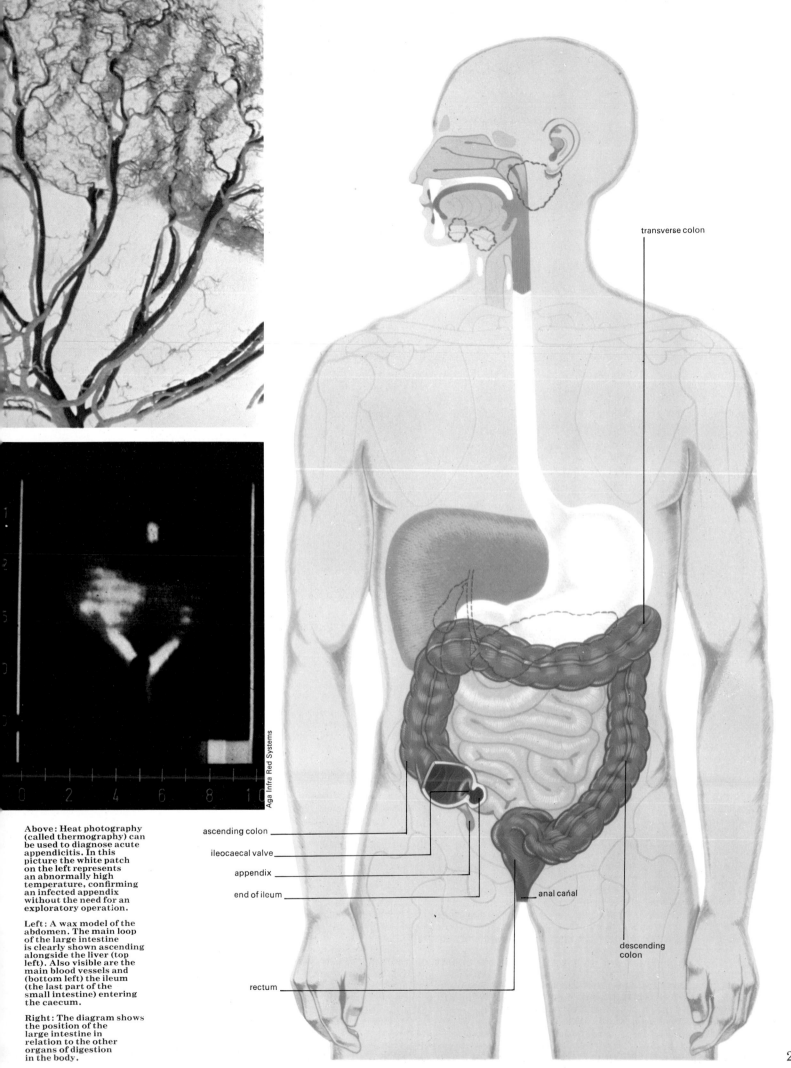

transverse colon

ascending colon

ileocaecal valve

appendix

end of ileum

anal canal

rectum

descending colon

Above: Heat photography (called thermography) can be used to diagnose acute appendicitis. In this picture the white patch on the left represents an abnormally high temperature, confirming an infected appendix without the need for an exploratory operation.

Left: A wax model of the abdomen. The main loop of the large intestine is clearly shown ascending alongside the liver (top left). Also visible are the main blood vessels and (bottom left) the ileum (the last part of the small intestine) entering the caecum.

Right: The diagram shows the position of the large intestine in relation to the other organs of digestion in the body.

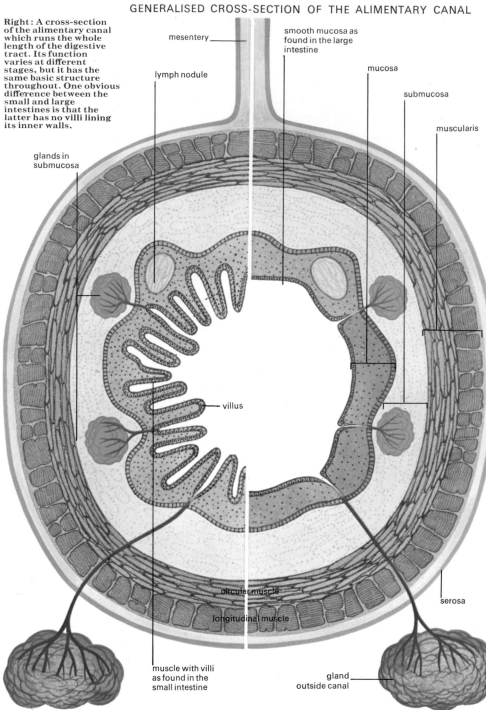

Right: A cross-section of the alimentary canal which runs the whole length of the digestive tract. Its function varies at different stages, but it has the same basic structure throughout. One obvious difference between the small and large intestines is that the latter has no villi lining its inner walls.

mesentery

smooth mucosa as found in the large intestine

mucosa

submucosa

muscularis

lymph nodule

glands in submucosa

villus

circular muscle

longitudinal muscle

muscle with villi as found in the small intestine

gland outside canal

serosa

goblet cells

mucous pit

mucus

folded mucosa

muscular layer

connective tissue

capillary

red blood cells

Biophoto Associates

break down any remaining proteins into amino acids and then into simpler substances, such as indole, skatole, hydrogen sulphide and fatty acids. Much of the indole and skatole is transported to the liver, where it is converted into less poisonous compounds and passed out of the body in the urine, but some remains in the faeces and is the chief cause of their distinctive smell.

Remaining carbohydrates are fermented by bacteria, releasing hydrogen, carbon dioxide and methane gas. A variable amount of gas is found in the colon, which may be released explosively when the pressure inside the colon and rectum forces the anal sphincter open. The bacteria also decompose bilirubin (the pigment produced by the breakdown of red blood cells) which is excreted in the bile, and the presence of this in the faeces gives them a brown colour.

By the time the faeces reach the rectum they are approximately 70 per cent water. Bacteria represent 10 per cent of the dry

weight and the rest is made up of food residues (mainly cellulose from plant sources which cannot be digested or absorbed by man), a certain quantity of the breakdown products mentioned above, intestinal secretions and dead cells from the lining of the intestine. An average adult on a normal diet will excrete 70 to 170 grams (2½ to 6 oz) of faeces daily.

Expelling the waste
It usually takes from 12 to 24 hours for the chyme to travel from the caecum, turn into faeces and reach the point where it accumulates at the end of colon, but this can be longer, depending on the amount of roughage in the diet. The colon works best when it is moderately full, so the indigestible material found in roughage is useful in increasing the bulk of the contents of the colon. The movement of faeces into the rectum prior to being expelled is not stimulated until the colon is relatively full. The longer this takes, the more water will be absorbed. making

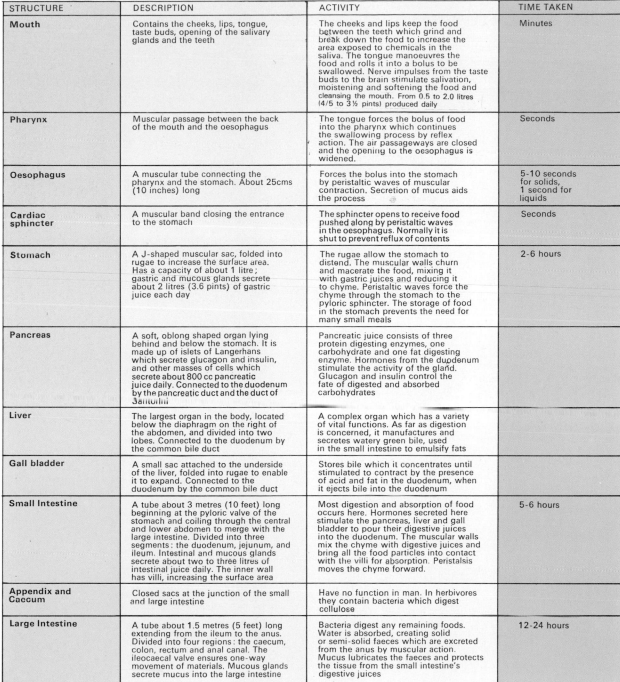

STRUCTURE	DESCRIPTION	ACTIVITY	TIME TAKEN
Mouth	Contains the cheeks, lips, tongue, taste buds, opening of the salivary glands and the teeth	The cheeks and lips keep the food between the teeth which grind and break down the food to increase the area exposed to chemicals in the saliva. The tongue manoeuvres the food and rolls it into a bolus to be swallowed. Nerve impulses from the taste buds to the brain stimulate salivation, moistening and softening the food and cleansing the mouth. From 0.5 to 2.0 litres (4/5 to 3½ pints) produced daily	Minutes
Pharynx	Muscular passage between the back of the mouth and the oesophagus	The tongue forces the bolus of food into the pharynx which continues the swallowing process by reflex action. The air passageways are closed and the opening to the oesophagus is widened.	Seconds
Oesophagus	A muscular tube connecting the pharynx and the stomach. About 25cms (10 inches) long	Forces the bolus into the stomach by peristaltic waves of muscular contraction. Secretion of mucus aids the process	5-10 seconds for solids, 1 second for liquids
Cardiac sphincter	A muscular band closing the entrance to the stomach	The sphincter opens to receive food pushed along by peristaltic waves in the oesophagus. Normally it is shut to prevent reflux of contents	Seconds
Stomach	A J-shaped muscular sac, folded into rugae to increase the surface area. Has a capacity of about 1 litre; gastric and mucous glands secrete about 2 litres (3.6 pints) of gastric juice each day	The rugae allow the stomach to distend. The muscular walls churn and macerate the food, mixing it with gastric juices and reducing it to chyme. Peristaltic waves force the chyme through the stomach to the pyloric sphincter. The storage of food in the stomach prevents the need for many small meals	2-6 hours
Pancreas	A soft, oblong shaped organ lying behind and below the stomach. It is made up of islets of Langerhans which secrete glucagon and insulin, and other masses of cells which secrete about 800 cc pancreatic juice daily. Connected to the duodenum by the pancreatic duct and the duct of Santorini	Pancreatic juice consists of three protein digesting enzymes, one carbohydrate and one fat digesting enzyme. Hormones from the duodenum stimulate the activity of the gland. Glucagon and insulin control the fate of digested and absorbed carbohydrates	
Liver	The largest organ in the body, located below the diaphragm on the right of the abdomen, and divided into two lobes. Connected to the duodenum by the common bile duct	A complex organ which has a variety of vital functions. As far as digestion is concerned, it manufactures and secretes watery green bile, used in the small intestine to emulsify fats	
Gall bladder	A small sac attached to the underside of the liver, folded into rugae to enable it to expand. Connected to the duodenum by the common bile duct	Stores bile which it concentrates until stimulated to contract by the presence of acid and fat in the duodenum, when it ejects bile into the duodenum	
Small Intestine	A tube about 3 metres (10 feet) long beginning at the pyloric valve of the stomach and coiling through the central and lower abdomen to merge with the large intestine. Divided into three segments: the duodenum, jejunum, and ileum. Intestinal and mucous glands secrete about two to three litres of intestinal juice daily. The inner wall has villi, increasing the surface area	Most digestion and absorption of food occurs here. Hormones secreted here stimulate the pancreas, liver and gall bladder to pour their digestive juices into the duodenum. The muscular walls mix the chyme with digestive juices and bring all the food particles into contact with the villi for absorption. Peristalsis moves the chyme forward.	5-6 hours
Appendix and Caecum	Closed sacs at the junction of the small and large intestine	Have no function in man. In herbivores they contain bacteria which digest cellulose	
Large Intestine	A tube about 1.5 metres (5 feet) long extending from the ileum to the anus. Divided into four regions: the caecum, colon, rectum and anal canal. The ileocaecal valve ensures one-way movement of materials. Mucous glands secrete mucus into the large intestine	Bacteria digest any remaining foods. Water is absorbed, creating solid or semi-solid faeces which are excreted from the anus by muscular action. Mucus lubricates the faeces and protects the tissue from the small intestine's digestive juices	12-24 hours

Above: The inner surfaces of the colon (the second region of the large intestine) magnified x 60 by an electron microscope. The folded inner layer is covered in mucus secreted by the goblet cells. This provides lubrication for movement of the intestinal contents.

Below left: The muscular layer of the colon magnified x 600. Layers of muscle responsible for peristalsis have been cut through, and a capillary is visible (with red blood cells inside). The connective tissue is at the bottom of the picture.

Below: A section through the mucosa (inner layer) of the colon showing the mucous pits magnified x 10. The goblet cells are stained purple.

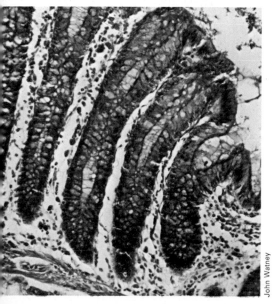

the faeces compacted and hard, so it is increasingly difficult to expel them.

The process of expelling waste through the anal sphincter is known as *defaecation*. Pressure of faeces in the rectum is the main stimulus, causing a peristaltic movement of the muscular wall of the rectum. This is under a certain degree of voluntary control which has to be learnt in early childhood and is largely absent in babies.

To expel the faeces, a conscious effort is made to force the diaphragm down thus increasing pressure in the abdominal cavity and propelling the faeces into the rectum. Once this process has begun, the rectum stretches to receive the entire contents of the lower part of the colon. The stretching triggers off the reflex contraction of the rectal muscles, the anal sphincter relaxes, and the faeces are pushed out of the body.

Neglecting the urge to defaecate, as well as eating foods that have insufficient roughage, will lead to constipation—the contents of the colon become hard and can only be passed out with some difficulty. Laxatives, taken as a cure for constipation, either act to increase the amount of water retained by the contents of the colon, so that the muscles find the waste softer and easier to propel, or some, like liquid paraffin, act as a lubricant for the passage of the faeces. Other drugs directly stimulate the gut walls to contract and expel the faeces. Doctors disapprove of the frequent use of laxatives, as it is easy to grow so dependent on such drugs that the bowel function becomes permanently abnormal.

Diarrhoea—the frequent expulsion of liquid faeces—can be produced by a number of factors, such as nervous stress, excessive use of laxatives or infection. Infection may prevent the large intestine from doing its job of reabsorbing water from the gut contents, so the faeces remain in a semi-liquid state, making the conscious control of defaecation much more difficult.

The Kidneys

The solid appearance of our bodies belies the fluidity of our internal environment. Inside we are awash with fluids: something like 60 per cent of our body weight is water, over half of which is contained inside the cells. The rest is mixed with salts (rather like diluted seawater) and bathes all the cells of the body.

The importance of the surrounding fluid can be demonstrated by the fact that the cells of a drop of blood placed in tap water will swell and burst. Placed in a five per cent solution, on the other hand, they will shrink and wrinkle up. In the first case water is rushing into the cells by osmosis, and in the second it is rushing out of the cells. In the body such gross changes in cell volume would be fatal to the functioning of cells. So it is vital that the bathing fluids are maintained at exactly the right concentrations.

The internal sea

Nearly every cell of the body is surrounded by a network of tiny capillaries, from which blood plasma diffuses into the internal sea. This salty fluid carries nutrients to the cells and removes their waste products, diffusing back through the capillary walls to mix with the other blood constituents. One particularly dangerous waste product is ammonia, produced when proteins are broken down to provide energy. This is a highly poisonous gas which dissolves readily in water. One thousandth of a milligram of

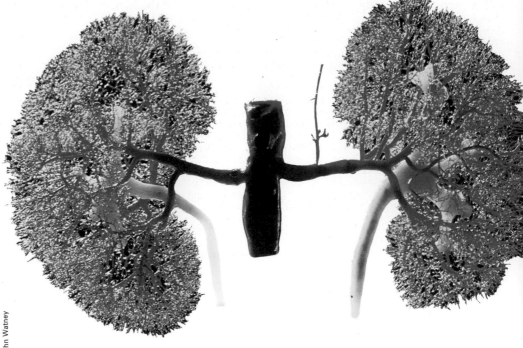

John Watney

Above: Human kidneys treated with resin to show the blood vessels. Each of the kidneys contains about one million nephrons—twisted hollow tubules through which the blood is filtered.

Right: Diagram showing the position of the kidneys, ureter and bladder.

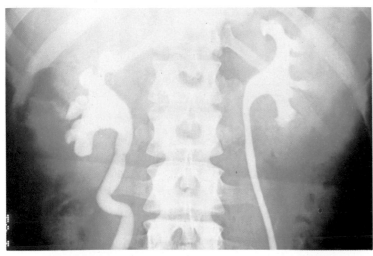

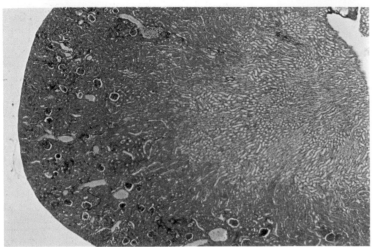

Biophoto Associates

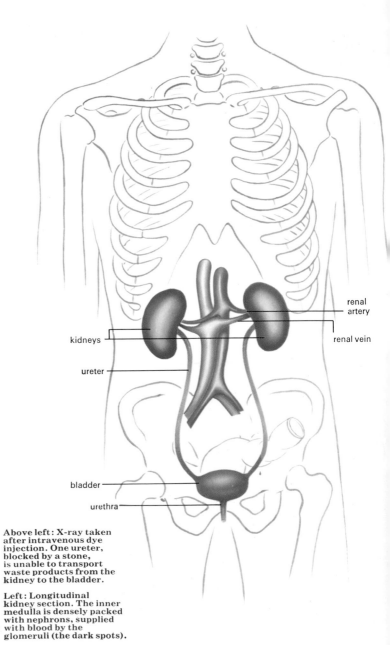

renal artery

renal vein

kidneys

ureter

bladder

urethra

Above left: X-ray taken after intravenous dye injection. One ureter, blocked by a stone, is unable to transport waste products from the kidney to the bladder.

Left: Longitudinal kidney section. The inner medulla is densely packed with nephrons, supplied with blood by the glomeruli (the dark spots).

ammonia per litre of blood is sufficient to kill a man, so the body must eliminate this as fast as possible. It is sent to the liver to be converted into a substance called urea which is still poisonous, but can be tolerated by the body in quantities one hundred thousand times greater than ammonia.

It is vital that the urea be eliminated and the salt concentration of body fluids balanced. It is also essential for the body to regulate the acidity of the bathing solution and control the volume of circulating water which will dilute the body fluids. All of these important functions are performed by the kidneys, which exert a fine degree of control over the substances comprising our internal sea. They chemically process and filter our body fluids and produce urine containing unwanted substances, which is then eliminated from the bladder.

Kidney structure

The two kidneys are attached to the abdominal wall and their surrounding structures by a layer of fibrous connective tissue. This holds them in place, one on either side of the backbone, above the small of the back just behind the stomach and liver. They are bean-shaped and engorged with blood brought to them by the large renal artery.

Microscopic examination of the kidney reveals a complex system of tubes, capillaries, arteries and veins, carefully packed together to form approximately one million identical units known as *nephrons*. The nephrons are miniaturized chemical filtration plants: they balance the composition of the blood and form urine which

collects in the renal pelvis, a large cavity in the centre of the kidney. From here the urine drains out through the ureter to the bladder.

The filtration units

The nephron is a twisted, hollow tube surrounded by a network of blood vessels. Each of these tubules is about 31 mm (1.25 inches) long, compacted into the smallest possible space. If placed end to end, the two million tubules of the two kidneys would form a pipe about fifty miles long.

At its closed end, the nephron has a cup called the *Bowman's capsule* which encloses a dense ball of blood capillaries. The tubule leading away from here immediately convolutes itself into a complex, twisted shape. Together with the Bowman's capsule they constitute the outer reddish-brown layer of the kidney—the *cortex*. The tubule straightens out and descends into the medulla, or interior of the kidney. Here it bends back on itself forming a hairpin bend (the *loop of Henle*) and ascends to the cortex again, makes another series of twists and joins up with a straight urine-collecting duct. This goes down through the medulla collecting urine from several nephrons, and discharges it into the pelvis of the kidney.

Below left: A cross section through the kidney showing the cortex, medulla and position of the nephrons.

Below: Diagram showing the arrangement of the kidney filtration units and the vessels which supply them. The renal artery divides into arterioles which subdivide into a spherical cluster of capillaries (known as the glomerulus) at the end of each nephron. Large molecules (protein and blood cells) are filtered out by the pressure of blood in the departing arteriole. Salts in solution are passed along the tubule for reabsorption by the cells lining the walls. Unwanted products (urine) are passed to the bladder.

The nephron is the centre of chemical balance and filtration in the body. To understand how it works it is necessary to follow the path of the blood which transports materials to the kidney.

One quarter of the total blood output from the heart comes to the kidneys along the renal arteries—approximately 1,200 cc (about 2 pints) every minute. The incoming artery divides up repeatedly inside the kidney, eventually forming arterioles, each one of which leads to a Bowman's capsule.

The arteriole splits into tiny, thin-walled capillaries which form a ball known as the glomerulus (little ball). These capillaries reunite to form the arteriole which leaves the capsule. The departing arteriole is narrower than the incoming one, which has the effect of increasing the resistance to the blood flow. This, in turn, increases the pressure in the glomerulus to something like three times the normal pressure, so that the blood is pressing very hard against the thin walls of the capillaries.

The capillary walls are riddled with minute pores which are so small that they act, in effect, like a miniaturized filter, allowing the water, glucose, salts, amino acids, vitamins and urea from the blood to pass through into the tubule, but preventing the passage of blood cells and proteins. The amounts of substances passed through are quite amazing: 125 ccs ($\frac{1}{4}$ pint) of fluid is filtered every minute, 180 litres a day, about four times the amount contained in an average size car petrol tank. This fluid contains something like one kilo ($2\frac{1}{2}$ lbs) of sodium chloride (common salt), .45 kilo (one lb) of sodium bicarbonate, .15 kilo ($\frac{1}{3}$ lb) of glucose.

Obviously the body cannot afford to lose such large amounts of these substances, so it reabsorbs about 99% of the fluid back into the bloodstream. In fact, the kidneys filter and reabsorb our entire internal sea nearly fifteen times every day, which amounts to a remarkably thorough cleansing operation.

The reabsorption process

Once it has passed out of the blood vessels of the glomerulus the fluid enters the tubule of the nephron. This is surrounded by a network of capillaries whose function is to reabsorb the valuable and useful blood components, leaving excess and waste products inside ready to be discharged as urine (about one per cent of the total filtered fluid).

During its passage through the first twisted part of the tubule (the *proximal convoluted tubule*) about 85 per cent of the water, sodium chloride and bicarbonate, together with virtually all the glucose, vitamins and amino acids, are reabsorbed. This is accomplished by the millions of cells lining this part of the tubule which have millions of microscopic villi—minute protrusions similar to those found in the lining of the small intestine—vastly increasing their surface area, so that they can absorb quickly and easily.

Most of the water passes through the tubule walls by osmosis, the process by which water is passed through a semipermeable membrane to equalize two different concentrations; other materials such as glucose, amino acids and vitamins have to be actively transported back into the blood by special carrier molecules. These pick up a particular molecule and carry it across the tubule cells and into

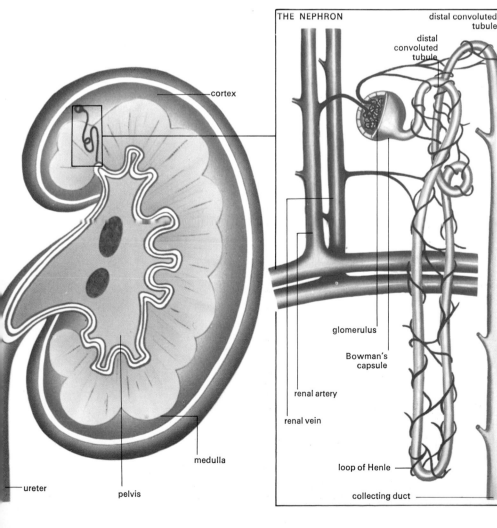

cortex

medulla

ureter

pelvis

THE NEPHRON

distal convoluted tubule

distal convoluted tubule

glomerulus

Bowman's capsule

renal artery

renal vein

loop of Henle

collecting duct

263

beating heart gives blood pressure

Biophoto Associates

glomerulus

fluid forced into Bowman's capsule

glucose, vitamins, amino acids

sodium (Na)

sodium (Na)

blood vessel

water

water

impermeable to water

collecting duct

Na   Na   Na

water   Na   Na   Na

Na   Na   Na

water   Na   Na

Na

high sodium concentration

loop of Henle

water

Above: The beating heart provides the pressure to filter the blood through the Bowman's capsule. The high concentration around the loop of Henle causes recycling of the sodium from the limbs of the tubule, so removing as much sodium as possible without losing water.

ACTIVE TRANSPORT FROM TUBULES

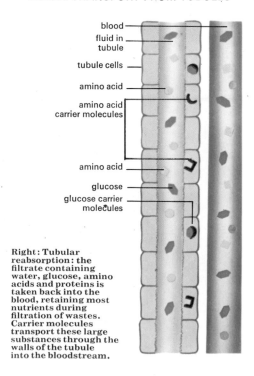

blood
fluid in tubule
tubule cells
amino acid
amino acid carrier molecules
amino acid
glucose
glucose carrier molecules

Right: Tubular reabsorption: the filtrate containing water, glucose, amino acids and proteins is taken back into the blood, retaining most nutrients during filtration of wastes. Carrier molecules transport these large substances through the walls of the tubule into the bloodstream.

the blood. Active transport needs energy, so the cells of the tubule have large numbers of mitochondria, the 'powerhouse' organelles in the cell, to produce the necessary ATP (adenosine triphosphate), 'high grade' energy fuel.

Water conservation

The remainder of the fluid passes down to the loop of Henle, and begins its ascent up the other limb towards the cortex. The ascending limb of the tubule does not allow water to pass through, but it actively absorbs sodium which it pumps out into the surrounding tissue. Since the descending and ascending limbs are very close together some of the sodium diffuses back into the descending limb to mix with the fluid coming from the capsule, hence recycling itself. The result of this is a very high concentration of sodium around the loop of Henle, and the more sodium there is, the more sodium will be pumped out of the ascending limb of the tubule. This is a method of removing as much sodium as possible in a very short tubule; the chloride follows the movement of sodium, enabling the body to retain its valuable salt.

The fluid travels up to the cortex in the

ascending limb into the twisted, *distal convoluted tubule* where water is once again absorbed. From here it enters the collecting duct which carries it down to the pelvis of the kidney. It again comes across a high concentration of sodium as it goes down through the inner area, the medulla, and past the region around the loop of Henle. This time, however, the walls of the tubule will allow water to pass through them by osmosis into the tissue and the blood. This rather complicated procedure is an ingenious method of concentrating the fluid to conserve water and keep as much salt as possible back from the urine.

Waste removal

The unwanted urea and excess materials pass straight through the tubule and into the collecting duct where they are then known as urine. A certain amount of water is essential to keep all these substances dissolved, which is one reason why we cannot survive for long periods without water. The body concentrates the urine to the maximum possible amount, but it must dispose of the poisonous urea, so urine must be expelled.

Besides removing substances from the blood, the kidney can also contribute small, but significant amounts of materials. Into the first twisted part of the tubule from the surrounding capillaries it secretes substances such as hydrogen ions which keep the acidity of the blood at a constant level (adding hydrogen ions will increase the acidity, and taking them away will decrease the acidity). The kidneys' efficient filtration system, however, also means that certain drugs, such as penicillin and one of the anti-malarial drugs, are immediately secreted into the urine. In order for them to be effective in the fight against invading bacteria, they must, therefore, be taken regularly.

The kidney is a very discriminating processing plant, carefully regulating our internal sea. Survival of the whole body relies on the delicate balancing processes of these two organs, each no bigger than the size of a clenched fist.

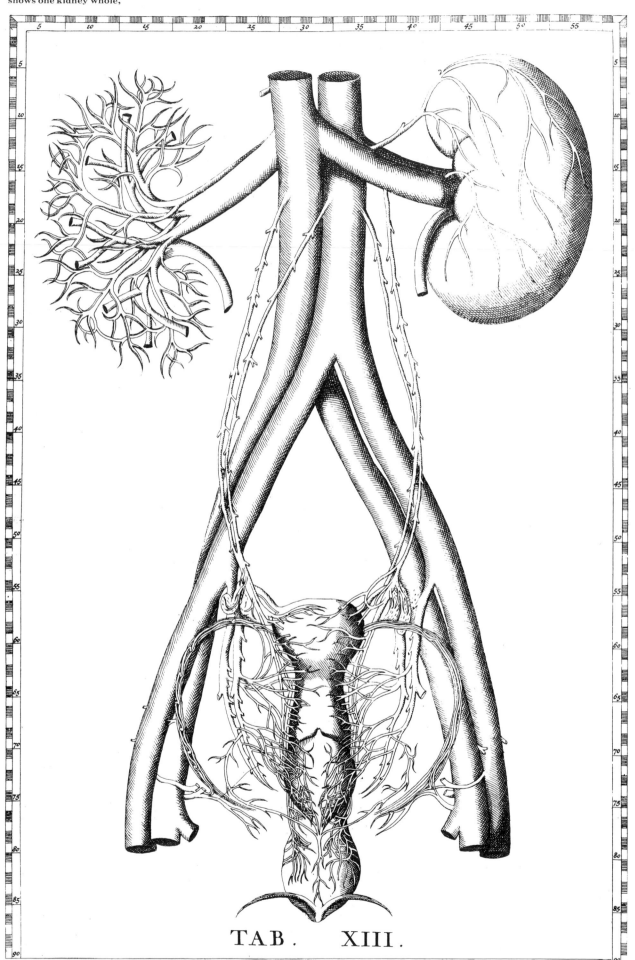

TAB.   XIII.

Skin

The skin is rightly described as the largest functional organ of the human body, since it covers an area of 1.5 to 2 square metres in an average adult person. Throughout life, the skin has a wide variety of tasks to perform in protecting the internal environment of the human body from the ravaging effects of the outer environment and in maintaining communication between the two.

The evolution of skin

During the course of evolution, this outer covering developed to protect the organs engaged in the basic tasks of survival—ingesting food, respiration and excretion of waste products. Since these interactions were no longer taking place on the surface because of increasing complexity—the elongation and convolution of the digestive tract, for example—less and less of the outer area was in direct contact with these processes and the outer layers of the body, like other organs, became specialized. Although responsible for a number of other activities, the skin is primarily involved in protection and communication and the two principal layers, the *epidermis* and *dermis*, are specifically adapted to carry out these tasks.

The skin layers

The *epidermis* is the outer layer of skin and is itself made up of some five layers of cells. The innermost layer of the epidermis, the *stratum basale*, or basal layer, of cells, formed in a column-like structure, is continually dividing and pushing toward the surface, during which time the nuclei degenerate and the cells die. This forms the outermost *stratum corneum*. This layer, 25 to 30 dead cells deep, contains an insoluble, indigestible protein called *keratin*, which is the main component of hair and nails. Keratin production varies throughout the body: it is much thicker, for example, on the palms and soles of the feet where pressure and friction is greater. This is what forms the *stratum lucidum*, a fifth layer, which is seen only in these thickened areas. The cells of this layer contain *eleidin*, a clear or 'lucid' substance formed from *keratohyaline* from which keratin is produced.

The keratin lies in a loose, basket-weave pattern allowing great mobility (particularly on the bodies of animals, where it forms scales) but nevertheless preventing the entry of bacteria, the absorption of water from outside or the loss of body water through evaporation.

Just above the innermost layer of the epidermis, the *stratum spinosum* (prickly layer) is formed from 8 to 10 rows of polygonal (many-sided) cells which have a prickly appearance. Like the stratum basale, this layer contains the pigment, *melanin*, which forms granules. These are gradually broken down as they are carried towards the surface with the basal cells and are finally shed with the keratin. Melanin protects the skin from excessive exposure to ultra-violet radiation: the light energy is absorbed by the melanin, the pigment becomes oxidized and therefore darker. This is what produces a 'sun-tan' when skin is exposed to the sun only for short periods. If the epidermal cells are damaged by excessive exposure, the melanocytes are stimulated to produce more melanin and thus a darker tan.

Melanin appears in the first two layers in the fair skin of northern peoples and in all the epidermal layers of the dark skin of peoples originating from tropical climates. Some oriental peoples, such as the Chinese, have an additional pigment called *carotene* in the corneum and the dermis giving the skin its characteristic yellow colour.

The third layer of the epidermis is formed from two or three layers of cells which are the source of keratin production. These cells contain granules of keratohyaline which give this layer its name, *stratum granulosum*. The epidermis is always busy rebuilding its cast off layers—this is an important factor in healing after disease or injury or in regrowing if transplanted to a new site in a skin graft. The epidermis is purely cellular. Nourishment of the five layers is provided by tissue fluids diffusing up from the spaces among the cells of the dermis, the area below.

The dermis is more active than the epidermis since it contains the skin's means of nourishment, communication and temperature control. The dermis has two layers, the upper one of which is rich in blood vessels that weave in and out of the tough *collagen* and *elastin* connective tissue. Collagen is formed from bundles of fibrous protein, in some of which the protein elastin, which gives the skin its elasticity, is present. The spaces between the bundles are thought to be filled with a watery substance. This upper layer is known as the *papillary layer* because its surface area is greatly increased by *papillae*, small, finger-like projections similar to the villi in the small intestine. Since the layers of the epidermis are built on top of these projections, the outer layer is structured in a series of hollows surrounded by ridges, known as the *epidermal* ridges, which change the outer appearance of the skin. These are what provide the easily recognizable differences between individuals in the patterns called fingerprints.

Dennis Stock/Magnum

John Watney

Above: The skin has to withstand a lifetime of wear and tear not least of which is the process of ageing. Although the epidermal, the outer, layers are constantly being shed and replaced from the inner dermis, the dermis itself gradually deteriorates. By the early 50s, the absence of the hormone oestrogen reduces the skin's bloom; elastin, the protein which gives the skin its elasticity, wastes away by the age of 60, and by the age of 70, the activity of the sweat glands is considerably reduced, probably due to the narrowing of the blood vessels. But despite these changes the skin retains its marks of individuality.

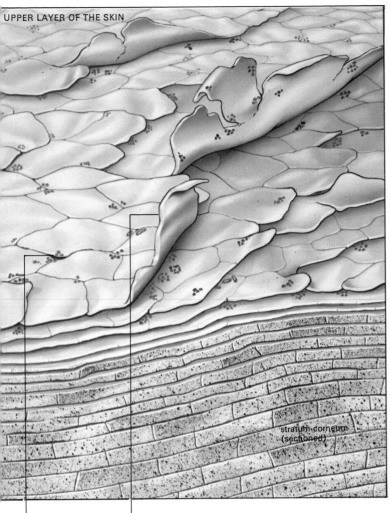

UPPER LAYER OF THE SKIN

stratum corneum
(sectioned)

bacteria
living on
the surface

flat dead cells
containing keratin,
continually
peel off

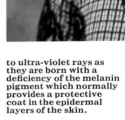

Below left: Fingerprints, the most distinctive characteristics of the skin, are formed by layers of cells built on tiny projections called papillae. The outermost layer is structured in a series of hollows and ridges, which are profusely covered with sweat, leaving impressions on all objects they touch.

Above: Diagram to illustrate a section of the epidermis, the outer layer of the skin. The constant shedding of dead cells allows bacteria to penetrate under the surface where they feed off the oily sebum secreted by the sebaceous glands.

Above right: Albinos are extremely sensitive to ultra-violet rays as they are born with a deficiency of the melanin pigment which normally provides a protective coat in the epidermal layers of the skin.

Below: Skin section stained to show blood vessel supply (pink) and the elastic fibres (red) in the two layers of the dermis.

Communication and protection

Capillary blood vessels loop in and out of the papillae. Together with the arterial supply and venous drainage network, they provide a certain amount of control over heat loss and retention by altering the flow of blood to the skin. They also facilitate the healing process by ensuring a prompt supply of nourishment since the blood transports a variety of nutrients: fatty acids, glucose, amino-acids and various types of salts. There are some nerve endings present in this layer which are receptive to touch (Meissner's corpuscles), pressure (Pacinian corpuscles) pain and temperature. They communicate the presence of potential danger in hot, cold, heavy or sharp objects, by transmitting signals to the brain via the spinal nerves. The muscles are then directed, via the transmission of impulses from the brain, to remove the endangered body area—a hand from extremely hot water, for example—instantly.

Below the papillary layer of the dermis lies the *reticular region*. This also contains collagenous and elastic fibres and blood vessels, but the spaces in between the bundles are occupied by the accessory organs: sweat glands, hair follicles and sebaceous glands. The reticular region is joined to the skeleton and muscles by the *subcutaneous layer*, throughout which fat cells, collected together to form *adipose tissue*, provide a cushioning layer. The adipose tissue not only acts as an emergency fuel store, but insulates the body from the cold by preventing heat loss.

Further protection is provided by the *sebum*, an oily substance secreted by the *sebaceous glands*. The sebum constantly flows along the ducts which connect it

Dumas/Fotogram

John Watney

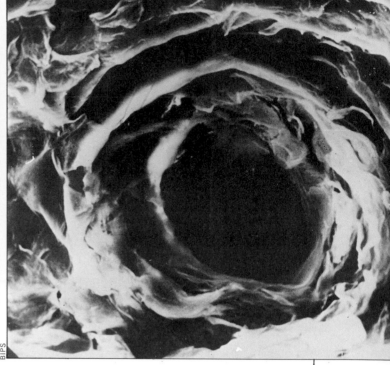

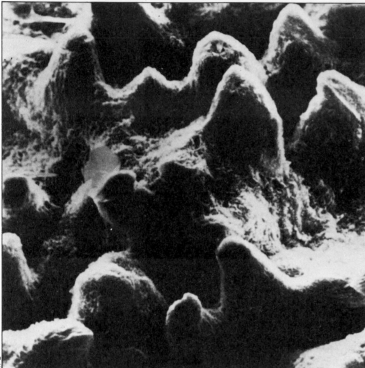

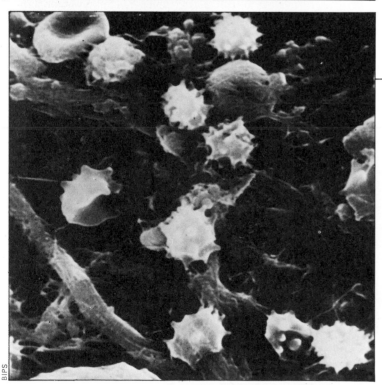

Above: A sweat pore magnified x 150. Sweat glands develop in the embryo as tubular downgrowths of the epidermis, ending in a spiral in the dermis from which the sweat is actually produced. Millions of these ducts open out as pores on the surface of the skin— they are more numerous in some areas: the palms, for example, have 350 per sq cm, while the backs of the hands have 200. Sweat glands can pour out as much as 1,500 millilitres of sweat in an hour which can enable the body to lose nearly 1,000 calories of body heat.

A SECTION THROUGH THE SKIN

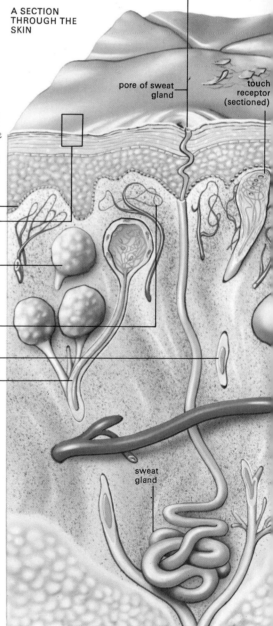

pore of sweat gland

touch receptor (sectioned)

see enlarged section (on previous page)

cold receptor (external view)

nerve fibres

sweat gland

Top left: Electron-micrograph of the outer layer of skin magnified x 90. It shows the epidermal ridges, or fingerprints, formed by the papillary projections in the upper region of the dermis.

Above left: Electron-micrograph of papillae, tiny projections in the outermost layer of the dermis which gives the outer layer its uneven, ridged surface.

Left: An electron-micrograph of the dermis, the inner layer of the skin, magnified x 2,200. It shows the disc-like red blood cells, the spiky platelets which form to seal damaged areas, and the collagen (connective fibres) in the background.

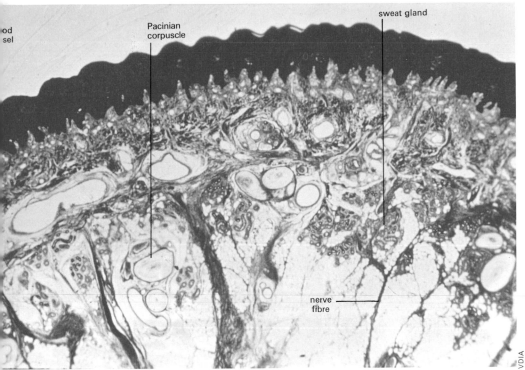

Pacinian corpuscle

sweat gland

od sel

nerve fibre

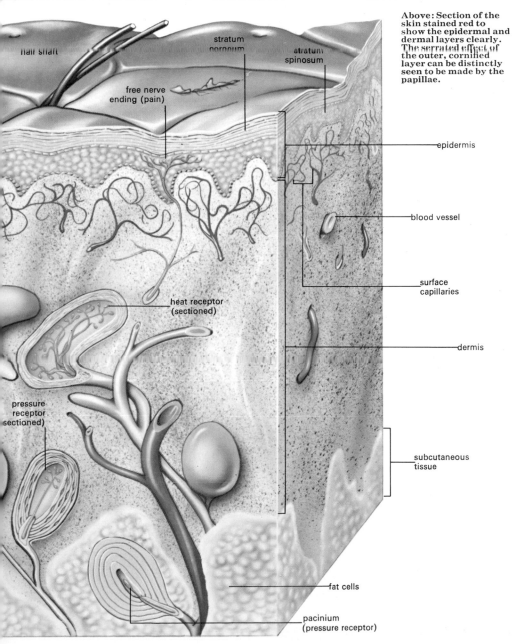

hair shaft

stratum corneum

stratum spinosum

free nerve ending (pain)

Above: Section of the skin stained red to show the epidermal and dermal layers clearly. The serrated effect of the outer, cornified layer can be distinctly seen to be made by the papillae.

epidermis

blood vessel

surface capillaries

heat receptor (sectioned)

dermis

pressure receptor (sectioned)

subcutaneous tissue

fat cells

pacinium (pressure receptor)

with the dip in the epidermis known as the *follicle* (little bag) in which each hair is rooted. Sebum is described as a *holocrine* type of secretion as the cells of the gland itself are broken down and form part of the secretion. After lubricating the hair in the follicle, the sebum flows over the skin surface, mixing with the outer keratin layers and so helping to protect against physical damage. The sebum also provides the first line of defence against invasion by bacteria as it is slightly antiseptic.

The secretion of sebum is particularly important in tropical climates where the surface layer is constantly being dried out and rubbed off. Without this slightly greasy protective lubricant, the skin would not be able to withstand daily wear and tear and the natural moisture of the skin would be lost, constantly endangering the body through dehydration.

Temperature regulation

The reticular region of the skin also contains the sweat glands which are vital to the regulation of body temperature. Unlike the sebaceous glands, the sweat glands are true or *eccrine* glands since the secreting cells do not form part of the secretion. The clear watery fluid known as sweat is produced by the cells lining the lower portion of a coiled tube embedded in the dermis. It flows along a straight duct which becomes spiralled (to control the amount of secretion) as it penetrates the epidermis before opening into a pore on the surface of the skin. Sweating enables the body to lose excess heat as the moisture evaporates into the atmosphere. Sweat glands are distributed throughout the body, particularly on the soles of the feet and palms, in the armpits and on the forehead. Another set of glands, the *apocrine glands*, similar to the sweat glands, are also present in the dermal layer. They are only found, however, in special sites related to the sexual areas—on the pubis, around the genitalia, in the axillae (armpits) and around the nipples. Like the sebaceous glands, the apocrine gland pours its secretion into the hair follicle rather than directly onto the surface of the skin.

The feedback system

Control of body temperature is very finely balanced in all warm-blooded mammals. This remarkable ability to maintain the internal environment of the human body at a constant 37°C (98.6°F) relies on a complex and delicate feedback system involving skin receptors, nerves, control centres in the brain and sweat glands.

A rise in external temperature is sensed by the specialized nerve endings in the skin, which relay the message to the hypothalamus, the temperature-regulating area of the brain. The brain sends nerve impulses to the sweat glands stimulating them to release sweat until the skin receptors detect that the skin temperature has returned to normal. They inform the brain accordingly and it ceases its messages to the sweat glands.

These adjustments to changes in the outer environment could not be made without the specialized organ we know of as skin. Without its protection we could not survive dehydration, abrasion or bacterial invasion encountered in daily activities in temperate climates, let alone survive the extreme conditions of desert or arctic regions.

269

Hair and Nails

Both our hair and our nails are essentially waste products. They are made by specialized cells but, because of our evolutionary development, they are no longer needed to carry out specialized tasks. Our nails were once used as claws and were particularly useful in grubbing for food. The function of the luxurious covering of hair possessed by our ancestors was to trap tiny pockets of warm air around the body, thereby conserving heat.

Although we have now discarded this thick coat of hair, it still grows strongly in one or two places, notably on the head, under the armpits and around the genital areas. Most of the human body is, in fact, still covered with hair, although it is mainly very fine. The only parts which are now entirely hairless are the lips, the nipples, the palms of the hands, the fingers from the second joint to the tip, the penis, and the soles of the feet.

Despite its decrease, the hair does still perform some useful functions. For instance, it protects the head from the harmful effects of the sun's rays. Certain brain proteins are particularly susceptible to heat and excessive exposure to the sun will affect the brain and cause sunstroke. The even, wool-like growth of hair covering the heads of African people is especially effective in this respect. In addition, the hair of the brows and lashes protects the eyes, and hair in the nostrils and the external ear filters out large dust particles to stop them entering the body.

One protective, but now ineffectual, device is still retained from the days when thick hair covered the human body. It can be compared with a parallel reaction in animals. In response to cold, the fur of animals puffs out, creating a thicker, more insulating layer; this also occurs in response to fright, as can be seen when a cat's fur stands on end. (The intention is presumably to make the animal, in a confrontation, look larger and more terrifying.)

In humans, under the stresses of cold or fright, the arrectores pilorum muscles lying near the surface of the skin, can tighten the skin and pull the hairs into a vertical position. This results in goose-flesh because of elevations of the skin around each hair.

The first growth of hair occurs while a baby is still in the womb and is a down-like covering of very fine hair called *lanugo*. By the time the baby is born, this has usually disappeared, although it may sometimes be seen in premature babies. Lanugo is replaced by stronger, though still soft, hair called *vellus* which normally has no colouring pigment and seldom grows much longer than 2.5 centimetres (1 inch). This then gradually begins to thicken and coarsen into the type of hair which will last through adult life, and it is at this stage that the hair takes on its true colour.

All hair growth does not, however, begin before and at birth, and later growth is largely associated with sexual development. At puberty, major changes in the sex hormones in both males and females stimulate the growth of hair under the armpits (*axillary hair*) and around the genital areas (*pubic hair*). In the later teens, males also begin to grow hair along

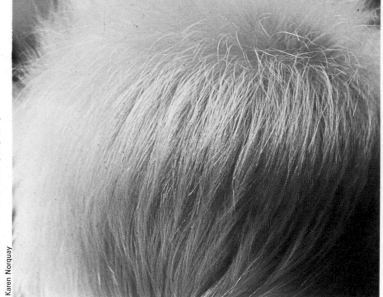

Karen Norquay

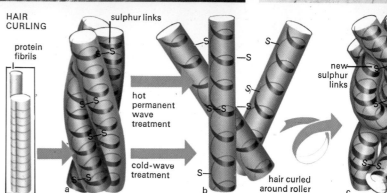

Above: The fine hair of an infant. Hair is essentially a waste product which in later life may serve the purpose of sexual attraction as much as any practical function like conserving heat.

Right: Hair is made up of twisting protein chains coiled round each other and linked together. *Denaturation*, by permanent waving, destroys the structure of the protein chains in hair. (A) shows normal coiled protein fibrils; (B) fibrils separated; (C) fibrils recoiled.

HAIR CURLING — protein fibrils — sulphur links — hot permanent wave treatment — cold-wave treatment — new sulphur links — hair curled around roller — a — b — c

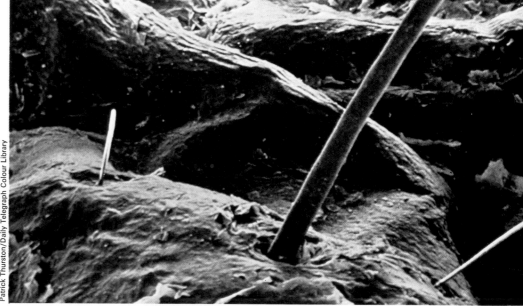

Patrick Thurston/Daily Telegraph Colour Library

Above: A magnification of a hair in a man's beard. Beard growth is a sexual characteristic, and scientific tests suggest that sexual activity, anxiety and mental fatigue may accelerate such growth.

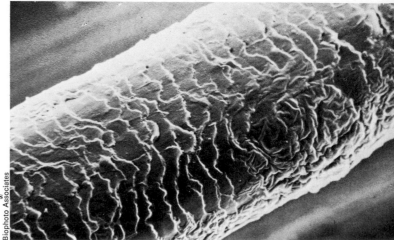

Biophoto Associates

Right: Each hair is covered with overlapping scales of keratin. Our reptilian ancestors adapted the keratin in the epidermis to form a protective coating of scales, and the scale has continued in specialized form on birds' legs and in the human nail. The hair of mammals and the feathers of birds also developed the scale, making it looser and so more able to trap warm air round the body and insulate it.

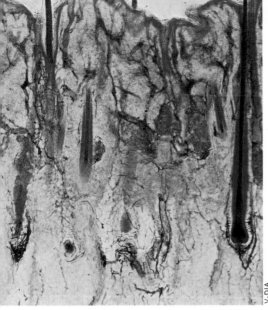

Left: A cross-section of the skin, showing hairs growing out of the follicles embedded in the dermis. See diagram below.

Right: The picture shows a broken hair, which can result both from over-washing and from over-brushing. Too frequent washing removes the film of sebum, the oily secretion from the sebaceous gland, which lubricates each hair and keeps it from drying out and becoming brittle. While occasional brushing is beneficial to stop the hair becoming matted, too vigorous brushing can knock the keratin scales off the hair, which will then split or break more easily, leaving the hair vulnerable to invasion by bacteria.

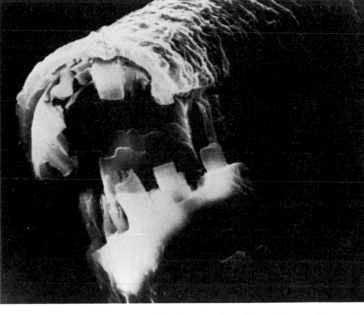

IR IN THE SKIN

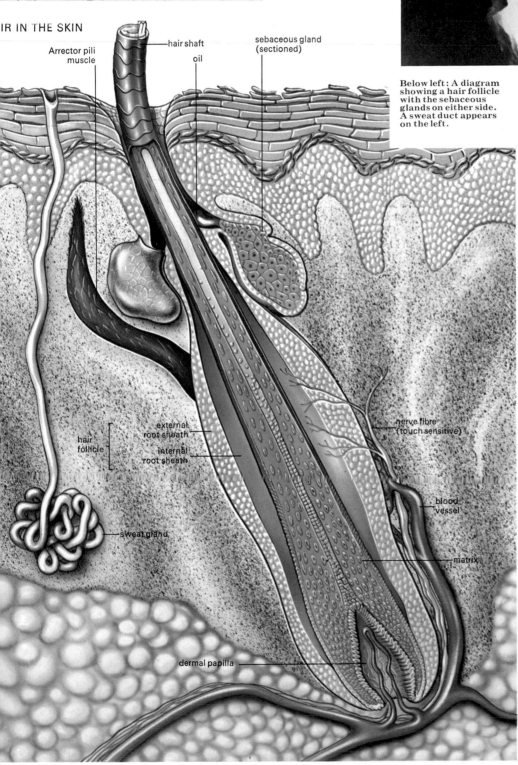

Arrector pili muscle

hair shaft

oil

sebaceous gland (sectioned)

Below left: A diagram showing a hair follicle with the sebaceous glands on either side. A sweat duct appears on the left.

hair follicle

external root sheath

internal root sheath

nerve fibre (touch sensitive)

blood vessel

sweat gland

matrix

dermal papilla

the cheeks, under the chin and on the upper lip, and also to develop longer hairs on the chest and shoulders. Since these features do not serve any vital purpose (although hair around the mouth may provide some protection for it), they are generally classified as secondary sexual characteristics, which distinguish the male from the female.

Hair growth

Each of us possesses between 100,000 to 200,000 hairs on our heads, which grow at the rate of about 1.25 centimetres ($\frac{1}{2}$ inch) a month. All hair grows out of the *hair follicles*, specialized pockets in the skin. These are actually cells from the upper skin layer—the epidermis—which have penetrated back into the lower layer, the dermis. The number and distribution of the follicles, and therefore the thickness of the hair, is a matter of heredity, being determined by our genes. All the follicles are established when in the womb, between the second and fifth months of pregnancy. Hair colour is genetically determined too, although a child does not necessarily inherit the hair colour of its parents: it could be a throwback from several generations.

One further aspect of hair is also determined by heredity: whether it will be curly, wavy or straight. This depends on the cross sectional shape of the hair which is in turn dependent on the cross section of the follicle. Round hairs grow straight while oval or flattened follicles produce curly or wavy hair. There are broad differences in follicle shape between ethnic groups. Races such as the Chinese, the Mongolians and the North American Indians tend to have coarse, straight hair almost circular in cross section, and almost always black in colour. Most of the negroid races have short, crisp wool-like hair with an elliptical or kidney-shaped cross section, again invariably black. European hair tends to be silkier and to be wavy or curly, due to its oval cross-section, and although fair colours predominate there is a wide variety from light blonde through flaming red to deepest black.

The structure of hair

Hair is composed of a number of parts. The lower end of each follicle is enlarged

271

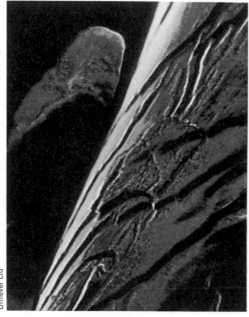

Above: A hair magnified and colour-coded according to brightness—light areas are shown as orange and dark areas as dark green and black—so that contours and dimensions can be more readily seen. The cuticle cells are shown as black criss-crossed lines and a particle of skin is attached to the left of the hair.

Below: A human hair with nits—the eggs of a louse. Several species of these insects are parasitic to man and they can infest either the head, the body or the pubic hair. In the past lice were wrongly associated with a lack of hygiene, but it is now known that they can also affect those who are very clean.

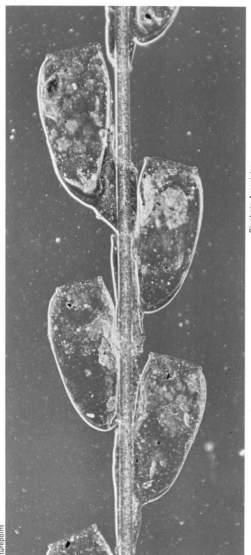

to form a bulbous shape which holds the *papilla*, a section of loose connective tissue. The papilla is richly supplied with dendrites, branch-like nerve endings, and with blood vessels which nourish the growing hair. The hair itself is actually formed by the division of cells in the *matrix*, a region of cells around the papilla. The basic material of which hair is comprised is a tough protein called *keratin*, produced in the fluid layer of the epidermis from a granular substance called keratohyaline. The centre of most hairs is hollow although some have a central pith of softer cells. The outer surface is covered with overlapping scales of keratin.

From the matrix, the hair moves as a shaft towards the skin's surface. Curiously, when it begins to grow it moves downwards in the follicle but after a few days the confined space forces it upwards. By the time the hair reaches the surface of the skin the cells comprising it are dead.

Hair does not grow continuously out of

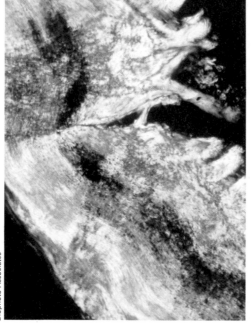

Above: Section of a human nail, viewed with a polarized light technique, in which all the light waves are vibrating at the same frequency so giving a prism effect under the electron-microscope. It shows the only layer of living cells which forms the quick or nail-bed.

Below: Diagram showing the layers which make up the nail.

SECTIONED FINGER TO SHOW THE NAIL

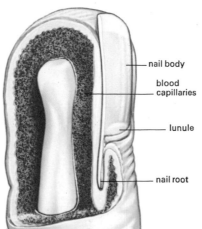

- nail body
- blood capillaries
- lunule
- nail root

each follicle: there is a distinct pattern of activity. First, there is the active phase with the hair steadily pushing itself out of the follicle, which usually lasts for between two and four years. Then there is a period of withering, lasting a few weeks, after which the hair falls out. The follicle may then be dormant for three or four months before hair growth begins again. As each hair has its own life cycle, independent of its neighbours, hair is actually being shed all the time, at an average daily rate of between 40 and 100 hairs. Similarly, some hairs are always being replaced, so, in general, the thickness of the hair remains fairly constant.

The rate at which hair grows varies from person to person, as it does from one part of the body to another. The average rate for hair on the head is about 15 centimetres (six inches) a year, and since the active period is usually only up to four years it is difficult for the average person to grow tresses more than a few feet long.

Both skin and hair are kept supple by a substance known as *sebum*, a mixture of fats, cholesterol, proteins, and inorganic salts. Sebum is secreted by the sebaceous (grease) glands, which lie at the side of each follicle, and are connected to the latter by short ducts. The glands vary in size and shape in different parts of the body, and are absent in the palms of the hands and the soles of the feet.

Hair loss

Just as increased growth of hair in adolescence is more a male concern, so loss of hair is also predominantly a male problem. Women rarely go bald. Some thinning of the hair may occur after the menopause, however, and excessive hair loss may also be experienced after giving birth. During pregnancy, changes in hormone levels cause the hair to grow luxuriantly, but after the birth the follicles become dormant and hair loss reaches as much as tens of thousands of hairs per week. Within six months, however, the follicles regain their rhythm.

Baldness in men is dependent both on a hereditary predisposition in each man, and on an overproduction of *androgens*, the group of male sex hormones.

Alopecia areata is a form of nervous illness characterized by sudden loss of hair in patches. In *alopecia universalis* all body hair is lost and in *alopecia totalis* all hair on the head including eyelashes and eyebrows.

The nails

Like the hair, the nails are made of keratin and are simply adaptations of the skin's outer layer. They consist of four parts. The first is the outermost layer of the epidermis which protrudes a short way above the nail and is known as the scarf nail or the cuticle. The nails themselves are formed by a specially thickened and so more protective layer of keratin, which exists only in those parts of the body where pressure and friction is greatest, such as the soles of the feet.

Below the nails lies a white granular layer made up of a different cell. It ends abruptly just above the point where the nail emerges, and can be seen in the white, semi-circular section at the base of each nail, known as the lunule or half-moon. Finally a layer composed, unlike the others, of living cells forms the nail bed or quick of the nail. It takes about six months for the nail to grow out from its base to the fingertip.

Unilever Ltd

Biophoto Associates

Picturepoint

PART 2
SCIENCE
AND
TECHNOLOGY

MATTER
AND
ENERGY

Atoms and Molecules

Everyone nowadays has at least a vague idea of the atomic theory of matter. The theory gives a picture of all matter as being composed of basic building blocks, the 92 different sorts of naturally-occurring atoms corresponding to the 92 different naturally-occurring chemical elements. In addition, there are over a dozen man-made elements.

At the centre of each atom is a tiny *nucleus*, very heavy and positively charged, which is made up of particles called *protons* and *neutrons*. The nucleus is surrounded by a cloud of much smaller particles, the negatively charged *electrons*.

The 92 natural elements have from one to 92 protons in the nucleus and these protons carry its positive electric charge. But while the number of electrons surrounding the nucleus corresponds to the number of protons, the number of neutrons can vary. These particles carry zero electric charge (although of approximately the same mass as a proton). The protons attract the electrons because they have opposite electric charges, as unlike charges attract each other whereas like charges repel each other. Overall, each atom is electrically neutral, as the positive charges in the nucleus are balanced by the negative charges of the electrons.

The difference between an atom of one element and an atom of another lies simply in the numbers of protons, neutrons and electrons they each contain. For example, an atom of helium has two protons, two neutrons and two electrons, while a carbon atom has six protons, six neutrons and six electrons. The particles are exactly the same in each case, it is only the numbers that are different.

Atoms can combine together to form *molecules*, such as the two-atom gas molecules of hydrogen (H_2) and oxygen (O_2) and the three-atom molecule of water (H_2O). Molecules may be much bigger than this however, and some which occur in living or organic substances contain thousands of atoms.

An atomic theory of matter had been conceived by early Greek philosophers, notably Democritus (about 420BC) and Epicurus (about 300BC). This atomic theory was not accepted by many other important philosophers, however, and Aristotle (384-322BC) rejected Democritus' theory in favour of the view that all matter was composed of different combinations of the 'four elements'—earth, water, air and fire.

This concept displaced the atomic theories and formed the basis of alchemy, the study of matter that dominated science up until the seventeenth century. Alchemy was widely practised in Arabia, China and Renaissance Europe, and two of its main objectives were to find a way of turning a base metal, such as lead, into gold and to find a 'elixir of life'.

Alchemy was supported by religious leaders of the time, whereas atomic theories with their implied atheism were suppressed by Jewish and Christian teachers. Many earlier texts survived, however, including the *De rerum natura*

Drawn & Etch'd by J. Stephenson.

Mary Evans

Above: An atomic model of a crystal of common salt, sodium chloride. The shape and the physical properties of a crystal are determined by the forces which bind the atoms together, forces which include ionic and covalent bonds, the metallic bond and the van der Waal's forces. The ionic bond is the electrical attraction between charged atoms and the covalent bond involves pairs of atoms sharing electrons. The metallic bond occurs in crystals of metals, where the positive metal ions are neutralized by a cloud of electrons which move freely throughout the lattice. This arrangement gives metals their characteristic physical properties, including their ability to conduct electricity. Van der Waal's forces are weak bonds caused by momentary disturbances in the electron clouds within the lattice.

Right: There are a large number of crystal shapes, which arise from the way in which the atoms are grouped together. This hexagonal shape is a model of a zinc crystal.

Above: John Dalton, the English philosopher who devised the first scientific theory of the atomic structure of matter. He was born at Eaglesfield, Cumberland, in September 1766, and by the age of 12 he was teaching at his local school. He had a life-long interest in meteorology, and kept a daily record of the local weather from his early childhood to his death in July 1844. This interest in the weather led him to study the atmosphere and subsequently the nature of gases and their properties. Through his experiments with gases, he arrived at the conclusions which formed the basis of his atomic theory. When he died over 40,000 people filed past his coffin.

Below: A molecule of nucleic acid, a heavy, complex organic acid which combines with a protein to form a nucleoprotein, an important part of the nucleus of a living cell. The helical bands represent chains of a compound called a nucleotide, and carry four other compounds, adenine (A), thymine (T), cytosine (C) and guanine (G). Bonding between T and A and between C and G holds the chains together.

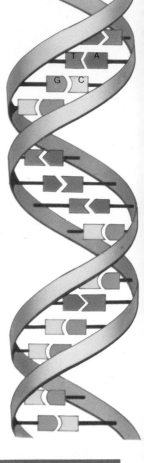

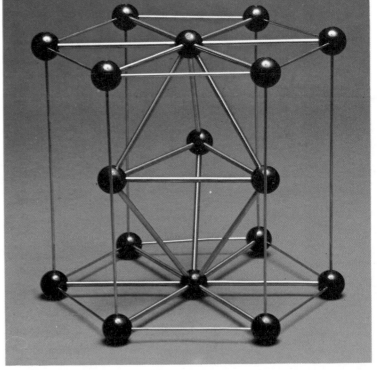

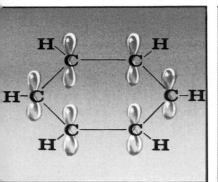

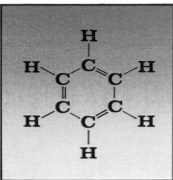

Tear shaped electron orbits of carbon atoms

Alternate single and double bonds between carbon atoms

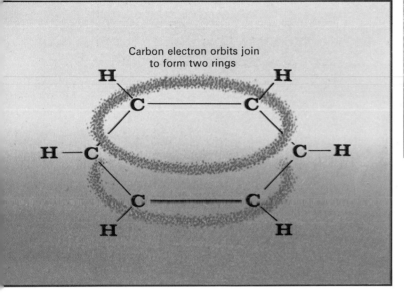

Carbon electron orbits join to form two rings

Messer, Griesheim

Left: The structure of benzene (C_6H_6) was a mystery for over a century, because its chemical properties were not consistent with its presumed structure of single bonds linking the hydrogen atoms to the carbon atoms, and alternate single and double bonds linking the ring or carbon atoms. The explanation was that some of the shared electrons travel in tear-drop shaped orbitals at right angles to the carbon atoms and, because these atoms are so close together, these orbitals overlap to form ring-shaped orbitals above and below the carbon ring. Benzene is used in making aspirin, aniline dyes, and some types of plastic.

Above: This sheet of clear plastic was charged up by bombarding it with electrons. When it was discharged at one edge, the departing electrons created this pattern in it.

Below: This cutting torch uses a stream of plasma (ionized gas) carrying a current of about 250 Amps.

('On the Nature of Things') written in the first century BC by the Roman poet Lucretius. In the first half of this six-volume poem, Lucretius described and defended the theories of Epicurus, and it was used as a source of reference by several seventeenth and eighteenth century philosophers.

At the beginning of the nineteenth century, John Dalton (1766-1844) produced the first atomic theory to be backed up by experimental evidence. Following on from the work of A. L. Lavoisier and J. L. Proust, Dalton investigated the way that elements forming chemical compounds combine in definite proportions by weight. He was then able to work out the relative weights of the atoms of various elements, including hydrogen, oxygen, nitrogen and sulphur.

For example, he calculated that when hydrogen and oxygen combine to form water they do so in the ratio, by weight, of one part hydrogen to seven parts of oxygen (it is actually eight parts of oxygen, Dalton's analysis was slightly incorrect). From this he deduced that an oxygen atom was seven times heavier than a hydrogen atom, because he assumed that a water molecule contained only one atom of each. In fact, a water molecule contains two hydrogen atoms and one oxygen atom, and oxygen is about sixteen times heavier than hydrogen.

Despite these errors, however, the theory formed the basis for a serious scientific study of the atomic structure of elements, and during the nineteenth century scientists were able to identify about 90 (out of 92 naturally-occurring) different sorts of atom.

Inside the atom

Investigations of the structure of atoms themselves began in the late nineteenth century. The crucial experiments involved investigation of the nature of the 'matter' taking part in electrical discharges in sealed tubes not unlike fluorescent lighting tubes.

Before 1890, rays streaming from the negative electrode or *cathode* of such tubes had been observed and were named *cathode rays*. The physicist J. J. Thomson (1856-1940) showed that the rays, when subjected to magnetic or electrostatic fields behaved exactly as negatively charged particles would be expected to.

These electrons, as the cathode rays were renamed, were assumed to be constituents of atoms. However, because it was difficult to separately measure either their electric charge or their mass, no-one knew how they fitted into the atom or how important they were.

Thomson proposed a model of the atom, the 'plum pudding atom', consisting of a not very massive sphere of positive charge in which thousands of plum-like electrons rotated in rings. This model needed a very large number of electrons in the atom because it was thought that they accounted for most of the atom's mass.

New experiments soon made Thomson's model unrealistic. When positively charged *alpha particles* (each comprising two protons and two neutrons) were directed on to thin films of atoms, a significant number bounced backwards. This could not have happened if Thomson's model had been correct; the positively charged 'pudding' would not have been able to repel the particles because it

Paul Brierley

was too light. Additionally its positive charge would have been neutralized by the electrons and so would not have repelled the positively charged particles.

Ernest Rutherford (1871-1937) proposed a different model which explained the backward scattering, and this model has been the basis of our understanding ever since. If the positive charge in the atom is heavy and concentrated, not light and diffused as in the Thomson model, then the experimental results can be explained. Rutherford's atom consists of a small (10^{-13}cm) heavy nucleus with a positive charge, surrounded by a diffuse cloud (10^{-8}cm) of light electrons.

It is tempting to visualize Rutherford's atom as a miniature solar system, with the nucleus as the sun and the electrons as the planets. In place of gravity, the attraction between the oppositely charged nucleus and electrons would hold the atoms together. But, according to the old laws of electromagnetism, even this picture would have been impossible. If the electrons revolved around the nucleus they would radiate electromagnetic waves, lose energy and spiral into the centre, attracted to the nucleus by its positive charge. According to the old laws, the atom could not be stable.

An excellent, though temporary, solution to the problem was provided by Niels Bohr (1885-1962). Instead of radiating continuously and spiralling in to the centre the electron, according to Bohr, could travel only on certain discrete closed orbits. The electron would radiate but it would do so suddenly, and at the same time jump between one orbit and another of lower energy (as if the Earth suddenly jumped into Venus' orbit).

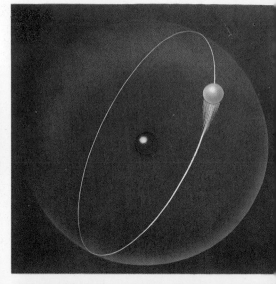

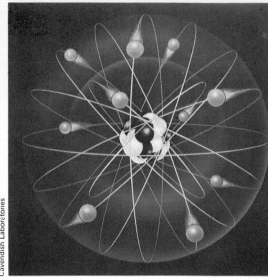

Cavendish Laboratories

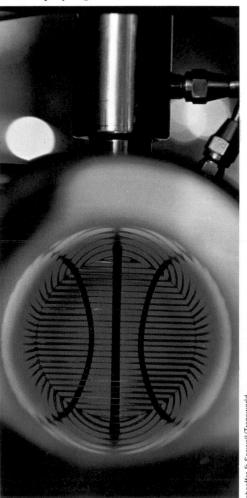

Above: Sir Ernest Rutherford, Lord Rutherford of Nelson (right), the founder of nuclear physics. He was born near Nelson, New Zealand, in 1871 and went to Cambridge University in 1895 to work with J. J. Thomson. He investigated radioactive decay, which led him to the discovery of alpha and beta radiation.

During his experiments with alpha rays he came to the conclusion that the atom had a heavy central nucleus surrounded by electrons. In 1918, at Manchester University, he discovered the proton when he 'split' nitrogen atoms by bombarding their nuclei with alpha particles. Rutherford died in October 1937.

ELECTRON SHELL

O shell (max 23)

P shell (max 10)

nucleus

K shell (max 2)

L shell (max 8)

M shell (max 18)

N shell (max 32)

Above (left to right): The first diagram shows the maximum number of electrons which can occupy electron shells K to P. The second diagram shows hydrogen, which has a single electron which occupies one of the available energy states in the K shell, and the third shows helium, whose two electrons fill its K shell.

Left: Prospecting for uranium using an instrument called a spectrometer, which detects any radiation from the rock which would indicate the presence of uranium ore. Uranium atoms emit alpha particles and thus gradually decay into 'daughter' elements, which in turn decay until they eventually become lead.

Far left: The ripple patterns in the light given off by an electrical discharge depend on the atomic structure of the electrodes between which the discharge occurs. The study of these patterns has helped scientists understand more about the structure of atoms and molecules.

Schaeffer & Seawell/Transworld

UKAE

278

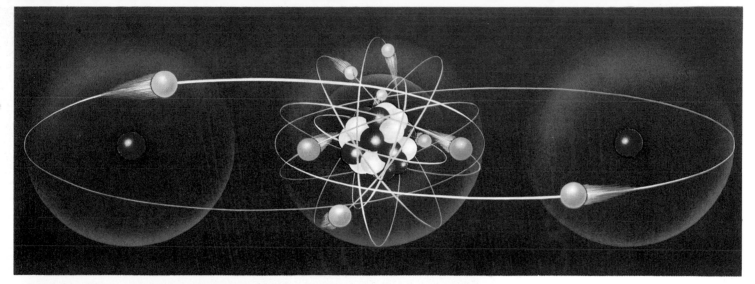

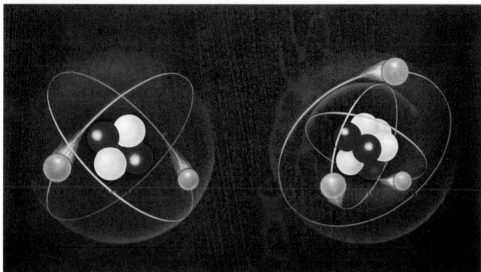

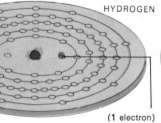

HYDROGEN

(1 electron)

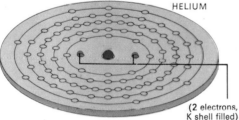

HELIUM

(2 electrons,
K shell filled)

Top, far left: Hydrogen has a single proton in its nucleus, orbited by one electron.

Above: When two hydrogen atoms combine with an oxygen atom to form a molecule of water, the hydrogen atoms share their electrons with the oxygen atom which has two unfilled states in its outermost shell.

Far left: Neon, like helium, is inert because its outer electron shell is filled.

Left: An atom of helium, on the left, has two protons and two neutrons in its nucleus, and two electrons. Lithium-7 (right), an isotope of lithium, has three protons, four neutrons, and three electrons.

Left: The chemical properties of an atom depend on the number of electrons and unfilled energy states in its outermost shell. Helium has its outermost shell filled by its two electrons and so, having no spare electron or energy state which it can share with other atoms, it cannot react or combine with them.

Finally, there was an orbit of minimum energy (like Mercury's orbit), from which the electron would not radiate. Once the electron reached this *ground state* it was stable.

Within a dozen years, the physical results of Bohr's model had been refined and justified by a new physical theory, *quantum mechanics*. Through this, nature was viewed in quite a different way. In the new theory, a particle's position and velocity could not simultaneously be measured with absolute precision (*Heisenberg's uncertainty principle*) and the concept of force, as it had been known, disappeared.

Our present understanding of electron structure in atoms is based on the system of discrete energy levels (like Bohr's orbits) that quantum mechanics allows, together with a new principle discovered in 1924 by Wolfgang Pauli (1900-1958): the *exclusion principle*.

The exclusion principle forbids more than one electron being in any possible 'state' of an atom or molecule. The states are sub-divisions of the energy levels, which surround the nucleus like a series of concentric shells and are known as the K, L, M, N, O, P and Q shells respectively, the K shell being the innermost. In naturally-occurring elements, the maximum numbers of states, and thus electrons, which can exist in these shells are 2, 8, 18, 32, 23, 10 and 2 respectively.

If it were not for the exclusion principle all electrons would fall to the lowest state, the level of minimum energy. The chemical properties of atoms are determined by the electrons in the outermost (highest) energy levels.

Molecular bonds

The way in which chemical behaviour, that is, the formation and properties of molecules, is determined by the electrons in the atom's highest energy levels, can be described in terms of different sorts of molecular bond.

The *ionic bond* occurs when one atom in a two-atom molecule has only one or two electrons in its outermost level, and the other atom has room for one or two more in its outermost level or *electron shell*. The electrons pass from the first atom to the second, so the first atom becomes positively charged because it has lost electrons and the second atom becomes negatively charged because it has gained electrons. These *ions*, as the charged atoms are now called, attract each other with their opposite charges, forming a stable molecule. One example is salt where sodium atoms lose their highest electrons to chloride atoms.

The other simple sort of bond is the *covalent bond*. This occurs when similar atoms form molecules, such as the gas molecules hydrogen (H_2), oxygen (O_2) and nitrogen (N_2). The electrons are shared between the two atoms, being clustered between the two positively charged nuclei and attracting them both.

Isotopes

The amount of positive charge on a nucleus is determined by the number of protons within it. The number of protons in the nucleus is the *atomic number* of the atom, and this is also the number of electrons the atom possesses.

The mass of the nucleus is determined by the number of protons plus the number of neutrons. The mass of a proton is about the same as the mass of a neutron and over 1,800 times the mass of an electron.

The atomic weight of an element should be just the number of protons and neutrons together, but some elements were found to have atomic weights which are not whole numbers. This was an unsolved problem for more than a century until it was realized that although atoms of a given element had a fixed number of protons, the number of neutrons was variable. The different forms were called *isotopes*, and the elements found in nature are mixtures of different isotopes.

The discovery of isotopes ushered in the nuclear age, an age of the study and application of nuclear forces. It was found that nuclei heavier than uranium could be built up and that nuclei could be broken apart. Nuclear bombs have been made, but the question of why the nucleus does not fly apart on its own, as it might be expected to due to the positively-charged protons repelling each other, has not yet been really answered.

But the questions the Victorians asked, 'Are atoms real? Can they be seen?' have been answered. Photographs of atoms taken by electron microscopes and field emission microscopes, in which streams of electrons take the place of the visible light used in optical microscopes, are as real as the pictures on a television set.

Elementary Particles

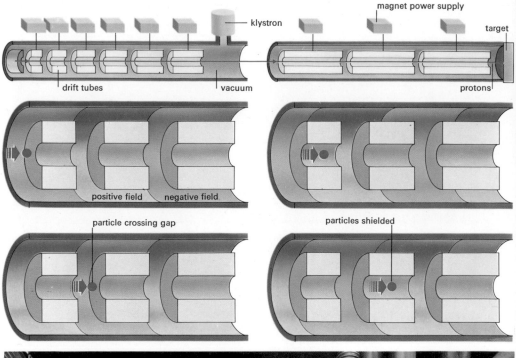

All matter, living or dead, is composed of atoms, which were originally thought to be solid and indivisible. Towards the end of the nineteenth century, however, scientists began to realize that the atoms themselves were made up of even smaller particles. The physicist J. J. Thomson established that electrons were constituents of atoms, then in 1911 Ernest Rutherford proposed the theory that the atom had a central nucleus around which the electrons were grouped.

The idea of the nucleus led to the science of nuclear physics, the study of the nucleus and its components. Rutherford suggested the existence of the proton in 1914 and in 1932 the neutron was discovered by James Chadwick. Particle physics, the study of matter at its deepest, most fundamental level, is an extension of nuclear physics and developed from it almost by accident.

In 1934 the Japanese physicist Hideki Yukawa suggested that the force keeping the protons and neutrons together in the nuclcus was due to a new particle, which came to be called a *meson*.

A systematic search for new particles began and about 30 were discovered during the next two decades, including one with the properties Yukawa had predicted. But the hope that the new particles would provide a detailed explanation of the structure of the nucleus was not completely realized. Emphasis shifted to the problem that seemed more basic, namely, the ways in which the new particles interacted with each other. Experiments designed to investigate this question revealed an embarrassing number of new particles and particle-like phenomena.

Gravity and electromagnetism

Following the discovery of the electron it was possible to think of atoms as being made up of electrically charged particles between which two types of force acted. One force was electromagnetism, due to the electric charges of the particles, and the other was gravity, although its effects were only slight.

The presence of gravitational forces on this scale was in accordance with Sir Isaac Newton's universal law of gravitation. This states that between any two objects in the universe, even such small objects as particles, there is an attractive force proportional to the masses of the objects and inversely proportional to the square of the distance between them.

In this idealization, the particles created smooth, continuous electromagnetic and gravitational *fields* or areas of influence around them. If a particle moved, the fields would change and the forces on other particles would consequently be altered.

Quantum theory

Einstein upset this simple picture of particles and fields. He found a circumstance in which it was more sensible to regard light, one of the forms of electromagnetic radiation, as being composed of a stream of particles rather than being a

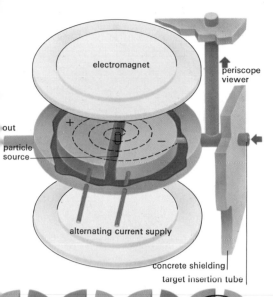

out

particle source

electromagnet

periscope viewer

alternating current supply

concrete shielding

target insertion tube

Left: A cyclotron has a pair of hollow, D-shaped units mounted in a vacuum chamber between the poles of a powerful electromagnet. These units are alternately charged positive and negative, so a particle put into the centre will spiral outwards and accelerate until it reaches the outer edge and hits the target.

Below: The Van de Graaff generator produces a very high voltage by accumulating an enormous amount of electrostatic charge and this voltage can be used in a laboratory to accelerate particles. This picture shows the top of the six million volt generator at the nuclear laboratories at Aldermaston in England.

Above left: In a linear accelerator, particles such as protons are accelerated along a tube by high frequency alternating electric fields supplied by a device called a klystron. A proton is accelerated when there is a negative field ahead of it. As the field is alternating —constantly changing from negative to positive and back—the protons have to be shielded from the positive field so that they are not decelerated by it. They travel through a series of 'drift tubes' which provide this shielding. The timing of the field and the lengths of the tubes are arranged so that the field is negative when the protons cross the gaps between the tubes and positive when they are within the tubes and shielded by them. When the protons hit the nuclei of the target atoms they break them up into particles.

Left: The interior of a linear accelerator.

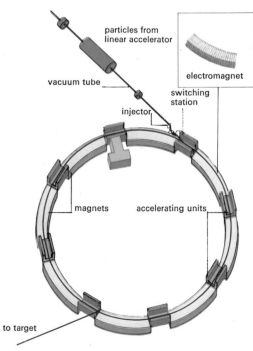

particles from linear accelerator

electromagnet

vacuum tube

switching station

injector

magnets

accelerating units

to target

Left: A 7 GeV proton synchrotron.

Above: A synchrotron is fed with accelerated particles from a linear accelerator and as they travel round the machine they are further accelerated each time they pass one of the accelerating units. When they reach a high enough velocity they are diverted out of the synchrotron to the target. The energy a particle possesses depends on the accelerating voltage. Particle energies are thus expressed in terms of 'electron volts'. For example, the tube of a television is a simple form of accelerator, accelerating electrons with a voltage of about 10,000 V. Thus each electron hits the screen with an energy of 10,000 electron volts or 10keV. Accelerators commonly operate at MeV (mega, or million, electron volt) and GeV (giga, or 1,000 million, electron volt) energy levels.

smooth, continuous field of energy.

The circumstance in question was known as the *photoelectric effect*. It had been discovered that, under certain conditions, light shining on a metal surface caused electrons to be emitted from it. The effect would occur only if the light was towards the blue end of the spectrum. A red light, even if it were intense or left on for a long time, would not cause the emission.

Einstein's explanation was that light was composed of particles called *photons*. The energy of a photon was proportional to the frequency of the light, and so was higher for blue light than for red light because blue light has a higher frequency. The emission of an electron from the metal surface was due to it being struck by a photon. A blue photon had sufficient energy to do this, but a red one did not.

The explanation of the photoelectric effect in terms of discrete bundles or *quanta* of energy carried by photons was in fact the second time such an idea had been used. Five years before, in 1900, Max Planck (1858-1947) had introduced the idea of discrete quanta of energy in his discussion of the spectrum of energy emitted by objects heated to incandescence.

Planck and Einstein forced physicists to accept that the electromagnetic field sometimes behaved like an assembly of particles (the photons) and sometimes like a continuous wave.

Quantum mechanics

In the 1920s, Prince Louis de Broglie suggested that the wave and particle aspects of light had to be considered together, not separately, since the energy of the particle depends on the frequency of the wave. In addition, he proposed that other particles besides the photon could also behave like waves. If this were so, electrons would be expected to exhibit characteristic interference patterns such as occur when two stones are dropped into a pond and the spreading ripples overlap. Three years later precisely such an effect was found.

The next step was taken by Werner Heisenberg, Wolfgang Pauli and Max Born, who developed a form of *quantum mechanics* which gave a complete understanding of the structure of stable atoms. Quantum mechanics predicted stable energy states for electrons in the presence of a positively charged nucleus. With the help of Pauli's exclusion principle, Bohr's theory of the atom was given a firm basis.

Paul Dirac applied the new quantum mechanics to the electromagnetic field and showed how it could be regarded as an assembly of photons. The resolution of the wave-particle paradox was that the intensity of the wave could be regarded as the density of particles in it. In certain situations the density would be so high that the grainy nature of the wave could be overlooked. In other situations, with low density, the fact that there was a wave at all might be neglected.

Almost all physics was explained by quantum mechanics. The structure of the atom and the formation of molecules could be understood, and electromagnetic radiation (such as light, radio waves and X-rays) was emitted and absorbed in accordance with Dirac's theory. All physics and chemistry, for example the formation of crystals and magnets and the action of solvents and adhesives, could be described in terms of particular effects of electromagnetic radiation.

In the stage of understanding reached by 1930, the original two long-range forces ruled all nature: gravity for very large masses on an astronomical scale (its effects being so weak at atomic levels that it could be ignored) and electromagnetism operating everywhere else. By analogy with the concept of the photon as the quantum (or particle) of electromagnetic radiation, many people suppose that the gravitational field is also composed of particles, which are called *gravitons*. As yet, however, there is no experimental evidence for them.

Strong and weak forces

After the discovery of the neutron, and the realization that the nucleus consisted of a collection of positively charged protons and uncharged neutrons, it became clear that a third basic force must exist in nature. This force was necessary to overcome the repulsive forces between the positively charged protons that would tend to push them apart. In addition, this *strong* or *hadronic force* would have to be very attractive and very short range to explain the small size of the nucleus (10^{-13} cm) as opposed to the overall size of the atom (about 10^{-8} cm), and to explain the fact that the nuclei, shielded by the electron clouds, seem to have no effect on one another.

Yukawa suggested that this strong force was transmitted by mesons, the mesons carrying the strong force in the way that photons carry electromagnetism.

There is one further force in nature, the so-called *weak force*. It is not thought responsible for creating any 'bound

Below: A storage ring collects bursts of particles from an accelerator and builds them into two intense beams of particles travelling in opposite directions around the ring. The beams are then fired at each other so that very high energy collisions occur between the particles, and new particles are created by the break-up or combination of the original particles. This diagram shows the rings at the European Centre for Nuclear Research (CERN) near Geneva. Protons from a linear accelerator are further accelerated in a synchrotron then directed into the rings.

Right: Setting up the complex equipment for a particle collision experiment at CERN.

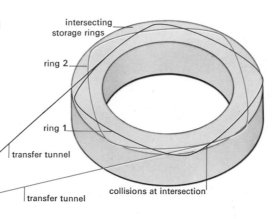

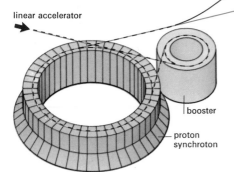

Below: Used to detect and identify particles produced by accelerators, the bubble chamber contains liquid hydrogen kept under pressure by a piston. The particles are fired into the chamber, the pressure is momentarily released and the particles leave a trail of bubbles in the liquid as they pass. The chamber is surrounded by powerful electromagnets; the size and charge of a particle can be found from the curve and the direction of the path it takes under the influence of the magnetic field.

Right: Part of the CERN apparatus. The proton smasher consists of a vast ring of magnets that are used to accelerate particles to great speeds before they are smashed into each other.

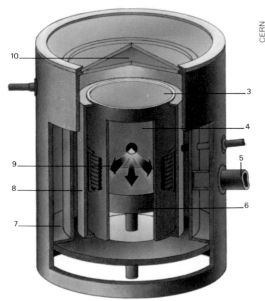

1 Camera
2 Lights
3 Bubble chamber window
4 Liquid hydrogen
5 Pipe to vacuum pump
6 Piston
7 Radiation shield
8 Liquid hydrogen chamber cooling tank
9 Beam of particles
10 Radiation shield window

Right: An aerial view of the proton smasher on the border between Switzerland and France.

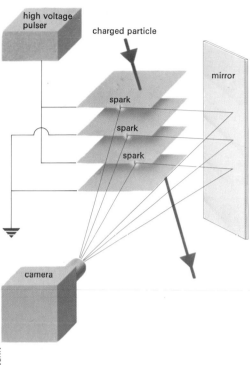

CERN

CERN

Above and above right: In the spark chamber particle detector, a stack of aluminium foil sheets, separated from each other by a gap of about a centimetre, is enclosed in a chamber containing an inert gas such as argon. A high voltage is applied to the plates and any charged particle passing through leaves a track of ionized gas in its wake. The ionized gas is electrically conductive and allows a spark to jump from one plate to the next along the route taken by the particle. The sparks are observed by a film or television camera. The photograph above shows the two mirrors of a spark chamber used at CERN in studying leptons—which include electrons, muons and neutrinos.

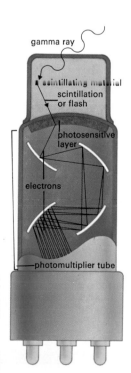

Above and left: The rate at which particles are being produced in an experiment can be measured by a scintillation counter. Some materials, such as certain types of plastic, give off a flash of light when a high-energy charged particle passes through them. The top of the counter, on the right in the photograph, contains a block of one of these scintillating materials. When a particle passes through it, the flash of light is picked up by the photomultiplier tube, a device which converts it into an electrical pulse. This pulse is relayed to a computer which counts and times the pulses. The accuracy is within a thousandth of a millionth of a second.

states' like the solar system, the atom or the nucleus, as gravity, electromagnetism and the strong force do. It is, however, thought to be responsible for the decay of many particles, in particular for the decay of a free neutron into a proton, an electron and a neutrino (a particle with no charge). The weak force is held responsible for all interactions involving neutrinos. A neutrino has so little mass, and such a weak interaction with matter, that only rarely will it disturb it as it passes through.

It is believed that the weak force may be transmitted by a particle called the *intermediate vector boson*, W, which was predicted by Yukawa in 1938.

Antiparticles

Conservation of energy is one of the principles of physics which, it is assumed, is never violated. Energy may change its form—it may reside in the mass of a particle at rest, and then become partly rest mass and partly the kinetic energy of the particle's decay products—but it is never created or destroyed. Energy is thus conserved absolutely.

Another quantity which is conserved absolutely is net electric charge, Q. This is slightly more subtle than energy

conservation, because electric charge can in fact be created or destroyed, but only in pairs of opposite charges. For example, pairing a negative electron with a positive electron produces a zero electric charge, and it is the net charge which never changes.

The positive electron or *positron* is the *antiparticle* of the ordinary negatively charged electron. It has the same mass as an electron, only it is oppositely charged. The electron pairs gave rise to the idea of antiparticles generally and so, when sufficiently powerful particle accelerators became available in the 1950s, there was great interest in whether an antiproton could be created. This was much more difficult than creating the electron pairs because the rest mass energy required is nearly 2,000 times greater.

Particle accelerators are machines which accelerate particles to enormous velocities. These particles then bombard target atoms to break up their nuclei and create new particles. The antiproton was found and it then became possible to conceive of an 'antiworld' made up of antiatoms—antiprotons surrounded by positrons. Such a world meeting ours would annihilate both in a great flash of light.

The existence of the antiproton brought into the open another absolutely conserved quantity, *baryonic charge* B. Like the electric charge, it is conserved net. It allows creation or destruction of proton-antiproton or neutron-antineutron pairs, but forbids their creation in single particles. The baryonic charge of electrons and mesons is zero, and it can be said that protons do not decay into positrons because the baryonic charge would not be conserved. If it were not for the conservation of baryonic charge, atoms would disintegrate into light and a flux of neutrinos.

Isomultiplets and strangeness

The discovery of the mesons and higher mass particles with baryonic charge +1 disclosed two further patterns or symmetries. Every particle had a place in a group called a *charge multiplet* or *isomultiplet*, each group consisting of particles having approximately the same mass but differing electric charges. For example, the proton and neutron form a multiplet. Their masses are nearly the same, but their electric charges are different, being one and zero respectively. Another example are the pi mesons or *pions*, the mesons predicted by Yukawa; their masses are the same but they can have either a positive, negative or zero charge.

The other pattern that was discovered was the operation of yet another kind of charge conservation, but this one was peculiar. The accelerators, by banging protons together, created many more particles. Some of these had a baryonic charge of +1 but were more massive than pions, and these higher mass particles were never produced singly. This suggested that a new sort of charge, which was termed *strangeness*, S, was being conserved. It would be zero for pions and nucleons (protons and neutrons), but possibly different for the heavier particles.

Quarks

Quarks are a class of elementary particle, smaller than *protons* and *neutrons* in an atomic nucleus – they are point masses

Right: The blue glow of Cerenkov radiation in a pool of water containing used fuel rods from a nuclear reactor. This radiation is caused by particles travelling faster through the water than light can. As the particles travel through the water they make its atoms give off this characteristic blue glow.

Above: A bubble chamber photograph showing the spray of mesons given off when a 20 GeV proton beam hit the stationary protons of the hydrogen atoms in the chamber.

Below: A beam of deuterons, each comprising one proton and one neutron, emerging from a cyclotron.

Below: Some of the known particles shown in an imaginary accelerator beam. The lightest particles are at the top; those on the left are positively charged, those in the centre neutral and those on the right are negatively charged. Also shown are a hydrogen atom and its corresponding anti-hydrogen atom.

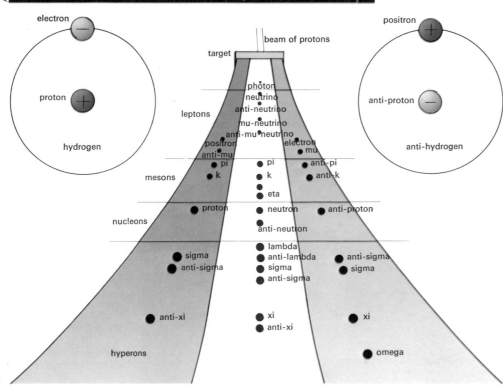

with no internal structure whatsoever. Quarks and *leptons* (a second class of elementary particle) are the building blocks out of which all ordinary matter is ultimately made.

In 1963, Murray Gell-Mann and George Zweig proposed that protons and neutrons were composite particles, each made of three quarks. The beauty of their scheme was that all particles subject to nature's *strong* nuclear force, known as *hadrons*, could also be assembled from quarks. In 1969, another experiment in California showed that six (not three) different types of flavours of quark were needed to build all hadrons – in order of increasing mass, the *up* and *down* quark, the *strange* and *charmed* quark, and the *top* and *bottom* quark – and, seemingly, there was a striking similarity between quarks and leptons (which also came in three pairs).

Supergravity, a theory still in its infancy, boldly asserts that quarks and leptons are different faces of the same subatomic coin. A curious fact about the Universe is that all ordinary matter is made from the two lightest quarks (the up and down) and the two lightest leptons (the electron and its *neutrino*). Quarks are peculiar in having fractional electric charge, but the dominant force between quarks is the strong or 'colour' force. The six quarks carry a colour charge as well of either red, green or blue, but physicists have assigned colours to quarks so that all hadrons are 'colourless'. All quark triplets, collectively known as *baryons,* conform to the same colour code – when quarks stick together in pairs, to form *mesons,* they do so in such a way as to hide their naked colours (an example of a meson would be a blue up-quark combined with an antiblue down-quark). An antiquark is the antimatter counterpart of a quark, a sort of mirror-image particle.

Quarks are influenced by all three forces in nature – the gravitational, electroweak and strong – and each force arises through the exchange of a different kind of 'messenger' particle. The carriers of the strong force are called *gluons* (which provide the 'glue' which binds quarks together). The messenger gluons carry colour charge and so the theory which describes their interaction with quarks is called Quantum Chromodynamics (QCD). The effect of the absorption or emission of gluons is to change the colour of quarks, which are also subject to the electroweak force (when a quark absorbs or emits a weak messenger its flavour is changed). Free or lone quarks do not seem to exist in nature, as gluons bind quarks so tightly inside hadrons that no force in the Universe can break the bonds and free them. The force between quarks, therefore, is very odd, as distance actually makes this force grow stronger – physicists refer to this as quark 'slavery'.

Despite the fact that hundreds of particles have now been discovered, many of them only relatively recently, the answers to the original questions about the nature of energy and forces, and just what exactly the smallest constituents of matter are, have still not yet been fully answered. The new and immensely powerful particle accelerators that are being constantly improved and refined may provide us with some of the answers; but one can safely say that there is still a great deal that remains beyond our understanding in the field of quantum mechanics, which may never be resolved in the lifetime of the current generation of physicists.

Electro-magnetism

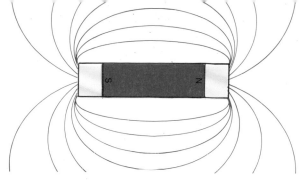

If a permanent magnet attracts a piece of iron or steel, that is a purely *magnetic* action. If a battery sends electric current through a wire so as to heat it, that is an *electric* effect. But wherever an action takes place involving both magnetism and electricity, such action is said to be *electro-magnetic*. There are therefore many manifestations of this phenomenon which was first discovered by the Danish scientist Oersted and greatly enlarged by the subsequent work of the British physicist Michael Faraday in the first part of the 19th century.

One common manifestation of electromagnetism is that a current flowing in a wire produces a magnetic field – this is the operating principle of an electromagnet, and can be harnessed to produce motion in electric motors through the attractive and repulsive forces of magnet fields.

When a magnet (either a permanent magnet or electromagnet) is moved near an electrical conductor, turbulent *eddy currents* are induced in the conductor and it experiences a 'dragging' force. This dragging force can be used to produce motion and, conversely, the eddy currents can be harnessed to produce a useful electric current (such as in alternators and dynamos). This is an example of a moving magnetic field producing an electric current.

A more complex example of electromagnetism is found in devices such as *transformers* where a *changing* magnetic field produces a current. Here, two coils of wire are placed close together. When a changing current (changing in amplitude and/or direction) flows through one coil a changing magnetic field is produced, which induces a voltage in the second coil. If this second coil is included in any kind of electric *circuit* a current flows.

Understanding by analogy
These phenomena are not fully understood.

Below: Michael Faraday was born in September 1791, and after a very basic education he was apprenticed to a London bookbinder. While working there he read an article on electricity in a copy of the *Encyclopaedia Britannica* and this interested him so much that he decided to take up the study of science. In 1812 he went to work for Sir Humphry Davy at the Royal Institution, and this was the beginning of his scientific career. In 1823 he discovered methods of liquifying gases; in 1825 he discovered benzene. His most important work, however, was his study of the relationship between electricity and magnetism.

Ferrofluidio Corp.

Below: The induction coil is a device for producing high voltage pulses. There is a soft iron core, around which is wound a primary coil and a secondary coil. Interrupting the electrical current in the primary coil creates a very high voltage in the secondary which has many more turns of wire wound on it.

Right: The disc dynamo built by Faraday in 1831. The copper disc is rotated with its edge between the poles of the magnet, so that it cuts through the lines of flux. This causes electric currents to be set up within the disc—and the electricity is collected by copper brushes which rub against the disc.

Above: The magnetic field of a bar magnet can be represented by lines of force which form closed loops around it, leaving the magnet at one pole and joining it again at the other. If a magnet is placed under a piece of paper, and iron filings spread on top, the filings will group together along the lines of force.

Below: The Earth's magnetic field may be caused by electric currents, circulating horizontally, within the liquid rock between the core and the crust. These currents may be produced by friction within the planet due to its rotation and they produce a magnetic field at right angles to their plane of rotation.

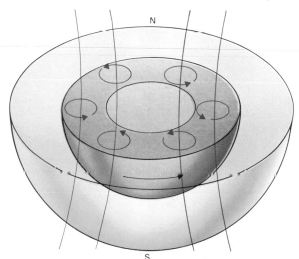

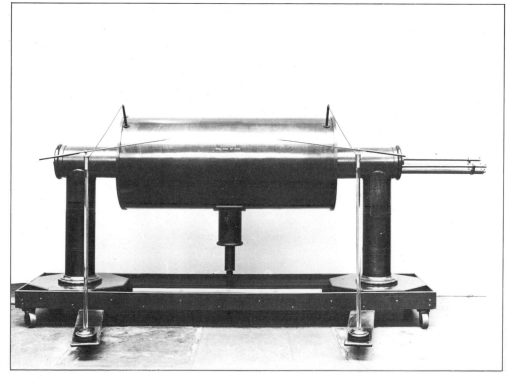

Michael Holford

But in order to exploit them, we devise mental models called *analogues* to help us to obtain at least an appreciation and a hope that through this means we may learn to design better machines by using a phenomenon which is no more understood than is gravitation. It helps to imagine something intangible as something we can see and feel.

For electric circuits we imagine that electrons flow in wires in much the same way that water flows in a pipe. We know that pressure is needed to make water flow so we invent an electrical pressure and call it *electromotive force* (emf) or voltage. The convenience of this analogue is that it allows us to use the equivalent of the frictional resistance in the water pipe which increases in proportion to the length of the pipe but decreases in proportion to its cross-sectional area. Then, by another analogy, we can invent a *magnetic circuit,* in which the driving pressure is called *magnetomotive force* (mmf) and the substance which it drives around the circuit is even less real than the flow of electrons in an electric current. This substance is known as *magnetic flux.*

Many authors and teachers declare that, despite its name, flux does not flow. The fact is that it does not exist, except as a human concept, and the only right or wrong about its flow is to be judged on whether the concept is useful to a particular individual. For some, it is more profitable to think of flux as merely being set up because it represents only *stored* energy, and not a continuous loss of power as is the case when electric current flows in a wire. For others, however, the analogue becomes more profitable if flux is considered to be a more precise analogue of electric current so that

Above and left: These two pictures show the spikes formed on the surface of magnetic fluids (also called ferrofluids) when subjected to a vertical magnetic field. Ferrofluids contain particles of ferrite, a ceramic material made from an iron oxide and small quantities of other metal oxides. The particles are coated with a type of plastic so that they can slide over each other with virtually no friction, and the fluid is made by suspending the particles in water. Because the particles are so small, they do not settle at the bottom of the water and the resulting fluid still has almost the same consistency as water. Despite appearances the spikes are fluid.

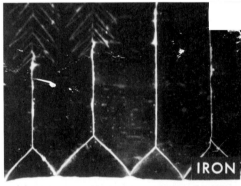

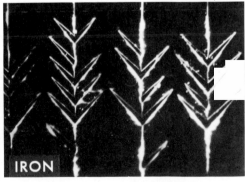

Left: Iron filings spread on top of the windings of a linear electric motor show the nature of its magnetic field. The motor is constructed so that its magnetic field travels along it, and so any metallic object placed on top will be carried along by the moving field while also supported by it.

Top and above: These two pictures show how crystals of iron behave when they are magnetized. The upper picture shows a sample which is not very highly magnetized, and the lower one shows the internal strains created when the magnetization is increased. This causes the crystals to deform as the atoms re-align.

Paul Brierley

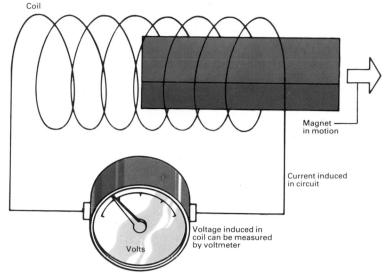

Coil

Current induced
in circuit

Magnet
in motion

Voltage induced in
coil can be measured
by voltmeter

Volts

Left: Moving a magnet
through a coil of wire
induces a current.
Below left: A transformer
consists of two coils
wrapped around a ring of
iron.

Right: Some of the wide
range of resistors used
in electronic circuits.
The resistance of these
devices is utilized to
reduce the current
flowing in a particular
part of a circuit, or to
reduce the voltage level
at a given point in a
circuit. The commonest
types are made of carbon
powder mixed with clay
and resin.

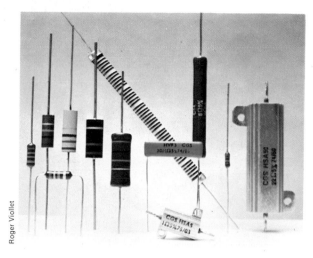

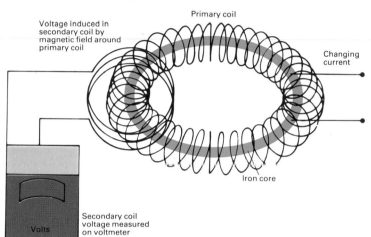

Voltage induced in
secondary coil by
magnetic field around
primary coil

Primary coil

Changing
current

Iron core

Secondary coil
voltage measured
on voltmeter

Volts

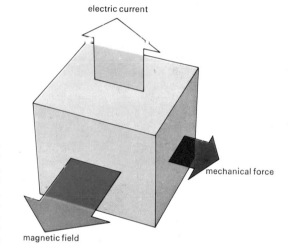

magnetic circuit

electric circuit

electric circuit

Left: This diagram
illustrates the way in
which the electric and
magnetic circuits of a
transformer are
interlinked. The current
in the primary electric
circuit, on the left,
sets up a magnetic
circuit, centre, which
then causes a current
to flow in the secondary
electric circuit on the
right.

Right: In an electro-
magnetic machine,
the forces involved act
at right angles to each
other. In a motor, for
example, the current in
the rotor will set up a
magnetic field at right
angles to its direction
of flow, and the turning
force on the rotor will
be at right angles to
both the current and the
magnetic field.

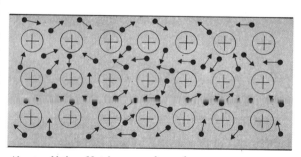

electric current

mechanical force

magnetic field

a magnetic circuit can then be given the
properties which are appropriate to those of
inductance and *capacitance* in an electric
circuit.

Linking electric and magnetic circuits

When discussing electric motors, generators and transformers, it is essential to
note that each machine includes at least
one electric and one magnetic circuit. Since
there is no simple equivalent in magnetic
circuits to the insulating materials of electric circuits, it is usual to design a machine
with only one magnetic circuit but two or
more electric circuits. Indeed, the design of
magnetic circuits has been likened to
attempting to design an electric circuit
which must work when immersed in sea
water so that although most of the energy
flows along the designated paths, an
appreciable proportion will follow other
routes. For the same reason, electric circuits found in machines are usually multi-
turn coils of relatively thin, insulated wire.
Magnetic circuits, on the other hand, are
most likely to be single-turn, short and
fat.

The subject of electromagnetism can
therefore be expressed as the *linking* of
electric and magnetic circuits. In such a
linking the driving pressure from one circuit is seen to be derived from the flow in
the other, and vice versa. For example, in a
transformer an alternating voltage (emf)
across the primary windings produces an
alternating current in the windings. This
produces an alternating mmf in the magnetic circuit, which creates an alternating
flux. The alternating flux induces a high
voltage in the secondary windings, which, if
connected in an electrical circuit, produces
current.

Vector quantities

The commodity we seek to produce in an
electric motor is force which arises as the
result of multiplication of flux by current,
but it is no ordinary multiplication, for the
only quantities of flux and current which
are effective are those which cross each
other at right angles. Quantities which
have both magnitude and direction are
called *vectors*, and when determining the
interactions of vectors with each other the
direction as well as the magnitude must be
taken into account. In the above example,
the force vector is the result of the *vector
multiplication* of the flux and current vectors. Where the flux and current vectors are
not at right angles to each other they must
be resolved into parallel and right-angular
components, but it is always the right-
angular components which produce the
force vector. Furthermore, the force vector
is always at right angles to both the flux
and current vectors.

Vector multiplication and, more generally, vector mathematics is only a form of
shorthand for handling quantities which
have been shown experimentally to interact in this unusual way. This is another
example of an analogue.

Electromagnetic radiation

The principles of electromagnetism are not
limited to electric motor and generator
design. Electromagnetic radiation is the
name given to a variety of phenomena to
which we give different names depending
on the context in which we study them.
Thus gamma rays, X-rays, ultraviolet
radiation, visible light, infrared (heat
radiation) and wireless (radio) waves are
all of the same nature and can all be
expressed in terms of a continuous inter-

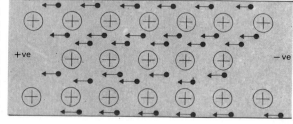

Above and below: Metals
are good conductors of
electricity because of
the way in which
electrons are free to
move around within their
crystalline structures.
When no voltage is
applied to them they
move around at random,

as shown above.
However, applying
voltage makes them drift
towards the positively
charged end, as in the
diagram below. This
electron drift is what
constitutes an electric
current in solid
conducting materials.

+ve   −ve

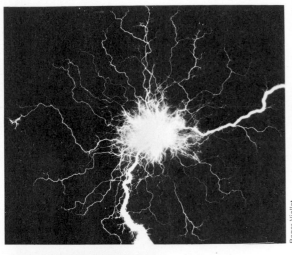

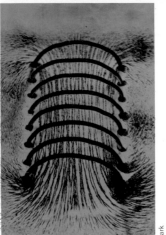

Above: A lightning flash is a very powerful discharge of static electricity. The thundercloud's charge is created by friction, caused by powerful air currents within it. This charge eventually becomes so great that a massive discharge occurs between the cloud and the ground or objects on it, such as trees.

Left: Iron filings show the pattern of the lines of force around a coil carrying a current.

Below: An electromagnet consists of a soft iron bar with a coil wrapped round it. When current flows in the coil, the bar acts like a permanent magnet because of the magnetic field passing through it.

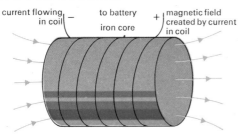

current flowing in coil — to battery + magnetic field created by current in coil
iron core

Below: This diagram represents the inseparable nature of electric and magnetic circuits. The designers of electromagnetic machines aim to make both of these as short as possible, with large cross-sectional areas, to minimize the losses of energy due to resistance and reluctance within the circuits.

electric (copper) circuit

magnetic (iron) circuit

Above: A 'flashover' discharge during the testing of an insulator of the type used in high voltage electricity supply systems. The voltage at the top of the insulator is steadily increased, until it becomes so high that it breaks down the resistance of the air around it and causes a discharge.

change of magnetic and electric energy, each of which pulsates in a plane at right angles to the direction of travel of the radiant waves. All travel at the same speed, about 186,000 miles per second (3×10^8 m/s). The only thing which distinguishes one kind of radiation from another is its wavelength (or frequency). The whole spectrum of radiation extends from very low frequencies which have wavelengths of many miles, to incredibly high frequencies of the order of over 10^{22} Hz (1 Hz = 1 cycle/second) and wavelengths barely measurable at less than a millionth of a millionth of an inch.

The study of electromagnetism is therefore basic to the whole of physics, if not to the whole of science. The Earth receives most of its energy from the Sun by electromagnetic radiation. The average private family house in the UK contains between 30 and 150 electromagnetic devices (although the higher numbers generally occur when there are several children, each of whom has battery-powered toys). Electromagnetism is the basic force behind the operation of radio and television sets, automobile ignition systems, radar, electric systems, electron microscopes, electric motors and generators, telephones and countless other well-known inventions.

Left: The ribbed glass insulators on a 400 kV transmission line. The insulators hold the lines, which are uninsulated themselves, away from the steel tower which is carrying them. The sections of line on either side of the tower are connected by lengths of line which bypass the insulators and the tower arms.

Light and Sound

Much of our awareness of the world around us comes from information received by our eyes and ears. Our eyes respond to visible light, which is one of the many forms of *electromagnetic radiation* (other forms include radio waves and X-rays), and our ears respond to sound or *acoustic radiation*. Electromagnetic and acoustic radiation can both be thought of as travelling in waves. The waves on the sea are the most familiar examples of waves, but light and sound also reveal a wave-like nature when studied closely in the laboratory.

Sound

When we hear a sound it is because the air is vibrating, alternately pushing and pulling our eardrums and forcing them to vibrate. So to make a sound that can be heard by others we must obviously make the air vibrate somehow. This is not difficult; any object that vibrates, such as a drumskin or a vocal cord, pushes and pulls at the air which surrounds it. Every time it moves forward it presses against the air in front and when it recedes again the air has to rush back to fill the partial vacuum thus created. In other words the air in front of the vibrating object (which can be called a *sound source*) is subjected to an alternating pressure.

The air of course is composed of separate molecules, many millions of them in every cubic centimetre, and the molecules next to the source are unhappy at having to suffer the alternations in pressure, so they pass the strain on to their neighbours, who pass it on to their neighbours in turn. In this way the pressure alternations at the source are passed through the air. Every time the source vibrates another cycle of alternating pressure is passed along and the succession of these pressure cycles moving through the air constitutes a sound wave.

Such a wave moves through the air at a fixed speed—the velocity of sound, which in dry air at sea level is about 344 metres/sec (770 mph). Sound waves can travel through almost any gas, liquid or solid but they cannot travel through a vacuum, because in a vacuum there are no molecules to transmit the pressure to their neighbours. In liquids and solids sound waves move faster than in gases like air about 1,400 metres/sec (3,130 mph) in water and 5,000 metres/sec (11,180 mph) in steel.

The number of vibrations made by the source in a second (the number of *cycles* per second) is known as its *frequency*, and since all the molecules affected by

Above: This device, in a Tokyo street, is indicating the sound level in the vicinity. The number it is displaying represents the local sound level in decibels. The formula for decibels is $10 \times \log E_N/E_R$, where E_N is the sound energy present and E_R is the energy of the quietest sound the ear detects.

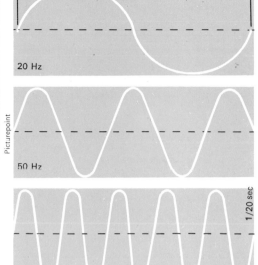

Right: Sound waves can be represented by graphs, with the vertical axis representing the intensity or amplitude of the sound, and the horizontal axis showing seconds. The frequency of the wave is the number of complete cycles per second. One cycle per second is known as 1 Hertz (1 Hz).

1 cycle

20 Hz

50 Hz

100 Hz

1/20 sec

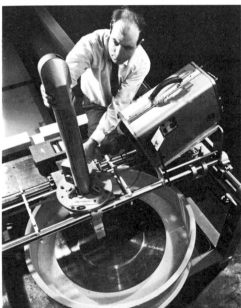

Left: Ultrasonic waves are used to detect flaws in engineering materials. The test sample is scanned with pulses of very high frequency sound which normally travel right through it. If they meet a flaw in the material, however, they are reflected back again. The machine will detect these reflections and thus record the presence of the flaw.

Above: High levels of sound are dangerous to health, causing hearing defects and creating fatigue which can lead to accidents. This picture shows sound level monitoring apparatus analyzing the noise in a workshop.

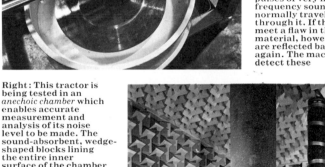

Right: This tractor is being tested in an *anechoic chamber* which enables accurate measurement and analysis of its noise level to be made. The sound-absorbent, wedge-shaped blocks lining the entire inner surface of the chamber are designed to eliminate any echoes within it which would result in incorrect measurements.

Below: Echoes occur when sounds strike a hard surface and are eventually reflected back to their source.

ECHOES

reflections

original sound

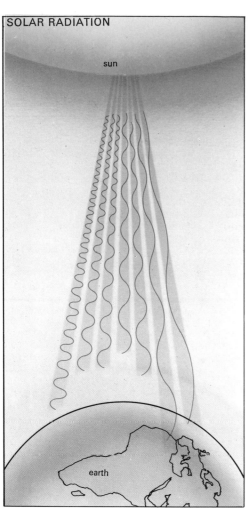

sun

earth

THE ELECTROMAGNETIC SPECTRUM

ultra violet

infra red

x-rays

microwaves

visible

gamma rays

| EHF | SHF | UHF | VHF | HF | MF | LF | VL |

radio waves

| 0.01 nm | 0.1 nm | 10 nm | 100 nm | 0.01 mm | 0.1 mm | 1 cm | 10 cm | 10 m | 100 m | 10 km | 100 |

0.001 nm   1000 nm   1 m   1 km   10

Far left: The sun sends a wide spectrum of electromagnetic radiation to the earth, much of which is absorbed by the atmosphere. The sun's radiation includes low frequency radio waves (on the right) and high frequency X-rays and gamma rays (on the left). Microwaves, infra-red rays, visible light and ultraviolet rays are in between.

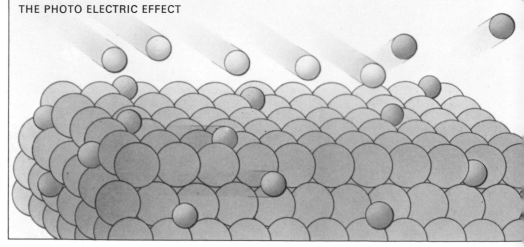

Snark

Left: This enormous structure is a radio telescope, used by astronomers to detect the radio waves emitted by stars. The energy of the waves reaching the earth is extremely low, and the dish-shaped part of the radio telescope acts as a reflector, focussing the waves on to the actual aerial so that a stronger signal is obtained.

Right: Rainbows are the result of a phenomenon called *refraction*. When light passes from one medium, such as air, to another, such as water, its angle is altered slightly. The size of this change depends on the light's wavelength, red (long wavelength) light being affected less than blue (short wavelength) light. Sunlight passing through raindrops will, if the angle is correct, be split into its component colours by the raindrops in such a way as to form a rainbow.

Below: Photons (blue) striking a photoelectric material, dislodge electrons (red), creating an electric current.

the wave it produces vibrate at the same frequency we can talk of the frequency of the wave. Frequencies are measured in *Hertz* (symbol *Hz*), one Hertz being one complete cycle of vibrations (from maximum to minimum and back to maximum) per second.

The speed at which sound travels is independent of its frequency, and so the peaks of high frequency sound waves are closer together than those of low frequency waves. The distance between successive wave peaks is known as the *wavelength*, and the wavelength of any type of wave can be calculated by dividing its velocity by its frequency.

Speech and music are a mixture of frequencies from about 20 Hz to 20,000 Hz (20 kHz). The higher frequencies are heard as treble notes and the lower as bass. Frequencies below 20 Hz are felt rather than heard; a large part of the vibration caused by earthquakes is in fact due to low frequency sound waves moving in the Earth's crust. Sounds above 20 kHz cannot be detected by human ears, although they are audible to other animals such as dogs and bats.

Electromagnetic waves

Electromagnetic radiation can be thought of in two ways, either as continuous waves of energy or as streams of 'particles' or pulses of energy known as *photons*. Whether it is considered as waves or as particles depends on which particular properties of it are under discussion; in some cases its behaviour is best explained by its wave-like properties, and in others it is better to think of it as streams of photons.

THE PHOTO ELECTRIC EFFECT

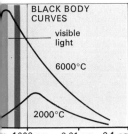

visible
light

6000°C

2000°C

1000 nm   0.01 nm   0.1 nm

Above: 'Black body
curves' show the
distribution of energy
radiated at various
frequencies by heated
objects. These curves
show how an object at
6,000°C radiates more
energy, at higher
frequencies, than one
at 2,000°C.

Right: A microwave
antenna. Microwaves,
because of their high
frequencies, can be
made to carry more
information than lower
frequency radio waves.

Left: The whole
electromagnetic
spectrum, from gamma
rays, through the
visible region, to the
longest radio waves.

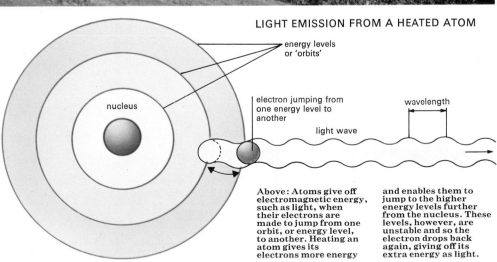

The optical properties of light, for
example, such as reflection and refraction,
are related to its wavelength and so in
these aspects light is best thought of as
waves. The photoelectric effect, on the
other hand, where light falling on to
certain materials causes an electric
current to flow in them, is best explained
in terms of high-energy photons striking
electrons in the material, freeing them
from their atoms so that they can travel
through the material as an electric
current.

Unlike sound, which is propagated by
the mechanical vibrations of the molecules of substances, electromagnetic radiation originates at a sub-atomic level
and travels most easily in a vacuum
where there are no atoms or molecules to
impede its progress. An electromagnetic
wave has two components, an electric
field and an associated magnetic field that
travels along with it.

Anything which produces either an
alternating electric field or an alternating magnetic field is also a source of
electromagnetic radiation. An alternating
electric current flowing in a wire, for
example, creates both an alternating electric field and an alternating magnetic
field around it, and these two fields spread
out together from the wire as an alternating electromagnetic field. This alternating
field travels as a wave-like series of
alternations in the strengths of the electric and magnetic fields, the 'peaks' of
the waves being at points where the field
strengths are greatest. As with sound,
the frequency of the wave equals the
frequency of the source, and the wavelength, that is the distance between two
successive points on the wave where the
fields are equal, is found by dividing the
velocity by the frequency. The higher the
frequency, the shorter the wavelength.

The velocity of electromagnetic waves
in a vacuum, as calculated by James Clerk
Maxwell who first suggested their existence in 1864, is an incredible 299,792·458
km/second (186,282 miles/sec, or
670,615,200 mph). This is the same as
the measured velocity of light, a coin-
cidence which persuaded physicists to
accept the existence of electromagnetic
waves long before their transmission was
first demonstrated by Heinrich Hertz in
1887. It was also obvious that one of their
forms is visible light itself.

Visible light, however, is only the most
obvious form of electro-magnetic radiation, which can be observed also as
radio waves, microwaves, infra-red and
ultraviolet light, X-rays and gamma rays.
All these differ from each other only in
wavelength and frequency, and there is a
certain amount of overlap between these
different groups, the highest frequencies
of one group being the same as the lowest
of the next.

The longest wavelengths are those of
radio waves, which range from over
1000 km down to about 10 cm, and these
are the simplest to generate artificially.
An alternating current of the right
frequency is passed through a straight
wire aerial, creating an alternating
magnetic field around the aerial which
radiates the waves into the air. An
equally simple aerial can be used to detect
radio waves, which induce a tiny alternating electric current in any wire which
points at the same angle and direction as
the transmitting aerial.

Shorter electromagnetic wavelengths,

LIGHT EMISSION FROM A HEATED ATOM

energy levels
or 'orbits'

nucleus

electron jumping from
one energy level to
another

wavelength

light wave

Above: Atoms give off
electromagnetic energy,
such as light, when
their electrons are
made to jump from one
orbit, or energy level,
to another. Heating an
atom gives its
electrons more energy

and enables them to
jump to the higher
energy levels further
from the nucleus. These
levels, however, are
unstable and so the
electron drops back
again, giving off its
extra energy as light.

unlike radio waves and microwaves, cannot be produced electronically. Infra-red radiation, which covers the wavelengths from 1 mm down to 1 micrometre (a millionth of a metre), is produced by the natural vibrations of atoms, particularly those in solids. Atoms are composed of electrically charged particles, and when these vibrate they create alternating electric and magnetic fields which project themselves away as infra-red rays. The hotter an object gets, the faster its atoms vibrate and the higher the frequency (hence the shorter the wavelength) of their radiation.

Since it is generally true that any emitter of waves will also absorb them, infra-red waves readily give up their energy to the atoms of any solid they encounter. This raises the temperature of the absorbing solid, so that infra-red can also be considered as radiated heat.

If an object is heated above about 530°C (986°F), it begins to radiate appreciable amounts of radiation at wavelengths as short as 750 nanometres (1 nm is 1 thousand millionth of a metre), which human eyes can detect as red light. Visible light wavelengths range from this down to 390 nm for violet light. Anything heated above about 1,200°C (2,192°F) radiates a mixture of visible light wavelengths which appears white to our eyes. This is the physical meaning of the terms 'red hot' and 'white hot'.

Shorter still than visible light is ultraviolet light, a term used to describe electromagnetic radiation with wavelengths from 390 nm down to 1 nm. Ultraviolet waves can be produced, like infra-red, by atomic vibrations, but the temperature must be about 5,000°C (9,032°F) before a significant amount is produced. The sun and other stars are at higher temperatures than this and consequently radiate a good deal of ultraviolet, but the bulk of their output is still in the visible range. However, ultraviolet and some visible light can also be produced at much lower temperatures by changes in the energy of electrons in atoms and molecules.

According to the *quantum theory*, electrons orbiting atomic nuclei can only have certain definite energy levels, and each time an electron changes from one energy level to another it emits a short burst of electromagnetic radiation called a photon. The frequency of the photon is directly proportional to the change in the electron's energy, and the possible energies of electrons are such that the emitted photons are visible or ultraviolet light. The higher the frequency of the photon, the more energy it possesses.

Black Body Radiation

The relationship between frequency and energy was first explained by the German physicist Max Planck (1858-1947) in 1900. The explanation was contained in Planck's quantum theory, which he formulated when studying the spectrum of radiation emitted by heated objects. Physicists had been unable to explain why, when an object was heated, it gave off much less high-frequency energy than they expected it to.

Planck's explanation was that the energy was emitted in discrete bundles or *quanta* (photons), and that a quantum of high frequency contained more energy than a low frequency one. Consequently the energy needed to enable an object to

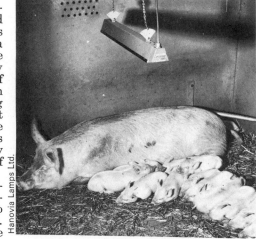

Hanovia Lamps Ltd.

Picturepoint

IMAGE INTENSIFIER

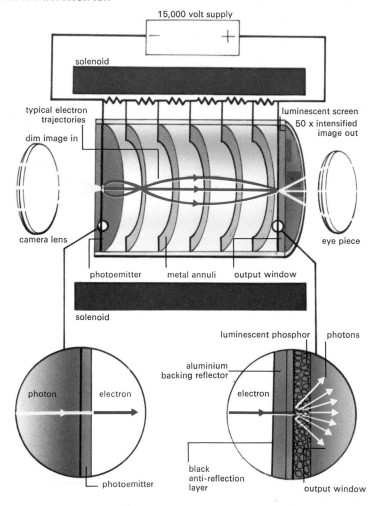

15,000 volt supply

solenoid

typical electron trajectories

dim image in

luminescent screen
50 x intensified image out

camera lens

eye piece

photoemitter   metal annuli   output window

solenoid

luminescent phosphor   photons

aluminium backing reflector

photon   electron

electron

photoemitter

black anti-reflection layer

output window

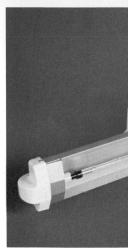

Above: Over 80% of the light emitted by an ultraviolet bactericidal lamp is 254 nm ultraviolet, which kills most kinds of germs.

Left: An image intensifier takes a dim image and focusses it onto a *photoemitter*. This emits electrons in proportion to the pattern of light of the image. These electrons are accelerated by the 15,000 volt supply, and focussed by the solenoid's magnetic field, and when they hit the luminescent screen they give off photons, creating a bright picture of the original scene.

Below left: An image intensifier gun sight and (below) Stonehenge viewed at night through an intensifier.

RCA

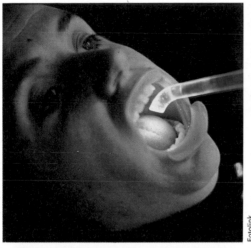

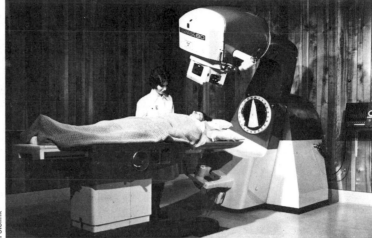

Far left: A litter of young pigs and their mother being kept warm by an infra-red heater. Infra-red radiation raises the temperature of any solid object on which it falls, but passes through air without heating it. Infra-red heaters such as this one provide ample warmth for the objects they are intended to heat, but do not waste energy by heating up the air around them.

Left: Banknotes can be 'marked' with Anthracene, which does not show up under ordinary light, but when lit with ultraviolet light it absorbs it and re-emits it as visible light. This effect is called *fluorescence*.

Above left: Ultraviolet light is the component of sunlight which causes sunburn. Its effects on skin tissue can be used medically: this picture shows a powerful ultraviolet lamp being used to seal a patient's gum tissue after a tooth has been extracted. The light also kills any germs present.

Above: Gamma rays can be used to destroy the cells of tumor tissue. This machine uses radioactive cobalt as a gamma ray source.

Left: Gamma ray and X-ray photography are used to study the internal structure of machinery. Here, a jet engine is being studied with X-rays.

form and emit high frequencies was greater than that needed for the formation of low frequencies. In the case of a heated object, the higher its temperature the more energy was available for the emission of radiation. Thus a relatively moderate amount of heat was required to make the object give off low frequencies (in other words to make it red hot), but a great deal more heat was needed to make it give off higher frequencies (to make it white hot). This is why a piece of metal can be made to glow red at about 530 °C, but must be heated to around 1,200 °C or more to make it glow white.

The energy levels at different frequencies, radiated by an object heated to a given temperature, can be predicted by using data based on the behaviour of the theoretical 'black body'. This theoretical body, being perfectly black, absorbs all the energy from all frequencies of radiation falling on it, but it radiates this energy at different frequencies. The amount of energy it emits at a given frequency depends on its temperature.

X-rays and gamma rays

X-rays have extremely short wavelengths, from 10 nm down to 0.001 nm. The longer X-rays are called 'soft' and the shorter 'hard'. Some soft X-rays are produced by electron energy changes in atoms, but they are usually generated by firing high speed electrons at a metal target. The sudden deceleration of a charged electron when it hits the target causes a very rapid change in the electric field surrounding it, which leads to the emission of radiation in the form of an X-ray photon.

Gamma rays, shortest of all electromagnetic radiation, are emitted as a result of energy changes in the elementary particles which comprise an atomic nucleus. They can be generated, somewhat haphazardly, in the core of a nuclear reactor, but are produced naturally in any radioactive process such as the disintegration of radium. Some gamma rays have wavelengths in the hard X-ray range—others are as short as 0.0001 nm (one billion billionth of a metre).

THE DOPPLER EFFECT

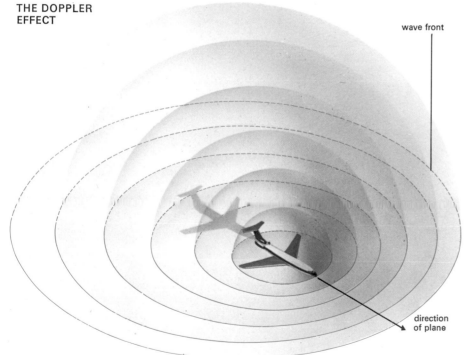

wave front

direction of plane

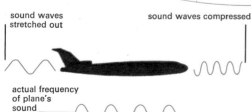

sound waves stretched out

sound waves compressed

actual frequency of plane's sound

Left: The pitch of the sound of an object travelling towards an observer sounds higher than it really is because it 'compresses' the sound waves in front of it. The sound appears lower when the object is travelling away, because the sound waves are 'stretched out'. This is called the *Doppler effect*, and

at extremely high speeds it has a similar effect on the frequency of light coming from an object. The light from an approaching object appears bluer than it is, as its frequency is higher, and conversely that from a receding object appears redder. The effect was discovered by C. Doppler in 1842.

The Foundations of Chemistry

We take the world around us very much for granted. But do we know what the wallpaper, the paint, the furniture, the transistor radio and the man-made fibres in our clothes are made of? Even if we were given the basic ingredients we would still need to know how to change them into the final product.

Chemistry is largely concerned with finding out more about substances, including their components and structure, their properties and how they can be made. The chemist's job is to analyse and synthesize things. In the past 30 years this has led to a vast range of new products: plastics, man-made fibres, dye-stuffs, fertilizers, medicines, synthetic rubbers, refrigerants, detergents, fire-fighting chemicals and rocket fuels, the list is endless. Chemistry has also gone hand in hand with physics; for example, in the development of the semiconductors used in transistors and integrated circuits.

The building blocks
All these achievements depended on a knowledge of the basic chemical *elements* or building blocks of matter. For about 1,600 years it had been left to the alchemists to try to untangle these secrets. Misguided by Aristotle's philo-sophic theory that all matter was com-posed of 'four elements'—earth, air, fire and water—and dedicated to the pursuit of turning base metals into gold and finding the 'elixir of life', they actually halted the progress of science.

However, in 1661 Robert Boyle correctly defined an element as 'a substance which cannot be split into anything simpler by a chemical change'. The search for elements began and within 100 years Antoine Lavoisier, the brilliant French chemist, had listed 27 of them. Today all 92

Derby Museum

Above: White phosphorus was unwittingly discovered by a German alchemist, Hennig Brand, in 1669, while looking for the elixir of life. He filled a retort with urine and heated it. The glowing residue was the element phosphorus. It was not until 100 years later that the search for elements began seriously.

ELEMENTS SHOWN IN THE PERIODIC TABLE

Ar	Argon	H	Hydrogen	O	Oxygen	Ta	Tantalum
Ac	Actinium	Ha	Hahnium	Os	Osmium	Tb	Terbium
Ag	Silver	He	Hellium	P	Phosphorus	Tc	Technetium
Al	Aluminium	Hf	Hafnium	Pa	Protactinium	Te	Tellurium
Am	Americium	Hg	Mecury	Pb	Lead	Th	Thorium
As	Arsenic	Ho	Holmium	Pd	Palladium	Ti	Titanium
At	Astatine	I	Iodine	Pm	Promethium	Tl	Thallium
Au	Gold	In	Indium	Po	Polonium	Tm	Thulium
B	Boron	Ir	Iridium	Pr	Praseodymium	U	Uranium
Ba	Barium	K	Potassium	Pt	Platinum	V	Vanadium
Be	Beryllium	Kr	Krypton	Pu	Plutonium	W	Tungsten
Bi	Bismuth	La	Lanthanum	Ra	Radium	Xe	Xenon
Bk	Berkelium	Li	Lithium	Rb	Rubidium	Y	Yttrium
Br	Bromine	Lu	Lutetium	Re	Rhenium	Yb	Ytterbium
C	Carbon	Lr	Lawrencium	Rf	Rutherfordium	Zn	Zinc
Ca	Calcium	Md	Mendelevium	Rh	Rhodium	Zr	Zirconium
Cd	Cadmium	Mg	Magnesium	Rn	Radon		
Ce	Cerium	Mn	Manganese	Ru	Ruthenium		
Cf	Californium	Mo	Molybdenum	S	Sulphur		
Cl	Chlorine	N	Nitrogen	Sb	Antimony		
Cm	Curium	Na	Sodium	Sc	Scandium		
Co	Cobalt	Nb	Niobium	Se	Selenium		
Cr	Chromium	Nd	Neodymium	Si	Silicon		
Cs	Caesium	Ne	Neon	Sm	Samarium		
Cu	Copper	Ni	Nickel	Sn	Tin		
Dy	Dysprosium	No	Nobelium	Sr	Strontium		
Er	Erbium	Np	Neptunium				
Es	Einsteinium						
Eu	Europium						
F	Fluorine						
Fe	Iron						
Fm	Fermium						
Fr	Francium						
Ga	Gallium						
Gd	Gadolinium						
Ge	Germanium						

1st period

2nd period

3rd period

4th period

5th period

6th period

7th period

Left: In 1940 scientists found they could make synthetic elements by bombarding uranium with atomic nuclei. Shown here is plutonium, atomic number 94. It is being handled by remotely-controlled tongs. A radioactive metal of the actinide group, it was used in some of the first atomic bombs instead of uranium.

Below: Many compounds in our world occur as mixtures which can be separated in various ways; by filtering, by gravity differences and by distillation. Air can be separated into its gases by liquefying and distilling it. Here salt is being extracted from sea water simply by letting the water evaporate off in the sun.

naturally-occurring elements, of which about 70 are metals, have been identified. In addition, about 14 artificial ones have been made during nuclear reactions, but being radioactive they are often short-lived.

If a massive chemical analysis of the Earth's crust was possible, the abundance of elements would be approximately 50 per cent oxygen, 26 per cent silicon, 7 per cent aluminium, 4 per cent iron, 3 per cent calcium, 2.5 per cent sodium, 2.5 per cent potassium, 2 per cent magnesium and all the other elements together 3 per cent.

Relatively few elements are found 'free' in nature; most occur chemically combined with one or more other elements, forming *compounds*. There are, however, rules governing which elements combine and the proportions in which they com-

bine. A compound is a pure substance with its own properties, often widely different to its constituent elements. For example, when sodium, a soft, highly reactive metal, is burned in chlorine, a poisonous choking gas, a harmless compound is produced, sodium chloride or household salt.

There is a further complication; in the world around us most compounds and any 'free' elements exist as *mixtures*, which are held together by physical rather than chemical means. The air, sea water, soil, rocks and crude oil are all mixtures of this kind. The separation of mixtures is important to many industries, for example, in oil refining, in the desalination of sea water, in the extraction of metals from mixed ores, and in brewing.

Atoms and the Periodic Table

Each element is, in fact, made up of millions of tiny particles known as *atoms*. The structure of these atoms helps to explain the chemical and physical properties of the various elements and how they form compounds.

At the heart of the atom is a cluster of positively charged protons and uncharged neutrons, which together form the nucleus. Surrounding the nucleus is a cloud of negatively charged electrons. These electrons are so light in comparison to the nucleus that an atom of hydrogen could be compared to a pea orbited by a speck of dust. In reality electrons are very important as they alone are responsible for chemical changes, but only the outermost ones are involved in these changes.

The electrons have to go into particular energy levels or concentric 'shells' around the nucleus and there is a maximum number of electrons which can exist in each shell. There are never more than eight electrons in the outermost shell. Those with the full complement of eight are chemically very stable. They are the rare or 'inert' gases; neon, argon, krypton, xenon and radon.

In all atoms the number of protons in the nucleus equals the number of elec-

rare (inert) gases

electropositive metals

non metals

transition metals

hydrogen

rare earths and actinides

elements with both metallic and non-metallic properties

Left: A modern Periodic Table. Above the symbol for each element is its atomic number, equal to protons in the nucleus. In each period all elements have the same number of electron shells. Broad classes exist, but sometimes they include smaller families having the same number of electrons in their outermost shell.

8	9	10					
O	F	Ne					
16	17	18					
S	Cl	Ar					

29	30	31	32	33	34	35	36
Cu	Zn	Ga	Ge	As	Se	Br	Kr
47	48	49	50	51	52	53	54
Ag	Cd	In	Sn	Sb	Te	I	Xe

72	73	74	75	76	77	78	79	80	81	82	83	84	85	86
Hf	Ta	W	Re	Os	Ir	Pt	Au	Hg	Tl	Pb	Bi	Po	At	Rn

104	105	106
Rf	Ha	

Above: In a solid the atoms stack in an orderly fashion, giving rise to beautiful crystalline forms. This applies equally to atoms of the same kind (as found in elements like iron, copper, sulphur and iodine), or different kinds, as in this compound, a natural mineral form of calcium carbonate, called calcite.

295

trons, making them electrically neutral. For example, the second lightest element is the gas helium which has two protons and two neutrons surrounded by two orbital electrons which fill the K shell. This makes helium as stable as the inert gases, which is why it is much safer to use helium in balloons than highly inflammable hydrogen. On the other hand, lithium, the lightest solid element, has three protons, four neutrons (the number of neutrons does not have to equal the number of protons) and three electrons. It is highly reactive because the third electron has to go into the second shell where it is loosely bound and easily lost to another atom.

Each element is assigned an *atomic number* based on the number of protons in the nucleus. It is also given an *atomic weight*, which is equal to the total number of protons and neutrons in the nucleus. (The electrons are so light they can be ignored.) Naturally this does not say how many grammes an atom weighs, but is useful for comparing the relative weights of elements.

Apart from the atomic numbers of elements, some system of classification other than metal or non-metal was sought. The first successful attempt to place the elements in some order was made by a Russian chemist, Dmitri Mendeleyev, in 1868. He noticed that when elements were listed in order of increasing atomic weight there was a definite periodic repetition of those with similar properties. He placed the elements in rows and columns and, as only about 60 elements were then known, left spaces and predicted the properties of the 'missing' elements. Today, this *Periodic Table* is complete and slightly more complex.

Elements may be grouped together on the basis of having the same number of electrons in their outermost shell. For example, all the halogens—fluorine, chlorine, bromine, iodine, and the unstable radioactive member, astatine—have seven electrons in their outermost shell. Elements can also be arranged in horizontal rows or periods. All the

elements in a period have the same number of electron-shells, but they themselves may differ widely chemically because they have different numbers of electrons in the outermost shell. For example, in the third period we find the highly reactive soft alkali metal sodium, plus aluminium, sulphur, the reactive gas chlorine and the inert gas argon.

In broader terms elements may be classified as being rare gases, electropositive metals, non-metals, transition metals, the rare earth elements and the actinides or radioactive elements—uranium, thorium, plutonium and so on. The transition metals are interesting as they have two unfilled electron shells—normally elements only have the outermost shell unfilled—and this gives them the ability to form a wider range of compounds. Iron, chromium, and copper are transition metals.

Symbols are widely used in chemistry. The Swedish chemist Berzelius first suggested our short-hand way of writing down elements and their compounds. The symbol for an element is usually an abbreviation of its present or original name: P for phosphorus, Zn for zinc, but Fe for iron from the Latin *ferrum*, and Na for sodium from the Latin *natrium*. The subscript numbers in a molecule or compound represent the numbers of atoms of each element present.

A molecule of water, whose symbol is H_2O, has two hydrogen atoms and one oxygen atom. Sulphuric acid, H_2SO_4, has two hydrogen atoms, one sulphur atom and four oxygen atoms. This universal chemical shorthand comes in very useful when describing chemical reactions. For example, when dilute sulphuric acid is poured on to a small piece of zinc, hydrogen gas bubbles off and the zinc dissolves, forming zinc sulphate, or, as in this equation:

$$Zn + H_2SO_4 = ZnSO_4 + H_2\uparrow$$

The arrow pointing up indicates a gas, while one pointing down would indicate a precipitate (or insoluble solid) forming in a solution, rather than the new compound remaining in solution.

HYDROGEN BONDS

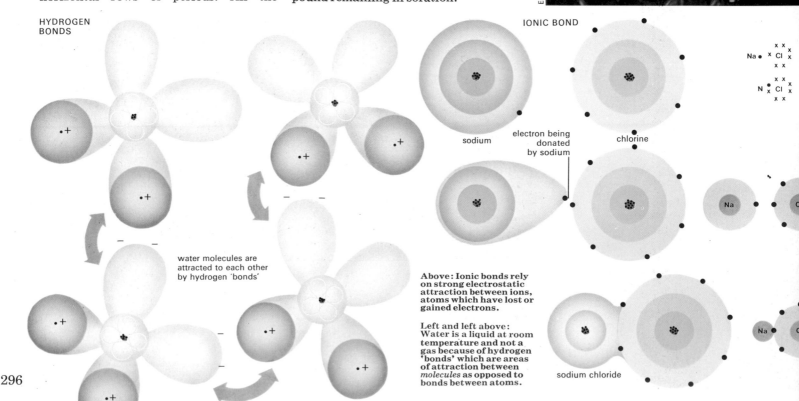

water molecules are attracted to each other by hydrogen 'bonds'

IONIC BOND

electron being donated by sodium

sodium   chlorine

sodium chloride

Above: Ionic bonds rely on strong electrostatic attraction between ions, atoms which have lost or gained electrons.

Left and left above: Water is a liquid at room temperature and not a gas because of hydrogen 'bonds' which are areas of attraction between *molecules* as opposed to bonds between atoms.

296

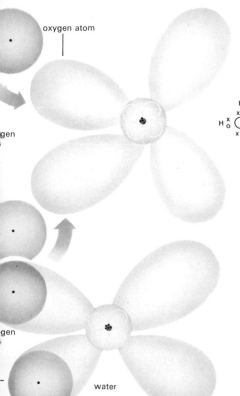

Valency and bonds

When elements form compounds the *valency* or combining power of one element with another is determined by the number of atoms of hydrogen that will combine with one atom of the element. For example, oxygen has a valency of two because two atoms of hydrogen combine with it to form water. But the full story of combining or bonding is more complex than this. Atoms tend to be able to combine by forming the stable inert gas configuration of eight electrons, and there are two ways of doing this.

In an *ionic* or electrovalent bond, such as that formed by sodium chloride, the sodium atom readily loses its single outer electron. This leaves it with a proton in the nucleus which is now unneutralized as it no longer has a negatively charged electron to balance its own positive charge, and the sodium atom then becomes a special type of atom—a positive *ion*, or *cation*. Chlorine, however, has seven outermost electrons and willingly accepts another to achieve the stable eight electron state, becoming a negative ion, or *anion*. The sodium ion, Na+, and the chloride ion, Cl-, are held together by a strong electrostatic attraction. Ionic compounds are usually solids, the ions being packed together in a stable pattern called a crystal lattice.

Apart from losing and gaining electrons, bonds may be formed by sharing electrons between atoms. These are known as *covalent* bonds. For example, in the gas methane, CH_4, the carbon atom has four electrons in its outermost shell and each hydrogen atom has one electron. By mutual sharing of electrons each hydrogen atom can have the stable two electron state, while the carbon ends up with a stable eight electron state. Sometimes more than one electron pair is shared between atoms, forming a 'double' bond or sometimes a 'triple' bond, as in acetylene. Both these bonds are less stable than a single bond. Covalent bonding is widespread in carbon compounds found in plants and animals. Some elements arc also covalent bonded: oxygen, O_2; nitrogen, N_2; and chlorine, Cl_2. Only covalent compounds or elements form these discrete particles of two or more atoms known as *molecules*.

All chemical bonds have two things in common; they arise from a stable arrangement of electrons around the atoms involved, and they result in more stable 'low energy' compounds being formed. This means that energy is required to break the bonds, but when they are being formed it is released, often as heat. For example, a tiny piece of sodium dropped on to water vigorously reacts with it to give the compound sodium hydroxide, and much heat is produced in the process of forming bonds.

Chemical reactions often only occur at high temperatures; copper reacts with oxygen to give black copper oxide only if they are heated together. However, extra heat is produced as the result of bond formation between the copper and the oxygen. Thus, to recover pure copper from its oxide, that much energy would need to be absorbed before the bonds could be broken. It is this release of energy during chemical bonding that provides the heat when fossil fuels are burned. Indeed, knowledge of such chemical changes can provide chemists with the key to the search for new materials.

BSC

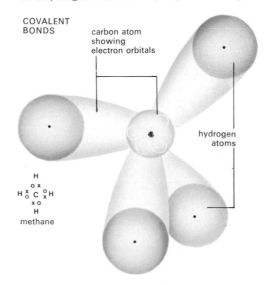

Left and below: Covalent bonds link atoms in molecules by sharing electrons, to give strange shapes where orbitals overlap. In water the two hydrogen nuclei are held at a 105° angle, keeping one side of the molecule positive and the other negative, which is useful for hydrogen bonding. Below, the gas methane.

Above: A selection of catalysts used in the oil and chemical industries. Chemical reactions are often difficult to get started or very slow, so to speed things up catalysts are used. They do not chemically change themselves. The black coal like lumps are iron oxide, used for making ammonia from hydrogen and nitrogen.

oxygen atom

gen

gen

water

H
$H_O^X \overset{X}{\underset{X}{O}} \overset{X}{\underset{X}{O}} H$

COVALENT BONDS

carbon atom showing electron orbitals

hydrogen atoms

H
$\overset{O X}{H \underset{X}{\overset{X}{O}} \underset{X}{C} \underset{X}{\overset{O}{X}} H}$
$\underset{H}{O}$

methane

Elements
of Nature

The usefulness of the various naturally-occurring chemical elements varies almost as much as their chemical and physical properties. Some, such as the gases oxygen and nitrogen, are essential to living creatures, while others, such as astatine, have little or no practical importance. This article deals with the nature and properties of some of the most important elements and the ways in which they are used.

Oxygen and nitrogen
Oxygen (O) and nitrogen (N) are the two main constituents of the earth's atmosphere. Pure dry air contains, by volume, approximately 21 per cent oxygen and 78 per cent nitrogen, the remainder being a mixture of other gases, including hydrogen and inert gases such as argon and helium.

In addition to the vast amount of oxygen within the atmosphere, it is also the most abundant element within the crust of the earth, where it occurs in combination with other elements such as iron, silicon and aluminium. Water, which covers over 70 per cent of the earth's surface, is made up of oxygen in combination with hydrogen.

Oxygen is an *electronegative* element, accepting electrons from other elements (which, in giving electrons away, are thus *electropositive*) when it combines with

them to form compounds. Pure oxygen can be obtained in small amounts by heating certain of these compounds, such as potassium chlorate and manganese dioxide, but on a commercial scale it is extracted from air.

Oxygen and water are both essential to living creatures, but oxygen also has many industrial uses. One of the most important is in cutting and welding metals, where it is burned together with acetylene gas to produce a very hot flame which melts the metals. It is also used in making iron and steel, where it is used to help burn away impurities in the molten metal. Liquid oxygen is used in rocket engines, where it is burned with a second fuel, such as kerosene, to produce the powerful stream of exhaust gases which drive the rocket.

Nitrogen, the principal constituent of air, occurs in combined form as Chile saltpetre (sodium nitrate, $NaNO_3$) and, in addition, it is a constituent element of proteins and so is a part of all living organisms.

Nitrogen is a very stable, non-reactive gas at normal temperatures, but at high temperatures the bonds holding the atoms within the nitrogen molecules break up, and the freed nitrogen atoms become very reactive. In a pure form it can be obtained either by heating suitable nitrogen-containing compounds or by extracting it from air.

Nitrogen is prepared industrially by the fractional distillation of liquefied air. The boiling point of liquid oxygen is 90°K (−183°C) and that of liquid nitrogen is 78°K (−195°C), so the two gases can easily be separated by controlling the temperature of the liquid air so that the

nitrogen 'boils off' leaving the oxygen behind. One of the most important uses of nitrogen compounds is in the manufacture of fertilizers, while others are used in making explosives. Liquid nitrogen is widely used as a coolant.

Silicon
After oxygen, silicon (Si) is the next most abundant element in the earth's crust. It occurs mainly as *silica* (SiO_2), which is the main constituent of sand, and as metallic silicates such as $K_2Al_2Si_6O_{16}$, a compound of potassium, aluminium, silicon and oxygen which is one of the group of rocks known as *feldspars*. Silicon is also found in *kaolinite* ($Al_2O_3.2SiO_2.2H_2O$), which is one of the main ingredients of china clay.

Silica occurs in either crystalline or *amorphous* (noncrystalline) forms. A good example of crystalline silica is quartz, while the precious stone opal is composed of amorphous silica.

Silica is the main ingredient of glass and silicon itself is used in many important synthetic materials such as synthetic rubbers. These *silicone rubbers* are more resistant to chemical attack than other rubbers. The enormous range of silicon-based products includes oils, greases, waxes and polishes, and solid resins such as those used for electrical insulating materials.

Sand, which is mostly silica, is used in large quantities for making concrete and mortar. *Kieselguhr* or *diatomaceous earth* is a type of silica formed in the earth from the skeletons of tiny organisms called diatoms. It is used in making fireproof cements and clays, as a filtering medium,

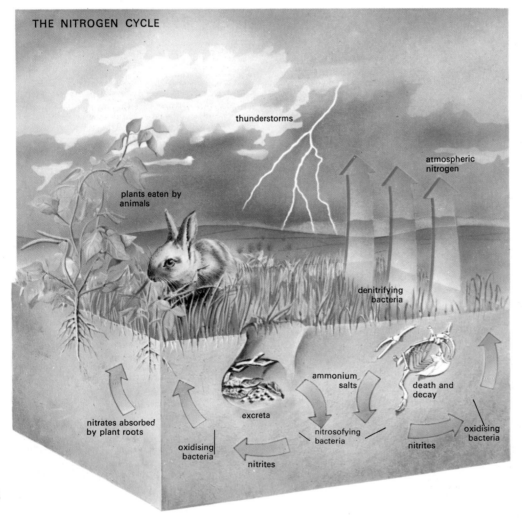

THE NITROGEN CYCLE

thunderstorms

atmospheric nitrogen

plants eaten by animals

denitrifying bacteria

ammonium salts

death and decay

nitrates absorbed by plant roots

excreta

oxidising bacteria

nitrosofying bacteria

nitrites

oxidising bacteria

nitrites

Paul Brierley

Left: The *nitrogen cycle*, the natural circulation of nitrogen compounds between plants, animals, the soil and the air. Nitrogen from the atmosphere is converted into various nitrogen compounds within the soil by the action of bacteria living in the roots of plants such as peas and beans. In addition, some nitrogen compounds are formed during thunderstorms. Nitrogen compounds in the soil are absorbed by plants, and then by animals which eat the plants, being returned to the soil in excreta or by the decay of dead animals and plants within the soil. Some nitrogen is returned to the atmosphere by the action of denitrifying bacteria.

Left: Diamond, one of the allotropes of carbon, is the hardest substance found in nature. Carbon will only crystallize into diamond at very high temperatures and pressures. Synthetic diamonds are now produced in large numbers, using apparatus capable of producing over 90,000 times atmospheric pressure at over 2,000°C (3,630°F), developed in 1953.

Below: The hardness of a diamond is due to the way in which the atoms are arranged within the crystal structure.

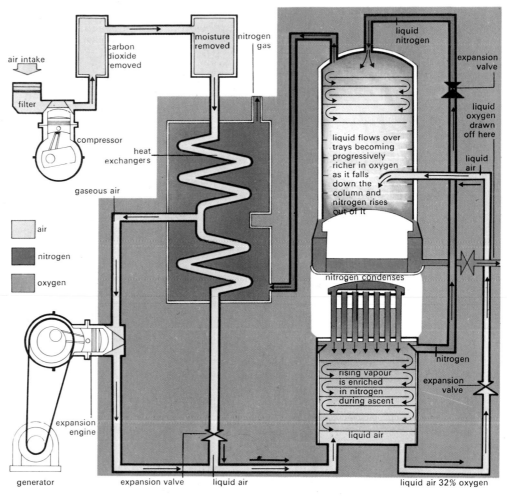

air

nitrogen

oxygen

air intake

filter

compressor

carbon dioxide removed

moisture removed

nitrogen gas

heat exchangers

gaseous air

expansion engine

generator

expansion valve

liquid air

liquid nitrogen

expansion valve

liquid oxygen drawn off here

liquid air

liquid flows over trays becoming progressively richer in oxygen as it falls down the column and nitrogen rises out of it

nitrogen condenses

nitrogen

rising vapour is enriched in nitrogen during ascent

expansion valve

liquid air

liquid air 32% oxygen

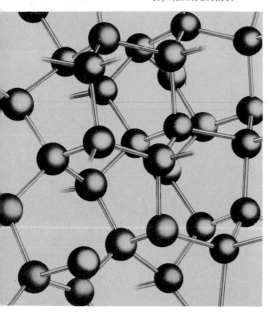

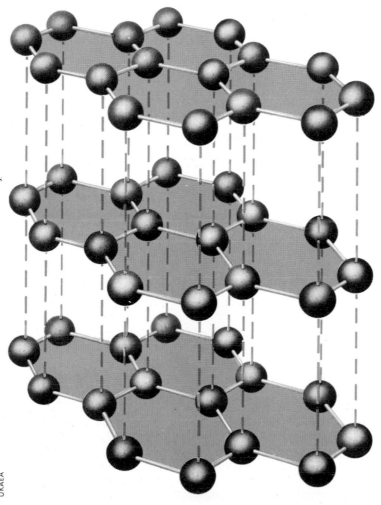

UKAEA

Right: Graphite, the second main form of carbon, has its atoms bonded together in layers. These layers can slide easily over each other, and this gives graphite its soft, slippery nature.

Left: A synthetic crystal of quartz, a form of silica (silicon dioxide, SiO_2). Silica occurs widely in nature, one of the commonest forms being sand.

Below: The rate of chemical decomposition of radio active compounds is reduced at low temperatures, and so they are stored in liquid nitrogen. This keeps them at below 78°K (−195°C), which is the boiling point of liquid nitrogen.

Above: Oxygen and nitrogen are obtained by the distillation of liquid air. Air is compressed and passed through absorbent materials which take away the carbon dioxide and moisture, then it is cooled in the heat exchangers. Next it is expanded so that its temperature drops further and it liquefies. Some of this expansion takes place in an expansion engine, which drives a generator to provide some electricity for the plant. In the distillation column the nitrogen boils out of the liquid first, as it has a lower boiling point than oxygen. The remaining liquid is almost pure oxygen.

and in the manufacture of explosives. Dynamite, for example, is made by absorbing nitroglycerine into a keiselguhr base.

Carbon

Compared with the great amounts of oxygen and silicon within the earth's crust, the amount of carbon (C) within it is very small—it comprises only about 0.3 per cent of the crust. This relatively small quantity, however, belies its extreme importance to living creatures. The molecules that form the basis of life, such as RNA and DNA, are based on carbon, and animals obtain their energy by the oxidation of the *carbohydrates* (compounds of carbon, hydrogen and oxygen) contained in the food they eat.

Carbon is also important to industry, being the basis of fossil fuels such as coal, and occurring in combination with hydrogen to form the *hydrocarbon* fuels such as oil and natural gas.

There are two naturally-occurring forms of crystalline carbon, both of which are pure carbon despite the great differences between them. These two forms or *allotropes* of carbon are diamond, a clear, very hard crystal, and graphite, a soft, smooth, black substance.

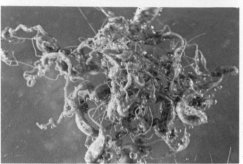

James Blake

James Blake

James Blake

The differences between diamond and
graphite are due to the way in which the
carbon atoms arrange themselves within
the crystal structures. In diamond, the
atoms are arranged in a tetrahedral
pattern in which the bonding between the
atoms is very strong in every direction.
The atoms in graphite, however, are
arranged in sheets or layers, each layer
being a network of hexagonal patterns of
atoms. The bonding within these flat
layers is strong, but the forces holding
the layers together are weak and so the
layers can easily slide over each other.

The structure of diamond accounts for
its hardness and transparency, and also
for the fact that it will not conduct
electricity—its electrons are held tightly
within it. On the other hand the ability of
graphite layers to slide over each other
gives this form of carbon its characteristic
softness and also makes it a good lubricant. It is a good conductor of electricity
and has many applications in the electrical
industry. Another very common use of
graphite is for the 'lead' of pencils.

Carbon and its compounds are so
important that a whole branch of
chemistry is devoted to the study and uses
of these substances. This is known as
organic chemistry, its name deriving from
the role that carbon plays in the structure
and life of plants and animals.

Sulphur
Sulphur (S), a hard, yellow substance,
has been known for over 3,000 years. It
was widely used by the Mediterranean
civilizations in various medicines and the
sulphur dioxide (SO_2) fumes given off by
burning sulphur have been used for

J. F. Millies/ZEFA

Left: Incendiary bombs often use a material called *thermite*, which is a mixture of magnesium, iron oxide and aluminium powders that reaches a temperature of 2,500°C (4,500°F) when it ignites. Napalm, an incendiary oil, contains petrol, polystyrene and white phosphorus.

Below: Sodium, one of the alkali metals, is so intensely reactive with air or water that it must be stored under paraffin oil. If it is exposed to air it rapidly oxidizes to sodium oxide, and if it comes into contact with water it reacts violently to produce sodium hydroxide and hydrogen gas.

Right: The violent reaction created when a piece of sodium metal is placed on a wet surface. The hydrogen gas given off is ignited by the heat produced during the reaction. When this reactive metal is combined with the poisonous gas chlorine, the result is harmless common salt.

centuries for bleaching cloth.

Deposits of pure sulphur occur in many areas, including the southern USA and Sicily. It also occurs in combined states such as the sulphides of zinc (ZnS), lead (PbS) and iron (FeS$_2$), and sulphates such as *gypsum* (CaSO$_4$.2H$_2$O, hydrated calcium sulphate). Sulphur may also be present in crude oil.

The principal industrial use of sulphur is for making sulphuric acid (H$_2$SO$_4$), which is used in the manufacture of fertilizers, paints, detergents, plastics, synthetic fibres and dyes. Sulphur is also used in making rubber during the *vulcanization* process which makes the rubber stronger and more durable, and many drugs, such as the antibiotics penicillin and sulphonamides, contain sulphur compounds.

The halogens

The name 'halogen' comes from the Greek words meaning 'salt producer', as these elements will readily combine with other elements to form salts. The original members of this group were chlorine (Cl), bromine (Br) and iodine (I), which occur as salts in sea water, and later on the elements fluorine (F) and astatine (At) were added to the list. Fluorine and chlorine are gases at room temperature, bromine is a liquid and iodine and astatine are solids.

The chief characteristic of the halogens is the fact that they each have a valency of 1, their outer electron shells being one electron short of the number needed to give them the stable eight electron configuration.

Their compounds are known as the halides, and those formed with the more electropositive metals are held together by ionic bonding. Halides formed with non-metallic elements and the less electropositive metals have covalent bonding.

The halogens are highly electronegative, having a great affinity for electrons and readily forming negative ions. This is what makes the halogens so reactive. Their high electronegativity also makes them powerful oxidizing agents; it is this

property which makes chlorine, for example, effective as a bleach and as a disinfectant.

The most common chlorine compound is ordinary salt, sodium chloride (NaCl), and other chlorine compounds are used in plastics (polyvinyl chloride, pvc), weedkillers, insecticides and drycleaning fluids. The bromine compound silver bromide is one of the light-sensitive compounds used in photographic film, and ethylene bromide is added to petrol to prevent lead (from the anti-knocking additive tetraethyl lead) from building up within the engine.

Iodine is widely used as an antiseptic and within the human body small quantities of iodine are essential for the proper functioning of the thyroid gland. Fluorine is the most active chemical element and one of its best-known uses is in the production of compounds used to make teeth more resistant to decay. Other fluorine compounds are used as refrigerants, aerosol propellants, firefighting chemicals and anaesthetics. Non-stick pan coatings are made of the fluorine-based plastic called *polytetrafluoroethylene* (PTFE). Astatine is the least important of the halogens and also in fact one of the least important of all elements, as its most stable isotope is very short-lived, having a half-life of only 8.3 hours.

Alkaline earth metals

The alkaline earth metals are a group of very reactive metals, namely beryllium (Be), magnesium (Mg), calcium (Ca), strontium (Sr), barium (Ba) and radium (Ra). The most important are calcium, which makes up about 4 per cent of the

earth's crust, and magnesium, which accounts for about 2 per cent of the crust. Being so reactive, none of the alkaline metals occurs in an uncombined state.

The chief sources of calcium are calcium carbonate (CaCO$_3$), which occurs in many forms such as limestone, marble and calcite; gypsum and fluorspar (CaF$_2$). Natural chalk is a form of calcium carbonate, but the manufactured chalk used for writing on blackboards is calcium sulphate (CaSO$_4$). Calcium is an important constituent of bones and teeth, but the metal itself is not widely used in industry in its uncombined form. Calcium compounds, however, have many applications, a good example being limestone, which is used in cement making. Limestone is also used in steelmaking, where it acts as a flux which absorbs impurities from the molten metal.

Two important ores of magnesium are *dolomite* (MgCO$_3$.CaCO$_3$), a combination of magnesium and calcium carbonates, and *carnallite* (KCl.MgCl$_2$.6H$_2$O), potassium magnesium chloride, which is also an important source of potassium salts. *Chlorophyll*, the green colouring material in leaves, is a mixture of two substances known as chlorophyll-a and chlorophyll-b. These are complex compounds of carbon, hydrogen, oxygen, nitrogen and magnesium, their respective chemical formulae being C$_{55}$H$_{72}$O$_5$N$_4$Mg and C$_{55}$H$_{70}$O$_6$N$_4$Mg. Magnesium also occurs in sea water, constituting about 0.5 per cent of it by weight.

Magnesium compounds are used in medicines, and the very light but strong magnesium alloys have many applications in the engineering industries.

TRANSPORT
AND
TECHNOLOGY

Aircraft

To defy the force of gravity and take to the air was for many centuries one of man's greatest ambitions. From the end of the eighteenth century, there were a number of successful attempts at flight —in balloons, gliders and a variety of strange flying machines—but in 1903 the dream finally seemed to have come true. In that year the Wright brothers made the first-ever 'sustained' flight in a powered airplane. The freedom of long distance flight, and ultimately space-travel, was then only decades away.

The essential principle involved in flight is the need to create enough force to overcome gravity and lift a craft into the air. Then this force must somehow be maintained, otherwise the aircraft will sooner or later be pulled back to earth.

An airplane which is unpowered, like a glider, is given the initial force required to launch it by the pull of a towing truck or light aircraft. This gives it sufficient *lift,* the force which keeps it in the air, until it picks up a rising air current or 'thermal' upon which it can soar. Without this fresh impetus from air currents, the glider will slow down and sink because of the combined effects of air resistance, or *drag,* and gravity.

Powered aircraft, however, can overcome drag and gravity through the force of their engines. It is these that provide the necessary forward motion to generate lift on the wings.

Newton's laws of motion

The laws of motion, first formulated by Sir Isaac Newton in the seventeenth century, explain why a lifting force is necessary for flight. The first law of motion states that a force must be applied to any object before it will change its position, its speed or its direction of travel; thus an object will remain quite still or continue moving in a straight line at a constant speed unless some external force acts upon it. This tendency to oppose any change in its state of rest or motion is called the object's *inertia.*

The second law of motion states that, providing the *mass* of a body remains constant, a force acting on it will produce an *acceleration* which is proportional to that applied force. The mass of a body is a measure of the amount of matter it contains. This is not necessarily the same as a body's weight, which is a measure of the pull exerted on it by the force of gravity. The difference is easily demonstrated in space flight, where a body becomes increasingly weightless the further it travels into space, as the force of the earth's gravity gets weaker; the body's mass, however, remains constant.

The third law of motion states that action and reaction are equal and op-

Hit a ball into the air with a racket and it climbs for a while before gradually falling back to earth. In so doing it is obeying Newton's first law of motion, which states that an object stays still or continues to move in a straight line at a constant speed unless it is interfered with in some way by an external force. In other words, the ball would not have climbed into the air spontaneously. It required an initial external force from the movement of the racket by the arm to launch it. Once in the air, in the absence of any external forces, the ball would continue on and up along its original course. Instead it follows a smooth curve because the invisible force of the earth's gravity pulls it down all the time while the air friction slows it. The action of these external forces constantly and subtly modifies the direction and speed of the ball, eventually bringing it back to earth. When the ball is given a light tap with the racket it does not travel as high or as far as when it is

posite. According to this law, when an aircraft is standing on the ground the ground is providing an equal and opposite reaction to its weight—otherwise it would either sink into the ground or rise into the air. In flight, however, the air itself must be made to provide the necessary reaction to the action of the aircraft's weight. This reaction or upward force is provided by the lift, a force created largely by the wings as the aircraft is pushed or pulled through the air by its engines.

Any structure, such as an aircraft wing or tailplane, which is shaped to produce aerodynamic lift is known as an *aerofoil* (airfoil). Looking at an aircraft wing in cross-section, the upper surface is curved slightly upwards, while the lower surface is almost flat. As it moves through the air, the wing's rounded front or leading

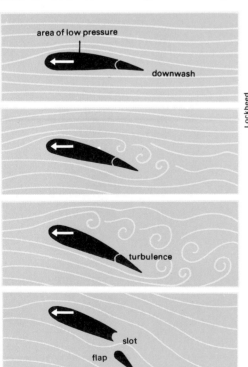

area of low pressure

downwash

turbulence

slot

flap

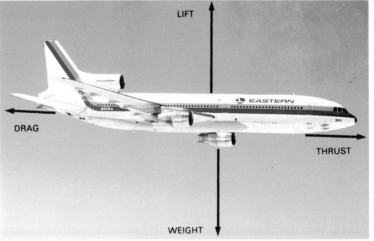

Lockheed

LIFT

DRAG

THRUST

WEIGHT

Left: The way an aircraft moves in the air depends upon the action of four basic forces. When an aeroplane is flying at a constant speed along a perfectly straight course these forces are in equilibrium. The lift from the wings exactly matches the weight; the forwards thrust balances the air resistance or drag.

Below: A model of an aeroplane in a wind tunnel shows the formation of turbulence. A swirling mass of air is created when the smooth airflow breaks away from the wings. Wind tunnels are used to test the airflow over new aircraft designs. Smoke is introduced into the tunnel to make the airflow visible.

Left: The airflow over a level wing or aerofoil is smoothly curved downwards, giving good lift. Tilting the wing up slightly boosts its lift. At larger angles the airflow starts to break away from the wing. As it is tilted further the turbulence moves forwards so that less of the wing gives lift. Eventually a critical angle of attack is reached when the airflow separates from the wing completely. Then so little of the aerofoil is creating lift that the aircraft 'stalls' and drops sharply.

Bottom left: Lowering the flaps on the wing exaggerates the profile of the whole aerofoil, increasing its lift and the critical stalling angle.

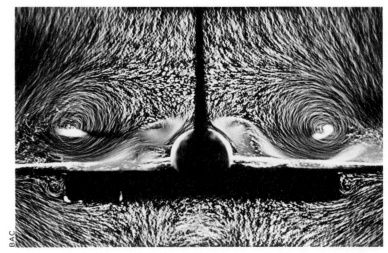

BAC

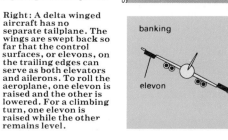

given a much stronger hit. According to the second law of motion, provided the mass of an object is kept constant, the force applied to it is proportional to its acceleration. While the mass of the ball is the same, the force applied by the racket in each case is different. The greater the force, the further the ball flies because of its greater acceleration.

When the ball lands, it bounces up again in accordance with the third law of motion. This states that to every action there is an equal and opposite reaction. As it hits the ground, the ball depresses the earth fractionally, but because the earth is so much larger than the ball, this dent is invisible to the naked eye. The earth reacts, however, by pushing back with exactly the same force as the force of impact, trying to return to its original shape. If the ground is soft, a slight depression might be visible where the ball landed because the soil was not strong enough to resist the sudden rapid acceleration of impact.

edge deflects the air into two streams, one of which passes over the wing and the other under it. Early attempts at heavier-than-air flight used wings with a flat cross-section, but designers soon realized that much more lift could be obtained if suitably curved aerofoil surfaces were used.

The shape is specifically designed to create lift, and is effective for two reasons. Firstly, as the aircraft moves forward, air has to rush in behind it to prevent a vacuum forming. Secondly, because the curved upper surface of the aerofoil is longer from front to back than the relatively straight lower surface, the upper airstream must travel faster than the lower airstream, in order to reach the trailing edge of the wing at the same time. That these actions create lift is explained by a principle discovered by the eighteenth-century Swiss scientist Daniel Bernoulli.

According to Bernoulli's principle, if the speed at which a *fluid*—that means a gas or a liquid—flows across a surface is increased, the pressure which it exerts on that surface will decrease. The faster airstream over the top of the aerofoil therefore exerts a much lower pressure than the slower one under it. This situation of reduced pressure above a wing creates a very powerful upward force, or lift.

The flow of air over the curved wing surface is known as *laminar flow;* it is made up of successive layers of air flowing smoothly over each other. The layers next to the surface of the wing, known collectively as the *boundary layer,* travel more slowly than the rest of the laminar flow, because of the friction between them and the wing. This boundary layer is very thin, less than a fraction of a millimetre thick.

The *angle of attack,* that is the angle at which the wing meets the airstream, has an important bearing on the amount of lift the wings generate. The wing meeting the air at a slightly up-turned angle gives a slightly increased pressure on the underside, which backs up the effects of the low pressure above the wing in creating lift. Increasing the angle of attack increases lift—up to a certain critical angle of about 15°. After that point, lift falls off sharply and the result can be a *stall.*

Turbulent air

The fall-off in lift is caused by *turbulent* air. At small angles of attack the boundary layer leaves the upper surface of the wing at or near the trailing edge; this is the *separation point.* Behind the separation point, the air flowing over the wing is no longer streamlined—in line with the direction of the wing—but *turbulent,* breaking up into swirling vortices. Turbulent air creates a lot of drag but very little lift. As the angle of attack increases, the separation point moves further and further forward on the wing, so that an increasingly small area of the wing is producing lift. Finally when the critical angle is reached, so little of the wing is contributing lift that the aircraft stalls and drops sharply. Similarly, when a plane runs into weather conditions that are causing turbulent air, this disruption of the smooth airflow can produce the same stalling effect. To correct a stall in mid-air the pilot needs to level-off the angle of attack and increase lift; the usual manoeuvre is a shallow dive, which will help the aircraft pick up speed and generate more lift.

Alternatively the lift of a wing can be increased at low speeds by extending different types of slats and flaps that effectively change the whole profile of the aerofoil. A small, adjustable aerofoil, or *slat,* positioned in front of the main wing with a small gap, or *slot,* between the two

CONTROL SURFACES

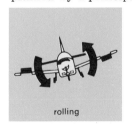

rolling

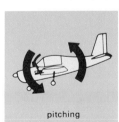

pitching

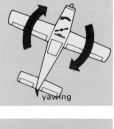

yawing

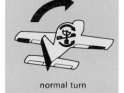

normal turn

pitch axis

yaw axis

elevator

rudder

aileron

flap

elevator

control column

rudder pedals

flap

aileron

roll axis

Above and left: A normal aircraft is manoeuvred about three axes by three sets of control surfaces.

Rolling: Turning the control column in the cockpit moves the ailerons, causing the aircraft to roll. When an aileron is lowered the wing creates more lift and rises. Raising the aileron on the other wing reduces its lift.

Pitching: Pushing the control column moves the elevators, tipping the aircraft up or down.

Yawing: Turning the rudder makes the aeroplane yaw, or turn. A normal banking turn combines yawing the aircraft and rolling it in to the turn.

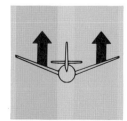

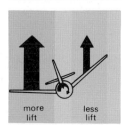

more lift   less lift

Left: The upwards tilting, or dihedral, of the wings stabilizes the aircraft. When equally inclined to the horizontal, both wings create equal lift. As the aircraft rolls, a sideways airflow hits the lower wing at a larger angle than the upper wing, so that it generates more lift, righting the aeroplane.

Right: A delta winged aircraft has no separate tailplane. The wings are swept back so far that the control surfaces, or elevons, on the trailing edges can serve as both elevators and ailerons. To roll the aeroplane, one elevon is raised and the other is lowered. For a climbing turn, one elevon is raised while the other remains level.

Saab

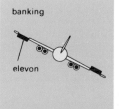

banking

elevon

banking and climbing

Left: Cargo-only Boeing 747. These aircraft are specifically designed for commercial freight loads, and have articulating nose cones.

Rolls Royce Ltd

Alphabet & Image

Right: BOEING 767 200 Cutaway view of a Boeing 767 medium range airliner, which first entered service in 1982.

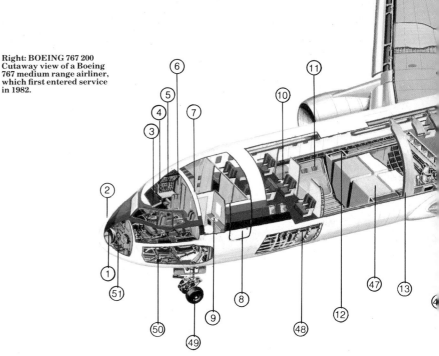

Left: A World War 2 Supermarine Spitfire XVI of the RAF, one of the most famous aircraft of the period.

so that it continues to produce lift until a greater stalling angle is reached.

The lift produced by the wing will vary with the speed of the aeroplane and its area. The slower an aircraft flies the greater the angle of attack its wings must have to create enough lift to keep it in the air. The faster it goes the more lift it will produce. Doubling the airspeed will give not twice but four times the lift.

This explains why an aircraft has to attain a considerable speed on the ground before it acquires enough lift to take off. At first, as the aeroplane accelerates along the runway, all the weight is borne by the wheels. The pilot watches the airspeed indicator and when the aeroplane is travelling fast enough he pulls back on the control column. This raises the elevators on the trailing edge of the tailplane or stabilizer which decreases the lift on the tail and rotates the nose upwards. Such tilting of the aircraft increases the angle of attack of the wings until the lift can support the weight so that the aeroplane rises into the air.

The aeroplane is usually allowed to reach a slightly higher speed than the minimum required for flight so that it does not have to be tilted to the maximum angle of attack before lift off. This would leave little margin for early flight manoeuvres. Sometimes in large jet aircraft flaps are lowered for take off to increase the lift of the wings and enlarge the angle of attack the aeroplane can reach safely before stalling.

Raising these flaps prematurely after take-off can have tragic consequences. For if the aeroplane is still climbing steeply when the flaps are raised, the wings may be inclined at an angle of attack greater than the critical stalling angle. In which case the aircraft stalls and, because it may not have gained sufficient height to give the pilot time to correct the situation by tilting the nose down into a glide until it has picked up enough airspeed to restore lift, it plummets to the ground out of control. Fortunately the chances of this error occurring are extremely slight because of the numerous warning systems built into the control panel in the cockpit.

Since lift also depends on the mass or density of the air, airports at high altitudes and in tropical countries where the air pressure is lower than at sea level or

1 Radar dish
2 Radome
3 Captain
4 1st officer
5 Engineer
6 Engineer's panel
7 Jump seat
8 Entry doors (port and starboard)
9 Forward toilet
10 1st class cabin (18 seats)
11 Forward freight door
12 Electronics bay
13 Air conditioning riser ducts
14 Leading edge slat (extended)
15 Vent surge tank
16 Integral fuel tank (starboard)
17 Spoiler (deployed)
18 Toilets
19 Inboard double slotted flap
20 Rear spar fuselage frame
21 193 tourist seats
22 Open cargo door (rear)
23 10 cargo containers in rear freight hold
24 HF antenna
25 TV antenna
26 Tail VOR antennas

27 Auxiliary power unit (APU)
28 Honeycomb construction
29 Static dischargers
30 Tail logo light
31 Rear galley
32 Rear toilet
33 Pressurization unit
34 Undercarriage mounting beam
35 Wheel bay
36 Hinge link fairing
37 Inner aileron
38 Flap hinge fairings
39 Outer aileron
40 Stringers
41 Main undercarriage
42 Pratt and Whitney JT9D-7R4D engine
43 Engine mounting pylon
44 Slat drive motor
45 Air conditioning distribution ducts/manifolds
46 Landing and taxiing lights
47 Cargo containers
48 Electronics cooling plant
49 Nosewheels
50 Nosewheel bay
51 Glideslope antennas

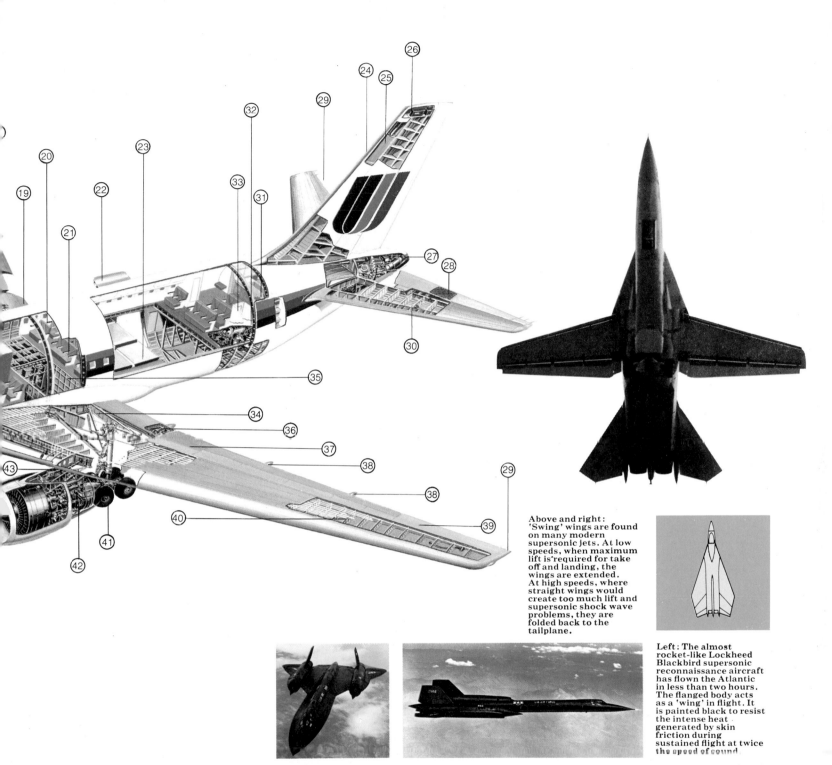

Above and right: 'Swing' wings are found on many modern supersonic jets. At low speeds, when maximum lift is required for take off and landing, the wings are extended. At high speeds, where straight wings would create too much lift and supersonic shock wave problems, they are folded back to the tailplane.

Left: The almost rocket-like Lockheed Blackbird supersonic reconnaissance aircraft has flown the Atlantic in less than two hours. The flanged body acts as a 'wing' in flight. It is painted black to resist the intense heat generated by skin friction during sustained flight at twice the speed of sound.

Left: The Russian Tupolev Tu-144 has a pair of retractable foreplanes behind the cockpit to improve its stability at low speeds.

Right: The streamlined Concorde is designed to cruise at supersonic speeds. The droop nose is lowered for landing to increase the pilot's visibility.

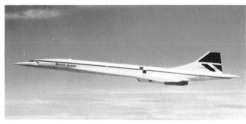

in temperate regions have longer runways. This allows the aeroplane more room to build up the slightly higher speed it needs before it can generate an equivalent amount of lift. Similarly, after take off, as the aeroplane climbs into thinner air at high altitudes, it must either go faster or fly at a greater angle of attack to maintain lift.

For landing, the elevators are lowered to tip the nose down into a gradual descent to the runway. On the final approach, the aeroplane adopts an increasingly nose-up posture, giving the wings a high angle of attack to sustain lift at the reduced speed. Flaps are also lowered during landing to boost lift. One potential danger in landing is that the nose will tip back so far that the aeroplane will stall and drop on to the runway. Depressed flaps help to minimize this risk of stalling by increasing the operative angle of attack of the wings.

Landing transfers the lift from the wings to the ground again. The pilot aims to bring the aeroplane into contact with the runway at the slowest possible vertical velocity and a low ground speed. Aircraft usually land into the wind in order to cut their ground speed. After landing, the aeroplane is slowed rapidly by raising air brakes or *spoilers* to increase drag and cut lift and by reversing the engine thrust.

Helicopters and Autogyros

A conventional fixed wing aircraft is able to fly because of the lift generated on its wings as they move forward through the air. On a helicopter or autogyro, however, the fixed wings are replaced by a set of thin wings called *blades* attached to a shaft. The rotation of this set of blades, or the *rotor*, through the air creates the lift necessary for flight.

An autogyro or a helicopter will climb when the total lift of the rotor exceeds the weight of the machine. The helicopter will hover when the sum of all the lift forces on the rotor blades is equal to the weight of the machine.

A helicopter has a rotor which is driven by an engine, but an autogyro has a rotor which gets its power from the motion of the airstream blowing through it, rather like a windmill. Thus the autogyro needs some other device, usually an engine-driven propeller, to pull or push it through the air horizontally.

Hovering and climbing

As the rotor turns, it traces out a circle in the air which is known as the *rotor disc*. The total lift generated by the rotor acts through the centre of this disc and at right angles to it. This means that when a helicopter is hovering the lift forces are acting vertically upwards through the centre of the rotor. To make the machine climb, the lift generated by each blade must be increased. This is done by increasing the *angle of attack*—the angle at which the leading edge meets the airstream—of each blade equally, thus increasing the total lift without changing the direction in which it acts. The pilot controls this by means of a lever known as the *collective pitch control*.

In order to make the helicopter fly forwards the rotor disc must be tilted forwards slightly, so that part of the rotor acts to pull the machine in that direction. The rotor disc is tilted forwards by increasing the angle of attack of each blade as it travels around the rear of the disc, and decreasing the angle as each blade travels around the front of the disc. As a change in the angle of attack means a change in lift, the lift is increased at the rear of the rotor disc and decreased at the front, causing the disc to tilt forwards.

These changes in the angle of attack of the blades can be made to occur at any point around the rotor disc, tilting the disc accordingly. This enables the helicopter to fly in any direction. The pilot controls the tilt of the rotor disc by means of the *cyclic pitch control lever*.

The importance of blade speed

When a helicopter is hovering, the speed of the blades through the air is due to their speed of rotation and is constant at all points around the rotor disc. When the helicopter is moving forwards, however, the speed of a blade through the air changes as it travels around the disc. When a blade is travelling towards the front of the disc, its air speed is its speed due to its rotation plus the speed of the aircraft (just as a bullet fired forwards

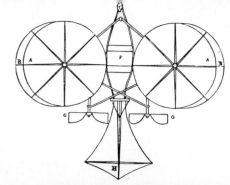

Right: Designed by Sir George Cayley in 1843, this early idea for a vertical take-off and landing aircraft used two sets of rotors to provide lift, and two propellers to provide forward thrust. It was intended that the fan-like rotors would fold flat to form circular wings to create lift during forward flight.

Below: This helicopter was built in France by Paul Cornu in 1907 and during several short flights in November of that year it reached a height of almost 2 m (6 ft). It was powered by a 24 hp Antoinette engine driving a pair of rotors mounted in a tandem configuration, and the pilot sat next to the engine.

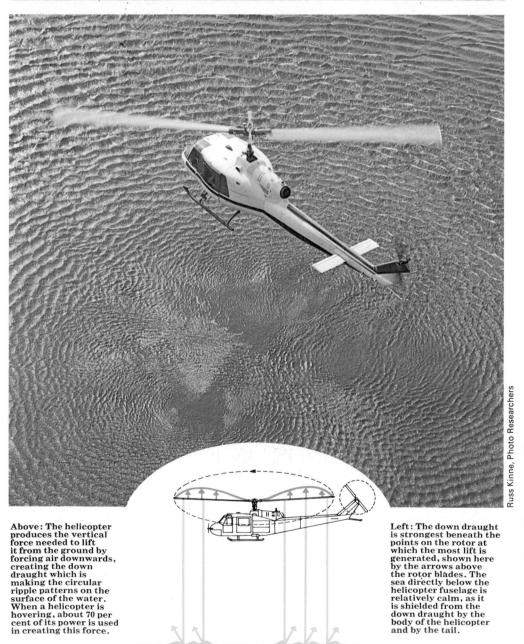

Above: The helicopter produces the vertical force needed to lift it from the ground by forcing air downwards, creating the down draught which is making the circular ripple patterns on the surface of the water. When a helicopter is hovering, about 70 per cent of its power is used in creating this force.

Left: The down draught is strongest beneath the points on the rotor at which the most lift is generated, shown here by the arrows above the rotor blades. The sea directly below the helicopter fuselage is relatively calm, as it is shielded from the down draught by the body of the helicopter and by the tail.

Radio Times Hulton Picture Library (above also)

Russ Kinne, Photo Researchers

Gazelle helicopters escorting army scout cars in Germany. In 1907 Paul Cornu had built the first helicopter capable of carrying a man.

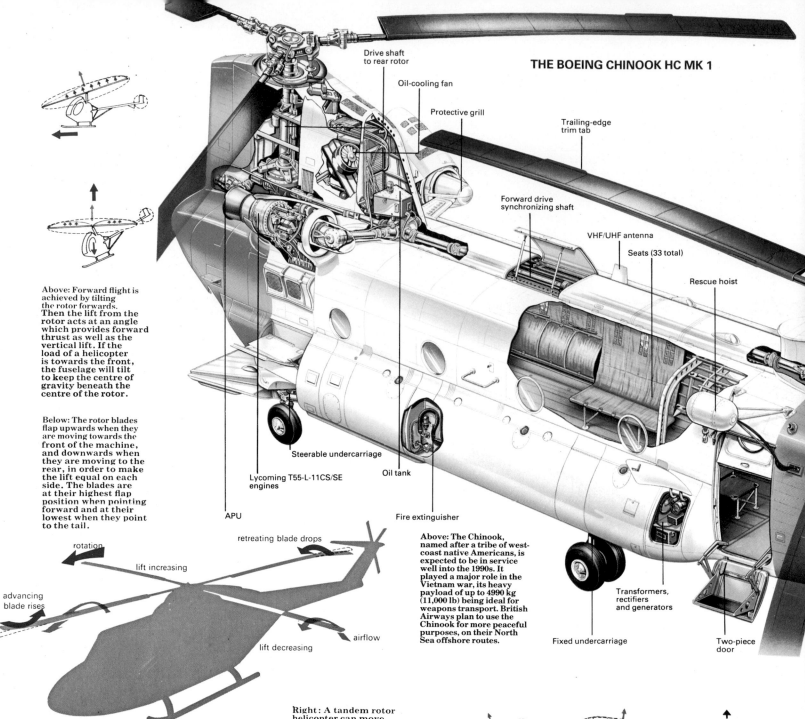

THE BOEING CHINOOK HC MK 1

Drive shaft to rear rotor

Oil-cooling fan

Protective grill

Trailing-edge trim tab

Forward drive synchronizing shaft

VHF/UHF antenna

Seats (33 total)

Rescue hoist

Steerable undercarriage

Lycoming T55-L-11CS/SE engines

Oil tank

APU

Fire extinguisher

Transformers, rectifiers and generators

Fixed undercarriage

Two-piece door

Above: Forward flight is achieved by tilting the rotor forwards. Then the lift from the rotor acts at an angle which provides forward thrust as well as the vertical lift. If the load of a helicopter is towards the front, the fuselage will tilt to keep the centre of gravity beneath the centre of the rotor.

Below: The rotor blades flap upwards when they are moving towards the front of the machine, and downwards when they are moving to the rear, in order to make the lift equal on each side. The blades are at their highest flap position when pointing forward and at their lowest when they point to the tail.

rotation

retreating blade drops

lift increasing

advancing blade rises

airflow

lift decreasing

Above: The Chinook, named after a tribe of west-coast native Americans, is expected to be in service well into the 1990s. It played a major role in the Vietnam war, its heavy payload of up to 4990 kg (11,000 lb) being ideal for weapons transport. British Airways plan to use the Chinook for more peaceful purposes, on their North Sea offshore routes.

from a gun on a moving train will travel at the speed at which it left the gun plus the speed of the train on which the gun was travelling).

When a blade is travelling towards the rear of the disc, however, its air speed is reduced by the speed of the aircraft, which at that point is effectively travelling in the opposite direction to it. As the lift on a blade varies according to its speed through the air, the forward-moving blade has more lift than the rearward-moving one.

If the rotor was a completely rigid structure, these differences in lift would cause it to tilt towards the rearward-moving side, and the helicopter would tend to fly sideways instead of straight ahead. To overcome this problem, the rotor blades are hinged at the roots to allow them to flap up and down a certain amount. This allows the forward-moving blade to rise slightly, in effect reducing its lift. The blades thus rise when moving forwards and drop again when moving backwards in order to keep the actual lift on them constant.

Right: A tandem rotor helicopter can move sideways by tilting both rotors towards the appropriate side. In order to turn the helicopter, the rear rotor is tilted to one side and the forward rotor to the other, so that the nose and tail of the craft are moved in opposite directions, causing it to turn.

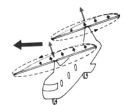

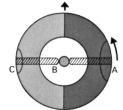

rotation

flapping hinge

lag hinge

hub

rotor blade

feathering hinge

control link

rotor shaft

flap

rotating plate

non-rotating plate

connection to pilot's controls

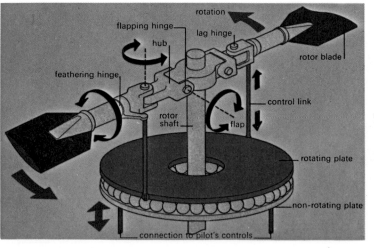

Above: A plan view of a rotor shows the points at which problems can occur when travelling at speed. At point 'A' the blade speed nears the speed of sound and drag is high; at 'B' the airspeed is too low for useful lift; and at 'C' the blade tip stalls as the pilot increases blade pitch to maintain lift.

Left: Changes in rotor blade pitch angle are transmitted by the swash plate which moves up or down for collective pitch changes, and tilts to give cyclic pitch changes. Blade pitch angle depends on the swash plate height. If it is tilted the pitch of a blade is increased as it passes the high side.

Changing direction

Newton's third law of motion states that every action produces an equal but opposite reaction. In other words, if a body exerts a force on another in one direction, it will itself be subject to an equal force acting in the opposite direction. Thus a main rotor which is rotated by an engine in the fuselage will set up a reaction which will result in the fuselage rotating in the opposite direction. To prevent this, a torque, or twisting force, compensating system is installed, such as the small anti-torque rotor at the tail of single main rotor helicopters.

Directional control can be achieved by varying the amount of torque compensation applied. Over-compensating turns the fuselage in the same direction as the main rotor, and under-compensating allows it to turn in the opposite direction. Where compensation is by means of an anti-torque rotor, the amount of compensation is controlled by varying the *pitch*, or angle of attack, of the blades.

What type of engine?

Helicopter rotors are usually driven through a shaft fitted to the rotor hub (shaft drive), but some have been built with small jet thrust units fitted at the rotor blade tips (tip drive).

Shaft drive rotors can be driven by any form of aero engine. Originally all helicopters were powered by piston engines, but the *turboshaft*, or gas turbine, engine is now used on all but the smallest machines. Rotary engines, like the Wankel engine invented in Germany, are being considered for these small machines.

Dealing with engine failure

In the event of engine failure, the rotor rapidly slows down and loses lift, but it is possible for the pilot to land safely by use of *autorotation*. By rapidly lowering the collective pitch lever the pilot can set the blades so that their leading edges are pointing slightly downwards from the horizontal. As the aircraft is descending, the new position of the blades means that a positive, or upwards, angle of attack is maintained against the upward flow of the airstream. This generates forces on the blades to keep them spinning, and as the helicopter nears the ground the pilot raises the collective pitch lever slightly, so that the spinning rotor provides enough lift to slow down the machine before it lands.

Helicopter speed limits

The conventional helicopter cannot fly at more than about 400 km/h (250 mph) because at high speeds the air speed of the forward-moving blade approaches the speed of sound and that of the rearward-moving blade is very low. The result of this is that the drag on the forward-moving blade is greatly increased and it begins to lose lift because of the break-up of the airflow over it. The rearward-moving blade loses lift because of its low air speed. At a critical speed, when pointing directly to the tail of the aircraft, the blade stalls, because air is flowing from the rotor hub to the blade tip—not across the blade to give lift.

A partial solution to this problem has been put forward by the Sikorsky Company. This is the Advancing Blade Concept (ABC) which uses two identical rotors, positioned one above the other and turning in opposite directions. The system balances the forces on the advancing side of each rotor, thus balancing the helicopter by cancelling out the loss of lift on the rearward-moving side of each rotor.

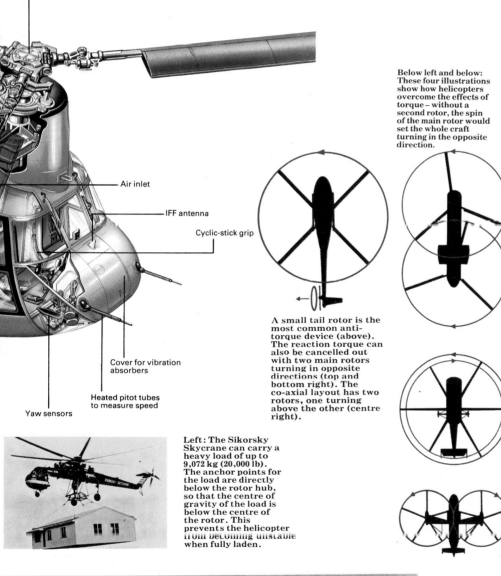

Rotor hub and oil tank

Air inlet

IFF antenna

Cyclic-stick grip

Cover for vibration absorbers

Heated pitot tubes to measure speed

Yaw sensors

Below left and below: These four illustrations show how helicopters overcome the effects of torque – without a second rotor, the spin of the main rotor would set the whole craft turning in the opposite direction.

A small tail rotor is the most common anti-torque device (above). The reaction torque can also be cancelled out with two main rotors turning in opposite directions (top and bottom right). The co-axial layout has two rotors, one turning above the other (centre right).

Left: The Sikorsky Skycrane can carry a heavy load of up to 9,072 kg (20,000 lb). The anchor points for the load are directly below the rotor hub, so that the centre of gravity of the load is below the centre of the rotor. This prevents the helicopter from becoming unstable when fully laden.

Left: The rotor of an autogyro is turned by air blowing through it. Lift is only created when the rotor is spinning, and so an autogyro must be moving forwards before it can take off.

Right: Autogyro rotor blades, like those on a helicopter, flap up and down to maintain equal lift across the rotor. Autogyros use propellers for forward thrust and are steered by rudders.

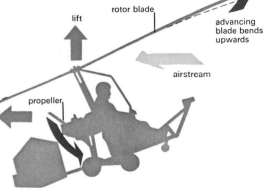

lift

rotor blade

advancing blade bends upwards

airstream

retreating blade springs down

propeller

thrust

Russ Kinne, Photo Researchers

Hovercraft
and Hydrofoils

In 1953 the British inventor Christopher Cockerell began investigating methods of making boats go faster. It was one of his successful experiments that gave the first real impetus to the development of vehicles supported by a layer of air. A number of names are used to describe air cushion supported craft, including *hovercraft, air cushion vehicles* (ACV), *ground effect machine* (GEM) and *surface effect ships* (SES).

Cockerell's idea was to trap air beneath the hull of a boat, thereby eliminating the friction between the hull and the water which slows down conventional craft. Originally this was achieved by blowing air into a shallow upside-down hull at a pressure slightly higher than atmospheric and trapping it by means of a curtain of very high pressure air around the edge of the hull. This *air cushion* trapped within an *air curtain* provided two to three times more lifting force than if the same air was simply directed downwards as an even jet of air. Cockerell produced a free-flight model using this system, followed by the construction of a full-scale manned hovercraft.

Flexible skirts

One of the disadvantages of the early system was that it required an excessive amount of power to generate the air curtain. The next important step in the development of an economic hovercraft was the introduction of a *flexible skirt system* in 1961. This is a rubberized material fringe that hangs down around the edge of the vessel. The skirt serves the same function as the air curtain in containing the air cushion.

In marine vehicles the air cushion permits speeds three times faster than a ship, with relatively low water resis-

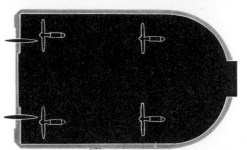

Above and right: The SR.N4 hovercraft travels on a 2.5 m (8 ft) deep cushion of air and is powered by four Rolls-Royce Marine Proteus gas turbine engines. The SR.N4 is 39 m (130 ft) long with a beam (width) of 24 m (78 ft). Overall height on its landing pads is 11.5 m (38 ft), and it weighs 160 tons.

Below and right: Air blown into the space between two cans creates a curtain of air around the lower rims. This traps a cushion of air below the inner can which gives the needed lift. On measuring the pressure on a scale Cockerell proved that the force of lift was greater than that achieved by one can.

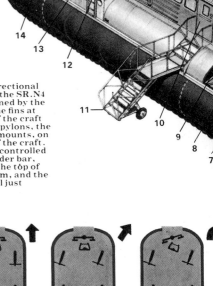

Below: Directional control of the SR.N4 is determined by the angle of the fins at the rear of the craft and of the pylons, the propeller mounts, on the roof of the craft. These are controlled by the rudder bar, shown at the top of the diagram, and the handwheel just below it.

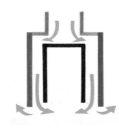

National Research Development Council

Right: Hovercraft are used to provide ferry services in many parts of the world. SR.N6s, the world's largest amphibious hovercraft, operate a regular service across the English Channel, each carrying 424 passengers and 55 vehicles, while the smaller SR.N4s carry 270 passengers and 35 vehicles.

Left: The world's first hovercraft, the SR.N1, was built by aircraft makers Saunders-Roe and financed by Britain's National Research Development Corporation. SR.N1 made the first hovercraft crossing of an open body of water when it crossed the English Channel from Calais to Dover in 1959.

Popperfoto

British Hovercraft Corporation

TYPES OF HOVERCRAFT

air fan air
plenum chamber

air fan air

air fan air
inner skirt outer

OPEN PLENUM

PERIPHERAL JET

FLEXIBLE SKIRT

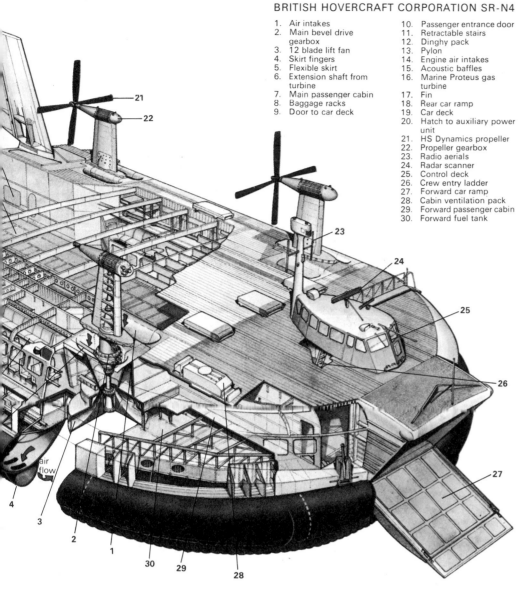

BRITISH HOVERCRAFT CORPORATION SR-N4

1. Air intakes
2. Main bevel drive gearbox
3. 12 blade lift fan
4. Skirt fingers
5. Flexible skirt
6. Extension shaft from turbine
7. Main passenger cabin
8. Baggage racks
9. Door to car deck
10. Passenger entrance door
11. Retractable stairs
12. Dinghy pack
13. Pylon
14. Engine air intakes
15. Acoustic baffles
16. Marine Proteus gas turbine
17. Fin
18. Rear car ramp
19. Car deck
20. Hatch to auxiliary power unit
21. HS Dynamics propeller
22. Propeller gearbox
23. Radio aerials
24. Radar scanner
25. Control deck
26. Crew entry ladder
27. Forward car ramp
28. Cabin ventilation pack
29. Forward passenger cabin
30. Forward fuel tank

tance. Craft using a full peripheral skirt can travel from one kind of surface to another with little perceptible change in the craft's motion. This means that amphibious movements — travelling from land to sea — and over-ice operations are possible. Non-amphibious marine hovercraft have been developed with side walls or keels immersed in the water, sealing the sides of the cushion, with the ends sealed by flexible curtains. These craft offer greater economy of power as far as the cushion is concerned but require relatively higher driving power because of the sidewall resistance in the water.

Moving forwards

Hovercraft can be propelled by a variety of means, including ducted or unducted propellers, with low tip speeds for quietness, and centrifugal fans. Propulsive devices which operate by contact with the ground are being considered for use in Arctic regions where the sloping terrain demands substantial side forces to control the craft effectively.

Redirection of the propulsive thrust is one common steering method. Many craft employ rudders operating in the fan or propeller slipstream to swing the craft into a turn. Sideways facing air nozzles are also used on some designs to help turn the craft at low speeds. For purely marine hovercraft, control can be very effectively obtained by the use of conventional rudders, and craft with immersed sidewalls can be steered by turning the sidewalls.

Braking of amphibious hovercraft is not as effective as for wheeled land vehicles unless a surface contacting device is used. Cutting off the lift-creating air to stop the craft by letting it settle on the surface is only advisable over water or smooth surfaces. Drawing to a halt is thus a very gradual process for amphibious craft — reverse thrust of the propellers is used, which provides only about one third of forward thrust.

Hovercraft are now used quite extensively as passenger and cargo ferries, and many are also in military use as patrol craft and troop carriers. *Hovertrains*, running along concrete tracks have been developed — but the future here seems to be with levitation by magnets (maglev) rather than air cushions. Another proposal, by the French company Bertin, is the use of air cushion landing gear for heavy freight aircraft, and SEDAM are presently building 225-ton air cushion ferry craft.

Rapid progress has been made in the development of air cushion platforms and strap-on skirt systems for the movement of large, heavy items such as oil storage tanks and electrical transformers. Air cushion platforms range in size from small ACV pallets a few feet square to large ACV platforms capable of handling loads weighing hundreds of tons. Basically these consist of flat boxes, sealed except for an inlet at one edge which is connected to an air pump and vents in the bottom through which the air escapes to form the air cushion. The use of these ACV pallets hovering a few inches above the ground means that heavy items like aero-engines or large castings can be easily be moved around by hand.

Ice-breaking is another dramatic role for ACV platforms. The reasons why ice-breaking occurs beneath an air cushion are not yet fully understood, but in

Left: Fixed sidewall hovercraft ride on 'captured air bubbles' and are nicknamed CABs. Thin but solid sidewalls extend into the water to block air leakage from the chamber beneath the hovercraft deck. Increasing the air pressure lifts the craft, thus reducing water drag.

Below: ACV pallets are used to move heavy loads. Air is pumped into the pallet and, as pressure builds up, escapes through thin lubricating seals. This creates an air cushion between the pallet and the ground, making the pallet and its load airborne. It can then be moved with little effort.

Beken of Cowes

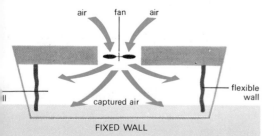

air — fan — air

captured air

flexible wall

FIXED WALL

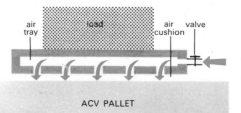

air tray — load — air cushion — valve

ACV PALLET

Canada 69 cm (27 in) thick ice has been broken by the passage of a 220–ton ACV.

Hydrofoils

A hydrofoil boat works on the same principle as an aircraft. It has a boat-shaped hull to which 'wings', or *hydrofoils,* are attached at the front and back by means of vertical, leg-like struts. As they travel through the water these hydrofoils produce lift in the same way the aerofoil shape of an aircraft wing provides lift in the air.

A stationary hydrofoil boat floats on the surface of the water like a conventional boat. As it gathers speed it begins to rise in the water until, when it is travelling fast, the lift created by the flow of water over the hydrofoil is sufficient to raise the hull clear of the water. A hydrofoil boat in full flight looks rather like an ordinary boat on water skis. Once out of the water the hull no longer suffers resistance from friction between the hull and the water or from waves in rough water and therefore gives a faster, smoother ride.

Water wings

The thicker the medium through which a foil is travelling, the more lift it can produce. As water is several hundred times denser than air, hydrofoils can be much smaller than an aircraft's wings and yet still create considerable lift. An aircraft's wings, however, operate in air whose density changes little over the range of altitudes at which they fly. The hydrofoil boat's 'wings' are working very close to the surface of the water where there is a massive and abrupt change in density between air and water. If the foils break through the surface a large drop in lift occurs because the pressure difference between its upper and lower surfaces is destroyed when the water no longer flows over the top.

The upper and lower limits of the depth within which the foils must operate are too fine to be controlled by hand. To ensure a nearly constant flying height, the foils need some form of automatic control. This in-built stability is achieved differently by the two principle types of hydrofoil design.

Surface piercing hydrofoils

In the *surface piercing* hydrofoils, the foils actually break the surface of the water as the craft moves forward. When lift is lost due to the hydrofoil breaking through waves, the craft sinks deeper into the water, thereby immersing a greater foil area which in turn creates more lift. This very simple design is used in almost all the commercial hydrofoil ferries in the western world.

Fully submerged hydrofoils

In the *fully submerged* hydrofoils, the foils are completely immersed in water all the time. The amount of lift produced is controlled by altering the angle of attack of the foils with hydraulic rams. These are rods moved by liquid under pressure which press down on or pull back from the hydrofoil to change its angle of inclination.

The movement of the hydraulic rams themselves is directed by signals from a sonic device in the bow which sends out pulses of high-frequency sound waves and listens for echoes from on-coming waves in order to assess the wave's height. It then automatically instructs the hy-

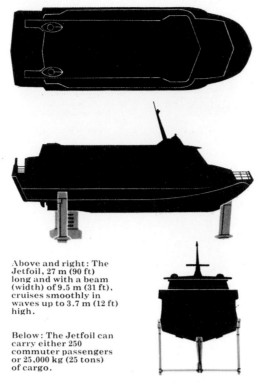

Above and right: The Jetfoil, 27 m (90 ft) long and with a beam (width) of 9.5 m (31 ft), cruises smoothly in waves up to 3.7 m (12 ft) high.

Below: The Jetfoil can carry either 250 commuter passengers or 25,000 kg (25 tons) of cargo.

Below: The torpedo-shaped HD4 hydrofoil boat was designed by Alexander Graham Bell and Casey Baldwin. Nicknamed the 'Water Monster' and weighing over 5,100 kg (5 tons), it achieved lift even at low speeds. In 1918 it reached a world speed boat record of 114.4 km per hour (70.86 mph).

Right: The Tucumcari, a Patrol Gunboat Hydrofoil, was designed to United States Navy specifications under a programme initiated in 1965. Its maximum foilborne speed of 50 knots made it ideally suited to Vietnam war service. The craft was scrapped in 1972 after running aground in the Caribbean.

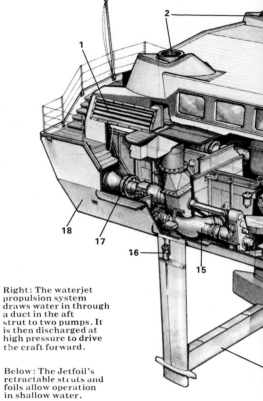

Right: The waterjet propulsion system draws water in through a duct in the aft strut to two pumps. It is then discharged at high pressure to drive the craft forward.

Below: The Jetfoil's retractable struts and foils allow operation in shallow water.

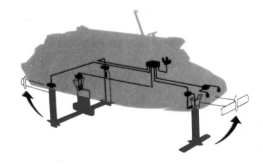

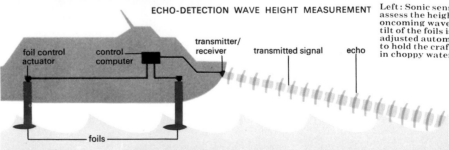

ECHO-DETECTION WAVE HEIGHT MEASUREMENT

foil control actuator — control computer — transmitter/receiver — transmitted signal — echo — foils

Left: Sonic sensors assess the height of oncoming waves and the tilt of the foils is adjusted automatically to hold the craft level in choppy water.

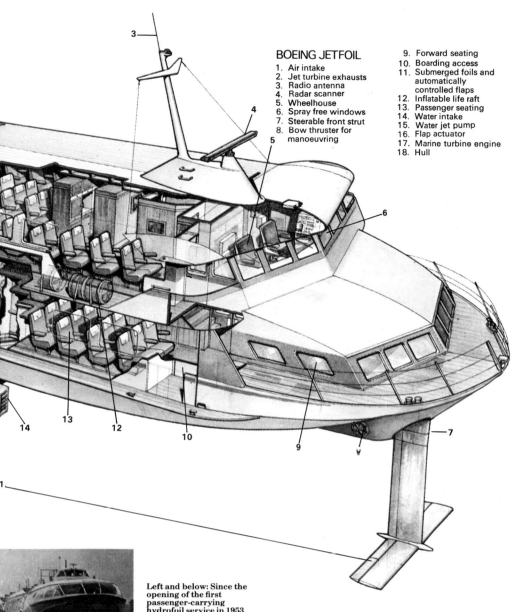

BOEING JETFOIL

1. Air intake
2. Jet turbine exhausts
3. Radio antenna
4. Radar scanner
5. Wheelhouse
6. Spray free windows
7. Steerable front strut
8. Bow thruster for manoeuvring
9. Forward seating
10. Boarding access
11. Submerged foils and automatically controlled flaps
12. Inflatable life raft
13. Passenger seating
14. Water intake
15. Water jet pump
16. Flap actuator
17. Marine turbine engine
18. Hull

Left and below: Since the opening of the first passenger-carrying hydrofoil service in 1953 many commercial routes have been developed, including a large fleet in Russia (left). The picture below shows a Swedish ferry to Oland.

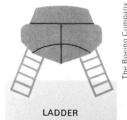

Above: The Boeing Jetfoil, operating regularly between Dover and Ostend, carries 280 passengers at a cruising speed of 80 km/h (50 mph) in one hour and 40 minutes. It is propelled by two gas turbines, of 3780 horsepower each, driving two water-jet pumps which expel 90,000 litres of water per minute.

Right: The Little Squirt in full flight can do 50 knots. Built in 1962 as a research vessel it was the first craft to be fitted with a waterjet system of propulsion. Trailing edge flaps were fitted to the foils and foil controls introduced both features used in later hydrofoil designs like the Jetfoil.

TYPES OF HYDROFOIL

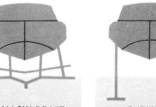

SURFACE PIERCING

SHALLOW-DRAFT

SUBMERGED

LADDER

draulic system to make the appropriate adjustments to the angles of the hydrofoils so that the hull is held steady. Gyroscopes in the hull which sense the craft's pitch, roll and heave motions also feed information into this control circuit and help to keep the hydrofoil boat level. These systems are very expensive; the principal user of fully submerged hydrofoils is the US Navy.

Propulsion systems

An early type of hydrofoil arrangement was the 'ladder' type, in which the amount of lift generated depends on the number of rungs immersed — the greater the number of rungs covered, the greater the lift.

Some designs of either type of hydrofoil have most of the weight carried by a large foil or foils at the front while on others the main foils are placed towards the rear. The smaller foil which carries the remaining weight is usually pivoted for steering the craft.

Commercial hydrofoil boats are usually powered by marine diesel engines, but high speed military craft often use gas turbine engines. There may be two separate propulsion systems, one for use when the craft is being carried by the foils and another for when it is moving very slowly and floating on its hull.

Problems at high speed

At speeds above 50 knots, hydrofoils can suffer from the effects of *cavity flow*. As a result of increasingly turbulent water flow across the top of the foil, cavities are formed along the foil surface which cut its lifting force. These cavities subsequently fill with air or water vapour.

When the craft is travelling very fast, the water pressure on the upper foil surface may drop below atmospheric pressure. Under such circumstances, air from above the surface of the water may be sucked down the strut and along the foil to fill the cavities. This effect is called *ventilation* and again causes a variation in lift.

If the pressure across the top of the foil falls low enough, the water will vaporize, forming bubbles of water vapour which break up the smooth flow of water over the upper surface, thereby reducing lift. This phenomenon, known as *cavitation*, not only upsets efficient lift production but can also seriously erode the foil over a period of time. As the bubbles burst they smash minute jets of water against the foil surface with sufficient force to damage the metal.

Bicycles and Motorcycles

The bicycle is a very efficient form of personal transport. Its history dates back over 200 years to the early designs of the second half of the eighteenth century. The most famous of the early machines was the 'Célerifère', later named the 'Vélocifère', built by the Comte de Sivrac in France in 1791. This was a two-wheeled wooden horse, propelled by the rider pushing his feet against the ground, and it must have been difficult to steer as the front wheel was not pivoted.

The first machine with a steerable front wheel was demonstrated by the German Baron von Drais de Sauerbrun in 1818. Known as the Draisienne or 'hobby-horse', it had a simple wooden frame and two large, spoked wooden wheels fitted with iron tyres. The hobby-horse was enormously popular during the following 20 years, but interest declined and production ceased about 1830.

The next development was the pedal operated bicycle invented in 1839 by Kirkpatrick Macmillan, a Scottish blacksmith. The pedals were fitted to the ends of two levers pivoted at the front of the frame above the front wheel, and the forward and back motion of the levers was transmitted by connecting rods to cranks driving the rear axle. Little progress was made in the development of drive mechanisms until the 1860s, when Pierre and Ernest Michaux of Paris fitted pedals and cranks to the front wheel of a hobby-horse type machine, which they called a 'vélocipède'.

During the 1860s, wire-spoked wheels and rubber tyres were introduced, and this led to the evolution of the 'Ordinary' or 'Penny-farthing' bicycles of the 1870s. This type of bicycle had a large front wheel, driven by pedals and cranks fitted to its axle, and a small rear wheel about half the diameter of the front one. The frame was a single metal tube and the saddle was mounted on it above the front wheel, close to the handlebars.

The forerunner of the modern design was the 'Safety' bicycle developed between 1870 and 1890. This type of cycle had two wheels of approximately equal diameter, with wire spokes and rubber tyres and a chain drive to the rear wheel. By 1895 the diamond-shaped frame was standard, as were pneumatic (air filled) bicycle tyres which had been patented in 1888 by J. B. Dunlop. Pneumatic tyres had, in fact, been invented in 1845 by R. W. Thompson, but were not adopted at that time and were forgotten.

The basic design of bicycles changed little during the first quarter of the twentieth century, but in the late 1920s improvements in materials and construction methods permitted the development of lightweight sports and touring machines.

One of the most radical changes in bicycle design came in 1962, with the introduction of the small-wheeled Moulton cycle and its many successors. These small-wheeled machines soon became popular, and contributed to the general revival of interest in cycling during the 1960s and 1970s.

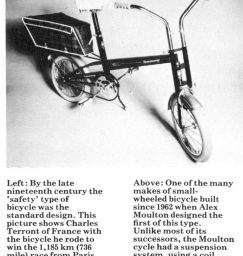

Above: An 'ordinary' or 'penny-farthing' bicycle, built in 1878 by Bayliss Thomson.

Left: The first pedal-driven bicycle, built in 1839 by Kirkpatrick Macmillan. He was also the first person to be fined for a cycling offence, after knocking over a child in Glasgow in 1842.

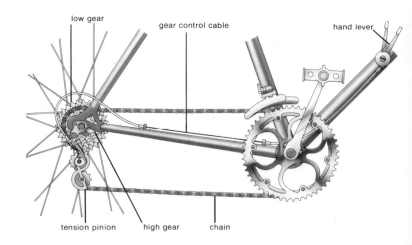

Left: By the late nineteenth century the 'safety' type of bicycle was the standard design. This picture shows Charles Terront of France with the bicycle he rode to win the 1,185 km (736 mile) race from Paris to Brest and back, in September 1891. He completed the course in under three days.

Above: One of the many makes of small-wheeled bicycle built since 1962 when Alex Moulton designed the first of this type. Unlike most of its successors, the Moulton cycle had a suspension system, using a coil spring on the front and a rubber shock absorber at the rear.

Below: A derailleur gear mechanism. Operating the hand lever moves the change mechanism towards or away from the wheel. As it moves, it transfers the chains from one sprocket to another. The system shown has a double chainwheel, which doubles the number of gear ratios available.

Right: A modern lightweight sports bike. Competition cycles can be very expensive, due to the high standards of workmanship employed, the small numbers produced and the use of expensive materials such as titanium. The frames are usually made of manganese-molybdenum steel.

low gear   high gear

low gear   gear control cable   hand lever

tension pinion   high gear   chain

With their chunky tyres and robust construction, BMX machines are designed for the roughest of cross-country track racing. These bicycles are now made by many manufacturers worldwide.

Left: The motorcycle built by Gottlieb Daimler in Germany in 1885. The drive from the single cylinder petrol engine was transmitted to the rear by a belt and pulley arrangement. A small gear fixed to the driven pulley turned the ring gear attached to the spokes of the rear wheel.

Right: Early machines were basically strengthened pedal cycles fitted with engines. This 1903 Triumph has an ordinary pedal drive on one side for starting and to assist the engine on uphill runs, and the belt drive from the engine on the other side.

Above: In 1988 Honda launched its most powerful road bike ever, the CBR1000 F. The four-cylinder, liquid-cooled engine produces 132 hp at 9,500 rpm (max), with a theoretical top speed of 273 km/h (170 mph) and a basic weight of 232 kg (511 lb). Over the last decade, the Japanese, headed by Honda, have acquired 90 per cent of the world market.

Right: This unusual motorcycle and sidecar combination was photographed in Berlin in 1928. The bike is an NSU, and the sidecar carries a duplicate set of controls and handlebars so that the combination can be driven from the sidecar or from the bike itself.

Above: Speedway bikes are single cylinder, single gear machines. They have no brakes or gearchange, the only controls being the clutch and throttle.

Below: Cross-country racing is a popular sport in many countries, using tough, purpose-built bikes. This one is a Spanish Bultaco.

Modern mass-produced bicycle frames are made from high-quality lightweight steel alloy tubing, with steel or light alloy handlebars. The wheels have steel or alloy rims and hubs, with steel wire spokes.

The pedals and cranks are fitted to a short axle running through the bottom bracket of the frame; this axle also carries the chainwheel. The chain is made of steel and connects the chainwheel with the rear drive sprocket mounted on the hub of the rear wheel. Except for track racing bikes, this rear sprocket incorporates a freewheel mechanism which allows the rear wheel to turn freely, enabling the rider to coast downhill without having to keep pedalling.

Many bicycles are fitted with gears, either the fully-enclosed type built into the rear wheel hub or the derailleur type comprising a set of rear sprockets of different sizes. The enclosed type is a miniature form of the epicyclic gearbox, the type of gearing used on many vehicle transmission systems, and gearchanges are accomplished by engaging different combinations of gear wheels within the hub.

Gear changing on a derailleur system is achieved by shifting the chain from one sprocket to another, the smallest sprocket giving the highest gear ratio.

Motorcycles

The first motorcycle was built in Germany in 1885 by Gottlieb Daimler, but the motorcycle industry did not really begin until the end of the nineteenth century. Early motorcycles were modified bicycles fitted with engines, but manufacturers were soon designing and building frames especially for motorcycles.

Most modern bike frames are made of steel tubing, with the engine mounted on twin tubes which form the bottom section of the frame. Suspension is provided for both wheels to give greater comfort to the rider and to improve the roadholding of the machine. The front suspension is by coil springs and telescopic hydraulic damper units incorporated in the front fork legs. The rear suspension uses a pair of spring and damper units. With one on each side, the upper ends are fixed to the frame below the saddle and the lower ends to the rear fork. The rear fork extends back almost horizontally from the frame, and it is pivoted to allow it and the wheel to move up and down under the control of the spring units.

The hydraulic damper units, or shock absorbers, regulate the up and down motion of the suspension. For example, when the wheel hits a bump in the road it is pushed upwards, compressing the spring. The spring pushes it back down on to the road again and it then tends to rebound back up, starting the whole process over again. If no dampers were fitted, this wheel bounce would make the machine uncomfortable to ride and difficult to control, especially at high speeds. The dampers smooth out these unwanted oscillations of the suspension by resisting the up or down movement of the spring.

The upper part of the damper is in effect a cylinder of oil, fixed to the frame in the case of rear dampers or to the upper part of the forks in the case of front dampers. The lower part, which moves up and down with the wheel, is connected to a piston within the oil cylinder. This piston has small holes drilled through it and as it moves the oil has to pass through these narrow holes. This means that the speed at which the piston can move is limited by the speed at which the oil can pass through the holes.

The speed at which the suspension unit can be compressed or expand again is thus limited to that of the piston, and this prevents the oscillations of the spring that could cause wheel bounce.

The wheels themselves have steel rims and spokes, except for motor scooter wheels which are usually made of pressed steel. Aluminium alloy rims and cast magnesium alloy wheels are also now frequently used.

Engines and transmissions

Modern motorcycle engines range in capacity from just under 50 cc (3 in³) to over 1200 cc (73 in³). They may be two or four-stroke petrol engines or rotary Wankel-type engines, either air cooled or water cooled. Some small electrically-driven machines have been produced for town use.

The crankshaft motion is transmitted to the gearbox via the primary drive, which is either a chain drive or a set of gears, and the clutch. The final drive from the gearbox to the rear wheel is usually by chain, but some of the more expensive machines use a drive shaft.

Most two-stroke bikes have magneto ignition systems, self-contained units driven directly from the engine that generate the power to run the ignition, lighting and horn circuits. The ignition coil and the contact breaker are built in to the unit.

Four-stroke machines use battery and coil ignition systems, with either a dc dynamo or an ac alternator, driven by the engine, to keep the battery charged and provide electrical power when the engine is running. Many bikes now use electronic ignition systems in place of the conventional mechanical contact breaker sets.

Brakes and controls

Motorcycles nowadays are fitted with disc brakes on both front and rear wheels, but older models have disc brakes on the front and drum brakes on the rear. (A drum brake consists of a brake drum built into the wheel hub and a pair of brake shoes lined with an asbestos-based material, which press against the inside of the drum when the brake is applied.)

The disc brake is a steel disc mounted on the wheel hub, with a pair of brake pads which are pushed against the disc from either side to grip it as the brake is applied.

The front brake is operated by a lever mounted on the right of the handlebars, the rear brake by a foot pedal, on the right hand side on modern machines. Drum brakes are usually operated mechanically, by cable on the front and by a rod on the rear, but disc brakes use hydraulic systems.

Engine speed is controlled by a twist-grip control on the right hand side of the handlebars, connected to the carburettor or carburettors by a cable. The clutch is operated by a lever on the left of the handlebars and smaller machines and motor scooters often use a twistgrip control, also on the left, to operate the gearchange.

Above: 250 cc (15.25 in³) racing bikes at the Daytona racetrack in Florida, USA. The technical experience gained from racing is of great benefit to the designers of ordinary machines.

Below: Competitors in a sidecar race at Brands Hatch racetrack in England.

Below right: The K 100 LT is BMW's latest, luxurious touring bike. The 987 cc four cylinder engine develops 66 kW (90 hp) at 8000 rpm, and from 1989 there will be front and rear disc brakes. Top speed is 215 km/h (135 mph) and it weighs 263 kg (579 lb).

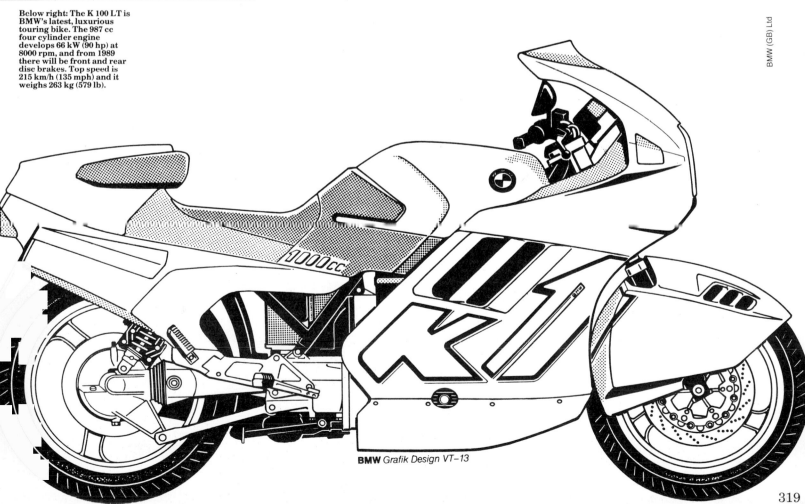

BMW Grafik Design VT–13

Cars, Trucks and Buses

1875 Marcus

1886 Benz

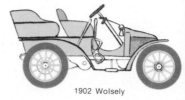

1902 Wolsely

The idea of using an engine to drive a wheeled road vehicle first became a practical reality in Paris in 1769, when Nicolas Cugnot built a steam powered carriage that ran at about 4 kph (2½ mph). Many steam cars and trucks were built during the following 150 years, and in 1906 a steam car designed by the Stanley brothers in the USA reached a speed of 204 kph (127 mph).

By this time, however, the more efficient internal combustion engine was rapidly taking over as the source of power for road vehicles. Condensing steam cars had been built in the US between 1900 and 1911, but by the middle of the 1920s steam vehicle building had virtually ceased.

Battery-operated cars outnumbered cars with gasoline engines in the US at the turn of the century. In 1909 939 gasoline-engined cars were built, compared with 1575 electric cars. In 1899 an electric car had been the first to break the 100 km/h (60 mph) barrier during a record run at Achères near Paris.

However, in the next decade or so electric cars are unlikely to become a viable alternative to conventional vehicles, although in cities large numbers of battery vehicles are used where high speeds or long distances are not involved, for example in delivering milk.

The main area of research has been to replace the conventional lead-acid battery with a smaller, more efficient unit. New plastic materials called electrically-conducting polymers, or symnetals, could be used to make lightweight batteries that deliver twice the power of conventional car batteries. Such plastic batteries could be repeatedly charged and discharged without degradation.

Mains-type electric vehicles, such as trolley buses and tramcars, do not have the problem of carrying their energy around with them since they pick it up as they go. Many cities are now building tramway systems again, in some cases less than 30 years after abandoning trams in favour of ordinary buses.

Cars

Although the credit for the building of the first automobiles powered by internal combustion engines is usually given to Karl Benz and Gottlieb Daimler, several such machines were built during the previous 60 years. Benz and Daimler produced their first cars in 1885 and 1886 respectively, but a car running on hydrogen gas had been built by Samuel Brown in London in the early 1820s. The Belgian engineer J. J. E. Lenoir built a car in 1862, and this was followed by the two built by Siegfried Marcus in Austria in 1864 and 1875.

The achievement of Daimler and Benz, however, is important because they envisaged the use of the car as a popular means of transport, and their efforts led directly to the creation of the motor industry. The earlier pioneers appear to have had little real interest in the future possibilities of their inventions, and did not persist in their development.

The drawings above and at the bottom of the page show how the shape of car bodies has evolved since the nineteenth century. Top row: Early cars were open vehicles with no weather protection, but body design progressed rapidly during the 1900s. The mass-produced Model T Ford was introduced in 1908 and over 15 million were built in its 19-year production run. The move towards fully enclosed designs continued during the 1920s, and in the 1930s body lines became more graceful and flowing. Bottom row: Designs changed little during the 1940s, but the introduction of unitary construction in the 1950s allowed designers to produce longer, lower and more adventurous shapes. Small cars like the Mini became very popular in the 1960s, and during the 1970s the clean, efficient 'wedge' shape evolved.

Right: A drawing of a 1903 Mercedes.

Below: A 1909 Buick, with a front-mounted engine driving the rear wheels through a chain and sprocket final drive.

Above right: The 1955 Lincoln is a good example of American car design of that period. The body is long and low, and the large windows and windshield give the driver excellent visibility.

Right: During the 1920s mass production techniques enabled manufacturers to build large numbers of cheap and reliable cars. The relative affluence of the period provided them with large sales, particularly in the US and western Europe, until the economic collapse of the early 1930s.

1948 Vauxhall

1954 Oldsmobile

1908 Ford

1922 Austin

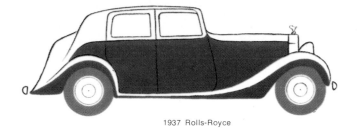
1937 Rolls-Royce

Michael Holford

Right: The operation of a four-speed manual gearbox. The gear lever moves the yokes to lock the required gears to the drive shaft. Here only one of the two yokes is shown at a time, and the line of power transmission is shown in red. The drive from the engine enters the box through the clutch shaft which drives the layshaft. First, second and third gears are selected by locking the required gear to the transmission shaft, taking up the drive from the layshaft. Top gear is selected by locking the clutch shaft directly to the transmission shaft. Reverse gear, not shown, is selected by connecting the transmission shaft to the layshaft via a separate idler gear.

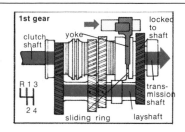
1st gear — clutch shaft, yoke, locked to shaft, R 1 3 / 2 4, sliding ring, transmission shaft, layshaft

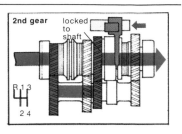
2nd gear — locked to shaft, R 1 3 / 2 4

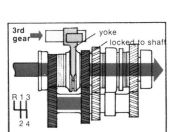
3rd gear — yoke, locked to shaft, R 1 3 / 2 4

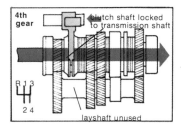
4th gear — clutch shaft locked to transmission shaft, R 1 3 / 2 4, layshaft unused

Michael Holford

Daymark

Left: Racing cars have evolved into highly specialized designs. On this one the engine is sited between the driver and the rear wheels. The cowling above and behind the driver's head is the air intake for the carburettors. Aerofoils at the front and back keep the wheels firmly on the ground at high speeds.

Top: Most car suspensions use coil springs, as in this example, but hydraulic or pneumatic systems are also used. The horizontal rod with the rubber dust seal is one of a pair linking the front wheels to the steering mechanism. When the steering wheel is turned the rods move sideways to pivot the front wheels.

Above: The rear suspension and drive shafts of a Lotus car.

Right: A cutaway of a Chevrolet Stingray, a powerful American sports car of the 1970s, which has a lightweight body built on to a steel girder chassis. The use of chassis-type construction has continued for a number of sports cars despite the use of unitary construction for most modern cars.

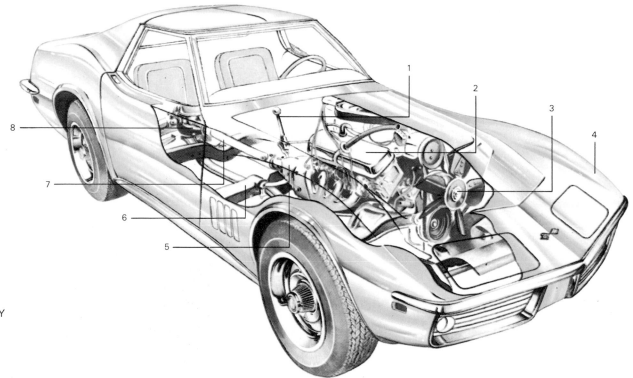

CHEVROLET STINGRAY
1 gearshift
2 engine
3 cooling fan
4 lightweight body
5 gearbox
6 chassis
7 drive shaft
8 differential

1955 Citroën

1959 Mini

1988 Ford

The early Benz and Daimler cars used single cylinder engines. But engine design progressed rapidly and by 1900 multi-cylinder engines were well established. During the first decade of the twentieth century, the design practice of putting the engine at the front of the car and taking the drive from there to the rear wheels was adopted by most manufacturers. Today's family cars have front-wheel drive, sun roofs, central door locking, power-assisted windows and electronic management systems to show up any faults.

The drive from the engine is taken via the clutch to the gearbox, and from there by drive shafts to the driving wheels. The clutch used with manual gearboxes has three main components: the clutch plate, the pressure plate and the flywheel on the end of the engine crankshaft. When the clutch is engaged, the pressure plate presses the clutch plate against the face of the flywheel. As the flywheel turns, the clutch plate turns with it, and so the drive is transmitted into the gearbox.

When the clutch pedal is depressed, the pressure plate is forced away from the clutch plate by hydraulic pressure. The clutch plate is then no longer being pressed against the flywheel and turned by it, and so the drive from engine to gearbox is disconnected.

Automatic transmission systems use hydraulic couplings in place of the friction type clutch. The flywheel drives a saucer-shaped impeller which is enclosed within a casing full of oil. As the impeller turns, oil is flung outwards by radial vanes on its inside face. The oil is deflected against similar vanes on the inside of another saucer-shaped unit, the turbine, which faces it. The force of the oil turns the turbine, which is connected to the gearbox by a shaft.

The various combinations of gears within an automatic gearbox are selected by clutch mechanisms within it. The clutches are activated hydraulically or electrically by devices which sense the engine and car speeds, and the position of the accelerator pedal, to determine the correct ratio required. These devices can be over-ridden by the driver, using the gear selector lever, so that the car can be held in any particular gear or put into reverse or neutral.

Cars use disc or drum brakes, or a combination of both with discs on the front and drums at the rear. The brake pedal operates all four brakes via a hydraulic system, but the handbrake operates only the brakes on the two non-driving wheels. The handbrake lever is linked to the brakes by steel cables or rods, and as it is independent of the hydraulic system it can provide some braking if the main brake system fails.

Until the 1950s, almost all cars had a steel girder chassis on to which the pressed-steel body was built, but during this period mass-produced cars were beginning to be built without a chassis. This method is called *unitary construction*.

The body and chassis parts are built together as a single unit from welded steel pressings. The method is lighter and cheaper than chassis type construction, and better suited to mass production techniques. Apart from this and styling considerations, body designers also have to take into account such factors as passenger safety and the aerodynamics of the body shape.

Above: The petrol-engined Albion of 1914. The development of trucks was stimulated by their use during the First World War. After the war the large numbers of surplus military trucks which were sold did much to encourage the spread of motor transport in Europe and the US.

Right: This ancestor of the modern double-decker bus is a 1910 type 'B' which belonged to the London General Omnibus Company. There is no roof to the upper deck and the wooden seating accommodates thirty passengers. The tyres are solid rubber, and its speed was 20 kph (12 mph).

Top: A large articulated truck with a twin-axled semi-trailer.

Above: A heavy duty articulated low-loader carrying a motor grader, a large earthmoving machine. Special low-loaders have been built which can carry loads of over 400 tonnes.

Right: A cutaway drawing of a three-axle rigid truck, showing the strong ladder-type steel chassis, the engine, the transmission and suspension. The drive is transmitted to both rear axles, and the use of double wheels on these axles allows heavier loads to be carried.

FODEN TRUCK
1 driver's cab
2 engine and gearbox
3 fuel tanks
4 drive shaft
5 final drive gearboxes
6 frame chassis
7 brake drum
8 rear suspension
9 front suspension
10 steering box

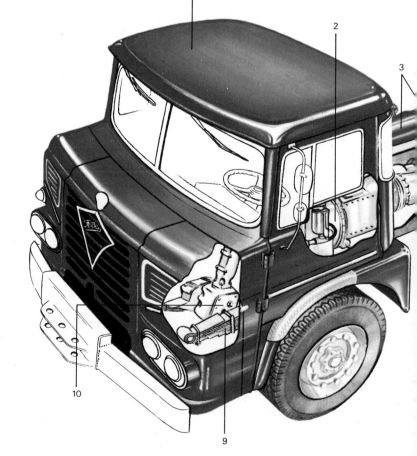

Japanese Tourist Board

Above: A rear-engined tour bus. Bus safety is improved by using multiple braking circuits. Many buses are also fitted with electro-magnetic retarders which exert a strong magnetic force on the vehicle's drive shaft to slow it down, thus supplementing the action of the brakes.

Below: A one-man-operated London bus. The driver collects the passengers' fares as they enter, and it has seats for 68 passengers with room for 21 standing. The six-cylinder 114 kW (153 hp) diesel engine and the four-speed gearbox are mounted across the rear chassis.

London Transport

Right: A pair of four-axled rigid tipper trucks used for carrying quarried stone. The tipper body is mounted on pivots at the rear, and the front end can be raised by hydraulic jacks to tip the load off at the back. The hydraulic system is driven by the truck's engine.

Fodens

Below: The triple-circuit braking system of an articulated tractor unit. The tractor and semi-trailer brakes are independently operated by compressed air from a compressor driven by the engine.

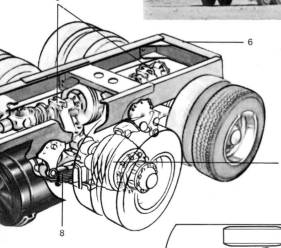

- air from compressor
- tractor pressure line
- tractor brake line
- trailer pressure line
- trailer brake line
- park brake pressure line
- park brake line
- emergency line
- anti-compounding line

During the development of a new model, extensive testing of mock-ups and prototypes is carried out. The design has to comply with international safety regulations, which cover many aspects including the size and position of the lights and the height and strength of the bumpers.

Prototypes are crashed into walls and other vehicles in order to evaluate the strength of the passenger compartment, and the ability of the front and rear body sections to absorb the impact created by a collision.

Wind tunnel testing is also used to improve the aerodynamic qualities of the body shape. This leads to better road-holding and acceleration, higher top speeds and greater fuel economy.

Commercial vehicles

Commercial vehicles are an important part of the transport systems of most of the countries of the world, particularly since the comparative decline of the railways. Early commercial vehicles were powered by steam, electricity or petrol engines, but most are now diesel powered.

The diesel engine was invented by Rudolf Diesel in Germany in 1897. Despite its success in marine propulsion, however, satisfactory road vehicle versions did not appear until 1922. On most commercial vehicles today the engine is mounted at the front, ahead of or beneath the driver's cab. Some manufacturers fit the engine beneath the chassis, and many buses and coaches use this layout or have the engine at the rear.

There is a wide range of commercial vehicle diesel engine, both two-stroke and four-stroke. Most are water-cooled, the main exceptions being the air-cooled engines produced by Magirus Deutz in Germany.

Light vans and some buses are often of unitary construction, without a chassis, but larger vehicles usually have a ladder-type frame chassis on to which an enormous variety of bodies can be built. Trucks may be either rigid or articulated. The rigid type has a single chassis carrying the cab, engine and body or load platform, and can have from two to four axles.

The articulated truck consists of a short tractor unit comprising the cab, engine and transmission. There is a 'fifth wheel' or turntable on top of the chassis, above the rear axle or pair of axles, to which the trailer is attached. The articulated trailer unit, called a semi-trailer, has no wheels at the front, being supported by the tractor, but one or more axles at the rear. Rigid units are often used for drawbar operation, towing trailers which are linked to them by a steel towing bar.

Most truck gearboxes are manually operated, and the number of gears available from the main gearbox can be doubled by means of an extra set of gears called a 'range splitter', or by using a two-speed driving axle. Automatic or semi-automatic transmissions are used on some heavy trucks and many buses.

Until recently, truck cabs were designed to be purely functional, unlike cars where driver comfort and convenience have always been carefully considered. Modern truck cabs, however, incorporate similar standards of seating, sound insulation and easily operated controls to those used in cars. This type of ergonomic design helps to reduce the driver fatigue which is a potential cause of accidents.

Railways

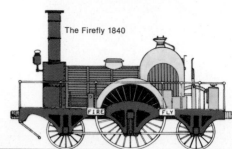
Trevithick's engine 1803

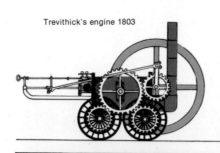
The Firefly 1840

On August 31, 1975, a grand cavalcade of locomotives was held to mark 150 years of rail travel in Britain. Since the opening of the Stockton and Darlington Railway in 1825, railways have become one of the most widespread forms of transport, serving almost every country in the world.

At the beginning of the nineteenth century Britain was still in the throes of the Industrial Revolution. Manufacturing industry, with its demand for power and raw materials, and its output of mass-produced goods, was altering the pattern of life. Not only merchandise but people also needed to be transported all over the country to help weave the web of commerce. The rutted and muddy roads were totally unable to meet this demand, while the canals were handicapped by the need for locks to overcome changes in water level. But by 1800 the public was already familiar with the two elements that were to combine to make the steam railway the transport of the future.

Railways had already existed in Britain for over 200 years, the first examples being wooden trackways along which horses could haul wagons of coal from the mines to the nearest water transport—canal, sea or navigable river. In time the wooden rails changed to iron, and the flat 'plateways' changed to edged rails along which flanged wheels were guided.

The other vital element was steam power, the moving force. This too had been developed as an adjunct of the mining industry, where low pressure steam engines were used to pump water from the underground workings. The Cornish mining engineer, Richard Trevithick, was the first to conceive the idea of building a high pressure engine and mounting it on wheels.

Trevithick's first two steam locomotives were in fact road vehicles: the idea of a steam engine running on rails only came about as the result of a wager. Much impressed by the potential of this new invention, Samuel Homphray, a South Wales iron master, bet a friend that a railway engine could be built to haul a ten ton load along the newly opened Penydarren Tramway at Merthyr Tydfil, a feat which Trevithick's specially built locomotive duly performed on Tuesday February 21, 1804.

In the years that followed, experimental railway engines were tried on various mineral railways. George Stephenson, the giant among the early railway builders, was, like Trevithick, a mining engineer. His particular achievement was to synthesize the best available knowledge and thus develop not only a serviceable and reliable locomotive but also the concept of the steam-worked railway.

1825 was the year of his first great triumph, the opening of the Stockton and Darlington Railway, the first public railway to be worked by steam traction. The opening train was hauled by Stephenson's *Locomotion*, preceded by a mandatory horse rider bearing a red flag.

Such exploits were at first regarded as highly dangerous by the general public, but in spite of widespread suspicion the construction of new railways proceeded apace and by 1841 the skeleton of Britain's railway network was already in existence.

Adam Woolfitt/Susan Griggs

Below: Steam engines are sturdy and reliable, but of the total heat energy supplied to them from the burning fuel only about six per cent is converted into useful mechanical energy. The unused energy escapes as heat in the exhaust steam and smoke.

Below right: A cutaway drawing of a steam engine. The steam from the boiler passes into the steam chest, and when the valve is opened it enters the cylinder. In the cylinder it expands, forcing the piston along. The piston's motion is transmitted to the driving wheels by the connecting rod.

American History Library

Above: These drawings show how steam locomotives developed from 1803 to the beginning of the twentieth century.

Left: The *Locomotion* was built in 1825 by George Stephenson, and in that year became the first steam engine to haul a train on a public railway, between Stockton and Darlington.

Right: The Furness Railway's locomotive number 9, built in 1855 by Fairbairn and Company. Steam engines can be classified by their wheel layouts; this one is an 0-4-0, having no wheels in front or behind its four driving wheels. These classifications do not include the wheels of the tender.

Ronan

ZEFA

STEAM LOCOMOTIVE
1. Cylinder
2. Smoke deflectors
3. Steam chest
4. Piston
5. Chimney
6. Valve gear
7. Connecting rod
8. Coupling rods
9. Sanding pipes
10. Water injector
11. Safety valve
12. Boiler tubes
13. Fire box
14. Regulator
15. Steam brake lever
16. Whistle
17. Vacuum brake lever
18. Reversing gear
19. Sand lever

Right: The *Dolbadarn*, a small, narrow-gauge locomotive on the Llanberis Lakeside Railway, Wales. Steam engines need to take on water frequently, either from trackside tanks, as in this case, or by scooping it up from troughs—between the rails at intervals along the track—as they travel.

Below: Southern Pacific locomotive number 2372 was the first of the twelve Class T-32 4-6-0 engines which were built at Sacramento, California, during the First World War. This particular locomotive was completed in 1918 and remained in use until it was scrapped in 1956.

Picturepoint

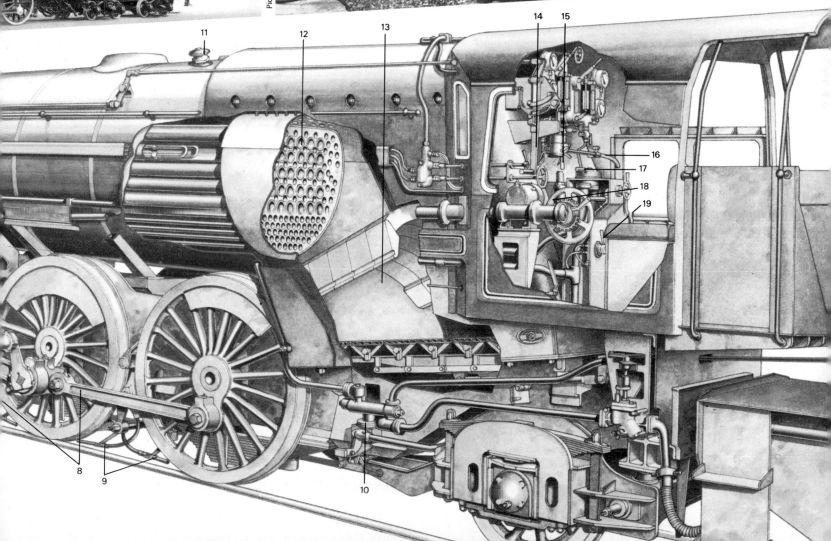

Above: Three twentieth-century steam engines. The streamlined *Mallard* set the world steam engine speed record of 202.8 kph (126 mph) in 1938. *Evening Star* was the last steam locomotive to be built by British Railways.

Left: The A-3 class *Flying Scotsman*, built in the 1920s and now restored. The extra tender was added to carry water, as watering facilities no longer exist on the British Rail network.

Right: A powerful diesel locomotive used for hauling trains along the line from Whitehorse in the Yukon Territory, Canada, to the port of Skagway in Alaska.

Railway construction had by this time spread to Europe and North America. The first lines on the continent were built by British engineers and used British-built locomotives. In France the first public steam railway was the 61 km (38 mile) long Lyons and St. Etienne line, opened in 1828. Germany followed a few years later with a short line from Nuremberg to Furth. Its first locomotive, Der Adler, was delivered complete with a British driver, William Wilson, who had been one of Stephenson's pupils.

British engineers later pioneered lines in many other European countries. Thus the 1.435 m (4 ft 8½ in) gauge adopted by Stephenson eventually became standard in most of the world.

Railways in the Wild West

In the United States and Canada, railways were built largely across virgin territory, where few restrictions of private ownership applied. North American railways were thus built to one of the most generous loading gauges in the world, even though the track was the standard 1.435 m (4 ft 8½ in). In the West, lines were built to open up the country, the towns arriving after the railway rather than vice versa. Many such lines converged on Chicago, which became the greatest railway town in the world. On May 9, 1869, a golden spike was driven to mark the completion of the first transcontinental railroad.

By 1850 some 10,460 km (6,500 miles) of line were in operation in Great Britain. Subsequent lines were generally of lesser importance, being either branch lines or competing routes. The working life of many of these has been relatively short, the rule of 'last opened, first closed' seeming to apply.

On the continent the railways were generally state owned rather than under private ownership. Lines were built for strategic or economic reasons, and on the whole a less dense but more efficient network has resulted.

The First World War left the European railways battered, and it was some time before pre-war standards were regained. However, the war had also encouraged the mass production of motor vehicles, and for the first time the dominance of the railway was challenged. During the depression of the 1930s there was little money available to carry out much-needed modernization plans and in only a few countries such as Switzerland and France was progress made with electrification. Experiments were made with diesel traction, including the high-speed *Flying Hamburger* from Hamburg to Berlin, but steam remained the dominant form of power.

The Second World War once again put enormous strains on Europe's railways, which suffered severely from bomb damage. In the post war era, car ownership came within the reach of most families, while an increasing proportion of freight traffic was carried by road. British Railways were nationalized and subsequently modernized. Many branch lines were closed and steam was replaced by diesel and electric traction.

The handling of individual wagon loads of freight began to be phased out in favour of bulk train loads, with automatic loading and unloading at terminals. Freightliner container trains now travel at speeds of 113 kph (70 mph) between most parts of the country. On the passenger side the emphasis is on fast and frequent services linking major cities, while suburban and minor cross-country trains are given lower priority.

Rolling stock

Steam power was the force that made the railways great, even though it has now been almost entirely replaced by diesel and electric traction. Steam locomotives can still be found at work in South Africa, India and China and eastern Europe, while in Britain various branch lines such as the Severn Valley Railway have been reopened by railway enthusiasts in order to run steam trains.

The steam locomotive is a robust and simple machine. Steam is admitted under pressure from the boiler to the cylinders.

Above: a double-headed steam train on the Pretoria-Rustenberg rairoad in South Africa.

Below: A French electric locomotive. The power is picked up from the overhead cable by the pantograph on the top of the locomotive. The voltages used by electric trains vary from one railway system to another, from 600 V (direct current) to 25,000 V (alternating current).

Evening Star — Last British Steam Locomotive 1960

Picturepoint

In the cylinder, steam expands and pushes a piston to the other end. On the return stroke a port opens to clear the exhaust steam. By means of mechanical coupling rods, the travel of the piston turns the driving wheels of the locomotive.

Diesel locomotives are of three main types: diesel-electric, diesel-hydraulic and diesel-mechanical. In the diesel-electric locomotive, the diesel engine drives a dynamo, and the electrical output from the dynamo powers electric motors which drive the wheels. In the diesel-hydraulic, the engine drives a hydraulic transmission, which turns the wheels by a form of miniature turbine, while in the diesel-mechanical locomotive the transmission is by a gearbox, just as in a diesel road vehicle. Diesel-electrics are by far the most common type, although diesel-mechanical locomotives are often used for shunting.

The third main form of motive power is electric traction. The first electric locomotives were powered by batteries, but modern locomotives take current from overhead wires or from a third rail. On the third rail system the current is supplied via the third rail and returned via the running rails. Four-rail systems are also used, on underground railways for example, which have two conductor rails for the supply and return of the current. Modern transmissions and traction motors are small enough to be housed in the bogie of the locomotive, rather than above footplate level as in older designs. Electric locomotives have a very high power-to-weight ratio as they do not have to generate their own power or carry fuel.

The latest passenger carriages are air-conditioned, have provision for the disabled and the Intercity 125s travel at speeds of around 200 km/h (125 mph). In 1989, the new Mark IV with a design speed of 224 km/h (140 mph) will be in operation between London and Edinburgh. Modern bulk freight vehicles have much greater capacity than the old loose-coupled freight wagons (each has its own brake but is controlled from the locomotive) and they travel at much higher speeds – up to 120 km/h (75 mph). Modern freight terminals have been specially built to accommodate these vehicles. The track and signalling equipment have also been improved to cope with faster and more frequent train services.

One-man, semi-automatic trains with sliding doors, first introduced on London Transport's Victoria Line in 1968, are in operation on local commuter trains, with the guards being replaced now by conductors. London's new Docklands Light Railway is electronically controlled with no driver but with a conductor.

In 1991 the Networker, a new type of suburban train, will be in operation, offering greater speed, acceleration and seating capacity. From 1993 the Channel Tunnel, jointly owned by the British and French governments, will carry an estimated 15 million passengers and 6 to 7 million tonnes of freight annually.

Above: Mountain railway cars may be self propelled, the driving wheel being a large cog that engages with a toothed rack between the rails, or they may be pulled along by a cable from a fixed winch.

Left: Monorail trains, running on single overhead rails, are used in some cities as an alternative to underground railways.

Below: A British Rail Intercity 125 train which travels at 200 km/h (125 mph) on scheduled services. A locomotive of this type holds the world speed record for diesel-electric propulsion of 230 km/h (143 mph).

ZEFA

British Railways Board

Rockets and Missiles

Of all those confusing and remote doctrines of the classroom, Isaac Newton's Third Law of Motion must surely rank among the most well remembered. This 300-year-old law stating that 'every action must have an equal and opposite reaction' has maintained a dramatic significance on world events through its most direct application—the rocket.

A rocket is simply a device or vehicle propelled by the expulsion of a stream of matter (usually gas) from it. The emerging surge of matter imparts an equal and opposite force to the vehicle itself. The inflated balloon or the garden hose nozzle are everyday examples of the principle—both come to rather eccentric (unguided) life when released. The escaping jet of air or water generates a *reactive thrust*.

'Rocket' applies both to any nonair-breath-ing engine and to the vehicle it propels. A thrown ball continues until air resistance (*drag*) and gravity overcome its projected force. Likewise, a rocket will continue to ascend for a little while after its engine cuts out, and then the combination of drag and gravity will slow it so that it falls back to Earth in an arc corresponding to that of its ascent. This is called a *ballistic* course or trajectory and can be used as a means of delivering a warhead from one part of the Earth to another in the shortest possible time.

The more a rocket accelerates and the higher the speed attained, the farther it will be 'thrown' before it falls back to Earth. Eventually it will reach a speed where its fall will take it constantly beyond the Earth's curvature and it will continue to fall around the Earth for ever, or until slowed by rocket thrust or fringe atmospheric particles. It is then in orbit. The minimum speed necessary for this is nearly 7,925 metres per second (26,000 ft/sec.). In this application the rocket is usually called a *launch vehicle*.

Rocket development

The rocket owes its development largely to the needs of war. Its first known use was to provide power assistance to the arrows and spears of the thirteenth century Chinese against the Mongols who, in turn, developed it for use against

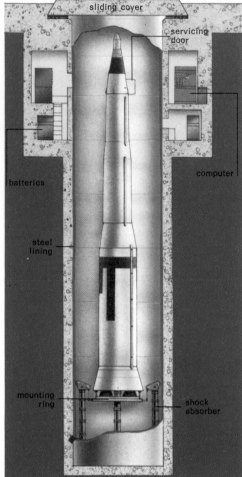

Above: Many long-range missiles are launched from underground 'silos'. The US, for example, houses its Minuteman III intercontinental ballistic missiles in silos 24.4 m (80 ft) deep. The Minuteman III can be equipped with MIRV (multiple independently-targetable re-entry vehicle) warheads, which contain several separate nuclear warheads that spread out to attack several targets at once.

Right: The land-based MX-1 Peacemaker missile being launched from its silo. This ICBM, which can carry up to ten independently targeted nuclear warheads, is scheduled to be based in the hardened silos originally designed for the Minuteman missile system, which it is replacing. The missile is an integral part of the Triad system, also comprising manned strategic bombers and missile-armed submarines.

the Arabs, who then introduced it warmly to the French Crusaders. Brought to Europe, the rocket was used by the French against the British at Orleans in 1429.

The emergence of the more accurate cannon reduced the rocket's military value for 300 years until the late eighteenth century, when British troops fighting in India found themselves once again on the receiving end of fiery salvos. This time they took notice, and the early nineteenth century saw extensive efforts, notably by Sir William Congreve and later by William Hale, to produce effective war rockets. Their work led to a naval bombardment weapon, to marine distress and rescue rockets, and to the crude anti-airship missiles of the First World War.

The birth of modern rocketry, however, is generally associated with Russia's Konstantin E. Tsiolkovsky (1857-1935) who, as early as 1883, began expounding on the potential and means of using rockets as launch vehicles. In 1929 Russia became the first nation to offer official, albeit military, status to rocket research. In Germany the theories of

Left: A ground-to-ground rocket fired from a self-propelled amphibious launching pad.

Above: The Russian rocket pioneer Konstantin Tsiolkovsky (1857-1935), working on a model of one of his rocket designs.

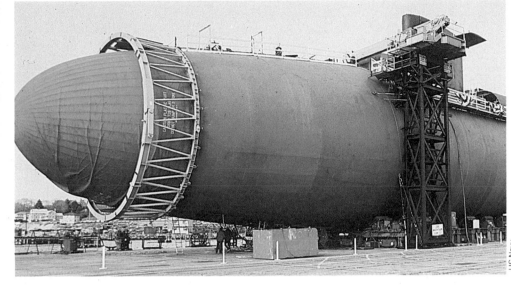

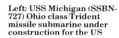

Navy. Trident has been chosen as the British Royal Navy's strategic deterrent.

Hermann Oberth stimulated the formation of the celebrated Society for Space Travel (VfR), itself succumbing in the mid-1930s to the opposition of the Nazi party. Military work absorbed some of its members, notably Wernher von Braun, whose efforts led to the world's first ballistic missile—the V-2. In the US, Robert Goddard independently covered much pioneering work in practical research.

As well as the V-2, used against Britain in 1945, small tactical missiles, fired by aircraft or from ground batteries, were used with reasonable effect in the Second World War. Since then the missile has really come into its own. The growth of the Cold War in the 1950s gave rise to the *strategic* missile, the intercontinental carrier of nuclear bombs. America delayed its development programme slightly to await the perfection of the compact hydrogen bomb, and the consequent reduction in launcher size. Russia, however, went straight ahead with the construction of large missiles to carry the massive atom bombs. Soviet scientists saw, too, that the same missile could place a smaller payload in orbit—and in October 1957, Sputnik 1 soared into space.

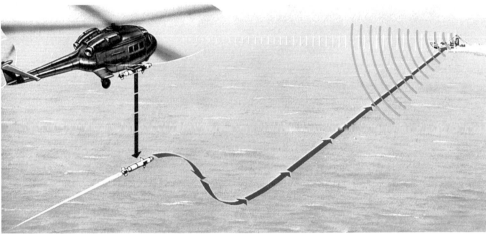

Left: The Sea Skua, the only one to be launched from helicopters, is designed to counter the threat of fast patrol craft before they get close enough to use their own weapons.

Below: The Pershing II intermediate-range nuclear missile has a two-staged launch vehicle. It can be deployed as a Multiple Independently targeted Re-entry Vehicle (MIRV) that can attack several targets from a single launch.

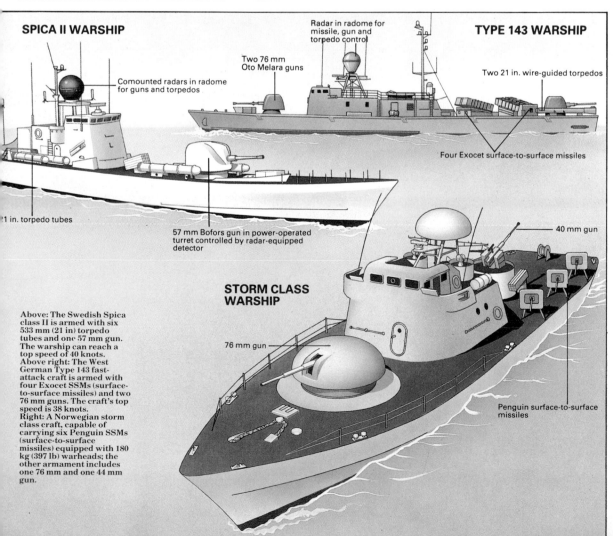

SPICA II WARSHIP

Comounted radars in radome for guns and torpedos

Radar in radome for missile, gun and torpedo control

Two 76 mm Oto Melara guns

TYPE 143 WARSHIP

Two 21 in. wire-guided torpedos

Four Exocet surface-to-surface missiles

1 in. torpedo tubes

57 mm Bofors gun in power-operated turret controlled by radar-equipped detector

40 mm gun

STORM CLASS WARSHIP

76 mm gun

Penguin surface-to-surface missiles

Above: The Swedish Spica class II is armed with six 533 mm (21 in) torpedo tubes and one 57 mm gun. The warship can reach a top speed of 40 knots.
Above right: The West German Type 143 fast-attack craft is armed with four Exocet SSMs (surface-to-surface missiles) and two 76 mm guns. The craft's top speed is 38 knots.
Right: A Norwegian storm class craft, capable of carrying six Penguin SSMs (surface-to-surface missiles) equipped with 180 kg (397 lb) warheads; the other armament includes one 76 mm and one 44 mm gun.

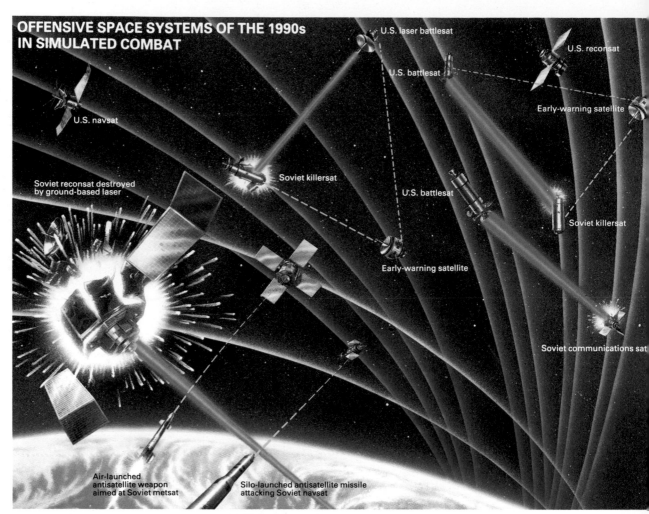

U.S. laser battlesat

U.S. reconsat

U.S. battlesat

Early-warning satellite

U.S. navsat

Soviet killersat

U.S. battlesat

Soviet reconsat destroyed by ground-based laser

Soviet killersat

Early-warning satellite

Soviet communications sat

Air-launched antisatellite weapon aimed at Soviet metsat

Silo-launched antisatellite missile attacking Soviet navsat

Right: 'Star Wars' presupposes a space-missile attack by the USSR on the USA.

Below right: A Polaris A-3 strategic nuclear missile launched from a submarine. The Polaris has a range of 4630 km (2875 miles), and is equipped with multiple nuclear warheads. It has two stages, each of which is powered by a solid-propellant rocket motor.

America's belated response four months later was due not just to the deliberate 'missile lag' but also to an inter-service rivalry over launch vehicle development, of which the winner, the US Navy, had far from the best programme in hand. Later, as the Thor, Atlas and Titan missiles became obsolete they formed the core of the development of 'medium' launchers, while the diminutive Scout and the mighty Saturn rockets were civilian programmes.

Specific impulse

The fundamental key to rocket propulsion is still Tsiolkovsky's *Ideal Rocket Equation* ('Ideal' because it ignores atmospheric drag) which says that total increase in vehicle velocity is equal to the exhaust velocity times the natural logarithm of the *mass ratio* (launch weight divided by empty weight). The greater the required acceleration, the higher must be either or both of the exhaust velocity and the mass ratio. Mass ratio can be improved by minimizing structural weight so that fuel burn-off plays a maximum part in allowing speed to increase. The exhaust velocity can be improved by increasing the efficiency of the *propellant* (fuel mixture).

Propellant efficiency is defined as the number of pounds of thrust that can be developed per second out of each pound of fuel (using a maximum efficiency engine). It is called the *Specific Impulse* (Isp) and the units in which it is measured are called *seconds*. Obviously, the faster the gases are emitted the greater the value of thrust per second, so that high speed/low volume tends to be more efficient than the reverse. There is thus a

Right: A prototype Air Launched Cruise Missile (ALCM) being launched from the weapons bay of a B-52G bomber. The ALCM is a new breed of small, cheap and very accurate nuclear missile.

Below: One of the most widely-used forms of rocket is the *sounding rocket*, a small, lightweight vehicle, usually solid-fuel propelled, used for scientific experiments in the upper atmosphere. This diagram shows some of their many uses.

Boeing Aerospace

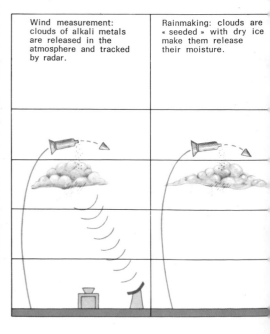

Wind measurement: clouds of alkali metals are released in the atmosphere and tracked by radar.	Rainmaking: clouds are « seeded » with dry ice make them release their moisture.

Photri

330

direct relationship between Isp and exhaust velocity, and an Isp of about 102 seconds provides an exhaust velocity of 1 km/sec. As a result, the higher the rated Isp, the lower the fuel mass needed for any specific acceleration, or the greater the acceleration obtainable from any given fuel mass.

Today's chemical propellants have a relatively low Isp and therefore present a severe weight penalty. Without the techniques of *staging* it would be impractical to accelerate a payload to orbital velocity. Any increase in propellant mass to prolong acceleration reduces the *rate* of acceleration—and therefore cancels out the value of the extra propellant. The extra mass can be used more effectively, however, if it is placed in separate tanks and given its own engine, forming an upper stage. It then becomes an extra rocket launched at altitude. In the vacuum of space, the Isp is measurably increased and the smaller mass needs only a small and less thirsty engine to maintain acceleration.

Guidance systems vary according to the degree of accuracy required. A general environment-measuring satellite intended for an orbit of 560 km (350 miles) will not suffer from a moderate variation from its course, provided that it can be accurately tracked. A pre-programmed autopilot would probably provide adequate positioning, while engine cut-out at the required velocity is obtainable by radio signal or pre-determined fuel supply. For pin-point aiming of a missile, or the injection of a deep-space probe into interplanetary trajectory, a very much higher degree of accuracy is required. A sophisticated inertial guidance system is now usual with gyroscopes sensing minor variations from the programmed path and correcting them by vectoring the main thrust.

This can be backed up by ground-based navigation and control. A short-range combat missile may often be wire-guided, an operator 'flying' it by sending corrective signals along a wire that is drawn out behind. Others are controlled by radio signals, with visual directions supplied to the operator by a television camera in the nose of the missile. Still others have automatic homing devices using radar, infra-red or visual contact.

Rocket engines

A basic characteristic of the modern rocket is its ability to operate independently of atmosphere. Rocket propulsion consists of burning a chemical in a confined space and allowing the gases to escape through a restricted nozzle. As oxygen must be present for combustion, a large supply of oxidizer must be carried. In modern liquid-fuel engines the fuel, such as kerosene or liquid hydrogen, and the oxidizer, now often liquid oxygen, are pumped separately into a small combustion chamber.

The second type of high-thrust rocket is based on solid-fuel; the solids basically are powder-packed squibs, the *charge* being a mix of dry fuel and a dry, oxygen-rich chemical (such as a mix of polyisobutane and ammonium perchlorate). They offer simplicity and reliability, but a lower Isp and a heavy structure and they cannot be controlled except by altering the burn rate.

Some form of nuclear propulsion is seen as the high-thrust system of the future. Solid-core devices which release heat from a fission reaction have already been ground-tested in Russia and America. However, greater attention is being given to the idea of streaming nuclear bomblets behind a thrust shield where they are positioned by a magnetic field and detonated by laser beam. Also, scaled-down chemical rockets are used to power orbit change, interplanetary course corrections and, in miniature form, for attitude control of probes and satellites and for rocket-stage and payload separation.

The most promising of the low-thrust rockets is the *electrostatic* or *ion* rocket, which works by isolating mercury or caesium ions and accelerating them to produce exhaust. The thrust is tiny, but with its compact fuel load and nuclear generator, an oil-powered space craft could keep accelerating gently for months and years, eventually developing phenomenal speeds. Deep-space missions are the main application, but Earth satellites will also be carrying ion engines for orbital positioning and attitude control before too long.

In the still theoretical electromagnetic or *plasma* rocket, a fuel such as hydrogen is converted to an electrically ionized gas by an electric arc, then accelerated out by a magnetic field. Nuclear fission is also under study for this category, in the form of a gaseous core rocket where fuel is passed through a gaseous reactor, suspended in the chamber by magnetic fields.

Fuze electronics
Safe and arm electronics
Command decoder
Autopilot electronics power supply
Safe and arm
Sustainer nozzle and jet deflector
Beacon antenna
Destabilizing fin
Proximity fuze antenna
Warhead
Command receiver antenna
Beacon transmitter
Tube liner segments
Booster nozzle

Above: The Roland SAM (surface-to-air) missile is designed to protect fast-moving armoured columns. Both Roland I and Roland II employ radar for target acquisition and IFF (Identification Friend or Foe). Roland I has an infrared guidance system optically aimed by the operator and steered automatically along the line of sight. Roland II is guided by tracking radar, although it can also be sighted optically.

...spheric temperature ...pressure information ...ed to ground ...on by instruments ...e rocket and in ...rated instrument ...age.	Electrical and magnetic properties of the upper atmosphere measured by instruments in nose cone.	Cosmic rays detected by geiger counters.	Atmospheric absorption of solar radiation measured by infra red spectrometers.

altitude in kilometres
250
200
150
100
50
0

APPLIED
SCIENCE
AND
TECHNOLOGY

Spaceflight

Space activities are generally divided into two categories: manned and unmanned spaceflight.

The majority of space activities have been confined to a small sphere of space enclosing the Earth and broadly termed Earth orbit. Orbit is achieved when the speed of a body produces a momentum that balances the force of gravity and therefore continues literally to fall round the Earth. An almost infinite variety of orbits is obtainable from a permutation of factors such as the *altitude*; the *velocity*, which, by Kepler's laws, is dependent on the altitude; the *inclination*, which is the angle the orbit makes with the equator; and the *eccentricity* or *ellipticity* which is the degree by which the shape of the orbit differs from circular. All these factors can be adjusted to give the right orbit for the particular scientific mission.

Orbital speed at low altitudes of about 190 km (120 miles) is about 4,755 m/sec (15,600 ft/sec). Acceleration pushes the orbit higher and, if speed is increased to about 10,670 m/sec (35,000 ft/sec) it will raise the orbit to the distance of the Moon. This is the method used for lunar travel. Arrival speed is invariably too high for orbital capture by lunar gravity, and so a braking rocket must be fired to slow the craft and achieve orbit, and then fired again if a soft landing is required, there being no atmosphere to slow the craft.

Return flights require an escape velocity of only about 2,377 m/sec (7,800 ft/sec) to overcome the low gravity. Apart from landing missions, lunar orbit has also been used for lunar surface photography as an 'anchor' for a few satellites.

For interplanetary travel, a spacecraft must break out of Earth orbit and enter an elliptical orbit around the Sun which will intersect with that of the destination planet. Initial speed required for this is about 11,580 m/sec (38,000 ft/sec). Missions to Venus are launched 'backwards' in relation to the Earth's motion around the Sun, so that their relative speed is slower and they drop towards the Sun. Missions to Mars and the outer planets are launched ahead of the Earth for the opposite effect.

Known as a *Hohmann ellipse*, this technique reduces the power required from the launch vehicle, and so although it is not the fastest route, it permits the use of much smaller and cheaper launch vehicles. It also requires specific positioning of the departure and destination planets at launch, usually near the period of closest approach. Such approaches occur at short and infrequent intervals, and the associated launch opportunities are called 'launch windows'. For Venus this occurs every 583 days, and Mars every 280 days.

America's Mariner 10 reached Mercury in 1975 by flying close to Venus and using the force of that planet's gravity to accelerate and re-direct the spacecraft to its destination.

Spacecraft

The term 'spacecraft' usually applies to any self-sustaining, active device operating for extended periods beyond the Earth's atmosphere. Spacecraft designed to leave Earth orbit and explore planets or adopt solar orbits of their own are known as *space probes*. Their designs vary considerably according to their particular destination, duration of mission and objective—whether they are supposed to fly-by, enter orbit or release

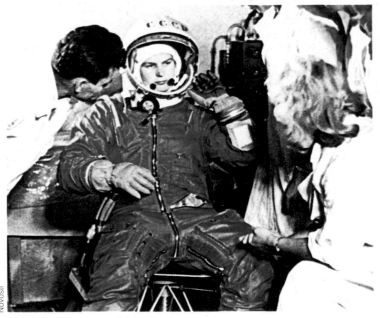

Left: Valentina Nikolayeva-Tereshkova, the first woman to make a spaceflight. Her Vostok-6 spacecraft, launched from Baikonur cosmodrome in Central Asia on 16 June 1963, made a total of 48 orbits during its 70 hour 50 minute flight, covering a distance of 1,970,990 kilometres (1,224,084 miles).

Below left: The first man in space was the Soviet cosmonaut Yuri Gagarin (1934-1968). His 108 minute flight, during which he made one complete orbit of the Earth in his Vostok-1 spacecraft, took place on 12 April 1961. In this picture, Gagarin is talking to Soviet rocket designer Sergei Korolyev.

Below: This multiple exposure shows the launch tower dropping away as the American Gemini-10 lifts off on 18 July 1966. Gemini-10, which used a Titan launch vehicle, was crewed by John Young and Michael Collins, and successfully docked with an Agena target vehicle orbiting at 298 km (185 miles).

Novosti

Photri

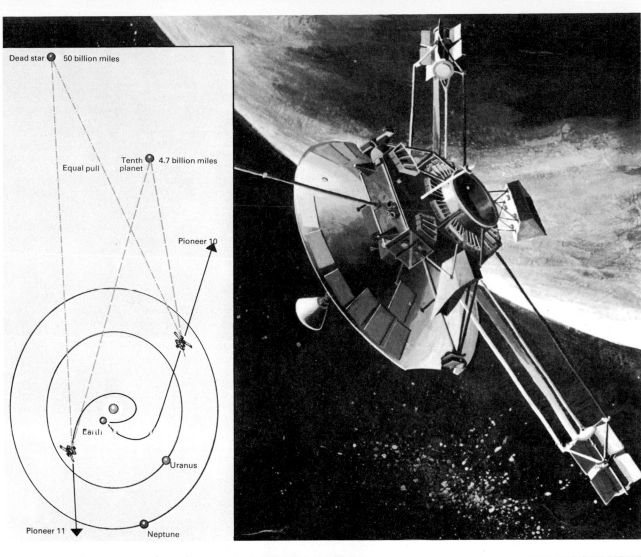

Left: Pioneer 10 became the first craft to pass into interstellar space in 1983. The diagram (inset) shows the path of the two Pioneer probes.

Bottom: Lunokhod 2, the second of Russia's remotely-controlled lunar exploration vehicles, was landed at the edge of the Sea of Serenity on 16 January 1973. Lunokhod 2's equipment included:
1. directional antenna;
2 and 8. tv cameras;
3. photoreceptor;
4. solar panel;
5. magnetometer;
6. laser reflector;
7. astrophotometer;
9. soil analysis unit;
10. telephotometers;
11. soil mechanics probe.
The vehicle covered a total distance of 37 km (23 miles). A similar Mars explorer was planned, but the USA got there first with the 1976 Viking probe.

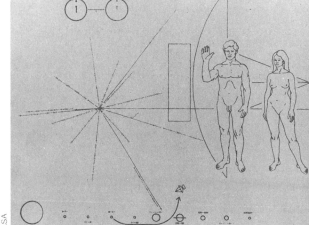

Left: Apollo 15 astronaut James Irwin with the electrically-driven Lunar Roving Vehicle, which enabled the astronauts to explore a wider area of the Moon than they could cover on foot. In the background is Mount Hadley.

Right: The pictorial plaque carried by Pioneer 10 contains information about Earth and humanity.

a landing craft. The operational and environmental demands placed on these craft has led to their development into some of the most sophisticated robots yet devised.

The general design of a spacecraft is dominated by three main considerations —intended purpose of the mission, launch vehicle compatability and, usually most important, weight reduction. The peculiarities of its operational life require a spacecraft to protect and support its payload over a wide range of extreme conditions. At launch it may experience acceleration forces 10 to 15 times that of gravity, atmospheric pressures which fall rapidly from that at sea level to a vacuum, plus heavy vibration.

In space it meets a considerable range of temperatures according to its position and attitude in relation to the Sun, and must also survive micrometeoroid impacts and solar and cosmic radiations normally screened by the atmosphere. If a survivable Earth landing is required, it must absorb the shocks of deceleration, pressure change and landing and survive air friction temperatures as high as 3,000°C (5,400°F).

The conditions of spaceflight dictate a basically common complement of subsystems. Unmanned craft consist of a simple open-frame structure to which subsystems are individually attached in separate boxes, or a sealed container enclosing most of the systems together. Manned spacecraft, with their need for living and working quarters for their crews, demand a very large sealed structure, usually large enough for the

Above: Soviet Venera probes have supplied much information about Venus; they took photographs and analyzed the soil. The American Pioneer Venus Orbiter has also mapped the surface.

Below: The spacesuits worn by Apollo astronauts comprised over 20 layers of different materials.

Above: The European Space Agency's Giotto space probe which, in 1985, was launched on the eight-month journey culminating in its encounter with Halley's Comet in March 1986.

Right: Apollo 15 astronauts, surrounded by technicians, undergoing space suit pressure checks.

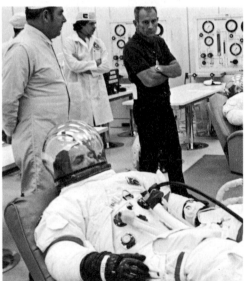

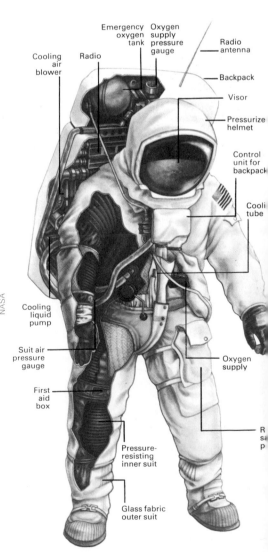

subsystems to be distributed widely in and around it.

The basic elements of any spacecraft are power supply, temperature control, communications, data processing, stabilization, attitude control equipment and, if required, navigation and propulsion systems. Power is usually supplied by panels of solar cells which convert the Sun's energy. As far from the Sun as Mars, solar arrays are efficient enough to be kept manageably small.

Short-life craft, notably the early satellites and some of the Soviet lunar probes, carry only simple chemical batteries. In all other cases, however, the generated raw power is conditioned and stored in batteries before delivery to components. Most spacecraft require between 100 W and 500 W. Large solar arrays developed for high-power comsats (communications satellites) can produce 1.5 KW. Some US manned spacecraft— the Apollos and later Geminis—depended on fuel cells in which hydrogen and oxygen were processed to generate electricity, supplying drinking water as a by-product.

Temperature control is often the most challenging element of a spacecraft, involving the appropriate distribution of cooling and heat with minimal power use. Some craft now use controllable louvres to exploit the Sun's heating. Rotation of the craft, or positioning of reflective thermal blankets and sunshields, keeps temperatures down. Numerous techniques, some ingenious, include relative positioning of hot- and cold-running components, heat sinks and direct electric heating.

Communications involve several essential links between controllers and craft, each link operating at a different frequency through its own type of aerial. One receives commands from Earth, while another feeds out telemetry data

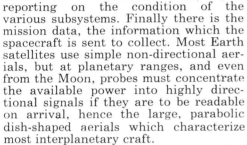

California Institute of Technology

California Institute of Technology

reporting on the condition of the various subsystems. Finally there is the mission data, the information which the spacecraft is sent to collect. Most Earth satellites use simple non-directional aerials, but at planetary ranges, and even from the Moon, probes must concentrate the available power into highly directional signals if they are to be readable on arrival, hence the large, parabolic dish-shaped aerials which characterize most interplanetary craft.

Even then there is such a heavy flow of information that some form of data processing becomes necessary. Normally this involves equipment which can selectively sample the telemetry or payload data on a command from Earth or from an on-board sequencer. Earth satellites often have to select data and store it on tape recorders while out of sight of a control station, and transmit it all on the next pass.

Like an aircraft, most spacecraft need to be able to change attitude at will and to keep stable at any particular attitude. Attitudes and navigational positions in space are identified by light sensors graded to specific objects such as the Sun, the Earth's horizon or, for interplanetary craft, the conveniently positioned bright star Canopus. Attitude is changed either by small gas jets or inertial wheels aligned along all three axes, both methods using reaction to turn the craft. Stabilization can be maintained most simply by spinning the entire spacecraft to create gyroscopic forces which keep it stable. For more accurate stability a system of three gyroscopes is required.

Many satellites spend their operational lives in the orbits into which they were first launched. Any manoeuvring, however, means that a rocket motor must be carried. For example, if recovery is intended, then the craft must have a braking rocket. Geostationary satellites are first launched into elliptical orbit with apogee (highest point) at 35,900 km (22,300 miles).

Above left: NASA's Galileo spacecraft, with its atmospheric probe (lower left). Galileo was launched on its journey to the planet Jupiter in May 1986 and began its detailed 22–month study of the planet and its four moons in 1988.

Above: An artist's impression of Voyager 1 as it passed through the flux tube of Io – the region between Jupiter and its satellite, Io – in 1979.

Below: Rescuing the communications satellite, Westar VI. One astronaut inserts a stinger in the rocket nozzle of the satellite. Another is moved to it by the Shuttle's remote-controlled arm. He grasps the antenna, and they are pulled back to the cargo bay where they secure the satellite.

Bottom: A model of France's proposed Hermes mini shuttle which should be launched in the late 1990s atop an Ariane 5 booster. At 17.9 m (59 ft) long and weighing about 17 tons, it could transport a satellite into orbit, ferry passengers to a space station or carry out space repairs.

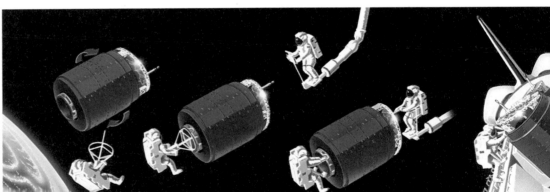

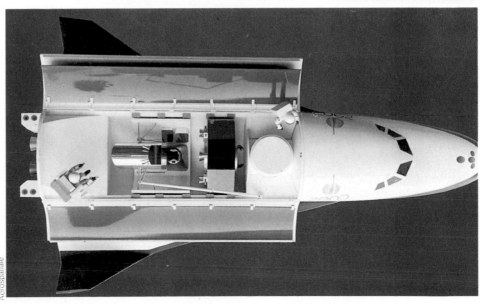

Aerospatiale

Space Shuttle

Behind the low scrub that binds the sands of Cape Canaveral to the Florida coastline lies a unique runway, a 4.5 km (15, 000 ft) long concrete strip designed to take the world's first reusable spacecraft – the Space Shuttle.

Space flights – manned or unmanned – are expensive, and no longer is it good enough to plead that money must be spent in the interests of scientific research. More and more, space rockets are used to launch satellites into orbit – satellites that carry out commercial tasks and, therefore, have to prove commercially economic.

Multiple use

One of the reasons for the great expense is that, until now, space rockets were not reusable – they mostly burned away during or after launch. By contrast, most of a Space Shuttle is designed to be used up to 100 times, with a great saving of money. Initial Shuttle plans were for a fully recoverable vehicle, consisting of a winged *orbiter* to carry payloads such as satellites into space, and a system of *rocket boosters* to help launch it. One proposed design was for a 12-engined booster vehicle 70 m (230 ft) long, carrying a 60 m (179 ft) orbiter to a height of 75 km (47 miles), at which point the orbiter would propel itself on into space. The payload cost was expected to be very small – around $135 a kilogramme, against the $10,000 a kilogramme typical of non-reusable launch vehicles. But the max-

imum payload was only about 11 tons, and the development cost would have been a prohibitive $10 billion.

So NASA decided to go for a reusable orbiter with conventional rocket boosters, although that meant the launch cost per kilogramme would be two or three times more. The size of the orbiter was reduced, and its carrying capacity increased, by storing its fuel in a disposable external tank. In place of the large manned booster, two strap-on solid fuel rockets were added. Thus the Shuttle evolved to its current well-known configuration.

The orbiter itself is the size of a DC9 jet airliner, 37.2 m (122 ft) long and with a wingspan of 23.8 m (78 ft). The astronauts who pilot the Shuttle ride in the nose of the orbiter, as in an ordinary aircraft. Half the orbiter's length is taken up by a cargo bay capable of carrying 29 tons into orbit, and of bringing 14 tons back to earth.

At the rear of the orbiter are three large rocket engines; during launch these are fed with fuel from an external tank strapped to the orbiter's belly. This external tank, 47 m (159 ft) long and 8.4 m (27.5 ft) in diameter, falls away as the Shuttle reaches orbit, burning up in the atmosphere. Weighing over 30 tons, the empty tank is

Right: The external fuel tank of a Space Shuttle. This is lowered into place on the mobile launcher platform where it will be mated with the two solid rocket boosters prepared for the mission.

Opposite: The launch and landing sequence – the large external fuel tank is the only part which is not recovered and used again. The Space Shuttle lands safely one hour after its de-orbit burn.

Above: After a seven-day orbit in space, Columbia begins its first touchdown on a concrete runway at Edwards Air Force Base, California.

Right: The flight deck of Space Shuttle Columbia. Immediately in front of each crew member is a hand control which is directly linked to the Shuttle's computer (seen here, between the two positions for the crew members). Three cathode ray tubes (CRT) display computer data and information for the crew. On either side of the CRT are flight instruments such as the altitude direction indicator as well as speed and direction finders. For orbital flight test missions, the Columbia's ejection seats (on each side of the circle) can accommodate emergency exits from the craft.

External tank separation. OMS engines take the Shuttle into its operating orbit

Main engine cut-off after 8½ minutes

3-g throttling to maintain moderate acceleration

Separation of solid rocket boosters

Burn out of boosters two minutes after takeoff

Ascent stage using booster rockets and main engines

Splashdown of solid rocket boosters

Recovery of rockets for refurbishment

Prelaunch stage, controlled from launch site

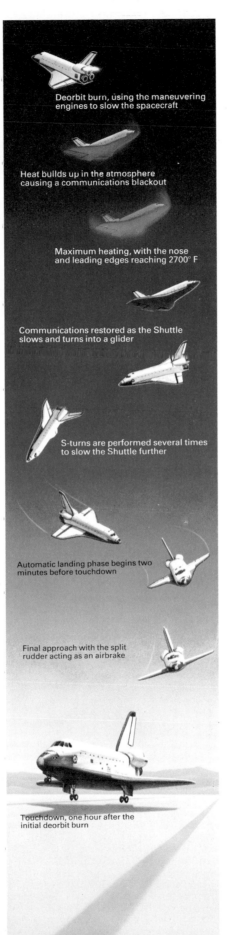

Deorbit burn, using the maneuvering engines to slow the spacecraft

Heat builds up in the atmosphere causing a communications blackout

Maximum heating, with the nose and leading edges reaching 2700° F

Communications restored as the Shuttle slows and turns into a glider

S-turns are performed several times to slow the Shuttle further

Automatic landing phase begins two minutes before touchdown

Final approach with the split rudder acting as an airbrake

Touchdown, one hour after the initial deorbit burn

heavier than the orbiter's payload, and it is the only part of the system not designed for reuse.

Getting away

To boost the Shuttle at launch, two large solid-fuel rockets are strapped to the sides of the external tank. These strap-on boosters fall away as the Shuttle ascends, parachuting into the sea to be recovered for reuse. Overall, the Shuttle stands 56 m (184 ft) tall and weighs 2000 tons.

Development costs for this design were estimated at around $5.5 billion, but problems and delays eventually increased this figure to $8 billion. One problem was that the engines, which burn liquid hydrogen and liquid oxygen, work at significantly higher pressures and temperatures than in previous rockets, and of course they have to withstand being fired for up to 100 missions. During the rigorous engine testing programme, cracks appeared in fuel pumps and in fuel pipe lines, valves failed and fires broke out. Another problem lay in heat shield tiles that protect the orbiter during its fiery re-entry into the atmosphere. Each of the 31,000 tiles had to be individually shaped and glued to the orbiter's surface; to do this properly took longer than expected.

One vital part of the test programme did go successfully: the approach and landing tests, in which a prototype space shuttle orbiter was released from a carrier aircraft over the Mojave Desert, California, and was piloted down to the ground. This was more difficult than it appeared. The orbiter's engines do not operate during the descent, making it less like an aircraft than like a 100-ton glider. For its atmospheric flight tests, the orbiter, named Enterprise after the spaceship in the TV series *Star Trek*, rode on the back of a modified Boeing 747 jumbo jet.

The Enterprise was then taken to the Marshall Space Flight Center in Huntsville, Alabama, for vibration tests to confirm that the orbiter's structure would withstand the force of launching. Following these tests, it was ferried to Cape Canaveral where it was mated with a dummy external tank and dummy rocket boosters. On 1 May, 1979, Enterprise was rolled out to the launch pad in a rehearsal of launch procedures.

While this was going on, the orbiter scheduled actually to make the first launch, Columbia, was undergoing the final stages of construction at Cape Canaveral. Other orbiters in the fleet were named Challenger, Discovery and Atlantis. Enterprise itself will never make a trip into space. A plan to bring it up to flight standard was abandoned as too costly. Instead, Enterprise was stripped down to provide parts for building other orbiters.

The first launch

Launch facilities for the Shuttle at Cape Canaveral have been modified from those built originally for the Apollo programme. Shuttles are assembled inside the 160 m (525 ft) tall vehicle assembly building which once housed Saturn rockets. The completed Shuttle is rolled out on its mobile launch platform by crawler transporters to launch pads 39A and 39B from which astronauts once left for the Moon.

After an initial computer hitch, the very first Space Shuttle flight was planned for 7am on Sunday 12 April, 1981. Right on time, the three liquid propellant engines roared into life and for nearly six seconds burned a transparent flame while compu-

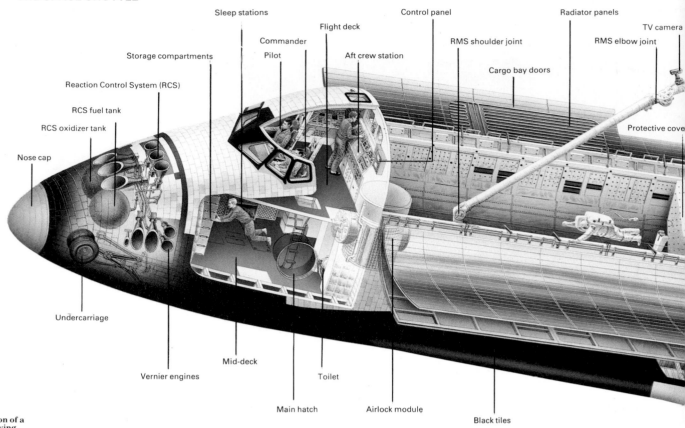

Sleep stations
Flight deck
Control panel
Radiator panels
TV camera
Commander
RMS shoulder joint
RMS elbow joint
Pilot
Aft crew station
Cargo bay doors
Storage compartments
Reaction Control System (RCS)
Protective cove
RCS fuel tank
RCS oxidizer tank
Nose cap
Undercarriage
Vernier engines
Mid-deck
Toilet
Black tiles
Main hatch
Airlock module

Above: A cross-section of a Space Shuttle. The living compartment for the crew takes up less than a quarter of the Shuttle's area. A large part of the remaining space is occupied by a cargo bay in which stray satellites can be stored.

ters on the ground examined thousands of separate items aboard the 2000-ton spacecraft. At the moment of ignition, astronauts Young and Crippen were slammed forward as the nose of Columbia pressed 480 mm (19 in) towards the big external propellant tank.

Computers then ordered the large solid rocket boosters to fire, which they did – spectacularly. Less than one minute after launch the Shuttle had turned to its proper heading for orbit, gently twisting around its long axis. Two minutes after liftoff the big boosters stopped burning and were jettisoned into the Atlantic, their descent rate arrested by three parachutes. The boosters would be recovered and towed ashore for use on up to 20 further flights. Meanwhile, Columbia moved out across the Atlantic, and six minutes later separated from the now empty liquid tank. Columbia was on its own, coasting upwards towards a high point of 136 km (84 miles) before thrusters fired to push it into a circular orbit 182 km (113 miles) above Earth.

Back over the US at the end of the first orbit, Young and Crippen opened the large cargo bay doors; a vital operation because radiators used for removing excess heat from Columbia were mounted on the inner face of each panel. It could not remain in space for long without the cooling system.

For two days Young and Crippen checked out Columbia's systems, and slept in their flight seats. The cubicles designed into the living quarters below the flight deck were not installed for this maiden flight. On board, the atmosphere was a comfortable oxygen-nitrogen mixture at one-third sea level pressure.

Then it was time to set up the four general purpose computers for the autopilot re-entry that would make the complex

landing operation look so easy. Columbia would be gliding back from space at 27,358 km/h (17,000 mph), more than three times faster than any previous winged vehicle, building up a temperature of 1482°C (2700°F) on the wing edges and on the nose of the space vehicle.

There was little room for error, but the complex slowing-down manoeuvre and looping glide to landing were achieved perfectly.

Regular operation

Columbia's first flight was the stuff that spectacular new stories are made of. But public interest in the Shuttle has not diminished despite many dozens of launches. Even before the first Shuttle had flown into orbit, it was virtually fully booked for 37 flights, covering three years of operation. The Shuttle can carry several satellites at once in its cargo bay 18.3 m (60 ft) long by 4.6 m (15 ft) wide. In orbit, the doors of the cargo bay swing open and an astronaut on flight deck uses a remotely-controlled arm to pick out the required satellite and release it into space. The same arm can be used to retrieve satellites for inspection and repair, or simply to bring dead satellites back to Earth, thereby helping clean up the orbital junkyard above our heads. Since the shuttle has a limited altitude, satellites destined for high orbits

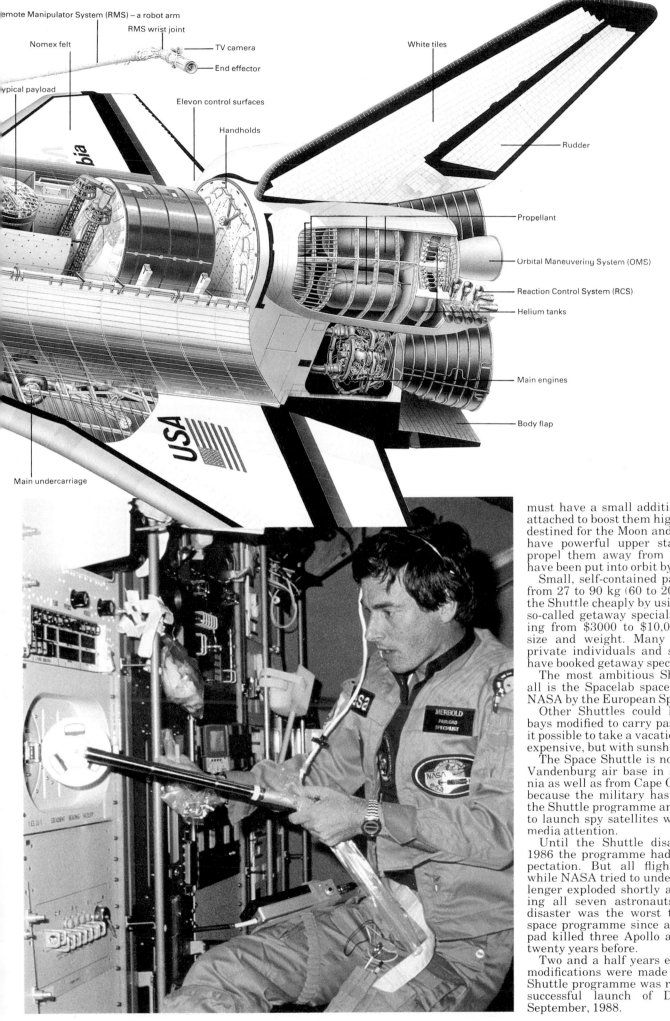

Remote Manipulator System (RMS) – a robot arm

RMS wrist joint

Nomex felt

TV camera

End effector

Typical payload

Elevon control surfaces

Handholds

White tiles

Rudder

Propellant

Orbital Maneuvering System (OMS)

Reaction Control System (RCS)

Helium tanks

Main engines

Body flap

Main undercarriage

must have a small additional rocket stage attached to boost them higher. Space probes destined for the Moon and planets will also have powerful upper stages attached to propel them away from Earth after they have been put into orbit by the Shuttle.

Small, self-contained payloads weighing from 27 to 90 kg (60 to 200 lb) can ride on the Shuttle cheaply by using one of NASA's so-called getaway specials, at prices ranging from $3000 to $10,000 depending on size and weight. Many users, including private individuals and small businesses, have booked getaway specials.

The most ambitious Shuttle payload of all is the Spacelab space station built for NASA by the European Space Agency.

Other Shuttles could have their cargo bays modified to carry passengers, making it possible to take a vacation in orbit – brief, expensive, but with sunshine guaranteed.

The Space Shuttle is now launched from Vandenburg air base in southern California as well as from Cape Canaveral. This is because the military has a large stake in the Shuttle programme and may often wish to launch spy satellites without attracting media attention.

Until the Shuttle disaster of January 1986 the programme had exceeded all expectation. But all flights were stopped while NASA tried to understand why Challenger exploded shortly after launch, killing all seven astronauts on board. The disaster was the worst to strike the US space programme since a fire on a launch pad killed three Apollo astronauts almost twenty years before.

Two and a half years elapsed and many modifications were made before the Space Shuttle programme was resumed, with the successful launch of Discovery on 29 September, 1988.

341

The Nature of Mathematics

To ask the nature of mathematics is to pose a question to which the answer is by no means clear. The reason for this strange state of affairs is to be found in the historical development of the subject.

The origins of counting and number systems are lost in antiquity, but as long as 4,000 years ago the Akkadian arithmetic was a high point of Babylonian culture. Unlike most modern counting systems, including our own, where the number 10 plays a basic role, this Babylonian system was based on the number 60. Irrespective of the actual symbols used, or the numbers upon which they are based, all developed counting systems are precise formulations of the concept of the *natural number*.

To the obvious natural numbers, such as 1, 2, 3, 4 and so on, we now usually add the *zero*, 0, which did not in fact appear as a genuine number (as distinct from a sign to indicate a space) until the Hindu arithmetic of the ninth century AD.

In due course the ideas of space and length, that is of *geometry*, were added to those of counting. Geometry arose as a practical subject, out of such problems as those involved in the surveying of the land around the Nile delta which was subject to annual flooding, but from about 500 BC onwards it was developed as a theoretical subject by the Greeks.

Pre-eminent in early Greek geometry was the proof of the theorem of Pythagoras, which stated that the square of the longest side of a right-angled triangle was equal to the sum of the squares of the other two sides. Thus for a triangle whose sides are 3, 4, and 5 units long, the square of the longest side is 25, which equals $3^2 + 4^2$, or $9 + 16$, the sum of the squares of the other two sides.

Calculus

To the Greek mathematicians such as Pythagoras, the concept of 'number' meant natural number. Fractions were only used in commerce; in geometry a ratio was not a fraction, but a separate entity. Later mathematicians, however, adopted a more general idea of number, considering first the *rational numbers* or fractions, and then the *real numbers*, those involving decimals instead of fractions.

Whereas the natural numbers increase in definite steps of one at a time (1, 2, 3 etc), any two rational or real numbers always have a range of other numbers in between. For example, between 1 and 2 lie other real numbers such as 1.3, 1.5 or 1.875. It is thus possible to think of a *continuously varying* real number.

This opens the way for the development of *calculus* and *mechanics*, two branches of mathematics which developed together during the seventeenth century. In mechanics, the basic idea is not the *point*, as in geometry, but the *particle* or *moving point*, whose position changes with time. The new mathematics of the seventeenth and eighteenth centuries expressed this in terms of the idea of a *variable*, such as the time or the distance of a particle from a fixed reference point.

	EGYPTIAN	BABYLONIAN	GREEK	ROMAN	MAVAN	II WEST ARABIC	HINDU
1	I	▼	A	I	·	1	۱
2	II	▼▼	B	II	··	2	۲
3	III	▼▼▼	Γ	III	···	₮	۳
4	IIII	▼▼▼▼	Δ	IIII	····	௴	۶
5	III II	▼▼▼ ▼▼	E	V	—	9	౬
6	III III	▼▼▼ ▼▼▼	F	VI	·⁻·	6	౬
7	IIII III	▼▼▼▼ ▼▼▼	Z	VII	·⁻··	7	౬
8	IIII IIII	▼▼▼▼ ▼▼▼▼	H	VIII	···	8	౮
9	III III III	▼▼▼▼▼ ▼▼▼▼	Θ	IX	····	9	౯
10	∩	◄	I	X	=	1·	౹౦

Above: The modern numerals for 1 to 10, used by western cultures, compared with their counterparts from older civilizations.

Below: Three counting systems—decimal (based on the number 10), binary (based on 2) and hexadecimal (based on 16).

DECIMAL	BINARY	HEXADECIMAL
1	1	1
2	10	2
3	11	3
4	100	4
5	101	5
6	110	6
7	111	7
8	1000	8
9	1001	9
10	1010	A
11	1011	B
12	1100	C
13	1101	D
14	1110	E
15	1111	F
16	10000	10
8 +4 ___ 12	1000 +100 ____ 1100	8 +4 ___ C

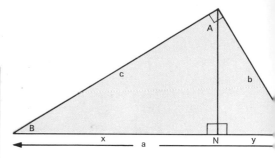

Above: Triangles ABN and ABC are *similar* triangles. Although they are different sizes, they each contain the same angles between their sides— ABC is simply a larger version of ABN.

Below: Pythagoras, one of the most famous Greek mathematicians, was born on the island of Samos in about 572 BC. He is best known for his theorem concerning right-angled triangles.

Below: The Egyptians constructed right angles by laying out a knotted rope into a 3, 4, 5 triangle, which includes a right angle.

Below: Pythagoras' theorem states that the square of the longest side of a right-angled triangle equals the sum of the squares of the other two sides.

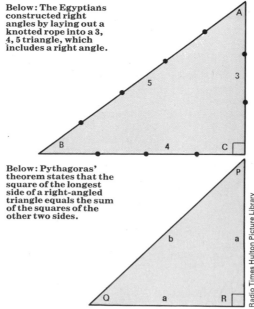

Radio Times Hulton Picture Library

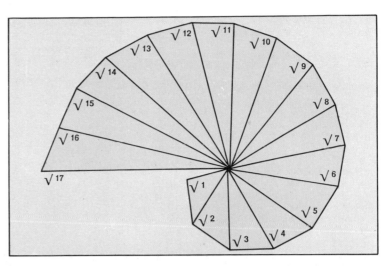

Right: A Greek geometrical construction based upon lines, radiating from a common point, whose lengths represent the square roots of the numbers 1 to 17. The lines joining the ends of these lines are all the same length, which gives the construction its shell-like shape.

Below: The shell of the pearly nautilus has a similar form of construction to the type of figure shown on the right. These creatures, which grow up to 20 cm (7.8 in) long, are found in the Indian and Pacific oceans, and as they grow they add new chambers to their shells. The animal's head is at the wide end of the shell.

Above: The work of the Greek mathematicians was known to the Arabs. This is part of a 15th century commentary on Euclid by Al-Tusi.

Below: An example of a natural geometrical construction—the cell wall structure of a micro-organism called a diatom.

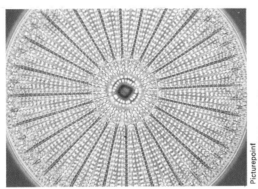

The dependence of one variable upon another, say of variable 'x' upon variable 't', was expressed in the form 'x is a *function* of t', which was written 'x = f(t)'.

The idea of *velocity* (the speed of an object *in a given direction*), which had given great difficulty to mathematicians during the thirteenth century, was now much easier to handle, for a function can be represented by means of graph. It was then possible to understand the velocity, at any instant, of a particle moving in a curved path, as that which it would have were it to continue in a straight line moving just as it was at the instant under consideration.

The velocity would be a function of the time, and if a graph showing the particle's position at various times were drawn, the velocity at any instant could be found by drawing a tangent to the curve of the graph at the time under consideration.

Infinite series
Many of the problems of calculus thrown up by mechanics would have proved too difficult without the use of the mathematical device of an *infinite series*. Some such series had been known for some time: the series '$1 + \frac{1}{2} + \frac{1}{4} + \frac{1}{8} + \ldots$', where

each term is half the preceding one, is one example. This series may be said to have a 'sum' of 2 in the sense that, however many terms are added together they will never reach 2, but on the other hand they will get as near to 2 as desired.

But the original idea that it was sufficient for the terms to decrease in order to be able to associate a sum with a series was shattered by the series '$1 + \frac{1}{2} + \frac{1}{3} + \frac{1}{4} + \ldots$'. In this series, the third and fourth terms together add up to more than $\frac{1}{2}$, as do the fifth, sixth, seventh and eighth. Therefore if a sum were to be associated with such a series it would be more than '$1 + \frac{1}{2} + \frac{1}{2} + \ldots$', and so it would, in effect, have no upper limit.

Despite the difficulties involved in determining the sums of infinite series, such series were often found to be useful in solving practical problems. During the eighteenth century it was suggested that the value of an infinite series should be defined in terms of the value of the function which gives it, the term 'function' in this case meaning an algebraic expression.

The general idea of a function did not evolve until the nineteenth century, when the intuitive but clumsy idea of a 'variable' having values expressed, by an algebraic formula, in terms of the values

of another variable, was finally displaced by that of a *mapping* between two *sets*.

In mechanics, for example, the relationship between time and the position of a moving particle could be expressed in this manner. The time would be represented by the set of all real numbers, and the distance at any one time between the particle and its starting point by the set of distances that it was possible for the particle to have. The mapping would then associate a unique member 'f(t)' of the second set with each member 't' of the first.

Reductionism
The concept of set was first clearly formulated by Georg Cantor in 1872, and it influenced the discussions about the philosophy of mathematics which arose in a gradual way as part of a general *reductionist* programme in the nineteenth century.

One instance of this programme is the clarification of the status of *non-Euclidian geometry*, a form of geometry not based upon the traditional form of geometry established by the Greek mathematician Euclid around 300 BC. Such geometries had been produced in earlier times, and the question arose whether it was con-

343

sistent to suppose, for example, a plane geometry in which from a point outside a line, no parallel to the line could be drawn.

This can be seen to be consistent (if ordinary geometry is consistent) by exemplifying it as the geometry of *great circles* on the surface of a sphere. A great circle is one whose diameter is the same as that of the sphere itself, and it is impossible to draw two great circles on the surface of a sphere without them intersecting. For the reductionist programme, the consistency problem in non Euclidian geometry was *reduced* to that of ordinary, Euclidian geometry.

There were other fields in which a reductionist programme was carried out. For example, ordinary geometry can be reduced to algebra by the use of a *co-ordinate system*. In this system, which was largely due to the French philosopher René Descartes (and is thus known as *Cartesian*), the position of any point can be fully described by means of its distances from two lines or *axes*, one vertical and one horizontal. Using Cartesian co-ordinates, any geometrical relationship between two points can be expressed in terms of algebra.

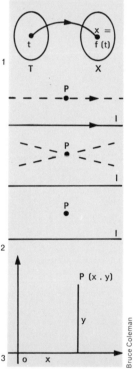

Left: 1. A graph of the position, x, at any time, t, of a moving particle which was originally at rest at x = 0, and then gradually accelerated. The velocity at point T can be thought of as that which the particle would have if its position graph were a straight line at a tangent to the curve at point T.
2. In a velocity/time graph of a moving particle, the shaded area is of size hv, and represents the approximate distance the particle travelled during time h.
Right: 3. The reduction of geometry to algebra employs a pair of fixed co-ordinate lines to describe the position of any point 'P'.

Right: The curved path of a jet of water from a fountain forms a type of curve known as a *parabola*, and the outline of each group of jets is itself a parabola.

Below: 1. Instead of the older, graphical representation of a function, the modern picture is of two *sets*, T, called the *domain*, and X, the *range*, with a *mapping* 'f = T — X' between them.
2. Three possible geometries of parallels. Top: Euclidian—only one possible parallel to a line can pass through point 'P'. Centre: hyperbolic geometry— two parallels can pass through 'P'. Bottom: elliptic geometry—no parallel can be drawn.

G. F. Allen/Bruce Coleman

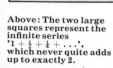

Above: The two large squares represent the infinite series '1 + $\frac{1}{2}$ + $\frac{1}{4}$ + $\frac{1}{8}$ + ...', which never quite adds up to exactly 2.

Bruce Coleman

ZEFA

344

Syndication International

Left: The woman's body and its distorted mirror image are *topologically* identical because the 'surface' of the image, although

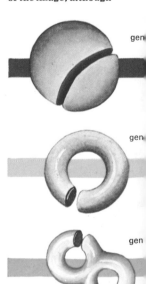

gen

gen

gen

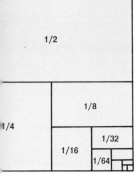

1/2
1/4
1/8
1/16
1/32
1/64

Below: Parallel lines often appear to converge, but, like an infinite series and its 'sum', they never actually do.

Left: Albert Einstein (1879-1955), whose mathematical theories of relativity were proven only later by practical experimental results. The concept of relativity is an example of the way in which mathematics is used to discover more about the physical universe.

Right: Academician Andrei Kolmogorov of the Soviet Union, a prominent modern mathematician who devised an abstract calculus for use in probability theory.

Below: A drawing by Leonardo da Vinci (1452-1519) which illustrates the geometrical nature of the proportions of the human body.

Radio Times Hulton Picture Library

Novosti

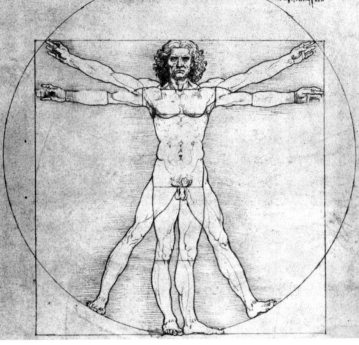

Mansell

distorted, has the same mathematical properties as the body's surface.

Below: the topological *genus* of an object is the number of times it can be cut without dividing it into two parts—none for genus 0, one for genus 1, and two for genus 2.

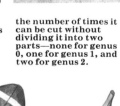

Set theory

Every attempt at a thorough reductionist programme since the work of Gottlob Frege in 1879 has depended upon the idea of a set. A set is simply a collection of all its members, and its members themselves may be sets. For example, the set of all people includes the set of all men, the set of all women, and the set of all children—and these in turn can be sub-divided into other sets.

Cantor had concluded that every well-defined decidable property defines a set, that is, the members of a set are just those possessing that property. In 1899, however, Cantor discovered to his surprise that his theory was plagued with contradictions. Russell attempted to resolve these contradictions in 1903, but with no real success.

The foundations of mathematics had suddenly been shown to be quite unsure. Russell and Whitehead, in 1919, suggested that a sure foundation was to be found in logic, but when they looked for it there they found that the logic which was taught at the time was a tissue of trivialities and nonsense that had been handed down almost unchanged from the Middle Ages, and so they had to begin again.

Their greatest triumph was the precise formulation of arithmetic, including a formula for the definition of the number 1. Another approach to the problems of the foundations of mathematics was begun by Hilbert in 1899. He was able to formulate geometry in better terms than those used by Euclid, and he turned his attention to the concept of truth, which is essential to both mathematics and logic.

The difficulties encountered in discussions about truth are exemplified by: (The sentence in these brackets is false). If we suppose this sentence to be true, then it asserts its own falsehood, which contradicts our supposition; but if we assume it to be false, this assumption is exactly what the sentence is saying, so that the sentence is therefore true and our assumption is again contradicted.

During the first 30 years of this century it became apparent that the consistency of much of classical mathematics depended upon the corresponding result for the arithmetic of natural numbers. As a result of this, Gödel, in 1929, devised a way of expressing the letters of the alphabet, and combinations of them such as words and sentences, by a numerical code. By this means, the truth or falsity of sentences could be determined arithmetically.

Gödel was able to prove that any system that was rich enough to describe elementary arithmetic, the arithmetic of natural numbers, would inevitably be either inconsistent or incomplete. Using his numerical code, he could construct an arithmetic statement which was essentially equivalent to: (The statement in these brackets is unprovable.)

There is no paradox as there was in the previous example. But if the sentence is true, it is an example of a true but inprovable sentence, so the system is uncomplete. If, on the other hand, it is false, it is an example of a false but provable sentence, and so the system is inconsistent. So, although the technical achievements of mathematics are not in question, its real nature still remains in doubt.

Scientific Analysis

Scientific analysis represents a composition of procedures and techniques associated with man's enquiry into the physical substance of his environment. Early practical demands probably originated from metallurgists needing some method of determining the percentage purity of gold and silver. Since then a wide variety of analytic instruments of observation and measurement have been developed to satisfy the demands of all branches of science. These may be of direct application such as the chemical balance and the microscope, or they may use some property of matter to provide results indirectly—for example, the spectrometer.

Analyses fall broadly within two categories: *qualitative* analysis which encompasses the detection of what a material is made of; and *quantitative* analysis which determines how much of the material is present.

Microscopy

Microscopy is an analytic process which had its origins among biologists, although its potential in the fields of crystallography and metallurgy was soon realized. In 1683, Anton van Leeuwenhoek (1632-1723) was the first to set eyes on bacteria, using a *simple microscope*, one fitted with a single lens.

There is a limit to the magnification obtainable with a simple microscope, however, and for further resolution of detail a *compound microscope* is necessary. The compound microscope, which is the type generally used, consists of two powerful converging lenses of short focal length.

Microscope use is very diverse; from its origins as a tool of direct observation it is now essential in many fields of qualitative and quantitative analysis. Physical observations are generally of colour, optical density, size, shape and surface characteristic. Chemical observations are mainly the study of precipitation reactions where a material is brought into solution and the colour and form of the precipitate crystals are noted when a test reagent is added.

Electron microscopes

No matter how well an optical microscope is made, there is a limit to the amount of detail it can resolve, and this limit cannot be overcome optically because it is due to the nature of light itself. In order to be able to distinguish between two closely-positioned particles, the light source used must have a wavelength of not more than twice the distance between them.

Visible light is restricted to a small band of wavelengths of the electromagnetic spectrum, its wavelength being of the order of about 0.5 microns (1 micron = 1 millionth of a metre). This means that an optical microscope cannot resolve details of less than about 0.25 microns. During the 1920s it was discovered that when electrons are accelerated, they travel with a wave-like motion similar to that of light, but with a wavelength over 100,000 times shorter.

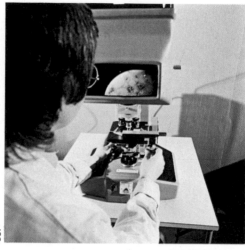

Above: The microscope is one of the basic tools of scientific analysis. This one is fitted with an optical projection system which projects the image of the specimen on to a screen, instead of the user having to peer into the eyepiece. This makes it easier to use and produces a clearer image.

Right: Crystalline tartaric acid (dihydroxy-succinic acid) viewed through a microscope at x 30 magnification in polarized light. The polarized light creates these coloured effects in the crystal which enable its structure to be seen more clearly than in ordinary non-polarized light.

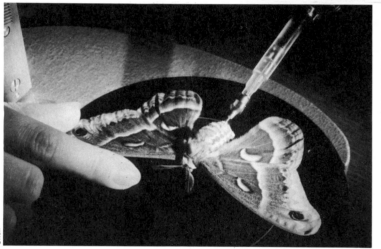

Left: A male silkmoth being injected with a radioactive substance as part of a biochemical analysis of its metabolism. The way in which the substance is broken down or metabolized, and distributed through the insect's tissues, can subsequently be analyzed by tracing the radioactivity.

Right: This apparatus is used for the microdistillation of weighable amounts of substances. This involves heating them to separate off their constituents, which vaporize at different temperatures and so can be collected separately for subsequent analysis. This enables the composition of the substances to be found.

This led to the invention of the electron microscope during the 1930s. The electron microscope uses a beam of electrons in place of light, and the beam is either directed right through the specimen, or reflected off its surface.

In the *transmission electron microscope*, an ultra-thin specimen is placed in the path of an electron beam, which passes through it and produces an image of it on a phosphorescent screen. The *scanning* electronic microscope, on the other hand, scans a fine beam of electrons across the surface of a specimen. As the beam hits the surface of the specimen it drives off 'secondary' electrons from it, which are drawn towards a detector. The detector produces a signal which is amplified, and used to drive a cathode ray tube that produces an image of the specimen.

A third type of electron microscope, the *scanning transmission electron microscope*, uses a similar scanning and detection principle to the scanning instrument, but the electrons are beamed right through the sample as in the transmission instrument. Modern electron microscopes can resolve details as small as 0.0002 microns.

Chromatography

Chromatography was initially developed as a means of separation of complex mixtures in the fields of organic chemistry and pharmacology, where chemical differences are so slight as to be insufficient to afford a means of separation, whereas molecular physical differences exist which are used as a means of resolution. Although several investigators applied chromatography more or less accidentally during the nineteenth century the Russian Mikhail Tswett (1872-1920) was the first to appreciate the underlying principles.

Chromatographic techniques involve manipulation of a few of the general properties of molecules. These are: first, solubility, the tendency of the molecule to dissolve in a liquid solvent; secondly, adsorption, the tendency for a molecule to attach itself to a finely divided solid; and thirdly, volatility, the tendency for a molecule to evaporate.

Tswett was interested in separating the pigments contained in the leaves of plants which he dissolved in ether. He then poured this solution into a vertical glass column filled with calcium carbonate and, as he continued to wash the solution through the column with more solvent, he found that it separated into a series of coloured bands which travelled slowly down the column to the bottom, where

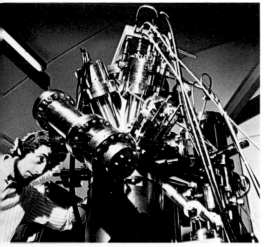

Left: Optical microscopes are limited to a useful maximum magnification of about x 2,000 because the wavelength of visible light prevents the resolution of details below 0.25 microns apart. Electron microscopes, on the other hand, can produce magnifications as high as x 1,000,000.

Right: A small transmission electron microscope like this one is usually mounted on a desk-type console. The electron beam, generated by a 60 kV electron gun, passes through the specimen and creates an image of it on the screen. The largest transmission microscopes, nearly three storeys high, operate at 3 MV.

CQI

ELECTRON MICROSCOPE

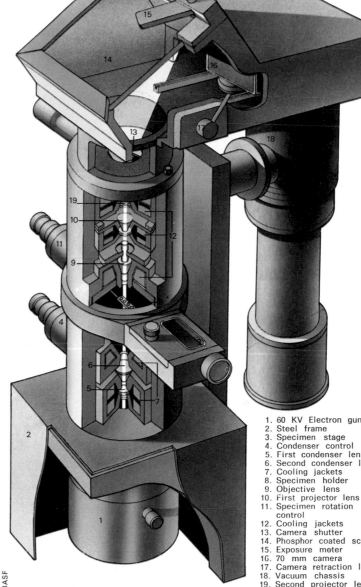

1. 60 KV Electron gun
2. Steel frame
3. Specimen stage
4. Condenser control
5. First condenser lens
6. Second condenser lens
7. Cooling jackets
8. Specimen holder
9. Objective lens
10. First projector lens
11. Specimen rotation control
12. Cooling jackets
13. Camera shutter
14. Phosphor coated screen
15. Exposure meter
16. 70 mm camera
17. Camera retraction lever
18. Vacuum chassis
19. Second projector lens

BASF

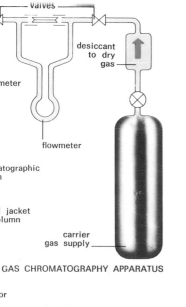

sample injection point

valves

desiccant to dry gas

manometer

flowmeter

chromatographic column

heated jacket for column

carrier gas supply

GAS CHROMATOGRAPHY APPARATUS

detector unit

Left: A basic gas chromatograph. The gas is dried by the dessicant, and its flow rate and pressure are monitored by the flow meter and manometer. The constituents of the sample are identified by the different times at which they emerge from the column. Gases used include argon, nitrogen and hydrogen.

Below: Chromatographic equipment in use in an oil company laboratory. Chromatography, particularly gas chromatography, is used extensively in the petrochemical and pharmaceutical industries, and throughout the chemical industry generally. It also has applications in forensic science.

Shell

they could be individually collected.

As the dissolved chemical compounds constituting the pigments were washed through the column, the ones that had an affinity for the large surface area of the finely divided calcium carbonate, the *adsorbent*, had their progress delayed. The ones completely inert to the surface passed through the column at the same rate as the solvent.

Not only do different substances have widely varying adsorption characteristics but differing solubility tendencies as well. As it is highly unlikely that two different substances will exhibit quantitatively the same pair of physical propertics, an interaction of these features will lead to the band separation of the compound, which will have their own characteristic rate of downward migration. These bands can be detected as they emerge from the column, isolated, and identified. Modern column chromatography, as it is called, is little different from the method used by Tswett, but alumina and silicia gel are the most commonly used adsorbents.

Since its inception chromatography has been continuously modified but the basis remains the same, that of two *phases* with a substance distributed between them, separation requiring one of the

347

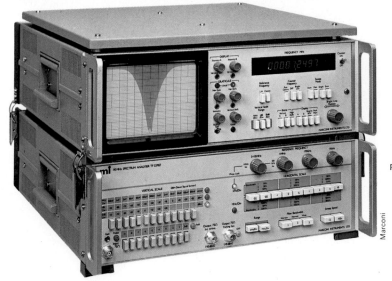

Right: This electronic spectrum analyzer is used to examine the component frequencies and waveforms of electronic signals.

Below: The *nuclear magnetic resonance* (NMR) spectrometer is used to analyze the structure of molecules. The sample to be analyzed is placed in a strong magnetic field and exposed to radio-frequency radiation. It will absorb radiation energy at frequencies corresponding to the magnetic resonance frequencies of its atomic nuclei, those at which they change their direction of orientation within the magnetic field. The frequencies at which energy is absorbed indicate the types of atoms present.

VIKING BIOLOGICAL LABORATORY

pyrolytic release illuminator assembly

labelled release carbon-14 detector

PYROLYTIC RELEASE EXPERIMENT

dump cell

test cell

organic vapour trap

dump cell

heaters

test cell

LABELLED RELEASE EXPERIMENT

nutrient reservoir

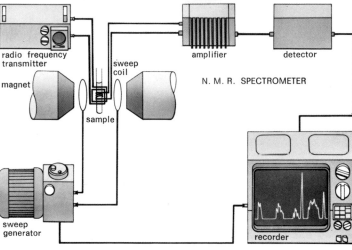

radio frequency transmitter

amplifier   detector

magnet

sweep coil

sample

N. M. R. SPECTROMETER

sweep generator

recorder

module enclosure

Right: The equipment used in the life detection experiments carried out by the Viking 1 and Viking 2 spacecraft on soil taken from the surface of Mars. There were three sections to these experiments: the *pyrolytic release* experiment, which looked for evidence of photosynthesis; the

labelled release experiment, which looked for signs of metabolic activity; and the *gas exchange* experiment, which looked for changes in the composition of the gases surrounding a soil sample that would indicate that some form of respiratory activity was taking place within the soil.

phases to be moving over the other, stationary phase. The moving phase may be a liquid or a gas; the stationary phase may be a solid adsorbent or a liquid film, the former being called *adsorption chromatography* and the latter *partition chromatography*.

Partition chromatography depends on the difference in solubility a compound may have in two different liquids. One of the liquids is kept stationary as a liquid film by impregnating it in an inert support, such as kieselguhr, cellulose or some other finely divided solid. The substance to be separated is dissolved in the moving phase, its progress being delayed according to its relative solubility in each of the liquids. Substances with different solubilities may be separated, the solutes more soluble in the moving phase progressing faster.

Gas-liquid chromatography (a form of partition chromatography) apparatus consists of a liquid film support packed in a small diameter tubular column, usually several metres long. The moving phase, an inert gas such as argon, is allowed to flow through the column, which is generally placed in an oven so that it can be heated to facilitate separation of high boiling point materials. The sample mixture is injected into the head of the column and passes down the tube under the influence of the carrier gas.

The individual compounds proceed at a rate dependent upon their affinities for the stationary phase, those with a strong affinity being retained longer than those with a weak affinity. A detector at the column exit produces a signal as the compounds emerge, which is amplified and displayed on a chart recorder.

Right: The size of the equipment used by the Viking landers in their search for life on Mars can be seen from this picture of the assembly of one of the complex miniature laboratories. Each one contained three automated units which performed the life detection experiments, plus associated equipment for handling the soil samples and a computer. The soil samples were dug from the Martian surface by a telescopic digging device and transferred automatically to the three experiments. The control analysis was carried out by repeating the experiments with soil samples that were sterilized to kill off any organisms present.

TRW Inc

Below left: The biological experiments performed by the Viking spacecraft. In the pyrolytic release experiment, a soil sample was kept in a container in which the Martian atmosphere was supplemented with carbon dioxide containing ('labelled with') radioactive carbon-14. The sample was bathed in light similar to Martian sunlight then the gases surrounding the sample were removed. It was then heated to see if it gave off any carbon-14, which would indicate that carbon had been removed from the gases by a photosynthetic organism. In the labelled release experiment, the sample was treated with a nutrient containing carbon-14, so that any living organism present to absorb the nutrient would give off carbon to the surrounding air, including carbon-14 which could be detected. In the gas exchange experiment, a gas chromatograph was used to detect any changes, caused by the respiration of a living organism, in the gases around the sample.

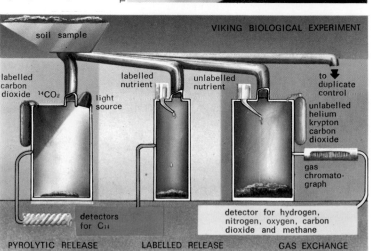

soil sample

VIKING BIOLOGICAL EXPERIMENT

labelled carbon dioxide $^{14}CO_2$

light source

labelled nutrient

unlabelled nutrient

to duplicate control

unlabelled helium krypton carbon dioxide

gas chromatograph

detectors for C14

detector for hydrogen, nitrogen, oxygen, carbon dioxide and methane

PYROLYTIC RELEASE   LABELLED RELEASE   GAS EXCHANGE

Perkin-Elmer

soil distribution assembly

soil entry port

nutrient valve block assembly

He/Kr/CO₂ reservoir

GAS EXCHANGE EXPERIMENT

heater

test cell

dump cell

thermostat

gas chromatograph

stainless steel tubing (15.24 m, 50 ft.)

electronic subsystem

Right: An NMR spectrometer, a very useful analytical instrument which can quickly determine the molecular structure of a sample.

Below: In *mass spectroscopy*, chemical compounds are analyzed by *ionizing* their atoms (removing electrons from them to make them positively charged), then accelerating them through a magnetic field so that they are deflected on to a photographic plate or electronic detector. The amount by which a particle is deflected depends on its atomic weight, and so the elements present can be identified by the position at which they strike the plate or detector.

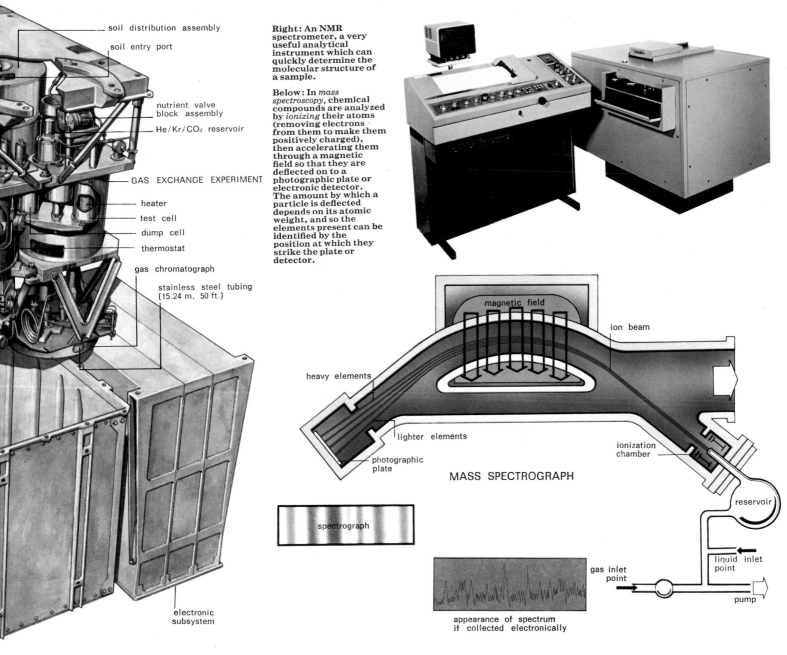

magnetic field

ion beam

heavy elements

lighter elements

photographic plate

MASS SPECTROGRAPH

ionization chamber

reservoir

spectrograph

liquid inlet point

gas inlet point

pump

appearance of spectrum if collected electronically

This display is called a *chromatogram* and ideally takes the form of peaks, each indicating the presence of a particular component. The retention time in the column is characteristic for each compound, allowing qualitative analysis to be made upon comparison with a standard sample chromatogram.

Spectroscopy

Newton was the first to discover that when a beam of white light strikes one of the faces of a triangular glass prism, the beam is bent or deviated from its straight path and resolved into a series of rainbow-coloured bands called a spectrum. Newton's spectrum, however, was impure, as the colours overlapped. An instrument for producing and measuring a pure spectrum is called a *spectrometer*, which by focusing the light admitted via a narrow slit or *collimator* on to the prism produces a series of distinct or *monochromatic* colours.

The spectrum produced by the white light of the Sun is a series of closely-adjacent radiations called a *continuous spectrum*. By contrast elements, when incandescent, produce light of distinct colours of particular wavelengths called a *line spectrum*.

The study and analysis of spectra is called *spectroscopy*, which involves observing and measuring the radiations emitted by atoms and molecules when they are excited by means of energy which is normally thermal or electro-magnetic in nature. Atoms consist of a nucleus surrounded by electrons moving in certain orbits corresponding to levels of energy. If supplied with an amount of energy at an appropriate frequency the electron will jump to another orbit, where it will have a higher energy level.

The difference between the energy states is equal to the energy supplied. Conversely, under favourable circumstances an electron may jump from a high to a low energy orbit, emitting energy in the form of electromagnetic radiation. The frequency of this radiation is proportional to the amount of energy it contains.

In a hot body, thermally excited atoms emit and absorb visible and invisible radiation of discrete and characteristic wavelengths due to energy changes between electron orbits, normally producing a radiation spectrum of more than one wavelength.

The first known spectroscopic observations to distinguish individual atomic transmissions were those of Josef von Fraunhofer (1787-1826) in 1814. Fraunhofer developed a spectrometer capable of resolving the spectral lines named after him, which arise from the absorption of solar radiation by the atoms in the cooler gas surrounding the Sun and by atoms in the Earth's atmosphere. The same spectroscopic techniques were soon applied to the analysis of other atomic emissions, for every element has a unique electronic structure, capable of producing a specific and identifying spectrum. Furthermore, the intensities of the lines of emission indicate the concentrations of the atoms present in the sample, so that a quantitative analysis is possible.

Any substance will absorb radiation of the particular wavelength that it emits at a high temperature. Thus, if radiation from a hot source emitting a continuous spectrum is passed through a transparent sample or vapour, the *absorption spectrum* is deficient in the wavelengths that the sample would emit if it were raised to the same high temperature. Absorption spectroscopy is a valuable analytic tool as it is easy to control and does not destroy the sample. By measuring the proportion of incident light absorbed the molecular concentrations may also be determined.

349

Optics

As you look at this page, you are actually observing a certain type of reflection. Almost everything we can see, except for actual sources of light such as the Sun or a light bulb, is visible only because of reflection. We normally think of reflection as being a property of mirrors or shiny objects, but the kind of reflections which produce images, such as those in a mirror, are really just one type, known as *specular* reflection.

Far more common is *diffuse* reflection, which causes this page to be visible. A beam of light striking the paper is reflected by it in all directions. Whichever angle you look at it from, it appears equally as bright. The printer's ink does not reflect as much light as the white paper—it absorbs some of it—so it appears darker by comparison. The coloured ink in the pictures absorbs some colours more than others, so only these others are reflected.

If you experiment by holding the page so as to catch the light from a table lamp in an otherwise dark room, you will find that at a certain angle it reflects slightly more light, as if it were behaving a little like a mirror. That is, the paper is not giving completely diffuse reflections—there is, in effect, also a slight specular component.

A mirror, however, gives purely specular reflections—the beam of light is reflected in one direction only, so that only when you are looking at the correct angle to the mirror will you see a particular object reflected in it. This, and the fact that light always travels in straight lines, accounts for the way a flat mirror produces reflections.

What makes some materials give diffuse, and some specular, reflections? The answer lies in the roughness of the material. If a light beam strikes a surface which is rough on a scale comparable with the wavelength of light (about 0.5 thousandths of a millimetre), then it may be reflected in any direction. But if the surface is within a few wavelengths of being flat, the beam will be reflected at a definite angle. The situation is comparable with throwing a tennis ball at a wall—if the wall is very rough, the ball may come off at any direction, but if it is smooth the ball will be 'reflected' at a predictable angle as long as it has no spin.

To make a mirror, therefore, one has to produce a very smooth surface. For normally rough surfaces, this can be done by applying a coating, such as the layer of varnish or wax on wood, or by including china clay in glossy paper. If the surface itself can be polished, as can glass or metal, so much the better. Glass can be made smooth fairly easily; to produce a mirror a sheet of glass is coated on the back with a thin layer of metal such as aluminium or silver, which reflects all colours equally well and therefore does not give a noticeable tint.

Specular reflection always obeys certain laws. In particular, the angle at which the beam strikes a surface (the *angle of incidence*) is always equal to the angle at which it is reflected (the *angle of reflection*). These two angles are measured from a line perpendicular to the surface, called the *normal*. The angles of incidence

and reflection and the normal are always in the same plane. Using these laws, we can easily predict how a ray will be reflected, just as a billiards or pool player can predict how a ball will bounce off the cushion at the side of the table.

Refraction

Although light normally travels in straight lines, it sometimes appears to bend. This occurs when it passes from one medium, such as air or water, into another, such as glass or clear plastic, which has different optical properties. The obvious example of this is when a stick is put into water at an angle—it appears bent where it enters the water.

This phenomenon is called *refraction*, and the optical property which causes it is called the *refractive* index. We can see its effects if we watch a beam of light passing into a glass block from air. Instead of carrying on in a straight line, it deflects towards the normal as it enters the block. The refractive index is a measure of the light-bending ability of a medium, usually compared with that of air, and is expressed as a number.

When light enters a parallel-sided glass block, the refraction at the first surface deviates the beam. As it emerges from the

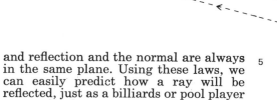

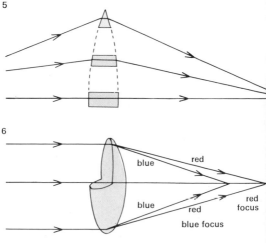

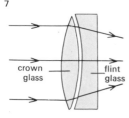

Left: These drawings show several aspects of the reflection and refraction of light.
1. When light strikes a smooth surface, such as a mirror, it is all reflected in the same direction, producing a reflected image of the object from which it is coming. This is known as *specular* reflection. If the surface is rough, the light is scattered in all directions. This *diffuse* reflection does not create a reflected image.

2. Light passing from one medium to another of different density is deflected or *refracted* slightly. Light passing through a piece of glass with parallel sides is refracted twice, by equal amounts but in opposite directions. Its direction of travel remains the same, but it is shifted slightly to one side.

3. Light passing through a prism is refracted twice in the same direction. The different wavelengths of light are refracted by different amounts, long wavelength (red) light being refracted the least and shorter wavelengths, such as blue, the most. White light passing through a prism is split into its component colours.

4. A mirage like this, an apparent reflection of actual objects, is caused by some of the light from them being refracted as it passes from cool air into hot air of lower density.

Radio Times Hulton Picture Library

Below: 5. and 6. A convex lens is, in effect, a series of prisms, each deviating light by a different amount, arranged so that light passing through them is all deviated to the same spot. As there is a different focus for each colour of light, the image formed has coloured fringes around it.

Left: 7. The *achromatic* lens produces an image with no colour fringing. The lens has two elements, made of two types of glass, and the colour dispersion caused by the first is corrected by the second. This eliminates the fringing effect or *chromatic aberration* which occurs with simple convex lenses.

other side, the beam is refracted back by an equal amount so there is no overall change in direction. But if the block does not have parallel sides, the result is an overall deviation in the light's direction. A triangular block of glass, usually called a *prism*, does this—but with one other important effect.

Unlike the law of reflection, which applies to all colours of light equally, the refractive index changes with the colour —blue light is refracted more than red when it enters a medium with a higher refractive index. For the parallel block, this *dispersion* into colours is cancelled out, just as the deviation was. But in the case of a prism, the dispersion is also increased with the result that white light is split up into all its colours, forming a *spectrum* of the colours of the rainbow.

(White is simply the visual appearance of all the rainbow colours seen together). This property is exploited in *spectroscopes*, which are used to analyze the colours in a source of light.

Diffraction

There is another way in which light can be bent and split into colours—by *diffraction*, which occurs on such a small scale that we rarely observe it in everyday life. It happens more obviously with sound waves. Imagine a band marching, hidden by buildings. To start with, you hear only the bass notes. When the band emerges into full view, you can hear the high notes as well. Long waves (deep notes) can bend round corners, while short waves (higher pitched) can do so less easily.

Left: Spectacles, pairs of lenses for correcting sight defects, have been in use for over 700 years. This picture shows a 17th-century Dutch spectacle shop.

Right: A selection of high quality prisms.

Below left: The way a pair of contact lenses fit onto the eyes can be checked by dropping a special fluid into the eyes and shining ultraviolet light onto them. The fluid glows brightly and any irregularities in the fit of the lenses can easily be seen.

Below: Photo-elastic stress analysis is a method of determining the stresses within a structure subjected to a load. A model of the structure is made from clear plastic, and loads are applied to it. When viewed under *polarized* light, light in which all the waves are vibrating in the same direction, patterns are produced which correspond to the area of stress. The brightest areas of the pattern are those where the stress within the model is at a maximum.

TERRESTRIAL TELESCOPE

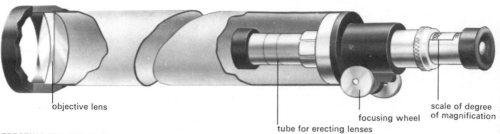

objective lens

focusing wheel

scale of degree of magnification

tube for erecting lenses

ERECTING THE IMAGE IN A TERRESTRIAL TELESCOPE

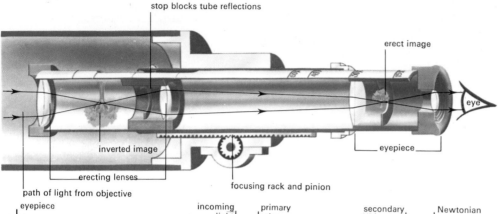

stop blocks tube reflections

erect image

eye

inverted image

eyepiece

erecting lenses

path of light from objective

focusing rack and pinion

Hale Observatories/Alphabet & Image

Left and below: The large diagrams show the basic design of a terrestrial telescope and the way in which an upright image is obtained. The smaller drawings show the principles of the optical systems of four types of astronomical telescope: the refracting, Newtonian, Cassegrain and coudé.

Above: An observer sitting in the prime focus cage within the 200 inch (508 cm) telescope at the Hale Observatory on Mount Palomar, USA. The prime focus is the point where light reflected from the primary mirror first comes to a focus, and the largest telescopes have cages at this point.

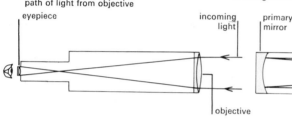

eyepiece

incoming light

primary mirror

secondary mirror

Newtonian focus

primary

Cassegrain secondary

objective

prime focus

Cassegrain focus

REFRACTING

NEWTONIAN

CASSEGRAIN

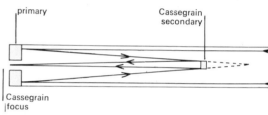

Coudé focus

primary mirror

COUDÉ

Coudé secondary

Below: A Questar *catadioptric* telescope. Catadioptric telescopes use a combination of refraction and reflection to form an image. Light enters through a large concave lens, and a concave mirror at the rear reflects it on to a small reflective spot on the rear of the lens. From here, it is

reflected down a central tube to a 45° prism, which directs it up to the eyepiece on top of the rear of the instrument.

Right: A pair of prismatic binoculars, which use pairs of Porro prisms to 'fold' the light path and make the system more compact.

William MacQuitty

A similar thing happens with light waves. They will bend—very slightly—round obstacles, the long waves (red light) more so than the shorter ones (blue). If a regular series of obstacles is used, the effect can be seen by eye. This accounts for the colours seen in the grooves of an LP record. Lights seen through finely woven fabric also show spikes caused by this diffraction effect. A spectroscope may use a surface with finely ruled grooves, called a *diffraction grating*, in place of the prism.

Lenses

Imagine a series of prisms one on top of the other, each deviating light to a different extent and arranged so that the top one deviates the light most, while the bottom one does not deviate the light at all—that is, it is parallel-sided. Clearly it is possible to arrange the prisms in such a way that all the light coming from any particular source is deviated to the same spot.

This, in effect, is what an ordinary *convex* lens is—a series of piles of prisms, arranged in a disc so that light entering it from any direction can be deviated to one spot. This is why lenses form images. If an object is very distant—effectively 'at infinity'—its light will be refracted to form an image at a *focal point* a certain distance from the lens. This distance is called the *focal length*. A fat lens, with steeply curved sides, has a short focal length compared with its diameter while a thin one, whose sides are almost parallel, has a long focal length.

The image-forming properties of a simple convex lens allow it to be used as a magnifying glass. A short focal length

lens will always magnify more than a long focal length one, whatever their diameters. In a telescope of the simplest type, one lens of long focal length (the *objective*) is used to form an image. This image can then be looked at with a shorter focal length lens which acts as a magnifying glass, called the *eyepiece*. The magnification is simply given by dividing the focal length of the objective by that of the eyepiece. Eyepieces of different focal lengths give a range of magnifications.

Astronomical telescopes

Telescopes with just two convex lenses are simple astronomical telescopes: they give upside down images, which is no great drawback in astronomy. But they have one more serious disadvantage. Just as a single prism gives colour dispersion, so a single lens has a different focal length for each colour. This results in images with coloured fringes. The longer the focal length of the lens, the less obtrusive this false colour is for a given magnification. Consequently, early astronomical telescopes had to be made impractically long to give good results.

Isaac Newton applied himself to this problem in 1668, and decided that the best solution would be to form the image not with a lens but with a mirror. A concave mirror behaves just like a lens in that it focuses light to a point—but with the advantage that since all colours are reflected equally, there is no false colour. The only drawback is that the image is formed in the path of the incoming light. To overcome this Newton placed a small flat mirror to intercept the light just before the focus and reflect it through 90° so that the image was formed outside the

352

Left: An aerial view of Mauna Kea, Hawaii, showing (from left to right) the 3 m NASA infrared telescope, the 3.8 m British infrared telescope (in the building with the dome shutter opened), the 2.2 m University of Hawaii telescope, and the 3.6 m telescope jointly funded by Canada, France and Hawaii (housed in the large onion dome). The summit of this extinct volcano (seen to the extreme right of the picture) is 4300 m (14,000 ft) above sea level – well above the clouds, which usually lie at about the 3000 m (10,000 ft) level.

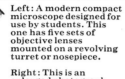

Left: A modern compact microscope designed for use by students. This one has five sets of objective lenses mounted on a revolving turret or nosepiece.

Right: This is an enlarged photograph, taken through a microscope, of a section of a porpoise's tooth. The tooth was illuminated with light polarized in one direction, and viewed through a filter polarized in another. Normally this would mean that no light could pass through the filter, but the material of the tooth has rotated the direction of polarization of the light falling on it so that some of it can pass through the filter.

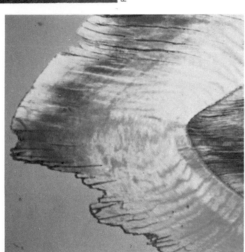

Above: The structure of the tooth is such that different wavelengths or colours of light are rotated more than others, so the original white light is split up to give a coloured image, which shows the structural detail more clearly than if it were viewed under non-polarized white light.

tube. There it can be viewed with an eyepiece, just as in a refractor except that the observer looks at right angles to the tube. These *Newtonian* telescopes, as they are called, are fairly easy to make and are popular with amateur astronomers.

Meanwhile, others studied the same problem and came up with the *achromatic lens*—a combination of two lenses of differing refractive index which are able to *deviate* light without *dispersing* it into colours. Achromatic lenses are now used in all high quality optical instruments.

The larger the diameter—or *aperture*—of a telescope, the more light is focused to an image and the brighter the view. For this reason, telescopes are described by their aperture rather than by their magnification (which is variable anyway). The largest optical telescope in the world is currently being built by Keck in Hawaii.

Terrestrial telescopes and binoculars

The upside down images given by astronomical telescopes are awkward when the telescope is to be used for everyday purposes. *Terrestrial telescopes*, the ordinary type used for viewing distant objects on land or sea, get over this by means of additional lenses which erect the image. Alternatively, the image can be reflected upright by a pair of *Porro prisms*, using the phenomenon of *total internal reflection*.

Because light 'bends' as it goes from a more dense medium into a less dense one, it is possible for the emergent light to be bent so much that none of it escapes from the prism at all. In this case, all the light is reflected from the surface inside the glass. In Porro prisms the light enters at right angles to one face, is totally internally reflected twice through 90° by the other two sides of the prism, and emerges at right angles to the original face, thus not suffering dispersion but turned through 180°. These prisms are used in *prismatic binoculars* to erect the image: they have the advantage over mirrors of never being able to tarnish, while their use shortens the tube length required by 'folding' the light path. Prismatic binoculars are thus two achromatic telescopes side by side, using Porro prisms to erect the image.

Simple binoculars, such as opera glasses and field glasses, are basically two-lens telescopes mounted side-by-side. These telescopes are known as *Galilean* telescopes, being based on the design invented by Galileo Galilei (1564-1642). The Galilean telescope uses a convex objective lens, but the eyepiece is *concave*. Concave lenses have one or both faces curving inwards, instead of outwards as they do on convex lenses.

Microscopes

While a simple magnifying glass can be used to give an enlarged image, it has the drawback that a high magnification would require a lens with an extremely short focal length. This would have to be so fat that it would be spherical; furthermore, it would have to be very small and it would be difficult to use. So in *compound* microscopes, the same ploy is used as in the telescope—one lens forms an image, which is then magnified by a second lens. The lenses have the same names of objective and eyepiece, but this time the objective has a short focal length and the eyepiece a longer focal length.

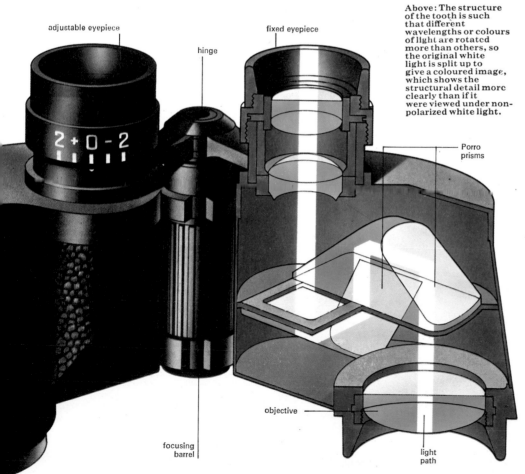

adjustable eyepiece

hinge

fixed eyepiece

Porro prisms

objective

focusing barrel

light path

353

Radar

Radio waves, like light waves, are reflected by obstacles in their path. The detection of these reflections enables such objects to be located. This is the basis of *radar*, a word coined from Radio Detection and Ranging. The phenomenon of reflection was known from the earliest days of radio communications, but was often only regarded as a nuisance.

The development of radar in Britain arose from a suggestion by Sir Robert Watson-Watt who had been carrying out research on the ionized layers in the earth's upper atmosphere. This work involved using pulses of radio waves to measure the height of these layers and Watson-Watt saw that the same principles could be applied to the detection of distant aircraft. The outcome was the rapid development of a chain of early warning radar stations round the coasts of the British Isles. They were in operation in time for the start of World War II and contributed greatly to winning the Battle of Britain.

Having started under the impetus of a defence need, radar has developed enormously and its uses now extend to a wide range of both civil and military applications.

Basic principles

Acoustic echoes are a familiar phenomenon. Knowing the speed of sound through air one can measure the distance of a remote cliff or high building by

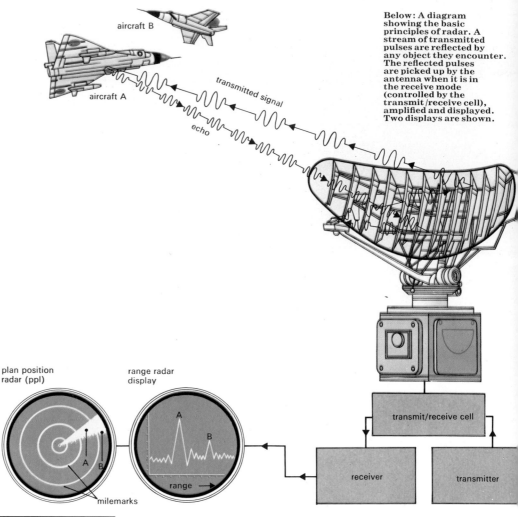

Below: A diagram showing the basic principles of radar. A stream of transmitted pulses are reflected by any object they encounter. The reflected pulses are picked up by the antenna when it is in the receive mode (controlled by the transmit/receive cell), amplified and displayed. Two displays are shown.

aircraft B

aircraft A

transmitted signal

echo

plan position radar (ppl)

range radar display

A

B

range

milemarks

transmit/receive cell

receiver

transmitter

Left: CH (Chain Home) towers near Dover, England. These were part of a long range, early warning system developed prior to the Second World War. By the beginning of the war the whole of the east coast of Great Britain was covered by this system. It could detect aircraft taking off in Germany.

Bottom left: An air defence station used during the Second World War. The plan position indicator on the left gave the range of approaching aircraft. Aircraft altitude was determined using the right hand display by adjusting the angle of the aerial until a maximum return signal was received.

Below: A radar controlled searchlight. This one was an experimental model with four Yagi receiving aerials around the searchlight and a folded dipole transmitter aerial mounted further back. This apparatus was extremely advanced for its time because it could automatically lock on to, and track, a moving target.

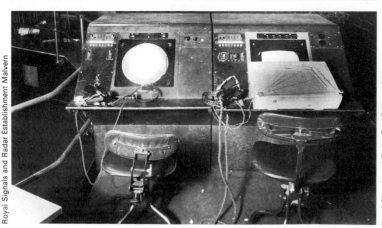

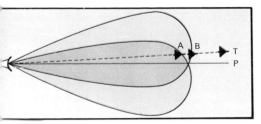

Above: Direction can be accurately determined in radar by using two partially overlapping beams. A target lying on the line of beam intersection (OP) produces an echo containing the two signals at equal strength. For a target at T, the ratio of signal strengths provides an accurate measure of the angle TOP.

Below: The Plessey ACR 430 airfield control radar system. This employs microwaves in the X-band frequency range (8,200 to 12,400 MHz). It uses a two-beam aerial system—each beam derived from a separate transmitter and fed via a waveguide to a separate horn. One of the beams is pencil-shaped for accurate surveillance.

ZEFA

Above: A radar tower with primary and secondary radar facilities. Secondary surveillance radar (SSR) allows extra information (such as flight data) to be returned to the flight controller along with ordinary data obtained from the primary radar system. Special apparatus is needed in each aircraft to obtain this information.

Right: A US tactical air control system with primary and secondary surveillance radar facilities. This control centre provides commanders with computerized tactical air control capability. Radar and other information can be rapidly exchanged between this and other command centres.

Hughes Aircraft Co.

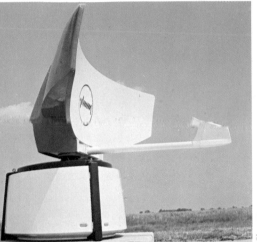

Below: A resonant cavity magnetron. The development of this device revolutionized radar, permitting the use of high frequency (short wavelength) radio waves at high powers. A waveguide is attached to the rectangular section on the front to channel the radio waves to the aerial. The fins cool the device.

Right: The Plessey WF-3 primary windfinding radar system. This operates in the X-band microwave frequency range. The antenna has automatic tracking facilities and a digital readout device for displaying range, azimuth and elevation. This particular version is of a portable design and is simple to instal.

Plessey

Plessey

EMI

observing the time that an echo takes to return. This is how radar works but using radio waves which travel at a speed of 300,000 km/sec rather than sound which only travels at about 340 m/sec. If both the total time of travel of the transmitted/reflected beam and its direction are measured the position of the distant reflecting object is obtained.

Either *continuous* waves, such as are used in broadcasting, or interrupted (*pulsed*) signals can be used, but the principles of radar are easier to understand in the case of the latter. Imagine a radio transmitter sending out a train of short pulses of radio energy. Each pulse may be a few millionths of a second long; the time interval between successive pulses is arranged to be longer than it would take for radio waves to travel out to any distant object of interest and back.

If these pulses meet an object (the *target*) they are reflected and some of this reflected energy is picked up by a receiver alongside the transmitter. The train of received pulses will be slightly retarded relative to the transmitted pulses by an interval corresponding to the out and return time of the waves. If directional aerials are used for transmitting and receiving then both the distance (range)

and direction of the target are obtained.

Usually the same aerial is used for transmitting and receiving. The receiver is protected against damage from the powerful transmitted pulses by being *suppressed* during the brief periods when they are emitted but *re-activated* in time to detect any reflected pulses. The rapid acting switch used for this protection of the receiver is known as *Transmit-Receive* (or *TR*) *Cell*.

The aerial directional pattern used depends on the purpose of the radar. For general surveillance as in Air Traffic Control a common pattern is the 'fan beam'. This is typically 1° or 2° wide in azimuth and 15° or 20° wide in elevation. With such a pattern, range and bearing can be measured quite accurately but no elevation information is available. This is adequate for many purposes.

It is possible to obtain full three dimensional information by using a 'stack' of beams each of which is narrow in both azimuth and elevation. The stack is arranged so that all beams lie in one vertical plane but pointing at different elevations. An alternative arrangement is to scan a narrow beam very rapidly in elevation while it scans much more slowly in azimuth. The rapid elevation scan is sometimes done by varying the frequency, the aerial having been designed so that its elevation angle is dependent upon the radio frequency.

Normally, direction is obtained as the angle at which maximum signal is received. This occurs when the peak of the aerial beam points at the target. If more accurate directional information is required the principle of overlapping beams is employed. In this arrangement the receiving aerial has two partially overlapping narrow beams. The exact direction of the target relative to the centre line of the system is obtained from the ratio of the signals in the two beams. Along the central cross-over line of the beams the signals are equal. The principle can be extended to measure two orthogonal angular co-ordinates, for example, elevation and azimuth.

Left: The Sea Cat, a direct predecessor of the Seawolf tracking radar, is an elderly but effective system that was introduced in 1962 to counter low-flying supersonic aircraft.

Below: The Norwegian coast-guard vessel, K/V Nordkapp, equipped with the Plessey AWS-4 radar.

A close relative of this form of aerial is the *conical scan* aerial in which a narrow pencil beam is caused to rotate at high speed about a line slightly displaced from the axis of the beam maximum. When a target lies exactly on the axis of spin, the echo has constant amplitude, but if it lies slightly off this axis the amplitude of the echo varies in sympathy with the rotation of the beam. Missile fire control radars use these principles.

Radar waves are essentially confined to line of sight although the atmosphere does produce a small amount of downwards bending. Thus radars do see marginally beyond the horizon. For practical purposes, however, the range of a radar is determined ultimately by geometrical considerations. High-flying aircraft can be seen at considerable range but to detect distant low targets the radar must be raised to extend the horizon.

Subject to these considerations it is possible to see aircraft up to 300 km (approx 200 miles) away. A typical modern long range air traffic control radar uses a wavelength of about 25 cm, a peak power of 2 MW and an aerial some 12 m wide by 5 m high scanning at a rate of 10 rpm.

Generation

At the heart of a radar equipment is a powerful radio-frequency generator. While radar is possible over a wide range of wavelengths, the most common lie in the range from about 25 cm to 3 cm (corresponding to frequencies of 1,200 MHz to 10,000 MHz). The most common radars are of the pulsed variety in which the transmitted signal consists of short pulses of radio-frequency energy, about 1 to 5 microseconds long, emitted in a stream at intervals of between 1 to 4 milliseconds. The peak power in the pulse may lie typically in the range of a few kW to a few MW, depending on the purpose of the radar. But the mean (average) power is less since the transmitter operates only during the short pulses. The ratio of mean to peak power is the *duty cycle* and for the figures quoted is about 1/1000.

Two types of microwave transmitting tubes are particularly important. In one, the *cavity magnetron*, a beam of electrons circulates under the influence of a powerful transverse magnetic field inside a metal structure which has cavities of a particular size. Radio energy is generated at a frequency determined by the dimensions of the cavities. The pulses are created by switching the electron beam on and off by a suitable high speed switch known as the 'modulator'. This is the commonest generator in current use.

The other important transmitting tube is the *klystron*, in which a beam of electrons passes through a series of metallic cavities 'tuned' to the required frequency. The velocity of the beam varies in sympathy with the radio frequency voltages within the cavities. The interaction between kinetic energy of the electrons and radio frequency energy in the cavities is used either to generate oscillations or to amplify oscillations already present. The tube is normally used as an amplifier, the short pulses being generated initially at quite low power.

Detection and display

The detection of the pulses returned from targets is carried out in a receiver similar to the vision receiver of a television set. Nowadays this is almost always a *solid-state* receiver. The output of the receiver is a stream of video pulses which have to be displayed suitably.

The most important display device is the *cathode-ray tube* (CRT), similar to the tube in a TV set. In the earliest radars the display tube was arranged to indicate directly the delay time of the echo pulses as follows. The cathode-ray beam is deflected across the screen of the tube at a steady rate commencing at the moment a pulse is transmitted. This produces a bright line across the tube face. Any returned pulse is arranged to cause a momentary upwards deflection of the beam thus producing a characteristic mark or 'pip'. If the speed at which the beam moves across the CRT is known, the distance of this mark from the commencement of the trace provides a direct measure of the time delay of the echo pulse and hence of the distance of the target.

In an alternative arrangement the cathode-ray beam, initially of reduced intensity so as to produce very little fluorescence on the tube face, traverses a line starting from the centre of the screen.

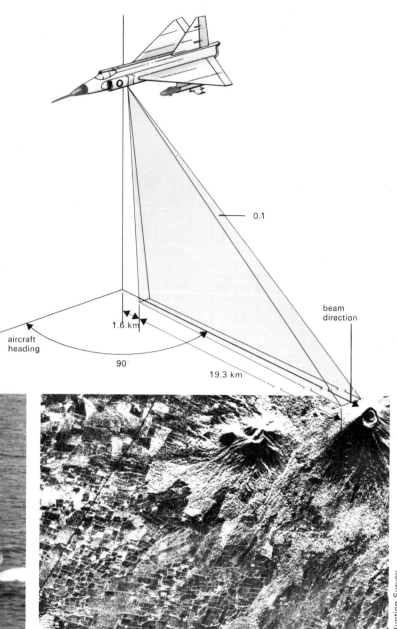

0.1

beam direction

aircraft heading

1.6 km

90

19.3 km

Photri

Hunting Survey

Jerry Mason

Plessey

Above: An airborne radar system. Because radio waves travel in straight lines, ground radar systems are limited in range to the horizon (except for small bending effects caused by the atmosphere). To increase the range of a radar system it is necessary to use airborne radar.

Above left: A side-looking radar system for mapping ground features. This uses a sharp and highly directional beam from a fixed antenna on the aircraft. The motion of the aircraft itself provides the scan across the earth's surface.

Left: A reconstructed image of Chinandega and the San Cristobal volcano area of western Nicaragua taken by side-looking radar (SLR). This system has the advantage that it can be used at night, in fog or cloud and any adverse conditions that prevent normal photography.

Below: Height-finding radar determines aircraft altitude using trigonometry. As it nods up and down when transmitting its beam, the relationship between antenna angle and the distance of the plane is used to compute altitude.

Right: The slab-faced planar array antenna of the Plessey AR3D long-range defence radar.

Returned pulses are made to momentarily intensify the beam and so produce a bright spot on the tube face at a distance from the centre corresponding to the distance of the target. If the line across the tube face is made to rotate about the centre in sympathy with the rotation of the aerial beam a map-like picture is produced on the tube face showing the position of reflecting targets around the radar. This is the well-known *Plan Position Indicator* or PPI.

Doppler radar

When a source of sound is approaching or receding, its apparent pitch is raised or lowered. This is the *Doppler Effect*. Similarly, radio waves reflected from a moving target have their frequency raised or lowered according to whether they are moving towards or away from the observer. One important use of this is to distinguish moving from stationary objects. In air traffic control, for example, reflections from buildings, trees or high ground may obscure the returns from moving aircraft. However, the latter reflections exhibit a Doppler shift in frequency.

In *Moving Target Indication* or MTI this shift is detected, causing only moving targets to be displayed. Another important use of Doppler is in airborne navigational radar, enabling an aircraft to measure its speed relative to the ground by the Doppler shift of the waves reflected by the ground.

Applications

From its birth as an early warning device against air attack, radar has expanded to a very wide range of applications both civil and military. It is the basis of air traffic control in all areas of dense traffic and is indeed essential for safety in air transport. It is used in aircraft to detect high ground and storms and to measure relative speed over the ground. At sea, the majority of merchant ships of any size carry a navigational radar enabling them to navigate in bad visibility, while land-based radar is used in busy ports to supervise and control movements in the shipping lanes. Radar also has many meteorological uses, such as detecting and tracking storms and hurricanes.

357

Navigation

Navigation probably originated on the waterways, such as the Nile and the Euphrates, around which the first major civilizations developed. From these simple beginnings, navigation became steadily more complex as the distances travelled and the speeds and numbers of craft increased with the spread of civilization and trade. Although the basic principles remain the same, the intervening centuries have provided a host of navigational aids and techniques to match the development of transport technology.

Navigation is a composite problem requiring the establishment of position, speed and direction. It is characterized by four main aspects: the determination of the destination; the choice of a suitable route; the estimation of course and speed; and a regular or continuous monitoring of the progress of the craft.

Early navigation

Early navigation in rivers, or in coastal waters in sight of land, was a relatively simple process, using landmarks and coastal features as visual references. Out at sea, however, the early mariners used the Sun and the stars to determine the direction in which they were heading.

The mapping of the heavens was started by the Babylonians, who regarded the heavenly bodies as being mounted on a celestial sphere, a hollow globe of great size which surrounded the Earth and rotated around it from east to west. In the north of the celestial sphere, around its upper pivot as it were, the stars did not change position as much as stars at other parts of the sphere, so a bright star near the centre of this pivotal area could act as an almost-stationary visual reference. In the northern hemisphere, the star occupying this position at present is the Pole Star (Polaris), which is part of the constellation of the Little Bear (Ursa Minor).

Gradually, the positions of celestial bodies were tabulated, and in conjunction with a calendar men could make observations with simple instruments to ascertain their latitude. One of the earliest instruments was the Greek astronomers' *astrolabe*, simplified for use by mariners and developed by the Portuguese in the 15th century for their oceanic voyages. Latitude could be found by observation of the angles between the horizon and the sun or certain stars, the simplest being the angular altitude of the Pole Star, as this angle approximately equals the latitude of the place of observation.

Solar observations were also useful in determining the time, the sun reaching its highest altitude at noon. This altitude also provided latitude, if combined with data (listed in simplified astronomical tables) concerning the angles and position of the Sun throughout the year. By comparing the local latitude with that of an already tabulated latitude of their destination, they were able to deduce their distance north or south of the destination. This furnished them with the rudiments of setting and maintaining course by sailing to the appropriate latitude and then running east or west to their destination, but without a knowledge of longitude a 'fix' of position was impossible.

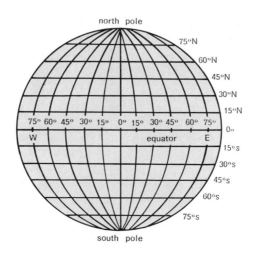

Above: Any point on the Earth's surface can be identified by its latitude and longitude. Lines of latitude are imaginary circles drawn round the Earth, the *Equator* being the line of zero latitude (0°). Lines of longitude are circles drawn through the poles, zero longitude (0°) being the *Greenwich Meridian*.

Right: A pair of seventeenth century Arabian *astrolabes*. The astrolabe had many uses including finding the time of day, and the rising and setting times of the Sun and stars. The Portuguese version, the *mariner's astrolabe*, measured the angle of the Sun or stars to indicate latitude.

Radio Times Hulton Picture Library

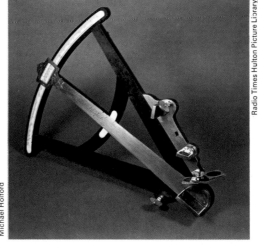

Michael Holford

Above: James Hadley's *octant* enabled navigators to make accurate measurements of the altitude of the Sun or stars, so that they could find their latitude. The observer viewed the horizon through a sight, and adjusted the movable central arm of the instrument until the reflected image of the

Sun or star appeared in a mirror placed in line with the horizon. The altitude was indicated on the curved scale.

Below: A *sextant* made by Hadley in 1785. The sextant, a more accurate version of the octant and capable of measuring a greater angle, was invented in 1757 by John Campbell.

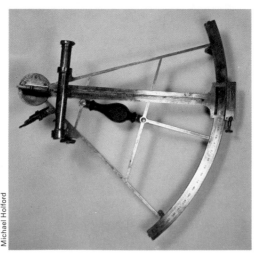

Michael Holford

SHIP'S COMPASS

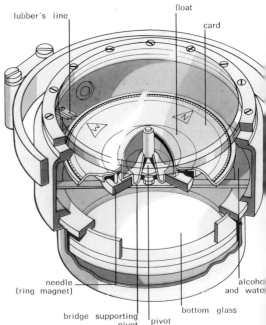

lubber's line

float

card

needle (ring magnet)

alcohol and water

bridge supporting pivot

pivot

bottom glass

Above: A mariner's compass. A magnet is attached to the bottom of the compass card, which is mounted on a float in water and alcohol so it stays horizontal as the ship moves. The 'north' on the card points to magnetic north, and the ship's direction is indicated by the *lubber's line*.

Right: The type of gyroscope used in many gyrocompasses. The gyroscope is a rapidly-spinning wheel which is controlled in such a way that it keeps itself pointing towards true north (the geographic north pole, as opposed to the magnetic one). It is unaffected by movement or by magnetism.

Left: The D-shaped scanner of a ship's radar system. Radar is a valuable navigation aid, providing information on the range and bearing of the coastline and other vessels. It is particularly useful at night and in bad weather when visual observations are not possible.

Right: Checking the accuracy of the *precision approach radar* at an RAF airfield in England. Precision approach radar is one of the many navigational aids used to guide aircraft safely down to the runway; the most advanced *instrument landing systems* can land an aircraft fully automatically.

Right: The operations room of the Thames Navigation Service in Gravesend, which is run by the Port of London Authority to ensure the safe navigation of vessels using the River Thames. The operations room is equipped with seven radar sets and several vhf radio consoles. Tide gauge readings obtained automatically from five separate points are displayed on tv monitor screens. The service broadcasts half-hourly bulletins on the state of the tides, the weather, ship movements and other navigational information. Over 1,000 ship movements per week are monitored and assisted by this service.

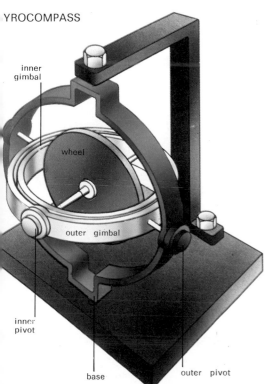

GYROCOMPASS

inner gimbal

wheel

outer gimbal

inner pivot

base

outer pivot

Dead reckoning

The mariner's compass, first known in Europe in the 13th century, introduced navigation as a science. The discovery of the directional properties of the lodestone, or of a magnetized needle, which if freely suspended appeared miraculously to point towards the Pole Star, even when she was invisible, made all-weather voyages possible. The compass depends upon the horizontal component of the attraction of the earth's magnetism for its directive force and thus by being free to rotate in a horizontal or *azimuth* plane determines bearing relative to the magnetic pole.

As the magnetic poles are moving slowly about the geographic poles, the compass does not show true North but aligns itself at an angle to it. This difference is called the *magnetic variation* and alters daily, but it is predictable and is listed in almanacs.

The discovery of the compass facilitated steering a course but ignored the vagaries of the wind, the tide and the current. It was therefore impossible to reckon accurately how far and on what bearing the ship lay from its destination.

The process of estimating position based on a record of known progress is known as *dead reckoning*, from the practice of throwing a log overboard (from the bow of the ship) which was assumed to be 'dead' in the water. By noting the time for the log to pass the length of the ship an estimate of speed could be made.

The English adapted this to the *log and line*. A log thrown overboard into the water was attached to a line knotted at regular intervals, and the line was paid out for about half a minute, timed on a sandglass. The length between each successive knot was chosen so that during the timed interval the number of knots paid out represented the number of nautical miles per hour (Knots) at which the ship was travelling. The speed was regularly recorded so that the distance travelled could be calculated. A record of the ship's direction of travel was also kept, and so by drawing a line on a chart which corresponded to the direction and distance travelled, the ship's position could be ascertained.

The ambitious voyages resulting from the expansion of trade created a demand for accurate maps, so that bearings from port to port could be known with some precision. Sailor's charts at this time mapped the world as plane and flat, and

359

marked with *rhumb lines*. A rhumb line, also known as a loxodrome, is a line which crosses every line of longitude at the same angle. Lines of latitude are rhumb lines, as they cross every line of longitude at an angle of 90°. By using the rhumb lines, routes could be planned along lines of constant direction.

The inaccuracies caused by ignoring the convergence of the meridians at the poles was acceptable in the low latitudes of the Mediterranean, but introduced large errors when sailing further North or South.

The great Flemish mathematician Gerardus Mercator (Gerhard Kremer, 1512-94) devised a projection in which straight line rhumbs were true. In this projection, while the meridians remained parallel and equidistant the lines of latitude, although parallel, were spaced in inverse ratio to the convergence of the meridians. Rhumb lines drawn between points with a ruler were correct, crossing every meridian at an equal angle. Such routes could be simply maintained using a compass on a constant course.

The position of a craft is known when both its latitude and longitude have been defined. Latitude and longitude are both measured in *degrees*, and for greater accuracy one degree can be divided into 60 *minutes*, and each minute into 60 *seconds*. The determination of longitude is inseparably associated with the measurement of time. As the earth rotates on its axis, successive meridians pass beneath the sun at an interval of four minutes for every degree of longitude. By comparing local time with a standard time at a reference meridian, say Greenwich at 0° (Greenwich Mean Time), the time divergence gives the difference in longitude, one hour forward or backward equalling 15° East or West.

Astronomical observations give local time but to deduce standard time some predictable phenomenon was required, which was independent of, and could be seen from, the observer's position on earth. The obvious answer was a clock, although it was not until the eighteenth

century, when John Harrison succeeded in designing a marine timekeeper (or chronometer) that was sufficiently accurate, that one could be carried on ship.

In addition to the chronometer, a method involving lunar distances relative to celestial bodies was proposed, for in principle any fast-moving object can be used for timekeeping provided its motion is predictable and it can be accurately observed. However, the existing instruments lacked the precision required and the method only became practicable with the invention of James Hadley's *octant* in 1731. The octant was the fore-runner of the modern sextant, and was designed for measuring the angle between a celestial body and the horizon to determine latitude.

It could also measure the angle between the Moon and a given star, and once this angle was known the exact time, and the longitude, could be calculated from astronomical tables.

Radio navigational aids

As radio waves, under perfect conditions, travel as a wave about a straight line axis their reception with a suitable receiver, or *Direction Finder* (DF), may be considered analogous to a line of sight bearing. By noting the bearings of two or more shore based stations a position fix may be obtained.

If a loop aerial of a receiver is placed at right angles to the direction of radio waves, the wavefront will strike each side of the loop simultaneously and there will be no signal. If the loop is aligned parallel to the path of the wave it will strike the two sides at slightly different instants of time and a difference signal

Above left: A Decca Navigator Mk21 receiver in use on a lifeboat. The Decca system uses groups of 'master' and 'slave' transmitters, operating in the 70-130 kHz band, which are positioned so that phase differences are created between the signals from the master and those from the slaves.

Above: The signals from a Decca master/slave combination produce hyperbolic lines along which the signal phase differences are zero. The receiver detects these phase differences and also responds to signals which are transmitted at one minute intervals to identify the individual Decca 'lanes', the areas between the hyperbolic lines. The receiver displays the Decca co-ordinates and lane numbers, which are then used in conjunction with a lattice overlaid on a standard navigational chart to establish the ship's exact position. The Decca system has a range of about 480 km (300 miles).

Below: A map display of an aircraft *inertial navigation* (IN) system. An IN system computes an aircraft's speed and position by data obtained from *accelerometers*, which register its horizontal and vertical accelerations, and gyroscopes, which register changes in direction and attitude.

Right: The Transit satellite navigation system is based on several satellites travelling in polar orbits around the Earth (orbits which pass over the north and south poles). As a satellite passes overhead, a ship using the system receives three separate transmissions from it. As the satellite's

position changes during the intervals between the signals, the receiver can compute the ship's position in a similar way to taking a fix from three separate ground-based transmitters. The ground system computes the details of the satellite's orbit and transmits this data to it every 12 hours.

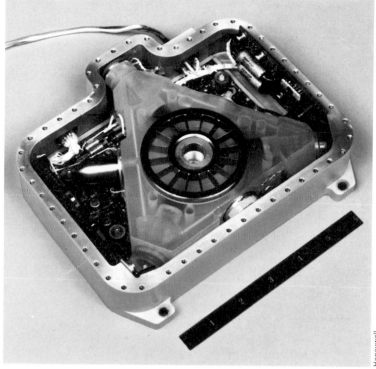

Honeywell

Above: A laser gyro developed for use in navigation systems. Instead of using a rapidly-spinning wheel, the laser gyro has two laser beams, one moving around clockwise and the other one anti-clockwise. If the gyro is rotated about its axis, the frequencies of the beams alter, and these changes in frequency are used to compute rotation rate.

Left: The sensing element of the inertial guidance system was built by Ferranti for the European Launcher Development Organization satellite launch vehicles. The element contained three gyros and three accelerometers which sensed the vehicle's motion.

Ferranti

will appear. Thus the signal intensity in the receiver alters from a maximum to a minimum as the aerial is rotated relative to the bearing of the transmitting station. Marine radio beacons along the coast or in lightvessels transmit a steady signal on which the bearing is taken, and a morse signal for identification.

A sophisticated omnidirectional version of marine DF is *vhf omnirange* (VOR). A beacon transmits two signals, one omnidirectional and one rotating, and the bearing of the beacon relative to the receiver is indicated by phase differences between the two received signals.

Most civil air traffic is routed along busy airways in controlled airspace. These airways are separated into height bands as well as different headings. The position of the aircraft in space is prescribed by ground authorities by means of radio and radar contact. At present the most widely used navigation aid is VORTAC, a radio system in which numerous ground beacons along airways send out signals that enable aircrews to check their bearing and distance to the next station. The bearing is checked against a VOR transmitter while distance is estimated using *Distance Measuring Equipment* (DME), which transmits a pulse from the aircraft to interrogate a responsive ground beacon called a *transponder*, which in turn transmits a signal back to the 'plane. The total time (measured from the aircraft) for the sequence to occur defines the distance from the plane to the beacon.

More flexible use of the total airspace is obtained with a phased group of ground stations that send out interlocked signals to create a hyperbolic pattern of position lines. There are a variety of systems available, which are in wide use by both shipping and aircraft. *Decca*, highly accurate to within a few yards up to 480 km (300 miles), from a Decca transmitting station, covers busy coastal shipping areas but is not suitable for ocean position finding and *Loran C*, although primarily designed for aircraft, can be used by ships.

Transit ' satellite

satellite orbit

position 3

position 2

position 1

tracking station, Minnesota

injection stn. California

time signal from US Naval Observatory, Washington DC.

computer centre at Point Mugu, California

ship's aerial receiving unit

TRANSIT SATELLITE NAVIGATION SYSTEM

Courtesy of Redifon

Nuclear Power

The energy produced by a nuclear reactor is released by the fission, or splitting, of atomic nuclei in a controlled and self-sustaining manner, and appears as heat which is then converted to electricity using more or less conventional steam turbine generators. Nuclear fission occurs when the nucleus of an atom splits into two parts, and some nuclei can be made to split by bombarding them with neutrons. More neutrons are produced as a result of the splitting process and under the right conditions go on to split further nuclei, giving a continuous chain reaction. Generally speaking, the chances that a neutron will interact with a nucleus are much higher when the velocity of the neutron is slow than when it is moving fast. For this reason, a moderator is used in the *thermal reactor* to slow down the neutrons emitted by the fuel to the velocities of thermal agitation. The most commonly used moderators are graphite (a form of carbon) and water.

The effect of neutron capture depends on the type of nucleus involved. The atomic nuclei of uranium, the most common reactor fuel, are of two types, or isotopes, containing different numbers of nucleons (neutrons and protons). About 99.3 per cent of the atoms have 238 nucleons, but 0.7 per cent have 235, and it is the uranium-235 that is the active, fissile fuel. Some thermal reactors are fuelled with uranium of natural isotopic composition, but, for the most part, the uranium is first *enriched* by being put through an isotope separation process which will remove some of the uranium-238.

Capture of a neutron by uranium-238 yields, as compound nucleus, uranium-239. This does not split, but it undergoes spontaneous radioactive transformations, increasing the positive electric charge of its nucleus by emitting two beta rays and so becoming plutonium-239. Plutonium isotopes are much in demand for making nuclear bombs.

Reactor design

In some reactors the fuel is uranium metal, but uranium oxide and carbide stand up better to high temperatures and to the accumulation of fission products. Rods or pellets of fuel are sealed into thin-walled metal tubes which, in some designs, are grouped into clusters of 36 to form a fuel element. For the highest temperatures, graphite is used instead of metal for cladding the fuel.

The first elements are assembled to form a core along with the moderator material and control rods. These control rods are made from a material that absorbs neutrons and can be moved in and out of the core to regulate the speed of the reaction. With the control rods in the core they absorb neutrons, so reducing the speed of the chain reaction. In addition there are shut-down rods which can be inserted into the core to absorb enough neutrons to stop the chain reaction totally. Heat produced by the nuclear reaction is removed by a coolant — either gas or liquid — which is circulated through the core and then through heat exchangers where the heat is used to boil water into steam for driving electricity-

Above: Assembling a cluster of fuel pins for use in a Fast Breeder reactor.

Below: A diagram showing how the fuel, moderator and control rods are arranged in a nuclear reactor. The moderator slows the fast neutrons so that they react more readily with the fuel, and the neutron-absorbing control rods control the speed of the reaction. The diagrams at the bottom show six types of nuclear power station.

UKAEA (American EP Co/Donald C. Cook)

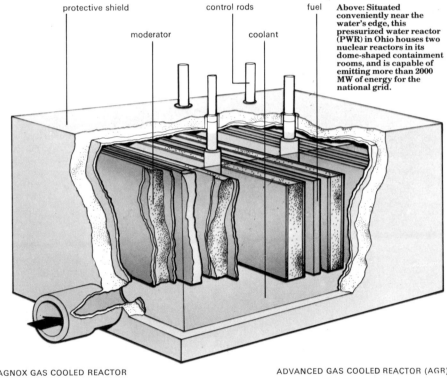

protective shield   control rods   fuel

moderator   coolant

Above: Situated conveniently near the water's edge, this pressurized water reactor (PWR) in Ohio houses two nuclear reactors in its dome-shaped containment rooms, and is capable of emitting more than 2000 MW of energy for the national grid.

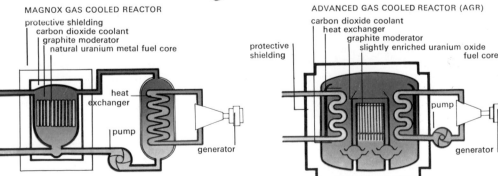

MAGNOX GAS COOLED REACTOR
protective shielding
carbon dioxide coolant
graphite moderator
natural uranium metal fuel core

heat exchanger

pump

ADVANCED GAS COOLED REACTOR (AGR)
carbon dioxide coolant
heat exchanger
graphite moderator
slightly enriched uranium oxide fuel core

protective shielding

pump

generator

generator

generating plant. Normally, the coolant is circulated under high pressure so the core is enclosed in a pressure vessel made from steel or prestressed concrete. Surrounding the core assembly is a safety vessel or biological shield to contain the radioactivity of the working core.

A number of different designs of thermal reactors are in common use, the main differences being in the cooling arrangements and the types of fuel elements (see diagrams). They include two types of light (ordinary) water reactors, the PWR or Pressurized Water Reactor, and the BWR or Boiling Water Reactor. HWRs or Heavy Water Reactors use the form of water containing heavy hydrogen or deuterium, which is a poor absorber of neutrons and this allows the HWR to use natural (non-enriched) uranium as a fuel.

Gases can also be used as the cooling medium, with designs such as the British Magnox Reactor using carbon dioxide under high pressure with a graphite moderator and natural uranium fuel. As with PWRs, the heat from the coolant is used to generate steam in a heat exchanger. More efficient steam generation can be achieved by the use of higher temperatures and this

Above: The enormous machine at Hinckley 'B' nuclear power station used for refuelling the reactor.

is achieved in the AGR or Advanced Gas-cooled Reactor, which uses uranium oxide fuel in stainless steel casings.

Fast reactors

An alternative design of reactor, the Fast Breeder Reactor, uses the fast neutrons produced by fission without slowing them down as in the thermal reactor. The fuel is usually plutonium-239 and uranium-235, in high concentration, allowing a lower core size. Coolants such as molten sodium or high-pressure helium, which offer good heat transfer efficiency and do not absorb or slow down the fast neutrons, are employed. By surrounding the core of a fast reactor with fertile material, such as uranium-238, the excess fast neutrons from the core can be used to breed more fissile plutonium-239 so that the reactor makes more fuel than it burns. By reprocessing the fuel burned in

this type of reactor, it becomes possible to use up to 60 per cent of the energy in the uranium, as opposed to a few per cent as is the case with thermal reactors, thus making Fast Breeder Reactors more economically desirable.

Safety

One of the main factors restricting the expansion of nuclear power reactors is public fears about the safety of reactors. These fears have been intensified recently by a near catastrophe, the partial melt-down of the Three Mile Island plant at Harrisburg, Pennsylvania, in 1979; and an actual catastrophe, the explosion at the Chernobyl plant in south Russia in 1986. This released a highly radioactive cloud that covered large parts of Europe, killed many people who were in the immediate vicinity, caused thousands to be evacuated, and led to the destruction of thousands of animals which were being bred for meat and found to have excessive radiation levels. Long-term effects may be worse.

Even under normal operating conditions, nuclear reactors produce waste products that are highly radioactive and so difficult to dispose of safely. Radioactive *isotopes* gradually decay as they emit radiation, the level of activity falling until the material becomes stable and non-radioactive. The time that it takes for the level of radioactivity of a substance to fall to half of its initial level is known as the half life of the substance.

The half life may be many thousands of years. For example, plutonium-239 has a half life of 24,000 years. In general, ten half lives of a highly radioactive element have to elapse – reducing the radioactivity to less than one-thousandth of the original level – before a material is no longer considered dangerous. The rate at which radioactive particles are emitted varies considerably according to the element concerned; short-lived, highly active isotopes give out many particles over a short period. The same amount of a longer lived isotope would emit fewer particles per second and so is less likely to cause damage. The cumulative effects of such radioactive decay over a long period, however, are extremely undesirable, evidence suggesting that prolonged exposure is likely, for example, to damage a living cell, perhaps causing cancer or mutation.

Nuclear waste is generally divided into three categories according to the amount of radioactivity in the waste, these being: low-level waste with a gross radioactivity of up to 100 curies per cubic metre (3 curies per cubic foot), intermediate-level waste of up to 10,000 curies per cubic metre (380 curies per cubic foot), and high-level waste which may have a radioactivity level of up to 10 million curies per cubic metre (203,000 curies per cubic foot).

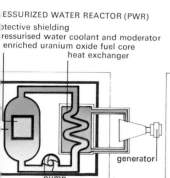

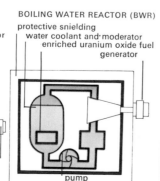

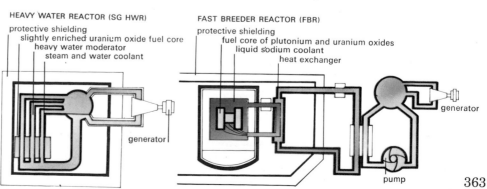

PRESSURIZED WATER REACTOR (PWR)
protective shielding
pressurised water coolant and moderator
enriched uranium oxide fuel core
heat exchanger
generator
pump

BOILING WATER REACTOR (BWR)
protective shielding
water coolant and moderator
enriched uranium oxide fuel
generator
pump

HEAVY WATER REACTOR (SG HWR)
protective shielding
slightly enriched uranium oxide fuel core
heavy water moderator
steam and water coolant
generator

FAST BREEDER REACTOR (FBR)
protective shielding
fuel core of plutonium and uranium oxides
liquid sodium coolant
heat exchanger
generator
pump

Low-level waste

By far the greatest volume of nuclear waste is low-level and consists of materials such as slightly contaminated protective clothing and equipment, for example glassware and pipework. This type of waste is disposed of by sealing it into steel drums and burying it in shallow trenches at special sites. Sea dumping at depths of 4 km (2.5 miles) or more has also been used for the disposal of low-level wastes, but this was discontinued in 1985 following concern about the environmental impact of this practice.

Intermediate waste

Much of the intermediate-level waste is produced by the irradiation of reactor components and includes the remains of fuel element cladding materials, together with exchange resins used in fuel processing and contaminated equipment. A particular type of intermediate-level waste is the transuranic waste, which consists of elements above uranium in the periodic table. These transuranic wastes are generally poisonous and highly radioactive and are separated out during the reprocessing of spent fuel.

The higher level of radioactivity from intermediate-level waste makes it necessary to shield it during handling (low-level waste does not require such shielding). In some cases the intermediate-level waste is disposed of by burial in concrete-lined repositories, and underground dumps in deep mines have also been used. Pending the development of suitable disposal sites, most intermediate waste is being held in store at fuel reprocessing plants and nuclear power stations.

During the early development of nuclear power and military nuclear establishments intermediate waste was not treated as a separate category, being handled with the low-level wastes. This resulted in long-lived (transuranic) intermediate wastes being dumped in shallow surface trenches so that in the US, for instance, there is an estimated one million cubic metres (35 billion cubic feet) of such waste in unsuitable dumps. According to the US authorities, much of this waste will have to be dug up and put into storage until safer burial grounds have been found.

High-level wastes

Most of the radioactivity in nuclear waste is in the high-level waste products, and it is the disposal of this type of waste that has aroused the greatest controversy. This waste is the result of reprocessing spent fuel from reactors and is highly radioactive. The decomposition of short-lived isotopes generates considerable heat, particularly during the first few years after removal from the reactor. In the US the used fuel elements from reactors are not reprocessed but simply stored in water-filled holding pools on the reactor sites. At a number of the power plants the storage pools will reach the limit of their capacity by around 1990 and so permanent means of disposal have to be found. Similarly, substantial amounts of high-level wastes are held at military reprocessing plants, although these are mainly in liquid or solid form.

Reprocessing of fuel from power reactors is being carried out in various countries, notably in Britain and France, which are developing techniques for high-level waste disposal commercially, and other countries, such as Sweden, Australia and West Germany, are also in the process of developing disposal techniques.

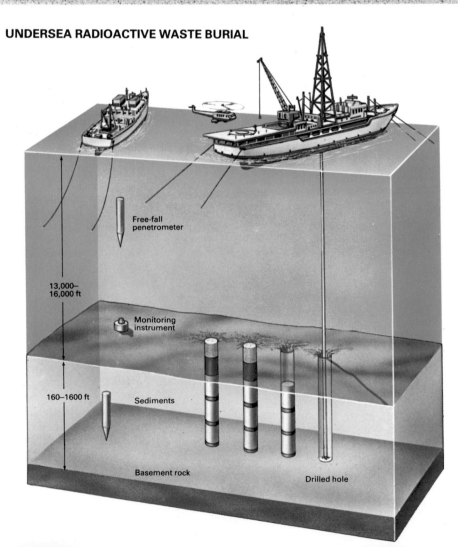

THE URANIUM–PLUTONIUM CYCLE

UNDERSEA RADIOACTIVE WASTE BURIAL

In reprocessing, the spent fuel elements are first split to separate the casings from the fuel itself, which is then submerged in concentrated nitric acid. The acid dissolves the uranium, plutonium and the fission products, leaving any solid wastes, and the resulting solution is put through a separation process. The unburned uranium and plutonium are recovered from the solution for reuse and the highly radioactive fission products remain as a hot, acid liquid which is concentrated by evaporation. This liquid is held in storage tanks for a period of several years to allow the initial high levels of heat (produced by the decay of short-lived isotopes) to fall and radioactivity to decay to more manageable levels.

The volumes of waste involved are relatively small. For example, the entire British nuclear power programme had produced about 1000 cubic metres (35,000 cubic feet) of concentrated wastes by the mid-1980s and these wastes are stored in stainless steel tanks at the Seascale processing plant. Various methods have been proposed for the eventual disposal of the waste – the techniques used have to take into account both the level of radioactivity and the continuing heat of the products.

Two main approaches are proposed: to deposit the material in mined cavities or bore holes in stable geological structures below ground, and to deposit it beneath the sea bed (see diagrams on this and facing page). The first alternative includes mining access tunnels or using old galleries, about 500 m (1600 ft) deep, these then being sealed off by backfilling. The prime requirement for underground storage is that the chosen site is geologically stable, because of the long storage time that is needed for the waste to decay to safe radiation levels (comparable with natural background radiation). In addition the material of a suitable site should be resistant to the action of ground water, and able to withstand the heating effects of the wastes. Formations under investigation include salt domes, clay beds, and granite, basalt and other hard rocks. Alternatively bore holes up to 4km (2.5 miles) with a diameter of about 1 metre (3 ft) would be sunk. Penetration of ground water to the bore hole would cause the mineral packing used to swell, so sealing any cracks in the walls

Above: Nuclear fusion is the joining together of two nuclei of light atoms to form the nucleus of a heavier atom, a process which releases energy. Experiments in controlled

nuclear fusion are continuing; nuclear fusion reactors could one day provide an inexhaustible source of energy, without any of the problems of nuclear fission.

Left: This diagram shows the uranium-plutonium cycle from the early mining, conversion, processing and enrichment stages to the production of fuel, nuclear

waste and atomic bombs. Strict safety precautions must be adhered to during this production cycle to prevent the leakage of radioactive materials.

Below left: The potential of nuclear energy is enormous, but its production generates radioactive nuclear waste, which is difficult to dispose of safely. Canisters of high-level nuclear waste have been disposed of at sea by drilling holes in silt on the

ocean floor, dropping the canisters in and capping the holes with concrete plugs. A support vessel drops penetrometers over the area to monitor the radioactivity around the site and check for possible leaks.

Below: How nuclear waste could be buried underground: (1) Galleries excavated and diggings conveyed to surface dumps (2). Canisters of waste travel from receiving station (3) via entry shaft (4)

for deposit in newly-cut galleries (5). Once filled, gallery is packed with diggings (6). Formations would have to maintain stability for centuries while all radioactive isotopes decay

and preventing further ground water from entering. Sea bed storage techniques also involve the use of bore holes, drilled by floating rigs, into clay beds to a depth of around 100 m (330 ft) beneath the sea bottom below 4 km (2.5 miles) of water.

It has also been suggested, however, that a better approach is to store the material above ground for tens of years while the long-term stability of possible burial sites is investigated, and to allow further reductions in the rates of heat production and radioactivity. Above-ground storage has the additional advantage that the wastes are readily accessible if improved means of treatment are developed in the meantime.

Solidification

Several processes have been developed to reduce the liquid wastes to a solid form for easier handling and reduced risk of leakage, with one of the favoured techniques being vitrification, by which the wastes are incorporated into glass. In this process, the liquid waste is sprayed into a high-temperature furnace where it is dried and oxidized to give a calcine similar to fine sand. The calcine is then mixed with borosilicate glass-forming materials, melted and cast to form borosilicate glass blocks.

The glass blocks retain their properties well at high temperatures, resist radiation damage and are generally insoluble. Radioactive elements, however, can be leached out of the blocks and into the surrounding soil by water, so the blocks are packed in corrosion-resistant canisters before being disposed of. Further protection is given by surrounding the containers with overpacking material to prevent ground water from reaching the waste canisters in geological depositories. In one process, the glass blocks are loaded into steel casks and the lids are welded on, then the casks are stored in concrete vaults with forced cooling to keep their temperature down. In another solidification technique, the liquid wastes are mixed with a mineral base, calcined and packed into stainless steel cans and pressed into a ceramic (Synroc) said to be stable under the action of heat and radioactivity and resistant to leaching of the radioactive elements.

UNDERGROUND RADIOACTIVE WASTE BURIAL

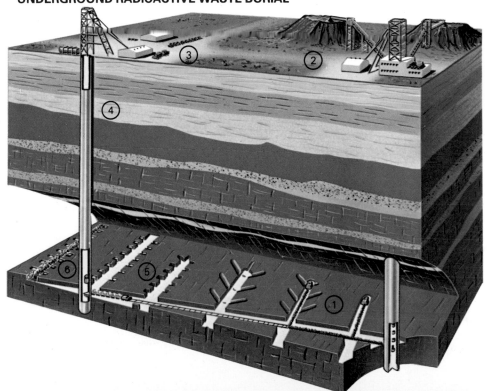

Gas Production

The modern gas industry has its origins in the late eighteenth century development of gas lighting, but the use of gas for heating and cooking did not become widespread until the second half of the nineteenth century. The first company to manufacture and supply equipment for using coal gas on a commercial basis was Boulton and Watt, of Birmingham. In 1814 the development of the industry was continued by the Gas Light and Coke Company in London which developed the system of distributing gas by pipeline from a central gasworks. Two years later, the American gas industry began in Baltimore, Maryland.

The modern use of natural, rather than manufactured gas began in the middle of the nineteenth century, when the Fredonia Gas Light and Water Works Company was formed in 1858, and there are now over 100,000 natural gas wells in the US alone. The general distribution of natural gas in Britain began in the 1970s, after discoveries of major gas reserves under the North Sea.

The three major types of gas in domestic and industrial use are coal gas, oil gas, and natural gas which is now the most important of the three. Liquefied petroleum gases (LPGs) such as butane and propane, are also distributed in some areas, but these are less common.

Coal gas
Coal gas is made by the carbonization of coal, a process which involves heating the coal in the absence of air, to drive off the gas, and which also yields several useful byproducts. The most important constituent elements of coal are carbon, hydrogen, oxygen, nitrogen and sulphur, and it is the hydrogen and carbon which form the basis of coal gas.

The crude gas obtained from the coal is passed through several purification stages to remove unwanted constituents such as ammonia, hydrogen sulphide, hydrogen cyanide, tars, and various hydrocarbons, before it is suitable for use. A typical purified coal gas may contain approximately 50 per cent hydrogen (H_2), 25 per cent methane (CH_4), and 10 per cent nitrogen (N_2), together with, for example, carbon monoxide (CO), carbon dioxide (CO_2), ethylene (C_2H_4), benzene (C_6H_6) and oxygen (O_2).

In processes employed in the USA until the 1930s, and in Britain until about 35 years later, coal was usually brought from the mines to the gasworks, where it was first broken down to a size suitable for distilling in the particular system of carbonization employed. From the breaker, the coal was conveyed to the overhead storage hoppers of the retort house in which the retorts were situated, and subsequently fed into the retorts. The retorts, either horizontal or vertical, were surrounded by a heating chamber which was heated by producer gas, a cheap low-grade gas used in many industrial processes. Producer gas, which is also known as Siemens' gas, can be made by many different processes, all of which involve blowing air or air and steam through a bed of heated fuel such as coal, coke or lignite.

The retorts, made of a refractory mate-

Gas Council

Above: One of the last British plants for making gas from oil-based feedstocks. In 1968 oil gas plant accounted for 73.1% of the total British gas-making capacity, and coal gas plant for only 11.2%. By the middle of the 1970s, however, natural gas had almost completely replaced other forms of gas.

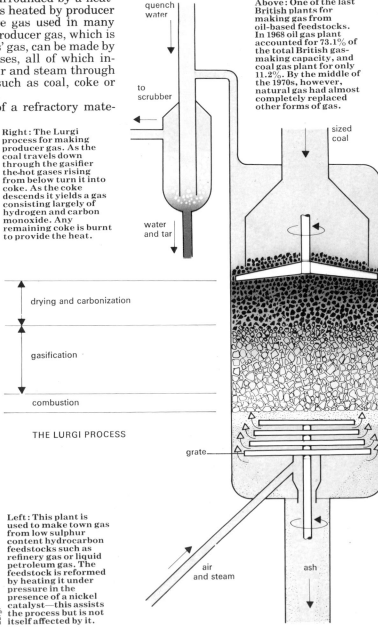

Right: The Lurgi process for making producer gas. As the coal travels down through the gasifier the hot gases rising from below turn it into coke. As the coke descends it yields a gas consisting largely of hydrogen and carbon monoxide. Any remaining coke is burnt to provide the heat.

quench water

to scrubber

water and tar

sized coal

drying and carbonization

gasification

combustion

THE LURGI PROCESS

grate

air and steam

ash

Left: This plant is used to make town gas from low sulphur content hydrocarbon feedstocks such as refinery gas or liquid petroleum gas. The feedstock is reformed by heating it under pressure in the presence of a nickel catalyst—this assists the process but is not itself affected by it.

Lurgi

Left: When a system is converted from town gas to natural gas, the pipes must be cleared of the town gas they contain before the natural gas is put into them. This picture shows town gas being burned off from a pipe in the street during North Sea gas conversion work in London.

Above: The first commercial gas installations had their own gas-making equipment as there was no piped distribution system. An alternative to having an individual gas plant was to have a gasholder to which gas was delivered when needed; this picture shows a French gas delivery cart.

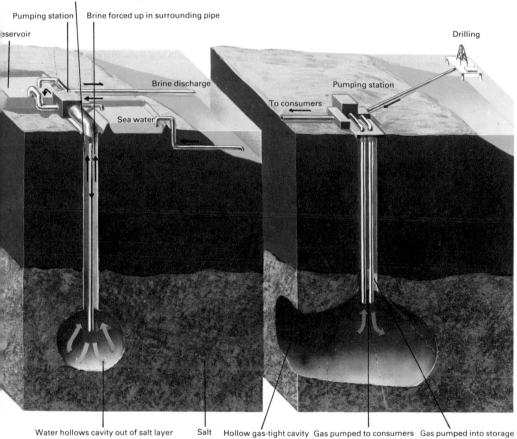

Sea water forced down under pressure

Pumping station

Brine forced up in surrounding pipe

Reservoir

Brine discharge

Sea water

Drilling

Pumping station

To consumers

Water hollows cavity out of salt layer

Salt

Hollow gas-tight cavity

Gas pumped to consumers

Gas pumped into storage

Above: An underground storage scheme for natural gas. A gas-tight cavity is hollowed out in a layer of rock salt, by washing out the salt with sea water. When a large cavity has been made, the pumping system is removed and replaced by gas equipment. Gas comes from a drilling rig and is pumped into the cavity and stored under pressure.

Left: A coal gas works. In many countries coal gas production at such plants has ceased because of the availability of natural gas which also has a higher calorific value.

rial, heated the coal to a temperature of around 1350°C (2462°F). On being subjected to heat, the coal gave off gases, steam and tarry vapours, and passed through a plastic stage during which the evolution of gas through the plastic layers of coal formed the porous structure of the solid residue, the coke.

From the retorts, the gas, steam and tarry vapours passed into a collecting main where a considerable quantity of the tarry vapours was deposited. From the collecting main the gas and impurities went into a condenser, where the temperature was reduced, and the tar and ammoniacal liquor condensed and ran off into a well. The ammoniacal liquor was formed by the condensing steam dissolving in the gas, and consisted of ammonia, phenols, and various sulphur and hydrogen compounds. The tar produced in this way contained pitch, creosote, carbolic and other oils, naphtha, and a small amount of water.

The gas was then pulled forward by an exhauster which fed it through the rest of the washing and purifying plant and into a gasholder. In the first washer, the gas was bubbled through weak ammoniacal liquor to remove any residual tar and some of the remaining ammonia, which was completely removed in a second washer.

The next purification stage removed the hydrogen sulphide (H_2S) from the gas by passing it over grids covered with hydrated iron oxide. The iron oxide absorbed the hydrogen sulphide and was converted to iron sulphide. The final stage involved washing the gas with oil to remove naphthalene and benzole, and it was then treated in a drying plant to extract any remaining moisture so as to reduce corrosion in the distribution pipes to a minimum.

Oil gas

The first applications of petroleum oil for the manufacture of gas were those in which crude oil was thermally 'cracked' with steam at atmospheric pressure and at temperatures of between 1000° and 1100°C (1832° and 2102°F). This was known as the noncatalytic process.

Subsequently the range of process materials was extended to include most liquid hydrocarbon 'feedstocks', but this purely thermal cracking process was superseded by a more efficient cyclic catalytic process, and eventually a whole range of cyclic and continuous processes (reformers) were devised.

Oil gas processes lent themselves more readily to full mechanization and automatic control. The purification of oil gas compared with coal gas is simplified owing to the absence of ammonia and hydrocyanic acid, and the overall result of changing to oil gas was a relatively lower capital cost and lower operating labour costs. The introduction of oil gas was the first large-scale revolution in gas-making technology since the first commercial applications of coal gas manufacture.

The objects of catalytic processes are twofold: firstly to produce gas from hydrocarbon feedstocks with a reduced yield of byproducts; and secondly to obtain higher gas yields compared with those attainable by unaided thermal cracking in steam.

Large-scale cyclic and continuous reformers do not differ greatly in terms of capital cost and thermal efficiency, but the pressures achieved in continuous reformers are very much higher, resulting in a greater gas yield. This increased production

367

represents the greatest single advantage of the continuous process.

Natural gas

Natural gas, of which the main constituent is methane (CH_4), is usually found in the same type of geological strata as oil, and is often found in association with oil deposits, the oil being driven to the surface by the pressure of the gas. In the early days of oil production the gas was regarded as a nuisance and was merely piped clear of the oil lines and burned away. The Chinese were using natural gas to evaporate brine for salt production as long ago as the first millennium BC.

Natural gas became the major source of gas in the US in the 1930s, following the discovery of extensive deposits and improvements in pipeline technology. In Europe, one of the most significant finds was made at Groningen, northern Holland, which strengthened the opinions of many geologists who believed that there was gas, and possibly oil, in vast quantities under the North Sea between Britain and the Netherlands.

The first commercial find in the North Sea was in 1965. Exploration and discovery made steady progress, and it was soon being piped ashore for use in Britain. There was a problem, however, in that the calorific value of natural gas is about twice that of manufactured gas. The calorific value of gas is the amount of heat available from a given volume, the figure for manufactured gas in Britain being $14.94 kJ/m^3$ (500 Btu per cubic foot). All of the 40 million gas appliances in the country were designed to burn manufactured gas and could not burn natural gas safely or efficiently without some modification.

ZEFA

Geroif Kalt/ZEFA

Left: A natural gas flare at a German gas processing plant. Natural gas is composed primarily of methane and ethane, and is found beneath the earth either alone or with crude oil. There are extensive natural gas deposits in north Africa, the USSR, the USA and beneath the North Sea.

Above: Storage tanks for liquefied natural gas. Liquefication of the gas greatly reduces its volume, making it easier to store and transport in large quantities. One of the major exporters of liquid natural gas is Algeria, and this gas is carried in the pressurized holds of specially built tankers.

Lurgi

There were two solutions to this problem: to use natural gas as a feedstock for the manufacture of gas by an adaptation of the oil gasification methods available (reforming); or, and this was the solution chosen, to convert the whole gas supply system of the country to handle natural gas. This decision was taken mainly for economic reasons.

The North Sea gas is brought by pipeline from the offshore drilling rigs to coastal reception terminals and distributed by a 3219 km (2000 mile) long high-pressure pipeline network, operating at up to 68.95 bar (1000 psi). The gas is taken from the main grid and distributed locally at less high pressures. By 1974 90 per cent of the conversion work had been completed, and because of the increased calorific value of natural gas, the existing pipelines were automatically doubled in energy-carrying capacity.

Natural gases vary in content, and some contain amounts of heavier hydrocarbons which are removed to produce liquefied petroleum gases, and other gases must be treated to remove unwanted sulphur compounds and carbon dioxide. A typical treated natural gas contains over 80 per cent methane (CH_4), together with ethane (C_2H_6) and about 1 per cent nitrogen (N_2). Natural gas has no appreciable smell of its own, so to prevent accidents a small amount of a liquid odorant is added which can be detected when accidental leakage occurs.

Other processes

There are several other important gas-making processes. The water gas process involves blowing first steam and then air through a bed of heated coke. The gas produced is often called 'blue water gas' because it burns with a characteristic blue flame. Carbureted water gas is produced by using the hot gases from the water gas generator to crack oil, producing an oil gas which is mixed with water gas before use in order to enrich it.

The Lurgi process, introduced in Germany in 1945, uses steam and oxygen under pressure to make gas from lignite or low-grade coals. Liquefied petroleum gases, chiefly butane (C_4H_{10}) and propane (C_3H_8) are byproducts of oil refinery processes and natural gas treatment. Coke oven gas is a byproduct of industrial coke making. Yet another type, blast furnace gas, is produced during the iron smelting process and is used at the works for steam raising, power generation, and preheating the blast air for the furnace.

Biogas, chiefly methane (CH_4), is a byproduct of sewage treatment, used to fuel pumps on sewage plants. Further development of fermentation processes to produce fuel gases is undoubtedly a major energy resource of the near future. Such processes will employ microbes, genetically engineered to break down all kinds of organic waste materials, to produce fuel gases and useful, non-toxic byproducts such as organic fertilizers.

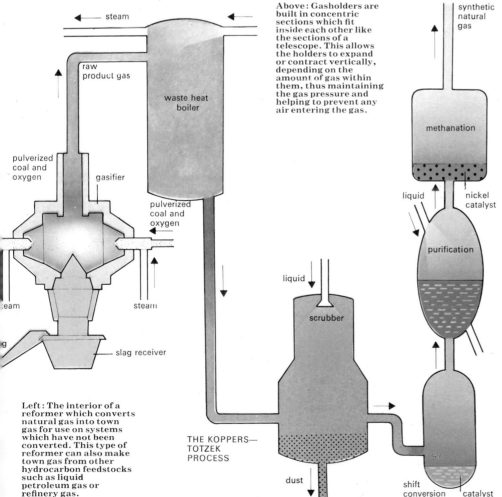

Above: Gasholders are built in concentric sections which fit inside each other like the sections of a telescope. This allows the holders to expand or contract vertically, depending on the amount of gas within them, thus maintaining the gas pressure and helping to prevent any air entering the gas.

THE KOPPERS— TOTZEK PROCESS

Left: The interior of a reformer which converts natural gas into town gas for use on systems which have not been converted. This type of reformer can also make town gas from other hydrocarbon feedstocks such as liquid petroleum gas or refinery gas.

Left: The Koppers-Totzek process makes producer gas from powdered coal by gasifying it with oxygen and steam. After the gas has been cooled and the dust removed, it passes through a catalytic conversion process which turns it into substitute or 'synthetic' natural gas.

369

Electricity Supply

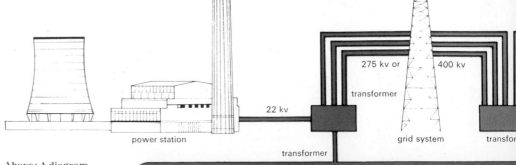

The first public electricity supply systems came into operation in the late nineteenth century. They were owned and operated by private companies or by local authorities such as city councils. There was little co-ordination between these individual undertakings; inter-connection between these many different systems was often economically impractical because they operated not only at different voltages but also at different alternating current (ac) frequencies, and in fact many were direct current (dc) systems.

As the use of electricity grew, it became obvious that voltages and frequencies should be standardized on a national level. This would not only permit the easy transmission of power from one part of a country to another, but it would also simplify the design and construction of electrical equipment. With a wide range of supply voltages in use, any electrical apparatus had to incorporate circuitry which enabled it to be adjusted to accept as many different supply voltages as possible.

In many countries, such as Britain and France, the establishment of national supply networks was followed by state ownership of the supply companies. In others, for example the USA or Switzerland, the national network interconnects a combination of both private and public systems.

The largest power system under centralized control anywhere in the world is in England and Wales. Operated by the Central Electricity Generating Board, this system supplies power to local Electricity Boards who in turn supply nearly 21 million consumers.

The system now comprises 74 power stations with powerful generators able to meet a simultaneous demand of around 54,000 MW (millions of watts). These are all interconnected by means of a system of high voltage transmission lines – the Grid system.

Power is transmitted over the Grid at three different voltages. The 400/275 kV network, often referred to as the Supergrid, extends over nearly 1600 km (1000 miles) and will remain adequate for system loads up to at least 110,000 MW up to the year 2000. The rest of the grid comprises transmission at 132 kV, carrying electricity to a multiplicity of substations.

Using high voltages for power transmission has two advantages: firstly it reduces the power loss along the cables, and secondly it increases the amount of power that a given size of conductor can carry. For example, a 400 kV line has three times the power-carrying capacity of a 275 kV line and eighteen times the capacity of a 132 kV line.

Circuit breakers

Three-phase electricity is usually produced in the stator windings of large modern generators at up to about 25 kV, and this is directly connected by heavy cables to a generator transformer in the adjoining main Grid substation. This steps up the voltage to 132 kV, 275 kV or 400 kV. From here conductors carry it to

Above: A diagram showing how electricity is brought from the power station to the consumer. The windings of the power station alternators are arranged so that they produce three separate alternating voltages, which are out of step with each other by 120° of rotation of the alternator rotor. One end of each of these phase windings is connected to a common point, the neutral point, which is connected to earth. The voltage between any two of the phases is about 1.73 times the voltage between any one of them and earth. Large consumers are provided with a three phase supply, but small ones, such as houses, are supplied with one phase and a neutral line. This carries the return current to the substation where the transformer secondary windings have an earthed neutral point. In this diagram, these local low-voltage systems provide 415 V phase to phase, and 240 V phase to neutral or earth.

Right: An 18/400 kV transformer at a power station in Venezuela.

Above: The 400-275 kV main transmission network operated by the CEGB in England and Wales. The CEGB generates power and transmits it over 400 kV, 275 kV and some 132 kV circuits to the 12 Area Electricity Boards. It is then distributed to the consumers at voltages down to 415/240 V.

400kV lines
275kV lines

John Topham

Above right: The cable ship *Dame Caroline Haslett* laying the cable which links the CEGB network with that of Electricité de France.

Right: The approximate route of the ±100 kVdc submarine cable which can transfer up to 160 MW of power either way between England and France.

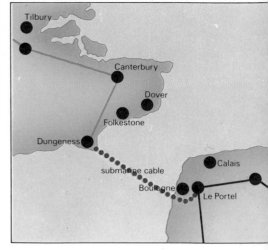

Tilbury
Canterbury
Dover
Folkestone
Dungeness
submarine cable
Calais
Boulogne
Le Portel

370

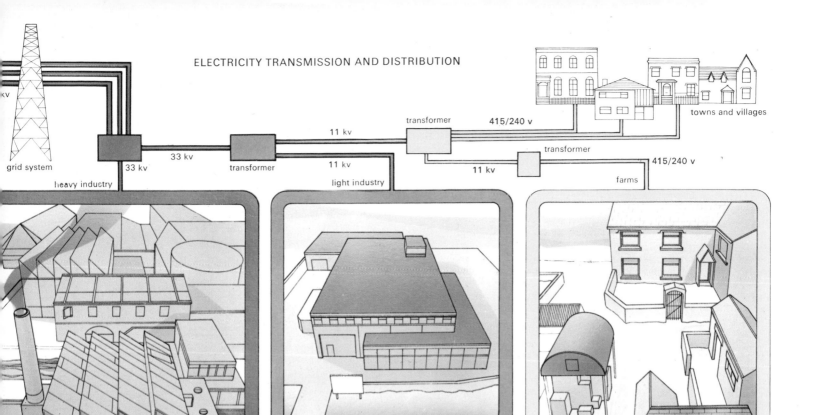

grid system

33 kv

heavy industry

33 kv

transformer

11 kv

light industry

11 kv

transformer

11 kv

transformer

415/240 v

farms

415/240 v

towns and villages

Paul Brierley

CEGB

CEGB

Above: 275 kV oil filled circuit breakers in the switching compound of a large power station.

Above left: Many circuit breakers can be isolated from the supply by lowering them so that they 'unplug' from the circuit. This picture shows the spiked connectors on the top of a circuit breaker, and the sockets they plug into. The breaker can only be isolated after it has switched off the circuit it controls.

Left: The control room of the CEGB's National Control Centre in London. This control centre supervises the seven Area Control Centres of England and Wales, and plans the transfer of power from one area to another.

a series of three switches, comprising an *isolator*, a *circuit-breaker* and another isolator, which are used to connect or disconnect the transformer with the transmission lines. There are three groups of such switches for each generator transformer—one for each of the three phases of the power supply.

The circuit-breaker is a heavy-duty switch capable of operating in a fraction of a second, and is used to switch off the current flowing to the transmission lines. Once the current has been interrupted the isolators can be opened. These isolate the circuit-breaker from all outside electrical sources, so that there is no chance of any high voltage being applied to its terminals. Maintenance or repair work can then be carried out in safety.

From the circuit-breaker the current is taken to the *busbars*—conductors which run the length of the switching compound—and then to another circuit-breaker with its associated isolators before being fed to the Grid. Each generator in a power station has its own transformer, circuit-breaker and isolators but the electricity generated is fed onto a common set of busbars.

Circuit-breakers work like combined switches and fuses, but they have certain special features and are very different from domestic switches and fuses. When electrical current is switched off by separating two contacts, an arc is created between them. At the voltage used in the home, this arc is very small, and only lasts for a fraction of a second. At the very high voltages used for transmission, however, the size and power of the arc is considerable and it must be quickly quenched to prevent damage.

One type of circuit-breaker has its contacts immersed in insulating oil so that when the switch is opened, either by powerful electromagnetic coils or mechanically by springs, the arc is quickly extinguished by the oil. Another type works by compressed air which operates the switch and at the same time 'blows out' the arc. These *air-blast* circuit-breakers are almost universally employed on 275 and 400 kV circuits.

Control centres

Power stations generate electricity most economically when they operate 24 hours a day, but as the demand for electricity is never constant, changes in consumption have to be balanced by starting or shutting down some of the generators in the power stations. The cost of generation is the main factor that guides the control engineers in deciding which power stations to operate. Large modern stations have the lowest running costs, while the older, smaller ones away from fuel sources are the most expensive to operate.

The operation of power stations must therefore be co-ordinated on both a regional and a national basis. In England and Wales there are seven areas, each with its own control centre, which are co-ordinated by the National Control Centre in London. These control centres, in conjunction with the engineers in the power stations, are also responsible for ensuring that the supply frequency, which is 50 Hz in Britain, is maintained at all times.

Distribution

The main 400/275 kV transmission system, or Supergrid, is connected to a total of 219 *grid sub-stations*, which accommodate heavy-duty transformers and associated switchgear. These grid sub-stations in turn are connected via 132 kV lines to a much larger number of sub-stations also incorporating transformers and switchgear, which effect further reductions in voltage to 66 and 33 kV. From these sub-stations bulk supplies of electricity are taken for distribution to particular towns and industrial areas, groups of villages and so on. The lines are fed into more local sub-stations where transformers again reduce the voltage, to 11 kV.

The transformers in these substations are usually equipped with automatic or remotely operated *tap changing* gear to ensure that consumers always have the correct supply voltage, within the statutory limits of plus or minus 6%. As the load on the system increases, the voltage tends to drop. The tap changers compensate for this by changing the ratio between the primary and secondary transformer windings to keep the supplied voltages within the legal limits.

Secondary distribution lines radiating from these substations carry the power into the areas to be supplied, and terminate at local distribution substations. Here the voltage is reduced to its final level of 415 V three phase (the voltage between any two phase lines) and 240 V single phase (the voltage between a single phase and earth) for use in small factories, shops, offices, schools and homes.

Some consumers use electricity in such large quantities that they are supplied at a higher voltage than that used in the home. Heavy industries may have their own connections direct to the grid, taking power at 33kV or even higher,

Picturepoint

Above: The copper conductors which route the power around this 400/275 kV substation are hollow tubes. There is no need for them to be solid, because at these voltages electromagnetic effects cause the current to flow near the surface of a round conductor, and very little flows through the centre.

Right: The demand for electricity varies throughout the day, and the year. This graph shows the average demands during winter and summer in England and Wales plus the days of maximum and minimum demand during 1984/85. Peak daily demand in summer is at about 9 am, and in winter at about 6 pm.

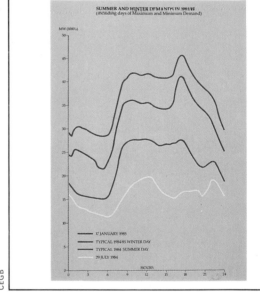

CEGB

CEGB

Above: To avoid any interruption of electricity supplies a great deal of repair work and routine maintenance is carried out without switching off the power. This picture shows men working on a live high voltage line, using insulated glass fibre equipment to handle the conductors.

CEGB

Right: Live line repairs can be carried out on lines operating at as much as 400 kV. The linesman wears an electrically conducting protective suit, which dissipates any electric charges, such as static electricity, which may occur. The sling carrying him is insulated from the tower.

Above: This local substation consists of a transformer, switchgear and fuses, enclosed in a module of aluminium slats coated with coloured pvc. This type of substation is an alternative to the ordinary 'outdoor' substation, which has the equipment mounted on a concrete plinth and surrounded by a fence.

Right: Pole-mounted transformers are widely used on overhead distribution systems. They are connected to the high voltage lines, and the low voltage supply to the consumers is taken from them either by overhead lines or underground cables. Fuses and isolators may also be mounted on poles.

Above: This old type of underground power cable has conductors made of copper wire, with rubber insulation. Rubber has been replaced by special oil-impregnated paper on modern cables. These are often enclosed in a lead sheath, protected by steel wire or tape and a canvas outer layer impregnated with pitch.

Below: Copper wire conductors are not always used on modern cables. This one has solid aluminium conductors, which are lighter and cheaper than copper although they have to be larger in cross-section to provide the same current-carrying capacity. This one uses a plastic insulating material.

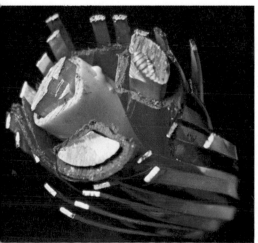

while hospitals, factories and large office buildings are often supplied directly from intermediate substations at 11 kV.

Railways have special substations alongside the tracks, drawing electricity directly from the Grid; the latest rail electrification schemes work at 25 kV.

Where existing power stations are already close to consumers, as in London, the power is often fed into the local primary distribution network at 66 kV or 33 kV, connections to the Grid system also being made in case of breakdown

The distribution of electricity is arranged so that, as far as is practicable, supplies are not interrupted if there is a fault in one section of the system. In a typical case this is done by running separate 33 kV lines from the Grid supply point to the intermediate substation feeding the town and the substation serving heavy industry. A further 33 kV line connects these two points together to form a ring so that if the direct connection to either substation breaks down, supplies can still be maintained through this connecting link. This arrangement for ensuring the security of supplies is in widespread use throughout all transmission and distribution networks.

There is no fixed pattern for local distribution, the arrangement of substations and transmission lines being developed as a result of the particular requirements of the area. Sometimes an intermediate substation may be built alongside a bulk supply point, and occasionally, even the bulk supply point may be in the town centre.

The above survey necessarily presents a rather simplified view of the power distribution system. As can be imagined

an enormous amount of equipment and resources are employed to ensure that a reliable supply of electricity is available to all consumers. At present, the final distribution network operated by the Electricity Boards in England and Wales comprises hundreds of thousands of substations and well over half a million kilometres of mains. These mains are operated at voltages ranging from 132 kV down to the 415/240 V of the local low-voltage distribution networks.

The whole network is fully protected by automatic circuit breakers, lightning arresters, fuses and other devices to prevent overloads damaging the system. In the event of a fault, the line or equipment concerned can usually be isolated and power routed over alternative lines, so that interruptions to consumers are kept to the minimum.

This vast network of overhead and underground cables, substations, transformers and switchgear represents a considerable financial investment and it must all be kept in working order to ensure continuity of supply. At the same time, modifications are continuously being made to reinforce supplies to particular areas, such as new housing estates, office buildings, and expanding or new factories. All this must be done with the minimum of interruption to supplies.

In fact, a great deal of work is carried out without switching off the power. Techniques of live-line working using special insulated tools have been developed in recent years which enable modifications, repairs and connections to be made to overhead lines while they are on load.

Water Supply

As soon as men began to settle into large communities they were faced with the problems of ensuring an adequate fresh water supply. The small settlements of the Neolithic age had successfully relied on natural springs and simple wells, but such sources were simply not capable of satisfying the towns and cities which began to develop about 4000 BC. At first, as in the cities of Mesopotamia, open conduits were used to channel water from distant springs and lakes. The ruins of Mohenjo-Daro in the Indus Valley, which date from about 2500 BC, boast the earliest known enclosed system.

The ancient Greeks made considerable use of conduits, pipes and tunnels to supply water to their cities, and their techniques were refined and developed by the Romans. Imperial Rome enjoyed a water system unrivalled at the time and unsurpassed for many centuries after. It has been estimated that enough was supplied by the Roman systems to give every urban inhabitant some 225 litres (50 gallons) per day. This is as much as many modern municipalities provide.

Water quality

Groundwater sources are usually less contaminated than surface waters because they have had less contact with possible impurities. Surface water may have flowed through hundreds of kilometres of stream and river before it reaches the lake or reservoir from which a public supply is taken. In the course of its journey it will have picked up a quantity of minerals, some of which may be poisonous industrial waste, and an assortment of plant and animal matter, including sewage, in various states of decomposition. In addition, lakes may become infested with algae, which give the water an unpleasant taste and smell.

A water treatment works aims to supply water that is safe and pleasant to drink. A number of simple tests are performed on the treated water to ensure that this is the case. Perhaps the most important of these is the *coliform bacteria count*. Coliforms, such as *Escherichia coli*, which is also widely cultivated for use in research, live naturally in human intestines and are excreted in large quantities into sewage. In themselves they are harmless, but the presence of such bacteria in a water sample indicates that other, more dangerous bacteria and viruses may also be present.

The *biochemical oxygen demand* (BOD) test is a useful measure of the amount of decomposing organic material present. Decomposition uses up oxygen, and the BOD test measures the amount of oxygen used up in this way by a sample of water which is maintained at 20°C (68°F) for five days.

The total amount of solid matter suspended in a water sample, which also includes inorganic matter such as clay, can be estimated by measuring the *turbidity* (cloudiness) of a sample. This can be done quite simply by shining light through the water and measuring the proportion of light scattered by the suspended particles.

The presence of an appreciable quantity of nitrogen in water is a good indica-

Above: A Roman aqueduct at Segovia in Spain, built during the reign of the Emperor Trajan (53-117 AD) and still in use today. It carries water from the Rio Frio for about 823 m (2,700 ft) to the old town, its maximum height being about 28.5 m (93.5 ft).

Above right: Laying a pipeline to carry water from a reservoir to a treatment works. The pipes are made of iron lined with concrete.

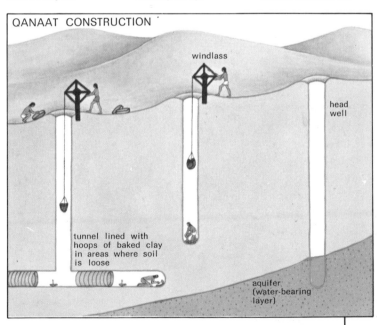

QANAAT CONSTRUCTION

windlass

head well

tunnel lined with hoops of baked clay in areas where soil is loose

aquifer (water-bearing layer)

Qanaats, widely used in Iran and other Middle Eastern countries, are inclined irrigation tunnels which carry mountain groundwater to arid plains.

QANAAT

farmland   canal   ventilation shafts

soil

aquifer

impermeable layer

rock

Left: The first step in building a qanaat is the digging of a head well down into the water-bearing strata in the hills, and then the tunnel is dug from the downhill end up to the head well. Ventilation shafts are dug at intervals of about 50 m, and the total tunnel length is usually about 10 to 16 km (6-10 mi).

water intake area

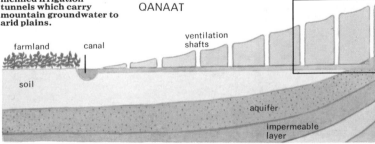

374

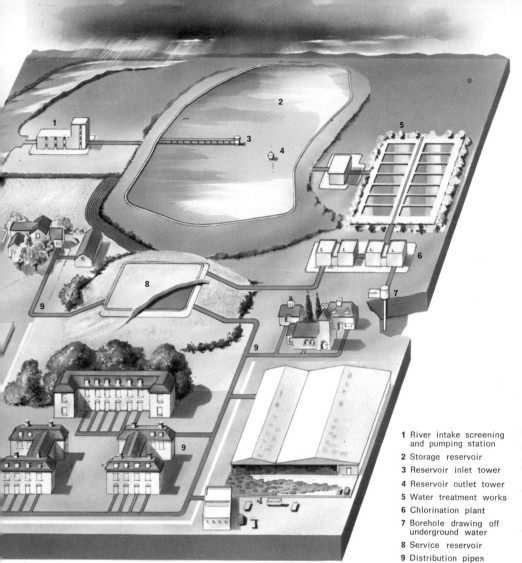

1 River intake screening and pumping station
2 Storage reservoir
3 Reservoir inlet tower
4 Reservoir outlet tower
5 Water treatment works
6 Chlorination plant
7 Borehole drawing off underground water
8 Service reservoir
9 Distribution pipes

Above: A typical water supply system. Here, water taken from a river is screened to remove debris and pumped into a storage reservoir. It is then filtered, purified and chlorinated before distribution to the consumers. Water pumped up through boreholes drilled into underground water sources needs only chlorination before it is distributed.

Left: Part of Israel's National Water Carrier, which carries water to the Negev desert.

Weir Pumps Ltd

Above: Three *pumpsets*, each consisting of a pump and an electric drive motor, at the Ross Priory pumping station in Scotland. These pumpsets, which have a total capacity of 227 million litres (50 million gallons) of water per day, pump water from Loch Lomond for distribution to reservoirs and treatment works supplying central Scotland.

Left: A reservoir in North Wales. Reservoirs play an important part in the purification of water. While the water is standing in the reservoir, the larger solid impurities settle to the bottom, the large surface area allows the oxygen in the air to attack other impurities, and the various physical, chemical and biological conditions set up within the water during storage have a destructive effect on any harmful bacteria.

Picturepoint

tion of possible contamination. Combined with hydrogen (forming ammonia, NH_3), it indicates pollution by organic matter. In the form of nitrites and nitrates, it points to inorganic pollutants such as fertilizers and chemical wastes.

Water treatment

Before it can be distributed to consumers, water must undergo a series of physical and chemical treatments to remove the impurities. The number and nature of the cleaning processes varies from one works to another, because some sources of raw water are much cleaner than others. The following is an exhaustive series of treatments, not all of which will be necessary in every case.

The first treatment is quite simple—the water is stored in large reservoirs or settling basins for several weeks. This allows the larger particles to sink to the bottom of the basin. During this period chemical reactions, which take place naturally and slowly in the water, tend to neutralize any acidity or alkalinity. The most important advantage of storage, however, is that the number of toxic bacteria in the water is strikingly reduced. Shortage of suitable food, a low temperature in the depths of the storage basin, the effects of sunlight, and the competition from harmless micro-organisms all contribute to the decline in the bacterial population.

The next stage in the treatment is to pass the water through a fairly coarse screen which removes leaves and other debris. At this stage chlorine is usually added to kill off the remaining bacteria. Chlorine is not the only possible disinfectant. Some European countries use ozone (O_3), which is rather more expensive, and in some small plants the water may be sterilized by irradiating it with ultra-violet light. A second screening usually follows, which removes algae and small particles. This is done by a *microstrainer*, a rotating filter drum covered with a very fine stainless steel mesh. The holes in the mesh are less than one micron (one millionth of a metre) in diameter, and the water passes through them from the inside of the drum outwards.

Even after passing through the extremely fine mesh of the microstrainer, water still contains many small suspended particles. Some of these are insoluble minerals, others are dead bacteria, and all make the water look cloudy and sometimes discoloured. They can be trapped by a process known as *coagulation and flocculation*.

In cloudy water the suspended particles are in continuous rapid motion and are never in close contact with each other for long enough to stick together. If a chemical coagulant such as aluminium sulphate ($Al_2 (SO_4)_3 . 14H_2O$) or ferric sulphate ($Fe_2 (SO_4)_3 . H_2O$) is added, the particles can be trapped by it so that they slowly aggregate together and eventually form a single, amorphous mass, leaving the water clear. This coagulated mass has a woolly appearance and settles in a sort of blanket about halfway down the tank; it is called a *flocculent precipitate* or *floc* for short. A small residue of the coagulant remains dissolved in the water and may make it harder and more corrosive.

By this stage the water is considerably purer than it was at its source, but it

MULTI-STAGE FLASH DESALINATION PLANT

sea water for cooling and feed

condenser

condenser

uncondensed gases

vapour condensing

product water

brine flows from left to right

chemical dosage tank

steam to heat brine

cooling sea water for discharge

heat exchanger

recirculating brine

condensed steam from heat exchanger

Top: A *multi-stage flash desalination* plant in Abu Dhabi, capable of producing over 9 million litres (2 million gallons) of fresh water per day.

Above: The multi-stage flash desalination plant distils fresh water from salt water by heating it and then reducing the air pressure around it. Sea water is heated by steam, and then passed through a series of chambers in which its pressure is progressively reduced. This causes fresh water to 'flash' (evaporate because of the low pressure) out of it and condense onto the condenser tubes.

Left: The *reverse osmosis* process is a potentially important desalination method. In this process, salt water is forced against a *semi-permeable membrane*, one which allows the solvent of a solution to pass through it but not the dissolved substances, in this case pure water and salt respectively. The membranes are made from suitable polymer materials such as cellulose acetate.

must still undergo further cleaning in filter beds. Filtering is one of the most important processes of all. There are two main methods of filtration. *Slow sand filtration* may be used for water which comes from a relatively pure source and has not undergone any previous treatment. The water flows into beds of fine sand, and seeps through the sand and an underlying bed of gravel into an underground drainage system.

Rapid sand filters are filled with coarser sand, often with a layer of crushed anthracite below and sometimes with a layer of fine sand above. Rapid sand filters are the most commonly used because they allow faster rates of flow, but they are generally suitable only for water that has been previously cleaned to some extent by coagulation and flocculation. Rapid filters are cleaned daily by *backwashing*, passing water through them in the opposite direction to the normal flow. Slow filters are cleaned about once every two months by removing the top layer of sand and replacing it with clean sand.

After filtration, water is usually *aerated* to increase the amount of dissolved oxygen it contains. This improves the colour and freshness of taste as well as reducing acidity by eliminating dissolved carbon dioxide. There are several different types of aerator. One, the *spray aerator*, forces the water through fine nozzles into the air. Another, the *cascade aerator*, has a series of steps over which the water falls.

No amount of filtration, sedimentation or coagulation, however, will rid water of substances that are completely dissolved in it, and a large group of such substances—the salts of calcium and to a lesser extent magnesium—are responsible for the 'hardness' of water. Hard water makes washing with soap more difficult, hinders the extraction of meat and vegetable juices in cooking, and deposits scale in kettles, boilers and pipes, and chemical treatment is often necessary to reduce hardness to an acceptable level. In areas where the water is exceptionally hard, a softening process may be carried out at the treatment works if costs permit, but it is usually left to individual consumers to install their own softening units if they require soft water. There are two kinds of hardness, *permanent* and *temporary*.

Temporary hardness is due to calcium bicarbonate ($Ca(HCO_3)_2$) and magnesium bicarbonate ($Mg(HCO_3)_2$), and causes scale when the water is heated because the bicarbonates break down into insoluble carbonates which settle out of the water and stick to the surface of the container. This kind of hardness can be removed by treating the water with lime (calcium hydroxide, $Ca(OH)_2$), which reduces the bicarbonates to carbonates, so that they precipitate out without the need for heating.

Permanent hardness cannot be removed by boiling. It is caused by sulphates and chlorides of calcium and can be reduced by treatment with sodium bicarbonate ($NaHCO_3$). This leads to an *exchange reaction*, in which the carbonate group of atoms is transferred from the sodium to the calcium atoms to make an insoluble compound which settles out of the water. The sodium atoms receive in exchange the chloride and sulphate groups, making salts which do not contribute to hardness.

The Lower Laithe
Reservoir at
Stanbury, Yorkshire
— a stunning example
of modern techni-
logical achievement.

Batteries and Fuel Cells

An electricity battery consists of one or more electric *cells*, which are devices for producing electric currents directly from chemical reactions. Electricity made in this way is much more expensive than that made by mechanical generators, but batteries, being compact and portable, are a better choice for many applications. The chemical generation of electricity is possible because many chemical reactions involve simply an exchange of electrons between atoms of different kinds.

The electrical nature of such reactions can easily be shown by passing a direct current through distilled water to which a little acid has been added to improve its ability to conduct electricity. The result is that the water splits up into bubbles of hydrogen and oxygen gases which can be collected separately.

This process of breaking down liquids by electricity is known as *electrolysis* and is widely used in industrial chemistry for separating many different compounds into their simple constituents. An electric cell performs electrolysis in reverse, forming compounds from simpler constituents in such a way that electricity is produced by the chemical reactions taking place.

In principle the action of an electric cell is simple. A current is created in a wire by feeding in electrons at one end and sucking them out at the other, causing the electrons to flow through the wire as an electric current. This is accomplished by attaching each end of the wire to a metal plate which is immersed in an *electrolyte*, a chemical solution of some *ionic* compound. When such a compound is dissolved, its molecules split into two or more parts which are kept apart by the molecules of the liquid it is dissolved in. Some parts of the dissolved molecule have a positive electric charge and are known as *positive ions;* other parts have a negative charge and are called *negative ions.*

For example, when sulphuric acid (H_2SO_4) is dissolved in water, the two hydrogen atoms are separated from each other and from the rest of the molecule. Because each loses an electron in this process, they become hydrogen ions and are denoted by the symbol H^+ to indicate that they have a positive charge. The rest of the molecule stays together as a sulphate ion, which is negative because it has gained two extra electrons (from the hydrogen atoms), and it is denoted by the symbol SO_4^-.

Sulphuric acid in water was used as the electrolyte in the first modern battery, invented by the Italian physicist Count Alessandro Volta (1745-1827) in 1800. The basic electric cell of this battery is perhaps the simplest of all. One end of the wire in which the current is to flow is connected to a plate made of zinc and the other to a copper plate. Both the plates, which are known as *electrodes*, are immersed in the electrolyte but do not touch each other.

The electrolyte reacts with the plates, feeding electrons to the zinc and extracting them from the copper in the following manner. The hydrogen ions from the sulphuric acid capture electrons from the

Ronan

Left: This battery, comprising 200 cells, was built by Sir Humphry Davy in the basement of the Royal Institution, London, to provide electricity for experiments and demonstrations. The picture is from a French book of 1870.

Below: A battery of silver-zinc cells built for use in a satellite. Silver-zinc cells have an alkaline electrolyte and their electrodes are made of silver oxide and zinc. They give high power in relation to their size and weight when compared with other types of battery, and their high cost is considered worthwhile for such items as satellites. These batteries provide power for the satellite when it is in the earth's shadow and there is no light to drive its solar cells—or they take over if the solar cells break down.

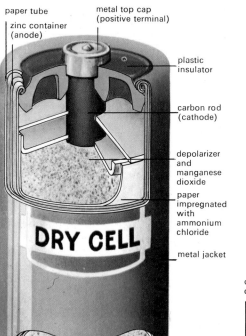

paper tube
zinc container (anode)
metal top cap (positive terminal)
plastic insulator
carbon rod (cathode)
depolarizer and manganese dioxide
paper impregnated with ammonium chloride
metal jacket

DRY CELL

metal base (negative terminal)

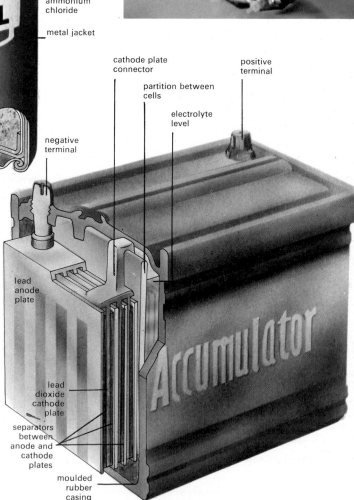

Paul Brierley

cathode plate connector
partition between cells
electrolyte level
positive terminal
negative terminal
lead anode plate
lead dioxide cathode plate
separators between anode and cathode plates
moulded rubber casing

Accumulator

Above: A dry cell of the kind used in radios and flashlights. This particular design has a carbon rod surrounded by a depolarizer and the manganese dioxide which forms the cathode (positive electrode). The rod and cathode are surrounded by paper impregnated with ammonium chloride electrolyte, and are contained within the zinc cup which is the anode (negative electrode). During operation, electrons travel from the anode, through the external circuit and into the cathode via the carbon rod.

Right: This car battery has a lead anode, a lead dioxide cathode, and a dilute sulphuric acid electrolyte.

atoms of the copper plate and change into hydrogen atoms, which are insoluble and escape from the solution as gas. Sulphate ions capture zinc atoms to make molecules of zinc sulphate. The zinc atoms each abandon two electrons in favour of the two spare electrons on the sulphate ion. These two abandoned electrons move through the wire, as an electric current, to replace those lost at the copper plate.

If the external wire connection between the plates is broken (which is in effect what happens when, for example, a radio or a flashlight is switched off), so that electrons cannot travel from plate to plate via the wire, the reactions will soon come to a halt. This is because a layer of electric charge, caused by an excess or deficiency of electrons, builds up on each plate and prevents the ions of the electrolyte from approaching the plates closely enough to capture electrons or atoms. Thus the available chemical energy is held in check until the circuit is completed again and electrons can again flow through the wire.

Primary cells

The arrangement just described can only produce current as long as there is zinc available to be converted into zinc sulphate. Once the zinc plate has completely disintegrated, the reactions which drive the current can no longer proceed as there is no 'fuel' left to feed them. Such a cell, which can be used only once, is known as a *primary cell*. The commonest primary cell is the familiar 'dry' cell, which is almost universally used to power flashlights, transistor radios and other devices which need only a small amount of power.

This cell, also known as a *Leclanché* cell after its inventor, Georges Leclanché (1839-1882), is not really 'dry' at all. The active ingredient is still a solution of an ionic compound (ammonium chloride, NH_4Cl) in water, but there is so little water present that the solution is a thick paste. Into this paste is inserted a rod of carbon, which is a good conductor of electricity, and the whole is enclosed in a casing of zinc. As long as the carbon and zinc are unconnected no reactions take place in the cell, but as soon as they are connected by an external circuit a current begins to flow as electrons are extracted from the paste via the carbon rod and fed through the circuit into the zinc casing.

One product of the reactions in the Leclanché cell is hydrogen gas and, as this accumulates at the carbon rod, it begins to interfere with the operation of the cell if current is allowed to flow for very long. This phenomenon is known as *polarization* and is partly offset by including some manganese dioxide (MnO_2) in the paste. This *depolarizer* reacts with the hydrogen to remove it from the carbon surface.

Secondary cells

The principal disadvantage of a primary cell is its short life. Obviously it would be more useful to have a cell which could be restored to its original condition once it had discharged all the available chemical energy stored in it. Fortunately it is possible to do this with some types of cell. Other electric cells, however, rely on reactions which are reversible. In these, the chemical compounds whose formation gives rise to the current can be changed back to their original components simply by passing a current through the cell in the opposite direction. They are then free to recombine as before to make current.

Such cells are called *secondary cells* and a set of them is called a *storage battery* because it enables charge produced by other means (usually generators) to be 'stored' for later use.

Storage batteries may be divided into two types, acid and alkaline, according to the nature of the electrolyte. The principal acid battery is the familiar lead-acid *accumulator*, almost universally used in motor vehicles. Each cell of this battery consists of a plate of lead (Pb) and a plate of lead dioxide (PbO_2) both immersed in an electrolyte of dilute sulphuric acid.

At the positive plate, the lead dioxide reacts with the hydrogen and sulphate ions of the acid to make lead sulphate ($PbSO_4$) and water, extracting two electrons from the external wiring to balance the reaction electrically. At the negative plate, the lead metal reacts with the sulphate ions to make lead sulphate and feeds two electrons to the external wiring to maintain the electrical balance. The net effect of this is to produce a current of electrons from the negative to the positive plate.

When no more lead or lead dioxide remains the cell is exhausted. It can be regenerated (recharged) by passing a direct current through the cell from the negative to the positive plate. This induces the lead sulphate to break down again to lead on the negative plate and to lead dioxide on the positive.

During the recharging, the electrical energy put into the cell creates the chemical energy that breaks the lead sulphate into lead and lead dioxide, and combines the sulphate ions (freed from it) with the water to form dilute sulphuric acid. When the cell is subsequently used, these chemical reactions are reversed and the chemical energy is turned back into electrical energy. The electricity used in recharging the cell can thus be thought to have been 'stored' by the cell.

Alkaline batteries, as the name implies, have an alkaline electrolyte, usually

Above: Francis Bacon, who designed the first efficient fuel cell. The idea of combining hydrogen and oxygen in an electrolytic cell, producing water and electricity, was first demonstrated by Sir William Grove in 1838. Bacon began working on this idea in the 1930s, and in 1959 he introduced a hydrogen-oxygen cell capable of producing 6 kW of power. Bacon's work was taken up by Pratt and Whitney in the USA, who built the fuel cells used in the Apollo moon missions. Fuel cells are now being built for large-scale power production.

Below: Bacon's 6 kW fuel cell, built in 1959.

Paul Brierley

Francis Bacon

Right: Hydrogen gas, which can be used to run fuel cells producing electricity for domestic and industrial premises, could be produced by the electrolysis of water. The electricity required for the electrolysis could be generated by using natural energy sources such as the wind, waves or sunlight. The energy available from these sources is variable and unpredictable—there may be times when demand for electricity is low, and little when demand is high. Electricity itself cannot be stored, so it cannot be generated during periods of low demand and kept until it is needed. If it is used to make hydrogen, however, the gas, and in effect the energy used to make it, can be stored almost indefinitely, and distributed by pipeline in the same way as natural gas and town gas are conveyed.

Below: When dc electricity is passed through water, hydrogen gas collects at the cathode and oxygen gas at the anode.

ELECTROLYSIS CELL

dc supply

+ −

hydrogen gas

oxygen

+

cathode (electrodes)

anode

sea water

wind powered generators supply dc current

river water electrolysis plant

hydrogen pipeline

hydrogen storage and pressurization plant

sea-water electrolysis plant

hydrogen pipeline

wave powered generators

hydrogen distribution network

hydrogen pipeline

solar powered river water electrolysis plant

Right: In a hydrogen-oxygen fuel cell the two gases react with the electrolyte, producing water and electricity.

Below: These two diagrams show how fuel cells, running on hydrogen produced by the system shown on the left, could replace the existing electricity supply system. The cycle of events would be as follows: natural energy sources produce electricity, which is used to obtain hydrogen from water. The hydrogen is then distributed to fuel cell units, on the consumers' premises, which produce electricity by combining the hydrogen with oxygen from the air to make water.

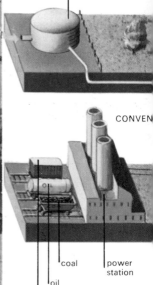

local gas storage tank

G

CONVEN

coal

power station

oil

nuclear fuel

---

potassium hydroxide (KOH). A common type of alkaline cell has one plate made of an oxide of nickel (Ni) and one of iron (Fe), and for this reason it is often known as the *NiFe* battery. Each cell weighs less than a lead cell but gives out only 1.2 volts. So for a 12 volt battery ten cells are needed as against six lead cells, which means that a NiFe battery ends up no lighter than a lead accumulator. Another type of alkaline cell, which has plates of silver oxide (AgO) and zinc (Zn), can give from two to ten times as much electrical energy for the same weight, but it is not widely used because of the high cost of silver.

Fuel cells

Even a secondary cell, however, cannot be used continuously. Its ability to be recharged is certainly a considerable advantage, but recharging takes several hours during which the cell cannot be used to provide current. So to obtain an uninterrupted current at least two batteries are needed and some means of recharging. All these problems are overcome in the *fuel cell*. In this, unlike any of the cells described above, the substances whose reactions drive the current are not contained within the cell but are

fed into it as required to sustain the reaction.

The first efficient fuel cell was produced, after many years of development work, by the English engineer Francis Bacon in 1959. Fuelled by hydrogen and oxygen gas, it is still the most reliable and widely used type and was chosen for the Apollo space missions.

The Bacon cell is filled with an alkaline electrolyte, potassium hydroxide in water, which is bounded by two very special electrode plates. They are made out of porous metal into which the electrolyte can penetrate, although it cannot pass right through. On the other side of one electrode is hydrogen gas, at a pressure which is carefully controlled so that the gas also can only penetrate part way into the plate. The other electrode is fed with oxygen gas in the same way.

The chemical and physical properties of the electrodes are crucial to the operation of the fuel cell, for it is only in the pores of these that the gases come into contact with the electrolyte. At the negative plate hydrogen molecules combine with *hydroxyl* ions (OH—) from the electrolyte and release electrons into the electrode. At the positive plate oxygen atoms capture electrons from the electrode

metal and combine with water molecules to make hydroxyl ions which dissolve in the electrolyte.

If the electrodes are connected outside the cell, the reactions will continue and current will flow through the external circuit as long as hydrogen and oxygen are supplied. To encourage the reactions to proceed at a reasonably rapid rate, the electrodes are made of a metal which acts as a catalyst. The best for this purpose is platinum, but since this is expensive Bacon cells use nickel which works very well at a temperature of about 200°C (392°F).

Another very promising type of fuel cell uses a metal carbonate as electrolyte. At the operating temperature of 700°C (1,292°F) the electrolyte separates into metal and carbonate (CO_3-) ions. The fuel is carbon monoxide (CO) at the negative plate, which reacts with carbonate ions to make carbon dioxide gas (CO_2) and supplies electrons as a result.

At the positive plate, oxygen combines with the carbon dioxide, extracting electrons from the plate as it does so, to make more carbonate ions. Fuel for this cell is cheap because the higher temperature allows air to be used at the positive electrode to supply oxygen, so a supply of

FUEL CELL

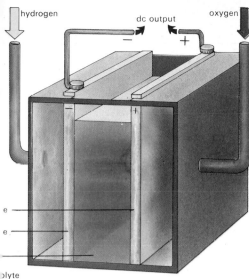

hydrogen

oxygen

dc output

− +

e

e

lyte
(ion of potassium hydroxide)

RVICE

fuel cell
located
on site

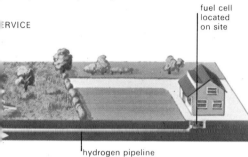

hydrogen pipeline

R SUPPLY

substation

transformer

Below: An aluminium air
fuel cell, being developed in
the US for use as a
rechargeable energy
source for silent and
pollution-free road
vehicles. Fuel cells are also

in use in spacecraft,
submarines and other
small-scale applications. In
larger units, such as in
power plants, their much
higher cost outweighs their
greater efficiency.

United Aircraft Corporation

Electricity Council

Above: One of the fuel cell
elements used in a 25 MW
power unit capable of
supplying the electricity for
a town of 20,000 people. The
power unit consisted of a
fuel conditioner, which
produced hydrogen from
natural gas, hydrogen-
oxygen fuel cells, and an
inverter which turned the
dc output into alternating
current.

Left: A great deal of work is
going into the development
of electric cars. At present
these are powered by
batteries, but future
designs may use fuel cells
running on fuels such as
liquid hydrogen, hydrazine
(N_2H_4), or powdered
metal-hydrogen
compounds (hydrides).

Lawrence Livermore National Laboratory

pure oxygen is not required, and carbon
monoxide is obtained as an inexpensive
by-product in the distillation of coal tar.

The working efficiency of fuel cells is as
high as 75 per cent, estimating efficiency as
the ratio of free electrical energy to heat
energy lost. Figures of around 95 per cent
can be achieved, but in practice some of the
generated electrical potential is used in
continuing the reaction, and all electrical
cells have an internal resistance, and these
factors reduce the working efficiency.

However, several limitations remain.
The electrolyte will eventually decompose –
as will the electrodes – although much less
quickly than in conventional batteries, because they are not consumed by the cur-
rent-generating process. Also the pressure
of the gases acting behind porous electrodes
is critical to efficiency and power. Too little
will allow the electrolyte to escape, too
much will blow it out of the pores, reducing
the vital contact area.

There are limits to the use of large fuel
cells for domestic power generation. For
100 MW stations, fuel cells are little more
efficient than steam turbines, and are much
more expensive to run. Figures are good,
however, for smaller applications of less
than 1 MW. For spacecraft and submarines,
the fuel cell is often chosen.

The Internal Combustion Engine

The internal combustion engine was one of the most important inventions of the nineteenth century. Its development and its applications have had far-reaching effects throughout the world—its use has revolutionized transport, its manufacture has spawned vast new industries and its technology has inspired developments in many other fields of engineering.

The internal combustion engine is so called because the heat energy that it converts into mechanical energy is produced within it by the repeated explosion of a mixture of fuel and air. For instance, if petrol gasoline vapour is mixed with the right proportion of air, the resulting mixture can be ignited by means of a spark. As it explodes it expands rapidly, and this expansion is what drives the pistons.

Early designs of these engines used coal gas as the fuel and were based on steam engine technology. The first reasonably successful engine was built by the Frenchman J. J. E. Lenoir in 1859. The Lenoir engine, however, suffered from a low power output and high fuel consumption, so many attempts were made to produce a more efficient design. This was eventually achieved in 1876 by Nikolaus Otto in Germany and his company, Otto and Langen, produced about 50,000 engines during the following 17 years.

Petrol engines

The basic components of an internal combustion engine are the cylinder, closed at the top by the cylinder head, and the piston which moves up and down within it. The piston is connected to a crankshaft by a connecting rod, so as the piston moves up and down the crankshaft is turned.

The fuel and air are mixed by the carburettor and this mixture is then drawn into the cylinder by the suction created during a downward stroke of the piston. When the piston rises again, the mixture is compressed as the space between the top of the piston and the cylinder head decreases. This compression raises the temperature of the mixture, making it more explosive.

Just before the piston reaches the top of its travel, the mixture is ignited by an electric spark created by current jumping across the gap between the two electrodes of a spark plug, screwed into the cylinder head.

By the time the piston has reached the top of its travel, the explosion which began in the mixture around the spark plug has spread rapidly throughout the rest of the mixture in the cylinder. The resulting expansion of hot gases created by the burning mixture drives the piston down again.

The power of the explosion is thus converted into a downward movement of the piston, and this motion rotates the crankshaft. The rotation of the crankshaft is then used to drive, for example, a car or a motorcycle.

The simplest form of petrol engine is the two-stroke engine, in which there are

Above: A two-stroke outboard motor engine. It is a V-6 engine, having two banks of three cylinders set at an angle to each other to form a V-shape. The total cylinder capacity is 2448 cc (149.9 in³), and the power output is 149 kW (200 hp).

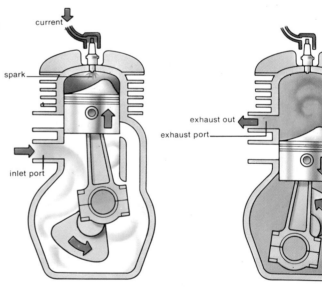

Right: The two-stroke cycle. As the piston moves up to compress the fuel/air mixture in the cylinder, the next charge of mixture is drawn into the crankcase via the inlet port. After the compressed mixture in the cylinder has been ignited by the spark plug, the expanding gases drive the piston down the cylinder. As the piston descends it pushes the mixture in the crankcase up the transfer port and into the cylinder. The mixture entering the cylinder pushes the exhaust gases out through the exhaust port, then the piston starts to rise and the cycle begins again.

two strokes of the piston, one up and one down, for each ignition of fuel. On a two-stroke engine the mixture is drawn into the cylinder via the crankcase, the casing below the cylinder which encloses the crankshaft.

As the piston rises to compress the mixture in the cylinder, the low pressure created in the crankcase below it sucks in fresh mixture through an opening, the inlet port, in the side of the bottom of the cylinder where it meets the crankcase.

Meanwhile, the mixture already in the cylinder has been compressed and ignited, and the piston is on its way down again. As it descends it uncovers two other openings in the cylinder wall, which were closed off by the sides of the piston during its upward compression stroke.

One of these ports is the exhaust port,

through which the burned exhaust gases escape, and the other one, on the opposite side of the cylinder, is the transfer port. The transfer port is the top opening of a passage leading down to the crankcase, and as the piston moves down it pushes the mixture in the crankcase up the transfer port and into the cylinder. As the mixture enters the cylinder it pushes the remaining exhaust gases out through the exhaust port.

The piston now rises again, covering the exhaust and transfer ports and so sealing the cylinder, compressing the mixture ready for ignition. The impetus required to push the piston back up the cylinder is provided by a relatively heavy flywheel, fitted to the end of the crankshaft, whose inertia keeps it turning after it has been set moving by the down-

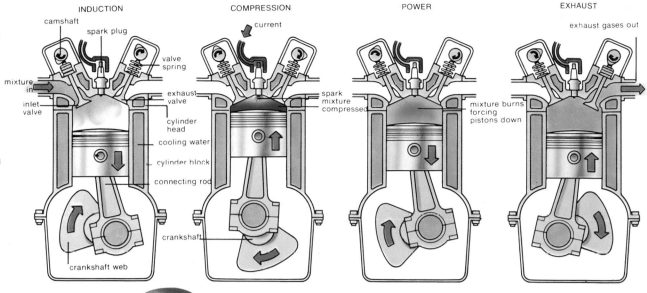

INDUCTION | COMPRESSION | POWER | EXHAUST

Right: The four-stroke cycle. On the first stroke, the induction stroke, the piston moves down and the inlet valve opens, allowing mixture to enter the cylinder. On the second stroke, the compression stroke, both valves are closed and the piston moves up to compress the mixture. After the mixture has been ignited the piston is driven back down on its power stroke. As it rises again on its exhaust stroke the exhaust valve opens and the exhaust gases are driven out of the cylinder. The exhaust valve then closes, the inlet valve opens, and the next induction stroke begins.

Below: A cutaway view of a four-cylinder engine with a belt-driven overhead camshaft.

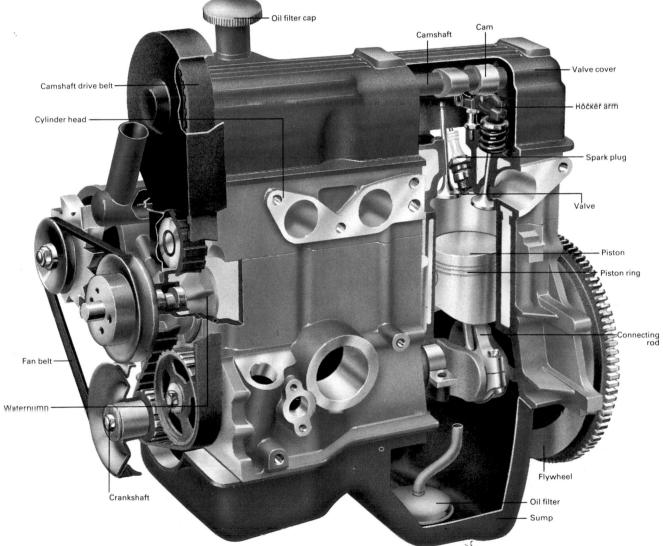

ward power stroke of the piston.

The four-stroke engine is more complicated than the two stroke because there is a separate stroke of the piston for each of the four stages of the combustion cycle. In addition, cam-operated valves are used to control the entry of the mixture and the exit of the exhaust gases, the mixture entering the cylinder directly and not via the crankcase.

The first stroke of the cycle is a downward stroke of the piston, during which the inlet valve is open to allow mixture to

be drawn into the cylinder. The inlet valve then closes and the piston moves up on the second stroke, the compression stroke, to compress the mixture which is then ignited by the spark plug. The expansion of the burning mixture drives the piston back down on its power stroke.

The cycle is completed by the next upstroke of the piston. As the piston rises, the exhaust valve opens and the exhaust gases are forced out of the cylinder. Then the exhaust valve closes and the cycle begins again.

Carburation

As the air is drawn through the carburettor by suction from the engine, it passes through a narrow passage called a *venturi* or *choke* (barrel). This narrowing of the air's path causes an increase in its velocity, and this increase in velocity causes a decrease in the air's pressure.

A small nozzle or *jet*, connected to the fuel supply, is positioned at the venturi, and the low pressure air flow sucks a fine spray of fuel out of the jet. This fine spray vaporizes and mixes with the air, in a ratio (by weight) of approximately 15 parts air to 1 part fuel. The amount of mixture drawn into the engine, which determines its speed, is controlled by a flap-like *butterfly valve* or *throttle* connected to the accelerator control.

On engines with more than one cylinder, the carburettor feeds the mixture into a *manifold*, a set of pipes connecting it with each of the cylinder inlets. Each cylinder draws mixture from the carburetor in turn. Many large engines have more than one carburettor, or a carburettor with more than one choke, to improve the flow of mixture to the cylinders.

Fuel injection systems use a high-pressure pump and injection nozzles to supply measured amounts of fuel to the engine.

A high voltage of up to 30,000 volts is needed to create the spark across the spark plug gap, and this voltage is supplied by the *ignition coil*. Current from a low voltage supply (such as the 12V supply from a car's battery) is fed into the low tension (lt) winding of the coil, which consists of a few hundred turns of copper wire wound on a soft iron core.

The flow of current sets up a magnetic field in the coil. When the current flow is switched off by a set of contact breaker points, operated by a cam driven by the engine, this magnetic field dies away or 'collapses'. The collapsing magnetic field creates or *induces* flow of current in the high tension (ht) winding of the coil. In comparison to the few hundred turns of relatively heavy wire which make up the lt winding, the ht winding consists of many thousands of

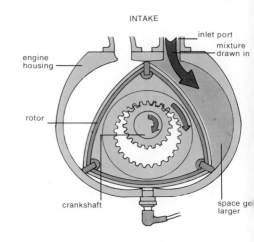

turns of fine copper wire. This also is wound around the soft iron core.

When one coil induces a current in another, as in an ignition coil, the ratio of the initial voltage to the induced voltage is the same as the ratio of the number of

ROTARY MOTOR CYCLE ENGINE

1. Air intake for carburettor
2. Carburettor
3. Cooling passages in rotor housing
4. Thermostatic switch for radiator fan
5. Inlet port (exhaust port below)
6. Wax thermostat
7. Rotor set trochoid pump for metering oil
8. Coolant pump rotor
9. Coolant pump volute
10. Ignition contact breaker (3 sets of points)
11. Oil filter
12. Oil sump inlet strainer
13. Chain tensioner
14. Multi-plate clutch
15. Twin drive chains from engine to clutch
16. Kick starter shaft
17. Kick starter freewheel mechanism
18. 5 speed gearbox
19. Chain lubricator
20. Drive chain to rear wheel
21. Electric starter
22. Spark plug
23. Tip seal
24. Rotor
25. 3 phase alternator
26. Combustion chamber

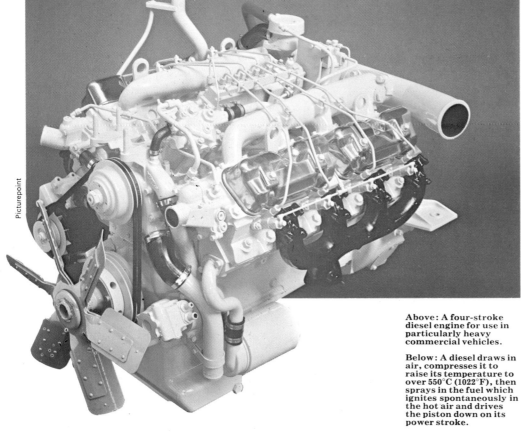

Above: A four-stroke diesel engine for use in particularly heavy commercial vehicles.

Below: A diesel draws in air, compresses it to raise its temperature to over 550°C (1022°F), then sprays in the fuel which ignites spontaneously in the hot air and drives the piston down on its power stroke.

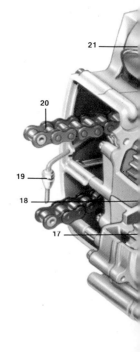

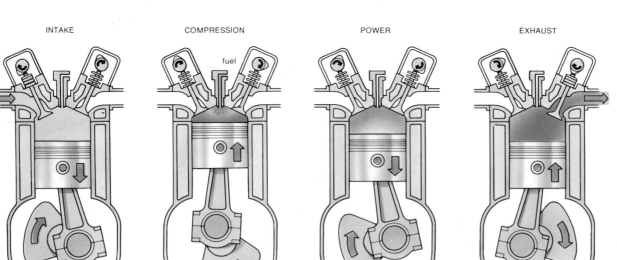

INTAKE   COMPRESSION   POWER   EXHAUST

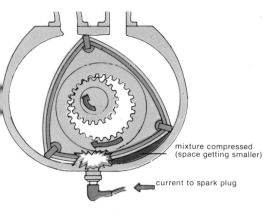

COMPRESSION AND IGNITION

mixture compressed
(space getting smaller)

← current to spark plug

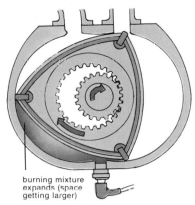

POWER

burning mixture
expands (space
getting larger)

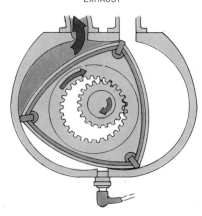

EXHAUST

turns of wire on the first coil to the number of turns on the second coil. This means that if the second coil has a thousand times more turns than the first, the induced voltage will be a thousand times greater than the initial voltage.

The high voltage pulse created by the coil is fed to the spark plug, where it travels down the centre electrode to its tip, which is inside the cylinder, and then sparks across to the other electrode. On multi-cylinder engines the pulses from the coil are fed to the *distributor*, which then distributes them to each cylinder in turn.

On many modern engines the current in the low tension circuit is controlled by an electronic circuit instead of by a mechanical contact breaker unit. Some also use fuel injection systems instead of carburettors, the petrol being sprayed directly into the cylinder instead of being mixed in a carburettor.

Diesel engines

The first diesel engine was built by Rudolf Diesel at Augsburg in Germany in 1897. Diesel engines, which may be either two-stroke or four-stroke, differ from petrol engines in several important respects. Only pure air is drawn into the cylinder on the induction stroke of the piston, and it is compressed to a much greater degree than is the fuel/air mixture of a petrol engine.

This high compression of the air raises its temperature to well over 550°C (1022°F). As the piston nears the top of its travel a measured amount of fuel is sprayed into this hot air by an injector nozzle fed by a pump unit.

The air is so hot that the fuel ignites spontaneously as it mixes with it, without needing a spark to set it off. As there is no carburettor, the speed of a diesel engine is controlled by altering the amount of fuel delivered to the injector by the pump. There is an injector in each cylinder of a multi-cylinder diesel engine, and the pump delivers a shot of fuel to each injector. Diesel engines can be modified to run on almost any kind of inflammable fuel, but most of them run on diesel oil.

Cooling

The combustion process inside the cylinders of an engine creates a large amount of heat, so without some form of cooling the temperature of the engine would rise rapidly. This would lead to a loss of performance and possibly internal damage due to the expansion of engine components; for instance the pistons could jam or 'seize up' within the cylinders.

Air-cooled engines have cooling fins on the outside of the cylinders, which increase their surface area so that the heat is carried away quicker by the surrounding air. Greater cooling is achieved by using a fan, driven by the engine, to blow air through the fins.

Water-cooled engines have water circulating in passageways around and between the cylinders to carry the heat away, and the water itself is cooled by passing it through a radiator. Most water-cooled engines have fans to draw air through the radiator and so increase the rate of cooling of the water.

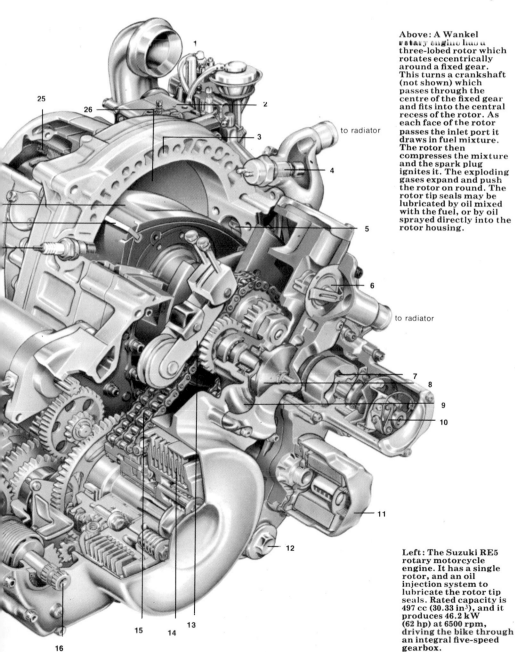

to radiator

to radiator

Above: A Wankel rotary engine has a three-lobed rotor which rotates eccentrically around a fixed gear. This turns a crankshaft (not shown) which passes through the centre of the fixed gear and fits into the central recess of the rotor. As each face of the rotor passes the inlet port it draws in fuel mixture. The rotor then compresses the mixture and the spark plug ignites it. The exploding gases expand and push the rotor on round. The rotor tip seals may be lubricated by oil mixed with the fuel, or by oil sprayed directly into the rotor housing.

Left: The Suzuki RE5 rotary motorcycle engine. It has a single rotor, and an oil injection system to lubricate the rotor tip seals. Rated capacity is 497 cc (30.33 in³), and it produces 46.2 kW (62 hp) at 6500 rpm, driving the bike through an integral five-speed gearbox.

Steam Engines and Turbines

Despite a tendency to regard steam power as a symbol of obsolescence, it continues to provide much of the energy used in modern society and there is, as yet, no practical alternative. Indeed, even the most advanced nuclear power station reactor is merely a source of heat to produce the steam which drives the generator turbines. Steam engines and turbines are good examples of energy conversion systems, in this case converting heat into mechanical energy.

The heat energy in steam is in a very convenient state for conversion into mechanical energy. Steam engines and turbines do this by expanding a supply of steam from a small volume at high pressure to a large volume at low pressure, with a corresponding fall in temperature. In steam engines this expansion moves a piston to-and-fro in a cylinder; turbines use it to give velocity to a flow of steam which then turns a rotor. Both machines are *external combustion heat engines*, that is, their fuel is burnt outside the working section. This permits better control of the combustion, and so the fuel can be burned under optimum conditions for avoiding atmospheric pollution.

Steam is generated in boilers heated either by furnaces fired by any convenient fuel such as oil or coal, or by some flow of hot fluid like the coolant from a nuclear reactor or the waste gases from a metal-smelting furnace.

The main types of boiler are the *shell* boiler, the *fire-tube* boiler and the *water-tube* boiler. The shell type boiler is cylindrical with internal flues, and is often set in brickwork containing *return flues* which carry the heat round to heat the outside of the boiler shell. The 'Lancashire' boiler, with two furnaces, is typical of this class.

In fire-tube boilers, as used on locomotives, the hot gases from the furnace pass through an array of small tubes immersed in water. In the water-tube boiler, on the other hand, arrays of small tubes carry the water through the combustion chamber. Although this type is more expensive to build, it is the most suitable for high pressure work, and is commonly used to supply turbines.

Steam engines

Most steam engines are *double acting*, that is, both sides of the piston are used to produce power, one side of the piston making a power stroke during the exhaust stroke of the other. The sequence of events during one revolution begins when steam is admitted to the cylinder just before the end of the previous stroke.

Next, the inlet port closes (known as *cut-off*) and the steam expands, driving the piston back down the cylinder. Just before the end of the power stroke the exhaust port opens, (known as *release*), and on the return stroke most of the steam is driven out of the cylinder. Finally the exhaust port closes and the remaining steam is compressed until admission begins again.

In most engines the whole sequence of events for both sides of the piston is

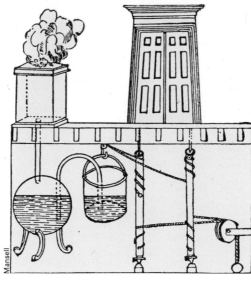

Above: The fact that heat could be converted into mechanical energy was known almost 2,000 years ago. This system, devised before 100AD by Hero of Alexandria, used the expansion of hot air beneath the fire on the hollow altar to drive water from the container into the bucket—which then descended and opened the temple doors.

Right: Newcomen's 'atmospheric' engine of 1710. Steam from the boiler 'a' was admitted to the cylinder 'c' and this pushed the piston up. A jet of cold water was then sprayed into the cylinder, condensing the steam, and the piston was driven back down by atmospheric pressure acting on its top surface.

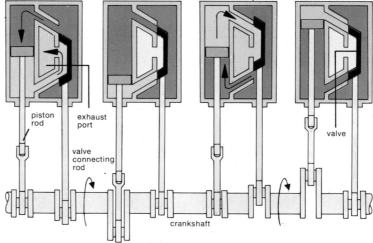

piston rod

exhaust port

valve connecting rod

valve

crankshaft

FOUR CYLINDER DOUBLE-ACTING STEAM ENGINE

high pressure cylinder

medium pressure cylinder

inlet

pis rod

crankshaft

COMPOUND (TRIPLE EX STEAM ENGINE

Above left: The operating principles of a double-acting steam engine, showing the action of the slide valve which controls the supply of steam to the cylinder.

Above: In a triple expansion engine the steam is passed from one cylinder to the next as its pressure drops.

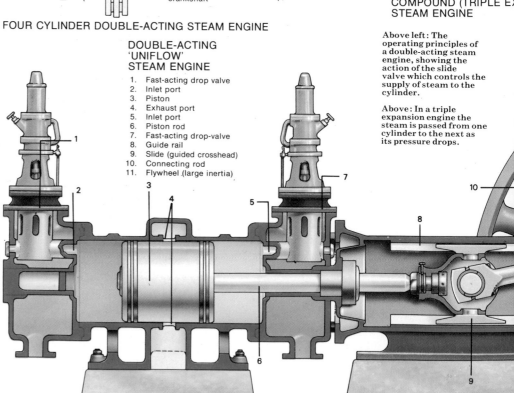

DOUBLE-ACTING 'UNIFLOW' STEAM ENGINE

1. Fast-acting drop valve
2. Inlet port
3. Piston
4. Exhaust port
5. Inlet port
6. Piston rod
7. Fast-acting drop-valve
8. Guide rail
9. Slide (guided crosshead)
10. Connecting rod
11. Flywheel (large inertia)

Left: James Watt was working as an instrument repairer in Glasgow University in 1763 when he was given a model Newcomen engine to repair. It occurred to him that the alternate heating and cooling of the cylinder was very inefficient, and so he designed an engine with a 'separate condenser'. This was a separate chamber into which the steam was led for condensation, so that the cylinder could be kept hot, and this greatly improved the engine's performance. He went on to design engines which drove rotating shafts instead of rocking beams, and he also invented the double-acting engine. The *watt*, the metric unit of power, is named after him.

Mansell

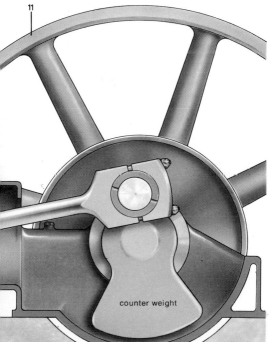

Radio Times Hulton Picture Library

John Watney

Above: A two-cylinder high pressure steam engine which was installed in a small cargo boat.

Left: An early pioneer of the French motor industry, the Marquis de Dion, driving a steam tricycle which he built in 1897. The engine is at the front and drives the rear wheel.

11

counter weight

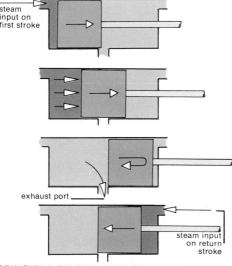

steam input on first stroke

exhaust port

steam input on return stroke

PRINCIPLE OF THE UNIFLOW STEAM ENGINE

Left: A diagram of a uniflow steam engine, which has an inlet valve at each end of the cylinder and a ring of exhaust ports half way along it.

Above: In the uniflow engine, steam is admitted at each end in turn, driving the piston up and down the cylinder and escaping through the exhaust ports.

controlled by a single D-shaped valve, which slides along the cylinder to open and close the ports in sequence. Some large stationary engines have separate inlet and exhaust valves for each side of the piston.

The to-and-fro motion of the piston is converted into rotary motion by a crank linked to the piston rod by a connecting rod. The inertia of a flywheel carries the crank on round past the places where the rod is in line with the crank arm and has no turning effect on it.

As the crank turns, the angle between the connecting rod and the piston rod is constantly changing. To allow for this, the connecting rod must be pivoted where it meets the piston rod. The most common arrangement uses a metal block which slides along guide rails at the end of the cylinder and connects the piston rod to the connecting rod. This sytem, the *guided crosshead*, is the one used on steam locomotives and in marine engines.

Some *single-acting* engines, where one side of the piston is used to produce power, have the connecting rod attached directly to the piston by a metal pin, the *gudgeon pin*, as in a petrol engine or diesel engine.

Compound engines

In a single cylinder, if the difference between the volume of the steam at cut-off and its volume at release is very large, the temperature variations of the cylinder wall which result will cause heat losses. These are unacceptable because the lost heat has to be replaced by burning more fuel, or else the temperature variations must be reduced by limiting the pressure of steam admitted to the cylinder to such an extent that the power of the engine is greatly reduced.

A solution to this was found by using a small, high pressure cylinder whose exhaust steam was passed into a larger, low pressure one. Such combinations are called *compound engines* and were made in several forms, some of which are still found in industrial engine-houses.

Triple expansion engines, with high pressure (HP), intermediate (IP), and one or two low pressure (LP) cylinders were used extensively in ships. The Atlantic liner *Olympic* (1911-36) had two such engines, each with a 1372 mm (54 in) HP cylinder, a 2134 mm (84 in) IP cylinder, and two 2464 mm (97 in) LP cylinders. Each engine developed 11,185 kW (15,000 hp) at 75 rpm.

Quadruple expansion engines were also used at sea, particularly in German ships around the turn of the century. One example, the *Kaiser Wilhelm II* built in 1902, had a total of eight cylinders and produced 16,033 kW (21,500 hp).

Uniflow engines

Uniflow engines are double-acting engines which release most of the expanded steam through a ring of exhaust ports in the cylinder wall. The ports are about half way along the cylinder, so that during most of the power stroke of either side of the piston, the piston is either between the inlet valve and the exhaust ports or closing off the exhaust ports.

A total expansion greater than in most compound engines is achieved in one cylinder at an almost constant wall temperature. Many large engines were built on this principle between 1908 and

Below: The upper drawing shows the steam path through a compound turbine which has six high pressure and four low pressure stages. The lower drawing shows the steam flow in a radial flow turbine. A rotating disc carries rings of blades which move within the fixed blades, and the steam flows outwards through them.

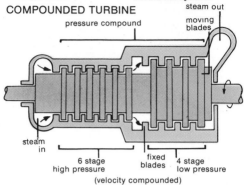

COMPOUNDED TURBINE

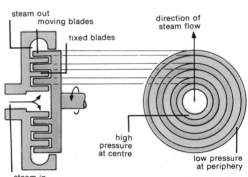

PRINCIPLE OF RADIAL-FLOW TURBINE

Right: Another of Hero's inventions, the 'Aeolipile', a kind of steam turbine. The tubes fixed to the hollow sphere had their ends bent over in opposite directions. The sphere was mounted over a boiler. Steam passed into it through the hollow bearings, to escape through the tubes and rotate the sphere.

Radio Times Hulton Picture Library

Below right: A single stage velocity-compounded turbine. The steam enters through the admission valve, and passes into the nozzle passages where it expands as its pressure drops. This expansion increases its velocity and it then passes rapidly through the blades, turning the rotor as it goes.

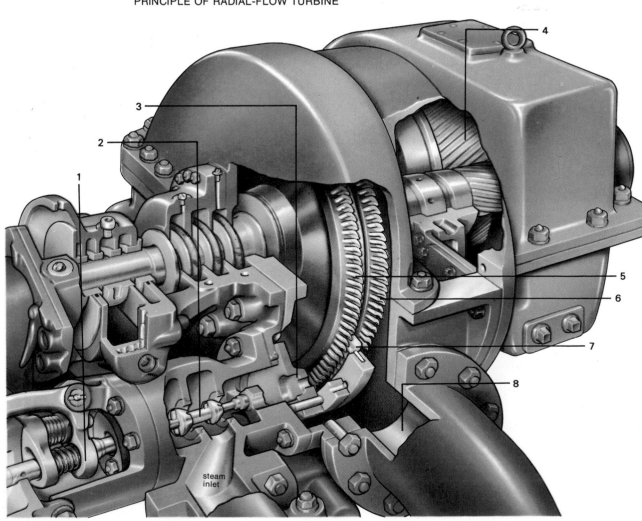

SINGLE-STAGE VELOCITY-COMPOUNDED TURBINE

1. Inlet valve governing mechanism
2. Inlet valve
3. Steam nozzle
4. Speed reduction gears
5. Moving blades (first set)
6. Moving blades (second set)
7. Intermediary fixed blades
8. Steam outlet

Above: The rotor and blades of the first turbine built by Sir Charles Parsons in 1884. The steam entered at the centre and flowed outwards towards the ends, turning the rotor at 18,000 rpm. The turbine was used to drive an electricity generator on board a ship and it remained in use for 16 years.

Below: This miniature turbine set was used in the Second World War to provide electricity for paratroops' radio and signals equipment. A fire was lit beneath the boiler to the left, and the steam was passed through the hoses to the generator turbine on the right. Power output was about 48 watts (8 amps at 6 volts).

Right: The rotor of a large power station turbine. As the blades used in the low pressure stages are so long, at a speed of 3000 rpm the tips of the blades may be moving at over 1½ times the speed of sound. The blades are made of high grade steel alloy to withstand the speed, heat and erosion by the steam.

1958, several uniflow cylinders being used in parallel for the largest. A five-cylinder German engine of the 1930s produced 22,371 kW (30,000 hp) to drive a rolling mill in a steelworks, and was the most powerful steam engine ever built.

Steam engine applications

Almost every type of machine that moves has at some time been driven by steam, either directly or through shafts and belts. In Victorian times the steam engine provided the power to print newspapers, spin and weave textiles, pump water, and power washing machines in 'steam laundries'. Portable steam engines ploughed and drained the land, threshed corn, drove fairground machines and even vacuum cleaners for cleaning-contractors. There were even steam driven scalp massage brushes in some barbers' shops.

Most of these applications will never return, but one which may be revived is the steam car. Several types were built in considerable numbers before the First World War, but went out of favour as the petrol engined car grew more efficient.

Steam turbines

The first practical steam turbines were built in the late nineteenth century by Carl De Laval in Sweden and Sir Charles Parsons in England. The main working part of a turbine is a rotor, which carries a set of blades, and is contained inside a casing which has a set of fixed blades to direct the flow of steam. A rotor can be regarded as a sort of windmill, each blade being a sail and the flow of steam acting like an enormously strong wind.

Expanding steam moves very fast: for example, expansion from a pressure of about twelve times atmospheric pressure down to about half atmospheric pressure produces a velocity of about 1100 m/sec (3600 ft/sec). The optimum speed of the moving blades for the transfer of kinetic energy from the steam to the rotor is half that of the steam. For instance, in the above example the ideal rotor speed would be 550 m/sec (1800 ft/sec). This is not always possible to achieve, however, and so the turbine may not be able to extract all the available energy from the steam.

Excessive steam speeds which can lead to this kind of energy loss are often avoided by using several sets of fixed and moving blades, and allowing only a fraction of the total pressure drop to occur in each set. Such turbines are said to be pressure-compounded. The blades are made progressively longer from the inlet to the exhaust end to allow room for the greater volume of steam at the lower pressures. This is comparable to the progressive increase in the size of the cylinders of a compound steam engine, where the high pressure cylinder is smaller than the intermediate and low pressure cylinders.

When a large pressure drop cannot be avoided, the steam leaving a row of moving blades is often re-directed on to a second, and sometimes a third, row of moving blades without further expansion. This sytem is called velocity-compounding.

There are two basic classes of turbine blading: impulse, in which the steam expands only in the fixed blades, and reaction, in which the steam expands in both the fixed and the moving blades. Steam has to be admitted to the whole circumference of the rotor when reaction blading is used, but impulse blading can be worked with some of the inlet nozzles shut off if required. Large turbines often have both types of blading, carried by several rotors in separate casings.

Power station turbines

The very large turbines used in power stations run at constant speeds, the speed being determined by the mains frequency of the system for which they are generating electricity. In most European countries, for instance, the frequency is 50 Hz (50 cycles per second) and the speed of the turbines is 3000 rpm. In North America, the frequency is 60 Hz and so the turbine speed is 3600 rpm.

A single line of rotors driving one alternator (ac generator) is used for powers up to 300 MW (300,000 kW). Two lines, interconnected on the steam side but with separate alternators, are used for greater power, sometimes as much as 600 MW. Such turbines are called cross-compounded.

Double-flow rotors, in which steam is admitted half-way along the cylinder and expands outwards towards both ends, are often used. These avoid excessive blade lengths for handling the large volumes of steam at the low pressure end and balance the pressure thrusts of reaction blading. The low pressure ends of the largest turbines comprise several double-flow rotors working in parallel.

Marine turbines

Smaller turbines are used in ships than in power stations because their size and speed must suit propeller requirements. The turbine may drive the propeller shaft through a set of reduction gears, or it may drive a generator which powers an electric motor that in turn drives the propeller shaft.

Large marine turbines are cross-compounded to save length. For example, the Queen Elizabeth II has two turbines, each developing 41,013 kW (55,000 hp) from two cross-compound rotors, one impulse and one double-flow reaction.

389

Jets and Gas Turbines

The invention of the jet engine had a tremendous impact on aviation. The world's first military jet was the German Messerschmitt Me 262, which went into service as a light bomber in 1944, and the first jet airliner was the de Havilland Comet, which made its first commercial flight on 2 May 1952. The jet engine is now extremely important in the field of aviation, but the gas turbine engine from which it was derived is also important in many others areas, including marine propulsion and electricity generation.

In both the gas turbine and the jet engine, air is drawn in at the front and compressed. Then fuel is burned in the compressed air, and the resulting gases expand rapidly through a turbine section.

One of the earliest patents for a gas turbine engine operating on similar principles to modern ones was that issued to John Barber in England in 1791, but the first successful engines were not built

Dave Hoskings

Right: The Rolls-Royce Pegasus vectored-thrust turbofan used by the Harrier vertical take-off jet. The jet exhaust is emitted through the ducts at the sides of the engine, which can be angled to direct the thrust downwards for take-off, to the rear for forward flight, or to the front to make the plane fly backwards.

Left: The Concorde uses four Rolls-Royce/SNECMA Olympus 593 Mk 602 turbojet engines, each developing 17,260 kg (38,050 lb) thrust.

Right: An Olympus 593 engine. The original Olympus engines were developed in the early 1950s, and turboshaft versions are used in ships and generators.

Right: The Vickers Viscount airliner uses four Rolls-Royce Dart RDa 7/1 Mk 525 turboprop engines, each developing 1484 kW (1990 hp).

Far right: A Pratt and Whitney JT9D turbofan on a Boeing 747 airliner. The JT9D-7W version of this engine produces 21,320 kg (47,000 lb) of thrust.

Picturepoint / ZEFA

Left: A Lynx helicopter is driven by a pair of Rolls-Royce BS 360 Gem turboshaft engines mounted side-by-side behind the main rotor shaft. The engines, capable of producing 670 kW (900 hp) each, drive the rotor via a reduction gearbox, and a transmission shaft takes the drive to the tail rotor.

Right: The McDonnell Douglas DC-10 airliner is powered by three General Electric CF6-50A turbofans, two of which are mounted under the wings with the third, shown here, in the tail.

Below: Checking a Rolls-Royce RB211 turbofan with an X-ray camera mounted on a fork lift truck.

ZEFA

Rolls Royce

until the early twentieth century.

The Swiss firm of Brown-Boveri ran a successful gas turbine in 1906 which was identical in principle to modern engines. This engine had an *axial* compressor, so named because the air enters and flows through it parallel to the axis of rotation of the compressor. The compressor consists of a series of discs or rings, each carrying blades projecting radially like spokes, which are assembled into a strong, light drum capable of rotating at high speed.

This compressor *rotor* revolves inside a closely fitting casing which has sets of stationary blades (*stator* blades) which just fit between the revolving blades of the rotor. When the rotor is spinning at high speed, air is drawn in and compressed as it passes through the sets or *stages* of fixed and moving blades, before being discharged at the rear of the compressor.

In early engines as many as 20 stages of blading were needed for a pressure ratio of 3:1, that is, for the outlet air to be at three times the pressure of the inlet air. Today it is possible to build compressors of much higher efficiency, which can achieve a pressure ratio of 30:1 with twelve stages.

With such high compression the air

John Ross/Robert Harding

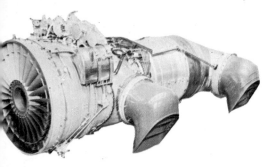

becomes so hot that the downstream stages have to be made of *refractory* (heat resistant) alloys.

From the compressor, the hot, high pressure air is fed through the combustion chamber where the fuel is added to it. A few gas turbines have run on pulverized coal or peat, but almost all use liquid fuels. An advantage of these engines is their ability to run on a wide range of fuels and, although most run on kerosene, it is possible to run gas turbines on heavy oils, high-octane petrol or natural gas.

An enormous amount of heat energy can be generated within the combustion chamber of a modern engine. As much as 37,350 kW (50,000 hp) can be produced in a combustion chamber whose volume is less than that of a briefcase.

From the combustion chamber the gas, now at perhaps 1300°C (2372°F), flows at high speed through the turbine section of the engine. Like the compressor, this consists of several axial stages, each separated by a row of stator blades which direct the flow on to the row of rotor blades immediately downstream, causing the rotor to revolve at high speed.

The rotor drives the compressor, usually by means of a simple drive shaft. It may also drive the machinery that the turbine is powering, or additional turbines may be used for this purpose.

Turboprops and turboshafts

The *turboprop* engine is a gas turbine engine which drives an aircraft propeller. The drive is taken from the turbine to the propeller via a gearbox because of the great difference in the rotational speeds of the rotor and the propellor.

For example, the Canadian Pratt and Whitney PT6 engine, used on many light transport planes such as those built by de Havilland of Canada, has a drive ratio of 15:1, linking a 33,000 rpm turbine with a 2,200 rpm propeller. The latest version has a 22.74:1 gearbox ratio, the 30,017 rpm turbine driving a larger propeller at only 1,320 rpm for lower noise.

In some engines, instead of having one turbine to drive both the compressor and the propeller, there are two turbines. The gas from the combustion chamber passes first through the compressor drive turbine, and then through the *free turbine*, which is mounted on a separate shaft to the compressor and its turbine. The propeller gearbox drive is taken from this shaft.

Sometimes a free-turbine type of turboprop is installed 'back to front', with the compressor at the rear and an arrange-

Right: The Rolls-Royce RB211 turbofan has three shafts or 'spools', carrying the low, intermediate and high pressure turbines and compressors (the low pressure compressor being the fan). The Lockheed L-1011-200 TriStar is powered by three RB211-524 engines, which deliver 21,775 kg (48,000 lb) thrust each.

Rolls-Royce RB-211
1 ip turbine
2 lp turbine
3 hp turbine
4 annular combustors
5 bleed air cooling
6 hp compressor discs
7 hp compressor blades
8 ip compressor discs
9 ip compressor blades
10 fan casing
11 guide vanes
12 33-blade titanium fan
13 inlet guide vanes
14 lp (fan) shaft
15 shaft coupling
16 engine core
17 ip shaft
18 hp shaft
19 rear shaft bearings
20 turbine discs
21 tail cone

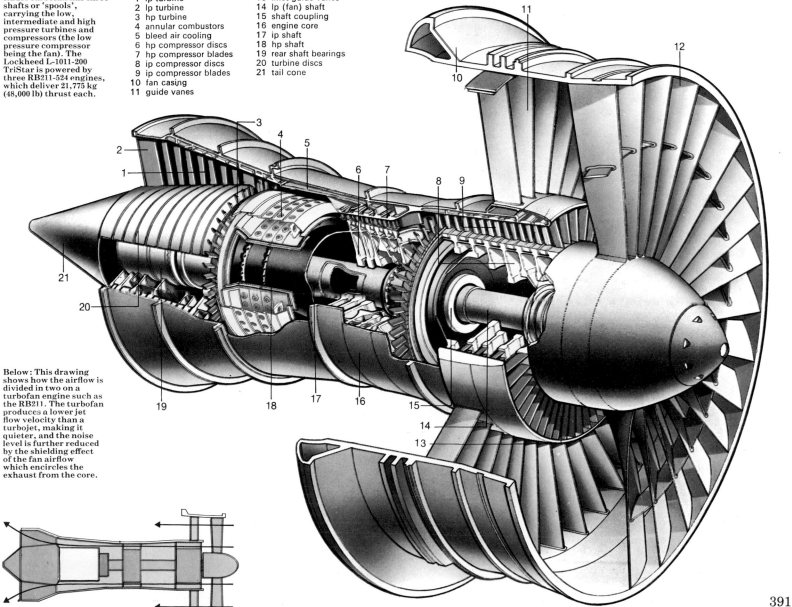

Below: This drawing shows how the airflow is divided in two on a turbofan engine such as the RB211. The turbofan produces a lower jet flow velocity than a turbojet, making it quieter, and the noise level is further reduced by the shielding effect of the fan airflow which encircles the exhaust from the core.

ment of ducts and vents to guide the inlet air into the compressor and deflect the exhaust gases away from the inlet. This simplifies the drive shaft arrangements which would be necessary to drive a front propeller if the engine were installed in the normal way.

Turboprops are nowadays used mainly for smaller military, private and business aircraft. The need for a reduction in noise levels in some areas, for example at inner-city airports, has led to the development of the *prop fan* engine, in which rear-mounted propellors have fewer blades but are more aerodynamically efficient, with the result that performance is quieter and therefore more acceptable.

Turboshafts are gas turbines used as a source of shaft power. They are used to drive naval craft of all kinds, fast container ships, hydrofoils, hovercraft, trains, electricity generators, and large-scale oil and gas pumping units. They are also being developed for use in heavy road trucks and other vehicles.

Turbojets and turbofans

The first jet engines were developed independently in the 1930s by Frank Whittle in England and Dr. Hans von Ohain in Germany. The jet is basically a gas turbine engine; the essential difference is that the turbine section extracts only a part of the energy of the gas flow. This extracted energy is just sufficient to drive the compressor in a *turbojet* or the compressor and a fan in a *turbofan*. The rest is used to accelerate the gas out through a nozzle at the rear of the engine —so driving the aircraft forward.

Newton's third law of motion states that for every action there is an equal but opposite reaction. In the case of the jet engine, pushing large amounts of gas rearwards at high velocity is the action, and the reaction to this is the forward thrust on the engine.

Whittle's first engine ran in April 1937, and the first British jet plane the Gloster E28/39 flew in May 1941. By the end of the Second World War, refined forms of this engine had been built in Britain and the USA for use in fighter aircraft.

Whittle's engine used a *centrifugal* compressor, because despite being fatter and less efficient than an axial compressor it was already well developed and easier to make. This type of compressor is essentially a spinning disc on which curved walls fling the airflow outwards at high velocity. Around the disc, often called the *impeller*, is a fixed deflector or *diffuser* in which the airflow is turned rearwards and slowed down. Its pressure rises as it is slowed.

Centrifugal compressor technology has since developed greatly, and almost all gas turbines designed for light planes, road vehicles, and small stationary power units use these cheap and robust compressors. At speeds higher than 30,000 rpm they can develop a pressure ratio exceeding 7:1.

Whittle's engines used an array of separate combustion chambers or 'cans' and expelled the gas discharged from the turbine through a simple short nozzle. Such an engine is called a *turbojet*. It is the simplest of all gas turbines, but tends to be noisy and is less efficient in aircraft propulsion until supersonic speeds are reached.

Since 1950 the gap between the noisy, high-speed turbojet and the quieter low-speed turboprop has been filled by a broad range of engines at first called *ducted fans*, but today called *turbofans*. Some early types were aft-fan engines, in which an additional turbine was added to the rear of the jet and provided with very long blades, which acted on the air flowing past the outside of the engine, rather like a multi-bladed propeller.

Nowadays the fan is mounted at the front of the engine, and it is essentially an oversized axial compressor, usually having one (but often as many as four) stages. The air it compresses is divided into two parts. That compressed by the inner part of the fan enters the main compressor and passes through what is known as the 'core' of the engine.

The core consists of the compressors, combustion chamber and turbines. In the Pratt and Whitney TFE 731 engine, for example, there is a four-stage low pressure axial compressor, a single stage high pressure radial compressor, an annular combustion chamber, then a single stage high pressure and a three stage low pressure turbine.

The rest of the fan airflow, which is usually from two to six times greater than that passing into the core, is discharged through a separate outer fan duct and used to provide forward thrust, rather like the rearward airflow from a propeller. If the fan is designed to run at a lower speed than the turbine, it is driven from a reduction gearbox mounted in front of the compressor.

The turbofan creates a greater rearward flow than the turbojet, but at a lower velocity. This reduction in the jet flow velocity makes it very much quieter. The turbofan is today by far the most important aero engine (except for light aircraft). The latest designs have three separate shafts, each rotating at its own best speed. One carries the fan, one an intermediate pressure (ip) compressor, and the third the high pressure (hp) compressor. Each shaft has its own turbine and the shafts are concentric (mounted one within the other), with the hp shaft outermost.

Afterburners

Engines for supersonic aircraft need to be slim but powerful. Most modern military aircraft compromise by using a turbofan with a low *by-pass ratio*—the ratio of the fan or secondary airstream to the core or primary airstream. In these military engines the fan airflow is not much greater than the core airflow.

Virtually all supersonic aircraft have an afterburner which adds fuel to the gas flow downstream of the turbine. The fuel burns in the gas, giving a much higher jet velocity and temperature. This gives extra thrust, but at the expense of greatly increased fuel consumption, and so it is used mainly for take-off and in the case of military aircraft, to give more engine power during combat manoeuvres.

An engine which has an afterburning or *reheat* system has to have a propelling nozzle whose diameter can be reduced when afterburning is not in use. As the nozzle is a large item, subject to severe stresses at about 1200°C (2200°F), it is not easy to make it open and close. The most common method is to use rings of inner and outer 'petal' flaps which are accurately positioned by hydraulic or pneumatic actuators located in cooler areas away from the nozzle.

The series of six diagrams on the right show the underlying principles of the gas turbine engine, and the way it can be used to drive a car or a truck.

In the first diagram, an electric fan is drawing in air and blowing it through a hollow cylinder, rather like a turbine compressor blowing air through the engine core. If a freely mounted fan is placed at the end of the cylinder, as in the second drawing, the airflow from the electric fan will make it rotate, like a turbine rotor. If heat energy is added to the airflow between the two fans, the air will expand and accelerate, creating enough energy to enable the second fan to drive the first, as in the third diagram, and the electric motor can be dispensed with.

In a turbine, this heat energy is supplied by burning fuel in a combustion chamber between the compressor and the rotor, and the engine is started by an electric starter motor or by blowing compressed air through it. If sufficient energy is produced by heating the air between the fans, only part of it will be needed to drive them.

The remaining energy can be used to drive a third fan, shown in the fourth diagram, and a load. In a gas turbine, this third fan is the free or power turbine and it is used to drive, for example, an aircraft or ship propeller, the wheels of a car or a truck, or an electricity generator. Any heat energy remaining in the gas after it has driven the third fan can be used to help heat the air from the first fan before fuel is burnt in it, and thus less fuel has to be burned to raise the turbine gas to its working temperature.

The heat from the exhaust gas is transferred to the air from the first fan in a device called a heat exchanger, as in the fifth drawing. The final drawing shows how the simple fans and other components shown in the other drawings relate to the components of an actual gas turbine engine. The advantage of having the power turbine on a separate shaft is that the speed of the compressor is unaffected by the load on the power turbine.

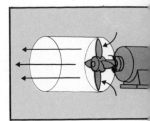

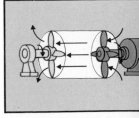

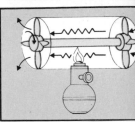

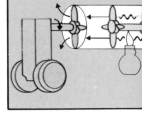

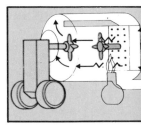

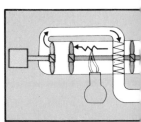

British Leyland

Left: The experimental Rover-BRM gas turbine engined sports car taking part in the Le Mans 24-hour race in 1965. It finished the race with an average speed of 160.6 kph (99.8 mph).

Right: A gas turbine powered frigate. Gas turbines are used in many types of ship, and are usually adapted from aero engines.

Below: A mobile gas turbine powered generating unit used to provide emergency electricity supplies.

British Leyland

Vosper Thorneycroft

Centrax

Right: The British Leyland LG 800R gas turbine truck engine. It is started by a 24 V electric starter motor, which accelerates the compressor while fuel is sprayed into the combustion chamber and ignited by an electric ignitor plug. Once the engine has reached a quarter of its top speed the starter and ignitor are switched off, and the engine accelerates up to its idling speed, which is half its top speed.

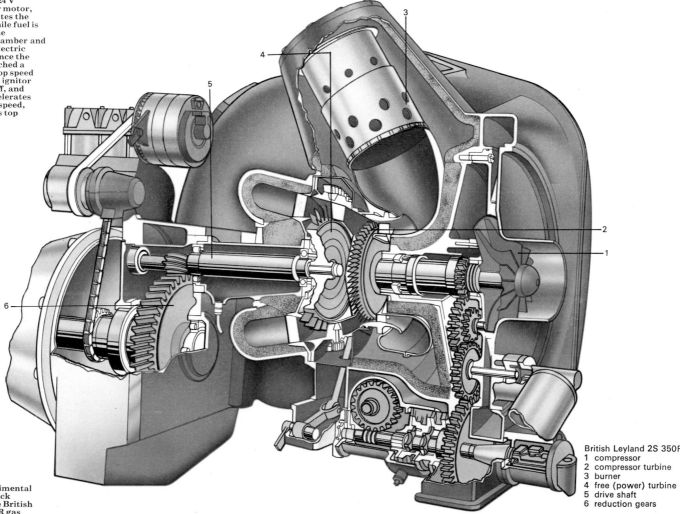

Left: An experimental articulated truck powered by the British Leyland 2S 350R gas turbine engine, a cutaway drawing of which is shown above right. The engine produces 260-300 kW (350-400 hp), can run on either petrol or diesel oil, and is designed for a life of 12,000 hours without major breakdowns.

British Leyland 2S 350R
1 compressor
2 compressor turbine
3 burner
4 free (power) turbine
5 drive shaft
6 reduction gears

Medical Technology

Doctors have always sought to use physical and engineering principles to help their patients. By their own ingenuity, or with the help of craftsmen or engineers, they have devised mechanisms like splints or 'peg-legs' which would help in times of injury or allow the patient to cope with handicap. The enormous progress made in the last few decades is, however, largely due to the emergence of a new profession, the bioengineer or medical physicist, working in close conjunction with medical personnel to use the potential of modern technology in the fields of health care. This has led to a whole range of developments, from the most complex achievements to such simple innovations as the plastic disposable syringe—which have had a major impact on practical medicine.

X-rays and nuclear radiations

X-rays, also called Roentgen rays after their discoverer, are a type of penetrating electromagnetic radiation which is created when electrons, accelerated in a vacuum by very high voltages (20,000 to 1,000,000 volts), are suddenly arrested by impact into a target. Their extraordinary usefulness in diagnosis is due to the fact that their absorption varies from tissue to tissue, being least in air-containing structures and greatest in bone. Thus the

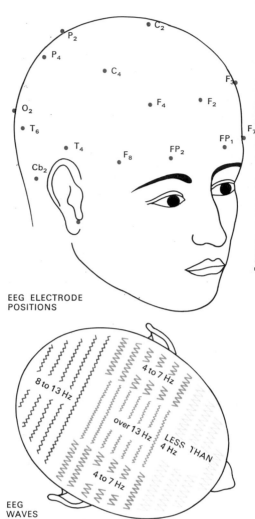

EEG ELECTRODE POSITIONS

EEG WAVES

8 to 13 Hz
4 to 7 Hz
over 13 Hz
LESS THAN 4 Hz
4 to 7 Hz

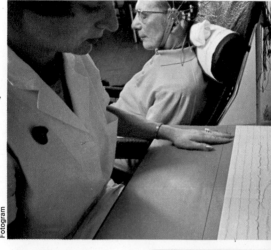

Fotogram

Above: The electrical activity of the brain can be examined by an electroencephalograph (eeg). The minute electrical impulses produced in the brain are picked up by electrodes attached to the scalp, and the eeg produces a chart which shows the waveforms detected from various parts of the brain.

Left: The upper diagram shows points on the scalp at which the electrodes are placed, and the lower shows the typical frequencies of brain waves detected at various areas around the scalp. If a patient's waves differ significantly from those expected, then some form of brain malfunction or damage is indicated.

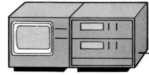

bedside instrumentation
ECG pulse rate blood
pressure temperature etc)

PATIENT MONITORING SYSTEM

bedside instrumentation

STARPAHC HEALTH SYSTEM

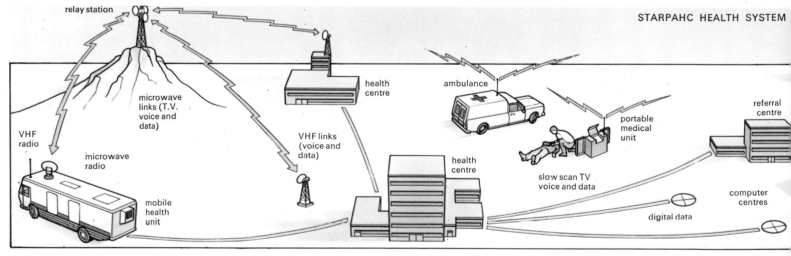

relay station

microwave links (T.V. voice and data)

VHF radio

microwave radio

mobile health unit

VHF links (voice and data)

health centre

ambulance

health centre

slow scan TV voice and data

portable medical unit

referral centre

computer centres

digital data

Lockheed

Above: The STARPAHC (Space Technology Applied to Rural Papago Advanced Health Care) system provides medical services to the Papago Indian reservation in Arizona, US. Mobile medical teams visit villages on the reservation. They are linked by VHF radio to health centres and computer centres which provide them with specialist information and advice. STARPAHC was developed initially by NASA and Lockheed in order to evaluate health care systems for use by astronauts during long missions.

Left: A STARPAHC Mobile Health Unit.

Right: A physician's console at one of the Health Centres.

Lockheed

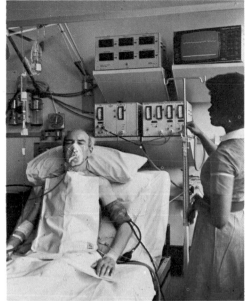

normal ECG trace

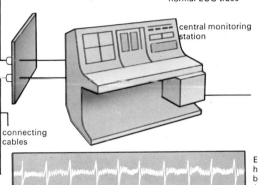

central monitoring station

connecting cables

ECG of heart beating very fast (120 beats per minute)

Below: An EMI-Scanner CT1010, a computer-assisted tomography unit which produces X-ray images of cross-sections of the brain and skull. The X-ray tube and detectors surround the patient's head and are rotated 3° at a time. The machine produces images of two cross-sections during each scan, which takes 60 seconds. Three scans are needed to image the whole brain, which takes a total of about 10 minutes. Whole-body scanners are also now in service.

remote monitor

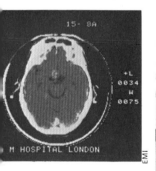

M HOSPITAL LONDON

Above: A scan taken by an EMI-Scanner at the Atkinson Morley's Hospital, London.

Below: The scanning pattern and basic system of an EMI-Scanner CT1010.

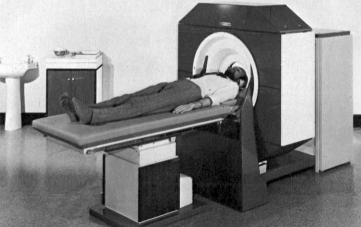

EMI-SCANNER CT1010

X-ray tube steps round 3° at a time

reference detector

scan detector array

monitor

control and viewing console

keyboard

X-ray control

line printer

computer and electronics unit

magnetic tape unit

data transfer module

diagnostic display console

disc store

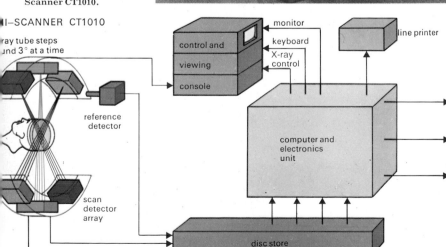

shadowgraph picture, produced by interposing part of the body between the X-ray tube and a photographic film (which is darkened by X-rays), will show fractures in bones, wear in joints or abnormalities in the lungs.

A different application of X-rays, and of the even more penetrating gamma-radiation given off by radium or artificial radioactive isotopes, is in the treatment of cancer. The destructive effect of these rays in high dosage is much greater for some tumours than for the surrounding healthy tissues. Careful adjustment of dose and concentration of the radiation in the tumour area, by the use of different but overlapping approach routes, will arrest the growth of a tumour, or destroy it altogether with minimal effect on surrounding tissue.

The equipment for generating X-rays consists of a high-voltage generator connected to the X-ray tube by heavily insulated cables. In this vacuum tube, the electrons given off by a heated filament are accelerated towards a spot on a target, where some of their energy is converted into X-radiation when they strike it. The tube is heavily shielded by lead cladding to confine the emission of X-rays to the wanted direction. Much of the bulk of modern machines is made up of equipment for adjusting the patient's position so that the beam is correctly directed and by provision for holding the photographic plates or direct-viewing devices.

To produce the most penetrating radiation, the electrons must be accelerated to energy levels greater than those which can be conveniently provided by a transformer power supply. When this type of radiation is required, the electrons are accelerated in particle accelerators such as betatrons or travelling-wave linear electron accelerators, devices in which a relatively low voltage is used over and over again in accelerating the electrons.

Computer-assisted tomography is a special X-ray technique capable of imaging cross-sections of the head or body with good contrast between tissues which cannot be visualized by conventional techniques. The X-ray source and a radiation detector, which measures the intensity of a narrow beam of X-rays as it emerges after passage through the tissues, are moved in a compound pattern so that each part of the section is traversed by the beam in several directions.

Measurements of the absorption experienced by the ray in its various directions of transit are fed into a computer which forms part of the machine. This calculates with great accuracy how much of the beam was absorbed in each minute region. The local brightness of a cathode ray tube display is then modulated so as to map the pattern of absorption in the cross-section. Organs having slightly different X-ray absorptions can be visualized and abnormalities of, say, the blood content of the different tissues noted. This powerful technique has greatly extended the range of conditions in which X-rays can give diagnostic information.

Isotope scanning is another technique used for similar purposes. Diseased tissue will often take up disproportionate amounts of compounds containing radioactive isotopes, which are introduced into the patient's circulation. As these emit X-rays or gamma-rays to the outside, regions where concentration has taken place can be detected by passing Geiger counters or other radiation-sensitive devices over the patient and noting where increased activity is present.

Ultrasonics

Ultrasound or ultrasonics, sound vibrations at frequencies beyond the upper limit of human hearing, is used in medicine in three different ways: as a therapeutic (healing) medium, for soft tissue imaging and for observing the motion of the heart or blood. Quartz or other piezoelectric materials are used to turn a high-frequency electrical oscillation (1-10 MHz) into a mechanical vibration at the same frequency. Devices such as these which convert one form of energy into another, in this case electrical into mechanical, are known as *transducers*. The beam of ultrasonic vibration is then transmitted into the body via a thin film of oil or aqueous (water-based) jelly.

In therapeutic applications, power levels of the order of a watt per square centimetre are used to produce accelerated healing of injuries, but just how this happens is still not fully understood. In the other two applications, the power levels are too low to have any effect on the tissues. The transmitting transducer, or a separate receiving transducer, translates some of the energy which is reflected by the tissues in the path of the beam into electrical waveforms.

For soft tissue visualization, the transmitting transducer is energized periodically and emits brief bursts of waves. Reflections from interfaces at increasing depths will be received with increasing delays from the time of their transmission. A map of the interfaces encountered in a section of the body is produced as follows. A spot on the cathode ray tube is deflected from a starting position, representing the position of the transducer, in the direction of the beam at a speed which corresponds to the speed of the ultrasound in tissue. The spot is brightened up whenever reflections are received. As the clinician moves the transducer so as to sweep the beam through the section, the pattern of brightness on the oscilloscope tube shows the position of organ boundaries and changes in tissue density. A common application of this technique is to follow the development of the foetus in the mother's womb.

If the reflecting interface is moving, the frequency of the reflected ultrasound will differ slightly from that of the transmitted beam. This phenomenon, the *Doppler effect*, permits the detection of moving interfaces within the body and also under favourable circumstances allows the speed of motion to be measured. The beating of the foetal heart can thus be detected by ultrasonic Doppler instruments from the tenth week of pregnancy.

An expanding use of this principle is in the measurement of the speed of blood flow in various vessels, the red blood cells acting as ultrasonic reflectors. Abnormalities of the pulsating pattern of flow in limb arteries points to the presence of obstructions. Cardiac function may also be monitored by Doppler measurements of blood velocity in the aorta, the main artery leading from the heart.

Electrophysiological instruments

Much useful information can be obtained about function in certain parts of the body

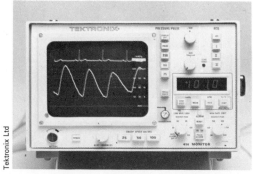

Tektronix Ltd

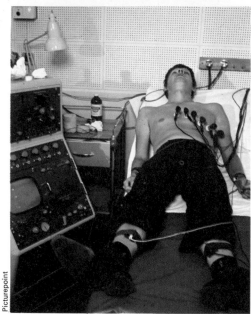

Picturepoint

Above: A patient connected to an electrocardiograph machine. The electrodes on the chest pick up the signals from the heart, and those on the arms and legs provide reference voltages that enable the heart signals to be correctly interpreted. The lead on the right leg is an earth connection.

Below: A diagram of a heart-lung machine, with an exploded view of the oxygenator on the left. The heart-lung machine takes over the functions of the heart and lungs during major heart surgery. The oxygenator removes carbon dioxide gas from the blood and adds oxygen to it before it returns to the patient.

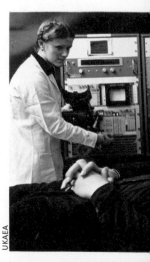

Left: The Tektronix 414 Portable Monitor has a dual-trace oscilloscope display which shows the patient's ecg pattern (upper trace) and blood pressure (lower trace). The digital display can show either heart rate, blood pressures or blood temperature.

Below: An MEL SL75-20 linear accelerator which produces high-intensity radiation for the treatment of cancer tumours. Many forms of tumour tissue are much more susceptible to high doses of radiation than are the healthy tissues surrounding them, and so they can often be destroyed by radiation therapy. This machine operates at an energy level of 20 million electron-volts (20 MeV).

UKAEA

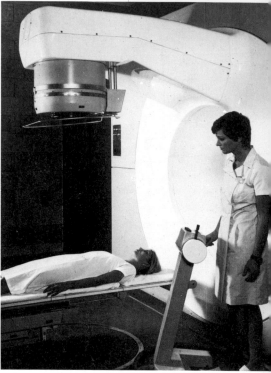

M.E.L. Equipment Ltd

HEART-LUNG MACHINE

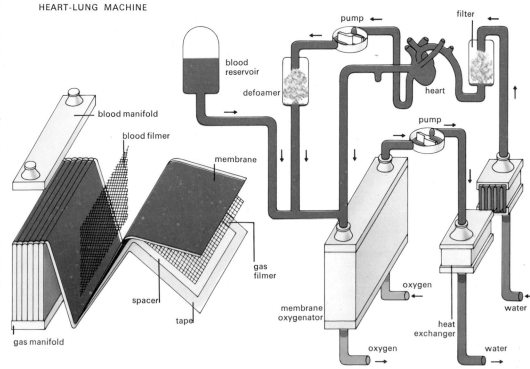

blood manifold

blood filmer

membrane

spacer

tape

gas manifold

gas filmer

blood reservoir

defoamer

pump

filter

heart

pump

membrane oxygenator

oxygen

heat exchanger

oxygen

water

water

396

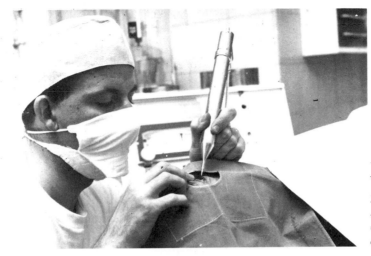

Above: Holography is a three-dimensional photographic technique originally based on interference patterns between two laser beams. This machine uses ultrasonic waves in place of lasers to produce holographic pictures of the eye for diagnostic purposes.

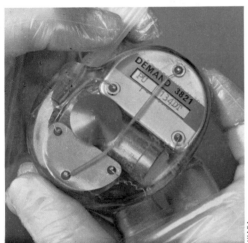

Above: This instrument developed for eye operations has a metal probe which is cooled by liquid helium to —120°C. Used like a scalpel, it can remove cataracts and 'weld' back detached retinas, operations which can also be performed by using heat created by laser beams.

Left: A heart pacemaker powered by a nuclear battery, which is implanted into the patient and maintains regular heart operation by stimulating it electrically.

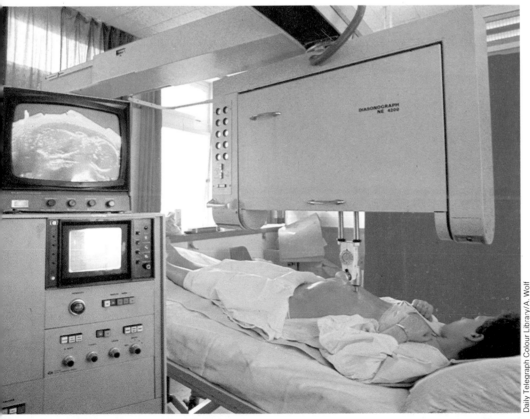

Above: A woman undergoing an ultrasound scan during her later stages of pregnancy. The outline of the womb and foetus can be seen on the screen (left) and any visible abnormality can be detected. This is a less invasive and so generally safer technique than the use of X-rays.

by observing the minute voltages which accompany muscle contractions and the passage of nerve impulses. *Action voltages* of about 1/20 volt can be picked up in their immediate vicinity, but it is also possible to sense the much smaller voltages which are transmitted to the body surface by using electrodes applied to the skin to determine the activity of underlying nerves and muscles. Specially constructed amplifiers are used to display the observed waveform by deflection of the spot on a cathode-ray tube or of the pen in a paper recorder.

A widely used electrophysiological instrument is the *electrocardiograph* (ECG) which gives information about activity of the heart from voltages picked up on the chest wall or even from the extremities. A comparison of the waveforms recorded from various electrode positions is useful in determining the location and extent of damage which may have occurred in, for example, the muscular wall of the heart. It is also possible to observe whether the muscle mass of the heart contracts in regular sequence, so that defects in the nervous pathways which co-ordinate the atrial and ventricular contractions may be detected.

Another application of electrocardiography is to the detection of rhythm disturbances (*arrythmias*). Occasional irregularities occur in normal health—'when I saw it happen, my heart missed a beat'—but potentially life-threatening ones may develop during a heart attack. Electrocardiographs are therefore widely used in coronary care units for patient-monitoring. Treatment of arrythmias in the early stages often prevents them from progressing to *asystole* (total stoppage of heart action) or a condition known as *ventricular fibrillation* in which the co-ordination of different parts of the ventricular muscle is totally lost and effective pumping stops.

A *defibrillator* can be used to restore co-ordinated contractions in the latter case. As Galvani showed when he applied a battery to a frog's leg—or anyone who has experienced an electric shock will remember—powerful muscular contractions are produced by currents which pass through the body. A defibrillator applies an electric shock of controlled magnitude, from a capacitor which has been charged to a high voltage, to the patient's heart via large electrodes placed on the chest. If the current is sufficient to cause the whole of the cardiac musculature to contract strongly at the same instant, synchronous contractions will often continue, so that co-ordinated heart action is restored.

The instrument which is used to record electrical activity from the brain is called an *electroencephalograph* (ecg). This differs from the electrocardiograph in that a number of recording channels are used simultaneously to display the electrical activity picked up by electrodes applied to various regions of the scalp, and that more sensitive amplifiers are required to amplify the weaker signals which reflect neuronal activity in a broad region underneath the electrodes. The waveform shape and frequency content of the recordings gives information on the nature of brain activity in alert, sleeping or unconscious subjects and allows regions of abnormal activity to be identified.

Calculators

One of the most widely-used calculating machines, the *abacus*, is also the most ancient. In one form or another it has been around for thousands of years, and millions are still in use all over Asia and the Soviet Union. The abacus consists of rows of beads, which represent the numbers, strung on rods or wires set in a rectangular frame, and although its operations are limited to basic arithmetic a skilled operator can use it, for the purposes needed, as fast as most people can use a modern electronic calculator.

The first real advances in calculating, after the abacus, came in the seventeenth century. In 1614, John Napier invented the system of calculating by means of *logarithms*. Ordinary logarithms are calculated as *powers* of the number 10, for example $100 = 10^2$, or 10 to the *power* of 2, and so its logarithm (to base 10) is 2.0000. The number 3, on the other hand, is $10^{0.4771}$, and so its logarithm is 0.4771.

Sets of tables, known as *log tables*, have been drawn up for use in calculations, and by using these it is possible to perform complicated multiplication and division by simply adding or subtracting logarithms. As a simple example, to multiply 3 by 4 the logarithms of 3 and 4, which are 0.4771 and 0.6021, are added together. This gives 1.0792, which, by reference to the tables, we find is the logarithm of 12, and so the result is 3 x 4 = 12. Division is carried out by the subtraction of logarithms; 12 divided by 3 would be 1.0792 − 0.4771, which is 0.6021, the logarithm of 4. The adding or subtracting of logarithms to perform multiplication or division is based on the *exponent law*, $10^a.10^b = 10^{a+b}$.

The invention of logarithms led to the development of the *slide rule* by Edmund Gunter and William Oughtred during the first part of the seventeenth century. In its simplest form the slide rule has two scales, one fixed and one moving, which are marked off in distances which are proportional to the logarithms of the numbers they represent. Adding or subtracting these distances, by sliding the moving scale along the fixed one, effectively adds or subtracts the logarithms of the numbers indicated on the scales, and so multiplies or divides them. The modern version of the slide rule is based on a design by Amédée Mannheim in 1859.

Mechanical calculators

The first mechanical calculating machine was invented by Blaise Pascal in France in 1642. This machine used the rotation of gear wheels to represent the numbers, and its design was subsequently refined by Gottfried Leibniz in 1671. Leibniz was the inventor of the *stepped wheel*, a device which was still used in certain types of mechanical calculator built as recently as the 1960s.

The ideas of Pascal and Leibniz were later bettered by the work of Baldwin, Odhner and Burkhardt in the late nineteenth century, who developed more compact and efficient designs. The design of mechanical calculators was steadily refined during the first half of the twentieth century, and electro-mechanical machines, which used an electric motor

Picturepoint

Erich Lessing/John Hillelson Agency

Above: The abacus is a form of calculating machine that has been in use for thousands of years. The original version, which was used in ancient Babylon, was probably a tray or board covered in sand, in which marks were made to perform the calculations. This picture shows a modern Japanese abacus.

Below: The first practical mechanical calculator was built by the French mathematician Blaise Pascal (1623-1662) in 1642. It consisted of a system of gears and numbered wheels. Although it could perform addition and subtraction it could not do multiplication or division.

Right: The linear slide rule consists of two sets of fixed scales, with a sliding set of scales in between them. The scales are calibrated logarithmically, so that multiplication and division are performed, in effect, by the addition or subtraction of lengths along the scales.

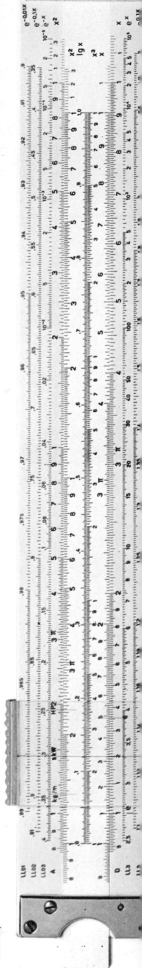

Dave Kelly

Left: A late 19th century adding machine.

Below: The upper two drawings show how a slide rule is used for multiplication. The top drawing shows how a slide rule multiplies 3 by 2; the *unity* ('1') mark on scale C is set at 2 on scale D. The cursor is placed over the 3 on the C scale, and the answer, 6, is where the cursor crosses the D scale. The middle drawing shows 5 x 3, and the way in which the position of the decimal point must be assessed by common sense—the answer is 15, not 1.5 as shown on the scale. The bottom drawing shows how D gives the square root of A, and C_1 gives the reciprocals of scale D.

to turn the gears that performed the calculations, were introduced.

Electronic calculators

The electronic calculator developed as a result of advances in electronic computer technology. The first computers were developed during the 1940s, and were enormous devices containing thousands of electronic valves. However, following the invention of the transistor in 1948, the size and power consumption of computer circuits decreased dramatically while reliability and complexity increased.

The first electronic calculator as such, based on computer circuit technology, was the Bell Punch Anita machine produced in Britain in 1963. It used thousands of discrete transistors in its circuitry, and by today's standards it was a cumbersome machine, but it marked the end of the era of the mechanical calculator based on the gear wheels of Leibniz and Pascal, as well as that of the slide rule based on Napier's logarithms.

With the introduction of integrated circuits by Fairchild and Texas Instruments in the early 1960s, the success of the electronic calculator was assured. An integrated circuit contains the equivalent of many thousands of transistors and their associated components, and is built up from a single chip of silicon which is about 0.3 cm square. The first compact calculator, based on an integrated circuit and using a light-emitting diode (led) readout display, was introduced in 1971, and since then calculator production has expanded enormously. Advances since then have produced calculators little bigger than credit cards, and prices are at almost throwaway levels.

Basic principles

The actual way in which an electronic calculator works is quite complex, but the basic principles can be explained by reference to the way in which simple calculations are performed.

The operation of a calculator is regulated by a *clock* circuit which, as its name implies, generates timing pulses that are used to synchronize the operations of the other sections of the machine. In a simple calculator the clock may operate at a rate of about 250,000 pulses per second, which would enable it to perform 250,000 operations in one second.

Calculators use a form of binary arithmetic to perform their calculations since, being based on the number 2, all binary numbers can be represented by

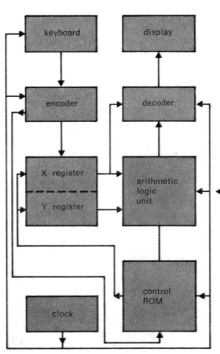

Left: A block diagram showing the relationships between the main sections of an electronic calculator. In the latest calculator designs, all the components apart from the keyboard, display and batteries are incorporated into a single integrated circuit chip about 0.3 cm square.

Far left: The latest space-age technology to affect the pocket calculator is a solar cell pack, which replaces the battery so the unit can be slimmer.

combinations of '1s' and '0s'. In a calculator, a '1' is present when a circuit is 'on', and a '0' when it is 'off'.

The form of binary arithmetic used by calculators is known as *binary coded decimal* (BCD), and the calculator contains an *encoder* which translates the decimal information from the keyboard into BCD, and a *decoder* which translates the BCD into decimal form to drive the output display.

In ordinary binary coding, the number '1010' represents the decimal number '10'; when read from right to left it represents no '1s', one '2', no '4s' and one '8'—a total of ten. In BCD, however, each *digit* of a decimal number is represented by a four-*bit* (binary digit) binary code, for example '87' would be 0001 1110 in BCD, which is read from left to right.

Simple calculations

Suppose we wish to do the calculation '5 + 9 = '. On each clock pulse the keyboard is *scanned*, and if there is a valid input present due to a key having been pressed it is sensed by the encoder, which then produces the BCD equivalent of the number.

The first number to be entered, 5, is encoded and then transferred to, and stored in, the *X register*, and it is also shown on the display. The next item to be entered from the keyboard is the *operator*, the ' + ' in this case, which is sensed by the encoder and sent to the

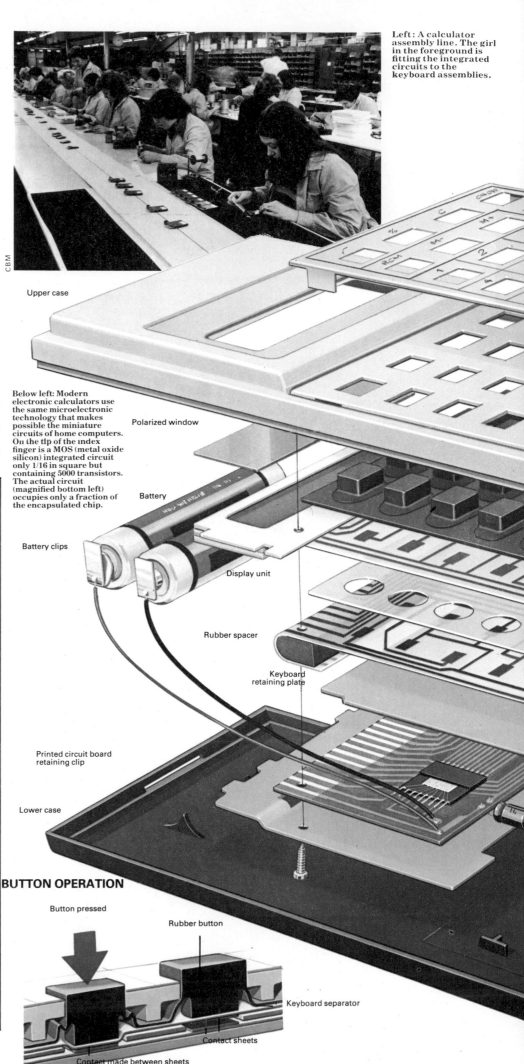

Left: A calculator assembly line. The girl in the foreground is fitting the integrated circuits to the keyboard assemblies.

CBM

Upper case

Below left: Modern electronic calculators use the same microelectronic technology that makes possible the miniature circuits of home computers. On the tip of the index finger is a MOS (metal oxide silicon) integrated circuit only 1/16 in square but containing 5000 transistors. The actual circuit (magnified bottom left) occupies only a fraction of the encapsulated chip.

Polarized window

Battery

Battery clips

Display unit

Rubber spacer

Keyboard retaining plate

Printed circuit board retaining clip

Lower case

BUTTON OPERATION

Button pressed

Rubber button

Keyboard separator

Contact sheets

Contact made between sheets

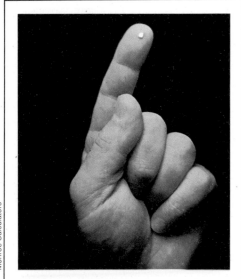

Monroe Calculators

Monroe Calculators

Burroughs

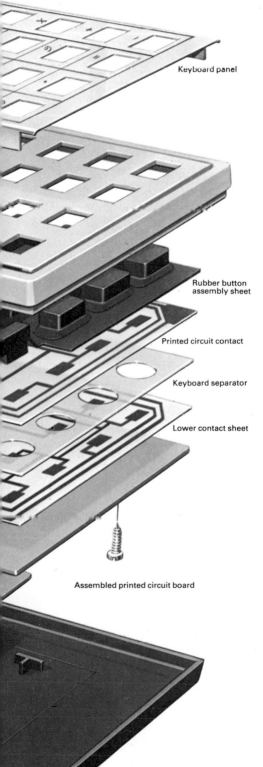

Keyboard panel

Rubber button assembly sheet

Printed circuit contact

Keyboard separator

Lower contact sheet

Assembled printed circuit board

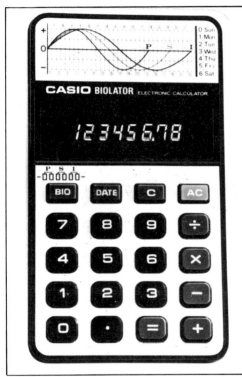

Automatic Business Machines Ltd

control ROM (Read-Only Memory) where it is stored. The control ROM is the 'brain' of the whole calculator, and it controls the operations of the *arithmetic logic unit* which performs the actual calculations.

The next number, 9, is then entered, and after encoding it is put into the X register, displacing the previous number, 5, into the *Y register*. The number 9 is shown by the display. When the 'equals' key is pressed to complete the calculation, the contents of the X and Y registers are read into the arithmetic logic unit where they are processed according to the operator stored in the control ROM. The answer, 14, is decoded and shown in the display.

Other forms of calculation, such as multiplication, subtraction and division, are carried out in a similar manner, under the control of the pre-programmed instructions of the ROM.

Complex calculations

When we consider more complex functions of a calculator, such as the calculation of square roots or trigonometrical ratios, the computing power of the calculator becomes apparent. Once again, these are done by addition-type processes, but the

numbers may pass through the arithmetic logic unit many times, with intermediate results being stored and recalled as required. These operations are controlled by built-in instruction programs called *algorithms*, the exact details of which are kept as trade secrets by the manufacturers. The better the algorithms used, the more accurate the calculator.

Simple calculators often have a *memory*, which is just another storage register similar to the X and Y registers, that can be controlled from the keyboard. A *constant* feature is often provided, which acts as a sort of limited memory in that the number is retained automatically in the Y register, and can thus be used for subsequent calculations without having to be re-entered through the keyboard each time it is needed.

On the newer and more advanced 'scientific' calculators, many extra features such as means, standard deviations, linear regression, combinations and factorials are available, in addition to logarithms, trigonometrical ratios and powers. These do not represent the peak of calculator design, however, because programmable machines, into which the user can program his or her own instructions to control the arithmetic logic unit, are also available (though threatened since the advent of 'home' computers).

In the less sophisticated programmables, the manufacturers have provided extra memory spaces so that a sequence of keystrokes for the solution of a particular equation can be 'remembered' and will operate on any number entered. This procedure saves time if the calculation has to be performed repetitively.

Unfortunately, the program is lost once the machine is turned off, and so they must be programmed each time they are used. This drawback may, however, be overcome by the development of new forms of memory circuits which retain their information even when the power supply has been switched off.

The more advanced programmable calculators have the programs retained on a small magnetic card which is put into the machine when required, the information on it being read and stored by the machine. With this type of machine, computer-like techniques can be used since calculation methods such as looping and conditional statements are possible. These pocket-sized machines are so powerful that their computing capacity far exceeds that of the first-generation computers, which occupied whole rooms and consumed tremendous amounts of electrical power.

Computers

Throughout history, man has attempted to produce mechanical aids to assist in the organisation and processing of information. The requirements have been for the storage of information, the processing of it in the form of sorting and arithmetic, and rapid retrieval of selected information.

Where the information to be processed is numeric, it can be represented either by a physical quantity, such as length or voltage, or by a combination of digits. In the first of these two methods, the physical feature used is said to be an *analogue* of the number. Possibly the best known example of this is the slide rule, in which a number is represented by a length proportional to its logarithm. This choice of representation enables the multiplication of two numbers to be performed by the addition of two lengths.

The modern analogue computer generally uses variable voltages to represent quantities, and it is particularly suited to performing computations on quantities which vary with time, and require the solution of differential equations.

In *digital* device, numbers are represented by positions on wheels, the fingers of the hands, or by a row of lights which represent the number in binary arithmetic. In the latter case, a light switched on would represent a binary '1' and a light switched off would represent a binary '0'.

Most examples of information processing do not require the particular aptitudes of analogue machines. They do, on the other hand, require an extensive storage capability and an ability to handle literal information, and for these requirements digital representation is appropriate. For this reason, the word 'computer' generally refers to the digital computer.

Personal computers.
Many people are now more familiar with computers than they ever thought they would be. In recent years, costs have fallen so dramatically and technology increased so rapidly that computers are now no longer room-filling monsters requiring numerous skilled staff to operate them. Instead, the *personal* or *home* computer is now a reality. Personal computers are widely used for playing sophisticated electronic games, but they are also capable of being useful round the house — helping with the homework, keeping the family budgets, maintaining names and address records for clubs and so on. And their use is widespread in business, too, for accounting, stock control, data management and word processing (producing letters and reports in electronic form so that they can be easily corrected and amended before being finally printed). It is not only small businesses that use personal computers — many large businesses use fleets of the machines for individual tasks, as well.

Personal computers form the *micro* end of the market. Slightly larger systems are referred to as *mini* computers, and for the largest tasks giant conventional computers — known as *mainframes* are still needed.

For any process to take place, with or without a computer, there must be some

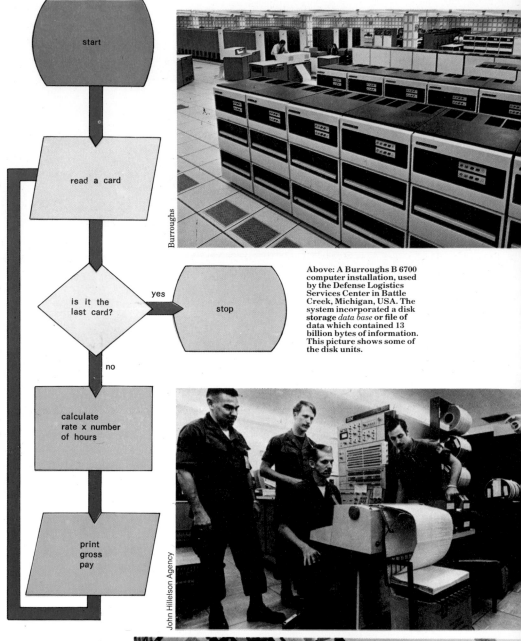

Burroughs

Above: A Burroughs B 6700 computer installation, used by the Defense Logistics Services Center in Battle Creek, Michigan, USA. The system incorporated a disk storage *data base* or file of data which contained 13 billion bytes of information. This picture shows some of the disk units.

John Hillelson Agency

Above: Programs are the computer's operating instructions. This simplified flow chart shows some of the steps of a payroll calculation program.

Above right: A computer used by the US Army to try and evaluate their progress during the war in Vietnam. This is an example of the use of a computer 'model' of a situation such as war; the machine analyzes changes in various aspects of the situation, and predicts their probable consequences.

Right: The computer of the Skylab 3 orbital laboratory. Computers have been essential to the development of spaceflight, not only by making it possible to perform all the necessary navigational calculations, but also by their ability to supervise functions such as spacecraft life-support systems.

Aspect

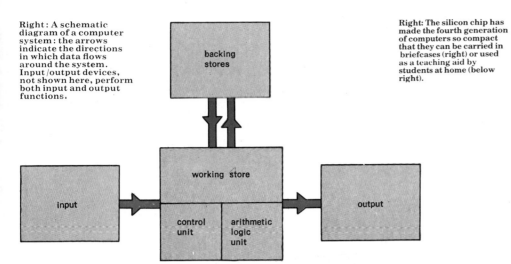

Commodore Electronics Ltd.

Photri

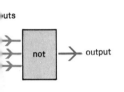

inputs			output
A	B	C	put
0	0	0	0
0	0	1	0
0	1	0	0
0	1	1	0
1	0	0	0
1	0	1	0
1	1	0	0
1	1	1	1

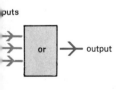

output			inputs	
A	B	C	or	ex or
0	0	0	0	0
0	0	1	1	1
0	1	0	1	1
0	1	1	1	0
1	0	0	1	1
1	0	1	1	0
1	1	0	1	0
1	1	1	1	0

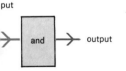

input	output
0	1
1	0

Commodore Electronics Ltd.

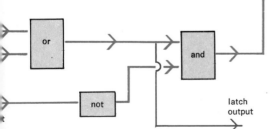

form of *input* to the process, the processing itself, and some result or *output*. The computer — whether micro, mini or mainframe — will always follow this essential pattern.

Input
The commonest form of input these days, whatever the size of computer, is the *vdu* (visual display unit) or *terminal*. Operators type in their information at typewriter-style keyboards and see their commands, and the feedback from the computer, displayed on a television-like screen. Changes and corrections to the information being fed in can be easily made, before the data are assimilated by the computer.

Processing
The input signals, which may represent data or instructions, pass as a pattern of pulses to the heart of the computer, the *central processing unit* (cpu). Here, the patterns are stored in an *immediate access* or *working store* which employs a two-state system — a pattern of 'ons' and 'offs' — to represent the data and instructions.

The main form of working store, or *memory*, is based on solid-state electronic circuits. Hundreds of thousands of these logic circuits form the storage in each computer — a density of electronics made possible only by the use of integrated circuits, popularly known as 'chips'.

In addition to the working store, the cpu has two other main components: the *control unit* and the *arithmetic logic unit* (alu). The control unit takes procedural instructions from the store, and sets up circuits to enable each instruction to be carried out, for example the transfer of data from an input device to the store, or from the store to the alu. A complete set of instructions is called a *program*, and the control unit will action each instruction of a program until an instruction indicates that it is a final one.

The arithmetic logic unit is the part of the cpu where the actual computation takes place. Words from store are passed to the alu so that, for example, they may be added or subtracted, multiplied or divided, compared or modified, according to the program instructions from the control unit. Comparison is one of the most important features of the alu; one simple example is to determine which of two names is alphabetically earlier so that sorting can take place.

Output devices
The purpose of an output device is to communicate information to the operator in a usable form. Output devices

403

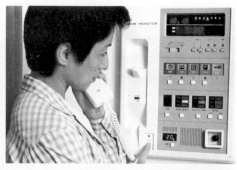

Above: Japan is well known for its wide range of electronics and gadgets. Home and office environments are controlled electronically (top), and traffic control systems are used to plan the smooth flow of traffic and to help prevent accidents (above).

British Steel Corporation

currently in use include graphic display units, high-speed line printers, specially adapted typewriters, daisywheel printers, dot-matrix printers, laser printers, and pen plotters. Each of these different kinds of printer and plotter has its own particular advantages and disadvantages.

Probably the most common output devices in large commercial and scientific installations is the line printer, so called because it prints a complete line at a time, working at a speed of around 2000 lines per minute. Even the fastest output devices are far slower in operation than the computer itself, so the CPU may put the information into a storage device known as a *buffer*

Above: Today most industrial processes are controlled or monitored by computers. Here, a computer calculates the optimum oxygen flow and temperature in a steel-making plant.

Below: Fifth generation computers will have three basic systems – user interaction and input, software modelling and the processing and support hardware. Some progress

has been made with the first two of these – for example, experiments with voice and pattern recognition machines, and programs.

store. The output devices then read from the buffer store at their own speed, thus leaving the processor itself free to commence other work.

Programming

To enable the user to instruct and communicate with the machines, it has been necessary to invent new languages. As machine language is based on the binary arithmetic system the first program languages tended to be mathematically based. In FORTRAN (FORmula TRANslation), for example, most commonly used for scientific and mathematical applications, an instruction might say 'ADD X to Y at Z,' where X

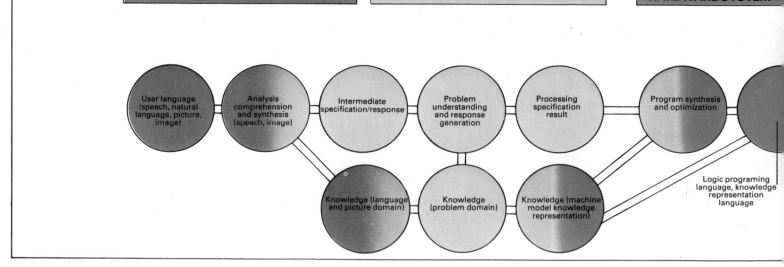

HUMAN APPLICATION SYSTEMS

MODELING SOFTWARE SYSTEM

MACHINE HARDWARE SYSTEM

User language (speech, natural language, picture, image)

Analysis comprehension and synthesis (speech, image)

Intermediate specification/response

Problem understanding and response generation

Processing specification result

Program synthesis and optimization

Knowledge (language and picture domain)

Knowledge (problem domain)

Knowledge (machine model knowledge representation)

Logic programing language, knowledge representation language

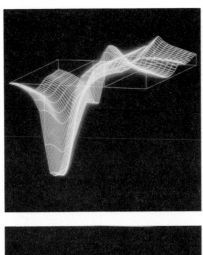
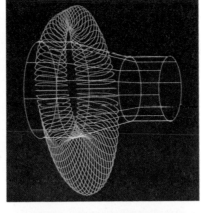
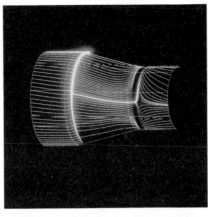
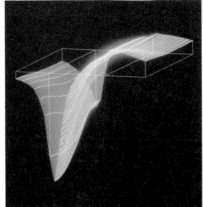
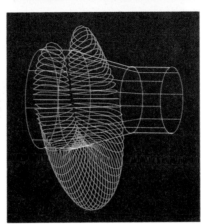
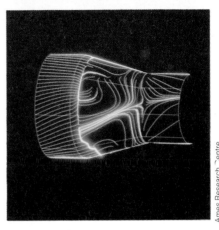

Right: A computer can simulate the flow of air over a missile. These projections (by supercomputer Illiac IV) show the aerodynamics of part of a missile, attacking at (top) a four-degree angle, and (bottom) 12 degrees.

Ames Research Centre

and Y are numbers and Z is an accumulator or register. Another common scientific language is ALOGOL (ALGOrithmic Language), taking its name from ALGORITHM, a set of instructions for solving a specific problem.

COBOL (COmmon Business Oriented Language) was developed at a later stage as a more alphabetically-based language, so that instructions written in this language came nearer to ordinary language. It has therefore come to be one of the most widely used of the commercial programming languages, enabling people who are not trained programmers to participate in the writing of fairly simple programs. A typical COBOL statement may simply be something like 'SUBTRACT TAX FROM GROSS GIVING NET.' Computer languages are often referred to as being either high level (near to humans), or low level (near to machine).

The most common computer language is BASIC (Beginners' All purpose Symbolic Instruction Code), which is a general-purpose language and has gained greatly in popularity alongside the personal or home microcomputer. There are also several other languages in more select use. Pascal is a computer language which has found many uses in many educational and commercial establishments, and is an example of a *structured* programming language. Logo has found favour among educationalists, when used in conjunction with Seymour Papert's Turtle teaching aid. Application in list processing and artificial intelligence projects find LISP an ideal tool. Experts are still experimenting with ways to improve and clarify computer language so that it is as clear, understandable and accessible as possible for all users.

The basic software of a system comprises the machine language programs, *compilers* and *assemblers* to translate high-level language to machine code, and a program library of commonly-used basic programs (*routines* and *subroutines*) that are frequently employed by a particular user. The main *applications programs*, written to instruct the machine to do specific tasks, are sometimes referred to as *middleware*, and are not generally classed as software. The programs, with the exception of the main *supervisory program*, are usually kept in the backing store. The main supervisory program is loaded permanently into the main store, and it controls the other programs, bringing them temporarily from the backing store into the main store when they are needed.

A suite or group of computer programs combine to perform one specific job, for instance a payroll. A software system is a combination of various suites of programs to perform a broader task. For example, it will take several programs to evolve a production control system for a factory, include reports on stock movement, work in progress, purchasing, production line workloads and availability of raw materials. A *systems analyst* will examine the total problem, divide it into subgroups and assign programmers to each subgroup to write the software for each sequential step of the operations.

Hybrid computing

There are situations when analogue data has to be fed into a digital computer, and others when digital data has to be fed into an analogue machine. This is done by feeding the data through analogue-to-digital converters and through digital-to-analogue converters. An example is in electrocardiogram analysis: heartbeat measures are taken in analogue form, after which they are converted to digital form and fed into a digital computer where they are then analyzed.

When digital machines are used for controlling production processes they are often dealing with continually changing quantities, temperatures and pressures for example, and this analogue data is converted into digital form to enable the machine to process it. On the basis of the data it receives the computer can make the required decisions, which are then converted back into analogue form in which they can control the machinery, pumps and actuator of the manufacturing plant.

The hardware used in mixed analogue and digital computing may consist either of separate analogue and digital computers, connected through a hybrid interface which does the conversions, or of a digital computer which has analogue units incorporated in the CPU.

405

Telephone and Telegraph

The technology of telecommunications is concerned with the transmission and reception of information using electricity and electromagnetic waves (such as light and radio waves). It involves many different disciplines from electrical engineering to electronics, signal analysis and information theory. The information itself may be printed news, speech, television pictures or telegraphic messages.

The early telegraph

The basic components of a telegraphic system, such as sources of direct (dc) current (batteries), electromagnets (solenoids) and current-carrying metal wires, all existed by about 1830. Of the numerous designs invented during this period, many were concerned with methods for displaying the characters (letters, numbers and punctuation) at the receiver after their transmission in an electrical form.

One of the most important telegraph systems of the nineteenth century was that invented in America by an artist called Samuel Morse. The Morse telegraph was attractive because of its simplicity—requiring only one wire (and a return) for the transmission of any character. Each character was represented by a combination of two simple signals: a dot (short burst of current) and a dash (a current of longer duration). The complexity of each coded character was chosen according to its frequency of use. Thus, for example, the most common English letter, 'e', is a single dot, while an 's' is three dots and an 'o' three dashes. The international distress call 'SOS' is simply · · · — — — · · ·.

Automatic telegraphy

The speed and accuracy of the Morse system was determined by the operator's skill rather than any technical limitations of the apparatus itself, and with the growth of telegraphic traffic, ways of using existing telegraph lines more efficiently were sought.

Michael Holford

Bell Labs

Top: A replica of a 19th-century Morse telegraph receiver.

Above: *Frequency division multiplexing*, a method of sending more than one message simultaneously down a single wire by superimposing each one on to a different carrier frequency, was first suggested by Elisha Gray in the late 19th century. These diagrams show a carrier wave (top) and a carrier wave modulated by a Morse code signal of one dot and three dashes; this gives one short and three long pulses.

Above: Bell's telephone transmitter (left) and receiver (right) which on 10 March 1876 carried the first sentence ever spoken over a telephone. The sentence, spoken by Bell to his assistant Thomas Watson, was 'Mr Watson, come here; I want you.'

Left: A teleprinter produces electrical pulses, based on a 5-unit code, which represent the various characters typed by the operator. These pulses are transmitted to the receiving teleprinter, which decodes them and types out the message.

Right: This chart shows the international code used for punched paper tape telegraphy, plus the Morse code. The patterns of holes in the tape code mean either letters, or other characters and instructions, depending on whether they were preceded by a 'letters' or a 'figures' code.

combination nos	Figures & symbols	5	4	3	2	1	letters	Morse Code
1	—				•	•	A	• —
2	?	•	•			•	B	— • • •
3	:		•	•	•		C	— • — •
4	who are you	•				•	D	— • •
5	3				•	•	E	•
6	(optional)	•	•	•		•	F	• • — •
7	(optional)	•	•		•		G	— — •
8	(optional)	•		•	•		H	• • • •
9	8		•	•	•		I	• •
10	bell		•		•	•	J	• — — —
11	(	•	•	•		•	K	— • —
12	)	•		•	•	•	L	• — • •
13	.		•	•	•		M	— —
14			•			•	N	— •
15	9	•	•			•	O	— — —
16	0	•		•	•		P	• — — •
17	1	•	•		•		Q	— — • —
18	4		•	•	•		R	• — •
19				•	•	•	S	• • •
20	5	•					T	—
21	7	•	•		•	•	U	• • —
22	—	•		•			V	• • • —
23	2	•			•	•	W	• — —
24	1	•	•		•		X	— • • —
25	6	•			•	•	Y	— • — —
26	+		•		•	•	Z	— — • •
27	carriage return			•				
28	line feed		•					
29	letters	•	•	•	•	•		
30	figures	•	•	•		•		
31	space			•	•			
32	all space			•				

Punched paper tape code and Morse code

ITT

406

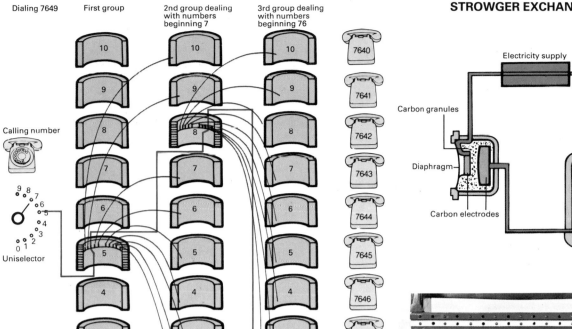

Dialing 7649

First group

2nd group dealing with numbers beginning 7

3rd group dealing with numbers beginning 76

Calling number

Uniselector

5th selector free in 1st group

Dial 7 goes to level 7, finds 8th selector free in 2nd group

Dial 6 goes to level 6, finds 2nd selector free in 3rd group

Dial 4 goes to level 4, dial 9 turns to contact 9

Called phone

STROWGER EXCHANGE SYSTEM

Electricity supply

Carbon granules

Diaphragm

Carbon electrodes

Magnet

Diaphragm

Michael Holford Library/British Museum

Above: Local telephone exchanges are designed to suit local conditions and may vary in size from 600 to 20,000 subscribers. When a caller lifts the handset in a Strowger system, a uniselector finds a free first selector, and so on until the required telephone is obtained. The telephone microphone and speaker are of a simple, sturdy construction.

Above: An 1879 switchboard. An undertaker named Strowger invented automatic switching after he lost business due to operator errors.

British Telecom

Left: Examining an elbow-joint X-ray transmitted via a facsimile machine. The picture is enlarged and has a high resolution for easy viewing. Telexes, too, can transmit information, but fax machines have the advantage as diagrams, plans and photographs can be sent either short distances, from one building of a complex to another, or to the other side of the world.

407

LONG-DISTANCE AND LOCAL LINKS

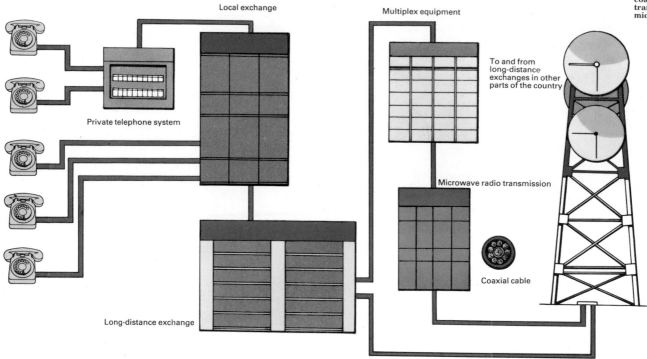

Local exchange

Private telephone system

Multiplex equipment

To and from long-distance exchanges in other parts of the country

Microwave radio transmission

Coaxial cable

Long-distance exchange

Below left: Telephones are connected either directly to a local exchange or via a private exchange. Long-distance links may be via coaxial cable or can be transmitted over a microwave system.

Charles Wheatstone provided a simple solution to this problem by designing a mechanical Morse sender which converted messages, stored in the form of holes punched in paper tape, into electrical pulses. At the receiver, an inker recorded these pulses on another reel of paper. The speed limitation of this device was determined solely by the reading and recording speeds of the terminal equipment. Whereas an expert Morse operator could send only 30 to 35 words a minute, the paper tape system could transmit at speeds up to 600 words per minute.

The telephone
Although others before him had succeeded in using electricity to transmit sounds

and musical notes over a wire, in 1876 Edinburgh-born Alexander Graham Bell was the first to patent a device capable of sending and receiving recognisable words. While the device worked well as a receiver, its performance as a transmitter was less successful.

An improved transmitter was developed almost simultaneously by Edison and Hunnings in 1878. This was the *carbon granule transmitter*. The modern version consists of an aluminium alloy diaphragm which is attached to a dome-shaped piece of carbon, anchored in such a way as to be free to move in and out of another cup-shaped piece of carbon, filled with carbon granules. Electrical connections are made to the carbon electrodes at the front and

back and the current flows from one, through the granules, to the other. The rapid changes of air pressure set up by speech cause the granules to be alternately compressed and released, so altering their electrical resistance. The current flowing through the granules thus fluctuates in the same way as the air pressure, so that the original sound can be faithfully reproduced at the distant end.

Bell's original earpiece worked on the principles of a combined permanent magnet and electromagnet acting on an iron diaphragm. A similar system is used in modern receivers, in which a thin metal diaphragm is made to vibrate by variations in the magnetic field of an

Standard Telephones & Cables Ltd

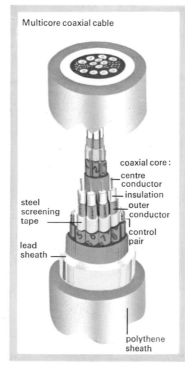

Multicore coaxial cable

coaxial core:
centre conductor
insulation
outer conductor

steel screening tape

lead sheath

control pair

polythene sheath

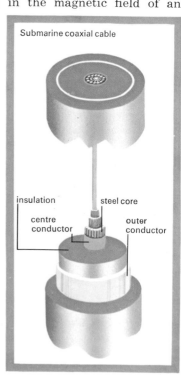

Submarine coaxial cable

insulation
centre conductor

steel core
outer conductor

Thomp=n CSF

Cabl= & Wireless plc

Edward Allington

Philips

electromagnet. These variations are set up by the varying electrical current carrying the incoming voice signal.

Telephone exchanges

The first telephone exchange opened in Connecticut, USA, in 1878, followed a year later by the first European exchange in Coleman Street in the City of London. The earliest exchanges were all manual, with operators physically placing and removing plugs to complete circuits. The first automatic telephone exchange was installed at La Porte, Indiana, USA, in 1892. It was based on a system invented in 1889 by Almon B. Strowger, an irascible American undertaker so irritated by inefficient operators that he developed his

own automatic switching board.

An automatic exchange is simply a set of apparatus to which all the telephones in a neighbourhood are connected, with a switching network that will interconnect any two of them. Interconnection is achieved by a series of signal pulses, transmitted by the dial mechanism of the sender's telephone, which control the switching network.

Strowger's invention consisted of a metal arm, rather like a windscreen wiper, which was driven around a series of numbered contacts (arranged in a semicircular form) by the dial pulses. The modern version of this *selector* is a two-motion type which first moves the wiper vertically to select one of ten sets of

contacts, and then sweeps it in a horizontal arc to select one of the ten individual contacts in that set.

When dialing the first digit of a telephone number, say 6, six pulses are sent to a *first selector* in the exchange. The wiper moves vertically to the contacts on the sixth level, corresponding to all telephones beginning with the number 6. Then to find a *second selector* to handle the second digit, the first selector wiper moves in a horizontal arc 'searching' for a free contact. If the next digit dialled is 2, the second selector wiper moves up to the second level and then sweeps horizontally until a free third selector is found (corresponding to all telephone numbers beginning with 62). This third selector deals with the third digit (vertical

Below: A communications station in the United Arab Republic. A large number of information channels can be carried by microwaves, and they are widely used instead of cable transmission systems. Because microwaves travel in straight lines and cannot bend around obstructions or over the horizon, the transmitter and receiver must normally be in 'line of sight' of each other. This can be overcome by beaming them up to a satellite, which then re-transmits them to distant stations, or by *tropospheric scatter*, bouncing them off the layers of air in the lower atmosphere. The large dish shown here is for satellite communications.

pulse code modulation

Left: The principles of *pulse code modulation* (PCM). This is a system for transmitting information so that it arrives with a minimum amount of distortion caused by electrical 'noise'— unwanted voltages picked up as it passes through the system. The first graph shows the waveform of the original signal.

This is how the original wave might look after being transmitted in an unmodulated form. The instantaneous values are the same, but it is very distorted. A wave reconstructed from a PCM signal would be free from this distortion, being based only on the instantaneous values.

time intervals →

This graph shows how the modulator measures the amplitude of the wave at regular intervals, and then produces electrical pulses whose amplitudes correspond to those of the original wave at those intervals. At the receiving end the demodulator uses these pulses to reconstruct the original wave.

Cable & Wireless

Left: The crossbar system, like Strowger, is electro-mechanical, but faster and more reliable. Crossbar switches have contact assemblies arranged in a grid pattern. Connections are made by electromagnets which make a row of input contacts intersect with a column of output contacts.

Below left: The Transaction Telephone is used for automatic verification of credit card transactions. Two cards are inserted into the machine; a dialling card which instructs it to dial the computer at the credit company's data centre, and the customer's credit card. The amount of the transaction is entered via the keyboard.

GEC

movement) and fourth digit (horizontal movement) and at this point the required telephone is interconnected.

A *uniselector* precedes the first selector, and this hunts for a free first selector. Consequently, no selector 'belongs' to a particular telephone but can be allocated to one for the duration of the call. This reduces the amount of equipment necessary in an exchange—the only equipment which does belong to each telephone is the uniselector, and this is relatively simple and cheap. If at any stage a free selector cannot be found, or if the telephone sought is in use, an 'engaged' tone is transmitted to the sender.

Since Strowger's invention, other switching systems have been developed, some of them electro-mechanical and others electronic. In the electronic

Bell

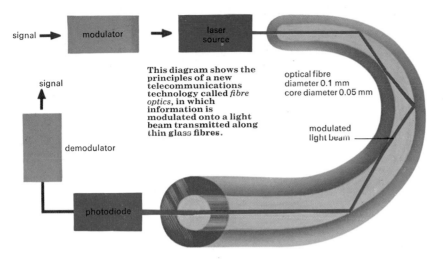

signal → modulator → laser source

signal ↑

demodulator

photodiode

This diagram shows the principles of a new telecommunications technology called *fibre optics*, in which information is modulated onto a light beam transmitted along thin glass fibres.

optical fibre diameter 0.1 mm core diameter 0.05 mm

modulated light beam

Above: Light is a form of electromagnetic radiation. It has a very much higher frequency than radio or microwaves, but it can be modulated in a similar fashion. In a fibre optic system, the light from a laser is modulated by an information signal such as a telephone conversation. The modulated light is beamed into the inner core of the fibre, which has a higher refractive index than the outer cladding layer. The light is reflected from side to side along the fibre by the core/cladding interface which acts as a sort of pipe to carry the light along. At the receiving end, a photodiode produces an electrical output signal when the light strikes it, and this signal is demodulated to reproduce the original signal.

exchanges the switching is performed by electronic circuits which are faster, more compact and less prone to failure than electro-mechanical systems such as Strowger or the 'crossbar' system widely used in many countries.

Multiplexing techniques
If one pair of wires were necessary for every telephone conversation going on in the world then we would either be queuing to use the phone or the world would be a veritable maze of copper wires. These problems are avoided by the use of transmission methods known as *multiplexing*. These methods allow us to transmit hundreds and sometimes thousands of conversations along one pair of wires.

One common multiplexing method, *frequency multiplexing*, uses a similar technique to that used in radio transmission, where it is necessary to be able to distinguish one signal from the hundreds of radio signals received by an aerial. This is achieved by a process known as *modulation*, whereby every broadcast is superimposed on a unique 'signature tone' or *carrier frequency*. At the radio receiver, a particular broadcast is obtained by selecting its associated carrier frequency and *demodulating* the incoming signal.

The use of carrier frequencies enables the capacity of a telephone network to be greatly increased. Between exchanges, for example, where the communications traffic is most dense, each conversation to be transmitted can be modulated on to a unique carrier frequency and at the receiving end a demodulater can extract any one of the conversations to the exclusion of all the others.

Frequency and bandwidth
The most important frequencies making up speech lie between 400 and 4,000 Hz, and if these are present the words and the person speaking them are recognizable. Thus a telephone line (and the associated transmitter and receiver) must be capable of handling these frequencies without losing too much of their strength (amplitude).

Unfortunately, a simple pair of telephone wires impedes high frequency alternating currents more than lower frequencies—a situation exacerbated by long distances. Consequently, the frequency bandwidth which the wires can handle decreases with distance. With a simple telephone conversation, this can be overcome by attaching inductive filters to the 'line which 'boost' the higher frequencies of the electrical signal. When, however, a modulated signal is transmitted down a telephone line other techniques must be sought.

When a speech signal, with frequencies from 400 to 4,000 Hz, is modulated on to a carrier frequency (which is much higher and beyond the audible range), the whole signal is moved up to the region of the carrier frequency. For example, if the carrier frequency is 100,000 Hz then the modulated signal occupies a bandwidth of 8,000 Hz about the 100,000 Hz mark (that is from 96,000 to 104,000 Hz). This presents a problem in telecommunications because ordinary wires will not handle such high frequencies.

Two inventions eventually came together to overcome the problem of transmitting high frequency modulated signals over long distances—these were the *coaxial cable* and the *telephone repeater*.

Modern coaxial cables will handle frequencies up to 10 MHz (10 million Hertz). If each signal occupies a bandwidth of 8,000 Hz about its own carrier frequency then approximately 1,000 different conversations can be transmitted along it.

However good a cable is, it will still attenuate (reduce) signals over long distances. To overcome this, amplifiers were developed which could be placed periodically along the cable to boost the signals—these are called *repeaters*. As low frequency currents (and especially dc) are attenuated less than high frequency ones, it was found to be possible to power all the repeaters on a cable from the terminal exchanges by passing direct current along the cable.

Opposite page, below right: Cassettes have made answering machines more versatile. The messages can be varied from 30 seconds to three minutes in duration, so goods or services are easily listed. Messages can be picked up by calling in and sending an electronic signal to the machine to start it playing back its recorded messages.

Left: The natural progression of the telephone is the videophone. First-generation videophone systems, such as this experimental arrangement, Siemen's Bigfon, in Germany, use fibreoptic cables. These systems require the laying of a nationwide network of optical fibres and the use of relatively expensive light-emitting and light-sensing devices at each end of the cable. The cables can, however, also carry videotext, radio and TV programmes.

Siemens

411

Radio

The invention of radio, at the end of the nineteenth century, marked the beginning of the era of mass communications. It was soon possible to broadcast the details of events, as they happened, directly to people's homes, and to communicate directly with ships at sea or moving aircraft. The development of radio also paved the way for the advent of television, which has had an even greater impact on home entertainment. Military operations have been affected by radio, and space exploration, both manned and unmanned, would be impossible without it.

Radio waves are a form of *electromagnetic radiation*, which consists of a combination of alternating electric and magnetic fields. Radio waves travel at the same speed as light, and the peaks of the waves are the points at which the values of the electric and magnetic fields are at their maximum.

The *frequency* of a radio wave is the number of times per second that these fields reach a maximum in one direction, reverse to a maximum in the other direction, and then return to the original maximum. The distance between two successive maximum values in the same direction is known as the *wavelength* of the wave, and the higher the frequency of a wave the shorter its wavelength.

Radio waves range from the very low frequency (VLF) waves having wavelengths of between 1,000 km and 10 km, up to the very high microwave frequencies which have wavelengths of from 1 m down to less than 1 mm.

The invention of radio

The existence of electric and magnetic fields was first recognized by Michael Faraday in 1845. Faraday's concepts were taken up by James Clerk Maxwell, who went on to predict the existence of electromagnetic radiation and calculated that electromagnetic waves could travel through space at the speed of light.

The German physicist Heinrich Hertz devoted much time to the study of Maxwell's theory—although it was generally not accepted by other scientists at that time—and in 1887 he succeeded in demonstrating the generation, transmission and reception of electromagnetic waves. He produced his waves by making a spark jump across a small gap in a loop of wire. A similar loop, with a small gap in it, was placed nearby, and when the spark was created in the first loop, a spark also appeared at the gap in the second. The current flowing in the first loop had created electromagnetic waves, which radiated away from the loop and were picked up by the second loop, causing a current to flow in it.

The work of Hertz was studied by researchers in many countries. Sir Oliver Lodge in England, Alexander Popov in Russia, Edouard Branly in France and Augusto Righi in Italy are among the most notable of these. Their work on methods of generating and detecting radio waves was studied by Guglielmo Marconi, who took out the first patent for wireless telegraphy in June 1896.

Marconi began his experiments in 1894, constructing a transmitter and receiver

Above: Guglielmo Marconi (1874-1937), the son of an Italian father and an Irish mother, was only 22 years old when he patented the first wireless telegraph in 1896. He was a joint recipient of the Nobel Prize for physics in 1909, and received other honours from both Britain and Italy.

Right: This 1927 radio is a *superheterodyne* receiver. It contains circuits which mix the modulated signal with an unmodulated one to produce a lower, intermediate frequency signal. This signal is then demodulated to produce the audio frequency signal that is used to drive a speaker or headphones.

Above: George Bernard Shaw broadcasting from a studio in Plymouth, England, in 1929. The microphone is contained within the 'meat safe' housing; it comprised a flat aluminium coil mounted within the field of an electromagnet and held in place by cotton wool pads covered in petroleum jelly.

Below: A 'crystal set', a popular form of cheap radio during the 1920s. The crystal set had a coil and a variable capacitor for tuning, and a silicon or germanium crystal which, when contacted with a wire probe called a 'cat's whisker', demodulated the signal by rectifying it.

Right: Radio waves can be transmitted considerable distances around the earth because the electrically-charged layers in the upper atmosphere, known collectively as the *ionosphere*, reflect them back down to distant receivers. The ionosphere is a series of layers, known as D, E, F_1 and F_2, consisting of ionized gas molecules with free electrons which were liberated when the molecules were ionized by the action of solar radiation. The height at which radio waves are reflected depends on their frequency, and the highest frequencies are not reflected at all. At night, the F_1 layer merges with F_2.

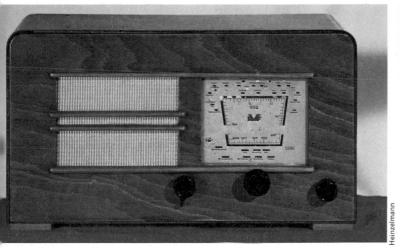

Left: The 'Heinzelmann' radio of 1948 was the German Grundig company's first product. It was supplied initially in kit form, but no valves were provided; customers were advised to buy the valves from army surplus stores.

Right: Low and very low frequency radio waves can travel around the earth in the region between the earth's surface and the ionosphere. This region acts as a kind of natural waveguide for waves of these frequencies. Short wavelength, high frequency waves, with frequencies up to 30 MHz, are bounced around the world between the ionosphere and the surface.

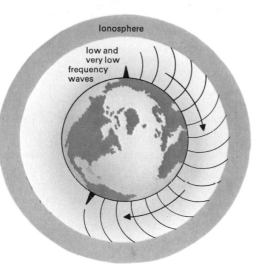

BEHAVIOUR OF RADIO WAVES IN THE ATMOSPHERE

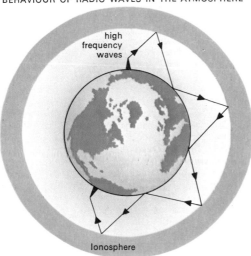

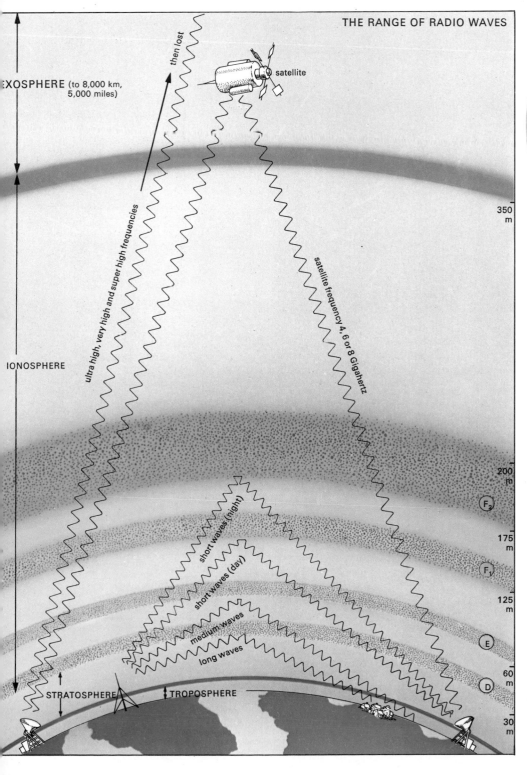

THE RANGE OF RADIO WAVES

at his father's villa near Bologna, Italy. His receiver was a detector of the 'coherer' type, invented by Branly, in which metal powder inside a glass tube stuck together when magnetized by a spark appearing across a gap in the adjacent aerial circuit. When the powder stuck together it allowed a current to be passed through it, and this current operated a telegraph receiver. By transmitting Morse Code signals in the form of pulses of radio waves, similar pulses of electric current were made to flow in the coherer and so the message was recorded by the telegraph receiver connected to it.

Post Office backing

Marconi approached the Italian government for backing, but they were uninterested and so he went to England, where Sir William Preece, the Engineer in Chief of the Post Office, put full facilities at his disposal. His system was successfully operated between the Post Office headquarters and the Thames Embankment in 1896, and the following year a 13 km (8 mile) circuit was set up across the Bristol Channel.

By removing the spark gap from the aerial circuit to a closed circuit—which acted as a reservoir of energy—long trains of waves were produced and very soon distances of several hundred miles could be covered. After building links to the Isle of Wight and to France, in 1901 Marconi successfully transmitted the first transatlantic signal, an 'S' in Morse Code, from Poldhu in Cornwall to St John's in Newfoundland.

The Marconi system only transmitted telegraphic messages in the form of pulses of radio waves, and it was not until 1906 that a method of transmitting speech was developed. This method was the work the Canadian physicist Reginald Fessenden, who invented the technique of *modulating* radio waves.

Fessenden used a continuous signal or *carrier*, with the speech signal superimposed on it in such a way that the amplitude of the waves varied with the variations in the speech signal. At the receiver, these variations in amplitude were used to produce a varying electrical signal which corresponded to the original signal with which the carrier was modulated. This signal was then amplified and put through a loudspeaker to reproduce the original sounds.

This method is known as *amplitude modulation* (AM), and it is the modulation technique used for long, medium and short wavelength radio broadcasts. One major drawback to AM radio, however, is that the wave can be modulated by unwanted electrical signals such as those produced by thunderstorms and some types of electrical equipment. This means that the signal can arrive at the receiver modulated not only with the original signal but also with these unwanted ones, which produce the background noise or 'static' often heard on AM radio.

A solution to this problem of static interference was found in 1939 by Edwin Armstrong in the US. Instead of using the sound signal to vary the amplitude of the carrier wave, he used it to vary its frequency. The signal produced by the receiver varied according to the variations in the frequency of the incoming carrier wave. This method is known as *frequency modulation* (FM), and it is used for transmissions in the higher frequency wavebands such as the VHF (very high frequency) band and the microwave bands.

Static interference still creates variations in the amplitude of FM signals, but as the receiver only responds to variations in the frequency of the signal these amplitude variations do not affect the reproduced sound.

Tuning

When a radio is tuned to a particular station, its tuning section is set to accept only the carrier frequency of that station. The tuning circuit contains, in its simplest form, a coil and a capacitor that together constitute a *resonant circuit*, one that offers very little impedance to a current whose frequency is the same as the *resonant frequency* of the circuit. This resonant frequency is determined by the values of the inductance of the coil and the capacitance of the capacitor.

The capacitor in a simple radio tuning circuit is variable, and when the tuning knob is turned the value of the capacitor is altered, so altering the resonant frequency of the circuit. The radio will now be tuned to the station whose frequency is the same as the new resonant frequency of the circuit.

Radio transmitters operate by amplifying the modulated signal and applying it to the transmitting aerial from which the radio waves are emitted. At the receiving end, the radio waves coming into contact with the aerial create tiny currents in it which are then passed through the tuning stage, demodulated, and amplified. Finally ,the signal is played through the loudspeaker to reproduce the

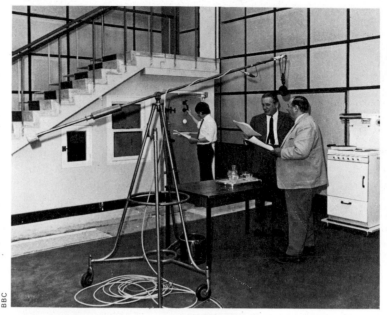

BBC

Left: Actors rehearsing an episode of a radio serial. The studio is equipped with various items for producing sound effects, including three types of stairs; two types of window; a door with a knocker, bell, latch, three types of lock and a bolt; and kitchen equipment including a stove.

Cable & Wireless

Above: A studio control booth. The signals from the studio, on the other side of the glass screen, pass through the control console

before being sent to the transmitter.

Below: Part of the output stage of a large radio transmitter.

Paul Brierey

Below: Radio waves are either *amplitude modulated* (AM) or *frequency modulated* (FM). In both cases, the variations in the modulated carrier wave correspond to the variations in the original sound signal. In the case of AM, the wave's amplitude varies; in that of FM its frequency varies.

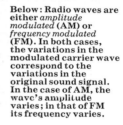

RADIO WAVE MODULATION

(1) original sound wave (2) carrier wave (3) amplitude modulated wave (4) frequency modulated wave

Marconi

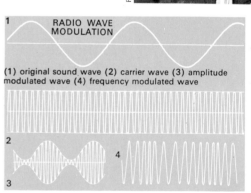

master volume control

studio control booth

faders

studio

preamplifiers

faders

final volume control

control room

programme selector

INSIDE A RADIO STUDIO

Above: A studio and control room arrangement. The studio has its own control booth where the signals from its microphones are amplified and then combined, using faders to adjust their relative volumes. The combined signal is then sent to the control room, which controls the output from several

studios, before going on to the transmitter.

Right: At the transmitter, the carrier wave is modulated with the signal from the studio then transmitted. The receiver retrieves the sound signal from the modulated wave and plays it through the loudspeaker.

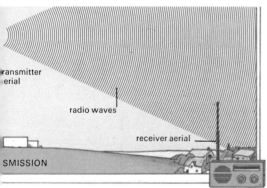

Above left: Radio waves are among the many types of electromagnetic radiation that reach us from outer space, so telling us of the existence and properties of objects which may not otherwise be detectable. The picture shows the largest fully steerable radiotelescope dish, at Effelsburg, West Germany.

Above: A Los Angeles police patrol reporting an accident to the central control room over their radiotelephone. Radiotelephones generally use the VHF (30 MHz to 300 MHz) and the UHF (ultra high frequencies – 300 MHz to 3000 MHz) bands, with the frequency spectrum being divided into channels and allocated to specific categories of user, which helps prevent interference.

Above: The signal applied to the transmitter aerial creates the radio waves which spread out in all directions. When they are picked up by the receiver aerial they set up a corresponding signal in it.

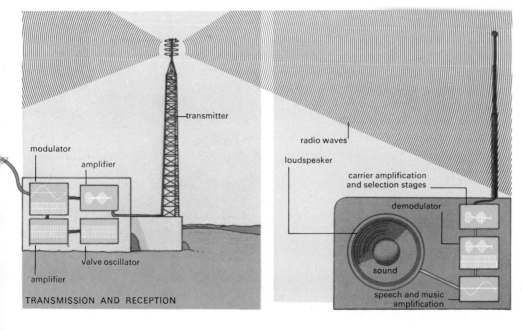

TRANSMISSION AND RECEPTION

broadcast sound.

An aerial transmits and receives radio waves most efficiently when its length is the same as the wavelength of the waves it is handling. This is usually quite feasible with a single frequency radio transmitter or receiver using the shorter wavelengths. An aerial will also operate quite effectively when its length is an even sub-multiple, such as a half or a quarter of the wavelength, and in many cases this may be more convenient. However, aerials designed to handle a wide range of wavelengths, such as those in domestic radio sets, cannot be accurately matched to all the wavelengths and so a loss of efficiency is unavoidable.

Broadcasting

The wavelengths of all radio stations are determined in accordance with the rules laid down by the International Telecommunications Union. These rules are intended to prevent transmissions from one station interfering with those from another. For stations not transmitting to other countries, the most widely used frequencies are between 150 and 550 kHz (long wave), 550 and 1660 kHz (medium wave) and 87.5 and 100 MHz (VHF). Most overseas broadcasts use the 2.2 to 30 MHz region of the short wave band. Amplitude modulation is used for long, medium and short wave broadcasts, and frequency modulation for the VHF transmissions.

The VHF frequencies (30 to 300 MHz), together with the UHF (ultra high frequency, 300 to 3,000 MHz) band, are also used for two-way radio systems such as those used by aircraft, ships, the armed forces, the police, and other operators such as taxi services.

The lower end of the long wave band, below about 100 kHz, plus some of the very low frequency band (3 to 30 kHz), is used for marine communications, radio navigational aids, and for long-range military communications.

Microwaves are radio waves with frequencies between 1,000 MHz (or 1 gigahertz, abbreviated 1 GHz) and 300 GHz. They are widely used in telecommunications because they can be modulated in such a way as to enable them to carry, for example, up to about 1,000 simultaneous telephone conversations on a single carrier wave.

Microwaves cannot be handled in the same way as lower frequency radio waves, because at frequencies above 1 GHz a current cannot be passed along a cable from one point to another, such as from the modulator to the transmitter, without it radiating all its power away or losing it due to capacitive effects. Instead of using cables, microwave transmitters use *waveguides*, hollow tubes which channel the microwaves from their source to the aerial. The aerial is a dish-shaped structure, and the microwaves are beamed into the centre of it so that it reflects them away in a narrow, straight beam.

Microwave receiver aerials are of similar construction, with the dish serving to reflect the incoming beam into the open end of a waveguide situated at the focus of the dish. In addition to their use in ordinary telecommunications networks, microwaves are used for space vehicle communications links and are the type of radio waves employed by radar systems.

415

Cameras and Film

The first photograph was taken as long ago as 1826, by the French engineer J. N. Niépce (1765-1833). Niépce died before he could perfect his process, but his work was carried on successfully by his partner, L. J. M. Daguerre (1787-1851). Daguerre produced a photographic plate coated with light-sensitive silver iodide, and his process, known as the *Daguerrotype* process, was what made photography a commercial proposition.

The earliest cameras were very simple. A lens at one side of a box threw an image on to the box's opposite wall, where the photographer would have his light sensitive plate. The other essential was a means of controlling the exposure time. A top hat could be used just as well as any more elaborate device: it covered the lens until you wanted to take the picture. By taking it off the lens for a few minutes, you admitted light into the camera. After a suitable length of time, you replaced the top hat and the exposure was complete.

The improvement which, more than any other, brought photography within everyone's reach was the invention of film, first introduced by George Eastman in 1889. Although glass plates and single sheets of film are still used for special purposes or for studio work, the use of lengths of film, giving 12, 20 or 36 shots in rapid succession, is practically universal.

The 'top hat' aspect has also changed. Instead of many minutes' exposure, modern films usually need just a few milliseconds; but a complete range from perhaps 1/1000 sec to a minute or longer may be required. The *shutter* which achieves this has to be designed so that no part of the frame area receives more exposure than any other part.

The easiest way to accomplish this is to put the shutter at a point where it is completely out of focus—as close to the lens as possible. Most modern lenses have several components, so if a camera has a non-interchangeable lens the shutter can actually be located inside the lens, between the components. It consists of two sets of thin metal blades or leaves, which are pivoted so that one group moves out of the light beam to start the exposure and the other moves in to end it. The timing of these actions is done simply by the tension in the spring which causes them to move. The shutter is usually *cocked*—tensioning the spring—when the film is wound on.

If the camera has an interchangeable lens, however, it is most likely to have a *focal plane shutter*. This consists of a pair of blinds which move across the frame immediately in front of the film. As long as the blinds move together, all parts of the film will be exposed equally. By changing the distance separating the blinds, rather than their speed, different exposure times are possible.

Choosing the lens

Lenses range from simple plastic ones for mass-produced cameras to expensive interchangeable multi-element ones. A very wide range of lenses are available.

There are two factors which the photo-

Radio Times Hulton Picture Library

Above: A replica of a camera used by William Fox-Talbot (1800-1877), who invented the negative/positive photographic process. His photographs were taken on paper impregnated with silver chloride, which gave negative images when developed. Positive prints were then made from the negatives.

Right: A cutaway drawing of a typical 35 mm single lens reflex (SLR) camera. These cameras have interchangeable lenses, and built-in exposure meters. The exposure meter shows the user whether or not sufficient light is entering the lens for a satisfactory image to register on the film.

SLR CAMERA

cocking lever

shutter release

shutter speed control

frame counter

main spring

self time

self time mechan

film take-up spool

film transport sprocket

Spectrum

Left: A Kodak 'Brownie' box camera, an easily-operated camera that was very popular in the 1950s. The main lens is the large one in the centre, and the two smaller ones are the viewfinder lenses, one for use with the camera upright and the other with the camera on its side. It took eight shots per roll of film.

Below: A Mamiya twin lens reflex camera, with a light meter (right) and two pairs of interchangeable lenses. Unlike an SLR, where the main lens is also the viewfinder lens, this type of camera has separate main and viewfinder lenses, so both must be changed if a different focal length is needed.

250 mm (10 inch) TELEPHOTO LE

depth of field scale

diaphragm setting ring

helical focusing

rear le group 3 elen 2 grou

Photri

Agfa-Gevaert

416

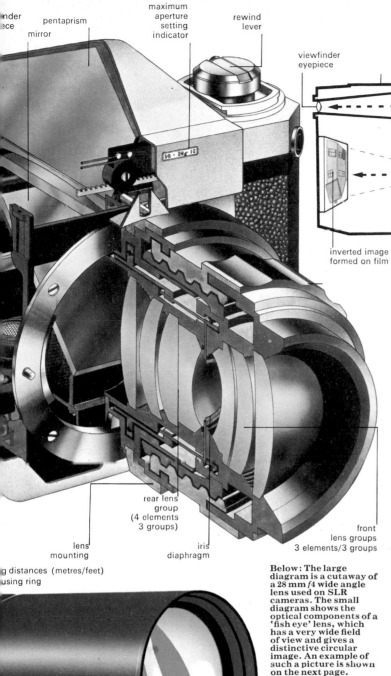

finder
piece

pentaprism

mirror

maximum
aperture
setting
indicator

rewind
lever

rear lens
group
(4 elements
3 groups)

lens
mounting

iris
diaphragm

front
lens groups
3 elements/3 groups

viewfinder
eyepiece

viewfinder
lens

light entering viewfinder

shutter

light entering main lens

main lens

inverted image
formed on film

iris
diaphragm

Above: This diagram shows how the image is produced within a camera. Light enters the lens, and passes through the diaphragm which controls the amount of light entering the camera. An inverted image is produced on the film when the shutter is opened, usually by a spring mechanism.

Right: Two 'instant picture' cameras. The Kodak Disc 4000 uses a negative disc which has 15 frames, each measuring 8 by 10 mm. It has fixed exposure and focus which make it easy to use. The Polaroid 660 produces excellent instant prints, each one measures 8 by 8 cm.

Rank Audio Visual Ltd.

Below: The large diagram is a cutaway of a 28 mm f4 wide angle lens used on SLR cameras. The small diagram shows the optical components of a 'fish eye' lens, which has a very wide field of view and gives a distinctive circular image. An example of such a picture is shown on the next page.

Right: This picture of a Rolleiflex SL 86 camera was taken by means of a new technique called *Neutrography*. This process is similar to X-ray photograph, but it uses beams of neutrons instead of X-rays. The image is much more detailed than those produced by X-ray photography.

General Electric Co.

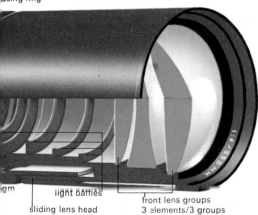

g distances (metres/feet)

using ring

light baffles

sliding lens head

gm

front lens groups
3 elements/3 groups

Above: A diagram of a typical telephoto lens design. This one has a focal length of 250 mm and a focal ratio of f4, and would be used on a single lens reflex camera. The light baffles within the unit prevent reflections from the inside of the tube, which would lower the contrast of the image.

Left: A Nikkormat EL 35 mm SLR made by Nippon Kogaku K.K. (Nikon) of Japan. This camera has an electronic exposure control system, which automatically adjusts the shutter speed to give the correct exposure time for a given aperture setting. The camera shown here is fitted with a 50 mm f1.4 lens.

WIDE ANGLE LENS

FISHEYE
LENS

iris
diaphragm

focusing
ring

aperture setting

depth of field scale

grapher considers when selecting a lens. First, the *focal length* – the distance between the lens and the image it produces. It is not really so much the actual distance that is important as the scale of the image produced. For an ordinary single lens reflex (SLR) camera using 35 mm wide film, a typical standard lens has a focal length of about 45 mm to 55 mm, and produces a field of view suitable for general photography. A longer focal length – up to 400 mm is common, and press photographers may use 1000 mm – gives a more magnified image, although taking in only a small field of view: these are called *telephoto lenses*. Lenses with shorter standard focal lengths, say 28 mm, are called *wide angle lenses* since they give a much wider field of view. Extreme versions, with focal lengths of 6 mm or so, are called *fish eye lenses*. *Zoom lenses* have a variable focal length and are used to 'move in on' a distant object to make a close-up shot.

The second consideration is the *focal* 417

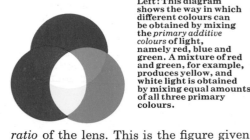

Left: This diagram shows the way in which different colours can be obtained by mixing the *primary additive colours* of light, namely red, blue and green. A mixture of red and green, for example, produces yellow, and white light is obtained by mixing equal amounts of all three primary colours.

Science Museum

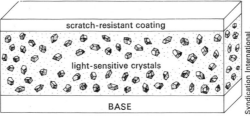

Left: The first colour photograph, of a piece of tartan ribbon, which was taken by James Clerk Maxwell (1831-1879) in 1861. The picture was made up of three negatives, each corresponding to one of the primary colours. Projecting these onto a screen, using coloured lights, produced a full colour image.

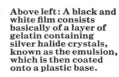

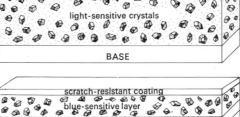

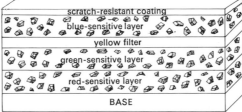

Syndication International

Above left: A black and white film consists basically of a layer of gelatin containing silver halide crystals, known as the emulsion, which is then coated onto a plastic base.

Left: A colour film has three separate emulsions, each sensitive to one of the primary colours.

Above: The Olympic swimming pool, Munich, taken with a fish eye lens.

Below and below left: Two pictures taken from the same position using lenses of different focal lengths. The picture on the left was taken with a normal lens, and the other with a telephoto lens.

ratio of the lens. This is the figure given by dividing the focal length by the maximum *aperture*—the clear diameter of the lens. Thus a 40 mm focal length lens with a full aperture of 10 mm has a focal ratio of 4—usually written *f*4. By cutting down the aperture of the lens, using an *iris diaphragm* (an arrangement of metal blades), the focal ratio can be altered, reducing the amount of light passing through the lens. The focal length remains the same, but if the area of the lens has been reduced by half (an aperture of 7.14 mm instead of 10 mm) the focal ratio is now 5.6. The difference between *f*4 and *f*5.6 is called one *stop*—because the ring which controls the iris diaphragm usually has click stops at each halving of the lens area. A full range of stops thus runs 1.4, 2.0, 2.8, 4.0, 5.6, 8, 11, 16, 22 and so on (some of these numbers are rounded off).

The lens' basic *f*-number is when it is wide open, letting in most light. Thus taking pictures in dim light requires a lens with a small basic *f*-number used at full aperture. But at full aperture any imperfections in the lens will be most obvious, so for perfect definition it is best to use a smaller aperture than the maximum possible on any given lens. In addition, the *depth of field* is smallest at full aperture. That is, the range of sharp focus is very small, so that only objects at the exact distance for which the lens is set will be perfectly sharp.

Shutter speeds are also arranged to vary by a factor of 2 between the click stops. So an exposure that was correct at 1/125 sec and *f*8 on a given film can be matched by one at 1/500 at *f*4, trading depth of field for a fast shutter speed which will 'freeze' movement.

If the lenses are to be interchangeable, giving different fields of view in each case, the photographer needs to know how much of the scene is appearing on the film. With non-interchangeable lens cameras, a *viewfinder* is quite adequate—a simple lens system, showing the field of view of the main lens. A development of this is the *twin lens reflex*, in which the viewfinder lens is similar to the main lens and is focused by the same mechanism. Its image is thrown on to a ground glass screen, so that the photographer can both focus up and frame the picture knowing that the main lens is seeing almost exactly the same image.

Many cameras are of the *single lens reflex* (SLR) type, where the image produced by the main lens is reflected by a mirror (placed within the camera, immediately in front of the shutter) up to a ground glass screen. The mirror swings out of the way just before the picture is taken. The photographer views the ground glass screen by means of a *pentaprism*, a prism with a pentagonal cross-section, which reflects the image so that it can be seen the right way round and in the same direction as the view being photographed. The viewfinder thus shows exactly the same scene as the lens.

Syndication International

Films and emulsions

The image from the lens is recorded by a light-sensitive layer called the *emulsion*, which is coated on to the film or plate material. The word 'emulsion' applies to any mixture consisting of fine particles distributed evenly throughout a liquid. The particles are thus suspended, rather than dissolved, in the liquid. In photographic emulsions, the liquid is gelatin and the particles are crystals or *grains* of silver halide. The emulsion is dried after being coated on to the film or plate, producing a solid coating of gelatin with halide grains dispersed evenly throughout.

Gelatin is made from the hooves and hides of animals. It has the almost unique property of being able to absorb water, so that it swells to several times its original size, and then dries to a solid again. It is also nearly transparent, and has chemical properties which improve the final emulsion.

Silver halides are the *salts* of silver and the *halogen* gases; chlorine, iodine and bromine are the common halogens. The grains are formed chemically in a warm solution of gelatin. The exact rate of addition of the chemicals and the temperature determine the final grain size and emulsion properties.

When a photograph is taken, there is no visible change in the emulsion's appearance. The action of light on a grain is to form a minute speck of metallic silver out of the silver halide. There is a range of sensitivity to light among the grains, so not all will be affected equally and thus subtle gradations of tone are possible. If there is a comparatively large amount of light, then a large number will be affected; if a small amount, only a few will contain the silver specks. Thus an invisible *latent image*, a pattern of halide grains containing silver specks which corresponds to the original pattern of light and shade of the image from the lens, is produced by the exposure in the camera.

This latent image is made visible by a process called *developing*. The developing agent is a chemical, such as *hydroquinone*, which will reduce silver halide to silver. The silver halide grains which have been exposed to light are more susceptible to conversion to silver, and during the carefully timed development process only the grains affected by light are converted to silver, in the form of tangled, fibre-like particles which appear black in colour. The developer is usually diluted with water, which makes the

POLAROID SX-70 CAMERA

eye piece

taking mirror

,000 r.p.m.
otor drives
xposed film
om camera

film pack

L/D control
controls
exposure
time

flash socket

photocell

lens

gear train

printed circuit

battery

shutter blades

FILM PACK

final images

diffuse
ghout reagent

black   white blue green   red

processing rollers

shutter button

developing film

clear
plastic
layer

acid
polymer
layer

timing layer

positive image
in receiving
layer

aspheric
mirror

spacers

mirror

light path

negative
base

yellow

magenta

cyan

exposed regions trap
dye developer in
molecules

in unexposed regions the
dye-developer molecules
diffuse upward unhindered

sensitized layers with negative
images in complementary colours

dye-developer
layers

processing
rollers

rubber
seal

Fresnel
mirror

hinged
carrier

film pack

Polaroid

**Above: The SX-70
Polaroid camera.**
Polaroid film contains
layers of chemicals
which develop the
exposed film, and the
image is chemically
transferred onto the
print paper. The
exposed film is passed
between two pressure
rollers which burst the
envelope containing the
chemicals, initiating
the developing and
printing processes.

Left: This series of
pictures shows the
gradual development of
an image on Polaroid
colour film after it
leaves the camera.

gelatin swell so that all the suspended grains are accessible to the developing agent.

Once the development has proceeded far enough, the film is washed to remove all traces of the developing agent. The next step is to 'fix' the film by immersing it in a chemical such as *ammonium thiosulphate* or *sodium thiosulphate* ('hypo') which makes the unwanted silver halide (which has not turned black) soluble in water. The developed silver is not affected by this, so after a final wash to remove the dissolved halides the film can be dried.

The result is an image in which the brightest areas of the scene are dark, and the darkest are light—a *negative*. To make a positive print, this must be projected on to photographic paper using an enlarger. The paper is also coated with emulsion, and it is processed in the same way as film.

The sensitivity of an emulsion to light is called its *speed*. Fast films are the most sensitive, and slow films the least. There are two main systems for measuring film speed, ASA (American Standards Association) and DIN (Deutsche Industrie Normen). In the ASA system, a doubling in film sensitivity gives a doubling in the speed figure, while in the DIN system the figure increases by 3 for every stop. Thus a film of speed 200 ASA corresponds to 24 DIN, while one of 400 ASA is 27 DIN.

Colour and reversal film

A colour film is essentially three black and white emulsions together (a *tripack*), each sensitive to a different colour of light. These colours are usually red, green and blue, since by adding different amounts of these almost any colour can be produced.

An emulsion is normally only sensitive to blue light, but by adding certain dyes which absorb light of other colours, the grains can be made sensitive to other colours as well. Since they are still blue-sensitive, a yellow filter (which cuts out blue light) is deposited in the tripack above the red- and green-sensitive layers.

To make the black and white emulsion yield colour images, dyes have to be substituted for the developed silver. In the case of colour negative films, used for making colour prints, the colours opposite to the layer's sensitivity are used—that is, yellow in the blue layer, magenta (pinkish) in the green layer and cyan (bluish-green) in the red layer. When the negative is enlarged on colour paper, which also produces colours opposite to those it sees, the original colours are produced. The negative film often has an orange 'mask' or overall colouring to correct for colour bias in the printing paper.

This two-stage process is not necessary if a transparency, rather than a negative, is required. The system by which positive transparencies are produced from the original film is called *reversal processing*.

After development and washing, the film carries a developed image consisting of silver, but also a reverse image consisting of undeveloped silver halide—those parts of the image which received little or no exposure. If the negative silver image is first bleached out, these areas can themselves be developed up so as to give a positive image. In the case of colour film this image can be dyed in the original colours—blue in the blue-sensitive layer, and so on.

419

Sound Recording

The first recorded sounds, traditionally supposed to have been the words 'Mary had a little lamb', were made in 1877 on the *phonograph* invented by Thomas Edison (1847-1931). This device recorded sound vibrations as indentations in a cylinder covered in tinfoil, although later models used a wax surface. The next significant development was the *gramophone*, invented some 10 years later, which registered the vibrations in a spiral groove on a flat circular disc. Neither of these machines used any method of amplifying the sound before recording it, except for a resonating sound box which acted in the same way as the body of a violin or guitar, and it was mainly for this reason that their performance was relatively poor.

Good quality recorded sound only became possible in the 1920s, when the first electrically assisted recording techniques were developed. The gramophone had by then established its superiority over the phonograph, and for the next 20 years professional organisations such as radio stations recorded entirely on discs.

The possibility of using metal wire or tape to store sounds magnetically had been recognized as early as 1880 by Alexander Bell (1847-1922), the inventor of the telephone. Bell, however, abandoned the idea as impracticable with the technology then available. Then, in 1898, Valdemar Poulsen (1869-1942) demonstrated a working wire recorder which he called the *telegraphone*, and for the next 40 years work proceeded in several countries with the aim of developing a high fidelity magnetic recorder.

The big breakthrough came in Germany during the 1930s with the development of plastic tape coated with iron oxide. The process of recording on magnetic tape involves a series of conversions of the sound energy into different forms. The first of these, performed by a *microphone*, translates the fluctuating sound vibrations into an electric voltage which fluctuates in exactly the same way. Next, this signal is fed to an amplifier, which increases its strength to a level suitable for use by the recording head, which converts it once again, this time into a fluctuating magnetic field. This field aligns particles of iron oxide (or chromium dioxide in the latest tapes) on the surface of the tape (which is driven past it) to produce a pattern of magnetization on the tape which reflects the sound pattern at the microphone.

Microphones

There are several different types of microphone, each of which has its particular advantages. One of the cheapest and most robust is the *crystal microphone* which relies on the *piezoelectric effect*, whereby certain crystals generate an electric voltage whenever they are bent or twisted. This voltage is proportional to the extent of the bending. The crystal in such a microphone is firmly clamped at one end and attached at the other to a flexible diaphragm.

Sound waves make the diaphragm vibrate and in doing so it bends the crystal back and forth, giving rise to an oscillating voltage which is picked up by leads attached to the crystal surface. The

Left: These Dictaphone machines worked on the same principle as Edison's phonograph. The machine on the right is a Type A recorder; when dictating a letter, the user spoke into the tube and the sound vibrations moved a cutting stylus that made impressions on a wax cylinder. When the letter was to be typed, the secretary used the machine on the left, a Type B transcriber, to play the cylinder.

Right: A tape cassette. The tape is contained within the cassette, each end being fixed to a small spool. Tape speed is 4.75 cm/sec (1.875 in/sec), and a pressure pad (bottom) keeps it in contact with the heads.

Right: This recorder, invented by Valdemar Poulsen in 1900, used a steel tape wound around a cylinder. The record/replay head was driven along by the leadscrew as the cylinder was rotated, so that it tracked along the length of the tape. The microphone is on the left, and replay was via the pair of telephone earpieces on the right.

Below: One of the first tape recorders to use a non-metallic tape coated with iron oxide. The first tapes of this kind were made of paper, but were soon replaced by coated plastic tapes. The machine shown here was built by AEG in Germany in 1936, and the tape was made by BASF.

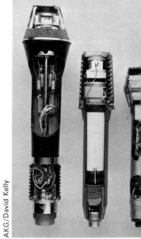

Above: Cutaway models of three types of cardioid microphone. These respond well to sound coming from in front of them, but less well to sound coming from the rear. They are commonly made by building a ribbon and a dynamic microphone into the same case. In such a microphone the ribbon element responds only to sounds coming from in front of it.

Left: A wire recorder of the 1930s. Steel wire is still used as a recording medium today, in aircraft flight recorders which record details such as the airspeed, altitude and control settings. Steel tape and ordinary plastic-based tape are also used in flight recorders.

Philips

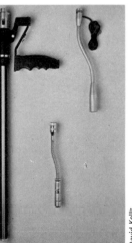

Left: A cardioid microphone (top right), an omnidirectional dynamic microphone (bottom right), and a 'rifle' type of directional microphone. The rifle microphone has a large number of narrow parallel tubes in front of the actual microphone element. Sounds entering the microphone from the front all have the same distance to travel along the tubes, and so they reach the element in phase with each other. Sounds entering from any other angle travel different distances along the tubes, and so reach the element out of phase with each other, effectively cancelling each other out. This makes the microphone highly directional.

David Kell

Ferrograph

EMI Ltd

Left and above: So sudden and increasingly rapid are the advances in stereophonic tapes and systems that relatively recent breakthroughs can look dated very quickly. Shown left is a standard high quality tape recorder, fitted with the Dolby noise reduction system; it is a half-track recorder and its versatility revolutionized recording. Immediately above is a modern Sony Stowaway, which is so small that you can carry your favourite music around in your pocket – and yet expect to hear it reproduced in exceptionally high quality.

response, however, is by no means perfect, treble (high) frequencies responding far better than any other frequencies. It is not consistent either, and tends to vary with changes in temperature and humidity.

The *moving coil microphone*, also called the *dynamic microphone*, is a far superior device. It consists essentially of a coil of wire attached to a diaphragm. As the diaphragm vibrates in response to the sound, the coil slides up and down the centrepiece of an M-shaped permanent magnet. The coil thus cuts through the magnetic field lines, which induce a fluctuating voltage in it. This fluctuating voltage faithfully represents the variations in sound pressure.

Both crystal and moving coil microphones respond equally well to sound from all directions and are consequently called *omnidirectional*, but this may not always be desirable as they tend to pick up unwanted background sounds too clearly. Often a microphone which detects better in one direction than others is more suitable, and this is a characteristic property of the *ribbon microphone*. A thin corrugated aluminium ribbon is suspended in the field of a permanent magnet and the sound arriving at the front or back of the ribbon causes it to move in the magnetic field. This induces a current along its length which is picked up by connecting leads. Sound waves impinging from the sides have little effect because they meet the thin edge of the ribbon. Strictly speaking this is a *bidirectional* microphone because it responds equally well to sound from in front or behind.

If a ribbon is combined in the same case as a moving coil the result is a *cardioid* type microphone which responds well to sound from roughly in front of it but less well to sound which approaches from the rear.

Recording

The electrical signal from the microphone is boosted by an electronic amplifier and applied to the *record head* of the tape recorder. This is basically an electromagnet, formed by a circular core of magnetic alloy in which is cut a small gap about 0.025 mm (one thousandth of an inch) wide. This is energized by the signal current from the amplifier which passes through a wire coil wrapped around the core.

The magnetic field produced in this coil is channelled around the core and can only escape at the gap. And it is just in the area of this gap that the tape makes contact with the head, so that as the tape moves past the head it cannot avoid the effect of the magnetic field. In consequence the oxide particles of the tape are magnetized either along or against the direction of tape travel according to the direction of the magnetic field when they were passing the gap. The strength of the magnetization also varies with the intensity of the field. So a small area of tape carries a complete magnetic record of the sound pressure at the instant it passed the gap.

Unfortunately the recording produced in this straightforward manner would not satisfy even the least discriminating listener. This is because the tape is not constantly magnetized in simple proportion to the magnetic field in the gap. Although for very small fields it is, as the field increases the magnetization is more nearly proportional to the square of the field. Beyond about half its maximum (or saturation) value the magnetization is once more simply proportional to the field. In short, the tape magnetization is a very poor representation of the field in the recording head gap, and hence it is a poor record of the sound and introduces frequencies which are not present in the original.

Such distortion (a form of *harmonic distortion*) must obviously be prevented and the only way to do this is to ensure that the tape magnetization is always high enough to keep it out of the region where it is not proportional to the field. One solution is to superimpose the amplified microphone signal onto a very high frequency current which is called a *bias signal*. This keeps the tape magnetization out of the danger area but still allows it to be magnetized in both directions, thereby reducing the noise problem.

The tape must of course be completely unmagnetized when it reaches the record head, because any superfluous magnetization appears as noise when the tape is replayed. This is achieved by an *erase head*, which is constructed in the same way as the record head but with a larger gap. The coil of the erase head carries a rapidly varying current of sufficient strength to magnetize the tape to saturation, first in one direction and then in the other, several times as it passes the gap. Any initial magnetization of the tape is thus completely swamped.

The large gap of the erase head allows its field to extend some distance beyond it, so that as the tape leaves the gap it still undergoes cycles of magnetization which become weaker and weaker as it

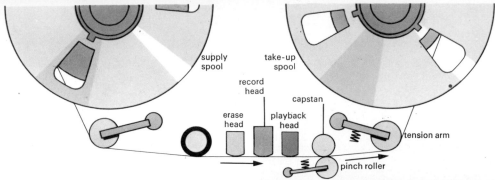

supply spool · take-up spool · record head · capstan · erase head · playback head · tension arm · pinch roller

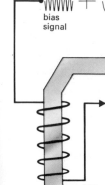

bias signal + sound signal

gap

Right: Two different ways of applying the bias signal to the tape. The conventional head arrangement feeds both the bias and the sound signals to the record head. The Akai Crossfield system uses a separate head to apply the bias in order to reduce the possibility of sound distortion.

Above: The tape drive and head layout of a high quality reel-to-reel tape recorder. The tape first passes the erase head, which wipes it clean of any previous magnetism, and then passes the record head which records the signal on to it. The playback head picks up this signal during replaying of the tape.

Right: The first step in record manufacture is the recording of the music. This picture shows three musicians recording at the EMI studios. Studio tape recorders use tape up to 5.08 cm (2 in) wide, and have 8, 16 or 24 tracks, compared with domestic machines which usually have only two or four tracks.

EMI Ltd

Decca/Photo: John Goldblatt

Far left: After the recording has been completed, the *master tape* is used to drive the cutting lathe (in the background) which produces a lacquer *master disc*. This is the last time the master tape itself will be used in the record manufacturing process. Moulds can now be taken from the master disc, and these will then be used in the record presses.

Left: The next step in record manufacture is the production of a *master shell* from the master disc. This picture shows the master disc after it has been given a very thin coating of silver. This silver coating then has 0.625 mm (0.025 in) of nickel deposited on top of it, to form the master shell which is finally separated from the master disc.

Below: A master shell about to have a further nickel shell, the *positive shell*, electroplated on to its silver face. The shells are then separated, and the positive shell goes on to the next step in the process.

recedes, vanishing to zero after a short distance to leave the tape completely demagnetized.

When the tape is replayed it is run past a *replay head* (or *playback head*), which is really only a record head operating in reverse—indeed many domestic machines use the same head for both purposes. As the magnetized tape passes the gap in the replay head, the tiny magnetic field which surrounds the tape surface is channelled around the core and hence through the surrounding coil. The alternations in this field, corresponding to the recorded sounds, generate a matching current in the coil (by electromagnetic induction, the same process which on a much larger scale is used to generate current in power stations). The current in the coil is then magnified in an amplifier which is usually the same one used when recording, and fed to a loudspeaker which converts it once again into sound.

Tape drive

For faithful reproduction of the sound it is essential that the tape is played back at the same speed as it is recorded and that this speed never fluctuates. In the earliest machines one of the two spools on which the tape is wound was directly driven by a motor and dragged the tape past the heads. But this led to unacceptable variations in speed which could be heard as *wow* and *flutter*. These are the sound engineers' names for audible fluctuations in the reproduced sound, wow referring to slow and flutter to rapid fluctuations.

On all modern machines it is the tape itself that is driven, by a spindle (often called the *capstan*) which is rotated by an electric motor. The tape is squeezed between this spindle and a rubber roller and is thus driven along at constant speed. The spools are also electrically driven via friction clutches which are adjusted to slip whenever the tension of the tape rises too high. This ensures that the tape does not break from being pulled too hard onto the spool or spill out of the machine from not being pulled fast enough.

To a large extent, the speed at which the tape moves determines the quality of the recording. If the tape moves too slowly it will not record high frequencies satisfactorily because too short a length of tape passes the head to accommodate the many thousands of oscillations which occur in the space of, for example, one second, when a high-pitched note is recorded. On the other hand, if the tape moves too quickly an inconveniently large reel of tape will be required for a given length of recording. In professional sound studios this does not matter and master recordings are made with the tape moving past the heads at a speed of 79 or 38 centimetres per second (30 or 15 inches per second). For domestic recorders a compromise is sought between quality and bulk so that 19 and 9½ cm/sec (7½ and 3¾ in/sec) are the common speeds.

Decca/John Goldblatt

Transworld

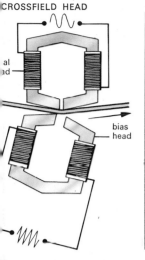

CROSSFIELD HEAD

al
ad

bias
head

Decca/Photo: John Goldblatt

Decca/Photo: John Goldblatt

Decca/Photo: John Goldblatt

Above: One of the later stages of record making is the production of the *matrix shell*, by depositing nickel on to the positive shell. Here, the two shells are being separated. The matrix shell is the one which will be used to press the actual records, having a spiral ridge which forms the groove of the record when it is pressed.

Right: Pressing a record. A 'biscuit' of extruded pvc, with the labels in place, is squeezed between two matrix shells (or stampers), one for each side of the record. 7-inch records are usually made by injecting hot plastic under pressure into a mould, instead of by this method which is used for 10 and 12 inch LP records.

Left: This machine trims excess plastic from the edges of the records after pressing.

Below: This series of diagrams shows some of the main stages involved in the recording and manufacture of long playing records.

Cassette recorders

The major difference between cassette recorders and normal reel-to-reel machines is that the tape is permanently contained within a plastic box, the cassette, which includes both a storage and a take-up spool. The tape passes through guides along the edge of the box in which there are apertures which allow contact with the erase and record/replay heads.

Irregularities on the tape surface give rise to a slight hissing noise and if the high frequencies are boosted to compensate for loss of high frequencies due to the slow speed (4.75 cm/sec, 1.875 in/sec) of the cassette, this noise is also increased so that it tends to drown out soft passages of music or speech, particularly if they are predominantly low-pitched. There is, however, a method of overcoming this difficulty.

It is known as the *Dolby system*, after its inventor, and relies on sophisticated electronic circuitry to detect low level passages. These are given extra amplification so that they are recorded at as much as ten times their normal intensity and when they are played back they are *attenuated* (reduced in volume) by an equal amount. The result is that these quiet passages replay at their proper level but the tape noise is only a small fraction of the total sound.

Manufacturers have developed the cassette format in other areas — notably in the coatings used on the tapes. The best machines and tapes are now capable of making recordings that are only a little poorer than those made by high-quality professional reel-to-reel recorders — with much greater convenience and at a far lower cost.

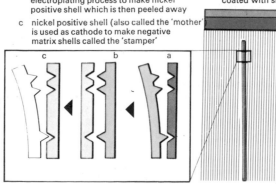

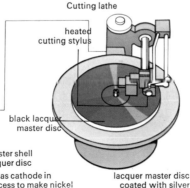

Cutting lathe

heated cutting stylus

Master tape

black lacquer master disc

lacquer master disc coated with silver

Performance

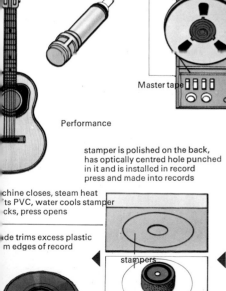

stamper is polished on the back, has optically centred hole punched in it and is installed in record press and made into records

chine closes, steam heat 's PVC, water cools stamper cks, press opens

de trims excess plastic m edges of record

a negative silver master shell is peeled from lacquer disc

b silver shell is used as cathode in electroplating process to make nickel positive shell which is then peeled away

c nickel positive shell (also called the 'mother' is used as cathode to make negative matrix shells called the 'stamper'

c   b   a

stampers

'biscuit' & labels

press

Sound Reproduction

Since the 1940s the techniques of sound reproduction have developed at an amazing pace. Today's amateur enthusiast can enjoy a quality of sound which would have astonished even a professional sound engineer before the Second World War.

Sound is usually encoded in one of three forms—in the grooves of a disc, in the magnetized oxide particles on the surface of a tape, or as variations in the amplitude or frequency of a radio wave—and the first stage in reproducing it is to convert it into an electric signal whose variations correspond to those of the original sound signal. The next step is to boost this signal to a more manageable level in a *preamplifier*, which at the same time compensates for any distortion which may have been accidentally or deliberately introduced. Controls for volume and tone are usually incorporated in this section of the equipment.

The signal is then in the right form to operate a loudspeaker, but it lacks strength and must therefore be amplified once again by a *power amplifier*. The loudspeaker is the final link in the chain and serves to convert the amplified electrical signal into vibrations of the air, thus reproducing the original sound.

Most equipment made today reproduces sound *stereophonically*. Stereophonic or stereo recordings and radio programmes are designed to give a more natural effect when replayed by taking into account the ability of our ears to detect the direction as well as the intensity of sounds. If directional information is absent in the reproduced sound it appears somewhat incomplete. When a stereo recording is made, two microphones (or two sets of microphones) are used, one of which receives more sound from the left and the other more from the right. The sounds detected by each are kept entirely separate and are encoded in two completely independent 'channels' of the recording or programme. Stereo reproducing equipment is really only a duplication of ordinary single channel (*monophonic*) equipment, with independent amplifiers and speakers for each channel.

Record Players
When a disc recording is made, a master disc coated with lacquer is rotated at constant speed on a turntable. A heated cutting stylus travels slowly from the rim to the centre of the disc and cuts a spiral v-shaped groove in the lacquer. The walls of this groove are normally at 90° to each other when no sound is being recorded, as in the run-in and run-out grooves at the start and finish of every record. But the cutting stylus is also moved magnetically in response to electrical signals from the master tape recording. This leads it to cut undulations in the groove walls which encode the sound, with the left channel registered entirely on the inner groove wall and the right entirely on the outer.

The stylus moves much more for a low frequency sound than for a high frequency sound of the same intensity, so much so that it is necessary to deliberately decrease the intensity (or *attenuate*) bass

Left: A turn of the century Edison phonograph. The records were wax cylinders, rotated by a clockwork motor, and as they turned they vibrated a needle connected to a diaphragm within the unit at the bottom of the horn. The sound created by the vibrating diaphragm was amplified by the horn.

Above: The phonograph was eventually replaced by the gramophone, invented by Emile Berliner in 1887. The gramophone used flat discs instead of cylinders, and was the ancestor of today's record players. The first commercial gramophones and records were produced in Germany in 1889.

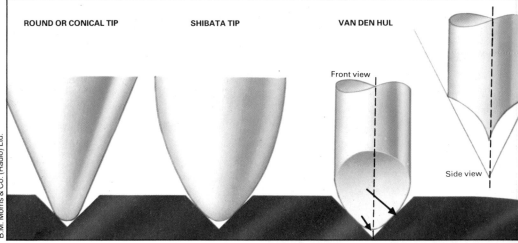

ROUND OR CONICAL TIP SHIBATA TIP VAN DEN HUL

Front view

Side view

sounds to avoid wide undulations of the stylus which would lead it to cut into adjoining grooves. In the final stage, the master disc is copied and any number of records can be manufactured from it.

Playing a record on a record player attempts to reverse the process by which the master disc was produced, translating the groove wall code back into electrical signals without loss of quality. However, there are two main reasons why this can never, even in the most expensive equipment, be achieved to perfection. The first is that it is not possible to use a stylus of exactly the same shape as the cutting stylus, because it would itself cut and damage the record. So a stylus with a rounded tip must be used and this cannot follow the undulations of the walls with complete accuracy because it cannot penetrate the recesses completely.

The more important difficulty is that the stylus, unlike the cutting stylus, cannot be mechanically driven across the record as it rotates. The reproducing stylus must therefore be pulled along by the forces exerted on it by the groove, and this means that the pressure of the stylus on the groove walls will vary. It is just feasible to suspend the stylus, like a travelling crane, from a rail which it

Below: In the ceramic pick-up cartridge, voltages are produced by the piezoelectric ceramic elements when they are bent by the motion of the stylus. In the magnetic cartridges, the output voltages are produced in the coils when the stylus motion creates changes in the magnetic field passing through them. This is done by moving the coils within a magnetic field (moving coil), moving an armature which links the field of a fixed magnet with a pair of coils (induced magnet), or by moving a magnet next to fixed coils (moving magnet).

CERAMIC

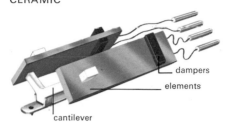

dampers
elements
cantilever

MOVING COIL

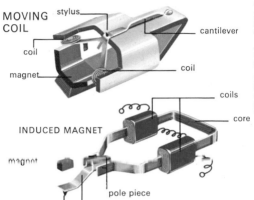

stylus
cantilever
coil
coil
magnet

INDUCED MAGNET

coils
core
magnet
pole piece
stylus
cantilever

MOVING MAGNET

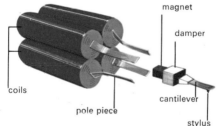

magnet
damper
coils
cantilever
pole piece
stylus

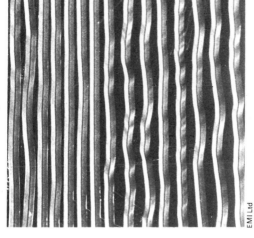

EMI Ltd

These four close-up photographs show the grooves of mono, stereo and quad records.

Above: The constant-width grooves of a mono record.

Below: A 45°/45° stereo record. The grooves are much more complicated, and their widths vary because the stylus must be moved vertically as well as laterally.

Above right: The grooves of a matrix quadraphonic disc are cut in the same way as those of a stereo disc.

Right: A discrete quadraphonic disc has a high frequency sub-signal cut on each wall of the groove.

Far left: Quality of sound reproduction depends on the accuracy with which the stylus traces the groove contours, and a variety of shapes are now available, all claiming improved contact. The simplest shape is conical, while the Shibata stylus gives a finer tracing radius. The Van den Hul stylus has a contact radius of only 0.00018 in. In addition, it has a straight contact line, or footprint, and is free of any tendency to twist on its own axis.

Below: This modern turntable, the Kenwood L-07D, features a highly rigid construction to eliminate signal loss caused by vibration.

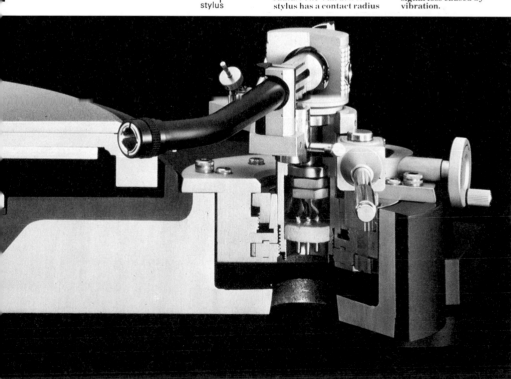

B M Morris & Co (Radio) Ltd

traverses from the rim to the centre of the record. This is the ideal because it ensures that the force pulling the stylus is always directed along the groove, but it is extremely costly to manufacture such a system to be neither so massive that it cannot follow the groove undulations quickly enough nor so weak that it sways and wobbles, introducing worse distortion than that which it was designed to prevent. The usual solution is to mount the stylus on a pivoted arm, known as the *tone arm*. Again, there are problems: however cunningly the tone arm is shaped it can never be exactly parallel to the groove over the whole width of the record. This introduces an unwanted force called *bias* which leads the stylus to press more against the inner than the outer wall. In practice bias can be compensated for by attaching a small weight to the other end of the tone arm in such a way that it tends to pull the stylus towards the rim.

The translation of the motion of the stylus into an electrical signal is accomplished by the *pick-up cartridge* which forms the business end of the tone arm. There are two main types of stereo cartridge, *ceramic* and *magnetic*. In the former, the stylus vibrations are transmitted by a connecting rod to two elements made of a crystalline ceramic material such as barium titanate, one of which is bent or twisted by vibrations in the plane of the inner groove wall and one by those of the outer wall. These elements thus produce, by the *piezoelectric effect*, two electrical signals which represent the left and right sound channels respectively.

In a magnetic *moving coil* cartridge the stylus is attached to two small wire coils, at 90° to each other, each of which

425

vibrates in the field of a permanent magnet. By electromagnetic induction, this produces in each coil a voltage which represents the left or right sound channel. *Moving magnet* cartridges have this arrangement reversed, with the magnet attached to the stylus in such a way that it induces voltages in stationary coils as it moves.

Tape recordings are very easily made in stereo, because all that is necessary is to devote one half of the tape width to each channel of sound. This of course produces a tape which must be rewound after each playing, so it is common to divide the tape width into four, using the first and third quarters for the two channels of one recording and the other two for a second, which is played in the reverse direction. The output from the tape replay heads is, like that from a record player cartridge, in the form of a weak electrical signal.

Amplification

Although records, tapes and radio programmes are all translated into electrical signals these are not all of the same strength. Consequently, if the same preamplifier is to be used for all three it must be equipped to amplify each signal to a different degree. A preamplifier consists of several transistor amplifier stages in sequence, with the output of each fed to the input of the next in line. Very weak signals like those from a magnetic cartridge are switched through all the stages and the strongest, those from ceramic cartridges, perhaps only through the last stage.

The different types of input also require different degrees of *equalization* to correct for the attenuation of the bass when recording discs or replaying tapes. Radio signals do not need any equalization, nor does the output from a ceramic cartridge because the ceramic elements themselves, when connected to a suitably high impedance, produce a higher output voltage at low frequencies than at higher. Equalization is achieved by taking advantage of the properties of capacitors, which impede low frequencies more than high. If these are inserted in appropriate places in the circuit, either bass or treble can be boosted or attenuated as required.

Nerve

Right: Combining the signals from several microphones. For mono, the signals are combined and reproduced in a single channel. With stereo (far right), the signals are combined into two channels.

Above right: The Nerve 8108 sound mixer. Features include: (1) Control of incoming signals from studio. (2) Filters to eliminate unwanted sound. (3) Parametric equalizers. (4) Auxiliary assignment and multi-track controls. (5) Secondary fader to adjust approximate sound. (6) Mix down control with pan potentiometers. (7) Primary fader to control the main sound balance and volume. (8) Interrogation switches to determine which microphones are feeding which tracks. (9) Remote control panel. (10) Touch pad facilities panel for quadraphonic listening.

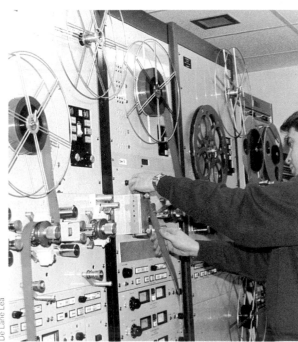

De Lane Lea

Right: A radio studio's magnetic tape recorder, which records the output from the mixing desk.

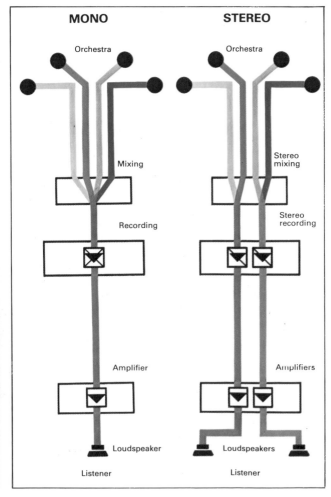

MONO | STEREO

Orchestra | Orchestra

Mixing | Stereo mixing

Recording | Stereo recording

Amplifier | Amplifiers

Loudspeaker | Loudspeakers

Listener | Listener

Capacitors are also used as part of the bass and treble tone controls, which divert a fraction of the signal through a network of capacitances and resistances which attenuates either the bass or the treble. A variable resistance, whose variation is controlled by a knob on the casing, determines what fraction is diverted. Filters are included in the better preamplifiers to eliminate very low-pitched sounds, like the 'rumble' which is caused by mechanical vibrations from the turntable or drive mechanism, and the 'hum' caused by stray radiations at the frequency of the mains supply, and also the very high-pitched noise which sometimes accompanies radio programmes. These filters are like fixed versions of the tone controls, consisting of capacitive networks which effectively cut out all frequencies below about 60 Hz or above about 10,000 Hz. The filters can be switched in or out of the circuit as required.

The power amplifier is often contained in the same case as the preamplifier. Its sole purpose is to amplify the signal from the preamplifier to a level at which it can drive the loudspeakers. It usually has two or more stages to achieve the necessary amplification, and each stage consists of two transistors because one alone has not enough range to accommodate the large current difference between the peaks and troughs of the signal at these stages.

Loudspeakers

The final stage of sound reproduction is the conversion of the electrical signal into sound waves by the loudspeaker. There are two main types of loudspeaker, *moving coil* and *electrostatic*. The most common are the moving coil speakers, in which the electrical signal is passed through a wire coil attached to a paper or plastic cone. The coil is free to slide over the centrepiece of an M-shaped permanent magnet which alternately repels and attracts it as the coil becomes magnetized in one direction and then the other. The cone is thus pushed and pulled against the air, creating sound waves.

One such speaker cannot faithfully reproduce the whole spectrum of sound for two reasons. One is that the coil impedes high frequencies more than low; the other is that the cone is mechanically more efficient at producing sound whose wavelength is roughly the same as its own diameter. A small cone is better for high frequencies and a large cone for low. Thus for good reproduction two or three or sometimes more speakers of different sizes are combined for each channel. An electronic *crossover network* of capacitors, inductors and resistors splits the amplifier signal current into separate frequency ranges and feeds one to each of the appropriately sized speakers. The bass speaker is often called a 'woofer' and the treble a 'tweeter'.

Electrostatic speakers work on a different principle. They move the air by means of a flat flexible diaphragm which is coated with electrically conductive material. This is fixed at a small distance from a metal plate of the same area to which the amplifier signal is applied. A small permanent polarizing voltage is maintained between the two, which induces opposite electric charges on the surface of each (making in fact a parallel plate capacitor). Applying the amplifier signal between the two causes the diaphragm to vibrate as it is alternately attracted and repelled by the plate. This principle is widely used for tweeters and occasionally for full-spectrum speakers, in which case the diaphragm is usually fixed between two perforated plates.

Headphones, which are miniature loudspeakers mounted in a lightweight headset, may also be of the moving coil or the electrostatic type. As is the case with loudspeakers, the majority of headphones in use at present are based on moving coil drive units. Electrostatic headphones, like electrostatic speakers, give a very clean sound, but most types must be connected to the amplifier via an adaptor unit which supplies the polarizing voltage.

Left: These bookshelf-sized speakers come with newly developed Polymer Graphite (PG) cones in the woofer and midrange units, and beryllium ribbon tweeters.

Below left: The look of today's computer-controlled receiver. This model offers a power output of 80 watts per channel. The built-in microcomputer controls the graphic equalizer and the tuner, and when the signal is very weak it automatically reduces the background noise. The liquid-crystal display shows the operating status of the receiver.

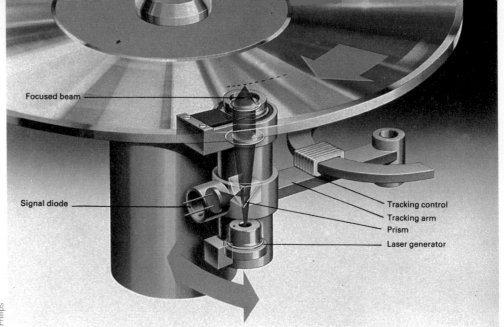

Focused beam

Signal diode

Tracking control

Tracking arm

Prism

Laser generator

Philips

Above: Part of the servo system in the Philips laser disc player which keeps the laser tracking the disc correctly.

Right: An analogue recording signal (top) is converted to a digital code (centre) and then back to analogue form as an output to the amplifier.

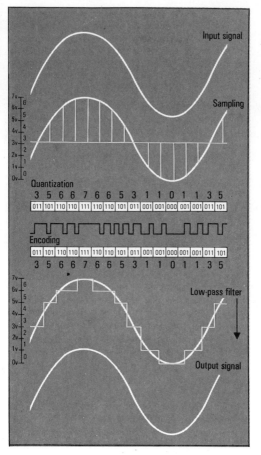

Input signal

Sampling

Quantization

Encoding

Low-pass filter

Output signal

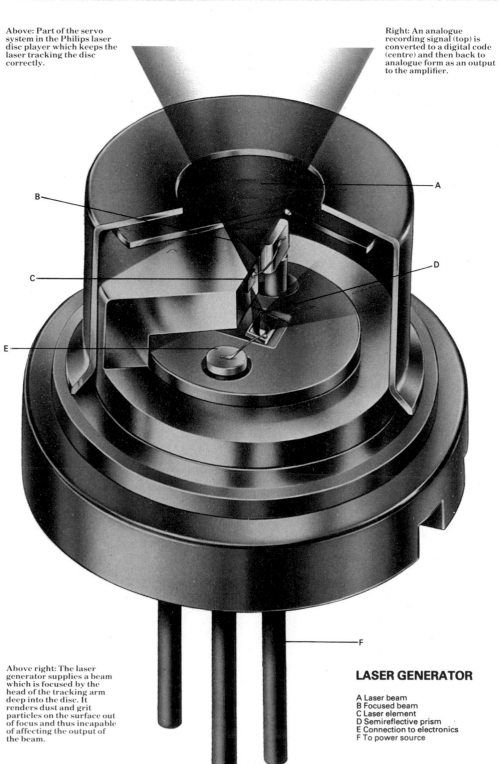

A
B
C
D
E
F

Above right: The laser generator supplies a beam which is focused by the head of the tracking arm deep into the disc. It renders dust and grit particles on the surface out of focus and thus incapable of affecting the output of the beam.

LASER GENERATOR

A Laser beam
B Focused beam
C Laser element
D Semireflective prism
E Connection to electronics
F To power source

Digital sound

The sound recording and reproducing methods and equipment described in this and the previous chapter have all been of the *analogue* type. The sound is encoded onto a record disc or a magnetic tape in wave forms that match (or are 'analogous' to) the original sound waves.

Though this system has the beauty of (relative) simplicity, there are many ways in which the analogue wave pattern that is created and reproduced can fall short of exactly matching the original, and there is a limit to how far faults can be corrected.

The way forward is to use computer techniques. During recording, the amplitude (i.e. volume) of the sound waveform is measured or *sampled* many thousands of times a second. Each of those measurements is converted into a number, and those numbers are recorded and stored in the form of a fast-flowing stream of computer *digits* — hence the term digital sound.

The advantage of digital recording is that the various distortions that would have been present on an analogue recording can be corrected for using computer-like techniques to a far higher degree of accuracy — so the sound you hear should be closer to perfect hi-fi than ever before.

The main problem is that the rate at which the digital numbers are produced is far too fast for them to be stored and reproduced using conventional audio equipment. However, *video* tape recorders and players are capable of handling these much faster flows of information, and it is derivatives of these pieces of equipment that are used for digital audio.

Some studios have been using digital tape recorders for some years — often these are simply professional video recorders with a special *analogue to digital converter* unit fitted that takes the

The Hollywood Bowl has the natural accoustic quality of the amphitheatre. Seating 3,000 people, it is used mainly for musical performances — notably 'Symphonies Under the Stars' in summertime — and has its own orchestra

(analogue) electrical signal from the recoding amplifiers and turns it into the string of digits that are stored on the recorder. Ordinary black vinyl LPs that are made from these recordings are often called 'digital', in fact they are made in the normal analogue way — the output from the digital recorder being passed through a *digital to analogue converter* first. This can certainly help sound quality, because all the processing, mixing and so on can be done in the studio with the sound in its digital form, and quality can be main-

tained. But it is only a half-way house.

Compact Discs are unlike conventional LPs because the sound pattern engraved on them is still in digital form. Instead of a wiggly spiral groove cut into the surface of the disc, a Compact Disc has innumerable microscopic metallized pits—each less than one-millionth of a metre in length—etched into its surface. The length and spacing of these pits carries the audio information. A special Compact Disc player is used to read the information off the disc, using a laser

beam rather than a conventional stylus. The beam is aimed at the pits, and is reflected off them in varying ways depending on the 'sound' contained within them. And it's only after reading the disc in this way that the information is converted into an analogue form so that it can be amplified and converted back into sound by conventional hi-fi amplifiers and loudspeakers. All the distortions introduced by conventional record players are eliminated, and the resulting sound quality can be much higher.

Cinema

Draw a little 'matchstick man' on the edge of a page of a book. On subsequent pages, draw similar men with slight differences, so that the movement of arms or legs is split up into individual steps. Now flick the pages so that the individual steps join up into a continuous movement and the man becomes animated.

If your eye and brain were remarkably alert, you would still be able to discriminate each individual step. But this is usually impossible as a result of *persistence of vision*. This is an effect of the eye and brain combined, and means that we do not see separate images if they occur more rapidly than about 12 times per second.

The earliest attempts at making moving pictures, during the second half of the 19th century, used the book page principle, or else consisted of a rotating cylinder with slots, each of which showed for an instant a slightly different picture on the inside of the cylinder. But the real breakthrough came in 1895, when the Lumière brothers in France demonstrated the forerunner of the modern cinema, taking photographs on a long strip of film and projecting each one for a split second.

Because each individual picture, or *frame*, needs an exposure time of about 1/50 sec, the film has to be motionless for a brief period in the film *gate*, to avoid blurring the image produced by the camera's lens. Then it must be moved on very quickly and brought to rest in time for the exposure of the next frame. This *intermittent motion*, first invented by Etienne-Jules Marey in the 1880s, was the secret of the success of the Lumière brothers' technique, and today's cameras work on the same principle. The usual method is to engage a claw in the sprocket holes of the film. This jerks the film along, then extracts itself and moves along to the next set of holes while the film remains stationary as the exposure is made. Meanwhile, a sector cut out of a disc rotating in front of the gate admits light only for a fraction of a second, cutting off the image while the film is being moved.

This procedure occurs at a standard rate. The normal shooting rate for cinema films is 24 frames per second, while amateur films are usually shot at 18 frames per second for greater economy of film.

Professional motion picture cameras generally have a viewfinder which, by a reflex system, shows the image as seen through the camera lens, rather than using a separate viewfinder system. A common way of doing this is to make the rotating shutter disc reflective, viewing the image mirrored in it except when the shutter is open.

There are four main film widths currently in use: 8 mm, 16 mm, 35 mm and 65 mm. The first is mainly for amateur film making, while the others are for professional and feature film work. Most television news or documentary films are on 16 mm film, while feature films for TV and cinema are on 35 mm. The 65 mm film size is used for major cinema films, often wide screen spectaculars, and the image

Science Museum

Left: An early movie camera, made in 1896. Thomas Edison, in the USA, produced the first commercial motion pictures in 1891, but these were viewed in a sort of peep-show machine rather than projected on a screen. The first motion pictures intended for viewing on a screen were produced in France by Louis and Auguste Lumière, whose camera, which also served as a projector, was patented in February 1895. This machine, called the 'Cinématographe', had its first public demonstration in Paris on 28 December that year.

Below: An Arriflex 35 mm movie camera, mounted on a tripod. The film is carried in the *magazine* on top of the camera body, and there are three lenses, of different focal lengths, mounted on a *turret* at the front of the camera. The turret is rotated to bring the required lens into position.

is transferred to 70 mm film for projection to include the soundtrack.

Sound recording
In some 16 mm movie cameras used for TV news filming, the signals from a microphone are recorded directly on to a strip of magnetic oxide 2.54 mm (0.1 in) wide coated down one edge of the film, a method which ensures that the sound and vision are kept precisely synchronized with each other. Most professional equipment, however, does not use this system. Instead, the sound is recorded separately on a good quality tape recorder and later transferred, along with music and other effects, to the sound track of the finished film.

Editing
Film scenes are very rarely shot in the same order in which they are shown. For example, all shots made at one particular location will be taken together, even though they may appear in different parts of the finished film. Since only one camera is normally used, many sequences will have to be repeated from different angles —if two people are talking together each actor's part may be filmed separately from over the other's shoulder. For action scenes, however, another camera may be used to provide 'cuts' or alternative views, as it would be difficult to repeat the same events exactly.

The job of putting all this together in the right order, along with titles, special effects and background music, may take several months for a full length film. Much of the work is done using a machine called a *Steenbeck* or *Moviola*, which enables film and soundtrack to be run

Right: A sequence of frames from a cartoon film. The amount of work involved in drawing and then photographing a cartoon film can be considerable; for example, this entire sequence would provide only about one third of a second of viewing time at a speed of 24 frames per second.

The reflex viewfinder of a movie camera uses light reflected from the shutters

1 shutter motor
2 vertical driveshaft
3 helical gear
4 reflective shutter blade
5 stock of film
6 film plane
7 camera lens
8 focussing screen
9 field lens
10 prism
11 viewfinder optics

Below: A cutaway drawing of a professional movie camera. The *matte box* in front of the lenses is used to hold mattes during special effects filming. The small diagram on the left shows the optical components of the reflex viewfinder system used on such a camera.

1 Locknut
2 Matte support bar
3 Front effects stage
4 Front adjustment
5 Matte box
6 Rear adjustment
7 Prime lens
8 Front filter rack
9 Rear filter rack (revolving)
10 Ground glass screen
11 Rear of prime lens
12 Centre turret pivot

13 180° mirror shutter at 45° to the film plane
14 Intermittent film claw
15 Mount for lens 3
16 Alternative lens (2nd)
17 Neck strap lug
18 Field lens
19 Focussing levers
20 Prism
21 Film plane
22 Registration pin
23 Filmgate
24 Film stock
25 Lens barrel locks
26 Turret shift tabs
27 Pressure rollers
28 Viewfinder optics (10x)
29 3 lens divergent turret
30 Feed film spool
31 Geared sprockets
32 Take-up film spool
33 Viewfinder focus
34 Eyepiece cup

Left: An early system for producing optical soundtracks, which could also be used as a sound recorder during location filming. Some of the first 'talking pictures', introduced in the 1920s, had the sound recorded on gramophone records, but these were soon superseded by films with soundtracks.

Science Museum

Right: Special effects man Ray Harryhausen arranging a scene for the Columbia film 'Jason and the Argonauts'. The scene was shot in a large tank of water, using models for the cliffs and for the boat and its occupants. The wave effects in the water were created by a wave-making machine at the edge of the tank.

Grange Calverly/Bob Godfrey Films Ltd

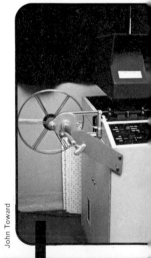

together, frame by frame, for matching and cutting purposes. The film which is used for preliminary cutting is not the original black and white or colour negative, which is unsuitable for viewing anyway. Instead, prints (positive copies) are made and the original is kept until the editing has been finalized. When the editing is completed, the original negative is cut and the final prints made. This involves *grading* the colour—making sure that the exposure and colour balance are the same from shot to shot.

Music and other sounds can now be added. Quite often it is necessary to match the music to the film, so the musicians perform in a studio with a projector so they can link the two. In many cases extra sounds are added in this *dubbing studio*, such as suitably satisfying cracks, thuds and howls during fight scenes which may well be filmed without the sound being recorded.

Finally a master soundtrack is mixed together, using multitrack facilities similar to those in recording studios. There are two ways of adding sound to a film—by *optical* or by *magnetic* soundtracks. It was the optical system which first came into general use, and is still commonly employed today. Alongside the picture area of the film are two continuous clear lines on a black area, whose width variations correspond to the soundtrack signal like the wiggles in the groove of a record. To play the soundtrack requires a photocell which responds to the variations in the intensity of light passing through the soundtrack, and produces a correspondingly varying electrical signal which is then amplified and passed to the cinema's loudspeakers.

The alternative system uses a stripe of the same type of magnetic oxide as used on recording tape. This is coated down both edges of the film, so that the extra thickness does not cause the film to wind unevenly on the spool.

Special effects
As well as the wide range of mechanical effects used to make films, such as the small explosive charges which produce realistic bullet wound effects when detonated beneath an actor's clothes, there are *optical effects* which are only possible on film. In the early days such tricks as double exposure were used, but now there are a wide range of specialized techniques, some of which require extensive laboratory facilities.

Some effects, such as the destruction of cities, are carried out using models, with no other illusion than that caused by the lack of scale. Where some monster or mythical creature is required, it will often be made as a model with flexible limbs. These are filmed frame by frame, with slight movements between each frame. Where the model is to be combined with human action, the model can be placed in front of a screen on which is projected, again frame by frame, previously-shot film of the actors. The screen may be translucent with the film projected from behind (back projection) or it may be highly reflective with the film projected from the front. The image from the projector also strikes the model, but as it is not so reflective as the screen it does not show it. These two projection techniques are also widely used at full scale with actors, for example to make it appear that they are in a moving car or perhaps in a desert.

Another method of faking a background is the *glass shot*, which uses a sheet of glass close to the camera on which details are painted. The camera views the scene through the glass, but the aperture is chosen so that both the glass painting and the scene are in focus. This may be used on location to add some landscape details or remove others by obscuring them.

One widely used method of superimposing one scene on another or achieving special effects is by means of the *matte* technique. In its simplest form, this involves masking out part of the scene being photographed by a piece of black card, the matte, right in front of the camera. Then another piece of card, which masks out the rest of the picture but leaves the originally masked area clear, is

This series of pictures shows the main stages involved in making a film.
1. Shooting a scene in a studio. The camera is mounted on a *camera crane*. The picture to the right shows a Panavision camera, mounted in an aircraft, which was used in filming aerial action for the film 'Battle of Britain', and the top picture is a set used in François Truffaut's 'Day for Night'.

2. After shooting, the film is processed in an automatic developing machine.

3. Sound recorded during shooting is transferred from tape to magnetically coated film.

4. The sound and picture are edited.

5. Music and sound effect tracks are added to the dialogue track.

6. These tracks, with the picture, are then played through the dubbing console, where the tone and volume of each track are adjusted to give the correct sound balance.

2

3

4

5

6

7. The magnetic recording of the mixed soundtrack is run on the *replay machine* (on the right), whose output signal drives the camera unit (left) which produces the optical soundtrack.

8. The brightness and colour balance of the picture are adjusted on a *visual colour grader*. The control settings are recorded on punched paper tape, then used to control the machine that produces the final prints.

9. The picture negative and the negative of the optical soundtrack are loaded into this printer, which produces the final combined picture and sound prints that are later distributed to cinemas.

8

7

9

substituted, the film is wound back in the camera and the scene is shot again to fill in the new part of the scene.

Alternatively, the new piece of action, photographed separately, is added in an *optical printer*, which enables two separate pieces of film to be photographed together on to a third. This allows the use of *travelling mattes*, which can change shape and move. Sometimes the mattes are prepared photographically by lighting the unwanted part of the film set in a hue which affects only the blue-sensitive layer of the colour film. This region can then be turned black by photographic techniques.

Cartoons are made by drawing each frame separately and projecting them in sequence, just as in the matchstick man technique. To save a lot of time the backgrounds are prepared separately and the moving characters are painted on transparent overlays called *cels*. The limbs of cartoon characters are painted on separate cels so that their positions can be changed easily. Usually the soundtrack is recorded first and the drawings made to match it.

Projectors

Projectors are mechanically quite similar to cameras—in fact, the Lumières used their cameras as projectors by placing a lamp behind the processed film as it passed through the gate. Modern projectors, however, are purpose built.

The light source used in amateur projectors is a tungsten or quartz halogen light bulb. In large cinema projectors, arc lamps, or more recently xenon discharge tubes, are used.

In order to even out the coverage of light across the film, projectors use a *condenser* system. This usually consists of a concave mirror placed behind the light source, to make use of the light given off to the rear of the lamp, and a lens in front of the source which concentrates the light on to the film area. The main projector lens, which beams the film image on to the screen, is situated in front of the film.

In the case of CinemaScope or Pana-

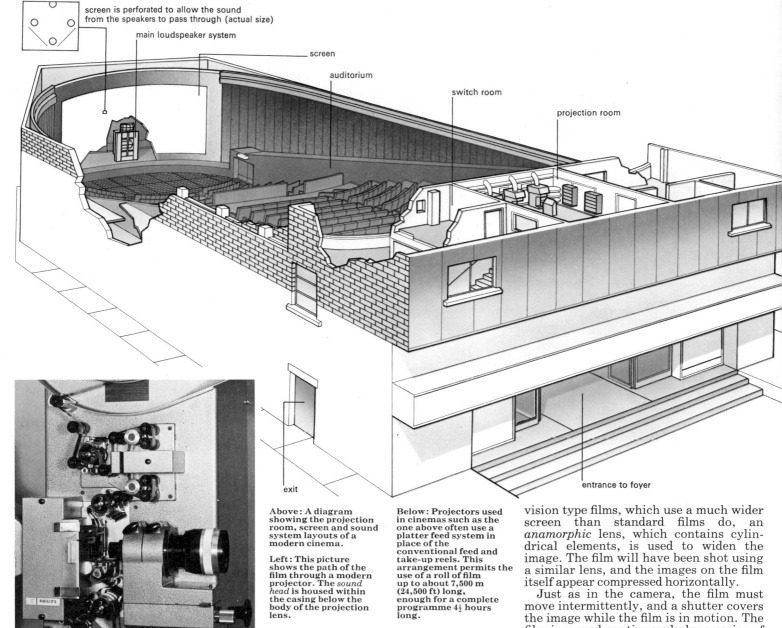

screen is perforated to allow the sound from the speakers to pass through (actual size)

main loudspeaker system

screen

auditorium

switch room

projection room

entrance to foyer

exit

lamphouse ventilation flue

Platter Feed System

projection room window

projection lens

gate

lamphouse

pedestal

feed disc

take-up spool

projector

third disc carries additional programme

PHILIPS

EMI

Above: A diagram showing the projection room, screen and sound system layouts of a modern cinema.

Left: This picture shows the path of the film through a modern projector. The *sound head* is housed within the casing below the body of the projection lens.

Below: Projectors used in cinemas such as the one above often use a platter feed system in place of the conventional feed and take-up reels. This arrangement permits the use of a roll of film up to about 7,500 m (24,500 ft) long, enough for a complete programme 4½ hours long.

CINEMA PROJECTOR WITH PLATTER FEED SYSTEM

vision type films, which use a much wider screen than standard films do, an *anamorphic* lens, which contains cylindrical elements, is used to widen the image. The film will have been shot using a similar lens, and the images on the film itself appear compressed horizontally.

Just as in the camera, the film must move intermittently, and a shutter covers the image while the film is in motion. The film is moved continuously by a series of sprockets; its intermittent motion is made possible by loops of free film above and below the gate. These allow the film to be stopped and started in the gate without interfering with its continuous motion through the rest of the mechanism.

The soundtrack is recorded continuously, and not intermittently like the pictures. For this reason the part of the soundtrack which relates to a particular frame is separated from it by an exact number of frames. At the sound head itself, where the film's movement has to be completely even, it passes round a heavy 'sound drum' whose inertia damps out any remaining ripple in the motion.

The length of film on one reel is limited by bulk—a reel carrying more than about 1,800 m (6,000 ft) of film, lasting about an hour, is difficult to lift up on to the projector. Until the introduction of automated projection equipment, most films had to go on two or more reels, and cinemas needed two projectors for a continuous performance.

Modern cinemas use automated systems, which can often accommodate a whole programme of films over four hours long on a single projector, or on two projectors, operating under automatic control, which can hold about 150 minutes of film each.

Lasers

Lasers are devices which encourage atoms to emit visible light in a regular manner, rather than the sporadic and random emission which normally occurs in nature. Masers operate on the same principles as lasers but produce microwaves rather than light. The unique properties of lasers and masers have already been applied in many fields, including industry, communications, and medicine, and new applications are continually being developed.

Light and microwaves are both forms of *electromagnetic radiation*. The only difference between them is the frequency (and hence also wavelength) of the radiation—light is of a much higher frequency (shorter wavelength) than microwaves.

Electromagnetic radiation is produced when electrons, which move in orbits or 'levels' around the nucleus of an atom, give up some of their energy. But to understand how this happens, and how lasers harness this energy into a regular, ordered form, it is necessary to explain the mechanisms of the atom.

Electrons in orbit

Whether in molecules or atoms, electrons are not free to move as they please but are confined to relatively few distinct orbits, which are always the same for any two atoms of the same element but can vary widely between elements. Electrons in each orbit have a fixed energy, those closest to the nucleus having low energies and those further out have higher. Only one electron can occupy any orbit at a time.

Electrons can move from their orbit to any empty orbit, but in so doing they must also obey the law of *conservation of energy*. So electrons wanting to move outwards from the nucleus must somehow gain enough energy to make the jump and those moving inwards must lose energy. They can do this by emitting or absorbing light in the form of small 'packets' known as *photons*. Photons are the smallest possible packets of light that can exist and the light we see consists simply of vast numbers of individual photons whose abundance gives the impression of a continuous stream of light.

Each photon has a fixed energy and a wavelength which is inversely proportional to this energy. When an electron moves from an outer to an inner orbit it emits a photon whose energy equals the energy difference between the two orbits. The reverse process, in which an electron jumps from the lower to the higher level (from the inner to the outer orbit), requires that the electron gain the same amount of energy. One way of achieving this is for the electron to absorb a passing photon of exactly the right energy and wavelength.

Spontaneous emission

The lowest energy state of an electron is called the *ground state* and all others are known as *excited states*. Electrons may be excited to higher states by several methods other than the photon absorption process just described. Heating a substance will excite the electrons of its atoms or molecules as will subjecting it to an

Photri

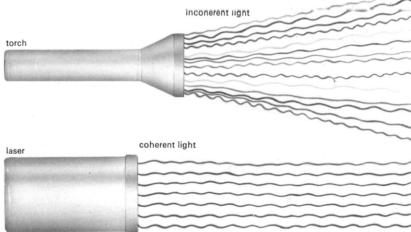

Above: A photograph of Washington monument illuminated by lasers.

Right: The important difference between a laser and, say, an electric torch is that the laser produces *coherent* light. Ordinary light contains a jumble of light waves with different frequencies (between red and blue). These are randomly generated and scattered in all directions: it is the torch reflector that organizes these waves roughly into a beam. Such light is termed *incoherent*. With coherent light, the waves have exactly the same frequency and are in step with each other. That is, the 'crests' of the waves line up to form a *wavefront*. Laser beams are also nearly perfectly parallel.

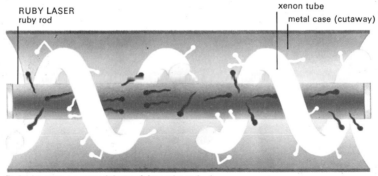

RUBY LASER
ruby rod

xenon tube
metal case (cutaway)

flashtube pumps energy (photons) into ruby rod

Left and below: A diagram showing the mechanism of a ruby laser. The electrons in the chromium atoms are excited into higher energy levels by the light from a powerful spiral flashtube. As these electrons drop back to their ground state (lowest energy level) they each emit a photon of light of the characteristic ruby red colour. This is spontaneous emission. To produce laser action, the crystal is cut to a special shape to enhance stimulated emission along the ruby crystal axis.

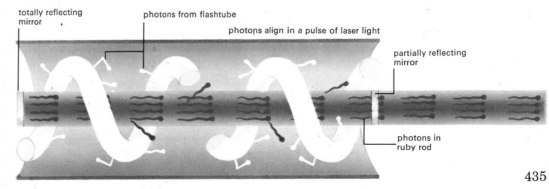

totally reflecting mirror

photons from flashtube

photons align in a pulse of laser light

partially reflecting mirror

photons in ruby rod

Left and right: Laser light is nearly perfectly parallel. To demonstrate this fact, a laser beam was directed from this window in a city centre (left). When viewed directly from a distant hill (right), the beam is much brighter than the surrounding street lamps even though the laser produces about 1/1000 of their power.

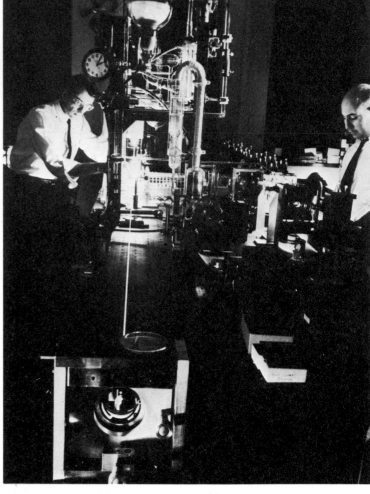

Left: This green beam of laser light is produced by an argon laser. The specific colour of a laser depends on the electron configuration of the element employed to initiate stimulated emission. The larger the energy difference between the ground state and excited state of these electrons, the higher the frequency of emitted radiation (and smaller wavelength).

Right: This was the first gas laser to produce a continuous beam of visible light. Present day lasers produce a vast range of frequencies from microwaves (masers) through infra-red and the visible spectrum to ultra-violet. Theoretically, even higher frequency laser radiation is possible. Scientists are considering the possibility of using it for X-rays and even gamma radiation.

Below left: The inventor of the ruby laser, Theodore Maiman, with one of his instruments. The spiral flashtube can be clearly seen and inside this is the cylindrical ruby crystal with machined and silvered ends.

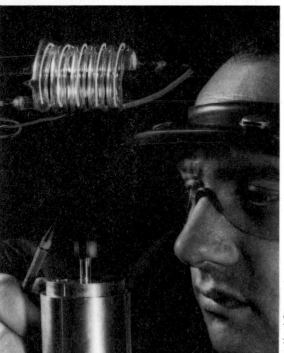

intense electric field or bombarding it with free electrons.

Electrons which have been excited to higher states by any method are, however, not stable. They spontaneously drop back to any empty lower level, emitting the appropriate photon as they do so. This *spontaneous emission* is quite random and there is no way of telling when the photon will be emitted or what direction it will move in, although for a large number of excited atoms it is possible to predict quite accurately how many photons will be emitted in a given time.

Spontaneous emission by excited electrons produces all the light that we normally see—the various light sources differ only in the method used to excite the electrons, for example nuclear heating in the sun, electric heating in a light bulb and electron bombardment in a neon tube. Because of the random nature of spontaneous emission these sources all emit light in all directions and the component photons are out of step with one another. Such light is *incoherent*.

Stimulated emission

We have seen that an electron can be excited to a higher state by the impact of a photon of the right energy. But what happens if the electron is already in the excited state when it is struck by the photon? Common sense suggests that it will be unaffected but common sense is no guide in atomic physics. In fact what happens is that the excited electron drops back to the lower state emitting a photon as it goes. This process, called *stimulated emission*, was first predicted on theoretical grounds by Einstein in 1917.

Even more interesting, the photon emitted in this process moves in the same direction and exactly in step with the stimulating photon (that is, they are *coherent*). The two identical photons are now free to stimulate further emission of photons from any other excited electrons they encounter and these photons too will match the original. Thus, if conditions are right, the original photon will be amplified again and again by each successive stimulation of an excited electron. The word laser was coined to describe this process by its initial letters which stand for Light Amplification by Stimulated Emission of Radiation.

One factor prevents laser action under normal circumstances, namely the possibility that photons, instead of stimulating emission from electrons in the higher state, will encounter electrons in the

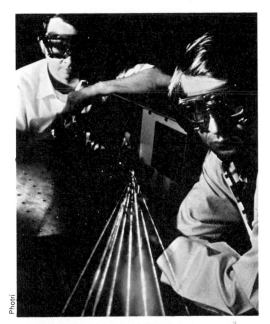

Left: This *dye laser*, produces a range of colours from ultra-violet to yellow. One device of special interest is the argon/krypton gas laser whose output of mixed radiation gives the appearance of white light.

Right: A portable laser microwelder. Because the beam from a laser is almost perfectly parallel, the focal point of the beam when focused by a lens is extremely small and distinct. Therefore the intensity of light at the focus is very high high enough to be used in welding applications. Theoretically, a perfectly parallel beam aimed at a perfect lens will produce a *point* of light (of zero area and infinite intensity). A conventional source of light produces a large and hazy spot. More powerful types of laser, such as the carbon dioxide version, can cut through sheet metal. Such welding devices are gas jet assisted.

Photri

IRD

Howard Sochurek/John Hillelson Agency

Scientific American

LASER-FUSION REACTOR

high-intensity laser light

hot expanding surface of disintegrating pellet

laser beams focused onto fuel pellet

containment vessel (cutaway)

heat given off by fusion reaction is removed by heat exchangers, and used to raise steam which powers turbogenerators

➔ 'hot' electrons
➔ alpha particles
➔ neutrons

Above: Detecting an art forgery using laser techniques. One way to achieve this is by detecting the undulations of the paint surface, by which means the number and thickness of paint layers underneath can be determined. The technique employed is similar to that used in holography where the depth nature of a scene (in this case the paint undulations) modifies the laser beam reflected from the surface.

Right: Using laser light to illuminate a scene for television. The principle is not to flood the whole scene with laser light, but to scan across the scene in a manner similar to that used in a television camera and receiver.

Howard Sochurek/John Hillelson Agency

Above: How lasers could be used to create the energy source of the future—nuclear fusion. If a very short but intense burst of laser light could be focused from all sides onto a frozen pellet of deuterium and tritium (isotopes of hydrogen), the nuclei would fuse together to form helium with a large release of energy. As the light strikes the pellet, the surface temperature rises and becomes ionized. 'Hot' electrons move inwards, carrying energy with them and heat the interior. As this happens, neutrons and alpha particles explode outwards causing an equal and opposite implosion of the interior which creates sufficiently high temperatures and pressures to cause fusion.

437

Above, right and below: Even if laser 'death rays' are at present confined to the realm of fiction, the uses of lasers in military applications have not been slow in developing. The apparatus above can aim a laser beam precisely at a target. The light scattered from this is registered by apparatus in the nose of the strike aircraft (right) and used to 'home in' on the target. Similar devices can also be fitted to missiles. Below the diagram shows how the apparatus is used. The aircraft receptor filters out all light except that from the laser and so this system can be used in daylight although this is much brighter than the laser light. The equipment can also be used for rangefinding. Systems such as this were used by the Americans in Vietnam. Even such sophisticated technology marks only the beginning of its military uses.

Ferranti

lower state and be absorbed by them. Since there are normally more electrons in lower states than higher, this means that emitted photons are annihilated more rapidly than they can breed. For amplification it is necessary to ensure artificially that the majority of electrons are in the excited state, which will tip the balance in favour of creation rather than destruction of photons. Such a situation is called an *inversion*.

The ammonium maser

The first ever maser used a very simple method of obtaining an inversion in molecules of ammonium gas. These molecules have many different energy states but the ammonium maser uses only two of these, which differ in energy such that when an electron drops from the upper to the lower it emits a photon of wavelength 1.2 cm. If ammonium gas is passed through an electric field the molecules in the upper of these two states will be deflected in one direction and those in the lower state in another, giving two beams of molecules, one predominantly upper state and the other lower. The beam of excited molecules in the upper state is then a suitable medium for laser action, until spontaneous emission degrades it once again to the lower state.

The excited beam is directed into a metal box or cavity where it is exposed to a weak microwave signal of 1.2 cm wavelength. This stimulates emission of 1.2 cm photons from some of the molecules, which quickly avalanches to full maser action. Provided a continuous supply of excited molecules is fed to the cavity, the ammonium maser will emit a continuous coherent microwave beam from a small hole in the cavity. The power is not great, being less than 1 microwatt (10^{-6} watt), but the frequency of the radiation is so stable that it is used as a standard for measuring time.

In most cases it is not so simple a matter to create an inversion as it is with the ammonium maser. The energy levels of interest cannot usually be separated by electric fields and in any case this method is obviously useless if the atoms form part of a solid. Several other methods have been developed for obtaining an inversion, each of which is appropriate for a different lasing medium.

Types of laser

The first laser (producing visible as opposed to microwave light) used a crystal of ruby as the medium and employed a process known as *optical pumping* to excite the electrons to an inverted condition. Ruby is a regular crystal form of aluminium oxide in which are embedded some chromium atoms. The chromium atoms are really only impurities in the crystal but they are responsible for the characteristic red colour light which is produced naturally by spontaneous emission from their electrons. The ruby laser produces the same colour light in coherent form by stimulated emission. To do this it makes use of *three* of the energy levels of the chromium atoms.

The middle and lower levels are those used in the laser action. The upper level really consists of a large number of levels so closely spaced that they are effectively a broad band of energy which many chromium electrons can occupy. The principle of optical pumping is to flood the crystal with light from a xenon flash lamp.

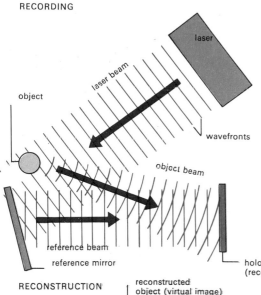

laser

laser beam

object

laser beam

wavefronts

object beam

reference beam

reference mirror

holographic plate
(recording pate)

reconstructed
object (real image)

reconstructed
object (virtual image)

screen

RECONSTRUCTION

laser

eye sees
virtual image

the laser beam travels to the hologram
and is split into two beams

Above: How lasers are used in *holography* to record and reconstruct a 3D image. A normal photograph only records the intensity of a scene, but a holographic record or *hologram* also records phase information of the impinging light waves. This is possible because laser light is coherent. For this, a standard is necessary—achieved by directing part of the laser light directly on to the hologram (this is the reference beam). To reconstruct the image, the hologram is viewed in laser light— the image appears beyond it.

Right: A typical layout for holographic recording. On the right is the laser which floods both the scene to be recorded (bottom left) and a mirror (top left) which directs the reference beam on to the hologram.

Below: Here, the laser beam is split into two. One is aimed at the mirror, the other at the object to be recorded. The shape of an item can be checked against a standard by replacing the mirror with the standard. The hologram records the *differences* between them.

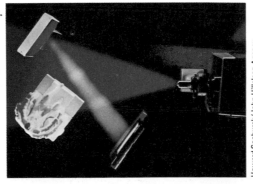

Howard Sochurek/John Hillelson Agency

Photri

Electrons in the lower level absorb photons of this light and jump directly to the upper band. Once in this band they soon lose energy to the atoms of the crystal and decay to the middle state.

If more than half the chromium electrons can be pumped like this to the upper levels, then an inversion exists with more in the middle than in the lower level. The middle level electrons will start to spontaneously emit, in all directions, photons of wavelength 0.6943 micrometres (which is 0.6943 millionths of a metre or 6943 A and corresponds to light in the red region of the spectrum).

The crystal is specially shaped to ensure that some of these cause the system to lase. It is cut in the form of a long rod and the ends polished and silvered. When a spontaneous photon is emitted along the axis of the rod it is reflected back along its path whenever it reaches one of the ends, ensuring that it travels a very long path which gives it a high probability of encountering a chromium electron in the middle state. As soon as this happens the laser avalanche is initiated. One of the ends is made less than 100% reflective so that part of the laser light can escape.

There are now many similar lasers which use a variety of crystals. One, which relies on neodymium impurities in a crystal of yttrium aluminium garnet, is of interest because its energy levels are so spaced that it can be pumped by sunlight.

Another large class of lasers uses gases as the lasing medium. Perhaps best known of these is the helium-neon laser which emits coherent neon light. The initial excitation is produced by passing an electric current through a mixture of helium and neon gas. This raises the energies of the helium electrons and as these collide with neon atoms the neon electrons are in turn raised to excited states. The gases are contained in a long tube with mirrors mounted at either end so that an initial spontaneous emission from an excited neon along the axis causes the whole system to lase back to a lower state.

Gas lasers give the most coherent light, but they are generally quite inefficient, requiring about a thousand times as much energy to be fed in as is extracted in the form of laser light. An exception is the carbon dioxide (CO_2) laser which emits up to 15% of its energy input as light. Another interesting gas laser contains a mixture of argon and krypton and is capable of lasing at several different wavelengths at the same time so that its mixed output appears as white laser light.

Applications

Because stimulated emission creates new photons which move in exactly the same direction, the beam of light from a laser is almost perfectly parallel. This means that it can be focused by a lens into an extremely small area. In this area the intensity of the light is so high (even if the unfocused beam is weak) that it can easily vaporize metals and even diamond. This has made the laser a useful tool for all sorts of cutting, drilling and welding operations, especially for small scale work where accuracy is very important. Perhaps the most spectacular application in this field is the use of a laser by surgeons to weld back a detached retina. The laser beam can be precisely aimed at the spot where the retina is detached and the eyeball itself is used to focus the beam.

The unvarying wavelength and frequency of lasers means that for the first time visible light can be manipulated in a similar way to radio waves and much research is now going on to develop a communications system based on laser light. The main advantage of using visible light is that its very high frequencies enable millions more telephone or television channels to be carried on the same beam than on a single radio wave. Also the highly directional beam means that less power is required to communicate between two points as energy is not wasted in other directions. This also means that a laser is useless for general broadcasting, which requires an aerial that will radiate in all directions. And laser light cannot penetrate cloud any better than normal light can usually.

Satellites

Since the Earth's first artificial satellite, Spuknik 1, was launched by the USSR in 1957, several hundreds of satellites of increasing size and complexity have been put into orbit, mostly around the Earth. Craft have been orbited around the Sun, Moon and Mars, but these are generally known as space probes.

The use of Earth satellites has many practical benefits to humankind. The world's meteorological services depend increasingly on satellite photographs of cloud cover and on measurements of atmospheric properties made from space. Communications satellites are of great importance, not just for relaying live pictures of sporting events but mainly for providing telephone and data links for governments and industries. The data gathered by scientific satellites have greatly increased our knowledge of the world and its surrounding environment. Major powers use satellites to gather military intelligence.

A satellite must reach a velocity of 41,000 km/h (25,000 mph) to escape from the Earth's gravitational pull, and continue at 30,000 km/h (18,000 mph) to stay in a low orbit. The US has launched satellites as part of its Space Shuttle programme, while the USSR and Europe have so far used unmanned *staged* rockets. In the US and Europe satellites are an important commercial concern. Asia, Japan, China and India have ambitious satellite programmes, and many other countries of the world will soon put satellites into orbit using rocket vehicles of their richer neighbours.

Working environment

Satellites have to operate in a harsh environment which cannot totally be simulated in ground tests. Equipment must work in zero gravity, under high vacuum conditions and with wide temperature variations. During launch, the vibrations transmitted from the launch vehicle and shock loadings as the upper stages take over are severe. To add to the problems, some materials can emit gas or give off particles of their substances under a vacuum, and have to be avoided, as the particles could confuse star sensors or contaminate solar arrays. Two similar metal surfaces may weld together under pressure in a vacuum, and conventional lubrication systems would not work as the oil would evaporate. Surfaces which have to touch each other are made of dissimilar materials, and solid-film lubrication systems using lead or PTFE (Teflon) are needed.

Construction

The design of a satellite involves a number of subsystems: structure, thermal control, attitude control, power, electricity distribution, telemetry and command, and an operational payload. The payload may be a number of scientific instruments, or cameras to photograph the terrain below.

So that the satellite can carry the maximum payload, its construction must be as light as possible, yet it must maintain its integrity under the strains of launch. Aluminium alloy and conventional aerospace building techniques are generally employed. Floor panels, side walls and solar array frameworks are made from aluminium or glass-fibre laminate-faced honeycomb panels. Threaded inserts fitted to

Above: One of the first living creatures to orbit the Earth and return alive, the Russian space dog Belka together with its companion Strelka was launched into orbit on 19 August 1960. Another dog, Laika, had made the first spaceflight by a living creature in the Russian satellite Sputnik 2 in 1957.

Below: The first satellite to go into Earth orbit was 'Sputnik 1', launched by the Russians on 4 October 1957 from their launch site at Tyuratam in Kazakhstan. Sputnik 1 carried a radio transmitter which transmitted a series of 'bleeps' so that the satellite could be tracked.

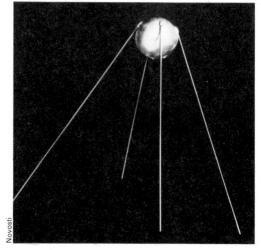

Novosti

medical data impulse converters

ground station

breathing | heart rate | blood pressure

transmitter

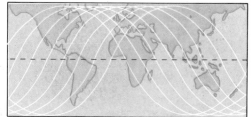

medical data recorders

Above: Sputnik 2 was launched to investigate the effects of solar and cosmic radiation and weightlessness on living creatures. Its occupant, the dog Laika, was connected to instruments which monitored its breathing, heartbeat and blood pressure.

Below: The path of Sputnik 1 across the face of the Earth during a 24-hour period. The lines of the path are the result of the rotation of the Earth and the orbital direction of the satellite. Sputnik 1 burned up on 4 January 1958.

the honeycomb are used to mount the equipment. Machined parts are made from aluminium alloy, titanium or beryllium – materials chosen for their nonmagnetic properties as well as for their strength and thermal stability. The satellite has to stay correctly balanced under all configurations and conditions; and any spin-stabilized satellite must be designed to be stable in one axis only.

Electronic equipment is sensitive and usually operates within the spacecraft at a temperature of approximatley 25°C (77 °F). Variations will be just a few degrees from this. The satellite's environment, however, can vary from full sunlight to full eclipse, and it may or may not be illuminated by light reflected from the Earth; surface temperatures on the satellite body exterior can be as high as 160°C (320°F) and as low as -140°C (-220°F). The apparatus on board can vary in its heat output as well, and yet the interior of the satellite must be kept in thermal balance. If the experiments are not too demanding a *passive* control system may be used: the exterior finish of the satellite is chosen to absorb or emit radiation and no further temperature control is needed. For example, a light or shiny finish will neither absorb or emit very much radiation, whereas a black finish will. Ther-

mal blankets of crinkled multilayer aluminized plastic film are used to insulate some areas.

For complex satellites, an *active* thermal control system is used. A louvre system on the spacecraft wall can control the inside temperature, or alternatively heat pipes may carry excess heat away from localized hot spots to the wall of the satellite.

Attitude control

Satellites usually have to be pointed in space in some way so that the solar arrays are always pointing at the Sun. Simple satellites are *spin stabilized* like a gyroscope about one axis, while others are oriented by a system of control jets fixed to the body – *three-axis stabilization*. With this system, the satellite's orientation has to be measured, so that corrections can be made, and this is carried out by sensors which are designed to observe the position of astronomical bodies such as the Sun, Earth and certain stars. The attitude control system receives this information or an overriding ground command and demands pulses from the control jets to realign it as required. These control jets once used hydrazine as a fuel – a single propellant which does not have to be mixed with anything else, but which decomposes

Left: an early tracking antenna at a ground station. Multiple exposure photography shows the complicated movements of the tracking dish as it followed a satellite's path.

Right: A Russian satellite tracking ship that saw long service: the *Yuri Gagarin*, named after the USSR's – and the world's – first astronaut.

Below: European satellites were at first carried into orbit by US rockets. This GEOS scientific satellite, shown being tested at BAC Electronic and Space Systems in Bristol, carried seven separate experiments designed to investigate the *magnetosphere*, the area of space influenced by the Earth's magnetic field.

Below: Three types of orbit. In a *polar synchronous* orbit the satellite appears to follow a figure-of-eight path over the Earth and can observe most of it over a period of time. Satellites in *retrograde* orbits travel against the Earth's spin, those in *direct* orbits with it.

Right: Satellites quickly grew in size and complexity, as this picture shows. The smaller satellite is a model of 'Early Bird' or Intelsat I, dating from 1965. The larger satellite, Intelsat IVA, dates from ten years later. Both satellites were powered by *solar cells*, which show up as their shiny dark surfaces.

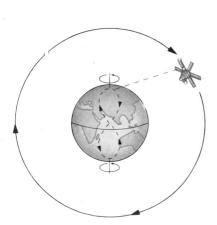

polar-synchronous orbit

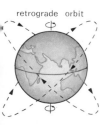

retrograde orbit

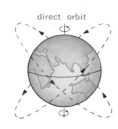

direct orbit

on contact with a catalyst, but most modern satellites under construction use a bi-propellant system using nitrogen tetroxide and monomethylhydrazine as the fuel. Future satellites may use *ion propulsion* for the same purpose. Using these systems, a satellite can be pointed with high accuracy – an orbiting craft can be pointed at a selected spot on the ground below to an accuracy of 10 m (33 ft), for example.

Electric power

Satellites in Earth orbit have almost unlimited supplies of power available from the Sun. Solar cells are either mounted around the body or are on panels which can be extended from the sides of the satellite on light spars. Since there is no air in space, and since the satellite is weightless with hardly any strain imposed on it, these panels can be very lightly constructed. A panel of 2 sq m (21.5 sq ft), the size of a tabletop, can generally provided 500 watts of power all the time it is in sunlight. A battery provides power for emergencies and for when the craft is in the Earth's shadow.

Satellites have a limited lifetime for a number of reasons. The output of the solar cells decreases with time, a fact which can be allowed for by producing excess power to start with which is reradiated as heat into space from special panels. The attitude control systems have only a certain amount of fuel; and the satellite itself may encounter sufficient air resistance to bring the craft out of orbit to burn up in the atmosphere in a comparatively short time. Lifetimes of two to ten years are common, but as space travel becomes more commonplace, maintenance programmes will become possible.

Below: Enviromental monitoring is an important task for satellites such as Landsat. On the left is a Landsat image of a forest area near Harrisburg, Pennsylvania, taken in 1976 to show the extent of defoliation by gypsy moths. The image on the right, photographed one year later, reveals increased areas of defoliation, showing up as dark patches, caused by spread of the gypsy moths.

NASA

Photri

Daily Telegraph Colour Library/Space Frontiers Ltd

Science Photo Library/Dr S. Gull

Left: Vast structural satellites are a sure thing for the future. To build them, however, more economic transporters of material into space than the present space shuttles will have to be devised.

Above: A microwave beam transfers solar energy to Earth. This could be a solution to all our fuel problems, but there remains the problem of danger to all life under the beam.

Applications

The first large communications satellite to be orbited was Echo 1, in 1960. This was a *passive* satellite – it had no electronics on board, but simply reflected signals. It was a 32 m (100 ft) aluminium-coated Mylar balloon in an orbit 1610 km (1000 miles) above the Earth's surface. Echo reflected any signal beamed at it, but at greatly reduced power. Despite its simplicity, the power problem and the fact that space particles eventually punctured and distorted it made the passive satellite of limited value, and none are now used.

Active satellites, on the other hand, are booster or repeater stations – they receive signals from ground stations, amplify them and re-transmit them to other ground stations. This system offers much greater efficiency, and only with satellites of this type is it possible to handle television broadcasts, which nowadays comprise one of the most common uses for satellites.

Communications satellites are an important part of the information revolution. Telephone calls, computer data, TV and still pictures can be transmitted across the world via satellite. Cheaper global communications are becoming available as each new satellite is launched.

Weather satellites are in constant use providing pictures of cloud cover over the Earth. By observing infrared wavelengths, they can operate at night, since there is a temperature difference between cloudy and clear areas. One system transmits pictures continuously so that anyone with a suitable receiver on the ground can pick up signals and convert them on a facsimile machine to a photograph of the region as seen from space. Other satellites have been proposed which will carry out tasks more economically than ground systems – for example, to help oceanographers construct accurate profiles of currents, temperatures and densities of the ocean, a task which would be almost impossible by conventional means. Such information, together with satellite data on the polar caps, is of great value not only to the meteorologist and hydrologist but also to such people as deep-sea fishermen.

The Earth's resources can be studied from space far more effectively than from ground level. By using cameras which take images in several different colour bands, potential diseased crop areas can be spotted as a result of the effect on the reflectivity of the plants. Mineral resources, cattle grazing densities, forestry and water supplies can all be surveyed rapidly from space. An experimental satellite, the Earth Resources Technology Satellite, has proved remarkably successful in this respect: its images show ground features as small as 90 m (300 ft) from an altitude of 914 km (570 miles). Such a satellite can also detect pollution sources: oil tankers are now under surveillance and can no longer risk prosecution for illegal tank washing and dumping oil at sea.

New roles for satellites seem assured in the future – commercial, scientific and military. Some scientists envisage manufacturing in space, although a plan to manufacture biomaterials there has recently been postponed by the drug company involved. Astronomers are planning large satellite-based telescopes; these will be able to observe the heavens in far more detail than ever before.

In the USA, despite the ever-increasing importance of commercial satellites, the military still provide most of the cash and impetus behind satellite programmes. The traditional role of satellites where high-quality pictures are relayed back to Earth to be analysed seems to be about to be supplanted by a new role. President Reagan's Strategic Defense Initiative (SDI), or Star Wars, is still in its infancy, but billions of dollars have been promised to scientists who can develop this nuclear defence system. Highly sophisticated computer-controlled laser satellites are being planned which could destroy incoming missiles. Some scientists have great reservations about whether SDI can ever work properly, but the funding given to scientists working in the satellite field can only make these devices more common.

Neutralizer cathode

Electromagnet producing magnetic field

Discharge chamber

Electrons

Mercury atom

Flow of neutralized ions

Keeper anode

Hollow cathode

Mercury ions

Plasma arc

Accelerator grid

Mercury vapor feed

Main ionization region

Main anode

Electron trajectories

Above left: A schematic view of the interior of the T4 ion propulsion motor, which was designed for use on a European communications satellite. Ion motors are best suited to applications where a small thrust is needed over a long time, as the thrust available is very low = 10 millinewtons in the case of the T4. Positive mercury ions and electrons from the mercury propellant are created in the motor, and these are accelerated through the negatively charged acceleration grid, applying a reactive thrust to the motor.

US Department of Defense

Left: A US anti-satellite system using a rotating mirror for targeting a laser weapon. This scenario from Star Wars involves tests that use the space shuttle as a target.

INDEX

Page numbers in *italics* indicate illustrations in addition to text matter on the subject

A

abacus *398*
abdomen *258–259*
Acacia 76
acanthodes *44*
acceleration, Newton's
    law 304
accelerators
    known particles *284*
    nuclear *280–282*
accelerometers *360–361*
accumulators, lead-acid *378*, 379
acetylcholine *217*
achromatic lenses *350*, 353
acorn worm *44*
    larva *100*
acoustics *429*
ACTH *see* adrenocorticotrophic
    hormone
actin *216*, 217
action potential 205
ACV pallets *313*, 313–314
adding machine, 19th century *399*
adenosine triphosphate 264
ADH *see* vasopressin
adipose tissue 267
adrenal gland 234, *235*, 236
adrenalin *222–223*, 234, *235*
adrenocorticotrophic hormone 236
advanced gas cooled reactor *362*
aeolipile *388*
aeration, water supply 376
aerials, radar *354*, *355*, *356*
aerofoils, lift effect *304–305*
afterburners, supersonic 392
agar-agar 69
agate, Mexican Lace *29*
ageing
    eyes 192
    hearing 200, 201
    skin *266*
Agfamatic 2000 camera *416–417*
agglutinogens 245
ailerons, aircraft *305*, 307
air, ancient element 294
air cushion vehicles (ACV) 312,
    313
air-launched Cruise missile *330–
    331*
air resistance (drag) 304
air traffic control *355*, *357*
aircraft *304–307*
    helicopters *308–311*
    navigational aids *359*, 361
    power units 390–392
    radar use *357*
    supersonic 392
airflow
    aircraft wings *304*
    helicopters *310*
airmen, pressure problems 226
Akai crossfield recorder head
    422–423
Alaska, earthquake in *16*, *17*
albatross, wandering *(Diomedea
    exulens) 117*
albinos *267*
albumin 218
alchemy 276
    'four elements' 294
alcohol
    liver breakdown 253

metabolism 249
alder *(Alnus glutinosa)* 77
    nodules on root of 77
aldosterone 222, 236
Aleutian trench, earthquake in 15
algae 58, 60, 62, 63, 66–69, 74
    blue-green *58*, 58–59, 74, 77
    brown *Pohaeophyta* 60, 67
    green 60, 66, 67, 74, 77
    red 58, 67, 69
algal bloom *66*, 67
algebra
    geometric conversion *344–345*
    variable concept 343
alginates, uses of 69
ALGOL computer language 405
alimentary canal 242, *248*, *260*
alkaline earth metals 301
Allen, Joe, astronaut *442*
allergy, food 256
alligator *154*
    American *(Alligator
    mississippiensis) 154*
allotropes 299, 300
alopecia 272
alpha particles 277
alternating current (ac) 370
altitude sickness 226
aluminium 31
    power cables *373*
alveolar walls 241
alveoli 238, *240*
American missiles *328–331*
amino acids 254, 256, 260, 263–
    264
ammonia, breakdown 262–263
ammonites *43*, 46, *46*, 99
ammonium lasers 438
Amoeba 96, 99
amphibians 101, 156–158, 159,
    160
    characteristics 157
    see also caecilians; frogs; newts;
    salamanders; toads
amphioxus *44*, *99*
amplifiers, sound 426–427, *427*
amplitude modulation (AM) 414
amylase 244, 253
anachromic lens 434
anaemia 219, 220
Anak Krakatoa *21*
anal canal 258, *259*
    sphincter 258, 260
analogue computers 402, 405
analysis, scientific *346–349*
Anas, genus 112
Anchorage, earthquake in *16*
androgen 272
angaran flora 64
angina pectoris 223
angiotensin 222, 223
angle of attack
    aircraft 305–306
    helicopters 308
angles
    incidence *350*
    reflection *350*
animal kingdom, division of 96, 99
animals, ancestry 96, 99
anions 297, 378
annelids *98*
annularia *62*
antacids 248
anteater numbat, marsupial

(Mrymecobius fasciatus) 121,
    122–123
antelope 99
anthers 61, *84*, 86, *87*
anthracite 35, *35*
antibodies 218
antidiuresis 237
antidiuretic hormone *see*
    vasopressin
anti-haemophilial globulin 220
anti-malarial drugs 264
antiparticles 283, 284
ants *103*
Anurans 156, 157
    see also frogs; toads
anus 258
aorta 230
apatite 212
apes 178, 179, 181
    see also individual names
aphids, migration method 110
aplastic anaemia 220
apnoea 240
apocrine glands 269
Apoda 156
    characteristics 160
Apollo spacecraft *335*, *336*
    metals used in *33*
Appalachian Mountains 24, *24–
    25*
appendicitis 258, *259*
appendix 258, *259*, 261
apples *59*
aqueducts, Roman *374*
aqueous humour 190, *191*
arbuscules 77
arch, natural *50–51*
archaeocyatha 46
archaeopteryx *44*, *45*
argon 295
Aristotle 276, 294
arithmetic 342, 345
arithmetic logic unit (alu) 401,
    403
Arriflex movie camera 430, *431*
arterial vessel resistance 225–226
arteries 221, *224*
    blood clotting *225*
    bronchial 239
    coronary *232*, 233
    damage 223
    hardening 223
    hepatic 252
    pulmonary 230, 238–239
    renal *262*, 263
arterioles 221, 222, 225
Arthropoda 46
arthropods 96, *98*, 100
    characteristics 100
    see also centipedes; insects;
    invertebrates; millipedes;
    spiders
Artiodactyla 140, 144
    see also hippopotamuses;
    peccaries; pigs
asbestos suit *29*
asci (sporangia) 59
ascomycetes *see* fungi, cap; lichens
ascospores 73
ascus 70
astatine 301
asteroxylon *62*
asthma 241
astigmatism *190–191*

astrolabes 358
astronauts *334–337*
astronomy
    satellite instruments 441–443
    telescopes *352–353*
atherosclerosis 223
Atlantis space shuttle 339
atlas 212
atmospheric engine *386–387*
atmospheric pollution 228
atomic bombs 341, 362
atomic number *294–295*, 296
atomic weights 277, 296
atoms 276–279
    chemical elements 295–296
    energy, electrons 435–439
    infrared emission 292
    light emission *291*, *292–293*
    nuclear fission 362
    particles, sub-atomic 280–284
    structure *277–279*, 295–296
atrium 230–231, 232
atropine 248
attrition (river) 47
auk, razorbilled *(Alca torda) 113*
auricle 198, *199*
Austin car (1922) *321*
Australopithecus *45*
autogyros 308, *311*
automobiles *see* cars; vehicles
autonomic nervous system 222,
    226
autoregulation 222
axillary hair 270
axis 212
axolotl *(Ambystoma mexicanum)*
    159, *159*
axons 202, *203*, *204*, 210

B

B (baryonic charge) 283
babirusa *(Babyrousa babyrussa)*
    141
    characteristics 143
baboons 181, 183, *183*
    characteristics 183
    Papio anubis 181
backwash 50
Bacon, Francis, fuel cell *379*
bacteria *58*, 58–59, 76–77
    fighting 220, 228
    large intestine 258–260
    symbiotic 256
    water supplies 374
bactericidal lamp *292–293*
bacteriods 77
badgers *167*
    common *(Meles meles)*,
    characteristics 167
    Taxidea taxus 167
Balanophoraceae see plants,
    parasitic
baldness 272
baleen 177
bandicoots 121, 122
    long-nosed *121*
    rabbit *(Macrotis encula) 121*
banking control, aircraft *305*
Barbary ape *(Macaca sylvana)*
    181, *182*
Barber, John, gas turbine 390
barbiturates 253

barium sulphate 256
bark beetle (Scolytus scolytus) 91
barnacles 98
baroreceptors 226
baryonic charge (B) 283
baryons 284
BASIC computer language 405
basidiomycetes and toadstools see
  mushrooms
basilar membrane 200
Bates, H.W., and mimicry 109
bath white butterfly (Pontia
  deplidice) 109
bats 99, 128, 129
  Bechstein's (Myotis bechsteinii)
    130
  bulldog (Noctillio leporimus)
    131
  characteristics 128
  development in 129
  diadem round-leaf
    (Hipposideros diadema) 131
  dog-faced fruit (Cynopterus
    brachyotis) 131
  flight in 129, 130–131
  fruit-eating, characteristics 128
  ghost (Macroderma gigas),
    characteristics 131
  horseshoe (Rhinolophidae) 130
  insect-eating (Vesperti liandae)
    128, 130–131
  leaf-nosed (Hipposideridae
    phyllostamatidae) 130
  long-eared (Plecotus auritus)
    130
  long-tongued fruit
    (Macroglossus logi chilus)
    128
  nectar (Leptonycteris sanborni)
    129, 129
  pipistrelle (Pipistrellus
    nonulus) 130
  short-nosed fruit (Cynopterus
    sphinx) 128
  sonar 129, 129–130, 131
  tomb (Taphozons melanopogon)
    130
bats, false vampire
  (Megadermatidae) 131
  characteristics 131
  Lavia frons 131
bats, vampire (Desmodontidae)
  129, 131
  characteristics 131
  common (Desmodus rotundus)
    131
  Vampyrum spectrum 129
  see also flying fox
batteries 378–380
battery-powered vehicles 320
bauxite 30
bays 48
beaches 48–49, 50–51
  changing appearance of 48–49
  shape of 50–51
  types of material 50
beans 80
beards 270
Becquerel, Henri 10
beeches 60, 90–91
bee hawk moth (Hermaris tityus)
  110
bees 103
beetles 98, 103
  Goliath, breathing method 100
  see also invertebrates
behaviour, greeting 206–207
belching 247–248
belemnites 46
Belka, space dog 440
Bell, Alexander Graham 314, 408,
  420
Bell Punch Anita calculator 399
bends 226

Benioff, Hugo 17
Benioff zones 17
Benz, Carl, cars 320, 322
benzene
  structural models 277
Bernoulli, Daniel, aerofoils 305
beryllium 301
Berzelius, J.J. 296
bicarbonates 254
bicycles 316, 318
'Big Hole', Kimberley 28
bikes, racing 318–319
bile 250, 252
  acid 250
  duct 250, 252
  salts 250, 252, 254
bilrubin 250, 252, 260
binary coding calculators 399–
  400
binary number system 342, 403
bindweed 79, 80
binoculars, structure 352, 353
Biogas 369
biorhythms calculator 401
birches (Betulaceae) 92
bird kingdom, the 114–115
  groupings in 112, 113
bird of paradise (Diphyllodes
  magnificus) 113
birds 101
  evolution of 101
  migration of 116, 117, 118
  moulting 118
  navigation 118–119
  number of species 113
  see also individual names
bird's nest orchid (Neottia
  nidus-avis) 79
bit term 403
bitumen, use of 38
bivalves 46
blackberries 59
Blackbird aircraft 307
black body radiation 291, 292–
  293
blackouts 226
bladder 262
bladderworts 81, 82, 83
blades, helicopter 308–311
blast furnace gas 369
blastula 98
blindness
  colour 193
  taste 194
blood 218–226
  acidity 264
  agglutinogens 245
  artificial 220
  circulation 221–223
  clotting 218–219, 220, 223, 225,
    258
  contents 219
  count 220
  flow 225, 226, 230
  letting 218
  nutrient absorption 249, 254,
    255
  osmotic pressure 218
  plasma see plasma
  pressure 223
  sugar level 210, 235, 236, 237,
    253
  supply 221
    bone 212, 214
    brain 210, 222, 225
    heart 221, 225, 232, 233
    kidney 221, 222, 263
    large intestine 258–259
    liver 224
    lungs 238
    skin 221, 225, 267
  volume 228
  water content 235
blowhole 48, 51

bluebottle 98
bluethroat (Luscinia svecica) 112
BMW K100 LT touring bike 319
boar, wild (Sus scrofa) 140, 141
boas (Boinae), food-gathering 150
BOD tests, water supply 374
body cavity, development of 99
body fluids 227, 262–265
  heat, regulation 227, 269
    smoking effects 222–223
body scanning instruments 395–
  396
Boeing 747 306
Boeing 767 200, plan 306–307
Boeing Chinook helicopter, plan
  310–311
Boeing Jetfoil hydrofoils 314–315
Boerhaavia repens 89
bog myrtle (Myrica gale) 77
Bohr, Niels 278–279
boilers, steam engines 386
boiling water reactor (BWR) 363
bollworm, pink (Platyedta
  gossypiella) 111
bombs (volcanic) 20
bonds, chemical 279, 296–297
bone
  composition 212–214
  fracture 214
  growth 214
  marrow 220
  pressure 213
  structure 212, 213
    abnormal 237
  types 212, 213
booby, blue-footed (Sula nebouxii)
  112
Boomer Beach 48–49
boreholes 37
Boswellia thurifera, resin from 93
Botrytis 70
boulders (in ocean) 53
bowel, large 258
Bowman's capsule 263, 264
Boyle, Robert, chemical elements
  294
brachiation 179, 184
brachiopods 42, 43, 46, 46, 98
  see also crustaceans
braille 208
brain 209–211
  arterial circuit 226
  blood supply 210, 221, 222, 225
  disorders, diagnosis 237
  electrical activity 209–210
  nervous system 202, 211
  neurones 210
  stem 209
  waves, EEG tests 394
brakes
  motorcycles 317, 319
  road vehicles 322, 323
branch-tendrils 80
Brand, Hennig 294
Branly, Edouard, radio 412
Braun, Werner von, rockets 329
breasts, milk production 236, 237
breathing 88–91
Brehm, C.L. 113
bristlecone pine 10
bristle-tails 102, 103
  characteristics 102
  Petrobius maritimus 102
broad bean (Phaseolus vulgaris),
  root of 76
broadcasting wavelengths 413,
  415
bromine 301
bronchi 238, 240
bronchial arteries 239
bronchioles 238, 240
bronchogram 238
bronchoscope 241
Brontosaurus 148

broomrape 79
Brown, Samuel, gas car 320
bryozoan 98
bubble chambers, accelerator 282
bud scales 90
buffer store, computers 404
buff-tip moth (Phalera
  bucephala), head of 111
Buick car (1909) 320
bulb, structure of 87
Burgess Shale 42
burnet moth, use of colour in 109
Burroughs 6700 computer 402
buses 320, 322–323
bushbaby 99
butane 369
buttercups (Ranunculaceae) 89
butterflies 98, 103, 108–109, 110,
  110–111
  Charaxes saturnis 110
  migration, method of 110
  peacock, use of 'eye spot' 109
  Precis octavia, colour in 109
  structure of head 109
  see also individual names;
    Lepidoptera
butterfly valve, petrol engines 384
butterwort 81, 82
  pink (Pinguicula lusitanica) 83
bytes (8 bits) 403

C

CBR1000 F motorbike (Honda)
  318
cabbages (Cruciferae) 89
cabbage white butterfly,
  caterpillar 108
cable systems, telephones 408
cables, electric power 372–373
cacomistle, North American
  (Bassariscus astutus), habitat
  168
Cactoblastis cactorum 111
caddis flies, on geological
  timescale 103
caecilians 156, 160
  Caecilia thimpsoni 160
  Ceylonce (Ichthyophis
    glutinosus) 160
  Seychelles 160
  South American (Siphonops
    annulatus) 160
caecum 258, 261
caiman
  Caiman palperbrosus 154
  head shape 154
  spectacled (Caiman solaropo)
    154–155
Cainozoic era 46
Calais, beach at 50
calamites 63
calcareous ooze 55
calcite 30
  crystal 295
calcium 301
  water hardness 376
calculators 398–401
calculus 342–343
caldera 20
callous 214
Calystegia sepium 80
calyx 84
cambium 88, 91
Cambrian period 13
  fossil record 42–45
camera obscura 192
cameras 416–419, 430–432
Campbell, John, sextant 358
cantharidin (poison) 125
Cantor, Georg, set theory 345
canyons, submarine 54

445

capacitance, electromagnetism 287
Cape Cod 49
Cape Hatteras 54–55
capillaries 218, 221, 222, 224, 225, 240–241, 256
  lymphatic 227
capitulum 86
Caprimulgiformes 115
cap rock, types of 39
carageenin 69
carapace 152
carats 29
carbide 362
carbohydrate 299
  breakdown 252
  digestion 244, 254, 256, 260
carbon 299–300
  and age of earth 12
carbon dating 12
carbon dioxide
  diffusion 225
  exchange 221, 222, 231, 238
  exhalation measurement 238–239
  intestinal 260
  stimulation of respiratory centre 240
Carboniferous period 13
  formation of coal 34, 34
  fossil record 42–45
  plants of 62, 63
carburation, petrol engines 385
carburettors 383, 384–385
cardiac cycle 230–231
  output 225
  sphincter 247, 249, 261
cardioid microphones 420–421
cardiovascular system 224–226
Carnivora 161
carotene 266
carpus 213
carrot (Daucus carota) 88
cars, vans 320–323
  electric power 295
  gas turbine engines 393
  petrol engine 383
  steam power 387, 398
Cartesian co-ordinates 344
cartilage 212
  production 237
cartoon movies 430–431, 433
cartridges
  recording tape 423
  sound pick-up 424–426
casein 248
Casey, Baldwin, hydrofoil 314
Casio Biolator 401
cassette recorders 421–422, 423
Casuariiformes 114
Casuarina 77
catadioptric telescopes 351
catalysts 297
cataract 192
Cathaysian flora 64
cathode rays 277
cathode-ray tube (CRT) 356
cations 297, 378
catkins 90
cats (Felidae) 161, 162, 163
  Australian native 122
  characteristics 162
  types of 161
cauterizing 247
caves 48
cavitation, hydrofoils 315
cavity magnetron 355, 356
Cayley, Sir George, aircraft 308
CEGB control centres 371, 372
Célerifère bicycle 316
cells 58, 68, 88
cellulose 258, 260
  effect of enzyme on 73
centipede 98

central nervous system 202, 203
  muscle control 215
central processing unit 402–403
Cephalopods 43, 46
ceramic pick-up stylus 425
cerci 105
cerebellum 203, 209, 210
cerebrospinal fluid 210
cerebrum 203, 209, 210–211
Cerro Negro (volcano) 19
chalk 43
Challenger, HMS 52
Challenger space shuttle 339, 341
chameleon, European (Chamaeleo chamaeleon) 150
Channel Tunnel 327
Charadriiformes 114
chassis, road vehicles 320–323
cheetah (Acinonyx jubatus) 101, 162–163, 165
  characteristics 165
cheirolepis 44
Chelonia 148, 152
chemicals, fossil products 64
chemistry 294–301
  analytical methods 346–349
Chernobyl 363
Chesil Beach 50
Chevrolet Stingray car 321
chief cells 248
child development
  bone 212
  hearing 200, 206
  sight 206
  touch 207
childbirth 214
chimpanzees (Pongidae) 98, 185, 186, 186, 187, 187,
  Pan paniscus 186
  Pan troglodytes 186
  skull of 184
Chinook helicopter 310–311
Chionochloa flavescens 60
chitin 81
chitons ('coat of mail' shells) 98
Chlamydomonas 60
Chlorella 67
chloride 264
chlorine 295, 301
  sterilizer, water 375
chlorophyll 58, 59, 60, 66, 67, 78
chloroplasts 66, 66, 67, 68
cholecystokimin 250, 254
cholera 254
cholesterol 250
chorda tympani 244
chordae tendineae 231
Chordata 46, 96, 99
chromatography 346–349
chromatophores 66
chronometers 360
chrysotile 29
chyle 228
chyme 248, 249, 250, 253, 254, 258
Ciconiiformes 114
cilia 99
  nasal 238
ciliary muscle 191
cinema 430–434
cinema theatre 434
Cinemascope films 433–434
Cinematographie camera (1895) 430
cinnabar 30
cinnabar moth (Hypocrita jacobaeae), colour in 111
circuit breakers 370–372
circuits
  calculators 400, 402–403
  loudspeakers 427
  pick-up cartridges 425
  record players 426
  telephones 407–409
circulation 218–237

cirrhosis 253
Citroën car (1955) 321
classification, system of animal 112
clavicle 213
cliffs 47–48
  low-tide 51
  scenery 50–51
climbers, methods of twining 80
climbing control, helicopters 308
climbing effect, aircraft 305
climbing plants, disadvantages of 80
club moss 42, 59, 60, 62
clutch mechanisms, cars 322
coagulation, water supply 421
coal
  bituminous 35, 35–36
  cyclic sedimentation 35
  deposits 35
  electrical logging 37
  formation 34–35, 34–35
  fossils 34
  humic 35
  in-seam gasification 37
  longwall extraction 37
  measures 36–37
  mining methods 36–37, 37
  rank of 35
  remaining resources 37
  sapropelic 36
  search for 37
  types of 35, 35–36
coal gas 367–369
  history 366
coatimundi (Nasua nasua) 168
coaxial cable 408, 411
cobalt, radioactive 293
COBOL computer language 405
cobra 99
  African spitting (Nija nigricillis) 148
  king (Ophiophagus hannah) 148
coccolithophores 55
coccyx 213
cochlea 198, 199, 200
cochlear duct 200
Cockerall, Christopher 312
cockle 98
cockroaches 103, 106
  American (Periplaneta americana) 106
  British 106
  common (Blatta orientalis) 106
  German (Blatta germanica) 106
cocoa (Theoibroma cacao) 92
codling moth (Cydia pomonella) 111
coelacanth 44
coelenterata 46
coelenterates 98
  see also corals; jellyfish
coelom 99
coke oven gas 369
colic 256
Coliiformes 115
collagen 212, 214, 266, 268
collateral circulation 223
Collins, Michael, astronaut 334
colobus (Colobidae)
  black and white (Colobus polykomos) 183
colon 258, 259, 260, 261
colour blindness 193
  light components 350–351
  spectrum 193
  television receiver 193
  vision 192, 193
colour photography 418–419
Colugo (Cynocephalus volans) 127
Columbia ice fields 10
Columbia space shuttle 338–340
Columbiformes 115

comma butterfly (Polygonia c-album) 109
commercial vehicles 322–323
communications satellites 440–442, 443
compact discs 429
compasses, navigation 358–359
compound steam engines 386–388
compounds, chemical 295
  radioactive 293, 298–299
compressors, gas turbines/jets 390–391, 392
computer mechanism 211
computers 402–405
Concord aircraft 307
condensers, steam engines 387
cones
  cinder 20
  eye 192, 193
  parasitic 18
  spatter 20
Congreve, Sir William 328
conida 73
conifers (Coniferales) 63
conga eels 160
conjugation 69
conservation, energy law 435
constipation 261
contact lenses 351
continental drift, and climate 64
continental rise 52, 54
continental shelf 52, 53
continental slope 52, 54
contractile vacuole 66
contraction, muscle 215, 217, 227
  uterus 237
control rods, nuclear plant 362
convex lenses 350, 352
Convolvulaceae 78
convolvulus hawk moth (Herse convolvuli) 110
Cook, Captain James 120
Cooksonia 62
Cooma (wreck) 55
coordination 212–217
copepods 98
  see also crustaceans
copper 30, 31
  ingot 30
  mine 32–33
  ore 30
  power cables 373
Coraciiformes 115
coral 43
  limestone 43
  stony 98
core samples 33
cork 91
cork oak (Quercus suber) 90
cornea 190, 191
Cornu, Paul, helicopter 308, 309
corolla 84
coronary arteries 232, 233
corpus callosum 124
corpuscles
  Meissner's 207, 267
  Pacinian 206, 207, 267
  red 218–219, 252, 260, 268
  white 219–220, 228
cortex 263
corticosteroids 235
cortisol 237
Corylaceae, members of 92
cotyledons 61
cough reflex 241, 245
covalent bonds 279, 297
coves 48
cpu, computers 402, 403
cranium 212, 213, 214
creeping willow (Salix repens) 90
Cretaceous period 13, 64, 84
  fossil record 42–45
crickets 104, 105, 106
  characteristics 106

mole 106
  structure *102, 105*
crinoid *42, 43*
crinoidea (sea-lilies) 46
Crippen, astronaut 340
crocodiles 99, 154, 155, *155*
  characteristics *154,* 154–155, *155*
  esturine (*Crocodylus porosus*) 154
  long-nosed *see* gharial
  Nile (*Crocodylus niloticus*) 155, *155*
  see also alligators; caimans; gharials
Crocodilia 148
cross-pollination 84, *84*
Cruise missile *330–331*
crystals 26, *26, 27*
crystal lasers *435,* 439
crystal sets *412*
cuckoos (*Cuculus cnaorus*) 118, *119*
Cuculiformes 115
cucumber, sea 99
Cugnot, Nicolas 320
curare *217*
curlew sandpiper (*Calidris ferrugines*) *118*
curves, graphical 343, *344*
cuscuses 121
cuticle 98
  cells 272
cycads (*Cycadales*) 63, 64, 77, 84
cyclotron *280–281*
cysts, hydatid *253*

D

Daguerre, L.J.M. 416
Daguerrotype process 416
Daimler, Gottlieb 318, 320, 322
daisies (*Compositae*) 61
Dalton, John 276, 277
damping-off disease 70
damselflies *102, 104*
Dana (geologist) 24
danger signals, in body 267
Darwin, Charles 45
Dasyuridae 121, 222
Davy, Sir Humphrey *378*
DDT storage, in body 253
deafness
  conductive 200
  perceptive 200
death's head hawk moth (*Acherontia atropos*) 110
Decca navigational system 360–361
decibels *289*
decimal number system *342*
defaecation 261
defibrillators, heart 397
dehydration 237
delta wing aircraft *305*
Democritus, atomic theory 276
demodulation process 411, *412*
denaturation 270
dendrites 202, *203, 204,* 210
Dendrohyrax 133
derailleur gears *316,* 318
dermis 155, 266, 268
desalination, water supply *376*
Descartes, René 344
desmids, structure of 68
deuterium, fusion reactions 363
deuterostomis 98
Deutz, Magirus, engines 323
developing process, films 418–419
Devonian period 13
  evolution during *62, 63*
  fossil record *42–45*
dialling systems, telephones

407, 409–410
diamond drilling 33
diamonds *299–300*
  in Kimberlite *29*
  mine shaft *32*
  panning for *29*
  polishing *28*
diaphragm 239, 240
diarrhoea 254, 261
diastole 230
diastolic blood pressure 223
diatomite 67
diatoms 55, 58, 60, 67, 68
  Navicula monilifera 60
dicots *see* herbaceous dicots
Dictaphones *420*
Dictyoptera, characteristics 106
Diesel, Rudolf, engines 323, 385
diesel engines *384,* 385
  locomotives 326, *327*
  road vehicles 323
diffraction, light 351–352
diffusion 225, 256
digestion 252–261
digestion juices 236, 254
digital computers *402–405*
digitalis 233
digits *213*
dinoflagellates 67
dinosaurs
  eggs 45
  types of 148
Dion, Marquis de *787*
diplopia *192–193*
direct current (dc) 370
Direction finders (DF) 360–361
disc brakes *317, 319,* 322
Discovery space shuttle *339, 340, 341*
disease, fighting 220, 228
distributors, ic engines 383, *384–385*
diuresis 237
divers, pressure problems 226
Docklands Light Railway 327
dodders 78, *78*
  development of 79
dog-rose (*Rosa canina*) *59*
Dolbadarn locomotive *325*
Dolby system, recorders *421,* 423
dolphins 175, *175,* 176
  Amazon river (*Inia geoffrensis*) *176*
  black and white (*Cephalorhynchus commersoni*) *176*
  bottlenosed (*Tursiops truncatus*) *175*
  section through skin *174*
domain set 344
domes 20
Doppler effect *293*
  body scanners 396
  radar 357
drag effect
  aircraft *304*
  helicopters *310,* 311
dragonflies *103, 104*
  Aeshna cyonea 102
  Borneo (*Tetracanthagyna plagiata*) *104*
Drais de Sauerbrun, Baron von 316
Draisienne, hobby-horse 316
Drake, Edwin L. 38
drilling bits *37*
drilling rigs *39*
drinking *244*
drinking water *374–375*
drug, metabolism 264
drum brakes *319,* 322
duck-billed platypus 45
ducks (*Anatidae*) 112
  pintail (*Anas acuta*) *116*

duct of Santorini *250*
dugongs (*Dugongidae*) 172
  Dugong dugon 173
Dunlop, J.B., tyres 316
duodenum 250, *251, 254, 255*
durain 36
Dürer, Albrecht, woodcut of rhino 136, *136*
'Dutch' elm disease (*Cerotocystis ulmi*) 91
Dutchman's pipe *see* pitcher plant
dwarfism 237
dynamic microphones 421
dynamite 299
dynamos 11–12
dyspepsia *246,* 248

E

eagle, golden (*Aquila chryseatos*) 113
ear
  canal 198, *199*
  structure 198, *199, 200–201*
eardrum 198, *199*
Early Bird satellites *441*
early warning stations *354,* 356, 357
earth
  age of 10–12
  ancient element 294
  chemical composition 295
  magnetic field *283*
  radio waves *413*
  satellites *440–443*
earthquakes
  course of waves 16–17
  distribution *14–15,* 17
  epicentre 16
  intensity *15*
  man-made 17
  measurement of *16,* 16–17
  prediction and control 17
Earth Resources Technology Satellite 443
earthworm (*Lumbricus terrestris*) *96, 98*
  characteristics 99–100
earwigs *103*
Eastman, George, films 416
ebony (*Diospyros elenum*) 93
eccrine glands 269
ECGs *395, 396,* 397
echinodermata 46
echinoderms 99, *100, 101*
echinoidea (sea urchins) 46
echoes *289*
  radar principle *354*
echo-sounding *54*
  deep-sea 52
  machine *54*
Edison, Thomas
  movie camera *430*
  phonograph 420
  telephones 408
editing, film scenes 430, 432
eddy currents 285
EEGs *394–395, 396–397*
Einstein, Albert *345*
  photoelectric effect 280–281
elastin 266
Elborz Mountains 23
electricity 285–288
  battery sources *378–380*
  current 285–288
  electromagnetic radiation 287, 288
  electromotive force (emf) 286, 287
  fuel cells *379, 380–381*
  magnetomotive force (mmf) 286, 287
  photoelectric effect 290, *290,* 291

  supply *370–373*
  transformers 285, 287
  vectors 287, 288
  wavelengths 288
electric locomotives *326–327*
electric motors, field effect 287
electric vehicles 320
electrocardiographs *395–397*
electroencephalographs *394–397*
electrolysis 378, *380–381*
electromagnet *288*
electromagnetism 280, *285–288*
electromagnet radiation 287–293, 415
  lasers *435–439*
  spectrum *290*
  velocity 291
electromotive force (emf) 286, 287
electronic calculators *399–401*
electron microscopes 346, *347*
electrons
  baryonic charge 283
  excited states 435–438
  fusion reactions 362–363, *365*
  negative charge 276
  orbital energy 290–291, 435–439
  particle decay 283
  photons emission 280–281, 435–439
  structure, atomic 277–279, 295–297
electrostatic engine 331
gloidin 266
elementary particles 280–284
elements, chemical 294–297
  allotropes 299, 300
  atomic number 296
  atomic theories 276–277
  isotopes 279
  names 294
  periodic table 294–296
  symbol abbreviations *296*
  valency and bonds 279, *296–297*
elephants (*Proboscidea*) 132, 133, 135
  African (*Loxodonta africana*) *132, 133, 134, 135*
    characteristics 134–135
    structure of *132*
  Indian (*Elephas maximus*) *132, 133, 135*
    characteristics 134–135
  structure of herd *133*
elevators, aircraft 305
elliptic geometry *344*
emulsification 250
emulsions, photographic *418–419*
end plate 215
endocrine glands 234–236
energy
  black body radiation 291, 292–293
  chemical reactions 297
  conservation 283, 328
  electron changes 435–439
  electron shells *278–279,* 295, *296–297*
  fossil fuels 366
  fuel cells *380–381*
  heat radiation 292–293
  nuclear power 362–365
  quantum theory 280–281
  release in body 217
engines
  aircraft 306–307
  gas turbines 390–393
  helicopters *310–311*
  hydrofoils *314–315*
  internal combustion *382–385*
  jets 390–392
  motorcycles 319
  petrol *see* petrol engines

railway *324–327*
road vehicles 320, *322–323*
rockets *328–331*
steam *386–389*
Enterprise space shuttle 339
enzymes 218
digestion 242, 245, 248, *251*
Ephemeroptere 104, 105
Epicurus, atomic theory 276
epidermal hairs *84*
epidermal ridges 266
epidermis 60, 88, 155, 266, *267*
epiglottis 238, *243*
epiphytes *76–77*
equalization, sound 426
erasure heads, sound tapes 420–421
Erinaceidae, members of 124
erosion 25
eructation 247–248
escape velocity, rockets 328, 334
Esso scotia 41
Eucalyptus 90
characteristics 93
Euclidian geometry 343–344, 345
eukaryotes 62
Euramerican flora 64
Eustachi, Bartolommeo *265*
Eustachian tube 198, *199*
evaporites 28
Evening Star locomotive *327*
evolution
explosive 45
progressive 45
rates of 45–46
evolutionary convergency 46
exchanges, telephone *407, 408,*
409–411
exclusion principle 279
exercise
blood flow 221
carbon dioxide exhalation *238–239*
energy use 217
heart effects 230
Exocet missiles *329*
exocrine gland 234, 236
exosphere, Earth *413*
expiration 239–240
explosives 299, *300–301*
extension, muscle *215*
extracellular fluid 204–205
eyed hawk moth (*Smerinthus ocellatus*) 109
eye muscles
protection 190
retinal vessels *223*
structure 190, *191*
eye-spot (in algae) 67
'eye spots' 109

F

Fabre, J.H. 111
facsimile machine *407*, 443
factor VIII 220
factories, electricity 372–373
faeces 258, 260–261
fainting 226
Falconiformes 114
falcon, peregrine (*Falco peregrinus*) *112*
families, animal 112
family tree, evolutionary animal 96, *98–99*
Faraday, Michael *285*, 412
Farancia 149
fast breeder reactors 362, *363*
fat
breakdown 250, 252–253, 256
conversion 217
production 237
transport 228, 256

fatty acids 254, 260
Fawley oil refinery *40*
femur 212, *213*, 214
ferns *59, 63*
Filicinae 60
ferrets, habitat 166
ferries
hovercraft *312–313*
hydrofoils *314–315*
ferromagnetic materials *286*
fertilizers, nitrogen compounds 298
Fessenden, Reginald, radio 414
fibre optics, telephones *411*
fibrin *219*, 220
fibrinogen 218, 252
fibula *213*
fig tree chert 62
films
cinema 430
photographic 416, *418–419*
filtration, body 120–123
filtration, water supply 375, 376
fingerprints *266–267, 268*
fire, ancient element 294
firebrats 102, 104
Firefly locomotive *324*
fireworks *300*
firs 61, 63
fish
bony groups of 101
cartilagenous 100–101
fish eye lenses *417, 418*
fissile materials 362
flagella 67
flaps, aircraft *305, 306–307*
flatworms 98
fleas 98, *103*
Archaeopsylla erinacei 125
flexion, muscle *215*
flies, scorpion *103*
two-winged *103*
flint axes 28
flocculation, water supply 375
flowering cherry (*Prunus* 'Kanzan') *93*
flowers 84, 86, 87
fluids
interstitial 227
kidney action 262–265
fluorescence 28
phenomenon 292, 293
fluoride 256
fluorine 301
fluorite 28
flutter (record player term) 422
fly agaric (*Amanita muscaria*) 77
flycatchers (*Muscicapidae*) 116
pied (*Ficedula hypoleuca*) 116
flying foxes *128*, 130
characteristics 130
structure 128–129
Flying Scotsman locomotive *326*
flying techniques *304–307*
focal ratio, lenses (f) *417–418*
Foden truck design *322–323*
foetus
circulatory system *222–223*
foramen ovale 231
respiratory system 241
foils, hydrofoils *314–315*
folds
crustal *23, 24, 24–25*
recumbent 24, *24*
folic acid 219
follicle 269, 273
-stimulating hormone 236
food
allergy 256
appearance 194
chain 96
digestion 252–261
poisoning 254
tasting 194

texture 194
transport 228
types 247
foramen ovale 231
foraminifera 46, 55
Foraminiferida 99
Ford cars *320–321*
foreland, cuspate *50*, 51
forties oil platform *40*
FORTRAN computer language 404
fossil fuels 38, 366
fossil record
adaptive radiation 45
assemblages 45
chemofossils 46
and evolution 45–46
evolutionary convergence 46
extinction of species 46
iterative 46
pre-Cambrian 62
through time 46
trace fossils 42
zone fossils 45
see also individual names
fossils, and animal ancestry 99
four-stroke engine cycle *383*
fovea 192
Fox-Talbot, William, photography *416*
fragmentation 74
frames
bicycles 316, 318
heavy road vehicles 323
motorcycles *318–319*
France, Anatole 209
Fraunhofer, Josef von 349
Frege, Gottlob, logic 345
frequency
measurement (Hz) 289–290, 382–383
modulation (FM) 414
radar 356
radio waves 412, 413–415
telephone transmissions 410–411
frogs 99, 156, 157, *157*, 160
Argentine horned (*Ceratophrys ornata*) 156
Borneo flying (*Rhacophorus pardalis*) 159
common (*Rana temporaria*) 156, 158
giant goliath (*Gigantorana goliath*) 159
hairy (*Trichobatrachus robustus*) *158*, 159
in Venus flytrap *82*
marsupial, and young 159
Phyllobates trinitatis, tadpoles *160*
propulsion *156–157*
Rana wittei 157
Seychelles 159
tree
Asian (*Rhacophoridae*) 158
Hyla arborea 156
Phyllobates bicolor 156
Phyllomedusa trinitatis, eye of *156*
fructose 256
fuchsia, cross-section of *85*
fucoxanthin (pigment) 60
fuel cells, electric *379, 380–381*
fuel injection, petrol engines 384
fuels, fossil sources 366
fumaroles *19*
functions, mathematical 343
fungi 58, 59–60, *63*, 70, 71, 72–73, 74
algal (*phycomycetes*) 59, 70, 71
cap (*ascomycetes*) 59–60, 70, 72–73
mycorrhizal 77

parasitic 72
see also mushrooms; toadstools; 'water moulds'
fusain 36
Fuscarium graminarium in human food 73
fusion reactions 362–363, 437

G

Gagarin, Yuri, cosmonaut *334*
Gaiadendron 79
Galen 224, 230
Galileo Galilei 353
Galileo space craft *337*
gall bladder 250–252, 254, *261*
Galliformes 114
gallstones *251*, 252
gametophytes 68, 87
gamma globulin, ray scan *237, 252*
gamma rays 288, *290, 292, 293*
ganglia 254
Gardna, Dale, astronaut *442*
gas
burning 38, 40, *40–41*
natural *see* natural gas; petroleum
gas chromatography *347–348*
gas cooled reactors 362
gases
coal *see* coal gas
fuel cell source *380–381*
lasers 437, 439
nitrogen 298
oil sources 366, 367
oxygen 298
gasholders *369*
gas turbine engines *390–393*
gastric glands 248
secretion 248–249
ulcer *247*
gastrin 249
gastropods *43*, 46
gastrula 98
Gaviiformes 114
Gazelle helicopters *309*
gearboxes
cars *321*, 322
trucks 323
gears, bicycle *316*, 318
geckos (*Gekkonidae*)
characteristics 151
Phelsuma madagascariensis 151
Gemini spacecraft *334*, 336
gemstones
distribution 29
weight of 29
genus, topological 345
geodes 28
geological column 12
geological timescale *103*
geometries 342–344, 345
geomorphology
geophones 37
geosyncline 24–25
gernierite deposits 32
GEOS satellite *441*
gharial (*Gavialis gangeticus*) *154–155*
giant atlas moth (*Attacus atlas*) 111
gibbons (*Hylobatidae*) 178, 180
characteristics 178–179, 180
hoolock (*Hylobates hoolock*) 180
Hylobates klossi 180
Hylobates lar 178, 180
propulsion *178–179*, 180
skeleton 178, *184*
giddiness 222
ginkgo *63*
ginkgoales 64

Giotto spacecraft *336*
giraffes (*Giraffa camelopardalis*)
144, *144*, 145, 146, *146*, *147*
blotched 145–146
characteristics 144
Helladotherium 147
Masai *146*
reticulated 145
short-necked *144*
Sivatherium 144
white *147*
glandular fever 228
glaucoma 191
globigerina ooze 55
globulin 218
glomeruli *262*, *263*, *264*
glossopteris flora 64
glucagon *235*, 237, 253
glucose
breakdown 217, 253, 256
release 252
storage *250*
transport 263–264
gluons 284
glycerides 254
glycogen
breakdown 253
storage 217, 252
goblet cell *255*, *261*
Goddard, Robert, rockets 329
Gödel's theorem 345
gold *31*, *33*
mines 32
golden emperor moth *110*
gonadotropins *235*, 236, *237*
goose, greylag (*Anser anser*) 118
goosegrass (*Galium aparine*),
hairs on stem of 80, *80*
goose pimples 270
gorillas (*Pongidae*) 178, 184,
184, 185, *185*, 186
characteristics 185
Gorilla gorilla 186
skull of *184*
gossons 32
gramophones 420, *423*
Grampian Mountains 25, *25*
granulocytes 219–220
grape vine (*Vitis vinifera*) 80
graphite *299–300*
graphs 343, *344*
graptolites 46, *98*
grasses (*Graminae*) 61
grasshopper *98*, *103*, 105, 106
African 106
long-horned *see* crickets
lubber (*Phymateus
purpurascens*) *104*
structure of *105*
toad *105*
gravitational force 226, *244*
gravity
Newton's law 280
specific 27
grayling (*Thymallus thymallus*)
101
grayling butterfly (*Eumenis
semele*) 108
grey mould *70*
Grid system, electric *370–373*
groove systems, records *425*
ground effect machines (GEM)
312
ground-to-ground rockets *328*
groundwater supplies 374
Grove, Sir William 379
growth hormone *234*, 237
groynes 51
Gruiformes 114
guenons 181
guidance systems, missiles 331
gun flint chert 62
Gunter, Edmund, slide rule 398
gymnosperms *see* trees, coniferous

gyrocompasses 358, *359*
gyroscopes 360, *361*

H

Hadley, James 358, 360
hadrons 284
haemoglobin 218
haemolytic anaemia 219
haemophilia 218, 220
haemmorhage 220, 222
haemorrhoids 258
hair 270–272
growth 271
loss 272
lubrication 269
raising 270
structure *271*, *272*
Hale, William, rockets 328–329
Half Dome (mountain) *22*
half life, radioactivity 363
Hall, geologist 24
halogens 301
electron distribution 296
hand
massage *208*
sensitivity *208*
hand axes, flint 28
handbrakes, cars 322
handsets, telephone *409*
hardness, water supply 376
Harrison, John 360
Harvey, William *224*, 230
haustoria 78, *78*, 79
haustra 258
Haversian canals 212
hawk moth (*Deilephila merii*) 111
hawthorn 42
hazel (*Corylus avellana*) 92
headlands 48
head movement 212
headphones 427
heads, sound recording *421–423*
health systems 394
hearing 198–201
differentiation 201
loss 200–201
heart 221, 230–233
blood pumping 224–225, 230,
233, *239*
blood supply 221, 225, *232*, 233
failure 223
hole 231
instruments *395–396*
lung machine *232*
muscle 215, 217, 231, 233
safety factors 232–233
structure 230–231
surgery 232–233
valves 230, 231–233
heartwood *91*
heat
infrared radiation 292
natural gas *366–369*
heather 92
heavy water reactor (HWR) *363*
hedgehogs 124, 125, *125*
characteristics 125
European (*Erinaceus
europaeus*) *124*, 127
height-finding radar *357*
Heisenberg, Werner, uncertainty
279
helicopters *308–311*
helium
atomic structure *279*
fusion reactions 363
heparin 223, 252
hepatic artery 252
duct *250–251*
portal vein 252, 256
see also liver
herbaceous dicots 61, 63, 88, 89

herbivores 247, 258
Hering, Ewald 193
Hermes mini space shuttle *337*
Hero of Alexandria 386, 388
heron, purple (*Ardea purpurea*)
112
herring *44*
Hertz (Hz) *289*, 290, 382–383
Hertz, Heinrich 412
heterohyrax 133
hexactinellida *99*
hexadecimal number system *342*
hibernation, in snakes 150
Hilbert, David, mathematics 345
hills, abyssal 52, 54
Himalayas *22–23*
Hinckley 'B' nuclear power
station *363*
hip joint 212
hippopotamuses *142*, 143
characteristics 143, *143*
common (*Hippopotamus
amphibius*) *142*, 143
pygmy (*Choeropsis liberiensis*)
142, 143
characteristics 143
hobby-horse bicycles 316
hog
pygmy (*Sus salvanius*) 143
wart (*Phaecochoerus
aethiopicus*) *140*, 143
characteristics 143
Hohmann ellipse techniques 334
holdfast (seaweed structure) *67*
hole in the heart 231
Hollerith, Herman 402
Hollywood Bowl theatre *429*
holocrine secretion 269
holography *396–397*, 439
Homphray, Samuel 324
honey badger *see* ratel
honeysuckle (*Lonicera
periclymenum*)
method of climbing 80
hop (*Humulus lupulus*) 80
hormones 218, 234–237
digestive 248, 250, 254
hornbeam (*Carpinus betulus*),
appearance of 92
hornets *see* wasps
horse chestnut (*Aesculus
hippocastanum*) 90
horsetails (*Sphenopsidae*) 59, 63
Horst 25
hovercraft *312–314*
hovering effect, helicopters 308
hovertrains, development 313
Hoy, Old Man of 48
humerus *213*
hummingbird, ruby-throated
(*Archilochus colubris*) 116
hummingbird hawk moth
(*Macroglossum stellatarum*)
110
humus 34
Hunnings, telephones 408
hybrid computing 405
hydatid cysts *253*
hydrocarbons 38
hydrochloric acid 248, 254
hydrofoils *314–315*
hydrogen 260
anti-hydrogen model *284*
atomic structure *278–279*
electrolysis production *380–381*
fusion reactions 363, 384
ions 264
isotopes 362, 363
sulphide 260
hydrozoan *98*
Hymenoptera 111
see also ants; bees; wasps
hyperbolic geometry *344*
hypermetropia *191*

hypertension, ideopathic 223
hyphae 70, 74, 76
hypothalamus 211, *234*, *235*, 236–237
hyraxes (*Hyracoidea*) 133
Cape (*Procavia capensis*) 135
characteristics 132–133
rock, habitat 133–134
tree 133
common (*Dendrohyrax
arboreus*) 135

I

ichthyosaurs *44*
Ichthyostega *44*, 156
ignition coil 384
iguana, marine (*Amblyrhynchus
cristatus*) 149
ileocaecal valve 255, 258, *259*
ileum 254, *255*, *258–259*
imago (mayflies) 105
immunity 218
incendiary bombs *300–301*
incidence, angle of 350
incoherent light *435–436*
Indian leaf butterfly 108
indole 260
inductance 287
induction coil *285*
inert gases 295
inertial navigation 360
infection
appendix *259*
intestinal 261
lymph nodes 288
infinite series 343, *344–345*
influorescences 87
information processors *402–405*
infrared radiation 290, 292
infrared wavelengths 288, 443
inlets 48
input, computer systems *402–403*
insectivores 124
characteristics 124
see also hedgehogs; moles;
shrews
insects 102, *103*
characteristics 102
exopterygote 105
social *see* Hymenoptera
stick *103*, 106, *106*
winged (*Pterygota*) 102, 104
wingless (*Apterygota*) 102
inspiration 239–240
instruments
analytic *346–349*
laser *436–437*, 439
medical *394*, 397
navigation *358–361*
optical *351–353*
insulation, electricity *373*
insulators, electric 288
insulin 235, 236, 253
integrated circuits 399
telephones *408–409*
Intelsat satellites *441*
intercostal muscles 239, 240
internal combustion engines *382–385*
internodes 80
Intercity 125 train *327*
interstitial fluid 227
intestine
large 258–261
small 254–257, *261*
villi 228, 254, *255*, *256*
intracellular fluid 204–205
invertebrates 46
number of species 96
see also arthropods
iodine 237, 301
iodopsin 192

449

ion engines 331
ion propulsion 441, *443*
ionic bonds 279, *296–297*
ionosphere, Earth *413*
ions 279, 297
  electrolytes 378
iris, eye 190, *191*
irises (*Iridaceae*) 89
iron 31
  body requirements 219
  magnetized *286*
  meteoric *33*
  storage by body 253
Irwin, James, astronaut *335*
islets of Langerhans 253
Isoetes see club moss
isomultiplets 283
isotopes 10, *10*, 11, 279
  scanning *395–396*
Isp ratings, propellants 330–331

J

jaguars (*Panthera onca*) 98, 162,
  163, *163*
jaundice 220, *251*, 252
jaws, chewing action 242
jejunum 254, *255*
jellyfish *43*, 98
jet engines *390–392*
jetfoil hydrofoils *314–315*
jewel anemones (*Corynactis
  viridis*) 96
Johnston, Sir Harry, and okapis
  146–147
joint, structure 214
Jurassic period *13*
  fossil record *42–45*

K

kangaroos 99, 120, 121, *122–123*
  characteristics 121
  great grey (*Macropus
    giganteus*) 121
  Matschie's tree (*Dendrolagus
    matschiei*) 123
  red (*Macropus rufus*) 121
katydids 105
keratin 155, 266, *270*, 272
keratohyaline 266, 272
keratosa *99*
kidneys 262–265
  blood supply 221, 222, 263
  damage 223
  lymphatic drainage 229
  salt balance 263
  structure 263
  water balance *235*, 237
  see also renal artery
kinkajou (*Potos flavus*) 169
  characteristics 168
kittiwakes (*Rissa tridactyla*)
  migration 116
klystron radar generator 356
knee jerk *203*
  joint *212*
koalas (*Phascolarctos cinereus*)
  120, 121, *121*, 122
Kodak 'Brownie' camera *416*
Kohinoor (diamond) *29*
Kolmogorov, Andrei, calculus 345
komodo dragon (*Varanus
  komodoensis*) 151
Koppers-Totzek process *369*
Korolyev, Sergei, rockets *334*
Kartland, Adriaan, and
  chimpanzees 184
krait, banded (*Bungarus
  fasciatus*) 150
Krakatoa 20, *20–21*
Krause end bulbs *207*

Kremer, John 360
krill 171, 177
kryton 295

L

laboratory, space vehicle *348–349*
Labyrinthodontia 156
lachrymal glands 236
lacteal *228*, *255*, 256
lactic acid 217, 223
lacundae 212
Laika, space dog 440
Laminae 69
lamprey (*Petromyzon marinus*) 99
landing spacecraft *334–336*
landing technique, aircraft 307
Landsat satellites *442*
languages
  analysis 201
  computer programming 404–
    405
  logical use 345
lanugo 270
lapilli 20
lapwing (*Vanellus vanellus*) 62
larynx 238, *243*, *244*
laser disc players *428*
laser gyros 361
lasers *435–439*
  printers 404
  telephone links *411*
  weapons *443*
latimeria *see* coelacanths
latitude *358*, 360
Lauraceae 78
lava
  types of 19
  lead 31
  lepidodendron *42*
lava bread 69
Laval, Carl de 389
Lavoisier, A.L. 277, 294
laxatives 261
lead-acid accumulators *378*, 379
leaf 80, *88–89*
leaf-curl disease *72–73*
Leclanche, George 379
leech *98*
legumes (*Leguminosae*) 76, 80
Leibniz, Gottfried 398, 399
Lenoir, J.J.E., car design 320, 382
lenses *350–353*
  cameras *416–418*
  cine-camera *431*, 434
  concave spectacle *190*
  convex spectacle *191*
  eye 190, 191
Lentibulariaceae see plants,
  carniverous
Leonardo da Vinci, drawings *345*
leopards 162, *164*
  Panthera pardus 162
  clouded (*Neofelis
    nebulosa*) *163*, 165
    characteristics 165
  snow (*Panthera uncia*)
    162, *164*
Lepidoptera 108, 110, 111
  caterpillars 108, 111
  Geometridae caterpillar 108,
    109–110
  see also butterflies; moths
Lepospondyli, characteristics 156
leptons 284
leukaemia 220
leukocytes 219–220
lichens 67, 74, *74*, *75*, 76
  crustose (crusty) 74
    Lecanora conizaeoides 75
    Xanthoria aureola 75
  foliose (leafy) 74
    Parmelia caperata 75

    Parmelia saxatilis 75
  fructicose 74, *76*
  shrubby
    Evernia prunastri 75
    Usnea subfloridans 75
    Xanthoria parietina 75
lift effect
  autogyros *311*
  helicopters *308*
  hydrofoils 314
lift principles, aircraft *304–305*
ligaments 214
  suspensory 191
light 289, *290–292*
  and algae 67
  coherent *435–439*
  image intensifiers 292
  incoherent *435–436*
  lasers *435–439*
  Maxwell's discoveries 291
  optics *350–353*
  photoelectric effect 280–281,
    290
  polarized *346*, *353*
  refraction 290
  sight and 190–191, *193*
  spectrum *290*, 349
  ultraviolet *290*, *292–293*
  velocity 291
lighting, gas 366
lightning flash *288*
lignin *91*
lignite 35, *35*
lilies (*Liliaceae*) 89
  calyx in 84, *86*
  'Royal Gold' *61*
  sea *99*
limb, artificial *213*
lime, common (*Tilia* x *europea*)
  90, *93*
limestone, shelly *43*
Linné, Carl von, and animal/
  plant classification 112
lions (*Panthera leo*) 97, 162, 163,
  164, 165, *165*
lipase, gastric 248, 253
lipid transport 256
lips, function 242
liquified petroleum gases (LPGs)
  366, 369
LISP computer language 405
lithium
  atomic structure 279
  fusion reactions 364–365
liver *251*, *258–259*, 261
  bile secretion 250
  blood supply 221, *224*
  cysts *253*
  damage 253
  fat accumulation *252*
  breakdown 256
  function 252–253
  lymph 228
  protein breakdown 260
  scan *252*
liverworts 59
  Hepaticae 60
  Marchantia polymorpha 59
lizards 99, *150*, 151
  bearded (*Amphibolurus
    barbatus*) 149
  characteristics 150–151
  flying (*Draco volans*) 150
  monitor 151
  zebra-tailed (*Callisaurus
    draconoides*) 151
lobster 42, *43*, *98*
lobules 252
locomotives, railway *324–327*
locusts *104*, *105*, 110
Lodge, Sir Oliver, radio 412
log, ship's 359
logarithms 398
Logo computer language 405

London plane (*Platanus
  acerfolia*) *63*, *92*
longitude *358*, 360
longshore drift 48, 49, 51
long-sightedness *191*
loop of Henle 263, *264*
Loranthaceae see plants,
  parasitic
loudspeakers 427, *427*
louse *98*
  eggs 272
Lucretius, atomic theory 276–277
Lumière brothers, cinema 430,
  433
lunar hornet moth (*Sphecia
  bembeciformus*) *111*
Lunar Roving Vehicle *335*
lungfish *44*, *99*
lungs
  blood supply 238
  foreign bodies 238, 241
  structure 238, *239–240*
  volume 239–240
Lunokhod 2 spacecraft *335*
Lurgi process 366, *369*
luteinising hormone 236
L-waves 16
Lycopersicum esculentum 58
Lycopodium see club moss
lymph 228
  flow 227
  node 228, *229*
  vessel 255
lymphatic capillaries 227, 256
  duct *227*, 228
  system 219, 227–229
lymphocytes 219–220, 228, *229*,
  256
lymphocytosis 228
lymphopenia 228
lysozyme 244, 245

M

macaques 181, 183
  characteristics 181
  pig-tailed (*Macaca hemestrina*)
    181
machine codes, computers 405
mackerel 99
Macmillan, K., bicycles 316
macrophage 228
Macropodidae 121
magma, chamber 18
magnesium 301
magnetic flux 286
magnetic tape, manufacture *421*
magnetic tape recorders *420–423*,
  426
magnetism 285–288
  computer stores *402–403*
  ferrofluids, response *286*
  fields *285*, *286*, *383–384*
magnetite 28
magnetomotive force (mmf) 286,
  287
magnolia family (*Magnoliaceae*),
  characteristics of 90
Magnox nuclear reactors *362*, 363
mahogany (*Swietenia mahogani*)
  93
maize stem borer (*Busseola fusca*)
  111
malachite *30*
mallards (*Anas platyrhynchos*)
  112, 113
  Greenland (*Anas platyrhynchos
    conboschas*) 113
Malpighi, Marcello 224
mammals 101
  placental 124
mammoths 133
  Mammuthus imperator 133

450

woolly (*Mammuthus primigenius*) 133, *134*
man 96, *98*
  skeleton of *179*, *184*
  see also skeleton
manatees (*Trichechidae*) 172
  Amazonian (*Trichechus inuguis*) 173
  characteristics 173
  Florida (*Trichechus monatus*) 173
  West African (*Trichechus senegalensis*) 173
mandible 213
mandrill (*Mandrillus sphinx*) 183
  characteristics 183
manifold, petrol engines 384
Mannheim, Amédée, slide rule 398
mantids *103*, 106
mantis, praying 106
mapping 343, *344*
  historical notes 358–360
  radar methods *357*
Marconi, Guglielmo, radio *412–414*
Marcus, Siegfried, cars 320
Marey, Etienne-Joules, cinema 430
marine engines
  gas turbines 392, *393*
  outboard in engine *382*
  steam engines *387*
  steam turbines *389*
Mariner spacecraft 334
marrow, bone 212
marsupials 120, 121
  American 123
  Australian 121–122
  carniverous 121, 122
  characteristics 120
  Diprotodan 120
  Thylacosmilus 122
  see also individual names
marteus, arboreal 166
  hunting 166
masers 435, 436, 438
mass spectroscopy *349*
master gland *see* pituitary gland
mastigophora *99*
mastodons 133
mathematics 342–345
  logarithms 398
matrix 272
matter
  atomic theories 276–277
  chemical elements 294–295
  'four elements' 294
maxilla 213
Maxwell, James Clerk 291, *412*, 418
mayflies (*Ephemera danica*) *103*, *104*, 105
meadow vetchling (*Lathyrus aphoca*), method of climbing 80
mechanics 342–343
medicine 394–397
medulla
  brain 226
  kidney *262*, *263*
  oblongata 240
Megachiroptera 128, 129, 130
meganeura monyi *43*, *103*
Meissner corpuscle *207*, 267
melanin 266
membrane
  basilar 200
  potential 205
  semi-permeable 225
  tympanic 198, *199*
memory
  calculators 401
  computer stores 402–405

Mendeleyev, Dmitri 296
menopause 272
mercalli scale 16, *16–17*
Mercator, Gerardus 360
mesoderm 99, *100*
mesons 280, 284
Mesozoic era 46
  reptiles in 101
metacarpus *213*
metallurgy 30
metal ores
  detection of *31*
  hydrothermal solutions 31
  impregnations 31
  magmatic segregations 30
  major deposits *31*
  pegmatite deposits *31*
  pneumatolytic deposits 30–31
  secondary enrichment 32
  see also individual metals; minerals
metals
  alkaline earths 301
  chemical names 294–295, 296
  electric conduction *287*
  metamorphism 25
metatarsus *213*
meteorite *11*
methane 34, 266
  natural gas source 369
mica, atom of *28*
Michaux, Pierre and Ernest 316
Microchiroptera 128, *129*
microcirculation 225
microphones 420–421
microscopes 352, *353*
microscopy 346–347
microwaves 290, 291
  beams *442*
  masers 435, 436, 438
  telephony *410*
  transmission *415*
midland hawthorn (*Crataegus oxycanthoides*) 92
migration
  bird 116, *117*, 118–119
  Lepidoptera 109–110
mildews
  downy 72
  Peronospora parasitica 71
military equipment
  Gazelle helicopters *309*
  missiles 328–331
military use
  computers *402*
  lasers *438*
  radar *354*, *356–357*
  satellites 443
milk
  curdling 248
  breast, production 236, 237
milkweed butterfly (*Danaus plexippus*) 110
millipede *43*
minerals
  alluvial deposits 29
  atomic structure 26–27, *26, 27*
  characteristics 27
  classification 26–27
  colour in 27, 29
  deposits 27–29
  effect on light 27
  elements in 26
  eluvial deposits 29
  exploration for 32–33
  hardness 27
  hydrothermal veins 28
  magmatic 27–28
  metamorphic deposits 28
  native 29
  occurrence of *28–29*
  placer deposits 29
  precious 29, 30
  production by weathering 31

residual deposits 29
sedimentary deposits 28, 31
systems 26–27, *26–27*
weight 29
see also individual names; crystals; gemstones
mining
  open-cast *32–33*, 33, *36*, 37
  retreat 37
  underground *36–37*
minks 166
mirage effect *350*
mirrors, light reflection *350*
missiles *328–331*
mistletoe
  European (*Viscum album*) 61, *79*
  characteristics 79
  tropical (*Viscum minimum*) 74
Mitchell, John 16
mites *98*
mitochondria 264
modulation
  radio waves *414*
  telephones 411
Moeritherium, characteristics 133
moho 16
Mohorovicic (seismologist) 16
Mohs (mineralogist) 27
Moh Scale 29
molecules 276–279, 296–297
moles (*Talpidae*) 125, *126*, *126–127*
  Cape Golden (*Chrysochloris asiatica*) 125, 127
  common (*Talpa europaea*) 124, 125–126, *126–127*
  marsupial 120, 121, 122
  characteristics 122
  Old World 125
  shrew 125
  star-nosed (*Condylura cristata*) *124*, 125, 126
molluscs 46, *98*, *100*
moloch (*Moloch horridus*) 151
monaxonida 99
monitor, giant (*Varanus giganteus*) 150
monkeys 181
  see also individual names
monocotyledons *see* plants, flowering
monosaccharides 256
mono sound system *426*
monorail train 327
moon, escape velocity 334
morse code *406*, 413–414
Morse, Samuel, telgraphy 406
morula *98*
mosses (*Masci*) 58, 60
moths *103*, 108–109, 110, 111
  Operophtera brumata 109
  structure of head *109*
  Syssphinx molina 110–111
  Theria rupicapraria 109
  see also individual names; *Lepidoptera*
motion, Newton's laws of *304–305*, 310, 328
motor cortex, nerve pathway *211*
motorcycles *317–319*
  engines 384–385
moulting, in arthropods 100
Moulton, Alex, bicycles 316
mountain sickness 226
mountain building
  erosion 25
  movement in Earth's crust 22, *22*, 24
  recumbent folds 24
  roots 25
  in Tertiary era 17
mountains
  angry 20

great chains 22
see also specific names
mouth *244*
  digestion 242–245, *261*
  mucous lining 238
  temperature receptors 194
movie cameras *430–432*
moving coil microphones 421
moving coil pick-up *425–427*
moving magnet pick-up *425–427*
mucilage *66*, *67*
mucin 245
Mucor see pin mould
mucous cells, stomach 248
  membrane, gall bladder 250
  large intestine 258
mudflats, tidal 48
mud puppies, development in 159
multiplets 283
multiplex telephony *411*
muscles 191, 215–217, 227, 231, 233, 239, 241, 242, 258, 260–261
mushrooms and toadstools 59, 60, 70, 72–73
  and orchids 77
Mustela 166
mustelids, characteristics 166
mycelium 70, 74
Mycena inclinata 58
mycorrhizas 77
myelin sheath 202
myopia *190*
myosin *216*, 217
Myrmecobiidae 121

N

nails, human 270, 272
Napier, John, logarithms 398
narwhal (*Monodon monoceros*) 175
  characteristics 176
nasal bone 213
natural gas 366, *368–369*
natural number concept 342
nautilus *98*
navigation *356–361*
  radar use 357
nectar *84*
nectarines *84*
negative ions (anions) 378
negative photographs 418
nematodes *98*
neon 295
  atomic structure *278–279*
neotemy 159
nepenthesin 81
nephrons *262*, *263*
Nerva nuclear engine 331
nerve bundle *204*
  cells 202
  endings *204*, *206*, *207*, 267
  fibres 202, *205*, 207
  impulse *204–205*
  optic 190, *191*
  parasympathetic 244–245
  somatic 207
  sympathetic 245
  vagus 248
nervous system 202–205
  circulation control 222
neuroglia 202
neurone 202, *203*, 204–205, 209–210
neutrinos 283, 284
neutrography 417
neutrons 276, *279*
  fusion reactions 362–363
  nuclear fission 362
  particle decay 279
Newton, Sir Isaac *193*
  gravitation law 280

motion laws 304, 310
  spectrum discovery 349
  telescopes 352–353
newts 156, 159
  Alpine (Triturus alpestris) 159
  characteristics 159
  palmate (Triturus helveticus) 159
nickel mining 32
nicotine 253
Niepce, J.N., photography 416
Nikolayeva-Tereshkova, V. 334
nitrogen 298
  coal gas 366
  'fixation' 76
  manufacture 298, 299
  narcosis 226
  natural gas 366, 368–369
nitrogenase 77
nits 272
nodding thistle (Carduus nutans) 86
nodes, stem 88
nodules, root 76
noise chart 199
  monitoring techniques 289
  pollution 201
    control 289
noradrenaline 222
nose, structure 194–195, 196–197, 238
  see also nasal
notochord 96
Notoryctidae 121
nuclear fission 362
nuclear particle accelerators 280–281
nuclear power 362–365
nuclear reactors 362–365
  gamma ray emission 293
nuclear rocket engines 329, 331
nuclear waste disposal 64–65, 363, 364–365
nucleic acid molecule 276
nucleons 362
nucleus 66
  atoms, splitting 362
number concepts 342, 343

O

oak 60, 90
  number of species 91
Oberth, Hermann, rockets 329
obsidian 20
ocean floor
  composition of 55
  profile of Atlantic 54–55
  provinces of 52, 54–55
  submarine density current 54
Odonata, characteristics 104
  see also damselflies;
    dragonflies
oedema 228
Oedogonium 68
Oersted, scientist, electro-magnetism 285
oesophagus 238, 243, 244, 247, 261
oestradiol 236
oestrogen 235, 266
Ohain, Hans van, jet engine 392
oil
  crude see petroleum
  gas synthesis 366, 367
  shales 41
  well, first 38, 38
  see also petroleum
okapi (Giraffidae) 144, 146, 146, characteristics 147
  Okapi johnstoni 146, 147
olfactory area 194–195
  hair 197

olingos 168
olm (Proteus anguinus), habitat 160
Olpidium brassicae 70
omnivores 247
Omomyidae, history of 181
ootheca 106
opossums (Didelphidae) 123
  common (Didelphidis marsupialis) 120
  rat (Caenolestidae) 123
  thick-tailed (Lutreolina crassicaudata) 123
  water (Chironectes minimus) 123
opponent-process theory 193
optic nerve 190, 191
optics 350–353, 435–439
orang-utan (Pongo pygmaeus) 178, 179, 180, 180
  skull of 184
orbicularis oris 242
orbits, satellites 440–441
orchids (Orchidaceae) 81
orders, animal 112
Ordovician period 13
  fossil record 42–45
organelles 59, 66
organ of Corti 200, 201
Orobanchaceae see plants, parasitic
orogeny see mountain building
Orthoptera 105, 106
  see also crickets; grasshoppers
oscilloscope 198
osier (Salix viminalis) 90
osmosis 225, 263
osmotic pressure, blood 218
ossicles 198, 199, 200
osteoblasts 212
osteocytes 212, 214
ostracoderms, headshield of 45
ostracods 46
otosclerosis 200
otters
  Canadian (Lutra canadensis) 166–167
  clawless (Aonyx capensis) 167
  European (Lutra lutra) 168
  giant (Pteronura brasiliensis) 168
  sea (Enhydra lutris) 167, 168
Otto, Nikolaus 382
Oughtred, W., slide rule 398
outboard engine 382
output, computer systems 403–405
ova development 236
oval window, ear 198, 199
ovaries, plant 61, 86, 87
ovipositer 106
ovules 86, 87
owls (Strigiformes) 112
  North American screech (Otis asio) 118
oxygen 298, 299
  in body
    diffusion 225
    exchange 221, 222, 231, 238
    starvation 231
    supply to muscles 217
    transport 218–219, 221, 222
    use 238
oxytocin 234, 237
ozone sterilizer, water 375

P

pacemakers, heart 397
Pacinian corpuscles 206, 207, 267
pain
  heart 223
  sensation 204, 207, 208, 210
palaeocologist 45

palaeontologists 42
Palaeoptera 104, 105
  see also damselflies;
    dragonflies
Palaeozoic era 46
palate, soft 238
palms (Palmae) 63
Panavision films 433–434
pancreas 235, 236, 250–251, 253
pancreatic duct 253
  juice 253
pancerozymin 253, 254
pandas, giant (Ailuropodidae) 168, 169, 169
  classification of 168
  red (Ailurus fulgens) 169, 169
    characteristics 169
panthers, colour in 162
papain 92–93
papaya (Carica papaya), cultivation of 92–93
papillae, skin 266, 268, 272
  tongue 195
papillary layer 266
parabolas 344
parallels, geometries 344
paralysis 217
paramylon (stored carbohydrate in plants) 66
parasites
  hair 272
  intestinal 253, 256
parasitism, plant 59, 74, 80
parasympathetic nervous system 244–245
parietal cells 248
parotid gland 244
Parsons, Sir Charles 389
particles 280–284
Pascal, Blaise 398, 399
Passeriformes 115
passion flower 80
patella 213
Pauli, Wolfgang, exclusion principle 279
peat 34
pearl-bordered fritillary (Argynnis euphrosyne) 110
pears 59
peas (Leguminosae)
  Pisum sativum 80
peccaries 143
  characteristics 143
  collared (Tayassu tajacu) 141
    characteristics 143
  white-lipped (Tayassu pecari), characteristics 143
pedunculate oak (Quercus robur), fruit of 91
pegmatite 30
Pelecaniformes 114
pelican, brown (Pelecanus occidentalis) 113
Pelsaert, Francisco 120
pelvis 214
pendular movements 254
peneplain 25
penguins, Adelié (Pygoscelis adeliae) 119
penicillin 264
Penicillium
  killing bacteria 71
  Penicillium glaucum, reproduction in 73
  Penicillium notatum 60, 71
penny-farthing bicycles 316
peppered moth (Biston betularia) 109, 110–111
pepsin 81, 246, 248
pepsinogen 248
peptones 248
Peramelidae 121
Père David, and giant panda 168
perianth 86

periodic table 294–295, 296
peripatus 98
peripheral nervous system 202, 203
peripheral units, computers 404
Perissodactyla 138
  characteristics 136
  see also rhinoceroses; tapirs
peristalsis 247, 249, 254
  mass 258
peristome 81
Permian period 13
  fossil record 42–45
pernicious anaemia 219
Pershing II missile 329
petals 84, 87
Peters, J.L., classification of birds 113
petiole 88
petrol 99
petrol engines
  cooling systems 385
  four-stroke 383
  road vehicles 320, 322, 323
  rotary 384–385
  two-stroke 382–383
petroleum/crude oil/gas
  distillation 41
  drilling for 41
  fields 39, 39
  migration 39
  North Sea sites 40
  origins 38
  production platform 40
  quantity of 40–41
  seepages 38
  seismic surveys for 41
  sources 39–41
  supply 38–39
  see also oil; gas
Peyer's patches 256
phaeochromocytoma 223
Phalangeridae 121
phanerozoic time see Cainozoic era; Mesozoic era; Palaeozoic era
pharynx 243, 261
phases, electricity supply 370, 372–373
Phasmida, characteristics 106
phenylthiocarbamide test 194
pheromones 197
phloem 88
Phobosuchus ('terror crocodile') 154
phonographs 420, 424
phosphorus discovery 294
photoelectric effect 280–281, 290
photoemitters 292
photography 416–419
  X-rays 293
photons 281
  electric current effect 290, 291
  engines 331
  fusion reactions 362–363
  laser light 435–439
  nuclear decay 362
photosynthesis 67
phycoerythrin (pigment) 67
phycomycetes see fungi, algal
Phyla 96
Phylloglossum see club moss
Phyllorhynchus 149
Piciformes 115
pick-up cartridges, sound 425
piezoelectric effect 420–421, 425
pigs 140, 141
  Bornean (Sus barbatus) 140, 140, 143
  bush (Potamochoerus porcus) 143
    characteristics 140
  domestic 141, 143
  Javan (Sus verrucosus) 143
  see also babirusa; boars; hogs

piles 258
pillow lavas 52
piloting techniques
  aircraft 304–307
  helicopters 308–311
pines (Pinaceae) 61
pin-mould 72
  reproduction in 59, 70–71
pinnipeds 170
Pioneer spacecraft 335
pisiform 212
pitch, helicopter blades 308, 310
pitch discrimination 200
pitcher plants 81
pitching control, aircraft 305
pituitary gland 211, 234–235,
  236–237
placenta 120
placoderms, characteristics 100
plains, abyssal 52, 54
Planck, Max 281, 292–293
Plan Position Indicator 357
plant kingdom, the 58–61
  division of 58, 58–59
plant life, first evidence of 62–63
plant partnerships 74, 76–77
plants
  carniverous 81–83
    catching mechanism 81, 82,
    83
  climbing 78, 79, 80
  consumers 78
  evolution of 62–64
  flowering 59, 61, 84, 86–89
    stem of 88
    types of 60, 61, 61, 62
  land 58–59, 60–61
    gametophyte generation 60
    sporophyte generation 60
    of the past 63–64
  parasitic 78, 79
    Rafflesia arnoldii 79
  procedures 78
plasma 218, 228, 229, 262
plasma engines 331
plastron 152
platelets, blood 220, 223
platypus 99
Plethodontinae species of 160
pleura 239
pleural cavity 239
pleurisy 239
plexi 254
plovers, golden (Pluvialis
  apricaria) 116
plume (volcanic) 21
plutonium 295
  fissile isotopes 362
pneumatic tyres, bicycles 316
podetia 74
Podicipediformes 114
polarization phenomenon 379
polarized light 346, 353
polecats 166, 166
  European (Mustela putorius)
    distribution 166–167
poles, geographic 358, 359
pollen 61, 86, 87
  grain, fossil 64
  tube 86, 87
pollination, importance of 86
pollution, atmospheric 228
  noise 201
  tests, water 374–375
poplars 90
  black (Populus nigra) 90
polyhydric alcohol 74
Popov, Alexander, radio 412
poppy, field (Papaver rhoeas) 61
Porphyra 69
porpoises 175
  common (Phocaena phocaena)
    166
Porro prisms 353

Poseidonia 61
positive ions (cations) 378
positrons 283
possums
  Australian (Trichosurus
    vulpecula) 120
  dormouse 121
  flying 121
  gliding 120
  ringtail 120
potato blight, history of 72
Poulsen, Valdemar 420
power 362–393
power stations 370, 372
  nuclear reactors 362–365
  steam power 389
power systems, electricity 370–
  373
Pratt & Whitney jet engine 306–
  307
pre-amplifiers 424, 427
pre-Cambrian era 13
  fossil record 42–45
  North America in 11
Preece, Sir William, radio 413
pressoreceptors 226
pressure sensation 206
pressurized water reactors
  (PWRs) 363
primary cells (batteries) 378, 379
printers, computer output 404
printing calculators 401
printing process, films 432–433
prisms, light behaviour 350–351
privet hawk moth (Sphinx ligusti)
  109
  caterpillar of 109
Procavia 133
Procellariiformes 114
processing, computer systems
  402–405
producer gas 366
programmable calculators 401
programs, computer 404–405
projectors, cinema 433–434
prokaryotes 59, 62
prolactin 234, 236, 237
propane gas 369
propellants, rockets 329, 330–331
prop fan engine 392
prosobranchs see gastropods
proteins
  digestion 248, 252–253, 254,
    256, 266
  lymph 228
  plasma 218, 228, 229
  production 237
proteoses 248
ptyalin 248
pubic hair 270
pulmonary artery 230, 238–239
  vein 231, 238
protons 276, 279
  electric charge 276
  fusion reactions 362–363
  particle decay 283
proton smasher 282
protostomia 98
protosuchus 44
protozoa 46, 99
Proust, J.L. 277
psilophyton 42
Psittaciformes 115
pteraspidomorph 44
Pteridophyta 59, 60, 63
  see also club moss; ferns;
    horsetails
Pteridospermae 63, 84
puffin (Fratercula artica) 100
pulse code modulation (PCM) 410
pumice 20
pumpsets, water supply 375
pupil, eye 190, 191
purity tests, water supply 374–375

pus 220
puss moth (Cerura vinula),
  caterpillar of 110
P-waves 16, 17
pyloric sphincter 249, 254
pyramidal cells 209
pyrenoids 66, 68
Pyrethrum, pickling 89
pyroclasts 20
Pythagoras, mathematician 342
Pythium, reproduction of 70, 72
pythons (Pythoninae) 150
  royal (Python regius) 148

Q

qanaats 374
quadraphonic sound 428
quantum mechanics 279, 281
quantum theory 280–281, 292
quarks 283–284
quartz 298, 299
Quaternary period 13
  fossil record 42–45
Questar telescope 352

R

raccoons (Procyonidae)
  characteristics 168
  North American (Procyon lotor)
    168, 168
radar 354–357
  navigational aid 359
radiation
  light 289, 290–292
  radioactive elements 362–365
  sound 289, 290, 293
  spectroscopy 348–349
radio 412–415
  Doppler effect 357
  navigational aids 360–361
  satellite systems 441–443
  telescopes 290
  velocity 355
  waves 288, 290, 291–292
radioactive compounds 293, 298–299
radioactive decay 10, 10, 363–365
radioactive elements 10
  half-life of 10, 10, 363
radioactive radiation 293
radiocarbon dating 12
radiolarians 55
radiotelephone 409, 415
radium 301
radius 213
radon 295
Rafflesiaceae, see plants,
  parasitic
ragworm 98
railways 324–327
  electricity supply 373
rainbow plants 82
rainbows 290, 291
range set 344
raphe slit (diatom) 66
rare gases, laser light 437
raspberries 59
ratel (Mellivora capensis)
  characteristics 167
rats, moon 124, 125
rattlesnake, American (Crotalus
  cerastes) 149
receivers
  radio 412, 414–415
  telephone 409, 411
receptors, nerve 204
record heads 421–423
record players 424–427
recorders, sound 420–423
records, manufacture 422–423
rectum 258, 259

red admiral (Vanessa atalanta)
  110
red blood cells see corpuscle
red horse chestnut (Aesculus x
  carnea) 93
redout 226
reductionism 343–344
redwood (Sequoia sempervirens)
  65
reflection 350
reformers, town gas 368–369
refraction, light 350–351
reindeer moss (Cladonia
  rangiferina) 74
relativity 345
renal artery 262, 263, 264
renin 222, 223, 248
repeaters, telephone 409, 411
reproductive system, hormones
  236
reptiles 101, 152
  characteristics 155
  extinction of giant, fossils
    46
  see also individual names
reservoirs, water supply 375
resistors, electric 287
respiration 238–241
  inhibition 245
respiratory centre 240
  distress syndrome,
    organs 239–240
reticular formation 210
  region 267
retina 190, 191, 223
reversal film 418
Rheiformes 114
rhesus monkey (Macaca mulatta)
  181, 183
rhinoceroses 136, 139, 139
  black (Diceros bicornis) 136,
    137, 139
    characteristics 137
  characteristics 137
  Indian (Rhinoceros
    unicornis) 138, 139
    characteristics 139
    skeleton of 136
  Java (Rhinoceros sandaicus)
    138, 139
  square-lipped (Ceratotherium
    simum) 137, 138
    characteristics 136, 137
  Sumatran (Dicerorhinus
    sumatrensis) 138, 139
    characteristics 139
  woolly 138
rhizoids 60
Rhododendron 92
rhodopsin 192
rhumb lines 360
Rhynchocephalia 148
rhythmic segmentation 254
rib cage, human 212
Richter, C.F. 16
ridges, mid-oceanic 54
Righi, Augusto, radio 412
rocket boosters 338
rockets 328–331
rocks
  age of 11–12
  Bulawayan group, evidence of
    plant life in 62
  cap 39
  igneous 18
  reservoir 39
  source 39
  see also individual names
rods, eye 192
rolling control, aircraft 305
Rolls-Royce engines
  helicopters 310
  hovercraft 312
ROM, calculators 401

roots, plant 76–77, 87
roses (Rosaceae) 59
rotary engines 384–385
rotifer 98
rotors
  autogyros 308, 311
  gas turbines 390
  helicopters 308–311
round window, ear 200
royal fern (Osmunda regalis) 59
rubber 301
ruby lasers 435, 438–439
Ruffini corpuscle 207
rugae
  gall bladder 250
  stomach 247
runner beans (Phaseolus multiflorus), method of climbing 80
Russell, Bertrand 345
Rutherford, Sir Ernest 10, 278, 280

S

Saccharomyces cerevisiae 73
sacrum 213
salamanders 99, 156
  Asian, development in 159
  cave, characteristics 160
  fire (Salamandra salamandra) 158
  giant 159–160
  lungless 160
  Pyrenean (Euproctes asper) 158
  see also axolotl; mud puppies
saliva 194, 236, 244–245
salivary glands 236, 243, 244, 244–245
salt (sodium chloride)
  atomic model 276
  balance in body 235, 236, 263
  deposits 28
  dome 40
  halogen compound 301
  seawater extraction 295
  structure 26
  X-ray 28
San Andreas fault 14–15
saprophytes 78
saprophytism 59
sapwood 91
satellites 337, 440–443
  navigational aids 360–361
  radio links 413
  telephone links 410
Saturn V launcher 330
scanning instruments, body 395–396
scapula 213
scarlet windowed moth 111
Schwann cells 202, 205
scientific methods 342–348
sclera 190, 191
scorpions 43, 98
scots pine (Pinus sylvestris) 42, 77
scutes 152
sea buckthorn (Hippophae) 77
sea cows (Sirenia) 132, 172
  characteristics 172–173
  Steller's (Hydrodamalis stelleri) 173
sea lions (Otarunae) 170, 171, 172
  Californian (Zalophus californianus) 171
  characteristics 171
  Steller's (Eumetopias jubatus) 171–172
seals 170
  Alaska fur (Callorhinus ursinus) 172
  crab-eating (Lobodon carcinophagus) 170, 171

eared (Otarriidae) 170, 171
  elephant (Mirounga leonina) 170, 171
  fur (Archtocephalinae), characteristics 171
  grey (Halichoerus grypus) 171
  harbour (Phoca vitulina) 171
  harp (Payophilus groenlaudicus) 173
  hooded (Cystophora cristata) 172
  leopard (Hydrurga leptonyx) 173
  South African (Arctocephalus pusillus) 172
  true (Phocidae) 170, 171
  Weddell's (Leptonychotes weddelli) 171
seamounts 55
searchlight, radar controlled 354
Seascale nuclear power plant 365
Sea Skua 329
sea squirt (Giona intestinalis) 44, 96, 99, 101
sea urchins 99
seawater, desalination 376
seaweeds
  brown
    Fucus vesiculosus 69
    Laminaria digitata 69
  green 68
    Caulerpa prolifera 68
  habitat of 67
  infra red photo of 68
  reproduction in 69
  shore
    Fucus 68, 68
    Laminaria 68
sebaceous gland 236, 267, 272
sebum 267–269, 271, 272
secondary cells 378, 379–380
secretin 253, 254
sedge grass 63
seismic profiling 54
  continuous 52
seismic regions 14
seismic surveying, 37, 41
seismograph 16
Selaginella see club moss
sensation
  brain transmission 211
  pain 204, 207, 208, 210
  phantom 208
  pressure 206
sensory nerve pathway 211
sepals 84, 87
septum 155, 230–231
Sequoia fossils 65
serotonin 220
serum 220
sessile oak (Quercus petraea), fruit of 91
set theory 343, 345
sex glands 234, 237, 270
sextants 358, 360
sharks (Selachii) 44, 99
shark's tooth 55
Shaw, George Bernard 412
shield areas 11–12
shingles 48
ships
  navigation 358–361
  radar use 356, 357
shock 220
shock absorbers, motorbikes 318–319
shore platforms 50, 51
short-sightedness 190
shoulder joint 212
shrews (Soricidae) 126
  African otter (Potamogale velox), characteristics 127

elephant (Elephantulus brachyrhynchus) 125, 127
  characteristics 127
  otter (Micropotamogale) 127
    Potamogalidae 127
  pen-tailed tree (Ptilocerus lowii) 125
  white-toothed (Crocidura leucodon) 125
    common European (Crocidura russula) 126
shutters, camera 416, 418
siamang (Symphalangus symdactylus) 178
sidecars, motorcycles 318, 319
'side-winding' 149
Siemen's gas 366
Sierra Nevada 22
sight 190–193, 210–211
silica 26, 298–299
silicon 298, 299
silicones 298
silk moth (Bombyx mori) 111
Silurian period 13
  fossil record 42–45
silver 31
silver fir 59
silverfish 98, 102, 104
  characteristics 102
silver Y moth (Plusia gamma) 109, 111
single lens reflex cameras 416–417
sinuses, facial 238
  lymph node 228
sinusoids 228
Sirenia 172
Sivrac, Comte de, bicycles 316
skatole 260
skeletal muscle 215, 217
  blood supply 221
skeleton
  arthropods 100
  human 212–214
skin 267–269
  blood supply 221, 225, 267
  lymph 228
  moisture 269
  sensory receptors 206–207
skirts, hovercraft 312–313
skull x-ray 242
skunks 167, 168
  spotted (Spilogale putorius) 168
Skycrane helicopter 311
slide rules 398–399
sliding filament theory 216
slow worms (Anguis fragilis) 149
SLR camera, diagram 416–417
slugs, sea 98
smell 194–197
smoking, effects on body heat 222–223
smooth muscle 215, 217
snails 98
snakes 148, 149, 149, 150
  American mud 149
  characteristics 150
  corn (Elaphe guttata) 148
  desert leaf-nosed 149
  egg-eating 149
  grass (Natrix natrix) 100, 148
  sand (Psammiphis sibilans) 149
  sea (Hydrophiinae) 150
  shield-tailed (Uropeltidae) 149
  see also individual names
sneezing response 241
sodium 264, 301
  bicarbonate 253
  chloride 276, 301
  see also salt
solar energy
  calculators 399

satellites 441, 442
solenodons (Solenodontidae) 127
  characteristics 127
  Solenodon paradoxus 126
solidification, nuclear waste 365
somatic nerves 207
  nervous system 202
sonar, sidescan 52
sound 289, 290, 293
  distinguishing 200
  echoes 354–355
  localization 198, 201
  pollution control 289
  recording 420–423
    movies 430, 431
  transmission 198–199
sound mixer desk 426
sound reproduction 424–429
soundtracks, movies 430, 431, 432–433
space flight 226, 245, 334–341
Spacelab I 340, 341
space probes 334
space shuttles 338–341, 442, 443
space suits 336
space vehicles
  computers 402
  manned 334–341
  navigational aids 360–361
  rocket launchers 328–329, 331
  satellites 337–338, 440–443
  Viking laboratory 348–349
spark plugs, petrol engines 382–385
special effects
  cinema 431–433
  radio 422
species, classification of animal 112
spectacles 190–191, 350–351
  bifocal 192
spectra
  electromagnetic 290
  light 290, 350, 351
  measurement 349
spectrometer, mass 10
spectroscopes 351
spectroscopy 348–349
specular reflection 350
speech frequencies 411
speed
  camera shutters 418
  films, photographic 419
  movie film 430
  sound recording 422
speedway motorcycles 318–319
spermaceti 175
spermatophores 159
Spermatophyta 59
spermatozoa, development 236
spermatozoids 60
Sphemsciformes 114
sphincter
  anal 258
  cardiac 247, 249, 261
  oesophageal 247
  of Oddi 250
  pyloric 249, 254
spiders (Arachnids) 98
  Misumenops nepenthicola and pitcher plants 81
spinal column structure 203, 212
  cord 203
spit (of sand) 51
splitting, nuclear fission 362
sponges 99
sporangia 59, 63, 71
sporophyte 68, 87
sporopollenin 64
sporozoa 99
springtails 102, 103
  characteristics 102
  green (Sminthurus viridis) 102

Podura aquatica 102
spring wood 90
Sputnik 1 spacecraft 329
Sputnik space vehicles *440*
spruces, growth in 61
Squamata 148
squid *98*
squirrel *99*
stack (coastal) 48, *50*
staged rockets 440
stall effect, aircraft *304, 305–306*
stamens 86, *87*
Stanley, Henry, and okapis 146
Stanley brothers, steam cars 320
starfish *99*
Starling's law 233
starlings (*Sturnus vulgaris*) and navigation *118*
STARPAHC health system 394
stars
    navigation use 358
'Star Wars' *330, 443*
static electricity *288*
steam cars 320
steam locomotives *324–327*
steam power *386–389*
stems
    inside of herbaceous *87*
    structure of 88
Stephenson, George, railways 324
stereoscope *192*
stereophonic sound (stereo) 424
stereo sound systems *425, 426*
sterilization, water supply 375
sternum *213*, 238
stigma 61, *84*, 86, *87*
stipules 80
stoat (*Mustela erminea*) 166, *166*
stomach, anatomy 247–249, 261
stomata 88–89
stoneflies *103*
    nymph *104*
stork, European white (*Ciconia ciconia*) 119
strangeness charge (S) 283
Strategic Defense Initiative (SDI) *330, 443*
stratigraphy 42
straum basale 266
    corneum 266
    granulosum 266
    lucidum 266
    spinosum 266
Strelka, space dog *440*
stretch receptors 241
striated muscle 215, 217
stridulation 106
Strigiformes 115
stromatolites 62
strontium 301
Strowger, Almon B. 407, 409
Struthioniformes 114
strychnine 253
studios
    cinema *432, 433*
    radio *414*
    sound recording *422*
sturgeon *99*
style 61, 86, *87*
Stylites see club moss
styluses, sound pick-up *424–425*
sub-atomic particles 280–284
subcutaneous layer 267
subimago (mayflies) 105
sublingual gland 244
submandibular gland 244
submarine cables 370, *408*
substations, electricity *372–373*
sugar, blood levels 210, *235*, 236, 237, 253

sulphur *300–301*
sulphuric acid 296, 301
    formula *296*
    lead-acid batteries 378
sundews 81, 82, 83
    Drosera rotundiflora 82–83
sunstroke 270
supergravity 284
superheterodyne radio *412*
supersonic aircraft *307*
surface effect ships (SES) 312
surface piercing hydrofoils 314, *315*
surfactant, alveolar 241
suspension
    bicycles 316
    cars *321*
    motorcycles 318–319
suspensory ligament 191
swallowing action *244–245*
swallows (*Hirundo rustica*) 119
swallowtail butterflies
    Papilio dardanus 109
    Papilio machaon 108
S-waves 16
sweat glands 197, 269
    pore *268*
sweating 269
sweet chestnuts 90
sweet pea (*Lathyrus odoratus*) 80
swifts (*Apodidae*), reasons for migration 116
swing-wing aircraft *307*
switching systems, electric *370–373*
sycamore (*Acer pseudoplatanus*) *92*
symbiosis 74, 77
symbols, chemical use 296
sympathetic nerve 245
synapse *204*, 205
synaptic cleft 205
Syncardia 98
synchotrons *281, 282*
Synchytrium endobioticum 70, 72
synovial fluid 214
syringomyelia 207
systole 230
systolic blood pressure 223

T

tabulate animals *98*
tail rotor, helicopters *310–311*
taipan (*Oxyuranus scutulatus*) 150
tape recorders *420, 423*
tapeworm *98*, 253, 256
Taphrina deformans 72
    sexual reproduction in 72–73
tapirs 136, 137, 139, *139*
    Central American (*Tapirus bairdi*) 138
    characteristics 136
    Malayan (*Tapirus indicus*) *139*
    mountain (*Tapirus pinchaque*) 138
    South American, characteristics 137
    Tapirus terrestris 139
tap root 88
tar sands 41
tarsus *213*
tartaric acid *346*
Tasmanian devil (*Sarcophilus harrisi*) 122, *122*
taste 194–197
taxonomy 58
tea (*Camellia sinensis*), types of 92
teak (*Tectona grandis*) 93
tea rose (*Rosa odorata*) 59

tears 236
tectonic events 14
teeth
    carnassial 161
    development in humans 242–244
    fluoride 256
    molar *244–245*
telecommunications *406–415*
telegraph, wireless (radio) 412
telegraphone invention 420
telegraphy 408
telephone exchange 33, *205*
telephony *406–411*
telephoto lenses *416–417*
teleprinters *406*
telescopes
    astronomical *352–353*
    radio *290*
    satellite-based 443
television, colour 193
Temnospondyli 156
temperature receptors in mouth 194
tendrils 80
tenrecs (*Tenrecidae*) 127
    Tenrec ecaudatus, characteristics 127
    lesser (*Echinops telfairi*) 125
'tepus' plant 139
terminal growth 90
termites *103*
tern, Arctic (*Sterna paradisaea*) *117*
terrapin (*Pseudemys dorbicny*) 152
Terront, Charles *316*
Tertiary period 13, *64*, 84
    fossil record *42–45*
testosterone *235*, 236
Teton range *23*
thalamus 211
Thallophyta 58
thallus 74
    in algae 60
thermal reactors 362
thermite *300–301*
thermography *259*
Thompson, R.W., pneumatic tyres 316
Thomson, J.J. 277, 280
thoracic cavity 240
    duct 227, 228
thorax *239*, 240
Three Mile Island 363
threshold 82–83
thrips, on geological timescale *103*
thromboplastin *219*
thrombosis 223
throttle, petrol engines 384
thrush, rock (*Turdus saxatilis*) 112
thyroid gland 234
    disorder, diagnosis 237
    stimulating hormone 236
thyroxine *235*
tibia *213*
tigers (*Panthera tigris*) 161, 162, *162*, 163
    sabre-tooth (*Machairodus lapidens*) 161
    skeleton of *161*
'tiger cat', Australian (*Dasyurus maculatus*) 123
tiger moth (*Arctia caja*) 111
time
    mathematics 342, 343, *344*
    progress of life through 46
tin 31
    dredging for *32–33*
    mining 33
Tinamiformes 114
tissue, vascular 60

Titan/Centaur rocket 330
Titan launch vehicle *334*
toads 156, 159, *159*
    Bufo bufo, mating *158*
    Bufo periglines 101
    European midwife (*Alytes obstetricans*) 158–159
    neotropical (*Bufo marinus*) 157
    Surinam (*Pipa pipa*) 159
toadstools see mushrooms and toadstools
Tokyo, earthquake in 17
tombolo 48
tomography units 395
tongue *243*
    papilla *195*
    taste mechanism 194
toothwort 79
topology *344–345*
torque effects, helicopters *310–311*
tortoises *99*
    giant (*Geochelone elephantopus*) 153
    Indian star (*Testudo elegans*) 153
    see also turtles and tortoises
touch 206–208, 211
trachea 238, *240*
track improvements, railways 327
Tradescantia leaf, close-up of 88
trains, railway *324–327*
transducers 396
transformers, electrical 285, 287, *287, 370–373*
transmission, electric power *370–373*
transmission systems, vehicles 321, 322, 323
transmitters
    microwaves *410, 413*, 415
    radio *414–415*
    telephone *410*
transpiration 89
transport
    aircraft *304–307*
    helicopters *308–311*
    hovercraft *312–314*
    hydrofoils *314–315*
    of nuclear fuels *364–365*
    railways *324–327*
    road vehicles *320–323*
transuranic nuclear waste 364
traps
    adhesive 82
    anticlinal 40
    fault 40
    lobster-pot 83
        Genlisea, description of 83
    snap 82
    structural 40
    suction 82–83
treatment, water supply *375–376*
tree-ferns 63
trees
    coniferous 61, 63–64
    families, temperate 90–92
    flowering, description of 90
        growth in 90
        uses of 92–93
    growth in *11*
    tropical and sub-tropical types of 93
    tropical food 92
trenches 52, 55
Trevithick, Richard, locomotives 324
triangles, Pythagorean *342*
Triassic period *13*
    fossil record *42–45*
tribe (unit of classification) 58

trilobites *42, 43,* 46, *46*
Trichoderma virde, effect on
   cellulose 73
tricycle, steam *387*
Trident missile *329*
trigger hairs 82
triglycerides 256
Trogoniformes 115
trucks *322–323*
truth, mathematical concepts 345
trypsin 253
Tsiolokovsky, K.E. *328,* 330
Tsunami 14–15, *15*
Tswelt, Mikhail,
   chromatography 346
tubellaria *98*
tulip tree *(Liriodendron
   tulipfera)* 86
   leaf of *88*
tuning process, radio 414–415
Tupolev Tu-144 airliner *307*
turbidity, water supply 374, 375
turbines, marine engines *389*
   steam-powered 386, *388–389*
turbofan engines *390–391,* 392
turbojet engines 392
turboprop engines *391–392*
turboshaft engines 310, 311, 392
turning control, aircraft *305*
turtles *44*
   alligator snapping
      (Macroclemys temminckii)
      153
   green *(Chelonia mydas)* 153,
      153
   leatherback *(Dermochelys
      coriacea)* 152, *153*
   Mata-mata *(Chelys fimbriatus)
      152*
   sea 152, *152,* 153
      characteristics 152, *152*
turtles and tortoises 152, 153,
   153, 154
   structure *152*
   see also terrapins
twin lens reflex cameras *122,* 124
two-stroke engine cycle *382–383*
tympanal organs 110
tympani 106
tympanic canal 200
   membrane 198, *199*
typhoid fever 256
typhus 254, *272*
Tyrranosaurus rex 148

U

ulcers, stomach *246, 247,* 248
Ulmaceae 91–92
ulna *213*
ultrasonics, medical use *396–397*
ultrasonic waves *289*
ultrasound scan *397*
ultraviolet radiation 288
ultraviolet light 290, *292–293*
   bactericidal use *292–293*
Umbelliferae, inflorescence of *87*
uncertainty principle *279*
uniflow steam engine *386–387,
   388–389*
uranium 31, 278
   and age of earth 10–11
   enrichment 362
   fissile isotope 362
   uranium-plutonium cycle *364*
urea 253, 263, 264
ureter, stone *262*
urethra *262*
urine production 237, 263, 264
urodeles 156, 159
   see also newts; salamanders
uterus, contractions 237

V

vacuole *68*
vagus nerve 248
valency of elements 297
valves 67
   heart *230,* 231–233
Van de Graff generator *281*
Van de Waal's forces 276
vans 323
variables, mathematical 342–343
varicose veins 223
vascular bundles *87,* 88
vascular plant, oldest known *62*
vascular tissue 88
vasoconstriction 225
vasodilatation 225
vasopressin 234, 237
vectors 287
veins 221, *222,* 224, 225
   damage 223
   hepatic portal 252, 256
   pulmonary 231, 238
   renal *262*
vellus 270
Velocifere bicycle 316
Velocipede bicycle 316
velocity 343, *344*
venom *see* vipers
ventricle 230–231, 232, 239
venules 221, *222*
venus flytrap *(Dionaea
   muscipula)* 82
vertebrae 212, *213,* 214
vertebrates 42, 96, 100–101
vertical take-off aircraft *311*
Vesalius, Andreas *221*
vesicles 77
vestibular canal 200
Vesuvius (volcano) 20
vibration frequencies (Hz)
   289–290
videophone *411*
Viking spacecraft *328*
villi *228,* 254
vipers and venom 150
Virginia creeper *(Ampelopsis
   veitchi),* method of climbing
   80
visceral nervous system 202
vision
   accommodation 191
   acuity 191
   blind spot *192–193*
   colour 192, *193*
   double *192–193*
   peripheral 192
   stereo *192*
vitamin A 253
   B 258
   B12 253
   D 253
   K 220, 258
   transport, in body 263–264
vitrain 36
vitreous humour 190, *191,* 192
volatiles 34
volcanoes 18, 19, 20, 21, 22–23
Volta, Count Alessandro 378
voltages, electricity supply
   286, *370–373*
Vombatidae 121
vomiting 248, 254
von Drais *see* Drais
von Hemlholtz, Hermann 193, 206
Vostok spacecraft 334
Voyager 1 spacecraft *337*
vugs 28
vulcanization process 301

W

W (intermediate vector boson) 283
wallabies 121
   albino bush 122
wallaroo *(Macropus robustus)* 121
walruses *(Odobenus rosmarus)*
   170, *170, 171,* 172
   characteristics 172
Wankel rotary engine *384–385*
Wankel-type engines 319
warbler, willow *(Phylloscopus
   tronchilus)* 118
'wart disease' in plants 70, 72
wasps *98, 103, 108*
   ichneumon *(Rhussa
      persuasoria)* 111
waste disposal, nuclear 363, *364–
   365*
water
   ancient element 294
   chemistry of 67
   in body
      conservation 264
      evaporation 269
      excretion 234, 237
   molecular structure *296*
   nuclear reactor coolant 362–
      363
   supply *374–377*
water-lilies *(Nymphaeceae)* 90
'water-moulds' 70
Watson-Watt, Sir Robert 354
Watt, James *387*
wavelengths
   light *350*
   photons, laser 438, 439
   radar 356
   radio 412, *413–414*
waves
   electromagnetic 288, 290–293
   frequency (Hz) 289–290, 291
   in sea 47, 50, 51
wax 236
weasels *(Mustelidae)* 166
   characteristics 166
weather satellites *442*
weightlessness 226
welding, laser light *437,* 439
whales *(Cetacea) 99,* 174, 175
   baleen 175, 177
      characteristics 176–177, *177*
   beaked 175
   blue *(Balaenoptera musculus)
      176–177,* 177
   bowhead *(Balaena mysticetus)*
      177
   characteristics 174–175
   flipper structure *176*
   grey *(Eschrichtius gillosus)
      177*
   humpback 175
   killer *(Orcinus orcas) 175*
      characteristics 176
   pilot *(Globicephala
      scammoni) 174*
   right 175
      characteristics 177
      skeleton *177*
   rorqual 175
      characteristics 177
      lesser *(Balaenoptera
         acutorostrata) 177*
   sperm *(Physeter catodon)
      174–175,* 175
      characteristics 175–176
   toothed 175, 176
      characteristics 175
   white *(Delphinapterus
      leucas) 174*
wheatear *(Oenanthe oenanthe)*
   116, *116*

Wheatstone, Charles 408
wheels
   bicycle *316*
   motorcycles *317, 318–319*
whinchat *(Saxicola rubetra) 119*
white blood cells *see under*
   corpuscle
Whitehead, A.N., logic 345
Whittle, Frank, jet engine 392
wide angle lenses *417*
Williams, C.B., and butterfly
   migration 110
wings
   hydrofoil likeness 314
   lift effect *304–305*
winter buds 90
wireless telegraphy *see* radio
wire sound recorders *420*
wiring, telephone *407–411*
Wohler, Friedrich 380
wolf, marsupial *(Thylacinus
   cynocephalus)* 122
   characteristics 122
wolverine *(Gulo gulo) 166*
   characteristics 166
wombats 120, 121
wood
   petrified *63*
   structure of *91*
woodlice *(Porcellio scaber) 98*
woody nightshade *(Solanum
   dulcamara)* 80
'woolly bears' 111
worm, nematode *(Mermthoidea)
   98*
wow (record player term) 422
Wright brothers, first flight
   304

X

xenon 295
x-ray examination
   head and neck *242*
   large intestine *258*
   skull *242*
   small intestine *256*
x-rays 288, *290, 293, 394–396*
xylem 88
   of *Lupinus 91*
   parasites and *79*

Y

yawing control, aircraft *305*
yeast 60
yellow underwing moth
   (Triphaena comes) 108
Young, John, astronaut 334, 340
Young-Helmholtz theory 193
yucca moth *(Pronubia yuccasella)
   111*
Yukawa, Hideki 280, 283

Z

zinc 31
   crystal model *276*
zoom lens 417
zoospores 59, 68, 70
zorilla *(Ictonyx striatus)* 167
zygospore *67, 71*
zygote *71*